THE EVE OF CONFLICT

STEPHEN A. DOUGLAS
THE LITTLE GIANT IN HIS PRIME
From a photograph made in 1859

THE EVE OF CONFLICT

STEPHEN A. DOUGLAS AND
THE NEEDLESS WAR

BY GEORGE FORT MILTON

WITH ILLUSTRATIONS

1969
OCTAGON BOOKS
New York

Reprinted 1963, by special arrangement with Alice Milton Dwight

OCTAGON BOOKS
A DIVISION OF FARRAR, STRAUS & GIROUX, INC.
19 Union Square West
New York, N. Y. 10003

LIBRARY OF CONGRESS CATALOG CARD NUMBER: 63-14346

Printed in U.S.A. by
NOBLE OFFSET PRINTERS, INC.
NEW YORK 3, N. Y.

TO HER
WHO AGAIN HAS GIVEN ALL HER TIME
STRENGTH AND THOUGHT
IN THE BUILDING OF THIS BOOK
ALICE WARNER MILTON
I DEDICATE IT

ACKNOWLEDGMENTS

WITHOUT the co-operation and generous assistance of a great many people, it would have been impossible for me to have written this book. In the apposite footnotes, and personally, I have extended appreciation to the many who have aided the determination of specific incidents. In addition I must acknowledge aid and comfort extended throughout my four years of labor by other scholars and friends.

This present glimpse into the gestation of the Civil War, and the effort of Stephen Arnold Douglas to prevent it, could never have been more than hinted had it not been for the discovery, by Mr. Robert Dick Douglas, of Greensboro, North Carolina, a grandson of the Little Giant, of an old box which contained more than twenty thousand letters, and illumined the portion of Douglas' life which was of high national significance. Mr. Douglas' generous kindness in permitting me to make use of this treasure-trove cannot adequately be acknowledged.

Mr. Martin F. Douglas, of Greensboro, likewise a grandson of the Senator from Illinois, has been equally cordial and gracious in making available another body of manuscript material in his possession, including a delightful series of letters which Douglas wrote home in his first few years in Illinois.

The rich correspondence of Charles H. Lanphier, editor of the *Illinois State Register*, of Springfield, has been put at my disposal by his grandsons, Mr. William L. Patton and Dr. Charles L. Patton, of Springfield. Next to the Douglas manuscripts, this is the richest known source of primary material about the Little Giant and his Illinois and Washington campaigns. Mr. George H. Sheahan, of Chicago, the son of James W. Sheahan, editor of the Chicago *Times* and Douglas' first biographer, very kindly lent me the original letters of Senator Douglas to his father.

Miss Mary Erwin, of Athens, Georgia, with characteristic graciousness, has permitted me to examine a large body of heretofore unused letters written by and to her distinguished grandsire, Howell Cobb. These have permitted an understanding and reflection of the Southern point of view in the 'Fifties which otherwise could not have been attained. Dr. Julian P. Boyd examined for me the manuscript remains of Hendrick B. Wright, a prominent figure of Wilkes-Barre and Pennsylvania politics of the 'Fifties. His selections and transcripts have been of great assistance.

In the preparation of the manuscript itself, I have had the constant co-operation of Mr. Paul M. Angle, Librarian of the Illinois State Historical Library, and a highly distinguished student of Abraham Lincoln's career; Dr. Roy F. Nichols, of the University of Pennsylvania, an authority on the administration of Franklin K. Pierce; Dr. Charles W. Ramsdall, of the University of Texas, one of the South's shrewdest students on ante-bellum economics and politics; Professor P. L. Rainwater, of the University of

Mississippi, whose studies in the folk movements of the Cotton South are penetrating; Dr. James G. Randall, of the University of Illinois, whose incisive and sympathetic understanding of the making of the West has led him to give me many enlightening suggestions and encouragement; Dr. Frank H. Hodder, of the University of Kansas, a pioneer in putting Douglas in his true place in our history; Dr. Avery Craven, of the University of Chicago, a skilled interpreter of Southern emotional developments, and Dr. Harry E. Pratt, of Blackburn College, whose aid in manuscript material has been especially valuable.

Mr. David Rankin Barbee, of Washington, out of his immense store of information as to the State's Rights side of the pre-war controversy, has been of invaluable assistance as to many matters.

Dr. Henry Steele Commager, of New York University; Dr. Benjamin B. Kendrick, of the University of North Carolina; Dr. William B. Hesseltine, of the University of Wisconsin; Dr. Richard R. Steenberg, of the University of Texas; Dr. Thomas D. Clark, of the University of Kentucky; Dr. Culver H. Smith, of the University of Chattanooga; Mr. Glenn H. Seymour, of Charleston, Illinois, and Mr. Oswald Garrison Villard, of New York City, have given me many useful and pertinent suggestions and criticisms.

In the consideration of the Dred Scott case I am indebted to Judge Horace H. Hagan, of Tulsa, Oklahoma, and to Dr. Carl E. Swisher, of Columbia University. In Lincoln matters I have been greatly aided by the suggestions of Mr. William H. Townsend, of Lexington, Kentucky, and Mr. F. Lauriston Bullard, of Boston.

Dr. Thomas P. Martin, of the Manuscript Division of the Library of Congress, has been continuous in his suggestions and assistance. In the reading of the manuscript for general content and style, Mr. Marquis James, of Pleasantville, N.Y., and Mr. Gilbert E. Govan, of Chattanooga, have given generously of their time and talent. Miss Nora Crimmins, Librarian of the Chattanooga Public Library, has conferred many favors.

I cannot close this note without acknowledging most particularly the unflagging energy and attention of my efficient secretary, Mrs. Ellen Douglas Pennington, whose time and devotion to this task has been even greater than my own.

GEORGE FORT MILTON

CHATTANOOGA, TENNESSEE
September 12, 1934

CONTENTS

ILLUSTRATIONS

SIGNIFICANT DATES IN THE CAREER OF
STEPHEN A. DOUGLAS

1813   Birth, at Brandon, Vermont
1828   Cabinet-maker, at Middlebury, Vermont
1831–32   Student at Canandaigua Academy, Canandaigua, New York
1832   Emigrates to the West
1832–33   Schoolmaster at Winchester, Illinois
1834   State's Attorney
1836   Elected to Illinois Legislature
1837   Register of Federal Land Office at Springfield, Illinois
1838   Candidate for Congress; lost by 37 votes
1841   Secretary of State of Illinois
1841   Associate Justice, Illinois Supreme Court
1843   Elected to Congress
1847   Elected to the Senate
1847   Marries Martha Martin
1850   Effects Compromise of 1850
1852   Seeks Democratic Presidential nomination; re-elected to Senate
1854   Passes Kansas-Nebraska bill, with repeal of Missouri Compromise
1856   A second Presidential effort
1857   Breaks with Buchanan over Lecompton and Kansas
1858   Seeks Senate, against Republicans and Buchanan men; the Great Debates with Lincoln; Douglas wins
1859   Debates with Southern Ultras; organizes for a Presidential candidacy; Harper's Ferry
1860   The Charleston Convention; the second halt at Baltimore; Douglas seeks to save the Union; Secession and efforts to compromise
1861   The Cotton States withdraw; Douglas' peace efforts fail; holding Lincoln's hat; the war begins; Douglas goes West to rouse the people; illness and death

THE EVE OF CONFLICT

.: .

CHAPTER I

PORTRAIT OF A SENATOR

ALL over the globe the 'Forties and 'Fifties registered the impress of the Industrial Revolution upon man's economic and social patterns. Not only did the changes born of Watt's singing kettle and Stephenson's iron horse fashion a new economic world of *laissez faire*, but also it loosed the leash upon emotions and the ensuing ferment had vast consequence.

Within a single decade Darwin disturbed the Scriptural story of man's genesis; Marx questioned the social value of private ownership; Britain abandoned her corn laws and her old parties; nationalism flamed across the face of Europe and there was fighting in the streets of Paris and revolution in Budapest.

While America escaped bloodshed at the barriers, thought and feeling waged an increasing struggle to control her development. From the middle 'Forties forward, the concepts of the Founding Fathers were increasingly neglected, while emotional currents excited the feelings of her people and rendered them susceptible to the ministrations both of zealots urging abstract causes and of manipulators who knew what they wanted and employed the tools needed to secure it. This sharpening duel between emotion and intelligence marked the real beginning of the great American crisis, that constitutional debate which ended in a war of brothers and a peace of desolation and despair.

No more then than now could such changes come in man's life patterns without the forms of his political expression and the human symbols of control being profoundly affected. By the 'Forties the gods of the beginning were no more. The Father of his Country, the Author of the Declaration, the shapers of the Constitution were now statues rather than puissant men.

And the half-gods who succeeded them — Henry Clay, John Randolph and the War Hawks; Andrew Jackson, hero of New Orleans; Daniel Webster, the orator of the Constitution; John C. Calhoun, prophet of the slave-expanding South — these men, with their ruffled shirts, powdered hair and well-turned periods, had their day, but were now in the twilight and lighted only fitfully the descending dusk. Some of them lingered on in House and Senate but new men had come into the councils: virile, ambitious fellows who felt their elders had had glory and power enough and that the time had come for the new generation to take command. The dying giants launched with stately prose the great debates of peace or war which their successors concluded with sabers flashing in the air.

This record will be set before the reader — the history of America's great decision, of the forces which operated to produce it, the chief actors in the drama and how they played their parts. It shall be my attempt to inquire whether or not it was inevitable that the sword decide the dispute between the sections and to assess certain responsibilities for the decision when that fateful hour came.

The facts of this epoch, and the truth behind them, deserve retelling, for they suggest with tragic clearness that this particular war need not have been fought — at that time, at least. They suggest likewise that the war marked the defeat of a brave body of patriots and statesmen who had striven to keep the peace.

This book seeks to recapture the personalities of these men — and of those who balked their efforts — to reveal the high points of their struggle, and particularly to describe Stephen Arnold Douglas, the chief among them. Great in friendship, great in mind, great in purpose, his was the greatest effort to make intelligence the arbiter of American affairs. In the end his plans crashed down in ruin, inflamed minorities called upon the god of battle and the America of peace and concord had a requiem of battle-fire. But it was not of Douglas' causing — and the guns at Sumter quite broke his heart.

Before entering the narrative, we had better glance at this man they called 'the Little Giant,' note his stature, his interests and his traits, and gain some idea as to what manner of man he was. Certainly there was no obscurity about him. From his election to the Senate, in 1847, visitors to the gallery would remark the Lilliputian member. And yet, despite his height of five feet four inches and his age of thirty-four, this new Senator from Illinois did not look a boy; while his slight stature was constantly surprising his associates, it did not diminish his essential dignity or strength.[1]

As a youth Douglas had been slender but by the time the Illinois Legislature elected him to the Senate he had fleshened up considerably and was almost stout. His head was huge, so large that it seemed quite out of proportion to his body. By 1847 his thick, deep brown hair, slightly curly, began to be sprinkled with gray. His forehead was broad, more full than high, his round face had neither moustache nor beard and he kept it clean shaven. His complexion was rich and dark.

Douglas' eyes were probably his most striking feature. Large, steady and dark blue in color, set deep beneath dark eyebrows of great width, they impressed people with a peculiar quality of depth. A thick and pugnacious nose was placed above an arched, clear-cut mouth. His chin was square but full of eddying dimples. His ears were small and white. This

[1] Major O. H. P. Belmont, in conversation with the author, Washington, D.C., January 14, 1928. Sixty-odd years later the son of August Belmont remembered a carriage ride down the streets of Newport. Douglas, the elder Belmont and the boy had ridden together. 'My feet did not reach the carriage floor,' Belmont recalled, 'and neither did those of Mr. Douglas.'

heavy and impressive head and face was connected by a short neck to a pair of strong, square shoulders. Douglas' chest was full and his body was not unduly short but his lower limbs were very much so; his hands were small and chubby and his feet very small.[2] He dressed with neatness, 'though not always in good taste.' All in all, he looked the part of a great man.[3]

And then there was a peculiar fascination to the voice of Douglas, a quality it did not lose with passing years. While not a loud talker, his tones were marked with a deep, vibrant energy and were effective not only in the legislative hall but also in the open air, where his voice would rise and fall with the fluctuations of the winds, seeming to have the effortless volume of a great organ tone. Round, deep and sonorous, his words reached his remotest hearer and yet did not come as an ear-splitting tempest upon those immediately at hand.

In his boyhood, Douglas wrote poetry and he was the author of one or two good poems in his later life.[4] In addition, he seemed attracted by the pictorial and plastic arts, and from 1845 onward took an especial interest in young artists. In the 'Fifties, at a time when he was under a heavy financial strain, he provided the funds to send Leonard Volk to Rome to study sculpture and the young American became a noted sculptor. A few years later Governor Matteson of Illinois commissioned him to make a statue of the Little Giant and Volk carved a noble figure which can still be seen in Springfield. Many impecunious young painters secured commissions from Douglas to do his portrait, in addition to which he had several fine portraits by Healy and other American portraitists of the Middle period.[5]

Douglas' religious interests were no less characteristic than his artistic. A Congregationalist by inheritance, as a young man in central Illinois he made it a point to go to Peter Cartwright's revivals. A few years later he came to have some distaste for preachers in politics, especially because this breed in the North seemed determined so to inflame popular emotions over slavery that friendly settlement would be impossible. Early in 1850, however, he wrote an Illinois friend who had recently embraced the ministry that his mind had undergone 'material changes upon the nature and importance of our religious duties.... You have my prayers for your sucess and may I ven-

[2] Joseph Wallace, *Illinois State Register*, Springfield, Ill., April 19, 1885; *The Vermonter*, XI, No. 6, 93 *et seq.*

[3] Joseph Wallace, *Illinois State Register*, April 30, 1899.

[4] I am indebted to Miss Adelaide Jackson for the privilege of viewing the school-girl copy-book of Douglas' sister Sarah, in which young Stephen had written several juvenile sets of verse. Mr. Eugene F. Hoyt, of Savona, N.Y., has furnished a clipping from Chicago *Courier*, 'The Late Senator Douglas as a Poet,' giving poem entitled, 'Bury Me in the Morning.'

[5] *Journal*, Illinois State Historical Society, VII, No. 2, 74–75. In 1860, Douglas had some statuettes made of himself, and gave them to friends who had loyally supported him. One given to Mrs. Hendrick B. Wright, wife of a loyal Pennsylvania friend, is at present in the possession of Mr. George B. Wright, of Dallas, Pa. Leonard Volk, Rome, Nov. 2, 1855, Douglas MSS.: 'You desired me to let you know in time when I wanted more money.' Volk was Douglas' cousin by marriage.

ture to ask yours for my salvation.' [6] But in 1854 his irritation against religion in politics flamed again over the Northern evangelicals' strictures upon the repeal of the Missouri Compromise. Rebuking such critics sternly, he bade them keep to their cloth.

There is little further evidence of any inclination toward the creeds of his childhood. The lovely Adèle Cutts, his second wife, was a Catholic. The Senator, by nature tolerant of all faiths, permitted her to send the two children of his first marriage to Georgetown, a Catholic school, and they later embraced their stepmother's faith. Bishop Duggan, the Catholic Primate of Chicago, preached his funeral sermon, and the Douglases of the third generation are Catholic. While the Little Giant himself was not particularly devout, undeniably he did believe in a Supreme Creator.

His experiences as a schoolmaster his first winter on the Illinois prairie made Douglas a lifelong friend of public education. Again and again he sought to strengthen the State's school system; his interest in college development was evidenced both by honorary degrees showered on him and by his sponsorship of the foundation of a great University for Chicago. Donating the land upon which it was built, so long as he lived Douglas pressed the cause of this first Chicago University and looked to it to light a lamp of learning for the West.[7]

His efforts to encourage higher education afford but another index to the man's wide horizons. When a student at the Canandaigua Academy, in up-State New York, in the late 'Twenties, he had been an inveterate reader of the classics. In 1833, his first winter in Illinois, he invested in good books a part of the few dollars he painfully acquired teaching school. During his years in Washington the Senator made constant demands on the Congressional Library. Not only did he pursue such utilitarian subjects as electricity and telegraphy, but he read the sources of the constitutional debates, carefully examined Calhoun's dialectics, sought statistics about slavery and the slave trade and relaxed himself upon the poetry and romance of the day.[8]

[6] Douglas to the Reverend William S. Prentice, Washington, Jan. 16, 1850. Original owned by Miss Bertha Kimble, Springfield, Ill. I am indebted to Mr. Paul M. Angle for this copy.

[7] In 1844, Norwich University, of which Douglas had Vermont boyhood memories, conferred on him the degree of Master of Arts. T. B. Ransom, Norwich, Vt., Aug. 14, 1844; M. F. Douglas MSS., announced its conferring. President Charles A. Plumley, present head of this institution, now at Northfield, Vt., has kindly had records examined for me. The Board of Trustees, Aug. 14, 1844, voted this degree to Douglas and others. Seven years later Middlebury College in Vermont conferred on him an LL.D. degree. He attended the commencement, speaking for half an hour in a 'pleasing and impressive manner.' A year later he volunteered a gift of $500 to the college. Middlebury *Register*, Aug. 20, 27, 1851; *The Vermonter*, XI, 93 *et seq.* I am indebted to Mr. Harry F. Lake, of Concord, N.H., for certain verifications as to Middlebury. A. D. Eddy, Chicago, March 31; S. Y. McMasters, Alton, April 21, 1856, Douglas MSS., show the Senator's Chicago University efforts. Carlinville, Ill., *Free Democrat*, Sept. 3, 1857, sneered that 'Senator Douglas has made $20,000 by his gift of land for a Baptist University at Chicago. The surrounding lots have been much increased in value. So much for giving.'

[8] While the fight over the Compromise of 1850 was at its height, he was reading Vail's book on the magnetic telegraph, Espy's book on storms, several numbers of Silliman's *American Journal*, and Sturgeon's *Annals of Electricity*. A little later he called for Mrs. Trollope's *Paris and the Parisians*, Shee on Physical Science, Sherwood's *Gazetteer of Georgia*, a biography of Benedict

But Douglas' force and vigor seem all the more surprising when one takes into account the physical frailties to which he was subject. In his boyhood he had a breakdown; on his first trip West a siege of fever brought him close to death's door, and ten years later his health was so bad that he thought of giving up his new position on the Illinois Supreme Court. A Southern electioneering trip in the Summer of 1848 led to a severe attack of bilious fever, and the next Summer he suffered 'an attack of cholera, followed by bilious diarrhea,' which for a time was believed to have permanently impaired his health.[9]

Nor was this the only frailty; almost every year his throat required treatment, at times his vocal cords were affected. In December, 1855, while Douglas was in the midst of a campaign to vindicate his Kansas-Nebraska Bill, he was stricken in Terre Haute, Indiana, and after several weeks' illness made his way to Cleveland, Ohio, for a delicate operation by a noted surgeon.[10]

Douglas was always impatient when illness interfered with his duties, for enormous energy was a mark of his whole career. As a Judge of the Illinois Supreme Court he was termed a veritable 'steam engine in britches,' and this same habit of hard work persisted during all his years in Washington. His growing importance in national affairs soon expanded the range of his public interests. His committal to the doctrine of Manifest Destiny brought contact with engineers, explorers and settlers in the new Territories of the Pacific Coast; his zeal for railroad building and commercial expansion added a large national acquaintance to his list.

From 1847 onward, the Senator's correspondence exhibited this widening of horizons. He was asked to recommend applicants for jobs, look up bounty claims, file patent applications, give letters of introduction and speeches and documents, secure printing for friendly papers, work confirmations through the Senate, and secure appropriations for a 'full outfit' for a newly confirmed

Arnold, and several volumes of the works of Edmund Burke. From 1857 to 1861, the Library records charged him with Lipsius' *Egypt and Ethiopia*, Millinger's *History of the Church*, Shakespeare's plays, some of Scott's and Cooper's novels, Bancroft's *American History*, Martin's *British Colonies*, Doran's *Habits and Men*, Newman's Lectures on Catholics in England, Chatham's *Works*, Las Cases' *Journal*, Halleck's *Poems*, Maria Edgeworth's productions, the *Federalist* and innumerable copies of the *Congressional Globe*. Edwin B. Stelle, Assistant Librarian, to Mrs. Stephen A. Douglas, Washington, June 27, 1861, M. F. Douglas MSS., indicates that at Douglas' death he had about twenty books borrowed from the Library. The volumes here mentioned are upon the pages of the Congressional Library's register of withdrawals, an old book kept during the late 'Forties, 'Fifties and 'Sixties. Mr. F. M. Roberts, superintendent of the reading room has been good enough to furnish me the photostats of the entries for withdrawals by Johnson, Douglas, Lincoln and other great figures of the epoch.

[9] Eugene S. Didier, *Greenbag Magazine*, XV, 459; *Illinois State Register*, Sept. 10, 1849.

[10] Douglas to H. M. Rice, Cleveland, Ohio, Dec. 28, 1855. For copy of this letter I am indebted to Mr. W. H. Townsend, of Lexington, Ky. 'Doct. Ackley performed his first operation day before yesterday,' Douglas wrote Rice. 'The passing of an instrument down the throat and some distance into the wind-pipe, with the view of injecting nitrate of silver into the ulcerated parts, is not enjoyable, although not a very painful operation, if it did not stop your breathing for a few minutes. The next step is to cut off the nerves or lower Pallet and after that to cut the tonsils. Doct. Ackley thinks he will put me in condition to travel in less than two weeks, although I would *not be of much account in a senatorial fight for some time.*'

American envoy abroad. To all of these he handsomely responded, especially so when requests came from dear friends of his early years.[11]

But while Douglas continually sought appointments for friends whom he thought competent for the tasks, he set his face sternly against dragging relatives into office with him. 'Judge Douglas, when elected to office, considered that the people voted for him — they did not vote for the whole family of Douglasses and their collaterals,' a political opponent testified. He never 'put his hand upon a recommendation for one of his relatives.' [12]

In appraising Douglas' traits mention must be made of his amazing capacity for friendships. After 1850 thousands of the emerging generation, who called themselves 'Young America,' regarded Douglas almost as a demigod. George N. Sanders, of Kentucky; August Belmont and Dean Richmond, of New York; John W. Forney and Hendrick B. Wright, of Pennsylvania; 'Lean Jimmy' Jones, of Tennessee; Robert Toombs and Alexander H. Stephens, of Georgia, and Pierre Soulé, of Louisiana, had faith in Douglas and his political philosophy.

When Alexis de Tocqueville, the famous French political scientist, visited America in 1831–32, he spent some time with the Spencers at Canandaigua, New York. Douglas, then a student in a law office there, remembered through the years de Tocqueville's reference to the strange anomaly that in a democratic country some States required a voter to possess a freehold estate. In 1850 Douglas' friend David Settle Reid became Democratic candidate for Governor of North Carolina, then firmly Whig. 'Make the issue free suffrage,' Douglas urged him. 'Call upon the people to put an end to the disfranchisement of an intelligent man because he does not own land, you will have the issue that will make you Governor and give the Democratic party control of North Carolina.' Reid took this advice, lost his first campaign by only 854 votes, and two years later, on the same issue, became Governor.[13]

But Douglas did not permit the acquisition of new friends and interests to cause him to neglect the associates of his early Illinois years.[14] Nor did he overlook the power of the press. One of the first things he did on settling in central Illinois in 1833 was to cultivate Jacksonville's Democratic editor, and when he moved to Springfield he established close relations with the

[11] J. S. McConnel, Jacksonville, June 30, 1848. This letter was written in behalf of Major Murray McConnel, who wanted a West Point appointment for his son George, whom Douglas had dandled on his knee. 'Our congressman is a Whig, and rather a bad specimen of even that species,' wrote McConnel. This application added as the reason why Douglas was asked to help. The man in question was Abraham Lincoln; C. Eames, Baltimore, Feb. 18, 1849, Douglas MSS., asking for outfit.

[12] *Missouri Republican*, St. Louis, Jan. 28, 1862.

[13] Governor Clark of North Carolina told Joseph Blount Cheshire, venerable Episcopal Bishop of North Carolina, of the de Tocqueville origin of Douglas' suggestion; see letter Bishop Cheshire to author, Raleigh, N.C., April 14, 1931, and the Bishop's book, *Non Nulla*, Chapel Hill, N.C., 1931. The Honorable Josephus Daniels has furnished me with memorandum of statement W. W. Holden made him as to Douglas' agency. I am indebted to Professor George Wilson Pierson, of Yale, for certain information about de Tocqueville's visit to Canandaigua.

[14] Douglas to Colonel A. G. Herndon, Washington, April 14, 1846, quoted Joseph Wallace, *Transactions*, Illinois State Historical Society, VI, 113, shows that for all this Douglas was careful not to attempt to claim credit for appointments to which he had no agency.

party organ there. In the 'Forties, when young Charles H. Lanphier took over the editorship of the *Illinois State Register*, the most intimate and affectionate relations grew up between Douglas and the editor, and the columns of the *Register* came to reflect the Little Giant's views on public questions almost as accurately as did his own speeches in House and Senate.[15]

In Quincy, Douglas had real friends in Austin Brooks and J. M. Morris, proprietors of the *Herald*, and on occasions assisted them financially. In the 'Forties he had Chicago press support, both from 'Long John' Wentworth's *Democrat* and from the *Tribune*, but both papers began to incline toward Free Soilism.[16] Thus by 1850 a friendly Chicago paper became almost a political necessity and Douglas and his friends began to discuss the establishment of a proper organ there. Efforts were made to interest Edmund Burke, of the Washington *Union*, to found one, but it was not until 1855, when James W. Sheahan, an experienced Eastern journalist, was induced to come out to edit the Chicago *Times*, that the Douglas men secured the needed organ. The Little Giant kept his finger on the paper's financial pulse, and from his sick-bed wrote its editor, 'Let me know the worst, and it shall be provided for.'[17]

From the days of his first coming to Illinois the Little Giant had been land-hungry. During 1836's boom times he bought unwisely, the next year's general crash wiped out his equities and left him with a load of debt which, for several years thereafter, absorbed everything he could make. But in the early 'Forties, with the economic recovery of the Western country the land fever seized him once more.

When Douglas went to Washington he managed to clear up his past debts and soon began to plunge in real estate again. Even before his removal to Chicago he started picking up property in that city. It was his custom to scrape up the cash some way or other to make a down payment, and then to expect that the land's increase in value would enable the mortgage debt remaining to be wiped out by the sale of a portion of it. After he became a Senator, Douglas gave freer rein to these speculative propensities and confidently looked forward to making a large fortune through Chicago's growth.

Moreover Douglas was a good business man and the future verified his judgment of Chicago values. His land there was worth a million at the time of his death and today would be worth tens of millions. While he was often comfortably off during his lifetime, there were occasions of business

---

[15] Douglas to Lanphier, Quincy, Ill., Aug. 22, 1845, Washington, Jan. 9, 1847; Patton MSS. Incidentally, the letters from Douglas to Lanphier, the largest single body of Douglas letters extant, constitute one of the best historical sources for the presentation of his career. For their use I am indebted to Mr. William L. Patton and Dr. Charles L. Patton, of Springfield.

[16] Austin Brooks of the *Herald*, to Douglas, Quincy, Ill., June 9, 1856; Douglas MSS.: 'You are the first public man who has ever offered to assist me in a substantial way, and I shall be slow to forget it.' *Transactions*, Illinois State Historical Society for 1924; 105.

[17] Governor A. C. French, Springfield, Ill., June 21; Isaac R. Diller, Springfield, Ill., Sept. 16; 1850; Douglas MSS. Douglas to Sheahan, Cleveland, Ohio, Jan. 11, 1856; Sheahan MSS. in possession of Mr. George H. Sheahan, of Chicago, to whose kindness I am indebted for its use.

crisis or political emergency when his financial resourcefulness was taxed to the breaking point. But always he worked his way out.

Not only was Douglas alert to personal business opportunities, but he was concerned over the general prosperity of the region, and this gave him a keen interest in betterment of agriculture. In the late 'Forties, learning that Cyrus H. McCormick, a young Virginia mechanic who was the 'inventor of a machine known as the Virginia reaper,' wanted to go West with it, the Senator introduced him to Messrs. Peck and McDougall, leading Chicago business men. McCormick soon settled in that city, establishing what has since become one of the Nation's greatest enterprises.[18]

About the time Douglas became a Senator the Government began to implement James Smithson's great endowment and in 1854 Douglas was named a regent of the Smithsonian Institution. In a few years' time he became a devoted friend of Professor Joseph Henry, the great scientist who headed the undertaking, faithfully attended regents' meetings and evinced an understanding of the problems and an aid in their solution such as is seldom elicited from a politician. It was not without reason that on Douglas' death the Smithsonian Board of Regents held a special memorial service to testify to his services as friend of science and patron of the arts.[19]

Transportation and communication enthralled the Little Giant, the scientific details of the railroad and the telegraph particularly enlisting his attention and the records of the Congressional Library show how he pored over books about the magnetic telegraph. But his interest in these practical aspects was overshadowed by the rôle his imagination told him these agencies could play in the development of a great continent-girding Union. He expected the railroad and the telegraph to be of immense importance in mingling the populations of the sections, in giving them better understanding, in promoting trade and increasing understanding, thus cementing the union of the States.

An illustration that his railroad interest was more practical than scientific was his part in building the Illinois Central system.[20] Railroad lines to join the Great Lakes to the Southern Gulf and to link the mid-continent with California and Oregon were indispensable to his great economic program for the Mississippi Valley and the West. Geography had made Illinois the key to Middle-Western railroad development and from 1835 forward, Douglas was in the forefront of the fight to bring it about along sound lines. Illi-

---

[18] Douglas to Peck and McDougall, Washington, May 7, 1848; original owned by Mr. Oliver R. Barrett, of Chicago, to whom I am indebted for a photostat.

[19] A. Wetmore, Acting Secretary of the Smithsonian Institution, to author, Washington, Aug. 27, 1932. Douglas was first appointed by the President of the Senate, Feb. 25, 1854. He was reappointed Jan. 28, 1860. The memorial services were held May 1, 1862, S. S. Cox, of Ohio, delivering the eulogy.

[20] Douglas to C. R. N. Patterson, Washington, Feb. 4, 1850, Illinois State Historical Society MSS., Douglas to Elisha Whittlesey, Washington, June 16, 1860, Chicago Historical Society MSS., reveal that at the height of the 1850 turmoil over slavery in California, and while he played a rôle of commanding importance in fashioning and passing 1850's Compromise, his heart was equally set on Federal legislation to aid the building of a railroad from Great Lakes to Gulf.

nois succumbed to the internal improvement fever of the 'Thirties, but promoters' promises went unfulfilled and, until 1849, the Northern Cross, from Naples to Springfield, was the only railroad in the State.

By 1850, however, a shift from south to north of Illinois population and wealth divided the State increasingly into two antagonistic social, political, and economic communities. Douglas wanted a central railroad, both because the consequent increase in the intercourse between the sections of the State would lessen sectional division, and because such a railroad, linked at the Ohio with another to the Gulf, would be an immense economic stimulus to Illinois and the entire nation.

Such a central railroad had long been projected by the speculators. After the panic of 1837 had deflated their scheme they asked the Federal Government for large grants of public land to enable the road to be built.[21] Darius Holbrook, a daring promoter, led these efforts, in which the railroad project soon became an appendage of an enormous Cairo land boom. Important politicians, including United States Senator Sidney Breese, took stock in the gamble and exerted all their energy to persuade Congress to make the gifts.[22] The promoters also wanted to leave Chicago off the main line of their railroad.

Douglas was anxious for the road but felt that, in order 'to impart nationality' to the project and secure Northern and Eastern votes, the Federal grant should go to the State, not the promoters, and also that Chicago should be a northern terminus.[23] When he went to the Senate he introduced a bill along these lines. But Senator Breese would not yield and after his defeat for the Senate returned to Washington to lobby for his scheme.

In the Thirtieth Congress, Douglas' bill had to meet sharp attacks on its constitutionality by Senators King, of Alabama, and Davis, of Mississippi. These did not keep the last Senate from passing it, but their House delegations, following their lead and joining with the Holbrook efforts and Eastern jealousy, defeated it in the lower House. But the Holbrook cabal had not been sure of this and reinsured their speculation by bribing an engrossing clerk to smuggle into the Acts of the Illinois Legislature a formal transfer to their group of any rights the State might later get. On discovering this, Douglas pledged that he would defeat any Congressional grant of land 'to any one except the State of Illinois itself.' [24]

[21] For these efforts, see William Ackerman, *Early Illinois Railroads*, Chicago, 1884; 16 *et seq.* Howard G. Brownson, *History of the Illinois Central Railroad to 1870*, Urbana, Ill., 1915; chs. I and II, and Paul W. Gates, *The Illinois Central Railroad and Its Colonization Work*, Cambridge, Mass., 1934; 3–65. Professor Gates, who has studied the Illinois Central history carefully, and President L. A. Downs, of the Illinois Central, have through personal correspondence aided me greatly in unravelling the complexities of early Illinois Central politics. Sidney Breese, in 1835 a State Judge, later a United States Senator, claimed paternity of the Central Railroad scheme.

[22] J. Madison Cutts, *Constitutional and Party Questions*, New York, 1866; 188 *et seq.* Cutts, who was brother of Douglas' second wife, took down a great many of the Senator's reminiscences. Douglas to Breese, Lawrenceville, Ill., Jan. 25, 1851, printed in *Illinois State Register*, Springfield, Feb. 6, 1851.

[23] Douglas to Breese, Washington, Jan. 5, 1851, printed in *Illinois State Register*, Jan. 20, 1851.

[24] Cutts, 189–90.

The Senator early laid his plans to pass his bill through the next Congress. Knowing that King and Davis yielded a blind adherence to the doctrine of instructions, he undertook to stimulate the South's railroad magnates to have the Alabama and Mississippi Legislatures impose such instructions on their Senators. In November, 1849, he quietly visited Mobile, Alabama, headquarters of the Mobile Railroad Company, an ambitious but almost bankrupt project to build a road from the Ohio to the Gulf. Douglas proposed to its directors that they refinance through such a grant of Federal lands as he was seeking for Illinois. Jumping at the chance, they set to work to secure the necessary instructions.

The Senator now hastened to Washington, forced Holbrook to release Illinois from all claims on future Federal land and then introduced an Illinois Central bill. Soon the Alabama and Mississippi Legislatures instructed their Senators to urge similar land grants for the Mobile Railroad. King and Davis cursed their solons but asked Douglas to let them amend his bill by adding the Mobile grants to it. This done, the Senate passed it by an ample margin.[25]

Douglas' shrewd ministrations were also essential to the measure's passage in the House. Due to promoters' intrigues and sectional jealousies, Eastern Whigs and Democrats, together with many representatives from Indiana and Ohio, voted against it on an important test vote.[26]

The railroad bill leaders could only avert complete defeat by moving that the House go immediately into Committee of the Whole on the slavery question. Inasmuch as fifty members had speeches they wanted to make on the subject, this motion carried and the defeat was staved off momentarily. But the railroad bill, which went to the very foot of the calendar, had ninety-seven bills ahead and it seemed almost impossible for it to come up again that session.

According to one apocryphal account, the Senator finally determined that the same tactics which had deferred the railroad bill could be applied to the ninety-seven others, which would bring it back to the top of the calendar so that it could be brought to a vote. He devised an ingenious technique to do this, which worked like a charm. On September 17 the Illinois Central Railroad bill finally appeared at the head of the calendar again.[27] Now the Illinois men mustered their strength and Douglas' bill

[25] Ackerman, 33; Cutts, 19 *et seq.*; *Congressional Globe*, Thirty-First Congress, First Session, 904. It was known as Senate Bill No. 22, entitled 'An Act Granting the Right of Way and Making a Grant of Land to the States of Illinois, Mississippi and Alabama in Aid of the Construction of a Railroad from Chicago to Mobile.'

[26] Thomas L. Harris to Lanphier, Washington, July 23, 1850; Patton MSS.

[27] There is a great mystery as to the particular technique Douglas adopted to bring the Illinois Central bill back to the top of the House calendar. Cutts, 194, describes it, in words attributed to Douglas, as involving the making of ninety-seven separate motions to go into Committee of the Whole, each motion moving the bill then under consideration to the bottom of the calendar. Cutts also relates Douglas' triumphant disclosure of the manner in which he persuaded a friend from another section to make this motion again and again, thus removing from the immediate sponsors of the railroad bill any onus of responsibility for the defeat of each of these ninety-seven measures. A careful inspection of the House Journal for this Congress, from July 23 to Sept. 17, 1850, does not enable me to support Cutts' statements. The Honorable Sam D. Mc-

passed by a majority of three. 'If ever a man passed a bill,' Douglas said reminiscently a little later, 'I did that one.' [28]

The politicians' mouths were watering for the manna of the railroad speculation. John A. McClernand wanted Lanphier to go with him to Cairo 'and make each a big fortune,' and some of the Illinois delegation picked up a little land, but while Douglas bought some State of Illinois bonds, he purchased no land.[29] As soon as the bill had passed, the Senator took to his bed to recover from an operation on an abscess in his thigh. Darius Holbrook invaded the sick-room to propose that if he would surrender the release, the promoter would immediately deed him 'one-half of the lands granted, over two and a half million acres, and worth twenty millions.' The Little Giant jumped out of bed, seized his crutches and gave the would-be briber a blow on the head as he rushed through the door. 'It would disgrace the whole delegation in Congress,' he wrote Lanphier, 'to have Holbrook cheat the State out of those lands.' But it was with great difficulty that he finally persuaded the Illinois Legislature to accept Holbrook's release.[30]

Soon thereafter a group of Eastern capitalists offered to construct the Illinois Central and the road was chartered and built on terms most favorable to the State.[31] Douglas aided the construction of the road, performed favors

Reynolds, member of Congress from Tennessee, and Mr. Lewis Deschler, Parliamentarian of the House, have carefully examined the Journal, and considered the rule of the House in 1850 and have concluded that Cutts probably was in error. The bill was not a private but a public one. It was treated under 'morning hour' rules not now used in the House. A memorandum by Mr. Deschler states that the Journal entries show 'some discrepancies between Mr. Douglas' memory and the actual facts as they occurred.' Professor Gates writes me that he has 'never been completely satisfied. The more I study the bill the more complex its passage became to me'; letter to author Dec. 23, 1932.

[28] Cutts, 195–99. Thos. L. Harris to Lanphier and Walker, Washington, July 31, 1850; Patton MSS.

[29] McClernand to Lanphier, Washington, June 25, 1850; Patton MSS. *Missouri Republican*, St. Louis, Jan. 28, 1852, quoting Wentworth's speech. Gates, *op. cit.*, lists 'Long John' Wentworth, Governor A. C. French, Judge David Davis, Representative W. H. Bissell, Stephen T. Logan and Robert Smith as typical examples of the politician-speculator in lands made valuable by the Illinois Central. Douglas had already invested heavily in Chicago real estate, part of which the Michigan Central and Illinois Central had to buy to get lake shore entrance into the city. Before the Illinois Central bill he bought 2872 acres of land at Lake Calumet, paying $2.50 per acre for it. In 1855 he bought 4610 more acres near his other holdings, paying the Illinois Central $10 per acre for it. Later, when he was hard pressed and wanted release from some of the debt on this, the President of the road refused to give it. So far as I can determine, Douglas' sole financial transaction in 1850 was the purchase of Illinois State bonds. For this see Douglas to W. W. Corcoran, Washington, Dec. 10, 1850; Corcoran MSS., Library of Congress: 'I think the time has arrived,' he wrote the Washington banker, 'for purchasing those bonds according to the understanding between us. I fix no limit to the amount, for I am satisfied that it is a good investment and desire as many as you are willing to purchase and hold for me.'

[30] Cutts, 192–93; Douglas to Lanphier, Washington, Oct. 2, 1850; Patton MSS.

[31] The petitioners were George Griswold, Robert Schuyler, Gouverneur Morris, Franklin Haven, David A. Neal, Robert Rantoul, Jr., Jonathan Sturges, Thomas W. Ludlow, and John F. A. Sanford — names of respectability and financial strength, inspiring confidence and respect. They proposed to form a company under the laws of Illinois to build, in accordance with the act of Congress, and complete by July 4, 1854, 'a road which should be in all respects as well and thoroughly built as the railroad running from Boston to Albany, with such improvements thereon as experience has shown to be desirable and expedient.' The petitioners also agreed to

for its officers, and watched to see that the State secured its proper revenue therefrom. But his main care was that of economic betterment and social understanding. Senator Walker, of Wisconsin, had said in the Senate debate that the Illinois Central project was 'a great chain to unite North and South.' Douglas had had this in mind all through the struggle.

'There is a power in this nation greater than either the North or the South,' Douglas said, in that same Congress, in response to a Websterian slur on the West. 'A growing, increasing, swelling power, that will be able to speak the law to this nation, and to execute the law as spoken. That power is the country known as the great West — the Valley of the Mississippi, one and indivisible from the Gulf to the Great Lakes, and stretching, on the one side and the other, to the extreme sources of the Ohio and Missouri — from the Alleghanies to the Rocky Mountains. There, Sir, is the hope of this nation — the resting place of the power that is not only to control, but to save, the Union. We furnish the water that makes the Mississippi, and we intend to follow, navigate, and use it until it loses itself in the briny ocean. So with the St. Lawrence. We intend to keep open and enjoy both of these great outlets to the ocean, and all between them we intend to take under our especial protection, and keep and preserve as one free, happy, and united people. This is the mission of the great Mississippi Valley, the heart and soul of the nation and the continent.' [32]

Douglas' keen interest in matters of commercial and economic interest was in evidence on a tour he made of Europe, in 1853. The breakwater being constructed at Genoa fascinated him, he saw how its principles of construction could be applied to Chicago and carried home detailed maps and plans. The resemblance of Illinois prairies and Russian steppes likewise interested him and there is record of his renting a huge carriage, with sleeping-room and kitchen, to take him from Odessa to the confines of Tartary.

In Germany, he was attracted to the operations of the Prussian *Zollverein* or customs union. Ever after this trip he revolved the idea of an American continental commercial alliance, and just before Sumter thought of adapting this pattern of economic union and political separation to the United States. [33]

His attitude toward Europe, as expressed to the Senate shortly before departure, was one of anything but unmixed admiration. Its choicest products were 'relics,' 'sad memorials of departed glory and fallen greatness,' which 'bring up the memories of the dead but inspire no hope for the living.'

His description of England as 'a cruel and unnatural mother' was reported in London and he met a cold reception there. It was intimated that he could be formally presented to the Court but must don knee breeches, silk stockings

pay the State of Illinois a fixed percentage of the gross earnings of their railroad, 'without deductions of charge for expenses, or any other matter of cost.' The percentage was left blank in the offer, but Douglas suggested and the Illinois Legislature incorporated seven per cent as the figure.

[32] *Congressional Globe*, Thirty-First Congress, First Session, App., 365.

[33] Douglas' map of the Genoa breakwater is now in the possession of Mr. Martin F. Douglas, of Greensboro. Not long after his return to America, Senator Douglas became very active in

and buckled slippers for the occasion. Cocking a weather eye upon the effect back home, he asked to be allowed to appear in the ordinary dress of an American citizen and was refused. As a result, the Little Giant was not presented to the Queen. Many of his letters of introduction went unanswered and the Government and the nobility gave him the cold shoulder. But John Bright noted that he had met, at Richard Cobden's, 'a little, dark, firm built and intelligent looking person, called in his own country "The Little Giant," evidently a man of superior mental power.' [34]

From London Douglas journeyed by easy stages through France and Italy to Greece, Constantinople and Smyrna. All along the route he saw signs of the growing tension between Russia and Turkey, for the Crimean War was in its gestation stage. Reaching Smyrna at the time of the Koszta episode, when the excitement was 'beyond anything he had ever seen,' he upheld the course of Captain Ingraham, the American naval commander, in sustaining Koszta's American citizenship and in threatening to open fire on an Austrian brig to prevent Koszta's being seized. [35]

Next the Little Giant turned to Russia, eventually winding up at St. Petersburg, where Count Nesselrode treated him with extraordinary civilities and he was received at court 'in the same dress he usually wore at the White House.' The high point was sitting by the Czar at a great military review at which Douglas was treated like a Grand Duke. [36]

urging the Illinois Legislature to appropriate for modern harbor works at Chicago. For Russian journey from Odessa to Tartary, see Paris Correspondence, Cincinnati *Gazette*, clipped in *Illinois State Register*, Oct. 31, 1853. Douglas was amazed at the carriage clipping along at a rate of from eight to ten miles an hour. For German visit, David Smith, U.S. Consulate, Basle, Switzerland, March 11, 1854; Douglas MSS.: 'I can now understand your words uttered at Baden-Baden....' For American *Zollverein* project, see *infra*, Chapter XXX.

[34] *Congressional Globe*, Thirty-Second Congress, Special Session of the Senate of Mar. 4, 1853, 262–73, for speeches of March 10 and 17, 1853. James W. Sheahan, *The Life of Stephen A. Douglas*, New York, 1860; 443–44; Chicago *Times*, Sept. 7, 1866, sketch of Douglas; August Belmont, The Hague, Nov. 15, 1853; Douglas MSS. Secretary of State Marcy had instructed all American diplomats that the President wished they would wear only citizen's dress when they appeared at foreign courts. John Bright, *Diaries*, R. A. J. Walling, ed., New York, 1931; 146, 157.

[35] His route was from London, Paris, Genoa, Florence and Greece. There he was given a copy of a book of Byron's *Poems*, now in the possession of his niece, Mrs. Adelaide Jackson, of Rochester, N.Y., and inscribed in his hand: 'This is the first book ever printed in Greece in the English language.' In Constantinople he had a long conference with Reschid Pascha over the probabilities of a Turko-Russian War. Paris Correspondence, Cincinnati *Gazette*, clipped *Illinois State Register*, Oct. 31, 1853, and Usher F. Linder, *Reminiscences of the Early Bench and Bar of Illinois*, Chicago, 1879; 79. He also spent a night on Mount Olivet; Edward A. Gilbert to author, Long Beach, Cal., Nov. 18, 1931. James Schouler, *History of the United States*, New York, 1891; I, 275, for Koszta episode. This Hungarian-born Levantine had taken first papers to become a naturalized American citizen. Austria claimed him for military service. Ingraham, commanding an American ship, threatened to open fire on an Austrian brig unless he were given up. For Douglas' comment, see Cincinnati *Gazette*, *supra*, and 'Occasional,' Philadelphia *Press*, July 4, 1859.

[36] Linder, *loc. cit.*, 79, *et seq.*; George Murray McConnel, Illinois State Historical Society, *Transactions*, Springfield, 1901; 48; Sheahan, 444–45; Stevens, 639. 'That was a proud day for our country,' Douglas later told a friend. 'I was never vain enough to appropriate it to myself. When the little man in black was given the place of honor, it was a stroke of policy on the part of Nicholas.'

This was not the Senator's only court presentation. Visiting France, on his way back to America, he was presented at St. Cloud, to Louis Napoleon and Eugénie, who received him with 'marked distinction.' During the interview the Empress undertook to rebuke America's anxiety to acquire Cuba. 'Were I Queen of Spain,' she said spiritedly, 'I would spend the last coin and shed the last drop of Spanish blood before the United States should have even a foothold on that island.' The Senator bowed very low and answered: 'Madam, were you the Queen of Spain, it would not be necessary to spend money or shed blood, as love would keep all your subjects loyal.' Eugénie's beautiful face broke into a smile and the retort courteous was the talk of the court.[37]

These glimpses of the personality, traits and interests of Stephen A. Douglas are persuasive that he was the sort of man any of us would delight to have had the opportunity to know. Able, courageous, captivating in company, he was staunchly loyal as a friend. Yet neither his opportunistic genius nor his ability as a public speaker, nor his persuasiveness in court or Congress, chiefly distinguished him from the other politicians of his day and generation. More than all these, Douglas illustrates again that most satisfying of all human capabilities, the capacity of a man to have an organic growth of character.

In his first decade in Illinois he was little more than a bright and pleasant fellow who had learned the trick of getting on in the world. In Washington he felt the impact of mighty issues, the engaging politician grew under pressure and became a far-seeing, patriotic statesman. In the end Douglas employed his matchless talents for the glory of the Nation which gave him birth and the preservation of the Union that he loved. This change from attractive smallness to real nobility of conduct chiefly interests one in the Little Giant. This quality gave him dominance in the twilight years, and still makes him memorable in our history.

[37] Cincinnati *Enquirer*, Dec. 2, 1853, printing Paris Correspondence, dated Nov. 10; Donn Piatt, Paris, Nov. 28, 1853, Douglas MSS., admitted his authorship of the article, adding: 'If we cannot have officials to represent us as we are, it is well a Democrat gets abroad now and then.' Cf. also August Belmont, The Hague, Nov. 15, 1853; Douglas MSS. Cincinnati *Gazette*, *cit. supra*. Cincinnati *Commercial*, Dec. 22, 1870, gives Edwards Pierrepont's account of Douglas' interview with Eugénie. Douglas left Liverpool, Oct. 19, 1853, on the steamer *Arctic*, for New York.

CHAPTER II

THE PRAIRIE POLITICIAN

THERE was little hint of promised greatness in Stephen A. Douglas' immediate antecedents. His paternal grandfather, Benajah Douglas, was a Vermont farmer of some little substance; his large head and body and short limbs were doubtless the source of the grandson's physical characteristics. Benajah's son, the first Stephen Arnold, began practice of medicine in Brandon about 1810, soon thereafter marrying Sarah Fiske, a woman of courage and character.[1]

The young doctor and his bride established themselves in a little cottage in the village. On April 23, 1813, their second child, a fourteen-pound son was born; to him they gave the father's name. A few weeks later, as Dr. Douglas was sitting in his chair before the fire and fondling the babe, he suffered a sudden heart attack and dropped over dead. The infant rolled from his lap but a neighbor snatched him from the flames.[2]

The widow Douglas soon moved with her small daughter and infant son to the near-by farm of her bachelor brother, Edward Fiske. From the Fiske homestead Stephen could look over broad plains to Lakes George and Champlain, where the Revolutionary patriots had battled with the British, with Fort Ticonderoga in the background. There is no record as to what thoughts this historic vista inspired in the youngster's mind, but he was taught to welcome honest toil, and was equally ready to pitch hay into the loft, to go fishing with a pin hook or to play one-eyed cat.

The district school which he attended had but a three-months term; even so, the boy was reported 'the best scholar in his classes.' After a few years the bachelor uncle married, began to raise a family of his own, and grew colder to young Stephen's pleas for an expensive education.

Thereupon the impetuous lad undertook to make his own way in the world, apprenticing himself to Nahum Parker, a cabinet-maker in near-by Middlebury. There he learned to saw table legs from two-inch planks and many are the antiques which today are claimed to have been fashioned by his hands.

[1] Sheahan, 2; Allen Johnson, *Life of Stephen A. Douglas*, New York, 1908; 4; *Vermont Historical Gazette*, III, 457. The parents spelled the name Douglass, as did Stephen until about 1840, but for the sake of simplicity I am using the single *s* throughout. Mr. Wilder Foote, of the Brandon *Union*, has found for me that Benajah's estate was appraised at $4447.57.

[2] The Douglas birthplace, now maintained as a patriotic shrine by the Lake Dunmore Chapter of the Daughters of the American Revolution, is changed somewhat in its architecture from its original condition. I am indebted to Mr. Edward S. Marsh, the historian of Brandon, for many details concerning it. Stevens, 257, cites statement of Ann DeForest, the nurse at Douglas' birth, for his weight. Dr. Douglas died July 3, 1813; the neighbor who rescued young Stephen from the fire was John Conant, who entered the door just as the babe rolled from the physician's lap. Dr. Conant Wait, letter to author, Los Angeles, Cal., May 12, 1931, gives Conant family records on the incident.

The shop was also the scene of vigorous political argumentation between the master, a conservative Whig, and his mischievous young apprentices. At the time John Quincy Adams and his alleged 'corrupt bargain' with Henry Clay were greatly in the public mind, and these cabinet-shop debates fixed Douglas' politics; ever after Old Hickory was his idol and his star.[3]

In 1830 Stephen's mother remarried and the family moved to Clifton Springs, Ontario County, New York. Their circumstances were much bettered, for the Grangers were a family of some distinction and one cousin, in near-by Canandaigua, was a veritable seigneur. Entered in the Canandaigua Academy, a school of admirable parts, young Stephen soon made himself an excellent Latin scholar, showed proficiency in 'logic and abstruse mathematics' and became a voracious reader. He was always defending Old Hickory in the Academy debates. His affirmative that Andrew Jackson was a greater soldier, statesman and hero than Napoleon Bonaparte, seemed to the judges 'so eloquent, so fanciful, so captivating' that, although they were ingrained Whigs, they gave Douglas the prize.

In addition he became a student clerk in Walter Hubbell's law office. The training was more than legal; to be a hospitable gentleman and to interlard a conversation with wisdom, wit and repartee were equally necessary. Every so often the oldsters held dinners at which they quizzed each other's clerks on Greek, Latin, mathematics and philosophy as well as on Chitty, Blackstone and Coke. These professional activities were interspersed with gay parties and the lad was said to have been 'literally a pet of the petticoats.'[4]

But he was restless and ambitious, the stories which came back from the West set him on fire and he tried to persuade an uncle to move to the prairies. Soon he could be restrained no longer, and on the morning of June 24, 1832, set forth by himself. 'When will we see you again?' his mother asked as he departed on the stage-coach. 'I will stop by and see you on my way to Congress within the next ten years,' was his proud and confident reply.

[3] Stephen A. Douglas, 'Autobiography,' 58. The original MS. of this document, which was written about 1839, is now in possession of Mr. M. F. Douglas. A correct text was published in a Douglas memorial volume, Brandon, 1913. My references are to page number in the memorial volume. The Little Giant was bitter about his uncle's refusal. Stevens, 259, 262; Johnson, 8; Sheahan, 4, for apprenticeship episodes.

[4] The family shift was the unique one of a mother and daughter marrying a father and son. On Feb. 13, 1830, Sarah Douglas married Julius Granger; on Nov. 27, following, Mrs. Douglas married Gehazi Granger. Their new home at Clifton Springs was a place of considerable comfort. At Canandaigua, Gideon Granger, Gehazi's second cousin, had a château with courtyard, porter's lodges, and a library of more than a thousand volumes. In 1831, Henry Howe was superintendent of the Canandaigua Academy. Six years later Douglas wrote him to acknowledge 'that he is indebted to your instructions, your counsels and advice more than anything else for what little success he may have had in his outset in life.' Douglas to Henry Howe, Jacksonville, Ill., Jan. 14, 1836, letter owned by D. L. Mason Clarke, Dorset, Vt. Mr. Charles F. Milligan, of Canandaigua, has kindly furnished me a copy. For Academy and law clerk details see James G. Paine to John Wentworth, Denver, Col., May 1, 1881, printed in Chicago Tribune, May 13, 1882. 'Autobiography,' 65, lists Douglas' reading. Among the leaders of the Canandaigua bar were: John Greig, Judge Nat Howell, Harrod Wilson, Mark H. Sibley, John C. Spencer and Walter Hubbell. For debates see Paine, loc. cit., and Stevens, 265–66.

This journey had a somewhat ludicrous beginning. At an early stop he ate a currant pie, the handiwork of a girl he knew. But it seemed as if she 'had baked the pie before it was done rising. At least it kept rising after I ate it, so that the first time I opened my mouth it leaped out.' With this, vomiting became the 'business of the day,' and by the time the stage reached Buffalo the passengers all said 'that I had puked so much there was nothing left of me but my hat and my boots.'

Recovering, he went on to Cleveland, Ohio, where he secured a place as a student law clerk, but in a week or so was stricken with bilious fever. Soon his physicians abandoned hope. He himself felt that he was on 'the dividing line between this world and the next, must continue to exist in the one or the other, was willing to take either and felt no choice which.'[5] The lad's sturdy constitution, however, brought him through the crisis, a providential check from home enabled him to pay his debts and with thirty dollars in his pocket he set forth for the West.

Young Douglas could find a lawyer's clerkship neither in Cincinnati, Louisville nor St. Louis; in the latter place his money was almost gone, something had to be done, and that at once. As in those days teaching was the temporary recourse 'of four-fifths of the educated and nearly an equal number of the uneducated young men who came West,' it was not strange that Douglas determined to seek some small hamlet where he could get up a school and sustain himself through the Winter. Accordingly he made his way *via* the Illinois River to Jacksonville, Illinois, but no school was available there. Selling some schoolbooks for a little cash, he pushed on into the country and one November night came into the little town of Winchester with only three bits in his pocket. But there he made friends with Edward Miner, a fellow Vermonter who was running a store; next he earned $2.50 as clerk at an auction sale; soon his new friends helped him secure forty pupils, at $3.00 each, and he began his school.[6]

By the time Douglas had been in Winchester a week he wrote home that

[5] Beriah Douglas to Stephen A. Douglas, Albany, N.Y., June 10, 1832; M. F. Douglas MSS. He sent Stephen $170 for the journey. Eugene F. Hoyt, Savona, N.Y., April 25, 1931, giving me a story of Douglas' parting with his mother. Mr. Hoyt is a grandson of Sarah Granger. For trip details, Douglas to Julius N. Granger, Cleveland, Ohio, Aug. 6, 1833, M. F. Douglas MSS.; 'Autobiography,' 61–62.

[6] Stevens, 269–70; 'Autobiography,' 61; Sheahan, 8; Douglas to Granger, Winchester, Ill., Dec. 15, 1833; M. F. Douglas MSS., for recovery from sickness and journey to St. Louis. Miss Ainslee Moore, of Jacksonville, Ill., has kindly furnished me with a letter of Lila Chapman to Ensley Moore, Dec. 8, 1922, giving details of Douglas' first arrival at Jacksonville as related by her grandfather Robert Goudy. Joseph Wallace, *Illinois State Register*, April 19, 1885, tells of Murray McConnel's advice to Douglas to push on to Pekin. Winchester, Ill., *Times*, Jan. 22, 1909; July 4, 11, 1930, discuss Douglas' entry into Winchester. Douglas to Granger, Winchester, Ill., Dec. 15, 1833, *cit. supra*. 'Autobiography,' 64; Stevens, 273; Fritz Haskell, *Winchester Centennial Souvenir*, Winchester, 1930; 7–11; E. G. Miner, Winchester, Ill., Jan. 14, 1877, quoted *Proceedings*, Illinois Association Sons of Vermont, Chicago, 1877, 11–12, gives light on the getting up of the school. Joseph Wallace, *Illinois State Register*, Springfield, April 30, 1899, Stevens, 273–74, and Miner, *loc. cit.* for auction. The records of the administration of the estate of Elihu Martin show that Douglas was allowed $2.50, but had bought items totaling $1.76, including three linen collars at 18 cents each, nine magazines at 40 cents and a lot of old newspapers at 14 cents. Mr. Frank J. Heinl, of Jacksonville, and officials of Morgan County, aided in the inspection of these records.

already he had become 'a Western man, with Western feelings, principles and interests,' and had selected Illinois for his home. He spent his spare time 'either mingling with the people and forming acquaintances, or petti-fogging in the Justice court.' Through this technique he became 'popular among the Suckers' — as the inhabitants of Illinois, 'the Sucker State,' had dubbed themselves — and had money enough to pay his expenses and purchase a small library. That winter a lyceum was organized there. At one weekly meeting Douglas answered effectively an attack Josiah Lamborn, a Jacksonville lawyer and 'the greatest master of invective' in the region, made on Andrew Jackson; thereby the schoolmaster's prestige grew.

But Douglas' mind was still fixed on the law and he looked on Winchester as merely a good place where he could 'live cheap this Winter, do business enough to bear my expenses and pursue my studies until Spring.'[7] Miner tried to get him into Lamborn's law office but the latter refused, because the boy didn't 'know enough law to write out a declaration.' Naught daunted, the youngster applied to Judge Lockwood for examination for a law license, and as soon as he finished giving the term of school, packed up his grips and went to Jacksonville. The Judge agreed to give him a certificate but warned that 'he must apply himself closer to the study of the law.' The license, however, was enough. The new lawyer, still lacking six weeks of his majority, rented an office in the Morgan County Court House and hung his sign upon its wall.[8]

The beginning advocate was so pleased with this new home that he pressed his family to join him there. 'You can let out your money here to good advantage in almost any kind of business,' he wrote seductively; expenses run little more than a dollar a day, 'equality and equal rights prevail and no man acknowledges another his superior.' In these days in Jacksonville he went through the usual vicissitudes of early love affairs, but seemed to escape dangerous entanglements and all the while increased his popularity with the people.[9] And yet, while Jacksonville might have been 'the finest village in the State,' the eleven lawyers then at the Morgan County bar well absorbed all available law business. But if there were no law cases, there was always politics, and Douglas 'started at once for the Presidency of the United States.' In almost no time he 'doffed his Eastern dress and manners, and assumed a suit of Kentucky jeans,' together with a colorful frontier vocabulary. Before long he 'hobnobbed with the Border Democracy like one to the manner born.'[10]

[7] Douglas to Granger, Winchester, Dec. 18, 1835; Jacksonville, March 11, 1834; M. F. Douglas MSS.

[8] For application for law license, Miner, *loc. cit.*; Douglas to Granger, Jacksonville, March 11, 1834; M. F. Douglas MSS.; Johnson, 17; 'Autobiography,' 65; Sheahan, 16 *et seq.*; Stevens, 280.

[9] Douglas to Granger, Winchester, Dec. 15, 1833, Jacksonville, July 18, Nov. 14, 1834; July 24, Nov. 9, 1835; M. F. Douglas MSS. Jacksonville *Journal*, Oct. 17, 1931, gives incidents of his life and courtships there. Mrs. Margaret G. Devine, Altantic City, N.J., Jan. 10, 1932, has given me data concerning other episodes. Among girls Douglas went with were Mary Stice, 'the lily of the West,' and Margaret McMackin.

[10] Daniel Roberts, 'Recollections,' *Harper's Monthly Magazine*, LXXXVII, 957–58; Robert Roberts, Esq., of Burlington, Vt., has kindly furnished a confirming memorandum found in his

Douglas thought this new country the 'paradise of the world' but its frontier days were not far removed. At the time of his advent, 'the butcher knife boys' were still in prominence and the red-fringed hunting-shirt was only beginning to give way to the cloth coat, and boots to take the place of moccasins. Hunting and trapping were just being replaced by grain farming as the people's chief means of livelihood, the humble pig was present everywhere and land speculation was the order of the day.[11]

Politically the division was between the friends and enemies of Andrew Jackson. The repercussions of the struggle between the President and 'Emperor Biddle' were acutely felt, the 'Reign of Terror of the Bank' had depressed the county's Democrats and Jackson partisans were in despair. But Douglas soon set to work to reorganize the party structure, his first step being a county-wide mass meeting. This the opposition tried to capture, and Lamborn delivered a terrific tirade against Old Hickory as the author of the Nation's woes.

When Douglas jumped to his feet to repel these charges, the crowd responded with growing enthusiasm to his denunciation of Biddle and the Whigs. 'Give it to him!' shouted one delighted farmer. 'Go it, little game cock!' another called out. They howled down Lamborn's attempt to answer, hoisted the diminutive Democrat on their shoulders and paraded around the public square terming him their 'high-combed cock,' their 'Little Giant' and displaying him to a delighted populace.[12]

This incident, in addition to equipping Douglas with a lasting sobriquet, nerved the Jacksonians of the region to tremendous efforts to counteract 'the Distress, Pressure and Panic.' As a result they triumphed at the ballot box, both in Morgan County and over the whole State. But treachery was afoot, all but one of Morgan's Democratic House delegation succumbed to pressure and the Whigs jubilated 'that the Jackson party was used up.' Next they undertook to keep the upstart Douglas from getting any law cases and thus to starve him out. His answer was 'to carry the war into Africa, as of old.' He undertook to have the next Legislature repeal out of office John J. Hardin, the Whig State's Attorney, taking the place for himself.

Captain Jack Wyatt, the one faithful Democratic Representative, took to the idea and Douglas went with him to Vandalia to put the project through. The Captain was a huge man; ribald solons termed his diminutive candidate 'Jack Wyatt's tomtit,' but after a prolonged struggle the repealer became a law and Douglas was chosen for the vacated post. 'What business has such a stripling with such an office?' complained the Whig Judge who had given

father's papers. S. J. Clarke, *History of McDonough County, Illinois*, Chicago, 1878; 49. This frontier language has much of it remained in the American vulgate to this day. Because the fat of the opossum was the most fluid of oils known in Illinois, a slippery politician was said to carry a gourd of 'possum fat' with which he 'greased' the people. A victim of such artifice was said to have been 'swollered' and anyone who let himself be a tool in another's hands was 'used up' — that is to say, he had been used like soft soap until there was nothing left of him.

[11] J. M. Peck, *Gazetteer of Illinois*, Jacksonville, 1834; 21–47.

[12] Joseph Wallace, *Illinois State Register*, April 30, 1899; Douglas to Granger, Jacksonville, May 9, 1835; M. F. Douglas MSS.; 'Autobiography,' 65 *et seq.*; Stevens, 284; Winchester *Times*, July 11, 1930.

Douglas his license. 'He is no lawyer and has no law books.' But the new official wrote home that, thanks to 'the Lord, the Legislature, and General Jackson,' he was doing as well in his profession 'as could be expected of a boy of twenty-one.' [13]

One bright Sunday morning in February, 1833, the new State's Attorney, on a borrowed horse with a borrowed book on criminal law, set out for Springfield to assume the duties of his circuit. 'I find myself in a new theater of action and I may say a very important and critical one,' he wrote his brother-in-law, 'but I think I shall be able to give general satisfaction.'

His first real test came at Bloomington, when Major John T. Stuart, an opposing lawyer, moved with offensive sarcasm to quash the indictments Douglas had drafted, on the ground that the name M'Lean County had been written out MClean and there was no such place. The courtroom rocked with laughter and Douglas' heart sank within him, but he demanded that his antagonist procure the official act printing the statute creating the county, to see whether or not his indictment was in fact mistaken. A few days later Stuart's messenger returned with the volume of printed statutes. To everyone's amazement it read 'McClean.' Douglas thenceforth adopted as a rule of action: 'Admit nothing and require my adversary to prove everything.' [14]

His chief upsets as State's Attorney arose from his carelessness, but his quickness of wit generally repaired the damage. The offenses for which he must prosecute were those of a frontier environment: gambling, and open saloons on Sunday and assaults and batteries with such varied weapons as butcher knives and fence-rails. It was a world of rough and tumble, Douglas encountered some threats from evil-doers but went 'prepared' for such animals 'in real Kaintuck style.' [15]

Soon the young attorney was a candidate for the Legislature, 'found no difficulty in adopting the Western mode of electioneering or addressing the people from the stump,' and welcomed the combat, 'the warmer the better, for I like excitement.' In the outcome he led the ticket. [16]

[13] Douglas to Granger, Jacksonville, May 9, 1833, Sept. 1, 1834, Feb. 22, 1835; Douglas to Henry Howe, Jacksonville, Jan. 14, 1836; M. F. Douglas MSS.; 'Autobiography,' 66 et seq. Daniel Roberts, loc. cit.; Stevens, 290; Johnson, 22; Douglas to Granger, Jacksonville, Feb. 22, 1833, May 9, 1835; M. F. Douglas MSS.

[14] Roberts, loc. cit.; Douglas to Granger, Jacksonville, Feb. 22, April 25, 1835; M. F. Douglas MSS.; 'Autobiography,' 69-70.

[15] Isaac Arnold, Early Chicago and Illinois Bar, Chicago, 1880; 12; Morgan County Court House Records, Supreme Criminal File No. 0031A; Thos. Ford, History of Illinois, Chicago, 1854; 83 et seq.; Stevens, 292, for threats and Douglas' attitude. Douglas to Granger, Jacksonville, Jan. 7, 1835 (misprint for 1836); M. F. Douglas MSS.

[16] Sangamo Journal, Springfield, May 7, 1836; Stevens, 296; Douglas to Gehazi Granger, Jacksonville, Feb. 28, 1836; Douglas to J. H. Granger, Jacksonville, Feb. 28, 1836; M. F. Douglas MSS. Only one Whig was elected from Morgan County, this being the same John J. Hardin Douglas had ousted as State's Attorney. The canvass partook of the characteristics of the era; apparently an inescapable element of campaigning was to 'treat' all the voters, the liquor flowed freely, and after the voters had imbibed, then the candidate would mount a wagon or a newly cut stump to make his appeal. Generally such a meeting wound up with the Suckers throwing caps in air and screeching like infernal spirits.

DOUGLAS BEFORE HE WENT WEST

While the Legislature which met at Vandalia, December, 1836, contained many men destined to be prominent, its sessions were chiefly taken up with political feuds and with internal improvement legislation.[17] The pressure for public credit for wild bank, canal and railroad schemes was overwhelming, land speculation ran riot, new towns were springing up like mushrooms, 'the State was mad and the Legislature went mad with it.' Douglas fell in with the spirit of the times, although he did try to check its worst excesses.

Much of this jobbery was linked with Springfield's campaign to have the State Capital moved there, and this was accomplished by such barefaced log-rolling that it was estimated that the shift really cost Illinois $6,000,000. Abraham Lincoln and the others of the 'Long Nine,' as the delegation from Sangamon County was known, 'threw itself as a unit' into these Springfield maneuvers. Douglas, from near-by Morgan, voted for the change.

He took another step up the political ladder when he was named Register of the Federal Land Office at Springfield. The Whig organ there commented sarcastically that 'the *little man* from Morgan was perfectly astonished at finding himself making money at the rate of from $100 to $200 a day.'

Such prosperity, however, was short-lived, for the panic followed the boom and in a few months Illinois' house of cards collapsed. There were immediate ideas of repudiation of the State debt. This Douglas opposed, in one speech saying that 'the State should be honest if it never paid a cent.' Due to his and others' efforts the Democratic party was pulled out of the hole and once more carried the State.[18]

By this time Douglas was ready to go forward again, the proper wires were pulled and he became the Democratic nominee for Congress. 'Ask Mother what she would think if the people of Illinois should be so foolish as to send her prodigal son to Congress,' he wrote the home-folks; the people were thinking of doing so 'just for the fun of the thing.'

Many were the personal problems confronting candidates 'in beating up for votes.' Douglas' own technique was simple; 'I live with my constituents, eat with my constituents, drink with them, lodge with them, pray with them, laugh, hunt, dance and work with them; I eat their corn dodgers and fried bacon and sleep two in a bed with them.' One night he had to put up at a cabin with only one room. The jewel of his host's family was Serena, 'seventeen, plump as a pigeon and smooth as a persimmon.' The hour wore late but the young lady would not heed Douglas' hints that she retire

[17] Among the members were E. D. Baker, later Congressman, officer in Mexican and Civil wars, and only Senator killed in the latter conflict; Jesse K. Dubois; Ninian W. Edwards; Augustus C. French, a future Governor; John A. Logan, a future Representative, General and Senator; John A. McClernand, also to be a Congressman and General; James Shields, General in two wars and Senator from three States; William A. Richardson, future Speaker of the National House, and Abraham Lincoln, destined to be President of the United States.

[18] *Illinois State Register*, Vandalia, Dec. 12, 29, 1836; March 1, 1837; Ford, 169 *et seq.*; Davidson and Stuvé, *History of Illinois*, Springfield, 1873; 434 *et seq.*; Sheahan, 27 *et seq.* Douglas became Register of the Land Office on March 10, 1837. Sangamo *Journal's* comment, April 15, 1837. For panic, Sheahan, 33; Davidson and Stuvé, 432-41; *Illinois State Register*, Vandalia, Oct. 27, Nov. 4, 1837.

while he undressed. Finally in desperation he disrobed; she watched the process with fascinated eyes, and at its conclusion observed: 'Mr. Douglas, you *have* got a mighty small chance of legs there.' [19]

The nominee's campaign funds were so slight that he could not insure himself 'a proper degree of personal comfort,' but for funds he substituted hard work and personal charm. Campaign issues were few in number, and wit and drollery were the chief weapons he used against his Whig opponent, the same Major Stuart who had sought to humiliate him at Bloomington. The Major was termed 'the handsomest man in Illinois' and was a stout campaigner.

The district was full of Irish immigrants working on the Illinois and Michigan Canal. Stuart told them he was a Scotch immigrant, with a family kinship to the Irish. But Douglas portrayed himself as a real Irishman, descended from the McDouglases, and made such progress that Stuart accepted a challenge, earlier refused, for joint debate. The two canvassed the district together, becoming so unfriendly that on the eve of the election they 'fought like tigers' in a Springfield barroom.[20]

But for a trick the Little Giant would have won the election. In one county the Whigs substituted the name A. T. Douglas for S. A. Douglas on the poll books, in another they listed him as a candidate for the Legislature and not Congress, and in many other counties the Irish canal-builders could not spell his name and their votes were thrown out. As finally certified Stuart nosed him out by thirty-six votes in a total of 36,495 votes cast.[21]

'Mr. Douglas was elected by the people,' the *Illinois State Register* proclaimed; indeed, the evidence of fraud was such that the Little Giant began gathering data for a contest. But the cost was great, Stuart rejected all proposals of recount or new election and Douglas finally abandoned the idea. His prestige, however, was really enhanced by 'Stuart's steal.' [22]

Douglas now turned to the law again and for the next two years was busy finding clients, trying cases and preparing to renew his political career. Again his personal charm was most useful. He could always recognize old acquaintances, no matter how humble, by their proper names, and made

[19] *Weekly American Eagle*, Memphis, Tenn., Feb. 28, 1845, clipping 'Judge Douglas in Illinois,' correspondence of the New York *Evening Mirror*. Douglas insisted that 'there is not in Illinois a more modest or more sensible girl than Serena. It's habit, all habit. I think nothing of it now. Why, it's only last week I was at a fine wedding party, and a large and fine assembly of both sexes lodged in the same room, with only three feet or so of neutral territory between them.'

[20] *Illinois State Register*, Springfield, Oct. 13, 27, Nov. 4, Dec. 9, 1837; May 11, 1838; *Sangamo Journal*, Nov. 25, 1837; Johnson, 38–41; Douglas to Granger, Springfield, Dec. 18, 1837; M. F. Douglas MSS. *Missouri Republican*, St. Louis, Jan. 28, 1862; quoting Wentworth; Stevens, 315 *et seq.*; John M. Palmer, *Personal Recollections*, Cincinnati, Ohio, 1901; 24; Sheahan, 36–37; Ward H. Lamon, *Abraham Lincoln*, Boston, 1872; 230; Usher F. Linder, *Reminiscences*, Chicago, 1879; 348.

[21] *Illinois State Register*, Aug. 10, Sept. 28, 1838; Oct. 7, 1842; Sheahan, 37 *et seq.*; Linder, 347.

[22] Douglas to F. E. Blair, Springfield, Ill., Nov. 2, 1838, Historical Society of Pennsylvania MSS.; Benton to Douglas, St. Louis, Oct. 27, 1838; M. F. Douglas MSS.; Stevens, 320; Joseph Wallace, *Illinois State Register*, April, 1885.

even his humblest followers feel that 'he was the frank and personal friend of each.' His court presentation was bold and determined, but the most remarkable of his legal gifts was a 'wonderful faculty for extracting from his associates, from experts and others, by conversation, all they knew of a subject he was to discuss, and then making it so thoroughly his that all seemed to have originated with him.' He carefully prepared the cases he carried to the State Supreme Court, won ten of the thirteen, and it began to be said that 'in a bad case Douglas was the best lawyer Illinois ever produced.' [23]

He was also interested by Springfield's society, with its fifty 'really splendid carriages' and its fashionably dressed fair sex. His carelessness of dress began to disappear and his good humor and charm made him a general favorite. Joining the Masons in 1840, he soon became Junior Warden in Springfield Lodge No. 4. Becoming quite expert at little attentions to the ladies, he would sit on a red piano stool laughing quite as merrily as the girls, giving back jest for jest, never losing his temper and always master of the play of wit. It was no uncommon sight to find him surrounded by a bevy of girls and he paid marked attention to Sarah Dunlap, Julia Jayne and Mary Todd.[24]

An entrancing legend has grown up about his relations with the latter, chiefly because the spirited Kentucky belle later married Abraham Lincoln. The conventional story is that it was her ambition to marry a future President, and as early as 1840 she could see that Lincoln would win the White House, Douglas would fail and therefore refused the Little Giant.

The truth is that Douglas liked Mary but just as he did Sarah Dunlap, Julia Jayne and others. In the Summer of 1840, when Mary was in Missouri on a visit, she wrote a friend at Springfield that she thought he had forgotten her. A few months later he disclosed that his family back in

[23] For cases in 1839, see 'The Dockett of S. A. Douglas,' a little leather-bound book listing 64 cases in Sangamon and many in other counties, with charges against his clients and notes of the fees he had charged. It is now in the possession of Mr. Martin F. Douglas. His Springfield partner was John D. Urquhart, a Virginian, 'a gentleman of the old school, with too much refinement to adapt himself to Western methods.' This partnership was dissolved in October, 1839. *Illinois State Register*, Springfield, Oct. 26, 1839; *History of Sangamon County*, Chicago, 1881; 98; O. H. Browning to I. N. Arnald, Quincy, Ill., Sept. 15, 1880; Chicago Historical Society MSS. For Douglas' memory of names and faces see McConnel, *op. cit.*, 41–42; James Johnson, El Dorado, Cal., Jan. 18, 1859, Douglas MSS., enclosing a series of articles signed 'Fulton,' in El Dorado *Index*, describing Douglas' early years. Palmer, 30–31; Arnold, 146; Douglas' argument in Daniel Brainerd *vs.* Canal Trustees, 12 Illinois, 488, Arnold termed 'one of the ablest arguments I ever heard at any bar.'

[24] W. A. Lanphier to Mrs. Martha R. Ditty, Upper Alton, Ill., Sept. 28, 1838; Milton H. Wash, Springfield, Ill., May 6, 1839; Patton MSS. *Illinois State Register*, Springfield, Sept. 30, 1842; for Springfield society, Stevens, 323; McConnel, 45. I am indebted to the late Thomas Rees and Mr. J. B. Hildebrand for a copy of Douglas' Masonic application, dated June 11, 1840. He was passed June 24, became a Master Mason June 26, securing the Mark degree in Springfield, the Past Most Excellent and Royal Arch Degree in Quincy. *Illinois State Register*, Oct. 30, 1840, states that he was elected Grand Orator of the Grand Lodge, but could not attend. He seems to have attended Lodge meetings regularly at Springfield, Quincy and elsewhere on his judicial circuit. In 1849, when the Grand Lodge met in Chicago, Douglas, General James A. Shields and 'Long John' Wentworth attended its meetings every day.

New York remained 'the only persons on earth to whom I feel any peculiar attachment.' [25]

But neither law nor society could keep Douglas away from politics. The essence of the Illinois problem was financial. Ruin and dishonor impended and the surprised people of Illinois, astounded at their folly, looked about for a scapegoat. In the Spring of 1840, however, Douglas became chairman of the Democratic State Committee and undertook to organize and campaign Illinois so as to avert defeat. The Democrats were quite successful in shifting the issue from internal improvement to the alleged Whig bias of their Supreme Court. One or two apparently political decisions enabled their stumpers to rouse voters against 'life tenures for Whigs.' And so, despite the landslide to 'Tippecanoe and Tyler too,' Illinois went for Martin Van Buren and elected a Democratic legislature.

A first fruit of victory was Douglas' appointment as Secretary of State. On the heels of this, the Legislature added five new justices to the Supreme Court and Douglas was made one of the five.[26]

Only twenty-seven years of age, Douglas was the youngest Supreme Court member Illinois had had before — or has had since. His friends feared and his enemies expected that he would not make good and he himself was not in any too happy frame of mind. 'Office and honors have lost their charm,' he wrote home; he had so neglected his financial affairs that 'whatever of character and of fame I may have acquired are all I have left.' But with this change to a new theater of action he expected for the next few years 'to devote all the energies of my mind to my judicial duties and my private affairs.' [27]

For all these gloomy forebodings 'the baby Judge' made an excellent record on the bench. He retained his free and easy manner and visitors from the East were astounded to see him leave the bench during a trial and

[25] Stevens, 323: Douglas 'did not solicit the hand of Miss Todd in marriage.' Carlos W. Goltz, *Incidents in the Life of Mary Todd Lincoln*, Sioux City, Iowa, 1928; 13 *et seq.*, gives this episode, which he had second hand: One day when Mary was winding a wreath of roses, Douglas asked her to go with him for a dish of ice cream. 'I will come if you will wear this wreath of roses upon your head,' she answered, and the Little Giant took the dare. For Mary Todd's wanting to marry a future president, see Ward H. Lamon copy, Herndon Papers, 223, Huntington Library, San Marino, Cal., giving statement by Mrs. Ninian Edwards, Mary's sister, to Herndon; Mrs. Edwards also stated that Mary 'had gone with Mr. Douglas to several places; they were very well acquainted and were good friends.' *Ibid.*, 220, has J. F. Speed, of Louisville, saying that 'she refused Douglas on the grounds of his bad morals.' H. E. Barker, *Mary Todd*, Springfield, 1917; 4. These items were furnished by Dr. W. A. Evans, of Chicago. Mary's own letters were written between July, 1840, and June, 1841, from Columbia, Mo., to her friend Mercy Levering. That of July 23, 1840, intimated that, as to Douglas, '*There* I had deemed myself forgotten.' None of the other Levering letters mention Douglas at all. For these I am indebted to Mr. Paul M. Angle. For Douglas' own attitude, see his letter to Julius Granger, Springfield, April 2, 1841; M. F. Douglas MSS.

[26] Ford, 192, *et seq.*; Davidson and Stuvé, 445–49, for State debt problems. Two main charges were brought against the court; the case of the Secretary of State, and that as to voting rights of unnaturalized aliens. Stevens, 329–30; *Illinois State Register*, Nov. 13, 1840; Feb. 26, 1841.

[27] Chicago *American*, Feb. 18, 1841; Douglas to Granger, Lewiston, Ill., April 1, 1841; M. F. Douglas MSS.

take a seat on the knee of a friend. But while unconventional in his conduct, he was so expeditious in handling cases that the leisurely lawyers called him 'a perfect "steam engine in britches."' In every county on his circuit cases which had lingered for years were either tried or dismissed.

He did his full share of the decision work of the court *en banc*, taking exchange assignments to other circuits where, despite an initial adverse opinion, his grasp of legal questions soon conquered the admiration of the bar. 'I thought I could handle him,' exclaimed Justin Butterfield, greatest Whig and cynic of the Chicago bar, 'but damn that little squatty Democrat — he is the very best and most acute Judge in all this Democratic State. He listens patiently, comprehends the law and grasps the facts by intuition; then decides calmly, clearly and quietly and then makes the lawyers sit down. Douglas is the ablest man on the bench today in Illinois.' [28]

His circuit was in the west of the State, he established his home in Quincy and there made hundreds of enduring friends. His chief problem, political as well as legal, was the treatment of the thousands of disciples of the Church of Latter Day Saints, concentrated in that neighborhood. The worship and the wanderings of the Mormons between New York, Ohio and Missouri do not belong to this narrative. In 1839, when they fled Missouri and found asylum in Illinois, Joseph Smith — 'The Prophet of the Lord' — set them to building a fine city, which they called Nauvoo. The Illinois politicians, both Whig and Democrat, fell over themselves giving special favors in an effort to line up these new voters. Soon Nauvoo secured an extraordinary city charter from the Legislature, under which it set up its own militia, its own judges and courts and became almost a separate principality. But the Mormons' religion, their system of plural wives and other differences from the accepted social patterns embittered the old inhabitants, isolated crimes occurred on both sides and in two years' time the Saints and the Gentiles were at daggers' points.

Like the other politicians, Douglas was not above courting the Mormon vote. One of the Saints' General Orders testified their admiration for the 'able and profound jurist, politician and statesman.' Before long an old unexecuted Missouri warrant against the Prophet was returned before the Judge. Irate Gentiles packed his courtroom, summary vengeance was about to be executed on Smith's body, and the sheriff, a timid soul, quailed. Judge Douglas, however, took command of the situation and averted the threatened lynching. That Fall the Mormons voted for the Democratic nominees. A little later Joseph Smith told Douglas of the vicissitudes of the Saints, then warning him: 'Judge, you will aspire to the Presidency of the United States. If you ever turn your hand against me or the Latter Day Saints you will feel the weight of the hand of the Almighty upon you.' [29]

[28] Arnold, 145; *Law Reporter*, Boston, 1842; IV; Douglas to James Shields, Lewiston, Ill., April 2, 1841, Illinois State Historical Library MSS.; Quincy *Argus*, April 24, 1841; Quincy *Whig*, May 1, 1841. Stevens, 343–49; Chicago *Democrat*, quoted *Illinois State Register*, May 14, 1841; *Missouri Republican*, St. Louis, Jan. 28, 1862.

[29] For data on Douglas' relations with the Mormons I am indebted to the Historian of the Church of Latter Day Saints, at Salt Lake City, who has furnished me illuminating extracts

After Douglas went to Washington the Saints' quest for special privileges was unending. Joseph Smith announced his candidacy for the Presidency, and the Gentiles got the idea that there was a plot against the State. A body of masked men murdered the prophet and his brother, and the Gentiles announced 'a great wolf hunt.' The Governor called out the militia, and sent Douglas to Nauvoo to urge the Mormons to seek a new home outside the State. Brigham Young, the new head of the Church, agreed to move to 'some point so remote' that no difficulty could occur. Finally, in 1846 the main body of the Saints undertook their tragic march across the plains to Lake Deseret.[30]

When the 1842 election yielded a strong Democratic majority in the Illinois Legislature, Douglas became a candidate for the United States Senate. Sidney Breese, who had mounted the Supreme bench with the Little Giant, was the chief aspirant. He became so alarmed that he tried to make a deal to use his strength to elect Douglas to the next vacancy if only the Little Giant would now step aside. While pledges seemed to have been exchanged, it took nineteen ballots for the Democratic caucus to center on Judge Breese, who finally won with but 56 votes to 51 for Douglas. But for the fact that 'the baby Judge' would not quite have reached the constitutional age of thirty by March 4 next, the legal but not actual date for the next Senate term, it seemed he would have won.[31]

This contest warmed Douglas' blood and he set out to win a seat in the National House. The new Fifth District, containing the populous Democratic counties of his circuit, was ready-made for his ambition. Forty 'respectable Democrats' assembled in convention and nominated Douglas for the place. While Orville H. Browning, his Whig opponent, put up a stalwart battle and the Mormons were momentarily disaffected, the Little Giant's genius at campaign organization, together with his strength in a joint canvass of the district, gave him the victory.

That Fall he set out for the National Capital by way of Canandaigua, where he had a happy reunion with his mother and her family. Within eleven years he had been schoolmaster, lawyer, State's Attorney, Legislator, Secretary of State and Justice of the Illinois Supreme Court; he was now on

from the Manuscript History of the Church. For Nauvoo charter, see Davidson and Stuvé, 494 et seq.; MS. History, IV, 516. For approval of Douglas, ibid., IX, 49; IV, 356–57. For Missouri warrant trial, Joseph Wallace, Illinois State Register, April 19, 1899; Ford, 226; Quincy Whig, June 19, 1841; MS. History, IV, 380–81, 480. For Smith interview, William Clayton Journal, May 18, 1843.

[30] Davidson and Stuvé, 500 et seq. The actual inciting cause of the renewed hostility was an extraordinary ordinance passed by Nauvoo's special council providing that 'no writ issued from any other place except Nauvoo, for the arrest of any person in the city, shall be executed without the approval indorsed thereof by the Mayor.' William H. Carpenter and Timothy S. Arthur, History of Illinois, Philadelphia, 1854, 227–30, for murder of Joseph and Hyrum Smith; Stevens, 381–82; Sheahan, 51; Johnson, 90 et seq. for Douglas' part.

[31] Douglas to Col. Harry Wilton, Lewiston, Ill., March 27, 1842, Chicago Historical Society MSS., reveals the Judge's active campaign. Douglas to Breese, Springfield, Nov. 6, 1846, Breese MSS.: 'I remember well what you said to me on that subject four years ago and now have an opportunity of seeing the noble manner in which you are redeeming that promise.' Illinois State Register, Dec. 23, 1842.

his way to Congress. For a man of thirty, 'the widow's son' had done very well.[32]

The shadow of Old Hickory still hovered over the National Capital. The issues of the National Legislature were likewise chiefly those of the past: Internal Improvements, Sub-Treasury and the Bank. The Senate still had men in the uniform of the Founding Fathers, but the new House contained many who were soon to sow the wind of discord and reap the whirlwind of civil war.[33]

Douglas made his first real impact upon his colleagues early in January, 1844, when he delivered a strikingly effective speech urging a Federal appropriation to repay Andrew Jackson the $1000 fine a Federal District Judge had imposed after the Battle of New Orleans.

The theme was a familiar one for the Little Giant; he had rung the changes on a hundred stumps in Illinois, but it captivated the House Democrats to be told that, even if the General's acts had been unconstitutional, he had not been sentenced justly under the forms of law. Douglas' closing passage, reaching real eloquence, contributed measurably to the passage of the refunding bill. His name was on everyone's lips and the 'Elijahs marked him out as the Elisha upon whom their mantle was soon to fall.' [34]

As this was the presidential election year, most of Congress' time was spent in spade-work for the campaign. The Democrats must choose whether Martin Van Buren and his Nationalists or John C. Calhoun and his Southern Rights men would control their party. Calhoun had an ace up his sleeve in a thoughtless Andrew Jackson letter favoring Texas annexation and putting him in opposition to the announced views of his chosen heir-apparent. Shaken by this blow, and checkmated by the evil two-thirds rule, the Van Buren forces grudgingly joined in the nomination of the first 'dark horse' — James K. Polk, of Tennessee.

Well pleased with the nomination, Douglas accompanied an Illinois group to Nashville for a great ratification meeting. At a call at the Hermitage Douglas met the old General, who complimented him lavishly upon

---

[32] For campaign, see Johnson, 64; W. A. Richardson, II, Scrapbook, *Illinois State Register*, June 9, 16, 23, 1843; Isaac N. Arnold, Springfield, June 7, 1882; Chicago Historical Society MSS.; Alton *Telegraph*, July 20, 1843. Douglas' majority was 461. *Illinois State Register*, Oct. 27, 1843.

[33] Among Douglas' colleagues there were William L. Yancey, of Alabama, with an already well-developed secession complex; John Slidell, Louisiana's transplanted Tammany politician; R. Barnwell Rhett, a South Carolina disciple of Calhoun, but a few years removed from a Tennessee tailor shop; there too was Alexander H. Stephens, of Georgia, a worthy foeman of Douglas' steel. From the North were such men as Hannibal Hamlin, of Maine; John P. Hale, of New Hampshire; and Joshua Giddings, of Ohio, announced Abolitionist; and 'Old Man Eloquent,' the venerable John Quincy Adams, of Massachusetts.

[34] *Congressional Globe*, Twenty-Eighth Congress, First Session, 43 *et seq.*; *ibid.*, App., 112–15. Both print text of Douglas' speech. *Missouri Republican*, Jan. 28, 1862, for John Wentworth's statement of its effect upon the party leadership; Richmond, Va., *Enquirer*, Jan. 6, 1844. John Quincy Adams, *Memoirs*, Boston, 1885; XI, 478, termed it 'an eloquent, sophistical speech, prodigiously admired by the Slave Democracy in the House.'

his speech about the fine. 'I felt convinced in my own mind that I was not guilty of such a heinous offense,' Jackson told him, 'but I could never make out a legal justification of my course, nor has it ever been done, Sir, until you, on the floor of Congress, at the late session, established it beyond the possibility of cavail or doubt.'[35]

Now turning to his own re-election campaign, Douglas and his Whig opponent, D. M. Woodson, of Carrollton, made a joint canvass of the district. The Little Giant stressed the two Democratic issues, the 're-annexation' of Texas and the 'reoccupation' of all of Oregon. Both Douglas and the West believed in 'Manifest Destiny' and electric thrills went through the crowds as the Little Giant defied British aggression. After the votes were counted a Whig lamented that 'Coons' — the frontier name for Whig — 'are scarce indeed in the Sucker State, the boys went it strong for Polk, Dallas, Douglas and Texas.'

Freed from danger at home he responded to a call from Polk's own State, where Sergeant S. Prentiss' description of the Democratic nominee as 'a blighted burr that has fallen from the mane of the War Horse of the Hermitage' was being used with telling effect. To defeat the Whigs, then in control of the State, the Tennessee Democrats brought in a battalion of outside speakers. At the close of Douglas' two weeks' tour, a Nashville paper said that as a popular debater 'he was equalled by few men.' When he spoke in Missouri he won a similar tribute. In the event, Tennessee stubbornly rejected its own candidate, but the Democrats were successful in the Critical States of Georgia, Louisiana, Michigan, Pennsylvania and New York and Andrew Jackson was enabled to write gleefully, '"Who is J. K. Polk?" will be no more asked by the Coons.'[36]

Their zeal renewed by Polk's election, in the short term of Congress the

[35] Sheahan, 69–71; Douglas to Lanphier, Washington, Dec. 7, 1847, Patton MSS., asking the editor of the *Register* to send him clippings of the interview with Jackson; Lanphier to Douglas, Springfield, Dec. 20, 1847; M. F. Douglas MSS.; *Illinois State Register*, June 8, 1844; Orville H. Browning, *Diary*, Springfield, 1925, I, 300–01, claims that Walters, editor of the *Register* in 1844, later alleged that the story was a fraud, told merely to help Douglas. But by that time Walters had become bitter against Douglas because of a patronage disappointment. Blair MSS., Library of Congress, Washington, contains a copy of Douglas' printed speech endorsed in Jackson's hand: 'This speech constitutes my defense; I lay it aside as an inheritance for my grandchildren.' James Parton, *Life of Andrew Jackson*, New York, 1860, III, 641.

[36] David Davis to Julius Rockwell, Bloomington, Ill., May 14, 1844, original owned by Mr. F. W. Rockwell, North Andover, Mass.; this letter gives an insight into the effectiveness of the Manifest Destiny argument with the Illinois electorate. James Johnson, El Dorado, Cal., Jan. 18, 1859; Douglas MSS.; 'Fulton,' No. 13, gives Douglas-Woodson campaign incidents. The late speaker Henry T. Rainey, to author, Carrollton, Ill., Oct. 27, 1931, gives incident at last debate of Douglas and Woodson, in Carrollton, on Aug. 3, at which Douglas badly bested his opponent in the latter's home town. L. J. Woods to James McClure, Carlinville, Ill., Aug. 30, 1844, original owned by James McClure, of Carlinville, Ill., gives Whig reaction to election result; J. A. McCormac, *James K. Polk*, New York, 1918, 277, for Prentiss statement; James K. Polk to Cave Johnson, Columbia, Tenn., Aug. 20, 22, 23, 26, 1844, Polk-Johnson letters, Tennessee *Historical Magazine*, Sept., 1915, for Douglas speeches in the Volunteer State; Nashville *Union*, Sept. 2, 1844; *Missouri Republican*, clipped in *Illinois State Register*, Oct. 4, 1844, for comment on Douglas' speeches in Tennessee and Missouri; Andrew Jackson endorsement on letter of A. C. Flagg, Nov. 7, 1844; Polk MSS., Library of Congress.

Texas annexationists put through a joint resolution absorbing the Lone Star Republic. This step resulted from the junction of the extreme pro-slavery men and the proponents of Manifest Destiny. These first were re-acting to the new Abolitionist agitation, which had shifted the attitude of the slave-holding South from one of apology for its 'peculiar institution' to a bold declaration that it was 'a good — a positive good' and a de-termination to extend its area. The 're-annexation' of Texas also met with great favor from the Western people, who believed it was the 'manifest destiny' of the United States to be the sovereign of the entire continent, and were equally willing to expand south, north or west.

Douglas' course in the House was bottomed on this Western wish for empire.[37] His already demonstrated legislative skill was rewarded when the Democratic caucus of the Twenty-Ninth Congress chose him for Chairman of the House Committee on Territories. Douglas was happiest when he had the most work to do. His Committee promptly brought in and passed a bill bringing Texas into statehood.[38]

His Oregon position was extreme: he would never be satisfied while Great Britain held 'one acre on the Northwest coast of America.' The Democratic slogan in 1844 had been 'Fifty-four, forty or fight.' But when Polk looked at the realities and submitted a British compromise to the Senate, Douglas and nine other 'Manifest Destiny' Westerners marched by the House tellers crying: 'Fifty-four, forty forever.'[39]

With the coming of the Mexican War Douglas turned ardently to Polk's support, and soon was breaking oratorical lances with John Quincy Adams and other Whigs, who were terming it an 'illegal, un-righteous and damnable war.' Asserting that the President had made an honest effort to keep the peace, Douglas went over the 'catalogue of ag-gressions and insults; of outrages on our national flag and on the persons and properties of our citizens; of the violation of treaty stipulations and the murder, robbery and imprisonment of our countrymen,' which justified the war.[40]

Douglas now undertook to prove America's Texas boundary contention by a dispatch John Quincy Adams had written in 1819 as Secretary of State, holding that the American title 'as far as the Rio Del Norte was as

[37] Johnson, 88; *Congressional Globe*, Twenty-Eighth Congress, Second Session, 85 *et seq.*, App., 65–66, gives Douglas' speech for 'An Ocean Bound Republic.' He felt Texas no pawn in the battle between slavery and freedom but a 'theater for enterprise and industry.' The best treatment of the Texas matter is to be found in Justin H. Smith, *Annexation of Texas*, New York, 1913; 327–53. For Douglas on Oregon, see Sheahan, 92; *Illinois State Register*, Feb. 28, 1845; *Congressional Globe*, Twenty-Eighth Congress, Second Session, 173–198–202, 225–26.

[38] *Congressional Globe*, Twenty-Ninth Congress, First Session, 39–65.

[39] *Ibid.*, 258 *et seq.*; Johnson, 103; James Knox Polk, *Diary*, Chicago, 1910; I, 295–96, 478–79.

[40] Northern Whigs currently portrayed the Mexican War as an effort of the American 'slav-ocracy' to get new territory for shackles and lash. This tone runs through most of the subsequent historical treatments of the matter. But Justin H. Smith, *The War With Mexico*, New York, 1919, I, 58–101, presents an admirable statement of the facts as to anterior Mexican-American relations and the responsibilities for the conflict. Professor Smith, a New Englander who before this study had a prejudice against Polk, acquits the Tennessee President completely of the charges brought against him.

clear as to the Island of New Orleans.' Adams writhed in his seat and Douglas had a great triumph.[41]

The Congressman from Illinois sympathized with Polk, whose problem was one of extreme difficulty. While it was a Democratic war, Zachary Taylor and Winfield Scott, the leading generals in the field, were Whigs; were victories won the Whig Generals would get the credit; were battles lost the Administration would be blamed. Douglas wanted very much to go to the war himself, but Polk was loath to appoint any member of Congress to the Army.[42] Reluctantly yielding, Douglas worked in every way to strengthen the Administration.

Soon Taylor and Scott won decisive victories in Mexico, American troops also occupied California and large annexations of territory were clearly ahead. But now the Northern anti-slavery Congressmen undertook to exclude slavery from it. David Wilmot, of Pennsylvania, sought to amend a bill appropriating funds for negotiating peace by adding a proviso that whatever territory was acquired should be forever free. While the motion failed in the Senate, Pandora's box had been opened.

The chief agitator of the Congressional ferment, however, was not Wilmot but South Carolina's John C. Calhoun. After Andrew Jackson, he was the South's most extraordinary figure, and Webster regarded him as the greatest man he had ever met. By the late 'Forties Calhoun had become, not alone a politician but a missionary; not only the leader of a Democratic faction but, even more, the prophet of the slavery-extension South. In truth he was 'the impersonation of intellectual grandeur.' His face was almost Grecian, with square brow, fine forehead and resolute mouth. Power was in his aspect and force darted from his dark gray eyes. When he would fix the President of the Senate with his eyes, burning with a sort of icy fire, the effect was startling. He was no orator; it was not his words but his thoughts which were unsettling. If once the initial premise of his argument were admitted, 'he would carry you irresistibly along... until you would be puzzled to know the difference between your views and those of the South Carolina secessionist,' no matter if you were an Abolitionist in embryo.

And yet, if ever a man gave the impression of being a thinking machine, it was Calhoun. Even in private conversation he spoke like a college professor demonstrating a theorem to his class. One Illinois House member, upon whom the South Carolina sage had employed his powers, spoke of his pale but vivid countenance, his silvery, attractive voice, his eyes almost mesmeric in their power. To James A. Shields, 'there was not a mean, sordid, sensual feature in his whole countenance; his life was more like spirit life than worldly life. The intensity of his faith made him look further into the future. He saw with his soul as we see with the eyes.' Whenever Southern notabilities visited Washington they were asked, 'Have you seen Mr.

---

[41] *Congressional Globe*, Twenty-Ninth Congress, First Session, 816–17; John W. Forney, *Anecdotes of Public Men*, New York, 1861; I, 52–53; 'It was a bombshell. It was a new thing to see John Quincy Adams retreating before anybody.'

[42] Polk, *Diary*, II, 348. *Illinois State Register*, July 31, 1846; Douglas to Lanphier, Washington, July 20, 1846; Patton MSS.

Calhoun?' and again, 'Do you think of leaving without seeing Mr. Calhoun?' [43]

When the Wilmot Proviso was reoffered at the next session of Congress, Calhoun promptly took the warpath and the Southern Fire-Eaters rallied to his support. The situation soon grew so tense that Polk was extraordinarily alarmed. 'The slavery question is assuming a fearful and most important aspect,' he noted in his diary. 'It will be attended with terrible consequences, and cannot fail to destroy the Democratic party, if it does not ultimately threaten the Union itself.' The President believed that a few Ultra Northern members had introduced the Proviso mainly for political purposes, and that equally Ultra Southerners had seized upon it as a means of forming a Southern party. 'There is no patriotism on either side,' he said. 'It is a most wicked agitation that can end in no good and must produce infinite mischief.'

Douglas, too, regarded the Proviso as an act of folly, which would certainly lengthen the war and might have even graver consequences. He vigorously defended the Administration's right to organize temporary governments in California and New Mexico, and contended that the slavery question must not be permitted to prevent the ending of the war.[44]

But Congress was in a ferment, Northern objections held up the treaty of peace and Southern objections, based on slavery dialectics, interfered with all Douglas' and Polk's efforts to give Territorial government to Oregon. The session ended with confusion worse confounded.

While the Little Giant had an easy victory in his 1846 race for reelection to Congress, he had already made up his mind to go to the United States Senate. All Summer and Fall he waged an active campaign to win this seat. He was successful in keeping dangerous rivals out of the contest, in November wrote a friend that he had 'no opponent in the field,' and so it proved. When the Democratic members of the Illinois Legislature caucused in December, 1846, they nominated Douglas unanimously and the two Houses quickly elected him Senator.[45]

With this election he became the acknowledged leader of the Democratic

[43] Peter Harvey, *Reminiscences of Daniel Webster*, New York, 1880; 219; John Wentworth, *Reminiscences*, Chicago, 1889; 21; Henry S. Foote, *Casket of Reminiscences*, Washington, 1872; 214; Henry W. Hilliard, *Politics and Pen Pictures at Home and Abroad*, New York, 1893; 4; William L. Condon, *Life of General James A. Shields*, Chicago, 1902; 78.

[44] Polk, *Diary*, II, 305–48; 371; 426. He regarded Calhoun as the most dangerous of the Southerners, terming him 'the most mischievous man in the Senate.' The South Carolina Senator, 'an aspirant for the Presidency,' had been dissatisfied 'ever since I refused to retain him in my Cabinet,' and Polk concluded 'that he is governed more by his personal and political interests than by the public good.' *Illinois State Register*, Springfield, April 2, 1847; *Congressional Globe*, Twenty-Ninth Congress, Second Session, 1314.

[45] Douglas' opponent for Congress this time was Isaac Vandeventer. The Little Giant received 9629 votes to Vandeventer's 6864. For Senate election maneuvers, Stevens, 393–94. Douglas to Breese, Quincy, Ill., Oct. 30, Springfield, Nov. 6; Lawrenceville, Ill., Nov. 19, 1846; Breese MSS. Douglas to Harry Wilton, Charleston, Ill., Nov. 14, 1846; Chicago Historical Society MSS. Joseph McRoberts, Danville, Ill., Nov. 16, 1846; Douglas MSS. *Illinois State Register*, Dec. 18, 25, 1846.

party in his State. At first some contested his primacy but his rivals either became loyal followers or were defeated and destroyed. His firm establishment in Illinois equipped him to bid for national leadership.

No sooner had Douglas taken his seat in the Senate than his colleagues there recognized his merits and accomplishments by organizing a Committee on Territories, which theretofore the Senate had not had, and electing him chairman of it. Thus, before he was thirty-five years old, Douglas held the key Congressional position for directing the expansion of the United States.[46]

For some months, however, the Little Giant had been engaged in other maneuvers than those of Illinois politics, and had employed his deep, persuasive voice upon others than his colleagues. Thus, when Congress adjourned on March 4, 1847, Douglas did not hasten to the Illinois prairie but remained in Washington to transact some important unfinished business on his personal calendar.

The business was naught else than an affair of the heart. A political friendship had provided the occasion but Love itself had managed the campaign, and Douglas' heart and hand had been captured by Martha Denny Martin, a charming girl from Rockingham County, North Carolina, just south of the Virginia line.

The romance between West and South had begun four years before, shortly after Douglas first came to Washington. He soon formed a fast friendship with his House seat-mate, a brilliant young North Carolina Democrat named David Settle Reid,[47] and they became intimate and inseparable. Early the next Spring, Reid's uncle, Colonel Robert Martin, visited the Capital with his daughters Martha and Lucinda.[48] Douglas was especially attracted by Martha, who was gracefully formed, had an attractive, elfin face, fine hazel eyes and an unmistakable charm and wit. She was almost equally drawn to her new suitor from the West.

Under the influence of this new attachment, Douglas began to slough off the frontier ways which he had learned in the Illinois rough and tumble, and

---

[46] His election as Chairman of the Committee on Territories came on Dec. 18, 1847, on motion of Senator Mangum, of North Carolina. Douglas received thirty-three votes, to two for Corwin, of Ohio; two for Hunter, of Virginia; one for Chase, of Ohio; one for Turney, of Tennessee, and one for Daniel Webster, of Massachusetts.

[47] Frank E. Stevens, *Stephen A. Douglas*, etc., Springfield, Ill., 1923; 363. There were points of contact between them from the outset. Douglas' weight was 95 pounds; Reid weighed but three pounds more. Douglas and Reid were of about identical height. Furthermore, they had been born the same month and the same year.

[48] Harry E. Tucker, 'The Story of Lucinda and Martha Martin,' Greensboro, N.C., *Daily News*, June 19, 1932, quoting statement of Mrs. Mary M. Baker. The two girls, who spent several years at Miss Sigourney's select school for young ladies in Philadelphia, were accomplished on harpsichord and harp, read French and enjoyed Scott's novels. After Lucinda died in 1846, Martha became the very idol of her family and nothing was too good for her. The Colonel paid $700 in gold coin for a harpsichord for her, to say nothing of a gold table fork, a gold spoon, and a solid gold comb for her hair. The gold spoon is now in possession of Mrs. E. W. Myers, of New York, a granddaughter of Martha Martin.

became quite careful in dress and manner. Also he abated, for the moment, his keen relish for the luxuries of the table and for his normally ever-present cigar. Before and after he was a lover of good wines, importing his port direct from Oporto and drinking freely when under pressure, but these habits also went into eclipse during courtship.[49]

Soon he accepted Reid's invitation to accompany him home to North Carolina, and what had begun as a flirtation developed into a romance. After being tested by three years' devotion, on April 7, 1847, the marriage took place.

A few days after the wedding the newlyweds set out for Illinois in Mrs. Douglas' own private carriage. Their destination was Chicago, where they took a suite at the Tremont House. Hitherto the Little Giant had lived in central Illinois, at Winchester, Jacksonville, Springfield and Quincy, yet from 1833, his first year in the State, Chicago's potentialities had captured his imagination and now he chose it as his abode. He delayed formal announcement until May, 1849, yet henceforth Chicago was Douglas' home. Martha Douglas was interested in her new environment, did her best to adjust herself to the West's new ways and customs and delighted her husband's friends. After a prairie Summer the bridal couple came to Washington, where Martha Douglas made a delightful home and the Little Giant seemed to revel in domesticity. Late in January, 1849, his wife bore him a son, whom they named Robert Martin, after the good old Colonel. On November 3 of the next year, a second boy arrived, and him they called Stephen Arnold, Junior, soon corrupted into 'Steen.'

Douglas was a good husband and a good father. His attachment to his sons was such that, long afterwards, one of them termed him as 'my friend, my playmate and my chum, whom I loved and respected but never learned to fear.' Many were the occasions when the father would let one of the lads grasp a lock of senatorial hair in chubby fingers and lead him about the floor in a game of horsey.[50] And Martha was the love of his life. In January, 1853, when she died at childbirth, Douglas was grief stricken. Debate and politics proved poor anodynes, and the Senator sought forgetfulness in a European tour.[51]

[49] Joseph Wheeler, 'Life of Stephen A. Douglas,' MSS. found in the McDonald Bookshop, Springfield, Ill. For this I am indebted to Dr. Harry E. Pratt, of Illinois Wesleyan University, Bloomington, Ill. The few pages of this document which remain afford much useful information about Douglas' private habits and life. C. H. de la Figanure to Douglas, New York, June 13, 1850, Douglas MSS., notifies the Senator of the arrival of a schooner with casks shipped to him by Mr. Jinelli, wine merchant of Oporto. George T. M. Davis to Douglas, Jalapa, Mexico, May 9, 1847, Douglas MSS., quotes General James A. Shields as telling Davis, his aide, on hearing of Douglas' marriage, that it was all that Douglas required to make his ascent up the uncertain cliffs of political fame not only certain but rapid.

[50] Stevens, 648, quoting Stephen A. Douglas, Jr.

[51] Mrs. Douglas died Jan. 23, 1853; an infant daughter lingered a few months and then followed her. Martha was buried in the old Martin burying-ground on the banks of the Dan. The Senator brought his sister, Sarah Granger, to Washington to be mistress of his household and rear his two boys. She found eleven servants but reduced the staff, introduced economy and proved a capable and popular chatelaine. Cf. Stevens, 640 et seq.

But this marriage also meant for Douglas the introduction to a world with which he had been unfamiliar but which he now began to understand. This was the South, the land of tobacco and sweet potatoes and cotton, of great plantations, pleasant society and of masters and their property in man.

Before coming to Congress, Douglas had never been south of Louisville. His boyhood memories were of a bleak New England farm; his young manhood was taken up with unending struggles to get ahead in the world, and while there was much honest friendship and boisterous pleasure in the West when he moved there, it must be admitted that there was little of real culture or refinement in the prairie towns still redolent of the frontier's cutting edge. Southern society was differently organized and Douglas adapted his ways to this more courtly world.

Almost from the beginning his father-in-law had a great attachment for him. The Colonel had a plantation of eight hundred acres on the banks of the upper Dan, where he grew cotton, corn and tobacco, and under his prudent management it prospered greatly. In the 'Thirties, along with many other planters of the Southern Seaboard States, he had been attracted by the great new cotton empire opening up in the Southwest and purchased a large plantation on Pearl River, in Lawrence County, Mississippi, staffing it with an ample corps of slaves. This venture likewise proved profitable.

The day after the wedding, the Colonel handed his new son-in-law a package of papers, telling him that it was a wedding gift. It proved an absolute deed to the Pearl River plantation and all its slaves and equipment, easily worth $100,000.

Greatly affected by this generosity, Douglas thanked the Colonel, explained that he was no Abolitionist and had no sympathy with them, but still he was a Northern man by birth, education and residence; as such he was totally ignorant of that species of property, did not know how to care for it and could not accept the gift. The father-in-law honored the Westerner for his attitude and did not press the gift.

On Colonel Martin's death the next year, it was found that Martha had been willed the Mississippi plantation and its slaves but that the good Colonel had not been unmindful of Douglas' position about slavery. 'In giving to my dear daughter full and complete control over my slaves in Mississippi, I make to her one dying request,' his will set forth. 'That is, that if she leaves no children, to make provision before she dies to have all these Negroes, together with their increase, sent to Liberia, or some other colony in Africa.'

Then came this significant sentence: 'I would remind my dear daughter that her husband does not desire to own this kind of property, and most of our collateral connection already have more of that kind of property than is of advantage to them.'

Colonel Martin made a small cash bequest to Douglas, named him manager of the estate and directed that a fifth of the net income of the property left

Martha was to be paid the Senator as a management fee. The latter accepted the trust and administered it until his death.[52] At various times in the intervening years he was charged with ownership of slaves, but he indignantly denied it and his denial was correct.[53]

[52] Statement of Judge Robert Martin Douglas to F. E. Stevens, quoted, Stevens, 641–42.

[53] Probate court records, Rockingham County, North Carolina; a copy was probated in Lawrence County, Miss., June 26, 1848, Douglas being present; M. F. Douglas MSS. A separate will, dated May 29, 1847, and filed in Mississippi alone, named Douglas executor, and set his compensation for handling the Mississippi estate at one-third of its annual net income. For true copy, I am indebted to Mr. Martin F. Douglas. After the portion quoted in the text, the will continued that, in the event she did have children, and he trusted in Providence that she would, 'I wish these Negroes to belong to them, as nearly every head of a family among them has expressed a desire to belong to you and your children rather than go to Africa; and to set them free where they would entail on them a greater curse, far greater in my opinion, as well as most of the intelligent among themselves, than to serve a humane master whose duty it would be to see that they were properly protected in such rights, as yet belong to them, and have them properly provided for in sickness as well as in health.' Douglas to Chas. H. Lanphier, Washington, Aug. 3, 1850; Patton MSS. Lanphier, editor of the *Illinois State Register*, of Springfield, was an ever loyal lieutenant and friend of Douglas. 'It is true that my wife does own about 150 Negroes in Mississippi,' the latter wrote. 'My father-in-law in his life-time offered them to me and I refused to accept them. *This fact is stated in his will*, but I do not wish it brought before the public, as the public have no business with my private affairs, and besides anybody would see that the information must have come from me. My wife has no Negroes except those in Mississippi. We have other property in North Carolina, but no Negroes. It is our intention, however, to remove all our property to Illinois as soon as possible.'

CHAPTER III

CALIFORNIA

D OUGLAS' Senatorial service began when the Administration of James K. Polk was at its midway mark. By this time the President had suffered so many betrayals of his friendship that he was sick of politics and hungered for the fresh, clean air of Tennessee. Furthermore, his announcement at the time of his nomination that one term was all a President should serve, and that he would neither seek nor accept a second, was beginning to be believed by friends and enemies alike.

For the last two years John C. Calhoun had been nursing the hope that at last he might have a chance to become President. Martin Van Buren might have had hopes of his own, but a realistic examination of the situation apparently convinced him that his own future rôle in national politics would be negative rather than affirmative. Another aspirant was Richard Mentor Johnson, of Kentucky. He had been Vice-President during Van Buren's term, but his chief claim to fame was expressed in the 1836 campaign verse:

> ... Rumpsey, dumpsey,
> Colonel Johnson killed Tecumseh.

James Buchanan, of Pennsylvania, Polk's Secretary of State, was a more formidable aspirant. His White House ambitions led him into disloyalties to Polk, who bitterly resented them. Levi Woodbury, of New Hampshire, who had held Cabinet posts under both Jackson and Van Buren, likewise had high hopes.

The leading candidate, however, was Lewis Cass, of Michigan. For some years this General of the War of 1812 had hoped for the Democratic nomination. He had been in the lead in 1844, before Polk's dark-horse entry, and his election to the Senate by Michigan gave him further advantage. In 1846, he prepared a lecture, 'The Progress of Knowledge,' which caused some to deem him not only soldier and statesman but also 'one of the first literary men of the country.'[1]

The injection of the Wilmot Proviso issue into the last Congress, and its explosive results North and South, had shown nearly every politician of presidential pretensions that, to win, he must define his views on slavery. This Cass undertook to do late in 1847. The existence of slavery

---

[1] For Buchanan maneuvers, see John W. Forney to Buchanan, Philadelphia, Dec. 20, 1847; Jan. 4, Feb. 7, 20, June 25, Aug. 5, Oct. 9, Dec. 15, 1848; Buchanan MSS., Historical Society of Pennsylvania, Philadelphia. Forney was active building a Buchanan machine, bringing Buchanan into contact with George Law, a steamship and railroad magnate who was available for campaign contributions, etc. For the President's keen resentment, see Polk, *Diary*, I, 98, 104, 201, 297, 299; III, 209, 256, 257, 350, 355, 359, 362, 402–04. For Cass' lecture, see W. C. Whitthorne Diary, MS., entry for Feb. 28, 1846; for access to this Whitthorne material, I am indebted to his son, Judge W. C. Whitthorne, of Columbia, Tenn. Whitthorne, a Government clerk at Washington at the time, later a United States Senator, heard the lecture.

in those States where it was already established was not at issue. The most determined Abolitionists admitted the constitutional right of a State to elect or reject slavery within its own boundaries and that the Federal Congress could not interfere: hence their denunciations of the Federal charter as 'a league with death and a covenant with Hell.' The emerging contest concerned not this but the status slavery was to occupy in Territories prior to their admission as States. The large prospective additions from the Mexican War made the question one of actual and immediate, rather than merely theoretical concern. Furthermore there was room for constitutional argument. Cass' task was to evolve a formula which would convince all but the most Ultra-Southerners of his anxiety to protect their 'peculiar institution,' and to do this without alienating any important part of the Northern Democracy.

In December, 1847, the Michigan aspirant carefully phrased a letter addressed to A. O. P. Nicholson, a Tennessee lawyer, editor and politician, proposing that 'Popular Sovereignty' determine whether slavery should or should not exist in the Territories. So far as Congress' power was concerned, Cass took the position that the constitutional clause referred to 'territory' only as property, and conferred no right of Territorial political control upon Congress. Consequently the Federal legislative power in the Territories was strictly limited to the creation of proper Territorial Governments, and to making provision for their eventual admission into the Union as States. Other than this, Cass insisted, the people must be left to regulate their internal affairs as they themselves saw fit. Even if Congress had the right to regulate such internal affairs of a Territory, which he denied, he argued that for it to do so would cause discord, hamper the prosecution of the war and defeat the making of a treaty of peace.

This doctrine pleased the Democratic Moderates but both Ultra elements denounced it. Southern Rights men began saying that Cass' 'nomination would endanger our success in the Union' and took up Woodbury as their candidate. Their influence extended to the West, Woodbury delegations were selected in Missouri and Iowa and by March, 1848, the Cass campaign had slowed up.[2]

The Northern Free-Soil Democrats were also opposed to Cass' middle of the road position. The most active resentment was in New York State, where bitter feud seemed the normal Democratic lot. The desire of the Free-Soil group to extirpate slavery, whatever might be the cost of sectional hatred or war, had been likened to the state of mind of a farmer so determined to drive the rats from his barn that he would burn down the barn to do so. From this the group was nicknamed 'Barnburners.' The derisive label of 'Hunkers' was applied to the more conservative faction; a little later these split into the 'Hards,' who were unwilling to co-operate with Barnburners in any shape, form or fashion, and the 'Softs,' who wanted to win an occasional election, even with Barnburner votes.

Douglas was already emerging as a national leader, and New-Yorkers

[2] Samuel Treat to Douglas, St. Louis, April 8, 1848; Douglas MSS. John A. McClernand to Chas. H. Lanphier, Washington, March 4, 1848; Patton MSS., Springfield, Ill.

began laying their party situation before him. 'The bolting of the Barnburners last Fall,' he was informed, 'has created a degree of bitterness in
our ranks hardly to be conceived.' A little later, the Barnburners were
reported 'resolved to be content with nothing short of the interpolation of
the Wilmot Proviso into the Democratic creed,' otherwise they would
'pull the whole party to pieces.' [3] While not similarly bent upon mischief
and ruin, the Hunkers were sending a full delegation to Baltimore and predicted certain defeat for the national ticket should their rivals be seated.

The Barnburners were quite hostile to Cass but showed a disposition
to unite on Woodbury, the Southerners' candidate and Douglas was asked
how that would suit the West. It was a disturbing question, for the
Wilmot Proviso spirit had become active in Illinois, and 'Long John'
Wentworth, an important Chicago Democratic editor, was leading a
Free-Soil Democratic wing. This insurgence alarmed Charles H. Lanphier,
editor of the *Illinois State Register*, the Douglas organ at Springfield.
Lanphier thought the Ultras should be excluded from party management,
and sought to have the State's delegates to the approaching Baltimore
National Convention chosen, not by the districts but by the entire State
Convention. This effort 'to exclude fire-brands from the national convention and the bosom of Democracy of our State' won the approval of several Illinois House members at Washington, who thought it would 'purge
away the rank inflammation of politics and religious fanaticism.' [4]

The prevailing sentiment in Illinois was for Cass; Woodbury had some
support, and many of its Democratic leaders were anxious to compliment
Douglas. 'Your course as Senator satisfied us,' one wrote him, 'and we
know of no good reason why we should not present a candidate to the
Baltimore Convention. If unwavering Democracy with huge majorities
count anything, Illinois should be entitled to the next President.' [5] But the
Little Giant was under no illusions as to his own chances and sought no
premature compliment. Cass' Popular Sovereignty platform was not un-
akin to his own views, he thought the General's nomination inevitable
and informed his friends of his opinion. Thus when the Illinois Democratic
State Convention met in Springfield on April 25, 1848, the Wentworth
project was suppressed and a delegation of Cass men was chosen. [6]

The party warfare over slavery had bitter echoes in Washington.
Early in April, a mob attacked the printing plant of the *National Era*, a
paper the Abolitionists had recently established in the Capital. Senator
John P. Hale, of New Hampshire, an avowed Abolitionist, who was expected to be that group's presidential candidate the coming Fall, promptly

[3] D. L. Seymour, Troy, N.Y., March 25, 1848; Douglas MSS.; John W. Forney to James Buchanan, Philadelphia, March 26; New York, April 15, 1848; Buchanan MSS., Historical Society of Pennsylvania, Philadelphia.
[4] John A. McClernand to Chas. H. Lanphier, Washington, March 4, 1848; Patton MSS.
[5] E. S. Kimberly, Chicago, April 10, 18, 1848; Douglas MSS.
[6] James A. Shields, Springfield, Ill., April 25, 1848; H. S. Pierce, Rock Island, Ill., June 2,
1848; Douglas MSS.

introduced a bill to protect property in the District of Columbia. The Southern Ultras understood his purpose and were enraged. On April 20, some further remarks from Hale irritated John C. Calhoun and Henry S. Foote, of Mississippi. Displaying an excitement he had never before shown in the Senate, Calhoun said that he would as soon argue with a maniac from Bedlam as with Hale. Foote invited the Abolitionist Senator to visit Mississippi, and to 'grace one of the tallest trees of the forest, with a rope around his neck.' Hale irritated the Mississippian still further by saying that if he would come to New Hampshire, he would be guaranteed a respectful hearing in every town in the State.

Douglas undertook to call the Senators to their senses. The two Southerners had just done the Abolitionists the greatest favor they could have wanted, he exclaimed sarcastically; they had doubled Hale's vote in the Free States that fall; Foote's attack was worth not less than ten thousand votes to the Abolitionist: 'It is the speeches of Southern men, representing Slave States, going to an extreme, breathing a fanaticism as wild and as reckless as that of the Senator from New Hampshire, which creates Abolitionism in the North.' The Southerners instantly chastised this new critic. Calhoun was defending 'the Constitutional rights of the South,' he indignantly informed Douglas. Foote began to paint a blood-curdling picture of slaves rebelling against their masters, burning mansions, murdering the men and ravishing the women. His depiction of the future was so extreme that it brought rebuke from Jefferson Davis, who asserted that the slaves were happy and contented — slavery was 'a paternal institution.'

Foote returned to the assault. 'I must again congratulate the Senator from New Hampshire on the accession of five thousand more votes,' Douglas interjected a second time. This brought another storm, and Calhoun termed the course of the Senator from Illinois 'at least as offensive as that of the Senator from New Hampshire.'

'I have no sympathy,' Douglas countered, 'for Abolitionism on the one side, or that extreme course on the other which is akin to Abolitionism.' The Northern Democrats were not willing to be trodden down while the Southern Ultras hazarded nothing by their violence. Hale 'is upheld at the North because he is the champion of Abolition; and you are upheld at the South, because you are the champion who meets him; so that it comes to this, that between those two Ultra parties, we of the North who belong to neither are thrust aside.... I believe, Sir, that, in all this I have spoken the sentiment of every Northern man who is not an Abolitionist.'

Douglas took care to assure his colleagues that he was not unacquainted with life in the South, and understood Southern resentment against Abolitionism. 'We stand up for all of your Constitutional rights, in which we will protect you to the last... but we protest against being made instruments... puppets... in this slavery excitement, which can operate only to your interests and the building up of those who wish to put you down.'

Foote answered with 'the language of just indignation.' He recognized Douglas' usual fairness to the South, but warned him that he was mistaken if he thought he could be neutral in the conflict.

The Little Giant replied with dignity. He was not speaking for or against slavery. Where it existed, it was sustained by local opinion, and by this it would stand or fall. 'In the North it is not expected that we should take the position that slavery is a positive good — a positive blessing,' he warned them. 'If we did assume such a position, it would be a very pertinent inquiry, why do you not adopt this institution? We have moulded our institutions at the North as we have thought proper; and now we say to you of the South, if slavery be a blessing, it is your blessing; if it be a curse, it is your curse; enjoy it — on you rests all the responsibility! We are prepared to aid you in the maintenance of all your Constitutional rights; and I apprehend that no man, South or North, has shown more consistently a disposition to do so than myself... But I claim the privilege of pointing out to you how you give strength and encouragement to the Abolitionists.'[7]

Douglas was substantially correct in declaring that his attitude correctly reflected 'the sentiment of every Northern man who is not an Abolitionist.' Certainly it voiced the general sentiment of Northern Democrats, as was shown the next month at the National Convention in Baltimore. At the outset, the party strategists sidestepped the Hunker-Barnburner battle by seating both New York delegations, the State's vote split between them. 'By doing so,' one leader explained, 'the party at large avoided becoming the ally of either section, and thus avoided making the difficulty now local to New York common to all the Free States. Besides it leaves both sections upon the same ground, with an incentive to each to come into the support of the nominees.' But the companion effort to avert open conflict over the Territorial question was a failure. William L. Yancey, of Alabama, led the effort of the Southern Ultras to force the party to adopt the Calhoun platform. He was voted down and withdrew from the convention, uttering Cassandra-like prophecies of the Union's doom. After the platform battle, Cass was quickly named the Presidential candidate, with William O. Butler, of Kentucky, as his running mate.[8]

At first Cass' nomination seemed extremely popular, and Democratic leaders of his party persuaded themselves that he would carry Ohio against anyone, Tennessee against Clay, and could win even without New York. But a dark cloud soon loomed on the campaign sky. 'Certain Ultra pro-slavery men from the South have foreshadowed a disposition to break down our nominees in the South,' McClernand wrote his friend Lanphier, 'by urging the Calhoun standard of orthodoxy in relation to slavery.'

The Democrats feared that the Whigs would select not one but two candidates, one on the Northern platform of anti-slavery, the other on the Southern pro-slavery platform. This apprehension led Cass' lieutenants

[7] *Congressional Globe*, Thirtieth Congress, First Session, App., 506–07.

[8] John A. McClernand to Lanphier and Walker, Washington, May 30, 1848; Patton MSS. Yancey's plank, rejected 216 to 36, demanded 'non-intervention in the rights of property of any portion of the people in this Confederation, be it in the States or in the Territories, by any other than the parties interested in them.' For fuller account, see John Witherspoon DuBose, *The Life and Times of William Lowndes Yancey*, Birmingham, Ala., 1892; 217–20.

in the Free States to impress upon the party editors the need for extreme circumspection in the treatment of the slavery issue. John A. McClernand advised the editors of the *Illinois State Register* that the proper course was non-interference in the Territories. He did not agree that Congress had no power to govern the Territories, but felt that these theoretical differences need not be argued, for 'the reasonable and reliable men North and South can agree in the *practical* conclusion that we will refer the question of slavery in Territories upon both principles to the people immediately interested. This would be but an affirmance of the right and the capacity of the people to govern themselves.'

But Calhoun's platform, as put before the convention by Yancey, was 'wholly inadmissible.' Its assertion, in effect 'that the Constitution *per se* establishes slavery in the Territories,' McClernand held to have been denied by a Supreme Court decision that slavery could not exist in a Territory except by law. Inasmuch as Calhoun denied the right of the people of a Territory to decide the question, and also held that Congress possessed no power to legislate upon the subject, the Illinois Democrat termed the Southern Ultra claim a mere abstraction. If neither Congress, 'nor the people of the Territory, nor the Supreme Court may uphold slavery,' he asked, 'what public authority on earth remains to uphold it? Again, if as Mr. C. claims, Congress is required by the Constitution to enact remedies for the preservation of slave property in the Territories, then his position is not one of non-interference by Congress — not one of reference to the people of the Territory — but of positive interference by Congress to uphold slavery in the Territories. This will never do.' [9]

From the time of his first victory on the Rio del Norte, General Zachary Taylor had kept one eye on the presidential prize. Clay tried to persuade him to keep out and the General wrote back craftily that, while for President he preferred Clay to any man living, yet 'I could not avoid being a candidate if I would, and ought not if I could.' [10] By the fall of 1847, the shrewd politicians back of the General began undermining 'Our Harry.' Early in the year his fellow Kentuckian John J. Crittenden came over to Taylor and Clay stock fell rapidly. By convention time 'Old Rough and Ready' was irresistible. Again Henry Clay was balked of his dearest ambition, and again he could exclaim, as in 1840: 'I am the most unfortunate man in the history of parties; always run by my friends when sure to be defeated, and now betrayed for a nomination when I, or anyone, would be sure of an election.' As in 1840, an effort was made beforehand to persuade Webster to take the Vice-Presidential nomination; again he almost consented, then declined. After Taylor's choice, an obscure New York Congressman named Fillmore was put at the tail of the ticket.[11]

[9] McClernand to Lanphier and Walker, Washington, May 30, 1848; Patton MSS.

[10] Henry Clay, *Private Correspondence*, New York, 1856; 557–60. Zachary Taylor to Henry Clay, Baton Rouge, La., April 30, 1848.

[11] McClernand to Lanphier, Washington, March 4, 1848, Patton MSS., remarked of this, and added that Crittenden 'probably looks to be Secretary of State under Taylor, and his successor.' Henry A. Wise, *Seven Decades*, New York, 1870; 170 *et seq.*

While the hydra-headed Whig candidacy did not materialize, the convention effected almost the same political result by nominating Taylor on no platform at all! The General accepted their nomination, at the same time announcing that he was not willing to be 'the exclusive candidate of any party,' and so would accept the nomination of any other party that wanted to propose him. This had curious results. Some of Calhoun's Charleston friends held a great meeting, praised Taylor as a slavery champion and nominated him, an honor which the General readily accepted! Thus was notice served upon the Northern Democrats that the Southern Ultras preferred a politically inexperienced Louisiana Whig, on no platform at all, to such a champion of non-interference with slavery as Lewis Cass.

'Old Rough and Ready's' nomination also made a difference in the North, where the sponsorship of William H. Seward, of New York, gave him important aid. 'Long John' Wentworth proved the worst trouble-maker in Illinois. First he consolidated his own position, using 'the cut-throat system' to secure his own renomination.[12] Then he stirred all northern Illinois against Cass and Popular Sovereignty, and by mid-July the State was in doubt.[13]

Douglas, already in national demand as a party speaker, was anxious to do his part in the campaign and undertook a general speaking tour through the South.[14] On his New Orleans visit he was enabled to listen to the eloquence of Mississippi's Sergeant S. Prentiss. Douglas' own speech at New Orleans attracted wide attention. Coming from a Western man, and delivered to the citizens of the South, it bespoke the anxious solicitude of the middle part of the entire Union for the welfare of the common country. Through it the Illinois Senator helped make himself the champion of 'the rights of the States, and the States united' against the fratricide of faction. Next he went into Mississippi, and thence to Alabama, where he made a great Democratic speech in Montgomery on the 4th of July.[15] Then he returned to Washington to attend the closing weeks of Congress.

On August 17, immediately after the adjournment, a minor disagreement led Douglas to give way to a fit of ill temper and to speak offensively to the President. The latter found the Senator's conduct 'not respectful to my public station,... assuming and arrogant.'[16] Shortly afterwards, Douglas left the Capital for his wife's home in North Carolina. Already unwell when he left, in Richmond Douglas was 'attacked with an ague chill plus bilious fever,' which interrupted his journey and forced him to bed there. After a

[12] Joseph McRoberts to Chas. H. Lanphier, Danville, Ill., June 15, 1848; Patton MSS.

[13] James A. Shields, Chicago, July 12, 1848; Douglas MSS.

[14] John W. Forney to James Buchanan, Philadelphia, Dec. 12, 1847; Buchanan MSS.

[15] *Illinois State Register*, Springfield, July 28, 1848, quoting Washington *Union*, and Montgomery, Ala., *Gazette*.

[16] The Illinois Senator was trying to persuade Polk to order some money paid one J. Quinn Thornton for making a trip from Oregon to Washington. The President was, as usual, tracking the letter of the law, refused to pass on insufficient evidence, and required Douglas to give a binding certificate. Thereupon the Little Giant objected 'in an excited and offensive manner.' See Polk, *Diary*, IV, 80–83.

few days he continued to the Martins', but had to suspend his plans to get into the Illinois campaign.[17]

Thanks to the Barnburners, from August onward things went worse and worse with the Cass campaign. After their failure to secure all their wishes at the Baltimore Convention, the Proviso Democrats returned determined to upset the party program. Soon they called a national meeting of Free-Soilers. Barnburners, Free-Soil Democrats and 'Conscience Whigs' met at Buffalo on August 9, spoiling for the fray. It took little deliberation for them to draft Martin Van Buren for the head of the ticket. Henry C. Dodge, of Wisconsin, was selected for second place; when he declined, Charles Francis Adams, 'Old Man Eloquent's' able son, took his place. The platform was tersely stated: 'Free Soil, Free Speech, Free Labor, Free Men.'[18] Conscious of the impossibility of his own election, Van Buren believed that the national situation demanded a sharp rebuke to the Democratic party for ignoring the Free-Soilers' principles and undertook the fight.

Van Buren's entrance had an immediate effect. Fifty New York papers put his name at their mastheads. To the great irritation of the Cass press, they often quoted Andrew Jackson's letter: 'I cannot hope to be alive to witness the acclamation with which the people of the U.S. will call Mr. Van Buren to the Presidency at the end of Mr. Polk's term; but you will, and I know you will rejoice at it as a consummation of an act of justice, due alike to him and the honor and fame of the country.'

It seemed that Cass had been born under an unlucky star. His military glory, dating back to the War of 1812, could not stand up against Taylor's Buena Vista fame. In the South, the hostility of the Ultras sapped Cass' strength. In the East, still another new party aided the enemy — the Native Americans, born of intolerance to aliens, Catholicism and all foreign customs or ideas. Endorsing Taylor, this group was of considerable weight in several Eastern States. These developments foreshadowed the election outcome. Taylor won some Southern States, lost most of the Western ones, including Illinois, and was indebted to Van Buren for his victory, for the Free-Soil candidate led Cass in Massachusetts, Vermont and New York, the shift of whose electoral votes would have made Cass President.[19]

'I cannot find power of language to reflect my feelings on the recent hell-leap of Martin Van Buren,' a friend wrote Douglas, 'a man upon whom the Democracy of the Union have for years heaped honors, dignities and wealth — and now, on the brink of the grave, in a spirit of malevolent vengeance... draws from beneath his hypocritic cloak an assassin's stiletto to stab not only his party, but that glorious Union, the golden hope of the oppressed all over the world.'[20] But men of Douglas' political position realized that

---

[17] Douglas to Robert Smith, Rockingham County, N.C., Sept. 20, 1848, quoted *Illinois State Register*, Springfield, Nov. 3, 1848.

[18] Shields to Douglas, July 12, 1848; Douglas MSS.

[19] The electoral votes were Taylor, 163; Cass, 127; the popular votes, Taylor, 1,360,099; Cass, 1,220,544; Van Buren, 291,263. In New York Van Buren received 120,510; Cass, 114,318; the two combined exceeded Taylor's 218,603.

[20] Levi D. Slawson, U.S. Steamer *Alleghany*, at sea, Nov. 1, 1848; Douglas MSS.

there was a further and equally disturbing aspect to the election. It had been notice to Northern Democrats that their Southern associates were slave-holders first and Democrats second. Beset on both sides by the Ultras, Moderates found the going hard.

Nine days after the treaty of peace between Mexico and the United States was signed at Guadalupe Hidalgo, a great event occurred in California. Sutter's Creek was a rapid stream in the foothills of the Sierras; there, on January 24, gold nuggets were found. By May San Francisco was convinced of the truth of the reports and the fevered rush to the gold mountains denuded the town. Soldiers, sailors, clerks, none was exempt. By July all America was ablaze with excitement, and the adventurous set out for the new Golconda.

This rapid concentration of settlers in the gold fields, the appalling license and lawlessness which ensued, made more acute the already pressing problem of the establishment of a stable government for the people of the new Territory. Polk was alarmed by reports of this turbulence and crime and urged Congress to take action. But the Southern Rights men, debating a slavery formula for Oregon, which they knew was too far north for slavery to be economically possible, had not hesitated to force a two-year delay in its creation into a Territory. California was partly south of 36° 30′, and they were determined that its government be held up until they could make some bargain. So the session of Congress adjourned without taking action.

The California situation grew more and more serious. In August, Senator Thomas H. Benton, of Missouri, addressed a message to the Californians, telling them that, as Congress would give them no lawful government, they should go ahead and organize one of their own. About this time Attorney-General Toucey informed Polk that 'the government of the Territories rested in the people, and that they could, in the absence of action of Congress, govern themselves as they chose.'

When Douglas reached Washington in November, he went straightway to the White House to apologize to the President for his conduct three months before. Polk recorded that 'the explanations were cordial and mutually satisfactory, and it was agreed to suffer the matter to sleep in oblivion. Senator Douglas has been one of my most ardent and active political supporters and friends, and I am much gratified.' [21]

The President was well advised to have composed his differences with his lieutenant, for he had need of all available support. From the moment Congress opened the next month, the California issue was a powder mine and there was a lighted match in nearly every hand. Far-sighted Federal politicians realized that California must be given civil government. Polk feared that, unless something were quickly done to give the people the protection of law, they would organize an independent Pacific Republic.

Consequently he made herculean efforts to persuade the adoption of some form of government — either Territorial or State — for the Pacific Coast

[21] Polk, *Diary*, IV, 192–93.

community. In his annual message he outlined the importance of California to the Union, termed its situation 'the only dangerous question which is in our path,' and earnestly invoked Congress, 'for the sake of the Union, its harmony and our continued prosperity as a nation,' to adjust its differences and immediately provide organized Territorial Government. To this he added sharp rebuke for the folly of those who 'foment and excite geographical and sectional division,' and 'deliberately calculate the value of the Union.' He pointed out to the Southern obstructionists that, so far as California was concerned, the slavery issue was 'abstract rather than practical.' [22] In the larger part of the area, the nature of the climate and productions made it certain that slavery could not exist; in the remainder it was probable that it could not. If Congress would but abstain from forcing external rules upon the Californians, the people thereof could establish whatever system they wished, a course in conformity with the essence of American political philosophy.

Thus the President put his face 'alike against Southern agitators and Northern fanatics,' and did his utmost to have the recommendations carried out. In this he was warmly seconded by Senator Douglas. A week after his message had gone in, Polk became deeply disturbed over the way the slavery issue seemed to block every prospect of consideration. 'We have a country to serve as well as a party to obey,' he told callers, urging them to favor a California bill. [23] But it quickly became apparent that no satisfactory Territorial organization for California could be enacted, for the Northern Free-Soil majority controlling the House was determined to attach an anti-slavery proviso to whatever law was passed. Accordingly, Douglas shifted his efforts, and proposed to bring California in immediately as a State, thus skipping the Territorial stage completely, and 'leaving it to the inhabitants of the new State' to decide the question of slavery for themselves.

This ingenious device of the Illinois Senator was denounced by Ultra-Slavery men as a 'mere quibble.' But Polk, who called himself a Southern man, 'as much attached to Southern Rights as any man in Congress,' thought no Southerner ought to object to the plan and suggested only that Douglas had embraced too large an area in his proposed State. [24] After several conferences, the Senator agreed to cut it into two, the western portion to be admitted immediately as the State of California, while the eastern portion would become the Territory of New Mexico.

The President sought Calhoun's assent to this scheme but the South Carolinian refused. Soon Calhoun employed a House motion to abolish the slave trade in the District of Columbia, as an excuse to call a caucus of all Southern members, to issue an ultimatum to the North. If their advocacy for their 'rights' involved secession, Calhoun was ready for that final step.

[22] James D. Richardson, *Messages and Papers of the Presidents*, New York, 1901; IV, 635–43.
[23] Polk, *Diary*, IV, 231–32, *et seq.*
[24] Hopkins Holsey to Howell Cobb, Athens, Ga., Feb. 24, 1849; Toombs-Stephens-Cobb Correspondence, *American Historical Association Report* for 1911; II, 154, Polk, IV, 279 *et seq.*

Polk was outraged at this extremist stand. 'The agitation of the slavery question,' he noted in his diary, 'is mischievous and wicked.... It is a mere political question on which demagogues and ambitious politicians hope to promote their own projects.' He feared that events might occur which would make it his duty 'to incur high and vast responsibilities,' and was prepared to do so. On January 16, Calhoun called on him and they had a heated session. The South Carolinian was 'very earnest in the expression of the opinion that the South should no longer delay resisting the aggressions of the North.' The Southern slave-holding President again informed the Sage of Slavery that he deemed it 'of the greatest importance' that the slavery agitation be stopped, and urged the Douglas bill as an effective way to do so. Calhoun excitedly opposed this view and said the time had come for action. Thereupon Polk firmly announced that 'any movement which tended to violence or the disunion of the States' would find him fighting it with all the powers of the Government.[25]

Late in January Polk set his Cabinet to work to press through the California bill and had unexpected aid from the Southern Whigs, who had become highly suspicious of Calhoun's fundamental purpose. Alexander H. Stephens, of Georgia, wrote a friend that he believed the 'dissolution of the present Confederacy' the thing nearest 'Mr. Calhoun's heart.' Robert Toombs, of Georgia, pithily expressed this group's viewpoint as to California: 'It cannot be a slave country; we have only the point of honor to save.' Accordingly they embraced the Polk-Douglas bills as the way to save that point of honor, 'and rescue the country from all danger from agitation.' Furthermore, they felt that the Calhoun Southern caucus project was, inherently, 'a bold stroke to disorganize the Southern Whigs and either to destroy Gen'l. Taylor in advance or compel him to throw himself in the hands of a large section of the Democracy of the South.' Almost every man of the Southern Democrats, Toombs continued, had joined Calhoun's movement, their action based 'not on the conviction that Gen'l. Taylor can *not* settle our sectional difficulties, but that he *can* do it. They do not wish it settled.' Therefore the Southern Whigs went into the Calhoun caucus, 'to control and crush it.'

The meeting, which was held behind closed doors, proved an oratorical field day for the South Carolinian. An unfriendly Southern Whig, who attended, made note that Calhoun, 'always impressive, was never so impassioned and vehement as on that occasion. He was a lion roused.' As he described Northern aggression and demanded Southern resistance, he rose

---

[25] Polk, IV, 251–52; 284–88. Howell Cobb to Mrs. Cobb, Washington, Feb. 9, 1849, Erwin MSS., Athens, Ga.: 'The question will be settled at the present session on the basis of the Douglas bill,' unless prevented by Calhoun. 'It does not suit his purposes to get clear of it upon any reasonable terms. It constitutes his last hope of organizing a Southern party of which he shall be head and soul. God grant that we may be able to floor the old reprobate and thereby preserve the honor of the South and secure the permanency of the Union.' Calhoun's determination to make his political friends adopt his policies completely or break their friendship was thus put by Waddy Thompson, of South Carolina: 'When I say *go*, you are to *go*; when I say *trot*, you are to *trot*; and when I say *run*, you are to *run*.' For this, see Henry T. Thompson, 'Sketch of Waddy Thompson,' *Libertarian Magazine*, Dec., 1925, 358.

to Demosthenian ardor. His gestures were bold, and he was so moved that he forgot his usual impassivity and stamped his foot with angry emphasis.[26]

For all this, the conservatives in the caucus established control of its decisions. A little later, Toombs wrote Crittenden: 'We have completely foiled Calhoun in his miserable attempt to form a Southern party.'[27] But the success went no further; Calhoun's Southern party plans might be foiled but the California bill would not go through. Filibusters held up essential appropriation bills and the threat was angrily made that, unless California were side-tracked, no supply bill would be allowed to pass.

Unceasing in his efforts, Douglas 'tried to get up State bills, Territorial bills, and all kinds of bills in all shapes, in the hope that some bill, in some shape, would satisfy the Senate,' but failed in all. When the last day of the session came, and one of Calhoun's new aides, Jefferson Davis, of Mississippi, moved final non-concurrence, Douglas lamented that he had rather see the office-holders do without their pay than the Californians any longer do without protection from murder and plunder.[28] Southerners answered they would rather none were paid than for California to come in a Free State. As the hour of adjournment neared, excitement among Southern Representatives was particularly intense, there were fist-fights in both House and Senate, but there was no bill for California.[29]

[26] Henry Hilliard, *Politics and Pen Pictures, At Home and Abroad*, New York, 1893; 199. This stamping of the foot surprised Hilliard, who had never before seen Calhoun do so.

[27] Toombs-Stephens-Cobb Correspondence, 139, 140, 141.

[28] *Congressional Globe*, Thirtieth Congress, Second Session, 668; 685.

[29] Polk, *Diary*, IV, 366.

CHAPTER IV

THE TITANS' LAST STAND

ON MARCH 4, as James K. Polk and Zachary Taylor were riding down Pennsylvania Avenue on the way to the latter's inauguration, the retiring President was startled to hear his successor remark: 'California and Oregon are too distant to become members of the Union; it would be better for them to be an independent government.' This observation confirmed Polk in his belief that, while Taylor was well-meaning enough, he was 'uneducated, exceedingly ignorant of public affairs,' of only ordinary capacity and likely to be putty in others' hands.[1]

The old General was Virginia-born and Kentucky-reared, but for many years he had made his home at Baton Rouge, Louisiana, where he owned some large plantations and nearly three hundred slaves, and the Southern Rights leaders were especially confident that they could dominate him. About the time he began to angle for the Presidency, Taylor wrote his son-in-law, Jefferson Davis, already a rising Southern Rights politician, that should any actual attempt be made to deprive the slave States of their constitutional rights, the South should 'act promptly, boldly and decisively, with arms in their hands, if necessary, as the Union in that case will be blown to atoms, or will no longer be worth preserving.' Taylor's prompt acceptance of the endorsement by the Charleston Democracy had further reassured the Calhoun men.[2]

For all this their confidence was not well placed. Taylor could not have been elected without Northern Whig support, and when this support was effectually extended, the General's gratitude was enduring. William H. Seward and Thurlow Weed, partners in New York's most famous political union, supplied acumen and good sense to the Taylor management. The Whig victory in New York sent Seward to the Senate, in which post he further aided Taylor, who came to put great confidence in him and came generally to hold the Northern section of his party in high favor.

Southern Ultras thought that in his Inaugural General Taylor put far too much emphasis on the phrase, 'preserve, protect and defend' the Constitution, and was unduly emphatic in his declaration that he would not permit his Administration to be directed 'to the support of any section or merely local interest.' His description of the Federal Union as 'the paramount object of our hopes and affections' seemed another hint of an unexpected determination to uphold the Union even against Southern Rights.

---

[1] Polk, *Diary*, IV, 375–76. Cf. also William M. Gwin, 'Memoirs on History of United States, Mexico and California,' MSS., Bancroft Library, University of California, Berkeley, 1878; 5–6. Dr. Gwin was with Douglas in front of Willard's Hotel as the procession passed. 'Within a year of this time,' he informed Douglas, 'I will ask you to present my credentials as a Senator from the State of California.' Douglas was surprised but said he hoped Gwin would succeed.

[2] H. Montgomery, *The Life of Major-General Zachary Taylor*, Auburn, N.Y., 1854.

The new President's actions soon confirmed the Southerners' premonitions. As soon as he came into immediate contact with the realities of the California problem, he quickly dropped any ideas as to the creation of an independent Pacific republic. Before he had been President a month he dispatched Thomas Butler King to California, to hint to the Californians that they should act immediately, send delegates to a constitutional convention, draft a constitution, and ask Congress for admission as a State.[3]

When King reached the coast he found that the Californians, anticipating the President, had already elected delegates to a constitutional convention. These met in September; Southern men were as active and influential as Northern men, but the delegates unanimously approved a clause in the Constitution prohibiting slavery in the proposed State. They finished their task in October and the Constitution was overwhelmingly ratified at the polls. When Congress met, California was knocking for admission as a Free State.[4] While the Californians were adopting a free Constitution, New Mexico's inhabitants met and drafted a petition to Congress asking that slavery be legally abolished there.

The South was growing more and more apprehensive. In 1847, the Legislature of every Free State in the Union, plus that of slave-holding Delaware, endorsed the Wilmot Proviso, and Legislature after Legislature in the South passed counter-resolutions. The people of Virginia, its General Assembly declared, could have no difficulty in choosing between 'abject submission to aggression and outrage' and 'determined resistance...at all hazards, and to the last extremity.' [5] With a single exception, every Southern Legislature endorsed these drastic resolves. Even in Missouri the Calhoun men, anxious to hamper Benton with instructions, 'smuggled' a set of Ultra resolutions through a Legislature of the State.[6]

In April, 1849, steps began to be taken for concerted action by Ultras throughout the South. South Carolinians took the actual initiative, but thought it best for the first public steps to be taken in Mississippi, where a State Convention issued an address to the Southern people, calling a general convention of the South to meet in Nashville on June 1, 1850.

Soon these members of Congress who had resisted Calhoun's address to the Southern people were heavily attacked for alleged betrayal of the

---

[3] Richardson, V, 27 *et seq.* Taylor insisted, however, that he did not 'anticipate, suggest or authorize the establishment of any such government without the assent of Congress, nor did I authorize any Government agent or officer to interfere with or exercise any influence or control over the election of delegates or over any convention making or modifying their domestic institutions.' For instructions, see Secretary Clayton to King, House Executive Documents, Thirty-First Congress, First Session, No. 17, 9–11. Howell Cobb to Mrs. Cobb, Washington, July 12, 1850, Erwin MSS., says that King had expected to be elected to the Senate from California but 'he dropped his piece of meat in the vain effort to grasp the shadow.'

[4] Carl Schurz, *Life of Henry Clay*, Boston, 1889; II, 320–21.

[5] *Niles' Register*, LXXV, 73.

[6] James B. Bowlin to Howell Cobb, June 6, 1849; Toombs-Stephens-Cobb Correspondence, 159. Their purpose was 'to head Benton'; the latter fought back, 'made Calhoun's name odious there,' and Bowlin added, perplexedly, 'it is hard for an honest man with Southern feelings and principles and yet a devoted lover of the Union to know where he is.'

South. One branch of the onslaught was based on the claim that the Northern Democrats had fought their last battle for the constitutional rights of the States. Were this true the South could look for no external aid and must protect itself. Some of the Southern Conservatives appealed to their allies of the North for statements to be used to offset the charges. Others felt themselves forced to assume bold ground of defiance or separation. But Calhoun wrote a Mississippi Ultra that dissolution of the Union would please him better than submission to the North.[7]

When Congress met in December, this emerging sectional bitterness had immediate repercussion in the inability of the House to elect its Speaker. The Democrats had a majority and, under a strict party vote, Howell Cobb, of Georgia, the choice of the Democratic caucus, would have been elected quickly. But the specter of slavery shattered party lines. Northern Free-Soil Democrats would not vote for Cobb, Southern Ultras would not vote for the Southern Whig candidate because of his angling for votes from the North. Ballot after ballot was taken fruitlessly and the House was in complete turmoil. 'Talk, talk, talk' proceeded in the caucuses by night and on the floor by day.[8]

On December 13, when John W. Forney visited the House, he 'found there a terrible scene' and wrote James Buchanan that the crisis was at hand. 'Hilliard, Toombs, Stephens and other Southern Whigs declared, amid the huzzahs of the Democrats in the South, that they would secede if the Wilmot Proviso passed.' William A. Richardson, of Illinois, was so disturbed that he wrote despairingly to a constituent: 'There is a bad state of things here and, as little as is thought about it, I fear this Union is in danger. The bonds of Union are not what they have been. The feeling in the South is among the People. I once thought it confined to the Politicians. I fear I was mistaken. Still I think it strong enough to ride the storm that now threatens us. I pray God it may be so.' On December 22, however, the plurality rule was successfully invoked and Cobb was elected Speaker.[9]

The President's message, now officially received, brought no comfort to the Southern Rights men. 'Impelled by the necessities of their political condition,' Taylor advised Congress, the people of California had framed a constitution, and under its terms would soon ask admission as a State. He also expected that New Mexico would take similar steps, and Congress should admit them both. He discoursed gravely on the maintenance of the Union. 'Its dissolution would be the greatest of calamities: Whatever dangers may threaten it, I shall stand by and maintain it in its integrity, to the full extent of the obligations imposed and the power conferred upon me by the Constitution.' Upon this bold avowal Southern Rights leaders privately denounced what they termed Taylor's treachery to the South;

---

[7] Toombs-Stephens-Cobb Correspondence, 145–54. Calhoun to Tarpley, July 9, 1849; Southern Historical Society Publications, VI, 416.

[8] McClernand to Lanphier and Walker, Washington, Dec. 9, 1849; Patton MSS.

[9] Forney to Buchanan, Washington, Dec. 13, 1849; Buchanan MSS. W. A. Richardson to D. T. Berry, Rushville, Ill., Dec. 16, 1849; original in possession of Wm. H. Murray, Galesburg, Ill. Howell Cobb to Mrs. Cobb, Washington, Nov. 28, Dec. 8, 11, 15, 1849; Erwin MSS.

the Northern Free-Soilers were pleased, and the older Conservative leaders of both sections were greatly disturbed.

At first Douglas was only moderately impressed by these broils and alarums, which seemed more superficial than fundamental. He was working on plans to build railroads from the Great Lakes to the Gulf, and from the Mississippi to the Pacific, thus stimulating intercourse between the sections, and increasing their mutual understanding and good will. Furthermore, he had a plan for compromise. Soon he advised Lanphier that 'we will all be together in favor of the admission of California as a State.' Some months before he had predicted that, if left to themselves, the Californians would decide against slavery. The result had verified his belief, thus demonstrating the unreality of the Free-Soilers' fears, and the latter had now come to the support of his program. Within the next few days General Cass would 'take strong ground in favor of the State admission of California,' and Douglas believed that the 'Whigs and Abolitionists would be compelled to follow suit.'

But he was quick to perceive the changed situation. On February 4, he wrote candidly that nothing could be done with the Illinois railroad bill until slavery agitation ended. 'It now absorbs everything else,' he continued, 'and he must be blind who does not see that there is really danger in it. Yet my wishes and judgment concur in the belief that we will be able to save the Union.' [10]

In this he seemed too optimistic. In less than a month the California debate had raised the latent sectional animosities to fever heat. Daily there were verbal duels in House and Senate, with threats of physical violence and reprisal. House strife was renewed over the selection of the Clerk. Now the very Calhoun men who had 'turned up their chivalrous noses' over the efforts of the Southern Whig candidate for Speaker to get a few Northern votes, made a trade and put in a Northern Free-Soil man as Clerk. Indignant Democrats excoriated it as 'a bargain of the worst character,' the object of which was disunion.

'Hell is to pay and no pitch hot,' Thomas L. Harris, a new Democratic member from Illinois, wrote indignantly to Charles H. Lanphier. 'Broke loose and there is no hotter.... These Calhoun men are aiming to create a sectional division and to offset disunion.' They had proscribed the Northern Democrats; they had defeated Cass solely because he 'did not live in niggerdom.' Harris had concluded that the storm was at hand, immediately and at once, 'not by the act of the North but by the act of the South.' [11]

'The Union is in real, imminent peril. There is no use in denying the fact,' W. H. Bissell, another Illinois Congressman, wrote Sidney Breese. He was convinced that a large and influential Southern party wanted disunion for its own sake. 'Had they not a plausible pretext for forwarding their designs in the slavery question,' he declared, 'they would hunt for such a pretext elsewhere — or invent one.' [12]

[10] Douglas to Lanphier and Walker, Washington, Jan. 7, 1850; Patton MSS.; Douglas to C. R. N. Patterson, Washington, Feb. 4, 1850; Illinois State Historical Society MSS.

[11] Harris to Lanphier and Walker, Washington, Jan. 12, 1850; Patton MSS.

[12] Bissell to Breese, Washington, Jan. 17, 1850; Breese MSS.

It became apparent that the issue of events would chiefly depend upon the attitude of the leaders of the conservative Democracy of the North. As their views began to be advanced in the Congress, the public found them marked by a determination never before manifested. They considered the Union indissoluble and were determined to maintain it. They felt that California must be admitted as a State under the constitution the people had adopted. They would yield much to the South but not these two essentials.

During this six weeks a number of memorials, petitions, resolutions and bills dealing with the status of California and New Mexico had come before the Senate. Douglas was unceasing in his attempt to have them all referred to the Committee on Territories. On January 22, the last unreferred measure was turned over to the Committee, and the Little Giant now had in his charge the bringing forth of the legislation to calm the California storm.[13]

Douglas set to work on the details of the accommodation he had in mind. He still was not tremendously concerned by the developments, still believed the apprehensions of disunion unduly great, and many of the younger men in Congress were of a similar mind. But there were others, chiefly of the passing generation, who were very much alarmed.

Of these Henry Clay was conspicuous. Whatever might be said of his vanity and his ambition, Clay had a fundamental reverence for the Union of the Constitution which made him respond whenever he thought it in danger. After Taylor's nomination, the great Kentuckian had retired to Ashland to nurse the wounds of an indifferent, ungrateful party. But the developments North and South had alarmed him, and in 1849 he accepted another election to the Senate and returned to Washington to make one final effort to maintain the Union unimpaired.

The first six weeks of Congress so disturbed Clay that he determined on a desperate move to preserve the peace. On January 21, Taylor sent a special message reciting domestic turmoil in California and renewing his appeal for statehood. This raised new protest from the Ultras of both sections. Clay was quite unwell but that evening he braved the inclement weather to call upon Daniel Webster, whom he disliked but whose aid he felt essential.

The scene of this meeting in Webster's library of these aging giants of a generation on the wane, deserves to be re-created. When first they had come upon the national stage, Thomas Jefferson had been holding his republican court. They had seen the fathers of the Constitution laid in their simple graves, had heard John Marshall hand down *obiter dicta* shrewdly fashioned to change a confederation into a nationality, had battled 'Old Hickory' and his backwoods patriots, had frowned in vain on Texas annexa-

    [13] These were: 1. Memorial of the provisional government of the people of Deseret; 2. Senator Foote's resolution of December 27, for the establishment of suitable governments for California, Deseret and New Mexico; 3. Senator Sam Houston's resolutions covering State organizations; 4. Senator Thomas H. Benton's bill for reducing the west boundary of Texas, compensating that State, and making it possible later to divide Texas into two States; 5. Foote's bill of January 16 for Territorial Governments. For a sound and comprehensive discussion of the situation in Congress at this time, see George D. Harmon, *Douglas and the Compromise of 1850*, Lehigh, Pa., 1930; 14 *et seq.*

tion and the war, and now feared that the eruptive force of the slavery issue would imperil the Union itself.

The Senate still held others of the older statesmen but their number was fast decreasing. Death was not the only foe — a new generation had come upon the scene, a new and pushing breed of politicians, less courtly, more determined, men who looked askance at ruffled shirts and frilled-lace cuffs and indulged in contemptuous pleasantries about the dying gods.

Clay could have seen, in the man before him, little evidence of change from the Daniel Webster of years gone by. For age seemed to have had slight effect upon his appearance. His small hands and feet comported oddly with his more than ordinary height and portly form. But his great head was his most compelling feature — almost never had there been such a head on human shoulders. The brow was massive, Olympian; it overhung his eyes as the crag of a mountain-top. With the years his raven hair had grayed up perceptibly, but his dark, solemn, deep-set eyes, heavy eyebrows, and erect carriage resisted change. His countenance seemed stern to strangers but it was bland and agreeable when lighted up in conversation. He spoke slowly, and generally in low, musical tones, but when excited his words came like trumpet blasts. Now in his sixties, Webster was by long odds the most distinguished-looking man in Congress; an Englishman said he 'looked like a cathedral,' and thousands of Americans called him 'the God-like Daniel.' [14]

Time had not used Clay so gently and in 1850 he was quite another man from the fiery orator of the war with Jackson. Hot toddies and high stakes had sapped a much-enduring frame, his step had lost its usual spring and thwarted ambition had etched its lines upon his face. But still he stood erect and still high he held his head. Still he indulged in jocose sallies and charmed the hearts of men.

For thirty years these two had been standing in one another's way. To Clay had been given that gift of gifts for the politician, that inexplicable magnetic charm which caused men to forget his ugly angularity and drew them to him as with bands of steel — men who heard him on the hustings, men who chatted with him in hotel lobbies, men who merely knew the steel engravings of his face and brow. But he was irked by Webster's attitude of intellectual superiority and envied his mind and voice; while Webster sighed in vain for Clay's uncanny magnetism.

This evening, however, no hint of this rivalry cropped out. Clay, coughing badly and very feeble, outlined the main points of compromise he had in mind. After some talk, Webster said the plan 'ought to be satisfactory to the North, and to the reasonable men of the South.' Offhand, he believed he could himself endorse it all. Clay thought some Democratic Senators and nearly all the Whigs, except the Proviso men, would co-operate. At length the Kentuckian seemed exhausted and got up to leave. Then Webster promised that, if reflection did not change his view, 'I will devote myself to this cause ... no matter what may befall me at the North.'

[14] Charles Lanman, *Private Life of Daniel Webster*, New York, 1856; 179; *Century Magazine*, XXIII, 538; William L. Condon, *Life of General James A. Shields*, Chicago, 1902; 310–14.

When the visitor had gone, Webster remarked that Clay's objects were 'great and highly patriotic. Perhaps Providence has designed the return of Mr. Clay to the Senate, to afford the means and the ways of averting a great evil from our country.'[15]

Thus assured of Webster's mighty aid, Clay set to work on his compromise scheme and, on January 26, secured recognition in the Senate to offer a series of resolutions. These, in combination, were to effect 'an amicable arrangement of all questions in controversy between the Free and the Slave States, growing out of the subject of slavery.'

There were eight branches to his program. California should immediately be admitted as a State, with suitable boundaries, and 'without the imposition by Congress of any restriction in respect to the exclusion or introduction of slavery.' The second resolution declared that slavery did not exist by law and was unlikely to be introduced in fact into New Mexico; therefore it was 'inexpedient for Congress to provide by law either for its introduction into or exclusion from' any portion of the area. Congress should proceed to set up Territorial Government for New Mexico, without restriction or condition as to slavery.

The third resolution fixed New Mexico's eastern boundary, using the line agreed on by the United States and Spain forty years before. This involved a concession on the part of Texas of a part of her grandiose territorial claims. To quiet these demands, Clay's next resolution contemplated payment by the Federal Government of Texas' pre-annexation public debt.

The next two items treated slavery in the District of Columbia, long a sore spot with the Ultras of both sections. One resolution asserted that so long as slavery continued in Maryland, original donor of the District, it was 'inexpedient' to abolish it in the District 'without the consent of that State, without the consent of the people of the District, and without just compensation to the owners of slaves within the District.' By implication this phraseology asserted Congress' power to abolish in the Federal District, a power strenuously denied by the Southern Ultras; this in itself was sure to raise a storm. The companion resolution declared it 'expedient' to end the slave trade in the District.

The last two sections were definitely directed toward a mollification of Southern opposition. Clay's seventh resolution proposed an effectual Federal statute, 'according to the requirement of the Constitution,' for the recovery of fugitive slaves. His last one called for no legal enactment; it required a recital, by Congress, that the National Legislature lacked power to prohibit or obstruct the slave trade between the slave States themselves.

Adoption of this program, Clay said, would call for 'an equal amount of concession and forbearance on both sides.' He warned the Southerners that he had asked from the North 'a more liberal and extensive concession' than from the South. He warned the North that the concession demanded from her was of an abstraction, a sentiment, while in the Slave States 'the social intercourse, habit, safety, property, life — everything is at hazard.'

[15] George Ticknor Curtis, *Life of Daniel Webster*, Boston, 1878; II, 395 *et seq.*

He besought his colleagues to hold up general discussion of his proposals, but his wish was ignored. Rusk, of Texas, rebuked him for having taken one-half of the territory of Texas 'to make a peace offering to a spirit of encroachment on the constitutional rights of one-half of this Union.' Foote, of Mississippi, was in arms against the hint that Congress had power to legislate on slavery in the District. He thought a fugitive slave law the South's right, but did not want California admitted a Free State unless a new Slave State came in to balance it. Both Foote and Mason, of Virginia, remarked that it was strange for such a plan to come from a Senator from a Slave State. Butler, of South Carolina; Downs, of Louisiana; Berrien, of Georgia, and Davis, of Mississippi, were apprehensive, the latter acidly terming it no compromise at all but a settlement requiring all the concession from the South.

Clay felt forced to reply. 'Coming from a Slave State as I do,' he said, 'I owe it to myself, I owe it to truth, I owe it to the subject, to say that no earthly power could induce me to vote for a specific measure for the introduction of slavery where it had not before existed, either south or north of the Missouri Compromise line.' The resolutions were then set the special order of the day for February 5.

That day Clay was feeble and coughing badly from a deep-seated cold. As he ascended the long flight of steps at the Capitol, paroxysms of coughing made him pause repeatedly and a friend had to help him mount. But he would not listen to remonstrance against the day's exhausting task. 'I consider our country in danger,' he protested. 'If I can be the means in any measure of averting that danger, my health or life is of little consequence.' [16]

The notice of Clay's expected address had drawn hundreds from other cities. Something went wrong with the heating apparatus and the official thermometer stood at 100°.[17] By the time Clay arrived the Senate galleries were packed to suffocation, hooped ladies and perspiring gentlemen crowded the Senate floor and the corridors were filled with the overflow. When he rose to speak, the galleries burst into applause, the throng in the corridors cheered in turn.

Clad in his usual black, with a high black stock and a huge white collar reaching to his ears, Clay stood there waiting to be heard. He easily looked his seventy-three years. Bald on the top, his head was fringed with long iron-gray hair; his cheeks were sunken, his nose looked pinched, his wide mouth was wreathed in smiles. He began in a faltering voice, but the scene, the occasion and the theme inspired him and soon his periods began to ring with forceful grace.[18]

Securing the rapt attention of the Senate and galleries by a devout and appealing exordium, he proceeded to assess the responsibilities for the existing state of affairs. In working out any adjustment, he chiefly dreaded the violence of party spirit; 'it is passion, passion — and party, party and

[16] The Reverend C. C. Van Arsdale to Theodore Frelinghuysen, Albany, N.Y., Aug. 2, 1852, printed, Calvin Colton, *Last Seven Years of Henry Clay*, New York, 1856; 128–29.

[17] Harvey, 218.

[18] Ben: Perley Poore, *Reminiscences*, Philadelphia, 1886; I, 363.

intemperance — that is all I dread.' His advocacy of the eight resolutions was powerful, cogent and persuasive. Especially forceful was his appeal to the Free-Soil men to abandon the Wilmot Proviso, because a law of nature would keep slavery out of the territory acquired by the Mexican War. When the Proviso had first been agitated, the new areas were distant, conditions there little known and it was perhaps natural enough for the North to apprehend that slavery would move in bag and baggage unless specifically interdicted by law. Since then, however, the facts had become quite clear. Slavery did not exist by law in the new territory, while climate, geography and economic law made its establishment there unlikely. Within the last few months California had declared for freedom. New Mexico's soil was barren and natural law would prohibit slavery there.

If only the North had understood these facts at the time of the Proviso excitement, Clay declared, if the North 'had foreseen the excitement, the danger, the irritation, the resolutions which have been adopted by Southern Legislatures, and the manifestations of opinion by the people of the slave-holding States,' the Proviso agitation would have been still-born. What the North wanted was that slavery should not extend its area. 'Have not you got it in California, already, if admitted as a State?' he asked. 'Have you not got it in New Mexico, in all human probability also? What more do you want? You have got what is worth a thousand Wilmot Provisos. You have got nature itself on your side.' In view of this new condition of affairs, Clay earnestly appealed to the Northern members to act 'as patriots, as representative men, as lovers of unity and above all this Union.' [19]

He defended his Texas boundary provisions, destroyed the contention that the Federal Government had no power to affect slavery in the District of Columbia, pointed out the fairness of effective fugitive slave legislation, and then examined the renewed suggestion that the sectional questions be settled by extending the Missouri Compromise line to the Pacific.

Such a step would positively forbid slavery north of the line while south of it slavery could not be imposed by law. 'It is better for the whole South,' he pointed out, 'that there should be no action on both sides, than that there should be action interdicting slavery on one side, without action for the admission of slavery on the other side.' This principle of non-action, non-legislation, was the very essence of his program. If it implied slavery exclusion from California, this could not be helped and Congress could not be reproached for it. 'If nature has pronounced the doom of slavery upon these Territories,' he said, 'if she has declared by her immutable laws that slavery shall not and cannot be introduced there, whom can you reproach but Nature or Nature's God?'

Clay concluded with a great appeal for Union and for peace. What value would it be to the South even if she could peacefully withdraw from the Union? The only effect of such a success would be to make the recovery of fugitive slaves more difficult. But the South need not think that secession would be accomplished without the tramp of armies; in less than sixty days after it should be attempted war would blaze in every part of the land. And

[19] For text of this speech, see Colton, *Last Seven Years of Henry Clay*, 302-45.

if there were separation, America would be riven into three, not two, con-federacies — one for the North, one for the South Atlantic, and one for the Mississippi Valley, this last inevitably because the peoples living at the headwaters of the Mississippi would never consent for that river's mouth to be held in alien hands.

Clay himself intended to stand and die within the Union; he believed no State had any right of secession — it could only free itself by revolution. The South might as well be aware that secession and war were identical. Finally, he implored his hearers 'solemnly to pause at the edge of the precipice before the fearful and dangerous leap be taken in the yawning abyss below from which none who ever take it shall return in safety.'

The strain of this two-day appeal told visibly on Clay, and as he neared his close his energy was only sustained by his unfaltering will. As he con-cluded, hoarse and exhausted, there were tears in many eyes and he was overwhelmed with congratulations. Webster was particularly delighted. 'I never listened to him with so much admiration and favor,' he told an intimate. 'He is a very great man, there is no mistake about that; he is a wonderful man.' [20]

While Clay momentarily moved his hearers he neither altered the de-termination of General Taylor in the White House, nor of the Congressional Ultras of both sections. For the next three weeks frictions increased and dangers multiplied and House tensions reached the point that personal encounters were momentarily expected. When Clingman, of North Carolina, threatened violence, McClernand armed himself with a bowie knife and two revolvers, and Richardson and Harris equipped themselves for defense. 'The people at home little dream of the real state of feeling here,' Harris wrote Lanphier. 'Cass told me day before yesterday that he had given up all hope.'

'Slavery, Slavery, is the eternal word in Congress and in every circle of private conversation here,' Richardson wrote a friend. 'It is appalling to hear gentlemen, Members of Congress sworn to support the Constitution, talk and talk earnestly for a dissolution of this Union.' The Illinois Demo-crat had become satisfied that 'a large majority of the Southern men' were anxious for disunion *per se*. Should the Wilmot Proviso pass, trouble, per-haps civil war, would result.

But the Northwestern Democrats had no thought of yielding the Union. 'In every emergency, at all times, it is our duty to stand by the Union as it is, defend it to the last and if need be fall in its defense,' Richardson wrote. 'For one, this Union shall have my all — life, hope and expectations — freely, whenever and wherever she may ask them.'

President Taylor's plan for immediate grant of statehood without de-termining collateral questions had Seward's active support, and a large House majority favored it. When Doty, of Wisconsin, sought to instruct the House Committee on Territories to report such a bill, the Southern Whigs resisted violently, Stephens and Toombs, of Georgia, and Clingman,

[x] Harvey, 218.

of North Carolina, taking the lead. But the Western members were not daunted by secession threats and Bissell, of Illinois, denounced them to the House.[21]

At the height of the crisis Toombs, Stephens and Clingman told the President that if he persisted in his plan, disunion was at hand. The old General was 'very firm' and there was a stormy session. The Southerners inquired if he had expressed himself 'ready to maintain the Union at any cost.' He answered in the affirmative; in case of armed resistance to the collection of customs he would blockade every Southern port; he would not use the Regular Army, but would 'call for volunteers from the Northern and Western States, putting himself at their head, and would pour out his blood, if need be, in defense of the Union.' Furthermore, he thought the Southern people themselves would repress secession, while as to the departure of the Southern Congressmen, there would be enough more good men ready to come in their places. Finally, any men who led such a movement while he was President would 'be dealt with by law as they deserved, and executed.' Thurlow Weed, entering Taylor's study immediately after the Ultras' departure, was greeted with the oath-garnished query: 'Did you meet those traitors?'[22]

The Northern Ultras were no less unyielding: 'We are disunionists,' Wendell Phillips proclaimed in the *Liberator*. The adoption of the Proviso, Horace Mann admitted, would produce a Southern rebellion, but he insisted on it. 'Rebellion or not,' Edward Everett felt the catastrophe inevitable, and General Winfield Scott made up his mind that the country was 'on the eve of a terrible civil war.'[23]

With affairs at such a crisis, Senator Douglas undertook to pacify the House. First, he had his friend McClernand approach Stephens and Toombs to find out if compromise were possible. The Georgians answered that they would not yield California's admission unless Territorial questions be settled simultaneously. They insisted that Congress should not exclude slavery, that 'in organizing Territorial Governments, the people under each should be distinctly empowered so to legislate as to allow the introduction of slaves and to frame their constitutions in respect to African slavery, as they pleased; and when admitted as States into the Union, they should be received without any Congressional restrictions upon the subject.' At the Westerners' request, Stephens and Toombs put these terms in writing. Douglas studied them and concluded that agreement could be had.

[21] W. A. Richardson, Washington, Feb. 19, 1850, name of correspondent unknown. Original in possession of Wm. H. Murray, of Galesburg, Ill. Harris to Lanphier, Washington, Feb. 21, 1850; Patton MSS. Within a few moments after Bissell had concluded, enthusiastic Westerners demanded 50,000 copies of his 'glorious speech' for circulation back home.

[22] New York *Tribune*, Feb. 25, 1850, giving dispatch from its Washington correspondent, dated Feb. 23. Thurlow Weed Barnes, *Memoirs of Thurlow Weed*, Boston, 1884; II, 177–79. A. T. Bledsoe, *Southern Review*, IX, 805 *et seq*.: 'General Taylor ought to have been impeached.... If... the South, or only the Gulf States had stood together, a bloodless reformation would have saved the constitution, and have perpetuated the Union it established.'

[23] *Liberator*, March 22, 1850; Burke Hinsdale, *Horace Mann*, New York, 1898; 268; Claude M. Fuess, *Daniel Webster*, New York, 1930; II, 208; William T. Sherman, *Personal Memoirs*, New York, 1890; I, 82.

A conference occurred the next evening at the house of Speaker Howell Cobb. The Northwest was represented by McClernand and Richardson, of Illinois, and John E. Miller, of Ohio. The Southerners present were Cobb, Toombs and Stephens, the Georgia Giants, and Linn Boyd, of Kentucky. Douglas thought it best not to be at the meeting himself, but McClernand informed the group that he was authorized to say that Douglas would act in concert with him on any agreement he might make.

A compact was quickly reached: California should be admitted under its Free Constitution: Territorial Governments should be provided for the rest of the war-acquired area, slave owners being given the right to take their slave property into any of these Territories; finally, any attempt to abolish slavery in the District of Columbia would be opposed. Douglas at once prepared bills to effectuate the compromise, McClernand introduced their counterparts in the House, and the tension was relieved.[24]

During these exciting events in the House the Senate continued its debate. When the President transmitted the California Constitution, Senator Benton moved to refer it to a Select Committee, a move which would deprive Douglas' Committee on Territories of control of the situation. In the debate which followed, the Little Giant warned the Senate that unless the compromise measures were brought forward separately they would never pass. Admitting the force of Douglas' warning as to procedure, Clay declared it impossible that anybody could think he 'intended to embrace all this variety of subjects in one bill, and propose the passage of them all at once.' [25]

'If the people of California want slavery,' Douglas said, 'they have a right to it, and if they do not, it should not be forced upon them.' But the determination as to whether California should be a Slave or Free State depended not upon the South or the North, but upon the people of California themselves. The prohibition of slavery in the Territories, while violative of the great fundamental principles of self-government, would be 'no violation of the rights of the Southern States.'

'Talk to me about the rights of the North or the rights of the South,' he exclaimed dramatically. 'Neither has any right there so far as the institution of slavery is concerned. Why, Sir, the principle of self-government is that each community shall settle this question for itself; I hold that the people of California have a right either to prohibit or establish slavery, and we have no right to complain either in the North or in the South, whichever they do.'

Thus far Webster had not publicly discussed Clay's plan of compromise, but he was greatly alarmed by the House troubles and told the President that the admission of California without settlement of the other issues was likely to lead to civil war. He knew not how to meet the emergency, nor 'with what weapons to beat down the Northern and Southern follies,' but for him there was no weapon equal to the tongue, and so he determined upon 'an honest, truth-telling speech, a Union speech.' [26]

[24] Alexander H. Stephens, *A Constitutional View of the War Between the States*, Philadelphia, 1868; II, 201–04.
[25] Colton, *Last Seven Years*, etc., 156.   [26] Fuess, *Daniel Webster*, II, 207–10.

Before doing so he consulted John C. Calhoun, for whom he had great personal esteem. Once when Peter Harvey asked him whom he considered the greatest man he had ever met, he named Calhoun, 'long-headed, a man of extraordinary power.' This winter the Southern Ultra was at the very gates of death and Webster was much concerned. About the last of February he visited Calhoun in his room in the Old Capitol, talked freely to him of the troubled state of the Nation and outlined his own views. Calhoun expressed the greatest anxiety to be in the Senate to hear Webster's speech; and then shook his head sadly and said he feared he was on his death-bed.[27]

A night or two later, General James Hamilton of South Carolina called on Calhoun, who related Webster's plans. 'Suppose that Mr. Webster does... succeed in adjusting the question.... What shall we of the South do for him?' Hamilton inquired.

'Nominate him for President,' Calhoun responded, 'for he will deserve it for that single act.... I shall most probably never recover my health. But if I do, I will not only not allow my name to be used against him, but will regard it as a sacred duty to support him.'[28]

But while such was Calhoun's reaction to the compromise, as expressed in private conversation, publicly he yielded no jot or tittle of his adamantine insistence upon Southern Rights, and he saw to it that his own views were placed before the Senate before the date set for Webster's speech. On March 4, Calhoun was supported into the Senate Chamber and in a weak and faltering voice asked that his friend Senator Mason be permitted to read some remarks for him. The Virginian declaimed Calhoun's dolorous pronouncement. Profoundly silent, Senate and galleries attended this extraordinary spectacle, which had the impressive solemnity of a funeral ceremony. Wrapped in flannels, ghost as much as man, Calhoun lay back in his chair while Mason read. From time to time, better to emphasize some particular point which Mason had just read, Calhoun would turn from Senator to Senator, and fix upon him eyes glowing with the brilliancy of a meteor.[29]

'I have believed from the first,' his address declared, 'that the agitation of the subject of slavery would, if not prevented by some timely and effective measure, end in disunion.' The South was affected with an almost universal discontent because its States believed that they could not remain in the Union and retain honor and safety. This feeling arose because 'the equilibrium between the two sections... has been destroyed.' Had this come from natural causes the South could not have complained — but it was not so. Calhoun then made his usual statement of the nature of the Federal compact, renewed his complaint that the North had won ascendancy in every branch of the Federal Government, gave a vivid account of

[27] Harvey, 219–20; New York *Tribune*, Jan. 22, 1860.

[28] Waddy Thompson to Webster, Washington, March 2, 1850; Webster MSS., Library of Congress, XIV, No. 17255. Hamilton's conversation with Calhoun had taken place the night of March 1. Foote, *Casket of Reminiscences*, 43–44.

[29] Ben: Perley Poore, I, 365; H. Van Holst, *John C. Calhoun*, Boston, 1882; 338.

the rise of Abolitionism, and warned that unless something was done to arrest this evil agitation, the South would be forced to choose between Abolitionism and Secession. True, the sections were bound together by many cords and disunion could be effected by no single blow. Yet one by one the cords had been snapping, commercial, financial, religious ties had been severed. The political tie would be the next to go.

He grew satiric about Clay's program. 'The cry of "Union, Union — the glorious Union!" can no more prevent disunion than the cry of "health, health — glorious health!" on the part of a physician can save a patient lying dangerously ill.' The cause of the disease must be removed — the North must do justice by conceding the South an equal right in the new territory; she must perform her constitutional duty by returning fugitive slaves; she must cease to agitate the slavery question. As a guaranty of good faith she must procure the amendment of the Federal Constitution, thus reassuring the South by restoring the equilibrium of power and authority between the sections. 'Having faithfully done my duty to the best of my ability,' his address ended, 'both to the Union and my section throughout this agitation, I shall have the consolation, let come what will come, that I am free from all responsibility.' When Mason pronounced these words, Calhoun was lifted from his chair and tottered into the corridor.[30]

The South Carolinian seemed unconscious of the fatal contradiction of his position. The very next day, when Foote, of Mississippi, challenged his thesis, Calhoun said bluntly: 'As things now stand, the Southern States cannot remain in the Union.' But only a few minutes later, he insisted that 'if I am judged by my acts, I trust I shall be found as firm a friend of the Union as any man in it.'

Webster had given notice of his intention to speak on March 7. He was far from well that morning, had not slept the night before, and feared that the speech meant his political ruin, but was determined to go ahead. As always on a great day he donned the uniform of the Revolution — coat of blue, tie of white, vest of buff. Soon after breakfast, a Senate Sergeant-at-Arms rushed to his home to notify him that both Senate Chamber and corridors were crowded by an eager multitude.

Every vacant seat on the floor was occupied by a lady. Others of the fair sex commandeered piles of documents and even the steps beneath the presiding officer's chair. Members of the lower House packed the lobbies, diplomats were out in full force. Clay was there, weak and pale, eagerly awaiting Webster's words. Calhoun was the only conspicuous Senatorial absentee.[31]

Webster was calm and composed but his face was unusually stern. To Frederica Bremer, the world traveler, his eyes seemed 'catacombs of ancient wisdom.' He passed his hand across his brow and began to talk; the tone was low, clear, conversational. Then his voice began to swell and its volume grew, without shrillness, until it seemed a great organ gathering

[30] Von Holst, *Calhoun*, 338–47; Ben: Perley Poore, II, 366.
[31] Fuess, *Daniel Webster*, II, 210–12.

volume with the theme. It was not long until the chandeliers vibrated to his words, for his voice, 'like tones of muttering thunder, reached everywhere, filled everywhere, and the effect upon the audience was to chain them to their seats.'[32]

He opened with the words: 'I wish to speak today, not as a Massachusetts man, nor as a Northern man, but as an American.' Carefully he laid his historical foundation, and carefully he erected upon it a commanding edifice of argument and appeal. Excoriating the absolutists of both sections, those who thought right could be distinguished from wrong with the precision of an algebraic equation, he called for mutual charity, concession and compromise.

He had not been speaking long before a tall, emaciated figure, with deep, cavernous eyes and a thick mass of snow-white hair advanced with feeble step, and sank into a chair on the other side of the Chamber. It was Calhoun.

Webster, who had not seen him enter, pressed forward with his theme. He did not conceal his earlier attitude on slavery. He deemed it a great evil. When Wilmot's Proviso had first come up, he had approved it; he would rejoice to see freedom reign throughout the continent. But a new state of affairs had occurred. Nature had made slavery impossible in California and New Mexico. Therefore, he was now willing to abandon the Proviso doctrine; not only was it useless but it was a quite unnecessary indignity to the South.

'I would not take pains,' he cried, 'uselessly to affirm an ordinance of Nature, nor to re-enact the will of God.' No matter how much he personally abhorred slavery, the Constitution provided for it and the constitutional rights of the slave States must be acknowledged and maintained.

Next he turned upon secession threats, and opened his guns on Calhoun's recent avowal. As he mentioned the South Carolinian's prediction of peaceable secession, Webster's eyes glowed like balls of fire and his vigorous gestures denoted his emotional stress. Soon he referred to something Calhoun had once said in debate, terming it 'the utterance of the distinguished and venerable Senator from South Carolina, who, I deeply regret, is prevented by serious illness from being in his seat today.' Upon this, Calhoun moved nervously and bent forward as though to interrupt. Soon Webster referred again to Calhoun. The latter nervously grasped the arm of his chair, his black eyes glared, and half-rising, he exclaimed in a feeble, sepulchral voice: 'The Senator from South Carolina is in his seat.' Startled, Webster turned, bowed, smiled and continued his excoriation of disunion.[33]

He heard these threats of breaking up the Union with distress and anguish. He turned to Calhoun and exclaimed with profound emotion: 'Peaceable secession is an utter impossibility.' With telling blows he exposed the strife that would attend any dissolution effort. Referring to the threatened Southern Rights Convention which was to meet in Nashville three months thence, he ridiculed the very thought of 'hatching secession over Andrew Jackson's bones.' Finally, he appealed to his countrymen to cease this harmful

[32] Foote, *Casket of Reminiscences*, 36–37.
[33] Harvey, 221–22.

DANIEL WEBSTER
Defender of the Constitution and Fashioner of 1850's Compromise

debate over secession, and to come forth into the light of day and 'enjoy the fresh air of liberty and Union.'

When Webster sat down the applause could not be stilled; hundreds rushed to his side to wring his hand and express their thanks. But Calhoun checked the congratulatory chorus. In faltering tones he expressed vehement dissent. 'I cannot agree,' he shrilled, 'with the Senator from Massachusetts that this Union cannot be dissolved. Am I to understand him that no degree of oppression, no outrage, no broken faith, can produce the destruction of this Union?'

'Why, Sir,' he continued, 'if that becomes a fixed fact, it will itself become the great instrument of producing oppression, outrage and broken faith. No, Sir, the Union *can* be broken. Great moral causes will break it, if they go on, and it can only be preserved by justice, good faith, and a rigid adherence to the Constitution.'

As he took his seat, Webster arose to answer the question. 'I know, Sir,' he said, 'that this Union can be broken up — every government can be — and I admit that there may be such a degree of oppression as will warrant resistance and a forcible severance. That is *revolution* — that is revolution! Of that ultimate right of revolution I have not been speaking. I know that that law of necessity does exist. I forbear from going further because I do not wish to go into a discussion of the nature of this government. The honorable member and myself have broken lances sufficiently often before on that subject.'

'I have no desire to do it now,' Calhoun muttered.

'I presume the gentleman has not,' Webster answered, 'and I have quite as little.' Thereupon Calhoun arose from his seat, and, standing erect, walked out of the Senate Chamber. He was never to enter it again.[34]

But this final note of dissent did not alter the effect of Webster's effort. His audience had been profoundly moved and reverberations of his speech were heard for many months to come. In the South his new views gained him cohorts of stalwart friends. Many wrote that he had disarmed their apprehensions and they had nothing more to ask. But in the North there was bitter denunciation by the Abolitionists, sullen resentment by the Free-Soilers and only mild approval by the Conservatives.

In a sense, Webster's speech marked the end of an epoch. When 1850's dangers had become apparent, the aging giants girded their shriveled loins for one last battle for the Union of their fathers. Come what might, even in their twilight these dying gods stood upright to meet the foe.

[34] Hilliard, 226.

CHAPTER V

THE TRIUMPH OF THE LITTLE GIANT

BY MID-MARCH all the great figures had had their say. Benton, Clay, Cass, Calhoun, Webster and Seward had sustained their views by marshaling in serried ranks a great battalion of noble abstractions. Nature, Duty, State's Rights, the Constitution, Union, Peace, Good Will: all had been summoned for Senatorial aid. On March 13 Douglas of Illinois undertook to refocus Senatorial thought upon the practical situation, proposing a definite, articulate program to settle the difficulty.

The Little Giant did not begin by parading the Holy Ghost before his hearers but went immediately to points at issue. First he defended the policy of the Northern Democrats. Referring to Webster's recent discovery that an ordinance of God was interdicting slavery in California and New Mexico, he asked ironically why the Massachusetts statesman had not discovered this before. Cass had proclaimed it in 1848 but Webster had then opposed it with all his force and eloquence.

Douglas' own objection to the Wilmot Proviso was not because it violated any ordinance of God but because it denied the people the right of Popular Sovereignty. Not only did the Proviso ban slavery in Territories while they remained such, but it pledged the 'faith of the nation that slavery should *never* exist in the country acquired.' Thus it proposed to deprive the people 'of the right of moulding and framing their domestic institutions to suit themselves'; it proposed to 'destroy the constitutional right of one or more of the new States of this Union.' [1]

The Little Giant next turned his batteries on John C. Calhoun, and particularly on what he described as Calhoun's 'fundamental error,' that of supposing that his particular section had a 'right to have' a due share of the Territories 'set apart and assigned to it.'

'What share has the South of the Territories?' Douglas asked 'or the North? or any other geographical division unknown to the Constitution? I answer, none — none at all. The Territories belong to the United States as one people, one nation, and are to be disposed of for the common benefit of all, according to the principles of the Constitution. Each State, as a member of the Confederacy, has a right to a voice concerning the rules and regulations for the government of the Territories, but the different sections — North, South, East, and West — have no such right. It is no violation of the Southern rights to prohibit slavery, nor of Northern rights to leave the people to decide the question for themselves.'

[1] *Congressional Globe*, Thirtieth Congress, First Session, App., 366 *et seq.*, gives speech. William L. Marcy to James Buchanan, Washington, March 10, 1850, Buchanan MSS., expresses the Northern Democratic view thus: 'The whole people in the non-slave-holding States are decidedly opposed to extending slavery by the action of Congress.' 'But to conciliate and quiet the South the Northern Democracy are willing to protect slavery where it now is, to let the Territories, so far as this question is concerned, remain as they are, and to abstain from irritating agitation.'

He then sought to refute Calhoun's charge that the Ordinance of 1787 for the government of the Northwest Territory had deprived the South of its rights. Despite the Ordinance's restriction against slavery, he pointed out, there had been individual cases of slavery in Illinois. Nor had the Missouri Compromise been the agent which had excluded slavery from the region north of its line; on the contrary, prior to its passage, 'the laws of nature, of climate and production' had as effectually excluded it from the whole of that country as it was now excluded by an act of Congress.

The North was needlessly apprehensive over New Mexico. The only possible portion of the ceded area in which slavery had had a chance had been that in the Sacramento and San Joaquin Valleys, but California had already declared itself determined to be free. Climate, which regulated the matter, 'depends upon elevation above the sea as much as upon parallels of latitude.... The country is now free by law, by nature and in fact. It will be free under any bill you may pass, or without any bill at all.'

Calhoun's insistence upon an equilibrium between the sections was 'a moral and physical impossibility,' Douglas said. 'We all look forward with confidence to the time when Delaware, Maryland, Virginia, Kentucky, and Missouri, and probably North Carolina and Tennessee, will adopt a gradual system of emancipation, under the operation of which those States must, in the process of time, become free. In the meantime we have a vast territory, stretching from the Mississippi to the Pacific, which is rapidly filling up with a hardy, enterprising, and industrious population, large enough to form at least seventeen new free States, one-half of which we may expect to be represented in this body during our day.... I think I am safe in assuming that each of these will be free Territories and free States, whether Congress shall prohibit slavery or not. Now let me inquire where are you to find the slave Territory with which to balance these seventeen free Territories, or even any one of them?... There is none — none at all.'

After complimenting Clay's 'matchless moral courage in standing undaunted between the two great hostile factions, and rebuking the violations and excess of each,' the Illinois Senator declared that the people of the whole country had begun to see that there was nothing in the controversy seriously affecting the interest, invading the rights or impugning the honor of any section or State. 'The Union will not be put in peril,' he cried. 'California will be admitted; governments for the Territories must be established; and thus the controversy will end, and I trust forever.'

Douglas now applied himself with his usual aggressive vigor to securing definite action. He had already laid before his Committee bills to settle the difficulties on the lines of the agreement which on his initiative House members had made the month before. Now he spurred his Committee associates and two bills were perfected, the first to admit California with her Constitution as submitted, and the second to establish Territorial Governments for New Mexico and Utah, without prohibiting slavery, and to establish a western boundary for Texas.

Before reporting these measures Douglas consulted both Henry Clay and Lewis Cass as to whether he should bring in a single bill or should offer the two projects separately. Both advised him to keep them separate and a few days later publicly expressed their belief that this was desirable.[2] But the Chairman could not secure a majority of the Committee for his program. At length he made the best of a bad situation and, on March 25, reported two bills to the Senate, adding that the Committee was divided upon their propriety, and that each member of the Committee had reserved 'the privilege of stating his own opinions, and acting in accordance with it.'

The following week, while Calhoun lay at the door of death, his mind was much disquieted over the future of the South, which he believed he alone could save. A disciple remarked that never had his life been more precious or his counsel more needed. Tears gathered in Calhoun's eyes, and he replied: 'There indeed is my only regret at going. The South! The poor South!'[3]

He occupied his last days dictating resolutions to be introduced into the Senate representing the South's ultimatum. Visitors to his room were struck with its bare austerity. No touch of human heart or hand was observable in his quarters. On the narrow mantelpiece they saw a lump of cold boiled rice, a glass of water, some dried prunes and an ineffective tallow candle. On Sunday morning, March 31, he breathed his last.

Funeral ceremonies were held in the Congressional Chamber the next Tuesday. Clay, Webster, Mangum, Cass, King and Berrien were his pall-bearers, and the ceremonies were solemn and impressive.[4] He was temporarily laid to rest in the Congressional burying-ground, preparatory to being removed to Charleston, to become South Carolina's patron saint.

Calhoun's death only momentarily checked the senatorial debate. When the Chairman of the Committee on Territories made his report, Foote seized the evil omen of division and renewed his and Benton's plea for a Select Committee of Thirteen. Douglas strove desperately to persuade the Senate to vote upon the bills already placed before it. Clay admitted to him that he saw no need to change any single feature of the bills. Senatorial sentiment, however, fast drifted toward a Select Committee and Clay soon began to favor it. A fight commenced over Benton's motion to except the question of California statehood from the matters to be referred to the Select Committee, his object being to bring in California and leave the Territories out. In the debate preceding the defeat of this endeavor, Cass' firmness brought compliments from both Clay and Webster.[5]

[2] Douglas to Lanphier and Walker, Washington, Aug. 3, 1850. Original in possession of Dr. Charles L. Patton, of Springfield, Ill.

[3] Hunt, 312. At that, the South had not hearkened to the Calhoun program as promulgated in his speech of March 4. William L. Marcy to James Buchanan, Washington, March 10, 1850; Buchanan MSS.: Calhoun's speech had 'failed to take the South with him' and so Webster was 'lord of the ascendant.'

[4] Howell Cobb to Mrs. Cobb, Washington, April 21, 1850; Erwin MSS.: neither Cobb nor Fillmore nor the President knew how to follow the Episcopal service, 'a gloriously ignorant trio,' but the sermon, by Chaplain Butler, was 'very pretty... short and appropriate.'

[5] Douglas to Lanphier and Walker, Aug. 3, 1850, cit. supra; Thomas L. Harris to Charles H. Lanphier, Washington, April 11, 1850; Patton MSS.

On April 18 the Senate ordered and selected the Committee. The Chairman was Henry Clay. Lewis Cass gave added weight. Daniel S. Dickinson, of New York, had great prestige as an orator. Jesse D. Bright, of Indiana, was to represent the Democratic West. Daniel Webster, the leading member from New England, was offset by Phelps, a Vermont Free-Soiler. Cooper, of Pennsylvania, completed the Northern membership. In addition to Clay the South was represented by John Bell, of Tennessee, staunch Whig and advocate of Taylor's program; Berrien, of Georgia; Willie P. Mangum, of North Carolina, both doughty conservative Whigs; Mason, of Virginia, a disciple of Calhoun; King, of Alabama and Downs, of Louisiana. The group well reflected the variant sectional viewpoints represented in the Senate. But Douglas was not of the Thirteen.

There are various explanations for this omission. He had already impressed the Senate with his power and his chairmanship of the Territorial Committee gave him a certain right of courtesy to membership upon the Select Committee. Some authorities have suggested that the omission marked a direct snub by Clay. But Douglas himself wrote Lanphier that he had been offered membership, but had 'declined being a member,' because he did not believe that the Omnibus Bill had any conceivable chance of success and he wished to keep in a position to save something from the wreck.[6]

Not in the least taken aback, the Little Giant requested that his California bill be considered immediately and that it be made the special order of the day. Henry Clay supported his request, but inasmuch as he was among the Senators selected to accompany Calhoun's remains to South Carolina, asked Douglas for an understanding that the bill would not be brought to a vote before the committee returned. Douglas made it clear that his sole purpose was to expedite matters. When the bill was brought to the point of a test vote, he planned to defer it until the funeral committee returned. 'That is exactly in conformity with the liberal, manly course of the Senator,' Clay replied, serving notice that he intended to move to add Territorial and Texas boundary provisions to Douglas' California bill. On April 22 Cass remarked in debate that he thought it quite possible that the Thirteen would merely amend Douglas' measures.

In a fortnight the Thirteen's ideas changed, and on May 7 Clay told Douglas that the Committee would soon present an elaborate report but felt some embarrassment as to the bills. In their report, they would recommend that the Senate accept Douglas' California and Territorial bills and unite them into one act. Why did not Clay himself unite these measures and have them reported as the Select Committee's bill? Douglas inquired. Clay answered that this would be neither just nor fair to Douglas, especially as the latter had done all the labor on them and had put them 'in a form so perfect' that the Select Committee could not change them for the better in any point. In justice to Douglas they should be recommended to the Senate as they stood.[7]

[6] Douglas to Lanphier and Walker, Washington, Aug. 3, 1850, *cit. supra.*
[7] Sheahan, 131 *et seq.*

But the Little Giant insisted that he had no such pride in authorship as to desire that the Select Committee, out of regard to him, 'should omit adopting that course which would ... best accomplish the great object in view.' Douglas reiterated his belief that, if the measures were united, they would unite the opponents of the measures, and therefore fail. If this were true, it would be better to have the Committee report them together, so that Douglas himself could renew them separately after a failure. Clay thanked him but repeated that it would be unjust.

'I respectfully ask you, Mr. Clay,' Douglas countered, 'what right have you, to whom the country looks for so much ... to sacrifice to any extent the chances of success on a mere punctilio as to whom the credit may belong of having first written the bills? I, Sir, waive all claim and personal consideration in this matter, and insist that the Committee shall pursue the course ... best calculated to accomplish the great end we all have in view.' Clay was much touched. 'You are the most generous man living,' he exclaimed, stretching out his hand. 'I will unite the bills and report them; but justice shall never the less be done you as the real author of the measures.'[8]

The next day the Committee of Thirteen presented its compromise. The main measures were a bill for admitting California as a State and Utah and New Mexico as Territories; a provision for adjusting the Texas boundary dispute and a provision for abolishing the slave trade in the District of Columbia. A Fugitive Slave bill was already before the Senate and its passage was urged.

True to his word, Clay made it clear that the Committee's California bill was that reported by the Committee on Territories, and called attention to that body's 'arduous and valuable labors.' Indeed, the Select Committee's California bill literally consisted of copies of Douglas' two bills, joined together with a wafer. Only a single line had been added — a sentence prohibiting Territorial Legislatures from acting upon slavery.[9] Douglas could quite truthfully boast to Lanphier that 'the difference between Mr. Clay's compromise bill and my two bills was a wafer; he did not write one word of it, and I did write every word.'

Douglas immediately sought a test as to whether the Senate preferred to consider the measures separately or in a single bill. After the Senate decided in favor of the latter plan he loyally supported its every item. But its course was troubled. President Taylor sneeringly termed it an 'omnibus' and

[8] Sheahan, 132–34; see also Douglas to Lanphier and Walker, Washington, Aug. 3, 1850. In his life of Douglas, Professor Allen Johnson casts dubiety upon the conversation between Douglas and Clay, as reported by Sheahan. There is indisputable proof in my possession that Douglas scrupulously read proof-sheets of the Sheahan biography, and corrected error after error of fact. Furthermore, his letter of Aug. 3, 1850, outlines in compressed form just such a colloquy as Sheahan reported *in extenso*. There is no substantial doubt of the authenticity of Sheahan's account.

[9] Douglas to Lanphier and Walker, Washington, Aug. 3, 1850. Douglas added that 'this amendment was voted in the Committee in opposition to the wishes of General Cass and Mr. Clay and they gave notice that they should move to strike it out in the Senate, and it was stricken out.'

worked against it, while the Southern Ultras were no better pleased. On May 15 Jefferson Davis moved an amendment to prevent Territorial Legislatures from interfering 'with those rights of property growing out of the institution of African slavery as it exists in any of the States of the Union.'[10] He modified his proposal a week later to assert that such legislatures should not pass any law 'to introduce or exclude African slavery.'

Douglas now sought to have the Senate eliminate the single new clause incorporated in the Committee's wafer joining his two bills. Expressing his regret 'that a clause had been introduced into this bill providing that the Territorial Government should not legislate in respect to African slavery,' he renewed his insistence that 'this and all other questions relating to the domestic affairs and domestic policy of the Territories ought to be left to the decision of the people themselves.' The inclusion of this new clause constituted 'a violation of that principle upon which we have all rested our defense of the course we have taken on this question.'[11]

Davis responded that the difference between himself and Douglas was in their definition of a people. 'The Senator says that the inhabitants of the Territory have a right to decide what their institutions shall be. When? By what authority? How many of them? The difference then between the Senator from Illinois and myself is the point at which the people do possess and may assert their rights.'

Douglas took up the challenge. 'If, Sir, there are enough to require a government,' he replied, 'and to authorize you to allow them to govern themselves, there are enough to govern themselves upon the subject of Negroes as well as concerning other species of property and other descriptions of institutions. You will concede that government is necessary — a government founded upon principles of Popular Sovereignty and the right of the people to enact their own laws.... You confer upon them the right to legislate upon all rightful subjects of legislation except Negroes. Why except the Negro? Why except African slavery? If the inhabitants are competent to govern themselves upon all other subjects... they are competent also to enact laws to govern themselves in regard to slavery and Negroes.'[12]

Soon afterwards Douglas moved to strike out the clause forbidding Territorial Legislatures to establish or prohibit 'African slavery.' The first effort was unsuccessful but a few days later the Senate accepted the change, and the bill was again in the exact form that Douglas had drafted it in March.

As the critical votes approached, the tension between President Taylor and the Compromise Whigs increased and the President exerted himself to the utmost to defeat the Compromise. Despondent, Clay wrote his son that 'the Administration, the Ultra Southern men and the timid Whigs of the North' were all combined against it, and it would be 'wonderful if it should

---

[10] *Congressional Globe*, Thirty-First Congress, First Session, 1000 *et seq.*, gives Davis' speech about this time insisting that the climate and soil of New Mexico would permit slavery to flourish.

[11] *Ibid.*, 1114.

[12] *Ibid.*, 1115–16. Moreover, Douglas denied 'that to exclude any species of property by law from any Territory is a violation of any proper right to property.'

succeed.' Webster feared that the Administration was doomed, and the Whig party doomed with it. Cass, too, thought the Compromise doomed.[13]

From the start the Southern course generated resentment. 'We were actually goaded almost to madness,' Shields wrote a friend back home. 'They pounded on the North until it became insufferable.' The Western members were exasperated by the bitterness of the extremists North and South. 'The Ultra pro-slavery man is intolerable,' Shields declared. 'The Ultra Free-Soil man is still worse. It should be our effort to keep the middle course between two extremes. I am opposed to the extension of slavery. I believe Illinois opposed to it. But this opposition must be bounded by justice and moderation. There should be no "Wilmot," no attempt to interfere with the right of self-government in the Territories more than in the States. If the country keeps within the Constitution, they should be permitted to manage their own affairs. This is a sound principle but I am sorry to say it is not acceptable to the South.'

While provoked over the way the Compromise debate caused Congress to neglect 'the business affairs of the country,' yet Douglas came to Clay's aid on nearly every issue that arose.[14] When Berrien sought to delay the admission of California's Representatives into Congress, he defended their right to full and immediate representation. When Soulé, of Louisiana, sought to postpone California's admission until she had enacted an ordinance disclaiming all right to Federal public lands, Douglas spoke for two days in vigorous opposition. 'It is admitted on all hands,' Harris wrote, 'the ablest speech Douglas ever delivered.'[15]

On July 4, following imprudent exposure at Washington Monument ceremonies, President Taylor was suddenly seized with cholera morbus and in a few days was at the point of death. On July 9 Webster rose during the usual acrimonious Senate debate to announce that the President was dying.

The death-bed scene was touching. The old General gasped for breath, and exclaimed: 'I have endeavored to do my duty, I am prepared to die. My one regret is leaving behind me the friends I love.' In a few minutes he was dead. Soon after the funeral Webster ran across his friend Hilliard, of Alabama, and they fell into discussion of the late President. 'If General Taylor had lived,' Webster said, 'we should have had civil war.'[16]

Millard Fillmore's accession renewed Clay's hopes of passing the Compromise. The new President had long been a foe of Seward in New York politics, a fact which led him to become an advocate of Clay's Compromise. But these hopes proved illusory and Compromise hopes grew fainter and fainter. Jubilant, the Southern Ultras boasted that they would keep anything from being done; the Free-Soilers were equally pleased. Soon a great uproar

[13] Henry Clay to Thomas Clay, Washington, May 31, 1850; Clay MSS., Library of Congress. Webster to Hall, Washington, May 18, 1850; Webster MSS., Library of Congress. Thomas L. Harris to Lanphier and Walker, Washington, June 26, 1850; James A. Shields to Lanphier and Walker, Washington, June 29, 1850; Patton MSS.

[14] Douglas to Elisha Whittlesey, Washington, June 25, 1850; Chicago Historical Society MSS.

[15] Thos. L. Harris to Chas. H. Lanphier, Washington, June 20, 1850; Patton MSS.

[16] Hilliard, 229-31.

w,ould break out in the South, culminating in the much-threatened secession — such at least became the belief of Northern Democrats — and upon this, they felt sure, Free-Soilism, secretly pleased, would turn up pious eyes to say: 'It is not my work — these villains always had treason in their hearts, and wanted only a pretext to commit the overt act.'

In mid-July Harris had a long talk with Speaker Cobb. 'He understands the movements of the South perfectly,' the Illinois member noted, 'and is fixed in the opinion that an open attempt at Secession will be made... Georgia, Alabama and Mississippi are not quite up to South Carolina, but so incessant is the conspirators' urging that they are fast bringing the masses to their views. Cobb is determined to be silent no longer.' [17] This altered attitude among such leaders of the Southern Whigs, reflected also by Stephens and Toombs, was later to have a powerful moderating effect both in Congress and in the States.

On July 17 Webster made his last Senate speech before accepting from Fillmore the Secretaryship of State. His swan-song was an elaborate appeal for the Compromise. He favored every measure of the Omnibus but thought that, whatever might be the fate of the Compromise as a whole, California should be immediately admitted. Did Douglas think the admission of California would settle the irksome question? he inquired.

'If California should be admitted by herself,' the Illinois Senator answered, 'I should certainly feel it my duty as Chairman of the Committee on Territories to move and take up the Territorial bills at once, and put them through, and also the Texas boundary question, and to settle them in detail if they are not settled in the aggregate.' [18]

'If this bill should fail today,' Webster continued, 'would you bring in that bill tomorrow?'

'Yes,' was the laconic reply.

On July 25 Seward sought to have New Mexico admitted as a State, his speech evoking answering fury from the Southrons. Bradbury, of Maine, wanted the Texas line fixed by a joint commission of Texas and the United States, but would not have the new boundary operative until Texas had accepted it. All knew Texas would never do so and this scheme too was voted down.

By July 31 the whole matter was in such a tangle that motion was made that action on the Omnibus bill be indefinitely postponed. Marshaling his forces to oppose this, Clay was momentarily successful but the victory was short-lived. A few minutes later the New Mexican Territorial provision was eliminated. Next the Texas boundary provision was stricken from the bill. Then three attempts were made to eliminate the California bill, the final one successfully. Nothing was now left of the Omnibus except the establishment of a Territorial Government for Utah. The mountain had labored and had brought forth a mouse.

[17] Thomas L. Harris to Lanphier and Walker, Washington, July 19, 1850; Patton MSS. Howell Cobb to John B. Lamar, Washington, June 26, 1850, *Georgia Historical Quarterly*, September, 1921, 42: 'I... am prepared for the issue if forced upon me by the extremists.'

[18] *Congressional Globe*, Thirty-First Congress, First Session, 1266.

The defeat of the Omnibus marked the departure of all of the great triumvirate from the senatorial stage. Calhoun had been the first to go. Four months before, as if he despaired of securing from fleshly hands that perfect equilibrium for which he plead, his frail body had been consigned to the grave, and his weird logic willed to his lieutenants — a legacy destined to be paid in blood. Webster, too, had left his favorite forum. No more would the idle loiterers start up on seeing him approach in the uniform of the Revolution. He had had his last 'great day,' and now was again enjoying the comfortable office and pleasing dignity of Secretary of State. Clay was still a member of the Senate, but despondent, disillusioned and worn. He had poured all his energy and hope into the ill-fated Omnibus, it had failed, and the future seemed 'dark and portentous.'

On August 1 he rebuked the Senate for its course. 'We presented to the country a measure of peace, a measure of tranquillity,' he declared, 'one which would have harmonized all the discordant feelings which prevailed... The measure was defeated by the extremists on the other side of the Chamber, and on this.' He stood in his place, he continued defiantly, 'meaning to be unawed by any threats, whether they came from individuals, or from States.' Furthermore, 'if any one State, or a portion of the people of any State, choose to place themselves in military array against the Government of the Union, I am for trying the strength of the Government.' It was time to find out 'whether we have got a Government or not.'

His final salvo against disunion was that not his State but the Union was his country. 'Even if it were my own State,' he shouted, 'if my own State, lawlessly, contrary to her duty, should raise the standard of disunion against the residue of the Union, I would go against her. I would go against Kentucky herself in that contingency, much as I love her.' Soon afterwards he left for Newport to repair his health in the refreshing breezes of the New England coast.

On that same day Douglas took charge of the abandoned Compromise. During all the debates Clay's plan had received his 'active and unwavering support.' [19] His Illinois colleague, General Shields, had gone with him, as had all but two of the State's delegation in the House. From the start, Douglas had predicted that Clay would fail because it would unite the enemies of the various items. Harris believed that the Compromise had been 'dashed to pieces by the carelessness or over-carefulness of its friends,' but the Little Giant ascribed the defeat to 'a union between the Free Soils and Disunionists and the Administration of Gen'l. Taylor.' To accomplish it, 'all the power and patronage of the Gov't. was brought to bear against us, and at last the allied forces were able to beat us.' [20] Analyzing the votes upon the Compromise, he saw how the juncture of the measures had 'united the opponents of each measure, instead of securing the friends of each.' Similarly he saw how resolving the Omnibus bill into its individual components would enable him to secure the passage of each in turn.

[19] Colton, *Last Seven Years*, 389-96; Douglas to Lanphier and Walker, Washington, Aug. 3, 1850.

[20] Harris to Lanphier and Walker, Washington, Aug. 1, 1850; Patton MSS.

More than this, the Little Giant sensed the changing temper of the country. The much-advertised Nashville Convention had been expected to prove that the great mass of the Southern people were ready to break up the Union. When the delegates assembled, their Ultra and unrepresentative character was clearly apparent and the real strength of the Southern Unionists began to be revealed.

In the North, too, sentiment began to change. Developments in Illinois were indicative. Many of the Free-Soil Whig leaders, in and out of the State Legislature, who had been insisting on a Wilmot prohibition, saw the situation in a new light and came out for compromise. The Illinois Democrats in Congress were overjoyed at these developments. 'Now, by Saint Paul, the work goes bravely on!' Harris chortled. He believed a Whig schism had occurred, and that 'those profligate politicians, who have driven the country to the verge of dissolution were becoming conscious of their errors, and were seeking to save themselves from the consequences of their acts.' [21]

These shifts in public opinion North and South aided Douglas in his new task. He amended the caption of the ill-fated Omnibus so as to make it accurately descriptive of the Utah Territorial establishment. This done, he promptly reintroduced the bill for the admission of California as a State and asked that it be so amended as to reinstate a public land provision earlier stricken out. The Senate heeded Douglas' request and put the clause back in. Two hostile amendments were then offered, the first to divide the State into two parts, on a parallel of $35° 30'$, the second to divide it on the parallel of $36° 30'$. He opposed both.

He was immediately charged with inconsistency in opposing the extension of the Missouri Compromise line to the Pacific Coast. For three months he had been silent under similar attack. Now he undertook to meet it. He admitted that in 1848 he had offered a similar amendment to the Oregon bill. 'I was then willing to adjust this whole slavery question on that line and on those terms,' he said. 'If the whole acquired territory was now in the same condition as it was then, I would vote for it, should be glad to see it adopted. But since then California has increased in population, has a State Government organized, and I cannot consent, for one, to destroy that State Government... For that reason, and that alone, I shall vote against the amendment.' Then he forced the two proposals to a vote and was able to have both rejected.

At this period Douglas seemed quite concerned to prove his own consistency. He caused the *Illinois State Register* to answer the charge that he was a slave-owner, and to correct the charge that he was a Free-Soiler.[22] As the Springfield editor explained, under instructions, the Senator had opposed the Wilmot Proviso, had 'always advocated the right of the people in each State and Territory to decide the slavery question for themselves,' and only voted for the prohibition of slavery in 1850's Territorial bills in obedience to instructions: 'The vote was the vote of those who gave the instructions and not his own.' A little later, Douglas asked again that the paper make it plain that any vote which he had given or would give, seemingly inconsistent to that principle, was not his vote but 'the vote of those who gave the instructions.' [23]

Henry Clay had sought to float the Compromise to success upon a sea of stately speeches. During the five months from February to August he had been on hand every day the Senate was in session, had made several set speeches and had addressed the Senate more than seventy times. Indeed, so great were his oratorical exertions that, by the time of the defeat of the Compromise, his health had completely broken down.[24]

With Douglas' accession to command there came a distinct shift in strategy. A past-master of parliamentary procedure, the Little Giant had an uncanny knowledge of the various combinations he could devise to sustain the diverse items of his program. Already 'some of the chivalry,' alarmed at the result of their conduct, had begun to back down.[25] Well aware of the situation, and secure in his leadership, Douglas let others stalk the boards while he directed the stage.

The Senate responded readily to the new management. After his third day in command Douglas felt so confident of success that he wrote Lanphier sanguinely: 'We have the greatest confidence that we will yet be able to settle the whole difficulty before we adjourn.'

He then revealed his plans for the various items of the Compromise. The Senate was at the moment engaged on his California bill. 'I trust you will hear of its passage through the Senate before you receive this. We shall then take up a bill for the Texas boundary which Mr. Pearce of Maryland and myself are now preparing.... We shall then take up the bill for New Mexico and pass it just as I reported it four months ago. Thus will all bills pass the Senate, and I believe the House also. When they are all passed, you see they will be collectively Mr. Clay's Compromise, and separately the bills reported by the Committee on Territories four months ago.'

So far as earlier efforts had been concerned, Douglas felt that 'if Mr. Clay's name had not been associated with the bills, they would have passed long ago. The Administration were jealous of him and hated him and some Democrats were weak enough to fear that the success of his bill would make him President. But let it always be said of Old Hal that he fought a glorious and patriotic battle. No man was ever governed by higher and purer motives.' [26]

In accordance with Douglas' plan, on August 5 Pearce introduced his bill for the settlement of the northern boundary of Texas. During the ensuing four days' debate, except to answer questions, Douglas spoke only once.

---

[23] Douglas to Walker and Lanphier, Washington, Sept. 5, 1850; Patton MSS.

[24] Colton, *Last Seven Years*, 180.

[25] Harris to Lanphier and Walker, Washington, Aug. 1, 1850; Patton MSS.

[26] Douglas to Lanphier and Walker, Washington, Aug. 3, 1850. Douglas added: 'The same remark is true of Senator Cass. Many of our friends talk hard of Buchanan. It is supposed that he encouraged the nullifiers and disunionists to oppose the measures out of jealousy of Cass.'

This speech was to assure the Senate that any change made in this bill would automatically be incorporated in the New Mexico bill when that measure came forward. On August 9 the bill passed by a vote of 30 to 20.

Three days later Douglas spoke at some length upon the main measure. Answering attacks on the irregularity of the California constitutional procedure, he offered the illustration of Michigan. His advocacy was both compelling and successful, for the bill passed the Senate the next day and another item of Douglas' original measures to be enacted practically in the form of its initial draft.

The Little Giant at once called up his New Mexico bill, and moved to strike out all sections in it referring to the government of Utah and the solution of the Texas boundary. This was promptly done. Enemies of the measure then brought forward amendment after amendment, but each was defeated. The Illinois leader then brought the bill to a vote and it passed. Then he moved to change the title of the measure so as to omit the name of Utah — a small matter, but quickly voted, another illustration of his effective leadership.

Thus, under Douglas' leadership, in two weeks' time, the Senate had voted to admit California, to quiet the Texas boundary dispute and to give New Mexico Territorial Government. The Little Giant had proved his mastery.

But the passage of the measures through the Senate was only half of the battle. As late as June, Douglas' House associates had felt certain of their ability to pass the Compromise. In August, however, when the Senate bills started coming over, defeat stared the House managers in the face. The Senator gave the closest attention to the House progress of the various bills. He had great personal influence and prestige there, exercised it to the fullest and his leadership proved effective.

The danger in the House was the same that had been met in the Senate. Southern Ultras and Northern Free-Soilers, equally unwilling to yield to the idea of compromise, were not unwilling to join hands to negative a middle course. Of the two, the anger of the Southerners seemed the more intense, but the great strength of Wilmot Whigs made their attitude politically more dangerous.

By the last of August it seemed that the Texas boundary bill was sure to be killed in the House. The Northwestern Democrats were mainly for it but the Whigs were acting badly. 'No sooner do they see a prospect of settlement than they want to make the most they can of party capital out of it,' Harris wrote bitterly to Lanphier. 'Some of them now want simply to pass the California bill and the boundary bill, and to relieve the Administration of the troubles, and let the Territorial bills go.' [27] The plan of the Northern enemies of the Compromise — chiefly Whigs still anxious to carry out the Taylor scheme of six months before — was to pass a Texas boundary bill, admit California as a State, and do nothing further about the other elements of the Compromise.

[27] Harris to Lanphier and Walker, Washington, Aug. 23, 1850; Patton MSS. Howell Cobb to Mrs. Cobb, Washington, Aug. 10, 1850; Erwin MSS.

To counter this scheme, Linn Boyd, of the House Committee on Territories, had Douglas prepare a literal copy of the Senate's New Mexican bill
so that it could be offered as an amendment to the Texas boundary bill.[28]
Douglas did so. Boyd introduced the amendment, the Free-Soilers saw their
danger and factional turmoil broke out.

On September 1 the struggle began in earnest. Loyally following Douglas'
lead and constantly advised by him, the Western Democrats undertook
to carry through the Compromise as a whole. All that was needed, Harris
believed, was for the Territorial bill to pass; that done, the road lay open
for full adjustment.[29]

When Boyd's amendment was brought to a vote, the Northern Whigs
turned against it, and it was 46 votes short of passage. On September 4,
when the Texas boundary bill, shorn of Boyd's amendment, was brought
up again, enough of the Northern Whigs turned away to defeat it. 'Nothing
can effect a settlement,' Harris indignantly wrote, 'until Whiggery caves
in, admits its follies and its political wickedness, and strangles its Proviso
bantling.' They knew they could pass the bill with Boyd's amendment,
he added a little later, 'yet the cowardly tricksters voted against that amendment because it had not the Wilmot in it. They wanted it passed, and they
would then have voted for the bill in numbers sufficient to have carried it.
But they were committed, as they say, against Territorial Governments
unless the Proviso was on.'[30]

But the disappointment was short-lived. The Compromise leaders saw
that the defeat was solely technical and parliamentary and that, 'Lazarus
like,' the bills would come forth from the grave and be passed. The day
after the adverse vote Douglas wrote confidently that the bill would come
to life. Cobb stayed in the Speaker's chair 'during two days of the most
exciting scenes I have ever witnessed.'[31]

Early on the afternoon of September 6, these maneuvers had their effect,
and Harris was able to address a joyous note to Douglas: 'Boundary bill
and New Mexico bill just ordered to 1 reading by ten maj. All danger is
over — all's bright, and everybody but the Abolitionists or disunionists
glad. The sneaking, contemptible Whig pups of the North barked *No* at
the bill all through, with a few venerable exceptions.... Glory to God in
the highest.'[32]

Among spectators of this triumph were Lewis Cass and Henry Clay. The
latter, who had returned from Newport on August 28, was only moderately
pleased at Douglas' success. 'We can see no end yet of this fatiguing session,' he wrote his son soon thereafter. 'I am again getting very much
exhausted. I wish that I had remained longer at Newport.'[33]

---

[28] Douglas to Walker and Lanphier, Sept. 5, 1850; Patton MSS.

[29] Harris to Lanphier, Washington, Sept. 1, 1850; Patton MSS.

[30] Harris to Lanphier, Washington, Sept. 4, 1850; Patton MSS.

[31] Douglas to Lanphier and Walker, Washington, Sept. 5, 1850; Patton MSS. Cobb to Mrs.
Cobb, Washington, Sept. 6, 1850; Erwin MSS.

[32] Harris to Douglas [Washington] Sept. 6, 2 o'clock, 20 min. [1850]; Douglas MSS.

[33] Henry Clay to Thomas Clay, Washington, Sept. 6, 1850; Clay MSS., Library of Congress.

Clay had returned in time to take part in the debate on the two remaining items of the Compromise — the abolition of the slave trade in the District of Columbia and the enactment of a better Fugitive Slave law. During the debate on the first of these, Seward proposed to abolish slavery itself in the District, a motion which occasioned lurid fireworks but was rejected with only five affirmative votes.[34] After two weeks' general debate, the Senate passed the original measure by 33 to 19.

The other item of the program, a new Fugitive Slave bill, was also enacted into law. Originally fashioned by Mason, of Virginia, it was an integral part of the Compromise and had the general assent of the moderates. But while Douglas favored it, he was not on hand to vote, a circumstance which laid him open to the charge that he had tried to dodge.

Always adventurous in land speculations, Douglas' obligations were constantly maturing. In September, 1850, his note for $4000 was about to fall due in New York. He thought that he had made arrangements to meet it, but these fell through and he rushed to the metropolis.

Before he left, several Senators assured him that debate over the Fugitive Slave bill would continue for at least another week. But the Senate acted with unusual promptness. On Douglas' second evening in New York, while he was dining with some friends from Illinois, he was surprised to learn that the bill had already been ordered engrossed for its third and final reading. He left immediately for Washington but arrived after the vote had been taken and the bill had gone over to the House.

The Little Giant wished to explain the reasons for his failure to vote but Shields held him back. Everyone knew that Douglas favored the bill, the General said. Also, in all likelihood, it would come back from the House with amendments and Douglas would then get a chance to vote. The charge that he had sought to escape passing on this bill seemed absurd to Douglas, and appears equally absurd to the modern historical student. As he said later, 'Dodging votes, an attempt to avoid responsibility, is no part of my system of political tactics.'[35]

Finally these two measures likewise passed the House, and by the end of September every item which Douglas deemed necessary for the solution of the sectional difficulties had become a law. Convinced that the sectional disputes had been completely quieted, he 'resolved never to make another speech upon the slavery question in the Houses of Congress.'[36]

During the latter part of his labors for the Compromise, its new general had to contend against sickness as well as Abolitionists and Southern Ultras. For much of September he was crippled, 'and kept in constant torture by a very painful and deep-seated swelling on his hip.'[37] But, painful as this was, Douglas stayed at his task until the session ended.

[34] Sheahan, 156. These were Chase of Ohio; Dodge, of Wisconsin; Seward, of New York; Hale, of New Hampshire, and Upham, of Vermont.
[35] *Congressional Globe*, Thirty-Second Congress, First Session, App., 66.
[36] Speech in U.S. Senate, Dec. 23, 1851.
[37] Thomas L. Harris to Chas. H. Lanphier, Washington, Sept. 24, 1850; Patton MSS.

Nor was his agency in the success of the Compromise without notice. 'If any man has a right to be proud of the success of these measures,' Jefferson Davis, of Mississippi, an opponent of the Compromise, declared in the final debate, 'it is the Senator from Illinois.' Clay proclaimed the final success of the program as 'a triumph for the Union, for harmony and concord' and added that 'to Douglas, more than to any other individual,' was due the fact that disruption had been averted.[33] Douglas declared himself proud of having played 'an humble part in the enactment of all these great measures,' but said firmly that 'no man and no party has acquired a triumph except the party friendly to the Union.'

In essence, he felt that the great principle of the Compromise was its endorsement of 'the right of the people to form and regulate their own internal concerns and domestic institutions in their own way.'[39] A large group of Southern Compromise men were equally delighted with the outcome. They too felt that a great essential principle had been secured. But they saw the new principle not a national but a sectional one. Robert Toombs was again and again to proclaim that the Compromise upheld 'the principle of non-interference with slavery by Congress, the right of the people to hold slaves in a common Territory.'[40]

The discrepancy between these views of the basis of the Compromise was fundamental. Under Douglas' view, if they so determined, the people of the Territory could exclude slavery. Did Toombs and the other Southern Compromisers understand the measures of 1850 to embrace this right?

Here was a portent of further disagreement between the sections. The Missouri Compromise had failed to still the clash of sections and it had been necessary to abandon it. Perhaps this new Compromise contained within itself further seeds of strife. Would the new statesmanship prove equal to the task of continual adjustment? Upon this depended the Nation's peace.

[33] Sheahan, 158; *Congressional Globe*, Thirty-Second Congress, First Session, 1850. 'Savoyard,' Washington *Post*, Sept. 23, 1894, for Clay's tribute to Douglas.

[39] Sheahan, 169.

[40] Johnson, 189. This principle, Toombs and the Southern Compromisers insisted, had been unwisely surrendered by the South in 1820 through the adoption of the Missouri Compromise. Now this surrender had been undone, and the South had again secured and could maintain its rights.

CHAPTER VI

THE FIRST DEFEAT

BY THE time the Compromise succeeded, less than a year and a half after Zachary Taylor entered office, many shrewd observers saw that the Whig party would soon be dead. It had become an *omnium gatherum* of high-tariff devotees, Emancipationists, office-seekers and speculators. Defeat had kept the party whole but victory pronounced its doom.

Thus the next President was sure to be a Democrat and Douglas' friends insisted that the time had come for him to make a bid. Theirs was the initiative, and from this time until his death Douglas' own ambition was a less controlling force than was his friends' ambitions for him. This was a result chiefly of his amazing hold on the human heart. His friends, even to a Free-Soiler like 'Long John' Wentworth, adored the Little Giant and believed that there was no place he could not fill. With them *here* was always the place for Douglas and *now* always the time.[1]

At first the Senator felt that he could well afford to wait, but he allowed himself to be persuaded, and came to think that he had as good a chance as any living Democrat to become the next President of the United States. In 1851, however, nearly every Democrat of greater than gubernatorial stature — and some of less — looked toward the White House and there was almost a battalion of active aspirants: Lewis Cass, James Buchanan, William L. Marcy, Levi Woodbury, William O. Butler, Sam Houston and the Little Giant himself. Cass was sixty-nine, Marcy sixty-five, Woodbury sixty-two, Buchanan sixty, both Butler and Houston fifty-eight; Douglas alone did not belong to the generation on the wane.

The Southern Rights men had not forgiven Cass for the Nicholson letter, the Wilmot Proviso men continued hostile, and the Democratic Moderates of North and West were his dependence.

Taylor had not been in the White House six months before Buchanan began laying plans for 1852, with John W. Forney as his chief agent for the North and John Slidell, of Louisiana, his fugleman for the Cotton South. While Buchanan had a solid intellect, he was ponderous and unexciting. Andrew Jackson had known him but did not trust him. Polk made him Secretary of State, over Old Hickory's protest, and regretted it. During the California ferment Buchanan did nothing to allay Southern apprehensions; on the contrary, he expressed to Howell Cobb his 'desire that the South should show themselves to be in earnest.'[2] 'Many of our friends talk hard of Buchanan,' Douglas wrote when the Compromise was in

[1] *Missouri Republican*, St. Louis, Jan. 28, 1862; quoting Wentworth's eulogy of Douglas.

[2] Foote, *Casket of Reminiscences*, 110-12; Polk, *Diary*, I, 98, 104, 201, III, 403; Buchanan to Cobb, Wheatland, Nov. 10, Dec. 29, 1849; Erwin MSS.

the balance. 'It is supposed that he encourages the Nullifiers and Secessionists to oppose the measures out of jealousy of General Cass.'[3] When the
Compromise passed, Buchanan would not endorse it, a fact which operated
to make him the chosen candidate of the Southern Ultras.

Although William L. Marcy, of New York, is chiefly known in history as
the author of the phrase, 'to the victor belongs the spoils,' he was a shrewd,
well-poised man, with a sense of humor and a practical philosophy. He had
been a notable public figure, but was now weary of the shabby devices of
party politics and was practically in retirement. Yet the fact that Marcy
was the Softs' patron saint set the Hards unalterably against him, and
Daniel S. Dickinson, known both as 'Silver Dick' from his oratory, and
'Scripture Dick' from his prolixity of Bible references, held him in contempt.
When Dickinson evinced an unsuspected zeal in Cass' behalf, leading Softs
warned Marcy that if the National Convention dead-locked, Dickinson
would try to nominate himself. Chiefly to checkmate Dickinson Marcy
now became a candidate.[4]

Levi Woodbury, of New Hampshire, a 'learned and laborious' man, had
been a Senator, Secretary of the Treasury and for the last five years an
Associate Justice of the United States Supreme Court. Without bias on
the slavery issue, and with an energetic New England support, Woodbury
was well situated to make a bid.[5]

While Douglas was only thirty-seven, his youth made him the idol of
'Young America,' a large and growing group impatient with the 'old fogies'
who had so long monopolized the national stage. His shrewder advisers
wanted him to pay 'attention to the *real* business of a Senator, without
drawing any man's car or riding in it,' because '*Time* will do what exertion
cannot accomplish, as Clay, Webster, Calhoun and Cass have found out.'[6]

As the canvass neared, Douglas saw clearly that there would be a mad
scramble and that it was almost certain that the successful candidate would
win by maneuver in the convention itself. He made up his mind to show himself over the country, to make speeches on non-controversial subjects and
to cultivate the friendship of the leading men. He was determined, however,
to refrain from attack on any of the rival candidates, because the votes
to nominate him might come from Cass, or Marcy, or Woodbury, or
Buchanan, and all must be kept so that any could turn to him.

But first Douglas must defend 1850's Compromise against the resentment
of the extreme elements both North and South. There was bitter schism
in the South and the Compromise men from that section were denounced
as traitors to their States.

So inflamed was the South Carolina feeling that the State's Union party
disappeared. The agitation affected Georgia and Alabama, and Secession
was in the crucible all through the Cotton South. The Northern Ultras

[3] Douglas to Lanphier and Walker, Washington, Aug. 3, 1850; Patton MSS.
[4] Roy F. Nichols, *The Democratic Machine, 1850–1854*, New York, 1923; 92 *et seq.*
[5] Francis P. Blair to Martin Van Buren, Silver Spring, Md., Dec. 30, 1850; Van Buren MSS.
[6] E. H. Gillett to Douglas, New York, April 19, Sept. 15, 1850; Douglas MSS.

contended that the Compromise men had surrendered a great moral principle; not only had they failed to put a definite ban on slavery in the war-acquired Territories, but also they had made slave-catchers out of the Northern people.

Illness kept the Little Giant in Washington until October.[7] Then he set out for Chicago, where he arrived about the middle of the month. The city's Abolitionists and Free-Soilers had worked themselves into a rage over the great compromise over slavery, and on October 21, the Common Council of the City adopted resolutions denouncing the Fugitive Slave law and terming the Northern Senators and Representatives who had supported it men 'fit only to be ranked with the traitors, Benedict Arnold and Judas Iscariot, who betrayed his Lord and Master for thirty pieces of silver.' As the Fugitive Slave law was 'cruel and unjust,' the Council refused to 're-quire the city police to render any assistance for the arrest of fugitive slaves.' A great public mass meeting was called to ratify these resolutions. The next evening, while twenty-five hundred Chicagoans were applauding a speaker's appeal to defy 'death, the dungeon and the grave' in resisting the Fugitive Slave law, Douglas demanded permission to speak and announced that he would appear there the next evening to prove that he had been right.

At the time appointed, four thousand gathered, the members of the City Council were directly in front of the stand, and in the rear was a large body of armed Negroes, including many fugitive slaves. Douglas first explained the doctrine of Popular Sovereignty, upon which the Compromise had been founded. Then he turned to the Common Council, which had declared an Act of Congress void 'upon the ground that it violates the Constitution of the United States and the law of God,' and had called on the citizens and police to abstain from aiding in its execution. But the Senator had yet to learn that a subordinate municipal corporation could 'raise the standard of rebellion, and throw off the authority of the Federal Government at pleasure'; this was 'naked, unmitigated nullification.'

He then took up the specific objections to the law, answered them patiently, responded courteously to hostile questions, and declared: 'The real objection is not to the new law, nor to the old one, but to the Constitution itself.... The whole catalogue of objections would all be moonshine, if the Negro was not required to go back to his master. Tell me frankly, is not this the true character of your objection?' There was an affirmative shout from the audience, and Douglas read the slavery clause in the Constitution, binding on every citizen so long as the Constitution remained. This made it a question of union or disunion, because 'we cannot expect our brethren of other States to remain faithful to the compact and permit us to be faithless.' He himself was prepared 'to maintain and preserve inviolate the Constitution as it is, with all its compromises, to stand or fall by the American Union, clinging with the tenacity of life to all its glorious memories of the past and precious hopes of the future.'[8]

[7] Douglas to Lanphier, Washington, Oct. 2, 1850; Patton MSS.

[8] For full text of this speech as written out by Douglas the next day from notes, see Flint, App., 3–30.

The Senator then submitted resolutions which favored carrying into effect every provision of the Constitution and laws in regard to fugitive slaves. These were adopted unanimously, as was a formal repudiation of the Common Council's resolutions. Douglas now turned to the campaign elsewhere in the State, and the November result was generally satisfactory. The Illinois Legislature soon repealed its Wilmot instructions and passed resolutions warmly commending Douglas' Compromise stand.[9]

In the South the contest was sharpest in Georgia, Alabama and Mississippi. In Georgia's first test, in November, 1850, over the election of delegates to a State Convention to consider remedies for grievances, the Compromise leaders won a striking victory. But this meant, not 'unconditional submission' but that Georgia would abide by the settlement and the North must 'carry out in good faith her part of it.' [10]

The next year the Georgia State's Rights men renewed the struggle. Party lines were obliterated, the Ultras supported Charles J. McDonald, Union Whigs and Union Democrats formed a new Constitutional Union party, with Howell Cobb as their candidate for Governor, to whom Toombs and Stephens gave a mighty support. The Unionists brought forward the Georgia platform that the Compromise should be sustained but the South would resist any further encroachment upon its rights. After a campaign in which the State was stirred to the depths, the Union men won an overwhelming victory.

Hilliard defeated Yancey in Alabama, a result accepted by both sides as an endorsement of the Compromise. John A. Quitman ran for Governor of Mississippi on an extreme Secession platform. Henry S. Foote, his Conservative opponent, amassed such strong support that Quitman withdrew in favor of Jefferson Davis. Foote, however, was triumphantly elected. In these real tests, and with real leadership for the Union cause, the Southern foes of the Compromise were routed and sectionalism rebuked.

During this exciting Southern drama, the would-be Presidents began dealing one another stealthy blows. Young America wanted to put all the candidates into the same deck, believing that in the shuffle Douglas would 'come up trump.' About this time, however, Buchanan's willingness to 'unite with the Fire-Eaters' made him more formidable, and the Woodbury campaign also emerged as a real threat. This last was largely due to Thomas H. Benton's multiplying troubles in Missouri. For a decade a Southern Rights faction had sought to unseat him and now he needed a national campaign, preferably behind a Jackson man, to help him in his fight at home. Woodbury was the best available, 'Old Bullion' persuaded the Blairs and the Van Burens to take him up and the enterprise began to show real strength. In September, however, Woodbury died.[11]

[9] *Illinois State Register*, Nov. 5, 1851; Henry M. Flint, *Life of Stephen A. Douglas*, Philadelphia, 1863; 56.

[10] Luther J. Glenn to Howell Cobb, McDonough, Ga., Nov. 28, 1850; printed in *Georgia Historical Quarterly*, September, 1921; 43.

[11] Alfred Gilmore to Buchanan, Washington, Dec. 24, 1850; Buchanan MSS. Robert Toombs to Howell Cobb, Washington, Jan. 2, 1851; Erwin MSS. Nichols, *The Democratic Machine*, 81–82.

Here was a bolt from the blue; some Bentonians wanted to take up Sam Houston, but revelation of a mysterious correspondence linking Houston with Free-Soilers gave the *coup de grâce* to these plans. Benton eventually adopted General William O. Butler, of Kentucky, another follower of Old Hickory. Brigadier in the Mexican War and Cass' running-mate in 1848, the South knew that he owned a few slaves, the North that he favored gradual emancipation.

Douglas planned his own campaign shrewdly. He would cultivate the leaders of all sections and all factions and so conduct himself that a failure now would not impair his chances later. 'I do not consider myself a candidate in the field,' he wrote a Boston editor. 'I am young and can afford to wait.'[12] But this did not mean that he neglected practical steps. He made a plan to break Buchanan's Southern Ultra strength and to cut into Cass' Northwestern backing, while New York friends maneuvered for Tammany help.

Accordingly Douglas' Southern friends proposed that the ticket be made up of a Northerner who had supported the Compromise and a Southerner who had opposed it. After the Little Giant visited Richmond, Virginia, Buchanan leaders were aghast to find Senator R. M. T. Hunter 'willing to ride behind the Judge.' This was true, for he deemed Douglas 'one of the coolest observers, even when he himself is concerned, that I ever saw.' The Hunter project went forward during the Summer, and Buchanan's Virginia lieutenants were thoroughly alarmed.[13]

Douglas declined several invitations to public dinners, feeling that it was better for him to meet his friends 'in the private and social circles.' In this field, however, he was indefatigable, visiting New York repeatedly, and in the Summer going West to handle politics at home.[14] 'All the news I get in regard to politics is favorable,' he wrote Sanders from Chicago. His general policy in the West was to look with favor on favorite son delegations, with himself as second choice. When his Indiana manager proposed to have Indiana endorse a favorite son, with Douglas as second choice, the Senator answered that it would 'do equally as well as to instruct for me in the first instance.'[15]

Some of the support offered him had strings tied to it. George Roberts, of the Boston *Times*, was willing to play ball, but hinted that the candidate, if successful, should look after the editor's friends. But Douglas was not willing. 'I have not allowed myself to give the slightest promise or intimation to any man living of any personal advantage to be derived from my Administration in the event of my election,' he wrote Roberts. 'I have

---

[12] Douglas to George Roberts, New York, Sept. 8, 1851; photostat in author's possession.

[13] Wise to Buchanan, Richmond, Va., Feb. 20; John A. Parker to Buchanan, Ashland, Va., March 28, April 18, July 20, 1851; H. A. Wise to Buchanan, Richmond, Va., April 20, 1851; Buchanan MSS. Hunter to Sanders, Lloyds, Va., May 9, 1851; Sanders MSS., Library of Congress.

[14] Douglas to George N. Sanders, Washington, April 11, Manchester Center, N.Y., May 18, 1851; originals in Watertown, Conn., Library.

[15] Douglas to George N. Sanders, Chicago, July 12, 1851; original in Watertown, Conn., Library. Douglas to W. H. English, Washington, Dec. 29, 1851; Illinois State Historical Library MSS.

refused such intimations in cases where there was danger of disturbing old personal relations and friendships, and I place the refusal upon a principle from which I can in no instance depart. I have as strong attachments to friends as any man and am as likely to remember their services to me with gratitude; but in the performance of public trusts, favors to friends must be consistent with or subordinate to the public interests; and of this I must be allowed to judge from time to time as it becomes my duty to act.' [16]

Douglas' careful handling of the New York situation bore such fruit that Marcy became disturbed, and late that Fall sent an agent to Douglas with a message of friendship and a hint that New York was concentrating on its distinguished statesman. The Little Giant was forced to reply that he would leave the New York field to Marcy and expected the latter to leave Illinois to him. [17]

But there were few such strategic retreats. The Polk party became active in Douglas' behalf in Tennessee, Buchanan's supporters there tried to stop the swing by ridiculing him as 'a boy thirty-eight years old who wants to be President over us old fellows,' but it took more than irony to put him down. George Sanders visited Kentucky to torpedo the Butler boom. Andrew J. Donelson, Jackson's nephew, and editor of the Washington *Union*, concluded that the Little Giant's chances were better than those of either Cass or Buchanan. Douglas himself believed success in sight. 'Things look well and the prospect is brightening every day,' he wrote. 'All that is necessary now to insure success is that the Northwest should unite and speak out.' [18]

The assemblage of the Thirty-Second Congress, in December, 1851, brought forward another problem for the battalion of presidential aspirants. This was the demand of the Southern Unionists that the finality of the

[16] Douglas to George Roberts, New York, Sept. 8, 1851; *cit. supra*. The Boston *Times*, the first enduring penny paper in Boston, was founded in 1836 and was bought by the Boston *Herald* in 1857. From 1844 it was a strong Democratic paper, fighting the battles of George Bancroft and the Van Buren wing of the Massachusetts Democracy against the Tyler-Calhoun faction, of which Benjamin F. Hallett, Robert Rantoul, Jr., and C. G. Greene were prominent. In 1851 George Roberts and William H. Garfield were its proprietors. Douglas' manly letter to Roberts apparently did not alienate him, for early the next year the *Times* put the Little Giant's name at its masthead. I am indebted to Mr. F. Lauriston Bullard, of the Boston *Herald*, a Lincoln authority of note, for the background data as to the *Times* and for a careful reading of its files for 1851–52.

[17] W. L. Marcy, Albany, N.Y., Sept. 6; Barnabas Bates, New York, Sept. 24; John M. Slidell, New York, Sept. 29, Oct. 10; August Belmont, New York, Dec. 6, 1851; Buchanan MSS. Belmont, the budding New York financier, at the time a Buchanan man, heard reports from Washington 'that Douglas and his party will leave nothing undone this session which can in any way further their aspirations, and that the wildest schemes for appropriations for railroads, public works, distribution of public lands, etc., will be moved and advocated by them in order to secure popularity in the different sections.' Douglas was being called 'the steam-candidate.' Charles Eames, Washington, Nov. 11, 1851; Marcy MSS., Library of Congress. Eames, an assistant editor of the Washington *Union*, was Marcy's envoy to Douglas.

[18] Alfred Balch, Nashville, Tenn., Nov. 18; W. L. Marcy, New York, Nov. 24, 1851; Buchanan MSS.; J. P. Beckman, Washington, March 9, 1852; Van Buren MSS. A. J. Donelson to Howell Cobb, Washington, Oct. 22, 1851; *American Historical Association Report* for 1911, II, 262–63. Douglas to Lanphier, Washington, Dec. 30, 1851; Patton MSS.

Compromise should be recognized and that the Ultras should not dictate the nominations. This insistence seemed at one time to be leading to a new party. Under the leadership of a 'Committee of Safety' of a hundred New York business men and financiers, Whig and Democratic Compromise men made plans to this end. Southerners like Foote, of Mississippi, and Stephens, Toombs and Cobb, of Georgia, became interested and Henry Clay agreed to lead the new formation. But Cass declined to become Clay's running-mate and the movement collapsed.

The Ultras countered by a coalition between the Democratic extremes, and Alexander H. Stephens observed that, while the country was in a perfect calm, 'it is the interval which the tempest sometimes gives while it shifts its points and renews its energy and fury.'

True, the Compromise had won in the State elections in Georgia, Alabama and Mississippi, but this had been accomplished by fusion and the Democratic party machinery had generally remained in the Ultras' hands. When it came to electing delegates to a National Convention, as a Douglas lieutenant shrewdly observed, the State's Rights party '*is* the Democratic party of the South.' [19] Thus presidential aspirants who had aided the Compromise were eliminated before they started, unless some formula could be found to keep it from being made a general test of party faith.

Observing feverish moves to this end, Stephens concluded that the leading object of the Democrats was to find a way by which the Free-Soil Democrats of Ohio and New York could be readmitted. He thought it the work of Benton and Van Buren, who expected the Southern Fire-Eaters to reapply as a matter of course, as those of Georgia and Alabama had already done, 'without asking terms, qualifications or conditions.' Therefore those Southern Democrats who wanted to purge the party, so as to make it a sound national party, were highly obnoxious to the Ultras of both sections. Stephens, Toombs, Cobb and their group wanted 'a pure, sound . National party,' and did not care by what name it was called, but the presidential candidates were all calling for 'the old Democratic party,' without caring, so Stephens thought, what might be 'the sentiments or principles of the two great wings of which it is composed.' [20]

Soon after the session opened, Foote introduced a resolution pronouncing the Compromise of the year before a 'definite adjustment and settlement' of the issues between the sections. Douglas then gave his own platform, that the Compromise was final, and the slavery question should be excluded from political debate. 'The Democratic party is as good a Union party as I want,' he told the Senate, 'and I wish to preserve its principles and its organization, and to triumph upon its old issues. I desire no new tests — no interpolations into the old creed.'

[19] Stephens to Cobb, Washington, Dec. 8, 1851; Erwin MSS. W. L. Marcy to Buchanan, New York, Nov. 24, 1851; Buchanan MSS. R. Barnwell Rhett, of South Carolina, had just told Marcy that the South would not stand for Cass or any Compromiser. Thompson Campbell to Lanphier, Washington, April 4, 1852; Patton MSS.

[20] Stephens to Cobb, Washington, Dec. 23; Toombs to Cobb, Washington, Dec. 21, 1851; Erwin MSS.

At a great Democratic festival on the eighth of January, he declared that 'the North and South may quarrel and wrangle about a question which should never enter the Halls of Congress. But the great West will say to the South: "You must not leave us," and to the North, "You must faithfully observe the Constitution with all its Compromises."' [21]

With the turn of the year, Douglas' opponents became very active to off-set his unmistakable gains. Senator Hunter, of Virginia, who was up for re-election, preferred the certainty of another term to the uncertainty of being candidate for Vice-President. So when the Virginia 'Buchaneers' offered to 're-elect him at once,' Hunter capitulated, the bargain was carried through and Buchanan jubilated that Douglas was 'sinking as rapidly as he rose.' [22]

But this defection was not a fatal blow to the Little Giant. He won California, developed great strength in Ohio, and began to make progress in New England. The Boston *Times* termed Douglas talented, experienced and identified 'with the progressive spirit of the age and country,' and predicted that his nomination 'would be equivalent to an election.' [23]

At the Kentucky Democratic Convention, General Butler's foes inserted in the platform a statement that Congress had no power to keep a slaveholder from carrying his slaves into any Territory of the United States. General Butler, who was smarting under the charge that he was the Free-Soilers' candidate, ignored a promise not to commit himself on slavery and approved the Kentucky resolutions. When this fact became public, the Butler campaign blew up. [24] Douglas' chances now began to impress the knowing. Francis J. Grund, the veteran newspaper correspondent, concluded that 'if the State's Rights men of the South were sincere in their professions,' Douglas had an excellent chance. [25] But now the Little Giant was to pay dearly for his mistake in judgment in permitting George N. Sanders to take an active part in the campaign.

This eërie Young American was brilliant but unstable. Though Kentuckian by birth he was a world spirit by adoption, intrigued to precipitate revolution in half a dozen European capitals, and was said to have been in the fighting at the barricades in Paris in June, 1848. Sanders, who had great personal attraction, often boasted that no one ever controlled him. Calling the Old-Line politicians 'Old Fogies' and 'vile toads,' he liked

[21] *Congressional Globe*, Thirty-Second Congress, First Session, App., 68. J. Catron, Washington, Jan. 9, 1852; Buchanan MSS. Justice Catron reported the remark of the man who sat by him: 'How tediously and carefully he is digging his own grave.'

[22] J. A. Parker to Buchanan, Richmond, Jan. 22; Buchanan to Isaac Toucey, Wheatlands, Jan. 29, 1852; Buchanan MSS., retained copy, signed.

[23] S. L. Hunt, Warren, Ohio, Jan. 22; James O. Donnell, Portland, Me., Nov. 29, 1852; Douglas MSS.; S. W. Baker, San Francisco, Jan. 1; Alfred Gilmore, Boston, April 12, 1852; Buchanan MSS. Boston *Times*, Jan. 1, 1852; the same editorial said the 'nomination for Vice-President should go South,' and proposed R. M. T. Hunter. *Ibid.*, Jan. 2, 1851, had this ticket at the masthead and there it remained until June 5. Douglas editorials and news articles were published on Jan. 13, 23, 26; Feb. 10, 12; March 3, 22, 28, and May 3, 15, and 19.

[24] *Congressional Globe*, Thirty-Second Congress, First Session, App., 299–300.

[25] Grund to Cobb, Washington, Feb. 16, 1852; Erwin MSS.

Douglas' views on foreign affairs and pitched in to make him President. Douglas liked Sanders' candor and thought him an extremely useful ally.

In the Fall of 1851, Sanders became impatient over the slow progress of the campaign, and undertook to buy the moribund *United States Democratic Review* and to make it a Douglas organ. He asked the Senator for a loan, but the latter replied, 'I have already borrowed so much that I don't know where to apply.' But somehow Sanders found the money, assumed the editorship and began asking Douglas' assistance in many different lines.[26]

The Little Giant, who kept cautioning his friends to 'refrain from attack upon any candidates,' did not dream of the blow impending. But late in January the first copy of the *Democratic Review* under its new management had a savage attack on the Old Fogies. Butler, of Kentucky, was termed 'a judicious bottle holder,' and Cass was a 'beaten horse.' When Douglas protested the impolicy of these slurs, Sanders retorted that in his February number, he would 'make an attack on General Butler more terrific than was ever made against mortal man before... It will not be thunder, but it shall be an earthquake.' [27]

On this the Senator pointed out that the friends of other candidates held him responsible for Sanders' assaults; 'it is no answer to say that I am not responsible. You know and I know that my advice in this respect has been disregarded and yet they will not believe it.' The bellicose editor might reply, as formerly, 'that you are a free man, and have a right to do as you please and that I had better mind my own business.' This would be all very well if nobody were affected but Sanders himself. 'But when your active support of me leaves the world to suppose that I instigate these assaults, I submit to you whether my appeals to you to desist ought not to be respected.' [28] Receiving no reply, Douglas added a telegram, which brought the tart rebuke that 'the foggy atmosphere of Washington makes cowards of you all, and the sooner you understand that you cannot direct the columns of the *Review*, the better.' [29]

Sure enough the February *Review* protested against the nomination of any such candidate as Butler of Kentucky, 'a good sample of the no-policy statesman,' and launched a bitter attack on Butler's past career. Sanders did try to clear the Little Giant of any hand in the magazine, but Butler's partisans raged and John C. Breckinridge charged that Douglas was to blame.

The latter's lieutenants did the best they could to meet this frontal attack. William A. Richardson soon told the House that Douglas both had no interest in and no control over the paper and that he deprecated Sanders'

[26] Merle E. Curti, 'George N. Sanders — American Patriot of the Fifties,' *South Atlantic Quarterly*, XXVII, 80 *et seq.* Douglas to Sanders, Chicago, July 12, 1851; original in Watertown, Conn., Library; Douglas to Sanders, Washington, Dec. 29, 1851; Illinois State Historical Library MSS.; Sanders to Douglas, New York, Jan. 23, 1852; Douglas MSS.

[27] Douglas to Lanphier and Walker, Washington, Jan. 21, 1852; Patton MSS. *United States Democratic Review*, XXX, 12. George N. Sanders, New York, Feb. 3, 7, 1852; Douglas MSS.

[28] Douglas to Sanders, Washington, Feb. 10, 1852; Illinois State Historical Library MSS.

[29] Quoted by W. A. Richardson in a speech in the House of Representatives, March 10, 1852; see *Congressional Globe*, Thirty-Second Congress, First Session, 711–14.

assaults, and in proof of this last read Sanders' sharp message of February
20. The editor seemed to enjoy the havoc he had wrought, for the March
Review satirized Breckinridge's speech, poked fun at Cass, Marcy, Buchanan
and Butler and came out for Douglas for President. The latter kept a stiff
upper lip. 'Now that Butler is used up, will you support me?' he asked
Francis P. Blair one day. The old editor replied evasively that his support
would kill anybody. 'I've got a strong constitution,' Douglas answered,
'I can stand anything.' [30]

The truth was, however, that Douglas knew all too well that his friend
had slaughtered him. But he did make one last effort to stop the editorial
madcap. Sanders sent word that he intended to keep up his blasts against
Cass and the other candidates. 'I am held responsible for your attacks,' the
Senator wrote bitterly. 'If you cease now and make no more attacks upon
anybody, and especially none on Gen'l. Cass, possibly I may yet regain my
lost position. If these attacks are repeated, my chances are utterly hopeless and I may be compelled to retire from the field and throw my influence
in favor of one of these whom the *Review* strives to crush.' His prospects
had been blighted 'by this course which represents me as an Ishmaelite
with my hand against everybody and inviting everybody's hand to be
against me.' If Sanders would not cease his attacks on others, 'also assail
me with them, and at the same time select somebody else as your candidate
and bend all your energies to elect him.' [31]

The Little Giant had by no means overstated the damage the *Review* did
his prospects, for by mid-April the Old Fogy leaders were shouting joyfully:
'Douglas is out of the ring.' Louisiana, declaring for Cass, disappointed
both Douglas and Buchanan. Missouri, too, declared for Cass. The Tennessee delegation was evenly divided between Douglas and Buchanan.
The Polk coterie resolved to liquidate the failing partnership, and General
Pillow, who liked dark horses, journeyed to New England to talk to Franklin Pierce. Douglas' foes believed that these successive blows had laid him
prostrate. Andrew Johnson, of Tennessee, termed him a 'dead cock in the
pit.' [32]

---

[30] Nichols, *Democratic Machine*, 114 *et seq.* The attack on Butler was inspired by a family
feud. Many years before Sanders' father had been an applicant for a political job in Kentucky
and General Butler had not aided him in securing it. Father and son never forgot nor forgave
this action. *Congressional Globe*, Thirty-Second Congress, First Session; App., 299, for Breckinridge charge; *ibid.*, App., 711–14, for Richardson's rather uncandid explanation. F. P. Blair,
Silver Spring, Md., April 30, 1852; Van Buren MSS.

[31] Douglas to Sanders, Washington, April 15, 1852; Illinois Historical Library MSS.

[32] D. R. Porter, Baltimore, April 19; John M. Slidell, New Orleans, May 9, 1851, Feb. 26,
1852; Slidell to A. G. Penn, New Orleans, March 11, 1852, Buchanan MSS. Washington *Union*,
Jan. 11, March 11, 1852; Amos A. Ettinger, *The Mission to Spain of Pierre Soulé*, New Haven,
1932, 121–31. *Congressional Globe*, Thirty-Second Congress, First Session, App., 383–85; Baltimore *Sun*, April 12, 1852; Gideon Pillow to Edmund Burke, Sept. 4, 1852; cited in Nichols,
125. Jones to Cobb, Washington, April 14, 1852; *American Historical Association Report* for 1911;
II, 288. Andrew Johnson to D. T. Patterson, Washington, April 4, 1852; Johnson MSS., Library
of Congress. Johnson added that Douglas was a 'precocious politician, warmed into and kept
in existence by a set of interested plunderers that would, in the event of success, disembowel the
Treasury, disgrace the country and damn the party to all eternity that brought them into power.'

And yet Douglas' recovery in Virginia was marked. Senator King, of Alabama, advised Buchanan that high-minded, patriotic Virginians were joining in 'the efforts now being made by the supporters of that little whipster Douglas,' who was again becoming 'the dangerous man.' The Little Giant began opposing new party tests and urging readoption of the 1848 platform 'without addition or elimination,' while his aides wrote to Illinois that 'the less we say at this time about the Compromise, the better it will be for all concerned.' Cass' friends, however, were determined that the Baltimore Convention should endorse the Compromise and the Fugitive Slave law as finalities.[33]

Despite this partial recapture of lost ground, there was bitterness against Douglas in every candidate's *entourage*. His enemies charged that he promised every office in the Federal Government, from Cabinet to Clerk, and painted a most unpleasant picture of the campaign methods of his friends. 'Those arms thrown about his neck along the streets,' one wrote scornfully, 'reading pieces to him in an oyster cellar,... then a drink, next a haugh, haugh, then some claim to be discussed by which they expect to practice some swindle upon the Government.' But each of the other major figures had financial janissaries and made moves to retain their support.[34]

Early in May, Cave Johnson, the shrewdest of Tennessee politicians, thought Buchanan should offer Douglas the second place on the ticket, although probably the latter was 'so elated with his prospects of being second on everybody's ticket, and ultimately to be made the first on all, that his friends would not yield to such a suggestion now.' Sure enough, cautious inquiries by Buchanan agents revealed that the Little Giant's supporters would fight to the last for their man, and reported to Lancaster: 'Douglas is your most dangerous competitor,' Cass was out of the ring and the real struggle would be between Pennsylvania and Illinois. A final effort was now made to sidetrack Douglas by promising him that, if he would help Buchanan now, it would create 'an eternal debt of gratitude which... should be most scrupulously discharged at the struggle four years hence.' But Douglas had decided to chance the breaks of the game.[35]

By the first of June, Baltimore's hotels, boarding-houses, saloons and gambling-parlors filled to overflowing. Tobacco-spattered sawdust covered the floors; rye, Bourbon and good Maryland blend flowed across the polished bars; politics filled the air and politicians were everywhere. General Cass' interests were committed to the hands of Jesse D. Bright, of Indiana; Simon Cameron, of Pennsylvania, and Daniel S. Dickinson, of New York.

[33] James A. Seddon to R. M. T. Hunter, Richmond, Feb. 7, 1852; *American Historical Association Report* for 1916; II, 136–37. Henry A. Wise, Washington, March 3; W. R. King, Washington, March 6, 1852; Buchanan MSS. Thomas Campbell to Lanphier, Washington, April 4, 1852; Patton MSS. F. J. Grund to Howell Cobb, Washington, May 10, 1852; Erwin MSS.

[34] Johnson to David T. Patterson, Washington, April 4, 1852; Johnson MSS. G. W. Jones to Howell Cobb, Washington, May 18, 1852; Erwin MSS.

[35] Cave Johnson, Nashville, May 6; A. G. Penn, Washington, May 10; D. R. Porter, Washington, May 24, 1852; Buchanan MSS.

Buchanan's managers secured a back room at Carroll Hall and tried to establish liaison among his friends. Marcy's headquarters were at the Eutaw House, and his leaders set to work to convince the South that he was sound on the Compromise. Douglas' men were ubiquitous, and the Old Fogies charged that they were soliciting delegates through alcoholic entertainment, promises of jobs, hints of speculation and other underhanded means.[36]

The convention opened at noon Tuesday, its session being enlivened with a vain effort to drop the two-thirds rule. The next day the Buchaneers tried to postpone the balloting on candidates until after the adoption of the platform, hoping, through a floor battle on the 1850 Compromise, to fuse a Southern bloc solidly behind Buchanan. But their effort failed. The first ballot taken Thursday morning showed Cass in the lead and on the eighth ballot his total reached 119 votes. Buchanan, with 95 from Pennsylvania and an almost solid South, was second. At the outset Douglas had only 20, but Florida turned to him, soon followed by Vermont, Arkansas and most of California. Late Thursday the Little Giant's total reached 51.

Nearly all Thursday night was spent in caucus and Friday's sessions opened with heightened tension. The Douglas Virginia minority tried to break the unit rule. Cass' vote fell badly, and Rhode Island, Wisconsin, Iowa, Louisiana and majorities from Massachusetts and Tennessee turned to the Little Giant. Buchanan, too, gained greatly, and when he secured 104 votes his managers feverishly implored the Marcy men to come on over; but the New-Yorker's managers thought Buchanan already at his crest. That afternoon the Buchanan boom began deflating, Missouri returned to Douglas, who secured four votes from North Carolina and his total mounted to 92. The Maine delegation caucused and decided to substitute Douglas' name for Cass. These developments increased fears of a final Douglas swing. There was a last-minute effort to build back the Cass vote, as a result of which he recovered Maryland, Delaware and Ohio, won Tennessee and Indiana and reached 123 votes. This so alarmed the other candidates' managers that an adjournment was rushed through.

Everyone felt that the crisis was at hand. The Southern Ultras would not take Cass and 'Squatter Sovereignty.' The Buchanan men felt that they could not nominate their aspirant until every other candidate except Douglas had been tried out. So the Buchaneers met in their back room at Carroll Hall, conferring far into the night. The final scheme was to give General Butler a run for his money, to see what Marcy would do and also to try out a dark horse. They would split their vote; Pennsylvania, Georgia and Alabama would stand firmly by Buchanan, but Virginia, North Carolina and Mississippi would explore the field.[37]

A dark horse was all ready to be paraded for inspection — Franklin Pierce,

[36] Dr. Richard Arnold to John W. Forney, Savannah, Ga., March 30, 1858; Letters of Richard D. Arnold, Richard H. Shryock, ed.; Trinity College Historical Society Papers, XVIII–XIX, 87.

[37] James O. Donnell, Portland, Me., Nov. 29, 1852; Douglas MSS. Henry A. Wise to Franklin Pierce, June 22, 1852; quoted in Nichols, *The Democratic Machine*, 138.

of New Hampshire. No ancient, he belonged to Douglas' generation, and had been Nathaniel Hawthorne's classmate at Bowdoin. After some law practice, Pierce got into politics, came to Washington as Congressman and Senator. In the Mexican War he was a Polk brigadier, in one battle having the misfortune of being thrown from his horse into a muddy ditch, where he remained bogged while his men charged to victory. After the war the General plunged back into law and local politics, the Presidency being the last thing in his mind. But Fate or Chance played a prank on him. Woodbury's death and the collapse of Butler's campaign convinced the Concord cabal which ran Democratic politics in New Hampshire that the National Convention would be deadlocked and that Pierce would have a good chance to break it. These shrewd leaders set to work, Edmund Burke, maneuvering for Douglas in Washington, clambered on the new bandwagon, and New Hampshire's Democratic State Convention put forward Pierce's name 'as worthy...of high place,' this vagueness leaving them free to urge him either for head or tail. While the General wrote that such a candidacy 'would be utterly repugnant' to his wishes, the Concord cabal gave his views no heed.

After Butler had been blown out of the water by the Kentucky resolutions and Douglas had been scuttled by Sanders' folly, many men began looking to Pierce as a candidate by whose success they could advantage themselves. The schemers agreed that the dark horse would not run until the others had been lamed.[38]

On Saturday morning, June 4, the convention was angry, tired, dazed — almost anything could happen. The New York Hards believed the time had come to see if Daniel S. Dickinson could not be selected and persuaded the Virginians to turn to him. After the Old Dominion announcement, North Carolina started to cast her vote for Dickinson, but before she could do so the New York Senator took the floor to implore Virginia to support Cass rather than himself. Ladies in the gallery tossed Dickinson their bouquets but Virginia would not take his candidate. The Douglas men on the delegation made a final effort to secure the State, but she resolved to turn to New Hampshire rather than Illinois.

Marcy now had his run, but his managers' earlier unwillingness to help Cass or Buchanan caused the friends of these candidates to turn deaf ears to the New-Yorker's frantic pleas; his chances darkened and soon were forever gone. Little by little Pierce picked up votes. On the forty-eighth ballot the Douglas Virginians had that State trembling to turn to the Little Giant, but John S. Barbour saved the day for Pierce. North Carolina and Georgia were coming to him on the next ballot, he told his colleagues, a nomination was in sight and Virginia must not change.

[38] Burke to Douglas, Newport, N.H., n.d., 1853; Douglas MSS. At this time Burke had fallen out with Pierce and claimed to Douglas that he had always been for the latter, never for Pierce. Dr. Roy F. Nichols, letter to the author, New York, Aug. 30, 1932, is convinced that 'the Concord ring and the old Woodbury crowd got up the idea of Pierce and that Burke joined them when he found out what they were doing.' New York *Herald*, May 6, 1852; correspondence between Burke and Pierce, *American Historical Review*, IV, 110 *et seq.*

The roll began to be called for the forty-ninth time. When North Carolina was reached, James C. Dobbin burst into fervid oratory, starting a landslide for Pierce. State after State turned to the unknown. Marcy was withdrawn, Dickinson cast his minority for the General, Pennsylvania fell into line. Hoarsely but evangelically, the Chairman read the tally: Cass 2, Douglas 2, Butler 1, Houston 1, 'Franklin Pierce, of New Hampshire (God bless him), 282 votes.' Senator King, of Alabama, Buchanan's friend, was named Vice-President and the platform was brought in. The Compromise plank was full, clear and explicit, and Toombs felt that 'the Fire-Eaters have succumbed and Free-Soilers have flunked out.'

As the delegates turned homeward there was great rejoicing among the Old Fogies that the Little Giant had lost. Meeting a last time in their room at Carroll Hall, Henry A. Wise, of Virginia, rose and gave thanks that 'the brandy bottle is smashed, the Champagne bazaars are closed, and Douglas has crept out of town like a whipped dog with his tail between his legs.' [39]

But there was a more fitting epitaph to the Little Giant's campaign. 'Douglas' case has been overworked, and thus was spoiled,' W. H. Bissell wrote Sidney Breese. 'With one-fourth the effort on the part of his friends, and no more, he would have been the nominee. Henceforth he will have to *struggle*, like other aspirants to the Presidency, and like them take his *chance*. The prestige of *universal good feeling* has gone from him, and forever. But he will come up again.' [40]

While this contest left deep wounds on Douglas, Young America believed that they would heal with time, and many thought, with Senator Yulee, of Florida, that the Little Giant had crushed all the old combinations and organizations and thus opened the way 'to the dynasty of a new generation.' [41]

While Douglas' presence on the stump was not needed to influence an election predetermined by Whig impotence and dissension, the Pierce management was anxious to enlist him and the Senator embraced this opportunity to give a public sign of his party fealty. The nominee and his advisers felt that the great fight of the campaign would come in the West, but the Little Giant sent word that he planned 'to spend the whole vacation upon the stump,' and believed Pierce would 'not lose a Democratic vote in the whole Northwest.' [42]

[39] Nichols, *The Democratic Machine*, 143. Toombs to Cobb, Washington, June 10, 1852; printed in *Georgia Historical Quarterly*, Dec., 1921; 52. Dr. Richard D. Arnold to John W. Forney, Savannah, Ga., March 20, 1858; Letters of Richard D. Arnold, Richard H. Shryock, ed.; Trinity College Historical Society Papers, XVIII–XIX, 87.

[40] W. H. Bissell, Washington, June 10, 1852; Breese MSS.

[41] Cave Johnson, Washington, June 8, 1852; Buchanan MSS.; Edward Everett Diary, Feb. 28, 1853; MS. in Massachusetts Historical Society, quoting Marcy's statement to him. W. W. Paine to Howell Cobb, Washington, Feb. 26, 1853; Erwin MSS. D. L. Yulee, Margarita, Fla., Jan. 28, 1853; J. F. Donnell, Portland, Me., Nov. 29, 1852; Douglas MSS.; Bailie Peyton to Sanders, Santiago, Chile, Aug. 28, 1852; Sanders MSS.

[42] Charles H. Peaslee, Washington, June 8, 1852; Pierce MSS., New Hampshire Historical Society.

Democratic expectations as to Whig weakness were soon realized. This time Clay was not a candidate; as the Whig delegates gathered in Baltimore in mid-June, he lay at the National Hotel in Washington, near death from debility, and passed away soon after they adjourned. President Fillmore could not renominate himself. Webster was vetoed by Seward and his Free-Soilers; the Whigs seemed dazzled by the idea that only a General could win for them and so General Winfield Scott became their nominee.

Webster retired to Marshfield to mourn this last defeat. 'What pains me,' he told a friend, 'is that the South, for which I had done and sacrificed so much, did not give me a single vote.' He thought Scott a mere tool of Seward, and 'if I had a vote to give I would cast it for General Pierce.' But Webster himself did not vote in the election; on October 24, he raised himself in his bed, remarked solemnly, 'I still live,' and then his spirit sped.

While the Whig platform contained a definite declaration of the finality of the Compromise of 1850, and Scott was a Virginian, his choice was the result of the Eastern Abolitionists' determination to punish Webster. Scott's sentence, 'I accept the nomination with the resolutions annexed,' seemed equivocal; it was charged that Seward was responsible for the ambiguity, and he took the extraordinary step of saying that he would neither ask nor accept 'any public station or preferment whatever at the hands of the President of the United States, whether that President were Winfield Scott or any other man.' [43]

Many of the elder statesmen of Southern and Border States became very much worked up. 'The election of Scott under the lead of Seward and his Hellish apostates,' wrote the aging Richard M. Johnson, of Kentucky, 'would seriously jeopardize, if not destroy, the Union of the States.' [44] Georgia Whigs began to bolt the ticket, and Stephens, Toombs and three other Southern Whig Congressmen repudiated Scott.

Under such circumstances the Democrats began their campaign with real enthusiasm. Martin Van Buren announced for Pierce, William Cullen Bryant and the New York *Evening Post* adjourned anti-slavery views to support him, all over the country the welkin rang with Democratic oratory. From July until November Douglas was 'in the field with his armour on.' If General Taylor 'had lived for one year more than he did,' Douglas asked dramatically in a speech at Richmond, Virginia, 'would this Union be extant at the present time?' The Senator admitted Old Rough and Ready's patriotic purposes, but pointed out that, at the time of his death, the General 'had already committed himself to steps which would have led inevitably to a civil war.' It was the hand of Providence 'that saved us from our first and only military Administration.' But in the present campaign, the Senator charged, it looked as if the normal rôles had been reversed, and *Politician* Scott was under the command of *General* Seward.

The Richmond papers made a to-do over Douglas' shrewd passes at the Whigs and the speech was sent all over the country. In Illinois it evoked

[43] Fuess, *Daniel Webster*, II, 288–89; Henry B. Stanton, *Random Recollections*, New York, 1887, 180; Harvey, 199–202; William H. Seward, *Works*, III, 416.

[44] R. M. Johnson, White Sulphur, Scott County, Ky., July 23, 1852; Sanders MSS.

the wrath of Abraham Lincoln, who asked the Scott Club of Springfield to invite him to make a speech to answer Douglas.[45]

August and September State elections foretold November, but Pierce's friends bestirred themselves to make the victory overwhelming, and such it turned out to be, for he received 1,601,274 votes, to 1,386,580 for Scott. In electoral college strength, the contrast was more startling: 254 to 52. Scott carried only four States, and an Illinois aide wrote Douglas: 'Who could ever have dreamed that Whiggery would squat — and shrivel — and collapse — and die of over-feeding on its own element — humbuggery?'[46]

Pierce's election brought reappraisal of his qualifications. Richard H. Dana, Jr., of Boston, called him a 'doughface militia colonel, a kind of third-rate county, or at most, State politician.' Nathaniel Hawthorne, his indulgent friend, concluded that 'he is deep, deep, deep. But what luck withal! Nothing can ruin him.' In the beginning it seemed that Hawthorne was right. The politicians made a mad rush for Concord, but Pierce kept his own counsel, made few promises and seemed master of the situation.

Soon, however, there was a rift in the lute. Pierce undertook to knit the party together, recognizing all former factions. In his inaugural he would set a tone of expansion to please Young America; of Compromise finality for the Constitutional Unionists; of strict construction for the Southern Rights devotees, of economy and honesty as a side blow at the Whigs; of the need of having friends in office, a fillip for the hungering Democratic hordes. In his Cabinet he would pacify all major rivals by their own appointment or that of friends. The widespread report that Pierce believed it necessary to have 'extremity represented in his council' and that Jefferson Davis would be in the Cabinet dismayed the Unionists both North and South.[47]

Apparently Pierce neglected to consult Douglas, either directly or through mutual friends, as to the latter's wishes or suggestions, either for general Administration policy, Cabinet appointments, or even as to Administration leadership in Congress. Of the leading Northern Democratic Senators — Cass, Douglas, Bright, of Indiana — none was consulted, but the General picked Charles H. Atherton, of New Hampshire, a new member, for the post, a choice regarded as a snub to the existing leaders.

Soon after the President-elect reached Washington his Cabinet was revealed. Marcy was the choice as Secretary of State; James Guthrie, of Kentucky, was slated for the Treasury; Jefferson Davis for the War Office; Dobbin, of North Carolina, for the Navy; McClelland, of Michigan, for the Interior Department; James Campbell, of Pennsylvania, Postmaster-General, and Caleb Cushing, of Massachusetts, Attorney-General. Upon this balanc-

[45] Stevens, 426; Johnson, 207. 'Speech of Hon. Stephen A. Douglas, Richmond, July 9, 1852,' pamphlet; *Illinois State Register*, Springfield, Aug. 3, 1852, quoting Richmond, Va., *Enquirer*; Stevens, 427.

[46] Harris to Douglas, Petersburg, Ill., Nov. 11, 1852; Douglas MSS. Roy Franklin Nichols, *Franklin Pierce*, Philadelphia, 1931; 216.

[47] Charles F. Adams, Jr., *Richard H. Dana*, Boston, 1890; I, 226; Horatio Bridge, *Personal Recollections of Nathaniel Hawthorne*, New York, 1893, 131. Nichols, *Franklin Pierce*, 220 *et seq.* G. W. Jones to Howell Cobb, Washington, Feb. 20, 1853; Erwin MSS.

ing of extremes, the practical politicians at Washington predicted that within a year 'there must be a blow-up.'

During these three months of wire-pulling, Douglas was deluged with appeals for offices, perhaps a deserved retribution for his statement, not long after the election, that 'for every Whig removed there should be a competent Democrat put in his place.' Nearly everyone wanted at least a ministership abroad, although some would prefer 'a republic, if a republic only in name,' as more consonant with their democratic feelings.[48] The Illinois Democrats kept a keen weather eye on the loaves and fishes, and Douglas' presidential aspirations, past and future, laid on him the further burden of looking out for patronage requests of supporters in other sections.[49]

The Little Giant's most immediate interest, however, was in the new Illinois Legislature assembling in Springfield, for the time for his re-election was at hand. None the less, he expected no trouble. His hold on the Democratic organization in his State had grown so great that before Matteson, the new Governor, took office, he sent a draft of his inaugural message to Douglas for the latter's approval. The Democratic members met January 4, and promptly telegraphed: 'Your nomination in caucus was made this evening unanimously and by acclamation.' Two days later the legislators balloted and Douglas received seventy-five of the ninety-five votes.

With his re-election the Little Giant's word in the Illinois Democracy was law, and so continued until his death. There were insurgencies in the next few years caused either by personal ambition or difference on party policy. Whenever such occurred, 'Shoot the deserters,' Douglas would demand of the party and it was always ready to shoot. The foundations of this power were Douglas' miraculous energy, his vibrant, engaging, compelling personality, his sound judgment and clear vision as to the welfare of the party and the State. Not without reason was the Little Giant in command.[50]

Almost before Pierce's vote was counted, Douglas' friends were pressing the question: 'Do you intend to be a candidate for the succession?' He was warned that the next nomination would not 'go by chance,' and by January, 1853, his friends were generally determined that he must seek the 1856 Democratic presidential nomination. When the last term of the Thirty-Second Congress opened in December, 1852, the Little Giant received many

[48] Edmund Burke, Newport, N.H., Jan. 16, 1853; Douglas MSS. W. W. Paine to Cobb, Washington, Feb. 26, 1853; Erwin MSS.; Nichols, *Franklin Pierce*, 221-40.

[49] *Illinois State Register*, Dec. 23, 1852; David Sturgeon, Uniontown (Pa.), Nov. 29, 1852; Thomas L. Harris, Petersburg, Ill., Nov. 11, 1852; James S. Green, Canton, Mo., Nov. 15, 1852; J. B. Ingersoll, London, England, Jan. 28, 1853; Isaac R. Diller, Springfield, Ill., Dec. 6, 1852; D. L. Yulee, Margarita, Fla., Feb. 20; J. A. McDougal, San Francisco, Jan. 27, 1853; Douglas MSS.

[50] Douglas to Lanphier, Washington, Dec. 3, 1852; Patton MSS. David L. Gregg, Springfield, Dec. 27, 1852; J. A. Matteson, Springfield, Jan. 7, 1853; James M. Campbell, Springfield, Jan. 7, 1853; Douglas MSS. *Illinois State Register*, Springfield, Jan. 5, 1853; John M. Palmer, *Personal Recollections*, 64. James O. Donnel, Portland, Me., Nov. 29, 1852; Thos. L. Harris, Petersburg, Ill., Nov. 11, 1852; Douglas MSS.

hints as to those who would aid or harm another candidacy. Senator Jesse D. Bright, of Indiana, who was vastly jealous of Douglas' rise and reputation, had kept the Indiana delegation from coming to his support and had probably been the controlling influence in preventing his nomination. When Congress opened, Bright sought to make apologies and to effect a reconciliation.

'He is your enemy,' Senator Yulee, of Florida, warned the Little Giant. '*I know it*, and you can never make him otherwise, for you cannot serve the purposes he indulges.... Bright will defeat this desirable "solidarity" of the N.W. if he can;... He does not mean that you shall rise if he can prevent it — and his *professed friendship* will be more dangerous than his professed enmity.'

In addition, Douglas and his advisers made careful analysis of the problems which would have to be met in the next presidential bid. 'The plan which should mark our campaign is plain,' Senator Yulee advised. 'You stand well with the State's Rights men — with New England — with the South — and with the party at large.' The Northwest, powerful in numbers and wealth, had never had a President. If the Northwest were to be divided, Douglas' chances would depend upon the outcome of a battle-royal. But if the Northwest were united, her claim would be 'yielded to at once, and your nomination effected without contest.' Therefore it was highly important that Douglas' section be concentrated upon him.[51]

With this in view, and greatly to the delight of Young America, the Little Giant sought to strengthen his position in the Northwest and to array about himself a strong group which agreed both with his doctrine of Manifest Destiny and with his determination to link the United States together by a great economic program within its domestic confines. There was no question but that, after this first defeat, there had been real recovery for a second effort to win the prize.

[51] D. L. Yulee, Margarita, Fla., Jan. 28, 1853, Douglas MSS.

CHAPTER VII

THE RACE FOR THE PACIFIC

WHEN Congress opened in December, 1853, America was economically at high tide. Stocks were booming, railroads were being built in all directions, steamship lines were thriving, the cotton-grower was paying debts and buying slaves, the prairie farmer was shipping wheat and corn to New York by lake, railroad and canal and to New Orleans by river. The new President, who had not yet confronted the new Congress, was still 'Young Hickory' to Young America. In the Senate there were thirty-seven Democrats, twenty-one Whigs and two Free-Soilers, and in the House, the Administration ratio was even greater. Pierce, in his message, extolled the nation's prosperity, which would 'suffer no shock' during his incumbency.

This indication of strength, however, was merely superficial. Pierce's popularity had already worn thin with most first rank Democratic leaders and troubles were multiplying everywhere. Douglas was among those whom the new Administration had virtually ignored in dispensing of major patronage. When worth-while appointments did not come, Illinois Democrats bluntly expressed chagrin. John A. McClernand, who wanted to be Minister to Spain or Mexico, and had heard that, with the sole exception of Jefferson Davis, the whole Cabinet was unfriendly to Douglas, wrote the latter that 'If the Administration is against you, let your friends at home know the facts.... If it is with you, ought not the fact to be manifested in some way?' [1]

But the fact was not 'manifested,' and there was a growing expectation in Washington that Douglas was 'to be crushed' by Pierce. Buchanan's friends 'got all they want, and more,' but the general report was that Pierce planned to give Douglas' friends nothing. General Shields could not understand Pierce's motive. 'If it were to crush the Little Giant, I would think him more than mad.' [2]

Shortly before Douglas departed on his tour of Europe, he had a long conference with Shields, after which the latter made a temperately worded demand upon Pierce for the 'claims and expectations of our State for a reasonable share of the general appointments.' [3] Little heed was paid this protest, and the Little Giant's Illinois friends were ignored.

New York was the major seat of disaffection. When Pierce put Marcy in his Cabinet Dickinson was outraged. When minor appointments went

[1] J. A. McClernand, Jacksonville, Ill., March 22, 1853; Douglas MSS.

[2] J. A. Shields, Washington, undated; Douglas MSS.

[3] Shields to Pierce, Philadelphia, April 16, 1853. Copy sent to Douglas in letter cited in footnote 2. The two Senators thought Illinois should have two chargés or one full minister, three or four consuls of all grades, one comptroller, auditor or commissioner, and some moderate proportion of the minor clerkships at Washington.

to the Hards, both Softs and Barnburners prepared for war. Pierce's new, all-inclusive test of present attachment rather than past alignment proved an empty formula of words, and soon there was open rebellion in both New York Democratic camps. By Fall the battle was so bitter that the Whigs carried the State election.[4] The ensuing recrimination fed the flames of conflict. Soon after Douglas' return, a New York friend informed him 'that a war full of bitterness and personality, and looking to extermination of one or the other of the parties' was being waged.'

All over the country the Administration had 'played the devil with a vengeance.' General Cass, who had changed his opinion of Douglas and disclaimed any further Presidential aspirations, saw danger ahead. That shrewd political analyst, Samuel Treat, of St. Louis, wrote the Little Giant that already the public mind was nearly made up 'that cowardice, bad advice or something worse renders it impossible for any good to come out of this Administration.' All saw that Pierce's interference in the New York quarrel had been ill-advised. Lanphier wrote that 'If Mr. Marcy and Mr. Dickinson cannot heal up old sores, I can see no good reason why the Democracy of the other States of the Union should tear themselves to pieces.' [5]

The President's growing weakness encouraged Douglas' friends to make preparations for a new presidential candidacy, and his lieutenants counseled the Illinois House delegation so to conduct itself that his presidential hopes would be advantaged. W. A. Richardson was being discussed for Speaker, but 'Illinois should go for the man that brings the most available strength to you in 1856.' [6]

The Senator could see that Pierce was no Young Hickory but a riven scrub; even so the Little Giant was not yet ready to embark on a presidential venture of his own. 'The party is in a distracted condition,' he warned Lanphier, 'and it requires all our wisdom, prudence and energy to consolidate its power and perpetuate its principles.' Already the party press was holding him up as a presidential candidate. 'I do not wish to occupy that position,' he insisted. 'I do not think I will be willing to have my name used. I think such a state of things will exist that I shall not desire the nomination. Yet I do not intend to do any act which will deprive me of the control of my own actions. I shall remain entirely non-committal, and hold myself at liberty to do whatever my duty to my principles and my friends may require when the time for action arrives. Our first duty is to the cause — the fate of individual politicians is of minor consequence.... Let us leave the Presidency out of view at least two years to come.'

The Pierce Administration had made many mistakes in its appointments, but Douglas had not expected to be pleased and therefore was not dis-

[4] For the most revealing study of the New York schism, see Nichols, *Franklin K. Pierce*, 276–93.

[5] Edward C. West, New York, Nov. 15; Geo. W. Hughes, Baltimore, Nov. 16; Andrew Harvie, Chicago, Nov. 14, quoting recent interview with Cass; Samuel Treat, St. Louis, Dec. 18; C. H. Lanphier, Springfield, Nov. 21, 1853; Douglas MSS.

[6] Silas Ramsey, La Rose, Ill., Nov. 12, 1853; Douglas MSS.

appointed; 'If it stands firmly by the faith, if it is sound and faithful in its principles and measures, it will receive *my* hearty support.' But it must meet the difficulties ahead 'boldly and fairly,' the Treasury surplus must be disposed of and the tariff reduced 'to a legitimate revenue standard.' He felt that the Pacific railroad question would be a 'disturbing element'; it would never do to put the Federal Government into the railroad-building business; 'We can grant alternate sections of land, as we did for the Central road but not a dollar from the National Treasury.' [7]

The Little Giant was right that the Pacific railroad would prove a 'disturbing element.' He had fought for it from his first year in Congress.[8] When Asa Whitney memorialized Congress for the grant of a strip of land sixty miles wide, to aid in building a railroad from Lake Michigan, at or near Milwaukee, to the Columbia's mouth, Douglas alone of the 284 members of the House and Senate took public notice of the scheme, replying with an eight-page open letter offering a counter-program of his own.[9]

But this plan did not please the other Illinois politicians, who persuaded the Illinois Legislature to instruct its Senators to support the Whitney scheme. Within the next year or so rivers and harbors and railroad conventions all through the Mississippi Valley passed resolutions approving a transcontinental line. In 1848, Iowa and Missouri asked for Federal land grants for railroads between the Mississippi and the Missouri and Douglas again brought forward a bill for the Territorial organization of Nebraska.

Southern statesmen had long been concerned over the way their section was being distanced economically by the North. Robert Y. Hayne, of South Carolina, thought the South's insufficient railroad facilities were a chief cause and undertook to join Charleston with Cincinnati by a line through the Southern Appalachians. John C. Calhoun bent his energies to a rail connection of the Atlantic and the Mississippi.[10]

The Southern leaders of the 'Forties were equally keen for a road to the Pacific. In 1846, in giving instructions for the negotiation of a treaty of peace with Mexico, Polk's Secretary of State specifically sought the thirty-second parallel as a southern boundary, 'since Major Emory represents the necessity of being able at some points to run the railroad south of the Gila River.' While the American envoy did not secure this, he did get Mexican agreement to permit the road to be built south of the Gila.

The Southerners lined up allies for their project. Sidney Breese approached the Illinois Legislature on their behalf, portraying the beauties of a southern

[7] Douglas to Lanphier and Walker, Washington, Nov. 11, 1853; Patton MSS.

[8] In 1844, when the Texas and Oregon controversies were becoming heated, Tyler's Secretary of War had suggested that Nebraska be organized as a Territory, an initial step toward establishing military posts all the way to Oregon. Douglas, then a new Congressman from Illinois, embraced the idea, supported the Nebraska measure which the Committee on Territories had introduced and drafted a bill of his own for establishing the chain of posts.

[9] Douglas to A. Whitney, Quincy, Ill., Oct. 15, 1845; copy in possession of Martin F. Douglas.

[10] For an able account of Hayne's struggle, see Thomas D. Jervey, *Robert Y. Hayne and His Times*, New York, 1909. Ulrich B. Phillips, *History of Transportation in the Eastern Cotton Belt to 1860*, New York, 1908, gives an excellent general survey.

transcontinental railroad, and succeeded in procuring instructions in favor of the southern route. For some years these instructions halted Douglas' efforts to pass a central or northern Pacific railroad bill. They also removed his chief reason for seeking Territorial organization for the Indian lands of Kansas and Nebraska.[11]

The year 1849 gave further impetus to a Pacific railroad plan. The Missouri Legislature had passed State's Rights resolutions, professedly designed 'to instruct Benton out of the Senate.' He issued a dramatic 'Appeal to the People of Missouri' and made an unbelievably bitter assault upon the Missouri Ultras.[12] In addition, he projected the Pacific road issue into Missouri politics through a bill 'to provide for the location and construction of a central National road from the Pacific Ocean to the Mississippi River.' The route he urged was between the thirty-eighth and thirty-ninth parallels of latitude, 'the Buffalo trail.'[13]

During the Summer of 1849, advocates of a southern route to the Pacific held a railroad convention at Memphis. There must be no concession to a central or northern route, the delegates insisted. The protagonists of these other routes then issued a call for a rival convention of their own, to meet in St. Louis, in October. The people of Chicago urged Senator Douglas to represent them at the St. Louis Convention, but he felt that he must first remove an impediment. Calling a mass meeting, he reviewed his 1845 proposal for a road from Chicago to Council Bluffs and thence west through South Pass to the Pacific and pointed out that the Legislature's pro-southern instructions prevented him from urging this plan.

Thus prompted, the Chicagoans passed resolutions to untie his hands, on October 15 he was in St. Louis and was made president of the convention. His advocacy of the South Pass route, with connections with both Chicago and St. Louis, brought such criticism from the St. Louis press that he resigned his presidency. In the outcome, the convention declared in favor of 'a grand trunk railroad with branches to Saint Louis, Memphis and Chicago.'[14]

The Compromise of 1850 was of inestimable advantage to the advocates of a southern route, for New Mexico's Territorial organization enabled every mile of such a road to be built in organized territory, and thus the difficulties which confronted a southern route were physical, not legal. But railroads by the central and the northern routes must still pierce through a great unsettled and ungoverned area in the possession of Indian tribes.

[11] Hodder, 'The Railroad Background of the Kansas-Nebraska Act,' *Mississippi Valley Historical Review*, XII, reprint.

[12] P. Orman Ray, *The Repeal of the Missouri Compromise, Its Origin and Authorship*, Cleveland, 1909; 27-50. 'The right to prohibit slavery in any Territory,' the fourth of the resolves declared, 'belongs exclusively to the people thereof, and can only be exercised by them in forming their Constitution for a State government, or in their sovereign capacity as an independent State.' In his appeal, Benton said that if the people of Missouri sustained the instructions, 'I shall give them an opportunity to find a Senator to carry their will into effect, as I cannot do anything to dissolve this Union or to array one-half of it against the other.'

[13] *Congressional Globe*, Twenty-Ninth Congress, Second Session, 470, 625.

[14] Hodder, 'The Railroad Background,' *Mississippi Valley Historical Review*, XII, reprint; *Chicago Journal*, Oct. 12, 1849.

In 1852 Missouri was granted Federal lands to aid in building a road from Hannibal to St. Joseph. This would be a bridge from the existing mid-Western lines to the Missouri River points proposed as starting-point for a central Pacific route. The Senate passed a similar bill for an Iowa line from Davenport to the Missouri River. Whenever such a bill was introduced providing for a railroad which would reach unorganized territory, a companion measure would be brought in establishing a Territorial organization for the area in question. In April, 1852, when Douglas introduced a bill for the protection of the emigrant route, bills for railroads and Territorial organization were not far away.

With the December, 1852, session of the Thirty-Second Congress the Pacific railroad problem quickly came to the fore. Senator Gwin, of California, sought to amend Douglas' bill so as to procure Federal aid for the construction of a railroad and telegraph line to the Pacific. This the Senate referred to a special committee, which, on February 1, 1853, reported a bill for a road, leaving the route to the President.

Gwin thought the measure would pass, but at the last minute Shields, of Illinois, offered an amendment that none of the money appropriated in the bill should be expended within the limits of a State, and Cass, Douglas and Weller, of California, supported him. Probably both Douglas and Cass saw that Gwin's bill would be to enable the construction of a line from San Francisco to New Orleans, but the branches to St. Louis and Dubuque could not be built until the Indian areas had been organized into Federal Territories. Their amendment was a keen maneuver to prevent the Northwest from being disadvantaged in the race to the Pacific.[15]

When brought to a vote the amendment carried and Douglas thenceforth gave the bill a vigorous support. On February 22, when it was killed by a *viva voce* adjournment vote, the Little Giant, with a good deal of temper, insisted on a roll call. Gwin then offered an amendment to the Army Appropriation bill directing the Secretary of War to have thorough surveys made of the various proposed Pacific railroad routes, and to report the results to Congress by February next. Both Houses accepted it and Davis set his engineers to work.

While the Senate was debating the transcontinental railway question, the House was discussing a bill to organize the Territory of Nebraska. This action was the result of a number of diverse forces. The Northwestern members' anxiety for a Pacific railroad, the pleas of the land-hungry for virgin soil; the desire of the Wyandotte Indians for a share in the prosperity of the pale-face, the complexities of Iowa politics and the Missouri Democratic war — all these were factors and each determinatively influenced the result.

[15] Gwin, MSS. Memoirs, 85–88, asserts a belief that the sole purpose of Shields' amendment was to enable Douglas and Cass to curry favor with the Southern members, by giving them the chance to endorse the State Rights doctrine that in such matters as a Pacific railroad, Congress could not constitutionally appropriate money from the National Treasury to be expended within the borders of a State.

Missouri's party battles had been without respite since 1849. The fortunes of war had first favored Benton, then had inclined to the State-Righters, who were ably led by David R. Atchison and James S. Green. Modern psychographers might assert that the name of Atchison's Kentucky birthplace — it was Frogtown — had some effect on his character. In later life, he delighted to make rough jests about it and said he always was the 'big frog in the puddle.' Moving to frontier Missouri as a young man, he quickly jumped into the rough and tumble of politics, became State legislator and judge and was appointed to the United States Senate upon the death of Dr. Linn. The same Missouri Legislature that instructed Benton and provoked his famous Appeal re-elected his rival to the Senate.

In 1852 Atchison had had the longest continuous Senate tenure of any of the members, for that reason was elected its President *pro tempore*, and with the death of Vice-President King, was next in line for the Presidency. His personality suited a frontier politician. He was a man of bulk, florid, hot-headed, high-tempered, fond of rich food and hard liquor. In Washington he lived with the two Virginia Senators, the pompous, self-important James M. Mason, Chairman of the Senate Foreign Relations Committee, and the quiet, unobtrusive, able R. M. T. Hunter, Chairman of its Finance Committee, and with A. P. Butler, of South Carolina, head of the Senate Judiciary Committee.[16] This concentration under one roof of the leaders of the State's Rights faction gave Atchison a weight in Senate politics altogether out of proportion to his inherent abilities and he made full use of it in his struggle with Benton. James S. Green, a brilliant young lawyer, was a member of the Thirtieth and Thirty-First Congresses. In 1849 he arraigned 'Old Bullion' before the people of Missouri pitilessly and with compelling logic.[17] The excitement equaled that of a presidential election and the Democratic party was badly split. When the Legislature met Benton could not command a majority, and a Whig was elected in his stead.

But Old Bullion could not be thus summarily retired to private life. Organizing a revolt from the party he ran as an independent for the House. While he did not win that year, his revolt sent three Whigs to the House. James S. Green was among the State's Righters defeated. Two years later Benton was again a candidate for the House, won election from a St. Louis district, and at once launched a campaign for election to the Senate in place of Atchison, his arch-foe. While that election would not come until 1854, Benton was determined to destroy Atchison's political strength beforehand.

For this, a new issue was demanded, and late in 1852, Benton renewed his championship of a Pacific railroad and the organization of a Territorial Government for Nebraska, which last would put law and civilization into communication across the continent and through its center, make traveling safe, direct, speedy and cheap, and open up fresh land to settlers.[18]

Benton's purpose was to convince the Missourians of the intimate connec-

[16] Nichols, *Franklin Pierce*, 303–04; Forney, I, 57–58.

[17] James G. Blaine, *Twenty Years of Congress*, Norwich, Conn., 1884, I, 273; Green, he thought, had done more than any other in Missouri to break Benton's power in the State. Ray, 51–52.

[18] Speech at Jackson, Mo., Oct. 30, 1852; cited, Ray, 75–76.

tion between securing organized government for Nebraska and the building of a Pacific railroad by the central route. Once the public understood this, it would be highly embarrassing to Atchison, who was on record a hundred times as being unyieldingly opposed to any Territorial establishment to the west of Missouri that would not permit slave-holders to carry their slaves there. The Kansas-Nebraska land was all to the north of the Missouri Compromise line of 36° 30′; if admitted as a Territory it must be free. Benton was charging that Atchison was actively hostile, both to the road and to the organization of a Nebraska Territorial Government.

This sagacious campaign produced immediate results. In December, 1852, Willard P. Hall, one of Atchison's most active House lieutenants, reintroduced his bill for the organization of the Territory of the Platte, fought for it with almost frantic determination and Atchison himself began to show signs of change of base. Hall's bill was referred to the House Committee on Territories, of which Douglas' trusted lieutenant Richardson was chairman. On February 2, 1853, the Committee reported a substitute bill for the organization of the Nebraska Territory. Slavery was not mentioned, and the Southerners instantly objected to the wrong that would be done the poor Indian.

Richardson was provoked at a Texas member. 'He wishes to treat with those Indians,' the Chairman exclaimed, 'to go through that slow process, and in the meantime all the great objects of the bill will be lost and the emigration to the Pacific will be driven to another portion of the Union from the route that it now follows.' Hall excoriated such opposition as being based solely on the desire to defeat a northern route. 'Everyone is talking about a railroad to the Pacific Ocean,' the Missourian shouted bitterly. 'In the name of God, how is the railroad to be made if you will never let people live on the land through which the road passes?' [19] On February 10, the bill was carried, but nearly every negative vote came from the South.

Douglas, who was waiting for the House bill to come over, fortified himself with the facts as to the Indian argument, securing an official statement as to the actual number of Indians in the tribes 'south of the Missouri river and west of the boundaries of Iowa and Missouri.' Excluding the Cherokees, who were definitely domiciled in the Indian Territory far to the south, the entire region in question contained only 25,391 Indians, and the number actually affected by the proposed Nebraska Territory was much smaller.[20]

Armed with these facts, Douglas made repeated attempts to get the House bill to a Senate vote. At first Senator Atchison opposed it but before the end he came to its support, explaining that his initial objections had been two, that the Indian title to the territory had been insufficiently extinguished, and more important, the Missouri Compromise. 'Whether

[19] *Congressional Globe*, Thirty-Second Congress, Second Session, 558; 560–63.

[20] Statement of Office of Indian Affairs to Douglas, Washington, Feb. 13, 1853; Martin F. Douglas MSS. These figures excluded the Cherokee. They listed the numbers of the various tribes as follows: Omaha 1300, Pawnee 4500, Otoe & Misc. 1000, Halfbreeds 250, Ioway 437, Sacs & Fox of Mo. 200, Kickapoo 475, Delaware 1132, Pottawatomie 4300, Wyandot 553, Shawnee 931, Wea & Kaskaskia 255, Ottawa 247, Sacs & Fox of Mississippi 2173, Swan Creek & Black War Chippewa 30, Kanzas 1375, Miannes 250, Osage 4951, Quapaw 314, Seneca & Shawnee 290, Seneca (Sandusky) 177. Total, 25,391.

that law was in accordance with the Constitution of the United States or not,' Atchison said, he had felt that 'it would do its work, and that work would be to preclude slave-holders from going into that territory.' As the session proceeded, under pressure both at home and in Washington, he had thought further, and 'found that there was no prospect, no hope of the repeal of the Missouri Compromise excluding slavery from that territory....'

The freedom clause in the Ordinance for the Northwest Territory had been 'the first great error committed in the political history of this country,' the Missouri Compromise had been the next, but 'there is no remedy for them. We must submit to them. I am prepared to do it.' [21]

Douglas, greatly encouraged, strove with might and main to effect this plan. The object of the bill, he told the Senate, was 'to form a line of Territorial Governments extending from the Mississippi Valley to the Pacific Ocean,' to give 'continuous settlements from the one to the other.' [22]

But all the effort was in vain. On March 4, the bill was laid upon the table by a vote of 23 to 17, an almost exclusively sectional vote. Local necessities might have brought Atchison to time but there was no such pressure upon the other Southern Senators. If Nebraska were not organized as a Territory, the southern route would retain its advantage. Once more the Southern opposition kept a Territory from being organized. [23]

As soon as Jefferson Davis took up the duties of the War Department, he set engineers to work upon the surveys of transcontinental railroad routes. Pierce appointed Isaac Stevens Governor of the new Territory of Washington; he came to Washington and had a number of conferences with Senator Douglas about the surveys for a northern route, which would be made in Stevens' territory. The Illinois Senator went over a large-scale map with Stevens, pointing out the possibilities of gaps in the Rockies, the Cascades, and other ranges and evincing a 'special solicitude' over their particular exploration. [24]

Douglas' efforts in behalf of a central route for the Pacific railroad sprang almost wholly from his anxiety to build up the Chicago region economically and to secure it politically. His own real estate holdings in that city might have been a minor influence, but Chicago's growth thus far had already made these investments highly profitable. In the northern route, however, the Little Giant had a more definite prospect of financial reward. As Chairman of the Senate Committee on Territories he had perfected the organization of the Territory of Minnesota. His work gave him an intimate understanding of the geography and economic possibilities of the Northwest area and in 1853 he embarked on a large real estate speculation in the Lake Superior region, and undertook to organize a syndicate to handle it.

The particular land on which he had his eye was at Fond du Lac, at the

[21] Mrs. S. B. Dixon, *A True History of the Missouri Compromise and Its Repeal*, Cincinnati, 1899; 426–27.

[22] *Congressional Globe*, Thirty-Second Congress, Second Session, 1116.

[23] Dixon, *Missouri Compromise*, 423, 429.

[24] I. I. Stevens, Fort Benning, Upper Missouri River, Sept. 18, 1853, Douglas MSS.

head of Lake Superior, in whose immediate neighborhood he believed the northern transcontinental railroad would have its eastern terminus. He employed one D. A. Robertson, who was to secure the land. Robertson wrote, 'Know nothing — say nothing about our affairs to anyone.' [25]

Finally a tract of six thousand acres was rounded up and a little town established, under the name of Superior City. In less than a year it had five hundred inhabitants; soon thereafter the Sault Ste. Marie Canal was finished and land values grew amazingly. [26]

But the Little Giant was far from being greedy for all the profits from his speculation. He was fond of John W. Forney, the Pennsylvania editor-politician. 'How would you like to buy a share in Superior City?' he asked Forney one day in 1853. Before the editor could reply, Douglas clambered in a chair, pointed to a great map on the wall, and almost delivered a stump speech; from that point, or near it, he prophesied, would start 'the greatest railroad in the world.' When Forney pled poverty, the Senator told him he could get a share for $2500 and could then divide it with another investor. Forney had faith in Douglas' judgment, borrowed the money, bought the share, sold half as arranged and from what remained eventually realized a profit of $21,000! [27]

Douglas' anticipation as to the northern route to the Pacific was fully shared by that ubiquitous statesman-politician-promoter Robert J. Walker, who wrote the Illinois Senator that the construction of a road from the head of Lake Superior to Puget Sound was eminently practicable and would require only fourteen hundred miles of road. [28] Henry M. Rice, a former Indian trader who had secured election as Minnesota's Territorial Delegate to Congress, interested himself in this and other railroad schemes. In particular was he anxious for a road to be built from Lake Superior to Dubuque, Iowa, where it would link with the northwestern terminus of the Illinois Central. [29]

While a bluff, friendly man in outward aspect, Rice was an even more resourceful — and unscrupulous — politician. When Douglas' agent first went to Superior to acquire the land, he warned the Illinois Senator to beware of Rice, who had 'attempted to pirate' the Douglas acres. Gorman, Territorial Governor of Minnesota, warned Douglas that Rice had bad claims against the Winnebago Indians and the Government and had better be watched. [30] Rice's pretensions to the coveted land gave Douglas and his original associates some trouble and they had to admit the Minnesota Delegate to the syndicate, whose membership acquired a highly political tinge — Senators and Congressmen then, as now, not being averse to

[25] D. A. Robertson, Willow River, Wis., Nov. 21, 1853; Douglas MSS.

[26] Douglas to John C. Breckinridge, Indianapolis, Sept. 7, 1854; Breckinridge MSS., Library of Congress.

[27] Forney, *Anecdotes of Public Men*, I, 19–20.

[28] R. J. Walker, New York, Jan. 27, 1854; Douglas MSS.

[29] H. M. Rice, Washington, Dec. 8, 1853; Douglas MSS.

[30] D. A. Robertson, Willow River, Wis., Nov. 21, 1853; W. A. Gorman, St. Paul, Minn., Nov. 25, 1853; Douglas MSS.

speculative profits. The syndicate divided the ownership equally between Douglas; John C. Breckinridge, of Kentucky; Jesse D. Bright, of Indiana; H. M. Rice, of Minnesota, and D. A. Robertson. These shares quickly assumed a substantial cash value; by September, 1854, Douglas was asking $10,000 cash for a half share, and claiming it was worth double 'that sum today as an investment.' [31]

The Army Engineers surveying the northern route for the Pacific road discovered a thoroughly feasible route from The Dalles, on the Columbia River, to the headwaters of the Missouri, and Governor Stevens reported to Douglas: 'The question of the feasibility of a railroad to the Pacific Ocean is no longer a matter of doubt, and is a fixed fact. The route is eminently practicable and offers no serious obstructions. Each of the various mountain ranges afford two passes through which a railroad can be built. The intermediate country furnishes favorable connections, having inexhaustible supplies of wood and stone for building purposes, and being admirably adapted to settlement and cultivation. The amount of tunneling throughout the whole route is small, not probably exceeding two miles in all, and the rivers and streams are such as to be easily bridged. There are five harbors for the terminus of the route on Puget Sound.' But for all Douglas' private interest in Superior City and the northern route for a Pacific railway, it does not appear that he exerted his public influence in behalf of any other route than the central one he had been urging since 1845.

The Summer of 1853 saw an intensification of the efforts to have the southern route selected. With the approval of the President and in his presence, Jefferson Davis made a flamboyant speech in Philadelphia, insisting that a Pacific railroad was needed for national defense, and that, to procure one, 'the application of the war power of the Government... would be within the strict limit of the Constitution.' Guthrie, the Secretary of the Treasury, followed with the hint that, if sufficient funds remained in the national coffers after the debt had been paid, 'why, for purposes of self-defense, shall we not extend a railroad to the Pacific?' [32] In his first annual message the President urged the building of the road, and said he expected to have the Army Engineer survey reports ready for presentation by February next.

It was generally expected that these reports would recommend the southern route. Jefferson Davis, the controlling influence with the President, had steps afoot to secure from Mexico enough land south of the Gila to remove the last physical obstacle to the building of the road. On the other hand, while Manypenny, Pierce's Commissioner of Indian Affairs, visited the Nebraska region in the Summer of 1853, and purchased the title rights of some of the tribes, he neglected to extinguish titles to the west of Iowa

[31] Douglas to Breckinridge, Indianapolis, Sept. 7, 1854; Breckinridge MSS. Douglas needed $10,000, and wanted to sell so as to avoid having to sell a Chicago lot that had cost him $1600 five years before. Memoranda in Corcoran MSS. indicate that Douglas, Breckinridge and Rice each borrowed $5000 from Corcoran, Riggs and Company for the Superior speculation.

[32] I. I. Stevens, Fort Benning, Upper Missouri River, Sept. 18, 1853; Olympia, Oregon Territory, Dec. 5, 1853; Feb. 12, 1854; Douglas MSS. Nichols, *Franklin Pierce*, 282.

and provoked acute suspicions of his interest and good faith. Unless the Westerners could do something, and that immediately, it looked very much as if the southern route had won.

The peoples of Missouri, Iowa, Illinois were quite aware of the impending danger. The Missouri manifestations have already been described. In 1852, the Illinois Legislature repealed its instructions in favor of the southern route. There was an intense interest in Iowa, Senators Dodge and Jones became as busy as possible, bridge lines across that State from Davenport to Council Bluffs were pushed with vigor and Iowans took a very practical hand in the battle.

While the Nebraska lands were technically the roaming places of wild Indian tribes, actually they were controlled by the emigrant tribes, among whom the leaders were the Wyandotte Indians, a self-respecting, intelligent people, predominantly white in blood, with an organized government and a keen economic foresight. Originally an Ohio tribe, in 1843 the Wyandottes had been removed by the Federal Government and settled on the west bank of the Missouri, at the mouth of the Kansas River. Realizing full well that their tribal status was temporary, they themselves determined to end it, and in ending it to secure the highest possible price for their lands by locating there the eastern terminus of the Pacific railroad. In the Fall of 1852, the Wyandottes sent a delegate to Washington to urge the organization of their areas. In the Summer of 1853, the emigrant Indian tribes of the Nebraska region held a convention, favored Benton's central route for the Pacific railroad, asked for the Federal organization of the Nebraska Territory, established a provisional government of their own and called an election for a Territorial Delegate to Congress.

The election was duly held, and Thomas Johnson, a Methodist missionary to the Shawnees, was selected Delegate. But here a complication entered. When the people of the Iowa border learned of the election call, they feared that their own railroad interests would suffer if the Delegate selected were a man representing the southern or Kansas River part of the territory. Accordingly, on the day appointed the people of Council Bluffs crossed the river, went through all the forms of an election and chose one Hadley D. Johnson as Delegate. The two Johnsons proceeded to Washington and were there when Congress opened. Each vigorously urged that Nebraska be organized and each presented credentials for the mythical delegateship.[33]

The situation was not long in making itself manifest in the new Congress. Senator Dodge, of Iowa, introduced a bill to organize a Territorial Government for the Nebraska, it had two readings and was referred to Douglas' Committee on Territories and the Little Giant fell immediately to work upon it.

He knew there had been no substantial change in the Senators' minds upon the Territorial question. He knew of the impending recommendation of the Gila River route, of Gadsden's coming mission and of the nearness of

[33] Hodder, 'Genesis of the Kansas-Nebraska Act,' State Historical Society of Wisconsin, *Proceedings*, 1912, 75-76.

defeat for a central route. As a realist, never tremendously impressed with formulæ, he preferred to test their soundness by their applicability to facts. A student of the Constitution, he did not believe that the Missouri Compromise was valid; indeed a Douglas letter of November 30, 1852, is in print, though not thoroughly authenticated, stating that even then he planned 'to repeal altogether' the Compromise.[34] Active mover in the great Compromise of 1850, he believed new principles were now in effect: Popular Sovereignty, non-intervention, Congressional abstention from either establishing or disestablishing slavery in the Territories.

While no 'dough-face' — a Northern man with Southern principles — Douglas believed, with Clay and Webster, that a law of physical geography would keep slavery from any Territory of the United States in which it did not already exist. Therefore it was mere folly for the South to deny the Mid-West a transcontinental road merely because of adherence to an empty formula of words. At any rate it did not take him long to make up his mind to embrace the only feasible mode of organizing Nebraska.

Within a week of the reference of the Dodge bill, Douglas suggested that Lanphier hint in the *Illinois State Register* that the people of Nebraska might safely be left to act for themselves on slavery and other questions.

[34] Parmenas Taylor Turnley, *Letters of Parmenas*, London, 1863; 104–06, printing Douglas to Turnley, Washington, Nov. 30, 1852. The central statement reads: 'My plan now is to bring forward a Bill to repeal altogether that Compromise.... I have tried the extension of it, and have failed. I am now for its repeal. It was a compromise of principle in the Constitution in the first place, which was wrong; yet it was acquiesced in, and for that reason I was willing to continue it. But I am met in my efforts by the most violent opposition from Northern fanatics; so I will try to remove altogether the question.' Turnley, author of the volume in which the letter appears, was born at Dandridge, in East Tennessee, went through West Point, served in the Mexican War and at that period expressed active pro-slavery sentiments. During the Civil War he remained in the Federal Army. His sister, unyielding in pro-slavery attachment, emigrated from Tennessee to Canton, Mississippi. According to Mr. David Rankin Barbee, of Washington, she was there induced by Jefferson Davis to collect certain letters to and from her brother, and to have these published abroad, for possible effect on foreign sentiment.

My examination of Senator Douglas' papers, both the voluminous files at Greensboro and the scattered lots elsewhere, has disclosed a single letter from Captain Turnley to Douglas, written from Salt Lake City, Utah, in the Spring of 1861. In 1902, Captain Turnley published his reminiscences, based on voluminous diaries. The reminiscences do not reveal or refer to any communication between Turnley and Douglas between September, 1852 and November, 1854. I have made vigorous efforts both at Dandridge, Tenn., at Canton, Miss., and in Chicago, where Turnley lived after the Civil War, to discover the Captain's correspondence file and to find the original of the purported Douglas letter. But it cannot be found, nor does it comport with the Little Giant's character to have determined, as early as November, 1852, upon repealing the Compromise, and then not to have moved to do so during the Nebraska Territorial bill debates in the ensuing short term of the Thirty-First Congress. If, at any time in these debates, Douglas had proposed repeal of the Missouri Compromise restriction, as the printed letter to Turnley indicated, he could have easily won over the Southern votes and passed the bill. I am therefore highly dubious of the authenticity of this letter. My judgment is that, whatever might have been the Little Giant's earlier legal view as to the constitutionality of the Missouri Compromise, he had no plan to move its repeal until Jan., 1854, when Atchison, Dixon and Phillips insisted that it be done. For aid in seeking the Turnley papers, I am indebted to Mr. Barbee; Dean James D. Hoskins, of the University of Tennessee; Miss Minnie D. Goddard, of Dandridge, Tenn.; Miss Emma Gertrude Turnley, of San Francisco, and Milton Turnley Lightner of the same city.

'The Territories,' Lanphier soon said editorially, 'should be admitted to exercise, as nearly as practicable, all the rights claimed by the States and to adopt all such political regulations and institutions as their wisdom may suggest.' The next week the Washington correspondent of the New York *Journal of Commerce* predicted that Douglas' Committee would soon report a bill for three Territories, on the basis of the 1850 bills for Utah and New Mexico — in other words, without either expressly excluding or establishing slavery. 'Climate and nature,' the correspondent went on, 'and the necessary pursuits of the people who are to occupy the Territories will settle the question — and these will effectually exclude slavery.' [35]

On January 4, 1854, Douglas laid the Committee's report before the Senate, bringing in Dodge's bill with amendments. These last incorporated two clauses taken word for word from 1850's Utah and New Mexican Territorial Acts. 'When admitted as a State or States,' the first recited, 'the said Territory... shall be received into the Union with or without slavery, as their constitutions may prescribe at the time of their admission.' The second clause provided that all questions involving title as to slaves should be heard by the local courts of the Territory, subject to appeal to the Supreme Court of the United States.

The measures involved in the Compromise of 1850, the report declared, 'were intended to have a far more comprehensive and enduring effect than the mere adjustment of the difficulties arising out of the recent acquisition of Mexican territory. They were designed to establish certain great principles.' Consequently the Committee on Territories had deemed it a duty 'to incorporate and perpetuate, in their Territorial bill, the principles and spirit of those measures. If any other consideration were necessary to render the propriety of this course imperative upon the Committee, they may be found in the fact that the Nebraska country occupies the same relative position to the slavery question as did New Mexico and Utah when those Territories were organized.'

In 1850 it had been unsettled whether slavery was by law prohibited in the areas acquired from Mexico. Now the question was whether slavery was prohibited in the Nebraska country by *valid* law. 'In the opinion of those eminent statesmen who hold that Congress is invested with no rightful authority to legislate upon the subject of slavery in the Territories,' the report asserted, 'the eighth section of the Act preparatory to the admission of Missouri' — the teeth of the Missouri Compromise — 'is null and void; while the prevailing sentiment in large portions of the Union sustains the doctrine that the Constitution of the United States secures to every citizen an inalienable right to move into any of the Territories with his property, of whatever kind and description and to hold and enjoy the same under the sanction of law.'

But the merits of this controversy involved the same grave issues which had produced 'the fearful struggle of 1850.' Just as Congress then had not deemed it best itself to decide this issue, the Committee was not now

[35] *Illinois State Register*, Dec. 22, 1853; *Journal of Commerce*, New York, Dec. 30, 1853; *Herald*, New York, Jan. 2, 1854.

prepared to recommend a departure from the course then pursued. Instead, it urged that the basic principles of the Compromise of 1850 should again be put into practical effect. These principles it thus stated:

> First: That all questions pertaining to slavery in the Territories, and in the new States to be formed therefrom, are to be left to the decision of the people residing therein, by their appropriate representatives, to be chosen by them for that purpose.

> Second: That 'all cases involving title to slaves,' and 'questions of personal freedom,' are referred to the adjudication of the local tribunals, with the right of appeal to the Supreme Court of the United States.

> Third: That the provision of the Constitution of the United States, in respect to fugitives from service, is to be carried into faithful execution in all the 'organized Territories,' the same as in the States.[36]

The immediate reaction to these proposals was reminiscent of those of 1850's Compromise debate. Senator Mason, of Virginia, told a Northern Congressman that he did not want the Nebraska bill, was willing for things to stand as they were. Other Southern Ultra leaders were only mildly pleased, Northern Abolitionists and Free-Soilers were concerned, the chief support came from the middle-ground group which had welcomed 1850's Popular Sovereignty solution. A typical expression of this point of view came from Edmund Burke, of New Hampshire. 'I am glad to see,' he wrote, 'that you are not disposed to treat the principles of the late Compromise acts as nullities — mere expedients to escape the peril of the moment — but as practical things to be sacredly observed whenever occasions arise which demand their practical application.' [37]

When the text of Douglas' bill was first printed in the Washington *Sentinel* on January 7, it contained no reference to the Missouri Compromise, and had no definite suggestion that the Nebraska Territorial Legislature would have conferred upon it power and authority to determine whether or not slavery should exist there. The initial bill gave the impression that slavery would continue to be prohibited so long as Nebraska remained a Territory, except that the courts might in the meantime declare the unconstitutionality of the Missouri Compromise. Thus Douglas' initial concession to the South was actually no more than to limit the slavery prohibition upon a Territory to the period that it remained such.

Probably this concession failed to procure sufficient Southern support to pass the bill. What demands were made or arguments exchanged in these first few days are shrouded in silence. However, on January 10, the Washington *Sentinel* reprinted the text of the Committee's bill. This time it had a new section appended — Section Twenty-one, which, the *Sentinel*

---

[36] Senate Reports No. 15, Thirty-Third Congress, First Session.

[37] Chase to E. S. Hamlin, Washington, Jan. 22, 1854, *American Historical Report* for 1902; II, 255; Edmund Burke, Newport, N.H., Jan. 9, 1854; Douglas MSS.

asserted, had initially been omitted because of a 'clerical error.' 'In order
to avoid all misconstruction,' this new section set out, 'it is hereby declared
to be the true intent and meaning of this act, so far as the question of slavery
is concerned, to carry into practical operation' the propositions and principles
established by the Compromise of 1850, as given in the Committee report of
January 4.[38]

This new section represented a far step toward meeting the wishes of
the State's Rights Senators. Having gone this far Douglas had every reason
to believe that his bill would now be satisfactory to the dialectic Southrons,
while at the same time geography and climate would preserve freedom
for such new States as might come in from the Nebraska Territory.

At first the Little Giant's judgment seemed correct. Atchison, of Missouri,
believed that Section Twenty-One of Douglas' bill repealed the Missouri
Compromise and seemed satisfied with its form. Francis J. Grund wrote
the Baltimore *Sun* that while the Missouri Compromise *forever* prohibited
slavery, the new Nebraska bill permitted it under a certain contingency.
Thus the second bill was inconsistent with the first one, and inasmuch as
it would be the latter one, it would thus take precedence and so by inference
repeal the prohibition clause of the Missouri Compromise.

But this prospect of Southern acceptance was quickly shattered by a
Senator from a Border State and a Representative from the Cotton South.
The Senator was Archibald Dixon, of Kentucky; the Representative,
Philip Phillips, of Alabama, the first a Whig who had favored the Compromise of 1850, the second a Charleston-born State's Rights man who had
opposed it. While this was Phillips' first — and only — term in Congress,
he was a member of the House Committee on Territories and carefully
analyzed the text of the Nebraska bill. He had long asserted the belief that
the Southern slave-holder possessed full constitutional right to take his
property, of whatever sort, into any Territory of the United States.[39]

Therefore it seemed to him that Douglas' measure was but a delusion
to the South. He was exercised by the word *forever* in the Missouri Compromise. Under it, he insisted, no slave-holder could carry his slaves into
a Territory north of the line 36° 30'. Under Douglas' bill, this restriction
was to be lifted when the people of the Territory came to form their State
Constitution; then, and not until then, Phillips contended, the people
would be free to choose whether to prohibit or permit slavery in the new
State. Therefore, if the promoters of the Nebraska Act really desired to
recognize the equal rights of the slave-holding States in the common Territory, Douglas' bill did not go far enough. The South's rights could only

[38] Johnson, 233. Inspection of the bill as originally brought in shows the first twenty sections
had been written on white paper, obviously by a copyist. Then came a sheet of blue paper, with
the twenty-first section, in Douglas' own hand, and a rather hasty hand at that. This blue
sheet had been torn, pasted back together, and attached to the earlier sheet with sealing wax.
Furthermore, the last of the white sheets had penciled on it, at the end of the text of Section
Twenty, the words: 'Douglas reports Bill & read 1 & 2 reading special report Print agreed.'

[39] Phillips, a Charleston, S. C., Jew moved to Savannah, married a Miss Levy, who bore
him thirteen children. Phillips soon moved to Mobile, Ala., where his law practice made him
rich. He did not return to Alabama after his service in Congress.

be given by the repeal of the prohibition as contained in the Missouri Compromise Act. True, he thought it only '*a theoretical right*,' but believed the form in which Douglas' bill had it was 'delusive,' and determined to force a change. On the day after the bill was introduced, Phillips gave Senator R. M. T. Hunter, of Virginia, his view of the flaws in Douglas' bill. That evening Hunter related this conversation at his mess. The next day Atchison remarked to Phillips: 'Hunter tells me you say Douglas' bill does not repeal the Missouri Compromise Act. This surprises me.' When Phillips confirmed the statement, Atchison asked him to meet Douglas and himself in the Vice-President's room in the Capitol the next morning.

When the three met, Atchison asked Phillips to state his opinion of the effect of the measure. Phillips did so, adding that 'Repeal by implication was not allowed, but could only be effected by express words, or by the passage of an act so inconsistent with the former act that the two could not coexist.' The Little Giant 'seemed impressed' with Phillips' statement. There were other conferences, at which 'many of the most distinguished Southern members' were present, 'Douglas alone representing the Northern Democracy.' Lewis Cass was approached about this time and urged to move the repeal, being told that Douglas would do so if he did not.[40]

While Douglas was considering the Ultras' demands, the Gordian knot was cut by Senator Archibald M. Dixon. This Kentuckian was quite a man. Over six feet in height, his face while not handsome was attractive. He talked well, and when excited in debate his eyes blazed with fire. Lawyer, planter, successful business man, Dixon owned some hundreds of slaves, and was fixed in his belief that the owner of a slave had a basic constitutional right to take his property with him into any of the Territories of the United States. While a lifelong Whig, he was more doctrinaire than politician; once he had taken a position he would stand by it though the Heavens fell.[41]

Dixon had been elected on the death of Henry Clay, and when he came to Washington brought a letter of introduction to Douglas from a mutual Indiana friend.[42] Even so, he took his seat prejudiced against the Little Giant, but before long Douglas' affability and charm thawed him out and Dixon came to deem the Little Giant 'far the ablest Democratic member.' [43]

---

[40] Notes of Philip Phillips, Left for his Children, originals in Phillips MSS., Library of Congress. H. B. Learned, 'The Relation of Philip Phillips to the Repeal of the Missouri Compromise,' *Mississippi Valley Historical Review*, VIII, 303–17; Philip Phillips, in Washington *Constitution*, Aug. 25, 1860. Gideon Welles, 'Diary,' MSS. 'Library of Congress, entry for June 29, 1855, gives Cass statement to him that day on events of January, 1854.

[41] The Dixon family MSS. loaned me by Mrs. Julia Dixon Clarke, of Henderson, Ky.; these references are to pp. 20, 47.

[42] John Law, Evansville, Ind., Sept. 17, 1852; Douglas MSS. Law termed Dixon of 'superior intelligence and strict integrity.'

[43] Louisville *Democrat*, Oct. 3, 1858, containing text of letter, Dixon to Henry S. Foote, Henderson, Ky., Oct. 1, 1858. Douglas was 'sociable, affable, and in the highest degree entertaining and instructive in social intercourse,' Dixon wrote. 'His power as a debater seemed to me unequaled in the Senate. He was industrious, energetic, bold and skillful in the management of the concerns of his party. He was the acknowledged leader of the Democratic party in the Senate, and, to confess the truth, seemed to me to bear the honors which encircled him with sufficient meekness.'

When Dodge introduced his Nebraska bill, Dixon noted the absence of reference to slavery and determined to do something about it. At Christmastime, the Senator and his wife went to Philadelphia to spend the holidays with John Bullitt, the latter's brother. Startled at a hint that Dixon planned an amendment repealing the Missouri Compromise, Bullitt earnestly opposed it. While theoretically the Senator might be right, such a repeal could never be of any practical value to the South, but would 'be like a spark of fire to a train of powder' in the North and frightful havoc might ensue. Dixon was unimpressed. The proposition was right in itself, he answered; if strife should ensue the South could take care of itself; he only wished to assert the South's fair and constitutional rights.[44] When the Senator returned to Washington he began work on his amendment. On the evening of January 15, he had his wife get pen and paper, and dictated an amendment for the repeal of the Missouri Compromise.[45] She made many mistakes, reworked it 'innumerable times,' but finally it satisfied the Senator, who then copied it in his own hand.

The next morning Dixon showed the amendment to Senator Jones, of Tennessee, who read it with amazement but agreed. Soon the Kentuckian gave notice that when Douglas' bill should come up for consideration, he planned to offer an amendment repealing the Missouri Compromise. Dixon's amendment provided that 'the citizens of the several States and Territories shall be at liberty to take and hold their slaves within any of the Territories of the United States, or of the States to be formed therefrom,' as if the Missouri Compromise 'had never been passed.'

The Senators were startled and none more so than Douglas, who rushed to Dixon's seat and urged him not to insist upon this step: the bill as already introduced was almost in the words of the acts of 1850, and as a friend of that Compromise, Dixon should do nothing to weaken it before the country.

'It is precisely because I have been, and am, a firm and zealous friend of the Compromise of 1850, that I feel bound to persist,' Dixon answered. 'I am well satisfied that the Missouri restriction, if not expressly repealed, will continue to operate in the territory to which it had been applied, thus negativing the great and salutary principle of non-intervention, the prominent and essential feature of the plan of settlement of 1850.'[46] Douglas' hasty arguments did not alter these views.

All the next day the Dixon parlor was crowded with visitors, Whigs and Democrats alike, 'expressing a delighted surprise.' William Preston, the Louisville Congressman, opened the door about halfway, and with a broad smile exclaimed 'Eureka.' John C. Breckinridge took the Senator's hand and said impressively: 'Why did none of us ever think of this before?'[47]

Soon thereafter Douglas called and invited Dixon to take a carriage ride with him so that they could discuss this new development. They talked

[44] John C. Bullitt to Mrs. S. B. Dixon, Philadelphia, Dec. 13, 1894, printed in Dixon, *The Missouri Compromise*, 603 *et seq.*

[45] *Ibid.*, 442 *et seq.*

[46] *Ibid.*, 446–47. I have changed the tenses slightly.

[47] Dixon, *Missouri Compromise*, 444–45.

a long time; the Kentuckian was earnest, emphatic and unyielding. At last, realizing that the doctrinaire would not budge an inch, the Little Giant admitted that he thought the Missouri Compromise constitutionally invalid. The Kentuckian renewed his pressure for the flat, forthright repeal. 'By God, sir, you are right,' Douglas finally exclaimed. 'I will incorporate it in my bill, though I know it will raise a hell of a storm.' [48]

[48] Douglas' words, quoted by Dixon to his wife immediately after his return from the carriage ride. See Dixon, *The Missouri Compromise*, 445. In 1878, Dixon wrote Henry S. Foote, of Mississippi, about the Compromise repeal, and at this time he attributed more courtly language to Douglas, and had him saying: 'I have become perfectly satisfied that it is my duty, as a fair-minded national statesman, to co-operate with you as proposed in securing the repeal of the Missouri Compromise restriction. It is due to the South; it is due to the Constitution, heretofore palpably infracted; it is due to that character for consistency which I have heretofore labored to maintain. The Repeal, if we can effect it, will produce much stir and commotion in the free States of the Union for a season. I shall be assailed by demagogues and fanatics there without stint or moderation. Every opprobrious epithet will be applied to me. I shall be, probably, hung in effigy in many places. It is more than probable that I may become permanently odious among those whose friendship and esteem I have heretofore possessed. This proceeding may end my political career. But acting under the sense of duty which animates me, I am prepared to make the sacrifice. I will do it.' *Ibid.*, 447–48. The terse form seems more compatible with Douglas' conversational custom. The 1878 version seems to me probably Dixon's interpolation, in the manner of Thucydides, as to what Douglas should have said.

CHAPTER VIII

THE COMING OF THE STORM

DOUGLAS was not mistaken in his prediction. As soon as Dixon made his motion, there were premonitory lightning flashes, and the very next day Charles Sumner, of Massachusetts, offered a counter-amendment that 'nothing herein contained shall be considered to abrogate or in any way contravene' the Missouri Compromise.

For the moment, however, the more disturbing developments were among the Southern Ultras. On Thursday evening, January 19, Douglas and John C. Breckinridge called on Philip Phillips to discuss the form of a Compromise repeal. Finally Douglas asked Phillips to write out his own formula. The Alabaman wrote a few lines and handed them to the Senator.

Douglas read it, asked if this was satisfactory. Phillips said that it was so far as he was personally concerned, but he had no right to speak for the others. Thinking a minute, he added that on Saturday he would answer for the general body of Southern men. So he consulted several of his colleagues and had a particularly earnest conference with the members of the Atchison mess. He found 'a general concurrence in the propriety of the repeal,' and a disposition to accept his draft.

Until then apparently Douglas had not consulted the President or his Cabinet as to the Nebraska bill. When he had first reported it, the Washington *Union*, the Administration organ, most of whose important editorials were written by Caleb Cushing, the Attorney-General, had approved its principles. John W. Forney thought it 'a happy event for Pierce.' On Saturday, however, the *Union* took distinct ground against the expediency of the repeal, declaring that its benefits would not compensate the Administration for the embarrassment of a renewed anti-slavery agitation.[1]

This impressed on Douglas the necessity of forcing Pierce to make the Nebraska bill, with its Compromise repeal, an Administration measure and party test. Soon Phillips reported the general agreement of Southern members as to outright repeal. 'Very good,' Douglas said. 'Tomorrow night we will go to the White House and see President Pierce on the subject.' Surprised, Phillips pointed out that Pierce never did business on Sunday, but Douglas assured him that the visit would not be unacceptable. This Phillips took to mean that the interview had already been arranged.[2]

---

[1] Forney to Buchanan, Washington, Jan. 10, 1854; Buchanan MSS.: It would 'go far to help the Administration.' Claude M. Fuess, *Caleb Cushing*, New York, 1923; II, 146–47.

[2] Philip Phillips, Notes Left for His Children; Phillips MSS., Library of Congress. According to Henry Wilson, *The Slave Power*, II, 382–83, Marcy told Reuben E. Fenton, a New York member, that Douglas had seen Pierce on Saturday. Dr. Roy F. Nichols, Pierce's biographer, thinks Davis arranged the interview. Phillips' account, written in January, 1876, is in part based on a letter he wrote the Washington *Constitution*, Aug. 24, 1860, printed the next day. Phillips died in 1884.

The next morning Douglas assembled those most keenly interested in the matter — Senators Atchison, of Missouri; Hunter and Mason, of Virginia; Representatives Phillips, of Alabama; Breckinridge, of Kentucky, and Goode, of Virginia — and they went to see Jefferson Davis, Pierce's chief adviser. The group found him at home and stated the case.

The Committees on Territories of both House and Senate, they explained, had agreed upon a bill for the Kansas-Nebraska Territory, Douglas desired to report it to the Senate Monday morning and Richardson, Chairman of the House Committee, would simultaneously bring it in. But before either of them would move, the measure must 'receive the sanction of and be supported by the President.'

Davis carefully examined the bill, was quite pleased with it, but remarked to his callers that they were 'either a day too late or too early' — the President would receive no visitors on the Sabbath. Douglas explained that if the House Committee did not report Monday, there would be much delay. The Secretary of War must persuade General Pierce to see them on the Sabbath. After a moment's thought, Davis agreed.

Not without reason had Douglas sought the Secretary of War, who had far outstripped the more moderate Marcy as dominant figure in the Administration. Pierce loved and trusted Jefferson Davis, consulted him even on minor decisions, and, so followed his advice that enemies sneered that the Secretary of War was really President.[3]

The two Senators remained in the White House library while Davis invaded the President's private quarters to explain the necessity for the call. Soon thereafter Pierce came into the library.[4] There ensued a conversation between Pierce, Douglas and Atchison. Its purport is not known, but when the rest of the group, which had been walking to the White House, entered the library, the President and the two Senators were standing and Phillips was struck by the 'cold formality' which prevailed.

Almost immediately the subject of the repeal of the Missouri Compromise was broached. 'Gentlemen,' the President remarked, 'you are entering on a serious undertaking, and the ground should be well surveyed before the first step is taken.'[5]

There was no debate as to the propriety of the repeal but a long discussion ensued as to the precise phraseology to be employed. Finally, a formula was found to which all heartily agreed. Well aware of Pierce's vacillating character, Douglas insisted that the President take a pen and paper and write it out. The resultant draft was both guide for preparing the bill and the Little Giant's protection against a White House change. As the leaders

---

[3] In 1857, when Pierce went out of office, he said to Davis: 'I can scarcely bear to part from you, who have been strength and solace to me for four anxious years, and never failed me'; quoted, Varina Davis, *Memoir of Jefferson Davis*, New York, 1890; I, 530.

[4] Jefferson Davis to Mrs. Archibald Dixon, Beauvoir, Miss., Sept. 27, 1879, quoted, Dixon, *Missouri Compromise*, 457–60.

[5] Philip Phillips, Notes Left for His Children; Phillips MSS. The Alabaman's recollection was that the visit to the White House occurred about nine Sunday night. His memory on this point is doubtless in error, for Davis, in 1879, put it as having occurred Sunday morning. 'Savoyard,' 'Stephen A. Douglas,' Washington *Post*, Sept. 23, 1894, puts it as a Sunday morning call.

YOUNG HICKORY: FRANKLIN PIERCE
President of the United States, 1853–1857

left, Pierce requested that they call on Marcy and secure his approval. They did go to Marcy's house, found him dining out and did not go back.

Thus Douglas and his associates altered the political character of the Nebraska bill. No longer was it merely a proposal of the Senate's Committee on Territories, a project of Stephen A. Douglas.[6] Now it had become an Administration measure, a party test.

While Douglas was lining up Administration support for his Nebraska bill, the leading Congressional Abolitionists were preparing a great *coup de théâtre* to reawaken the anti-slavery passions of the North. This group's leaders in Washington — Salmon P. Chase, of Ohio; Charles Sumner, of Massachusetts; and William H. Seward, of New York — saw in Douglas' original Nebraska bill the chance to raise that storm of passion the Little Giant had foreseen. They had great ability along these lines. But for playing like virtuosi on the strings of popular passion, perhaps Chase and Sumner would never have gone to the Senate. All three recognized the political usefulness of emotional hysteria, and that the Nebraska bill had possibilities of adding to their group's strength in Congress. For these reasons, as well as because of their anti-slavery views, they began drafting a document.

Joshua Giddings, fanatical Free-Soil Congressman from Ohio, made the first draft, then Chase took it, rewrote it and impressed his stamp upon it. Sumner and Gerrit Smith made some verbal changes, but Chase considered it the fruit of his own pen, was quite proud of it and for some months thereafter held it 'the most valuable' of his works.[7]

Chase was tall, of good presence, with well-formed head and firm mouth. But one of his eyelids had a peculiar droop, lending a sinister touch to his countenance. A man of purpose, energy and ambition, he had ability to concentrate, analyze and organize, but his great failing was the lack of a sense of humor and a consequent lack of any sense of proportion. He had come to the Senate in 1849 as the result of a political brawl in Ohio. The 1848 State election had resulted in an almost even balance between Democrats and Whigs in the Legislature and a handful of Free-Soilers held the balance of power. These Abolitionists stubbornly refused to yield in the election of a Senator. Finally the Democrats coalesced with the schismatics and gave the senatorship to Chase, the latter's choice, in preference to a Whig. He was anxious for a new party on the platform, 'no more slave States — no slave Territory.'[8]

[6] Joseph Robertson to John H. George, Washington, Jan. 24, 1854; George MSS.: 'The bill ... embraces the views of the Pres. and will be sustained as an Administration measure.... The amendments... are in fact the President's.... He read me the day before from his own manuscript the amendment.... The general impression is that the bill will pass by a good vote.' Henry Wilson, *The Slave Power*, II, 382–83, quoting statement of Marcy to Reuben E. Fenton, New York Congressman and Marcy follower, on Monday, Feb. 23, 1854, that the party had called on Pierce Sunday, that Pierce had told them to see him, that they had called on him and he had been out at dinner. Marcy generally dined at three in the afternoon.

[7] Chase to E. L. Pierce, Washington, Aug. 8, 1854, *American Historical Association Report for 1902*; II, 263.

[8] S. P. Chase, Washington, Feb. 26, 1861, printed T. F. Madigan, *Autograph Album*, I, 30.

Charles Sumner, of Massachusetts, the only other avowed senatorial Abolitionist, was a psychic puzzle to contemporaries. Handsome, able, erudite, he was well aware of all three traits. He spoke too well; a consummate actor, he carefully modulated his voice, laid great stress on inflection, introducing appropriate, carefully rehearsed gestures. His addresses were opportunities to demonstrate an encyclopædic knowledge and were studded with quotations from Homer and Horace, Shakespeare and Milton, John Locke and Rousseau. And yet, few who ever sat in legislative halls have been so cordially despised as Charles Sumner. Without humility, without consideration for others, not only did he enrage his opponents but he irritated and alienated those who agreed with him. His truly colossal egotism, his extraordinary genius for antagonism caused party associates to sneer at him as 'a snob, a social flunky, a genus Yellow-Plush,' a man who would treat the unknown white man with haughty contempt but would bump his head on the floor in the presence of an English lord.[9]

William H. Seward, of New York, still technically a Whig, was the ablest of the three. A slight man, not so much taller than Douglas, he had a sedentary stoop and was more impressive sitting down than on his feet. His head was large and well-formed, his mouth large and flexible, his nose aquiline, his eyes cold gray, occasionally quizzical, his brow broad, crowned with a fine head of hair. A subtle, quick man, with a remarkable memory constantly displayed, he was anxious for power, fond of a jest, full of oracular utterances. Deep down, however, Seward was cold, without deep emotions or vivid imagination. He was facetious rather than witty, logical rather than of good judgment, plausible rather than truthful or profound.[10]

During the week, Chase polished up his appeal, it was viewed and reviewed by his chief associates, and by Saturday the powder-mine was nearly ready to be set off. That day Chase dined with Thomas H. Benton and noted Old Bullion's remark that 'Douglas has committed political suicide.'[11]

Early Monday morning Douglas had a meeting of his Committee on Territories, advised his colleagues of the week-end's developments and submitted a new bill he had prepared, incorporating the changes to which the President had agreed. The Committee quickly approved and Douglas brought the new measure before the Senate that day. There were two important changes. First, in place of the original provision for the establishment of a single Territory of Nebraska, the report of January 23 proposed the division of the area into two Territories, the southern one to be known as Kanzas or Kansas, the northern one as Nebraska.

---

[9] George Fort Milton, *The Age of Hate*, New York, 1930; 33–35; Cincinnati *Commercial*, Jan. 15, 1868, giving Don Piatt's letter, Washington, Jan. 13, 1868. Piatt illustrated Sumner's colossal egotism by this incident: During the Civil War, at a time of terrible excitement, a friend met Sumner walking slowly down a Boston street. He rushed up to the Senator and exclaimed in great excitement: 'Mr. Sumner, have you any news for us?' 'Yes, sir,' responded Sumner, 'Yes, sir, I am much better.'

[10] Milton, *The Age of Hate*, 18; Foote, *Casket of Reminiscences*, 124–26.

[11] Chase to E. S. Hamlin, Washington, Jan. 22, 1854, *American Historical Association Report for 1902*; II, 255–56.

The second change was in the provision affecting slavery. All questions pertaining to slavery in the Territories and in the new States which might be formed therefrom were to be left to the decision of the people through their appropriate representatives. 'All cases involving title to slaves' and all 'questions of personal freedom' were to be referred 'to the adjudication of the local tribunals, with the right of appeal to the Supreme Court of the United States.' Finally the Missouri Compromise Act, 'suspended by the principles of Compromise measures of 1850,' was expressly declared 'inoperative and void.' [12]

Douglas' substitute occasioned considerable excitement among the Softs in the New York House delegation, who dispatched Reuben Fenton to see Pierce and Marcy to ascertain the facts. When Fenton intimated that the Softs might bolt the Douglas bill, the President, excited, chided him, pointing out that the Softs had been shown 'at least equal consideration in patronage.' Marcy, who seemed agitated and depressed, told Fenton that as a fundamental principle the bill was Democratic; the only question was as to the appropriateness of its application. But 'every person must judge of his duty for himself, and walk in the light of his own convictions.' [13]

Caleb Cushing became one of the bill's most ardent advocates. His arguments, joined with those of Jefferson Davis, wrung a reluctant acquiescence from Marcy and the Cabinet presented a united front for repeal.

The Administration hastened to proclaim its adoption of the new Douglas bill. On Tuesday morning the *Union's* leading editorial, written by the President himself, announced that the new Kansas-Nebraska bill was an important part of the legislative program which the Pierce Administration had undertaken for the session, and support of it would 'be regarded by the Administration as a test of Democratic orthodoxy.' [14] With this forthright Administration endorsement, and after a further conference with the President, Douglas sought to push the bill along.

[12] Henry Wilson, *Slave Power*, II, 381–82. Phillips' amendment, which Douglas had requested but not used, was: 'and that the people of said Territory through the Territorial Legislature hereafter provided, may legislate upon the subject of slavery in any manner they may think proper not inconsistent with the principles of the Constitution of the United States, and all laws or parts of laws inconsistent with this authority or right, shall from and after the passage of this act, be and become, inoperative, void, and of no force and effect.' Dixon's amendment, adding a twenty-second section to the bill, explicitly repealed by chapter and title the Missouri Compromise. The new Kansas-Nebraska bill was a double bill of forty sections, against twenty of the original January 4 bill, the last twenty being identical with the first twenty, except that the word Kansas, in the first group, was made Nebraska in the second. There were slight changes in sections thirteen and twenty, due to the division of the Territory; section twenty-one of the January 4 bill was omitted, the new phraseology covering the matter being incorporated in section fourteen.

[13] *Ibid.*, II, 382–83. A few days later Marcy had a few of his personal and political friends in the New York delegation for a conference, bringing up the question of his resignation. But these Softs did not like the prospect of the Hards getting all the offices and urged Marcy to stay in, which he did.

[14] Washington *Union*, Jan. 24, 1854. Fuess, *Caleb Cushing*, II, 147, states that the original draft of the editorial, in Cushing's hand, proves an authorship which tone and style had indicated. But Joseph Robinson to John H. George, Washington, Jan. 24–25, 1854, John H. George MSS., states: 'The amendments as well as the arguments contained in the *Union* of yesterday (Jan. 24) are in fact the President's.'

During this discussion, Dixon, of Kentucky, declared himself thoroughly satisfied with the amendment Douglas had reported. 'The object of the Committee,' Douglas replied, 'was neither to legislate slavery in or out of the Territories; neither to introduce it nor exclude it; but to remove whatever obstacles Congress had put there, and to apply the doctrine of Congressional non-intervention, in accordance with the principles of the Compromise measure of 1850.' But Chase and Sumner asked that it be delayed for a few days, and the Little Giant courteously agreed.

That very afternoon, Douglas read with amazement and indignation in the columns of the *National Era*, the Abolitionists' Washington organ, a document entitled 'The Appeal of the Independent Democrats.' The first name signed to it was Salmon P. Chase who, with smiling face and pretense of friendship, had asked for delay in consideration of the bill. Other signers were Charles Sumner, Gerrit Smith, Joshua Giddings, Edward Wade and Alexander DeWitt, the last four being Free-Soil Congressmen.

The enactment of this Nebraska bill would 'open all the unorganized Territory of the Union to the ingress of slavery.' Because of this, it was arraigned 'as a gross violation of a sacred pledge; as a criminal betrayal of precious rights; as part and parcel of an atrocious plot to exclude from a vast unoccupied region immigrants from the Old World and free laborers from our own States, and convert it into a dreary region of despotism inhabited by master and slaves.'

Giving a typical Free-Soil account of the origin of the Missouri Compromise, the Appeal asserted that, for over thirty years, 'this compact has been universally regarded and acted upon as inviolable American law.' Therefore 'language fails to express the sentiments of indignation and abhorrence' aroused by this 'bold scheme against American liberty,' which was 'worthy of its accomplished architect of ruin.' The bill was a 'monstrous' plot against humanity and democracy, 'dangerous to the interest of liberty throughout the world.' 'The dearest interests of freedom and the Union' were in 'imminent peril' and the Appeal urged a universal protest by letters, newspapers, memorials, public meetings and legislative resolutions, and speeches in the pulpit to stop this 'enormous crime.'

A postscript described the substitute reported on January 23 as 'a manifest falsification of the truth of history.... Not a man in Congress, or out of Congress, in 1850 pretended that the Compromise measures would repeal the Missouri prohibition. Will the people permit their dearest interests to be thus made the mere hazards of a presidential game, and destroyed by false facts and false inferences?' [15]

This assault upon the Kansas-Nebraska bill incensed Douglas, for he felt it based upon ingenious but thoroughly false historical foundations.

---

[15] *Congressional Globe*, Thirty-Third Congress, First Session, 281. The *National Era* printed it on January 24, dating it the 22d. The New York *Times* printed it that same day, and gave it the Sunday date. The New York *Tribune* copied it from the *Times* and changed the date to the 23d. When the signers of the address put it in the *Congressional Globe*, they carefully avoided the Sunday date, dating it back to January 19.

The personal attack on him, however, made him fighting mad, the Appeal's outrageous adjectives and vindictive slurs made him resolve to give no quarter but to expose its signers in such a way that the country would understand their hypocrisy and thorough disrepute.

On the evening that the Appeal was published he called at a Congressman's room at the Brown Hotel. The man he wanted to see was not there, but another friend was in the room, young George Murray McConnel, the son of the Senator's old-time benefactor out in Jacksonville, Illinois. The two had a happy reunion, but as Douglas rose to go he saw on the table a copy of a paper containing the Appeal of the Independent Democrats. His whole aspect changed, and he termed it 'an unpardonable thing in many ways, and in nothing more than the duplicity of the way in which opportunity was secured to forestall public opinion, to say nothing of the vilification of me and my motives.'

Absently he took a cigar from the mantel, lit it and began to walk back and forth before the fire. The cigar went out, he chewed it into shreds, flung it into the fire. 'Stick to the law, my boy,' he told the startled lad, 'stick to the law! Never go into politics. If you do, no matter how sincere and earnest you may be, no matter how ardently you may devote yourself to the welfare of your country, and your whole country,... no matter how clear it may be to you that the present is an inheritance from the past, that your hands are tied, and that you are bound to do only what you can do with loyalty to institutions fixed for you by that past, rather than what you might prefer to do if free to choose; no matter for all this or more you will be misinterpreted, vilified, traduced, and finally sacrificed to some local interest or unreasoning passion. Adams, Webster, Clay, Wright and others, were victims, and I suppose I must be another.'

He went on that he thought slavery 'a curse beyond computation to both white and black.' But the only power that could destroy slavery was the sword, and if that were once drawn no one could see the end. 'I am not willing to violate the Constitution to put an end to slavery,' he said; 'to violate it for one purpose will lead to violating it for other purposes. To "do evil that good may come" is false morality and worse policy, and I regard the integrity of this political Union as worth more to humanity than the whole black race. Some time, without a doubt, slavery will be destroyed,' but he was not willing to set fire to the ship in order to smoke out the rats.

The Missouri Compromise repeal he termed a step toward freedom, because 'Slavery can no longer crouch behind a line which Freedom is cut off from crossing.' He had been surprised that the proposal to repeal came from the South, dreaded the effect, but what could he do? 'All my public life I have been among party men. For nearly twenty years I have been fighting for a place among the leaders of the party which seems to me most likely to promote the peace and prosperity of my country, and I have won it.'

That party had now decided on an unwise step, he had said so in the party councils but had been overruled. 'I must either champion the policy the party has adopted,' he said, 'or forfeit forever all that I have fought for — must throw away my whole life and not only cease to be a leader but sink into a nobody. If I retain my leadership I may help to guide the party aright in some graver crisis. If I throw it away, I not only destroy myself but I become powerless for good forever after.'

'But, Mr. Douglas,' young McConnel said, as the Senator paused, 'if you think it's right ——' 'Ah, my boy,' he broke in impetuously, 'I felt that way once. Felt that if I only thought anything right! But why should I or anyone oppose an individual judgment to that of a great party? Am not I at least as likely to be mistaken as the others? That is not politics, nor policy, nor wisdom.... I know I am politically right in keeping within the pale of the Constitution. I believe I am right as to the moral effect, and I know I am right as a party leader anxious to help in keeping his party true to the whole country.

'It is the vilification of my motives that most wounds.... No man loves his country better than I. I know she is not faultless. I see as clearly as they that she is afflicted with a dangerous tumor. But I believe she will slough it off in time, and I am not willing to risk the life of the patient by the illegal and unscientific surgery they demand. D—— them,' he added, furiously, 'they are the traitors to freedom, not I, if there be any treason at all. We may all be overwhelmed together in the storm they are brewing, but I, at least, shall stick to the old ship while there's a plank of her afloat.' [16]

This outburst to young McConnel may have relieved Douglas' heart of the anger the Appeal had occasioned, but it required all his patience and his courage to endure the ensuing storm, for the signers of this Appeal had calculated shrewdly as to the tumult it would raise. Throughout the North, Whig and Free-Soil papers accepted its assertions as fact, displayed it boldly, in large type, wrote heated editorials, set match to powder-train in every community. Greeley thundered in the *Tribune*, Henry J. Raymond denounced in the *Times*, William Cullen Bryant rang the changes in the *Evening Post*. Samuel Bowles was excited in the Springfield *Republican*, even James Watson Webb, of the *Courier and Enquirer*, became virtuously indignant and Thurlow Weed and his Albany *Journal* displayed an extraordinary concern over ethics and morality. In almost every hamlet from Maine to Michigan less-known editors followed their cue, Douglas was termed 'Agitator-General... the bully of slavery.' Mass meetings began to be held, resolutions to be adopted, anonymous letters to be showered on the Administration leaders. One kind soul in Ohio wrote anonymously that Douglas' loss of his wife was a judgment of the Almighty!

Because of his agreement Douglas had to wait a week to declare his views upon his assailants and the bill itself. On January 30, when the bill came up for consideration, he made a speech that stunned his foes and raised his friends to a frenzy of applause. The Little Giant, all admitted, was never so powerful as when 'baited by his enemies.' His self-confidence was supreme, his tones of defiance clear and ringing, he had an intellectual vividness 'nearly akin to eloquence, his intrepidity was like an inspiration.'

Douglas brought with him an armory of facts which astounded and

[16] George Murray McConnel, *Recollections of Stephen A. Douglas*, 48 *et seq.*

alarmed his antagonists, many of whom sought to meet him with high-sounding phrases, an equipment utterly inadequate. As a contemporary biographer of Jefferson Davis explained a Douglas triumph over the Southron, 'the finest orator in the Senate,' the Little Giant had 'that ready and intricate skill which comes from the close and narrow study of a specialty, an acuteness carried to the nicest point of perfection.' Douglas was constantly defeating antagonists 'by his superiority in facts; and his great power in debate was his minute and remote illustrations drawn from this special fund of knowledge. He had at his fingers' ends all the *Congressional Annals* and *Globes, National Registers*, and political encyclopedias of every sort from "Clusky's Text Book" to the briefest *vade mecum*. In this intricate field of knowledge he had no rival; his illustrations gathered there were weapons, and they sometimes bore down the most formidable arrays of the intellect, and scattered the literary ornaments and flowery language of his cultivated competitors.' [17]

On this occasion, the notice of the speech had filled the galleries with an expectant throng. Douglas began by explaining that when he had proposed on the preceding Tuesday that the Senate take up the bill, he had planned 'only to occupy ten or fifteen minutes in explanation of its provisions' relating to the Indians and its bearing upon the slavery question.

In drafting the bill, Douglas pointed out, he was mindful of the great anxiety some Senators had expressed about protecting Indian rights, and he believed that these had been carefully safeguarded. The Committee's intention as to slavery was to be equally definite. It had taken the principles of the 1850 Compromise as guide 'and intended to make each and every provision of the bill accord with those principles.' These he proclaimed as being 'that the people should be allowed to decide the questions of their domestic institutions for themselves, subject only to such limitations and restrictions as are imposed by the Constitution of the United States, instead of having them determined by an arbitrary or geographical line.'

When the Committee first reported its bill, Douglas continued, its members believed that it had accomplished this object. But inasmuch as its object had been 'to conform to the principles established by the Compromise measures of 1850, and to carry these principles into effect in the Territories,' when doubts were raised, the bill was changed so as to recite 'precisely what we understood to have been accomplished by those measures.'

Such, Douglas said, had been his intention on January 24. But he reminded the Senate that Chase had then objected to immediate consideration, 'on the ground that there had not been time to understand and consider its provisions,' Sumner had joined in the request, and Douglas had consented.

'Little did I suppose,' he went on, in tones of withering scorn, 'at the time that I granted that act of courtesy to those two Senators, that they had drafted and published to the world a document, over their own signatures, in which they arraigned me as having been guilty of a criminal betrayal of my trust, as having been guilty of an act of bad faith, and being engaged in an atrocious plot against the cause of free government. Little

[17] Edward A. Pollard, *Life of Jefferson Davis*, Philadelphia, 1869; 35-36.

did I suppose that these two Senators had been guilty of such conduct when they called upon me to grant that courtesy.'

The irate Senator hammered the point home. He had since discovered that on that very Tuesday morning the *National Era* contained an address to the people grossly misrepresenting the bill, grossly perverting the Committee's action, arraigning the motives and calumniating the characters of its members. Moreover, 'there was a postscript added to the address published that very morning, in which the principal amendment reported by the Committee was set out, and then coarse epithets applied to me by name.' Had he known these facts at the time, he would have responded to the request of the Abolition Senators 'in such terms as their conduct deserve, so far as the rules of the Senate and respect for my own character would have permitted me to do.'

Douglas then began reading from the text of the Appeal, commenting upon such phrases as 'criminal betrayal,' 'servile demagogues' and 'meditated bad faith.' 'That address,' he said, 'bears date Sunday, January 22, 1854. Thus it appears that on the holy Sabbath, while other Senators were engaged in divine worship, these Abolition confederates were assembled in secret conclave, plotting by what means they should deceive the people of the United States and prostrate the character of brother Senators. This was done on the Sabbath day, and by a set of politicians, to advance their own political and ambitious purposes, in the name of our holy religion.'

As Douglas warmed up to his theme, the auditors were quiet, preternaturally attentive. The scene was striking. The Senate Chamber was packed to suffocation. Old Sam Houston, wearing his famous panther-skin vest, was not whittling as was his usual wont, but was pacing restlessly to and fro behind the presiding officer's seat. Senator Butler, of South Carolina, a notable figure with long white hair flowing to his shoulders, was looking alertly over the assemblage. Sumner was pretending to read. The ominous quiet was broken only by the Little Giant's deep, sonorous tones.

At length, Chase rose, tall, cold, his bald head reflecting the flickering Senate lights, his eyes roving uncertainly. As Douglas paused for breath, the Ohio Senator sought to interrupt. 'Mr. President,' he began.

The Little Giant started slightly, his cheek paled a little, the lines about his mouth deepened and he responded, 'Sir, I do not yield the floor.' His tone was steady, even, but all could detect the intense feeling behind it.

'Mr. President,' the tall, cold Chase imprudently repeated.

Instantly the irate speaker turned squarely upon him.[18] 'I do not yield the floor,' he said, in words that rang like trumpet tones across a stricken field. 'A Senator who has violated all the rules of courtesy and propriety, who showed a consciousness of the character of the act he was doing by concealing from me all knowledge of the fact — who came to me with a smiling face, and the appearance of friendship, even after that document had been uttered — who could get up in the Senate and appeal to my courtesy in order to get time to give the document a wider circulation before

[18] George Murray McConnel, *op. cit.*, 46 *et seq.*

its infamy could be exposed; such a Senator has no right to my courtesy upon this floor.'

Chase still tried to interrupt, began that 'the Senator misstates the facts.' Douglas cut him off again and then Chase insisted on saying he would make his denial.

'If the Senator does interpose,' Douglas said with heat, 'in violation of the rules of the Senate, a denial of the fact, it may be that I shall be able to nail that denial, as I shall the statements in that address which are over his own signature, as a wicked fabrication, and prove it by the solemn legislation of this country.' Chase called Douglas to order, the presiding officer said he was certainly out of order, Douglas responded: 'Then I will only say that I shall confine myself to this document, and prove its statements to be false by the legislation of the country. Certainly that is in order.'

This Douglas next undertook to do, through an historical review made without notes or manuscript. He challenged the Appeal's basic assumption that the policy of the Founding Fathers 'was to prohibit slavery in all the Territories ceded by the old States to the Union, and made United States territory, for the purpose of being organized into new States.' While legally true in the case of the Northwest Territory, it was not true in the case of the Territory South of the Ohio River nor in that of the Territory of Mississippi. Indeed, he felt that the only conclusion that could be fairly and honestly drawn from that legislation was that the founders had sought to establish 'a line of demarcation between free Territories and slave-holding Territories by a natural or geographical line, being sure to make that line correspond, as near as might be, to the laws of climate, of production, and all those other causes that would control the institution.'

Soon he came to the conditions affecting the entrance of Missouri into the Union. In 1820, an Illinois Senator had introduced a bill for Missouri's admission, providing that, except for Missouri, slavery should be prohibited in all the Louisiana Purchase north of 36° 30′. The object of this, the famous Missouri Compromise, was 'to go back to the original policy of prescribing boundaries to the limitation of free institutions and of slave institutions by a geographical line, in order to avoid all controversy in Congress upon the subject.'

In 1845, when Texas was being annexed by joint resolution, he had himself sought to have the Missouri line extended 'indefinitely westward,' not because such an extension would have any practical importance but 'for the purpose of preserving the principle.' Upon the acquisition of California he had sought to carry the line to the Pacific. The Senate had adopted Douglas' proposal but it had been defeated 'by Northern votes' in the House. 'The first time that the principles of the Missouri Compromise were ever abandoned was by Northern votes with Free Soil proclivities.' This had 'reopened the slavery agitation with all its fury,' this had necessitated the making of 1850's new Compromise.

'Who was it that was faithless?' he asked. 'I undertake to say it was the very men who now insist that the Missouri Compromise was a solemn compact and should never be violated or departed from. Every man who is now assailing the principle of the bill under consideration, so far as I am advised, was opposed to the Missouri Compromise in 1848. The very men who now arraign me for a departure from the Missouri Compromise are the men who successfully violated it, repudiated it and caused it to be superseded by the Compromise measures of 1850. Sir, it is with rather bad grace that the men who proved themselves faithless should charge upon me and others, who were ever faithful, the responsibilities and consequences of their own treachery.'

Douglas now proved by citation after citation that the essential principle of the Compromise of 1850 was Popular Sovereignty, and pointed out that these measures and their basic principles had been solemnly ratified and adopted by both major parties. The Utah and New Mexico bills had been 'an express annulment of the Missouri Compromise; and as to all the other unorganized Territories, it was superseded by the principles of that legislation, and we are bound to apply those principles to the organization of all new Territories, to all which we now own or which we may hereafter acquire.' The legal effect of the Kansas-Nebraska bill was 'neither to legislate slavery into these Territories nor out of them, but to leave the people to do as they please, under the provisions and subject to the limitations of the Constitution of the United States.' Why should not this principle prevail? he asked. Why should any man, North or South, object to it?

When the colonies became free twelve of the thirteen were slave-holding. Since then six had become free. Had they done so in response to Abolition agitation in Congress or under the edict of the Federal Government? 'Not at all. They have become free States under the silent but sure and irresistible working of that great principle of self-government, which teaches every people to do that which the interests of themselves and their posterity, morally and pecuniarily, may require.'

'Where have you succeeded in excluding slavery by an act of Congress from one inch of the American soil?' he asked. While the Ordinance of 1787 had excluded it by law from the Northwest Territory, it had not been excluded in fact. So long as she was a Territory, and under this Congressional law of freedom, Illinois had slavery in fact, but when she went from under Federal rule and became a State and so her own master, then she excluded it herself and provided a system of emancipation.[19]

Soon he turned again upon his Abolition assailants, asked them to show him 'a man in either House of Congress who was in favor of those Compromise measures in 1850, and who was not now in favor of leaving the people of Nebraska and Kansas to do as they pleased upon the subject of slavery, according to the principle of my bill. Is there one? If so, I have not heard of him. This tornado has been raised by Abolitionists, and Abolitionists alone.'

While he wanted the bill pressed forward to a vote, he favored giving every enemy the most ample time and wanted them heard patiently.

[19] *The Nebraska Question*, New York, 1854; 37-46. This booklet, in addition to speeches by Douglas, Chase, Truman Smith, Edward Everett, Ben Wade, Badger of North Carolina, William H. Seward and Charles Sumner, contains a good factual history of the Missouri Compromise.

Still he reserved for himself, as he believed 'common courtesy and parliamentary usage awards to the chairman of a committee and the author of a bill, the right of summing up.' Those in favor knew that the principle on which it was based was right. 'Why, then, should we gratify the Abolition party in their effort to get up another political tornado of fanaticism, and put the country again in peril, merely for the purpose of electing a few agitators to the Congress of the United States?' [20]

[20] The United States Census for 1840 listed 331 slaves as still being held in Illinois. I am indebted to Dr. J. G. Randall, of the University of Illinois, for calling this to my attention.

CHAPTER IX

RIDING THE TEMPEST

BY FEBRUARY both North and South were deeply agitated over the proposal to repeal the Missouri Compromise. In the South, Douglas' doctrine of non-intervention was quickly and generally embraced. Such a staunch Unionist as Howell Cobb wrote the Little Giant that 'it is a doctrine worthy of the Democratic party. I hope to hear that the Administration and the entire Democratic party are united in sustaining your position. With this crisis in the National Democratic party, he who dallies is a dastard and he who doubts is damned.' [1] Moreover, 'every Southern Whig in the Senate' favored the bill because it offered 'the only possible mode of disposition' of the dangerous question of the status of slavery in the Territories.[2]

To this growing Southern determination the Abolitionists and Free-Soilers of the North opposed an almost frenzied resistance. In nearly every Northern State the 'tornado' increased in intensity and emotional excitement rose from height to height of fury. Whenever he had a chance to confront his detractors face to face, the Little Giant was more than a match for them, but he could not cope with the campaign outside. Douglas' experience demonstrated again the old adage that a lie wears seven-league boots, and travels round the world before the truth can get its breeches on.

From early January, his friends in Illinois advised that there was trouble ahead.[3] Douglas was particularly concerned over rumors that a coalition was being effected between Abolitionists, Whigs and disappointed office-seekers to procure instructions from the Legislature against the Nebraska bill.

'The object of the Whigs and Abolitionists is apparent,' he wrote Lanphier. 'They wish to divide the Democratic party and then elect a Whig Senator. Their only chance of success consists in our division. The Democratic party is committed in the most solemn manner to the principle of Congressional non-interference with slavery in the States and Territories. The Administration is committed to the Nebraska bill and will stand by it at all hazards. The only way to avert a division of the party is to sustain our principles.... The principle of this bill will form the test of parties, and the only alternative is either to stand with the Democracy or to rally under Seward, Yates, Van Buren and Co.' [4] These apprehensions proved unfounded, for early in February the Illinois Legislature endorsed his own course on the Kansas-Nebraska matter. None the less, the debate provoked schism in Demo-

---

[1] Howell Cobb, Athens, Ga., Feb. 5, 1854; Douglas MSS.

[2] Toombs to W. W. Burwell, Washington, Feb. 3, 1854; *Toombs-Stephens-Cobb Correspondence*, 342. Burwell was editor of the Baltimore *Patriot*.

[3] Murray McConnel, Jacksonville, Ill., Jan. 28, 1854; Douglas MSS.

[4] Douglas to Lanphier, Washington, Feb. 13, 1854; Patton MSS.

cratic ranks, and John M. Palmer, hitherto an almost idolatrous Douglas follower, was among the recalcitrants.[5]

Douglas' declaration that slavery had existed in fact in Illinois despite the prohibition of the Ordinance of 1787, cut at the foundations of the Abolition argument, and its historical accuracy was heavily assailed. But the Senator exposed the realities of slave-holding in early Illinois.[6]

By this time the Abolitionists had found a new contention with which to alarm the North. This was that Douglas' bill would absolutely insure the existence of slavery in the Territories, because the repeal of the Missouri Compromise would revive, in full force and effect, the pre-existing laws of the old Territory of Louisiana, which permitted and established slavery in that whole area. Several Northern papers withdrew their support from the Nebraska bill and charged that the only question was: 'Shall slavery be revived and re-established in Nebraska and Kansas?

Noticing such a change of front in a New Hampshire paper, the Little Giant addressed it a public letter denying that there was any basis in law for the belief, and pointing out the utter improbability in fact of Kansas becoming any other than a Free State. Every intelligent man knew that the proposed repeal was 'a matter of no practical importance,' so far as slavery was concerned. 'The cry of the extension of slavery has been raised for mere party purposes by the Abolition confederates and disappointed office-seekers. All candid men who understand the subject admit that the laws of climate, and production, and of physical geography... have excluded slavery from that country.' Had not Senator Everett, of Massachusetts, appealed to the South not to ask for this bill because it would not derive any advantage from it? Furthermore, Senator Badger, of North Carolina, had admitted that neither he nor his Southern friends expected slavery to go into Nebraska, because the region's climate and crop conditions did not encourage slave labor. They looked on the repeal 'as a matter of principle, and principle alone.'[7]

The Appeal of the Independent Democrats had been fashioned with an eye to Ohio politics, and that State became a vortex in the ensuing storm. A burning editorial of the Canton *Democratic Transcript* of February 3, illustrated the Free-Soil reaction. Entitled 'Senator Douglas — The Little Napoleon of America,' the editor termed him an ambitious, designing egotist. Richard the Third, 'who plotted in cold blood the assassination of Clarence and the two Princes'; Macbeth, who murdered Duncan; all others who 'dipped their robes in the blood of their fellows to mount to exalted station' — all these men were 'models of philanthropy' in com-

[5] Illinois State Historical Society, *Transactions*, 1901; 76. Palmer prepared and presented a substitute resolution, commending any restriction upon the introduction of slavery in the new Territories. His resolution was lost.

[6] Douglas to Edward Coles, Washington, Feb. 18, 1854; pamphlet in possession of Mr. Martin F. Douglas. The Illinois Senator filled his pamphlet with citations, such as that to the statutes, Indiana Legislature for 1807, 423, 'An Act Concerning the Introduction of Negroes and Mulattoes into This Territory.'

[7] Douglas to *State Capital Reporter*, Concord, N.H., Washington, Feb. 16, 1854; pamphlet, p. 7. The paper's statement, to which Douglas took exception, had been published Feb. 14.

parison with the monster from Illinois. The price of his ambition would be greater than Napoleon's payment for his imperial crown — 'the mangled corpses of thousands of Frenchmen on the battlefield.' There was no need to admit Nebraska. Let her stay out.

But Douglas and his measure were not without staunch defenders. When an anti-Nebraska meeting was held at Canton to denounce Douglas, opinion was found so mixed that resolutions of condemnation were laid on the table![8] After the first fury of the assault, and as accounts came from Washington of Douglas' Senatorial triumph over his foes, the Little Giant's advocates took fresh heart. 'You have made cords of friends here, notwithstanding all that is said,' Samuel S. Cox, the new editor of the Columbus *Statesman*, wrote him: 'The sentiment of this State is misrepresented. We can today whip the Whigs and Abolitionists out — niggers too.'[9]

The tornado raging the countryside affected the Congressional debate. As chief author of the Appeal, Chase took over the leadership of Senate opposition to the bill. As soon as Douglas had concluded his speech of January 30, the Ohio Senator tried to defend himself. On February 3, he added an elaborate formal defense under the moving title, 'Maintain Plighted Faith.' Summoning Henry Clay, Webster and others of the buried great as witnesses, he again denied that in 1850 anyone had 'ever intimated' that the new Compromise, even by implication, repealed the old one. The Missouri Compromise itself had been a bargain between the Free and Slave States, the latter had 'received a large share of the consideration coming to them paid in hand.... Every other part of the compact, on the part of the Free States, has been fulfilled to the letter. No part of the compact on the part of the Slave States has been fulfilled at all, except in the admission of Iowa and the organization of Minnesota.'

Chase's peroration was a highly emotional appeal to the Senators to reject the bill, 'as violation of the plighted faith and solemn compact which our Fathers made, and which we, their sons, are bound by every sacred tie of obligation sacredly to maintain.' The Ohio Abolitionist wrote an intimate that he had done better than he anticipated.[10]

Most of the other Northern Free-Soil Senators carefully followed the path Chase marked out. Seward, who had not signed the Appeal because the time was not yet ripe for a new party, could not conceal his Whig delight over the internecine Democratic war, and he backed the insurgents with a clever legal argument. His adroit reasoning had great effect upon the politically ambitious, for it disclosed to them the magnificent possibilities of forming a new and successful party upon this great emotional issue.

Sumner had carefully prepared and his speech rang the changes on the moral issue. His illustrations were fanciful and his quotations swept the

[8] Canton *Democratic Transcript*, Feb. 3, Feb. 24, 1854. For these and other quotations from this paper, I am indebted to Mr. J. W. Hughmanic, of the Canton *Repository*, who painstakingly and intelligently searched the files for me.

[9] S. S. Cox, Columbus, Ohio, March 24, 1854; Douglas MSS.

[10] Chase to E. S. Hamlin, Washington, Feb. 10, 1854; *American Historical Association Report*, 1902; II, 257.

whole field of literature. Edward Everett, conservative Massachusetts Whig, who had supported the Compromise of 1850, argued that, while the 1850 measures had gone against the Missouri Compromise restriction in a specific case, this had not established a new general rule negativing it.

But Senator Toombs, of Georgia, held with Douglas that, in the year of their adoption the Compromises of 1850 had been understood as an abandonment of the Missouri Compromise. In the ensuing Georgia campaigns, he recalled, he had been violently attacked for support of the Compromise, and had proclaimed throughout the State that it had repealed the Missouri Compromise: a great Southern right, he had said, given away in 1820, had 'been rescued, re-established, and again firmly planted in our political system.'

'If some Southern gentleman,' asked Badger, of North Carolina, 'wishes to take the nurse who takes charge of his little baby, or the old woman who nursed him in childhood, and whom he calls "Mammy" until he returns from college, and perhaps afterward too, and whom he wishes to take with him in his old age when he is moving into one of these new Territories for the betterment of the fortune of the whole family — why, in the name of God, should anybody prevent it?' 'We have not the least objection,' Ben Wade wittily retorted, 'and would oppose no obstacle to the Senator's migrating to Kansas and taking his old "Mammy" along with him. We only insist that he shall not be empowered to *sell* her after taking her there.'

Chase introduced amendment after amendment designed to produce a breach between the bill's Northern and Southern supporters. Chase's idea was shrewd. The Northern Senators supporting the Kansas-Nebraska bill believed that, in its practical operation, the legislation would result in the inhabitants of the Territories themselves protecting or prohibiting slavery. The Southerners, however, were contending for the Calhoun doctrine that slaves were property. Owners could take slaves into any Territory and no law could rightfully or constitutionally prevent them. They wished definition of the precise point at which a Territory would become governmentally competent. On this the Northerners were vague.

While the debate on the Senate floor was live and vivid, the real decisions as to the bill were made in the Senate Democratic caucus. The possibility of the two constructions was carefully considered, the caucus agreed to pass it and let the Supreme Court decide which was correct.

What position would Lewis Cass finally take? The original sponsor of Popular Sovereignty did not like the bill, said privately that he feared the Union could not stand the shock, and begged Pierce not to identify the Administration with it. But he had long doubted the constitutionality of the Missouri Compromise, and thought it his duty to vote to repeal it if ever it were brought to a vote.[11] Now he claimed to dislike the word 'in-

---

[11] Gideon Welles, 'Diary,' MSS., June 29, 1855, giving Cass' statement to him as to 1854 event. On his White House visit, Cass said Pierce said he agreed, 'but,' said Cass, with a heavy breath, 'the next man he saw had probably different views from mine, and the President doubtless agreed with him also.'

operative' in the repeal amendment and gave this as a reason for voting for one of Chase's amendments. Taking hold of this objection, the Little Giant once more changed the wording of this pivotal section. After referring to the Missouri Compromise Act, the bill was changed to read 'which, being inconsistent with the principles of non-intervention by Congress with slavery in the States and Territories, as recognized by the legislation of 1850, commonly called the Compromise measures, is hereby declared inoperative, it being the true intent and meaning of this act to preserve as a rule of action the principle that the people of all the States and Territories are to be left free to regulate their own domestic institutions in their own way, without any interference by Congress, and subject only to the Constitution of the United States.' [12]

Completely satisfied, Cass soon made an elaborate speech defending Douglas' bill. When the Abolitionists badgered him about the beginning point of Popular Sovereignty in a Territory, he testily exclaimed that he did not seek 'in the science of arithmetic the principles of the science of political institutions.'

Under the bill as Douglas originally brought it in, the privileges of suffrage and of holding office in the new Territory were to be confined to citizens of the United States, or to those who had 'declared their intention' to become citizens, and who in addition had taken 'an oath to support the Constitution of the United States and the provisions of this Act.' This clause had enabled the Abolitionists to portray the bill as 'an atrocious plot' to exclude immigrants from the Territories. Soon German protests against the bill began to roll into Washington.

On March 2 Senator Clayton, of Delaware, sought to confine these rights solely to citizens of the United States. To every Senator who came from a State containing immigrant groups this was a highly dangerous amendment, and Douglas, knowing that it sprang from the Know-Nothing movement, was apprehensive as to its effect.

But soon the Southern leaders, who had never liked immigration or homesteading, and believed that the slave system could not work side by side with a system of free labor, took up Clayton's amendment. On the vote, Douglas, Shields and every Northern Senator except its author and Brodhead, of Pennsylvania, voted against it, but the Southern phalanx carried it by the narrow margin of two votes.[13]

Douglas also had to meet Clayton's argument that, inasmuch as the Kansas-Nebraska bill specifically called for Congressional approval of Territorial laws, the doctrine of non-intervention was delusive, because any member of Congress could move to repeal any Territorial law. The Senator from Illinois had not insisted that the people of the Territory

[12] The original of this historic paragraph is in the manuscript collection of Mr. Oliver R. Barrett, of Chicago, who has kindly furnished me with a photostat. The reverse of the paper bears this statement: 'Hon. Stephen A. Douglas' original draft of the provision in his Nebraska Bill that has raised the furor. Given to me by Senator Gwin, 24 Mch. 1854, John S. Cunningham.'

[13] F. T. I. Herriott, 'Senator Stephen A. Douglas and the Germans in 1854,' Illinois State Historical Society, *Transactions*, 1912, reprint, 5. The vote was 23 to 21.

have complete right of self-government, without any Congressional supervision, had urged only a partial self-government, the power to regulate
their domestic institutions. Confronted with Clayton's shrewd thrust, he
eliminated from the bill the section requiring all Territorial laws to be laid
before Congress for its approval.[14]

Douglas knew that every day's delay would intensify the Abolitionist
storm. He was confident of a Senate majority of three to one, believed a
'decisive' majority would be obtained in the House, thought that this outcome would make the Democratic party stronger than ever, 'for it will
be united upon principle.'[15] But he found it almost impossible to hurry
the Senate. Upon his introduction of the final verbal change in the clause
repealing the Compromise, Senator Everett asked for delay so that he
could study it. This Douglas was reluctant to permit. When Clayton
labored under the physical strain of speaking Douglas urged him to go forward. This attitude, alien to his natural politeness and consideration, indicated the strain under which he labored.

Finally he secured agreement that the Senate vote should be taken on
March 3. As this date approached there was no check to the debate and
the morning session of the day appointed brought no diminution of oratory.
A night meeting was voted but still the torrent of words gushed forth. It
lacked but half an hour of midnight when Douglas secured the floor, determined to close the argument and force the vote.

As Douglas rose, Sam Houston called attention to the lateness of the
hour and sought adjournment. There was a shout of No; thereupon the
unruly Texan gave notice of his own intention to speak after the Illinois
Senator had finished, and Sumner too asked a final word.

Before entering upon his general argument, Douglas took up the objections
which had been offered by Senators Bell and Houston. Bell had heartily
endorsed the Compromise repeal, but was not satisfied as to its protection
of Indian rights and hence intended to vote against the bill. Douglas
pointed out that it had never been the custom to incorporate Indian provisions in Territorial bills. He expected that the Committee on Indian
Affairs would now 'propose such measures as will do entire justice to the
Indians.'

Turning to Houston's objections, Douglas pointed out that most of the
tribes about the sanctity of whose treaties the Texan had expressed deep
concern were not in the Kansas-Nebraska Territory. Indeed, there was but
one tribe affected, the Ottawa Indians, 200 persons owning 34,000 acres,
'less than two townships of land.'

Is it possible, he inquired, 'that a country, said to be 500,000 square
miles in extent, and large enough to make twelve such States as Ohio, is

[14] *Congressional Globe*, Thirty-Third Congress, First Session, 296–97; Douglas did not say,
however, whether this elimination took from Congress its power of revision.

[15] Douglas to Lanphier, Washington, Feb. 13, 1854; Patton MSS. Administration efforts
had already lined up a large Senate majority. Cushing sought the vote of Hamlin, of Maine;
Charles Eugene Hamlin, *The Life and Times of Hannibal Hamlin*, Cambridge, 1899, 270, gives
a highly colored account of Hamlin's refusal.

to be consigned to perpetual barbarism merely on account of that small number of Indians?' But Douglas did not intend his measure 'to invade the rights of even one Indian,' therefore he had put in the first section of his bill that none of the tribes with treaty rights should be embraced in the Territories except by voluntary consent, with new treaties. 'If any Senator can furnish me with language more explicit,' he offered, 'or which would prove more effectual in securing the rights of the Indians, I will cheerfully adopt it.'

Douglas then examined the assertion that there was no need to organize these new Territories. 'Senators seem to forget,' he said, 'that our immense and valuable possessions on the Pacific are separated from the States and organized Territories on this side of the Rocky Mountains by a vast wilderness, filled by hostile savages; that nearly 100,000 emigrants pass through this barbarous wilderness every year on their way to California and Oregon; that these emigrants are American citizens, our own constituents, who are entitled to the protection of law and government; and that they are left to make their way as best they may, without the protection or aid of law or government.'

His former efforts to afford such protection had been voted down, the excuse being that there were not enough white inhabitants in the area to require or sustain a government. 'You refuse to throw the country open to settlers,' he continued, 'and then object to the organization of the Territories, upon the ground that there is not a sufficient number of inhabitants.'

Now Douglas turned to 'the great principles involved in the bill.' The very Senators who were now proclaiming the sanctity of the 1850 compact, he declared, had predicted that all manner of evils and calamities would flow from adoption of the measures of 1850, had sought to repeal them and, after they had become the laws of the land, had even urged resistance to their execution. It was odd, therefore, to hear these same Senators unitedly attest Congress' wisdom and patriotism in passing the Compromise over their protest. Douglas knew that this change of front was only to give them a pretext to charge on him, as author of the Nebraska bill, 'the responsibility of the agitation which they are striving to produce.'

The Abolition Senators had charged that he wrote and introduced the Nebraska bill. 'That is true,' he admitted, 'but I was not a volunteer in the transaction. The Senate, by a unanimous vote, appointed me chairman of the Territorial Committee, and associated five intelligent and patriotic Senators with me, and then made it our duty to take charge of all Territorial business.' Similarly the Senate had referred the Nebraska Territorial bill to the Committee, and had required it 'to report specifically upon the question. I repeat, then, we were not volunteers in this business. The duty was imposed upon us by the Senate.'

The Little Giant went on that, in 1850, Congress had substituted the right of the people to decide this question for themselves, subject only to the Constitution, for the doctrine of Congressional intervention. So in 1854, he and his Committee on Territories were initially called upon to decide, 'and, indeed, the only question of any material importance in framing the bill, was: Shall we adhere to and carry out the principles recognized by the Compromise measures of 1850, or shall we go back to the old, exploded doctrine of Congressional interference?' The doctrine of 1820 or that of 1850 must prevail.

Douglas and his Committee could not hesitate in a choice between these two. Both great political parties stood solemnly pledged to adhere to the 1850 measures 'in principle and substance.' Every member of the Senate except Sumner and Chase, the two avowed Abolitionists, belonged to these two parties, 'and hence was supposed to be under a high moral obligation to carry out the "principle and substance" of those measures in all new Territorial organizations.' The Committee had reported in accordance with this obligation, and he would let the vote that night determine whether he had faithfully represented the Senate's will.

The Little Giant now undertook not only to punish his opponents for their opprobrious slurs upon him personally, but to overturn the very foundations of their argument. 'You have seen them on their winding way,' he said, 'meandering the narrow and crooked path in Indian file, each treading close upon the heels of the other, and neither venturing to take a step to the right or left, or to occupy one inch of ground which did not bear the footprint of the Abolition champion.' As he warmed up, onlookers could see Sumner's complacency deflate just a little, Chase's pendulous eyelid quiver and Seward's quizzical smile become frigid and set.

The principle in the bill Douglas thus described: 'Congress shall never legislate slavery into any Territories or State, nor out of the same; but the people shall be left free to regulate their domestic concerns in their own way, subject only to the Constitution of the United States.' He called attention to his introduction on March 25, 1850, of two bills for admitting California as a State, Utah and New Mexico as Territories, bills which 'proposed to leave the people of Utah and New Mexico free to decide the slavery question for themselves, *in the precise language of the Nebraska bill now under discussion.*' [16]

When Clay's Committee of Thirteen took the two bills and joined them with a wafer, one of the minor amendments added was that the Territorial Legislatures should not pass upon the subject of African slavery. 'I objected to that provision,' Douglas said, 'upon the ground that it subverted the great principles of self-government upon which the bill had been originally framed by the Territorial Committee. On first trial, the Senate refused to strike it out, but subsequently did so, after full debate, in order to establish that principle as the rule of action in Territorial organizations.' [17] Dodge, of Iowa, interrupted: 'It was done on your own motion.'

He now called attention to his speech in Chicago, October 23, 1850,[18] and

[16] Italics Douglas'. See pamphlet, Washington *Sentinel*, 1854; 6.

[17] See *supra* 69. On Aug. 3, 1850, Douglas wrote Lanphier and Walker that this objectionable amendment had been made over Clay's protest, and that Clay had been anxious for it to be struck out.

[18] For account of this speech, see *supra*, 81–82. In this last, he had said, 'these measures are predicated on the great fundamental principles that every people ought to possess the right

to resolutions the Illinois Legislature had passed in 1851, approving the Compromise, and in 1854, approving the Nebraska bill. All this he offered to show that, in his bill, he had only carried out 'the known principles and solemnly declared will' of his State.

The Little Giant next undertook to meet the charge, first made by Chase, then echoed by Smith, Wade, Seward and Sumner, that the initial bill did not intend to repeal the Compromise. What did Senators mean by such a statement? 'Do they mean to say that the adoption of our first bill would not have had the legal effect to have rendered the eighth section of the Missouri Act "inoperative and void"?... Will they rise in their places and inform the Senate what their meaning was?'

He turned appealingly to Chase, then to Sumner, but both remained mute in their seats. 'I despair of extorting a response from them,' Douglas went on, 'for, no matter in what way they may answer upon this point, I have in my hand the evidence over their own signatures, to disprove the truth of their answers. I allude to their appeal or manifesto to the people of the United States, in which they arraign the bill in coarse and savage terms, as a proposition to repeal the Missouri Compromise, to violate plighted faith, to abrogate a solemn compact.' This document, he pointed out, was signed by the two Senators before any amendment had been offered to the bill, a fact which completely met the charge.

Was the Missouri Compromise a compact? Douglas pointed out that, in 1820, it had passed the Senate by a vote of 24 to 20, but of the Northern Senators, only four voted affirmatively, eighteen were negative. 'If it was intended to be a compact,' he commented, 'the North never agreed to it. The Northern Senators voted to insert the prohibition of slavery in the Territories; and then, in the proportion of more than four to one, voted against the passage of the bill. The North, therefore, never signed the compact, never consented to it, never agreed to be bound by it.'

This had become apparent the very next year, when Missouri formed her constitution and asked for admission. The Senate voted to take her in but the House, by Northern votes, rejected her. 'Now, Sir, what becomes of our plighted faith, if the Act of the sixth of March, 1820, was a solemn compact, as we are now told? They have all rung the changes upon it, that it was a sacred and irrevocable compact, binding in honor, in conscience and morals, which could not be violated or repudiated without perfidy and dishonor.'

Seward winced under these blows, and announced the doctrine that, while the North had not voted for the Compromise, yet 'it was carried by a vote which has been held by the South and by the Honorable Senator from Illinois to bind the North. The South having received their consideration and equivalent, I only hold him, upon his own doctrine and the doc-

of forming and regulating their own internal concerns and domestic institutions in their own way.' He also called attention to his statement in that same speech that slavery and other domestic questions 'are all confided by the Constitution to each State to decide for itself and I know of no reason why the same principles should not be confided to the Territories.'

trine of the South, bound to stand to it.' Douglas asked him directly if he had not claimed the Missouri Compromise a compact between the sections, in which the North had faithfully performed its part for thirty years, the South receiving all the benefits, and that the moment these had been fully realized, the South disavowed its obligation.

Seward dodged and evaded. 'I choose to bring men directly up to this point,' Douglas said. 'The Senator from New York has labored in his whole speech to make it appear that this was a compact; that the North had been faithful; and that the South acquiesced until she got all its advantages, and then disavowed and sought to annul it. This he pronounced the bad faith.' Smith and Sumner and Chase had done the same and this was the great point to which the whole Abolition party had directed all its artillery. 'Now I propose to bring them to the point. If this was a compact, and if what they have said is fair, or just, or true, who was it that repudiated the compact? If it was a compact between the two parties and one party has been faithful, it is beyond recall by the other. If, however, one party has been faithless, what shall we think of them if, while faithless, they ask a performance?'

Seward was nettled. 'Show it,' he shot forth.

Show it Douglas did. He read to the group the amendment a Vermont member had sought on February 12, 1821, that Missouri should not be admitted unless she would ban slavery. Seward demanded the record of the vote. Douglas had that too. 'Sixty-one Northern men voted for that amendment,' he said, 'and thirty-three against it. Thus the North, by a vote of nearly two to one, expressly repudiated a solemn compact upon the very matter in controversy, to wit: That slavery should not be prohibited in the State of Missouri.'

Douglas' followers were wild with joy at the way he was transfixing the squirming Abolitionists. 'Let the Senator from New York answer that,' Weller, of California, shouted gleefully.

Seward haltingly tried to do so, but there was worse in store for him. Douglas next called his attention 'to the fact that his own State was the first to repudiate the compact, and to instruct their Senators in Congress not to admit Missouri into the Union in compliance with it, nor unless slavery should be prohibited in the State of Missouri.' Seward was forced to admit that that was so, and then Douglas turned the knife in the wound, reading the New York Legislature's resolutions and emphasizing significant phrases.

'Let me ask the Senator from New York,' the Little Giant shouted, 'by what authority he declared and published in his speech that the Act of 1820 was a compact which could not be violated or repudiated without a sacrifice of honor, justice and good faith.'

Seward next tried to maintain that, although the contract had been made against New York's protest, it had stood for thirty years, all of it save the part beneficial to New York and its section had been fulfilled, and now the North demanded the fulfillment of that part. But Douglas would not let him off. He offered a resolution the 1854 New York Legislature had passed, declaring the Missouri Compromise 'a solemn compact,' and saying that its repudiation would be regarded by New York 'as a violation of right, and of faith, and destructive of confidence and regard.'

'If such be a compact,' Douglas scornfully remarked, 'the State of New York stands self-condemned and self-convicted as the first to repudiate and violate it.'

Seeking to interrupt again, Seward said he hoped Douglas would yield for a moment, 'because I have never had so much respect for him as I have tonight.' Douglas brought laughter when he responded that he now could see what course he would have to pursue to command Seward's respect. 'Any man who meets me boldly,' Seward replied, 'commands my respect.' From this point Douglas drove Seward into unqualified admission that he had 'misapprehended' the facts.

Then Sumner sought to avoid responsibility for his own misstatements, but Douglas would not let him off so easily. These men had deliberately done him a great injury. 'You degrade your own State,' he pointed out, 'and induce the people, under the impression that they have been injured, to get up a violent crusade against those whose fidelity and trustfulness will in the end command their respect and admiration. In consequence of arousing passions and prejudices, I am now to be found in effigy, hanging by the neck, in all the towns where you have the influence to produce such a result. In all their excesses, the people are yielding to an honest impulse, under the impression that a grievous wrong has been perpetrated. You have had your day of triumph. You have succeeded in directing upon the heads of others a torrent of insult and calumny from which even you shrink with horror when the fact is exposed that you have become the conduits for conveying it into this hall.'

With this, he turned directly upon an unsmiling Chase. 'In your State, Sir,' he said, 'I find that I am burnt in effigy in your Abolition towns. All this is done because I have proposed, as it is said, to violate a compact! Now, what will these people think of you when they find out that you have stimulated them to these acts which are disgraceful to your State, disgraceful to your party, and disgraceful to your cause, under a misrepresentation of the facts, which misrepresentation you ought to have been aware of, and should never have made?'

Chase said he certainly regretted that anything had occurred in Ohio which should be otherwise than the disposition, which he trusted he had 'ever manifested,' to treat the Illinois Senator with 'entire courtesy.'

Douglas riddled Chase's disclaimer. 'Did he not say,' he asked, 'in the same document... that I was engaged, with others in "a criminal betrayal of precious rights," in an "atrocious plot"? Did he not say that I and others were guilty of "meditated bad faith"?... Did he not say everything calculated to produce and bring upon my head all the insults to which I have been subjected publicly and privately — not even excepting the insulting letters which I have received from his constituents, rejoicing at my domestic bereavements, and praying that other and similar calamities may befall me? And after all this, after having used such language, he says he meant no disrespect

— he meant nothing unkind! He was amazed that I said in my opening speech that there was anything offensive in this address; and he could not suffer himself to use harsh epithets, or to impugn a gentleman's motives! No! Not he!'

After this digression, which brought sustained applause from the galleries, Douglas returned to the thread of his argument. The Abolition speeches had been full to overflowing of the statement that Clay would turn in his grave if he knew that his Missouri Compromise was to be repealed. Did not these men know that Clay had not been the author of the Missouri Compromise which it was proposed to repeal? 'Do they not know that Mr. Clay never came into the Missouri controversy as a compromiser until after the Compromise of 1820 was repudiated and it became necessary to make another? How did they dare call upon the spirit of that great and gallant statesman to sanction their charge of bad faith?'

When Seward tried to defend the statement, Douglas called attention to Clay's speech in the Senate on February 6, 1850, in which the Kentuckian had said that it was an error to attribute to him the Act of 1820. Upon this Seward nodded his remembrance.

Soon the Little Giant returned to chastise Chase and Sumner for their impeachment of his motives by asserting that the Compromise repeal was an afterthought, a bid for the Presidency.

'I must be permitted to tell those Senators,' Douglas said, with intense feeling, 'that their experiences in seeking political preferment do not furnish a safe rule by which to judge the character and principle of other Senators. I must be permitted to tell the Senator from Ohio that I did not obtain my seat in this body either by a corrupt bargain or a dishonorable coalition. I must be permitted to remind the Senator from Massachusetts that I did not enter into any combinations or arrangements by which my character, my principles and my honor were set up at public auction or private sale, in order to procure a seat in the Senate of the United States! I did not come into the Senate by any such means.'

This direct, forceful and indignant thrust at Chase and Sumner produced a storm. Weller, of California, a former Ohioan, shouted out, 'But there are some men who I know that did.' Mason, in the chair, rapped fruitlessly for order. Chase snarled, 'Do you mean to say that I came here by a bargain?' Weller answered that he would tell what he meant, but Douglas refused to yield.

'He has arraigned me,' Douglas said, 'on the charge of seeking high political station by unworthy means. I tell him there is nothing in my history which would create a suspicion that I came into the Senate by a corrupt bargain or a disgraceful coalition.' Chase tried to deny it, Douglas said that he chose to maintain his own position and to leave to the public to ascertain how the Ohio Senator had been elected.

Chase quailed before this assault. Reciting the objectionable query at the end of the Appeal of the Independent Democrats, 'Would they allow their dearest rights to be made the hazards of the presidential game?' he tried to explain and excuse it by saying: 'I certainly did not intend to impute to the Senator from Illinois — and I desire always to do justice — any improper motive. I do not think it is an unworthy ambition to desire to be a President of the United States. I do not think that the bringing forward of a measure with reference to that object would be an improper thing, if the measure be proper in itself. I differ from the Senator in my judgment of the measure. I do not think the measure is a right one. In that I express the judgment which I honestly entertain. I do not condemn his judgment; I do not make, and I do not desire to make, any personal imputations upon him in reference to a great public question.'

The Lord had delivered his enemy into Douglas' hands. When Weller sought to interrupt, Douglas waved him aside, he would take care of Chase. 'I must remind him,' Douglas said, 'that, in addition to that insinuation, he only said, in the same address that my bill was a "criminal betrayal of precious rights"; he only said it was "an atrocious plot against freedom and humanity"; he only said that it was "meditated bad faith"; he only spoke significantly of "servile demagogues"; he only called upon the preachers of the gospel and the people at their public meetings to denounce and resist such a monstrous iniquity.' And now Chase said that he had not charged an unworthy ambition, that he meant no 'personal imputation' upon his motives or his character, or 'personal disrespect' to him! 'There is a very wide difference of opinion between the Senator of Ohio and myself in respect to the meaning of words.'

Then Sumner tried to interpose. 'I shrink almost instinctively from any effort to repel a personal assault,' he began, but added that he did not recognize the Senate's jurisdiction to try his election to it, denied that he had been a party in any way to any betrayal of principle at the time of his election by the Massachusetts Legislature.

If Sumner expected to benefit by such a plea, Douglas answered, 'he should act in accordance with his profound principles, and refrain from assaulting the character and impugning the motives of better men than himself. Everybody knows that he came here by a coalition or a combination between political parties holding opposite and hostile opinions.' It would not do for Sumner to deny being a party to it, thereby he betrayed a consciousness of the immorality of the proceeding without acquitting himself of responsibility.

'I must be permitted to remind him,' Douglas said, with a scorn that pierced even Sumner's complacency, 'that when he arrived here to take his seat for the first time, so firmly were Senators impressed with the conviction that he had been elected by dishonorable and corrupt means... that, for a long time, he was avoided and shunned as a person unworthy of the association of gentlemen. Gradually, however, these injurious impressions were worn away by his bland manner and amiable deportment; and I regret that the Senator should now, by the violation of all the rules of courtesy and propriety, compel me to refresh his mind upon these unwelcome reminiscences.' Sumner did not try to interrupt again.

Douglas now apologized for having taken so much of the Senate's time to repel the disreputable assaults upon him. He predicted that, despite Abolitionists' alarums and the misunderstanding of the measure in the North, yet when the principles of non-intervention and popular sovereignty were thoroughly understood, the bill would be as popular in that section as in the South. He felt sure the Northern people were attached to the principle of self-government and he was willing to stand upon this great principle of self-government everywhere. While the opponents of the bill had dealt entirely in sectional appeals, its advocates had maintained a great principle of universal application, which could be sustained 'by the same reasons and the same arguments in every place and in every corner of the Union.'

With this the Little Giant took his seat. All through the night a tense, excited throng had clung to their seats in the Senate galleries. Now it was five o'clock, the dark night was beginning to fade into a cold gray dawn, but wave after wave of applause thundered from floor and gallery over Douglas' triumph over his enemies.

Not without reason did they cheer him. In a single speech he had torn away the Abolitionists' foundations; he had shown and forced them to admit that their contention that the Missouri Compromise was a compact was a historical lie; he had proved that the North had repudiated it within a year of its making, that the faithless had no right to expect further compliance from the faithful. More than this, he had taken the measure of each of his three chief critics. He had forced Seward to admit that his whole contention was based upon a 'misapprehension,' Chase had been reduced to contemptible apology, Sumner's egotism had been pierced, his complacency shattered, his record exposed, and he sat stunned and speechless in his seat. The bill now came to a vote and the Senate passed it by a vote of 37 to 14.[19] Mason's gavel sounded and Senators and spectators streamed home, while guns at the Navy Yard thundered the victory.

Although he had won the struggle in the Senate, the bill must still run the gauntlet of the House. As Douglas had anticipated, it was here that the Abolitionist crusade had its chief effect.

As soon as the Senate bill was brought before the House, Richardson, of Illinois, Chairman of its Committee on Territories, endeavored to have it referred to his group. But Cutting, a New York Democrat, and a Hard, moved instead that it be referred to the Committee of the Whole; he himself favored the bill, but it was a 'grave and serious question'; since its introduction 'the North would seem to have taken up arms' and they must give it careful scrutiny. Richardson protested that this 'would be killing it by indirection,' but the motion carried by 110 to 95.

This seemed to have put an end to any hope during the session. The

[19] For text of speech, see *Congressional Globe*, Thirty-Third Congress, First Session, App., 325 *et seq.*

Negative Democratic votes were Dodge and Walker, of Wisconsin; Hamlin, of Maine; James, of Rhode Island; Houston, of Texas; Whig noes came from Fessenden, of Maine; Seward and Fish, of New York; Foot, of Vermont; Smith, of Connecticut; Wade, of Ohio; Bell, of Tennessee; Chase and Sumner, Abolitionists. Everett left at 3:30, did not vote; Clayton was ill.

Committee of the Whole had fifty other bills before it, each of which had precedence over the Nebraska bill and it looked as if Douglas' bill could never be brought up. But the Little Giant never quit. He now began to make use of Administration pressure. He had not so greatly needed Pierce's support in the Senate, but the House members were hungry for presidential morsels and the Administration did exert itself.

'Should the bill be defeated in the House,' Caleb Cushing wrote in an editorial in the *Union*, 'it will, it must be admitted, be a defeat of the Administration.' [20] Pierce himself wrote New England editors, urging them to defend a policy eminently just, wise and patriotic. He gave an interview, widely published, that the passage of the bill would aid the extension of freedom in the Nation. He applied pressure on Northern Democratic Congressmen and his Cabinet aides went even further along these lines. And never before were the Southern members so united. [21]

Through March and April Douglas and the Administration applied themselves to building up a safe majority. The wavering were made firm, many deserters were brought back into line and by early May the leaders in the House were confident that they had amassed the necessary votes. At every stage Richardson looked to Douglas for leadership and the Administration carried out his suggestions as commands.

At length he determined upon the final thrust. On May 8, Richardson moved that the House clear up the Speaker's table. This legislative device had worked for Douglas in 1850, in the Illinois Central bill; it functioned satisfactorily now. Richardson's preliminary motion to go into Committee of the Whole carried, 109 to 88. Then he moved to postpone bill after bill, and one by one the House laid aside the eighteen bills on the calendar of the Committee of the Whole. Then they came to Bill 236, the House edition of the Kansas-Nebraska bill; it was the Senate bill without the Clayton amendment, a change which largely increased House support.

After eighty speeches had been made, Richardson announced that only four more days would be given for debate. This drove the Free-Soil members almost frantic, there were scenes of wild excitement, weapons were drawn, fighting talk was heard and bloodshed on the floor was narrowly averted. By Douglas' prompting a longer debate was finally provided. On May 22, the bill came up for third reading and was passed by a vote of 113 to 100.

Throughout the battle in both Houses, Douglas 'had the authority and power of a dictator.' As he himself later said, 'the speeches were nothing. It was marshalling and directing of men, and guarding from attacks, and with a ceaseless vigilance preventing surprises.' Not without reason did he say, 'I passed the Kansas-Nebraska Act myself.' [22]

[20] Fuess, *Caleb Cushing*, II, 148.

[21] Nichols, *Franklin Pierce*, 337; Philip Phillips to Washington *Constitution*, Aug. 25, 1860. Cf. J. B. Bowlin to Buchanan, St. Louis, April 21, 1854, Buchanan MSS.: The Pierce Administration was in a dilemma; should the bill win, Douglas would reap 'the whole harvest of glory'; should it lose, the Administration would have lost its leading measure, incurring 'all the shame of defeat.'

[22] Cutts, 122-23.

'The great struggle is over,' Alexander H. Stephens wrote a friend; 'Nebraska has passed the House.' The Georgian predicted that the Senate would speedily agree to the House substitute.[23] This prediction was borne out. The only difference between the bill as it had passed the House, and the original Senate measure, was that it was without the Clayton amendment. After two days of debate, Douglas pressed the matter to the issue, the Senate receded from the Clayton amendment and adopted the House's Kansas-Nebraska bill. On May 30 Franklin Pierce affixed his signature.

Abraham Lincoln was attending court on the Springfield circuit when he heard the news that Douglas' bill had passed. That evening he perched his gaunt form on the edge of the bed and talked far into the night with Judge T. Lyle Dickey, who was sharing a tavern room with him. When Dickey awoke the next morning, he was surprised to find his roommate sitting up in bed, apparently in a brown study.

'I'll tell you, Dickey,' Lincoln observed, as though he were continuing the argument, 'this nation cannot exist half slave and half free.' [24]

[23] Alexander H. Stephens to W. W. Burwell, Washington, May 23, 1854; original in Watertown, Conn., Library.

[24] Horace White, 'Abraham Lincoln in 1854,' Address at Springfield, Ill., Jan. 30, 1908.

CHAPTER X

IN THE LIGHT OF HISTORY

WHY did Stephen A. Douglas procure the repeal of the Missouri Compromise? Why did he bend his efforts so determinedly to secure Territorial organization for Kansas and Nebraska?

These questions have occasioned one of the great debates of American historians. To reach a valid opinion on them, one must cut away a tangled undergrowth of time-hallowed misstatement, making allowance for inherited prejudices, and weighing the credibility of inferences as to motives. This requires not only winnowing of assertions from facts but, even more, a search for the truth behind the facts.

When Douglas brought his first Nebraska bill from the Committee on Territories, the Anti-Slavery group in Congress could discern its latent political possibilities. It should not be hard to persuade the North that the Missouri Compromise was a sacred compact between the sections, and that the effort at its repeal proved that an unprincipled slavocracy was determined to encroach on the area of freedom. Furthermore, they could convince the North that its leaders would not protest it, because the 'Northern men with Southern principles,' to subserve their own shabby ambitions, were actually leading the shameful conspiracy. Through this showing, they could convince the Northern people that a new and sectional party must be organized or the slavocracy would succeed.

As to result it made no difference whether this Abolition group sincerely believed its thesis or merely employed it as a pretense for its own aggrandizement. Doubtless men of both types were included in it; doubtless some of the leaders held a mixture of these variant views. And of course it took something more than factional interest of would-be leaders to bring the new party into being; Lincoln, Trumbull, Palmer and Arnold, to name Illinois men alone, would not have gone heart and soul into a merely partisan movement. And yet that it was present cannot be gainsaid.

At any event, as soon as Douglas reported his first bill, and before Philip Phillips or Dixon had objected, Chase, Sumner and the Abolitionist members drafted their Appeal to the country, employing a tone of moral exhortation to portray the bill as a breach of plighted faith, a new movement of the slavocracy, an assault on deserving immigrants, an encroachment on freedom which the North must resist with every ounce of strength. The Appeal's postscript disclosed it by its blunt references to Douglas and its charge that his bill was one of 'the hazards of a presidential game.'

These charges and inferences were quickly accepted as indisputable facts by the North's Free-Soilers and Abolitionists. Hundreds of thousands of Whigs, who formerly had held for Douglas only the normal disesteem which attached to any Democratic leader, now thought him a demon in human form; an equal number of independent Northern Democrats came to regard him as an Ishmael made despicable by his ambition. On such foundations a new party was builded, and eventually a war was fought through which the new party imposed its will upon America. In this tradition, party speakers, pamphleteers, politicians and historians described the Compromise repeal. Thus for forty years or more the conventional explanation was that Douglas had repealed the Missouri Compromise so as to get Southern votes for President.

In his mammoth work, *The Rise and Fall of the Slave Power*, Henry Wilson asserts that the Little Giant, 'simply selfish, ambitious and anxious to win,' was ready 'to disregard the rights of man, the enduring interests of the country and the sacred claims of the Christian religion.' Von Holst, the German interpreter of our American stream, asserts the same. James Schouler, a historian ordinarily temperate and cautious in his judgments, flatly terms the Compromise repeal a 'plot,' in which the chief conspirator was 'Stephen A. Douglas, ambitious, forceful, and subservient.' James Ford Rhodes, regarded by his generation as a calm, dispassionate and objective judge of historic truth, asserts without qualification that, in bringing in the repeal, the Little Giant was making 'a bid for Southern support in the next Democratic Convention,' a course which he was able to take because, for Douglas, 'moral ideas had no place in politics.' [1]

In the case of some of these historians, subjective feeling may have to some degree influenced the conclusion. Senator Henry Wilson became Vice-President by virtue of the Republican party's foundation and political success. Von Holst, whose philosophy smacked of Kant's categorical imperative, based his entire history on the thesis of the bitter moral wrong of slavery, the debased principles and unhallowed ambitions of the slavocracy, the abysmal subservience of the Northern Moderate leaders.

James Ford Rhodes offers no such obvious explanation. His father, Daniel Pomeroy Rhodes, of Cleveland, collaterally related to and an unyielding friend of Douglas all during the latter's life, believed in the principle of Popular Sovereignty as defined in the Nebraska bill. In 1856 he worked untiringly to secure Douglas the Presidential nomination. In 1860, he went to Charleston as Douglas' agent. His son, the historian, admitted that his father had been a friend and 'constant admirer' of the Little Giant. 'It has been a matter of regret to me,' James Ford Rhodes wrote privately, in 1914, 'that I could not see him with my father's eyes.' [2]

Perhaps certain events after Douglas' death may have had something to do with James Ford Rhodes' inability, in this instance, 'to follow his father's bringing-up.' On Douglas' death, Daniel P. Rhodes became executor of his estate, and during its administration Rhodes was, to say the least, negligent of the interests of Douglas' widow and his two sons. The

---

[1] Henry Wilson, II, 405; Von Holst, V, ch. vi–viii; James Schouler, *History of the United States*, New York, v.d.; V, 280–85; Rhodes, I, 430–31.

[2] Daniel P. Rhodes, Cleveland, Ohio, June 15, 1857; M. F. Douglas MSS.: 'I am resolved, Douglas, God sparing my life until the meeting of the Charleston Convention, to work for this object alone.' James Ford Rhodes to Edward S. Marsh, Boston, Nov. 5, 1914; original in possession of Edward S. Marsh, of Brandon, Vt.

great potential fortune which the Senator had accumulated in Chicago real estate was allowed to be foreclosed under dubious circumstances. Douglas' children were so bitterly disillusioned by Rhodes' stewardship of their affairs that they brought suit against him as executor, alleging that he had entered into conspiracy to defraud them of their patrimony. The suit was brought to trial in an Illinois court and the Douglas children finally recovered $30,000. Before the decision, Daniel P. Rhodes died, his son James Ford Rhodes became executor of the father's estate, and as such paid the reparation to the Douglas boys. It is barely possible that this experience of James Ford Rhodes the executor may have, unconsciously of course, colored the judgment of James Ford Rhodes the historian.[3]

But inferences as to possible subjective coloration on the part of some historians would be of no consequence should a painstaking examination of the facts develop that these men's statements were accurate.

Inquiry must be made as to the accuracy of the underlying assumption that, prior to December, 1853, Douglas had no purpose of repealing the Missouri Compromise. The only evidence to overthrow this assumption is the purported letter to Captain Turnley, dated Washington, November 30, 1852, declaring, as to the Missouri Compromise, that 'I have tried the extension of it, and have failed. I am now for its repeal....I will try to remove altogether the question.'[4]

In it, Douglas is made to say that Nebraska 'is large enough for three or four Territories, and we will certainly make two, or perhaps three, out of it in the first place.' This hints of composition after rather than before 1854; as will be seen, the original Nebraska bill called for a single Territory, and the separation came from Missouri and Iowa rivalries, not from Douglas.

Additionally, had Douglas written such a letter, in 1852, it would seem that he would certainly have published it in 1854, because it would have been added evidence for his plea that he saw that early that such action was necessary to carry out the principles of the Compromise of 1850. Finally, if at any time in the debates of 1852–53, Douglas had proposed repeal of the Missouri Compromise restriction, he could have broken the Southern opposition to the then Nebraska bill, and passed it. But he made no such move.[5] Whatever might have been the Little Giant's juristic

---

[3] Some historical student might readily write a fascinating brochure on the subject of the dissipation of the Douglas estate. The Pearl River plantation, and its slaves, in Mississippi, were a casualty of war and the Union soldiers. Long after the war, and after much litigation, the Douglas sons received a part of its value through a Federal payment for confiscated cotton. The Chicago land is treated in a volume by a Chicago real estate man, thoroughly familiar with the details: N. P. Iglehart, *History of the Douglas Estate*, Chicago, 1869. The original of the court order under which Rhodes the historian paid the Douglas boys the $30,000 is in the possession of Mr. Martin F. Douglas of Greensboro, N.C. I have a photostat copy of it. Professor Frank H. Hodder was the first to bring to light Rhodes' dubious position in regard to Douglas. His article 'Propaganda as a Source of American History,' appeared in the *Mississippi Valley Historical Review* in June, 1922.

[4] *Vide supra*, 108, and note, for text of statement and discussion of its authenticity.

[5] Dr. Richard R. Stenberg, of the University of Texas, has made me valuable suggestions as to this internal analysis of the purported Turnley letter. Dr. Stenberg is definitely of the opinion that it is a forgery.

opinion as to the constitutionality of the Missouri Compromise, he only moved its repeal when this step was essential to the accomplishment of some vital purpose.

Was this vital purpose that adduced by the Abolitionists and indorsed by Rhodes, a bid for Southern support for his Presidential aspirations? Rhodes contends that Douglas lost the Presidential nomination in 1852 because 'he had the smallest following' in the South of any of the leading aspirants for the prize.[6] This lack, Rhodes continued, 'had taught Douglas that he could not be nominated without the aid of Southern votes.'

But the fact was that all during the delegate campaign preliminary to the Baltimore Convention, and in that convention itself, Douglas did have a strong Southern support. Buchanan, Cass and Douglas were the three leading candidates before the convention, Buchanan's support came from only fifteen States, Cass had votes from twenty-one States and Douglas had votes from that same number. Buchanan was weakest in the North, Cass was weakest in the South but Douglas' weakness was not in the South but in the Middle States.

Almost from the outset Florida was for the Little Giant, Louisiana and Tennessee gave him a number of votes, and the Douglas minority in the Virginia delegation was so strong and determined that it appealed to the convention to break the unit rule. Near the end of the convention, Southern delegations were so inclining in Douglas' direction that the Buchanan managers took up Pierce in order to stop the Little Giant.

For Douglas, the lesson of the 1852 Convention was that, to secure the presidential nomination, the Northwest must be made a unit for him. Douglas' presidential situation did not change during 1853. In less than a year after Pierce became President, according to a shrewd political observer, 'every man of solid understanding both in Congress and elsewhere, who had aided this ill-starred scion of the Granite State in his efforts to reach the Presidency, became satisfied of his utter incompetency for the performance of the duties devolved upon him.'[7] From this, Democratic leaders knew that the ambitions of others need not be adjourned. Up to January, 1854, no event had happened to affect Yulee's estimate of Douglas' strength. Douglas' standing with the Southern Democracy had not been destroyed or impaired; on the contrary, his relations with their leaders had become even more cordial and his speeches on expansion had brought him new strength with their rank and file. Certainly there was no need for him to undertake a desperate adventure to secure an esteem already possessed.

There is strong contemporary evidence to this effect. In the fall of 1854, in a speech at Lexington, John C. Breckinridge took care to refute the charge that Douglas had urged the Kansas bill to make presidential capital for himself. On the contrary, Breckinridge 'knew of his own knowledge that

[6] Rhodes, I, 424.

[7] D. L. Yulee to Douglas, Margharita, Florida, Jan. 28, 1853; Douglas MSS. For a conclusive analysis of the 1852 Baltimore Convention vote, see Johnson, 206. For contemporary opinion as to Pierce's first year, see Foote, *Casket of Reminiscences*, 91.

Judge Douglas did not seek the introduction of this subject, but it was literally forced upon him.' [8]

But as proof and clincher for their argument that Douglas was seeking Southern support, the Abolitionists charged and historians in their tradition have almost uniformly asserted as a fact that, while Douglas had initially sought to incorporate all Nebraska into a single Territory, he had subsequently cut it into two Territories, for the sole purpose of making the southern one a slave State. What is the truth about this charge?

Reference has already been made to the presence in Washington in December, 1853, of two Delegates-elect from the uncreated Territory of Nebraska. Both of these Johnsons wanted to be seated, a desire that could most easily be satisfied if there were two Territories. Accordingly the two Johnsons petitioned that this division be made, and that the fortieth parallel be made the boundary between Kansas and Nebraska. This request was supported by the Congressional delegations from both Missouri and Iowa.

In addition to this, Hadley Johnson, the Iowa-elected Delegate, had been frightened by the failure of Pierce's Commissioner of Indian Affairs, an Atchison partisan, to extinguish the title of the Omaha Indians, who held lands directly west of Iowa. If the whole area of Nebraska were made a single Territory, the Iowa Johnson feared that its seat of government, the center of gravity of its population, and the Pacific road would be in its southern part and so Iowa's interests would be sacrificed to Missouri. He came to Senators Dodge and Jones, of Iowa, and poured out his fears. Jones, a member of the Committee on Territories, was sympathetic. Dodge brought Johnson to Douglas, the latter saw that the safest way to safeguard Iowa's interest was to divide Nebraska into two Territories, and did so in his new bill of January 23.

In a brief statement to the Senate, Douglas explained that the Missouri and Iowa delegations thought 'their local interests, as well as the interests of the Territory' required division. Dodge gave much the same reason. 'I favored the organization of one Territory,' Senator Jones, of Iowa, said, but representations from Iowa constituents, and a more critical examination

---

[8] Kentucky *Statesman*, Lexington, Oct. 31, 1854, giving outline of Breckinridge's speech. The Kentucky Representative further stated that 'so far from Douglas introducing this subject into Congress, it was one of those matters which, in the progress of our history as a nation and people, arose of itself, and from an intrinsic necessity forced itself upon the consideration of Congress.... The South and not the North was responsible for this question being brought before Congress and the country. It was the South and not the North who insisted that the unconstitutional Missouri restriction should be taken off.... The advancing wave of emigration had accumulated such a weight of population along the borders' of Missouri and Iowa 'that it threatened to break over, into the unoccupied territory immediately west of Missouri, regardless of all law and in open violation of Treaty Stipulations in the Indian tribes.' For this item I am indebted to Mr. C. R. Staples, of Lexington, Ky. J. B. Bowlin to Buchanan, St. Louis, Mo., April 24, 1854, Buchanan MSS., states that the bill was 'gotten up exclusively as an Administration measure.' After its introduction the Southerners' 'support was so cold, if it could be called support at all, that they lost their identity in the measure and it became apparent that the glory of success, if it succeeded, would all belong to the Little Giant.' For other viewpoint, see F. P. Blair to William Allen, Washington, Feb. 10, 1854; Allen MSS., Library of Congress: 'The whole work was done by the Southern plotters operating through their automaton.'

of the railroad problem convinced him that unless there were, for the great interests of the whole country, and especially of our State, two Territories, 'the seat of government and leading thoroughfares' would be to the south of Iowa.[9]

It is also pertinent to examine whether, in January, 1854, Douglas had any reason to believe that slavery could be established either in Kansas or Nebraska. Most contemporary evidence is to the effect that there was a general belief that slavery was highly unsuitable for the region's products and the climate. During the Senatorial debates Southern statesmen said that slavery could not go there; Clingman, of North Carolina, and Butler, of South Carolina, were blunt about it and Atchison expressed grave doubts, reflecting prevailing Missouri pro-slavery opinion.

Early in April, the St. Louis *Herald*, leading organ of the Atchison party, declared 'that the slave-holding emigration to Missouri entirely ceased three years ago. There is now a slave-holding emigration from Missouri,' and ten years thence there would be twenty free men to one slave. Moreover, 'both Nebraska and Kansas are less suited to slavery than Missouri,' and it was practically certain that both Territories were destined by economics, soil conditions and geography to be free.[10]

In view of the belief both in Congress and on the Kansas border that slavery could not be established there, Douglas' explanation of the separation of the area into two Territories would seem much more trustworthy than is the time-hallowed story that it was done so as to give the South a new Slave State. Probably he was much more concerned that it be a new Democratic State.

There remains another of Rhodes' statements, that Douglas believed 'moral ideas had no place in politics,' and hence was quite willing for Kansas to become a Slave State. His oft-quoted sentence, uttered during the Lecompton Constitution fight four years later, that he did not care whether slavery was 'voted up or voted down,' is offered as indisputable proof of this indictment. But the background and circumstances of this declaration vitally affected the meaning. At the time it was made, Douglas was engaged in a battle for the right of the people of Kansas to choose whether they would form a Free or Slave State. It was this right of choice, and not how this right was exercised, that immediately concerned him. During the heat of debate, and to emphasize this point, he made the statement.

Nor is evidence lacking that Douglas felt that slavery was ethically wrong. In 1848, when he called Foote, of Mississippi, to order for the language applied to Hale, he clearly expressed his position. He was not speaking for or against slavery, he said; where it existed it was sustained by local opin-

---

[9] *Congressional Globe*, Thirty-Third Congress, First Session, 221, 223, and App., 382. Hadley Johnson, Nebraska Historical Society, *Transactions*, II, 90. On this point, Allen Johnson, 239, says: 'Put in the language of the promoters of the Pacific railroad, one Territory meant aid to the central route; two Territories meant an equal chance for both northern and central routes. As the representative of Chicago interests, Douglas was not blind to these considerations.'

[10] Quoted, *Illinois State Register*, April 6, 1854.

ion and by this it would stand or fall. 'In the North,' he explained — and one would be blind not to catch the clear import of the words — 'it is not expected that we should take the position that slavery is a positive good — a positive blessing. If we did assume such a position, it would be a very pertinent inquiry, why do you not adopt this institution? We have moulded our institutions at the North as we have thought proper; and now we say to you of the South, if slavery be a blessing, it is your blessing; if it be a curse, it is your curse; enjoy it — on you rest all the responsibility!'

Even more revealing were Douglas' words to young George McConnel the day of the publication of the Appeal of the Independent Democrats. 'I am not pro-slavery,' he exclaimed. 'I think it is a curse beyond computation, to both white and black. But we exist as a nation by virtue only of the Constitution, and under that there is no way to abolish it. I believe that the only power that can destroy slavery is the sword, and if the sword is once drawn, no one can see the end.' Furthermore, the repeal of the Missouri Compromise would be 'a step toward freedom,' because after it Slavery could 'no longer crouch behind a line which Freedom could not cross.' [11]

There can be little doubt as to this clash of judgment in Douglas' mind. He might think slavery a curse beyond comparison and refuse to own slaves himself, but he knew the compromises of the Constitution and felt the Nation's existence under it of paramount importance. At the time of his rebuke to Calhoun and Foote, he had added, speaking for the Northern Democrats: 'We are prepared to aid you in the maintenance of all your constitutional rights.'

Furthermore, this point of view was thoroughly consonant with the Little Giant's political philosophy, which was clearly marked with the frontier tenet of the right of the individual community to direct its own destiny. This was the ideological foundation for Cass' doctrine of non-intervention. This was the underlying philosophy of Douglas' Popular Sovereignty. Be slavery right or wrong, the right of the people of any community to govern their own domestic affairs was fundamental and imperative, and Douglas was resolved to protect the people's right to choose.

This thesis Douglas had incorporated in the Compromise of 1850, as the principle upon which slavery agitation should be settled. In the Fall of that year he had announced that doctrine in Chicago and had convinced the people that it was right. The next year the Illinois Legislature had approved and affirmed his course and the principles upon which it was based. This doctrine made Douglas willing to accord the same right to the people of Nebraska and of Kansas, and undoubtedly it underlay his willingness to repeal the Missouri Compromise.

In recent years these rebutting facts have impressed many professional historians and they have sought to identify other factors which might have determined the Little Giant's plans. Of the new explanations, the most convincing is that the Little Giant was vitally interested in having the Pacific

[11] See *supra*, 39–40, 121–22.

railroad built by the central route, which could not be done unless the Nebraska area were given formal governmental organization.[12]

Another suggestion is that Douglas was really an unwilling mover in the repeal. In his death-battle with the turbulent Atchison, Thomas H. Benton had inflamed the imaginations of would-be settlers of Nebraska and thousands were in western Missouri clamoring to move onto the promised land. Therefore Atchison knew that, if his political life were to be preserved, Nebraska must be organized, so that settlers could go there, and so that a railroad could be built. But Atchison was the leader of, and was dependent for his office and influence upon, a vigorous championship of slavery and Southern Rights. To maintain his slave-holding support in his own State, he had been a hundred times on record that, unless the Missouri Compromise were repealed, the Nebraska lands should lie fallow for eternity. The thrusts by Benton put Atchison in a bad hole. He must firmly grasp both horns of his dilemma, and organize the Territory of Nebraska with the Missouri Compromise's slavery restrictions repealed.

Atchison made a speech, half drunk, in September, 1854, in which he claimed that he had threatened Douglas that, if he would not bring in a report from the Committee on Territories favoring it, the Missouri Senator would take its chairmanship and bring in the bill. According to this story, Douglas asked for a day to consider it and then agreed.[13]

Several variants of this story have been brought forward. In 1876, Henry S. Foote, of Mississippi, offered his opinion that Douglas 'only agreed' to accept the Compromise repeal after being solicited 'by certain gentlemen from the South, of extreme views,' one of whom was a member of Pierce's Cabinet. These men whispered to Douglas that if he would consent, Pierce and his group would support him for President.[14] Another story is that Davis devised the whole plan and then General Robert Armstrong, the proprietor of the Washington *Union*, 'bedeviled' Douglas into taking up the repeal, and procured Dixon, of Kentucky, to make the public move. But Senator Dixon is authority for the statement that he consulted neither the Administration nor Jefferson Davis nor General Armstrong about his own writing of the Compromise repeal or Douglas' acceptance thereof.[15]

A further tale was that Dixon's own intervention was the fruit of a shrewd Whig plot; that Seward thought the introduction of an amendment for

[12] See *supra*, 99–107. The Douglas papers contain a mass of correspondence adding weight to this theory.

[13] Atchison's speech was made on Sept. 26, 1854. New York *Tribune*, Oct. 10, 1854, contains an account of it copied from Parkville, Kansas, *Luminary*, Sept. 26, 1854. Professor Ray, chief protagonist of the Atchison theory, has collected a great deal of evidence on the matter, and lays great stress on it. See Ray, 'Genesis of the Kansas-Nebraska Act,' American Historical Association, *Annual Report* for 1914; I, 259–80.

[14] Foote, *Casket of Reminiscences*, 93–94.

[15] General Armstrong, an able and popular editor and politician, was father-in-law of Thomas L. Harris, Douglas' faithful friend. According to these versions, Davis had devised the entire plan, the Administration, Armstrong and Harris kept after the Little Giant, and finally dragged him in. Louisville *Courier-Journal*, Aug. 5, 1878, prints Dixon's denials. J. T. Dubois and G. S. Mathews, *Galusha A. Grow*, New York, 1900, 144–45, quote Dixon as having said that, when he introduced his amendment, he had no idea it would pass.

outright repeal of the Compromise would stimulate Free-Soil sentiment in the North and persuaded Dixon, a fellow Whig, to make the move. According to this ingenious story Dixon believed that to do so would strengthen him in the South and did as Seward wanted.[16] This Dixon bluntly denied.

Some of these imputations became current in the 'Fifties, and Douglas took occasion to give them specific denial.[17] 'The Nebraska bill was not concocted in any conclave, night or day,' he told the Senate on February 23, 1855. 'It was written by myself, at my own house, with no man present. Whatever odium there is attached to it, I assume it. Whatever of credit there may be, let the public award it where they think it belongs.' Even Rhodes admits that 'all the circumstances support the truth of this denial. Douglas was a man of too much independence to suffer the dictation of Atchison, Toombs or Stephens. He always wanted to lead and was never content to follow.' Jefferson Davis said later that Douglas had originated the bill, 'and for a year or two vaunted himself on its paternity.' [18]

During the 1860 campaign, William H. Seward charged that Northern Democrats had forced upon the South the 'great boon' of the repeal of the Missouri Compromise, but that the South had accepted it with 'hesitation and reluctance at the hands of their Northern allies.' As soon as Seward made this charge Philip Phillips challenged it in a public letter.

Upon the Senate Committee's first report, in January, 1854, Phillips had examined the bill carefully, and had concluded that Douglas' bill 'could not work out with the equality and fairness which on its face it promised, so long as the Missouri Compromise,' which completely excluded slave-holders from settling in the Territory up to the very period for inaugurating the State Constitution, 'remained unrepealed.' Therefore in a few days he 'submitted to a distinguished Southern Senator' — this was Hunter, of Virginia — 'a written proposition for the repeal.'

'This led to interviews with Judge Douglas and with the President,' Phillips' letter continued; both concurred in the propriety of this change and the bill was amended. While these negotiations were under way, Dixon, of Kentucky, acting independently, gave notice in the Senate that he would propose the repeal. While 'many of the most distinguished Southern members' were in the conferences, Judge Douglas was 'the only representative of his section' present at any of them.

'So far, therefore, as the *initiation* of the measure is concerned, there is nothing to justify Mr. Seward's statement,' the Phillips letter concluded. 'If you look to its *consummation*, the same conclusion must follow.... Never before did so important a measure receive so united a vote from the South. The strength of old party ties dissolved in its presence. In the Senate the voices of Bell and Houston were alone lifted against it; and in the House, in proportion to its numbers, the unanimity was equally as conspicuous.

[16] Montgomery Blair to Gideon Welles, quoted in the latter's article in *Galaxy*, July, 1873, cited Dixon, *Missouri Compromise*, 589.

[17] *Congressional Globe*, Thirty-Fourth Congress, First Session, 393.

[18] Rhodes, I, 432; Varina Davis, I, 671.

While this was the case at the South, there was a serious division among the representatives of the Northern Democracy. These indisputable facts show that the repeal originated with Southern members, and was perfected by their united action.' [19]

It must always be remembered, in fixing the responsibility for almost all great political decisions, that usually these come as the result not of one but of many factors. A President or Senator receives advice from many men, many factions. Diverse interests combine to urge or oppose a policy. Selection of any one element as the determining factor is hazardous.

Of course, the political turmoil in Missouri was a contributing factor to the repeal of the Missouri Compromise. Contemporaries were well aware that the death-battle was under way. Senator Jones, of Iowa, wrote Howell Cobb that their mutual friend John S. Phelps, a Missouri Democratic Congressman, 'and others are in a bitter fight with Old Bullion in Missouri, and the remark has been made that Benton came in on the Missouri Compromise and will go out on and with it.' [20]

Even so, the Missouri war probably was only a minor factor. Douglas liked Atchison although he did not greatly respect him. If he could have helped the Missourian without harm to himself, he would have done so. But he neither feared Atchison's power, nor was under any such obligation to him as to be forced to follow an unwelcome course. It so happened that Douglas' own plans for Pacific railroad-building could only be carried out by adopting the policy which would likewise aid Atchison in Missouri. [21]

Douglas' vital interest in the building of a Pacific railroad by the central route was well known to his intimates, and they believed it constituted his controlling purpose in the repeal. James W. Sheahan, one of the Little Giant's trusted lieutenants, his first biographer and understanding friend, pointed out that, after the Compromise of 1850, 'California had been acquired and a road to the Pacific was indispensable.' But the immense Nebraska area was, by law, closed to immigration and travel. 'Like a huge block, it barred the natural pathway to the Pacific. The South was

[19] Washington *Constitution*, Aug. 25, 1860, printing Philip Phillips' letter to the editor, dated Washington, Aug. 24, 1860. For interesting confirmatory evidence of Southern authorship, cf. P. R. Frothingham, *Edward Everett*, Boston, 1925; 345, 352–53; Dubois and Mathews, 138–40; Ray, *Repeal*, 232, M. W. Granger, *Washington vs. Jefferson*, New York, 1898, 71, quoting Benton: 'Douglas was driven into the Kansas-Nebraska bill by . . . the fire-eaters of the South.'

[20] G. W. Jones to Howell Cobb, Washington, Feb. 9, 1854; Erwin MSS.

[21] Chief protagonist of the Atchison theory is Professor P. Ormond Ray, who published *The Repeal of the Missouri Compromise, Its Origin and Authorship*, Cleveland, Ohio, 1909, a volume of 315 pages. The most stalwart champion of the railroad thesis is Professor Frank H. Hodder, of the University of Kansas. Professor Hodder has had a number of shrewdly reasoned, well-documented pamphlet presentations of the subject, including 'The Genesis of the Kansas-Nebraska Act,' *Proceedings*, State Historical Society of Wisconsin for 1912, 69–86; 'Propaganda as a Source for American History,' *Mississippi Valley Historical Review*, IX, No. 1; and 'A Famous Chapter in American Politics,' *The Dial*, Sept. 1, 1909. A careful judgment of the controversy leads one to believe that Ray's facts, and the general situation which he describes have not been seriously demolished; even so, they do not prove his contention that Missouri politics was the chief cause.

pressing a railroad from Memphis, and southwesterly across the continent. Mr. Douglas wanted a fair chance to have that railroad lead from the North, where it could find communication through Chicago to the Atlantic. Our railroads had already reached the Mississippi, and others were projected, extending to the Missouri. He wanted Nebraska and Kansas opened, and the country made free to the enterprise of the North.... That was the motive for organizing these Territories — a motive having its origin in the desire to benefit the whole nation, and especially to give the Northwest a fair opportunity to compete for the commerce of the great East.' [22]

Sheahan's statement suggests the best approach to Douglas' Territorial policy. The West had to develop, this required Federal action and for Territories to precede Statehood was the accepted procedure. By the 'Fifties the organization of the vast Platte country was long overdue. As soon as the question was raised, it became enmeshed with such troublesome complications as Chicago's growing ambitions; various schemes of Southern expansionists and the sectional conflict over the location of the railroad to the Pacific. Moreover, in the 'Fifties there could be no Territorial legislation which did not deal with slavery, not so much because of its consequence to the particular Territory but because it had become an intersectional issue of extreme sensitiveness and importance.

Douglas did not create the slavery issue. It was no fault of his that it divided the Democratic party and the country, but he dealt with the situation as he found it. Far from urging pro-slavery measures, he sought to subordinate the question to those larger issues he saw emerging. As Chairman of the Senate Committee on Territories, not only was he charged with framing a practical policy but also he was under heavy pressure from conflicting interests in the party and the country. Naturally he could not ignore the South; Abolitionists might do so but not Douglas. When events forced him to bring in a Territorial bill for Nebraska, he presented one which met the situation the best way that he knew — by applying the principles of local self-government.[23]

[22] James W. Sheahan, 'Eulogy on Stephen A. Douglas,' Chicago, July 3, 1861; reprinted, *Fergus Historical Series*, Chicago, 1881; XV, 120–205.

[23] In this judgment I am sustained by the concurrence of Dr. James G. Randall, of the University of Illinois, letter to author, Jan. 2, 1934. Some of his statements I have paraphrased. I am also indebted to Mr. Paul M. Angle, Mr. Marquis James, Dr. Roy F. Nichols, and Dr. Richard R. Stenberg, for their comment upon this chapter and substantial support in my conclusions.

CHAPTER XI

A REALIST IN AN EMOTIONAL AGE

AS THE historian follows the labyrinths of American national development, he becomes all too familiar with the politician's armory of pet phrases, with slogans skillfully designed to protect special interests and with constitutional interpretations which mask political ambition or predatory purpose. But amid the common cant and dialectic of the 'Fifties was a realistic statesman. By the time he was thirty years old, Stephen A. Douglas had begun to slough off intellectual immaturity. In the next decade he undertook to relate himself constructively to the social pattern of his age.

On occasion he indulged in dialectics and sought to buttress his policies of economic intelligence with formulæ of party doctrine and constitutional interpretation. In large part this was because he lived in an age when speech in any other vocabulary would not have been comprehended. And yet one cannot doubt the Little Giant's sincere effort to understand the *Zeitgeist*. 'I know not what our destiny may be,' he confided to a friend, 'but I try to keep up with the spirit of the age, to keep in view the history of the country, to see what we have done, whither we are going, and with what velocity we are moving, in order to be prepared for those events which it is not in the power of man to thwart.' [1]

And yet while such intelligence of purpose would generally constitute high merit in a statesman, there are instances when it occasions disaster and defeat. Douglas had premonitions of trouble over the repeal of the Missouri Compromise, but he saw so clearly the inevitable effect climate, soil and natural productions would have on human institutions in Kansas and Nebraska that he unduly discounted the effect on the emotions of men, of aroused fears, passions and hates.

Throughout the world the 'Forties and the 'Fifties were marked by disturbances in social, political, economic and emotional equilibrium. In 1846, Karl Marx wrote one of his most powerful pronouncements against the capitalistic system. In the middle 'Forties Great Britain abandoned her corn laws and her party system shattered into bits. In 1848 nationalism flared in vivid flame in Hungary, for a brief few weeks Germany was under revolutionary control and France installed the third Napoleon. All over the planet new currents were cutting new channels for men's faith and effort; the rivers of life were burdened with the flotsam of the past; the winds were laden with the whispers of the future. In America the epoch was one in which the people's traditional attachments were loosened, their new faiths not yet fixed. From 1850 forward, the American public mind was fluid,

[1] S. S. Cox, 'Eulogy on Douglas,' *Annual Report*, Smithsonian Institution, 1863; 121.

its intellectual concepts changing, its emotions sensitive and awaiting mobilization by master psychologists.

It was in this decade that the basic philosophical conflict of all American history, the battle between rational and mystic democracy, neared its climax. Even before the foundation of the Republic this strife of idea and emotion had been in progress. For the first forty years — and despite the glowing phrases of the Declaration of 1776 — intelligence had been dominant. True, there had been schism between the Jeffersonians and the Hamiltonians as to the national fiscal program and the nature of the Federal system. The Hamiltonians might design a program inuring chiefly to their own benefit, the Jeffersonians might prefer a more pervasive social purpose, but both upheld, in practice, the basic principle of rule by the intellectual élite. There had been general agreement that it was the function of the competent, the mentally alert and the socially responsible to conduct public affairs.

The Jeffersonian revolution of 1800 merely established a rational democracy. To these men, whose philosophy went back to Aristotle and John Locke, Liberty was evolutionary rather than revolutionary and men's rights had been painfully acquired by generations of effort, privation and sacrifice. Governments were shifted on issues, not impulses, and democracy involved reason and intelligence.

In the 'Twenties a new and rival spirit welled up from the West — in part, perhaps, the resentment of those who people a new land against those who live in complex and controlling areas — but at any event an emotional democracy, bottoming itself on Rousseau's mystic claims of innate rights, looking on Liberty as a spontaneous creation and asserting rights unconnected with responsibilities, among these the universal manhood competence for self-government. In 1828, under the leadership of Andrew Jackson, frontier aristocrat by birth but born leader for an emotional crusade, mystic democracy took command.

The Abolition movement, though reprehended by Old Hickory, was a manifestation of emotional democracy. The South sought to meet this wave of feeling by dialectic. It gave its intellectual sword so fine an edge that the Calhouns, Yanceys, Davises and Rhetts made reality keep its distance. These subtleties of unrooted logic led to solemn justifications of slavery as an ordinance of God, 'A positive good' to master and to slave. Similarly it encouraged a metaphysic contemplation of the Federal Constitution as a cadaver for verbal dissection rather than a living instrument, capable of organic growth.

This Southern defense mechanism was doomed to fail, because logical abstractions were no better counter to deep-seated passions than to economic realities. The acquisition of Mexican territory occasioned another great upsurge of feeling, which David Wilmot's Proviso raised to fever heat. This time, however, common sense took a hard grip upon the emotion of the two sections, found a basis of mutual concession and forced 1850's Compromise.

But the check upon the emotional flood was merely momentary. The

THE PRAIRIE POLITICIAN: STEPHEN A. DOUGLAS
In his early years in Illinois politics

psychic forces clamoring for expression soon broke all barriers and by 1854 were gushing in a dozen different streams. It was a time for untrammeled expression. There was a drive for reform, change, agitation, which boded ill for any arbitrament of intelligence.

The undertones of this great orchestration of agitation and dissent were interesting. Amelia Bloomer was preaching to her sex of the need for freedom from the thralldom of skirts. Lucy Stone was agitating the emancipation of women from the slavery of having to adopt their husbands' names. Channing, Parker, Horace Mann, each was seeking his heart's desire. Margaret Fuller was abetting a dozen unsettling movements. Thoreau was proclaiming the virtues of civic disobedience; Emerson was singing in transcendental strains and Poe was ignoring issues while he thrummed a mystic lyre.

These minor ebullitions sympathetically environed the three great ferments of the 'Fifties. Interestingly enough, each of the three — anti-liquor, anti-foreign, anti-slavery — was phrased in negative terms, and in none was there substantial trace of modern technique in social reconstruction, nor the proposal of a substitute mechanism to replace the organism to be destroyed. None the less, the moving spirits in these battles showed a remarkably keen insight into latent mass emotions and did not hesitate to employ appropriate devices to mobilize the mob mind.

The prohibition agitation of the 'Fifties was an outgrowth of the temperance movements of twenty years before, when Temperance societies had sprung up in all parts of the country, later forming an overhead organization known as the American Temperance Society, and becoming no mean political and social force. In the early 'Forties the Sons of Temperance was founded, 'to shield its members from the evils of intemperance, to afford mutual assistance in case of sickness and to elevate their character as men.' By 1850 it had almost a quarter of a million members.

At first moderation was advocated, then abstinence was voluntarily pledged, finally the more ardent drys began agitating for complete prohibition of the liquor traffic. In 1851, Neal Dow, of Maine, crowned a life's career of prohibition agitation by putting the famous Maine liquor law on that State's statute books. Two months after Maine's action, a National Temperance Convention attracted three hundred delegates from seventeen States. The next year Prohibition began its sweep over the country. The Massachusetts Legislature succumbed to a petition with 133,312 signatures. More than 600,000 asked New York and Pennsylvania to go dry.[2]

Vermont's experience illustrated the emotional basis of the new Prohibition drive. In 1852 the drys of the Granite State confronted the Legislature with a State-wide Prohibition petition bearing 38,000 signatures. That November, Neal Dow came from Maine to exhort the State's Legislature, and its solons enacted the Maine law with a referendum clause. Thereupon the drys inaugurated a vigorous campaign in the larger towns. In the vote, the larger cities' Prohibition majorities overcame the negative vote of the small towns and the country and by 22,215 to 21,045 Vermont went dry.

[2] Leigh Colvin, *Prohibition in the United States*, New York, 1926; 15-32.

The Prohibitionists had successfully aroused the group emotions of the city crowds but the people of the country, not subjected to these appeals, did not want this extension of group control of individual life.[3]

The next year the Legislatures of both Michigan and Wisconsin adopted Prohibition, with referenda, and the voters returned sustaining majorities. In that same year the Prohibition agitation began in Illinois, and Abraham Lincoln was one of the thirty-nine citizens to sign a public letter asking for the publication of a Prohibition sermon, because it was likely to be 'productive of good.' The next year the Illinois Legislature passed a Maine Liquor law, subject to a referendum in June, 1855. Quite a fierce debate ensued in which Lincoln took no part but Douglas opposed Prohibition with his usual forthrightness. The Connecticut Legislature also enacted State-wide Prohibition and only the veto of Governor Seymour prevented such a measure from becoming a law in New York.[4]

Like the Prohibition crusade, the anti-foreign, anti-Catholic frenzy of the 'Fifties was rooted in past agitations. Each new wave of European immigration seemed to provoke a new nativist agitation — as early as 1790, the original Society of St. Tammany had been founded as a nativist protest against the influx of foreign laborers into New York. In the late 'Thirties and early 'Forties, Irish immigrants flowed in to work on railroad- and canal-building projects and anti-foreign sentiment flared up again.

Ireland's great famine of 1846 renewed that country's heavy immigration to the United States and occasioned a new and virulent American nativist protest. Almost spontaneously, organizations under such titles as the Sons of '76, the Sons of the Sires, the United Americans, the American Republican Party, the Order of Free and Accepted Americans — 'The Wide Awakes' — sprang up over the country. These had their chief potency in

[3] Dow addressed the Vermont Legislature on Nov. 9, 1852; the Legislature, on Nov. 23, passed the act, which was entitled 'An Act to Prevent Traffic in Intoxicating Liquors for the Purpose of Drinking.' The vote was the following March. For these details I am indebted to Judge Charles H. Darling, of Burlington, Vt.

[4] Dr. James K. Pollock and Mr. Harold M. Dorr, of the University of Michigan, have checked up on the figures as to the 1853 Prohibition referendum in that State, and Dr. W. B. Hesseltine, of the University of Wisconsin, has done so for the results in that State. The Michigan Wets abstained from the referendum, which was later knocked out by the courts. The Wisconsin figures were 27,519 for Prohibition, 24,109 against. Governor Barstow vetoed the ensuing dry law. Mr. F. Lauriston Bullard, of Boston, has analyzed for me the conflicting evidence as to Lincoln's part in the 1854 and 1855 Illinois Prohibition battle. The only evidence that Lincoln publicly espoused the prohibition side in this fight was offered in 1906–10 by the Reverend James B. Merwin. Mr. Merwin, then in the eighties, claimed that in 1855 he and Lincoln had stumped Illinois together in the dry cause. But no private letters or public reports indicate or intimate anything of the kind. In 1917, Robert Todd Lincoln wrote that he 'never heard of James B. Merwin until a few months ago.... I was dumbfounded to know that my father had a friend who claimed such intimacy with him and of whom I knew nothing whatever.' Undoubtedly Lincoln avoided involvement in the Illinois Prohibition battle, because in 1855 he was already an aspirant for Douglas' Senate seat, and was discretion itself in refraining from tactics which might cost him votes. He would speak out with reasonable boldness on the slavery issue, but the Illinois anti-slavery men were divided on prohibition and on Know-Nothingism, and it is significant that Lincoln maintained a discreet silence on both issues. Cf. also Paul Angle, 'Lincoln and Liquor,' *Abraham Lincoln Association Bulletins*, Nos. 27 and 28.

such large cities as New York, Philadelphia, Boston, Baltimore, where the immigrant groups, with their alien tongues and customs, had largely concentrated. Nearly every nativist group, taking to politics to enforce its demands, was anti-Democratic, doubtless because of the manifest Democratic inclination of the Irish and German immigrants.

As the successive waves of immigrants flocked to the Democratic fold, the Whig leaders welcomed and encouraged the answering anti-foreign agitations, seeing in them possible offsets to the immigrant vote. William H. Seward of New York, a conspicuous exception to this tendency, was in 1860 to pay dearly for his dislike of proscription. But the Southern Whigs welcomed nativism, anti-catholicism, anti-foreignism and prohibition, and in the North, the party was equally receptive to the Abolition crusade.

The 1852 national election, giving notice that the Whig party was on its deathbed, quickened the growth of the possible substitute political group. The next Fall all the anti-foreign and anti-Catholic societies joined 'The Order of the Star-Spangled Banner,' in form a secret society with awesome secrets, private conclaves and an officialdom of extraordinary nomenclature. There were three degrees to the order, whose ritual impressed moron minds. Whenever members were questioned as to its secrets, they were oath-bound to answer: 'I know nothing,' whence Greeley dubbed them 'Know-Nothings.' [5]

Only a native-born citizen, 'a Protestant, born of Protestant parents, reared under Protestant influence, and not united in marriage with a Roman Catholic,' could become a member. The ritual further revealed the order's purpose: 'To resist the insidious policy of the Church of Rome, and other foreign influence against the institutions of our country, by placing in all offices in the gift of the people or by appointment none but native-born Protestant citizens.' [6]

'Americans must rule America' was the order's public slogan, to which was always added, 'No Papacy in the Republic.' Its national platform demanded that immigration be restricted; that before an alien could be naturalized, a residence of many years be required; that church schools be prohibited; that the Holy Bible be read and taught in the public schools, and that, above all else, Catholics be kept out of public office.

With this creed Know-Nothingism swept like a prairie fire across East, West, North and South. Whigs who saw their own party sinking beneath their feet rushed into its conclaves. By tens of thousands, Northern Democrats who did not like the Kansas-Nebraska bill switched over to the Know-Nothing fold. Most of the Northern preachers who urged prohibition, most of the pastors who sent petitions to Congress denouncing the

[5] James P. Hambleton, *Henry A. Wise*, Richmond, 1856; 43–54. Louis Dow Scisco, *Political Nativism in New York State*, New York, 1901, gives an excellent general account of the nativist movement in America. Channing, VI, 129–38, has a succinct statement.

[6] Hambleton, 47–54, prints the ritual in full; to the clause banning from membership anyone married to a Roman Catholic was added a proviso that local councils could waive this restriction, but 'no member who may have a Roman Catholic wife shall be eligible to any office in this Order.' Later, however, there were Catholic Know-Nothings in Louisiana.

repeal of the Missouri Compromise, joined the new secret order and advocated its proscriptive principles.

In 1854 there were riots against foreigners in Boston streets. The Know-Nothings secured control of the Massachusetts Legislature and elected their leader, Henry Wilson, to the Senate. In May, 1854, the Know-Nothings won a Philadelphia city election by a majority of 8000; while this was portrayed to the country as a great popular rebuke to the Kansas-Nebraska bill, in reality it was a Know-Nothing victory. The Order of the Star-Spangled Banner was received by Southern Whigs with great enthusiasm, acquiring such strength in Virginia that, in 1854, it undertook to capture control of the State and had an excellent chance to do so.[7]

As with the anti-liquor and anti-foreign movements, emotion was the basic quality of the renewed anti-slavery drive. While each of the three had social and economic background, especially was this true of the anti-slavery crusade. In its complex, one can discern social forces, economic determinants, differences in group cultures, religious factors and moral ideas. Running through all of these, translating the static into the dynamic and giving unity and coherence, was an overwhelming emotional drive.

This renewal of the anti-slavery campaign did not, however, represent a belated Abolition triumph. From the time of the Nat Turner insurrection, the Abolitionists' chief effect upon the North had been to excite distaste and opposition, while in the South they had aroused a frenzy of resentment and fear. William Lloyd Garrison's imprisonment in Baltimore gave satisfaction in Philadelphia, New York and Boston, as well as in Richmond, Charleston and Mobile. When William Lloyd Garrison denounced the Constitution as 'a covenant with death and an agreement with hell,' great Northern groups were horror-struck. Attempts to give political instrumentation to Abolition policies became increasingly ineffective, and after 1840, the word came to be used to represent a demand for solution of the slave problem by other than political means.

Examination of Abolition speeches, sermons, pamphlets and books during these 'Thirties and 'Forties affords a ready understanding of these reactions. For, in the deep black of Southern turpitude the Abolitionists could see no good, no redeeming trait, no shade of gray. The formula of attack was almost standard: The Negro was God's image in ebony. White and black were brothers, equals, and slavery was a sin against God. The Declaration of Independence asserted that all men were created equal, and so slavery was a breach of the Declaration as well as an affront to Almighty God.

There could be no honest slave-holder, the Abolitionist insisted, all such were thieves, robbers and man-stealers. The slave-holder underfed his chattels, housed them in hovels and punished them like wild animals. Tales of savage cruelty and bestial lust were eagerly repeated. Abolitionist lecturers went into every hamlet of the North painting tales of unmentionable

---

[7] Thomas J. Wertenbaker, *Norfolk, Historic Southern Seaport*, Durham, N.C., 1931, 219, relates how, in Norfolk, the Know-Nothings gained thousands of converts and for a time secured complete control of the City Government.

horrors in the South. The entire Southern social system was indicted along with slavery. All Southern white men were portrayed as lazy, drunken, lustful braggarts. Their society was an oligarchy, a slavocracy destructive of American democracy.

But the crowning indictment was that planters, overseers — in fact, all white men in the South — forced slave girls and women into adultery. 'The South is one great brothel, where half a million of women are flogged to prostitution,' Wendell Phillips thundered. The slave-holder would defile his daughter, others charged, and then sell her into infamy.[8]

A bitterly resentful Southern group answered each salvo of Abolition pamphlets with a cannonade of pro-slavery print. This battle of the books, from the Southern standpoint purely defensive, before long resulted in the equally extreme contention that slavery was not an evil to be endured, but, as Calhoun put it, 'the most safe and stable basis for free institutions in the world.' [9]

This contradiction of view as to the same institution arose in part from the antagonism of emotion and interest, but even more from the basic fact, still insufficiently understood, that the slave system in the South had two phases widely different in character and effect. The first of these may be termed feudal or manorial slavery, and the second commercial slavery.

The first system was built about the great plantation, often hereditary, almost a barony in miniature. The planter's social life struck Sir Charles Lyell, the great geologist, as that of the English country gentleman. He had a comfortable home, with pillared veranda, enclosed garden and spacious shade-trees. There were many clean, whitewashed Negro cabins, each with its little vegetable garden and its rollicking pickaninnies.

Self-interest as well as humanity led the master to deal kindly with his slaves. Harriet Martineau was struck by the patience of the slave-owners with their slaves. 'The first law of slavery,' said De Bow's Review, the great Southern economic journal, 'is that of kindness from the master to the slave.' Most of the great planters sought overseers who were humane and understanding. It was a part of the daily routine of 'Mistis,' the planter's wife, to see to the health and welfare of all the slaves, a duty never-ending and uncomplainingly performed. Expert medical attention was carefully provided; usually the same physician attended the 'Big House' and the cabins.

The slaves were not overworked. Planters would not set their bondmen to the most unhealthy types of labor, such as ditching and draining, but

---

[8] There is a world of Abolition literature making such charges. Typical specimens include Charles G. Parsons' *Inside View of Slavery, or A Tour Among Planters*, Boston, 1855; *American Slavery As It Is*, The American Anti-Slavery Society, Boston, 1839; Dr. John T. Kramer, *The Slave Auction*, Boston, 1859, pamphlet; Wendell Phillips, *Speeches, Lectures and Addresses*, Boston, v.d. (Phillips' statement about prostitution occurs on page 108); Stephen S. Foster, *The Brotherhood of Thieves*, Boston, 1844.

[9] Calhoun, *Works*, III, 180; cf. also Alexander H. Stephens, *Constitutional View*, I, 593: 'Slavery, so-called, because there was no such thing as slavery in the full and proper sense of the word,' was 'regulated by law to promote... the best interests of both races.' *Ibid.*, II, 25, terms slavery 'a political institution.' 'The slave, so-called, was not in law regarded entirely as a chattel... He had important personal rights secured by law.'

would hire white men for this work. Usually the task assigned each slave was easily carried out. Punishment was inflicted chiefly on the lazy or the vicious. If a slave repeatedly ignored a task assigned, or were unduly impudent or malingered, he might be whipped. But it was a matter of common observation that happy slaves worked best and frequently a master would sell a surly or dissatisfied slave, even at a substantial sacrifice.

If punishment was held in one hand, reward was held in the other. Quite often the planter paid a cash premium for a slave's additional performance. On many plantations, labor was cheerfully performed and the Negroes seemed gleeful and contented.[10] The field hands sang to the hoe hands, and these answered in song. There were gifts for all at Christmas and care for all through the year. There was happiness in the cabin and a sense of responsibility in the 'Big House' on the hill.

Many such planters looked on slavery as a sort of serfdom under which family life should be encouraged, with marriage, inheritance and opportunity for some measure of education and betterment. The great planters were not so anxious to perpetuate property in man as they were to maintain an ordered society and preserve a way of life.

Those who upheld this feudal slavery did so, with rare exceptions, in sincerity and good faith. They did not dislike the Negro; Henry A. Wise expressed a general feeling in terming them patient, faithful, brave 'and more disinterested than the white man.' Even so, they believed that the Negro was a child race and slavery was its training school for life. By it ignorant, idle Africans, barbarous and unmoral, were divested of their savage inheritance and gradually given the white man's superior civilization. To Jefferson Davis this feudal type of slave society represented a desirable social system. It was manorial slavery which Calhoun termed 'a good — a positive good!'

Such men did not contend that slavery would exist forever; they thought the Negro would eventually be equipped for and would be granted a qualified liberty. On his plantation of Briarfield, Davis sought to minimize external discipline of the Negroes and to build up in the slaves a desire to discipline themselves. If a slave could make money for himself, he was at liberty to do so, merely paying the master the wages of an unskilled laborer.

These men were convinced that the system was a substantial benefit to the slaves themselves.[11] But when they talked of the benefits of slavery they had in mind a slavery of the manor type. They ignored the Census figures, which revealed a different aspect of the slavery problem. There were, in the United States in 1850, some 347,000 slave-holders. Of this

---

[10] Harriet Martineau, *Society in America*, New York, 1837; II, 75. Two other of her books on American observations are worth reading: *Retrospect of Western Travel*, New York, 1838; *Views on Slavery and Emancipation*, New York, 1837. *De Bow's Review*, XV, 257, 277.

[11] Barton H. Wise, *Life of Henry A. Wise*, New York, 1899; 161, quoting Wise to the Reverend Nehemiah Adams; Ulrich B. Phillips, *Life and Labor in the Old South*, Boston, 1930, gives an appealing picture of slavery of the manor type. Nathaniel W. Stephenson, *Lectures on Typical Americans and Their Problems*, Claremont, Cal., 1932, 40–46, contrasts the two phases; for Jefferson Davis' attitude and experience, see Walter L. Fleming, 'Plantation Life in the Old South,' *Journal of American History*, II, 233–46. For a good summary see Beveridge, II, Chapter I.

entire number, less than 8000 slave-holders owned more than fifty slaves apiece.[12] Of the greater group, doubtless many thousand were city men who held slaves as house servants. The bulk of the remainder were small farmers. A large segment of these, however, were men on the make, men who saw in slavery not a feudal status of society but the chance to make a fortune through labor exploitation. They did not have manor houses — they envied those to the manor born — and sought similar estates of their own.

The great westward movement from the Seaboard South, a striking feature of the first few decades of the nineteenth century, was largely an index of this determination on the part of the ambitious, the bankrupt, the poor and desperate. They heard of the hundreds of thousands of fallow acres in Alabama, Mississippi, Louisiana, Arkansas and Texas, available at figures fantastically low in view of the prevailing demand for cotton. In the new Cotton Kingdom, they visioned a manor, broad acres and social status equal to that of the great planters at home. All these they saw — if only they had courage and willingness to exploit the slave system.

This dichotomy of Southern viewpoint made itself apparent in South Carolina with the turn of the Nineteenth Century. The Federal Constitution's ban on the importation of slaves was to date from 1808, but South Carolina passed a State law prohibiting it immediately. In 1804, however, commercial interests sought to reopen the State's slave trade. South Carolina's greatest planters fought desperately against it, but the movers of the scheme were not thinking about South Carolina but of profits from the labor demand for the great empire opening up in the Southwest. Joseph Alston and other great planters protested in vain, the law was repealed and for four years the State had a frenzied importation of slaves.

This episode throws into bold relief the clash between the feudal and the commercial concepts of the slave system, and slavery's legal status permitted either system: the man who owned the slave could be his lord protector or he could treat him as a mere beast of burden, a tool to till the soil. The laws often interfered with the best intentions; let the most humane of masters die, and his slaves might have to be sold and families separated, for a settlement of the estate. Extraneous considerations were constantly creeping in to prevent the South from probing its own problem and giving statutory authority to the feudal attitude.

Southern apologists were prone to look away from slavery's other face — as well they might, for an evil face it was. After 1808 the internal slave trade, commercial slavery's most hideous side, had a great increase. It made its way with coffles and slave jails; girls were exposed on auction blocks and occasionally the best-formed among them were purchased for love rather than for labor. Frequently wives were sold away from husbands and children away from mothers. The 'first law of slavery' might be the happiness of the slave, yet planters found it hard to secure good overseers, and a Virginian termed them 'the curse of this country, Sir, the worst

[12] U.S. Census, 1850. The exact number was 347,525. Of these 68,820 held only one slave apiece, 105,683 more than 1 and less than 5, and less than 8000 over 50 slaves.

men in the community.' Many slaves had kind and indulgent masters but tens of thousands were ruthlessly exploited, particularly upon the new plantations in the Southwest.[13]

Some States were charged with becoming almost a breeding-ground for labor for the Southwest. Virginia during the 'Fifties was selling about six thousand slaves a year to the Cotton Kingdom. These situations had great influence on the commercial system. If a Negro girl were just entering child-bearing age and had given proof of fertility by a pickaninny or two, she would bring more than the ordinary prime field hand.[14]

While the Abolitionists' chief charge that the South was 'one great brothel' was characteristically exaggerated, miscegenation was undoubtedly slavery's greatest evil. The mistress of a great plantation confided to Miss Martineau that 'a planter's wife was only "the chief slave of the harem."' William Gilmore Simms, one of the South's shrewdest defenders, admitted that the English spinster's observations on this evil phase of slavery were 'painful because full of truth.' [15]

The North was not altogether unaware of the two phases of the slave system. The commercial North had maintained for years intimate relations with Southern planters, factors and great cotton merchants. Many Northern bankers and merchants were familiar with Southern slavery at its best. This first-hand knowledge, joined to a financial interest in continuing prosperity for the Cotton Kingdom, conditioned the commercial North to a relatively unemotional attitude toward slavery. Indeed, the Abolitionists were about the only important Northern group which ignored all other than slave pen and auction block.

Furthermore, most of the Northern people retained respect for the State as a sovereign political unit. The Kentucky-Virginia Resolutions of 1798 were still occasionally read at Northern Democratic meetings, and some Northern college professors proclaimed the theoretical validity of Secession. In 1848, Douglas had expressed the attitude of the great body of Northern Democrats, when he informed Southern colleagues: 'We stand up for all of your constitutional rights, in which we will protect you to the last....

---

[13] Frederick Law Olmsted, *A Journey in the Seaboard Slave States*, New York, 1856. My references are from the 1904 Putnam reprint, I, 45. For unsparing pictures of commercial slavery, see Frederic Bancroft, *Slave Trading in the Old South*, Baltimore, 1931; Theodore D. Jervey, *The Slave Trade*, Columbia, S.C., 1920.

[14] Thomas Roderick Dew et al., *Pro-Slavery Argument*, Philadelphia, 1853; 358: 'Virginia is, in fact, a *Negro* raising State for other States; she produces enough for her own supply and six thousand for sale.' This volume, which contained essays by Dew, Simms, Senator James H. Hammond, of South Carolina, and Chancellor William Harper, is one of the strongest Southern defenses. Cf. Alexander Mackey, *The Western World*, London, 1849; II, 145: Virginia 'enjoys the unenviable notoriety of being the chief slave-breeding State.' For the two views as shown by modern historians, see Bancroft, *Slave Trading*, Chapters IV and V, and Beverly B. Munford, *Virginia's Attitude Toward Slavery and Secession*, New York, 1909; Chapters XX, XXI. In this same connection, however, it is well to remember that white women in the North and West were expected to bear enormous families, because a scarcity economy existed and each new child was a labor asset.

[15] Martineau, *Society*, II, 81. For Simms' admission, see Dew, 228–29.

If slavery be a blessing, it is your blessing; if it be a curse, it is your curse; enjoy it — on you rests all the responsibility.' [16]

And yet one of the chief instruments which altered the Northern attitude was fashioned by Southern hands. While the Federal Constitution had provided for the return of fugitives from labor, Congress' initial act had proved ineffective, several Northern States had forbidden local officers to give aid or protection and in some the owner of a fugitive slave was in danger of physical violence if he undertook to apprehend the fugitive. Not only the financial loss but this disregard of their constitutional rights irritated the Southerners, who insisted on a Federal Fugitive Slave Act that would work. With this instrumentation, an integral part of 1850's Compromise, owners of runaway slaves took heart and undertook the recovery of their property.

The chief effect of this endeavor was to convince large Northern groups that manorial slavery was a myth, and that commercial slavery, with all its pictured horrors, was a dragon which must be slain. The gross value of escaped slaves was far less than the annual increment in slave value due to births, the South could well have afforded to recompense each owner of an escaped slave from public funds. But it did not do so and almost every effort at recovery produced great turmoil in the North.

Whenever a fugitive was seized in Boston or in Lancaster, in Ohio or Wisconsin, hordes of new converts were made for Abolition. Thousands of conservative Northerners, hitherto but slightly affected by the Abolitionist propaganda, were brought face to face with one of the harshest and most repellent aspects of commercial slavery, and these attempted slave recoveries greatly increased the North's emotional temperature.

The publication, in 1852, of Mrs. Harriet Beecher Stowe's amazing antislavery novel, *Uncle Tom's Cabin* lighted a new Northern torch. The author, the daughter of one New England preacher and the wife of another, had easily excited sympathies, a flexible imagination and a Puritan conscience. The passage of 1850's Fugitive Slave Act filled the cup of her bitterness to overflowing, and she set to work upon a novel which would arouse the North. The plot creaked, the background was sketchy, her slaves were mere black-faced whites, but for all this, *Uncle Tom* proved one of the great human documents of the century, with emotional effects comparable to those roused by Rousseau or Paine.

She drew the contrast between manorial slavery in Kentucky and the commercial system in the deep South. Her villainous, lecherous planter was a transplanted Yankee, and so was Simon Legree. But in her picture of commercial slavery giving the setting for Legree, Little Eva, the bloodhounds and the ice, she found the material for an appeal to Northern emotion. Those who would admit only the slavery of the manor termed the book fantastic and unjust, but some Southerners confessed it occasionally skirted close to the truth. Moreover in recent months the Northern people had seen the slave-catchers at work, and *Uncle Tom* seemed to hundreds of thousands an unanswerable appeal to human heart and conscience.[17]

[16] See *supra*, 40.

[17] Vernon Louis Parrington, *Main Currents in American Thought*, New York, 1927; II, 376.

Within the year, over a hundred thousand copies were sold, it enjoyed an enormous English sale and was translated into all Continental languages. The following year it was dramatized and soon dozens of troupes were touring the North holding aloft this emotional firebrand.[18] When President Lincoln met Mrs. Stowe, ten years later, he remarked, 'So this is the little lady who brought on this great war.'

Thus the North's psychic equilibrium was deeply disturbed many months before Douglas brought in his Nebraska bill, and probably a sympathetic shift in political attachment was merely a matter of time.[19] Undoubtedly Chase, Sumner, Giddings and Gerrit Smith saw the possibilities of mobilizing and giving political effect to the North's new emotional current. At any event, their 'Appeal of Independent Democrats' acted as a catalytic agent, and the immediacy of Northern response attested their foresight.

The seizure in Boston of one Anthony Burns, a runaway slave, gave great stimulus to their campaign. His identification was absolute, his master was there, demanding him back and the Federal authorities prepared to carry out the law.[20] Aghast at the prospect, Boston's leading Abolitionists called a mass meeting and an enormous throng filled Faneuil Hall to hear Theodore Parker and Wendell Phillips excoriate the Federal Government as a vile catcher of slaves. Then a young minister, Thomas W. Higginson, leaped to the platform, secured recognition, and delivered a fiery harangue. Wild with emotion the audience was transformed into a frenzied mob and poured forth into the street with savage yells, 'To the court-house!'

A huge timber mysteriously passed over the heads of the crowd and the court-house door was burst open. The United States Marshal and an armed guard were ranged inside. A shot was fired, then a whisper ran quickly through the crowd that a man had been killed at the door. The rumor had been well-founded — one of the Marshal's deputies had been killed. The people melted away almost as if by magic and in five minutes the mob was gone.[21]

[18] George L. Aiken wrote one dramatic version of *Uncle Tom*, which was first produced at the Museum in Troy, N.Y. It ran there a hundred nights, and as many in Albany. Taken to New York, it ran two hundred nights continuously at the National Theater; at first two shows were given each day; but the public's demand was so great that a third was added, and the actors stayed from morning to midnight in the theater, eating their meals back-stage. Since then, *Uncle Tom* has never been off the boards. Interestingly enough, the 'Fifties also saw dramatization of the prohibition crusade. William W. Pratt dramatized T. S. Arthur's famous novel, *Ten Nights in a Bar-Room*, and this too had a phenomenal run. I am indebted to Dr. Frederick H. Koch, Director of the Carolina Playmakers, of the University of North Carolina, for reproductions of play-bills of both of these plays, and for data concerning their history.

[19] James Ford Rhodes, *Lectures on the American Civil War*, New York, 1913; 29. calls 1854 a year 'of political and moral excitement,' admits the Maine Law and Know-Nothing hysterias, but declines linking them up to the anti-slavery crusade.

[20] Channing, VI, 107–11. Burns' master, a Colonel Suttle, of Norfolk, Va., had put him in charge of hiring out himself and other slaves. Taking advantage of his opportunities, Burns had hired himself out upon a vessel bound for Boston.

[21] George Murray McConnel of Jacksonville, Ill., at the time a law student at Harvard, was in the audience, and was carried along, willy-nilly, in the mob. His recollections of the episode are recorded in an article which he wrote in November, 1921, for the Pi Alpha Society of Illinois College of Jacksonville. Mr. W. D. Wood, of that city, has furnished me a copy.

This tragedy deepened the determination of the Federal authorities to execute the law. Surrounded by police and marshals, and with an escort of eleven hundred soldiers, the Negro was taken to the wharf and his master carried him back to Virginia and to servitude. As the guarded slave was carried through the streets, the Abolitionists gave every exhibition of frenzied grief. Stores closed their doors; windows were draped in black; the American flag, bordered with mourning, was turned Union down; a coffin, labeled 'The Funeral of Liberty,' was suspended high in the air.[22] 'The Burns outrage' helped light the Northern flame.

One section of the Anti-Nebraska Manifesto had been especially designed to arouse ministers of the North. Chase, Sumner and their aides secured lists of all the Congregational, Presbyterian, Methodist and Baptist ministers in the Northern States, and sent each a copy of the pamphlet, together with the form of a petition to Congress.[23] These efforts soon bore fruit. On March 14 a monster petition was thrust into the hands of Senator Edward Everett, of Massachusetts, who sent it to the Clerk's desk.

His curiosity aroused, Douglas went to the Clerk's desk to look at the mass of papers. It was a petition signed by three thousand New England clergymen, who 'in the name of Almighty God, and in His presence,' did 'solemnly protest' the Nebraska bill. They looked on it as 'a great moral wrong, as a breach of faith eminently unjust to the moral principles of the community, and subversive of all confidence in national engagements; as a measure full of danger to the peace and even the existence of our beloved Union, and exposing us to the righteous judgments of the Almighty.'

The Little Giant had the memorial read to the Senate. 'It is our duty,' he said, indignantly, 'to expose the conduct of men, who, under the cloak of religion, either from ignorance or willful misrepresentation, will avail themselves of their sacred calling to arraign the conduct of Senators here in the discharge of our duties.' The ministers had been led by an atrocious falsehood 'to desecrate the pulpit, and prostitute the sacred desk to the miserable and corrupting influence of party politics.'

The dangerous thing about it was that it was part and parcel of the campaign the Senatorial Abolitionists were carrying on, not to influence their colleague's votes, but 'simply to furnish capital for organizing a great sectional party, and trying to draw the whole religious community in their schemes of political aggrandizement.'

Later Douglas added that the petition was evidence of 'a deliberate attempt to organize the clergy of this country into a great political, sectional party for Abolition schemes.'[24] He was particularly irritated by the fashion

[22] Pierce telegraphed the United States Attorney: 'Incur any expense deemed necessary... to insure the execution of the law,' Nichols, *Pierce*, 361. It was estimated that Burns' return cost the Federal Government $40,000. Before Suttle left, Abolitionists raised a fund of $1200 to buy the slave, but the United States Attorney refused to permit the sale to be made until the case had been heard and decided. After the Negro reached Norfolk, the sale was made. Burns went to Canada and became a preacher.

[23] *Congressional Globe*, Thirty-Third Congress, First Session, App., 636.

[24] Later it was found that Harriet Beecher Stowe had suggested and paid the expense of circulating the petition; Beveridge, II, 221, note.

in which the memorialists had protested 'in the name of Almighty God, and in His presence,' and thus had claimed 'to speak in the name of the Almighty upon a political question pending in the Congress of the United States.' 'I deny their authority,' he said; 'I deny that they have any such commission from the Almighty to decide this question. I deny that our Constitution confers any such right upon them.' [25]

As soon as the Chicago papers published the Senate debate, twenty-five Chicago preachers signed a petition, couched in terms identical with that from New England, but with even more definite assertion of Divine inspiration, and sent it to Douglas himself to present! This the Senator did, but immediately wrote a public letter to the 'Reverend Gentlemen,' appealing to their sober patriotism to cease attempts to interfere in government.

Douglas' friends in Washington praised him warmly for the courageous way he had brought the Abolition clergy to a sharp turn.[26] But the ministers were indignant that their plenary inspiration had been doubted, and described Douglas from their pulpits as an Apocalyptic beast. The Senator read his colleagues excerpts from the ministerial billingsgate, and used it as a further text for his war against parsons in politics. But the organizing group soon secured another petition of 504 Northwestern preachers, with an added resolution denouncing Douglas for his 'want of courtesy and reverence toward man and God.' This too he presented and rebuked.

The campaign among the preachers was next extended to the Northern Legislatures. Within three months' time the law-makers of Massachusetts, Vermont, New Hampshire, Connecticut, New York, Pennsylvania, Ohio, Indiana, Iowa and Wisconsin adopted resolutions and protests, all of which followed faithfully the theme of the Appeal of the Independent Democrats.

Before long every Southern Legislature endorsed the Repeal as an act of justice and reprehended Northern attacks. But at first this was the mere mechanical operation of conventional defense mechanisms and it was months before Southern leaders became really apprehensive. These leaders knew the political significance of these sermons, memorials, petitions and resolves, but did not believe the move could succeed. Toombs saw that 'Greeley, Seward and company are now endeavoring to raise a sectional party upon the ruins of the Whig organization.' But he did not fear it; 'they now look formidable,' he wrote, 'but it is in appearance only. They will die out after the Fall elections. The new organization will be more narrow, sectional, selfish and anti-Liberal even than the old one, and has no head to guide and direct it.' [27]

Southern statesmen greeted the passage of the Kansas-Nebraska Act as

[25] *Congressional Globe*, Thirty-Third Congress, First Session, 617 *et seq*. Douglas thought so much of his speeches in the debate that he had them reprinted in a pamphlet put out by Buell and Blanchard.

[26] *Illinois State Register*, April 20, 1854. Douglas' letter was dated April 6, and was published in the Washington *Sentinel*, April 11, 1854. For speeches, see *Congressional Globe*, Thirty-Third Congress, First Session, App., 654-61.

[27] Toombs to George N. Sanders, Washington, June 13, 1854; original in Watertown, Conn., Library.

a triumph all the greater because 'purely sentimental and intangible,' and expressed amazement that the North would take it as occasion 'for violent eruptions of sectional jealousy.' [28] Douglas was informed that his Nebraska course had put him 'far ahead of all the statesmen of the present day.' From Ohio came word that the agitation was breaking down, his stock was rising again and 'just you wait till '56.' Douglas' speech of March 3 was widely circulated. 'I have risen from its perusal with entire satisfaction,' wrote Horatio Seymour, of New York. Whatever losses the Democratic party in New York had sustained had resulted not from the Nebraska bill, but from the mistakes of the Pierce Administration, whose appointments in New York had 'abolitionized' the party.[29]

For all this, Douglas began to realize that, whatever might have been the intensity of his previous political struggles, he was now involved in a battle without quarter, the stakes of which were more than office, more than fame — the peace and orderly evolution of the Nation as a whole.

But he felt that, given time, and with the full facts before them, the people would make a wise and just decision. As Congress neared adjournment he girded up his loins for battle; now his combat would be transferred from the senatorial arena to the greater battleground of the country as a whole.

Incidentally, Douglas set out to fight the whole brood of emotion-born agitations. He thought Neal Dow's prohibition crusade bottomed on the same desire to interfere in the lives of others which conditioned the anti-slavery drive, and intended to set his face sternly against the Maine Law, and to seek its defeat at the polls in Illinois. His disapproval of the Know-Nothings was equally as determined. Invited to deliver the annual Fourth of July address at Independence Hall in Philadelphia, he accepted, on two conditions: he wanted to lay before the people the truth about the Kansas-Nebraska bill, and to pay his respects to the Know-Nothings. 'No principle of political action could have been devised more hostile to the genius of our institutions, more repugnant to the Constitution, than those which are said to form the test of membership in this Society,' he said. 'To proscribe a man in this country on account of his birthplace or religious faith is subversive of all our ideas and principles of civil and religious freedom. It is revolting to our sense of justice and right.' [30] Coupling Know-Nothings and Anti-Nebraska men as enemies of the public peace, he excoriated the leaders and flayed the purposes of the order.

As Philadelphia's city election had just gone for the Know-Nothings, this was a daring challenge. Douglas was the first American statesman with the courage to do so, and his speech sent a thrill through Democratic ranks North and South. The party press reprinted and lavished praise upon it. The speech encouraged others to take up the cudgels, and it marked the first real Know-Nothing set-back.[31]

[28] Alfriend, *Jefferson Davis*, 95.

[29] D. S. Reid, Raleigh, N.C., June 17; S. S. Cox, Columbus, Ohio, March 24; Horatio Seymour, Buffalo, April 14, 1854; Douglas MSS.

[30] Pamphlet Speech in possession of Mr. Martin F. Douglas.

[31] Memphis *Appeal*, Aug. 2, 1854, termed it a 'thrilling speech,' the best specimen of American eloquence.

For three months word had been coming to Douglas that there was trouble in Illinois, where the Nebraska bill had aroused opposition of an unexpected intensity and already there was talk of a new opposition party — the Anti-Nebraska men. If the Little Giant expected his course to be sustained by his own constituents, he must hasten home. But Douglas believed he could reason with the people of his State. He recalled a similar occasion four years before, when there had been great resentment against the Compromise of 1850. And yet, when he had bravely faced the people, he had forced them to hear the reasons for the measures of adjustment and finally Illinois had approved. He believed that he could once more appeal to the sober common sense of the people. With Congress' adjournment in August, he turned his steps toward Illinois.

CHAPTER XII

THE BLACK REPUBLICANS

FOR all Douglas' apprehensions, he seemed not to have comprehended that Illinois was being shaken to its political depths. From the beginning of the year, each of the major agitations had been flaming in the State. The Prohibitionists secured thousands of converts for their Maine law. Know-Nothing lodges sprang up as if by magic, and nowhere stronger than in Chicago. The excitement over the Nebraska bill was even more intense.

By February the evidences of Illinois' revolt were such that Douglas began to fear that the Legislature, which was in special session, would formally disapprove it. To his surprise and delight, the Legislature proceeded to endorse the Kansas-Nebraska bill, but this action was far from reflecting the temper of the State.[1]

In truth, not only had the Little Giant's bill shocked large masses of people of Illinois but also his enemies believed that he had made a fatal blunder. Sincere opposition to the Nebraska bill joined with an equally sincere desire to divide Douglas' political inheritance in spurring the Opposition leaders forward. Douglas' friends saw the danger; some felt that his course had made it impossible to follow him any farther, but most subdued their qualms and rallied to his cause.

Now, as for years past, the Old-Line Whigs — such men as Orville Browning, John T. Stuart, David Davis, Stephen T. Logan and Abraham Lincoln — were the backbone of the Opposition. Illinois Whiggery was made of sterner stuff than it was in many other places, and could still put up a respectable opposition. This year, too, the Whigs were to have three important accessions of strength — the insurgent Anti-Nebraska Democrats, the Know-Nothings and the German immigrants.

The Appeal of the Independent Democrats wreaked havoc on the Douglas party structure in the State. Such important leaders as Lyman Trumbull, Norman B. Judd, Sidney Breese, John A. McClernand and Gustav Koerner gave public expression to their dislike of the 'Nebraska humbug.' Meetings began to be called over the State, and the Anti-Nebraska Democrats were as zealous as Whigs and Free-Soilers in denouncing any policy which would permit extension of slave territory. Regular Democratic leaders undertook to counter this both by holding meetings of their own to influence the people, and by cracking the whip on the recusants. While often successful, more often these succeeded only in showing the depth of the party chasm.

In the revolt's incipient stages, Douglas felt that he could set up unqualified acceptance of the Kansas-Nebraska bill as a new test of party regularity,

[1] Lincoln to Joshua F. Speed, Springfield, Aug. 24, 1855, *Works*, II, 286, claims 'Douglas' orders came on to have resolutions passed approving the bill.' Actually Douglas' 'orders' had been that the Legislature, in special session, had no right to act on the matter, cf. Douglas to Lanphier, Washington, Feb. 13, 1854; Patton MSS.

and sent word that any who would not subscribe to the new faith were party deserters from the standard, and abettors of Abolitionism. Democratic county conventions passed stirring resolutions of endorsement and all the ordinary party machinery was put at work.

These tactics evoked strong resentment, and such a party stalwart as McClernand, in a speech at Alton, denounced Douglas' new test as 'simply an act of senseless and outrageous proscription,' instituted on the Senator's authority alone, and McClernand refused to 'bend the knee to Baal.' McClernand finally wheeled into line; others, like John M. Palmer, who was anxious to return to the State Senate, backed and filled for months, and finally took stand against the Douglas policy; still others, like Trumbull and Koerner, the Lieutenant-Governor, went completely beyond the pale.

'The Nebraska dose is a hard one to take by a good portion of the Locos,' an Opposition leader jubilated; 'Pierce, Douglas & Co., however, mean to compel them to swallow it without sugarcoating the pill. They must indorse the Measure from its inception.... Democrats are already predicting a visit to the head waters of Salt River in November.' [2]

By one of the anomalies of practical politics, the German immigrants and the Know-Nothings, whose interests and purposes were fundamentally antagonistic, joined in the Anti-Nebraska campaign. The Germans were alarmed over the bill's provisions as to citizenship and office-holding, they resented Clayton's amendment, and the Abolitionists convinced them its whole purpose was to exclude the foreign-born from the new Territories so as to establish slavery there. Chicago's immigrants were raised to a frenzy against Douglas and the Nebraska bill and they began holding protest meetings. On the night of March 16, one such group blackguarded Douglas for an hour and then marched to the public square, to burn him in effigy.

While the Little Giant's Chicago friends reported that the actual burning had been done by 'a few boys and drunken rascals,' and comforted him with the assurance that such excesses would react in his favor, and that the recoil would be 'terrible and complete,' it was an ominous incident.[3] When first Douglas and Shields canvassed the Democrats in the Illinois delegation, all agreed that the Nebraska bill was right. After the Chicago incident the more cautious Illinois Congressmen began to desert. But however much others might waver, Douglas would not shift. 'Let what may happen,' he wrote, 'I shall persevere and abide the consequences. I know the bill is right.' [4]

[2] McClernand speech, reprinted in Carlinville, Ill., *Free Democrat*, Oct. 27, 1859; also reprinted in pamphlet of speech of Congressman William Kellogg, of Illinois, before House, March 13, 1860, Buell and Blanchard, printers; 15–16; for other steps in his decision, see Alton *Courier*, Oct. 12, 19, *Illinois State Register*, Oct. 19, 1854; Palmer, *Personal Reminiscences*, 68–69; Alton *Courier*, Aug. 31, 1854; James Knox to Richard Yates, Knoxville, Ill., Sept. 4, 1854, Chicago Historical Society MSS. Browning, *Diary*, I, 129 *et seq.*

[3] Samuel Ashton, Chicago, March 18, Thomas Hoyne, Chicago, March 18, 1854; Douglas MSS.

[4] Douglas to Ninian W. Edwards, Washington, April 13, 1854; Chicago Historical Society MSS.

While the Germans denounced Douglas for his unfriendliness to the immigrants, the Know-Nothings charged him with the heinous sin of over-friendliness to the foreign-born. Even before the Senator's Fourth of July speech, the rumor was rife in Chicago that he would be mobbed when he came there.[5] After his blistering denunciation of the secret order, there was no limit to Know-Nothing wrath.

During the summer Illinois was beset with anti-slavery agitators. Chase and Giddings, of Ohio; Cassius M. Clay, of Kentucky; Ichabod Codding, the Chicago Abolitionist, and many others ranged the State, preaching the enormity of the Nebraska bill and the necessity of a new Northern party to halt slavery's extension, Giddings being denounced by the Democratic papers as an 'open-mouthed Abolitionist disunionist,' and Codding as an 'itinerant spouter of treason.' [6] A host of Illinois notabilities aided in the campaign, some championing Prohibition as well as Anti-Slavery, others speaking a good word for 'the Sons of Revolutionary Sires,' and still others playing on the Germans' racial pride. All, however, denounced Douglas, the slavocracy and the repeal of the Missouri Compromise. When Lyman Trumbull opened his campaign for Congress with a trumpet-blast against Nebraska, the Opposition's cup of joy overflowed. Theirs was the rising tide.[7]

Such conditions were not confined to Illinois, but were astir from Maine to Wisconsin. In the early Summer there was a general concentration of the elements opposed to the Democratic party and several great meetings were called to lay the foundation for a new party. At Jackson, Michigan, on July 6, in response to a call signed by ten thousand Michigan citizens, an immense body of men gathered in an oak grove, and with enthusiasm and determination adopted a platform and nominated candidates for a new political party, which they called Republican.

In August Iowa, so far a rock-ribbed Democratic State, elected James W. Grimes, a Free-Soil Whig, as Governor, by the close margin of 2000 votes. Overconfidence was partly responsible for this Democratic disaster, for party leaders so poorly sensed the situation that Dodge and Jones, the two Senators, remained in Washington during the campaign's critical stages. Also Grimes had cleverly inflamed the Iowa Germans over a chance remark Butler, of South Carolina, had made during the Senate debate. But the fact of defeat remained.[8] The next month word came that Maine, banner Democratic

---

[5] *Illinois State Register*, June 15, 1854.   [6] *Ibid.*, Sept. 7, 9, 1854.

[7] *Illinois Journal*, Springfield, Sept. 28, 1854.

[8] For the best analysis of the Iowa upset, see Professor F. I. Herriott, 'James W. Grimes *versus* the Southrons,' reprint from *Annals of Iowa*, XV, 323–57, and same author's 'A Neglected Factor in the Anti-Slavery Triumph in Iowa in 1854,' German-American Historical Society of Illinois, *Yearbook* 1918. Iowa had been settled chiefly from the South; its early population had left the South to get away from the slave system, but was bitterly hostile to Abolitionists. On Jan. 1, 1854, the opposition to the Democratic party in Iowa was discordant and disorganized. In the early months of the year, many of its nominees for State office refused to run. Grimes, who was eventually agreed on as candidate for Governor, was an able, forthright Free-Soil Whig. During the Senate debate on Feb. 24, 1854, Butler, of South Carolina, undertook to answer Abolitionist attacks on the Kansas-Nebraska bill. Among other things, he said: 'The slave-holder, with his slaves well governed, forms a relation that is innocent enough, and useful enough. I believe that it is a population which Iowa tomorrow would prefer to an

State of New England, had elected a Fusionist Governor, over a friend of Pierce.

The public saw the evidence of a political revolution and through the Northwest the damage was great.[9] The Illinois Opposition leaders renewed their efforts to find a common denominator. Whig papers urged a State Convention 'of all parties and divisions of parties, opposed to the repeal of the Missouri Compromise.[10] Early in August at a meeting at Ottawa, the name 'Republican' was adopted, soon the Whigs of the First Congressional District adopted the same name, and in September other conventions proclaimed themselves Republicans, and a call was issued for a State Convention at Bloomington on October 5. A new party was in birth.[11]

This appropriation of the name 'Republican' brought instant protest, for the word had treasured Democratic associations dating from Thomas Jefferson's founding title in 1800, of 'the Democratic-Republican' party. The clumsiness of the hyphen had caused dropping of the' word, but no new and sectional party could claim 'Republican' without contest.

This new Republican party, Douglas was soon to charge, was not national but 'a purely sectional party, with a platform which cannot cross the Ohio River and a creed which inevitably brings the North and South into hostile collision.' In view of the emphasis on the Negro, it should be called the Black Republican party, an adjective which should be insisted on.[12]

The defection of newspaper support also embarrassed the Democrats. Scores of editors who had hitherto followed Douglas foreswore their allegiance. 'If I am to be ruined at all,' John W. Scripps, of the Chicago *Daily Press*, wrote his father, 'let it be from meeting the responsibilities of my position with a conscience void of offense toward God and man.' 'Long John' Wentworth became a rabid Anti-Nebraska man and the Chicago *Democrat* teemed with articles abusive of the Little Giant. Joseph Medill, the new editor of the Chicago *Tribune*, sought to inflame every element against Chicago's Senator. Soon every Chicago paper was ranged against the author of the Kansas-Nebraska bill.[13] Douglas saw that he must correct

inundation of those men coming as emigrants from a foreign country, wholly unacquainted with the institutions of this country — and nearly all continental comers are of that class.' Northern Democratic Senators realized the dynamite in this. The next morning Butler sought to explain it as a 'playful remark' and denied any comparison of blacks and Germans. The incident attracted little notice, but the editor of the Burlington, Iowa, *Telegraph*, caught it up and on March 18 reprinted it. Grimes adopted the issue as one with election possibilities, and began denouncing Butler and the Southern slavocracy from the stump. The Germans in the State were set on fire. Prohibition and Know-Nothingism were also important factors. The Democrats did not realize their danger. On August 7, Grimes won by 2110 majority. Butler's 'playful remark' had lost the State.

[9] James Knox to Richard Yates, Knoxville, Ill., Sept. 4, 1854, Chicago Historical Society MSS.: 'The Iowa election *hurts* the Locos, and will help us...'

[10] Tazewell *Mirror* and *Illinois Journal*, quoted in *Illinois State Register*, Aug. 3, 1854.

[11] Beveridge, II, 264, quoting Rock River *Democrat*, Aug. 8; Ottawa Weekly *Republican*, Aug. 19, Sept. 16; Chicago *Free West*, Sept. 7; Aurora *Guardian*, Sept. 21; Ottawa *Free Trade*, Sept. 15, 1854.

[12] *Congressional Globe*, Thirty-Fourth Congress, First Session, App., 392.

[13] Illinois State Historical Society, *Transactions*, 1924, 105. The *Tribune* thoroughly convinced

this Chicago situation, and before leaving Washington, arranged for the establishment of a new daily in Chicago, and saw to it that presses, type and quarters were procured. He persuaded James W. Sheahan, an able newspaper man of Washington, to go to Chicago as its editor, and in August, the Chicago *Times* began publication, and at last assured the Little Giant of faithful and intelligent journalistic support in his home city.

When Congress adjourned late in August, Douglas started for Illinois. At first he was 'in fine spirits,' but the latter stages of his journey gave further evidence of his new opprobrium. In several cities he was greeted by denunciatory newspaper editorials; in one Ohio village a group of indignant women termed him a Judas and presented him with thirty pieces of silver. 'I could travel from Boston to Chicago by the light of my own effigy,' he was later to say. 'All along the Western Reserve of Ohio I could find my effigy upon every tree we passed.' [14] Announcing his arrival in Chicago, the *Tribune* warned that, if the Senator 'attempts to get up what he calls a "vindication" of his crimes, if he collects around him a crowd of Irish rowdies and grog-house politicians, and attempts to send forth their approbation as the "voice of the people of Chicago," it will not be our fault if he arouses the lion he cannot tame.' [15]

Despite the many evidences of the ugly temper of the crowd, Douglas was not daunted. Soon he announced that on the evening of September 1, he would address his Chicago fellow citizens on the subject of the Nebraska bill. Reports of plans to precipitate a riot did not change his plans. 'They threaten to mob,' he wrote Lanphier, 'but I have no fears.' [16]

There was, in fact, an organized effort to interfere with Douglas' meeting. The Abolition papers printed the most outrageous charges. Douglas had selected a bodyguard of five hundred Irishmen, all armed, one hinted. 'Every revolver and pistol in the stores of the city has been sold,' another warned. The Irish, it was claimed, would 'compel silence while Douglas spoke,' and 'a season of violence' was in store. All these publications were to arouse the anti-slavery partisans to humiliate the Little Giant 'and, if possible, to prevent his being heard.' [17] Douglas himself believed that the Know-Nothings had telegraphed to New York for arms.

At one o'clock on the afternoon of the day appointed, the flags on several vessels at the docks were half-masted. With twilight, church bells began to toll a funeral dirge which continued until the hour for the Senator's appear-

shipowners, shipmasters, sailors, and longshoremen that Douglas was an enemy of lake commerce, merely because of this vote. The innuendo was that his interest in the Illinois Central had caused him to oppose the development of the Port of Chicago.

[14] Daniel E. Sickles to Buchanan, New York, Aug. 17, 1854; Buchanan MSS. Sickles, who had ridden from Washington to New York with Douglas, reported his good spirits and optimistic attitude. For later trip details, see Philadelphia *Press*, Sept. 26, 1859; Rhodes, I, 496.

[15] Chicago *Tribune*, quoted in Washington *Sentinel*, Sept. 1, 1854.

[16] Douglas to Lanphier, Chicago, Aug. 25, 1854; Patton MSS.

[17] Sheahan, 271–72; Chicago *Daily Democratic Press*, Sept. 4, 1854. The Anti-Nebraska men made a desperate effort to convince the public that Douglas' cohorts intended to overawe the crowd by arms.

ance. The heat of the night was oppressive but an excited throng of eight thousand filled the Public Square, while hundreds were in windows, on balconies, and even on near-by roofs. Many in the gathering were Know-Nothings, 'armed to the teeth.'

Douglas began to speak amid an ominous silence. He had spoken but a few sentences when there was a 'storm of hisses,' but he calmly stood his ground.[18]

A temporary lull gave Douglas the chance to say a few more words; the audience did not understand the Nebraska bill, he began, because the papers which had so outrageously vilified him had never published it. Now cat-calls, boos and vile epithets were added to the hisses. The Senator's friends, wild with anger, wanted to fight, but Douglas would not let them — he would handle the mob. His 'bold, defiant manner' probably prevented a fearful riot.[19]

While the pandemonium continued unabated, the Little Giant read a letter warning that, if he tried to speak, he would be roughly treated. A chorus of groans, hisses and ribald shouts sought to drown his voice, but he shouted so that he was heard above the infernal din. Then he denounced Medill's *Tribune* for having precipitated the ruffianly proceedings. The crowd cheered lustily for the *Tribune*. He shouted that he had come there to speak and would stay until the crowd heard him. The rowdies chanted:

'We won't go home till morning, till morning, till morning,
'We won't go home till morning, till daylight doth appear.' [20]

Now the crowd's temper grew uglier, and it began to shout questions at the speaker it would not let speak. But Douglas would not be diverted from a denunciation of the Know-Nothings. When finally he got it out, there was a deep chorus of groans.

Douglas stood there for nearly four hours, hoping that the tumult would subside and allow him to finish his defense. But the din showed no sign of diminishing and finally he admitted defeat. He pulled his watch deliberately from his pocket and looked at it under the gaslight. Taking advantage of a lull in the din, he shouted in stentorian tones: 'Abolitionists of Chicago! It is now Sunday morning. I'll go to church and you may go to Hell.' [21] The crowd jeered as, guarded by friends, he made his way to his carriage and was driven to the Tremont House.

[18] Such at least was the account of the Chicago *Times*, and of Douglas' friends; Chicago *Tribune*, Chicago *Daily Democrat*, Sept. 2, 3, 4, 1854, claimed the Senator had been immediately enraged and had hurled insults at the crowd. These accounts, however, were highly colored, partisan and unreliable. New York *Tribune*, Sept. 7, 1854, has an interesting account.

[19] Sheahan, 272–73, reports that some of the armed Know-Nothings who were in the mob told him afterwards 'that nothing prevented bloodshed that night but the bold and defiant manner in which Douglas maintained his ground.' Horace White, who was on the platform to report for the *Tribune*, claimed years later 'there was nothing like violence at any time.' See Horace White, 'Abraham Lincoln in 1854,' Address, Springfield, Ill., Jan. 30, 1908; 8–9.

[20] Chicago *Free West*, Sept. 7, 1854.

[21] Sheahan, 271–73; Cutts, 98–101; Johnson, 259, quoting New York *Times*, Sept. 6, 1854, but Flint, 74, has him say '... while you can go to the devil in your own way.'

Thus opened Stephen A. Douglas' campaign for vindication in Illinois. The mob scene was a national sensation and most of the press condemned it in scathing words.[22] Indignation was particularly keen in the South. 'If your friends failed to make you President in 1852,' wrote Senator Brown, of Mississippi, 'your enemies will succeed in making you the first man in the Republic in 1856.'[23] Douglas' own determination was intensified. After speaking at a Democratic rally at Indianapolis, on September 6, he threw himself into the Illinois campaign.

His first engagements were in the Anti-Nebraska territory close to Chicago.[24] Everywhere he was met with a storm of abuse and 'Judas' became a byword, while 'Stephen Arnold Douglas, with the accent on the *Arnold*,' came from many pulpits.[25] Burning effigies, offensive signs and ugly placards greeted his eyes as he entered many towns. On several occasions Abolitionists attempted to repeat the tactics of the Chicago outrage but never again with success.

Douglas' basic theme was the fundamental American principle of self-government, and on it he built up his argument; he would tell of the development of the West, and the national problems caused thereby. He would recite the history of the Missouri Compromise, how it had been a sectional bargain, and how the Northern Whigs, Abolitionists and Free-Soilers had breached its spirit. He told of his own efforts, as a matter of good faith, to carry the line to the Pacific, efforts defeated by Northern votes. Then the Compromise of 1850 had altered the national policy; the idea of a geographical line had been dropped, and that of local control, of Popular Sovereignty, had been substituted. Then it was logic and good faith to apply the new principle to the Kansas-Nebraska territory. But soil, climate and natural products insured that slavery could not long exist there.

His excoriation of the Know-Nothings, was savage and unrelenting, and it had some effect upon the Germans, many of whom became restive over further alliance with their own worst enemies.

Such a speech and such an earnest, forceful speaker were bound to have effect and Douglas was quick to sense it. 'We have had glorious meetings at Joliet, Morris and Ottawa,' he wrote Sheahan from La Salle.

But his new Chicago organ must attack the Know-Nothings with real vigor, 'that will bring the Germans and all other Foreigners and Catholics to our side.' Furthermore, Sheahan must treat the *Tribune*, the *Daily Democratic Press*, and the *Democrat* all as organs of the Abolitionists without distinction.[26]

[22] Washington *National Intelligencer*, Sept. 16, 1854; the Washington *Union*, through September reprinted editorial denunciation by papers of all sections.

[23] A. G. Brown, Washington, Sept. 8, 1854; Douglas MSS.

[24] *Illinois State Register*, Springfield, Sept. 7, 1854, announced that he would speak at Joliet, Monday; Morris, Tuesday; Ottawa, Wednesday; La Salle, Thursday; and so on through the month.

[25] Rhodes, I, 496.

[26] Douglas to Sheahan, La Salle, Ill., Sept. 14, 1854; Sheahan MSS. The Senator knew further that, to have real influence, the *Times* must be something more than a political organ — it must be a real newspaper, and he insisted that Sheahan 'pay more attention to the market

Douglas could not deal such sturdy blows without being buffeted himself. The Know-Nothings charged that he believed Catholicism the only true faith; that he had said that ignorant foreigners should be dealt with better than 'descendants of Revolutionary Sires,' and his 'coarsest and most abusive epithets' had been applied to native-born patriots. He had 'cursed the Christian in the Senate,' and 'the true American' from the stump.[27]

The depths of the *argumentum ad hominem* were reached, however, in the persistent attack on the Senator's alleged personal interest in slaves. He had brought about the repeal of the Compromise so as to swell his own wealth, it was charged in Illinois and all over the North. A St. Louis paper printed a list of Douglas' slaves, analyzed their value, and said the repeal would add ten thousand dollars to their cash worth. Lincoln's organ, the *Illinois Journal*, demanded that the *Register* print the number of the Senator's slaves, to show his 'peculiar interest' in the peculiar institution.[28]

The Opposition also sought to make capital out of renewed Mormon flare-ups. This proud, unhappy sect, in its attempts to establish a new commonwealth on the Great Salt Lake, had come into conflict with the pioneers and trappers who theretofore had controlled the Deseret area.[29] Once more the Halls of Congress rang with denunciation of polygamy, and the Illinois Free-Soilers charged that Douglas' Popular Sovereignty would permit the Mormons to bring Utah into the Union as a polygamous State. Lincoln's Springfield organ called Thomas L. Harris, a Douglas follower who was seeking re-election to the House, 'Polygamy Harris.'[30]

The Opposition leaders also set their own speakers on Douglas' trail; at nearly every meeting one would ask to divide the Senator's time, and, if refused, would announce an answering speech a few hours hence. The speakers were shrewdly chosen to conform to local feeling. In the north of the State, avowed Abolitionists were set up against him; in the central portion, Old-Line Whigs; in the south, Anti-Nebraska Democrats. Douglas generally answered that the people had come there to hear him — let the Abolitionists get up their own crowd.

Toward the close of September the Little Giant went to Bloomington, where a great crowd had gathered. His hotel suite filled with callers. On the sideboard, as was the custom of the day, his host had placed a decanter

reports and the commercial articles. Let no expense be spared on this point. Tell Cook that he must furnish all necessary funds for the paper and I will furnish money soon. I am making arrangements for that purpose. Excuse my direct mode of talking, but these things are necessary.' Cook was Isaac Cook, a Chicago business man and postmaster.

[27] *Illinois Journal*, Sept. 25, 1854, quoting La Salle *Watchman; ibid.*, Oct. 2, 1854, quoting Bloomington *Pantagraph; Illinois State Register*, Oct. 3, 1854.

[28] *Illinois Journal*, Sept. 18, 23, 1854. The St. Louis *Intelligencer* had made the estimate.

[29] Brigham Young, Great Salt Lake, April 29, 1854, Douglas MSS., is a long and cogent letter of expostulation. Young sought to emphasize that the Mormons were not forgetting the interest or welfare of the people of the United States; on the contrary, 'we have already sent a large and new group of our elders to operate in the States east of the Rock Mountains, and to purchase lands and farm settlements in the neighborhood of Cincinnati, St. Louis,' etc.

[30] *Illinois Journal*, Sept. 14, 20, 23, 28; Oct. 30, 31, 1854. The *State Register* responded with denunciation of the 'Utah humbug.'

of 'red liquor,' a pitcher of water and glasses. Douglas was careful to invite his callers to have a drink, if they wished. Among those who paid their respects was Abraham Lincoln, who had come to Bloomington in the hope that Douglas would divide time with him. After chatting for a few moments, he arose to go.

'Mr. Lincoln, won't you take something?' Douglas then asked, according to a report which spread like wide-fire.

'No, I think not,' Lincoln answered.

'Why; are you a member of any Temperance Society?' the Senator persisted.

'No!' Lincoln answered. 'I am not a member of any Temperance Society, but I am temperate *in this*, that I don't drink anything.' [31]

Shortly after Lincoln's departure, Jesse E. Fell asked Douglas to divide time with Lincoln. The Senator seemed annoyed. 'No,' he said, after a brief hesitation. 'I won't do it. I come to Chicago, I am met by an Abolitionist; I come to the center of the State and am met by an Old-Line Whig; I come to the South and am met by a Democrat. I can't hold the Abolitionist responsible for what the Whig says; I can't hold the Whig responsible for what the Abolitionist says, and I can't hold either responsible for what the Democrat says. It looks like "dogging" a man over the State. This is my meeting. The people came here to hear me, and I want to talk to them.' [32]

That afternoon a huge throng heard the Democratic champion, whose speech was along the usual lines. That night an 'immense' audience at the court-house heard Lincoln.[33] Bloomington was 'dry' territory and the day's temperance story had swelled his crowd.

Douglas was to speak at Springfield on October 3. The State Fair was in progress, and because of the two events there was 'an unprecedented concourse of people.' [34] But the Opposition converged its speakers; Palmer, Breese, Taylor were there and Trumbull was expected. Douglas was greeted at the railroad station by a brass band and as he rode to his hotel, Hopkins' Artillery Company thundered its salutes. His meeting was to have been held at a grove where seats had been prepared for five thousand, but because of a downpour the meeting was changed to the Hall of Representatives.

Douglas was greeted with loud cheers — he was in the house of his friends. His speech was new to his hearers, who listened with growing sympathy. His telling blows at the Know-Nothings stirred the Democrats to a high pitch of delight. It was 'impossible to do justice' to the speech, the *State Register* exulted; it was 'unanswerable.' [35]

[31] James S. Ewing's statement, in *Abraham Lincoln, By Some Men Who Knew Him*, Bloomington, Ill. 1910; Jesse W. Fell MSS.; quoted by Beveridge, II, 241–42. Beveridge did not put great faith in the story, for he labeled it as a mere report. Its circulation, however, was immediate and its effect not inconsiderable. Ewing was among the callers on Douglas that day.

[32] James S. Ewing, in *Abraham Lincoln, By Some Men Who Knew Him*, 55–57.

[33] *Illinois Journal*, Springfield, Sept. 29, 1854.

[34] Herndon, II, 367.

[35] Issue of Oct. 4, 1854. While the *Register* printed no *verbatim* account, its references, and Lincoln's, establish the tenor as that of Douglas' general campaign speech.

While Douglas was speaking, one of his friends noticed Abraham Lincoln walking nervously back and forth in the lobby of the hall, all the while listening intently to every word that came from Douglas' lips.[36] When the meeting broke up, and the crowd was passing out of the hall, Lincoln's tall, gaunt figure appeared on the landing of a stairway and he announced that, the next afternoon, Lyman Trumbull would address the people there in the same hall, replying to Senator Douglas. But if anything happened to prevent Trumbull from coming, he himself would make the reply.[37] Trumbull was not there that next afternoon — but Lincoln was. He had prepared carefully for his address; it was his second bid for a place in the political sun.

When Douglas brought in his measure for the repeal of the Missouri Compromise, so shrewd a politician as Lincoln doubtless saw that the gates of opportunity were again opening for him. During the long debate in Congress, he read the *National Intelligencer*, scrutinized the debates and studied Douglas' powerful arguments. As soon as the Illinois campaign opened, Lincoln began to prepare to take part in it. 'He had been nosing for weeks in the State Library,' the *State Register* said, 'pumping his brain and his imagination for points and arguments.' He had studied census reports, reviewed the voluminous literature and tested out his ideas. On August 26, he made his speech for the first time, at Winchester, and repeating it for weeks, polished it, buttressed the arguments and gave his stories point.[38]

On the afternoon of October 4, Lincoln mounted the platform, clad in his shirt sleeves, without collar or tie, and his trousers were short and ill-fitting. Douglas, whom he had invited to reply if he wished, was in the front of the audience, well-clad, well-groomed and confident. Then, in a thin, rasping voice, Lincoln began a speech that opened a great career.[39]

Theretofore the Opposition had assumed solely sectional grounds. Chase, Sumner, Wade, Wendell Phillips and the whole brood of Abolitionists had assailed the Kansas-Nebraska bill as a plot of the 'Slave Power,' had accused Douglas of making a presidential bid and had attacked the South. Lincoln did none of these. He proposed to speak on the repeal of the Missouri Compromise, 'and the propriety of its restoration,' but he did not intend 'to question the patriotism or to assail the motives of any man or class of men, but rather, to confine myself strictly to the naked merits of the question. I also wish to be no less than national in all the positions I may take.' In addition, he wished 'to make and keep the distinction between the existing institution and the extension of it.'

His first attack was on Douglas' proclaimed neutrality as to whether the people of a Territory chose slavery or freedom. Lincoln termed 'this de-

---

[36] Memorandum left by Samuel S. Gilbert of Carlinville, Ill., a friend of Douglas, who was in Springfield for the occasion. This memorandum was found in Mr. Gilbert's papers after his death, and a copy has been furnished me by his son, Mr. Charles F. Gilbert of York, Nebraska.

[37] Gilbert, *Recollections*. The statement was that 'we' — the opposition leaders — had sent for Trumbull, and expected him to be there.

[38] Beveridge, II, 238; 243.

[39] For text of this speech, see Lincoln, *Works*, II, 198–248. It is known as the Peoria speech, for Lincoln did not write it all out until Peoria. For abstract, see Beveridge, II, 245–63.

clared indifference,' a form of covert zeal for the spread of slavery, and he hated it 'because of the monstrous injustice of slavery itself.' For this he did not blame the slave-holders, for 'they are just what we would be in their situation.' He could not blame them, for 'if all earthly power were given me, I should not know what to do as to the existing institution.' He favored settlement in Liberia, but this could only be done 'in the long run.' He hoped to see 'gradual emancipation' but would not condemn the South for not adopting it. He acknowledged the South's Constitutional rights, 'not grudgingly, but fully and fairly,' and would give them 'any legislation for the reclaiming of their fugitives which should not in its stringency be more likely to carry a free man into slavery than our ordinary criminal laws are to hang an innocent one.'

But he would not countenance permitting slavery to go into free territory; the repeal of the law forbidding slavery in Nebraska was no better than would be repeal of 'the law which forbids the bringing of slaves from Africa.' There was need for giving Nebraska some Territorial organization, but it could have been done without the repeal of the Missouri Compromise; in the preceding Congress, the bill, without any repeal provision, had been 'within an ace' of passing. The passage with it was a mistake, for the repeal was 'wrong — wrong in its direct effect, letting slavery into Kansas and Nebraska, and wrong in its prospective principle, allowing it to spread to every other part of the wide world where men can be found inclined to take it.' In handling the claim that 'equal justice to the South' demanded that Southerners be allowed equal privileges in the Territories for their property, he termed this 'perfectly logical if there is no difference between hogs and Negroes.'

Lincoln had admitted that the Slave States had a right to perpetuate the system indefinitely within their own borders. Now he undertook to show either that the Territories did not or ought not to have this same right. Douglas had insisted that the whites in the Territories were good enough to govern themselves; why, then, were they not 'good enough to govern a few miserable Negroes.' Lincoln answered 'that no man is good enough to govern another man without that other's consent.' Now he asked: 'Is not Nebraska, while a Territory, a part of us? Do we not own the country? And if we surrender the control of it, do we not surrender the right of self-government? If you say we shall not control it, because it is only part, the same is true of every other part; and when all the parts are gone, what has become of the whole? What is there left of us? What use for the General Government when there is nothing left for it to govern?'

His answer to Popular Sovereignty was that slavery in a Territory was not the 'exclusive concern' of those who lived there; the whole Nation was interested and wanted them for the homes of free men. 'You say this question should be left to the people of Nebraska,' he said, 'because they are more particularly interested.... What better moral right have thirty-one citizens of Nebraska to say that the thirty-second shall not hold slaves than the people of the thirty-one States have to say that slavery shall not go to the thirty-second State at all?' This gave Douglas the chance to answer that thirty-one citizens in a State or Territory might force the thirty-second into obedience to a local law or institution, but, save in matters granted by the Federal Constitution to the General Government, that number of States could not force another State.

The chief further argument in the speech was that, up to the time of the repeal of the Missouri Compromise, all legislation on slavery had treated the institution as though it would ultimately be extinguished. Douglas' Kansas-Nebraska bill had made it possible to extend slave areas and was a backward step, but the damage could be repaired by restoring the Missouri line.

Lincoln had become passionate in making this speech, sweat had poured from his brow, and he had quivered with emotion. His hearers, deeply affected, had been alternately still as death and wildly enthusiastic. Herndon, Lincoln's law partner, exulted that Douglas had been 'crushed.' [40]

But if Douglas had been 'crushed,' they had forgotten to tell him of it, for he leaped to the platform and spoke for an hour and a half. Lincoln had not forced him off his foundations. The Kansas-Nebraska Act had not been designed to increase the area of slavery and would not do so. Slavery had never been prevented anywhere by Congressional interference, but local self-government had done so in every free State — a principle which had begun when Man had first been given the choice between good and evil and had been held responsible for his choice. The Federal Constitution had provided for Congressional action to prohibit the external slave trade, but had no provision to permit Congress to exclude slavery from the Territories. The American Government had been made by white people for white people and not for Negroes.

Point by point, the Little Giant examined Lincoln's statements of fact, exposed the errors and overturned the logical slips. Douglas had demolished the Goliath of the Anti-Nebraska Black Republican Fusionists, the *State Register* ecstatically declared, and 'the thunders of the applauding multitude shook the State House from turret top to foundation stone.' A St. Louis correspondent reported that the Senator had 'flayed his opponent alive,' and even Herndon, Lincoln's Springfield partner, confessed that 'Douglas ... had power.... He is the grand master of human passion and rules the crowd with an iron rule.' [41]

Douglas turned from this encounter to a continuation of his canvass of the State. Lincoln turned from it to a hasty buggy ride to escape from a political dilemma. The radical element of the Opposition had called a State Convention for Springfield for October 6 and Ichabod Codding, Owen Lovejoy and men of that type would predominate in its attendance. Although an Abolitionist himself, Herndon told Lincoln to make an excuse and get out of town at once. So Lincoln found legal business in Tazewell County, 'hitched his horse to his ramshackle buggy and made off on the wobbly but effective wheels of political prudence,' staying away until the Abolitionists

---

[40] Editorial in *Illinois State Journal*, Oct. 5, 1854, which Herndon (II, 367–69) says was his own.

[41] For Douglas' rejoinder, see *Illinois State Register*, Oct. 6, 1854; *Missouri Republican*, reprinted in Washington *Sentinel*, Oct. 19, 1854; abstract of rejoinder in Lincoln Peoria speech, Lincoln, *Works*, II, 249–62. Herndon, in his *Journal* editorial, termed Douglas 'the greatest demagogue in America.'

had met, elected Lincoln a member of their committee, endorsed his speech and left.[42]

Herndon now got four friends to sign a petition asking Lincoln to keep after Douglas 'until he run him into his hole or make him holler, Enough!' Lincoln intercepted Douglas in Peoria on the afternoon of October 16. After the Senator's address the band struck up, the crowd shouted, and there were calls for Lincoln, who announced he would talk there that night. It was a rejoinder, the chief point being that Douglas had 'no very vivid impression that the Negro is human, and consequently has no idea that there can be any moral question in legislating about him,' while the great mass of mankind 'consider slavery a great moral wrong.' [43]

What was the basic difference between these two antagonists? In their speeches in 1854 were the fundamentals of their speeches in 1858. In the clash of viewpoint at Springfield and Peoria, one can find the philosophic conflict which four years later appeared at Ottawa and Freeport. These made up two sides of the triangle of which the Southern Rights theories formed the third side; in 1861, the two sectional sides overcame the national hypotenuse and the apex was Civil War.

On many points Douglas and Lincoln agreed. Each wanted to preserve the Union, and to protect the States in their Constitutional rights. Each felt that chattel slavery would eventually be extinguished, each wished this to occur. But Douglas believed in the operation of economic laws and felt that the climate, soil and other natural characteristics of the Western Territories would make them free. He thought the Missouri Compromise repeal would not extend slavery, but would reduce Southern opposition to the formation of new Territories. A series of new free Territories would be established, finally the South would find competition too unprofitable and severe, and slavery would die a natural death. But the South would have no legitimate complaint, for its honor would have been respected and its constitutional rights scrupulously offered and maintained. This, to Douglas, was national ground.

Lincoln, however, claimed that the end desired could only be attained by recognizing that slavery was morally wrong, with national legislation to prevent its spread. He insisted that the Kansas-Nebraska Act would cause a renewal of sectional agitation and strife, and hinted that Kansas might soon flame in civil war.

Lincoln said that slavery was 'a great moral wrong.' Douglas knew that Calhoun and many another from the South had regarded 'the conviction of the sinfulness of slavery in the North' as the seed of the difficulty between the sections. Douglas felt that the safety of the Union depended upon keeping the Democratic party a great national party, that the South would countenance no step of national policy premised on the sinfulness of slavery and that, if disunion were to be prevented, this expression of moral and emotional indignation must be stopped. Douglas had often privately termed slavery 'a curse beyond comparison, to both white and black,' but he could not publicly admit this — to do so would destroy the Democratic party as

[42] Beveridge, II, 265.   [43] Lincoln, *Works*, 261-62.

a national force, and he regarded 'the integrity of this political Union as worth more to humanity than the whole black race.' [44]

Most of the North's Democratic leaders were confronted with this same problem. During the 1854 campaign, the Richmond *Enquirer* and other extreme Southern papers began denouncing all Northerners who refused slavery public endorsement. Lewis Cass had no further political aspirations, but he reacted to the problem just as Douglas had done. While no man in a Free State could support the doctrine that slavery was 'a blessing,' Cass could support the defense of 'the Constitutional rights of the South because the Constitution guarantees them.' He was coming to Illinois to speak not 'as an advocate of slavery as one of the conditions of life, but as an advocate of those portions of the Confederation which choose to recognize slavery, as they have the right to do.' [45] But any Northern Democrat who publicly proclaimed his belief that slavery was a positive evil would go far toward rupturing the Union.

Moderate Southern leaders believed that Democratic victory in Indiana and Illinois would quiet Southern apprehensions. John C. Breckinridge, of Kentucky, saw that the Fusionists were playing the devil in the Northeast, 'but if we can save Illinois and Indiana all will be well.' [46] This was the reason Douglas proclaimed neutrality. But while Lincoln claimed that he sought to stand on national ground, he took sectional ground on the moral wrong of slavery, regardless of the effect on the South.

While the Springfield and Peoria speeches constituted a high point in Abraham Lincoln's career, to Douglas they probably represented little more than two arduous days in a State-wide campaign. The skies were looking darker. The October States, Pennsylvania, Ohio and Indiana, had just gone against the Democrats, who in these States lost 31 Congressmen, half their House majority. But Douglas interpreted these defeats as chiefly due to Know-Nothings and Prohibitionists, and campaigned with greater energy.

At Peoria, some Lincoln authorities contend, Douglas 'flattered' Lincoln as 'giving him more trouble than all his opponents in the Senate combined;' and proposed that neither should speak again. According to the story, Lincoln accepted, but two days later Douglas broke the faith and spoke. But Lincoln's most recent biographers term this tale thin. Certainly for Douglas to have sought such a truce with Lincoln would have been quite as uncharacteristic of the Little Giant as would have been his immediate breach of plighted word.[47]

[44] See *supra*, Chapter VIII.

[45] Lewis Cass to A. Harvie, Detroit, Oct. 1, 1854; Douglas MSS.

[46] Breckinridge to Douglas, Kentucky, Sept. 26, 1854; Douglas MSS. He offered to come to Illinois to speak.

[47] Beveridge, II, 270-71; Herndon, II, 373-74; Johnson, 266. Herndon said Lincoln told him this two weeks after the Peoria encounter. According to the story, neither spoke at Lacon on Oct. 17, but at Princeton on Oct. 18 Douglas spoke. Beveridge cites the evidence of another trustworthy Lincoln friend, Dr. Robert Boal, of Lacon, who drove Lincoln from Peoria to Lacon, a three hour drive, and who again was with Lincoln after his Lacon speech. During all this time, according to Dr. Boal's statement, quite positive and emphatic, Lincoln said nothing of any

Douglas' itinerary had already been planned, each day he visited a different place and made a major speech, with as many small side trips as time and geography would permit. In each place party leaders made elaborate plans for his coming, he would be greeted by an enthusiastic committee, the faithful would stream to his hotel quarters and party workers would bring those who were not quite so faithful. In such a campaign as this, Douglas was incomparable. He knew the people throughout the State, many thousands by name and circumstance. His memory of incidents was uncanny and his stock of stories full and pertinent. His willingness to laugh, even at himself, endeared him to the people.

For Douglas to be in a town, even if for a few hours only, was a campaign tonic. His cheery smile, his reminiscence, his hand-shake, his arm thrown about the shoulder, could in themselves upset the Opposition's best-laid plans. Then too he always made a sturdy, convincing, sledge-hammer speech, concluding his remarks with deep and resonant words about the Constitution, the Union, the Democratic party as a national institution and the fundamental right of self-government. When he would drive away behind the finest span of high-stepping horses in the country, many a waverer had returned to the fold and many a doubter had been steeled in the faith.

Had it not been for the Little Giant the result would have been a fearful Democratic rout. Such realistic lieutenants as Richardson saw the handwriting on the wall. 'The disasters in Pennsylvania, Ohio and Indiana have drawn from us every doubtful vote,' he wrote Douglas. 'The State is lost, at least for a time.' The Know-Nothings were more numerous than they had feared. In the Quincy district alone they knew of seventeen lodges, 'and the smallest number of Democrats in any of them is twenty, which makes the changes enough to upset our majority and lose the district.' [48]

The result was a Democratic defeat. It was not the year for the election of a Governor, but of the State's nine Congressmen the Democrats elected only four. There was some solace in the fact that Richardson, Harris, and the Democratic candidate for State Treasurer had won and 'Long John' Wentworth had been retired. But they had lost the next Legislature. Could they prevent the choice of an Anti-Nebraska Senator?

Democratic disaster had been general through the North, and the Democrats would be in a minority in the next House. New York's decision was inconclusive, but Michigan and Wisconsin had gone definitely Republican, while New Jersey and Delaware had elected Know-Nothing slates. The most extraordinary upset, however, had come in Massachusetts. In addition to sending a completely new Congressional delegation, the Know-Nothings elected every member of the Massachusetts Senate and all but three of the 379 members of the Lower House. These promptly chose Henry Wilson, a Know-Nothing, as Senator.[49] Of the Northern States, New Hampshire and California alone remained Democratic.

agreement with Douglas not to speak. Cf. also Paul M. Angle, 'The Peoria Truce,' Illinois State Historical Society, *Journal*, XXI, 500–05.

[48] W. A. Richardson, Quincy, Nov. 5, 1854; Douglas MSS.

[49] Channing, VI, 135. Of the three uncontaminated members, one was a Democrat, one a Free-Soiler, one a Whig. Wilson was elected on the third day of the legislative session.

The outcome was hailed by the Anti-Slavery people as a smashing rebuke to the Nebraska law. The Democrats, however, blamed it upon a veritable 'torrent of Abolitionism, Whiggism, Free-Soilism, religious bigotry and intolerance.' [50] In Illinois, many of the party leaders were staggered by the outcome, and some began to talk of ousting Douglas from leadership.[51] But the main body of Douglas' friends clove to him all the closer. Particularly was this true in Chicago, where a distinguished group held a great public dinner in his honor on the evening of November 9.

Speaker after speaker declared his profound admiration for Douglas as a man and his appreciation for his public service, and particularly the way in which he had guarded the right of Popular Sovereignty. Finally Douglas rose to respond to these glowing toasts. He had carefully prepared his speech. He admitted, with a wry smile, that 'the skies were partially overcast,' but the fight had been bravely fought and there had been a measure of victory.

More than this, the Democrats had fought a great campaign for principles and had established the greatest of these. In all his canvass of the State, nowhere had he found anyone to deny the great fundamental:

'That the people of each State of this Union, and each Territory, with the view to its admission into the Union, have the right and ought to be permitted to enjoy its exercise, to form and regulate their domestic institutions, and internal matters in their own way, subject only to the Constitution of the United States.' [52]

[50] Joliet, Ill., *Signal*, Nov. 14, 1854; Washington *Sentinel*, Nov. 22, 1854; Beverly Tucker, Washington, Dec. 12, 1854; Douglas MSS. Tucker was editor of the *Sentinel* and dependent on House printing for his payrolls.

[51] William H. Underwood to Lanphier and Walker, Belleville, Ill., Dec. 19, 1854; Patton MSS. Underwood urged the desirability of the Democratic party making its cruise in 1856 'with the old chart and compass, and Commodore Buchanan, an old seaman, for commander.'

[52] *Illinois State Register*, Springfield, Nov. 23, 1854, republished Douglas' banquet address.

CHAPTER XIII

BLEEDING KANSAS

DURING these dramatic scenes in Illinois, Popular Sovereignty was having its practical test upon the plains of Kansas — but a Popular Sovereignty different from any the Little Giant had foreseen.

Himself an immigrant from the East, Douglas had had more than twenty years' experience with immigration, land settlement and Territorial development. First there would be a rush of hunters, trappers and pioneers, followed by hardy husbandmen breaking the virgin soil. By slow degrees an indigenous society would develop, with customs suitable to its circumstance. During this incubation period it would remain a Territory; when its members became sufficient in number, it would ask and be accorded statehood.

He confidently looked forward to a similar experience in the two Territories created in 1854. In Nebraska his expectation was amply met; hardy settlers homesteaded her rolling plains in the normal way. But from the outset, Northern Free-Soilers made a determined rush to people and control Kansas, pro-slavery men, chiefly Missourians, opposed them savagely and the result was civil war and 'Bleeding Kansas.'

The activities of an imaginative Massachusetts legislator, Eli Thayer, played an important part in this upset. Before the Kansas-Nebraska bill passed, Thayer persuaded the Legislature of his State to charter the Massachusetts Emigrant Aid Company, with an authorized capital of $5,000,000, 'to plant a Free State in Kansas, to the lasting advantage of the country; and to return a handsome profit to the stockholders upon their investment.' [1]

Shocked at news of this charter, the South objected that the territory belonged to natural and not artificial settlers, a Virginia paper suggesting that such emigrants be met with tar and feathers.[2] But in the final Senate debate, and speaking for the North, Seward said he would accept the challenge, 'We will engage in competition for the virgin soil of Kansas, and God give the victory to the side that is stronger in numbers as it is in right.'

Thayer in Kansas would determine whether freedom or slavery would rule the country. A curse to the Negro, slavery was a much greater curse

---

[1] Eli Thayer, *A History of the Kansas Crusade*, New York, 1889; 27 *et seq.* Thayer was determined to make his venture 'return a profitable dividend in cash,' as well as to vote Kansas free. William L. Garrison and his Abolitionists reprehended the enterprise. One Abolitionist told Thayer that he would rather have Kansas given over to slavery 'than to make a cent out of the operation of saving it to freedom.' While the South never forgot the initial charter, with its figure of $5,000,000 capital, as a matter of fact, less than $200,000 was subscribed to its stock. Some of the incorporators became concerned over the possibility that some legal liability was attached to them and the initial company never functioned. For a year Thayer and one or two other leading spirits operated as unofficial trustees. In 1855 the enterprise was reincorporated as the New England Emigrant Aid Company, with the profit feature eliminated.

[2] Lynchburg *Republican*, July 1, 1854.

to the white man, and the way to overcome it was 'to go to the prairies of Kansas and show the superiority of free labor civilization; to go with all our free labor trophies; churches and schools, printing presses, steam engines and mills; and in a peaceful contest convince every poor man from the South of the superiority of free labor.' Moreover his scheme could profitably be applied from Kansas to the Gulf.[3] Let New England *go* and *do* something for free labor, rather than to be content to stay at home and 'make women and children cry in anti-slavery conventions.'

New England took to the scheme, subscriptions flowed in, Thayer enlisted Horace Greeley in his crusade and the *Tribune* sought to stir the North about 'the plan for freedom.'[4]   Recruiting the first emigrant band was hard; funds were slender, prospects remote and Southern threats deterred the faint-hearted. But the company subsidized a book about the new land of promise.[5] Adventurous youths glowed at the prospect of battle and many men saw visions of fortunes on the plains. In mid-July a band of twenty-nine men departed, singing Whittier's specially-written hymn:

> We cross the prairie as of old
> The pilgrims crossed the sea,
> To make the West, as they the East,
> The homestead of the Free![6]

Cheering crowds filled the Boston station and there was a reception at practically every stopping-place, but in Missouri it was a different story. Missouri was a slave-holding State; for thirty years western Missouri had marked the mid-continent frontier, and had remained a rough country. For years these people had hungered for the new lands to the west, and for the last few months river steamers had been unable to care for the throngs of land-hungry people coming from nearby States waiting for the barriers to go down.[7] In the Spring of 1854, the Government's Indian Agents redoubled their efforts to make treaties with the Kansas-Nebraska Indians, so as to put the area in condition for legal settlement. When Pierce signed the bill, the throng rushed the border to stake the good lands near by.

The Missourians greeted the first Massachusetts group, in August, with black looks, but did not interfere. Some of Thayer's band, however, distinguished themselves by torrid remarks about slavery, and the New York *Tribune's* Missouri correspondent warned that they must 'forbear uttering

---

³ Thayer, 59: 'Two years of such a company, in Virginia, would have made her as secure for the Union in 1861 as Massachusetts was.' But when his associates got cold feet, and the project went 'to the charity plan,' it was never half so efficient as the other mode would have been. 'We were full twice as long in determining the destiny of Kansas'; all the fine plans for Virginia had to be abandoned.

⁴ New York *Tribune*, May 29, 30, 31, June 1, 1854.

⁵ Edward Everett Hale, *Kansas and Nebraska*, Boston, 1854. Hale, a young clergyman, was a warm admirer of Thayer and his plan.

⁶ John Whittier, *Poetical Works*, Boston, 1888; III, 176–77.

⁷ Washington *Union*, March 29, 1854. Edwin McMahan, 'Stephen A. Douglas,' *Washington Historical Quarterly*, II, 310, notes that in the Spring of 1854, the St. Louis *News* counted eleven west-bound wagons in a day.

hot and angry words.'[8] But the group disembarked at Westport, went overland to the south bank of the Kansas River, selected a town site and erected a few huts, which they called Lawrence.

Soon a second party arrived, bringing a steam sawmill, a hand-press, some fonts of type and the first issue of the *Herald of Freedom*, already printed in the East.[9] Provocatively displayed in it and provocatively sung by these emigrants was 'The Freemen's Song':

> Traitors shaped in Southern mould
> Have our honest birthright sold;
> Wolves are set to guard our fold;
> Shame, Democracy!
> From our mountains in the North
> Freedom's legions sally forth,
> Shouting o'er the trembling earth
> Death to slavery!

With this group came Charles Robinson, whom Thayer had picked to head the emigrants. A California Forty-Niner, Robinson was experienced in frontier forays and had courage to achieve his goal, whatever it might cost. In September, a third band arrived, by the end of the year, the Emigrant Aid Company had dispatched two more parties. En route each band was doubled by accessions and the number which reached Kansas was at least 3000. When the Missourians moved to Kansas, they took their families with them, but the Emigrant Aid Society's parties were all of men, mostly young, and nearly all armed with Sharps' rifles.[10]

This steady influx shocked and startled the western Missourians, who saw their good lands being snatched from their grasp. Thayer's boasts of colonizing miracles on $5,000,000 capital, and his predictions of a cordon of free States from Kansas to the Gulf, threw fat upon the fire. Before long the Missourians began forming protective associations of their own — 'The Sons of the South,' 'The Self-Defensive Associates,' 'The Social Band,' 'Blue Lodges,' to name the chief one. Epithets flowed freely, 'nigger-stealers,' 'black-hearted Abolitionists,' 'blue-bellied Yankees' and 'Northern mud-sills' were mild.[11] 'We want no Negro sympathizing friends among us,' thundered the Kansas *Pioneer*. 'Their hearts are as black as the darkest

---

[8] New York *Tribune*, Aug. 12, 1854, Missouri correspondence dated Aug. 6. A large majority of Missourians, this correspondent added, were 'eager for Kansas to be secured for Freedom'; but if once they got the idea that companies were being formed in the East to interfere with their legal rights in Missouri, 'such an intense degree of excitement will be raised' as to defeat the plan.

[9] Noble L. Prentis, *Kansas Miscellanies*, Topeka, 1889, 81 *et seq.*, says the *Herald of Freedom's* first issue had been printed back in Medina, Ohio, and dated at Warushka, K.T., a town which did not exist. The second issue was properly domesticated at Lawrence.

[10] Channing, VI, 161, gives these figures. Thayer, 57, says 500 left Boston in 1854, but insists that many more joined each band as it made its way out. From beginning to end of the excitement 3000 went. But each company would be joined on the way by many more, so Thayer estimated about 8000. The maker of these rifles was one Christian Sharps, a Swiss immigrant in Connecticut. Some are still to be found in the Southwest.

[11] Irelan, *Pierce*, 23.

deeds of hell.' The new settlers were not backward in responding with 'nigger-whippers,' 'squatter sovereigns,' 'chivalry' and 'Simon Legrees.'

At first the pro-slavery men followed David R. Atchison's leadership. He left Washington before Congress adjourned, took part in the first land rush and a town was named after him. He showed great talent at drinking deep and talking loud, but as a leader he failed completely. 'Atchison promises everything,' an irritated Missourian wrote Douglas, 'but his indifference and want of energy, unless pushed into action, renders it almost as inefficient as no support at all.' The next year, after others took Atchison's place in Kansas, he toured the South seeking official aid in making the Territory a Slave State.

Still the pro-slavery party made some progress. A paper called the *Squatter Sovereign* was founded at Atchison. Its editor, one General Brindle, began denouncing Thayer's 'Abolitionists.' Meetings were held over western Missouri, and Atchison and Benjamin Franklin Stringfellow, an abler, virulent leader, whipped up the people's wrath. 'I tell you to mark every scoundrel among you who is the least tainted with Abolitionism or Free Soilism, and exterminate him,' Stringfellow said, at St. Joseph. 'Your rights and your property are in danger.... Neither give nor take quarter, as the cause demands it.' A little later the Missourians formed an association to 'hold itself in readiness together to assist and remove any and all emigrants who go there under the auspices of the Northern Emigrant Aid Societies.' [12]

Soon they barred the river route to the Emigrant Aid bands, one or two were disarmed and sent back, others warned to stay away. But Thayer worked out an overland route through Iowa and Nebraska and soon the chanting emigrants poured in again.

While the Free-Soilers and the Missourians were incubating mutual hatreds, the Federal Government's official representatives were making blunder after blunder in the organization of the Territory. Franklin Pierce had tried to set up competent Territorial Administrations, naming a Southern man as Governor of Nebraska, and a Northern man Governor of Kansas, but in the latter instance he made a bad guess in his man. His choice fell on Andrew H. Reeder, a lawyer from Easton, Pennsylvania, forty-seven, fat, slow-moving and untactful. The new Governor professed complete agreement with Pierce's policy and the Kansas-Nebraska bill, but the event proved that he was even more interested in land speculation.

Reeder, commissioned in June, reached Kansas in October. The Pro-Slavery leaders at once insisted that he have a census taken and order Territorial elections. But he refused — he must first make a 'tour of inspection' — he was looking for land. While on his 'tour' he bought lots in Leavenworth, Lawrence, Tecumseh, Topeka and other towns. But his chief feat was to pick a site on the Kansas River, about a hundred miles from the Missouri border, where he laid out the town of Pawnee City, making plans to run steamboats to it and to make it Kansas' capital.

[12] James B. Bowlin, St. Louis, June 30, 1854; Douglas MSS.; Gideon Welles, 'Diary,' MS., June 29, 1855, giving recent data from Lewis Cass as to Atchison's absence from Missouri and trip through the South. For Stringfellow speech, see Irelan, *Pierce*, 260.

But his town-site was located on the Government reservation at Fort Riley and his land purchases were made fraudulently from Indians unable to alienate their land. The fact that several other officials, including a judge or two and the commander of the army post, had joined the promotion, did not make it any more palatable to the authorities at Washington.[13] Reeder finally submitted his contracts, but the Commissioner for Indian Affairs held that the Governor was robbing the Indians and the papers were incomplete, and the President returned them unapproved.

Reeder was too busy with his town-sites to take a census that Fall, but he did call an election for a Delegate to Congress. Held on November 29, it precipitated trouble between Atchison's Missourians and the Lawrence men. If a set of fanatics and demagogues a thousand miles off 'could afford to advance their money' to abolitionize Kansas, Stringfellow flamed, the Missourians could well afford to cross the river and run the election. Several hundred young men, most of them armed, crossed over on election day, and voted for John W. Whitfield, the Pro-Slavery candidate. Among other places, the 'Border Ruffians' visited Lawrence, where Robinson was 'ready to meet the issue with powder and ball,' but there was no clash.[14] Thus Whitfield won by a large majority — but he had a majority of the legal votes and would have won without the invasion.

The North heard that the Southern slavocracy had raped the ballot-box, added proof that the 'nigger-drivers' were determined to conquer Kansas, using fraud and force, if necessary. Greeley's *Tribune* led in the demand that the Free-Soil settlers defend themselves with arms. A few days after the election Robinson and his men organized the Kansas Legion, a secret military organization, and sent for arms and ammunition.

In the Spring of 1855, after the tide of Free-Soil emigration had set in again, Reeder finally ordered the election of a Territorial Legislature. The date set was March 30, 1855, four months after Nebraska's election and two months after its Legislature had convened. The Pro-Slavery leaders believed that Reeder had decided that his land would have more value if the State were settled from the North and that he was conspiring with the Emigrant Aid leaders to this end.[15] Stringfellow and his groups began to exhort their followers to 'beat the Yankees at their own game.' The Blue Lodges swore fearful oaths that these 'foreigners' could not steal their land.

[13] Nichols, *Pierce*, 408–09. The Kansas Indian Treaty of 1825 had made this area a perpetual reservation for half-breeds. Attorney-General Cushing had ruled that speculations in these lands were unlawful and Indian Agents had been ordered to drive the squatters away. Reeder had been very secretive in his contracts, and protests against his deal were made by Indian Agents on November 6. He was charged with cheating the Indians. Richardson, V, 352–60. The officer, a Colonel Montgomery, was immediately court-martialed and cashiered.

[14] *Congressional Globe*, Thirty-Fourth Congress, First Session, App., 90. Speech of Senator Henry Wilson, of Massachusetts, who called Robinson 'the Miles Standish of Kansas.' The Pro-Slavery candidate was the Government's Indian Agent. Pro-Slavery papers charged that 150 Free-Soil voters left Lawrence the day after the election; in other words, they had been hired to come out and vote, after which their contract was concluded and they could go back East. Washington *Sentinel*, Jan. 12, 1855, quoting Stringfellow's letter to Southern Congressmen.

[15] For example, it was freely charged that the date of Reeder's election was known in Boston long before the Governor announced it in Kansas.

All this excitement was quite needless, for the Territorial Census, taken late the preceding winter, showed that the real settlers from the South, who had actually broken land, were greater in number than those from the North. Then too, not all the Northern settlers were Anti-Slavery men. All the Missouri borderers needed to do to win was to let Nature take its course.

But these men were fully as unreasonable as were Garrison and the Abolitionists, and they were determined to control the election by main force. So on election morning a veritable army of over five thousand Missourians marched over the Kansas plains. All were armed, some with muskets from a Federal Arsenal, and there were a few cannon. They came on with bands playing, fifes and bugles going and flags waving in the breeze. There were many kegs of whiskey, and it was freely drunk. This 'army' seized polling-places, overawed election officers and tried to make a joke out of their interference. After casting its enormous poll for the Pro-Slavery men, it marched gleefully back; women cheered the warriors' return.

This show of force led to disaster. The *Herald of Freedom* worked its presses overtime printing lurid accounts of this invasion and sent them over the North. Greeley invented the phrase 'Border Ruffians' to describe the Missourians involved, and the Northern papers depicted the Pro-Slavery men as savage, unkempt fellows, drunken braggarts with bowie knives and rifles: a lawless, uncivilized tribe in strong contrast to the industrious, sober, devout emigrants from the Free States.[16]

The truth was that western Missouri had been settled by just such folks as had settled Illinois and Iowa. Life in Kansas was hard, as it was anywhere on civilization's fringe, and all its settlers must accommodate themselves to Nature's severities. Whether from Massachusetts or Missouri, those who lived in sod houses and homesteaded the prairie looked and lived alike.

Robinson and the men at Lawrence converted the hotel then under construction into a military citadel, with loopholes for rifle-fire and embrasures for cannon. Robinson also asked Boston for more rifles. After a sermon by Henry Ward Beecher, Sharps' rifles were known as 'Beecher's Bibles,' and many thousand were shipped West in boxes and barrels labeled 'Bibles,' 'Boxes of Primers,' 'Revised Statutes,' 'Crockery,' and 'Hardware.' [17]

When Reeder got around to canvassing the election returns, heavily armed delegations from both Border Ruffians and Emigrant Aid men visited his official residence. Both sides charged, stormed and threatened. After examining the facts as to the various contests, Reeder issued election certificates to nearly all the men chosen on the face of the returns. In eight cases, however, he turned down the returns on the ground of fraud and ordered new elections. The Pro-Slavery party refused to take part in these, but three of the eight rejected were chosen again.

While the Governor's own act gave title to an overwhelming majority of the Legislature, the Emigrant Aid men were agreed to flout them. 'We repudiate and despise them and their authority,' the *Herald of Freedom*

---

[16] New York *Tribune*, April 10, 12, 1855.

[17] *Herald of Freedom*, Lawrence, June 16, 1855; Thayer, 45-46; William Lawrence, *Life of Amos A. Lawrence*, Boston, 1880; 96-98.

announced, the people of Kansas should 'spurn everything in the shape of laws' which this 'bogus legislature' might later pass.[18]

In April, 1855, Reeder went to Washington. At his home at Easton, where he first stopped, he made a speech asserting that the late Kansas election had been rotten with fraud, and the Border Ruffians were to blame for the Territory's troubles. Atchison was in Washington demanding the Governor's removal because greed and corruption had controlled his official actions, and at every point he had cheated the Pro-Slavery group. Atchison would not listen to reason: Reeder *must* be removed! Upset by the Easton speech, when Reeder reached Washington, Pierce challenged him about it. If it had been a fraudulent election, why had he accepted it? 'Which shall we believe,' Pierce asked pointedly, 'your official certificate under seal, or your subsequent declaration?' Reeder's explanations were halting and Pierce suggested that he resign, but the Governor evaded and at length the President weakly permitted him to go back.[19]

Three months after the legislative election, Governor Reeder called the Legislature to meet at Pawnee, his own town-site. The members protested that Pawnee was one hundred and forty miles away and there were practically no habitations there, but Reeder would not yield. So the members proceeded there and organized.

The Governor's message to the Legislature was as pompous, flabby, evasive and self-seeking as was the man himself. There was not an intimation that Reeder considered the ballot had been outraged. The Legislature could do what it wanted about slavery, he wrote, the spirit of 'Abolitionism' must not influence them, counties must be created, the members must select a State Capital and Pawnee should be the place.

Had the legislators only done this last, perhaps the 'crime against Kansas' would have been a mere misdemeanor. But Pawnee had only three houses, life there was vastly uncomfortable and the solons were indignant over Reeder's brazen scheme to use them to boost the price of his lots. Therefore the Legislature quickly adjourned to Shawnee Mission, whence they memorialized the President to remove the Governor.

But before this petition reached Washington, Pierce found the Pawnee City land speculations intolerable, and removed the Governor. Now Reeder cast off all disguises and joined forces with the Free-State men. The Northern press thundered that his refusal to 'do the dirty work of slavery' had caused him to be dismissed.[20]

The legislators at Shawnee Mission asked the Supreme Court of the Territory for an official opinion as to the transfer of the meeting-place, and received one upholding the legality of their action. The laws enacted were, in the main, those needed for building up a civilization on the frontier. County and local governments were set up, offices created, civil and criminal statutes enacted, and the mechanics provided for an ordered society. Much

[18] *Herald of Freedom*, Leavenworth, June 9, 1855.

[19] Nichols, *Pierce*, 411-15. ·

[20] Nichols, *Pierce*, 418; Beveridge, II, 318.

of this acquisition of law was by wholesale, for they took time by the forelock and adopted Missouri's complete civil and criminal code.

Thus the Territory of Kansas acquired a body of laws for the government of slavery. But Missouri's slave code was not harsh, and the intense Pro-Slavery legislators of the Territory enacted further statutes, one decreeing the death penalty for anyone found guilty of aiding a slave to escape and another declaring it a felony to deny the right of a slave-holder to hold his human property in bondage.

The fanaticism thus expressed measured the folly of Atchison and his leadership.[21] These acts disgusted the Moderates, contributed to the failure of a National Democratic movement and gave Robinson and Reeder valuable ammunition. While the Black Code proved a dead letter, the Emigrant Aid presses put it in pamphlet form and circulated thousands of copies through the North.[22]

The Legislature also chose a new 'permanent capital,' with similar auspices and about as little to recommend it as had the ill-fated Pawnee City, now razed by order of the President. This was Lecompton, a new town named for Samuel D. Lecompte, the Chief Justice of the Kansas Supreme Court, a man about as hungry for a land boom as was Reeder. The Judge and other Pro-Slavery leaders bought and laid out some land not far from Lawrence, called it a town and lobbied its selection as capital through the Legislature. This land-speculation fever was probably as baneful to Kansas peace as was slavery. An indignant Free-Soil settler expressed the substantial truth when he declared that had it not been 'for land and town lot speculation, there would have been no trouble in Kansas.'[23]

But there was another great author of the wrongs: the blundering course of Pierce, in Washington. As James A. Shields, now a 'squatter' in Minnesota, wrote Douglas, 'It took a world of mismanagement to turn poor, homeless squatters, who have fences to make and corn to raise and wives and children to feed, into rebels to be kept down with ball and bayonet... Border Ruffians and Abolitionists could not do it. If there had been no mismanagement the thing would have settled itself long ago.'[24]

The Emigrant Aid group had prepared to defy this Legislature before it met. A Free-State party was organized on military as well as political lines, and the legal Assembly was denounced as a 'bogus' body, which could pass no laws they would obey. 'WE ARE READY,' the *Herald of Freedom* thundered.

More military companies were enlisted and troops drilled from morning to night. On August 14, the Free-Soilers, in convention at Lawrence,

[21] For example, one of the last acts of the session was to pass a resolution that it was 'the duty of the Pro-Slavery party, the Union men of Kansas Territory, to know but one issue, slavery; and that any party making or attempting to make any other is, and should be held, as an ally of Abolitionism and disunion.'

[22] Oswald Garrison Villard, *John Brown*, Boston, 1910; 101.

[23] St. Clair, Ill., *Tribune*, May 31, 1856, quoted in Beveridge, II, 319. An Illinois emigrant to Kansas was the source of the statement.

[24] J. A. Shields, Faribault, Minnesota Territory, March 6, 1856; Douglas MSS.

defied the Territorial Government, and dedicated 'our lives, our fortunes and our sacred honor' to an unending 'resistance to tyrants.'

This announcement of virtual rebellion evoked a response in kind. Atchison and Stringfellow became almost insane with rage, and western Missouri held indignation meetings to ask if slave-holders must wait until the torch was applied to their dwellings and the knife held at their throats.

When Wilson Shannon, of Ohio, the new Governor, reached the Territory, he found a state of incipient civil war. He should have made a better executive than Reeder. Twice Governor of Ohio, he had held other posts of importance and had shown executive ability and tact. The anti-slavery press said he would be merely a 'bill-signing automaton for the Atchison and Stringfellow ruffians' but he seemed a good choice.[25]

Shannon's arrival made no difference to the Free-Staters. 'Come one, come all, slavocrats and nullifiers,' the *Herald of Freedom* invited, 'we have rifles enough and bullets enough to send you all to your (and Judas') own place.' On September 5, at another great convention at Big Springs, Reeder gained the nomination for Territorial Delegate to Congress by advocating armed resistance and quoting from Fitz-Greene Halleck:

> 'Strike — for our altars and our fires
> Strike — for the green graves of our sires;
> God and our native land!'

But Reeder paled into insignificance beside a newcomer to Free-State leadership, a tall lean Indianan with deep-lined face, thick black hair and hypnotic eyes named Jim Lane.

This extraordinary character had been a colonel in the Mexican War. War fervor brought him the Lieutenant-Governorship of Indiana and then election to Congress. In the Thirty-Third Congress he had voted for Douglas' Kansas-Nebraska bill and was a staunch Popular Sovereignty man. About this time he had trouble with his wife, the Indiana courts refused him a divorce and he emigrated to Kansas. Lane let it be known that he was going to Kansas to be elected to the United States Senate, but he also went there to seek the divorce he had been denied at home. For his first month he was active in the councils of the National Democratic movement, but then the Legislature refused him a divorce and he rushed over to Lawrence, where he was taken to the bosom of the extremest of the extreme Free-State men.

General Lane was poorly educated, coarse and uncouth. His hair stood out in every direction, his mouth suggested plug tobacco and heavy curses and his dress was almost as extraordinary as his appearance. But this was not all of the man. Positive, insistent, domineering and dominant, he commanded his fellows. His energy was amazing and his calfskin vest was likely to appear in any part of the wilderness.

It was when he talked that Jim Lane had his greatest power. When he would point a menacing forefinger and shriek 'Great God,' his hearers

[25] Nichols, *Pierce*, 418. Shannon was also brother-in-law of George W. Manypenny, Pierce's Commissioner of Indian Affairs. New York *Tribune*, Aug. 16, 1855.

would almost jump from their skins. John J. Ingalls thought his diction 'a pudding of slang, profanity and solecism.' And yet through 'the magnetism of his manner, the fire of his glance, the sudden earnestness of his utterances,' he swayed his audiences 'like a field of reeds shaken by the wind.' [26] Such was Jim Lane, now quickly to become king of Abolition Kansas. After his speech at the Big Springs Convention, resolutions were vociferously adopted promising: 'We will resist them to the bloody issue.'

The final step in defiance was taken at Topeka on October 23. Here the Emigrant Aid men and other delegates pretended to regard themselves as a State Constitutional Convention, debated and formulated a State Constitution, ordered an election both for its ratification and for the choice of a Legislature, State officials and a member of Congress. One provision of this Constitution prohibited slavery but inserted a clause for the voters' separate approval, to prohibit free Negroes, as well as slaves, from Kansas.[27]

On October 15 the regularly ordained election was held. The Free-State men stayed away and the Pro-Slavery party's candidate for Delegate received practically all of the votes. Eight days later the revolutionary Free-State election was held; Reeder was its unanimous choice.[28]

Thus began open rebellion, which Governor Shannon took active steps to check. A general convention of supporters of legal government was called for Leavenworth, for November 14. Not only the Pro-Slavery fanatics but conservative Free-Soilers who disliked 'these revolutionary speeches' took a hand. John Calhoun, of Springfield, who had been appointed Surveyor-General of Kansas and Nebraska Territories, kept Douglas advised.

Calhoun, whose main anxiety had been to make Kansas Democratic, had been provoked by the Legislature at Shawnee Mission. On returning to the Territory in November, he found a decided change in the attitude of the Pro-Slavery party, whose leaders now perceived the impossibility of their success. Moreover, Shannon, though a drunkard, was when sober a sensible fellow, his advice paralleled Calhoun's and finally the Pro-Slavery party leaders agreed to abandon any distinctive Pro-Slavery organization, and to seek ground 'which would enable all Democrats and State Rights Whigs to make common cause against Abolitionism.'

John Calhoun insisted that the Pro-Slavery party must agree 'to abandon any attempt to execute the odious provisions of their Fugitive Slave Law,' and to place it 'upon its true basis' at the next session of the Territorial Legislature. Again, all Pro-Slavery organization must be abandoned.

[26] John J. Ingalls, in letter from Topeka to the Leavenworth *Conservative*, in 1862, quoted Prentis, 111–12. Prentis' chapter on Jim Lane affords valuable material for this sketch. I have also found useful recollections of Mr. Archibald Shaw, a former citizen of Lawrenceburg, Ind., Lane's Indiana home. For these last I am indebted to Mr. E. Y. Chapin, of Chattanooga. For other accounts, see W. E. Connelley, *James Henry Lane*, Topeka, Kan., 1899.

[27] This was no new thing. Villard, *John Brown*, 104, recites a resolution of the Big Springs Convention demanding 'stringent laws excluding all Negroes, bond and free, from the Territory.'

[28] Victor of the legal election was Gen. J. W. Whitfield, with 2721 of 2738 votes. The illegal Free-State election gave Reeder 2849 votes.

THE PROPHET OF SECESSION: JOHN C. CALHOUN
Secretary of War, Vice-President, Senator, and
Patron Saint of the Slave-Expanding South

Calhoun felt it decidedly more important 'to make Kansas a Democratic State than a Free or Slave State.' While the Pro-Slavery party was struggling to make it a Slave State, it would probably 'throw the power into the hands of Reeder and the Abolitionists, and make it an Abolitionist State.'

The consequence was a great convention at Leavenworth, at which the Pro-Slavery party abandoned its program and framed an effective counter to the Topeka rebellion. Now the Pro-Slavery leaders were willing to broaden the base of the party to one of opposition to 'Abolitionism and its revolutionary designs.' Calhoun became the Moses of the new movement.[29]

His resolutions branded the Topeka movement as 'treasonable' and 'revolutionary' and called on all good citizens to support the legitimate Government. To this end the Pro-Slavery party was dissolved, the Law and Order party becoming the Free-Staters' sole political antagonist.[30] By these actions order and consistency had been established by the Democratic party in Kansas, and the 'extravagant follies' of Atchison and his associates were repudiated. Thenceforward Douglas could 'count Kansas right.'

On December 15 the Free-Staters held their election, overwhelmingly ratified their Topeka Constitution and voted that all Negroes should be excluded. From this day forward, the Free-Soilers consistently claimed that Kansas was an organized Free State ready for and demanding admission to the Union.[31]

Thus the stage was set for battle on the prairie. There were not a hundred slaves in all Kansas, and that question was little more than theoretically at stake. Even more involved were the basic issues of law, order and national authority. The brutal murder of a Northern settler in a land dispute was the spark which set off the conflagration. A Free-State settler was arrested under a peace warrant but his friends took him by force from a posse led by Sam Jones, who was both Sheriff of Douglas County, Kansas, and postmaster of Westport, Missouri. Thereupon Jones, who was a crude, boasting borderer and a violent pro-slavery man, swore revenge and demanded of the Governor 'three thousand men to carry out the laws.'[32]

Shannon acted hastily and called some troops 'for the sole purpose of aiding the Sheriff in executing the law.' In response came 1200 men, mainly from Missouri. Poorly armed and poorly drilled, they made up in liquor what they lacked in arms. The Free-Staters in Lawrence mounted a cannon, dug breastworks and drilled their companies day and night. Jim Lane

[29] John Calhoun, Wyandotte City, Kan., Nov. 27, 1855; Douglas MSS. Calhoun had employed Lincoln as a surveyor in the latter's youth. A brilliant orator, Calhoun was at one time thought the strongest man intellectually in the Illinois Democracy, but drink broke him down. Cf. Abraham Lincoln Association, *Bulletin*, No. 35.

[30] The name was a concession to the prejudices of Southern Whig emigrants. Next year, Calhoun assured Douglas, the Democratic title would be assumed in full time for the presidential canvass.

[31] Villard, *John Brown*, 105–08. The vote for ratification of the Constitution as a whole was 1931 to 46. The vote on the clause about the exclusion of Free Negroes was 1287 to 453.

[32] John H. Gihon, *Geary and Kansas*, Philadelphia, 1857; 50 *et seq*. Dow, a young Ohioan, who had settled on Wakarusa River at Hickory Point, was the victim of a brutal murder. Jacob Branson, Dow's friend, was the man put under peace warrant.

trained his men as sharp-shooters and the Free-Staters for whom the Sheriff had warrants were spirited out of town.

Thus began the Wakarusa War. The Free-Staters could probably have routed Shannon's militia, but both sides held off and the Governor sought to pacify the rival 'armies.' Finally a 'treaty of peace' was framed with the deliberate purpose of being susceptible of two interpretations. Lane and Robinson, who signed it for the Free-Staters, denied knowledge of any organization to defy or resist the laws. Shannon commissioned the Free-State 'generals' to use their forces as in their judgment would best secure peace and order.[33] The Free-State commissariat now produced its whiskey, Lawrence's Free-State Hotel was the scene of a 'grand peace party,' Sheriff Jones was too drunk to be indignant and the Wakarusa War was settled without a drop of blood.

But this fortunate outcome did not check the series of crimes which led the North to call the Territory 'Bleeding Kansas.' At that, the number of these crimes was greatly exaggerated; from the opening of the Territory to its statehood seven years later, the deaths by violence were officially estimated to have 'probably exceeded rather than fell short of two hundred' but not by much. Over half had arisen from normal frontier disputation over claim-jumping, land title, liquor jugs or jealous love. In the Winter of 1855–56 only two deaths were directly chargeable to troubles over slavery. 'I know of no one being treated unkindly who minds his own business,' a Boston emigrant declared.[34]

Of the outrages actually and truthfully chargeable to the slavery issue, only the hardiest partisans asserted that the Border Ruffians were the sole sinners. Members of Pro-Slavery and Free-State parties both burned houses and robbed and murdered unoffending people. The Pro-Slavery advocates had their Blue Lodges, the Free-State men their Kansas Legion. Major Jefferson Buford and his Alabama band marched into Kansas, but they were armed with Bibles from the Montgomery Baptist Church, 'Alabama for Kansas, Bibles for Rifles,' and declared that if only the Pro-Slavery party could keep the Constitution and the laws on their side, they could 'put to flight a host of Abolitionists with their Sharps' rifles.' But Jim Lane's 'Army of the North' left behind it a trail of ruin.[35]

Of all the crimes against Kansas, the 'Sack of Lawrence' and John Brown's cold-blooded murders were the most conspicuous. The first was the issue, if not the outcome, of the Free-State leaders' breach of the treaty of peace. Lane and Robinson had pledged to help execute the law but emissaries left for the North 'to ask appropriations of munitions of war and means of defense.' Inflammatory meetings were held all over the

[33] Lawrence *Herald of Freedom*, Dec. 15, 1855; Jan. 12, 1856. The Free-State 'Army' had eleven companies of fifty-four men each, cavalry troops, and batteries of artillery.

[34] Channing, VI, 172, quoting report of Commissioners of Claims Under Act of Congress of Feb. 7, 1859; Beveridge, II, 329; Howard Committee, 841–44; the testimony was that of John E. Ingalls, uncle of John J. Ingalls, a famous Kansas Senator.

[35] Channing, VI, 164–65; Beveridge, II, 332–33; Gihon, 47.

Free States, a Kansas Aid Society was established in nearly every hamlet and appeals for cash and rifles brought great response.

As soon as Governor Shannon realized how badly he had been tricked, he went to Washington to tell the President the condition of affairs. Laying the facts before Congress, Pierce asked for authority to prevent civil war, and announced that the full power of the Federal Government would be used to uphold the law. As first steps he issued a proclamation warning against the Topeka Legislature, and authorized Governor Shannon to call upon militia or Federal troops to suppress 'insurrectionary combinations or armed resistance to the laws.' [36]

But the Free-State Legislature assembled. Robinson, their pretended Governor, sent a formal message, Lane and Reeder were elected United States Senators and Congress was asked to make Kansas a State under the Topeka Constitution. Warrants were sworn out against Robinson, Lane and other Free-State leaders, but Sheriff Jones received a bullet in the spine when he tried to serve them. The United States District Court then indicted Robinson, Lane and Reeder for 'constructive treason,' presented Lawrence's two Abolitionist papers and Free-State Hotel as nuisances and issued writs for their destruction.[37]

Appeals were made for a marshal's posse adequate to the task. The Border Ruffians acted with alacrity, Major Buford's men were sworn in, Atchison headed a company of riflemen from Missouri, Virginians made up a band called 'the Red Shirts,' and five cannon were carried along. The army marched under a red banner on which were emblazoned the words 'Southern Rights.' On May 21, Lawrence was surrounded. The Free-State Council had decided not to resist, Lane's fighting men left town, the Marshal made a few arrests and the posse searched the town for arms.

When the extremists proceeded to the destruction of the papers and the hotel, Major Buford protested that they must uphold, not violate, the law. The posse, however, had got raving drunk on captured liquor, and the famous sack of Lawrence ensued. The newspaper presses were broken up and thrown into the street and type hurled into the river. Thirty cannon shot were fired against the hotel's stout walls, kegs of powder exploded in it and the building was set on fire. No longer a posse, but a mob, the torch was applied and the town was looted. Fortunately the terrified inhabitants were not physically harmed, but the proceedings were wanton and completely without warrant of law.[38]

A grim, cold-eyed old man heard the news about the sack of Lawrence, but it only strengthened a determination arrived at some time before. This was John Brown, a recent emigrant, who thought himself the Apostle of the Sword of Gideon and that the time had come to strike. When Brown discovered that the Almighty had specially commissioned him, he left a farm at North Elba, New York, gathered his four sons together and set out for Kansas to do the Lord's work. The party crossed the Missouri border early in October, took land on Osawatomie Creek and made a pretense of farming. The old man, who was in Lawrence when Shannon made his treaty, was

---

[36] Richardson, V, 390–91.   [37] Villard, *John Brown*, 142–43.   [38] Beveridge, II, 334–36.

indignant over the peaceful issue and mounted a dry-goods box to proclaim to an unheeding crowd that blood must be shed. On May 23, he decided to wait no longer for 'some killing.' Conferring with a troop of Free-Staters, he persuaded some to accompany him, and set out to the accompaniment of wild cheers from the whole camp. That night the band reached Pottawatomie Creek. All the next day it lay on its arms. Their victims were already selected and Brown planned to strike in the dark.

That night Brown's party was frightened away from the first cabin, but at the second, that of the Doyles, a poor family from Tennessee, they had a gory success. Doyle and his two sons were forced to surrender and the grim Free-State fanatic marched them into the night. The next morning Mrs. Doyle found them dead in the yard.

The murderous band next sought the habitation of Allen Wilkinson, 'a quiet man,' pro-slavery in views but not active or offensive. His sin had been 'membership in the Territorial Legislature.' Poor Wilkinson was tricked into leaving the cabin and killed. The Sword of Gideon now sought out 'Dutch William,' one of four German emigrant brothers. In later days the Shermans were called 'brutes and bullies,' but this seems merely part of the later martyr propaganda, for the Shermans were little more than rough settlers. But whatever they were, 'Dutch William' secured no mercy. Brown's party captured him and split open his head — the work of the Lord had been done.[39]

With this the immediate slaughter ended. The Free-Staters' first feeling was of deep outrage. 'You are a vile murderer, a marked man,' an Osawatomie preacher warned one of Brown's sons. Their actions were altogether inexcusable even to their neighbors and friends. Several months later, however, the Free-Staters began to find excuse for this murderous old maniac. Within a few years Charles Robinson and the Free-State men began to endorse the Pottawatomie outrage, and to call it a necessary and justifiable act. In less than a decade, soldiers marched to battle singing that John Brown's soul went marching on.

[39] Villard, *John Brown*, Chapter V, gives the various accounts of this brutal outrage, and a full bibliography. Mr. Villard's final judgment is that nothing avails to offset 'complete condemnation' for Brown's 'cruel, gruesome, reprehensible acts on the Pottawatomie.' The best explanation Mr. Villard has gotten was that John Brown came to Kansas determined to precipitate war. He had disguised himself as a surveyor, had found the views of each of the men he later murdered, believed 'each one committed murder in his heart and according to the Scriptures they were guilty of murder and I felt justified in having them killed.' His murders led to acts of reprisal, and many more Free-State men were killed afterwards than had been killed before Osawatomie and other settlements were burned. The old maniac often insisted that 'without the shedding of blood there is no remission of sin' but the blood that he had shed set men at each other's throats, and came near to making Kansas a charnel house.

CHAPTER XIV

THE PENDULUM SWINGS BACK

THIS tragic mixture of fanatical emigration, Missouri rage, official greed and organized rebellion profoundly influenced Stephen A. Douglas' career. But he did not suspect it in November, 1854, when he left for Washington, for the opening of Congress; his thoughts were on the coming Senatorial election. Not only was he extremely fond of General James A. Shields, his colleague, but Shields' defeat would be a body-blow to his own party power.

En route to Washington Douglas and Shields sent messages to party stalwarts: 'We must save the Legislature.'[1] Even after late returns made it certain that the Nebraska men would be in a minority on joint caucus, the Democrats did not lose hope; most of the Opposition were Old-Line Whigs, some were Anti-Nebraska Democrats, a few were Native Americans and it would be hard for them to center on a candidate.

When Abraham Lincoln saw that the Anti-Nebraska men would control the Legislature, he resigned the seat to which he had just been elected in the State Assembly and became an active Senatorial candidate.[2] The Democratic *State Register* promptly informed him that he had 'no chance,' and Sangamon County, at a special election, chose a staunch Douglas Democrat for the vacated Legislative seat.[3] And in truth many were the obstacles to Lincoln's election. The Anti-Nebraska Democrats remembered his Whiggery, the new Republicans and Abolitionists charged that he had not dared oppose the Fugitive Slave law and was a 'Compromise Whig.'[4] But Lincoln was hopeful and extremely active. Nearly every important Old-Line Whig in the State heard from him. He began making trips and pulling wires, 'always calculating and always planning ahead.' His ambition, Herndon relates, 'was a little engine that knew no rest.'[5]

Of the hundred members of the Legislature, the handful of Anti-Nebraska Democrats held the key to the election. Having campaigned to 'purify' the Democracy, they could not go to Lincoln and would not go to Shields. The Douglas Regulars studied the situation and concluded that Governor Matteson would get more votes than Shields, whose Irish birth and Catholic faith had concentrated the Know-Nothings against him. On the other hand, Joel A. Matteson was a popular and able executive. Farmer, manu-

---

[1] Shields to Lanphier, Baltimore, Nov. 23, 1854; Patton MSS.

[2] Sangamon County had elected him to the House, in November, by about 600 majority.

[3] *Illinois State Register*, Springfield, Dec. 2, 23, 24, 26, 1854; *Illinois Journal*, Springfield, Dec. 30, 1854; Jan. 6, 1855.

[4] Lincoln to Codding, Springfield, Nov. 27, 1854; Lincoln, *Works*, II, 264; Chicago *Free West*, Dec. 14, 1854.

[5] Lincoln to T. J. Henderson, Springfield, Nov. 27, 1854; Lincoln, *Works*, II, 263; Herndon, II, 375.

facturer, contractor, railroad promoter, he had touched many circles, had a large fortune, would make a strong personal appeal.

The suggestion that Matteson be made the candidate was promptly forwarded to Washington, but Douglas would have none of it. 'Our friends in the Legislature should nominate Shields by acclamation, and nail his flag to the mast, and never haul it down under any circumstances nor for anybody,' the Little Giant wrote Lanphier. He thought that the Whigs would stick to Abraham Lincoln, 'to the bitter end, even if it resulted in no choice this session and the consequent postponement of the election.' He expected that the Anti-Nebraska Democrats, with a candidate of their own, would try to force the Whigs to come to his support and would cling to him to the last.[6] Lincoln and his aides shared these fears.[7]

Let the focus of the fight be shifted from the Nebraska bill to the Know-Nothings, Douglas ordered, 'our friends must stand by Shields, and throw the responsibility on the Whigs of beating him *because he was born in Ireland*. The Nebraska fight is over and Know-Nothingism has taken its place as the chief issue in the future. If, therefore, Shields shall be beaten, it will be apparent to the people and the whole country that a gallant soldier and a faithful public servant has been stricken down because of the place of his birth.' There must be no compromise on issues, 'no bargains, no alliances, no concessions to any of the allied isms.' Thomas L. Harris, his trusted lieutenant, must 'take personal charge of everything, and in no event leave Springfield even for a day during the session.'[8]

Harris, Lanphier and other Democratic lieutenants at Springfield struggled manfully to carry out these instructions. The Regulars controlled the Senate by a single vote, and for a time it refused to go into joint session with the House, where the Fusionists had a large majority. But the Opposition weakened the resolution of two susceptible Regulars and on January 19 the Legislature took an unexpected recess. Harris feared that the result would prove 'destruction on our side and union and success on the other.'

By this time it was obvious that Shields could not win. Harris assured Douglas that he was doing all in his power for the General, but that 'stronger efforts were never made for any man than are now being made for Matteson,' who was gaining every day; 'Shields can count but 43 votes certain, and his best probabilities count but 48. If he can get another one I don't know where it is to come from. Matteson can get three votes neither one of which do I suppose Shields can receive.'[9]

Sheahan wrote Douglas that the shift must be made, but the latter insisted that the Regulars 'stand by Shields to the last and make no compromises.' Should the Legislature adjourn without electing a Senator, let

[6] Douglas to Lanphier, Washington, Dec. 18, 1854; Patton MSS.

[7] Davis to Julius Rockwell, Bloomington, Ill., Dec. 27, 1855; original in possession of F. W. Rockwell, North Andover, Mass.: 'There is an odor of sanctity about a Democrat that follows him in his new party relations.'

[8] Douglas to Lanphier, Washington, Dec. 18; Richardson to Lanphier, Washington, Dec. 17, 1854; Patton MSS.

[9] Harris to Douglas, Springfield, Jan. 25, 1855; Douglas MSS.

Sheahan and the other Democratic editors promptly hoist Shields' name to the masthead, 'Good faith, honor and policy all dictate this course.' [10]

There was an extraordinary fall of snow during the General Assembly's recess and members were two weeks delayed getting back. It was February 8 before the Senate met with the House to elect a United States Senator. In the gallery of the Hall of Representatives, Abraham Lincoln was an anxious spectator, while his wife was on pins and needles.

Shields had 41 votes on the first ballot, Lincoln 45, Lyman Trumbull, the Anti-Nebraska Democrats' choice, had five votes, eight were scattered and none had a majority. For four ballots, Shields' forces held firm and on the fifth he gained a vote. Lincoln lost steadily, dropping to 34 on the fifth ballot. John M. Palmer, Norman Judd, Burton Cook and two House members voted steadily for their fellow bolter.

Now Major Harris realized that he could no longer temporize and on the next roll call, the Regulars shifted from Shields to Matteson; to them were added three new votes. The next ballot brought Matteson to 46 votes — five more and he would be Senator. Lincoln's strength crumbled to 27 and Trumbull's mounted to 18. It seemed sure that Matteson would win on the next ballot unless there were a concentration of all opposition votes upon Trumbull, yet Lincoln made no move to withdraw. Sure enough, the Democrat's vote mounted to 47; Trumbull went up to 35, Lincoln's strength dropped to a humiliating 15. The Whigs decided to end the deadlock and approached Lincoln. It must have cost him a pang, but he said: 'Go for Trumbull, by all means.' [11] So on the tenth ballot, Lincoln's friends joined Trumbull's 35, an odd vote was picked up and the Anti-Nebraska Democrat had exactly the number to make him Senator. [12]

Lincoln's organ sent 'Greetings to the Anti-Nebraska men throughout our wide land!' 'ILLINOIS HAS SPOKEN!' [13] Greeley held 'this glorious result,' 'a fitting finale to the Repeal of the Missouri Compromise by Douglas & Co.' [14] But Lincoln himself found defeat a bitter dose, his only satisfaction being to see the Nebraska men 'worse whipped than I am.' [15]

His wife found no solace at all. Mary Todd and Julia Jayne had been inseparable friends in girlhood days; the affection was maintained after Mary married Lincoln and Julia married Trumbull. But on election night and for years thereafter Mary would not speak to her once dear friend. [16]

Douglas and the Nebraska men were the hardest hit. 'The deed is done,' Sheahan wrote the Senator despairingly; 'the severest blow we could have received has been given us.' He wished Shields had been 'one half as anxious and efficient in his own cause as you have been,' but that was

---

[10] Sheahan to Lanphier, Chicago, Jan. 17, 1855; Patton MSS.; Douglas to Sheahan, Washington, Feb. 6, 1855; Sheahan MSS.

[11] Herndon, II, 377, note.   [12] Sheahan, 255-56; Davidson and Stuvé, 689; 890.

[13] *Illinois Journal*, Feb. 9, 1855.   [14] New York *Tribune*, Feb. 9, 1855.

[15] Lincoln to Elihu Washburne, Springfield, Feb. 9, 1855; Lincoln, *Works*, II, 274-77.

[16] Beveridge, II, 286, says she never spoke to Julia again. There is evidence, however, that during the Civil War the two women called on one another; Paul Angle to author, Springfield, Ill., Feb. 9, 1933.

water over the dam. Wentworth, Palmer and the lot would now be 'bold and defiant in their treason.' Harris termed Palmer 'a Maine Law whiskey swiller, a Democratic Abolitionist, a tolerant Know-Nothing, a whited sepulchre.' Bitter at Douglas and Illinois, Shields emigrated to a Minnesota homestead.[17]

Lanphier promptly attacked the Senator-elect as a traitor who, months before, had 'plotted the overthrow of the Democratic party.'[18] The National Democracy regretted Shields' defeat. 'That gallant soldier and statesman,' mourned Beverly Tucker's Washington *Sentinel*, 'was one of the noblest victims of the traitorous coalition.' Shields had been doomed to defeat, Douglas told the Senate; 'he had been guilty of the crime of being born in Ireland.'[19]

When Trumbull took his Senate seat, Douglas repudiated his claim to have come as a Democrat. 'That fact will be news to the Democracy of Illinois,' said the Little Giant. 'Such a statement is a libel upon the Democracy of that State. When he was elected, he received every Abolition vote in the Legislature of Illinois. He received every Know-Nothing vote in the Legislature of Illinois. So far as I am advised and believe, he received no vote except from persons allied to Abolitionism and Know-Nothingism. He came here as the Know-Nothing-Abolition candidate, in opposition to the united Democracy of his State and to its candidate.'[20]

With the December term of Congress, 'Bluff Ben' Wade and other Abolitionist and Free-Soil members began flaunting their triumph. Douglas refused to concede that the Nebraska bill had been repudiated, insisting 'that in the Free States there has been an alliance,... a crucible into which they poured Abolitionism, Maine liquor-lawism, and what there was left of Northern Whiggism, and then the Protestant feeling against the Catholic and the native feeling against the foreigner. All these elements were melted down in that crucible and the result was what was called the Fusion party.' In every instance, the crucible was 'a Know-Nothing Lodge.'[21]

Let Wade name 'a man in any free State of this Union whom the Anti-Nebraska men have elected to either House of Congress who was not elected by the Know-Nothings.' For example, in Massachusetts 'a whole delegation, arraying themselves under the black banner of Abolitionism and

[17] J. W. Sheahan, Chicago, Feb. 8, 17, 1855; Douglas MSS. Harris to Lanphier, March 18, 1856; Patton MSS. J. A. Shields, Beltsville, Md., March 18, 1855, Douglas MSS., insisted that Douglas pay some notes he owed Shields. Shields to H. H. Sibley, Faribault Cy., Minn., June 26, 1856, Minnesota Historical Society MSS., expressed pleasure at Douglas' defeat for the 1856 nomination.

[18] *Illinois State Register*, Springfield, Feb. 10, 1855.

[19] Douglas, Pamphlet, *Execution of United States Laws*, Washington, 1855; 7. This was the text of his speech of Feb. 23, 1855, in answer to Wade, of Ohio.

[20] *Congressional Globe*, Thirty-Fourth Congress, First Session, 655.

[21] *Congressional Globe*, Thirty-Third Congress, Second Session, App., 216-30. Douglas had his speech of Feb. 23, with all the questions and passages at arms, put into a pamphlet, which was widely circulated. The legislative excuse for the discussion was a bill to transfer to Federal Courts State cases about the return of fugitive slaves.

fighting Nebraska were all swept away,' and a new delegation 'under a similar black banner' had been elected. Was this one of Wade's 'glorious victories'? In Ohio itself every Anti-Nebraska Democrat as well as every Nebraska man had been beaten 'because the Know-Nothings demanded other men.'

'Look over all the recent elections,' Douglas challenged, 'and wherever you will show me one Nebraska member of the House cut down, I will show you, I think, nearly two for one Anti-Nebraska men defeated at the same election by the same causes. Was it the Nebraska issue, then, that administered this rebuke, or was it caused by your secret conclaves, where you get men together at the dark hour of midnight and administer to them the most terrible oaths, that they, with a smile upon their faces and a friendly grasp... will strike down their neighbor in the dark?'

Wade asked offensively: 'Have the people of Illinois forgotten the injunction of more than Heavenly wisdom, that "where a man's treasure is, there will his heart be also"?'

Douglas replied that the insinuation was false and Wade knew it to be false. 'I am not the owner of a slave, and never have been, nor have I ever received, and appropriated to my use, one dollar earned by slave labor.' Then he revealed the story of the tender his father-in-law, Colonel Martin, had made him, his own refusal and the provisions of the Colonel's will. 'God forbid that I shall be understood by anyone,' he added feelingly, 'as being willing to cast from me any responsibility that does now, or has ever attached to any member of my family.... I implore my enemies who so ruthlessly invade the domestic sanctuary to do me the favor to believe that I have no wish, no aspiration, to be considered purer or better than she who was, or they who are, slave-holders.' At the same time, in order that his Illinois enemies could not question the correctness of his statement, the Senator sent Sheahan a detailed analysis of his Chicago realty investments, none of which had been purchased from his wife's estate.[22]

Douglas besought the Senate not to let Wade's slurs becloud the issue. The truth was that the North had not pointed a pistol of hatred at the South, for 'the North are a Union people, a law-abiding people, a people loyal to the Constitution and willing to perform its obligations.' It was true that, 'once in a while, a combination of factions, brought together under extraordinary circumstances,' might make a temporary majority and so send to the Senate a man 'who is as much a misrepresentative of the sentiment of the North as he is of all the courtesies and proprieties which should exist among gentlemen here as well as elsewhere.'

But such men had no right 'to speak in the name of the North or for the North. This Abolition faction, this disunion cabal, this set of men who make their reputation by slandering better men than themselves, have never been the true representatives of the North. They always come here by a bargain, and they go out at the end of the term at which they arrive.'

[22] Douglas to Sheahan, Washington, March 10, April 6, 1855; Sheahan MSS. For details see *supra*, 36–37; 73. It was 'Wentworth's unscrupulousness' which Douglas particularly desired Sheahan to be able to check by showing the source of the money Douglas had used.

Thus the Abolitionist Chase, author of the Appeal of the Independent Democrats, would be replaced in the next Congress by George Pugh, a Nebraska Democrat. No, this band of men 'who have in turn, joined and been kicked out of each of the great political parties because they were found to be unworthy to belong to either,' and who had since fused all the isms in the Know-Nothing crucible, could not speak for the whole North. Soon the Know-Nothing frenzy would die down and Democracy would come back.

Not without reason had Douglas emphasized the Know-Nothing menace. At the beginning of 1855, this secret order constituted the most perplexing problem in American politics. In 1854, Know-Nothingism had swept the North and early in 1855 Pierce's own State of New Hampshire went completely into their hands, and Connecticut and Rhode Island followed suit.[23] A little later in the Spring, news came from Cincinnati of a fearful riot in which armed Know-Nothings had attacked bands of Germans and nearly one hundred people had been killed. Now the Know-Nothings began girding their loins to cross Mason and Dixon's line. Marcy thought that the 'sudden rise and wonderful progress' of the Know-Nothings could be explained neither on the ground of the President's unpopularity nor that of the Kansas-Nebraska bill. The new party had beaten Whigs as badly as Democrats and Anti-Nebraska Whigs as badly as Anti-Nebraska Democrats. Like Douglas, this shrewd old campaigner thought that Know-Nothingism was an ephemeral development.[24] The Southern campaign would tell.

The first great Southern test came in Virginia, where the Know-Nothings undertook to capture the governorship, to control the Legislature and to elect a Know-Nothing Senator in Mason's stead. Henry A. Wise, the Democratic candidate for Governor, unleashed his scorpion tongue and the country breathlessly watched the campaign. The Virginians asked leading Northern Democrats for statements as to the Know-Nothing–Abolition fusion in their section. They managed to get a copy of the secret order's ritual, which made fine ammunition on the stump. The Old Dominion was in a ferment. Douglas, who was drafted into the campaign, spoke several times with great effect.[25] Wise uttered scathing denunciations of Know-Nothingism as an evil thing bred in stealth and darkness. The chief argument, however, was that the Northern Democrats were the South's only true friends, and the safety of the Union depended on Democratic principles being upheld. At the election, on May 24, Wise won by a substantial majority and the Legislature was safely Democratic. Virginia had stood fast.

This outcome revived Democratic hopes throughout the Union. Franklin Pierce promptly wrote Douglas that it had 'put a new face upon the prospects

[23] Nichols', *Pierce*, 389–90. The New Hampshire Democratic vote had decreased only 2000 under normal, but 32,000 Know-Nothings appeared as if by magic and the news went over the country that the President's State had repudiated him.

[24] Nichols, *Pierce*, 390.

[25] R. K. Meade to R. M. T. Hunter, Petersburg, Va., Feb. 10, 1855; Douglas MSS. B. H. Wise, *Henry A. Wise*, 174, says the Indiana Democratic State Committee furnished the copy of the Know-Nothing ritual. Rhodes, II, 44.

of the Democratic party... the only party which carries no dark lantern.'[26] Soon bitter dissension broke out in Know-Nothing ranks. When the Grand Council of the Order met in June, the Southerners seized control, ousted the founder, put a Kentuckian in the Presidency and forced through a resolution on slavery. 'The best guarantee of common justice and future peace,' it said, would be 'to abide by and maintain the existing laws' on slavery; Congress had no power to legislate on slavery and could not refuse to admit any State because its Constitution permitted or rejected slavery.[27]

While this action destroyed the Northern Know-Nothing cause, in the South it fortified the order for a season of fierce campaigning. The next great test came in Tennessee, where Andrew Johnson was the lion in its path. Seeking a second term as Governor, he campaigned the State arraigning the secret order for its signs, grips and passwords, its oaths and secret conclaves, its midnight gatherings. 'Show me a Know-Nothing,' he would exclaim, 'and I will show you a loathsome reptile, on whose neck every honest man should put his foot.'

The Know-Nothings threatened Johnson's life, but he would put a pistol on the stand beside him and dare them to shoot. These rural Protestant counties went heavily for the brave plebeian, who was re-elected by a large majority.[28]

Virginia and Tennessee were the forerunners of further Democratic triumphs in the South. Alabama repudiated the Know-Nothings and Cobb, Toombs and Stephens won a great victory in Georgia. After its magnitude was realized, they arranged a monster celebration at Atlanta, and asked Douglas to attend as a living exhibit that Democratic principles were the same everywhere.[29] Mississippi's Democratic stumpers all spoke armed, 'and it was not unusual to hear the clicks of a dozen pistols in the course of a speech,' but their unremitting onslaught on 'this mass of ignorance and corruption' had its effect and Mississippi went Democratic by 8000 majority. In every State save Kentucky the Know-Nothing attack on the South was repulsed.[30]

The North, too, was the scene of an intense Democratic effort. Every State in which the Fusionists had made inroads was organized and thoroughly canvassed. Better economic conditions helped in the Mid-West. Corn went up to thirty cents a bushel, wheat neared a dollar, hogs were bringing five dollars a hundredweight and the people were feeling better. The Indiana campaign illustrated the striking Democratic revival. On August 28, thirty thousand assembled at Indianapolis, where, from five speakers' stands in the Capitol grounds orators from Indiana, Illinois and Kentucky denounced the Know-Nothings and appealed for a return to Democratic principles.[31]

[26] Franklin Pierce, Washington, May 28, 1855; Douglas MSS.
[27] Channing, VI, 136. [28] Milton, *The Age of Hate*, 87–90.
[29] Douglas to Cobb, Lexington, Oct. 6, 1855; Erwin MSS.
[30] C. S. Tarpley, Jackson, Miss., Nov. 15, 1855; Douglas MSS.
[31] William Nye to John Nye, Clifford, Bartholomew County, Ind., Oct. 11, 1855, printed in *Driftwind Magazine*, VII, 109–11.

For Douglas the campaign began early. During May and June he was busy with the Illinois Prohibition referendum. While Lincoln's Springfield organ and many of his close political friends supported the Maine law, Lincoln himself kept clear of the struggle. But Douglas urged the State to 'bury Maine-lawism and Abolitionism all in the same grave.' [32] When the ballots were counted, it was found that the voters had followed his advice.[33] This outcome convinced Douglas that the Fusion cause was failing. Signs from other parts of the country convinced him that the reaction had extended over the whole Union.[34]

The Little Giant took the stump early in the Summer. He spoke throughout Illinois and Indiana and went to Kentucky in a vain effort to save that State.[35] His Illinois canvass was especially effective. Everywhere he portrayed 'Abolitionism, Know-Nothingism, and all the other isms' as being akin. His shafts sank home, and particularly those aimed at the Know-Nothings. 'The intelligent and right-minded and useful portion' of the Whigs regarded the Know-Nothing policy as 'mean, narrow and selfish' and drew apart. Fusion leaders privately predicted that next year the State would go for Douglas for President.

Lincoln, who was already a candidate for Douglas' seat in the Senate, was disturbed, and told one of his intimates that 'if the Know-Nothing movement was successful, he would no longer be of any use to his fellow men in politics.' None the less, he did not denounce them, but made a few speeches to offset Douglas' sledge-hammer blows against Republicanism.[36]

When Maine, in her September election, returned to the fold, Democratic campaigners redoubled their efforts in the October States. The line was strictly drawn in Pennsylvania and Indiana and the Democrats triumphed in both. The next month Illinois, Wisconsin and New Jersey went Democratic again; Know-Nothingism was routed, North as well as South; as one Indianan exulted, 'The dark lanterns are broken.' [37]

'The skies are now looking bright,' a leading Mississippi politician wrote Douglas. Let the Territories settle their own affairs without the interference of Congress and the whole land would 'be covered with peace and our hills and valleys will be vocal with the rejoicings of a prosperous people.' [38]

---

[32] Mr. F. Lauriston Bullard, of Boston, perhaps the outstanding authority in the country on this phase of Lincoln's career, is definitely of this opinion. There is no contemporary evidence to indicate that Lincoln took a hand in the campaign, or publicly expressed his views on it.

[33] Colvin, *op. cit.*, 34–36; the election was held June 4, 1855. The Maine law men carried the Abolition counties in the northern part of the State, but the central and southern counties went heavily against it.

[34] Douglas to Lanphier, Chicago, July 7, 1855; Patton MSS.

[35] *Illinois State Register*, Sept. 18, 1855, announced 21 Illinois appointments, from Springfield on the 19th to Ottawa on Oct. 24th. The *Register* of Oct. 11, announced further speaking dates to Nov. 1. On Oct. 6, he was in Lexington, Ky.

[36] David Davis to Julius N. Rockwell, Bloomington, Ill., Dec. 27, 1855; original owned by F. W. Rockwell, of North Andover, Mass.

[37] William Nye to John Nye, Clifford, Ind., Oct. 11, 1855, *Driftwind Magazine*, VII, 109–11.

[38] C. S. Tarpley, Jackson, Miss., Nov. 15, 1855; Douglas MSS. Tarpley was Jefferson Davis' right-hand man.

Douglas wrote Howell Cobb that 'Victories are crowding upon us on all sides. The tide is now completely turned. The torrent of fanaticism has been rolled back almost everywhere.' [39]

For all of his ardor and satisfaction, Douglas was a non-combatant in the closing week of the canvass. His reckless disregard of health and strength brought a day of reckoning — the wonder was that it had been delayed so long. For the past three years he had been going at top speed, and with his wife's death he had started drinking again. He kept late hours, made too many engagements and did not take care of himself. The campaign of 1855 proved especially demanding, for nearly every engagement was for open-air speaking and frequently he must ride across country in an open carriage.

On Saturday, October 27, Douglas was in Paris, one of the last of his Illinois engagements. But he was too hoarse to do aught else than bow to the crowd — another substituted as speaker.[40] Friends took him to Terre Haute, Indiana, and put him to bed in the home of Dr. Ezra Reed, a friendly old country practitioner. That night he had paroxysms of coughing and was speechless for hours at a time.[41]

For a time his life was despaired of, but Major Harris hastened to Terre Haute to nurse him and Dr. Reed treated him with great skill.[42] Convinced of the imperative need for surgical attention, a month later he made his way from Terre Haute to Cleveland, where he went under the care of Dr. Horace Ackley, acknowledged head of Cleveland's medical profession and 'one of the foremost surgeons on the Western Reserve.' [43]

But his severe illness did not preserve him from the calumny of faction. 'It is generally believed that Mr. Douglas was confined at Terre Haute by an attack of delirium tremens,' the Cleveland *Leader*, Wade's organ, declared. 'It is well known in Chicago that he is a drunken little blackguard.' The *Plain Dealer* promptly came to his defense against 'the demons of the reckless press willing to pursue him to the portals of the tomb.'

The day after Christmas, Dr. Ackley performed the first of a series of operations, passing an instrument down the throat and into the windpipe and injecting nitrate of silver into the parts affected. A couple of days later, he operated on 'the uvula or lower palate,' removed his patient's tonsils and put him to bed to recuperate. All this Douglas accepted philosophically

[39] Douglas to Cobb, Lexington, Ky., Oct. 6, 1855; Erwin MSS.

[40] *Illinois State Register*, Nov. 3, 1855.

[41] W. D. Latham to Chas. H. Lanphier, Paris, Ill., Oct. 30, 1855; Patton MSS.

[42] *Illinois State Register*, Dec. 1, 1855, quoting Harris' letter; Terre Haute, Ind., *Journal*, Dec. 14, 1855; Cleveland *Herald*, Dec. 20, 1855; Cleveland *Plain Dealer*, Dec. 31, 1855.

[43] E. Cleave, *Biographical Cyclopedia of the State of Ohio*, Cleveland (n.d.); 2; Howard Dittrick, compiler, *Pioneer Medicine in the Western Reserve*, Cleveland, 1932; 83–85; Wm. R. Coates, *History of Cuyahoga County and the City of Cleveland*, Chicago and New York, 1924; I, 463. Ackley moved to Cleveland about 1839, helped found the Cleveland Medical College, and held the chair of surgery there until 1858. Gifted as surgeon and anatomist, he operated boldly, coolly and with unusual success. He had to battle mobs aroused by the dissection of human bodies. He died April 24, 1859. For these details I am indebted to Dr. A. C. Cole, of Western Reserve University.

enough — he was ever willing to pay the piper when demand was legitimately made. The first operation would have been all right, he wrote a
friend, had it not shut off his breathing. He was touched by Dr. Ackley's
delight 'in running prolongs down the windpipe, and cutting off palates,
and clipping tonsils, and all such amusements.'[44] None the less, the Senator
fretted at his slow convalescence.

The past year's great Democratic recovery had worked a great change
in the political situation. For a year, Franklin Pierce had abandoned hopes
of re-election. Now he became 'very much excited, and sanguine,' and
hungered for a second term.[45] Douglas too had a recurrence of presidential
fever. Confidential friends gathered about his sick-bed, confidential letters
were dispatched, and finally, in February, he departed for Washington with
his mind made up for a second White House bid.

[44] Douglas to H. M. Rice, Cleveland, Dec. 28, 1855; original owned by Mr. W. H. Townsend,
of Lexington, Ky.; Douglas to Howell Cobb, Cleveland, Jan. 8, 1856; Erwin MSS.; Douglas to
David S. Reid, Cleveland, Jan. 11, 1856; North Carolina State Historical Commission, Raleigh.
[45] Nichols, *Pierce*, 426.

CHAPTER XV

THE SECOND EFFORT

IF DOUGLAS repealed the Missouri Compromise from any Presidential motive, Democratic politicians agreed that he had made 'an awful investment in it,' for the North would pursue him so bitterly as always to make him unavailable, while not only was the South 'not strong enough to make Presidents,' but also she had never 'worked hard for a Northern man who had no Northern availability.' [1] All thought the Little Giant had been 'postponed' as President.

James Buchanan was the chief gainer by Douglas' distress. Frequent were his protestations of loyalty to Pierce, but while at first these may have been sincere, at length they became the *pro forma* cover for his ambition.

Buchanan's 'availability' — the word politicians frequently employ to show why a weak man should be preferred to a strong one — arose almost exclusively from the fact that, as American Minister to the Court of St. James', he had escaped the struggle over the Nebraska bill. Immediately following its passage Pierce sent word that Buchanan was the only Democrat who could win the next contest and he himself would not be a candidate. [2] Douglas, too, decided he would not be 'in the field.' [3] After the disastrous Illinois campaign he asked Beverly Tucker, publisher of the Washington *Sentinel*, to print a card 'authoritatively' announcing his abstention, and after Tucker had done so, complained that the language was not strong enough, 'to make it more so.' [4]

He asked Sheahan to republish the *Sentinel* article, and to say 'that my determination not to be a candidate has been known to all my intimate personal friends since the nomination of General Pierce in '52, and will be resolutely adhered to.' [5]

But by the time of Wise's victory in Virginia, Pierce's ambition had completely recovered and he set out to secure a renomination. Among his first steps was to cultivate more cordial relations with Douglas. Throughout the latter's Summer sojourn in Illinois, the President wrote him repeatedly about Federal appointments, and his anxiety to conciliate was most apparent. He began calling at Douglas' Washington home, playing with the two boys,

[1] John W. Forney to James Buchanan, Washington, Jan. 10, Feb. 12, March 19, J. Glancy Jones to Buchanan, Washington, March 29, J. B. Bowlin to Buchanan, St. Louis, April 21, 1854; Buchanan MSS.

[2] Daniel E. Sickles to Buchanan, New York, Aug. 15; Forney to Buchanan, Washington, Nov. 27, Dec. 25, 1854; Buchanan MSS.

[3] Daniel E. Sickles to James Buchanan, New York, Aug. 15, 1854; Buchanan MSS.

[4] Beverly Tucker, New York, April 19, 1856; Douglas MSS. Justifying his own support of Buchanan, Tucker's letter gives a circumstantial account of Douglas' relation to a nomination candidacy.

[5] Douglas to Sheahan, Washington, Feb. 6, 1855; Sheahan MSS.

and otherwise making himself agreeable. When Julius Granger, Douglas' brother-in-law, had a bad accident, Pierce was first to inform Douglas of it. In July, Pierce made a point of naming Major Murray McConnel, Douglas' Jacksonville friend, Fifth Auditor of the Treasury.[6] This was not without its effect. Douglas thought Pierce would never be renominated, but counseled against interference with the latter's campaign and announced that he intended to treat Pierce's Administration 'kindly and well; to embark in no crusade against him; and to give it credit for its good deeds.[7]

His friends knew his purpose to 'remain in reserve,' although they hoped that when other aspirants had exhausted themselves, Douglas would become 'the common center of union for all.'[8] Howell Cobb wanted him to take steps to get Georgia's vote in the next national convention. 'I do not seek the nomination,' Douglas answered, 'do not ask it at the hands of our friends.' The first duty of these was to see to it that Democratic party organization was 'consolidated and placed immovably upon a sound, national, constitutional platform.' The platform 'must be bold, unequivocal and specific on all contraverted points. There must be no general, high-sounding phrases meaning nothing — no equivocal terms — no doubtful meaning — no double dealing for the benefit of timid and tricky politicians.'

Most of all, the platform must not be susceptible of one construction in the North and another in the South. 'We must make the next fight a fight for principles,' he wrote Cobb, 'and our triumph must decide the feeling and action of the Government for at least four years. The new Administration must not be a coalition of discordant materials nor a futile attempt to harmonize the chiefs of hostile factions; but it must be organized upon the Principles avowed in the platform, and composed of men who are identified and bound by every tie to carry out those principles in their appointments as well as by their measures.' As to himself, Douglas desired the party to assign him whatever position would make him most serviceable to the cause. The battle over the Kansas-Nebraska Act, 'and especially the course pursued by the allied factions and isms' toward him individually, would render the triumph of the cause a 'perfect and complete vindication.' He asked no other reward and he sought no higher triumph.

'From what I have said,' he advised Cobb, 'you will perceive that if my name shall be connected with the presidential election, it must be the voluntary act of our friends, prompted by the eye single to the success of the cause and the permanent triumph of our Principles, without any reference to my personal wishes or aggrandizement, and especially without any agency on my part, directly or indirectly, by word or deed.'[9] In the Fall of 1855, Douglas was reported inclined to Buchanan's nomination. The latter was beset by one group to urge restoration of the Missouri line and by another

[6] Franklin Pierce, Washington, May 3, 28, June 18, July 25, 1855; Douglas MSS.

[7] Forney to Buchanan, Washington, Aug. 12, Oct. 22–23, 1855. This policy was also that of Cass: 'I have this from the lips of the first [Douglas] and Nicholson has it by letter from Cass.'

[8] Samuel Treat, St. Louis, April 8, 1856; Douglas MSS., recounting 'our conversation last Fall.'

[9] Douglas to Howell Cobb, Lexington, Ky., Oct. 6, 1855; Erwin MSS.

to come out flatly for Popular Sovereignty, but Douglas had no hand in the efforts to embarrass him.[10]

But Douglas' long illness gave him ample time to analyze the probable effect of that Fall's Democratic triumph on his own political fortunes. His friends earnestly pressed his entry and undertook a good deal of preliminary work. Making up his mind while at Cleveland, from the turn of the year he employed all his resourcefulness in making his second bid.

Several factors probably entered into this decision. The year's Democratic victories convinced him the Nebraska bill had not 'postponed' him, his Know-Nothing diagnosis had been prophetic, the Prohibition tide was beginning to wane, and there remained no specific issue to render him 'unavailable.' Nor was Douglas impressed with the other aspirants. Pierce had alienated the most important politicians. Members of his Cabinet were showing signs of disaffection, and one of Jefferson Davis' Mississippi intimates suggested that while Pierce would not do, Douglas and Davis would be 'a great ticket,' which the Nebraska issue would carry 'in triumph over all opposition.' [11] The Little Giant saw that even if he remained on the sidelines, Pierce could not be renamed. R. M. T. Hunter, of Virginia, was a good man on the tariff, but without any broad support. The talk about Bright, of Indiana, was quite ridiculous. Buchanan, the only really formidable contender, was in Douglas' view a trimmer and a humbug. Then, too, there was hardly a State of the Union in which the Little Giant did not have a group of unquenchable supporters, determined that he get into the contest. They could give Douglas Ohio, wrote an Ohio editor; let him jump into the fight.[12] 'Douglas first' was his friends' motto and they would not be balked.[13]

During his convalescence at Cleveland, the Senator read the papers eagerly, followed the details of the Democrats' desperate and eventually unavailing battle to prevent the election of a Black Republican as Speaker of the House, wrote incessantly to party leaders in Washington and set his Ohio friends to work warming up important Democrats in other States.[14]

John C. Breckinridge was informed that the Little Giant had 'more confidence in your friendship, sagacity, and ability than that of any other man living' and was invited to become one of Douglas' chief advisers from the West.[15] Many other such letters went out, and progress was quickly reported. Douglas' Ohio friends secured 'the entire and absolute control' of the delegation to the Cincinnati Convention. 'Ohio is as sure for us as

[10] Forney to Buchanan, Washington, Oct. 29, 1854; J. Van Dyke to Buchanan, Philadelphia, Nov. 27; T. J. McCamant to Buchanan, Washington, D.C., Dec. 13, 1855; Buchanan MSS.

[11] C. S. Tarpley, Jackson, Miss., Nov. 15, 1855; Douglas MSS. Davis' friend mentioned several other Southerners who might go on the ticket with Douglas.

[12] James B. Steedman to Senator George E. Pugh, Columbus, Ohio, Nov. 29, 1855; Douglas MSS.

[13] Harris to Lanphier, Washington, Dec. 17, 1855, Jan. 8, 1856; Patton MSS.

[14] Douglas to Howell Cobb, Cleveland, Jan. 8, 1856; Erwin MSS.; Douglas to H. M. Rice, Cleveland, Dec. 28, 1855, original owned by Mr. W. H. Townsend of Lexington, Ky.; Douglas to D. S. Reid, Cleveland, Jan. 11, 1856; North Carolina State Historical Commission.

[15] H. V. Willson to Breckinridge, Cleveland, Jan. 21, 1856; Breckinridge MSS.

Illinois,' the Little Giant wrote Sheahan. Soon he heard that Iowa and Wisconsin had also named Douglas delegates. With this foundation he planned 'to combine the whole Northwest as a unit.' The President's entry would 'hold the South uncommitted for the present.' Let Sheahan push the Nebraska issue as vigorously as possible, for no man could be nominated who was not identified with it.[16] When Douglas reached Washington, on February 11, his throat was still so raw that he could not enter the Senate's debate, but intimates learned that he now felt that he must permit his friends to 'use his name or be driven to ignore the great act of his life.' [17]

In considering the ensuing struggle, one must keep in mind the nature of the then American political system; it was organized so as to maintain the semblance of popular domination, but the reality of control was from the top. This came both from the defense mechanism which powerful economic and social minorities maintained to control the operations of mystic democracy, and from aggrandizing ambitions of political leaders. Popular demand was forced to make its way up every step of a pyramid of political organization. Minority groups and politicians generally had their own way.

The control mechanism of the Democratic party encouraged such tactics. In each State there was a State Democratic Committee chiefly officered by the holders of public jobs, State conventions were usually controlled by patronage, past, present and future, and national conventions were largely made up of similarly chosen delegates. The vicious rule of senatorial courtesy in the confirmation of Federal appointments gave any Senator belonging to the party in power a whip hand in his State. All too often it was possible for a few men to negative the public wish. The Democratic party had an additional handicap, the two-thirds rule in its presidential selections, a throttling practice which implemented minorities with veto power and made patronage bosses practically supreme.

Well aware of the set-up, the Little Giant played the game according to the rules he found. In 1856 his task was twofold. Not only must he kindle the enthusiasm of the rank and file but also he must 'line up' a strong group of politicians. Particularly must the Northwest be measurably united behind him and New York's riddle solved. If he could handle these two situations, the rest would pretty largely manage itself.

But while he had been alternately advancing toward and retracting from a candidacy, the Buchanan men had been organizing the West. Jealousy of the vigor of Douglas' leadership had alienated many of Douglas' Western colleagues. For two years, however, he had sought to re-establish personal friendship with several of these men. In Indiana, which was highly important, the Democratic leader was Jesse D. Bright, a man of mediocre ability, who had a genius for political chicanery through patronage. In 1854, Bright was

[16] Douglas to Sheahan, Cleveland, Jan. 11, 1856; Sheahan MSS.; Willson to Breckinridge, Cleveland, Jan. 21, 1856; Breckinridge MSS.

[17] H. M. Rice to Breckinridge, Washington, Feb. 3, 12, 1856; Breckinridge MSS. Rice, who had been urging Breckinridge to be neutral, now asked him to join in the movement because the West 'is entitled to the next President.'

sending Douglas little notes and showing all manner of friendly attention.[18] But the Indiana Senator had Cæsarian ambitions himself. Douglas had been warned that, whatever might be the surface, Bright was only waiting for a chance to deal a death-blow. Douglas, however, undertook to conciliate and went so far as to put Bright into the land speculation at Superior. When Douglas determined to seek the 1856 nomination, Bright promised his own support and that of the State, and the Little Giant proceeded on that assumption.[19] The outcome, however, was to prove that Douglas had misplaced his faith.

Next to his own overweening ambitions, Bright's course was animated by a desire to help Buchanan and by a bitter hatred of Pierce.[20] The Indiana Senator explained to Douglas that his delegation would instruct for him as a favorite son but only as a compliment. In January, 1856, the Indiana Legislature re-elected him and Dr. Fitch, his pliant colleague, and the State Convention gave him Presidential instructions.[21]

The Douglas men in Indiana put no confidence in Bright's word. 'If the Northwest is divided,' one of them wrote Richardson, 'we have but little hope.' The Buchanan men reported that Bright preferred Buchanan to Douglas or Pierce, had Indiana in his hand, and 'the rest will be a stampede.' [22] In Michigan and Wisconsin too, the Buchaneers had shown 'great industry for months,' and their organization was 'extended and minute.' [23]

All this, however, was not immediately apparent. Douglas believed Bright's promise and thought old relations in Michigan and Wisconsin would assure a general Northwestern support. His Southern friends became active and began to get second-choice strength. If the New York question could be settled, success was close at hand. But as usual, Empire State Democracy was rent by faction and shattered by hatred and feud. Pierce's preferment of Marcy had intensified the long-standing schism between Softs and Hards, and Daniel S. Dickinson, the latter's leader, viewed Pierce

[18] D. E. Sickles to Buchanan, Aug. 15, 1854, Buchanan MSS.; George W. Jones to Bright, sent by Bright to Douglas, Dubuque, Iowa, May 6, 1855; Douglas MSS.

[19] While there is no direct documentary evidence of this agreement, Douglas' correspondence during January, February and March, 1856, was full of references to Bright's promise, and to whether or not this action or that on the part of the Indiana politician constituted a breach of faith. D. T. Disney, New York, Feb. 28, 1856: 'Bright is acting in good faith toward you.' Disney to Douglas, New York, undated, relating Benjamin's remark that Bright had said Buchanan would be nominated: 'Is there not some mistake about this in relation to Bright? Look into this without delay.' Disney asked Douglas to get Bright to write Daniel S. Dickinson to come out for Douglas, and pressed Douglas to get this letter.

[20] Forney to Buchanan, Philadelphia, Nov. 27, 1855; Buchanan MSS. During a Philadelphia city election involving Buchanan's prestige, Bright offered $1000 toward the campaign expenses — a good index of his basic intent.

[21] John L. Robinson to Howell Cobb, Indianapolis, Ind., Jan. 30, 1856; Erwin MSS. Governor Joseph A. Wright sought to defeat Fitch, saw he would be beaten in the Democratic caucus, withdrew for a diplomatic appointment and both Bright and Fitch were nominated unanimously.

[22] W. J. Brown to W. A. Richardson, Indianapolis, Feb. 17, 1856; Douglas MSS.; George N. Sanders to Buchanan, Washington, Feb. 16; J. Glancy Jones to Buchanan, Washington, Feb. 27, 1856; Buchanan MSS.

[23] D. A. Noble, Monroe, Mich., April 9, 1856; Douglas MSS.

with unquenchable hate. New York would present the usual contesting delegations to the National Convention.

Douglas had one gleam of hope in this situation. Marcy was reasonably friendly and the Softs might be secured. Dickinson so hated Pierce that he might look upon Douglas' nomination as a victory. Perhaps both groups could be brought to agree on the Illinois Senator. He dispatched confidential agents to Manhattan to see what could be done along this line.

Fortunately the Little Giant was now represented by men of more intelligence and poise than in 1852. George N. Sanders had magnified a fancied grievance against Douglas and become an active Buchanan man. With him went Daniel E. Sickles, John W. Forney, Beverly Tucker and many of the most radical Young America group. Buchanan lieutenants were startled as well as pleased to see Young America join the Old Fogy camp.[24]

As confidential men for the 1856 campaign, Douglas selected D. T. Disney, of Ohio, and General J. W. Singleton, of Illinois. Disney, an Ohio Congressman, Douglas considered 'a discreet man, full of talents and resources.' Singleton, a former Virginian, an Old-Line Whig and intimate of Henry Clay, had great strength in political maneuver.[25]

When the Buchaneers suspected Douglas' entry, Slidell advised his chief that the Little Giant would prove 'a more formidable competitor than Pierce,' a judgment in which Sanders agreed. But for the time being they 'would coax and not quarrel with him.'[26] In February, Douglas admitted that he was making the race so as to uphold the principle of Popular Sovereignty. Now the Buchaneers raged that Douglas was a 'dog in the manger,' 'he was too fast before — he is too late now.'[27]

Douglas' lieutenants were elated with developments. When Pierce's Administration support restored to A. O. P. Nicholson the Government printing which Beverly Tucker had taken away two months before, they thought it would 'throw Virginia clean for Douglas.' Then, too, 'Pierce admitted he

[24] In 1853, Pierce nominated Sanders American Consul at London. Sanders proceeded to his post and began sending back scurrilous news letters to Bennett's New York *Herald*, which Bennett unkindly printed under Sanders' signature. These dispatches contained reflections on several Democratic Senators, who put up a fight on Sanders' confirmation, resulting in the Kentuckian's defeat. Although Douglas had done the best he could, Sanders blamed Douglas for his rejection. Toombs wrote Sanders that his suspicions were untrue, but this had no effect. The hot-head wrote Douglas a denunciatory letter, terminating their friendship. Douglas did not grieve. Douglas to Sanders, Washington, March 27, 1854; Illinois State Historical Library MSS.; Robert Toombs to Sanders, Washington, June 13, 1854; original in possession of Watertown, Conn., Library; J. C. Van Dyke to Buchanan, Philadelphia, Feb. 23, 1855; Buchanan MSS.; Beverly Tucker, New York, April 19, 1856; Douglas MSS.

[25] Douglas to Singleton, Washington, March 16, 1856; Illinois State Historical Library MSS. In 1864, Abraham Lincoln drafted Singleton both to conduct political negotiations highly important to the Emancipator's re-election, and to go to Richmond to negotiate peace with Jefferson Davis. Linder, 245, for Singleton's Illinois career.

[26] Slidell to Buchanan, Washington, Feb. 7; George N. Sanders to Buchanan, Washington, Feb. 16, 1856; Buchanan MSS.

[27] Forney to Buchanan, Washington, Feb. 28; J. Watson Webb to Buchanan, New York, March 10, 1856; Buchanan MSS.

could not win without Douglas' support.' But the latter's aides felt themselves certain of the delegates from Ohio, California, Missouri, Minnesota,
Wisconsin, Virginia, Arkansas, Texas, Louisiana and Florida. Perhaps
they would have Michigan and Vermont, and they thought their chances
good in New York and Tennessee. The Buchananites heard that Douglas
was almost ready to give it up, but the actual feeling in campaign headquarters was quite different. 'He is gaining every day,' Harris wrote Lanphier, on February 28. 'His nomination is by most of our friends and many
of our enemies considered certain.' [28]

Disney went to New York City in January and his quarters at the Astor
House were filled with Hards and Softs; he set to work to establish a *modus
vivendi* between them. Douglas' agent pointed out to all that their political
future was closed unless their State was redeemed. An ardent Cass man in
1852, Disney intimated that if New York would move toward Douglas, the
Cass group would 'cordially surrender their preferences and unite and go
with New York.' [29]

Marcy, who hated Buchanan, saw that Pierce could not travel, and was
bringing the Softs into line. Soon they began to hearken to Disney's program
and he redoubled his work on the Hards. 'New York may now be the arbiter
of the convention,' Disney told Augustus Schell, a powerful Hard. She could
dictate the nominee but only if the Hards and Softs would join on the same
man for President. Schell urged Disney to see Dickinson, which he determined to do.

But first Disney wanted 'a Southern man of standing' to help bring the
Hard leader around. 'You know these New Yorkers,' he wrote Douglas.
'To reach them you must show them a future of promise — with that I can
get both sides... and thus end all doubt about the nomination.' [30] The next
day, after another interview with Schell, he wrote the Little Giant: 'Can
you not get *Bright* to write to Dickinson urging him to come into the move,
and to take the initiative in New York in your favor?' [31]

New York was not Disney's only worry. He interspersed his accounts of
these New York negotiations with reports of affairs in other States. He saw
Hale, one of the Detroit *Free Press* owners, a most important Michigan factor,
who was strong for Buchanan 'to benefit himself.' Disney knew he could
'be got,' and wanted to bid high. Virginia was moving toward Buchanan,
couldn't Hunter and Pierce be aroused? [32]

Disney's request for assistance and for specific authority to present at
Binghamton came at a very bad time, for Douglas had had a renewal of his
throat trouble and was ordered to his bed. Disney was nettled at the lack of
response from Washington. 'I have pushed the matter of union between the

[28] Harris to Lanphier and Walker, Washington, Feb. 6, 26, 1856; Patton MSS.; J. Glancy
Jones to Buchanan, Washington, Feb. 27, 1856; Buchanan MSS.
[29] D. T. Disney, New York, Feb. 2, 28, 29, 1856; Douglas MSS.
[30] Disney, New York, Feb. 29, 1856; Douglas MSS.
[31] Disney, New York, 1856; Douglas MSS. The letter obviously came between Feb. 22, and
March 1.
[32] Disney, New York, March 2, 1856; Douglas MSS.

Hards and Softs to the verge of action in your favor,' he wrote, there was a 'reasonable probability' of success, but where was the letter from Bright? [33]

When Douglas recovered, he did what he could to support Disney, but found difficulty in getting Bright to write the desired letter and became less sanguine of his good faith. As to the other branch of the request, sending a good Southern man to help Disney, he had none such available. But General Singleton, who had reached Washington in mid-February, and had been at work writing pro-Douglas letters to important Southern papers, was dispatched to New York. He agreed with Disney that 'a little management' would win Douglas the Empire State. 'Now is the time,' he wrote Douglas: either to send them a Southern man of position or come himself, even for a day, and the matter might be arranged.

But Douglas could not find 'any Southern man of the kind you wish,' nor could he come himself, for his throat was so bad that he could not even get to the Senate to lead a fight to prevent the seating of Trumbull. So he wrote encouragingly and left Singleton and Disney to do the best they could. [34]

They were unable to make an authoritative agreement with Dickinson and the Hard faction, and Douglas was forced to look to the Softs. Dean Richmond, Marcy's ablest lieutenant, wanted 'to be on some winning side,' and slipped down to Washington for a 'secret interview' with Douglas. This proved 'perfectly satisfactory' and he pledged Douglas his entire group's convention support. [35] This was all right, if the Soft delegation were seated. But if the Buchaneers controlled the convention, the Softs might be thrown out and Douglas would lose.

During these weeks there were encouraging manifestations of growing public support for Douglas and his issue. His friends and foes converted a Chicago city campaign into a referendum on the Little Giant. By mid-February, the Douglasites were 'in the midst of a glorious fight.' Medill's *Tribune*, Wentworth's *Democrat* and other hostile papers declared that victory for Douglas' ticket would result in his nomination at Cincinnati and the *Times* hoped that it would be so. An acrimonious quarrel between Sheahan and his partner Cook, who was putting up the money for the paper, but who now sued the paper, and tried to force Sheahan out as editor, failed to check the enthusiasm of the campaign. The Senator's friends left their business affairs and put their time in with the voters. Every night there were meetings and speakings, and Douglas' name was the battle-cry. At the

[33] Disney, New York, March 5, 7, 1856; Douglas MSS.

[34] Harris to Lanphier, Washington, Feb. 26, 1856; Patton MSS. Douglas to Singleton, Washington, March 5, 1856; original owned by Mr. W. H. Townsend of Lexington, Ky. J. W. Singleton, New York, March 5, 1856; Douglas MSS. Douglas to Singleton, Washington, March 16, 1856; Illinois State Historical Society MSS.

[35] A. P. Edgerton, Hicksville, Ohio, March 27; H. V. Willson, Cleveland, Ohio, May 29, 1856; Douglas MSS. Edgerton had an interview with Richmond at Albany, and wrote Douglas of it. Willson, a personal friend of the Little Giant, was Richmond's lawyer and friend. When the New-Yorker came through Cleveland en route to the Cincinnati Convention, he told Willson of the secret interview, and that the Softs intended to carry out the agreement in good faith.

election on March 4, the Douglas ticket won and the city was 'wild with excitement.' 'Chicago is redeemed,' a friend exulted. 'Your name is on the tongue of every man as the next President of the United States.' Harris wrote Lanphier that Chicago had done it nobly, the result was 'an earnest of the future.' Washington, too, was impressed.[36]

Events operated to strengthen the demand that the Cincinnati platform contain an unqualified Popular Sovereignty endorsement. This Douglas buttressed by his report to the Senate on the troubles in Kansas. As Chairman of the Committee on Territories, Pierce's special message on the extraordinary events at Shawnee, Pawnee, Lawrence and Topeka had come directly to him. He studied the available data and carefully prepared his report. Harris, who saw it in proof form, was in raptures; it was 'a crusher, and would cut down Pierce completely,' it would be a big campaign gun.[37]

On March 12, Douglas brought forward the majority, and Collamer made the Republicans' minority report. Douglas first developed his conception of Territorial rights, Federal relations, and constitutional derivations. Domestic slavery was a concern of the individual Commonwealth; when new States were admitted, they had an equal right with the original ones to decide whether to have or prohibit slavery, for the Federal Constitution was the 'only limitation upon their sovereign authority.'

Congress' power to organize a Territorial Government was inherent in the right to admit a new State, but only 'as a means of carrying into effect the provision of the Constitution for the admission of new States.' In view of the people's reserved powers, the organic act for a Territory 'must leave the people entirely free to form and regulate their domestic institutions and internal concerns in their own way,' subject only to the Federal Constitution; this was the only mode by which they could surely come into the Union 'on an equal footing with the original States in all respects whatsoever.'

Describing Thayer's Emigrant Aid Company enterprises, he grew satiric in his description of the people of a State 'so much enamoured with their own peculiar institution' that they would conceive 'the philanthropic scheme of forcing so great a blessing on their unwilling neighbors.' Without question, this would be 'an act of aggression, as offensive and flagrant as if attempted by direct and open violence.' No State had a right to pass a law

[36] J. W. Sheahan, Chicago, Jan. 28, Feb. 19, March 16; Samuel Ashton, Chicago, March 5, 1856; Douglas MSS. Harris to Lanphier, Washington, March 7, 1856; Patton MSS. For Sheahan-Cook controversy, see Douglas to Sheahan, Washington, March 28, April 9, 11, 1856, Sheahan MSS. D. Cameron, Chicago, April 5; W. J. Brown, Chicago, April 6; E. R. Hooper, Chicago, April 12; T. L. Harris, Springfield, May 16, 1856, Douglas MSS. Sheahan nagged at Cook, the latter entered suit. 'If you are my enemy,' the Little Giant telegraphed Cook, 'you will continue your suit against the *Times*; if you are my friend, you will dismiss it.' Cook would not budge, and Douglas found $18,000 to extricate Sheahan. The Cook-Sheahan war went on through 1860.

[37] Harris to Lanphier, Washington, March 7, 1856; Patton MSS. D. T. Disney, New York, March 7, 1856; Douglas MSS. The Opposition grew alarmed over these reports; George N. Sanders to Forney, Washington, March 10, 1856, Buchanan MSS., speaks of an effort of Brown and Quitman of Mississippi to have Douglas 'play a desperate game for the Southern vote.'

or do or authorize any act to influence or change the domestic policy of a sister State, but this was precisely what Massachusetts had sought to do with Kansas. True, Kansas was a Territory but the principle applied.

Douglas' report then examined the inflammatory emigration, the Missouri counter-organization, Reeder's speculations, election blunders and removal, the events of Governor Shannon's ill-fated régime. He dwelt particularly on the Free-State men's repudiation of the legitimate Government, their calling of the Topeka Convention, adoption of a Constitution and insistence on being admitted as a State under this instrument of rebellion.

This subversive movement was the natural fruit of the anti-slavery effort to circumvent the law's intent 'to leave the actual settlers and *bona fide* inhabitants perfectly free to form and regulate their domestic institutions in their own way, subject only to the Constitution of the United States.' The quiet in Nebraska was irrefragable proof that these schemes of foreign interference 'to stimulate an unnatural and false system of emigration' were responsible for Kansas' plight.[38]

Pierce's special message had asked that Congress enable Kansas, as soon as her population became sufficient, to elect delegates, frame a Constitution and 'prepare through regular and lawful means' to become a State. Douglas' report gave notice of his early intention to bring in such a bill. This he did, supporting it on March 20 with a powerful speech. Again he condemned schemes of subsidized, artificial emigration as an affront to the national peace. In Nebraska Popular Sovereignty was highly successful; in Kansas it would be so but for the Abolitionists and their Emigrant Aid.

Collamer demanded immediate admission for Kansas under the Topeka Free-State Constitution. Seward, Chase, Sumner and the other Abolitionists and Free-Soilers came to Collamer's support. Their thesis was that Douglas was wrong as to the trouble, that the basic error had been the 'experiment' of Popular Sovereignty, this 'vice of a mistaken law' which had led inevitably to a competition of social and economic systems, of which the natural consequences was bloodshed.

Douglas answered Collamer that, by the Nebraska bill, slavery had been 'left to the decision of the people.' How could that be subject to objection? Collamer said that Popular Sovereignty tended to bring opposing elements and inflammable materials into collision. 'Does not the same objection apply to all other questions which involve the interests and excite the passions of men?' Douglas countered. If valid, this objection applied to any other legislation, or action, with an emotional impact, was an objection 'to the fundamental principles upon which all free governments rest' and, if heeded, 'drives us irresistibly to despotism.'

How did Seward reconcile his constant portrayal of 'the beauties of Negro freedom and equality,' Douglas asked, with his advocacy of Kansas' admission under the Topeka Constitution, a clause of which permanently banned free as well as slave Negroes from the State. Seward was forced

---

[38] *Congressional Globe*, Thirty-Fourth Congress, First Session, 638–39; the report was printed separately as a Senate Document; Sheahan, 287–94, prints essential portions.

to admit that he sought the Kansas admission for the white man's benefit, not the Negro's. In conclusion, Douglas touched up the platform of the Black Republicans. They stood pledged to stop the admission of any more Slave States, to repeal the Fugitive Slave law, to abolish the internal slave trade, to ban slavery in the District of Columbia, to reimpose the Missouri Compromise on Kansas and Nebraska and to stop the acquisition of any further territory anywhere unless slavery should first have been prohibited.

The Little Giant hoped the Black Republicans, having promulgated this creed, would not dodge or evade. Let there be no lowering of the flag, 'let us have a fair, bold fight before the people, and then let the verdict be pronounced.'

'You will have it,' Seward shot back.

Douglas rejoiced in the assurance. But let the Republicans be sure they did not falter or retreat. Rumor said that, in picking a presidential candidate, they were planning to ignore their battle-scarred leaders and to take up a new man without views or enemies. 'Are the offices and patronage of government so much more important to you than your principles, that you feel it your duty to sacrifice your creed, and the men identified with it in order to get power?' he asked scornfully. He hoped they would not now throw overboard their trusted leaders, merely 'for the purpose of cheating somebody by getting votes from all sorts of men.' The galleries burst into wild applause.[39]

As his friends had expected, the Little Giant's report, together with his part in the ensuing debate, gave a powerful stimulus to his campaign. North and South, Democrats applauded. New York saw a rapid shift on Popular Sovereignty, and one confidant wrote Douglas that while it had seemed as if the people 'were never going to get through hanging your effigy,' at last they have regained 'an appetite for substantial food.' [40]

For a month Slidell, Buchanan's chief manager, tried to keep Douglas out for, if he could do so, 'then the game is safe.' There had been 'much conversation,' and Slidell thought he was making headway.

But after the Little Giant saw the reaction to his report, it was definitely understood that he would go on through with his race. The Kansas report, in English and German, was being spread through the North. Bennett had committed the *Herald*. 'Douglas keeps very quiet but *works*,' Rice advised Breckinridge, 'his friends do the same.' Harris wrote gleefully: 'Douglas will be the nominee.' [41]

Buchanan's lieutenants thought that, whatever other effect Douglas'

[39] *Congressional Globe*, Thirty-Fourth Congress, First Session, App., 365–78; 358–64. The various main speeches of the debate were put into pamphlets and sent out by tens of thousands.
[40] Stephen Dellaye, Syracuse, N.Y., March 22; E. C. West to Douglas, New York, April 8, 1856; Douglas MSS.
[41] Slidell to Buchanan, Washington, March 11; J. Glancy Jones to Buchanan, Washington, March 22, 1856; Buchanan MSS. Charles Mason MSS. Diary, entry for March 18, 1856; Rice to Breckinridge, Washington, April 7, 1856; Breckinridge MSS.; Harris to Lanphier, Washington, March 24, 28, 1856; Patton MSS.

entry might have, it eliminated Pierce. The President was bitterly resentful. 'Douglas being a candidate is very unexpected,' he told an Illinois caller. 'I have not been treated right.'[42] But for all his disappointment, the President and his aides kept up their efforts, the chief of which was to consolidate the South. But several delegations there determined that, after a few ballots, they would turn from Pierce to Douglas, and a number of others were set for Buchanan against both.[43]

'Much depends on Virginia,' Douglas advised Singleton, who went to see what he could do. The basic trouble was that, from Governor Wise to Beverly Tucker, the dominant Democratic element was bitterly hostile to Pierce, Douglas had been understood not a candidate, and 'Buchanan was taken up as the best man to break Pierce down.' Douglas' admission to Beverly Tucker that under certain contingencies he might back Pierce had caused Tucker to undertake to set Virginia against Douglas too. Singleton did what he could to set up a Douglas group but was not too hopeful.[44]

The Georgia prospect was also disquieting. During Douglas' delay, Howell Cobb had embraced Buchanan and had drawn most of the State's leaders with him. Toombs and Stephens were friendly to Douglas but inactive. The people might be for Douglas but the delegation was in doubt.[45] Mississippi went for Pierce right enough, but many of its delegates had Buchanan as second choice. Andrew Johnson, Tennessee's Governor, did not like Douglas, besides which he was proposed for Vice-President. Slidell seemed to have control of the Louisiana delegation. Douglas had problems to work out in the South.

Even after Disney's failure in New York, Douglas' friends kept up the effort to concentrate both Hards and Softs on him, but the undertow there was for Buchanan and Bright's intimacy with Dickinson inclined the latter that way. There was no open disclosure. Hard leaders warned Douglas that his hopes of the Softs were illusory, he must not be deluded by this 'drop game' — the Hards would first vote for Daniel S. Dickinson but they were the real Douglas men. But Douglas was undeceived by this smoke-screen. Dean Richmond and the Softs were acting in good faith.[46]

[42] J. Glancy Jones to Buchanan, Washington, March 24, 1856; Buchanan MSS. Mrs. Adeline Crenshaw to Mrs. Chas. H. Lanphier, Washington, April 20, 1856; Patton MSS. Mrs. Crenshaw had gone to Washington with her husband, William, who wanted a Kansas job. John Calhoun, of Springfield, for two years Federal Surveyor of the two new Territories, took him to see Pierce, who made the remarks above quoted, which I have put from third to first person. The interview took place April 18. The next day Pierce gave William Crenshaw a job at Topeka.

[43] John F. Poppenheim, Charleston, S.C., May 9; J. George Harris, New York, May 22, 1856; Douglas MSS. Harris, a Navy Paymaster from Tennessee, had recently been to that State.

[44] Douglas to Singleton, Washington, May 14, 1856; Illinois State Historical Society MSS.; J. W. Singleton, Winchester, Va., March 28; Beverly Tucker, New York, April 19, 1856; Douglas MSS.

[45] J. H. Steele, Atlanta, May 12, 14, 1856; John C. Mather, Athens, Ga., May 12, 1856; Douglas MSS. Steele was editor of the Atlanta *Examiner*. Mather, a New York contractor, said that Cobb 'could right matters at once. Why is he for Buchanan?' Why should the younger leaders, with the future before them, be for Old Buck?

[46] E. C. West, New York, May 10, 13; J. Kimball, Brooklyn, May 10, 1856; R. V. Connolly, New York, May 21; H. V. Willson, Cleveland, Ohio, May 29, 1856; Douglas MSS.

Douglas' Western efforts were checkmated by the treachery of Senator Bright. Slidell, who was in charge of the Buchanan negotiations with the Indiana Senator, found that his price was the control of all major Federal appointments for the Northwest. But it was not for nothing that Slidell had had a Tammany training. He accepted the proposition, the agreement was made, 'the patronage for the Northwest was disposed of,' then Slidell wrote his chief: 'We can rely on Bright.' This agreement was confirmed by Buchanan, when he became President, and a general patronage triumvirate of Slidell, the campaign manager, Bright, the glorious apostate, and Corcoran, the campaign's financial angel, was set up.[47]

Douglas probably suspected what had happened, but Bright did not disclose his hand and comforting reports continued to come from the Illinois Senator's friends in Bright's State. A scout wrote him that 'The *People* are for you and the Politicians know it'; Bright's name would not be presented to the Cincinnati Convention and perhaps Hunter's would not. By May, however, Douglas was advised of the exact nature of 'Bright's game' — to claim the right to control Indiana's vote all through the convention.[48]

Slidell was equally successful in Michigan, where Senator Stuart was 'thoroughly with us,' and Cass was quite sympathetic. Buchanan sentiment among the people was slight and at first Douglas men believed they could check the patronage machine. Late in May, however, Pierce vetoed a Michigan pork-barrel item and the Michigan delegates set to work lobbying for Buchanan as soon as they reached Cincinnati. Not without reason had Slidell written that he was sure of all of the Northwest except Illinois.[49]

But the record was not all one of disaster. California elected a delegation of 'out-and-out Nebraska Democrats,' believed favorable to Douglas. Buchanan had a good start in Wisconsin, but Douglas' advocates became active, Governor Barstow swung into line and friendly delegates were chosen.[50] Ohio Douglas men claimed twenty-six of its delegation. Missouri adopted a flat-footed Kansas-Nebraska, anti-Know-Nothing platform; as to its delegation, 'several of the best Douglas men in the United States were upon it, and not a single man opposed.'[51] But when the Illinois De-

---

[47] In February, 1857, Douglas pierced to the bottom of this deal and his indignation over it was the beginning of his breach with Buchanan the ensuing December. Douglas to Samuel Treat, Washington, Feb. 5, 1857; Missouri Historical Society MSS. Slidell to Buchanan, Washington, March 11; J. Glancy Jones to Buchanan, Washington, March 22; Forney to Buchanan, Washington, Nov. 12, 1856; Buchanan MSS.: 'To Bright's indomitable energy we are indebted for... the *coup d'état* which gave us the vote of Indiana in convention.'

[48] Winslow S. Pierce, Indianapolis, March 8; U. F. Linder, Terre Haute, March 15; Austin H. Brown, Indianapolis, May 3, 1856; Douglas MSS.

[49] Slidell to Buchanan, Washington, March 11, 1856; Buchanan MSS. D. A. Noble, Monroe, Mich., April 9, 19; H. V. Willson, Cleveland, Ohio, May 29; Daniel P. Rhodes, Cincinnati, Ohio, May 28, 1856; Douglas MSS.

[50] William Hull to Douglas, LaCrosse, Wis. Dec. 5, 1857; Douglas MSS. 'It was expected by most of our party that you, sir, would have received the unanimous vote of Wisconsin in the last national convention.' Hull was a Wisconsin Assemblyman, Democrats' choice for Speaker.

[51] T. D. Hayden, San Francisco, March 20; Daniel Read, Madison, Wis., April 27; J. Woodle, Janesville, Wis., April 26, May 18; J. W. Gray, Cleveland, Ohio, April 25; Samuel Treat, St. Louis, Mo., April 8; D. Kennet, St. Louis, April 24; Richard F. Barry, St. Louis, May 25, 1856; Douglas MSS.

mocracy met in Springfield in May, and instructed for Douglas, Harris wrote unhappily that it 'came near botching the whole business.' [52]

As always, high tensions developed just before the convention and candidates did foolish things. Buchanan's aides advised him that a public declaration for the Nebraska bill would reconcile Douglas. Buchanan responded, but his verb was 'acquiesce,' not 'approve,' and it did not meet the case. Slidell now demanded that Buchanan pledge himself against a second term and that he come out flat-footed on Nebraska. While Old Buck refused the first pledge, he did write a statement that, had he been in Congress, he would have voted for the Nebraska bill. The Douglasites made a minor maneuver by the suggestion of Hunter, of Virginia, for President and the Buchaneers countered with a trial balloon for Jefferson Davis.[53]

Pierce's Southern friends indignantly said that the sole purpose of the Cincinnati Convention was 'to set aside the will of the people.' The Buchaneers would first show Pierce's inability to get two-thirds, then would undertake to 'prostrate Judge Douglas, who is obviously the next strongest man,' then they would rush to Buchanan. 'Everything depends on the South,' shrewd old Samuel Medary, of Ohio, believed. 'If they come divided in sentiment and remain irreconcilable, we will have a lottery drawing before us.' Such considerations constrained Pierce and Douglas to effect 'a good understanding,' and Douglas' intimates were assured that Pierce would not be a serious candidate.[54]

Washington was filled with rumors that Douglas planned withdrawal and that he and Hunter had combined to nominate Pierce. Slidell had been so confident of Buchanan's victory that he had not intended to go to Cincinnati, but upon this report he hastened to the front. Corcoran, the banker, heard the same rumor and relayed it to Bright, who used it as pretext, and sent word to Douglas that Indiana would be for Buchanan 'from beginning to end.' [55]

The convention was to assemble on June 2, but candidates' headquarters opened two weeks beforehand. Slidell, Bright and Corcoran secured a large suite at the Burnet House and lavishly entertained in Buchanan's behalf. Coleman, the famous boniface, reserved his 'very best parlor' for the Douglas men, at a modest $150 per day and Washington McLean, proprietor

[52] J. W. Singleton, Quincy, Ill., May 16; T. L. Harris, Springfield, Ill., May 16, 1856; Douglas MSS. Singleton was excited as to the personnel and the folly of depending on instructions. 'He who goes to Cincinnati to oppose you is armed by instructions — he appears under the face of friendship, under which he conceals the poisoned dagger.'

[53] J. Glancy Jones to Buchanan, Washington, March 22; Slidell to Buchanan, Washington, May 2; Forney to Buchanan, Philadelphia, May 4, 1856; Buchanan MSS. Winslow S. Pierce, Buffalo, N.Y., May 22, 1856; Douglas MSS. Buchanan to Slidell, Wheatlands, May 28, 1856; copy in Breckinridge MSS.

[54] Wilson Lumpkin to Pierce, Athens, Ga., May 19; Samuel Medary to Douglas, North Wood, Ohio, May 25, 1856; Douglas MSS. Rice to Breckinridge, Washington, May 18, 1856; Breckinridge MSS.

[55] Slidell to Buchanan, Washington, May 26; Corcoran to Buchanan, Washington, May 27, 1856; Buchanan MSS.

of the Cincinnati *Enquirer*, almost took charge of the headquarters. James B. Steadman, the Ohio editor, led a group charged with greeting visitors and 'making themselves pleasant and courteously agreeable to all.' Daniel P. Rhodes was there doing what he could, but the big guns were William A. Richardson, chairman of the Illinois delegation; Major Harris, Douglas' trusted friend, and Disney and Singleton, his pre-convention strategists.[56] For local press support, in addition to the *Enquirer*, Douglas had the advocacy of the Cincinnati *Gazette*, which declared he could carry every Northern State that Buchanan could and would win the South without question. On the other hand, Buchanan's strength was among the 'weak-backed and weak-kneed syllabub politicians.' [57]

Even so, the 'weak-back portion of the party' went about its convention job quite competently. Slidell, Bright and Corcoran arranged for the Pennsylvania delegation to bring with it 'several hundred followers, to make an outside pressure,' which began to be vociferously exerted from Saturday preceding the convention. Some delegates objected that 'the noise they occasion resembles running water passing over rocks in shallow places,' but it had quite an effect.

Buchanan's imported noise-makers were supplemented by Cincinnati's ruling Democratic city machine, which had declared war to the death upon the Wash McLean *Enquirer*, and all candidates he supported. McLean's activity at Douglas' headquarters 'raised up the whole party' in Cincinnati, the city machine 'acted systematically, and detached the members in squads of fifty to each hotel in town to clamor for Buchanan.' This contributed no little to making 'the outside pressure ten to one for Buchanan.' [58]

To offset all this proved impossible. Pierce had very few enthusiastic supporters. About a hundred Illinois boosters came with the Illinois delegation, an even larger group came from southeastern Indiana, and these did the best they could to counteract the manufactured Buchanan enthusiasm. But they found it hard to meet the cry of 'availability,' 'Pennsylvania's last chance,' 'safe man,' 'prudent,' 'politic statesman,' 'he can carry the doubtful Northern States,' and the like. The Northern Buchaneers' 'pleading, wailing, womanly cry' dampened Southern enthusiasm. Deeper than this, there was a general wish for political 'pacification,' and Buchanan's age, supposed experience and well-advertised moderation of views brought this sentiment to his support. Whigs just coming over to the Democratic party, 'tender-toed' Democrats and 'all the unsound' moved toward Old Buck.[59]

The arriving delegations quickly caucused. On Saturday Alabama and Arkansas determined first on Pierce and then the Little Giant. The Pierce-

---

[56] E. C. West, Cincinnati, May 22; D. P. Rhodes, Cincinnati, May 28; T. M. Ward, Cincinnati, June 1, 1856; Douglas MSS.

[57] Cincinnati *Gazette*, June 4, 1856.

[58] T. M. Ward, Cincinnati, June 1; Charles P. Button, Cincinnati, June 1; D. T. Disney, Cincinnati, June 7, 1856; Douglas MSS.

[59] T. M. Ward, Cincinnati, June 1; D. T. Disney, Cincinnati, June 7; Isaac R. Diller, Springfield, Ill., June 10, 1856; Douglas MSS.

Douglas men in the Georgia delegation secured Pierce the full first vote. But Buchanan's leaders were confident they would break down Pierce in New York and New England and shatter Douglas in the Northwest.[60]

They began this program with Indiana's caucus. Despite Bright, Douglas' lieutenants in the State had been extraordinarily active, great meetings had demanded that the delegates vote for the Little Giant, and when the delegates left Indiana, a majority had expressed a 'determination' to go for Douglas, as desired by 'the Democratic masses throughout the State.' But Bright met them at Cincinnati, his persuasions were effective and the caucus vote Saturday night was Buchanan, 16; Douglas, 10. The majority clapped on the unit rule and the deed was done.[61]

This was a major disaster. Indiana's 'singular bolt' immediately upset Ohio, and cost Douglas the major portion of that delegation. The New York Hards reached Cincinnati about ready to vote for Douglas, 'with a card in reserve for Dickinson.' But the Indiana action disturbed them, Bright and Slidell applied pressure and bargained to go for Old Buck. 'Indiana is playing the very old Harry with us,' an aide reported to Douglas, whose managers, enraged and aghast, said the day would come to 'reward Indiana and Ohio for their treachery.' There was not 'a redeeming spot' in the entire Indiana delegation, 'not a star to light the darkness of her treachery'; she had deserted in 1852 and now she had 'closed the volume of ingratitude.'

But denunciations of treachery did not alter that Sunday's gloom and before long rumors of Douglas' withdrawal were flying about the hotels. Pressing their advantage, the Buchaneers proposed to the Douglas managers that whichever candidate had the largest first ballot vote should get the Douglas men's second ballot vote.

While this ingenuous offer was promptly rejected, the Douglas men were in despair. 'Indiana is all gone — and wrong,' Richardson sadly telegraphed his chief, and his judgment was against Douglas continuing a candidate; Buchanan had worked up 'forty candidates' for Vice-President and would 'cheat them all.' But the Senator had not provided him with a letter of withdrawal, the Illinois delegation was 'wild for your name to be presented,' and he could not veto the demand. 'Of one thing be sure,' Richardson concluded, 'I will take things in my own hands, if necessary, and if you don't get the nomination, you will be borne from the contest without dishonor.' [62]

The convention itself opened at noon Monday. Medary, of Ohio, was made temporary president, committees on credentials, resolutions, organizations and rules were selected and the delegates intrigued over the Presidency while awaiting reports. The Buchaneers had gotten control of

[60] J. L. Reynolds to Buchanan, Cincinnati, June 1, 1856; Buchanan MSS.

[61] Forney to Buchanan, Washington, Nov. 12, 1856; Buchanan MSS.

[62] T. M. Ward, Cincinnati, June 1; Charles P. Button, Cincinnati, June 1, 4; W. A. Richardson, Cincinnati, June 1; D. T. Disney, Cincinnati, June 7; Isaac R. Diller, Springfield, Ill., June 10; John Law, Evansville, Ind., June 20, 1856; Douglas MSS.

visitors' tickets and packed the galleries.[63] The platform was brought in Wednesday morning. Before reading it, the committee chairman announced that it was unanimous on the planks about Popular Sovereignty and Kansas, whereat the convention went wild. When he read the sentences recognizing the principles in the Kansas-Nebraska Act as embodying 'the only sound solution of the slavery question,' delegates threw their hats in the air and cheered and shouted. The platform was adopted by subjects; on Popular Sovereignty there was not a negative vote.[64]

That night the Buchanan pressure became tremendous. Kentucky was 'trembling in the balance.' Only John C. Breckinridge held out against Old Buck, and as he wanted to tail the ticket he could not resist much longer. The Georgia Pierce men were wavering and Buchanan had gained handsomely in Ohio. There were reports of Douglas' imminent withdrawal, that Pierce would get a fine first ballot compliment, then 'draw his toga about him with dignity and expire gracefully.'

Douglas' prospects looked 'dark, very dark,' and some of his supporters were 'fearful of results personally dangerous to themselves' if they declared for him. Richardson and Harris were discouraged but other leaders swore never to surrender. 'I never will,' Soulé pledged promptly — but Louisiana was under the unit rule. They hoped to keep Iowa from bolting and New York's Softs were still sound. Southerners kept urging Richardson to hold on, Colquitt maintained that the Georgia delegation would assist shortly; Kentucky would come after one ballot. The *Gazette* bravely proclaimed that delay was aiding Douglas' chances, Steedman and Medary got after Ohio, there were sudden hopes of Virginia and slowly the shattered lines were reformed.[65]

The next day brought the test that determined: the contest from New York. The Credentials Committee brought in two reports; the majority recommended giving the Softs the best of a division, but the minority asked an even split. The Buchaneers forced the issue and carried the minority report by 137 to 128. They had control of the convention by five votes.

The first ballot for Presidential nominee gave Buchanan the lead, with 131½ votes; Pierce had 13 less; Douglas had 33 and Cass 4. The President's

[63] Cincinnati *Gazette*, June 3, 1856; Charles P. Button, Cincinnati, June 4, 1856; Douglas MSS.

[64] Cincinnati *Gazette*, June 5, 1856. The convention turned down a plank for a Pacific railroad, adopted one favoring General Walker's Nicaraguan Government. Significant sentences in the slavery planks were: 'The American Democracy recognize and adopt the principles contained in the organic laws establishing the Territories of Kansas and Nebraska as embodying the only sound and safe solution of the "slavery question.".... — NON–INTERFERENCE BY CONGRESS WITH SLAVERY IN STATE AND TERRITORY, OR IN THE DISTRICT OF COLUMBIA.... We recognize the right of the people of all the Territories, including Kansas and Nebraska, acting through the legally and fairly expressed will of a majority of actual residents, and whenever the number of their inhabitants justifies it, to form a Constitution, with or without domestic slavery, and be admitted into the Union upon terms of perfect equality with the other States.'

[65] Charles P. Button, Cincinnati, June 1; B. B. Chapman, Cincinnati, June 4; Peter Gorman, Cincinnati, June 5, 1856; Douglas MSS. Sickles to Buchanan, Cincinnati, June 4, 1856; Buchanan MSS. Cincinnati *Gazette*, June 4, 1856.

strength came chiefly from his native New England, the New York Softs, and the South, where he had the solid votes of the two Carolinas, Georgia, Alabama, Florida, Tennessee, Arkansas and Texas. Buchanan, however, broke into Massachusetts, had all of Connecticut, the New York Hards, and most of the Middle States. In the South he had Virginia, under the unit rule, Louisiana, part of Kentucky; in the West, over half of Ohio, all of Indiana, all of Michigan and three from Wisconsin. Douglas had Illinois, Missouri and Iowa solid, four from Ohio, three from Kentucky, two from Wisconsin. To everyone's surprise, California went for Cass and never changed.[66]

There were no major shifts until the seventh ballot, when some of Pierce's Southern votes came to Douglas. Tennessee's whole delegation joined his column, Georgia shifted seven to him, more Kentuckians came, Arkansas wheeled to her second choice, and Douglas' total began to rise. The fourteenth ballot resulted in the Little Giant having 63 to Pierce's 75. But Buchanan had crept up to 152½.

Adjournment was then taken, and all night the leaders strove to move key delegations. Disney made progress with Virginia and believed he had a commitment. On a caucus, however, the Douglasites were two votes shy. Douglas managers also talked urgently with the Pierce leaders, and later the charge was made that an agreement was effected for Pierce's strength to be thrown to the Little Giant, who would stay in and fight Buchanan until a compromise candidate could be picked.[67]

The next morning bleary-eyed delegates responded to roll call. New Hampshire announced 'her vote for the man who most fully represents the principles of Pierce's Administration, Stephen A. Douglas,' others followed and his total mounted to 118.

But there was a critical defection. Tennessee, which had stayed with the Little Giant for ten ballots, now hastened to Buchanan. Had she kept the agreement, Douglas would have had 130 votes to Buchanan's 156. But with the Tennessee shift the Missouri and Kentucky delegations 'were demoralized by fear.' Then came the sixteenth roll call. Douglas gained four votes, Buchanan still lacked two-thirds.

As soon as the teller announced the total, William Preston, of Kentucky, mounted the platform. A staunch Douglas man, he had been advising with Richardson, who had shown him a telegram from Douglas in Washington. Preston thought another ballot would be fatal, and that Douglas had better 'end by a splendid retreat than perish by the secession of faithless adherents.'[68] He had spoken but a few words about a 'useless contest' when pandemonium broke out over the hall and there were loud shouts of 'No.' Then Richardson announced that he had a telegram to read to the convention and that then he would withdraw his candidate's name.

[66] Cincinnati *Gazette*, June 6, 1856.

[67] Benjamin F. Butler, speech at Lowell, Mass., Aug. 10, 1860, pamphlet. Butler made the speech to defend himself against charges of treachery to Douglas at the Charleston Convention. His mode of defense was to charge Douglas with a breach of faith to Pierce at Cincinnati.

[68] William Preston, Cincinnati, June 7, 1856; Douglas MSS.

'If the withdrawal of my name will contribute to the harmony of our party or the success of our cause,' — so ran Douglas' telegram — 'I hope you will not hesitate to take the step.... If Mr. Pierce or Mr. Buchanan, or any other statesman who is faithful to the great issues involved in the contest, shall receive a majority of the convention, I earnestly hope that all my friends will unite in insuring him two-thirds, and then making his nomination unanimous. Let no personal considerations disturb the harmony or endanger the triumph of our principles.' [69]

Richardson said a few more words, then there was bedlam and the convention rushed unanimously to the 'Squire from Lancaster. Three cheers were given, delegates jumped to their chairs and Old Buck had it at last. 'Bless God for Buchanan's nomination,' General James A. Shields, still sore at his Illinois defeat, wrote a friend, 'Pierce and his crew are floored and Douglas has met his fate.'

But as the disappointed Douglas men made their way back to Illinois, they were careful to shout for Buchanan at every Indiana station where the train stopped. To their surprise, the people gathered at the stations shouted back: 'Damn Buchanan, hurrah for Douglas.' [70]

[69] Sheahan, 448-49. B. F. Butler's Lowell speech, *cit. supra*, charged that the alleged Douglas deal with Pierce the night of June 5, and then Richardson's withdrawal of him the next morning, was but a ruse to get for the Little Giant the credit of being the only competing candidate at the time the nomination was made and of having magnanimously made Buchanan's victory possible by withdrawing.

[70] Cincinnati *Gazette*, June 6, 7, 8; D. T. Disney, Cincinnati, June 7, 1856; James A. Shields to H. H. Sibley, Faribault, Minn., June 2, 6, 7, 1856; Minnesota Historical Society MSS. Isaac R. Diller, Springfield, Ill., June 10, 1856; Douglas MSS.

CHAPTER XVI

NEARING THE CRISIS

THE ensuing presidential campaign opened with ominous portents. For the first time in American history there was danger that the candidate of a sectional party would be elected President, precipitating the secession of several slave-holding States. Had the issue been clean-cut between Democrats and Republicans, although the canvass would have been bitter, the Nation was still made up of Union-loving people and the final result would not have been in much doubt. But the entry of a Know-Nothing ticket triangulated the contest and made confusion worse confounded.

In February, 1856, the American Party, as the Know-Nothings now called themselves, met at Philadelphia to determine whether or not to nominate a presidential ticket. A minority insisted on an immediate declaration about Kansas and slavery extension, together with delay in choosing candidates until the situation was better revealed. But this was vetoed by a large majority, the American creed was readopted, and a ticket chosen then and there.[1]

Ex-President Millard Fillmore emerged from retirement to accept the presidential nomination. Andrew Jackson Donelson, of Tennessee, Old Hickory's nephew, was his running-mate. The Know-Nothing minority held a rump convention and named John C. Frémont, of California, for President.[2]

The Republicans too began their activities early in the year, holding a great conference in Pittsburgh, on February 22, to determine national plans. At it their leaders saw that the time had come to broaden the base of the party; therefore they called a convention for Philadelphia in June to name a presidential ticket. During the Spring the insiders debated party policy. They saw there was little chance to elect a Republican President that year. William H. Seward, the strongest man in the party; Chase, of Ohio, and Wilson, of Massachusetts, were unwilling to be drafted. Justice McLean, of Ohio, a hardy Presidential perennial, became a candidate but obtained no important support.

The leaders determined to select a candidate whose defeat in November would not harm the party's future. Thus the stage was set and the cue given for John C. Frémont's appearance in the campaign. A flashing, spectacular figure, his political asset was the fact that his wife was Tom Benton's daughter. Old Bullion's staunch friends the Blairs took the lead

[1] Typical platform planks were that Americans must rule America; Congress must not interfere with affairs in a State; citizens permanently residing in a Territory must have control of their own affairs; the naturalization period should be twenty-one years, and foreign paupers and criminals must be kept out.

[2] New York *Times*, Feb. 19-26, 1856. William F. Johnston, of Pennsylvania, tailed the Know-Nothing bolters' ticket.

in pre-convention maneuvers, Thurlow Weed and Horace Greeley fell in line, Republican papers began booming 'The Pathfinder' and delegation after delegation pledged support.

Radical anti-slavery men were in the saddle when the Republican Convention met, June 17, in Philadelphia. David Wilmot offered the platform, which excoriated the crime against Kansas and termed polygamy and slavery 'twin relics of barbarism.' The McLean men tried to head off the Frémont stampede, but the General won on the first ballot. Frémont himself wanted Simon Cameron, of Pennsylvania, for running-mate, and Illinois proposed Abraham Lincoln, but political geography sent the nomination to William L. Dayton, a New Jersey man. The adjourning delegates cheered the campaign slogan 'Free Men, Free Soil, Fre-mont.'[3]

The Republican papers now began to build up the Frémont legend, Greeley wrote of the Pathfinder's 'distinguished ability,' William Cullen Bryant discovered 'something heroic' in him, and soon he was portrayed as a combination of Lochinvar, Deerslayer and William Pitt, with a dash of George Washington thrown in. But there was something mechanical about this enthusiasm. The Old-Line Whigs had wanted McLean, and complained that Frémont's choice had betrayed them. A Native American Committee, which had been at Philadelphia hoping to arrange a fusion, was indignant at the selection of this son of a French musician, whom they believed to be a Catholic, and left Philadelphia 'cursing the corrupt sale of the "new party" by Blair, Greeley and Weed.'[4]

But the possibilities of catastrophe inherent in the three-cornered contest alarmed the nation's conservatives, who saw that the coming battle would be 'the most violent, desperate and bitter which the politics of the country has ever evoked.' Furthermore, the personal assault a South Carolina Congressman had just made on Charles Sumner was believed to have cost Buchanan 200,000 votes in the Free States.[5]

It must be said that this attack was not without some provocation. In the debates of 1854, Sumner's conduct toward all colleagues who had run counter to his ruling obsession had been conspicuously and personally offensive. Since then his popularity, even with his Republican colleagues, had not increased. Such men as Collamer, Foot and Fessenden were coming to believe him 'cowardly, mean, malignant, tyrannical, hypocritical, cringing and toadyish to everything and everybody that had the odor of aristocracy. Others thought that he was afflicted with a maggot in the brain.'[6] Toward opponents he was quite unbearable.

At this particular time Sumner's news from Massachusetts was not too good. His term expired March 4 next, the State Legislature was soon to

---

[3] Allan Nevins, *John C. Frémont*, New York, 1928; II, 474–91. Francis Preston Blair promptly vetoed Frémont's desire for Cameron; Beveridge, II, 300 *et seq.* Practical vote-getting planks included one for a Pacific railroad, another for high tariff and a third for 'local improvements.'

[4] Nevins, II, 488–89; Samuel Treat, New York, June 19, 1856; Douglas MSS.

[5] J. M. Clay to John C. Breckinridge, New York, June 11, 1856; Breckinridge MSS.

[6] Orville H. Browning, *Diary*, I, 587–88; Cincinnati *Commercial*, Jan. 20, 1869, giving statement of Donn Piatt.

meet and, despite his anxiety for a second term, it might elect another in his stead. For two years his own popularity had been waning, his Abolitionist appeals seemed losing their effect, the Know-Nothings were fading and Governor Gardner was anxious for Sumner's seat.

All these things, added to his near-mania on slavery, led him to plan an extraordinary speech upon slavery and Kansas. He wrote and rewrote his words, sharpened each barb in his quiver, searched out smutty Greek quotations, entitled the speech 'The Crime Against Kansas,' and put it in type for a pamphlet. In addition he rehearsed his words before close friends, 'with the effective accompaniment of clenched hands, raised voice, rolling eyes.'

It was said some warned him against particularly vicious passages but he did not change them. It was reported on the streets that he had said he would be responsible for anything he said, and that he would be armed when he spoke. Southern leaders came to believe that Sumner was well aware of the 'warm and sensitive material' upon which he proposed to work, and that what he actually was seeking was 'to be martyrized into a re-election to the United States Senate.'[7] On the eve of its delivery, he wrote a Boston friend: 'I shall pronounce the most thorough philippic ever uttered in a legislative body.'

On May 19 — by coincidence the very day that the Marshal's posse was marching into Lawrence — Sumner spoke to a crowded Senate. It was a bright sunny day, and he was garbed for the occasion in a light sack coat with white pantaloons. His linen was immaculate, his hair oiled and curled. He spoke easily, without notes. His commanding presence, his six feet four inches height, 'the vigor and grace of his motions, the fervor of his oratory,' riveted attention. Characteristically he sought to shock his hearers and readers, employing calculated obscenities, jarring metaphors and lurid phrases. The crime against Kansas was 'the rape of a virgin Territory, compelling it to the hateful embrace of Slavery.' Border Ruffians, whiskey bottles, bowie knives, vied with classical quotations unfit for the drawing-room. No horror, actual or imagined, was omitted, no offensive misrepresentation was left out.

Not satisfied with a general assault against ideas and policies, Sumner next directed his polished billingsgate against Senatorial opponents. Such tactics had been demanded by Abolitionist supporters in Boston, who believed that the personal vilification of strong and popular opponents damaged them and thus helped the Abolition cause. Accordingly Sumner carefully exhibited a personal contempt for all who differed with him about slavery. It was 'hardly possible for a defender of slavery to be a gentleman,' he wrote privately to a friend; all in this vile cause forgot 'honor, manhood, and manners.' Now he had determined publicly to apply these offensive expressions to certain colleagues. Butler, of South Carolina, and Douglas, of Illinois, were the chief targets for his attack.

At this time Andrew Pickens Butler was personally the most popular and highly respected member of the Senate. His gentleness, courtesy and

[7] New York *Herald*, May 23, 1856; Washington *Union*, June 19, 1856.

learning were celebrated among his colleagues. He had lately suffered a stroke of partial paralysis, a bodily infirmity which aroused the pity of his associates. At the time of Sumner's speech, Butler was on a visit to South Carolina, but neither his affliction nor his absence persuaded the Abolition Senator to omit 'the opportunity of exposing him.' Butler prided himself on being a chivalrous knight, Sumner sneered, and as a knight he had chosen a mistress who, though ugly to others was always chaste in his sight — 'I mean the harlot Slavery.' Butler's defenses of this vile strumpet surpassed 'the frenzy of Don Quixote in behalf of his wench Dulcinea.' As Butler was the knight, so Stephen A. Douglas was 'the squire of Slavery, its very Sancho Panza — ready to do all its humiliating offices.'

The most actually insulting slur on the absent Senator was Sumner's reference 'to the loose expectoration of Judge Butler's speech.' Like many aged persons, the lingual or labial paralysis with which he was afflicted made it difficult for him to control his organs of speech, and when he spoke he sprayed spittle all over himself. Sumner's gratuitous reference to this infirmity as 'the loose expectoration of speech' gave new edge to the indignation with which his remarks were received.[8] Douglas became quite irritated and began pacing across the rear of the Senate Chamber, pausing now and then to listen. Finally he remarked in an undertone to Donn Piatt: 'That damn fool will get himself killed by some other damn fool.' [9]

The next day Sumner attacked Butler's State as savagely as he had his person. Why should he be proud of South Carolina, 'by what title does he indulge in this egotism?' He must remember her 'shameful imbecility' during the War of the Revolution, for which slavery had been responsible. South Carolina's whole history could be blotted out and civilization might lose thereby 'less than it has already gained by the example of Kansas.' These were by no means the most offensive of his slurs on Senators and States.

As soon as he finished, Lewis Cass told the Senate that he deemed Sumner's speech 'the most un-American and unpatriotic that has ever grated on the ears of the members of this high body.' Mason reprimanded Sumner for using language 'to which no gentleman would subject himself elsewhere'; his colleagues must endure him in the Senate Chamber, but he was 'one whom to see elsewhere is to shun and despise.'

Douglas remarked that Sumner's arguments required no answer; he rose only to reprehend the offensive personalities. Sumner's reference to the classics had been 'distinguished only for their lasciviousness and obscenity'; at least a hundred times Sumner had used obscene, vulgar terms reputable men would not repeat in decent company. Why had he made such a speech? Was he anxious to turn the Senate 'into a bear garden'? Sumner had repeatedly imputed infamy and crime to three-fourths of his colleagues, 'how does he approach one of those gentlemen to give him his hand after that act? ... He would deserve to have himself spit in the face for doing so.' Did

[8] New York *Weekly Day Book*, June 7, 1856, article entitled 'An Insult to Age,' quoting from New York correspondence of the Cincinnati *Enquirer*.

[9] Piatt's dispatch, Washington, Feb. 26, 1869, Cincinnati *Commercial*, March 1, 1869.

Sumner want 'to provoke some of us to kick him as we would a dog, that he may get sympathy upon the just chastisement'?

Nor had his offensive references been provoked in the heat of debate. On the contrary, Sumner 'had his speech written, printed, committed to memory, practiced every night before the glass with a Negro boy to hold the candle and watch the gestures, and annoying the boarders in the adjoining rooms, until they were forced to quit the house.' These libels had been 'written with cool, deliberate malignity, repeated from night to night in order to catch the appropriate grace, and then he came here to spit forth that malignity upon men who differ from him — for that is their offense.'

Particularly did Douglas reprehend the scandalous slurs on 'the venerable, the courteous and the distinguished Senator from South Carolina.' Soon he would return to speak and act for himself, and when he did, Sumner would 'whisper a secret apology in his ear, and ask him to accept that as satisfaction for a public outrage on his character.' Douglas knew Sumner's shabby tricks, his habit of doing those things, for he had himself 'had some experience of his skill in that respect.'

Sumner replied that Douglas must remember that 'the bowie knife and the bludgeon are not the proper emblems of senatorial debate.' Douglas had made statements which he branded 'to his face as false.' Furthermore, 'no person with the upright form of man can be allowed...' Here Sumner faltered. 'Say it,' Douglas demanded. 'No person with the upright form of man,' Sumner went on, 'can be allowed to switch out from his tongue the perpetual stench of offensive personality. The noisome, squat and nameless animal, to which I now refer, is not a proper model for an American Senator. Will the Senator from Illinois take notice?'

'I will,' Douglas retorted, 'and therefore will not imitate you, sir.'

'Mr. President,' Sumner sneered, 'again the Senator has switched his tongue, and again he fills the Senate with its offensive odor.'

Douglas thus closed the interchange: 'I will only say that a man who has been branded by me in the Senate, and convicted by the Senate of falsehood, cannot use language requiring reply.' Sumner said no more.

This speech created a sensation. Anti-slavery papers called it 'a solemn, majestic anthem,' but people in Washington thought it unpardonably foul. Such words might have come forth upon the floor of Congress in altercation, but never before had a Senator carefully prepared personal slurs to heap on a colleague and insults to hurl at a State.[10] Soon the Senate adopted a new rule: 'No Senator in debate shall refer offensively to any State of the Union.'

In the Senate gallery during Sumner's delivery was a kinsman of the absent Butler; this was Preston S. Brooks. Tall, robust, a veteran of the Mexican War, some thought him 'a stupid, overgrown, good-natured fellow, liked by the women and popular with the men.'[11] Elected to Congress in 1853, Brooks bore himself quietly in Washington, and even Abolitionists

---

[10] For Sumner's speech and the ensuing exchange, see *Congressional Globe*, Thirty-Fourth Congress, First Session, App., 529–47.

[11] Cincinnati *Commercial*, March 1, 1869.

had praised his restraint during the Kansas-Nebraska debate. But when he heard Sumner's stinging slurs on a kinsman he loved and a State he revered, something happened to his self-possession; he felt that this 'traducer' must be punished. Two nights he brooded; on the morning of May 22, he strode into the Senate Chamber, carrying, as was his custom, a gutta-percha cane.

The Senate was not in session but Sumner was writing at his desk. Brooks walked up to him and said, in a restrained tone, that he had read Sumner's speech twice, and 'with great care and with as much impartiality' as he could. 'I feel it my duty to say to you that you have published a libel on my State and uttered a slander upon a relative who is aged and absent, and I am come to punish you.'

With this Brooks brought his gutta-percha cane down on Sumner's head. The latter tried to rise and broke his desk from the floor, but Brooks continued to rain blows. The cane broke into pieces. A moment later Sumner cried, 'I'm most dead! Oh! I'm most dead!' and fell in the aisle, his head bleeding profusely. It was all over in a minute, and when Senator Crittenden rushed up and seized Brooks, the latter exclaimed: 'I did not wish to hurt him much, but only whip him.' Sumner soon regained consciousness and was carried outside.

Later, Sumner said that, when he recovered consciousness, he recognized among those crowded up but not offering assistance, Senators Douglas and Toombs, and that Brooks was between them.[12] Douglas told the Senate that, when the assault occurred, he was in the reception room. Hearing the commotion, he rose and went to the door to enter the Chamber. When he saw that Sumner, who two days before had addressed him so offensively, was being attacked, it flashed upon him that if he rushed in it would be thought he was abetting the outrage. Therefore he did not enter until a crowd had come up. He had not been near Brooks at any time, he was not with Toombs and did not know that an attack had been planned on Sumner, 'then, or at any other time, here or at any other place.'[13]

The attack upon Sumner set the North on fire. The Senator's assailant became 'Bully' Brooks, a villainous assassin, the apotheosis of the brutality of the slavocracy. Bulletins from Sumner's bedside were eagerly read by the people, and there was an extraordinary wave of denunciation, from press, platform and pulpit, of 'Bully' Brooks and all he represented. All this set in motion the South's defense mechanism. Southern speakers and papers made much of Sumner's insults to Senator Butler and his State and

[12] New York *Herald*, May 23, 1856.

[13] Rhodes, II, 148; *Congressional Globe*, Thirty-Fourth Congress, First Session, 1305. New York *Herald*, May 23, 1856, reported that at the time of the attack 'there were probably fifteen or twenty persons present, including Messers Crittenden, Foster, Toombs, Fitzpatrick, Murray, Morgan, and other members of Congress, together with Gov. Gorman, several officers of the Senate and some strangers.' Douglas was not listed. Yet it must not be thought from Douglas' statement that he had any sudden access of good feeling toward Charles Sumner. See J. F. H. Claiborne, *Life of John A. Quitman*, New York, 1860, II, 318–20, for account of Douglas' presence, along with Jefferson Davis, Senator Clingman and Lane and a few others, at a small dinner on Aug. 6, 1856, at which Quitman presented a cane to Preston Brooks.

insisted that Brooks had ample provocation. Southern Rights societies cheered Brooks' 'defense of his State' and he received scores of handsomely engraved canes to replace that shattered on Sumner's skull. But Brooks himself did not like being the hero of the Hotheads.

A Senate committee reprehended the assault in stinging language but confessed absence of authority to discipline a Congressman. A House committee reported a resolution that Brooks should be expelled, which needed a two-thirds vote; the Southern members stood by their fellow and only a majority was secured. Then Brooks resigned, as did Laurence Keitt, a fellow South Carolina Representative who had gone with him to the Senate Chamber 'to see fair play.' Both were promptly and overwhelmingly re-elected.[14]

The day after the attack, Senator Wilson, of Massachusetts, denounced Brooks' action as 'a brutal, murderous and cowardly assault.' Butler, who had that morning returned, retorted, 'You are a liar,' and Brooks soon challenged Wilson to a duel, but he declined, as did a Connecticut Congressman. As Brooks challenged and Northern Senators and Representatives declined, the North grew restive and a young Massachusetts House member saw an opportunity. This was Anson Burlingame, an anti-slavery man ambitious to be elected to Sumner's Senate seat, of which there had been some chance. He now made a vitriolic speech denouncing Brooks' assault, concluding with the statement that, if challenged, he would fight.

Brooks challenged promptly, but Burlingame sought out Lewis D. Campbell, of Ohio, for help in devising an acceptance which would preserve his reputation but avert the duel. They finally picked the Canadian side of Niagara Falls, a ruse which worked. 'I could not reach Canada,' Brooks later said, 'without running the gauntlet of mobs and assassins, prisons and penitentiaries, bailiffs and constables.... I might as well have been asked to fight on Boston Common.' When Brooks asked that another place be selected for the meeting, the Northern papers spoke of his cowardice, and praised Burlingame to the skies. But they said nothing of Brooks' renewed insistence and Burlingame's stubborn declination to name a closer point. At length Burlingame left Washington secretly for the Middle West, thus avoiding further danger. A few months later Brooks died.[15]

When Sumner was carried home after the assault, Dr. Cornelius Boyle, one of the Capital's best-known physicians, who attended, found him suffering solely from flesh wounds. The next day Sumner told the Doctor that he had not lost a single day's session that Congress and he wanted to go to the Senate. Boyle said that he might take a carriage and drive as far as Baltimore without any injury, but there was so much excitement about town that he had better remain away a day or so and let it wear off. On May 26, Sumner appeared before the House Committee and testified.

[14] The vote was 125 to expel, 95 not to do so. The Southern members took the position that the House had no control over a Representative's actions outside of the Hall of Representatives itself. As Brooks left the House, a bevy of Southern belles 'smothered him with kisses.'

[15] Gov. James E. Campbell, 'Sumner-Brooks-Burlingame,' *Ohio Archæological and Historical Quarterly*, XXXIV, 435–73.

But Burlingame's comedy of dueling had a fine Massachusetts reaction; there was some talk of electing him to the Senate and Sumner's friends grew worried. His brother arrived and began playing up the gravity of Sumner's wounds. Articles began appearing in the *Intelligencer* that Sumner had had a relapse. Dr. Boyle, who was calling twice a day, never detected any sign of fever, nor a pulse-beat higher than 82 and gave the *Intelligencer* a correction. Soon thereafter he was discharged from the case. The anti-slavery surgeon then employed, understanding the situation, sent Sumner back to bed and published that his condition had become quite dangerous. The Senator came forth again to testify to the House Committee but soon left Washington.[16]

For two years there was a vacant seat in the Senate — Northern visitors to the galleries always marked it. Sumner's Northern admirers came increasingly to regard him as a noble sacrifice to Southern passion. He spent the first few months in Boston. In the late Fall of 1856, accounts appeared in Washington and New York papers that Sumner had completely recovered. In January, 1857, on being re-elected by the Massachusetts Legislature, his letter of acceptance spoke of his 'complete restoration to health.' A few days later he went to New York and was marked there walking the streets 'with accustomed ease and elasticity.' About this time Higginson met him in the Boston Athenæum and asked him what he proposed to do upon his return to duty. 'I will make a speech upon slavery,' Sumner answered, 'which those who heard what I said before will say is as first proof brandy to molasses and water.'[17] But he changed his mind and carried his martyrdom across the seas to European spas.

Man makes much of trifles and history must record the whims which move him. From emergence to final conclusion, the great American crisis quickened, changed its course and was given momentum by small events and chance occurrences, neither fated nor plotted nor of great basic weight. Much is made of the deep conflict of great social systems and yet, perhaps, six incidents, mere smudges on the face of history, did more to rouse and array the will and emotion of the two sections than did all the fundamental factors combined.

Uncle Tom's Cabin, 'Bleeding Kansas,' 'Bully' Brooks' assault on Sumner, the Dred Scott case, Buchanan's hate for Douglas, Harper's Ferry — but for these there might have been no Civil War. The philosopher looking speculatively at history muses on what might have been. If only Mrs.

[16] When Dr. Boyle was before the House Committee of Investigation, he was questioned by Representative Cobb as to the nature of Sumner's injuries. 'They are nothing but flesh wounds,' he answered and repeated. 'How long need he be confined on account of these wounds?' Cobb continued. 'His wounds do not necessarily confine him one moment,' Dr. Boyle answered. 'He would have come to the Senate on Friday if I had recommended it.... He could have come with safety, so far as the wounds were concerned.... Mr. Sumner might have taken a carriage and driven as far as Baltimore [47 miles] on the next day without any injury.' See also New York *Herald*, May 25, 1856; Washington *Union*, May 28, June 19, 1856.

[17] Washington *Star*, Jan. 6, 1857, quoting New York *Journal of Commerce*; Washington *Union*, Jan. 20, 27, 1857.

Stowe had not joined to her Abolition fanaticism a real ability to create pictures which gripped the heart — and this is no large if, for most Abolitionist writing was dull stuff — but 'the little woman' had the trick, and used it!

Or take the strange array of Kansas blunders. Suppose President Pierce had had an eye for real manhood; and his first Governor of the Prairie Territory had been something other than a greedy Pennsylvania lawyer; or even suppose that the Border Ruffians had mixed brains with boasting, and had kept hands off the ballot-boxes — 'Bleeding Kansas' might not have bled.

Several ifs in connection with Brooks' attack on Charles Sumner are patent to the speculative eye. Suppose Sumner had been more of a gentleman and in his speech had been content to argue his case, what change might have come to our history? If only Sumner had risen when Brooks first addressed him, and it had been Brooks who sprawled in the aisle...

While the Democrats had been meeting in Cincinnati, the papers had been full of scare stories about the sack of Lawrence and Sumner bleeding on the Senate floor. When Frémont's nomination was added to Fillmore's, Buchanan's friends examined the situation and were thoroughly alarmed.

In addition to external difficulties, they discovered that the Cincinnati struggle had left deep wounds within the party. The chief fears were as to Pierce and Douglas. Senator Slidell, the nominee's most trusted adviser, had the gravest apprehensions as to the attitude of the President. Pierce was 'very sore,' Slidell reported; 'at least one man in his Cabinet' was anxious for Buchanan to lose. The only way that Pierce's Administration could thus affect the outcome was through prolonging and intensifying the troubles in Kansas, but there was imminent danger of such a course.

In mid-June Stringfellow came to Washington to urge the withdrawal of all Federal troops from Kansas. If done, Buchanan's lieutenants were sure that it would quickly be followed by an immediate armed invasion from Missouri, with a counter-movement from the Free States, precipitating civil war on a scale hitherto unknown. In a Cabinet on June 16, Jefferson Davis 'warmly urged the withdrawal,' and none of the President's other Constitutional advisers save McClelland opposed. Frantic with fear, Slidell got Lewis Cass to protest to Pierce and asked Douglas to do the same.

Should the troops be ordered out of Kansas, Slidell wanted Buchanan immediately to denounce the President for his course. This would hurt the ticket in the South, but such a denunciation would be indispensable to keep the Democracy together in the North. But if only 'we can persuade Douglas to take the initiative, all will be right.' [18] Buchanan must write him at once.

Obese in body, obtuse in perception and obstinate in character, the nominee turned a deaf ear to this suggestion. A month after his nomination, he had not written a line to the President, any member of his Cabinet, Douglas, Cass or any Democratic Senator. When aides protested, Buchanan

[18] Slidell to Buchanan, Washington, June 17, 1856; Buchanan MSS. The Little Giant, however, declared that he had had a breach with Pierce, was without influence with him, and did not go.

replied that he wrote no letters because he was determined that no one should be able to say that he had implied any promise of future reward. Actually his course, which increased Pierce's irritation and was highly offensive to other party leaders, was but another index of the man's small stature.[19]

Fortunately for the party, Douglas did not join the malcontents but he made the best of the situation and set to work for the ticket's success. It was not an easy thing to do, for his mail teemed with indignant expressions from outraged supporters.[20] But the defeated aspirant neither encouraged his friends' disaffection, nor sulked in silence, but promptly pledged hearty support of the new ticket and urged his intimate friends to do the same.[21] Soulé, of Louisiana, Steedman, of Ohio, Rhodes, of Cleveland, and other confidential aides promptly heard from him, thanking them warmly and in each instance pointing out that his and their first duty was for 'all to make a good fight against the common enemy.'

Douglas pointed out that the Cincinnati platform vigorously and completely endorsed his great measure, the Kansas-Nebraska bill, with its principle of Popular Sovereignty. Moreover, the nominee for Vice-President, John C. Breckinridge, was his close friend, had co-operated loyally in the campaign for his nomination and his selection was a recognition of the Douglas group's party rights. Even more, and although Douglas did not put it on paper, all his friends should know that he was still a young man. He would be only forty-seven when the next campaign came around and would be young enough and vigorous enough to be nominated and elected President. Had he not withdrawn when he did at Cincinnati, Buchanan's nomination might have been blocked completely. Thus, in a sense, Buchanan owed his nomination to Douglas' magnanimity. Now Douglas would set his shoulder to the wheel and would have every right to expect the Buchanan men's support four years thence.

Nearly all to whom Douglas wrote replied that they would follow his lead. James B. Steedman added that he was rejoiced at 'the good feelings, the cheerfulness, which your letter indicates. I was fearful you would be chagrined at the result, and I cannot imagine, Judge, how a man who has been used as you have, who has been deceived and betrayed, as you have been, can feel as you do.' [22]

But Douglas was not over-sanguine. Washington was actively discussing the possibility that no one of the three nominees would have an outright majority in the electoral college, and therefore the House of Representatives

[19] J. B. Lewitt to John C. Breckinridge, July, 1856; Breckinridge MSS.

[20] John Pettit, Lafayette, Ind., June 10, 1856; Rhodes, Cleveland, June 17; Robt. Smither and R. W. English, Alton, Ill., June 17, 1856; John Law, Evansville, Ind., June 20; E. C. West, New York, June 26, 1856; Douglas MSS. West insisted that Douglas make no more statements commending Pierce, for all his force could not make people believe the president 'respectable or respected.'

[21] Washington *Union*, June 7, 1856; the pledge was made at a mass meeting in Washington the night of the nomination.

[22] J. B. Steedman, Toledo, Ohio, June 28, 1856; Douglas MSS. Internal evidence in this letter and in one to Douglas from Soulé enables me to reconstruct Douglas' letters to them and other confidential campaign aides.

would elect.[23] The Democratic campaign had other troubles than its sullen, obstinate nominee. One of Slidell's best cards at Cincinnati had been to pledge the 'haut commerce,' with assurances of large campaign contributions for Old Buck. But the large merchants and financiers of Philadelphia and New York subscribed thousands to Frémont's campaign fund and hooted at Slave State talk of Secession as 'mere Southern gasconade.' By mid-August the Democratic National Committee had raised only four thousand dollars, and the defeated Douglas himself paid, in cash, one-fourth of it![24]

None the less, by Midsummer Buchanan's managers whipped a campaign organization into shape, made arrangements for influencing public opinion through newspapers and speakers, and the presidential race began to move.[25] There had been some uneasiness about the South, but Cobb found that the Democrats would carry Georgia 'by the largest majority ever,' and this condition was generally reported from below the Mason and Dixon line.[26]

At the same time the agitation of the Southern people over the possible election of a Black Republican reached the boiling point. The Charleston Mercury, the Richmond Enquirer, the New Orleans Delta, teemed with warning editorials. If Frémont's election should occur, declared John Forsyth, of Alabama, 'the South ought not to submit, and will not submit.' When 'Bully' Brooks said the section's only hope was 'in separating the living body from the dead carcass,' a South Carolina crowd cheered wildly. If Frémont won, said Mason, there was but one course open — 'immediate, absolute, eternal separation.'[27] Before the election in the October States, Governor Wise, of Virginia, became alarmed and issued a call for the Governors of the South to meet in Raleigh on October 13, to counsel about their course should Frémont win.[28]

This was more than rhetoric — current feeling as well as the actual event four years later indicates this — and these warnings had a powerful effect upon Northern Union and conservative sentiment. Thomas H. Benton fully comprehended the danger. 'We are treading upon a volcano that is liable at any moment to burst forth and overwhelm the nation,' he declared,

---

[23] Beriah Magoffin to John C. Breckinridge, Washington, July 2, 1856; Breckinridge MSS. Magoffin, a Kentucky Democrat, also informed the nominee for Vice-President that great efforts had been made to poison Douglas' mind against Breckinridge, without success, and that also Pierce was very cold toward known Breckinridge friends. Magoffin and Pierce had passed one another just recently; 'he spoke to me formally (coldly) and I returned the compliment, God damn him.'

[24] Beverly Tucker to Buchanan, Washington, Aug. 13, 1856; Buchanan MSS. Wm. Preston to Breckinridge, Philadelphia, Sept. 19, 1856; Breckinridge MSS.

[25] Douglas aided Slidell in these arrangements, and particularly in enlisting the aid of Francis J. Grund, the veteran newspaper correspondent. Slidell to Buchanan, Washington, July 17, 18, 20, 1856; Buchanan MSS.

[26] Cobb to Col. John Lamar, Washington, July 18, 1856; Erwin MSS.

[27] New York Evening Post, Oct. 6, 1856, summarizes such statements.

[28] Gov. Wickliffe of Louisiana, to Wise, New Orleans, Oct. 9; John B. Breckinridge to John C. Breckinridge, New Orleans, Oct. 10, 1856; Breckinridge MSS. Some thought Jefferson Davis behind this plan and were, therefore, highly suspicious of it.

and publicly attacked his son-in-law's candidacy as an ill-advised movement accentuating sectional hate.[29]

Old Bullion expressed the sincere conviction of a multitude of Union-loving, anti-slavery Democrats of the North. The Old-Line Whigs, equally apprehensive, drew away from Fillmore and concentrated upon Buchanan as the surest answer to the sectional threat. In Kentucky they allied with the Democrats, with a resultant August State victory.[30] In Illinois, General Singleton expressed fears of 'the black and foaming flood of fanaticism,' and came out for the Democratic ticket as the best way to secure 'the sovereignty of the people, the equality of the States, the freedom of conscience and the preservation of the Union.'[31]

This feeling was impressively stated by Rufus Choate, of Massachusetts, Daniel Webster's devoted friend, in a strongly reasoned public letter pointing out that the Whigs' first duty was 'to defeat and dissolve the new geographical party' and that he would vote for Buchanan. Fletcher Webster, Daniel's son, endorsed this declaration, as did James B. Clay, the son of Henry Clay, Robert Winthrop and Amos A. Lawrence.[32]

These attacks embarrassed the Fillmore movement and crippled Republican efforts to recruit from the Whigs. And stories were afloat about Frémont. Know-Nothings whispered that he was a Catholic and had been married by a priest. Also he was accused of being a hard drinker, a slaveholder and a reckless and unscrupulous speculator.[33]

For all this, the Republican campaign in the North was extremely effective. Mobilized for 'the cause of freedom,' the preachers talked through the week and preached on Sunday against the Democracy. 'We have a most desperate set of political Hell-hounds to contend with,' a Michigan Democrat lamented. The preachers, 'confirmed political liars,' were retailing 'the most villainous falsehoods' in and out of their pulpits. Cass begged Breckinridge to come to Michigan to counteract them.[34] By late Summer it was apparent that Buchanan would carry the South, that Frémont was sure of New England, New York and the far Northwest. Thus Pennsylvania, Indiana and Illinois would determine, and the October State elections in the first two became of vast importance.

Douglas' chief concern was with Illinois. The Republicans spent much time selecting a strong candidate for Governor. Abraham Lincoln was talked of but Democrats thought he would not be dunce enough to run 'unless his wifes makes him.'[35] William H. Bissell, their final choice, an

[29] New York *Tribune*, July 2, 1856.

[30] James Guthrie to John C. Breckinridge, Washington, Aug. 10, 1856; Breckinridge MSS.

[31] Letter of response to invitation to speak, dated Quincy, Ill., July 7, 1856. I am indebted to Mrs. Singleton Osburn of Charles Town, W.Va., for a copy.

[32] Nevins, II, 506–07.

[33] Nevins, II, 499–500. Of forty Catholic papers, not one supported Frémont in July.

[34] Howell Cobb to Mrs. Cobb, Indianapolis, Sept. 5, 1856; Erwin MSS. A. Pratt to John C. Breckinridge, Marshall, Mich., Sept. 25, 1856; Cass to Breckinridge, Washington, July 31, 1856; D. B. Cook to Breckinridge, Niles, Mich., Aug. 18, 1856; Breckinridge MSS.

[35] Harris to Lanphier, Washington, March 7, 1856; Patton MSS.

able man and effective speaker, got off to a good start and never lost it. The Republican orators were 'in the field day and night,' and the State was canvassed with frenzied zeal. William A. Richardson, the Democratic nominee, found the going hard.

The Little Giant was pressed to hurry home as soon as Congress adjourned, to keep the Democratic ticket from being 'disgracefully beaten.' The Opposition thought its opportunity had come, concentrated against Douglas and his personal and political position was at stake. His friends wrote that if he were to survive, he must come home and carry his own State. When he announced a few speaking dates in Maryland, they warned that 'your future depends upon the perpetuity of your power in Illinois... Speakers is what we want, enthusiasm must be got up or... we are defeated.' [36]

Douglas soon hastened to the danger point. Through August and September, he stumped Illinois, encouraging and directing party leaders, renewing the enthusiasm of rank and file and dealing body blows at the hydra-headed Opposition. By late September he was able to write Buchanan that, while he was 'in the midst of the most exciting contest ever known' in Illinois, 'you may rely upon this State with entire certainty.... We shall give you a handsome and decided majority.' [37]

The Little Giant also saw the paramount necessity of carrying Indiana and Pennsylvania. He was anxious to get good speakers for the Indiana campaign and himself spoke at important points there.[38] Buchanan headquarters sent many Southern leaders into Indiana, where the preachers 'talk through the week and preach on Sunday against the Democracy.' But the efforts of the Democratic campaigners bore fruit and the State began to look reasonably safe.[39]

Indiana was important but Pennsylvania was indispensable. Douglas wrote Buchanan that Democratic effort must be concentrated on its October election; if it were won 'the battle is over.' The Democrats saw that Republican 'money flowed like water' in the Keystone State and became highly alarmed. Affected by the panic, Old Buck wrote frantically for Breckinridge, Cobb and others to enter the campaign.[40] By September Pennsylvania was flooded with outside speakers. While Buchanan stuck close to Wheatlands, he left no wire unpulled to carry the Keystone State. A heavy October snowstorm caused no holiday for stumpers and Howell Cobb talked an hour and a half to an audience of three thousand in a driving snowstorm.[41]

[36] Daniel McCook to Douglas, Springfield, Ill., Aug. 8, 1856; Douglas MSS.

[37] Douglas to Buchanan, Chicago, Sept. 29, 1856; Buchanan MSS.

[38] E. M. Burns to John C. Breckinridge, Springfield, Ill., Sept. 18, 1856; Breckinridge MSS., expresses Douglas' urgent wish for the nominee for Vice-President to join him at a meeting at Terre Haute on Sept. 30, because the Indiana election was 'more important than any other,' and help was 'much needed' there.

[39] Howell Cobb to Mrs. Cobb, Indianapolis, Sept. 5, 1856; Erwin MSS.

[40] Douglas to Buchanan, Chicago, Sept. 29, 1856; Buchanan MSS. He would insure Buchanan 'Illinois at all events,' but would promise no more.

[41] William Rice to Breckinridge, Philadelphia, Aug. 21, 1856; Buchanan to Breckinridge, Wheatlands, Sept. 2, 1856; Breckinridge MSS. Cobb to Mrs. Cobb, Philadelphia, Sept. 15, no place given; Sept. 21, Erie, Pa., Oct. 2, 1856; Erwin MSS.

But more than oratory was needed and John W. Forney began raising a special campaign fund. Douglas felt that the time had come to make sacrifices, sold a hundred acres on the western limits of Chicago 'for the round sum of $100,000,' and put most of it into Buchanan's Pennsylvania campaign.[42] These efforts had their effect in the supplemental registrations early in October. 'The results are glorious,' Forney wrote Buchanan. 'We have naturalized a vast mass of men, and assessed many of the native-born citizens.... The Opposition are appalled. They cry fraud. Our most experienced men say *all is well*.' [43] Writing to Douglas — whom he carelessly addressed as Samuel, not Stephen — Buchanan admitted that 'only within the last fortnight' had he felt 'the least degree of confidence' as to Pennsylvania. [44]

But the danger had passed. The Democrats carried Buchanan's State; true, only by a margin of six thousand, but still they had won in a straight-out contest. Indiana likewise registered a notable Democratic triumph, electing the whole State ticket by seven thousand majority, six Congressmen, and a firm control of the Legislature.[45] The tide had turned, the White House was made safe for Democracy.

Sure enough, in November Buchanan swept the South and the Border States, and won by fair margins in the pivotal areas of New Jersey, Pennsylvania, Indiana and Illinois. Frémont carried New England and the rest of the North, Fillmore's vote was close to 900,000, but he carried only Maryland. In electoral college strength, Buchanan won 174 votes to Frémont's 114 and Fillmore's 8.[46]

The President-elect gloried in the victory and visitors reported him 'heartier, rosier, heavier' than ever. Bright, of Indiana, crowed over the discomfiture of the 'hatchet-faced Puritans of the East,' whose faces had become so long that 'not one in a hundred could be drawn through an ordinary sized horse-collar.' Democrats also exulted that it had been a locust year for the Know-Nothings, 'they came out of the dark ground, crawled up to the sides of the trees, ate their foliage in the night, chattered with a croaking harshness, split open on their backs and died.' [47]

Even so, the shrewd politicians saw no cause for discouragement, when their candidate, admittedly weak, won all but four Northern States. An-

[42] Sheahan, 443, tells of the Chicago land sale, and adds that 'his contributions that year in aid of the election of Mr. Buchanan, particularly to aid the Democracy in carrying Pennsylvania, were liberal in the extreme. Forney raised the fund for the Keystone State. Douglas' contribution there was rumored to have been $80,000!'

[43] Forney to Buchanan, Philadelphia, Oct. 3, 1856; Buchanan MSS.

[44] James Buchanan to *Samuel* A. Douglas, Lancaster, Oct. 4, 1856; Douglas MSS.

[45] John C. Rives to J. C. Breckinridge, Washington, Oct. 18, 1856; Breckinridge MSS. W. H. English to Howell Cobb, Lexington, Ind., Oct. 28, 1856; Erwin MSS.

[46] The total votes were: Buchanan, 1,838,169; Frémont, 1,341,264; Fillmore, 874,534. Buchanan's plurality over Frémont was 496,905. Of the total vote, Buchanan received 45 per cent, Frémont 35 per cent and Fillmore 22 per cent.

[47] John S. Cunningham to Buchanan, Lancaster, Pa., Nov. 7, 1856; Buchanan MSS. Bright to Breckinridge, Washington, Nov. 10, 1856; Jeff Brown to Breckinridge, Morganfield, Ky., Nov. 23, 1856; Breckinridge MSS.

alyzing the election returns, they believed that four years thence they would elect a President.[48]

But the Democrats were not thinking about such long-range problems. Buchanan was on his way in, his friends gathered beneath the plum tree and woe to any Pierce or Douglas man who hungered for a Federal job. First on the list for major rewards was Jesse D. Bright, whose part in the Cincinnati nomination Buchanan never forgot. Others high on the honors list were Howell Cobb, of Georgia; Jeremiah Sullivan Black, of Pennsylvania, and Jacob Thompson, of Mississippi.

At first Bright was slated for Secretary of State, but Cobb wanted it too. Nettled, the President-elect wrote that 'One thing is quite certain — I shall select my own Cabinet.' But soon it was seen that while Bright's appointment would infuriate Douglas and divide the Northwestern Democracy, it would be of no help in the South. In addition the Northwest was upset by the continued Southern disunion threats. 'Wise and Rhett and the *Mercury* and *Delta* can send us to the devil as a party in six months,' warned one of Breckinridge's friends. 'Southern fanaticism no less than Northern leads us at once to disunion.' Would Buchanan let the country be governed by the 'Wise Council' of Richmond, or would he select sound, conservative, Union-loving men? [49]

Intimates urged him to pick his Northwestern Cabinet member so that neither Bright nor Douglas could claim triumph or defeat. Douglas began bringing what pressure he could to substitute R. J. Walker or Lewis Cass for Bright, and a boom for Cass ensued.[50] The alarmed Bright brought forward a fanciful plan for eliminating the Michigan veteran. First Cass must move to Indiana. Under its Constitution any inhabitant could be elected to the Senate, and so Bright would guarantee that its Legislature would elect Cass. But this scheme failed when Bright's control of the Indiana Legislature was challenged and opponents contested the election of both Bright and Fitch.[51] Slidell now advised Buchanan to throw Bright overboard and name Cass.[52] J. Glancy Jones thought 'It would be a Godsend to get rid of Indiana.' Howell Cobb sent word that he desired to relieve Buchanan of embarrassment, and withdrew. Late in February Buchanan cut the Gordian knot, tendering Cass the State Department and Cobb the Treasury.[53]

[48] Frémont failed badly in his home State of California, which Buchanan carried by two to one and even Fillmore led the General by 16,000 votes. The Illinois vote was: Buchanan, 105,000; Frémont, 96,000; Fillmore, 37,000; the Republican, Bissell, was elected Governor by 5000. Buchanan's Pennsylvania majority was only 1025. Frémont had 68,850 majority in Massachusetts, 80,129 in New York. In the slave States Frémont's votes were: Delaware, 308; Kentucky, 314; Maryland, 281; Virginia, 291. For other figures see John Robert Irelan, *History of the Administration of James Buchanan*, Chicago, 1888; 139 et seq.

[49] O. B. Ficklin to John C. Breckinridge, Charleston, Ill., Dec. 17, 1856; Breckinridge MSS.

[50] Buchanan to Forney, Lancaster, Dec. 13, 1856; Clement Clay, Jr., to Buchanan, Washington, Feb. 11, 1857; William Bigler to Buchanan, Washington, Feb. 12, 1857; Buchanan MSS.

[51] Forney to Buchanan, Nov. 12, 1856; Buchanan MSS.

[52] Slidell to Buchanan, Washington, Feb. 14, 1857; Buchanan MSS.

[53] Howell Cobb to Mrs. Cobb, Washington, Dec. 27, 1856, Feb. 10, 1857, Buchanan to Cobb,

On Inauguration Day Washington was thronged with expectant Democrats. After an elaborate parade, the 'Squire of Lancaster read his Inaugural from the East Portico of the Capitol. Not only was he determined not to be a candidate for re-election, but also no motive would influence his conduct 'except the desire ably and faithfully to serve my country.' The Nation was again becoming more composed; in its practical aspects the controversy over the status of slavery in the Territories was almost completely solved. The Congressional application of the 'simple rule that the will of the majority shall govern the settlement of the question of domestic slavery in the Territory' he termed 'a happy conception'; nothing could be fairer than to leave the people of a Territory, 'free from all foreign interference, to decide their own destiny for themselves, subject only to the Constitution of the United States.'

A difference of opinion had arisen as to the point of time at which the people of the Territory should thus decide, but this was 'happily a matter of but little practical importance.' Moreover, it was a judicial question legitimately belonging to and then pending before the Supreme Court of the United States, and would 'be speedily and finally settled.'

'To their decision, in common with all good citizens, I cheerfully submit, whatever this may be,' he emphasized. By the coming decision the whole Territorial question would practically be settled 'upon the principle of Popular Sovereignty, a principle as ancient as free government itself.' This gave real ground for hope, not only that the long agitation over slavery in the Territories was nearing its end, but even more, that geographical parties born of the slavery issue — 'sectional parties so much dreaded by the Father of his Country' — would speedily become extinct. These predictions echoed as James Buchanan swore to preserve, protect and defend the Constitution.

Two days later, the Supreme Court rendered its decision in litigation which Dred Scott, a Missouri Negro, had begun eleven years before, seeking his freedom.

That morning the Supreme Court's chambers on the ground floor of the northern end of the Capitol were crowded. All nine Justices were seated in their comfortable, high-backed chairs. From an alcove in the wall behind the Chief Justice's place a portrait of John Marshall beamed down benignantly. Facing the Judges was a marble plaque of the scales of Justice.

Wheatlands, Feb. 21, 1857; Erwin MSS. J. Glancy Jones to Buchanan, Washington, Feb. 14, 1857; Buchanan MSS. Cobb did not look with any pleasure on the Treasury, believed it 'An extremely laborious position, full of hard work and responsibility for which I have neither taste nor desire.' Yet if he did not accept it, the Cabinet would be organized without any representation for his friends. And when Buchanan pointed out that he and Cobb would 'get on together for the public good in peace, harmony and friendship,' without further hesitation, Cobb accepted the post. Cabinet members other than Cass and Cobb, not too greatly distinguished, were thus distributed over the country: John B. Floyd, of Virginia, at the War Department; Isaac Toucey, of Connecticut, was Secretary of the Navy; Jacob Thompson, of Mississippi, Secretary of the Interior; Aaron V. Brown, of Tennessee, Postmaster-General, and Jeremiah Sullivan Black, Attorney-General.

Almost never in its history had the Court's membership been more distinguished than it was on that March Friday when Roger Brooke Taney, the Chief Justice, rose to read his opinion in the case of Sanford *versus* Scott. His tall, lean figure was bowed, his eyes were deep-sunk in his sharp, keen face, for he was but a week removed from his eightieth birthday. For twenty-two years he had presided over the Court and had completely won his associates' affection and respect.

This was no triumph of personal appearance or magnetic bearing, for Taney was gaunt and unattractive. While his eyes were blue and mild, his mouth was over-large, his teeth irregular and discolored, his voice low and hollow, and with the passing years his countenance had become deeply furrowed. His hair hung carelessly over his high forehead and every few minutes he would wipe it away with a long, bony, hair-matted hand. Even so, this sallow, hard-featured man had about him 'an unmistakable air of intellect and authority,' and when he spoke, his clear, simple, admirably arranged words led auditors to forget his appearance and attend his thought. 'I can answer his argument,' a distinguished opponent had lamented early in Taney's career at the bar, 'I am not afraid of his logic, but that infernal apostolic manner of his, there is no replying to it.'

Taney's education was thorough, his reading voracious and of the best type of books, magazines and reviews. A devout Catholic, he was unfailing in his performance of his religious duties; each day, before joining his fellow Justices, it was his custom to fall on his knees to ask guidance from the Almighty. After being admitted to practice, he quickly forged ahead and from 1825 forward had been the leader of the Maryland Bar, only William Wirt disputing his primacy. On his first appearance before the Supreme Court Story marked him 'a man of fine talents.' Jackson first made him Attorney-General, then at the height of the Bank battle made him Secretary of the Treasury and Taney removed the Government's deposit from Biddle's bank. In reprisal, the hostile Senate, led by Clay, Calhoun and Webster, repaid him by rejecting his nomination. In 1835 the President named him Associate Justice, and the Senate again voted him down.

Upon John Marshall's death, Old Hickory nominated Taney to be Chief Justice. After a lengthy struggle, the Senate confirmed the selection, but the vote found the great triumvirate still recorded in the negative. Soon his ability, wisdom and acknowledged high character dissipated suspicion and disarmed criticism of the Court. Before five years, Clay went to the Chief Justice to confess that he was satisfied that 'no man in the United States could have been selected more abundantly able to wear the ermine which Chief Justice Marshall honored.' Late in 1856 Taney's wife and youngest daughter died of yellow fever, a double blow which prostrated and nearly killed the affectionate old man. Through the Summer and Fall his life was despaired of, and there was universal sorrow, even the New York *Tribune* declaring sadly that 'his loss would be a public calamity.' Late in the year he passed the crisis, but he went back on the bench 'with broken health and a broken spirit,' and when he read his views in the Dred Scott case, one spectator thought he resembled a skeleton in a shroud.

ROGER BROOKE TANEY
Chief Justice of the United States, 1836–1864

Even so, Judge Curtis wrote, the Chief Justice's sure and brilliant intellect showed not the slightest sign of becoming hesitant or dim.

Four of the eight Associate Justices came from the North, four from the South. James K. Polk had appointed Robert C. Grier, of Pennsylvania, who, with his expansive brow, blue eyes and fine Scotch face, made a pleasing picture as a judge. Samuel Nelson was equally imposing. At the time of his appointment by John Tyler he had served fourteen years on the New York Supreme Court, the last seven as Chief Justice. Short and slender, with handsome features and a dignified but easy deportment, he showed much energy and industry in his work and was thought 'the best commercial lawyer on the bench.'

John McLean, of Ohio, 'a large, noble-looking man' with a well-formed head and clear gray eyes, was often said to resemble Houdon's Washington. Urbane, energetic, reasonably gifted in the law, McLean's ambition was an engine which drove him to many curious deeds. As Postmaster-General under Monroe and John Quincy Adams, he had a fine record but kept intriguing for the Presidency. When Jackson told McLean he planned to name him to the Supreme Court, he added the warning that he had 'perhaps peculiar views in regard to the course to be pursued by judicial officers; that he considered them as Ministers of the Temple of Justice, and that as such they were necessarily separated from all party politics or feelings.' But the ambitious Ohioan soon resumed his political intrigues. Disappointed in 1856, he nursed hopes that in 1860 the Republican mantle would fall on him.

Benjamin Robbins Curtis, of Boston, whom President Fillmore had named in 1851, was the fourth Northern man. He had a well-knit figure, a wholesome complexion, square chin and fine eyes. A comparatively young man when appointed, Curtis had won a high professional reputation, well sustained during his short years on the bench. A decided Whig, he had applauded Webster's Seventh of March speech. A member of the Massachusetts Legislature at the time of the Know-Nothing bargain which made Sumner Senator, he had denounced it as a 'criminal proceeding, which subjected the parties to it to prosecution under the Massachusetts statutes against bribery.'

Two Southerners were from the Cotton States, two from the Border. A staunch Jacksonian, James M. Wayne had been a member of the Georgia Supreme Court and then a member of Congress. During the Nullification troubles he was an active Unionist, and in 1835 Old Hickory named him to the high court. 'An exceedingly handsome man,' Wayne had a stout but graceful figure, a ruddy complexion, fine teeth and 'clustering, wavy hair.' Courteous and refined in speech, he had an 'ingenious, copious mind.' Admiralty law was his specialty.

Pierce had appointed John A. Campbell, of Alabama, the youngest member of the Court. Leading the bar of his State before forty, the United States Supreme Court was so impressed by him as to urge his selection upon the President. Visitors marked that he seemed always absorbed in thought, while Whig papers likened his learning to that of Story. Campbell adhered to moderately advanced Southern political doctrines but had already haled the fire-eating Quitman before him for trial as a filibuster.

Peter V. Daniel, of Virginia, an appointee of Van Buren, a bony, angular man with high cheek-bones and dark complexion, had some resemblance to an Indian. All praised his personal character and his legal experience, and admitted his learning. Hostile critics, however, te med his mind 'narrow in its conception.' Recently Mrs. Daniel had been burned to death almost before his very eyes and he was frantic with grief.

John Catron, of Tennessee, was a stout, healthy man, respectable and solid in appearance, with a face and head indicative of urbanity and good feeling. With good sense, moderate learning, great benevolence of feeling and kindness of demeanor, he was universally regarded as a 'useful, unpretending, respectable Judge.' He had been nominated by Andrew Jackson as the old master was on his way to private life. Theretofore, as Chief Justice of the Tennessee Supreme Court, Catron had made a reputation as a master of the law of real property. A man of salty humor, Catron contributed much common sense to the Court's proceedings.[54]

The Chief Justice was seated in the middle of the nine; to his right sat McLean, Catron, Daniel and Curtis; to his left, Wayne, Nelson, Grier and Campbell. A common characteristic of the Justices was their advanced age. Curtis was but forty-eight and Campbell forty-five, but the average age of the entire membership was sixty-five, a fact which reflected itself in the intellectual outlook of the Court.[55] All but McLean and Catron were college graduates, all led fine private lives, all were of old American stock. Taney, Curtis and Campbell were jurists of great power, Nelson, Wayne and Grier had considerable ability and McLean's capacity was marred only by his ambition. While Catron and Daniel do not rank among the greatest of the Justices, neither do they among the worst.

This was the Court upon whose devoted heads in a very few days was to break an almost unparalleled storm of abuse. They were to be called the pliant tools of the slavocracy, and their majority opinion was to be termed the work of rabid slave-holders and spineless 'doughfaces.' The truth is that while the Chief Justice came from a Slave State, it had been decades since he had owned a slave, his personal kindliness toward the Negro was well known, and several episodes of his early career showed his basic disapprobation of the whole slave system. While Taney had inherited a few slaves

[54] These descriptions are chiefly drawn from Charles Warren, *The Supreme Court in United States History*, Boston, 1924; II, 153–54, 258, 284–90, 477–79; Forney, II, 226–27; New York *Tribune*, Washington correspondence, published Feb. 21, 1857; George N. Searle, 'The Supreme Court of the United States in 1853–54,' *American Law Register*, October, 1854. For Taney, cf. Samuel Tyler, *Memoirs of Roger Brooke Taney*, Baltimore, 1876; 447–516, and especially 477, 478. Mrs. Clement Clay, 74–76, says Taney was 'all mind and body.' I am also indebted to Dr. Carl E. Swisher, of Columbia University, a student of Taney's career, for suggestions in this description. For Curtis, see George Ticknor Curtis, [ed.], *A Memoir of Benjamin R. Curtis*, Boston, 1879.

[55] As has been said, Taney lacked but a few days of his eightieth birthday, Daniel was seventy-six, McLean seventy-two, Catron seventy-one, Wayne sixty-seven, Nelson sixty-four, and Grier sixty-three. Omitting Curtis and Campbell, the average age of the other seven would have been seventy.

as a young man, long before he became prominent he freed such slaves as he owned, and in addition provided funds to support the older freedmen until their deaths. While he thought the black race fundamentally inferior, and recognized slavery's deep-rooted economic and social involvements, still he was no friend to bondage. Thirty years before, in defending a Pennsylvania preacher charged with inciting Maryland slaves to insurrection, he expressed his grave condemnation of human bondage; it was 'a blot on our national character, and every real lover of freedom confidently hopes that it will be effectually though it must be gradually wiped away, and earnestly looks for the means by which this necessary object may be best obtained.' But as a Judge, Taney must distinguish between his private hopes and his seasoned judgment as to the Nation's basic law.[56]

Nor did any other member of the Court own slaves. Upon appointment, Campbell freed his few household servants.[57] Like Campbell, Daniel was vigorously pro-Southern, but it was a State's Rights, not a slavery attachment. Both Wayne and Catron were uncompromising foes of Nu lification and Secession. During the Civil War both maintained their unswerving loyalty to the Union of the Constitution, Wayne's property being confiscated by the Confederacy. Grier wrote the Court's five to four opinion in the prize court cases. Had Wayne not concurred with him in upholding the Government's position the result might have been fatal to the North.

The Chief Justice's opinion this Friday morning was in the case of Dred Scott, an illiterate Missouri slave who in 1846 had begun action in the Missouri Court to secure his freedom. His ground was that, years earlier, his then owner, Dr. John Emerson, an army surgeon, had taken him from St. Louis to an army post in Illinois, a free State. A little later the surgeon moved to Fort Snelling, in the Territory of Wisconsin. In 1837, when his master carried him back to Missouri, Scott seems to have made no protest. In 1843 Emerson died, three years later Dred entered suit against the widow. The Illinois State Constitution, so Scott contended, forbade slavery and his residence there had made him free. Furthermore, under the terms of the Missouri Compromise, slavery was prohibited in all of the Louisiana Purchase lying north of 36° 30' save Missouri, so his having been removed to the Territory of Wisconsin entitled him to freedom. The initial State Court upheld his contention but in 1852 the Missouri Supreme Court reversed this decision, on the ground that, by his voluntary return to Missouri, he had resumed his slave status.[58]

---

[56] Tyler, 127-31, 478.

[57] Henry G. Connor, *Life of John A. Campbell*, Boston, 1920; 71; Beveridge, II, 477, thinks that perhaps Daniel or Catron owned a family house servant or so but is not sure.

[58] Dred had been born on the Blow plantation in Virginia. After the death of Peter Blow, of St. Louis, the latter's daughter, Elizabeth, sold him to Dr. John Emerson. The removal to Rock Island was in 1834, that to Fort Snelling in May, 1836. Then in the Territory of Wisconsin, Snelling is now in Minnesota. While at this last post, Dr. Emerson bought a Negro girl, Harriett, and Dred married her. In 1837, during the steamboat trip back to St. Louis, and before the vessel reached the Missouri line, Harriett gave birth to a girl. A year later in St. Louis another girl was born. In 1844, Dr. Emerson died, and Dred and his family became Mrs. Emerson's property. She also was administratrix of the estate. For a careful review of this

In 1850 Dr. Emerson's widow married Dr. Charles C. Chaffee, of Springfield, Massachusetts, a Know-Nothing and an Abolitionist. Chaffee was later elected to the Thirty-Fourth Congress and served in the lower House while the Dred Scott case was before the United States Supreme Court. For Mrs. Chaffee and her husband to have manumitted Dred would have been easy, but instead they made a 'fictitious sale' of the Negro and his family to Mrs. Chaffee's brother, John F. A. Sanford, of New York. This fictitious sale enabled Scott to sue Sanford in the United States Circuit Court at St. Louis, claiming diversity of citizenship. Had he sued Mrs. Chaffee, wife of a Massachusetts Abolitionist, the moot nature of the case would have been exposed.[59]

Sanford, Scott's technical owner, filed a plea in abatement in 1854, denying the Federal District Court's jurisdiction, on the ground that 'the said plaintiff, Dred Scott, is not a citizen of the State of Missouri, as alleged in his declaration, because he is a Negro of African descent, his ancestors were of pure African blood, and were brought into this country and sold as Negro slaves.' Scott demurred, was overruled by the Court, and issue was joined on the facts. On these it came to the Supreme Court.

The case was first argued there in February, 1856. Curtis thought the Court would not decide the legality of the Missouri Compromise line, for a majority deemed it unnecessary to do so.[60] But some of the Justices asked for a rehearing, which came in that Fall. Now the country began to realize that the case was packed with dynamite, and anti-slavery politicians started threatening the Court. But the question before it was the strictly legal one as to whether or not the Court had jurisdiction to hear Dred Scott's appeal, and this turned upon the constitutionality of the Missouri Compromise and the citizenship of a Negro.

At the Court's first conference, a majority of the Justices informally concluded that a Negro was not a citizen and so had no right to sue in the courts of the United States, therefore these had no jurisdiction and the appeal must be dismissed. They discussed rendering a brief opinion to this effect without passing on the constitutionality of the Missouri Compromise, so as to get rid of the matter with as little furor as possible. Judge Nelson

cause célèbre, see Warren, II, chapter XXI. Judge Horace H. Hagan of Oklahoma City, Okla., *Georgetown Law Journal*, XV, 95–114, has a clear analysis of the legal points involved. For a legal report, see 19 Howard, 393 *et seq.*, Sanford *vs.* Scott. Here, curiously enough, Sanford is misspelled *Sandford*. For Missouri Supreme Court Opinions, see 15 Missouri, 577–92. John D. Lawson, *American State Trials*, St. Louis, vid., XIII, 220–41 gives the record of the cases in the lower Missouri States Courts.

Frank H. Hodder, 'Some Phases of the Dred Scott Case,' *Mississippi Valley Historical Review*, XVI, No. 1, pamphlet reprint, 4, points out that, from 1822 to 1837, the Missouri Supreme Court decided eight cases on circumstances similar to that of Scott, holding in each that the Negroes involved had acquired freedom.

[59] Warren, II, 281. But Dr. Hodder feels that the case was *bona fide*; 'its object in the State courts was to secure Scott's freedom. It was begun anew in the Federal courts because the parties agreed that it was desirable to get an opinion from the United States Supreme Court upon the issues in controversy.' Hodder, *cit. supra*, 5 *et seq.* and letter to author, Sept. 30, 1933. Such a situation would bear a close resemblance to a moot case.

[60] B. R. Curtis, *Memoir*, 180.

was assigned the writing of the Court's opinion affirming the lower court's decision but leaving untouched the two difficult questions.[61]

A little later, the majority found that McLean and Curtis 'were determined to come out with a long and labored dissent' sustaining both the constitutionality of the Missouri Compromise and the Negro's legal right to citizenship. Some feared this might force them into full expression on these points, but Nelson and Grier had not yet concluded they needed to go so far.

So things stood in February, when Buchanan was preparing his Inaugural. On February 3, he approached his old friend Justice Catron, to ask whether the Court's opinions would be delivered before Inauguration Day. Catron answered that the case had not yet come up in conference. Later in the month, after the conferences had begun, Catron wrote the President-elect that he might safely say that the Supreme Court would soon 'decide and settle' the legality of the Missouri Compromise. Would not Buchanan point out to his friend Grier who, although he agreed with the majority on the main question, desired 'to take the smooth handle for the sake of repose,' the necessity of settling the agitation 'by an affirmative decision of the Supreme Court the one way or the other.' Buchanan did so at once, and on February 23, Grier answered, admitting his anxiety that, in the coming decision, 'it should not appear that the line of latitude should mark the line of division in the Court.' These two letters were the basis of the hopeful Inaugural prophecy.[62]

About the time of Catron's letter, and before Buchanan had written Grier, McLean's and Curtis' continued insistence on argumentative dissent determined the Pennsylvania Justice to join with others of the majority in giving equally responsive opinions. In the Court's next conference, Wayne moved that, because of its grave importance, the opinion be reassigned to the Chief Justice. Taney was still extremely feeble, and had but two weeks until the next opinion day. But he agreed, by great power of will accomplished his task, and on that fateful Friday morning announced the Court's decision, together with his own opinion.

Two leading questions were presented, Taney began. Did the Circuit Court of the United States have jurisdiction? If so, was its judgment erroneous or not? The first depended upon whether Scott was a citizen of Missouri, to which point his owner had earlier entered a plea in abatement asserting that Dred, 'being a Negro of African descent, whose ancestors were of pure African blood, and who were brought into this country and sold as slaves,' was not a citizen of Missouri.

Scott and the defendant had joined in a demurrer but the Circuit Court had overruled it. Some of the Supreme Court Justices believed the plea in

---

[61] This intimate picture of the Court's operations is contained in a letter of Justice Grier to James Buchanan, Washington, Feb. 23, 1857; Buchanan MSS.

[62] Philip G. Auchampaugh, 'James Buchanan, the Court and the Dred Scott Case,' *Tennessee Historical Magazine*, X, 234–38, reveals Buchanan to Catron, February 3, 1857, and Catron to Buchanan, February 6 and 10, 1857. Catron to Buchanan, Washington, February 19, 1857. John Grier to Buchanan, Washington, February 23, 1857, Buchanan MSS.

abatement was not before them, but Taney thought it was, and proceeded
to the issue: 'Can a Negro, whose ancestors were imported into this country,
and sold as slaves, become a member of the political community formed and
brought into existence by the Constitution of the United States, and as such
become entitled to all the rights and privileges and immunities guaranteed
by that instrument to the citizen?'

This question, Taney continued, must be examined solely from the viewpoint prevailing when the Constitution was drafted, for 'it must be construed
now as it was understood at the time of its adoption.' [63] It was not the
Court's province to decide upon the justice or injustice, the policy or impolicy, of these laws, but 'to interpret the instrument and to administer it
as we find it, according to its true intent and meaning when it was adopted.'

Viewed in this light, Negroes 'are not included, and were not intended to
be included, under the word "citizens" in the Constitution... On the contrary, they were, at that time, considered as a subordinate and inferior
race of beings who had been subjugated by the dominant race.' It was difficult 'to realize the state of public opinion in relation to that unfortunate
race, which prevailed in the civilized and enlightened portions of the world
at the time of the Declaration of Independence, and when the Constitution
was framed and adopted.'

But for more than a century Negroes had been regarded 'as beings of an
inferior order and altogether unfit to associate with the white race, either in
social or political relations; and so far inferior that they had no rights which
the white man was bound to respect; and that the Negro might justly and
lawfully be reduced to slavery for his benefit. He was bought and sold, and
treated as an ordinary article of merchandise and traffic, whenever a profit
could be made by it. This opinion was at that time fixed and universal in
the civilized portion of the white race.' Such had been the British conception when America was colonized; such had been the Colonial attitude
through the War of Independence. In some States climate had made
Negro labor unprofitable and slavery there gradually died out. But the
reason was economic rather than moral and citizens of these very States
were especially active in the slave trade, the system's 'worst form.'

This historical statement, buttressed with a detailed citation of statutes
and court decisions, led Taney to the final opinion that 'Dred Scott was not
a citizen of Missouri within the meaning of the Constitution of the United
States, and not entitled to sue in its Courts.'

[63] 'No one, we presume,' he said further, 'supposes that any change in public opinion or feeling in relation to this unfortunate race... should induce the Court to give to the words of the
Constitution a more liberal construction in their favor than they were intended to bear when
the instrument was framed and adopted. Such an argument would be altogether inadmissible
in any tribunal called on to interpret it.... It is not only in the same words, but the same in
meaning, and delegates the same powers to the government, and secures the same rights and
privileges to the citizens; and as long as it continues to exist in its present form, it speaks not
only in the same words, but with the same meaning and intent with which it spoke when it
came from the hands of its framers, and was voted on and adopted by the people of the United
States. Any other rule of construction would abrogate the judicial character of this Court and
make it the mere reflex of the popular opinion or passion of the day.'

The Chief Justice next undertook to determine the merits of Scott's contention that he should be free because he had been taken to a Territory north of the Missouri Compromise line. This brought up the validity of the Act itself. From what clause in the Constitution did the Congress derive its power over a Territory? The Chief Justice thought that the grant to Congress of the power to make 'all needful rules and regulations respecting the territories or other property belonging to the United States' was intended to make the new Government the successor in power and authority to the old Confederation and to give it right and title to the commonly owned lands and facilities thereof. But it had no reference to areas thereafter to be acquired. Congress' specific power to admit new States implies the further power to acquire territory not then ready for admission as a State, to be held until it was in a suitable condition to become a State. Such right as Congress had to regulate a Territory was incident thereto. But after-acquired territory was held by the Government 'as the representative and trustee of the people of the United States, and it must therefore be held in that character for their common and equal benefit.' [64]

The Chief Justice next pointed out that Congress' power 'over the person or property of a citizen' was not discretionary but was clearly delimited and defined, and Congress could exercise no greater power over the citizen in a Territory than in a State. Moreover, 'the right of property in a slave is distinctly and expressly affirmed in the Constitution.' Therefore the Act of Congress prohibiting a citizen from holding or owning slaves north of the Missouri line 'is not warranted by the Constitution, and is therefore void.' [65]

The Chief Justice's was but the first of seven opinions, requiring two days for delivery. Nelson presented the brief statement he had initially prepared. Catron, Daniel, Grier and Campbell each went at considerable length into the two controlling questions. Curtis' dissent, which occupied fifty-nine printed pages, was able, strongly reasoned and considerably persuasive. McLean was quite rhetorical and his words delighted the Abolition North.

This efflorescence of opinions has given many students of the law considerable difficulty in ascertaining precisely what points actually did secure the agreement of five among the Justices and thus became the judgment of the Court. Recent critical analysis establishes that the main essential agreement of five or more Justices was that Dred Scott was still a slave and therefore not a citizen, from which fact the Federal Court had no jurisdiction.

Particularly significant is that fact that the Chief Justice's elaborate

[64] Taney's view as to the 'necessary rules and regulations' clause went considerably beyond Douglas' 1854 position. Douglas had said repeatedly that the 'subject to the Constitution' clause in the Kansas-Nebraska bill meant that completely, and had refused to be drawn into argument with either side. In 1859, when he did elaborate his views, he agreed with Taney that 'territory,' as used in the Constitution, meant only public lands, but Cutts, 51–54, quotes Douglas to the effect that the Supreme Court was wrong in holding that the clause in question gave Federal power only over those regions in our possession in 1789.

[65] The Chief Justice likewise dismissed Scott's contention as to his acquisition of freedom because of his residence in the free State of Illinois, holding that when Scott returned to Missouri, being brought back as a slave, 'his status as free or slave depended on the laws of Missouri, and not of Illinois,' and the Missouri Supreme Court had already passed upon this phase.

statement that a Negro could not be a citizen within the purview of the Constitution was *not* the opinion of the Court, for only four Justices held that the plea in abatement that Scott was a Negro was before the Court. McLean and Campbell held definitely that it was not, and Catron, Grier and Nelson were silent. A majority were agreed that the Missouri Compromise was unconstitutional. Not only did this mean that Scott remained a slave, but also that slavery had national constitutional establishment and Congress could not prohibit it in a Territory.[66]

Dred and his family were almost immediately emancipated by their owners; for an instant a fitful light had played upon them and then they passed into the twilight. But the Dred Scott case proved more than a nine-day sensation. For the Republicans to 'cheerfully submit' to it would mean that their party's sole excuse for existence had disappeared. But there was no thought of submission. Before Court adjourned Saturday afternoon the anti-slavery press began attacking Taney and his majority associates.

The sentence Taney had employed in his historical review of the attitude toward the Negroes before and up to the time of the American Revolution — that 'they had no rights which the white man was bound to respect' — was instantly detached from its context, warped from its meaning and made a stick with which to belabor America's highest judicial officer as a veritable Simon Legree.[67] The decision, thundered Greeley's *Tribune*, was entitled to just so much moral weight as would be the 'judgment of a majority of those congregated in any Washington bar-room.' 'The moment the Supreme Judicial Court becomes a court of injustice,' the *Independent* foamed, 'that moment its claim to obedience ceases.' This particular decision was deliberate iniquity, and if the people obeyed it they disobeyed God.[68]

---

[66] Hagan, *op. cit.*, 109 *et seq.*, has analyzed the agreements and lack of agreements of these opinions in an unusually cogent and incisive way. Undoubtedly the only essential agreement was that the Circuit Court had no jurisdiction because Scott, the plaintiff in error, was not a citizen of Missouri. Hagan also points out that in their opinions justifying the Court's decision, the members of the Supreme Court were entitled to give as many reasons as they wished for their opinion, so long as the matters discussed were in the record before the Court when it considered the case.

[67] That this attitude did so exist in 1787, and for decades before and at least two decades afterwards, few competent historians of the period would seriously question. For other discussions, see E. W. R. Ewing, *Legal and Historical Status of the Dred Scott Decision*, Washington, 1909; Julius Cohn, 'The Dred Scott Case, *American Law Review*, XLVI, 548–57. Lawson, *American State Trials*, XIII, xx; E. S. Corwin, *The Doctrine of Judicial Review*, Princeton, N.J., 1914; 133–40.

[68] New York *Tribune*, March 7, 9, 10, 11, 12, 16, 17, 19, 20, 21, 25, 1857; *Independent*, New York, March 12, 19, 26, 1857. It should be noted, however, that this was the first Supreme Court decision since that of Marbury *vs*. Madison holding an act of Congress unconstitutional. Probably the Dred Scott decision would, therefore, have been attacked even had it not been involved with an issue of such an explosive character.

CHAPTER XVII

DOUGLAS AND BUCHANAN

THE record does not disclose whether Douglas heard Chief Justice Taney read his opinion that March morning, and the Little Giant's first public comment came three months later. Yet this epochal decision marked the beginning of the final phase of his career.

Douglas contended that a people's right to direct their own affairs was so fundamental that they possessed it for some time prior to their readiness for statehood. 'Let the people rule' bottomed his Kansas-Nebraska bill — safeguarded, of course, by the clause 'subject to the Constitution of the United States.' Agreeing to the principle, Southern Ultras had insisted that it could not be applied until statehood. Up to then, they insisted, any citizen had a right to take his property with him to any Territory and to have it protected there. Now the Supreme Court had upheld that view. If the people of a Territory could not govern their own affairs sufficiently to limit or prohibit slavery, what was left of Popular Sovereignty? This development might well give the Little Giant pause.

In addition Douglas was vexed by growing evidence that Buchanan felt no gratitude at all for his voluntary withdrawal at Cincinnati. He had come to Washington, the preceding December, expecting cordial relations with the new Administration, and had pressed for two Cabinet appointments for his Northwestern friends.[1] But these were ignored and it began to be more and more apparent that the new President was hostile to him and his supporters. Such Federal offices or favors as the Douglas men secured were grudgingly bestowed and it looked as though Buchanan would like naught better than to destroy his upstart antagonist.

Then there was a third matter distracting the Illinois Senator's attention. Within a fortnight of the election he had taken to himself a bride, and that Winter and Spring the Douglas home on Minnesota Row was the scene of unwonted social activities.

Adèle Cutts, the Capital's reigning belle, was the second to capture Douglas' heart. Like Martha Martin, she was of Southern blood. Her father, James Madison Cutts, a nephew of Dolly Madison, had lived for years with the ex-President and his wife. Her mother, one of the Maryland Neales, a prominent Catholic family, had beauty and charm and was often mistaken for Mrs. Rose Greenhow, her more famous sister.[2] Cutts

[1] Douglas to Samuel Treat, Washington, Dec. 20, 1856; Missouri Historical Society MSS. Douglas wanted Treat and W. A. Richardson in the Buchanan Cabinet.

[2] The elder Cutts had also been a colonel in the Mexican War, and had published a volume, *The Conquest of California and New Mexico.* When he died, May 11, 1863, he was second Auditor of the Treasury. Adèle was born December 27, 1835. Even in the 'Fifties, the parlor of Adèle's aunt, Mrs. Greenhow, was a focus for the gatherings of extreme Southern Ultras, and the

spent most of his life as a department clerk in Washington, and the family
had to put up a brave front on a meager income, but Addie, who grew up
into one of the most beautiful girls in Washington, nearly always made
light of her poverty. Once she complained to Mrs. Clement Clay of the
cost of gloves, but the latter easily consoled her by asking what mattered
gloves upon hands 'which might have been chiseled by Phidias.'

Tall, gracious and unassuming, Adèle soon captured a high place in Capital society, which was struck with her 'sweet oval face, large brown eyes,
small Grecian forehead and braids of glossy chestnut hair.' Young Henry
Villard remembered her as 'a most lively and queenly apparition,' and Mrs.
Pryor thought her 'as beautiful as a pearl.' Papa Cutts often went with
her to Germans and balls and Adèle could be seen at band concerts on the
White House lawn, attired in the 'simplest of white muslin gowns,' with
japonicas in her hair.

A devout Catholic, Adèle had been educated in the Georgetown Nun-
nery and through life faithfully observed the duties of her church. A great
reader, she was especially gifted as a linguist; after their marriage Douglas
began to requisition book after book in the original French from the Library
of Congress. Julius Granger thought her the handsomest and most accomplished girl ever raised in Washington and 'as good as she is handsome.'
General Shields termed her 'a splendid person,' with 'good sense, exquisite
taste and a kind and generous disposition.' [3]

At the time of the wedding, the Washington correspondent for one of the
New York papers offered an interesting though unlikely account of the inception of the new Douglas romance. It seems that Cutts' home was immediately across the street from that of Senator Bright. One August night,
when Douglas called at Bright's home to discuss the campaign, Adèle
happened to be there. When she left Bright remarked, 'Douglas, it is really
a shame you are not married. You ought to find a wife at once, and there's
the lady for you.' According to the story, Douglas accepted the suggestion,
and Bright introduced him to the family. Then Douglas became a frequent
visitor at the Cutts' home and in a few weeks' time Adèle promised to be his
wife.[4] At any event, as soon as the Presidential election was over, Douglas
hastened from Illinois to Washington. Shortly after his arrival Adèle's

lady herself quite definitely disapproved of Douglas' political views, although as a person
she liked him. After Sumter Mrs. Greenhow became a Confederate spy. Certain of her early
exploits alarmed Seward, who had her confined in Old Capitol Prison for many months. Then
she was sent through the lines to the Confederates and went to England on their behalf. In
1864 she sought to return to the Confederacy, the blockade runner failed to get through the
Federal squadron north of Wilmington, Mrs. Greenhow sought to escape to shore in a rowboat,
which capsized and she was drowned.

[3] New York *Tribune*, Nov. 22, 1856, reprinting *Evening Post* dispatch dated Washington,
Nov. 20. Mrs. Clement C. Clay (Ada Sterling, ed.), *A Belle of the 'Fifties*, New York, 1905;
35, 106; Marion Gouverneur, *As I Remember*, New York, 1911; 218–21; Ben: Perley Poore, I,
490; Mrs. Roger S. Pryor, *Reminiscences of Peace and War*, New York, 1904; 68; Henry Villard,
Memoirs, I, 92; Julius N. Granger to David [A. Lisk], Washington, Nov. 19, 1856; James A.
Shields to H. H. Sibley, Washington, Dec. 23, 1856; Minnesota Historical Society MSS.

[4] Washington correspondence, New York *Evening Post*, clipped, New York *Tribune*, Nov. 22,
1856.

parents announced her approaching marriage to the Senator, which became 'the absorbing theme of conversation in fashionable and political circles.'[5]

On the afternoon of November 20, Thanksgiving Day, the wedding was solemnized in the Roman Catholic church, Father Byrne officiating. The church was full, the bride was attended to the altar by several bridesmaids and it was a great social event. Douglas, who had General Shields for best man, seemed to one observer ill at ease during the Catholic ceremonial.[6]

That evening the Little Giant and his bride, General Shields, Julius Granger and a servant left upon a leisurely wedding journey. First they went to Philadelphia, where there was a little sight-seeing, then on to New York City, and about a week later they paid a visit to Douglas' mother at Clifton Springs, then they went on to Chicago.[7] By Christmas they were back in Washington, and Douglas had established Adèle as mistress of his spacious, stuccoed house on Minnesota Row at the corner of New Jersey Avenue and Eye Street.

Since his first wife's death, Douglas' sister Sarah Granger, and her daughters, plain, unassuming ladies, but pleasant and attractive, had managed his *ménage*. Every week during the season Mrs. Granger had 'reception days,' and Illinois visitors reported that they had 'nearly as much company as the President.'[8] Upon Adèle's installation, Minnesota Row became even more a social center, the new châtelaine thought it well to refurnish the home, there was entertainment on a lavish scale, and it was not long until the Douglas home became a social White House.

One of the second Mrs. Douglas' principal charms was her ability to put the awkward or ill-at-ease person completely at his ease. Many stories are told of the lengths to which she would go to make people feel comfortable. On one occasion a guest eating at the Douglas table broke a cup and was overcome with mortification. Adèle assured him that the cups they were using were much too frail for any useful purpose and, to carry conviction, struck her own and shattered it.[9]

Soon she was setting the styles for Capital society. One season, at her Saturday afternoon at-homes, she draped curtains over her windows and lighted the house with candles. In no time at all the fashionable hostesses followed suit. When Adèle's marriage gave her the means to dress according to her beauty, her toilettes 'were of the richest and at all times were models of taste and picturesqueness.' The wife of the most powerful Sena-

[5] New York *Herald*, Nov. 21, 1856.

[6] Washington correspondence, New York *Evening Post*, clipped, New York *Tribune*, Nov. 22, 1856; Ben: Perley Poore, I, 490.

[7] J. N. Granger to David [A. Lisk], Washington, Nov. 19, 1856; James A. Shields to Henry H. Sibley, Washington, Nov. 20, 1856; Minnesota Historical Society MSS. Granger was careful to write a friend near Canandaigua to keep news of Douglas' coming to himself if there was any likelihood of 'a demonstration against the Judge.' If, however, it seems that 'there would be no disorder or violence among the Abolitionists,' the word could be passed around.

[8] Adeline Crenshaw to Mrs. Chas. H. Lanphier, Washington, April 20, 1856; Patton MSS.

[9] Family recollections as transmitted to me by Mr. Robert Dick Douglas of Greensboro, N.C., June 20, 1933.

tor, with wealth, prestige and position, she soon was regarded as the un-
crowned queen of Capital society.

This first season Mrs. Douglas sat for her portrait to the second Benjamin
West, also a famous portrait painter; he was so pleased with his handiwork
that he added a most unusual background feature, the capital of a pillar
which, on close inspection, proved to be West's own portrait in miniature.
This painting was hung in the Douglas dining-room, and the Senator
frequently pointed out this anomalous capital, and would say that West
had sought 'to immortalize himself on the same canvas with this beautiful
woman.' [10]

But for all this Adèle Douglas was as modest and considerate as she had
been as the daughter of a department clerk. The two Douglas boys, Robert
and 'Steen,' found her affectionate and understanding.[11] She told the Senator that she did not believe his boys were receiving the proper religious
training. He agreed and said he was entirely willing for her to raise them
in her own religion. Soon she placed the boys in Gonzaga, a preparatory
school at Washington run by the Jesuits and later they entered Georgetown.

In the 1860 campaign one of Douglas' advisers suggested that it would be
prudent to take his boys out of the Jesuit school. He answered that, while
he wanted the Presidency more than any other earthly thing and was willing
to pay any reasonable price for it, taking his boys out of a Catholic school
because of the effect keeping them there might have on his political fortunes
involved a surrender of principle which was too high a price to pay.[12]

Since Martha Martin's death, Douglas had grown quite careless in dress
and in habit. With his marriage to Adèle he returned to the mode, and his
impress upon society was almost as great as was that of his fascinating wife.
At this time the sobriquet the Little Giant was most fitting. Mouth, nose
and chin expressed boldness and power of will and 'broad, high forehead
proclaimed itself the shield of a great brain.' Douglas' hair was showing a
tinge of gray, but his brilliant black eyes beneath shaggy brows still fascinated women and compelled men. Young Henry Villard, who met him
during the Winter, testified that 'it took but a glance at his face and head to
convince one that they belonged to no ordinary man.' [13] Douglas' manner
had lost most of its flavor of arrogance; he had just about worked out his

---

[10] Lyman Trumbull, 'Celebrated Men of the Day,' *Belford's Magazine*, V, 226–28; that
Spring, Douglas, Rice and Breckinridge bought 'two blocks 315 feet square each,' near
Minnesota Row, agreeing to pay $51,000 for it, borrowing the down payment of $12,500. They
planned to build and sell; Rice to Breckinridge, Washington, April 6, 14, 1857; Breckinridge
MSS. In 1866, one of the three houses on Minnesota Row proper was occupied by General
Grant. Friends later paid off its mortgage for Grant. When he became President, it was pur-
chased from him and given to General Sherman. Douglas' home was later purchased by Justice
Bradley; for West portrait item, see Stevens, 648, quoting William W. Hoppin, 'The Peace
Conference of 1861,' paper read before Rhode Island Historical Society. Incidentally, it was
at this same time that Healy came to Washington and painted Douglas' own full-length picture.

[11] So Stephen A. Douglas, Jr., told Allen Johnson; Johnson, 317.

[12] Family recollections as transmitted to me by Mr. Robert Dick Douglas of Greensboro,
N.C., June 20, 1933.

[13] Stevens, 649; Villard, *Memoirs*, I, 54–55.

A STATESMAN'S BRIDES

Above: Martha Denny Martin, of Rockingham County, North Carolina, whom Douglas married in 1847; died, 1853
Below: Adèle Cutts, whom Douglas married in 1856

philosophy of life, knew the main tenets of his beliefs and could defend them, amiably but powerfully, against all comers. Those who met him at this epoch were instantly impressed with his sense of power and reserved force.[14]

But whatever might have been Douglas' rapture in the gracious and affectionate Adèle, for him there could be no long escape from politics. The bride and groom had no more than returned from their wedding journey than the Senator heard further disquieting reports about Buchanan's hostility. Soon he came to resent what seemed a deliberate policy of proscribing his friends and destroying his own future prospects. When Buchanan came to Washington, Douglas called on him and, after 'a full and free conversation,' felt the inference was 'irresistible' that the 'patronage for the Northwest had been disposed of before the nomination.' Not only would Bright, his bitter enemy, be the patronage referee for that section, but Bright was already making the preliminary motions toward a Presidential candidacy in 1860.[15]

'If this purpose is carried out,' Douglas wrote a Missouri friend, 'and I am the object of attack, I shall fight all my enemies and neither ask nor give quarter.... At present I am an outsider. My advice is not invited nor will my wishes probably be regarded, I want nothing but fair play. I ask nothing for myself. I want only a fair share for my friends. I desire the bold, true men who fought the battle to be sustained. If this can be done I am content. If, on the contrary, the power of the Administration is to be used either for plunder or ambition,' he would return their blows.[16]

This state of mind made Douglas irritable.[17] Slidell warned Buchanan that the Illinois Senator, in addition to deeming himself the chief Democratic representative of the entire Northwest, was 'in a very morbid state of mind' and he believed there was 'a general conspiracy to put him down.' Buchanan was asked about the trouble. '*I trust in Heaven I may be President myself,*' he answered, '*and think I shall be.*'[18]

The rumor became widespread in Illinois that damaging disclosures were about to be made about Douglas, who would not seek re-election. The Senator, however, made short work of this gossip.[19] Buchanan awarded

[14] Charles T. Congdon, *Reminiscences of a Journalist,* Boston, 1880; 286–87.

[15] C. W. Cotton, Indianapolis, March 23, 1857; Douglas MSS.

[16] Douglas to Treat, Washington, Feb. 5, 1857; Missouri Historical Society MSS.

[17] James S. Green, Washington, Feb. 25, 1857; Douglas MSS. In addition, Douglas was sick and his physician would not let him go out of the house; Douglas to Horatio King, Washington, March 27, 1857, Horatio King MSS., Library of Congress.

[18] Slidell to Buchanan, Washington, Feb. 14, Buchanan, Washington, Feb. 25, 1857, undelivered letter, copy sent Buchanan Jan. 11, 1859, by T. C. Young, Postmaster at Saratoga, N.Y., with request to let him make it public. Buchanan MSS.

[19] Douglas to Sheahan, Washington, Feb. 23, 1857; Sheahan MSS.; Douglas to J. W. Singleton, Washington, Feb. 14, 1857; Illinois State Historical Society MSS. He wrote Sheahan that he had 'no fears of any disclosures that anybody has to make,' and advised General Singleton that he was determined to submit his conduct 'for approval or disapproval of the Democracy of the State by seeking re-election.' A little later the reported 'damaging disclosures' were revealed; they were charges, laid before Buchanan by 'Long John' Wentworth, that in the pre-

minor posts to a few of Douglas' friends but the sum-total was quite small.[20]

Early in April, the Senator, his bride and the two boys left Washington for Illinois to spend the Summer months. Soon the second Mrs. Douglas was conquering the hearts of her husband's Illinois friends. She refurnished his handsome Chicago home and entertained a great deal.

The Senator, however, had other than social problems. Soon after reaching Chicago, he undertook to ascertain at first-hand the actual public temper, and set out upon a visit to key points in the State. In Springfield the Federal Grand Jury insisted that he address it upon the state of the Nation. Here, on June 12, Douglas first gave public expression to his views as to the Dred Scott case decision.

Whether the Congress had power over slavery in the Territories was a judicial question, he reminded them. Under the Kansas-Nebraska Act, its determination by Congress had expressly been left subject to the final decision of the Supreme Court. This had now spoken, it had held the Missouri Compromise unconstitutional and it was the duty of good citizens to heed its decision. Indeed, the Court was to be commended for having passed from mere technical issues to the true merits of the case.

As a practical matter, however, the right of Popular Sovereignty did persist unimpaired. It was true that a master's right to take his slave to any Territory continued in full force, and could not be divested nor alienated by any act of Congress. But 'it necessarily remains a barren and worthless right unless sustained, protected and enforced by appropriate police regulations and local legislation, prescribing adequate remedies for its violation. These regulations and remedies must necessarily depend entirely upon the will and wishes of the people of the Territory, as they can only be prescribed by the local legislatures.' Because of this necessity for a sustaining local law, 'the whole principle of Popular Sovereignty and self-government is sustained and firmly established by the authority of this decision.'

By this interpretation the Little Giant upheld the respect for established law which the opinion of the Supreme Court required. More important, he pointed out that such a right was barren and worthless unless protected by local laws. In other words, Popular Sovereignty still was the main factor in the equation with which Douglas hoped to solve the slavery question.[21]

---

convention campaign of 1856, Douglas had personally written and had published in the Chicago *Times* a letter offensive to Buchanan. D. Cameron, Jr., Chicago, March, 1857, Douglas MSS., shows that Douglas knew nothing of the incident, and the actual author of the slur was a Chicago lawyer Douglas did not know!

[20] Samuel Treat, St. Louis, March 10, 1857; Douglas MSS. Treat, whom the Little Giant had urged for the Cabinet, was named to a new Federal Judgeship; Governor Joseph Wright, of Indiana, was appointed Minister to Prussia and a few other minor jobs were dispensed to Douglasites. Treat was 'fully gratified.' Wright's selection was chiefly the result of Bright's and Fitch's desire to get an Indiana foeman out of the way; Douglas to McClernand, Chicago, April 26, 1857; original in possession of Major Wm. L. Butler of Springfield, Ill., shows that while the Little Giant kept pressing for some foreign post for John A. McClernand, he was completely in the dark as to Administration intentions.

[21] New York *Times*, June 23, 1857.

While Douglas was thus laying the groundwork for his re-election in 1858, the velocity of events in Kansas indicated that a final show-down there was close at hand. Douglas, Buchanan, Cobb, Jefferson Davis, Robert J. Walker, Robert Toombs — indeed, nearly all important Democratic leaders — conceded that the thorny problems of Kansas constituted the chief challenge to a continuation of their party's national control. All realized that the Administration would succeed or fall on Kansas.

In Kansas itself, leaders of the Democratic party, the outgrowth of the Law and Order group, seemed anxious to allay apprehensions. Under the malign influence of Atchison, Stringfellow and the 'Border Ruffians,' the last Territorial Legislature had passed a series of laws so extreme and un-wise that the North had rung with indignant protest. Now, however, cooler heads were running things. Douglas, who had privately insisted upon repeal of these mistaken measures, received assurances from John Calhoun that he need not be alarmed. There had not been a pro-slavery meeting in Kansas for a year, the Territorial Legislature would undertake all necessary changes in the laws and 'preserve from the touch of Congress the principle of the organic act.' Indeed, already 'all the laws which any but an Abolitionist could object to are repealed.' [22]

The last Kansas Legislature had districted the Territory preparatory to the registration of eligible Kansas voters, looking toward an election of a constitutional convention. The registration was to be taken in the Spring of 1857, the election of delegates in June and doubtless by the assemblage of Congress in December Kansas would be asking admission as a State. The legislative act did not specifically require that the Constitution be sub-mitted to the people but the Cincinnati platform as well as Buchanan's campaign pronouncements and Inaugural all pledged that this would be done.

The President, however, was disturbed by renewed activities of the Free-Staters, who had held a sort of election for a legislature of their own. Were this body permitted to assemble at Topeka in June, as scheduled, he feared that a sanguinary conflict would ensue, for it was unthinkable that there could be in operation in Kansas at the same time a State and a Territorial Government. The new Administration must act intelligently and promptly to discover a *modus vivendi* for the opposing groups, and to prevent the so-called Topeka Legislature from setting up a rival and unlawful government.

All this lent extreme importance to the President's selection of a new Governor for the Territory. While Geary, with whom Pierce had replaced the alcoholic Shannon, had restored good order, he was tired of his job. Buchanan looked about for an outstanding man.

His choice fell on Robert J. Walker. Pennsylvanian by birth, Mississippian by long adoption, Secretary of the Treasury under James K. Polk, and Senator from his adopted State, railroad-builder, financier, ranking lawyer at the bar of the Supreme Court, Walker was a man whose appointment should

---

[22] John Calhoun, Lecompton, Kansas Territory, Jan. 26, 1857; Douglas MSS. Moreover, Douglas' wishes in this matter 'have been more consulted than all things else,' and a suggestion from him would do more to remove a defect 'than could be done by the whole force of the Administration.'

win acclaim both North and South. When Cabinet-building, Old Buck had considered the dapper little Mississippian both for the State Department and the Treasury. Now he pressed the latter to accept the Kansas post.

On Territorial problems Walker was convinced that Douglas' views 'must ultimately prevail.' [23] The Little Giant on his part was delighted at the President's selection and urged his friend to accept. The amenities of cultured society, however, meant much to Walker and even more to his wife. Then, too, Walker still nursed White House ambitions and feared that Kansas would prove an overwhelming disaster to his hopes. So he promised that he would not accept the post without her consent.

Buchanan overwhelmed him with importunities, pledging the most unwavering determination to sustain the Popular Sovereignty pledges of the Cincinnati platform by securing a true and honest Kansas vote. He also argued that, should Walker deal successfully with the Kansas slavery problem, there would be no office to which he could not successfully aspire. After Walker had declined several times, Buchanan asked Douglas to intervene and the Senator solicited Walker 'earnestly and excitedly.' The latter finally agreed that, if his wife would consent, and if there were the most thorough concurrence between the President and himself as to submitting the prospective Constitution to the people, he would accept.

Buchanan said this program was 'the one under which his Administration would sink or swim,' and immediately called on Walker. The latter pointed out to him the 'very peculiar phraseology' of the Kansas-Nebraska bill, and said he believed its great principle was that 'the Constitution itself should be submitted by the convention to the vote of the people.' Buchanan, who 'very distinctly and unequivocally' concurred with these views, then set out to persuade the obdurate wife. There were peculiar reasons, he told her, why her husband 'more than all others might perhaps save the country' by preventing the impending revolution, and securing a peaceful settlement of the Kansas question. At length she reluctantly gave her consent. [24]

[23] R. J. Walker, New York, Jan. 9, 1857; Douglas MSS. Walker had added his hope that the Supreme Court would soon settle the question as to Congress' power over slavery in the Territories, by denying it, a result which 'would give renewed confidence at home and abroad in the stability of our institutions and insure another Democratic victory in 1860.'

[24] Douglas, in a speech in Milwaukee, Wis., Oct. 13, 1860, Chicago Times and Herald, Oct. 17, 1860, said Buchanan had told him Walker was 'the only suitable man in America to administer the office in such a juncture of affairs,' and therefore asked Douglas to intervene. When he did so, Walker said he would if the President put it on the ground that the Union was in danger, 'but that he would never go to Kansas unless the Administration stood pledged to the principle that the Constitution, whatever it might be... should be submitted to the people for acceptance or rejection.' Walker had also told Douglas the Administration's officers in Kansas, and particularly John Calhoun, must help. Buchanan thereupon asked Douglas to see Calhoun, who was then in Washington. The Senator told Buchanan to give his own orders. Calhoun later told Douglas Buchanan had sent for him, outlined the program and said Calhoun 'was expected to carry it out in good faith.' For other generally corroborative accounts, see also reports of Committees of the House of Representatives, Thirty-Sixth Congress, First Session, Washington, 1860, V, 105; this volume is the Report of the House Committee, which in 1859 and 1860 investigated Kansas and other Administration scandals. It is known as the Covode Committee, and subsequent references to this volume will be to Covode.

During the weeks of Walker's persuasion, the Capital was the scene of many conferences on Kansas. Several of the Territory's Administration leaders visited the seats of the mighty seeking a way out of their dilemma. In private conversation they made no bones of the fact that Kansas would almost inevitably become a free State. John Calhoun, whom Buchanan continued as Surveyor and instructed to carry out Walker's program in good faith, assured Douglas that his chief concern was to make it a Democratic State and to take care of the Little Giant's Kansas interests.[25]

This acknowledgment of Kansas freedom as a *fait accompli* alarmed Missouri's Pro-Slavery group, but it did not seem to disturb the South's Democratic leaders, and expressions from Senators and Representatives from the Cotton States indicated their acceptance of the realities of geography and settlement. The Administration's chief fears that Spring were that something would happen during the complicated process of registration, delegate election, constitution-making and submission which would enable the temporarily quiescent Republicans to reinflame the North with charges of Kansas fraud. Were this to occur, the Republicans would gain a new lease on life.

Such charges would have their chief impact upon the Democratic party in Ohio, Indiana, Illinois, Iowa, Wisconsin and Michigan. Party leaders through the Northwest pressed on Douglas, both as a matter of right and of party necessity, that faith be fully kept in Kansas. Senator Stuart, of Michigan, feared that the registrations would be unfair, and that for the Republicans to raise such a charge would prove disastrous. Whatever happened, Kansas must not be admitted until Congress had corrected sins of Administration partisans in the Territory.

'Utter destruction awaits the Democratic party in the North and Northwest,' Stuart predicted, 'unless this course is taken early and rigidly adhered to.' In addition to being right in itself, '*it is the only mode in which what there is left of the party in the Northwest can be saved....* Your fate and mine politically hang on this thread.' He conceded that for the Northern Democratic Senators to join in this policy might unite the Southern members against them, 'but why hesitate? We are annihilated if we do not and saved if we do.... On one side there is salvation, on the other inevitable ruin.'[26]

But Douglas was reassured by Buchanan's choice of a Kansas Governor, and as soon as Walker's acceptance was certain, Douglas left for Illinois. Walker, too, was quite conscious of the dynamite in Kansas, but believed he could nip the fuse. As soon as he accepted the appointment, the President drew up for him instructions which said that, when the Constitution was submitted to the Kansas people, 'the fair expression of the popular will must not be interrupted by fraud or violence.'

Walker drafted an inaugural address which he planned to make immediately upon his arrival in Kansas, in the hope that, through its assurances, he could prevent the assemblage of the pretended Topeka Legislature.

[25] John Calhoun, April 2, 1857; Douglas MSS. Calhoun knew that the two most important of these were that the voters be fairly enrolled and that the Constitution really reflect the public will.

[26] C. E. Stuart, New York, March 29, 1857; Douglas MSS.

The President visited Walker's home by appointment and the two spent several hours together upon the draft. Buchanan weighed every word and 'fully approved' Walker's remarks on the submission of the Constitution.[27] When the Governor had the presidentially-corrected draft in his pocket he set out for the West.

As Buchanan had asked, Walker stopped in Chicago 'to get the assent of Senator Douglas' to his inaugural. The Senator examined the document with great care; when he came to the portion stating that Walker was authorized by the President and each of his Cabinet to say that if the Constitution were not submitted to the people, it would not be accepted by Congress, Douglas asked if he had that 'distinct understanding.' Walker then exhibited his manuscript, with its interlineations in Buchanan's own hand. Douglas insisted on having satisfactory evidence that the Constitution 'was the act and deed of the people of Kansas, and a faithful embodiment of their will.' The two men were puzzled by the problem of establishing voting qualifications giving all *bona fide* residents their rights but preventing floaters from controlling the outcome. Douglas finally saw the way out: let the Constitution itself define the qualifications for voters for the Governor, legislators, etc. It could then be provided that the same person who could vote for State officers could also vote upon the Constitution.[28]

On May 27, the day after Walker reached Kansas, he published his inaugural, an appeal to both factions to cease their disturbances, to submit to the national authority, to settle their disputes through the ballot box and thus to permit a peaceful outcome to the strife upon the Kansas plains. In it he insisted that the new Constitution be submitted for ratification; he was a Southern man and believed in slavery — but Kansas must be a Free State if her people wanted it so. Next he undertook a tour to persuade the leaders of all factions to follow this program. The reaction of the Pro-Slavery group was all he could have asked, Walker became convinced that every effort to make Kansas a Slave State had been abandoned, and

---

[27] Walker to Buchanan, Washington, March 26, 1857, Kansas Historical Collections, I, 290, for Walker's acceptance. This recited that 'you and all your Cabinet' concurred in Walker's view 'that the actual *bona fide* residents... by a fair and regular vote, unaffected by fraud or violence, must be permitted, in adopting their State Constitution, to decide for themselves what shall be their social institutions.' And so he accepted, 'in the full confidence, so strongly expressed by you, that I will be sustained by all your own high authority, with the cordial cooperation of all your Cabinet.' For instructions, Cass to Walker, Washington, March 30, 1857; printed, Kansas Historical Collection, 322. Foote, *Casket of Reminiscences*, 114, says the instructions were in Buchanan's own hand. Walker testimony, Covode Report, 106–07. In Walker's reference to slavery, Buchanan modified the words of one sentence, without affecting its meaning.

[28] Douglas to Walker, Chicago, July 21, 1857; original in possession of New York Historical Society. In this letter Douglas outlined his Chicago conversation with Walker and the points agreed upon. Cutts, *Constitutional and Party Questions*, 111. In his Milwaukee speech, Chicago *Times and Herald*, Oct. 17, 1860, Douglas also outlined the Chicago conference with Walker. The Governor had also said that when one Cabinet member had been cold to the inaugural, he, Walker, told the President that he would not go to Kansas 'with any one member of the Administration against him.' The one man then withdrew his objection 'and they all pledged themselves to stand by him on the principle of submitting the Constitution to the people.'

that the Border Ruffians from Missouri would never vote in Kansas again, unless incited by 'that wretched hypocritical Emigrant Aid Society.'

The Governor found that most of the farmers — even those from the South — favored Kansas becoming a Free State. Many had come expressly to settle in a Free State and all thought freedom would help land values, a major consideration in a boom. The interest of Pro-Slavery men in the towns had shifted from slaves to railroad stock and town lots, and it was 'universally conceded' that Kansas 'could never be made a Slave State by a fair vote of the people.' The Territory seemed in the grip of a 'universal rage for speculation,' which amazed Walker but he would 'buy nothing in Kansas: lands, lots, railroad shares.' [29]

Walker agreed with Douglas, Buchanan and the Administration that the chief problem was that Kansas be made a Democratic State. This he hoped to accomplish by uniting the Free-State Democrats and the Pro-Slavery party, who thus would constitute a numerical majority. With the slavery issue eliminated there was a logical basis for this jointure, for Free-Soil as well as Pro-Slavery Democrats were economically and socially conservative and ill at ease with Radical Republicans. As late as June of the critical year there was real hope that this program could be carried out. Visiting the Territory, George Sanders found the people 'very quiet and in a most excellent good humor, the dollar having taken the bullet's place.' While Walker had a hard job, he was 'wide awake and indefatigable.' [30]

The followers of Jim Lane and 'Governor' Robinson viewed Walker's professions with unconcealed suspicion. To win their confidence, he went to Topeka, 'capital' of the Free State, and made a dramatic plea to Robinson's followers to participate in the delegate elections. 'What will you do if the coming constitutional convention refuses to submit the Constitution to the people?' he was asked.

'I will join you, fellow citizens, in opposition to their course,' he replied, 'and I doubt not that one much higher than I, the Chief Magistrate of the Union, will join you.'

But it seemed as though a malignant fate thwarted all plans for intelligent adjustment of the Kansas troubles. As early as 1856, a good majority of the Territory's actual settlers were against a Slave State. In the Spring of 1857 there was a tremendous rush of settlers from the Free States of the North. That Summer Walker reported that Kansas contained 9000 Free-State Democrats, 8000 Republicans, 6500 Pro-Slavery Democrats, 500 Pro-Slavery Know-Nothings — almost three to one of anti-slavery men.[31]

The Free-State men had only to reach out their hands and the constitutional convention was theirs. Yet they obstinately refused to participate,

[29] Walker to Buchanan, Lecompton, June 28, 1857; Buchanan MSS.; Covode Report, 115. Kansas Historical Collection, I, 292 et seq., for text of speech.

[30] George N. Sanders to Buchanan, Leavenworth, Kansas, June 23, 1857; Buchanan MSS.

[31] Walker to Buchanan, Lecompton, June 28, 1857; Buchanan MSS. Prentice, Kansas Miscellany, 84, states that, so far as any bloodshed was concerned, the Spring emigration from the North 'virtually ended the controversy.' The 1860 census showed that Ohio had sent 11,617 settlers to Kansas; Missouri, 11,356; Indiana, 9945; Illinois 9367.

on the excuse that the Territorial Legislature had wronged them in laying out the delegate districts. But such shrewd partisans as Robinson and Lane knew that, once they dropped their pentateuchical pose and joined in the legal election process, their martyrdom would be over and their agitation ended by the realities of victory. So Walker's urgings fell on deaf ears. The election was duly held on June 15, but of 9251 registered voters, only 2200 had voted for delegates.[32] This abstention of the Free-State voters enabled the Pro-Slavery group, a small minority, to name the delegates.

Too late the Free-State leaders realized the consequences of their fanatic aloofness. Senator Henry Wilson, of Massachusetts, who was visiting the Territory, promised a campaign fund and later persuaded them to go into the October elections so as to control the next Territorial Legislature.[33] But their immediate reaction was toward violence, and Walker was faced with an incipient revolution under Jim Lane at Lawrence. The Governor quickly rushed troops to the scene of trouble and issued an address, both insisting that the Free-Staters cease their treasonable conspiracies and reiterating his determination to have the Constitution, when framed, submitted to the vote of *bona fide* settlers. This appeal and the show of Federal bayonets impressed the Lane Radicals and trouble was avoided.

Douglas wrote the Governor that he had 'placed the rebels clearly in the wrong,' and the country would sustain him. Also he approved Walker's insistence upon referring the Constitution to the people. 'It is all-important,' Douglas added, 'that the convention shall make such a Constitution as the people will ratify, and thus terminate the controversy.' [34]

Through July, surface factors led Walker to hope that despite the Pro-Slavery composition of the convention, its members would respect pre-election pledges and draft and submit a fair Constitution.[35] Three weeks after the election, the Democrats held a Territorial convention. The attendants were almost all Pro-Slavery men but by unanimous vote they declared their thorough approval of Walker's course.

The practical fact, however, was that the delegate election gave the Pro-Slavery men an unexpected chance to go as far as their quite elastic consciences would permit. Furthermore, with Walker's Lecompton message and Topeka speech, the Fire-Eaters of the South had come to life. Anti-Buchanan papers became virulent; Walker had 'delivered Kansas into the hands of the Abolitionists,' shrieked the Richmond *South*; remove him, demanded the Vicksburg *Sentinel*.[36] Party conventions added their

[32] F. P. Stanton, Message to Territorial Legislature, Dec. 8, 1859.

[33] Henry Wilson, II, 537. None the less, John Brown's followers never ceased to oppose this policy, because they were reluctant to win Kansas except by the shedding of blood.

[34] Douglas to Walker, Chicago, July 21, 1857; New York Historical Society MSS.

[35] Covode, 109, 175. The Democrats of Douglas County had named a ticket of eight delegates, with John Calhoun at its head. The nominating convention formally instructed the candidates to sustain the submission of the Constitution, and soon thereafter the eight published a written pledge to do so. Only a day or so before the election they reiterated this pledge even more specifically.

[36] Quoted, New York *Times*, July 14, 1857.

insistence that Buchanan discharge him. Then, when these Southern hot-heads learned that, even though by fluke, an overwhelming majority of Pro-Slavery delegates had been elected, they promptly demanded that the Administration at Washington and the Pro-Slavery leaders in Kansas disregard all pledges, push through a slavery constitution, without referendum being taken on it, and ask Congress to admit Kansas under it.

But this Southern agitation, emanating from the anti-Administration leaders in the South, was directed not so much at Walker as it was to use his course in Kansas as a pretext to express dissatisfaction with Buchanan's Cabinet and patronage policies.[37] In Georgia and Mississippi, the focal points of disaffection, the chief mischief-makers were the anti-Buchanan elements. In Mississippi, both Jefferson Davis and Albert Gallatin Brown denounced Walker's 'treachery'; in Georgia, every foe of Cobb raised the alarum. Meetings and conventions charged Buchanan with base ingratitude to the South and threatened him with condign punishment for his political infidelity.

Nearly every Administration adviser in the North told the President it was vitally important to the Democratic party's continued Northern existence to have a full, fair vote of the actual settlers. Walker wrote that the Administration must sustain him thoroughly and cordially, otherwise he could not control the convention and 'anarchy and civil war' would result. 'If the convention fails to submit the Constitution to the people,' he warned, 'there will be a universal crash.' [38]

Buchanan was galled and mortified by the Southern blasts on him, but at first determined to uphold Walker's course. His Cabinet sought to stiffen his backbone. Jacob Thompson saw through the Mississippi furor, and Henry S. Foote, just back from California, was sent to his old State to offset the Fire Eaters. Cobb too analyzed the storm, and sneered that although 'all the Democrats and Pro-Slavery men of Kansas' were satisfied with Walker, the Georgia Democratic Convention had denounced him. None the less, he busied himself to rally the Administration forces in his State.[39]

Foote's speech at Memphis was well received and the President's course was endorsed. He arrived in Jackson the morning after a mass meeting in the State Capitol at which Davis and Brown had denounced the President. But a great throng turned out to hear Foote's defense of Walker and Buchanan and at its conclusion adopted resolutions supporting the Administration.[40]

Late June and early July likewise brought good news from Georgia. At first Cobb had expected they would have 1850's fight all over. His antagonists at home, insisting that Cobb was as much President as if he had been sworn in, demanded that he remove Walker. But by the middle of the month, Cobb's mail indicated that the Democrats of Georgia would 'stand

---

[37] Douglas to Walker, Chicago, July 21, 1857; original in possession of New York Historical Society.

[38] S. M. Johnson to Buchanan, Baltimore, June 20, 1857; Buchanan MSS.

[39] Cobb to John Lamar, Washington, July 10, 1857; Erwin MSS.

[40] Foote, *Casket of Reminiscences*, 114–16.

firmly by their principles,' and he wrote his wife that the storm would 'pass over without seriously disturbing the peace and quiet of the country.' [41]

Cass, too, had bestirred himself; and among other things, he asked Colonel John Parker, a Virginian holding a Federal job in Nebraska, to go to Virginia to convert the party there to friendliness to Walker, for 'everything that he was doing was by instructions from Washington.' Parker hastened to Washington, conferred with Buchanan and Cass, then went to Richmond where he filled the papers with articles sustaining Walker and the Administration.[42]

Early news from Kansas and subsidence of the Southern storm greatly encouraged the President. 'It is strange,' he wrote Walker on July 12, 'that people at a distance, who have no practical acquaintance with the condition of Kansas, should undertake to be wiser than those on the spot. It is beyond all question the true policy to build up a great Democratic party there to sustain the Constitution and the laws.' He gave no sign of faltering as to the necessity for a referendum on the Constitution. 'The point on which your and our success depends,' he impressed on Walker, 'is the submission of the Constitution to the people of Kansas.' This was a tenet in which he had utmost faith. 'It is the principle of the Kansas-Nebraska bill, the principle of Popular Sovereignty and the principle at the foundation of all popular government; on it 'we cannot fail.' [43]

Late in July, however, Buchanan began to retreat. Foote returned to Washington to find that the 'howlings of the bulldog of Secession had fairly frightened him out of his wits.' Soon the President went over to the Secession faction horse, foot and dragoons.[44] In August he wrote a public letter defending slavery in Kansas. At the time the Kansas-Nebraska Act was passed, he insisted, slavery existed 'and still exists, in Kansas, under the Constitution of the United States. This point has at last been finally decided by the highest tribunal known to our laws.' How it could ever have been seriously doubted is a mystery. If a Confederacy of sovereign States acquire new territory at the expense 'of their common blood and treasure, surely one set of the partners can have no right to exclude the other from its enjoyment by prohibiting them from taking into it whatever is recognized to be property by the common Constitution.' [45]

But Buchanan did not notify Walker of his change of front, and the latter went right ahead in his efforts to persuade the Free-Staters to enter the legislative election, and the Constitutional Convention to submit whatever document they framed to a vote. In late August the Free-State men held

[41] Zachary T. Johnson, *The Political Policies of Howell Cobb*, Nashville, 1928, 152; Cobb to Mrs. Cobb, Washington, July 11, 1857; Erwin MSS.

[42] John A. W. Buck, Aurora, Ill., Dec. 16, 1857; Douglas MSS. Parker was Registrar of the Omaha District and Buck had a Federal position there too. 'These letters I saw and read myself,' Buck wrote Douglas. The articles appeared during July, in the Richmond *Enquirer*, the Richmond *Examiner*, and a few in the New York *Herald*.

[43] Buchanan to Walker, Washington, July 12, 1857; printed, Covode Report, 112–13. This letter was in response to Walker to Buchanan, Lecompton, K. T., June 28, 1857, *idem*, 115–19.

[44] Foote, *Casket of Reminiscences*, 116.

[45] Senate Documents, Thirty-Fifth Congress, First Session, I, 74.

a convention, protested afresh against the 'wicked apportionment' of legislative districts, but took notice that the Governor had repeatedly pledged
'a full and fair vote, before impartial judges,' and agreed to enter the legislative election. The Constitutional Convention met at Lecompton early
in September, selected John Calhoun for president, spent five days in discussion and then adjourned until after the election of the Legislature.

This first direct election clash of the two parties resulted in a striking
triumph for the Free-State men, whose candidate for Delegate to Congress
triumphed by a vote of two to one, and unofficial returns showed that they
had also swept the Legislature. But with the official returns came a huge
'roll of paper, forty or fifty feet long,' purporting to be a list of 1628 Pro-
Slavery voters in Oxford, a tiny hamlet in Johnson County. If these 'votes'
were counted, eleven Pro-Slavery members would be chosen from that
county and the Pro-Slavery men would control the Legislature. From
sparsely populated McGhee County a similar list of 1200 voters was
sent in.[46]

When these extraordinary and highly suspicious returns were brought
before Walker and Stanton, his Secretary of State, the Free-State leaders
promptly charged fraud and the two officials investigated. They visited
Oxford, found it 'a village with six houses and stores, and without a tavern,'
and saw that such a vote was utterly without possibility. The spurious
names had been copied from an old Cincinnati city directory! On October
19, the Governor issued a proclamation throwing out the Oxford ballots
and giving certificates of election to the Free-State candidates.[47]

When the Constitutional Convention reconvened, the usual models for
constitutions for frontier States were followed in the general provisions.
But on slavery, the delegates sank the knife right up to the hilt. The
pivotal section declared that the 'right of property is before and higher than
any constitutional sanction, and the right of the owner of a slave to such
slave and its increase is the same and as inviolable as the right of the owner
of any property whatever.' Elsewhere in the instrument was a provision
that the Constitution could not be amended for seven years after its adoption, and even after 1864, no alteration should be made 'to affect the rights
of property in the ownership of slaves.'

The question of submission now came before the convention. Up to this
time most of the delegates had given lip service to their pre-election pledges.
Now, however, a group professed to be incensed by Governor Walker's
repudiation of the Oxford-McGhee frauds and refused to submit the instru-

[46] Covode Report, 109; F. P. Stanton speech, Philadelphia, Feb. 8, 1858, printed, Philadelphia
Press, Feb. 9, 1858.

[47] Senate Executive Documents, Thirty-Fifth Congress, First Session, I, 103, giving Walker's
Oxford proclamation of Oct. 19, 1857; *ibid.,* I, 104–06, gives his McGhee proclamation of Oct.
22. 'The consideration that our own party by this decision will lose the majority in the Legislative Assembly does not make our duty in the premises less solemn and impressive,' the proclamation pointed out. 'The elective franchise would be utterly valueless, and free government itself would receive a deadly blow, if so great an outrage as this could be shielded under the cover
of mere forms and technicalities.' Covode Report, 109, 'Not thirty votes were really given'
at Oxford and not twenty in McGhee.

ment to a vote.[48]   This change had not come by chance. Jacob Thompson and Howell Cobb, Southern members of Buchanan's Cabinet, had dispatched a clerk of the Interior Department to Lecompton, theoretically to examine the accounts of Indian Agents, but actually as an envoy to the convention. Thompson's agent was given a seat of honor and took part in secret caucuses.[49]

When the question of full submission was brought to a vote, it was defeated, John Calhoun making the gesture of voting for it. Then he brought forward a shabby scheme to submit, not the Constitution as a whole, as Buchanan and Walker had pledged, but simply the clause as to slavery. If 'the Constitution with slavery' were ratified, the section as to the right of property would be incorporated. If, however, the voters ordered the 'Constitution with no slavery,' then a provision would be substituted to the effect that slavery should 'no longer exist in the State of Kansas except that the right of property in slaves now in this Territory shall in no measure be interfered with.' And the instrument could not be amended until 1864!

Calhoun informed Governor Walker that this was the Administration program, and that instructions to this effect had come to him out of Washington. If only Walker would go along, he could make himself President. Walker said it was 'impossible' that the President had agreed to this trick, and showed Calhoun Buchanan's letter of July 12. The Surveyor-General said it made no matter — Buchanan had changed his mind.

Did Calhoun have a letter from Buchanan to this effect? Calhoun said no, but that the assurance came 'in such a manner as to be entirely reliable.' 'I consider such a submission of the question a vile fraud, a bare counterfeit,' Walker burst forth. 'I will not support it, but I will denounce it, no matter whether the Administration sustains it or not.'[50] The conspirators went forward boldly, their scheme of pseudo-submission was adopted, December 21 was fixed for the referendum and John Calhoun was instructed to transmit the Constitution to Congress.

Walker had been right that the President was not privy to Martin's mission. On October 22, he had written Walker of his own — and his Cabinet's — firm and continued support of the Governor's program, and of his pleasure at word that the Convention would 'submit the Constitution to the people,' a sign that the whole affair was 'gliding along smoothly.'[51]

[48] Covode Report, 157–72.

[49] Covode Report, 159. Thompson's agent, one Martin, of Mississippi, brought word that Thompson desired the full Constitution submitted, but that he would not oppose Kansas' admission, 'if a pro-slavery Constitution should be made and sent directly to Congress by the convention.' L. A. Bargy, Washington, Aug. 14, 1858, Douglas MSS., offered Douglas 'full proof that the Lecompton Constitution was prepared word for word in Washington, under the especial supervision of John Slidell and Mr. Senator Bright, that it was sent out to Kansas in the hands of a secret agent of the Interior Department and received in accordance with a preconcerted plan.'

[50] Covode Report, 110.

[51] Buchanan to Walker, Washington, Oct. 22, 1857; Nicolay and Hay, II, 110–12; Nicolay and Hay secured the letter from General Duncan S. Walker, Robert J. Walker's son. Governor Walker had sought a leave of absence, and Buchanan had granted it, but to begin only after the convention's adjournment, for while it was in session, Walker's presence would be 'too important to be dispensed with.'

But when news of the psuedo-submission reached the White House, Buchanan sought excuse to yield to the Southern cabal and soon it was known that he was preparing to uphold and defend the Lecompton fraud. Fear caused this surrender. Through his career, Buchanan had been a 'dough-face' — now the Fire-Eaters' threats filled him with unquenchable alarm. When Forney protested, Buchanan insisted that he had been forced to it; if he had not abandoned Walker, the Southern States would carry out their threats 'either to secede from the Union or take up arms against him.'[52]

It was a singularly inappropriate time for the Administration to have provoked a new storm over slavery, for it had just won laurels in the off-year State elections through the North, and the Republicans seemed on the wane. In addition, the failure, in August, of the Ohio Life Insurance and Trust Company, had diverted the attention of the people from slavery to bankruptcy, and only a major blunder could have given Bleeding Kansas a new lease of life as an instrument of Republican agitation.

At the outset of the Administration, prosperity had seemed widespread. But the collapse of the Ohio firm had far-reaching consequence. In the ensuing three months, banks failed, railroads went in receivership, insurance companies suspended all over the country. Furnaces and factories closed down and there were 40,000 out of work in New York City alone. The pyramiding of debt and the insubstantial and haphazard bank-note currency caused the whole edifice of good times to crumble as a house of cards.

Buchanan himself seemed to have expected this catastrophe to ease the pressure about Kansas, writing Governor Walker that the financial 'revulsion' had driven 'all thoughts of "Bleeding Kansas" from the public mind.' But the President's own course quickly brought it back.[53] News of this presidential shift of front filled the Northern Democrats with consternation and bitter anger. Especially was this the case in the Northwest.

None was more alarmed than was Douglas. It had not been a particularly happy Summer for him. In August he had been charged with using his chairmanship of the Committee on Territories to help his own land speculations, and particularly at Fort Snelling. He answered hotly that he did not then and never had owned any land in a Territory.[54] And in many other ways Douglas was more and more alarmed by multiplying evidences of friction with the Buchanan Administration.[55]

After ignoring most of Douglas' definite recommendations, the President quite cannily undertook to negative any public protest by naming the

---

[52] Foote, 113; Covode Report, 296.

[53] Schouler, V, 389; the Democrats carried Pennsylvania and New York, cut Republican majorities elsewhere in the North. For panic, *ibid.*, 389 *et seq.*, Rhodes, II, 237; Nicolay and Hay, II, 111; Philadelphia *Press*, Oct. 10, 1857; *Brother Jonathan*, New York, Dec. 12, 1857.

[54] Douglas to New York *Herald*, Chicago, Aug. 29, 1857, published, *Herald*, Sept. 1, 1857. When he became Chairman of the Committee on Territories, he had 'determined neither to purchase or own or become interested in any land, town lots or other property in any of the Territories of the United States, whilst I held that position. I have never departed from this rule.' He was not interested in any land bought from the Federal Government outside of Illinois.

[55] C. M. Hatch to Lyman Trumbull, Springfield, Sept. 11, 1857; Trumbull MSS., Library of Congress. Douglas to Horatio King, Chicago, Oct. 9, 1857; King MSS. Library of Congress.

Little Giant's new father-in-law, James Madison Cutts, to an important Treasury auditorship. Douglas indignantly wrote Buchanan that he had not requested the selection and distinctly did not desire Cutts' new relation to influence the matter. Buchanan replied with cutting sarcasm.[56]

This developing acerbity may have conditioned Douglas' attitude toward the Administration, but he had never ceased to insist that the Kansas Constitution must represent 'the act and deed of the people of Kansas.' After the Convention adjourned, a John Calhoun lieutenant wrote Douglas apologetically that the instrument 'was the very best that could be done,' but Calhoun himself never had the effrontery to write to him.[57] Douglas, however, had overwhelming evidence that the Kansas Pro-Slavery party was no longer worthy of the name of party, was 'hardly a respectable faction,' and that the Lecompton Convention was a mere farce so far as the voice and sentiment of the people of Kansas were concerned. [58]

The whole Northwest blazed with anger. Leading Michigan politicians had but one sentiment — 'Walker must be sustained.'[59] The issue was even sharper in Illinois. When Douglas 'discovered the trick by which the people were to be cheated,' he did not wait 'one hour, or one minute' to denounce it. He wrote McClernand that, 'of course, we must stand firmly by the principles of the Kansas organic act.' The Democrats of the Northwest 'must stand on this principle and go wherever its logical consequences may carry us, and defend it against all assaults from any quarter.' The only question involved was whether the Lecompton Constitution was 'the act and will of the people of Kansas,' or that, of 'some small minority who have attempted to cheat and defraud the majority by treachery.' If this latter, there was but one course to pursue: 'Reinstate the principles of the organic act and the Cincinnati platform by referring the whole matter back to the people.' [60]

Douglas authorized a newspaper statement of his attitude, which brought messages of praise from Northern Democrats. Illinois Republicans were disturbed. Late in November, some of their leaders advised Senator Trumbull that Douglas had pledged to resist the Lecompton Constitution in the Senate.[61] Every Democratic paper in the State denounced John Calhoun's

[56] J. N. Granger, Washington, Sept. 5; Douglas to Buchanan, Chicago, Sept. 6, 1857, M. F. Douglass MSS. *Illinois State Register*, Oct. 12, 1857, prints the correspondence.

[57] Col. A. I. Isaacs, Leavenworth, Nov. 16, 1857; Douglas MSS. Isaacs claimed that the compromise had been based on an article in the Chicago *Times*, which Calhoun had said represented Douglas' instructions to the convention!!! Even so, Isaacs feared lest Douglas had been put in a 'false position,' and apologized that the instrument had been 'the best that could be framed by that convention.' William Weer, Lecompton, K. T., Dec. 21, 1857; Douglas MSS. The Chicago *Times* article 'may therefore claim to itself the glory of all the present uproar.' 'Evidence' that Douglas had written John Calhoun suggesting partial submission was brought forward in the 1860 campaign by the Buchaneers; see New York *Herald*, Oct. 19, 1860, for claims of 'the Democratic Association of Leavenworth.' Chicago *Times and Herald*, Oct. 17, 1860, gives Douglas' Milwaukee speech exposing the flimsiness of the 'evidence.'

[58] Joel I. Fiske, Leavenworth, Kansas, Nov. 13, 1857; Douglas MSS.

[59] A. Logan Chapman, Detroit, Dec. 2, 1857; Douglas MSS.

[60] Douglas to McClernand, Chicago, Nov. 25, 1857; original in possession of Major Wm. Butler, of Springfield, Ill.

[61] N. B. Judd to Lyman Trumbull, Chicago, Nov. 21, 1857; Trumbull MSS. Without he did

Lecompton Convention and all insisted 'on sending the Constitution back.' Sheahan told Douglas that 'to admit Kansas as a Slave State would be destructive of everything in Illinois; we could never recover from it'; there must be 'no compromise' unless Calhoun's Constitution be fully submitted for popular vote — 'Remember that the only fight of 1858 will be in Illinois.' [62]

Word came from Washington that never had that city displayed 'such anxiety to see Douglas. The President is on thorns.' [63] On November 24, Douglas left for the Capital 'full of wrath.' Immediately Congress opened, his intention was to introduce an enabling bill for Kansas, in the terms of the Minnesota bill. 'By God, Sir, I made Mr. James Buchanan!' he is reported to have said, 'and by God, Sir, I will unmake him.' [64]

The day he reached Washington he went to the White House to talk to Buchanan about Lecompton, and advised him, 'as a friend,' not to submit the Constitution. Buchanan begged him to say nothing about it until news came of the vote in the Kansas election. The Little Giant asked if the President would, in turn, delay his recommendation until after the vote.

Buchanan said he must recommend it in his message. 'If you do,' Douglas replied warmly, 'I will denounce it the moment your message is read.' The two men already cordially disliked each other and the conversation became acrimonious. Buchanan admitted that he was determined to make Lecompton a party test and would expect every Democratic Senator to support it. Douglas sharply refused. The President grew more and more excited; finally he rose to his full height and declared, with freezing dignity: 'Mr. Douglas, I desire you to remember that no Democrat ever yet differed from an Administration of his own choice without being crushed.' Pausing a moment he added: 'Beware of the fate of Tallmadge and Rives.' The threat was direct and blunt. Tallmadge and Rives were Democratic Senators who had differed with Andrew Jackson, who had destroyed their careers.

But Douglas rose too, and looked full into Buchanan's threatening eyes. 'Mr. President,' his voice rang out sternly, 'I wish you to remember that General Jackson is dead.' [65] With this, Douglas turned on his heel and left. Both knew that thenceforward it would be war to the death between them.

so, Norman Judd wrote Trumbull, Douglas 'has not the ghost of a chance of being re-elected to the Senate, and without he can maintain himself in the State his hopes of the Presidency are all gone.' Judd related to Trumbull a rumor that Douglas had told his Chicago friends that the Kansas business had been concocted 'by certain members of the Cabinet to ruin him,' and that Douglas did not think Buchanan desired it but could not help himself. Douglas, Walker and Forney had been and were in close correspondence.

[62] J. W. Sheahan, Chicago, Dec. 4, 1857; Douglas MSS.

[63] Harris to Lanphier, Washington, Dec. 3, 1857; Patton MSS.

[64] C. H. Ray to Trumbull, Chicago, Nov. 24; Judd to Trumbull, Chicago, Dec. 1, 1857; Trumbull MSS. The Illinois Republicans feared Douglas would be aided in popular favor by his course, and suggested to Trumbull that he do this thing himself, thus compelling Douglas to follow his enemy's lead.

[65] Douglas speech in Milwaukee, Wis., Oct. 13, 1860; Chicago *Times and Herald*, Oct. 17, 1860; Nicolay and Hay, II, 120; Beveridge, II, 538; Johnson, 328; Stevens, 519.

CHAPTER XVIII

'OLD OBLIQUITY'

DOUGLAS prepared for this struggle with a fortitude surprising in one who had long urged scrupulous fealty to party. 'The battle will soon begin,' he informed an Illinois lieutenant. 'We will nail our colors to the mast and defend the right of the people to govern themselves against all assaults from all quarters.' Democratic Congressmen from Illinois radiated confidence that the Little Giant would 'whip out the whole concern.' Greeley's Washington correspondent predicted that 'the struggle of Douglas with the slave power will be a magnificent spectacle to witness.' [1]

The Northern Democracy responded with enthusiasm to the Little Giant's Chicago intimation that he would oppose Lecompton, and leaders besought him, 'in God's and our Party's name,' to keep up the fight, for he was 'leading a betrayed party by steady siege to certain but distant triumph.' Even Pro-Slavery men in Indiana felt that submission of the Kansas Constitution was 'a point of honor, a very tender one.' If Douglas kept up the fight, Michigan leaders said their State would be redeemed. The Illinois response was so overwhelming that the Senator's aides advised him it would never do for him to 'falter, hesitate, or back down one inch.' Chicago was bare of Lecompton defenders, and of the State's fifty-six Democratic papers only one dared to stand up for the President. McClernand pointed out that hitherto Douglas had urged Popular Sovereignty as a principle, now he could 'contend for it as a fact.' Let him introduce, the first day of the session, a proper Kansas enabling act and the Republican party would become extinct.[2] George Bancroft felt with Douglas that the Nebraska bill must not be made 'an imposture and a sham,' adding a clairvoyant warning that the effort 'to cheat the people of Kansas of their right' would leave 'any Administration that should attempt it helpless in Congress and hopeless with posterity.'

The tone from South and Border was of dismay rather than indignation. Kentucky Democrats seemed 'all upset' at the idea of Douglas differing with the President. Judge Treat, of Missouri, thought Walker was laboring 'for selfish ends,' and that the Lecompton Convention had the legal right to say whether and how it would submit the Constitution. But he proposed a plan by which the whole controversy could be side-stepped: Ignoring both the Lecompton and Topeka Constitutions, Congress should return to the proper starting-point and pass a new law providing for a new census, con-

---

[1] Douglas to Lanphier, Washington, Dec. 5, 1857; Harris to Lanphier, Washington, Dec. 3, 1857; Patton MSS. New York *Tribune*, Dec. 9, 1857.

[2] William Hull, LaCrosse, Wis., Dec. 5; E. M. Huntington, Terre Haute, Ind., Nov. 29; W. W. Wick, Indianapolis, Dec. 8; Daniel Mace, LaFayette, Ind., Nov. 28; A. Logan Chapman, Detroit, Dec. 2; J. W. Sheahan, Chicago, Dec. 9; John A. McClernand, Springfield, Dec. 2; Douglas MSS. Chicago *Times*, Dec. 24, 1857.

vention and submission. Under this plan Kansas would become a Free State, but if it were not followed the Democratic party would be torn apart.[3]

Knowing that Buchanan must make the next move, Douglas bided his time. The night after his White House visit he responded to serenaders but said no word as to Kansas. But while Buchanan's mail contained strong protests against Lecompton, several politicians insinuated that Douglas' course was bottomed on the fact that he was 'looking for the succession,' a hint which stiffened the President's obstinacy. Administration leaders held secret conferences with the Little Giant but wanted him to do all the yielding. He went to the White House again but the President was as obdurate as ever. 'Mr. Senator,' he demanded, 'do you clearly apprehend the goal to which you are now tending?'

'Yes, sir,' Douglas answered. 'I have taken a through ticket and checked all my baggage.' It was the Little Giant's last White House call while 'Old Obliquity' was there.

The Administration's machinery was set in motion. Bright and Fitch, of Indiana, wheeled into line. Bigler, of Pennsylvania, speaking in Kansas that Summer from the same platform with Governor Walker, had uncompromisingly endorsed full submission of the Constitution, but now he maintained that the President had acted in good faith. Green, of Missouri, a master of logic, and a force in debate, agreed to defend Lecompton's legality. And of course every Southern Democrat joined the presidential phalanx.[4]

Douglas, however, recruited few supporters. The power of patronage and the fear of the Administration axe kept all but three Northern Democratic Senators from braving Buchanan's rage. Staunchest was David Broderick, an eloquent, magnetic newcomer from California who clove to the Little Giant, and his battle brought him fame — and death. A second, steadfast only for the first three months of battle, was George E. Pugh, of Ohio. Third was Stuart, of Michigan, whose apprehensions of party disaster nerved him to the combat.[5] To these twenty Republicans would be added.

Now came fresh news from Kansas to add fuel to the flames. After the Lecompton Convention, Governor Walker left for the East and F. P. Stanton, the Territory's Secretary of State, became Acting Governor. In Washington Walker was thunderstruck to discover that Buchanan intended to back the Lecompton fraud and had instructed Stanton to prepare for the election.

[3] George Bancroft, New York, Dec. 2, 1857; Douglas MSS.; Bancroft to Buchanan, New York, Dec. 5, 1857; Buchanan MSS.; I. N. Knapp, New York, Dec. 10; S. T. Bailey, Macon, Ga., Dec. 5; J. H. Harney, Louisville, Dec., n. d.; Samuel Treat, St. Louis, Dec. 2, 1857; Douglas MSS.

[4] For advice to Buchanan, see Buchanan MSS., from Nov. 30, 1857, to Jan. 15, 1858, such as Daniel S. Dickinson, Dec. 26, 1857; Robert Tyler, Dec. 16, 1857. For last Douglas interview, Horace Greeley, *Recollections of a Busy Life*, New York, 1868; 356. For Bigler's Kansas speech, see P. A. Hackleman, Rushville, Md., March 1, 1858; Douglas MSS. Hackleman had been in Kansas and had heard the speech.

[5] Blaine, I, 272, as to Green. According to Blaine, Douglas disliked to meet Green more than he did any other of the Buchaneers; Fessenden he feared more than any Republican Senator. Gwin, Memoirs, MSS., 134; Douglas to Sheahan, Washington, Dec. 6, 1857; original in possession of Mr. George Sheahan, of Chicago; Sheahan to Douglas, Chicago, Dec. 9, 1857; Douglas MSS.

But evidence came to Stanton that the Free-Staters had 'designs of the most desperate character,' and he concluded that, unless something was done, and that promptly, civil war would break out. So he summoned the new Territorial Legislature into extra session and called for measures to quiet the people and prevent the outbreak.[6] His report of this to Washington threw the Administration into a ferment and he was hastily removed. Thereupon Robert J. Walker resigned in protest.[7]

The Territorial Legislature did not countermand the referendum of December 21, but called a second election on the Constitution, to be held January 4. The Free-State men generally abstained from the December test, and only 6226 pro-slavery votes were cast on badly padded voting lists. While the pro-slavery men boycotted the second election, 10,226 votes were returned against the Constitution with slavery. These comparative figures gave a true index of the real hope and will of Kansas.[8]

On December 8, the President finally sent his message to the Senate. Buchanan devoted much space to 1857's disastrous panic, filibustering in Nicaragua and a wide range of governmental problems. But his views on the Lecompton Constitution confirmed Douglas' fears. He referred gingerly to his initial instructions to Walker that the Constitution must 'be submitted to the people,' who must be 'protected in the exercise of their right of voting for or against that instrument,' and 'must not be interfered with by fraud or violence.' Despite plain words, he asserted that his only desire had been 'that the people of Kansas should furnish to Congress the evidence required by the organic act, whether for or against slavery.' So his unequivocal instructions for a vote on the whole Constitution were to mean only a vote on a single section.

This followed hollow praise of 'the great doctrine of Popular Sovereignty,' to which the Lecompton submission adequately complied; at the coming election the exciting question of slavery in Kansas could 'be peacefully settled in the very mode required by the organic law.'

Douglas promptly offered the usual motion to print, adding briefly that he totally disagreed with that portion of it which 'may fairly be construed as approving' the Lecompton Constitution, but would reserve his remarks until the next day.[9] Then the Senate galleries were packed to suffocation.

[6] Cass to Stanton, Washington, Nov. 30, Dec. 2, 1857; Buchanan's Secretary of State ingenuously argued that the election would settle Kansas' slavery question 'in the very manner contemplated by its organic law.' Two days later he sent Stanton so much of the President's message to Congress as related to Kansas, and ordered him to publish it 'extensively.' Stanton to Cass, Lecompton, Dec. 1, 1857; Kansas Historical Collection, V, 411-13 et seq.

[7] Ibid., 431. Walker's letter of resignation contained a strong defense of his Kansas course, with a scorching statement of Buchanan's vacillations. Responding, Cass denied that the President had ever entertained or expressed the view that the Kansas Convention should submit any part of the Constitution, except the slavery clause, to a vote of the people!

[8] When the Free-State men demanded of John Calhoun's chief clerk that they be allowed to examine these returns, the latter claimed he had sent the returns on to Calhoun, in Washington. Then the Free-State men had a tip that the returns were buried in a candle box under a woodpile back of the Land Office in Lecompton. They found them on Jan. 28, 1858, and the count revealed the full extent of the fraud. Dr. Frank H. Hodder to author, Oct. 12, 1933.

[9] Richardson, V, 449-54; Congressional Globe, Thirty-Fifth Congress, First Session, 5.

Adèle Douglas beamed down on her husband, and bent forward to catch his words. The latter rose, weak from illness, and began in low, hoarse tones. He spoke rapidly and without preparation; he was laboring under deep emotion but his words were dignified and restrained.

Taking advantage of Buchanan's characteristic vagueness of expression, the Senator insisted that neither had the President endorsed the Constitution nor had he asked Congress to accept it. On only one point did Douglas express a flat difference of opinion. The President's message had said that the Kansas-Nebraska Act required the submission of the slavery question alone. The Senator deftly pointed out that it had required that *all* domestic questions be determined by the people.

On the issue itself Douglas spoke forth bravely. He brushed aside questions of procedural legality, for the controlling point was whether Congress should approve or reject the Lecompton Constitution. His own view was that Congress should reject it, because it did not represent the will of the majority of the Kansas people, as the legislative election had definitely shown. Others might contend that the pending election on December 21 would give the people a free choice on slavery. Actually what would occur would be that 'all men must vote for the Constitution, whether they like it or not, in order to be permitted to vote for or against slavery.'

It was charged against Napoleon that, when elected First Consul, he reviewed his soldiers, and said: 'Now, my soldiers, you are to go to the election and vote freely just as you please. If you vote for Napoleon, all is well; vote against him and you are to be instantly shot.' '*That was a fair election,*' Douglas exclaimed; 'this election is to be *equally fair*. All men in favor of the Constitution may vote for it — all men against it shall not vote at all. Why not let them vote against it?' This question he had asked many who framed the Constitution, many delegates and members of the cabal and he had received the same answer from every one of them — 'if they allowed a negative vote, the Constitution would have been voted down by an overwhelming majority, and hence the fellows shall not be allowed any vote at all.' He asked the Senate: 'Will you force it on them, against their will, simply because they would have voted it down if you had consulted them? If you will, are you going to force it upon them under the plea of leaving them perfectly free to form and regulate their domestic institutions in their own way? Is this the mode in which I am called upon to carry out the principles of self-government and Popular Sovereignty in the Territories?'

Nor did it help matters for advocates of Lecompton now to assure him that the slavery clause would be voted down, for 'You have no more right to force a Free-State Constitution on Kansas than a Slave-State Constitution. If Kansas wants a Slave-State Constitution she has a right to it; if she wants a Free-State Constitution she has a right to it. It is not my business which way the slave clause is decided. I care not whether it is voted down or voted up. Do you suppose, after pledges of my honor that I would go for that principle and leave the people to vote as they choose, that I would now degrade myself by voting one way if the slavery clause be voted down, and another way if it be voted up?'

His final passage was strong and stirring. 'If this Constitution is to be thrust down our throats,' he said sternly, 'in violation of the fundamental principles of free government, under a mode of submission that is a mockery and insult, I will resist it to the last. I have no fear of any party associations being severed. I should regret any social or political estrangement, even temporarily, but if it must be, if I can't act with you, and preserve my faith and honor, I will stand on the great principle of Popular Sovereignty, which declares the right of all people to be left perfectly free to form and regulate their domestic institutions in their own way. I will follow that principle wherever its logical consequences may take me, and I will defend it against assault from any and all quarters. No mortal man shall be responsible for my action but myself. By my action I will compromit no man.'

The next day he instrumented his views through a proposed new enabling act for a new and fair Kansas election.[10] With this broke the Administration storm. Already there had been talk that the Democratic Senatorial caucus would read Douglas out of the party and replace him as Chairman of the Committee on Territories. At the caucus, on December 11, the Little Giant was 'treated with profound respect' and was not disturbed as Chairman, but the personnel of his committee was so changed as to leave him in a minority.[11]

Bigler, Green, Fitch and Bright advanced to the attack. Douglas was denounced as a trouble-maker, an unscrupulous demagogue of bad habits, a marplot and party-wrecker. Buchanan's consistency was defended. The legitimacy of the Lecompton Constitution was brilliantly presented. Douglas' own words of a few months back excoriating the Topeka rebels were dug from their context and thrown into his teeth. Several of the Southerners vilified him unrestrainedly and there were threats of personal violence.[12] 'Old Obliquity' exerted all his force to destroy Douglas as Old Hickory had destroyed Tallmadge and Rives.

The Little Giant repeatedly defended himself from the casuistry and the venom of quondam friends. Hinting offensively that Douglas himself had shifted on submission, Bigler alluded to secret meetings on Minnesota Row. Douglas absolved Bigler from any pledge of secrecy and demanded to know if the Pennsylvanian charged that he was ever 'privately or publicly, in my own house or any other, in favor of a Constitution without its being submitted to the people?' Bigler was forced to reply in the negative.[13]

Douglas met with contempt the reiterated charge of inconsistency. What had that to do with it, 'is it right to force a Constitution upon a people against their will?' This was the great point; he looked on the Lecompton scheme 'as a trick, a fraud upon the rights of the people' and senatorial

---

[10] *Congressional Globe*, Thirty-Fifth Congress, First Session, 14–18; for speech, *ibid.*, 24; for bill, which was not unlike the suggestions of John A. McClernand and Judge Treat, *ibid.*, 47. 'I spoke rapidly without preparation.' New York *Tribune*, Dec. 10, 1857; New York *Independent*, Dec. 12, 1857.

[11] Philadelphia *Press*, Dec. 11, 1857.

[12] New York *Tribune*, Dec. 11, 1857.

[13] *Congressional Globe*, Thirty-Fifth Congress, First Session, 21–22; see *ibid.* 47 *et seq.*, for answer to Green; 117 *et seq.*, for answer to Bigler; 140 *et seq.*, for answer to Fitch.

sophistry could not erase the fraud. Nor did it matter that he was called a party-wrecker. 'Call it faction,' he warned, 'call it what you please; I intend to stand by the Nebraska bill, by the Cincinnati platform, by the organizations and principles of my party; and I defy opposition from whatever quarter it comes.'

He called attention to the stream of abusive dispatches which Administration-subsidized correspondents were sending out, and to the general report 'that the President intends to put the knife to the throat of every man who dares to think for himself on this question, and carry out his principles in good faith.' In moving tones he exclaimed: 'God forbid that I should ever surrender my right to differ from a President of the United States of my own choice. I have not become the mere servile tool of any President.'

The picture Douglas presented, standing up to the Administration bullies and returning blow for blow, delighted the Northern people, and an avalanche of applauding telegrams and letters descended upon him. Governor Gorman, of Minnesota, wrote that '999 out of every thousand voters in our party, except the office-holders under the present Administration, are with you, and even the latter are divided.' When Detroit's Buchanan postmaster sought to stage a Lecompton mass meeting, hisses and groans silenced their speakers. Wisconsin's Democratic State Convention was almost a Douglas mass meeting. Ohio Democrats were wild with joy. If Douglas kept firm, Iowa would be restored to Democracy. The Illinois reaction was even more encouraging. A special edition of Douglas' speech took like wildfire, Chicago's Germans held a mass meeting to express their pride in the Little Giant. The regular Democratic Committee had its own mass meeting, 'a most complete success'; and the sentiment of Northern Illinois was being revolutionized.[14]

Douglas' courage gave new heart to the Democrats of New England. If he kept on, wrote a Rutland friend, he would carry Vermont in 1860. Gideon Welles said the popular heart would sustain him. Ben Butler, Militia General but not yet Beast, wrote in extravagant praise. Maine Democrats rejoiced that Douglas had about revived their party. 'Don't give an inch.' [15]

Many predicted that his hold on the Northern Democracy could never be broken and never must he let himself be driven from the party 'by a set of Negro drivers and Northern Pudding-heads.' 'Prince John' Van Buren thought Douglas would be the Andrew Jackson of the day. Petitions poured in assuring him that he reflected the real feeling in Buchanan's State. The paper in Jeremiah Black's home town denounced Lecompton; in Philadelphia Forney had to reprint Douglas' speech a second time.[16] His tilt with

[14] W. A. Gorman, St. Paul, Minn., Dec. 27; J. Logan Chapman, Detroit, Mich., Dec. 23; J. W. Sheahan, Chicago, Dec. 31; H. B. Payne, Cleveland, Ohio, Dec. 25; James D. Eads, Des Moines, Iowa, Dec. 13; R. T. Merrick, Chicago, Dec. 12; Chas. P. Button, Dec. 16; D. Cameron, Chicago, Dec. 16; Thomas Hoyne, Chicago, Dec. 24, 1847; Douglas MSS.

[15] John Cain, Rutland, Vt., Dec. 11; Thomas Yeatman, New Haven, Conn., Dec. 12; Gideon Welles, Hartford, Conn., Dec. 12; Benjamin F. Butler, Washington, Dec. 18; G. P. Sewall, Old Town, Me., Dec. 23, 1857; Douglas MSS.

[16] Martin Ryerson, Newton City, N.J., Dec. 18; W. W. Sanger, New York City, Dec. 14, 1857; John Van Buren, Newburg, N.Y., Dec. 13, 1857; Seymour Chase, Ballston, N.Y., Dec.

Bigler brought forth the fact that, ten years before, this now staunch Pro-Slavery man had worked hard for the Wilmot Proviso.[17]

Nor was all the praise from the North. Governor Henry A. Wise, of Virginia, sent Douglas his 'heartfelt approbation,' and protested publicly that, if Congress should approve Lecompton, 'Democracy is dead. The Administration can save it now; it cannot after that act.'[18] Other influential Virginians termed Lecompton 'a deliberate lie on its face,' and many Southerners wrote Douglas that the South still felt kindly toward him.

The Little Giant's course brought words of strong approval from still another quarter — the Black Republicans. Douglas' eyes must have opened wide to read the tributes of the anti-slavery press, for he had said quite bluntly that he cared naught whether slavery were voted down or voted up, and yet here was the *Independent* glorying that he had 'met the issue fairly and manfully, and acquitted himself triumphantly.' Here was the *Times*, Seward's New York organ, making much of his scornful defiance of 'Old Obliquity'; here was Greeley's *Tribune* lauding him to the skies, and its editor wanting a million copies of the speech 'distributed among Democrats by Republicans.'[19]

There was more behind these journalistic transports than colorful reporting. The Republican leaders saw a chance to annex Douglas, which would give the new party a masterly and much-needed leadership. He had always had an extraordinary appeal to young men; six years before, the Young Democrats had chosen him for their leader, two of the three Democratic Senators who now followed him were under forty and it was not surprising that the younger Republican leaders were anxious to proselyte the magnetic Democrat. In this they had the approval of many of the elder statesmen. Greeley, who was in Washington to testify before a House Committee, called on Douglas, the first time in a decade.[20] Senator Wilson, of Massachusetts,

19, 1857; John W. Forney, Philadelphia, Dec. 13, 1857; W. F. White, Pittsburgh, Pa., Dec. 16, 1857; Douglas MSS.

[17] The Pennsylvania House had passed a resolution, instructing the State's Senators and Representatives in Washington to vote for the Wilmot Proviso. On Jan. 26, 1847, Bigler, then a State Senator, had called this resolution up in the State Senate and had sought to pass it.

[18] O. Jennings Wise, the Governor's son, to Thomas Pitman, Richmond, Va., Dec. 31, 1857; P. H. Aylette, Richmond, Va., Dec. 18; R. R. Collier, Petersburg, Va., Dec. 13, 1857; Douglas MSS. *Mississippi Free Trader*, Jan. 8, 1858, refused to doubt Douglas' party fealty.

[19] Ovando James Hollister, *Life of Schuyler A. Colfax*, New York, 1886; 119.

[20] On Dec. 8, 1859, William Kellogg, a Republican Congressman from northern Illinois, charged in open House that 'that man Greeley, again and again, with others, in consultation in the parlor of Judge Douglas, planned and schemed the election of Judge Douglas to the Senate' from Illinois. Douglas promptly and categorically responded that the charge that he had 'ever formed or planned or contemplated or arranged with Mr. Greeley in regard to the Illinois election in my house or at any other place is an unmitigated falsehood.' Greeley had visited his home but once in ten years, on that occasion merely to pay his respects, and there 'the Illinois election was never alluded to.' Douglas to McClernand, Washington, Dec. 8, 1859. Greeley later wrote Kellogg that 'never did any letter, message or word pass between us implying a desire on his part that I should or a promise on my part that I would support him at any time for any office whatever.' Cf. also Greeley to McClernand, New York, March 25, 1860, McClernand MSS.: 'You may not be aware that I went to Washington at that time in obedience to a sum-

heartily applauded the bid for Douglas and Seward did not take unkindly to it.[21]

Doubtless Henry Wilson discussed these possibilities with intimates, for soon Anson Burlingame was having interviews with Douglas. Schuyler Colfax, a young Indiana Congressman, enthusiastically seconded Burlingame, while Frank Blair, stormiest petrel of a stormy family, flitted back and forth, Burlingame and Colfax called at Douglas' residence Monday evening, December 14, and did not depart until after midnight. The Illinois Senator announced that it was his settled determination to follow the principles set forth in his Senate speech, 'no matter where they led him.' He had been surprised at the opposition 'to the simple demand of justice he had made for the people of Kansas,' but intended to maintain his position inflexibly, 'making all else subservient to it, even if it drove him to private life.'

Recent events and disclosures had convinced Douglas that Jefferson Davis and other Southrons were 'really for Disunion and wished an opportunity to break up the Union — that they hoped and worked to unite the South.' The continuation of these efforts 'might compel the formation of a great Constitutional Union party' to resist them.[22] The general policy of the Opposition should be not to permit the Administration to put Kansas ahead of other matters. Minnesota must first be pressed for admission and 'let the South resist it if they dare.' Let the appeal for Treasury notes, appropriations and other normal business be disposed of before Kansas was acted upon. All their steps should be directed 'to put the Disunionists in such a position that, when the breach was made, as it would be, they would be in the position of insurgents instead of us, as they desired should be the case.' Thus, as they would be the rebels, 'the army and the power of the Nation would be against them.'

The visitors sounded the Senator on his personal future. Colfax said that theretofore, because of the Nebraska bill, he had opposed Douglas, but

---

mons from a Committee of Investigation.... Most certainly Judge Douglas had nothing whatever to do with any visit to Washington at that or any other time.'

[21] Frederick W. Seward, *William H. Seward*, New York, 1891; II, 330. 'The Administration and slave power are broken,' Seward wrote his daughter upon Douglas' speech. 'The triumph of freedom is not only assured, but near.'

[22] The episode so impressed Colfax that, immediately upon his return to his lodgings, he wrote out a full account of the interview. This document is now in the possession of the Indiana State Historical Association, at Indianapolis. I am indebted to Miss Esther McNeill, of the Association's staff, for a photostat. Colfax wrote it all in the third person. I have changed two quotations from third to first person. This was not Colfax's first visit — he had gone with Greeley and Clark B. Cochrane, of New York. Neither was it to be his last. Colfax must have written Joseph Medill of the interview, for Medill wrote him: 'If Douglas falters in this crisis, he is a *dead* man. Now is his time to make a ten-strike... Tell him and *rub* in the idea.' Medill, Chicago, December 22, 1857, Colfax MSS. Palmer, *Personal Recollections*, 89-90, relates that when he was in Washington in February, 1861, a delegate to the Peace Convention, Douglas said to him: 'You and your friends did me great injustice in the Lecompton controversy. If I had had my way, and Buchanan had not been a traitor, I would have compelled Davis to raise the standard of rebellion during the controversy, and then there would have been Union sentiment enough to put him down in thirty days.'

now the Republicans felt that a fair Kansas vote dwarfed all other issues. The Little Giant could place himself in the most commanding position of any statesman in the Nation, and could be the Silas Wright of his party.

The two Republicans mildly disclaimed any intention of committing themselves to Douglas for the Presidency but the disclaimer itself was an unmistakable hint. 'That is right,' Douglas exclaimed, cutting short their protestations. 'I ask no support except support in this contest now. If this issue is settled right, new issues will come up hereafter and we will all divide again, as I regard them favorably or unfavorably.' Should Kansas continue the dominant issue, the future would decide their positions. But the Republicans were bent on keeping the matter open. When they left, Burlingame asked the Senator to let Banks, of Massachusetts, consult him the next day so that 'a program of battle' could be arranged, to which Douglas 'cordially agreed.'

A few days later Burlingame told the House that while he still thought it 'the first duty of the Republicans to extinguish the doughfaces,' he felt it equally their duty to attest the way Douglas had kept the faith. That 'gallant and gifted leader' and his men had borne the brunt of the battle. Soon Colfax urged the young men of the Nation to 'stand by these men with all your young enthusiasm. Stand by them without distinction of party.'

Douglas told a Washington newspaper man that he had started his fight against the single measure of Lecompton and not against the Democratic party. 'But a blow at Lecompton was a blow at slavery and he soon found the whole slave power arrayed against him like a pack of wolves.' Shocked to find a Southern group determined either to control or break up the Government, he was resolved they should do neither. Nor did he intend to be driven from the party and if, after exposing Buchanan and the Disunionists, he determined to leave it, it should be of his own accord.[23] Buchanan's Washington organ had a strident editorial reading the Little Giant out of the party, which merely intensified his determination to give battle.[24]

Two months later, however, Colfax and Galusha Grow, a Pennsylvania Republican Congressman, had another long interview with Douglas at the latter's home. The three men examined the political future. Douglas asked no pledge for Illinois support, but said he intended 'to make this fight against the Lecompton villainy and the men who endorsed it one that shall live through history.' But he would not deny that in the future he might not act with his old party, and Colfax wrote jubilantly that the Little Giant was progressing very rapidly in the right direction; if this went on,

[23] Quoted, Kellogg Pamphlet, 7; Kellogg took his quotation from Burlingame's speech in the *Congressional Globe*. *Ibid.*, 12, quotes letter from Chicago *Journal* correspondent describing his talk with Douglas.

[24] Washington *Union*, Dec. 27, 1857. The *Union* was at this time run by Cornelius Wendell, an unusually sinister dispenser of public plunder, who never blushed to put up money by the thousands to influence Congressmen or corrupt newspapers needed for the party cause. See Covode Investigation, V, for revealing evidence by Wendell and by bribees as to his technique.

by the last of the year 'he will do to be baptized.'[25]   All through the Spring
Henry Wilson told friends that 'Mr. Douglas was all right,' and intended to
act with the Republicans. Greeley's editorial praise of the Little Giant,
echoed by the leading Republican presses in the East, grew stronger and
stronger. Douglas himself did not hesitate to tell Republicans, as he had
told Buchanan, that he had checked all his baggage and taken a through
ticket.

Leading Illinois Republicans, however, were noteworthily absent from
any part in all this endeavor to capture the Little Giant. Uneasiness rather
than elation was their portion. In 1858 Illinois was to elect a Senator;
Douglas had announced his candidacy, but his party gave signs of a split
and the Republican coterie in Springfield and the Illinois men in Washington
believed they could elect their own candidate. Promised the 1858 Republican nomination, Abraham Lincoln had been fixing his fences for the race
and was determined not to be passed up again. Chicago's enthusiasm
for Douglas' December speeches drove 'Long John' Wentworth almost
frantic. Senator Trumbull, too, was quite uneasy, and asked Lincoln to
set their Illinois party organs to work denying that Douglas was 'now
contending for the principles of the Nebraska bill.'

Everything was in confusion, Trumbull wrote Lincoln. 'Douglas does not
mean to join the Republican party, I presume'; yet if the Kansas issue were
kept open, he might be forced to do so, for once 'the African Democracy'
concluded they could do without him, they would drive him out. This
report in no wise quieted Lincoln's nerves.[26]

But the Little Giant's view was still national, and he had no more patience
with a program attacking the just rights of the Slave States than he had
with an attempt to trick a free people. Douglas papers in the South maintained that he had not arrayed himself 'in opposition to the general policy
of the Administration and the Democratic party,' and he himself assured
a Virginia editor that the Lecompton bill was no proper party test and he
was and hoped to remain a Democrat.[27] A firm and enduring political alliance between Douglas and the Republicans could only be secured by
establishing a Constitutional Union party, and to do that the Republicans
must embrace Popular Sovereignty.[28]

[25] Hollister, *Schuyler A. Colfax*, 121; quoting Colfax's letter to his mother, Washington,
Feb. 21, 1858. As to Illinois, Douglas said that, 'if the people don't want him, or if his name
proves a barrier to the union of the anti-Lecomptonites, he is willing to retire to private life.'

[26] Trumbull to Lincoln, Washington, Dec. 25, 1857; Jayne Collection, Illinois State Historical
Library. Hollister, *Schuyler A. Colfax*, 120, gives response Ray, of the Chicago *Press and
Tribune*, made to Greeley, as to Douglas: 'I think I see his tracks all over our State... Not
a single toe is turned toward the Republican camp. Watch him, use him, but do not trust
him, not an inch.'

[27] R. H. Glass, Jan. 8, 1858, Douglas MSS., elicited the Senator's answer, which I have reconstructed from references to it in Glass' letter of acknowledgment Jan. 21, 1858; Douglas
MSS. Glass, editor of the Lynchburg *Republican*, deplored the controversy but admired
Douglas' courage and firmness and found consolation in the fact that a true Democrat and statesman would rather believe himself right than be President, and hoped that in two years' time
'the clouds will have disappeared from the skies.'

[28] Douglas to Lanphier, Washington, Jan. 5, 1858; Patton MSS.

For a while there seemed some prospect that the Eastern Republican group would march to this meeting-point, and Seward joined with Greeley, Wilson, Burlingame, Colfax and Frank Blair in assailing the affront to Popular Sovereignty. But the Administration began to explore the possibilities of an alliance with Douglas' foes at home, and easily established a working relationship between the 'slavocracy' and the Illinois Republicans. At the same time the Buchaneers struck at the pocket nerve of Douglas' followers. The Chicago *Times*, the *Illinois State Register* and other Douglas papers in Illinois were deprived of official advertising and post-office printing. Buchanan's political jackals went to Illinois to throw out all Federal office-holders there who would not betray the Little Giant.

So desperate were the White House maneuvers that some of Douglas' followers thought the President had actually gone mad.[29] The New York *Times* correspondent reported that whenever Kansas was mentioned in Buchanan's presence, he would give way to 'eccentric outbursts of choler' and denounce Douglas violently. Alexander H. Stephens, who led the Lecomptonites in the House, thought Buchanan in danger of a breakdown.[30]

Democratic leaders in Illinois were enraged at the lengths to which the President was going. History affords no parallel to so shameless a turncoat, George McConnel wrote Lanphier, 'everything proves him to be a decayed, superannuated old imbecile, as senseless as a Hindu idol.' The Administration's villainies left the Douglas men but one course — they must fight the Buchaneers with their own weapons, 'meanness for meanness, lies for lies, spy against spy.'[31]

'Old Obliquity' might have all the machinery of government at his disposal, but the Little Giant was a powerful antagonist. Soon his instructions to lieutenants went out, and trusted aides hastened to State Capitals to stir the people to action. Legislatures were meeting — let them instruct their Senators to oppose Lecompton. Democratic State Conventions were assembling — let them pass 'milk and water' resolutions about the Administration, and other resolutions insisting that Popular Sovereignty be upheld. When Buchanan's postmasters called mass meetings, let Douglas men take charge. Editors received confidential letters, pamphlets went out by thousands and once more the Little Giant showed himself a master of political technique.

Had the people not been with him, these devices would have availed Douglas naught, but popular indignation against Lecompton increased every day. In Indiana, for example, where for a decade the Bright-Fitch machine had held a death-grip, the two Senators' support of Lecompton precipitated a party revolution. For weeks before its State Convention, Bright's henchmen shelled the woods for delegates. On January 8 a horde of postmasters, marshals and mail agents was in Indianapolis to applaud Buchanan, but were met by an even greater throng of indignant Democrats. Seizing the convention machinery, the Buchaneers tried to ride the storm,

---

[29] Harris to Lanphier, Washington, Jan. 21, 30, 1858; Patton MSS.

[30] New York *Times*, Jan. 30, 1858; Johnston and Brown, *Alexander H. Stephens*, 329.

[31] McConnel to Lanphier, Washington, n.d.; Patton MSS.

but Bright was booed when he tried to speak and the Lecompton platform brought hisses. Lew Wallace, a young insurgent, offered a substitute plank attacking the fraud, there was an hour's bedlam and at midnight his resolutions passed by more than three to one. 'Bright is no more,' one delegate jubilated. 'Let no stone mark the spot where a traitor fell.' [32]

When Ohio's Anti-Lecompton Democrats sought legislative instructions upon the Senators from that State, the Administration sent all its job-holders and job-seekers to Columbus to defeat it. But Ohio was with the Little Giant, the Democratic caucus unanimously backed and the Legislature passed the instructions.[33] All the threats and promises of Buchanan's New Hampshire agents could extort no more than a milk and water resolution from its convention. Connecticut's Democrats tabled a motion to endorse the Administration. Maine's Democratic legislators sent in a round robin protesting against Lecompton.[34]

The Democrats of the Northwest were so strong for Douglas' policies that it was predicted that, before long, Buchanan would not have enough friends left there to hold the offices. 'Agitate — rouse the people' was their program. Indiana's anti-Lecompton Democrats, determined that Douglas should not go into the Charleston Convention 'to be strangled by the two-thirds rule or sold by traitors,' issued a call for a great Democratic convention representing all the Northwestern States, to nominate Douglas for President on the single issue of Popular Sovereignty.

The Little Giant's program, however, was to act with and fight inside the party. In March, when Ohio's Democracy met in mass convention, Douglas leaders had telegrams from their chief warning against the proposed Northwestern Convention. The Ohioans reluctantly abstained from any step for creating a new party, but roundly denounced 'Old Obliquity.' [35] Kentucky's Democratic Convention did not endorse his policies. The Buchaneers sought endorsement from the North Carolina Legislature but secured 'two short resolutions meaning scarcely nothing.' In Louisiana, 'very mild' Buchanan resolutions were introduced, and ignored.[36]

Buchanan Senators repeatedly charged a general Southern hatred of Douglas, but George Bancroft was convinced that the South was not

[32] W. W. Wick, Indianapolis, Jan. 2, 9, 17, 19, 29; Edward J. Kerscheval, Indianapolis, Jan. 9; A. A. Brown, Indianapolis, Jan. 11; W. W. Drummond, Michigan City, Jan. 15; John P. Dunn, Indianapolis, Jan. 16; Lew Wallace, Indianapolis, Jan. 17; J. S. Buckley, Jan. 18; Ezra Reed, Terre Haute, Jan. 21; R. J. Ryan, Indianapolis, Jan. 27; 1858; Douglas MSS. Fitch tried to tell the Senate that the convention had endorsed Buchanan, but Douglas exposed the fraud, which further delighted Indianians, who wrote Douglas, 'don't spare the hound.'

[33] H. B. Payne, Columbus, Jan. 4; W. Griswold, Columbus, Jan. 9; G. F. Newton, Millersburg, Jan. 14; S. S. Cox, Columbus, Feb. 2; 1858; Douglas MSS.

[34] Solomon Parsons, Boston, Jan. 9, 14; Thos. Yeatman, New Haven, Conn., March 4, 1858; Douglas MSS.

[35] D. P. Rhodes, Cleveland, Feb. 21; John A. McClernand, Springfield, Ill., Feb. 17; W. M. McCarty, Indianapolis, Feb. 24; W. W. Wick, Indianapolis, Feb. 27; J. W. Forney, Philadelphia, Feb. 25; H. B. Payne, Cleveland, March 12, 1858; Douglas MSS. Toledo Blade, Feb. 24, 1858.

[36] John B. Cochran, Shelbyville, Ky., Jan. 15; J. B. DeCarteret, Raleigh, N.C., Jan. 20; James Dawes, New Orleans, March 21, 1858; Douglas MSS.

against him — only the Southern politicians. Governor Wise, of Virginia, predicted that if the Administration's plan succeeded, it would 'raise the Black Republican flag over the Capitol.' 'Lean Jimmy' Jones deprecated the party schism, but wrote Douglas that Tennesseans had no bitterness toward him. Douglas' Missouri strength was great and even the Border Ruffians had no kind word for Lecompton. It seemed that the Little Giant was in a strong position; let him remain calm and conciliatory and his Southern strength would return.[37]

Kansas' unanswerable repudiation of the Lecompton Constitution at January's election strengthened the feeling of Moderates in Southern and Border States that Douglas was right. Judge Treat deemed the late election 'a legal and authentic expression of the popular will against the Lecompton Constitution.' Congress might properly order a new census, registration, delegate election, convention and submission. If Douglas would sit down with Senator Green, of Missouri, and work out a proper bill, harmony could be restored.[38]

Douglas conferred with Green, but found 'no hope of an amicable adjustment of the Kansas question.' On the contrary, the Administration was more anxious for his destruction than 'for the harmony and the unity of the Democratic party.' Not only was it removing Douglas' friends from office and requiring pledges of hostility from all new appointees, but it was 'endeavoring to form an alliance with the Republicans of Illinois' to defeat him for the Senate. Douglas had no alternative but to accept the issue.[39]

And yet he kept up his spirits. 'I am not dejected nor discouraged in the least,' he wrote John W. Forney. 'We will fight the battle out boldly and gallantly and triumph in the end. Let the enemy threaten, proscribe, and do their best or worst, it will not cause any honest man to falter or change his course.... Let us stand by our colors and make no compromise — no concession, and all will end well.'[40] 'If you fight the battle boldly,' McClernand wrote, 'even a defeat will be a victory, but if you yield an inch you are undone.' Douglas answered that he had taken his stand, and would hold to it, 'let the consequences be what they may.'[41]

[37] George Bancroft, New York, Feb. 18; A. D. Banks, Petersburg, Va., Jan. 2; Henry A. Wise, Richmond, Jan. 14, 1858; Douglas MSS. B. H. Wise, 236–38, gives Gov. Wise's public letter, dated Feb. 6: 'If we are not willing to do justice, we can't ask for justice.... Every Southern man would have been in arms and would have been roused to the shedding of blood rather than submit to Congress fastening upon a majority of pro-slavery people an arbitrary rescript of a mere convention unauthorized to proclaim its constitution without an express grant.' John L. Peyton, Staunton, Va., Feb. 23; Victor C. Barringer, Concord, N.C., Feb. 19, 1858, Douglas MSS. 'We feel,' Barringer wrote, 'that if Lecompton is a fraud, it ought to be rejected, and that in such event it would be no legitimate cause for dissolution of the Union.' Hiram Martin, Richmond, Jan. 20; James C. Jones, Memphis, Jan. 3; office endorsement on letter of John J. Quarles, Carthage, Tex., Jan. 30, was that it was only 'unapprobatory' letter received; James J. McBride, St. Louis, Jan. 10, 18; W. A. Richardson, Omaha, N. T., Jan. 19, 1858; Douglas MSS. Richardson had just journeyed through Missouri.

[38] Samuel Treat, St. Louis, Jan. 12, 1858; Douglas MSS.

[39] Douglas to Treat, Washington, Feb. 28, 1858; Missouri Historical Society MSS.

[40] Douglas to Forney, Washington, Feb. 15, 1858; Historical Society of Pennsylvania MSS.

[41] J. A. McClernand, Springfield, Feb. 12, 1858; Douglas MSS. Douglas to McClernand, Washington, Feb. 21, 1858; McClernand MSS.

This firmness of spirit stood Douglas in good stead during the social war which supplemented the Congressional conflict. Minnesota Row now was almost besieged: everyone who came to Washington wanted to see the man who defied the President.[42] Douglas' home vied with the White House as the fount of social distinction, Douglas' dinners were far better than those at the White House and the lovely Adèle was more than a match for the handsome, tepid Harriet Lane, Buchanan's niece and châtelaine. The season's climax was a great ball at the Douglas home, for which over fourteen hundred invitations were issued, and which attracted the notabilities in Congress, the diplomats and the reigning chiefs of Army, Navy and public life. The Little Giant was supposed to be under the President's social as well as political ban, but Isaac Toucey, of his Cabinet, Cass' daughter, Aaron V. Brown's wife, and even 'Old Obliquity's' private secretary, were all present. Reports were that the Douglas ball 'had never been approached in style and success.' Great praise was lavished upon Adèle, who bore her honors 'most becomingly.' [43]

This scent of attar of roses was all very well, but in the actual Congressional struggle, Buchanan patronage proved much more potent than Popular Sovereignty. The Senate was made up of 39 Democrats, 20 Republicans, and 5 'Americans' from the South. Of Democrats, Douglas could count on only Stuart, Pugh, Broderick and himself; of Americans, he was sure of Crittenden, of Kentucky, and hoped for John Bell, of Tennessee. The Republicans were solid on the issue, but all these totaled only 26, against 37 for Lecompton. The House, however, gave real ground for hope. There the Republicans had 92 and the Americans 14, and while the Democrats, with 131, had a majority, their ranks were honeycombed with disaffection.

Douglas talked candidly with the Illinois Democratic Congressmen. They had approved his course, knew that its issues were 'those of life and death' for them all.[44] Through January they agitated among their Northern party associates, and soon an anti-Lecompton Democratic caucus was organized with Thomas L. Harris as its chairman. By January 30, they had commitments from over half the Northern Democrats and more were sure to come. James B. Clay, of Kentucky, thought they could get several Southern votes, and Harris was confident of victory 'by a decisive majority.' [45] Nor was this expectation unreasonable. Buchanan's only grip on the Democrats in Congress was political position and patronage. Andrew Johnson, of Tennessee, who thought Douglas a 'dead cock in the pit,' saw both that the President had 'no personal strength' in Congress and expected from him naught but 'Grannyism.' [46]

[42] Cleveland *Plain Dealer's* Washington correspondence, reprinted, Chicago *Times*, Jan. 29, 1858.

[43] Mrs. Roger A. Pryor, *Reminiscences of Peace and War*, Chapter V, 51 *et seq*. Washington correspondence, Cincinnati *Gazette*, copied Quincy, Ill., *Herald*, Feb. 8, 1858.

[44] Kellogg Pamphlet, 2.

[45] Harris to Lanphier, Washington, Jan. 30, 1858; Patton MSS.

[46] Andrew Johnson to Robert Johnson, Washington, Jan. 23, 1858; Robert Johnson MSS.,

Buchanan's message transmitting the Constitution was momentarily expected. 'Hold your breath,' Harris wrote. 'Douglas will shake the Capitol and the country.' [47] On February 2, the message came. Long, labored, highly biased, studded with misleading excerpts from Walker's reports, Buchanan laid the entire blame for the Lecompton Constitution on the Free-State men. When he had instructed Walker 'in general terms in favor of submitting the Constitution to the people,' he declared that he had 'no object in view except the all-absorbing question of slavery.' This the convention's submission had satisfied and the legal election of December 21 had overwhelmingly sustained Kansas' pro-slavery Constitution. Now he was 'decidedly in favor of its admission,' the happy consequence whereof would be peace and quiet, not only to Bleeding Kansas but to the entire Nation. He himself had 'no other object of earthly ambition' than to leave America peaceful and prosperous 'and to live in the affections and respect' of his countrymen.[48]

The Lecompton Constitution was referred to the Senate Committee on Territories and the Kansas question colored all Senatorial debate. Many of the Lecomptonites privately admitted that their hearts were not in the battle. 'Every intelligent man with whom I have conversed,' Governor Letcher, of Kentucky, wrote John J. Crittenden, 'thinks Douglas had the right on his side.' Henry J. Raymond found it almost impossible to find a Democrat who would attempt 'to vindicate the Lecompton movement *per se.*' Senator Hammond, of South Carolina, felt in his heart 'that the South itself should kick that Constitution out of Congress.'

But while the Southerners were ashamed of the flimsy fraud, they felt that slavery's status was deeply involved. Then, too, there were ten Southern Senators and four Cabinet members who wanted to be President.[49] So the die was cast. The Lecomptonites had a majority of the Committee on Territories and Green wrote their highly legalistic report. Collamer and Wade presented the official Republican contention. Douglas submitted a third report, insisting that the Constitution was 'not an act of the people of Kansas' and did not embody their will. The submission of these reports precipitated a warm debate.

The first test in the House, the real battle-ground, came on February 8. While the Anti-Lecomptonites expected a majority of about twenty, such was the Administration pressure that the antis barely won.[50] Thereupon the

Library of Congress. Johnson believed Douglas intended to bolt to the Republicans, and did not care if he did, 'the party would soon recover from the shock.'

[47] Harris to Lanphier, Washington, Jan. 30, 1858; Patton MSS.

[48] Richardson, V, 471–81.

[49] Coleman, *John J. Crittenden*, I, 141; New York *Times*, March 24, 1858; Hammond's speech at Barnwell Court House, S.C., Oct. 29, 1858; quoted, Pamphlet,'Popular Sovereignty — The Reviewer Reviewed,' by a 'Southern Inquirer,' Washington, 1859; 37 *et seq.* Foote, *Casket of Reminiscences*, 117, quotes Cass as having urged, with tears in his eyes, that Foote go to the White House to persuade Buchanan to abandon his 'mad course.' For the Presidential aspects, see Hammond to William Gilmore Sims, Washington, Jan. 20, March 24, 1858; quoted, Elizabeth Merritt, *James Henry Hammond*, Baltimore, 1923; 121.

[50] Harris to Lanphier, Washington, Feb. 9, 1858; Patton MSS.

Administration read the Anti-Lecompton Democrats out of the party, heads rolled from the official axe, promises were paraded before the uncertain and no stone was left unturned to carry Lecompton through.

Trumbull's arrangement with the Administration was in good working order, and he assured Slidell that he would vote for any men the President might appoint 'to replace anywhere one of Douglas' supporters.' Buchanan nominated Isaac Cook, Douglas' bitter foe, for Chicago's postmaster and the Senate Committee promptly approved him.[51] When one Dr. Leib, a well-known rascal, was made mail agent for Illinois and started on his rounds, Harris called on Lanphier to 'sound the tocsin that Kansas outrages are about to be transferred to Illinois.' Jobs and contracts were dangled before the noses of newspaper proprietors and several papers began to 'give Douglas the devil.' [52]

Lanphier, who came to Washington, was disheartened. 'I fear they have got Douglas down and that our party has gone to the devil,' he wrote his wife. The Little Giant had one of his frequent throat affections. Moreover, Adèle had had 'a slip-up.' But she recovered from the miscarriage, Douglas grew stronger and undertook to 'give them all the fight that is in him.' [53]

Even an ailing Douglas was a giant in debate. Brown, of Mississippi, insisted that, had Douglas not opposed, there would have been no Lecompton agitation and Kansas would have been admitted almost without an effort. But no, 'the Senator from Illinois gives life, he gives vitality, he gives energy, he lends the aid of his mighty genius and his powerful will.' Some of the Southerners advanced startling ideas. Toombs sneered at the constitutional discussions; 'there's a "nigger" in it' was his verdict.

Jefferson Davis left a sick-bed to enter the debate. Spare, erect and austere, the soldierly Mississippian was a commanding figure. To the haughty manner of a conscious aristocrat he added the intense eyes of a zealot. His voice was clear and firm but he often gave the appearance of being suffused with a passion he suppressed, and his very restraint often aroused his followers to intense passion.[54] The South wished to extend its slave system, Davis declared, 'simply because of the war that is made against our institutions, simply because of the want of security which results from the action of our opponents in the Northern States.... You have made a political war. We are on the defensive. How far are you to push us?' [55]

When some of the Senatorial Buchaneers renewed their attempt to read Douglas out of the party, he remarked with great disdain that he would return from Illinois a Senator for six years longer, and when he did so would make further reply to his enemies, preferring to save time and unnecessary

---

[51] Slidell to Buchanan, Washington, Feb. 17, 1858; Buchanan MSS.; Sheahan, Chicago, Feb. 10; R. T. Merrick, Chicago, Feb. 22, 1858; Douglas MSS.

[52] Harris to Lanphier, Washington, Feb. 27, 1858; Patton MSS. Peter Sweet, Peoria, Ill., Feb. 8; C. Ballance, Chicago, Feb. 11, 1858; Douglas MSS., tell how G. W. Raney, a Peoria editor, came back from Washington with a turned coat.

[53] Lanphier to Mrs. Lanphier, Washington, n.d.; Patton MSS.; J.W. Forney, Philadelphia, Feb. 14, 1858; Douglas MSS.

[54] Pollard, *Jefferson Davis*, 32–33.   [55] Rhodes, II, 250–51.

fatigue by 'firing upon them in a bunch.' Davis denounced this remark as unexampled insolence. Again Douglas commented ironically on the defection of certain Southern friends, and indicated conditions upon which he would allow them to be restored to the party. Quivering with anger, Davis jumped to his feet, struck his breast with his hands and raged against his foe. More than once in the debate Douglas toppled him off his balance, Davis 'lost his temper, and rushed at his antagonist with an ungovernable violence.' [56] After the last interchange, Douglas' lieutenants chortled that Davis was 'used up for the session at least.' [57]

The House contest was almost as sharp. On March 13, Harris made a motion to recommit, and on a test the Anti-Lecompton men had eight majority. 'We have got them,' Harris exulted. 'Lecompton is doomed.' Crittenden made a powerful attack on Lecompton, insuring the firmness of the Americans, and the Administration's hopes of House success were gone.[58]

Douglas made his final Senate argument on the night of March 22. Before the hour for the session a tremendous throng filled gallery and corridors, while Congressmen crowded the Senate floor and the crush was such that even telegraph boys could not get through. There was a shout of applause when Douglas entered.[59] Still was he weak and ill, still was his voice low and husky and still was he determined not to yield an iota of principle. He began with his customary account of slavery legislation. From time to time Stuart, of Michigan, would read excerpts from official documents, enabling Douglas to save his strength and voice. But fact was piled on fact and evidence on evidence, that the Lecompton Constitution did not represent the will or voice of Kansas. Douglas then turned the doctrine of State's Rights against those who had preached it so incessantly. The Federal Government could not undertake to construe State Constitutions; whenever it undertook to give a meaning to a clause of the State Constitution which that State had not given, 'farewell to State's Rights, farewell to State Sovereignty.'

To the solemn warning to the South he added another even more specific. Stuart read for him a recent statement of extreme Southern doctrine, to the effect that any State law which prohibited citizens of one State from moving into another with their slave property was a violation of the Constitution.[60] 'Illinois has the sovereign right to prohibit slavery,' Douglas thundered, 'a right as undeniable as that the sovereignty of Virginia may authorize its existence.' He would not admit that the right of property in slaves was higher than and above constitutional obligations, and the South should know that, when she went beyond the Constitution, no one could say where her safety was.

Toombs countered that Douglas had defended what no one assailed and had attacked what no one defended. But the Little Giant was announcing

[56] Pollard, *Jefferson Davis*, 34, 38, 39, 40.

[57] Harris to Lanphier, Washington, March 13, 1858; Patton MSS.

[58] Harris to Lanphier, Washington, March 13, 1858; Patton MSS.; Stephens to J. W. Duncan, Washington, March 17, 1858; original in Watertown, Conn., Library.

[59] New York *Herald*, clipped, *Illinois State Register*, Springfield, March 27, 1858.

[60] Washington *Union*, Nov. 17, 1857, contained this statement.

a platform upon which the Northern Democracy could endeavor to maintain itself. He recited five broad principles declared in the Cincinnati platform, upon which he stood. First, the importation of Negroes, prohibited since 1808, should never be renewed. Again, Negroes, while not citizens of the United States and not entitled to political equality with the whites, should be given all rights and privileges they were capable of exercising. Each State and Territory must determine for itself how far these privileges should go. Each Free State would scrupulously maintain the rights of the Slave States, but it would also uphold and defend its own sovereign right to establish its own domestic institution, subject only to the Federal Constitution. Finally, the Kansas-Nebraska Act was a declaration in the form of law of the elementary principles of self-government. 'Let each State take care of its own affairs,' he concluded, 'mind its own business and let its neighbors alone — then there will be peace in the country.' [61] It was a great speech, applauded through the North, but it did not change the view of a single Senator. The next day Lecompton won, 33 to 25.

In the House there were three reports. There, too, the tension had become almost unbearable. On one occasion Keitt, of South Carolina, and Grow, of Pennsylvania, had a personal encounter; on another, thirty men were in a battle-royal. But all of this merely strengthened the determination of the Douglas Democrats. On April 1, with the House considering the Senate's Kansas bill, Montgomery, a Pennsylvania Democratic member, offered an amendment similar to that Crittenden had vainly urged in the Senate; under it the Lecompton Constitution would have been submitted to a new vote of the Kansas people. If they should vote for it, Kansas would be admitted into statehood. If they declined it, the people of the Territory were empowered to frame a new Constitution under which they could become a State.

The Buchaneers vainly sought to defer the vote. Summoning a dozen members to the White House, Buchanan besought them, curses mixed with tears, not to forsake him. Cobb boasted that the Treasury Department was 'good for at least twenty votes.' Yet, when the roll was taken only a single member was absent, and the amendment won, 120 to 112.[62] Great was the rejoicing of Douglas' aides. 'Few in number,' one of them wrote Lanphier, 'yet by indomitable courage they have held this powerful and proscriptive Administration in check, and have forced the Black Republicans to the support of a bill embodying fully in every respect the great principles of the Kansas-Nebraska bill.' [63]

'The agony is over, and thank God the right has triumphed,' a Douglas man exulted. 'Poor Old Buck! Why don't his friends stand by their post?

---

[61] *Congressional Globe*, Thirty-Fifth Congress, First Session, App., 194 *et seq.*

[62] New York *Times*, Feb. 20, April 2, 1858; Johnston and Brown, 329. In the vote, 22 Democrats, 6 Americans, 92 Republicans voted for the Crittenden-Montgomery amendment; 104 Democrats and 8 Americans were against it. Foote, *Casket of Reminiscence*, 118–19.

[63] S. S. Marshall to Lanphier, Washington, April 1, 1858; Patton MSS.

Never President stood in such need of friends! Won't they give him anything? Poor imbecile old man, has he neither organ, nor Senate, nor House?' [64]

But this jubilation was premature. House and Senate named conferees and William H. English, an Indiana Democrat who had followed Douglas, brought forward a plan of compromise, which the Buchanan men eagerly embraced. The scheme was to refer the entire Constitution to the Kansas voters. If these accepted it, the Federal Government would admit Kansas to statehood, at the same time giving it the large grant of land usually given new States. But if a majority rejected the Constitution, Kansas should not be admitted as a State until its population reached that required for electing a Representative to Congress. [65]

This compromise put the anti-Lecompton Democrats on the spot. Douglas was personally embarrassed, for English was an old friend, and in 1856 had left Bright to support the Little Giant for the Presidential nomination. Beyond this there was embarrassment in the terms of the bill. Douglas had insisted that he opposed Lecompton because it was a fraudulent submission — the English bill called for a vote not only on the slavery section but on the Constitution in its entirety. Douglas had called for evidence that the Constitution would really be the act and deed of the Kansas people. Proponents of the English bill might claim that the election it proposed would afford such evidence. True, some thought the bill was a patent bribe; 'adopt Lecompton,' it seemed to say, 'and we will give you much Federal land. Reject it and we will deny you statehood.' Even so, it was a technical affirmation of Popular Sovereignty. Douglas could accept it as such and his breach with the Administration would be ended. [66] Small wonder that he was perplexed and troubled. Dozens who had followed his political fortune urged him to seize the substance and to let the shadow go. Full well he knew that if he rejected it, 'Old Obliquity' and his group would remain his eternal foes. It was reported that he 'wavered,' the press was full of rumors and his Republican associates exhibited their suspicions. [67]

But for every appeal for him to accept, Douglas had a dozen pleas not to budge an inch. 'For God's sake,' one Ohio friend exhorted, 'put your foot on every proposition looking that way.' 'Yield not one inch,' came a typical Illinois expression. His closest advisers in Washington felt that it was a 'miserable scheme,' [68] and the Little Giant's own love of fair play and honest dealing counseled him the same way.

[64] H. B. Payne, Cleveland, Ohio, April 9, 1858; Douglas MSS.

[65] Rhodes, II, 255.

[66] Though the statement was made at the time that the land offer was a bald bribe, it is not exactly correct. Frank H. Hodder, 'Some Aspects of the English Bill for the Admission of Kansas,' *American Historical Association Report*, 1906, I, 201–10, has shown that the area offered Kansas was at the most no more than was usually offered new Territories becoming States, and indeed was less than several had secured. The actual unfairness was rather that, if Lecompton were rejected, Kansas could not become a State for several years. Cf. Johnson, 343–44.

[67] Henry Wilson, *Slave Power*, II, 563–67.

[68] Daniel O. Morton, Cleveland, Ohio, Feb. 22; H. T. Wilson, Cleveland, Ohio, Feb. 26; J. W. Davidson, Chicago, April 27, 1858; Douglas MSS. Harris to Lanphier, Washington, April 29, 1858; Patton MSS.

On April 29, when he told the Senate of his decision, he showed the emotion under which he labored. He had studied the bill's provisions with an 'anxious desire' to find it acceptable; but he found in it not Popular Sovereignty but intervention by Congress — 'intervention with a bounty on the one side and a penalty on the other.' The bounty was not sufficient to determine the Kansas vote but it interfered with 'the principle of freedom of election.' Therefore, despite his anxiety to return to harmony with his friends in Congress, he could bring neither his judgment nor his conscience to the conclusion that it 'was a fair, impartial and equal application of the principle' of Popular Sovereignty.[69]

This decision made little difference in the Senate, on whose vote Pugh deserted the Little Giant — of the Democrats, Stuart and Broderick alone stood up. In the House, the Administration intensified its pressure. Federal jobs and contracts were carried about on Administration platters. Cornelius Wendell, Buchanan's corrupt Public Printer, spent money by the tens of thousands. Live-oak contracts had their usefulness and one New York Democratic member was offered a township of land.[70] These arguments proved more powerful than editorials, reports or speeches. Of the twenty-two Democrats who had voted for the Montgomery amendment, only twelve were steadfast. Thus the compromise was adopted by a vote of 120 to 112. 'Old Obliquity' had saved his face.

Lecompton's epilogue occurred on August 2, when the new election was held in Kansas. The total vote cast was 13,088. Of these, 11,300 were to reject the English proposition. Free lands did not lure Kansas to come into the Union as a Slave State.

[69] *Congressional Globe*, Thirty-Fifth Congress, First Session, 1869 *et seq.*

[70] Harris to Lanphier, Washington, April 29, 1858; Patton MSS. Foote, *Casket of Reminiscences*, 118. Covode Report, Wendell's testimony. Haskin, of New York, was offered the land, but rejected it; see his testimony, Covode Report, and letter; Philadelphia *Press*, Sept. 30, 1858; Henry Wilson, *Slave Power*, II, 65.

CHAPTER XIX

BUCHANEERS AND BLACK REPUBLICANS

THERE could have been no stronger endorsement of Douglas' stand against Lecompton than this Kansas election forever establishing freedom on the prairies. But news of the outcome came when the Little Giant was fighting for his life against an extraordinary alliance of Buchaneers and Black Republicans.

From the start of the Lecompton struggle, the Illinois senatorial election had been in the background. When Douglas first propounded his Nebraska policy, the Illinois Democrats had followed him with some reluctance. Their fealty had been strengthened in 1855 and 1856, and the Little Giant's recent battle against great odds strengthened their idolatry. As the year turned, nearly every Democrat outside the post offices was for Douglas.[1]

The Illinois Republican party was now some weaker than in 1854. The initial merger of Abolitionists, Free-Soilers, Maine Law men, immigrants and Know-Nothings was more mechanical mixture than chemical affinity. After the heat of the first contest the party's strength waned. The elections of 1855 showed Democratic recovery, Buchanan carried the State in 1856, the next year's by-elections were none too satisfactory to the Republicans and their leaders had no roseate expectations for 1858.

These highly practical politicians knew their future was bound up in their party and undertook desperate measures to sustain themselves. A Lincoln aide wrote Trumbull that they 'must have *money* to colonize some four or five districts... and the end justifies the means...'[2] With the Little Giant's break with Buchanan, the prospect of a split Democracy fired the Illinois Republicans with new hopes. Small wonder that Trumbull, Lincoln, Herndon, Medill and Ray frothed at the mouth when Eastern Republicans suggested that Douglas be not opposed.

The Democratic schism in Illinois greatly stirred the professional politicians. For a decade Douglas had been filling the Federal offices, and there was point to the jest that each appointment yielded nine enemies and one ingrate. When Buchanan sounded his tocsin, Douglas' personal enemies leaped to the attack and personal hostility to him was a principal force behind the cabal.[3] To these shock troops was quickly added a brigade of mercenaries. The State was still in the throes of the panic, its horde of place-hunters was quite famished and the rush of the needy and the greedy

---

[1] W. W. Drummond, Springfield, Jan. 19; J. A. Ettinger, Maryland, Ill., Jan. 25; J. M. Davidson, Lewiston, Feb. 12; Wellington Loucks, Peoria, Feb. 12; W. J. Ward, Greenville, Feb. 13; B. B. Howard, Galena, Feb. 14; W. B. Armstrong, Warsaw, Feb. 25; W. P. Bartlett, St. Charles, March 1; N. W. Edwards, Cairo, March 5, 1858; Douglas MSS.

[2] O. M. Hatch to Trumbull, Springfield, July 13, 17, 1857; Trumbull MSS. Hatch was Republican Secretary of State. The Republican State Committee duly named a sub-committee 'with full power' to get up the money. Lincoln attended the conference. Funds were raised.

[3] R. T. Merrick, Chicago, March 27, 1858; Douglas MSS.

delighted 'Old Obliquity.' Soon the cadence of the headsman's axe was heard through the State. The resultant retinue of postmasters, pap-editors and Douglas foes appropriated the title of the 'National Democratic Party,' and announced its intention of building a 'real' Democracy for Illinois. A first step was to run a full set of candidates for State offices and for the Legislature.

The Republicans cemented their alliance with the Administrationists. Every time Buchanan's Washington *Union* blasted away at Douglas, the Chicago *Tribune*, the Chicago *Journal*, the *Illinois State Journal*, and other Republican organs would reprint the fulminade, sometimes with crocodile tears of sorrow that this last-minute Lecompton foe was assailed, but always predicting that Douglas' days were done. When a postmaster-editor called Lanphier's *Register* a 'dirty blackguard and lying thief,' and the Douglas press responded, the Republican papers dutifully enlarged the Democratic schism.[4] Republicans padded the attendance at schismatic Democratic meetings. Matteson concluded that the Illinois Republicans really hoped the Lecompton bill would pass so that the odium for it could be put on Douglas.[5] The Republicans overestimated the voting weight of Illinois Buchaneers, the editor of the Chicago *Tribune* predicting that its ticket would poll as many votes as the Douglas slate that Fall.[6]

From the start the Douglas men had known that the contest meant life and death to them, but they were outraged beyond expression by the efforts of the plunderbund. 'By Douglas I stand to the bitter end,' exclaimed Augustus French, former Governor and important party figure. 'What a spectacle! A few graceless and mercenary scoundrels attempting to break down the Illinois Democracy!'[7]

One of their earliest problems was how to launch their ticket. In February, they decided on a State Convention and issued the call, but made the mistake of delaying its date until April, after Chicago's city election. During this two months Buchanan's executioners speeded up their work. Frantic Douglas job-holders wrote Washington, and Harris gave them but cold comfort: 'We are all to be struck down, if possible.'[8] Isaac Cook took over the Chicago post office, Dr. Leib toured the State, Douglas' private foes went on the Federal payroll and editor after editor succumbed to post offices.[9] So rapidly

---

[4] Cairo, Ill., *Times and Delta*, April 7, 1858; *Illinois State Register*, June 19, 1858.

[5] J. A. Matteson, Springfield, March 5, 1858; Douglas MSS.

[6] C. H. Ray, Chicago, March 9; Norman Judd, Chicago, March 19; Joseph Medill, Chicago, April 13, 1858; Trumbull MSS.

[7] A. C. French to Lanphier, Lebanon, Ill., June 14, 1858; Patton MSS.

[8] Sheahan to Lanphier, Chicago, Feb. 4, 19; Harris to Lanphier, Washington, Feb. 10, 1858; Patton MSS.

[9] John D. Phillips, Berlin, Ill., April 14: 'If Pine, the editor, had not have had the post office and been afraid of losing it, he would have still been your friend. He is *anything* for money.' T. Huling, Kankakee, Ill., May 14, 31, 1858, Douglas MSS., reported the coming, and then the actual defection of the editor of the *Democrat*. They could get him 'back again, cheap,' but doubted 'if he would stay bought.' I am indebted to Attorney General Homer S. Cummings, letter to author, Washington, Dec. 11, 1933, for the Department of Justice records as to Illinois changes in United States Attorneys and Marshals, 1855–1860.

did the Administration machine build up that Sheahan thought a party break-up momentarily at hand.

The Douglasites did the best they could to offset these onslaughts. Lanphier and McClernand in Springfield, Merrick and Sheahan in Chicago, McConnel in Jacksonville, Morris in Quincy were ceaseless in their efforts. Letters were dispatched to key men; whenever a Douglas editor sold out for a post office, efforts were made to establish a new Douglas paper. Mass meetings denounced Lecompton and lauded the Little Giant, an organization was set afoot to recover the German voters and the majority of the Democratic press ferociously returned the traitors' blows. Governor Matteson had not agreed, in 1854, that it was expedient to repeal the Missouri Compromise, but in April, 1858, he wrote Douglas that 'the principle was right, it was noble, it was true. You lay yourself upon the block, you have been mangled some, you will feel the effects for some time. But depend upon it... all will come right. You are the leading spirit of the age in this world.' [10]

Now it was noted that not all the defections were from the Douglas ranks. Many conservative Republicans reprehended what they regarded as Lincoln's excessive veering toward Negro equality issues. Judge T. Lyle Dickey, one of Lincoln's intimate friends, decided to support Douglas. Arnold Skinner and Norman B. Judd spoke privately of an inclination to support him. Old-Line Whigs became conspicuously scarce in Republican county conventions.[11] The fact was that Douglas was retaining his hold better than expected. While Buchanan expressed pleasure when the Republicans elected 'Long John' Wentworth mayor of Chicago, actually the outcome was an index of the public's hostility to Lecompton. If the Buchaneers found pleasure in 'having one's brains blown out if the same shot brings down an enemy,' one of Trumbull's aides advised him, they might rejoice over Chicago. When the Buchaneers called a mass meeting in Chicago late in March, ten to one of the gathering were for the Little Giant and the Administration speakers were howled down. Even though his brother Thomas was a Federal official, Philip Hoyne broke away to follow Douglas, announcing himself an Anti-Lecompton, Douglas-Harris Democrat and nothing else; 'I intend to follow you wherever you pitch your tent, for I know you are right.' The Germans, too, were warming up.

Elsewhere the evidence was equally striking. The Democrats won city elections in Elgin and Kankakee by unexpected margins. A referendum on Lecompton, held in connection with the Utah city election, yielded 161

---

[10] Joel A. Matteson, Springfield, April 23, 1858; Douglas MSS. The Governor was so proud of the Little Giant that he commissioned the latter's friend Leonard Volk to carve a statue of Douglas in Italian marble. He also asked Douglas to have his own and Adèle's portrait painted to be hung in a room in Matteson's new home — a room which should never be used except when the Douglases were in Springfield. Cf. also Leonard W. Volk, Chicago, April 14, 1858, Douglas MSS., asking for sittings for the figure; Volk had bust of Douglas the previous Summer. *Illinois State Register*, April, 29, 1858.

[11] W. B. Ogden, New York, April 12, 1858; Douglas MSS. Ogden had just returned from Illinois, where Dickey, Judd and Skinner had told him they were for Douglas. When Lincoln learned of Dickey's decision, he said he 'did not know of any of his friends he felt so badly about losing, as Dickey,' Beveridge, II, 555.

votes against it, none in favor.[12] County conventions began to be held. In many counties there was no opposition at all to Douglas delegates and instructions. In several others the only dissenters were 'a few postmasters who smuggled themselves in as Democrats.'[13] Lanphier's only fear was that the Douglas delegates would arrive 'too bitter for judicious or prudent action.'[14]

The State Convention duly met at Springfield on April 21. About a hundred Buchaneers were there, on mischief bent. In the van were John Calhoun of Lecompton fame, Cook, Leib, Carpenter, Dougherty and 'many more of the paid tribe,' mainly postmasters, whom the Douglasites denounced as 'hounds,' 'spaniels' and 'janizaries.'[15] Their efforts had but little effect, for nine-tenths of the delegates had come to cheer the Little Giant. There was an outburst of enthusiasm when a bust of Douglas was placed on the clerk's desk.[16] Every mention of his name brought cheers, and the Administration men soon made their exit from the convention to a chorus of boos and jeers.

Thereafter harmony characterized the session. Usher F. Linder, of Coles County, an outstanding Old-Line Whig who had not been able to stomach the Republican 'Negro equality' talk, made a speech which set the delegates on fire.[17] Merrick and Thornton followed with stirring talks. Peter Cartwright, the old Methodist circuit rider, Lincoln's opponent for Congress in 1846, was so outraged by charges that Douglas had gone Black Republican that he became almost incoherent.[18]

The platform was particularly significant. It declared for State's Rights, reprehended 'sectional strife,' proclaimed the Cincinnati platform the sole present test of Democratic loyalty and insisted that no earthly power, other than another Democratic National Convention, had the right to 'change or interpolate that platform or to prescribe new or different tests.' Endorsing with enthusiastic vigor the principle of Popular Sovereignty, the platform demanded that the Kansas Constitution should be 'submitted to the direct vote of the actual inhabitants of Kansas at a fair election.' Douglas and the House Democrats from Illinois were applauded for their stand, and the Administration's record approved only so far as its course had or would carry out Democratic faith and policies as set out in the Cincinnati plat-

---

[12] Mark Skinner to Trumbull, Chicago, March 8, 1858; Trumbull MSS.; John W. Bell, Chicago, March 31; Philip A. Hoyne, Chicago, March 27; Henry Bandt, Chicago, March 31; E. Wilcox, Elgin, March 30; T. Henling, Kankakee, April 29; H. M. Hogan, Utah, Ill., April 14, 1858; Douglas MSS.

[13] E. Wilcox, Elgin, April 17, for Kane County; D. S. Waggoner, Canton, April 12, for Fulton; John Riley, Utah, Ill., April 6, for Warren County; M. S. Maloney, Chicago, April 7, 1858; Douglas MSS., quoting Matteson, just back from Cairo. S. A. Buckmaster, Alton, Ill., March 15, 1858; Douglas MSS.

[14] C. H. Lanphier, Springfield, April 8, 1858; Douglas MSS.

[15] *Illinois State Journal*, April 23, 1858.

[16] *Illinois State Register*, May 4, 1858. The bust belonged to Tom Owen, a Springfield druggist, 'one of the best Democrats in the State, who wants no office.'

[17] Chicago *Times*, April 27, 1858, printed it in full.

[18] Chicago *Press*, April 23, 1858, called him an old Boanerges.

form.[19] 'It was indeed a proud day in Illinois history,' Douglasites rejoiced. Governor Matteson wrote Douglas: 'Keep in good cheer. The clouds... will surely clear away and the day will grow brighter and brighter.' [20]

The bolters sought another hall and Republicans were summoned 'to prevent their numbers from appearing too ridiculously meager'; they prudently did not undertake to hold their rump convention immediately but called it for June 9. Lincoln's organ, the *Illinois State Journal*, was given *carte blanche* to dress up their program.[21]

The convention had a good effect on Democrats over the State, and through May the Little Giant had notable adhesions of support. President Blanchard, of Knox College, who theretofore had opposed him, now favored his reelection to the Senate and his elevation to the White House. The opposition was split in Geneva and Douglas had hopes there. After three weeks' advance advertising of an Edwardsville affair where Lincoln and John M. Palmer were to speak, only thirty-two men showed up. Madison County was strong for the Little Giant; two true men would run. If only the people of the northern part of the State were left to carry out their real views without 'dictation or party drill,' Douglas members of the Legislature would be elected.[22] Sheahan of the Chicago *Times*, who kept in intimate touch with developments, concluded that, while probably no outstanding Republican leader would go with Douglas, there would be great accessions from the rank and file. The contest would be sharpest in the La Salle, Peoria, Madison, Macon, and Sangamon districts, and a thorough canvass by Douglas should assure them.[23]

The Republicans maneuvered desperately to offset their losses. Simeon Francis, ex-editor of Lincoln's Springfield organ, wrote Douglas to praise his stand on Lecompton, and to urge him to drop the Senate race and take Harris' seat in the Lower House.[24] External as well as internal disaffection vexed the Illinois Republicans. Henry Wilson never became altogether reconciled to Lincoln's aspirations, Colfax, Burlingame, Blair and other Republicans in Washington continued to hope that Douglas would come over. The talk of Douglas' Republican alliance grew so strong that Sheahan repudiated it in the Chicago *Times*. 'Those Republicans who will vote with us,' he wrote Lanphier privately, 'do not ask him to abate one jot of his Democracy.' [25] Greeley reiterated that the Little Giant had shown a devotion and

---

[19] *Illinois State Register*, April 22, 1858; Sheahan, 394.

[20] J. B. Matteson, Springfield, April 23, 1858; Douglas MSS.

[21] James A. Barrett, Springfield, April 22, 1858; Douglas MSS.

[22] J. Blanchard, Galesburg, May 1; F. D. Preston, Galesburg, May 20; C. V. Dodson, Geneva, May 24; W. N. Coler, Urbana, May 25; W. H. Snyder, Belleville, Ill., June 2, 1858; Douglas MSS. Isaac G. Wilson to John D. Caton, Geneva, May 27, 1858; Caton MSS., Library of Congress.

[23] Sheahan, Chicago, May 30, 1858; Douglas MSS.

[24] S. Francis, Springfield, May 3, 1858; Douglas MSS. Francis sold the *Journal* in 1855.

[25] Sheahan to Lanphier, Chicago, May 23, 1858; Patton MSS. Washington *Union*, April 22, 1858, clipped an item from the New York *Tribune*, signed 'Northwest' that 'the Republican Senators held a consultation last night, with Senator Douglas, at his home, which was satisfactory to both parties.'

heroism to principle which required that he be sustained. When the *Tribune* charged the Illinois Republicans with 'consorting with the Buchanan men' to defeat him, Lincoln papers were struck with consternation. Harris promptly called to Lanphier's attention that this was 'a strong point to use. It was written for that purpose, watch for more — Seward says the same thing, and that he shall not be beaten.' [26]

The New York *Tribune's* weekly edition was a political Bible in thousands of households in Illinois. One day Lincoln came into the Springfield office to complain to Herndon, junior partner in politics as well as law, that 'Greeley is not doing me right.' Lincoln had shown himself a true Republican and yet Greeley insisted upon 'taking up Douglas, a veritable dodger — once a tool of the South, now its enemy — and push him to the front.' [27]

Taking the hint, Herndon soon left for the East to see what he could do. More than anything else, he wanted to see Douglas himself, 'I want to look him in the eye.' In Washington, Herndon began telling it around among the Senator's intimates that 'Douglas is the biggest man on earth.' These, however, were not deluded. Douglas received Herndon and asked about Lincoln. 'He is not in anybody's way,' the junior partner ingenuously responded, 'not even in yours, Judge Douglas.' But the Senator, undeceived, said that he too was not in Lincoln's way, let Herndon give Lincoln his regards, and 'tell him that I have crossed the river and burned my boat.' [28]

Washington Republicans gave Herndon little encouragement. Trumbull alone was positive that Douglas did not intend to become a Republican. When Lincoln's partner bearded Greeley in his den, the latter said Illinois Republicans were fools to fight Douglas, the Little Giant should be returned to the Senate. Herndon asked hotly if Greeley really wanted Douglas to ride to power through the North, which he had so much abused and betrayed?' 'Let the future alone, it will all come right,' was the editor's response. 'Douglas is a brave man. Forget the past and sustain the *right-eous*.' [29]

But Herndon was not the only unsuccessful negotiator that Spring. An important group of Douglas' friends had been anxiously awaiting an opportunity to patch up a peace. Judge Treat had continuously urged the Senator 'to calm this storm and to turn aside, unhurt, the arrows aimed at you. If you are voted down you should submit gracefully to your political friends.' [30] Such advice was much more easily given than carried out, for Douglas had no option but to maintain himself. The introduction of the English bill brought another flood of cautions from his friends in South and

[26] R. W. Burton, Washington, May 29, 1858; Douglas MSS.; Harris to Lanphier, Washington, May 17, 1858; Patton MSS.

[27] Herndon, II, 390–91.

[28] Joseph Fort Newton, *Lincoln and Herndon*, Cedar Rapids, Iowa, 1910; 151; Herndon to Theodore Parker, Springfield, March 4, 1858; Harris to Lanphier, March 1, 1858; Patton MSS.; Herndon, II, 394.

[29] Herndon, II, 394–95. In Boston he had the same experience, and was asked by many leaders to sustain the Little Giant. Kellogg Pamphlet, 7: 'I was indignant, and told him we did not desire success upon such terms.'

[30] S. Treat, St. Louis, March 5, 1858; Douglas MSS.

Border. After he had taken his stand on it friends again hinted that the opportunity had come for peace.

The shrewder of Buchanan's aides saw that the Administration's opposition was making friends for Douglas faster than its friendship had ever done. 'Old Obliquity' found the South tepid to the English bill. Almost all of the Tennessee and Kentucky delegations joined the English opposition, there were mutterings of condemnation from Alabama, and word came that Douglas still stood well in the South. In the North it looked as if the Democratic ticket would lose Pennsylvania by 50,000; Indiana by 25,000 and Ohio by a heavy vote. If Buchanan openly acknowledged his war on Douglas, it would 'defeat every Lecompton man' in those three States, as the candidates there well knew. Illinois was the party's best chance that year; save her and there would be a rallying-point for 1860. When Sheahan addressed questions to the Washington *Union* to force it to avow the Administration's purpose, Northern Democratic candidates redoubled their peace appeals.[31] Cass wanted peace and so did Jeremiah Black; Aaron V. Brown, Jacob Thompson and Howell Cobb were for continuing the war. Buchanan oscillated between these two views.

Douglas and his lieutenants did not thrust aside the olive branch, but let it be known they were for peace on honorable terms. For a month the White House could not make up its mind. Early in May, Harris heard confidentially that the Administration would cease its Illinois decapitations and might even order its tools there to support the State ticket. The next day he heard the White House had determined to wield the knife. About a week later, Washington filled with the rumors that Buchanan had definitely given orders 'to call off the dogs.'[32]

Some of Douglas' intimates did not respond with excessive enthusiasm to the peace prospects. 'Any reconciliation between you and the Administration party,' wrote Usher F. Linder, 'soils you, yes, to be plain, degrades you and strikes you down from that high position where you have fearlessly and consistently battled.' H. B. Payne asked why Douglas attacked Bright and Slidell without touching the 'weak, selfish, jealous, cold-hearted, malignant old man who encumbers the presidential chair.' Sheahan thought that if the White House determined on war, the Douglasites should meet it boldly, perhaps concentrating their attack on Cobb as the real mischief-maker.

'We are quite indifferent which is chosen and so tell them,' Harris advised Lanphier. Their group could gain nothing by the compromise. The Administration was 'either a blunder or a crime, we might as well tie ourselves to a dead carcass with the expectation of restoring it to life.' Lanphier wrote a warning editorial that the Democratic party of Illinois would treat as enemies all 'outside meddlers' who essayed to defeat Douglas by defeating

[31] Sheahan to Lanphier, Chicago, May 23, 1858; Patton MSS. New Orleans *Courier*, clipped, *Illinois State Register*, May 6, 1858, refers admiringly to the way Douglas, in the final Senate debate on Lecompton, took his malignant critics one by one, 'demolished without an effort all these adversaries... kicked them carelessly aside, as a man would kick a clod out of his path.'

[32] Harris to Lanphier, Washington, May 1, 8; Sheahan to Lanphier, Chicago, May 23, 1858; Patton MSS.

'OLD OBLIQUITY': JAMES BUCHANAN
President of the United States, 1857–1861,
whose policies disrupted the Democratic Party

his party in the State. 'If treason from without does not thwart us, we shall elect our State ticket, a majority of members of the lower House of Congress, and a legislature who will return a Democratic Senator. If he lives ... that man will be Stephen A. Douglas.' [33]

Late in May something happened to renew Buchanan's anger against the Little Giant. In all probability letters which Buchanan, Howell Cobb and other Administration leaders received from one Ike Sturgeon, a Treasury politician in St. Louis, were decisive. Sturgeon charged that Douglas had promised Frank Blair that he would stay in the Democratic ranks until the next presidential election, but 'intended to be with the Black Republicans in 1860.' One of Sturgeon's friends claimed to have seen a letter from Blair to his cousin, B. Gratz Brown, editor of a Republican paper in St. Louis, describing this interview. While, alas, this friend had seen this letter under such circumstances that it could not be referred to, Sturgeon denounced Douglas as 'a black-hearted traitor,' who would 'destroy his government if it would only elevate S. A. Douglas.' Let the Buchanan men boldly charge this treason.[34]

During the next few months much was hinted of this reported Douglas pledge. When he took the stump in Illinois, Buchaneers were planted in the crowd, to hurl at him the question: 'What about your promise to Blair?' In the Summer Blair himself determined that he was for Lincoln, admitted the letter to his editor-cousin and the interview with Douglas, but stubbornly evaded its details or decisions. His responses were so ambiguous that, while not directly compromising the Little Giant, they might do so by indirection.[35]

An editorial in the Washington *Union*, Buchanan's organ, on May 27, gave notice to politicians everywhere, but most particularly in Illinois, that the White House had chosen war, not peace. While the initial salvo made no mention of any pledge to Blair, it did compare the Douglas Springfield Convention to the Buffalo Free-Soil Convention of 1848 and charged that Douglas, like Van Buren, was pulling down the pillars of the Democratic

---

[33] Harris to Lanphier, Washington, May 8, 17, 1858; Patton MSS. U. F. Linder, Charleston, Ill., May 15; H. B. Payne, Cleveland, Ohio, June 3; Sheahan, Chicago, May 30; Douglas MSS.; *Illinois State Register*, May 26, 1858.

[34] Isaac Sturgeon to Howell Cobb, St. Louis, May 17, 1858; Erwin MSS. Sturgeon to Buchanan, same date; Buchanan MSS. Sturgeon, a Kentuckian, Assistant Treasurer of the United States, was a shrewd, active pro-slavery politician, and a feverish Buchaneer. He hated Blair, had charged him with authorship of an abusive editorial, Brown's paper, the St. Louis *Democrat*, had about Buchanan on March 2 (Sturgeon to Buchanan, St. Louis, March 2, 1858; Buchanan MSS.), and wanted Blair formally read out of the party. Cf. William E. Smith, *The Francis Preston Blair Family in Politics*, New York, 1933; I, 418-19.

[35] See Kellogg Pamphlet, which has all through it references to the Blair-Douglas pact. Cf. particularly Blair to Sturgeon, St. Louis, Oct. 25, 1858, Kellogg Pamphlet, 12 *et seq.*: 'It has always been a principle with me to hold sacred every private conversation between any gentleman and myself, and this will forbid my saying anything in answer to the questions you have asked, although Mr. Douglas, by his conduct to me, and by the unscrupulous attacks of his partisans, has forfeited all claims on my forbearance.' As to the interview described in the letter to Brown, which Blair said 'was written in strict accordance with the wishes of Judge Douglas himself,' Blair 'deemed it to be the *single object of the interview ... to mitigate, through me, the hostility of the radical Democratic press of St. Louis towards him. I wrote for this purpose ...*'

temple. The headsman's axe quickened in Illinois, and Buchanan said
he would remove every Federal office-holder in Illinois who opposed him.[36]

This outcome the Douglas men accepted without repining. An ousted
postmaster felt proud that now he could pitch into the campaign. All
realized that Douglas now faced the test supreme. 'Now is the time he must
put forth his energies,' wrote Governor French, 'and if he falls let him fall
like the strong man. It is not only that he has Giant's strength but let him
use it as a Giant now.' [37]

The atmosphere was surcharged with feeling when the Buchaneers assembled at Springfield on June 9, for their 'State Convention.' Two weeks
before the assemblage Sheahan had thought its chief purpose to lay the
foundation for a contesting delegation to Charleston in 1860.[38] But he was
wrong about it. Isaac Cook wrote Buchanan that 'the strength and weight
of the contest for the next two years with us must be fought and won *now*.'
Therefore the National Democrats must have 'all aid and assistance which
your Administration in its wisdom can afford us *previous to June 9*.' [39]

Postmasters and marshals received their orders, and while only forty-eight
of the State's hundred counties were represented, the delegates from these
were out for blood. Some Douglas supporters began to harass the speakers;
noses were pulled, blows exchanged and the dissenters were expelled by force.
The patronage brigade denounced Douglas and his followers as 'rebels'
and 'enemies of Democracy.' It foamed at the mouth when the word
'compromise' was mentioned, and a full ticket of candidates was put in
the field. The convention ended, the Douglas papers charged, in 'drunken
orgies' by the delegates.[40]

Dougherty, the 'National Democratic' candidate for State Treasurer,
told Lincoln that the National Democracy was determined 'to run in every
County and District a National Democrat for each and every office.' Lincoln
answered that 'If you do this the thing is settled.' [41] And so, as the campaign
proceeds, we shall see the Republican newspapers and politicians working
with the 'National Democrats'; we shall see every evidence to sustain
Sheahan's 1860 charge — denied neither then nor later — that Lincoln's
organization had spent $60,000 to keep the bolters' organization on its legs.[42]

These proceedings afforded Douglas a rare opportunity. He rose in the
Senate to denounce the bolters' convention. It was a plot against him and
against the Democracy of Illinois, a dirty, despicable plot. Its purpose was
to divide the Democratic party in Illinois and elect Republicans to the

[36] Harris to Lanphier, Washington, May 21, 1858; Patton MSS.

[37] S. S. Brooks, Cairo, Ill., June 23, 1858; Douglas MSS. This was the same Brooks who, an
editor in Jacksonville twenty-five years before, had backed Douglas in his first political battle
in the State. Augustus C. French to Lanphier, Lebanon, Ill., June 14, 1858; Patton MSS.

[38] Sheahan to Lanphier, Chicago, May 23, 1858; Patton MSS.

[39] Cook to Buchanan, Chicago, May 10, 1858; Buchanan MSS.

[40] *Illinois State Register*, June 10, 1858; Chicago *Times*, June 18, 1858; Isaac Cook to Buchanan, Chicago, June 14, 1858; Buchanan MSS.

[41] Herndon to Trumbull, Springfield, Ill., July 8, 1858; Trumbull MSS.

[42] Belleville, Ill., *Advocate*, June 16; Alton *Courier*, June 16, 1858; Sheahan, 396-97.

offices, even including that of United States Senator. Particularly biting
was his scorn of the sorry pack the Administration had set upon his heels.
This Cook, the new postmaster of Chicago, had held that office once before
but had been let out as a defaulter.[43] The two United States Marshals were
time-serving rascals, the brigade of pap-editors exchanging support for post
offices was beneath contempt.

But it was Leib upon whom he loosed the vials of his wrath. The last
session of the Illinois Legislature Leib had been a Democratic clerk. On
the outbreak of the war on Douglas, the existing mail agent for Illinois,
a Douglas man, had been removed. Leib's first act on getting his place was
to telegraph the Republican Secretary of State at Springfield.[44] Thereafter
he was the active liaison between Buchaneers and Black Republicans. He
kept in close touch with Trumbull in Washington, with the Republican
State Chairman in Illinois and with Republican editors and local leaders
through the State.[45] Lincoln was supposed not to be aware of these intimacies,
and they may have been kept from him, for Herndon wrote Trumbull significantly that 'Lincoln does not know the details of how we get along. I do, but
he does not.' [46]

But Leib had an all-too-recent past. In 1854 he had gone to Kansas,
Reeder found him a man after his own heart and gave him a census job,
in which Leib distinguished himself by enrolling only Free-State men.
When Reeder was removed, Leib went with him to Lawrence.[47] There he
had become the 'grand paymaster' of the secret order of the Danites, a
private army Jim Lane had set up for revolutionary ends. In his Kansas
report in 1856, Douglas had 'exposed' Leib. Now he repeated the disclosures,
announcing scornfully that he found himself opposed by an 'unscrupulous'
combination of Black Republicans and 'Danite' Democrats, with this
notorious Leib as its most active agent.[48]

Trumbull was stung to denial: 'He is no man of ours!' [49] But Douglas
would not be turned aside. 'I will charge the alliance,' he went on, 'and
I will prove the alliance. Yes, I could here in the Senate, if I could make

---

[43] Chicago *Times*, March 9, 1858, printed details of Cook's theft. Cf. Sheahan, 385–90.

[44] Chicago *Times*, March 27, 1858, carries the wire, dated March 24.

[45] Beveridge, II, 588, is 'certain' of Leib's contact with Judd, the State Chairman, although
Judd's papers have been destroyed. Cf. M. W. Delahay to Trumbull, Alton, Ill., May 22, 1858;
Trumbull MSS.: 'Last night with Brown [editor of the Alton *Courier*] I spent several hours;
Leib is drilling the faithful…'

[46] Herndon to Trumbull, Springfield, Ill., June 24, 1858; Trumbull MSS. Herndon added:
'That kind of thing does not suit his tastes, nor does it suit me, yet I am compelled to do it,
do it because I cannot get rid of it.' He did not specify what he meant by 'that kind of thing,'
nor did he need to do so, for Trumbull was well informed as to Leib's work.

[47] George Gillespy, Ottumwa, Iowa, July 6, 1858; Douglas MSS.

[48] *Congressional Globe*, Thirty-Fifth Congress, First Session, pt. III, 3055–58. The speech
was delivered June 15, 1858. The title 'Danites' stuck to the Illinois Buchanan Democracy.
It had been assumed by a military order the Mormons raised at Nauvoo in the early 'Forties,
the members of which had pledged themselves to carry out any order, lawful or not, of Joseph
Smith.

[49] Lincoln to Trumbull, Springfield, Ill., June 23; Herndon to Trumbull, Springfield, June 24,
1858; Trumbull MSS., endorsed Lincoln's statement, adding the significant declaration quoted.

witnesses speak, prove this man Leib went to the other side of the Chamber'
— to the Republicans — 'and appealed to them to vote for the confirmation
of a certain officer in Illinois, in order to help the Republicans beat Douglas.'
Trumbull did not deny the incident, nor did any other Republican Senator.

But Douglas had other purposes in this speech than the denunciation
of the Danites. He had determined to afford Buchanan one further avenue
to peace. So he said that, in his opinion, the President himself had no hand
in the attacks upon him. Some of Buchanan's aides thought this heavy
irony; one or two took it at its face value and sought at least a surface
reconciliation.

The morning following Douglas' speech, the Illinois Republican Convention met at Springfield. The delegates were not quite happy about the situation, for in the last few weeks a new disturbing factor had arisen — 'Long
John' Wentworth, the new mayor of Chicago. He had won his race by the
largest majority Chicago had ever given — a fact which gave him a momentary note through the North, and encouraged his senatorial ambitions. 'Long
John' was a man of good background, considerable attainment, political
shrewdness and personal courage. In Congress a dozen years, he had fought
against the Missouri Compromise and aided in founding the Republican
party before Lincoln had dared join its ranks.

Illinois filled with reports that, regardless of Lincoln's general acceptance
as Republican senatorial candidate, 'Long John' intended to elect and control
a group which would constitute the balance of power in the Legislature's
joint caucus and so secure the Little Giant's seat. He himself became
a candidate for the Legislature, as did Norman Judd and Arnold. 'All of
them intend to cheat Lincoln,' Sheahan reported. 'They say that if he does
not carry middle Illinois, he forfeits election.' Wentworth had a very poor
opinion of Lincoln and saw no reason why the Springfield lawyer-politician
should have the prize. Through April and May, Wentworth was 'as busy
as the Old Boy in a high wind' and openly declared that Lincoln could
never get elected.[50]

These new dangers moved Lincoln's Springfield friends to prompt action.
Lincoln himself was privy to the plans but characteristically kept them
to himself. Before the State Convention met, Republican gatherings in
all but five counties responded to hints from Springfield by endorsing Lincoln's senatorial candidacy.[51] Thus the stage was set for action 'for the object
of closing down upon this everlasting croaking about Wentworth.'[52]

The convention opened with rousing speeches. A propitiatory gesture
was made to the Germans by the choice of Gustav Koerner as the chairman.
The Know-Nothings were pacified by the omission from the platform of
any reference to tolerance for foreigners or their creeds. Other than this
prudent silence, the platform touched nearly every issue or project the

    [50] James M. Thomas, Wyoming, Ill., May 28, 1858; Douglas MSS.; Sheahan to Lanphier,
Chicago, May 23, 1858; Patton MSS.
    [51] Rockford, Ill., *Republican*, June 17, 1858, quoted, Beveridge, II, 568.
    [52] Lincoln to Trumbull, Springfield, Ill., June 23, 1858; Trumbull MSS.

endorsement of which might gain a few votes. This *omnium gatherum* adopted and the State ticket named, Charles L. Wilson, editor of the Chicago *Journal*, more bitter enemy of Wentworth than friend of Lincoln, offered a resolution: 'That Abraham Lincoln is the first and only choice of the Republicans of Illinois for the United States Senate, as the successor of Stephen A. Douglas,' which was adopted without a dissenting voice.[53]

That evening Lincoln spoke to the convention. He had prepared carefully for the occasion. For days he had been scribbling down his thoughts on envelopes and scraps of paper and filing them away in his rusty top hat. These he put together, revised repeatedly and at length read the speech to his private cabinet. One paragraph startled his aides. Lincoln had written that 'a house divided against itself cannot stand,' that the Nation could not endure half slave and half free. It was 'a damned fool utterance,' one friend told him and nearly everyone said it was inexpedient. But Herndon exclaimed: 'Lincoln, deliver that speech as read and it will make you President.' Lincoln said he had thought about it long enough, the time had come to say it; 'if it is decreed that I should go down because of this speech, then let me go down linked to the truth.'

The high point of Lincoln's speech that night was this very declaration: 'A house divided against itself cannot stand. I believe this government cannot endure permanently half *slave* and half *free*. I do not expect the house to fall but I do expect it will cease to be divided. It will become *all* one thing, or *all* the other.' [54]

Other than this 'House Divided' argument, Lincoln brought laughter by his treatment of the contention that Douglas was the man now to lead the anti-slavery forces of Illinois. He admitted that Douglas might be a great man; however, 'a living dog is better than a dead lion,' and even if Douglas were not a dead lion for the work of freedom, he was 'at least a caged and toothless one.' This was an unfortunate comparison; in the months to come we shall hear much from Douglas partisans about the 'dead lion'; during the debates nearly every effective Douglas sally would bring shouts: 'The lion isn't dead,' and 'hit the living dog again.' Then, too, he brought great applause by his charge that Douglas had been a party to the slave-holder's plot by which the Supreme Court adjudged Dred Scott a slave. Reviewing pro-slavery events of a decade, he concluded:

'We cannot absolutely *know* that all these exact adaptations are the result

---

[53] *Illinois Journal*, June 17, 1858; Nicolay and Hay, III, 136. The 1858 platform insisted that State's Rights be maintained, it urged rivers and harbors and the building of the Pacific Railroad; it denounced impartially the Kansas-Nebraska Act, the Lecompton Constitution, the Dred Scott decision, insisted that Congress was sovereign over the Territories and should exclude from them 'the curse of slavery.'

[54] The remainder of the statement endeavored to qualify the harshness of the initial sentence, 'Either the *opponents* of slavery,' Lincoln added, 'will arrest the further spread of it, and place it where the public mind shall rest in the belief that it is in course of ultimate extinction or its *advocates* will push it forward, 'till it shall become alike lawful in *all* the States, *old* as well as *new* — *North* as well as *South*.' The italics I have used are Lincoln's. When the speech was through, he went to the *Illinois Journal* office, carefully proof-read the galleys of the speech and himself marked the italics; see *Journal*, June 16, 1858; Herndon, II, 398-400.

of pre-concert, but when we see a lot of framed timbers, different portions of which we know have been gotten out at different times and places and by different workmen — Stephen, Franklin, Roger and James, for instance — and when we see these timbers joined together, and see they exactly make the frame of a house or a mill... in such a case we find it impossible not to believe that Stephen and Franklin and Roger and James all understood one another from the beginning and all worked upon a common *plan* or draft drawn up before the first lick was struck.' [55]

With this nomination the Illinois campaign was launched. The issue, declared the *State Register*, 'is now plainly and squarely before the people of the State... Stephen A. Douglas on the one side and Abraham Lincoln on the other; the Democracy of the one against the Black Republican principles of the other.' [56] Douglas was under no illusions. 'I shall have my hands full,' he said of Lincoln. 'He is the strong man of his party — full of wit, facts, dates — and the best stump speaker, with his droll ways and dry jokes, in the West. He is as honest as he is shrewd, and if I beat him, my victory will be hardly won.' [57]

Congress soon adjourned, but before leaving Washington for Illinois, Douglas tried to complete his arrangements for the coming campaign. Traveling expenses had to be provided, friendly newspapers properly munitioned, special trains and transparencies, fireworks and saluting batteries, marching clubs and messengers — all the appurtenances of electoral combat had to be paid for. Usually assessments on office-holders and contributions from wealthy partisans made up much of the fund. Now, however, the Administration's proscription of his retainers and the panic's impact upon his wealthy friends cut off material outside aid. Moreover, the Little Giant disliked being under obligations to tarnished angels and preferred to put up most of the money himself.

The panic of 1857 found Douglas over-extended, with many real-estate notes outstanding and with almost no income other than his official salary. He made herculean efforts to keep his paper from protest, to refinance maturing mortgages and to get money for the campaign, but no loan was to be had in Chicago; Corcoran and Riggs had gone with Buchanan and New York was the only hope for cash.

But money was tight and lenders almost non-existent. The Little Giant finally brought himself to the point of offering to mortgage all his Chicago property which had not been hypothecated in 1856, when he had put up $80,000 for Buchanan's Pennsylvania fight. New York friends trying to help him with the problem met the constant objection that 'the property in Chicago was not productive' — let Douglas throw in his Washington home as added security. Finally a lender was found, a lien was clapped on the Chicago land and Douglas got his money.[58] These transactions,

[55] *Illinois Journal*, June 18, 1858; italics are Lincoln's. This charge was in line with, and obviously inspired by, recent Republican Senatorial speeches in Washington.

[56] *Illinois State Register*, June 17, 1858.   [57] Forney, II, 1790.

[58] Douglas MSS., Feb. 1, Oct. 15, 1858, are full of financial correspondence. See T. Rush

however, were not finished until Douglas was in the midst of his campaign at home.

A second highly important problem was that of a friendly paper in the National Capital. For five years Douglas had used the Washington *Union* to keep the party posted as to his plans and ambitions. But when he broke with Buchanan, the *Union* became a dangerous foe, and he sought another Washington connection. 'The *States* will be with us from this time on,' Harris soon advised Lanphier. John P. Heiss, its editor, had been Douglas' friend since the days of the Polk Administration.[59] His paper already had a strong circulation in the South and must be given one in the Northwest. 'We must kick the Washington *Union* aside and support the *States*.' Heiss thought 'every Douglas man in the Northwest' should subscribe for the weekly edition, hinted that twenty thousand subscribers 'might be of considerable service,' and wanted State and County Committees to get busy. Club subscriptions flowed in, particularly from Illinois. Later a New York friend put up three hundred dollars a week to keep the *States* afloat.[60]

Furthermore, Douglas had such warm friends in the Eastern centers as Forney and Raymond. The Cleveland *Plain Dealer* staunchly supported him; Washington McLean and George P. Buell, of the Cincinnati *Enquirer*, were so loyal that Buchanan's gift of the post office to a third partner did not wean the paper completely away. In the South, too, he had a real newspaper strength, nearly all of which he kept right through the Lecompton fight.[61]

Douglas added two experienced publicity men to his staff for the campaign. Francis J. Grund, the veteran Washington correspondent, preceded him to Illinois.[62] A little later he went over to the Danites. James B. Sheridan, recommended by Forney as reporter and shorthand expert, clerked

Spencer, Feb. 21, July 23, 27, 29; O. Bushnell, June 30; James L. Woodward, July 1, 9, 10; F. B. Cutting, T. A. Fozler, July 2, 12; John B. Murray, July 7, 15; Fernando Wood, July 8, Aug. 25. Apparently the total amount of the new financing was $100,000, $40,000 of which went into repayment of a maturing mortgage. Douglas seems to have escaped putting up his home on Minnesota Row. Wood made the final arrangement and loaned Douglas $13,147 on an open note.

[59] Heiss, who was in Central America in 1847–49, supplied Douglas with much information about British machinations in the Gulf of Fonseca and through Central America generally that Douglas later used in assailing the Clayton-Bulwer treaty. Like so many of Polk's Southern aides, Heiss looked upon Douglas as the Tennessee President's logical political heir.

[60] Harris to Lanphier, Washington, Jan. 21, 1858; Patton MSS.; A. F. Dow, Ottawa, Ill., March 24; John P. Heiss, Washington, July 7, 10, 24, 30. Heiss to Arnold Harris, Washington, July 15, 1858; Douglas MSS.: '$300 per week to keep up this paper is too much to come out of your pocket.'

[61] For evidence of this, see Henry P. Schalle, Pella, Ia., May 21; A. G. Southall, Washington, June 19, as to Richmond, Va., *Examiner*; George N. Hickman, Baltimore, July 17, says the *Daily Exchange* of that city was for Douglas; George Canning Hill, Boston, July 26, pledged the Boston *Ledger*; for *Enquirer* situation, see George P. Buell, Cincinnati, June 29, 1858; Douglas MSS. In the South, such papers as the Richmond *Enquirer*, the Augusta *Chronicle and Constitutionalist*, the Atlanta *Era*, the Mobile *Register*, the New Orleans *Crescent*, and the *True Delta*, the Memphis *Appeal* and the Louisville *Herald* supported Douglas right through 1858.

[62] Thos. H. Holbach, Freeport, Ill., June 8, 1858; Douglas MSS.

in Douglas' Washington office until June, and then went to Illinois for the campaign. There he rendered competent service, of which his *verbatim* reporting of Douglas' speeches was but a part. Added to these were such regular journalistic standbys as Sheahan in Chicago, Lanphier in Springfield, Morris in Quincy, Brooks in Cairo — men ever ready to drink or drive all night, fight or write all day, for the Little Giant. Nor did Douglas neglect the German press, securing a careful analysis showing which German editors were true, which the Republicans had bought, and which were struggling for support.[63]

But Douglas did not depend upon newspapers alone for his propaganda. Not overlooking the unbelievable readiness of a hardy and long-suffering people to pore over printed speeches and reports, he distributed many thousand copies of his committee reports and Senate speeches. A single bill from the publisher of the *Congressional Globe*, was for $2286, a second for $3739.[64] Douglas' friends similarly busied themselves. A New York publisher started on a book of speeches. Not all the pamphlets escaped the Buchanan post offices and in Chicago Douglas documents were 'generally laid aside for a convenient season,' but enough got through to have a powerful effect upon the people.[65]

As Douglas prepared for his homeward journey, there were multiplying indices that the Northern Democratic rank and file did not sympathize with Buchanan. The Iowa Democratic State Convention unceremoniously tabled an endorsement of the President. Raymond's New York *Times* spoke feelingly of the tremendous odds against Douglas; should he succeed, it would be 'the most brilliant triumph of his life.' [66] There was no mistaking the eager and sympathetic attention with which nearly everyone in the North regarded this new crisis in the Little Giant's career.

Nor were the Buchaneers any too happy in their position. For weeks there had been rumblings from the South and Douglas' speech of June 15 brought quick action. Governor Wise came up from Richmond to warn Buchanan of the danger ahead. 'You will be held responsible,' he bluntly informed the President.[67]

[63] A. V. Hofer, editor of the *Staats-Zeitung*, to Henry Koch, New York, July 1, 1858; Louis Didier, 'Report on the German Press,' no date, probably early July, 1858; Douglas MSS.; the *National Democrat* made money, but it had no public confidence. The *Wochenblatt* was firm for him, but very poor and needed help; the Peoria *Banner* was brave and good, as were the Quincy *Courier*, the *Bundesflagge* of Springfield, the Alton *Beobachter* and the Freeport *Anzeiger*.

[64] Receipted bills in possession of Martin F. Douglas.

[65] Washington McLean, Cincinnati, April 4; George W. Gray, Centralia, Ill., May 26; D. B. Cooke, Chicago, March 29, 1858; Douglas MSS. McLean and a few other Ohio supporters raised the money and printed and distributed 150,000 copies of Douglas' March 22 speech. Derby and Jackson were the publishers. Douglas suggested Sheahan as author of the sketch of his life. Sheahan started, the sketch grew into a book, Henry M. Flint wrote the sketch for the Derby and Jackson volume. Harper & Bros. brought out Sheahan's *Life*.

[66] George E. Hubble, Davenport, Ia., June 25, 1858; Douglas MSS.; New York *Times*, July 15, 1858.

[67] John A. Parker, Richmond, Va., June 10, 19, 1858; Douglas MSS. Even before the speech, Wise, John A. Parker, A. D. Banks and others had 'deliberately and openly' taken position for Douglas, notifying Buchanan thereof.

This may have determined Buchanan to renew the idea of peace with Douglas. At any event, on the morning of June 21, as the Senator was standing in the Washington railway station waiting to start on his homeward journey, James May, a friend of the President, approached to urge a reconciliation. While at first stiff and reserved, Douglas finally authorized May to say to Buchanan and his friends: 'There is, or will be, no difficulty or misunderstanding if the Administration will sustain the Illinois nominations.' His language and manner convinced May that he 'was decidedly in favor of conciliation,' and had 'clearly and unreservedly committed himself.'

May talked to Floyd, Secretary of War; Bigler; Jones, of Iowa, and other Buchaneers. Floyd eagerly embraced the idea. Bigler seemed disposed to treat. May found that even the *Union* was tired of the war and wrote Douglas that: 'The gate is wide open, very moderate authority in tangible shape' would bring an agreement.[68]

There must have been something to the negotiations, for on June 24, Papa Cutts wrote that he had it by grapevine that the White House had determined 'to touch no more of your friends in Illinois,' perhaps even to restrain the raging Cook. May's efforts were soon seconded by George N. Sanders and Senator Gwin. Sanders, whom Buchanan had just named Navy Agent for the Port of New York, began telegraphing Buchanan and Douglas.[69] The Washington *Union* suspended its attacks and began advocating a reunion in the party and one or two pro-Douglas appointments were made. The President cautiously hinted the English bill had brought peace to the country and he hoped the breach would be healed, but he waited to see whether the Douglas ticket endorsed the English bill 'in a decided and unequivocal manner.'[70] Thus it was neither war nor peace — merely armistice; Buchanan was waiting to see whether Douglas would confess his sin and repent.

When the Senator left Washington, the lovely Adèle was at his side. In May she had intimated that she might not come to Illinois, but her husband's friends there would not hear of it. One wrote her that her presence was most important. 'The quiet, dignified influence you will exert in his behalf,' he insisted, 'simply by your presence in society, the encouragement that presence will give to his friends, the restraint that will be upon his enemies, the enthusiasm you will awaken in the most of these to have the

[68] James May, Washington, June 21; Baltimore, June 22, 1858; Douglas MSS.; James May to Buchanan, Washington, July 4, 1858; Buchanan MSS. Thomas B. Florence, a Philadelphia Congressman, and J. Madison Cutts, Adèle's father, overheard the conversation. May was a Pittsburgh man who in the 'Fifties moved to Iowa. He received no offices but was always active in adjusting party difficulties. In the Douglas instance, he persisted until late in October, calling on the Little Giant in Bloomington on Oct. 23. Douglas told him the olive branch must come from Washington, May to Buchanan, Peoria, Ill., Oct. 23; 1858; Buchanan MSS.

[69] New York *Journal of Commerce*, June 5, 1858.

[70] J. Madison Cutts, Washington, June 24, telegram, July 1; John L. Peyton, Staunton, Va., July 8, 1858; Douglas MSS.; Washington *Union*, July 3, 7, 1858; Douglas MSS.; Buchanan to C. Farley, editor of the Joliet *Signal*, Washington, July 15, 1858; Buchanan MSS. But he added that as 'a large majority of the Democracy of Illinois condemn the [English] bill... you will have no difficulty yourself in deciding what is the duty of a Democratic Administration toward the Democracy of the Union in regard to its opponents in Illinois.'

feeling to appreciate so sweet a smile as you can't help smiling — such is the kind of aid you can give.'[71] It was an appeal she could not resist.

The journey was by easy stages. The first stop was Philadelphia, where the Douglases had the imperial suite at the Girard House. All afternoon their parlor was crowded; Forney's reporter found the Senator in 'excellent health and spirits.' After two days in Manhattan, one evening being spent at the Opera, they went to Clifton Springs for a real rest with Douglas' mother.[72] There were friends to see at Albany and Buffalo. On July 7, his Ohio supporters held a great reception at Cleveland, Rhodes, Willson, Payne, Jim Steedman, Wash McLean, Vallandigham and hundreds of others taking part in the welcome.[73] At every other train stop on the journey, Douglas was greeted by cheering throngs. The Democracy of Ohio and Indiana left no doubt of their views.

For days his friends in Chicago had been preparing an appropriate reception. Sheahan's *Times* had been full of committee lists, lines of march, of welcome and jubilee. Those who could gave funds for fireworks, and those who could not made plans to come out to cheer. Republican papers sneered at these preparations but could not dampen Democratic enthusiasm; for the Little Giant, the champion of Popular Sovereignty, would be welcomed by his own.[74]

Friday, July 9, was the great day. All morning the Douglas men checked up on details, the streets flamed with bunting and nearly every hotel and office building in the city was covered with streamers, pennants and flags. At one in the afternoon a special train bore a reception committee of four hundred to Michigan City, sixty miles away, to meet the Senator. There the Chicago delegation found a great Indiana throng which had accompanied Douglas from La Porte. While 'some malicious person' spiked Michigan City's only gun, the Douglas braves found a large anvil, put it in the middle of the street and for an hour and a half it orchestrated the celebration.

At five the joyous Democrats started for Chicago. When the train neared the outer station at Twelfth Street, the national flag was hoisted aloft and a saluting battery boomed a welcome. Thenceforward the train moved slowly along, women waved their handkerchiefs, men shouted joyfully. When the special stopped, Captain Smith's battery in Dearborn Park fired one hundred and fifty guns and other batteries answered from the north and west, but their sounds could hardly be heard above the people's shouts.

The Montgomery Guards, the Emmet Guards and other crack companies

[71] R. T. Merrick to Mrs. Douglas, Chicago, May 7, 1858; Douglas MSS.

[72] Philadelphia *Press*, June 23, 1858; Washington *States*, June 25, 1858.

[73] Cleveland *Plain Dealer*, July 8, 9, 1858; Madison Kelley, Cleveland,' July 10, 1858, Buchanan MSS., remarked on the 'headless' officials on hand.

[74] Chicago *Journal*, July 9, 1858, sneered that for weeks the Democracy had been 'begging and scraping together all the spare dollars, shillings, dimes and sixpence that could be obtained.' They had 'bought powder enough to supply the Utah War,' had lavished large sums for banners and devices, transparencies and had hired 'men and boys to make up a procession and make a big noise.'

presented arms and Douglas entered an open barouche drawn by six horses, the Senator being greeted 'with every demonstration of grateful welcome.' For an hour or more people from all parts of the city had been collecting in the square in front of the Tremont House. By the time of his arrival, over 30,000 were gathered to welcome him.[75]

At length Douglas appeared on the north balcony of the Tremont House. Immediately across the way was a splendid transparency, with the words illuminated: 'Welcome to Stephen A. Douglas, the Defender of Popular Sovereignty.' Charles Walker, well-known Democratic leader, gracefully referred to the Senator's long but glorious struggle and waved him to the front.[76] The Little Giant stepped forward and the milling thousands roared in ecstasy.

It was quite obvious that the Senator was tired, he spoke without manuscript — even without notes — but he was greatly moved as he looked out upon the tremendous throng. His first remark was that this great reception, 'so great in numbers that no human voice can be heard by all its countless thousands,' was not so much a tribute to him as it was the public approval of a basic American principle. Even as he deprecated his rôle, voices over the crowd burst forth: 'It is!' 'You have deserved it!' and there was immense cheering.

He had fought the Lecompton Constitution because it violated the fundamental right of self-government. With the aid of others who thought that way, he had 'forced them' to send it back to Kansas. Paying tribute to John J. Crittenden and some 'glorious Americans and Old-Line Whigs from the South,' he then drew tremendous shouts when he said that the Republican Senators had joined him in the fight and were as fully deserving of praise as he himself.

But he wanted to be quite explicit that he had opposed the Kansas fraud because it violated the great principle of Popular Sovereignty. Once in the Senate he had fought for it against Northern opposition. He had defended it here in Chicago against 'great dissatisfaction,' recently and despite the resistance of the South he had again insisted on this right of self-government, and he had pledged himself always to fight for it. 'Have I not redeemed that pledge?' he asked, to be answered with three resounding cheers.

His attack on Lecompton had been occasioned, not by its slavery clause, but because the Constitution as a whole had not been submitted to the people. If a Free-State charter had similarly been put forward, he would have opposed it, for he denied the right of Congress 'to force a good thing upon a people who are unwilling to receive it.' This was the meaning of Popular Sovereignty, the principle upon which American institutions rested. Its force could not be offset by the argument that slavery was evil

[75] Chicago *Times*, July 10, 1858; Chicago *Tribune*, July 10, 1858, estimated the crowd at only 12,000. The dense throng made it difficult for the procession to get to the hotel, the drivers stupidly drove into the crowd, and as Douglas' barouche reached the doorstep, some blockhead on the balcony touched off welcoming rockets, the crazed horses plunged frantically about and several spectators were bruised.

[76] Chicago *Times*, July 12, 1858.

and must not be tolerated. The people were allowed to determine for themselves whether they elected or rejected Prohibition, 'what sort of schools they would have, all types of family relationships,' therefore why not let them decide for themselves upon this question of slavery too?

Now Douglas began to make up the issues between Lincoln and himself. He began by several pleasant compliments to Lincoln. 'I take great pleasure,' he declared, 'in saying that I have known personally and intimately for about a quarter of a century, the worthy gentleman who has been nominated for my place, and I will say that I regard him as a kind, amiable, and intelligent gentleman, a good citizen and an honorable opponent. And whatever issue I may have with him will be of principle and not involve personalities.'

With this he turned to Lincoln's 'well-prepared and carefully written' Springfield speech; it set forth two distinct propositions upon which he intended to take 'direct and bold issue.' Reading the paragraph about the House Divided, Douglas said that, 'Scripture quotations and all,' it meant a denial that the Nation could endure half slave and half free. The clear implication was that there must be uniformity in the domestic institutions of all the States; that Lincoln would have conflict without end until slavery was either established or abolished throughout the Union, 'a war of sections, a war of the North against the South, of the Free States against the Slave States — a war of extermination to be continued relentlessly until the one or the other shall be subdued and all States shall either become free or become slave.'

Douglas denied that such standardization was necessary, right, possible or desirable. The Founding Fathers, recognizing the evils of uniformity, had endowed each State with sovereignty over its domestic affairs, clothing the Federal Government only with 'specified powers which were general and national,' but Lincoln had totally misapprehended this 'fundamental principle.' 'Uniformity is the parent of despotism the world over,' let Lincoln's plan be followed and 'you have destroyed the greatest safeguard which our institutions have thrown about the rights of the citizens.' Such uniformity could be had only by pooling 'the rights and sovereignty of the States in one consolidated empire, and vesting Congress with the plenary power to make all the policy regulations, domestic and local laws, uniform throughout the limits of the republic.'

This being done, forecast the Little Giant with prophetic vision, 'then the States will all be slave or all be free; then the Negroes will vote everywhere or nowhere; then you will have a Maine liquor law in every State or none; then you will have uniformity in all things, local and domestic, by the authority of the Federal Government. But when you attain that uniformity, you will have converted these thirty-two sovereign, independent States into one consolidated empire, with the uniformity of despotism reigning triumphantly throughout the length and the breadth of the land.' With each salvo from Douglas' great, deep voice would come an answering shout from the audience, and with his final words there was a tremendous applause.

Next he turned to his second 'direct issue' with his opponent — Lincoln's attack on the Supreme Court of the United States. The American system had been established on the idea that the courts had a duty to expound the Constitution and construe the laws, and that, whenever a case had been decided, the people must yield obedience. Inasmuch as 'our rights and our liberty and our property all depend' on this principle, Douglas derided the idea 'of appealing from the decision of the Supreme Court upon a constitutional question to the decision of a tumultuous town meeting.'

Therefore he was opposed to Lincoln's doctrine 'by which he proposes to take the appeal from the decision of the Supreme Court of the United States upon these high constitutional questions to the Republican caucus sitting in the country.' A voice shouted: 'Call it Free Soil,' the crowd cheered, Douglas went on: 'Yes, or to any other caucus or town meeting, whether it be Republican, American or Democratic.' The only doctrine upon which America could be maintained was to stand by the Constitution, observe the laws, respect and maintain the courts. Booming cheers came back from the throng.

But Lincoln's reason for opposing this particular decision of the Supreme Court, Douglas deemed equally bad. It was that in holding that a Negro of slave descent could not be a citizen, the Court had breached the constitutional guaranty that the citizens of one State should have all the privileges of citizens of the others. The Supreme Court had held that this guaranty covered white men only and Lincoln now claimed that it covered black men too. This led Douglas to his final theme — that he believed in a white man's government — a plea which fearfully embarrassed Lincoln. Our government, Douglas thundered, 'is founded on a white basis.' There were great cheers. 'It was made by white men, for white men, to be administered by white men.' The shouts renewed. He did not mean that the people belonging to an inferior race ought not to possess, indeed they should have all the rights that they could, so far as was 'consistent with the safety of society,' but 'each State must decide for itself the nature and extent of these rights.'

Illinois had determined that the black man should be neither slave nor voter, Maine gave votes to Negroes and neither State had the right to complain as to the other's stand. Each State had the right to govern its own views on its relationship to the inferior race: 'Virginia has the same power by virtue of her sovereignty to protect slavery within her limits as Illinois has to banish it forever.'

Here, as in other domestic matters, such uniformity as Lincoln wished was neither possible, right nor wise. 'I do not acknowledge,' Douglas added, amid great cheering, 'that the States must all be free or must all be slave. I do not acknowledge that the Negro must have civil and political rights everywhere or nowhere.' Thus the issues between Lincoln and himself were clear, 'direct, unequivocal and irreconcilable. He goes for uniformity in our domestic institutions, for a war of sections, until one or the other shall be subdued. I go for the great principle of the Kansas-Nebraska bill, the right of the people to decide for themselves.'

With this, the crowd burst forth into frenzied applause, rockets flung into the air, and fireworks blazed, the band played 'Yankee Doodle' and the whole scene, Sheahan wrote, 'was glorious beyond description.' At length, when the Little Giant could proceed, he hammered home his point. He was opposed to Negro equality. The citizens must preserve the purity of government as well as race and there must be neither physical nor political amalgamation. The dire results of such mixtures were apparent in the countries to the south of them. The only safe policy was to accord 'to dependent races' all privileges society's safety would permit, but never any social, political or other equality. With this pandemonium broke forth.

When quiet was restored, Douglas took advantage of the condition of his audience to attack the combination which had been made against him. 'The Republican leaders have formed an alliance,' he said, 'an unholy, unnatural alliance, with a portion of the unscrupulous Federal office-holders. I intend to fight that allied army wherever I meet them.' He branded 'these men who are trying to divide the Democratic party for the purpose of electing a Republican Senator in my place' as being 'just as much the agents, the tools, the supporters of Mr. Lincoln as if they were avowed Republicans.'

Exhausted, Douglas said that he must stop. The crowd shouted to go on. He insisted that he had not been to bed for two nights and deserved a little sleep. Again the throng cheered him and insisted on a continuance. In truth he was exhausted, and after saying that this great welcome repaid him for all he had ever done in the public interest, he waved his hand and was silent.

The crowd stood there in the Square, shouting for its champion. A great piece of fireworks was set off, its fiery letters spelling 'Popular Sovereignty,' with which the crowd cheered even louder. For an hour after Douglas had left the balcony, thousands remained shouting for the Little Giant and his cause. Thus opened the great Illinois campaign.[77]

[77] For text of Douglas' speech, see *Lincoln-Douglas Debates*, Columbus, Ohio, 1860. This publication followed the version of the Chicago *Times*, July 11. The Chicago *Press and Tribune*, July 10, published the speech in full. New York *Times* published it in full July 13; New York *Herald*, July 14. For attendant circumstances, see *Illinois State Register*, July 13, Chicago *Press and Tribune*, July 10, Chicago *Times*, July 10–11, 1858.

CHAPTER XX

THE LITTLE GIANT TAKES CHARGE

THE campaign thus inaugurated would both involve the Little Giant's Senate seat and the fate of Northern Democracy. A demonstration that the Conservative Democracy could not resist the peace-disturbing clamor of Abolitionist and Secessionist would break the last enduring link of Union. Douglas' battle was impressed with a real significance to the country as a whole.

During the canvass there were seven formal encounters between the Senator and his Republican antagonist, wherefore history has attached to the entire campaign the convenient label of 'the Great Debates.' And, indeed, the debates which began at Ottawa in August and ended at Alton in October had an extraordinary significance in Abraham Lincoln's career. Before Douglas made him famous, Lincoln was looked on at home as a good lawyer, not a great one; a man who, in his effort to serve the two masters of law and politics, ever had one foot in the courtroom and the other on the stump. Outside Illinois he was chiefly known as a local Republican politician, who relished telling a good story and had some competence in the rough and tumble of politics.

Douglas' fight in early 1858 against his oddly assorted foes had already attracted the country's attention. His opening of the campaign in Illinois was colorful; then were added the spectacular debates and papers the country over reported and discussed the two champions' personalities, records and speeches. Thus Douglas' antagonist projected himself beyond the narrow circle of political mechanicians who already knew him. The 1858 campaign established him in the hierarchy of national Republican leadership — not upon the pinnacle occupied by William H. Seward, Salmon P. Chase and Horace Greeley, but in the second level, along with such men as 'Bluff Ben' Wade, John Covode, N. P. Banks and Lyman Trumbull. These debates had a greater effect upon Lincoln's ambitions than did any event prior to the 1860 Democratic catastrophe at Charleston.

But in the case of the Little Giant, their career effect was no greater than the Compromise of 1850 or the repeal of the Missouri Compromise. Certainly they were not so determinative as Douglas' break with Buchanan. 'Old Obliquity's' refusal to maintain faith on Kansas initiated that turbulent stream of events culminating in the break-up of the Democratic party, the election of a Republican minority President and the secession of the Cotton South. Douglas' stormy White House interview in December, 1857, would seem the Serajevo of the Civil War.

Then, too, as debates, the encounters do not measure up to the picture conventionally given. On neither side did the dialectic compare with that in the debates between Webster, Hayne and Calhoun. Nor could one expect appeals to the emotion or the prejudice of the individual Illinois voter to reach the highest plane of constitutional debate. The legend that Lincoln demolished his great competitor and threw him to the winds is part of the stubborn mythology with which idolators have shrouded nearly every circumstance of the Emancipator's career. Subjecting it to proper tests, the mists dissolve and the Lincoln of the debates stands revealed as a strong antagonist at grips with one quite as strong. At times both men seem political wrestlers crafty in verbal clutches, who spent much time in fumbling about for or escaping from effective holds. At times Lincoln was evasive and unresponsive; at times he indulged in unjustified personal aspersions, often he was candid — and occasionally not; occasionally Douglas met him on the same plane. There is no escaping the fact that Lincoln was an adroit and ambitious politician who never forgot that he was after Douglas' Senate seat.

The campaign was a hot one and the press of the day was as deeply partisan as were the politicians. The picture of the conduct of the crowd, the relative volumes of applause and the elation or chagrin of the two competitors depends altogether upon whether the particular paper consulted happened to be Republican or pro-Douglas. The Chicago *Press and Tribune*, the *Illinois State Journal*, Quincy *Whig* or Peoria *Transcript* insisted that 'Douglas was overwhelmed,' 'Lincoln wiped up the ground with the Little Giant,' 'the crowd groaned at Douglas,' and 'at the end of the speech he fled a defeated man.' The Douglas press similarly portrayed Lincoln's defeat in each encounter. This divergence, not only of interpretation but of actual statement of fact, colors the reminiscences of onlookers, private letters of the day and every type of available evidence. It is no easy task for the historian to winnow this mound of fable and find the grain of truth.

It is equally difficult to proportion the debates to the campaign. Douglas met Lincoln in seven formal joint debates, but he spoke in fifty-seven counties, making fifty-nine set speeches of from two to three hours' length, seventeen shorter impromptu speeches and thirty-seven responses to addresses of welcome. All but two of these were in the open air and seven were made in heavy rain. He traveled over practically the whole railroad system of the State, a journey of over 5200 miles, to say nothing of the heavy, weary miles by horse conveyance; also he used steamboats to canvass all the western side of Illinois.[1] Everywhere he went, Douglas attended receptions, arranged finances, superintended election arrangements, reconciled differences between lieutenants and undermined the efforts of the Danites — in a thousand different ways energizing the Democracy. To him the debates were but a part of the day's work.

In 1858, Illinois' political pattern was almost a microcosm of that of the Nation. Stretching from the Great Lakes to the Ohio, its northern rivers were ice-bound in winter but the fields of Egypt were white with cotton. Climate, soil characteristics and prevailing routes and modes of transportation had much to do with settlement and economic structure. The northern areas had been settled chiefly by people from the Abolition States, the cultures of Missouri, Kentucky and Tennessee predominated in the southern

[1] *Illinois State Register*, Nov. 23, 1858, clipping from New York *Times* correspondence.

section, while central Illinois was a plexus of these variant customs, prejudices, emotions and ideals.

Free-Soil principles predominated in the north, with a substantial infusion of out-and-out Abolition feeling. In the south, and especially in Egypt, the people drank their liquor and played their politics straight and 'straight-haired' Democracy was the rule. The middle section, stretching across the State from Quincy through Springfield to Champaign, was an amalgam of Egypt and Canaan. Here the Old-Line Whigs still frowned upon Abolition doctrines and the Democratic voters took seriously the Jeffersonian idea of the right of choice.

These contrasts were not always sharp and distinct. A political map would show some clean-cut contrasts of black and white, but mainly gradual shadings of gray, with an occasional freakish plop of color reflecting some divergent group attitude. The Irish were chiefly Democratic and had tended to concentrate in the cities, so Chicago, although in the north of the State, was not hopelessly Republican. The Germans also tended to the cities, and their concentration near East St. Louis changed the normal expectancy in that area. Until 1854 they had mainly been Democrats but the Kansas-Nebraska Act had alienated a large part of them.

The central and southern portions of the State contained tens of thousands of former Whigs who, like James W. Singleton, Usher F. Linder and John T. Stuart, had refused to go into the Republican fold. Many had joined no party at all, nearly all of them worshipped the memory of Henry Clay and attached great importance to the opinions of John J. Crittenden, Reverdy Johnson and John Bell. These Old-Line Whigs constituted the balance of power in central Illinois.

Also significant were the old Know-Nothings of whom, in 1858, there were about thirty-five thousand in the State. Four years before Douglas had unloosed his wrath upon them, but Lincoln had not come to their defense, a silence they remembered. Just recently the Native American members of Congress had followed Crittenden — and Douglas — against Lecompton. The Little Giant's lieutenants thought that Crittenden could control twenty thousand American votes in central and southern Illinois.

One further thing should be remembered. Neither Douglas nor Lincoln had their names upon the actual ballots, for Illinois, as the other States of the Union, elected her United States Senators, not by the direct vote of the people, but by the Legislature. Technically, Douglas appealed to the voters to elect pro-Douglas candidates to the Illinois House or Senate and Lincoln asked for Republican legislative candidates. The apportionment of the State had been made in 1849. Since that time, the Republicans complained, the population growth had been greater in the northern or Republican sections, wherefore the old basis of legislative apportionment was unfair. But the actual point at issue was the election of enough members of the two Houses to produce a majority on joint caucus. If Douglas could do this, and could also checkmate Danite schemes to destroy his majority by seducing hold-over Senators, his battle would be won.

One is struck by the great changes in the State in the twelve years since

Douglas had gone to the Senate. The frontier had moved westward, butcher knives and hunting-shirts belonged to old men's tales and Democracy was subdued in society and at the ballot box. Illinois, as the whole Northwest, had experienced a steady growth of Free-Soil and anti-slavery sentiment. In the struggle over the Compromise of 1850, Douglas had momentarily checked it, but the repeal of the Missouri Compromise, in 1854, had renewed its zeal, and had added to it the turbulent emotional forces of Prohibition and Nativism. That year the Democratic nominee for State Treasurer secured fifty-one per cent of the vote, but the Democrats lost the Legislature and General Shields had to yield his Senate seat to a Republican.

The following year witnessed a back-swing, the Maine Law zeal diminished, secret conclaves began to lose their appeal and German indignation lessened. But in 1856, while Buchanan carried the State, he did so by a plurality, not a majority, and owed this to Douglas' unremitting efforts. The race for Governor, which was not triangular, presented a truer measure of the State, and in this the Republican candidate defeated William A. Richardson, a man of force and popularity, by almost five thousand votes.[2] Had the Little Giant faced the Republicans uncomplicated by his feud with the President, his task would have been most difficult. But he had to give battle to a segment of the Democracy as well as to the Black Republicans, and so was confronted with the most desperate fight of his career. Only a genius at public persuasion could overcome such odds.

As soon as Congress adjourned in June, Thomas L. Harris hastened to Illinois to size up the situation. Soon he sent Douglas a more optimistic picture than the latter had expected. 'We will lose nothing in the center or south, and of course we can win nothing in the north,' Harris reported. The Buchanan bolters were growing weaker. The Republicans were becoming distrustful and dispirited, and Douglas should undertake 'a *severe* canvass against Lincoln.' The center of the State would determine the election and Springfield should be the base for the campaign. If Crittenden could be gotten into Illinois, it would insure the Old-Line Whigs.[3]

Douglas made careful preparations for a thorough-going campaign. Remaining in Chicago the week following his home-coming speech, he found the time was none too much to attend to matters of business and finance, make

[2] For 1854, see Cole, *Era*, 132–33 and map. Figures supplied by Miss Margaret C. Norton of the Archives Division of the Illinois State Library, show that in 1852, Matteson received 80,789 votes, the Republican candidate 64,408, and an independent, 9024. In 1856, Bissell received 111,466 to Richardson's 106,769, a third party candidate securing 19,088. The presidential vote that same year was Buchanan 105,528, Frémont 96,278, Fillmore 37,531. The compilation of the total Democratic and Anti-Nebraska votes for State Senators and Representatives in 1854 are unsatisfactory.

[3] T. L. Harris, Springfield, July 7, 1858; Douglas MSS. The people were waiting for the Senator's speeches, Harris insisted, and these would have a powerful effect. Indeed, if Douglas would 'go down to Winchester and make a *personal* appeal to the people of Scott,' he would carry that county, where he had begun his Illinois career twenty-five years before, by at least five hundred majority. The pivotal counties would be Scott, Morgan, Sangamon, Macoupin, Madison, St. Clair, Randolph, Bond, Mason, Champaign, Logan, Macon, Peoria, Woodford, Marshall, Putnam and Coles.

a tentative itinerary for his down-State tour, receive lieutenants and stimulate his organization.

The Republicans were not idle spectators of the Senator's triumph. Lincoln had been careful to be in Chicago on the date of Douglas' reception there. Republican papers ingenuously explained that their nominee's presence was 'accidental,' that he was in the city trying a case in court, but the truth was that Lincoln wanted to hear, first-hand, 'what the Giant had to say.'[4] All the while Douglas was speaking Lincoln sat just within the window behind the balcony, and took careful notes of the Senator's remarks. At one point he offered an interruption which Douglas took good-humoredly. The following evening the Republicans did their best to drum up a crowd to hear Lincoln, to whose not wholly objective eyes, it seemed quite as large as that of Douglas 'and five times as enthusiastic.'[5]

Lincoln was on the defensive and wit and satire were his shield and buckler. Without returning the Senator's personal compliments, he fiercely ridiculed every Douglas statement he could twist. The crowd roared when he suggested that the Allies in Crimea had eventually captured Sebastopol and the Allies in Illinois would likewise win. But when he ridiculed Popular Sovereignty, and scoffed at Douglas' part in opposing the Lecompton Constitution, he was hectored by the crowd until he almost lost his temper.

Repeating his House Divided passages, he denied Douglas' implications. Certainly Lincoln wished neither a consolidating government nor uniformity of domestic institutions, and as to slavery in States where it did exist, 'we have no right to interfere with it.' Lincoln repeated this denial with varying emphasis, over the State. But it was ingenuous, for apart from logic, and despite Lincoln's denial, the actual event was close at hand. The Civil War, by which the House Divided became the House United, did set in train nearly every consolidating force which Douglas had predicted. The operation of this doctrine quickened and made final just such a shift from Federal Union to consolidated republic, just such an imposition of uniformity on American institutions and customs, as Douglas had warned would come. In their interchanges on the House Divided doctrine, it was Douglas, not Lincoln, who read the future aright.

Lincoln made heavy weather countering Douglas' statement that this was a white man's government. His answer that, because he wanted the Negro free, he did not necessarily want a Negress for a wife, brought applause in northern Illinois but did not meet Douglas' argument. The weakest point of all was that support of Douglas really meant support of slavery extension. 'If he be endorsed by Republican votes,' Lincoln asked, 'where do you stand? Plainly you stand ready saddled, bridled and harnessed, and waiting to be driven over to the slavery-extension camp of the nation.' Douglas' efforts tended 'to make this one universal slave nation,' and that was why Lincoln resisted him.

[4] Chicago *Daily Democrat*, July 9, 1858; Herndon to Trumbull, Springfield, July 8, 1858; Trumbull MSS.

[5] Lincoln to Gustave Koerner, July 15, 1858; Beveridge, II, 599–600. Chicago *Press and Tribune*, July 12, 1858, put Douglas' crowd at 12,000, Lincoln's at 9000.

Lincoln's climax, however, had an oratorical effectiveness which brought cheers 'like blasts of a thousand bugles.' 'Let us discard all this quibbling about this man and that man,' he shouted, 'this race and that race and the other race being inferior, and therefore that they must be placed in an inferior position. Let us discard all these things, and unite as one people throughout this land, until we shall once more stand up declaring that all men are created equal.'

But these cheers did not hide the fact that Lincoln was on the defensive, and his Chicago speech was probably as unhappy an effort as he made anywhere during the campaign.[6] Recognizing this, the Republican mechanicians publicly thundered that Lincoln had annihilated the Little Giant, but privately besought Trumbull to hurry home to prop up the campaign.[7]

Douglas' friends down-State matured arrangements for his progress to the State Capital.[8] On July 16 a private car covered with mottoes and flags was attached to the Illinois Central's regular train from Chicago for Bloomington, bearing the Little Giant's campaign party. In addition to the Senator and his wife, it consisted of James B. Sheridan, two stenographers and party officials. Leonard Volk was along, hoping for odd moments when Douglas could sit for him. Lanphier had come to Chicago, Sheahan came from that city, newspaper men were welcome to enter and local delegations were encouraged to visit the car.

Douglas, who believed that 'the great unwashed' wanted their public men well-dressed, wore a suit of blue broadcloth, well-cut and carefully brushed. On his head he had a wide-brimmed white felt hat, which set off his long, dark hair and swarthy complexion.

The private car was partly showmanship but mainly comfort. While the Republicans affected horror at the extravagance and pomp of a private car, it was a shrewd plan to save Douglas' strength and health in a campaign whose rigors could be estimated in advance. The opposition cried that the railroad had given him the car free, but in all probability the Senator paid in full for the conveyance, for the Illinois Central showed him no leniency in other financial transactions and no evidence suggests that it did so now.[9]

At Joliet the train picked up a flatcar bearing a brass cannon served by two stalwart young men in semi-military apparel. Whenever the train approached a scheduled stop, the gun was fired again and again, informing the people that the Little Giant was coming to town, and Douglas' artillery and powder added to the picturesqueness of the campaign.

Throngs collected along the route. At Joliet 'the earth was fairly shaken

[6] Seymour, 'Political Principles,' MSS., 268.

[7] Norman B. Judd to Trumbull, Chicago, July 16, 1858; Trumbull MSS.

[8] J. A. Matteson and C. H. Lanphier, Telegram, Springfield, July 10; Lanphier, Springfield, July 11, 1858; Douglas MSS.

[9] Osborn to Foster, Feb. 23, 1860, Illinois Central President's letters. 'Under no circumstances ought we to surrender the contracts to Judge Douglas. He is responsible and bought the lands with his eyes open....' For this reference, I am indebted to Professor Paul M. Gates, of Bucknell University.

by the cheers of the thousands.' At Bloomington, a heavily Republican town, over two thousand gathered to welcome him, and the salvos from the car were answered by saluting batteries in the town. When the Senator descended from his car, there was 'a very grand demonstration of public sentiment,' a band struck up 'Hail Columbia' and led a procession to the gaily decorated Landon House.[10]

On the same train was Abraham Lincoln, whom the Republican strategists gathered at Chicago had decided should stick to Douglas like a burr, going everywhere Douglas went and making answering speeches whenever he could. Volk observed his entrance to the Bloomington hotel, carrying an old carpet-bag, wearing an overgrown, weather-beaten silk hat, and a long, loosely fitted black alpaca suit. As he chatted with the hotel clerk, friends rushed up shouting, 'How are you, Old Abe?'[11]

Lincoln was given a seat on the platform when Douglas spoke at sunset at the court-house square to 'an immense concourse.' It was about ten when he finished but all the time he kept the crowd enthralled, demonstrating 'a power seldom ever surpassed.' It was his Chicago speech, clarified and organized, and it proved so effective that 80,000 copies were sent through the State.[12] Again he charged the alliance of Buchaneers and Black Republicans. Again he assailed Lincoln's House Divided doctrine; convince either section that it should act upon it and war would follow. Better to let each State do as it pleased about slavery and be accountable to God therefor — 'it is not for me to arraign them for what they do. I will not judge them lest I shall be judged.'

He riddled Lincoln's defense that he had not meant for the Free States to *enter into* the Southern States and interfere with slavery. 'Oh, no!' he said scornfully, 'they stand on this side of the Ohio River and shoot across.'

Douglas had not understood his competitor to assert that Negroes should be made our social equals. Even so, there was the plain meaning of Lincoln's tenet of racial equality — the right of suffrage, of office, of taking part in making, administering and judging laws — in the end, the right of racial amalgamation.

He pointed out the Dred Scott decision's practical ineffectiveness in establishing slavery in any Territory. 'Mr. Lincoln is alarmed,' he said, 'for fear that, under the Dred Scott decision, slavery will go into all the Territories of the United States. All I have to say is that, with or without that decision, slavery will go just where the people want it, and not an inch further.'[13]

Twice did he repeat this insistence that slavery was utterly dependent on local support. Why had slavery failed to secure a foothold in Kansas? 'Simply because there was a majority of her people opposed to slavery, and every slave-holder knew that if he took his slaves there, the moment that majority got possession of the ballot boxes, and a fair election was held, that moment slavery would be abolished and he would lose them.'

---

[10] *Illinois State Register*, July 19, 1858. W. P. Boyd to John J. Crittenden, Bloomington, Ill., July 17, 1858; Crittenden MSS., Library of Congress.

[11] Leonard Volk, 'The Lincoln Life Mask and How it Was Made,' *Century Magazine*, I, 233.

[12] Sheahan, 417.   [13] *Debates*, 51.

Such being the fate of slavery when local legislation sustained but local opinion opposed it, what chance would it have when there were no laws or unfriendly ones? It was 'impossible under our institutions to force slavery on an unwilling people.' Give Popular Sovereignty a fair enforcement and 'slavery will never exist one day, or one hour, in any Territory against the unfriendly legislation of an unfriendly people.' No matter how the Dred Scott decision might have determined the abstract question, in practical fact this was the situation. Not only did Douglas think this the case, but an eminent Southern Senator had declared that, 'without affirmative legislation in its favor, slavery could not exist any longer than a new-born infant could survive under the heat of the sun, on a barren rock, without protection. It would wilt and die for want of support.'

To this doctrine, which Crittenden was advised was such that 'no city in the South but would have responded... with a hearty amen,' the Bloomington crowd gave loud and frequent applause. But Bloomington was definitely Republican territory, and after he had finished, the crowd called for Lincoln. After a while he came forward, his partisans raised three rousing cheers for him, but he did not speak.[14]

Tremendous preparations had been made for Douglas' reception at Springfield.[15] Every care was taken that the speaking at Edwards' Grove should be the greatest event the Capital had ever witnessed. Leaving Bloomington Saturday morning, in a heavy downpour, Douglas was met at Atlanta by the Springfield committee. The rain ceased a little before the train neared Edwards' Grove, but the ground was steaming and soggy and the decorations droopy and forlorn. The thousands who had braved the rain hailed Douglas with frenzied enthusiasm, the greeting was 'impossible to describe.' The Senator was introduced by Benjamin S. Edwards, an Old-Line Whig and author of the State Prohibition Law Douglas had opposed three years before.[16] The Springfield speech showed that Douglas had further mastered, refined and clarified his points and his friends thought it the best of the entire campaign.[17] He himself was in unusual spirits, his delivery was firm, full, clear, emphatic, he kept the crowd in a fine humor and from first to last his telling points were punctuated with shouts, cheers and wild applause.

About the only new point Douglas made was to dismiss with contempt Lincoln's charge of a 'conspiracy,' a 'scheme of political tricksters' between 'Stephen and Franklin and Roger and James' over the Dred Scott case. 'If Mr. Lincoln deems *me* a conspirator of that kind,' he declared, 'all I have to say is that *I* do not think so badly of the President of the United

[14] Bloomington *Pantagraph*, July 17, 1858. Lincoln merely remarked that the meeting had been called for Judge Douglas, and 'it should be improper for me to address it.'

[15] Lanphier, Springfield, July 11, 1858; Douglas MSS.

[16] Sheahan, 418; *Illinois State Register*, July 10, 1858. Volk, *loc. cit.*, 223, tells how, when the train reached Edwards' Grove, a vast crowd was waiting. The passengers climbed over the fence across the stubble field to the Grove. Lincoln was alone, taking immense strides, a carpet-bag in one hand, an umbrella in the other, his coat-tail flying in the breeze. Coming to the rail fence, he hopped lightly over it, and went on to Springfield.

[17] Koerner, II, 64.

States and the Supreme Court of the United States, the highest judicial tribunal on earth, as to believe that they were capable in their action and decision of entering into political intrigues for partisan purposes.'[18]

Again he insisted that slavery could not exist unless supported by local legislation and local opinion. Again he ridiculed the doctrine of appealing from a Supreme Court decision to a town meeting. Again he pressed home telling thrusts against Negro equality, bringing wild applause from the crowd. Again he paid personal tribute to Lincoln: 'There is no better citizen and no kinder-hearted man.'

That night Lincoln spoke in the Hall of Representatives, adding little new to his former utterances, save that he tried to make it appear that the Republicans were laboring under many 'disadvantages.' As to one, the basis of legislative apportionment, 'perhaps there is no ground of complaint on our part.' A second was the contrast between Douglas and himself, and here he launched into a curious, half-humorous self-abasement. Douglas had a world renown and was by many expected to become President; the Democratic politicians had seen in his 'round, jolly, fruitful face, post offices, land offices, and marshalships and cabinet appointments, chargé-ships and foreign missions, bursting and sprouting out in wonderful exuberance, ready to be laid hold of by their greedy hands.' But nobody had ever expected Lincoln to be President; 'in my poor, lean, lank face nobody has ever seen that any cabbages were sprouting out.'[19]

Lincoln's friends had complained that he was too much on the defensive. He now drew a personal issue, charging Douglas with misquoting his House Divided speech, and making much of the fact that Douglas had not categorically denied the charge that Stephen had conspired with 'Franklin and Roger and James' to procure the Dred Scott decision. 'On his tacit admission, I renew the charge. I charge him with having been a party to that conspiracy ... for the sole purpose of nationalizing slavery.'

So little did the Democrats think of Lincoln's rejoinder that the *Illinois State Register* rushed it into type so that its subscribers could compare the two speeches and to judge for themselves. The Republican press glorified Lincoln's effort but the politicians kept writing Trumbull to hurry back to the State.[20]

Until he heard the Bloomington speech, and the sledge-hammer blows against the House Divided doctrine, a friend wrote Crittenden, he had deemed the Little Giant dead in Illinois. But now 'you may expect to hear of such a canvass in Illinois as will equal in excitement and interest the battles of the giants in days of yore.... The Democracy of Illinois will unite to a man on Douglas. Many of the old Whigs, having no shepherd and in doubt where to go will readily turn to his fold. The very necessities of the Democratic party here and generally over the South and West must impel them to unite

---

[18] Carlinville *Free Democrat*, July 22, 1858; its editor, a strong Abolitionist, thought Douglas 'less bloated and more reasonable' than he had been. Lincoln, *Works*, III, 121–22, for conspiracy answer.

[19] Lincoln, *Works*, III, 157–58.

[20] Jesse K. Dubois to Trumbull, Springfield, July 17, 1858; Trumbull MSS.

together on the Douglas platform.... Douglas is the only man who can do anything for them here; killing him, they die also.' [21]

The three speeches at Chicago, Bloomington and Springfield set Douglas before the people of his State. Their essence was a strict Popular Sovereignty position. Whatever leanings he might once have had toward Republicanism had been cast aside. The Republicans did not know whether to be pleased or concerned over his failure to use his Lecompton record to win Republican votes. And they were distinctly troubled by his failure 'to tread heavily on Buchanan's toes.' [22]

The country read Douglas' speeches and learned of his increasing success down-State with growing satisfaction. While Horace Greeley had finally promised the Illinois Republicans to do no more for Douglas, he could not restrain himself from writing an editorial about 'the well deserved' tribute at Chicago. Nine out of ten Northern Democrats endorsed the Little Giant's views, which offered a platform upon which any Northern Democrat could stand honorably, logically and perhaps with success. Some of the New York Hards lamented that Douglas had omitted to say that Lecompton was a past issue, but the Softs responded that if the Administration wanted it a dead issue, Douglas must be let alone.[23] The 'triumphant march' on Springfield encouraged the Democratic Northwest. Ohio's Anti-Lecompton Democrats promptly organized for battle and Indiana Democrats were stimulated to a new war on Bright and Fitch.[24]

Even stronger were the expressions from conservative Border leaders. Reverdy Johnson, of Maryland, publicly approved Douglas' course. Notable for learning in the law, sagacious public judgment and calm courage, Reverdy Johnson was a Whig of the old school. He still wore frilled shirts and lace cuffs, and his views had great weight with Old-Line Whigs and conservative Democrats. Buchanan's proscriptive policy was 'not only insolent party tyranny but the very essence of folly,' he wrote Douglas. By it the presidential group was doing all it could to elect to the United States Senate a man 'deeply and incurably dyed' in every one of the Republican party's 'false heresies.' Douglas' defeat would be hailed by Republicans every-

---

[21] W. P. Boyd, Bloomington, July 17, 1858; Crittenden MSS.

[22] Koerner, II, 59, for Republican concerns. New York *Tribune*, July 12, 1858, for Greeley's praise of Douglas.

[23] Joseph Lowe, Concord, N.H., July 4; George Canning Hill, Boston, July 26, Sept. 6. Hill, editor of the *Daily Ledger*, wanted no job; A. V. Hofer, New York, July 14; the *Staats-Zeitung* printed the Chicago speech July 15, pamphlets could be had for $12 per thousand; Arnold Harris, New York, July 16; J. B. Adrian, New Brunswick, N.J., July 21, 1858, Douglas MSS.

[24] H. B. Payne, Cleveland, July 24; Washington McLean, Cincinnati, July 27; they overwhelmed Buchanan's supporters in the northern part of the State. Pugh and Vallandigham took a hand in south Ohio and even the Cincinnati *Enquirer*, despite the postmastership of one of its proprietors, mildly urged a Douglas endorsement by the coming State Democratic Convention. But the *Enquirer* support was too tepid for George Buell, who denounced Farran, the postmaster-editor, and threw up his job. Buell to Douglas, Cincinnati, Aug. 6; A. H. Brown, Indianapolis, Aug. 5, 1858; Douglas MSS.: 'Everything looks well for the defeat of the Bright dynasty.'

where 'as the death-knell of the Democratic party.' The meanness of Buchanan's course excited general wonder, and his excuse that Douglas had not agreed with the President's incontinent Kansas policy was 'too flimsy to deceive an honest observer.' [25]

An ardent Kentucky State's Rights man informed Douglas that three-quarters of the South would endorse his Chicago speech as the proper 1860 program. Old-Line Whigs urged Democratic John C. Breckinridge to make public endorsement of Douglas' course. The Vice-President did not immediately do so, but in several speeches endorsing the Administration he was careful not to allude to Douglas in any way.

John J. Crittenden was anxious to aid the Little Giant. Lincoln realized the danger from this quarter and wrote Crittenden to forestall it. But when Judge T. Lyle Dickey, of Ottawa, made up his mind to stump the State for the Little Giant, and asked Crittenden's formal permission to repeat what the latter had told him in Washington in April, the Kentucky Senator promptly did so.

'The people of Illinois little know how much they really owe to Senator Douglas,' Crittenden had told Dickey. The Little Giant 'had not only had courage and patriotism to take his just and independent position on the Lecompton question, at the sacrifice of old party associations, in the face of the bristling bayonets of the Republicans and defiance of the power and patronage of the Administration, supported by the dominant party and wielding a patronage of some $80,000,000 a year, but also at a sacrifice of social relations of the most interesting character. The attack upon him has been terrible. Through the whole session, his surroundings have been such that he is compelled to enter the Senate Chamber every day with the consciousness that he is liable to be set upon in such manner that he can maintain his honor only at the hazard of his life. And through every phase of this trying ordeal he has borne himself gallantly, gallantly, gallantly. I say, Judge Dickey, there is a heroism about him that deserves the endorsement of all your people of every party.' [26]

While Crittenden answered Lincoln that he had no personal ill-will toward him, the letter was not such as to offset the Kentuckian's advocacy of Judge Douglas. However, the *Illinois Journal* printed an obscure editorial reference to a Crittenden letter, inferring that it endorsed Lincoln and repudiated Douglas. Reprinting this, other Republican papers made it an excuse for charging that Crittenden had never been for Douglas.

[25] Reverdy Johnson, Lindhurst, near Baltimore, July 29; George A. Hickman, Baltimore, Aug. 7; G. N. Sanders, Baltimore, Aug. 30, 1858; Douglas MSS. On Aug. 6, when Baltimore's Democracy held its convention, by a vote of more than two to one it tabled resolutions approving Buchanan's course.

[26] E. M. Bruce, Covington, Ky., July 15, 30; R. Kendall, Lexington, Ky., July 15, saw both Breckinridge and General Leslie Combs; S. B. Buckner, Cairo, Ill., Aug. 30; Blanton Duncan, Louisville, Aug. 18, 1858; Douglas MSS. Lincoln to Crittenden, Springfield, July 7, 1858; Lincoln, *Works*, III, 17-18. T. Lyle Dickey, St. Louis, Mo., July 19, 1858; Crittenden MSS. Judge Dickey quoted Crittenden's remarks as having been made to him 'in April last in conversation at the Capitol.' He quoted them partially in present tense, partially in past tense. I have changed them to present tense.

Blair's paper in St. Louis began ringing the changes on this purported repudiation; Crittenden's friends there became irritated at the report, 'unjust, false and injurious' to both Crittenden and to Douglas. Crittenden denied the *Journal* canard and wrote Lincoln sternly about it, and Herndon was put to it to explain the origin of the report.[27]

Douglas' speeches likewise made a powerful impression on the South. The papers friendly to Douglas became far more enthusiastic over his speeches than did any Eastern Republican papers over Lincoln's, while even the Ultra-Southern papers which had opposed him on Lecompton quieted their attacks and some began to talk of supporting him for President in 1860. One shrewd old Virginia editor wrote him that his Chicago speech was 'proper, right, just, equal, and the superstructure which you have raised is based upon the eternal rock of Truth and Justice.' 'For God's sake, carry the State,' another friend implored. 'Carry the State and by Christmas the hoary-headed old sinner at Washington will be at your feet a suppliant for mercy.' [28]

Soon the deep South recovered from the first shock of Douglas' frank statement that slavery could never go where people did not want it. A prominent Macon citizen wrote reprehending the Administration's course and wishing Douglas 'the most complete success.' George W. Lamar, of Augusta, sent sage advice: 'Be calm and prudent and always yourself and you will yet cause them to wilt like cabbage leaves before the fire.' A little later, the editor of the Augusta *Constitutionalist* gave it as his considered opinion that the Ultra politicians who had been urging that Douglas should be defeated, now saw that they had overshot the mark 'and would cry *Peccavi* did personal pride not forbid it.' [29] Thus the fight on Douglas won him warm sympathy and made him the rallying-point for the Democratic party, the symbol of hope against rival sectionalism and fanaticism.

At the start of the campaign, Buchanan was understood still to be pondering a peace with Douglas. Through July, the latter heard nothing to indicate the definite failure of James May's negotiations. After the Chicago speech, George Sanders went to the White House with Senator Gwin and had a long

---

[27] A. G. Cates, St. Louis, Nov. 4; Wm. H. Herndon, Springfield, Nov. 1, 1858; Crittenden MSS. Herndon insisted that Lincoln himself did not inspire the editorial in the *Illinois Journal*. 'The notice going the rounds of the papers is wholly unauthorized by Mr. Lincoln,' Herndon insisted. 'I speak from knowledge. I am the only person in the world who knows that you wrote Lincoln, and outside of us — you, Lincoln and myself — no person knows anything about the matter.' After this interchange, the St. Louis *Republican* stated with authority that Lincoln knew from his correspondence with Crittenden that the *Illinois Journal's* story was false, and by his silence in the matter was doing Crittenden an injury in order to serve himself.

[28] Richmond *Examiner*, July 14, James Spencer, Baltimore, July 15; J. P. Heiss to Arnold Harris, Washington, July 18, 23, 27; Harris to Douglas, New York, July 29; A. D. Banks to Douglas, Washington, Aug. 21; R. W. Latham, Washington, July 16; Aug. 9; W. T. Early, Charlottesville, Va., Aug. 25; E. H. Steinback, Petersburg, Sept. 2; Thomas Foster, Portsmouth, Sept. 16; O. Jennings Wise, Richmond, Sept. 27; John Kierans, Richmond, Oct. 3; J. A. de Carteret, Raleigh, N.C., Oct. 12, 1858; Douglas MSS.

[29] W. H. de Graffenreid, Macon, Aug. 12; Geo. W. Lamar, Augusta, July 31, Aug. 23; James Madden, Summerville, Aug. 20; G. W. Palmer, Augusta, Aug. 21; James Gardner to A. D. Banks, Augusta, Oct. 12, 1858; Douglas MSS. Gardner was editor of the *Constitutionalist*.

interview with Buchanan. 'The President satisfied with position you intend occupying at home,' Sanders telegraphed the Little Giant. 'Adherence to regular Democratic nominations everywhere, State and Federal, in Illinois, Pennsylvania, California, Kansas question left with people of Kansas, English bill rejected, Kansas not to come in without representative ratio. Federal officials of Illinois to abandon their organization.' [30]

Douglas had every right to believe this a statement of the terms upon which 'Old Obliquity' had agreed to cease the war. For the last four years Sanders had been in Buchanan's train, he had just been given the lucrative job of Navy Agent at New York and apparently the President was using him as peace negotiator. A New York friend who visited Washington the day of Sanders' visit, but without knowledge of it, reported the general rumor that the President had determined on peace. 'Dr. Leib will be removed at once,' he wrote. 'All are now anxious to bring about a reconciliation.' By a little management, Douglas' friend continued, '*you can control the affairs of your State by your former enemies coming to the rescue....* The South is not ungrateful, the past she will never forget.' Talking with Slidell, Douglas' friend had been astonished by the latter's determination to help Douglas. The Louisiana Senator would soon visit Chicago, and Bright and Fitch, of Indiana, would act with him.[31]

But these hopes proved abortive. Buchanan's hatred of Douglas could not be repressed; sending for Sanders, he ordered the withdrawal of the telegram to Douglas.[32] While there is no record that this was literally done, Sanders promptly wrote the Little Giant a rasping, hectoring letter, sending Buchanan a copy.[33] The Washington *Union* became even more energetic in its attacks on Douglas, and Heiss of the *States* knew that Buchanan was personally responsible for these new assaults. 'He hates you in the most bitter and unrelenting manner,' Heiss wrote, 'would sacrifice you if it would sacrifice the Democratic party in doing so.' [34]

Slidell excused the Administration's renewal of the war by saying that Douglas' Chicago speech had furnished no evidence of his 'repentant spirit.' Taking this cue, Administrationists proclaimed that Douglas himself had chosen and 'war is declared.' [35]

Senator Slidell did make his visit to Chicago, where he conferred with the patronage brigade and studied the political probabilities for 1860 as well as for the present campaign. He recommended that the President cut the throat of every Douglas sympathizer in Federal office in Illinois and the

[30] Sanders to Douglas, National Hotel, Washington, July 11, 1858; Douglas MSS.

[31] W. W. Churchwell, Washington, July 11, 1858; Douglas MSS.

[32] J. S. Wright, Washington, Aug. 23, 1858; Douglas MSS. 'Another thing Sanders told me' was the information above.

[33] George N. Sanders, New York, July 17, 1858; Douglas MSS.; copy in Buchanan MSS.

[34] Heiss to Douglas, Washington, July 15; Heiss to Arnold Harris, Washington, July 16; Harris to Douglas, New York, July 16; Heiss to Harris, Washington, July 18, 23, 27; Harris to Douglas, New York, July 29, 1858; Douglas MSS.

[35] H. B. Payne, Cleveland, July 24; W. W. Wick, Indianapolis, July 18, 1858; Madison Kelley, Cleveland, July 25, 1858; Buchanan MSS.; Payne talked to Slidell on the latter's stop in Cleveland.

Northwest: 'It is the only course which will afford us a chance of success' in 1860. In addition he supplied the Danites with funds and expressed anxiety to have Lincoln win.[36]

Nor was 'Old Obliquity' reluctant to follow this advice; removals began with new vigor. On vacation at Bedford Springs, Buchanan grew restive over Douglas' trenchant blows at the Black Republicans, and began drafting an attack on the Little Giant for the *Union*. Then he sent his notes on to Jeremiah Black, with instructions to whip them in shape for publication. 'Judge Douglas,' he complained, 'ought to be stripped of his pretensions to be the champion of Popular Sovereignty.' Acknowledging the instructions, Black responded that Douglas needed to be 'wiped as a man wipeth a plate, turning it over and wiping it.' [37]

But Douglas had said that he would take charge of the Illinois campaign and he had done so. His progress to Springfield was a triumph. Of Illinois Democratic papers, sixty-five swung to Douglas and only five blew uncertain trumpets for the Danites. The chief figures in the Administration cabal in Illinois strove more furiously than ever. Dr. Leib, 'not one of ours,' advised Trumbull that they had completed arrangements for Danite legislative candidates in each county of central Illinois; and established organs in Chicago, Springfield and Cairo.[38] But by late July their rank and file was melting away. The Old-Line Whigs in the central and southern sections proved as cold as ever to Lincoln's preachments and the Native Americans were turning toward the Little Giant.

In Springfield Douglas conferred with John Moore, Chairman of the Democratic State Committee, and other advisers, soon announcing a long schedule of speaking appointments, covering a large part of the State and mortgaging his time for weeks to come. The Republican State Committee continued their plan of having Lincoln cling to Douglas' coat-tail, issuing a list of their own which put Lincoln in the towns of Douglas' schedule — in many on the same day, in the others on the day succeeding. Their hopes were somewhat strengthened by the news that Trumbull had started for Illinois.[39]

Douglas now returned to Chicago to complete arrangements for the grueling campaign ahead. Again Lincoln followed to confer with his own man-

---

[36] Slidell, Saratoga, N.Y., Aug. 8, Atlantic City, N.J., Aug. 22, 1858; Buchanan MSS. Foote, *Casket of Reminiscences*: 135. 'John Slidell... openly confessed to me... on his return from Illinois,... that he used money freely for the overthrow of Douglas.'

[37] Buchanan to Black, Bedford Springs, Pa., Aug. 5, 1858; Black MSS., Library of Congress; Black to Buchanan, Washington, Aug. 7, 1858; Buchanan MSS.

[38] Charles Leib to Trumbull, Chicago, July 20, 1858, Trumbull MSS., as to the candidates. The Danite paper in Chicago was the *Herald*, in Springfield the *Courier*, in Cairo the *Star of Egypt*, Governor Reynolds' personal organ.

[39] *Illinois State Register*, July 24, 1858, published a list of engagements for Douglas from July 27 to Oct. 29 In New York, en route, Trumbull launched a mighty thunderbolt at his colleague, and the Republican papers in the East regarded him rather than Lincoln as the Little Giant's real antagonist. Sparks, *Debates*, 58, quotes this Boston *Traveler* headline: 'ILLINOIS, TRUMBULL AND DOUGLAS.'

agers, who were quite dissatisfied with the trend. The way Lincoln was 'trailing' Douglas lent color to the Democratic charge that Lincoln could not command the crowds for himself and so must depend on Douglas. There was no use denying the disappointing size of Lincoln's crowds.[40] None could doubt that Douglas had taken charge of the campaign and Lincoln must capture the offensive.

The Republican managers now insisted that Lincoln challenge Douglas to a State-wide joint debate, and the most important party organ called upon the two men 'to canvass the State together, in the usual Western style.' These qualms in the inner council occupied Lincoln in Chicago. On July 24, Norman B. Judd, who quieting his qualms, had become Chairman of Lincoln's campaign committee, bore Lincoln's challenge to the Little Giant.[41]

'Will it be agreeable to you,' Lincoln wrote, 'to make an arrangement for you and myself to divide time, and address the same audiences the present canvass?' If Douglas should consent, the note continued, Mr. Judd was authorized 'to enter into the terms of such agreement.' [42]

This could not have been other than an unwelcome development for Douglas. At this particular moment he held a larger share of public attention than any other American public man. It would be an extraordinary advantage to Lincoln to share this attention through a debate on equal terms. Lincoln had everything to gain and Douglas everything to lose. Douglas knew this — and so did Lincoln.

When Judd left Lincoln's letter, Douglas conferred with his aides. 'Between you and me,' he told them, 'I do not feel that I want to go into this debate. The whole country knows me and has me measured. Lincoln, as regards myself, is comparatively unknown, and if he gets the best of this debate — and I want to say he is the ablest man the Republicans have got — I shall lose everything. Should I win I shall gain but little.' [43]

But he answered Lincoln's challenge the day it came. The Democratic State Committee in Springfield, he pointed out, had made appointments for Democratic meetings 'covering the entire period until late in October.' These arrangements involved more than speeches by the Senator. In addition, Democratic nominees for Congress, for the Legislature and other offices had arranged to be present and address the people. Their speeches, with his own, would 'occupy the whole time of the day and evening, and leave no opportunity for other speeches.' Next he referred to the recent report that the Danites were putting Judge Breese formally into the field against him, a third candidate 'with no other purpose than to insure my

[40] Cole, *Era*, 169.

[41] Herndon, II, 401; James S. Ewing statement, Feb. 12, 1909; Jesse W. Fell MSS.; Chicago *Press and Tribune*, July 22, 1858. Stevens, 522, apparently accepted by Beveridge, II, 628, gives as another main reason for Lincoln's willingness to challenge, his displeasure that, with Trumbull's entrance into the campaign, 'so much of the Douglas attention and newspaper comment became centered upon Trumbull.' But Douglas had not mentioned Trumbull's name in his Chicago, Bloomington or Springfield speeches, he made no more long speeches before going to Chicago for his final preparations, his attention to Trumbull seems actually to have come after, not before, Lincoln's challenge!

[42] Lincoln, *Works*, III, 189.   [43] Stevens, 553.

defeat by dividing the Democratic party for your benefit.' Should Douglas accept Lincoln's challenge, perhaps this Danite 'candidate' might seek inclusion on the same terms. Furthermore, if Lincoln had originally intended to issue such a challenge, Douglas was surprised that he had waited so long to do so, particularly in view of the fact that they had been together in Chicago, Bloomington, Atlanta, Lincoln and Springfield, all prior to the announcement of the list of Douglas' campaign dates.

But while he would make no arrangements to deprive the other Democratic candidates of their share in the meetings the State Committee had arranged, 'I will, in order to accommodate you, so far as it is in my power to do so, take the responsibility of making an arrangement with you for a discussion between us at one prominent point in each Congressiónal District in the State, except the second and sixth districts, where we have both spoken, and in both of which cases you have had the concluding speech.' If Lincoln were to agree to this, Douglas would designate these places for the seven debates: Freeport, Ottawa, Galesburg, Quincy, Alton, Jonesboro and Charleston. He would confer with Lincoln as soon as possible about the mode of conducting the debates.[44]

Lincoln replied from Springfield, on July 29. The challenge had been sent, he answered lamely, 'as soon as I resolved to make it,' and he had waited 'respectfully' for Douglas to challenge him! After ingenuous argument on other points, he concluded by agreeing somewhat ungraciously to the seven meetings 'at your own times.' Douglas then appointed the dates and Lincoln accepted them. Republican papers charged that the Little Giant was in fact the Little Dodger, but the Democratic papers waxed ironic that Lincoln had had the effrontery to expect Douglas to challenge him. The stage was set for the 'Great Debates' — the partisan orchestra was tuning up.[45]

[44] Lincoln, *Works*, III, 189–92.

[45] Lincoln to Douglas, Springfield, July 29; Douglas to Lincoln, Bement, July 30; Lincoln to Douglas, Springfield, July 31, 1858; Lincoln, *Works*, III, 193–97.

CHAPTER XXI

THE GREAT DEBATES

DESPITE the impending debates, Douglas' major campaign task was to appear each day in a new town and county, to address a foregathering of the people. Announced by cannon, he would come in on his special train; or he would drive in behind a fine team of horses. Responding to a welcome of oratory, he would deliver his set speech of two hours, handle local jealousies and irritations and inspire his local leadership.

His hopes of winning his way back to the Senate rested upon the success of this program. The long grind began at Clinton, on July 27, four days before the debate compact was completed and there was no rest for the weary until election day. Outside correspondents found the campaign a great trial. The railroads were poorly constructed, the country roads nothing but mud, the taverns at which they stopped quite wretched and, except in Egypt, 'the food and lodging were nearly always simply abominable.' [1]

But Douglas, a seasoned campaigner, knew his people and his opportunities. His speech had already been tested, he knew its strong points and made the most of them. Carefully laying the historical foundation for his argument, he dramatized the fundamental issues between Lincoln and himself and made a strong presentation of the urgent national need for middle ground between sectional extremes. In beginning his speeches, Douglas nearly always sought to check demonstrations for himself, and would say, much as at Ottawa: 'Silence will be more acceptable to me in this discussion of these questions than applause. I desire to address myself to your judgment, your understanding and your consciences, and not to your passions or your enthusiasm.' Nor did he employ the orator's conventional devices of anecdote and shady humor. His presentation was a business-like recital of the facts as he saw them, a making-up of the issues and a relentless hammering upon them.

His arguments, however, provided enthusiastic adherents with occasion to shout with joy. Old-Line Whigs were afforded timely reminders of Clay's and Webster's policy of peace and conciliation. Native Americans were pleased by his unfailing tribute to Crittenden and other of their members in Congress, for their assistance in the battle against Lecompton. The descendants of the liberty-loving pioneers were warmed by his advocacy of the right of self-government. And then there was a binding tie for all save extreme Abolitionists in Douglas' declaration that the Negro was not the white man's equal and should not be put upon terms of political or social equality. Treat him justly, treat him kindly, but inferior he had been born and inferior he would ever be.

A part of his set speech was to read Lincoln's House Divided doctrine, which he would do from a little note-book in which he had pasted the statement as it had been printed in Lincoln's own organ, the *Illinois Journal*.[2] After reading Lincoln's words, Douglas would launch his powerful attack upon this doctrine so implicit of war. The speech was simple, direct and forceful. Rarely did it fail to consolidate his own partisans, to attract Old-Line Whigs and Native Americans and to appeal to the more moderate Republicans.

Douglas' meeting at Lewistown was typical. At daylight on August 16, a saluting battery fired thirteen rounds of welcome, and from sunrise until ten o'clock the people poured into the town. The Canton band headed a grand pageant of the 'invincible Democracy' from South Fulton. Wagon after wagon and carriage after carriage followed after it, nearly every conveyance bearing banners on hickory poles. One carriage bore aloft a beautiful silk flag with a life-like portrait of the Senator. Another banner proclaimed that:

THE CANTON DEMOCRACY PREFER

THE DEAD LION RATHER THAN THE LIVING DOG

About two o'clock, escorted by the band, Douglas drove toward the speaking-ground. Attempting three times to begin, each time he was 'greeted with prolonged, uncontrollable outbursts of enthusiasm,' which drowned his voice but brought a quiet smile of satisfaction to his face. Then he stilled the throng and his voice began to be heard, earnest, slow, heavy-toned, slowly gathering strength and vigor, until his words seemed verily to be 'stirring up the souls of the audience, which sat and stood spell-bound, in death-like stillness.' For two hours he held his hearers, and when he had done the enthusiasm was tremendous.[3]

Adèle had her own task to perform. At every stopping she would attend a reception to the ladies. She never attempted to dress down to the country women nor to act other than as a cultured, refined, infinitely agreeable lady accustomed to good society. But her exquisite tact and good breeding never left her. The Republicans deemed her 'a dangerous element' and sorrowfully confessed that her presence was most helpful to the Judge. The editor of a St. Louis German paper, theretofore strong for Lincoln, met Adèle at a reception at Belleville and was so attracted that he immediately switched to Douglas' support. On one occasion Douglas had gone ahead to a meeting, and Adèle was riding on a train to join him. Abraham Lincoln was a fellow passenger and the two had an amiable conversation. At their destination, Lincoln handed her to the platform and said to her husband, who was there awaiting her, 'Judge Douglas, here's your old 'oman that I brought along. She can do more with you than I can.'[4]

[2] Notebook now in possession of Mr. Martin F. Douglas.

[3] Fulton *Democrat*, Lewistown, Aug. 20, 1858; reprinted in that same paper Aug. 16, 1922. The meeting had been held on Aug. 16.

[4] Herndon, II, 103–04, quoting statement of Horace White; Beveridge, II, 633–44; Koerner, II, 65–66. Lincoln did not have similar assistance; while Mary Todd Lincoln attended the

For a while, Lincoln clung to Douglas' meetings. Once or twice, he 'concluded on' Douglas the same evening of the latter's speech, and again Lincoln would speak in the same place early the next day. On one occasion, of which note was taken, he arrived while Douglas was still speaking, and was noticed on the edge of the crowd. Thereupon Republicans near the speaker's stand raised a shout and rushed to Lincoln's side, creating a great commotion. Douglas thought these tactics unfair but seldom complained publicly about them. On the road from Monticello to Bement, he passed Lincoln, hastening to Monticello to answer him. Lincoln had better come on to Bement with him, Douglas hailed jocularly, he would give his rival a much bigger crowd than Lincoln could get 'on his own.'[5]

But this good humor did not extend to his lieutenants. R. T. Merrick, of Chicago, was highly irritated by the way Lincoln continued to 'hang about the tail-end' of Douglas' meetings. If it kept up, Merrick would take it upon himself to 'hang on to Lincoln and answer him" in a similar way. The Republican candidate must have been conscious of the impropriety of his tactics, for he appended to his letter of July 29 the promise that he would not be present at any more of Douglas' 'exclusive meetings.'[6] In September, when Lincoln was billed to speak in a circus tent, the *Illinois State Register* jeered that he was 'advertised to hold forth after the performance of Spalding and Rogers' clowns.' Another Democratic paper sneered that the circus was following Douglas to get advantage of the crowds which flocked to hear him, while Lincoln was following the circus 'to get the ear of the crowd assembled to witness the antics of the clowns.'[7]

Douglas' appointment at Clinton, the first on the long list arranged by his committee, was also the first opportunity he had had to speak in public since Lincoln's renewal, at Springfield, of the Dred Scott conspiracy charge. Then Lincoln had said: 'On his tacit admission, I renew the charge. I charge him with having been a party to that conspiracy... for the sole purpose of nationalizing slavery.' This had made Douglas realize that his antagonist would not hesitate to repeat this canard and to claim that Douglas' silence was almost a confession of guilt. So at Clinton he met it frontally.

'It is perfectly true that I have not contradicted it,' he said, 'and I have not done so for this reason: that I did not believe that any citizen of Illinois was so degraded in his soul as to believe it... I did not believe that Mr. Lincoln himself intended to give it the slightest audit.

'What reply to make to such a charge without characterizing it as it deserves, and breaking beyond that restraint to which a proper self-respect commands me to submit, I scarcely know. The accusation is unfounded and untrue from the beginning to the end of it. I have never interchanged a

Alton debate, she was at Springfield during the other six debates. For train incident, I depend on statement of Mrs. Douglas, then Mrs. Williams, to Robert Dick Douglas, of Greensboro.

[5] 'Piatt,' Monticello, July 29, in *Illinois State Register*, Aug. 12, 1858.

[6] C. B. Buckner, Chicago, July 30, 1858, Douglas MSS., conveying Merrick's proffer; Postscript, Lincoln to Douglas, Springfield, July 29, 1858; Lincoln, *Works*, III, 196.

[7] *Illinois State Register*, Sept. 10, 1858, quoting Litchfield *Journal*. Douglas spoke in a circus tent at Lincoln, Ill., on Sept. 4. Lincoln was billed for the same tent for Hillsboro on Sept. 9, but did not use it.

single word with Chief Justice Taney upon the subject of the decision in the Dred Scott case, either before or since that decision. I neither understood from Mr. Buchanan or Mr. Pierce nor anyone else what the decision would be, and until it was pronounced I was as perfectly ignorant of what was determined as anyone who hears me. I do not believe that Mr. Pierce or Mr. Buchanan or anyone on the face of the earth ever approached the Judges of the Supreme Court upon the subject of that decision, or dared to approach them upon that subject otherwise than as counsel in the case in open court. I have never entered into any conspiracy to perpetuate slavery in the Territories with the conspirators named and intimated by Mr. Lincoln, or with any other persons. Upon the subject of slavery in the Territories, I have advocated in private no other principle than that for which I have contended in public before the eyes of the whole of the American people.' [8]

Trumbull signalized his return to Illinois by a 'ferocious' attack on Douglas. Hardly a word did the Republican Senator say about Lincoln or in his behalf, but his vilification of the Little Giant was unrestrained. The theme was another Douglas 'plot' against Kansas. The time was 1856, the occasion the Toombs bill, originally providing for submitting to the people any constitution which might be framed. When the bill emerged from Douglas' Committee on Territories, Trumbull charged, this clause had been stricken from it and Douglas was responsible! 'I will force the truth down any honest man's throat until he cannot deny it,' Trumbull shouted, 'and to the man who does deny it, I will cram the lie down his throat until he shall cry enough.' Douglas had done this deed, and it was 'the most damnable effrontery that man ever put on, to concoct a scheme to defraud and cheat a people out of their right, and then claim credit for it.' [9]

Trumbull's charge had been made originally in the Senate eight months before, during the Administration's first bitter onslaught on the Little Giant. When Bigler, of Pennsylvania, had offensively intimated it, Douglas had promptly and insistently demanded that his assailant be specific. After a spectacular interchange, Douglas had driven Bigler to disavow all his hints and inferences and to make a full and complete retraction. Trumbull had said no word during these exciting colloquies.[10] Then Trumbull had been glad enough of Douglas' powerful leadership in the struggle against the Lecompton fraud. Now he did not scruple to rake up Bigler's retracted charges and to fling them into the Illinois campaign with a venom far surpassing that with which Bigler had made them.

The charges were bold, official documents seemed to sustain them and the Republicans whooped with joy. Sheahan, greatly disturbed, sent Douglas a full copy of Trumbull's speech, a part of which 'will require an answer, and it ought to be given at once.' The letter did not catch up with Douglas for several days and Sheahan worked up a defense of his own for the Chicago

---

[8] Language taken from draft in Douglas' hand; Douglas MSS.

[9] Chicago *Press and Tribune*, Aug. 8, 1858.

[10] See *supra*, 278 *et seq.*; cf. also *Congressional Globe*, Thirty-Fifth Congress, First Session, 21–22, 112, 113.

Times. 'The matter created so much noise here,' he advised his chief, 'that silence was considered guilt.' [11]

Douglas learned the full purport of Trumbull's charges at Beardstown on August 11, and was overcome with rage. Trumbull was a liar and a coward, the Little Giant shouted to his audience; 'the miserable, craven-hearted wretch, he would rather have both ears cut off than to use that language in my presence, where I could call him to account.' He pasted in his notebook two paragraphs of Trumbull's charges, which he would read carefully to the crowd each day, and would cap it with a blistering excoriation of his Republican colleague.[12] Lincoln too came in for sharp castigation. Despite Douglas' categorical and detailed denial, Lincoln day after day continued to repeat his Dred Scott conspiracy charge, which Douglas termed 'an infamous lie.'

At last the Republicans were happy. For a month they had been hoping to bring charges which would topple Douglas off his balance. A calm Douglas was an invincible campaigner; a Douglas flaming with rage might at any moment make some fatal break. The next day, at Beardstown, Lincoln renewed his familiar indictment, daring Douglas to deny a single count. 'Let him do so,' he boasted, 'and I will prove them by such testimony as will confound him forever.'

The Senator's wrath was slow to cool; Republicans said he must have been drinking at Havana, for he had there called Lincoln 'a liar, a coward, a wretch and a sneak.' The target of these remarks, following the next day, jibed that Douglas had been a 'little excited' and had wanted to fight him. When a Douglas partisan in the crowd offered to take the Senator's place, Lincoln countered that he would fight neither the Judge nor his second: a fight would not prove anything, and besides, 'he and I are about the best friends in the world, and when we get together he would no more think of fighting me than of fighting his wife.... We will call it quits.' [13]

By this time all thoughts began to turn from Trumbull and the Toombs bill and Lincoln's silly conspiracy charge to Ottawa, where, on August 21, the first of the joint debates was to be held. Douglas went from Havana to Bath, thence to Lewistown and from there to Peoria. But he had recovered his poise, found that Trumbull's slur could be offset and determined to force the fighting at Ottawa.

Seeking implements to aid this recovery of initiative, Douglas sought new materials with which to bombard Lincoln and through him the whole Republican party and idea. He had a vague recollection of a wildly

---

[11] J. W. Sheahan, Chicago, Aug. 13, 1858; Douglas MSS.

[12] The clipping, from the Chicago *Press and Tribune*, Aug. 10, 1858, quoted Trumbull thus: 'I make the distinct charge that there was a preconcerted arrangement and plot entered into by the very men who now claim credit for opposing a Constitution not submitted to the people. ... I charge it tonight that the very men who traverse the country under banners proclaiming Popular Sovereignty, by design, concocted a bill on purpose to force a Constitution upon that people.'

[13] Herndon, II, 95, quotes Horace White's claim that he heard Douglas' characterization of Trumbull and of Lincoln; *ibid.*, II, 102–03, for the Havana incidents.

radical platform the Illinois Republican party had adopted at its foundation. When he made inquiries, someone brought him the files of Lanphier's *Illinois State Register* for August, 1856, reprinting a speech Thomas L. Harris had made in Congress, terming the new party's doctrine revolutionary, and documenting his assertion by a set of resolutions which he said had been adopted at its 1854 State Convention in Springfield.

But Douglas did not intend to go off half-cocked. 'I desire to know the time and place at which that convention was held,' he demanded of Lanphier, 'and whether it was a mass meeting or a delegate convention, whether Lincoln was present and made a speech, and such other facts concerning the matter as you may be able to give.' This information was 'very important' and the Senator wanted it immediately, 'must have it before next Saturday.' Let Lanphier see Harris, hunt up the facts and write him instantly at Ottawa.[14] Harris was sick, but Lanphier consulted him, checked up on his recollections, examined the *Register's* files for the Fall of 1854 and brought them with him to the scene of the debate.

Ottawa, a town of some nine thousand people about seventy miles southwest of Chicago, had regional importance, and the Illinois Supreme Court met there once a year. Its senatorial district, made up of La Salle, Grundy and Livingston counties, had two members in the Legislature. Strongly anti-slavery in its sentiment, in 1856 the Republicans had carried the county by fifteen hundred majority. But its Democrats were nearly all Douglas men and they did not intend to be downed without a struggle.[15] The Little Giant's Ottawa friends made careful preparations for his reception. Particularly solicitous that the Senator arrive separately from Abraham Lincoln, the committee in charge made secret arrangements for Douglas' advent by special train and kept the Republicans in ignorance of their plans until it was too late for Lincoln to 'horn in.'[16]

The day before the debate, little work was done in the surrounding country and everyone was in holiday mood. The people streamed to Ottawa afoot, on horseback, in hay carts and in canvas-covered wagons. That night camp-fires surrounded the town. Saturday was clear, the little town was crowded and a rough, undecorated pine board platform was put up on the town's Public Square. There were no seats for the audience but the grass filled with determined early comers.

A reception committee met Douglas at Peru and escorted him to Ottawa — the Senator riding in a fine carriage drawn by four splendid horses. Four miles out he was greeted by a great throng, with a band at its head.

[14] Douglas to Lanphier, no place, Aug. 15, 1858; Patton MSS. Harris' speech had been made Aug. 9, 1856. Douglas also wanted Lanphier to telegraph him at Peoria the time and place of the convention 'which passed a resolution concerning no more slave States'; it must have been held in August or September, 1854.

[15] William Hettick, Ottawa, July 9, 1858, Douglas MSS., tells of Caffrey, their candidate for Congress against Lovejoy: 'Caffrey is a good speaker, he will spend his money, would be supported by Judge Dickey, Mr. Gray and many other good speakers in the Republican party.'

[16] C. Gillespie, Ottawa, Aug. 17, 1858; Douglas MSS. These plans were for Douglas to come to La Salle, on a river steamer Thursday night, to remain in Peru Friday and then to reach Ottawa Saturday on a special train.

Two brass twelve-pounders announced his arrival, and the shouts were ear-splitting. The welcoming address by Colonel Cushman affected Douglas deeply. A little later the Republican train of seventeen cars from Chicago and Joliet arrived, the rival bands blared defiantly at one another and the confusion was tremendous. About twelve thousand people had gathered, but it was a good-natured crowd.

The principals and their seconds reached the platform about two-thirty and took their seats along with the official moderators for the debate. Behind the moderators were the reception committees, popularly known as 'Shouters.' Some tables for the press, immediately to the left of the platform, were soon filled.[17]

The principals' debate agreement had not included provision of chairmen or presiding officers. At Ottawa, Douglas had the opening and rebuttal. He prefaced his argument with a brief statement that, by arrangement, Lincoln and himself, 'representatives of the two great political parties of the State and Union,' had arranged a joint discussion of the principles at issue between the parties. Fully two-thirds of the crowd was Republican but Douglas' opening salvos brought prolonged applause. This the Senator sought to still, remarking that he sought his hearers' judgment, understanding and consciences and not their passions or enthusiasms.[18]

Before 1854 he declared, two parties, Whig and Democratic, had divided the Nation. Whig principles were not confined by sectional lines but were applied and proclaimed South as well as North, just as were Democratic principles. But then came the Abolitionists' injection of sectionalism in American politics. After describing the genesis of the Kansas-Nebraska Act, Douglas charged that on its passage, Lincoln and Trumbull had 'entered into an arrangement one with the other, and each with his respective friends, to dissolve the old Whig party on the one hand, and to dissolve the old Democratic party on the other, and to connect the members of both into an Abolition party, under the name and disguise of a Republican party.' The terms of this arrangement, which James Matheny, one of Lincoln's close friends, had made public, were that Lincoln was to have Shields' place in the Senate while four years later Trumbull should replace Douglas.

What were the principles upon which this Republican party had been established in Illinois? Using the files of the *Illinois State Register*, Douglas read three resolutions which Lanphier's paper had printed as having been

[17] Philadelphia *Press*, Aug. 26, 1858, for Ottawa reception details; James B. Sheridan, who acted as the *Press* correspondent, thought twenty thousand people were there. Sheridan and Henry Binmore represented the Chicago *Times*; Binmore also sent an account to the Washington *States* and the *Missouri Republican*. Henry Villard was there for the New York *Staats-Zeitung*, and Chester P. Dewey for the New York *Evening Post*. Horace White wrote the running story for the Chicago *Press and Tribune*, and Robert Hitt took down the speech stenographically for it. Colonel H. W. H. Cushman was moderator for Douglas.

[18] *Missouri Republican*, Aug. 29, 1858, termed Douglas' speech 'a calm and logical argument,' and said the people listened with the same calmness. But one would not suspect it from the Chicago *Press and Tribune*, Aug. 23, 1858, which charged that Douglas' 'face was livid with passion and excitement.... He resembled a wild beast in looks and gestures, and a maniac in language and argument.'

adopted by the Republican State Convention in Springfield in October, 1854. The first announced that, 'when parties become subversive of the ends for which they are established,' the people had the right and duty to leave them and to organize new parties. The second proclaimed that, therefore, the Republican party was organized 'to restore Nebraska and Kansas to the position of Free Territories...; to repeal and entirely abrogate the Fugitive Slave Law; to restrict slavery to those States in which it exists; to prohibit the admission of any more Slave States into the Union; to abolish slavery in the District of Columbia; to exclude slavery from all the Territories over which the General Government has exclusive jurisdiction, and to resist the acquirement of any more Territories, unless the practice of slavery therein forever shall have been prohibited.' The third resolution announced that 'we will support no man for office, under the General or State Government, who is not positively and fully committed to the support of these principles.'

The Republicans in the audience cheered as each sentence was read. 'Yet I venture to say,' commented Douglas ironically, 'that you cannot get Mr. Lincoln to come out and say that he is now in favor of each one of them.' Douglas' purpose in reading them was to lay the foundation to ask Lincoln whether he was today, as in 1854, for the unconditional repeal of the Fugitive Slave Law. Did he stand pledged today against admitting any more Slave States into the Union, even if the people wanted them? Was he pledged 'against the admission of a new State into the Union with such a Constitution as the people of that State may see fit to make?' 'I want his answers to these questions,' Douglas went on, 'your affirmative cheers in favor of this Abolition platform are not satisfactory. I ask Abraham Lincoln to answer these questions in order that, when I trot him down to lower Egypt, I may put the same questions to him.'

The Senator was interrupted by cheer after cheer as he continued: 'My principles are the same everywhere. I can proclaim them alike in the North, the South, the East and the West. My principles will apply wherever the Constitution prevails and the American flag waves. I desire to know whether Mr. Lincoln's principles will bear transplanting from Ottawa to Jonesboro.'

In this he meant nothing 'personally disrespectful or unkind' to his competitor. They had both struggled with poverty in a strange land; Douglas had taught school in Winchester, Lincoln had been a 'flourishing grocery-keeper in the town of Salem.' This thrust raised a laugh, for in the early days in the West a 'grocery' was naught other than a frontier saloon. In the Legislature Douglas had met him again, and 'he was just as good at telling an anecdote as now. He could beat any of the boys wrestling or running a foot-race, in pitching quoits or tossing a copper; could ruin more liquor than all of the boys of the town together; and the dignity and the impartiality with which he presided at a horse-race or a fist-fight excited the admiration and won the praise of everybody that was present and participating.'

After their legislative terms together, Lincoln had 'subsided or became submerged, and he was lost sight of as a public man for some years.' At the time of the Wilmot Proviso agitation he had 'again turned up,' this time as a Member of Congress, where 'he distinguished himself by his opposition to the Mexican War, taking the side of the common enemy against his own country.' Because of this he was again submerged, but in 1854 had come up again to make this Abolition platform and to help found this sectional party.

The Little Giant now turned his batteries upon Lyman Trumbull, 'who first became noted for his scheme to repudiate most of the State's debts,' a scheme 'which, if successful, would have brought infamy and disgrace' upon Illinois. Douglas recounted how he had walked into a public meeting in the hall of the House at Springfield and had replied to Trumbull's 'repudiating speeches.' A resolution had been carried denouncing repudiation, and 'Trumbull's malignity has followed me since I thus defeated his infamous scheme.'

Returning to the Lincoln-Trumbull bargain, the Senator told how Trumbull had broken faith with Lincoln, seizing for himself Shields' seat, which had been meant for Lincoln, and forcing the latter to wait four years to try to get Douglas' place. Lincoln was now demanding that the 1854 arrangement be carried out, and this explained why the recent Republican State Convention had instructed for Lincoln as the party's only Senatorial candidate. Douglas devoted his remaining time to Lincoln's House Divided and Dred Scott decision doctrines, along the lines of the Chicago, Bloomington and Springfield speeches.

The Republicans in the crowd cheered vociferously for several minutes when Lincoln rose, but while jocular he was nervous and upon the defensive. Lanphier thought Lincoln had come 'crammed with a speech suited for a defensive one from Douglas,' and had been upset when 'he found himself with a fire in front, rear and on both flanks.' After he had talked about twenty minutes, he asked the timekeeper how near his time was up.[19] Bothered by the resolutions Douglas had read, he explained that he had not been in Springfield when the Republican Convention was held, that he had been named on the Republican State Committee without his authority and that he had never had anything to do with the convention, the resolutions or the committee. He denied any compact with Trumbull and insisted that Douglas prove the charge. To show what his sentiments had actually been in 1854, he introduced a long quotation from his Peoria speech of that year.

As he talked on, Lincoln began to interlard his argument with witty sallies, bringing laughter and applause from the crowd. But he did not answer Douglas' questions. 'I do not mean to allow him to catechize me,' he said, 'unless he pays back for it in kind.' The Peoria quotation gave his position on the Fugitive Slave Law. He would say that he had 'no purpose, directly or indirectly,' to interfere with slavery in the States where

---

[19] *Illinois State Register*, Aug. 24; Philadelphia *Press*, Aug. 26; 1858. But these jests did not always please his hearers. Villard, *Memoirs*, I, 94, tells of meeting Lincoln at the Freeport debate, but of disliking him, principally because of Lincoln's love of telling jokes, 'the coarser the joke, the lower the anecdote, and the more risqué the story, the more he enjoyed them, especially when they were of his own invention.' These anecdotes, however, were told in private.

it existed, and he did deny any wish to introduce political and social equality between the races, admitting that he recognized a physical difference between them which probably would 'forever forbid their living together upon the footing of perfect equality.' He only insisted that 'in the right to eat the bread... which his own hand earns, he is my equal, and the equal of Judge Douglas, and the equal of every living man.' He further denied that he had ever been a 'grocery-keeper' anywhere in the world, although he admitted that he 'did work the latter part of one Winter in a little still-house up at the head of a hollow.' He insisted that he had not opposed the soldiers fighting in the Mexican War and undertook to interpret and explain away his House Divided statement.

Popular Sovereignty Lincoln called a plan which allowed the people of a Territory to have slavery if they want to 'but does not allow them not to have it if they do not want to have it.' This led him into his standardized argument about the Dred Scott case and he renewed his charge about Douglas' part in the alleged conspiracy, ridiculing the Senator's categorical denial.

But the House Divided speech still bothered Lincoln and he reverted to it again. About making slavery national, he said jocularly, 'there is no danger that the people of Kentucky will shoulder their muskets, and, with a young nigger stuck on every bayonet, march into Illinois and force them upon us. There is no danger of our going over there and making war upon them.' A brief three years was to show the blind fatuity of this argument. Several minutes before Lincoln's time was out, he exclaimed, 'the Judge can take his half-hour,' turned and took his seat.

The Republicans gave three tremendous cheers thrice repeated but their candidate was, in the opinion of Douglas' aides, distinctly in an unhappy frame of mind. The Senator made the most of his discomfiture and, a St. Louis correspondent thought, 'carried with him almost the entire crowd.' With Douglas in rebuttal, 'not ebullitions of merriment but loud, long and sturdy shouts of triumph rent the air.' [20] Calling Lincoln's denial 'a miserable quibble,' he pointed out that the platform had not been denied, and repeated his demand for specific answers to his questions. 'I will bring Mr. Lincoln to his milk on that point.' It was 'a torrent of logic and sarcasm.' Lincoln's 'smiling face changed considerably,' he squirmed but did not answer.

Douglas added the personal reminiscence that in October, 1854, he had heard Lincoln make a speech in the Hall of Representatives at Springfield the morning of the Republican Convention and that, as the orator had concluded, one of the convention managers had announced that the Republican State Convention would meet immediately in the Senate Chamber. This recollection angered Lincoln, who interrupted, but Douglas coolly responded and Lincoln's friends quieted him down. Douglas declared that Lincoln's renewed conspiracy charge about 'Stephen and Franklin and Roger and James' was, 'in all its bearings, an infamous lie.'

He concluded by reiterating his belief that Lincoln's insistence 'that the Union cannot exist divided into Free and Slave States' inevitably meant

[20] St. Louis *Herald*, Aug. 24, 1858; *Missouri Republican*, Aug. 29, 1858.

ABRAHAM LINCOLN
THE LITTLE GIANT'S GREAT ILLINOIS ANTAGONIST
(From an ambrotype made by Alschuler in Urbana, Illinois)

sectional war. 'If it cannot endure thus divided,' he charged, then Lincoln 'must strive to make them all free or all slave, which will inevitably bring about a dissolution of the Union.' [21] The timekeeper announced that his half-hour had expired and Douglas took his seat amid tremendous shouts. The correspondent of the Philadelphia *Press*, a Douglas man, reported that hundreds who had applauded Lincoln all along turned and applauded Douglas, and that Lincoln was 'the worst used-up man in the United States.' [22]

Douglas left the stand and made his way toward the waiting train at the station. The enthusiastic crowd made a great rush for him and there was a shout 'that reverberated for miles across the prairies.' The Senator swung his hat from right to left, the throng cheered and thousands rushed after him. The Republicans did not neglect their champion, who had remained on the platform. In a few minutes a group rushed up to the stand, two strapping young farmers seized Lincoln and, despite his protests, put him on their shoulders and bore him toward the town. Onlookers were amused to see Lincoln's 'grotesque figure, holding frantically to the heads of his supporters, with his legs dangling from their shoulders, and his pantaloons pulled up so as to expose his underwear almost to his knees.' [23]

The vigor of Douglas' Ottawa attack upon the Springfield resolutions embarrassed Lincoln and his supporters. Soon, however, investigation by the Chicago *Press and Tribune* developed the fact that the resolutions actually adopted at Springfield in 1854 were not those Douglas had used. The Republican papers flared with charges of forgery and deceit; Douglas had manufactured the bogus platform out of whole cloth, they shrieked; it was not an honest mistake, he knew that they were forgeries and he had conspired four years before with his tool Lanphier to print them in the Democratic organ.

Douglas' new investigation revealed that the resolutions he had read actually had been passed by a local Republican convention at Aurora, in Kane County, far in the north of the State. How the mistake was made was not explained. Lanphier, who was responsible, would not take the Republican thunder very seriously. 'I can see that your quotation from our old file has made an uproar,' he wrote Douglas. 'I yet believe the resolutions there given to be the genuine ones. Whether so or not, the point you made is not affected by their denial of the "spot." The resolution in dispute, if I am not mistaken, stood at the head of the Chicago *Tribune* as its platform from the time of its adoption at Aurora.' [24]

[21] For debate text, I am using Dr. Edwin Earle Sparks' volume, *The Lincoln-Douglas Debates of 1858*, Illinois State Historical Library Collections, Lincoln Series, I, Springfield, 1908. Dr. Sparks has carefully prepared the texts, comparing and annotating them with scholarly fidelity. His main basis is the Follett, Foster and Company publication in 1860, at Columbus, Ohio. However, he has compared these texts with the stenographic reports, that of Douglas in the Chicago *Times*, that of Lincoln in the Chicago *Press and Tribune*. Sheridan wrote the first, Robert R. Hitt most of the last. In 1860, Lincoln himself went over the reports of his speeches for the Columbus house. Douglas was not accorded a similar opportunity.

[22] Philadelphia *Press*, Aug. 26, 1858.

[23] Philadelphia *Press*, Aug. 26, 1858; Villard, *Memoirs*, I, 93.

[24] C. H. Lanphier, Springfield, Aug. 26, 1858; Douglas MSS.

Douglas at once incorporated in his speech for his day-to-day campaign a statement that probably he had been mistaken. But while admitting the mistake in the *spot* of the adoption, he collected a dozen similar resolutions which had blossomed over Republican territory in the Fall of 1854, and insisted that the Kane County declarations actually represented the temper, feeling and purpose of the Republicans when they organized in Illinois. Thus, despite his honest error, the general tone of Republicanism in Illinois in 1854 justified the questions he had put to Lincoln. It was the best face that could be put on a costly blunder.[25]

The second debate was scheduled for six days later, at Freeport, in the State's extreme north. Lincoln made up his mind to respond to Douglas' questions, and to counter with some questions of his own, which he wrote out. On the train to Freeport, he handed them to Joseph Medill, of the Chicago *Press and Tribune*. The latter did not like the second proposed question, which read: 'Can the people of a United States Territory, in any lawful way, against the wish of any citizen of the United States, exclude slavery from its limits prior to the formation of a State constitution?' Medill's objection was that this would give Douglas a chance to get out of a tight place. Lincoln, however, was determined to 'spear it at Douglas that afternoon,' and would not yield. [26]

The day at Freeport was wet, cold and dreary but some fifteen thousand people gathered. The scenes of Ottawa were repeated. In the memory of one who was present as a boy of nine, the little town was a 'seething, surging mass.' Many had come in the evening before in big wagons, driving oxen, and had camped there all night.[27] Each champion was received with booming cannon and great enthusiasm. Douglas' committee had engaged a fine carriage to convey him to the stand. This the Republicans burlesqued by carting Lincoln in a Conestoga wagon, but the Little Giant foiled them by walking to the scene of the debate.[28]

The two men made quite a contrast. Douglas was well dressed, with a ruffled shirt, a dark blue coat with shiny buttons, and a wide-brimmed soft hat. Lincoln wore a rusty, high-topped hat, an ill-fitting coat with sleeves too short, and baggy trousers so short that they revealed his rusty

---

[25] Beveridge, II, 654; Johnson, 370; J. G. Holland, *Life of Lincoln*, Springfield, Mass., 1866, 185, gives the typical Republican declaration: 'The charge... that the resolutions he read were passed by the convention that was held at Springfield was false... Did Mr. Douglas know it to be so?... He ought to have known it to be so.'

[26] Chicago *Tribune*, May 9, 1895, quoting Joseph Medill's statement; Sparks, *Debates*, 203–06. Later the legend grew that in the hurried conferences of Lincoln's aides over these proposed questions, he was warned that it would cost him the Senate race. He was supposed to have replied, 'I am after bigger game. The battle of 1860 is worth a hundred of this.' Beveridge, II, 656, says that no evidence has yet been discovered that anything of the kind took place.

[27] Dr. W. Woodbridge to author, Central City, Iowa, Sept. 16, 1932. Young Woodbridge and his mother had accompanied Charles Sellen, editor of the Galesburg *Democrat*, to the Freeport meeting.

[28] Chicago *Times*, Aug. 29, 1858; New York *Evening Post*, Sept. 2, 1858; *Missouri Republican*, Aug. 31, 1858; Freeport *Journal*, Sept. 2, 1858.

boots.[29] There was further contrast in their speaking manner. Douglas talked fast and steadily, in a heavy voice. He would shake his long, black hair and walk back and forth across the platform with great effectiveness. Lincoln's voice was light, almost nasal, and at the start had an unpleasant timbre, but carried well. Both gave a sense of 'profound earnestness.' [30]

Lincoln now opened by chiding Douglas for his mistake about the Springfield resolutions. Then he read his answers to Douglas' questions. Constitutionally, 'the Southern States are entitled to a Fugitive Slave Law,' Lincoln did not propose to repeal the existing one, for he 'would not be the man to introduce it as a new subject of agitation upon the general question of slavery.' As to admitting any more Slave States, Lincoln 'would be exceedingly sorry ever to be put in a position of having to pass upon that question,' he would be 'exceedingly glad' if no new Slave State ever came forward, but should some Territory, from which slavery had been excluded until it became ready to become a State, did then, with its people's wish, apply for admission with a Slave Constitution, 'I see no alternative, if we own the country, but to admit them into the Union.'

But he was quite definite as to exclusion of slavery from Territories. It was the 'right and duty of Congress' to prohibit it, and he favored the exclusion of slavery from all the Territories wherever situated. 'I am not generally opposed to the honest acquisition of territory,' he said, answering the final query, 'and, in any given case, I would or would not oppose such acquisition accordingly as I might think such acquisition would or would not aggravate the slavery question among ourselves.' On these views he said he would stand in Jonesboro as in Freeport.

But Douglas himself must answer several questions. Would he vote to admit Kansas if its people adopted a State Constitution before they had the population called for by the English bill? Could the people of a Territory keep slavery out, lawfully, before it became a State? Should the Supreme Court 'decree' that the States themselves could not exclude slavery, would Douglas be willing to acquiesce in this decision 'as a rule of political action?' Did he favor acquiring new territory without consideration of how it might 'affect the Nation on the slavery question?'

Thus Lincoln took the offensive. The heavily Republican and Abolition audience shrieked with joy. Now Lincoln had turned the tables on the Little Giant. But when it came Douglas' time to reply, he said calmly that he was glad Lincoln had finally answered the Ottawa questions. He had asked them legitimately, for they were based upon Republican platforms and temper of the general attitude of the time, but there was no similar basis for Lincoln's questions — these had sprung simply from Lincoln's 'curiosity,' and represented nothing which had 'received the sanction of the party with which I am acting.' None the less, the Senator would satisfy Lincoln's 'curiosity,' and would not wait six days but would answer now.

As to the first question, he had often said before and he repeated it that

[29] Statement of Ingalls Carleton, Sparks, *Debates*, 206–07.
[30] Dr. W. Woodbridge to author, Central City, Iowa, Sept. 16, 1932.

as soon as Kansas 'had population enough to constitute a Slave State, she has people enough for a Free State.'

Lincoln knew quite well what answer Douglas would make to his second question. The previous year Lincoln had studied and replied to the Senator's June 12 speech at Springfield. Just two months before, he had been on the platform in Bloomington when Douglas vigorously proclaimed that slavery could not exist without sustaining local legislation and opinion. He knew that since then Douglas had been saying this same thing in nearly every speech. Probably the chief purpose of the question was to widen the existing breach between Douglas and the Danites.[31]

'I answer emphatically, as Mr. Lincoln has heard me answer a hundred times on every stump in Illinois,' the Senator began, 'that in my opinion the people of a Territory can, by lawful means, exclude slavery from their limits prior to the formation of a State Constitution.' Here Douglas was interrupted by applause so enthusiastic that it was several minutes before he could go on.

'Mr. Lincoln knew that I had answered that question over and over again,' Douglas continued. 'He heard me argue the Nebraska bill on that principle all over the State in 1854, in 1855, and in 1856, and he has no excuse for pretending to be in doubt as to my position on that question. It matters not what way the Supreme Court may hereafter decide as to the abstract question whether slavery may or may not go into a Territory under the Constitution, the people have the lawful means to introduce it or exclude it as they please, for the reason that slavery cannot exist a day or an hour anywhere, unless it is supported by local police regulations.

'These local police regulations can only be established by the local Legislature; and if the people are opposed to slavery, they will elect representatives to that body who will, by unfriendly legislation, effectually prevent the introduction of it into their midst. If, on the contrary, they are for it, their legislation will favor its extension. Hence, no matter what the decision of the Supreme Court may be on that abstract question, still the right of the people to make a Slave Territory or a Free Territory is perfect and complete under the Nebraska bill. I hope Mr. Lincoln deems my answer satisfactory on that point.'[32]

This forthright answer drew thunderous applause from the Democrats but the Republicans sat glum and silent. When the tumult had quieted, Douglas continued that he was amazed that Lincoln should have put his third question; 'a schoolboy knows better,' shouted a man in the audience.

---

[31] Lincoln to Henry Asbury, Springfield, July 31, 1858; Lincoln, *Works*, III, 197–98, pointed out that Douglas 'cares nothing for the South; he knows he is already dead there. He only leans southerward more to keep the Buchanan party from growing in Illinois. You shall have hard work to get him directly to the point whether a Territorial Legislature has or has not the power to execute slavery. But if you succeed in bringing him to it... though he will be compelled to say it possess no such power... he will instantly take ground that slavery cannot actually exist in the Territories unless the people desire it and so give it protection by Territorial legislation. If this offends the South, he will let it offend them, as at all events he means to hold on to his chances in Illinois.'

[32] Sparks, *Debates*, 161–62; for the entire debate, see *ibid.*, 148–88.

Douglas repeated this, adding that Lincoln well knew that the only man in America 'claiming any degree of intelligence or decency who ever for a moment pretended' that slavery could not be interdicted within a State was the editor of the Washington *Union*. When that worthy had said so, 'Lincoln's friends, Trumbull, and Seward and Hale and Wilson and the whole Black Republican side of the Senate were silent,' but Douglas had promptly denounced it. In that colloquy, Douglas continued, Senator Toombs, of Georgia, had rebuked him for having noticed any such absurdity, declaring that 'there was not one man, woman or child, south of the Potomac in any Slave State who did not repudiate any such pretension.'

His competitor's final question, about acquiring new territory, had been put 'very ingeniously and cunningly,' but the Little Giant refused to dodge. 'Whenever it becomes necessary in our growth and progress to acquire more territory,' he declared, 'I am in favor of it without reference to the question of slavery, and when we have acquired it, I will leave the people free to do as they please, either to make it slave or free territory as they prefer.'

Lincoln, in his rebuttal, did not undertake to analyze Douglas' answer to his questions but used his half-hour further to defend his own consistency. When the debate was over, Lincoln's best friends were dispirited, and they could not get out of their minds the feeling that Douglas had turned the tables on his questioner.[33]

All this time the Republicans and the Danites kept up their speaking concentration against Douglas. Lincoln's activities have already been noted. Trumbull continued his tour of vilification, Lovejoy stumped the Abolition sections, Chase came in from Ohio, Frederick Douglass, the famous Negro agitator, toured the northern tier and dozens of other Republican and Abolition speakers flooded the prairie State. The Danite activity was intense. Ex-Senator Sidney Breese, ex-Governor John Reynolds, Colonel Dougherty and Dr. Leib covered Egypt with a fine-tooth comb. Daniel S. Dickinson sent 'a thousand greetings' to a Danite meeting. In addition to the money he had supplied, Slidell furnished the Illinois Buchaneers with large sums of money, and also with some juicy rumors that the slaves on the Douglas boys' plantations in Mississippi were 'in every way so badly treated that they were spoken of in the neighborhood where they are held as a disgrace to all slave-holders and the system they support.' [34]

The fanatic Sturgeon wrote such 'ferocious' letters into Illinois that some Douglas men went to St. Louis and 'damned him into acquiescence.' [35]

[33] Herndon, II, 110, quoting statement of Horace White.

[34] Sheahan, 439–42; Herndon, II, 128–29. He denied their sponsorship — after the campaign.

[35] Henry Binmore, Alton, July 20, reported on a St. Louis visit in which he had forced Sturgeon to admit Douglas was not a *Black Republican*; C. H. Lanphier, Springfield, Aug. 26, 1858, Douglas MSS., telling of George McConnel's St. Louis visit, in which he 'damned Sturgeon into acquiescence.' Isaac Sturgeon to Buchanan, St. Louis, Oct. 22, 1858; Buchanan MSS.: 'I do not think our friends in Illinois worth hell-room,' Sturgeon complained to the President. 'They have no nerve or backbone.' Sturgeon had been endeavoring to get them to ask Douglas public questions about the Blair mystery, he had sent these questions to Quincy, he had gone

The Little Giant's friends wondered how he, single-handed, could stand up against so many, particularly when they followed him and seized his meetings at night when he was worn out. Usher F. Linder sent word that he would be glad to take the stump and share the burden. 'Can't he be employed?' a mutual friend wrote Douglas.[36] The latter's answer was a prompt telegram: 'The Hell-hounds are on my track. For God's sake, Linder, come and help me fight them.' A telegrapher sold the Republicans a copy of this message, which made much mirth, and its recipient was known ever after as 'For God's Sake Linder.' [37]

Cyrus Edwards, a Whig war horse; E. B. Webb, that party's last candidate for Governor; Buckner S. Morris, a strong Native American; James W. Singleton, Henry Clay's confidential friend — all these came out for Douglas. Then it was announced authoritatively for Major John T. Stuart, Lincoln's first law partner, the man who had defeated Douglas for Congress in 1838, 'that on the slavery question he coincides with Mr. Douglas — that he is wholly opposed to the Republican party.' [38]

The admittedly debatable territory was central Illinois and there Douglas concentrated his major activities. Within a radius of a hundred miles of the Capital was the battleground, between Ottawa on the north, Belleville on the south, Oquawka on the northwest and Paris on the east; Sangamon, Morgan, Mason, Logan and Madison counties were particularly important.[39] Only twice during the campaign did Douglas leave this area for any length of time — once to meet Lincoln at Freeport, again to encounter him at Jonesboro.[40]

The second point was Egypt. 'It will never do to let the Opposition get a foothold in Egypt,' an aide warned. 'If they do, the State is gone beyond redemption.' [41] The Danites constituted the menace in that region and the Douglas Committee moved Heaven and earth to checkmate them. John A. Logan and S. S. Marshall took the stump there and efforts were made to get Southern leaders into the section. Alexander H. Stephens went to Chicago for a last effort to compromise the Democratic schism, but the Danites there complained to Slidell and Buchanan that his plan to 'harmonize' merely meant their 'unconditional surrender,' and Stephens was rebuffed.[42]

Democratic leaders through the country watched the Illinois debates with bated breath. Democratic conventions in Ohio, New York, Massachusetts and other States passed resolutions either endorsing Douglas' stand or

himself to Alton, but could not get it done at all. He feared Douglas would win, in which event he trusted to God there would be *no yielding* in Buchanan's party.

[36] J. J. Brown, Charleston, Ill., Aug. 26, 1858; Douglas MSS.

[37] Linder, *Reminiscences*, 78.

[38] Cole, *Era*, 175; *Illinois State Register*, Oct. 8, 1858: 'We are authorized,' etc. But on account of Stuart's '*personal* relations to Mr. Lincoln, he is unwilling to take any part in the senatorial contest, and shall not vote for Representatives to the Legislature.'

[39] Cole, *Era*, 175.   [40] Johnson, 363.

[41] S. S. Marshall to Lanphier, McLeansboro, Ill., Oct. 24, 1858; Patton MSS.

[42] C. N. Pine to Slidell, Chicago, Aug. 17; Henry S. Fitch to Buchanan, Chicago, Aug. 17, 1858; Buchanan MSS.

altogether ignoring Buchanan's Lecompton test. While Douglas' Freeport doctrine inspired prompt fulminations by the Washington *Union* and led many State's Rights stalwarts to repudiate the Little Giant, it did not materially check the general drift in his direction. Judge Treat, of St. Louis, an excellent barometer of conservative Southern Democratic feeling, wrote Douglas that the Lecompton Constitution was no longer an issue; Buchanan and his advisers 'are fast losing the sympathy of the country, because the party sees that the only possible result would be to destroy its ascendancy not in Illinois alone, but in all of the non-slaveholding States.'

Two months earlier, Senator Green, of Missouri, had 'given up all hope' of Douglas, writing Bigler that he was minded to attack him. But in mid-September he sent word to Douglas that he was willing to come to Illinois to speak in favor of his election.[43] Senator Albert Gallatin Brown, of Mississippi, made a speech at Hazelhurst, in which he said that he hoped 'Douglas would whip Lincoln out of his boots.' [44] In a speech in New England, Jefferson Davis stated distinctly that local laws were essential for the maintenance of slavery in any Territory.[45]

Nor did Slidell's views completely represent those of his own State. The Democratic papers of New Orleans generally applauded Douglas' cause, as did a number of up-State journals. J. D. G. DeBow wrote that his group's sympathies were warmly with the Little Giant and other representative men tendered their support.[46]

Old-Line Whigs were equally pleased by Douglas' stand. Alexander H. Stephens kept up his urgings. 'Lean Jimmy' Jones, of Tennessee, cordially sympathized with Douglas, induced the Memphis *Appeal* to announce its unqualified support and came to Illinois to help keep Egypt safe. James B. Clay, son of the Great Pacificator, followed suit.[47]

John J. Crittenden sent more letters into the State. When Lincoln's aides made a frantic drive to capture the Know-Nothings, and Douglas was 'in great danger,' Crittenden co-operated effectively to repel them.[48]

Leading Kentucky Democrats, even close friends of Buchanan, inclined toward Douglas, who dispatched a confidential agent to Lexington to see what John C. Breckinridge was willing to do.[49] Douglas' envoy and two

[43] Samuel Treat, St. Louis, Sept. 27; O. B. Henderson, Louisville, Sept. 20, 1858; Douglas MSS. Henderson was quoting a recent talk with Green. For earlier attitude, Green to Bigler, Canton, Mo., Aug. 6, covered Bigler to Buchanan, Clearfield, Pa., Aug. 20, 1859; Buchanan MSS. But W. A. Richardson, Quincy, Ill., July 27, 1858; Douglas MSS., told of a recent talk with Green, whom he found 'anxious for your success and ready to do whatever he can to aid.'

[44] *Mississippian*, Sept. 14, 1858, quoted Sparks, *Debates*, 543.

[45] Sparks, *Debates*, 463, Douglas' Alton speech, quoting from Davis' speech at Bangor, Me.

[46] Thomas W. Homan, Donaldsville, La., Aug. 17, as to New Orleans papers; Ronald Jones, Shreveport, Sept. 20, enclosing favorable editorial of *Caddo Gazette*; J. D. G. DeBow, Washington, Oct. 23; F. L. Claibourne, Point Coulee, La., Oct. 26, 1858; Douglas MSS.

[47] A. Rush, Memphis, Sept. 25, B. G. Dill, Leon Trousdale, John R. McClanahan, editors of the *Appeal*, Memphis, Oct. 8; D. B. Henderson, Louisville, Sept. 20; J. A. McHatton, St. Louis, Sept. 28, 1858; Douglas MSS.

[48] Blanton Duncan, Louisville, Aug. 18, 1858; Douglas MSS.

[49] J. W. Stevenson to John Moore, Chairman, Covington, Ky., Oct. 12, 1858; Patton MSS.

friends saw the Vice-President, who '*unqualifiedly* stated to us that he was for your election, expressed great anxiety for your success' and asked them to repeat his declaration to the world.[50] The Little Giant's agent repaired to St. Louis, where he inspired an item in the *Republican* that Breckinridge 'not only declares openly that he desires the Judge's election, but says he is ready to go to Illinois to assist him in his canvass if his services are needed.'

A cautious invitation was dispatched to the Vice-President to come to Illinois to speak. In his answer, Breckinridge said that, while he did not 'propose to leave Kentucky for the purpose of mingling in political discussions in other States,' he had often 'expressed the wish that Mr. Douglas may succeed over his Republican competitor.'

'The Kansas question is practically ended,' he added. 'Mr. Douglas in recent speeches has explicitly declared his adherence to the regular Democratic organization, he seems to be the candidate of the Illinois Democracy and the most formidable opponent in that State of the Republican party, and on more than one occasion during his public life he has defended the Union of the States and the rights of the States with fidelity, courage and great ability.'[51] This letter did Douglas so much good in Egypt that a leading Danite wrote Buchanan in deepest indignation at Breckinridge's 'treachery.'[52]

Another letter, useful for Egypt, came from Governor Henry A. Wise, of Virginia. 'I see you standing alone,' he wrote Douglas' campaign chairman, 'isolated by a tyrannical proscription which would alike foolishly and wickedly lop off one of the most vigorous limbs of the National Democracy ... I see you, in spite of this imputation, firmly fronting the foe and battling to maintain conservative nationality against embittered and implacable sectionalism... Fight on, fight on, never yield but in death or victory.'[53]

About that same time Wise protested vigorously to Buchanan. Why did not the President tell the *Union* to keep quiet? It was idle for him to say it was not his organ, for everyone knew it was. Douglas' '*success* in Illinois *without* the aid of the Administration will be its rebuke; his defeat with its opposition will be the death of the Administration; and his success with the aid of the Administration might save it and the Democratic party.'[54] It

---

[50] The agent was J. A. McHatton, a Kentuckian, who for ten years had managed the Mississippi plantations of the Douglas children. He went to Lexington with his brother, C. G. McHatton, and their cousin, D. B. Henderson, of Louisville. I have constructed my account of this incident from J. A. McHatton, St. Louis, Sept. 24; D. B. Henderson, Louisville, Sept. 20, 1858; Douglas MSS.; J. A. McHatton, St. Louis, Sept. 28, 1858, Martin F. Douglas MSS., added 'I was satisfied by his statement of his anxiety to see you succeed.'

[51] Breckinridge to the Honorable John Moore, Chairman, Versailles, Ky., Oct. 21, 1858; Patton MSS. A draft of Moore's letter to Breckinridge, also in Patton MSS., is written in Douglas' hand.

[52] Isaac Cook, Chicago, Oct. 27, 1858; Buchanan MSS.

[53] Henry A. Wise to John Moore, Richmond, Va., Oct. 13, 1858; Patton MSS.

[54] H. A. Wise, Richmond, Va., Oct. 12, 1858; Buchanan MSS. Apparently this letter provoked Buchanan to reprisals against Wise, *National Intelligencer*, Oct. 12, 1860, prints Wise's speech at Norfolk, Sept. 27, in which he told of protesting, in 1858, against the White House

seemed, in truth, as if Thomas L. Harris was right about it. 'You are making the greatest canvass ever done by mortal,' he wrote Douglas, 'for while you are carrying your own State, you will carry the whole country.' [55]

A main reason for this influx of outside Democratic support was the uninterrupted vigor of the Little Giant's campaign, of which the five remaining debates with Lincoln were an integral but by no means controlling part. The truth is that the normal campaign speeches of both candidates generally surpassed those in the joint debates both in sheer power of statement and in logical development. The debates themselves involved charges and counter-charges, sharp attack and equally sharp defense, the beginning of the new debate being but the rebuttal of the concluding statement of the last one.[56]

During the three weeks after Freeport, Douglas worked his way down into Egypt. At Jonesboro, on September 15, a little town near Cairo, not even on the railroad line, the third debate occurred. The crowd was the smallest at any of the seven debates. Lincoln had few friends there but endeavored to maintain himself the best he could with jest and raillery. Douglas too was in difficulties in the very center of the territory which the Danites claimed. Here, for the first time, Lincoln challenged Douglas' Freeport doctrine, claiming that the Dred Scott case had shown it untrue. The Little Giant, however, answered that the Dred Scott case proved completely his contention as to slavery. 'If the people are opposed to it,' he countered, 'our right is a barren, worthless, useless right; and if they are for it, they will support and encourage it.' The fourth joint appearance was September 18, at Charleston, in central Illinois, doubtful territory, with the crowd divided rather evenly, and both men striving with might and main for the advantage. Lincoln had been smarting under Douglas' Negro equality charges. Now he undertook to offset them. At Chicago he had urged his hearers to end 'all this quibbling... about this race and that race and the other race being inferior,' to 'discard all these things, and unite as one people throughout this land, until we shall once more stand up declaring that all men are created equal.' [57] At Charleston he sought to water down this thick syrup, asserting that he was not 'nor ever have been in favor of bringing about in any way the social and political equality of the white and black races.' This statement he supplemented by saying that 'There is a physical difference between the white and black races which will forever forbid the two races living together on terms of social and political equality. And inasmuch as they cannot so live, while they do remain together there must be the position of superior and inferior, and I, as much as any other man, am in favor of having the superior position assigned to the white race.' Upon this tempering of doctrine to fit the audience, Douglas charged Lincoln with being 'jet black' in the north, 'a decent mulatto' in the center, and 'almost white' in lower Egypt.

policy; ' the answer was prompt. The telegraph conveyed instructions from Washington for my immolation.' But he continued to term Lecompton ' an infamous fraud.'

[55] T. L. Harris, Petersburg, Ill., Oct. 6, 1858; Douglas MSS.

[56] Cole, *Era*, 172–73.   [57] See *supra*, 320.

The fifth debate, three weeks later, was at Galesburg, an Abolition stronghold. Spectators noted that Douglas' voice was deep, hoarse and indistinct.[55] The strain of the daily receptions and speeches was telling on him. Douglas again pointed out the divergence of Lincoln's views at Chicago and at Charleston. Lincoln denied this warmly, but even the casual reader of the debates can note the marked difference in his emphasis in northern and southern Illinois. To men of anti-slavery views he emphasized the moral wrong of the system. In doubtful counties he emphasized with equal vigor that he thought the Negro inferior to the white man. Douglas had sound reason for saying of his competitor, 'he has one set of principles for the Abolition counties and another set for counties opposed to Abolitionism.'

At Quincy, the starting-point of Douglas' Congressional career, his legion of friends made the most of his appearance, on October 13, for the sixth debate. When Lincoln repeated his Dred Scott conspiracy charge, Douglas was much provoked at these 'gross personalities and base insinuations.' Relating his Ottawa blunder, he said: 'When I make a mistake, as an honest man I correct it without being asked to, but when he, Lincoln, makes a false charge he sticks to it and never corrects it.' To his rival's repeated charge that he cared nothing about the moral wrong of slavery, Douglas replied with good sense. 'I hold that the people of the slave-holding States are civilized men as well as ourselves,' he said, 'that they bear consciences as well as we, and that they are accountable to God in their posterity and not to us. It is for them to decide, therefore, the moral and religious right of the slavery question for themselves within their own limits.'

Two days later came the last debate, at Alton, again in the Danite section. Douglas came there by river steamer and more than a thousand St. Louis Democrats came up to hear him.[59] Here Douglas went after the Danites, that 'contemptible crew' trying to break up the party, and paid his respects to the Administration leaders in Washington, who had egged them on. 'Most of the men who denounced my course on the Lecompton question,' he said, 'objected to it, not because I was not right, but because they thought it expedient at that time, for the sake of keeping the party together, to do wrong.... There is no safety or success for our party unless we always do right and trust the consequences to God and the people. I choose not to depart from principle for the sake of expediency on the Lecompton question, and I never intend to do it on that or any other question.'

Here at Alton, in the last debate, the two men epitomized their points of view. Lincoln charged that the trouble with Douglas was *that he looks to no end of the institution of slavery.* Douglas, however, viewed the matter quite differently. 'I care more for the great principle of self-government,' he said, 'the right of the people to rule, than I do for all the Negroes in Christendom. I would not endanger the perpetuity of this Union, I would not blot out the great inalienable rights of the white man, for all the Negroes that ever existed.'

[58] William H. Gay, Illinois State Historical Society, *Journal*, VII, 250.
[59] Koerner, II, 67.

The close of the Great Debates did not end Douglas' campaign. At Alton his voice had been hoarse, at times 'almost extinct'; Gustave Koerner, who hated him, thought him haggard under bronze and bloated from drink or fatigue.[60] His old throat trouble was reappearing, but no matter, he kept up his daily meetings right until election day.

Election day, the second of November, dawned rainy, dreary and cold, but it did not keep the people from the polls. The Republicans took some comfort from having elected their two candidates for State office by a margin of less than four thousand — a victory they owed to the five thousand votes cast for the Danite ticket. But the important point was the election of the Legislature. Of the members of the House, the Democrats elected forty and the Republicans only thirty-five; of the State Senators, they won eight to Lincoln's seven votes. Of the hold-overs, six were Democrats, four Republican. Douglas had won his fight.

The Lincoln men protested that but for the rain on election day they would have triumphed. The weather had kept 10,000 ease-loving Republicans at home. Even more clamant was their insistence that the defeat was due to the unfair apportionment, that Lincoln's candidates had polled 190,000 votes to 176,000 for the Douglas men and he should have won. But for all this there was no blinking the central fact — it was a Douglas Legislature. When Lincoln was certain that the Democrats had won the Legislature, a friend asked him how he felt about it. 'Well, it hurts too much to laugh,' he said, 'and I'm too big to cry.' [61]

As yet, however, the Douglas men were none too certain. Buchanan's leaders in the State set to work to deprive the Little Giant of his prize by corrupting the hold-over legislators. In September a Douglas man in Washington heard that two hold-over State Senators, succumbing to offers of Federal patronage, had agreed to vote against Douglas.[62] To the very day of the joint caucus Sheahan and Lanphier remained apprehensive.[63]

In this they had good reason, for Isaac Cook, the President's chief Illinois agent, called a meeting of Danite leaders to see if they could not cheat Douglas. 'Lincoln is defeated beyond hope,' Cook wrote Buchanan, 'and as for Mr. Douglas he need not be elected.' A strong effort would be to

[60] Koerner, II, 67. This vigorous partisan also insisted Lincoln was as cool and collected as ever at Alton.

[61] Weber MSS., 44.

[62] McCook to Thos. L. Harris, Washington, Sept. 15, 1858; Patton MSS. One of these was Martin of the Twenty-Third District, 'one of the most reliable districts in the State.' This man, according to the report, was to secure the place of District-Attorney replacing Joshua Allen; should not Allen immediately resign, thus causing Martin immediately to resign also so that the promise of the White House could be made good. 'If they refuse to give it to him, he will remain in the Senate, denounce them and sustain the Judge.' Furthermore, as soon as the election was over, 'you will see a clean sweep made in Illinois, and all sympathizers in this city. The Administration and its organ are becoming desperate, they find that they cannot control the masses against the Judge; to equipoise this matter they will remove your friends.' An order had been issued to remove Murray McConnel from his Treasury post, but Breese stepped in and stopped it.

[63] Sheahan to Lanphier, Chicago, Dec. 28, Dec. 31, 1858; Patton MSS.

keep one House from joining the other in joint caucus and thus no election could take place.[64]

In the outcome, however, all these plans were fruitless. When the Legislature met, not a man dared change, and on January 6, the joint caucus was held and resulted in fifty-four votes for Douglas and forty-six for Lincoln.

Springfield Democrats went wild with excitement, the immense crowd in the Capital shouted with joy, and as one wrote Douglas, 'They hollowed, they chanted, the cannon roared, the music played, Democrat greeted Democrat while the Danites and their allies stood aghast.' The thunder of the saluting battery roused loyal partisans in the near-by countryside; these mounted their steeds and in spite of Hell and high-water galloped to town to join the jubilee. 'Glory to God and the Sucker Democracy,' Lanphier telegraphed the Little Giant. 'Let the voice of the people rule,' came Douglas' prompt reply.[65]

[64] Cook to Buchanan, Chicago, Nov. 28, 1858; Buchanan MSS.

[65] C. H. Lanphier, Springfield [Jan. 6, 1859]; J. W. Keener, Springfield, Jan. 7, 1859. Douglas MSS.; Douglas to Lanphier, Baltimore, Jan. 6 [1859]; Patton MSS.

CHAPTER XXII

THE AFTERMATH OF VICTORY

THIS 1858 election had a larger function than the choice of an Illinois Senator. After a campaign waged in some form in nearly every Northern State, the balloting constituted an unofficial referendum upon Buchanan's policies and furnished the Democratic party with an index of the public mood. The result should have frightened the blindest Northern Doughface and impressed the most sulphurous Southern advocate of reopening the slave trade.

In Pennsylvania, New York, New Jersey, all New England, such Middle States as Ohio and Indiana, practically every candidate tainted with Lecomptonism was badly beaten. Not only did Buchanan's policies fail to command a majority of the electorate but the Democratic rank and file had no heart in their defense.[1]

Viewing these results, B. F. Hallett, of Boston, former Chairman of the Democratic National Committee, thought the Eastern States were 'hopeless for the future,' thenceforward 'the National battle of the Union must be fought in the Northwest.' But he felt ground for hope, for 'in Illinois, Wisconsin and Michigan a light breaks.'[2]

A light had indeed broken in the Northwest. Not only did the Illinois Democrats re-elect Douglas but they won five of the State's nine seats in Congress, and the combined votes for the Douglas and the Danite candidates for State office slightly exceeded that for the Republican candidates.[3] Wisconsin Democrats elected one out of the State's three Congressmen and erased over half the Republican 1856 majority. In Michigan, Frémont had led Buchanan by almost 20,000 votes, but in 1858 Douglas' friend Stuart, seeking the governorship on a Douglas platform, cut the Republican lead to less than 10,000 and the Democrats won half of the State's seats in Congress. Iowa showed this same tendency.[4]

---

[1] In 1856, Buchanan had carried his own State of Pennsylvania by 230,722 votes, to Frémont's 147,963, and Fillmore's 82,202. The next year the Democratic candidate for Governor had 188,887 to the Republican's 146,136. In 1858, the State's Democratic candidates for the Supreme Court, the only State-wide contest, lost by 171,130 to 198,117 for the successful Republican. New York elected a Democratic Secretary of State in 1857, by 195,482 votes to 177,425 for the Republican candidate. In 1858, the Republican nominee for Governor secured 247,953 to 230,513 for the Democrat. In 1857, H. B. Payne, Democratic nominee for Governor of Ohio, a Douglas man on a Douglas platform, secured 159,060 votes to 160,541 for the Republican. In 1858, Democrats carried but six of Ohio's twenty-one Congressional districts. Indiana had gone Democratic in 1856. Two years later Republicans won eight of its eleven Congressional districts. *Tribune Almanac and Political Register, 1857, 1858, 1859.*

[2] B. F. Hallett, Boston, Mass., Nov. 6, 1858; Douglas MSS.

[3] *Tribune Almanac and Political Register, 1859,* gives French, Democratic candidate for Superintendent of Public Instruction, 122,413; John Reynolds, the Danite, 5173, as against Bateman, the Republican, with 124,566. The two Democrats together outweighed Bateman by 3030 votes.

[4] *Tribune Almanac and Political Register, 1859.* Michigan, 1856: Buchanan, 52,136; Frémont, 71,762; Fillmore, 1660. Chief Justice election, 1857: Republican, 50,729; Democratic, 39,002.

All through November, Northwestern Democrats celebrated Douglas' victory as a symbol of their strength. The Cleveland Democracy fired a salute and held a great mass meeting. A hundred guns thundered in Toledo and over twelve hundred Popular Sovereigns testified their delight. Mount Vernon's Democracy held a 'Douglas festival.' At Kalamazoo, Michigan, thirty-two guns of triumph sounded off, a prelude to a great banquet with Stuart in the chair. Indianapolis held a great assemblage and Loganport's mass meeting was 'tremendous.' 5

This silver lining to the cloud gave satisfaction to Eastern party leaders. 'All Democrats here are Douglas men now,' telegraphed a Hartford friend, and that city celebrated with saluting batteries and torchlight processions. Douglas represented 'most directly the great conservative sentiments of the people.' 6

Middle States' satisfaction was, if anything, more intense. 'The true interests and the safety of the country' were bound up in Douglas' success, Reverdy Johnson declared. Had Seward's doctrines prevailed, the Union would not have continued. Buffalo organized a Committee of Fifty to celebrate Douglas' victory. The Grangers, the Spencers, the Hubbells and other Canandaigua friends could not restrain their glee. 'Whipping Swamp may wax hot with rage,' a New-Yorker wrote him, 'and South Carolina in a body reach a white heat; but on your platform, with you to lead the columns, must the Democracy win, if at all.' In Pennsylvania plans were promptly set on foot for a State convention to nominate for President the man who had successfully defied 'Old Obliquity.' 7

The Northern Democracy now knew that one champion had found national ground upon which he could hold his own against the party of the 'higher law.' For almost a year it had been apparent that no trust could be rested upon Buchanan's twin policies of Lecompton and proscription. For almost as long there had been a growing belief that Douglas' formula of Popular Sovereignty offered an avenue of safety. Illinois had proved

---

Governor, 1858: Republican, 65,201; Democratic, 56,067. Wisconsin, 1856: Buchanan, 52,843; Frémont, 67,090; Fillmore, 580. Total Congress vote, 1858: Democratic, 61,356; Republican, 55,243. Iowa, 1856: Buchanan, 36,170; Frémont, 43,054; Fillmore, 9180. 1858, Secretary of State: Democratic, 45,748; Republican, 49,085.

5 H. B. Payne, Cleveland, Nov. 5; James B. Steedman, Toledo, Nov. 7; W. C. Gaston, Mount Vernon, Nov. 7; Charles Stuart, Kalamazoo, Mich., Nov. 6; N. B. Palmer, Indianapolis, Nov. 13; S. A. Hall, Logansport, Ind., Nov. 11; C. P. Pascall, Goshen, Ind., Nov. 11, 1858; Douglas MSS.

6 Julius S. Strong, Hartford, Conn., Nov. 4; J. C. Tanner, Hartford, Nov. 6; C. M. Ingersoll, New Haven, Nov. 6; William Faulkner, New Haven, Nov. 15; F. H. Forbes, Boston, Nov. 6; George Ashmun, Springfield, Mass., Nov. 6; Joseph Haynes, Lynn, Mass., Nov. 8; C. W. Payne, Andover, Mass., Nov. 9; Joseph Low, Concord, N.H., Nov. 5; A. G. Jewett, Belfast, Me., Nov. 5; Sam Lawrence, Lowell, Mass., Nov. 15, 1858; Douglas MSS.

7 Reverdy Johnson, Baltimore, Nov. 5, Washington, Nov. 13; C. W. Clinton, Washington, Nov. 2, Nov. 13; L. B. Smith, Buffalo, Nov. 11; H. Clay Mudd, New York, Nov. 5; S. W. Salisbury, Canandaigua, N.Y., Nov. 6; John T. Taylor, Oswego, N.Y., Nov. 6; W. H. Ludlow, Sayville, L.I., Nov. 6; Galen Wilson, Syracuse, N.Y., Nov. 17; Martin Ryerson, Newton, N.J., Nov. 19; John Davis, Davisville, Pa., Nov. 6; John C. Knox, Harrisburg, Pa., Nov. 4; W. A. Stokes, Harrisburg, Nov. 12; J. A. Fulton, Kittanning, Pa., Nov. 22, 1858; Douglas MSS.

the case, Michigan and Wisconsin had given added evidence and Democrats could now see that the Little Giant and his policies might save the party in the North.

But what of the South? Immediately after Freeport this whole section had been depicted as preferring a Black Republican to Douglas. Newspapers vied with one another in their adjectives and orators competed in excoriation.[8] But by mid-November these fires began to die. The most extreme State's Rights men were still bitter, the Ultra newspapers still assailed the Douglas doctrine, but there were signs that the pendulum of public opinion had started swinging back. One Mississippi paper might lament that he 'betrayed us at the critical moment, the only one in which he could have eminently served us,' and counsel, 'Let him go.' But another retorted boldly that, if Buchanan had meant what he said in his Acceptance in 1856, 'he meant just what Douglas does in his Freeport speech.'[9]

Well might the Lecomptonites bite their nails in anger, observed Governor Wise, of Virginia, for the South was beginning to see that 'its self-glorifying guardians poked their fingers in their own eyes.'[10]

'You had the world, the flesh and Buchanan to contend with,' rejoiced a North Carolina admirer; not only did Douglas deserve the Presidency but 'a seat in the Kingdom of Heaven.' Toombs and Stephens jubilated over Douglas' triumph. Banks and Pryor, of Virginia, Rust, of Arkansas, and Albert Gallatin Brown, of Mississippi, were 'joyous and enthusiastic'; the latter loaned his personal frank for circulating Douglas' speeches through the Cotton States. Green, of Missouri, insisted Lecompton was no sound party test. Some urged Douglas above all to stand by the National Democracy, others insisted that he run for President without the Charleston nomination and still others urged prompt announcement that he favored annexing Cuba, which would be as a platform to unite South and West.[11]

Likewise significant was a late October speech of Senator James H. Hammond, of South Carolina, kinsman of John C. Calhoun and advocate of that Sage's Southern philosophy. Hammond was a co-operationist, a

[8] Okalona, Miss., *Prairie News*, Sept. 16, 1858, termed him 'a designing, double-dealing demagogue, a silvery-tongued, slavery-crusted Abolitionist.'

[9] Port Gibson, Miss., *Daily Southern Reveille*, Sept. 17, 1858; Raymond, Miss., *Hinds County Gazette*, Oct. 13, 1858.

[10] John T. Reid, New Orleans, Nov. 13; H. A. Wise, Richmond, Va., Nov. 12, 1858; Douglas MSS.

[11] W. A. Albee, Olive, N.C., Nov. 21; James A. Nisbet, Macon, Ga., Nov. 5, for Stephens' views; Winslow S. Pierce, Washington, Nov. 9: Dr. Pierce, an Indiana friend visiting the National Capital, reported the attitude of Banks and Pryor, Rust and A. G. Brown; Daniel McCook, Washington, Nov. 7, told of the use of Brown's frank; S. C. Leland, Pinola, Miss., Nov. 6; Oliver Jones, Aberdeen, Miss., Nov. 15; W. H. Lyon, Demopolis, Ala., Nov. 2; W. M. Lowe to A. G. Brown, Florence, Ala., Nov. 18; J. D. Fuller, New Orleans, Nov. 8; Edward Delaney, New Orleans, Nov. 8; Henry O. Langdon, New Orleans, Nov. 8; H. N. Clark, New Orleans, Nov. 9; James Drew, Fort Smith, Ark., Nov. 12; John B. Ficklin, Fredericksburg, Va., Nov. 5; John Kierans, Weston, Va., Nov. 19, Samuel Treat, St. Louis, Nov. 17, 1858; Douglas MSS. Treat quoted Green as having said the Sturgeon charges in the late campaign were 'too insignificant for a moment's consideration.' There was no reason why Lecompton should be made a party test.

believer in Secession but only in co-operation with the other Cotton States. Never did he yield his belief that the black race was 'Providentially designed' to be hewers of wood and drawers of water; never did he abate his insistence, in and out of Congress, that the Southern States must have their 'Constitutional rights and equality in the Union.' Even so, he had a healthy dislike for shams, and frankly told his constituents that the slave trade could never be reopened without dissolving the Union. Furthermore, although he expected African slavery to extend over the world 'wherever climate and soil would warrant it,' he did not think there was any Territory then in the Union which was suitable for slavery. From first to last, the Kansas excitement had been 'the greatest imposition ever practiced on intelligent communities.' Never had he thought that the Territory could, under any possible contingency, become a Slave State — the whole idea was 'preposterous and delusive in the extreme,' and his view had been 'that the South herself should kick that [Lecompton] Constitution out of Congress.' He doubted 'if an affair so rotten from beginning ᴛᴏ end can have any principle at all.' Now, fortunately, Kansas was 'squeezed dry,' the agitation over slavery there was 'dying out for want of fuel.' Upon what measure could the Abolitionists ever again muster their legions as in 1858? 'Will anyone state the practical questions, if we offer them none — and we have none to offer — on which they are next to rally for the conquest of the South?... If the Abolitionists cannot unite the Free States as a purely Anti-Slavery party in the presidential election of 1860, and fail again in 1864, we shall never hear more of them as a political party.' [12]

This new note from the Cotton South caught the instant attention of Northwestern conservatives. 'Except for the bold stand taken by Mr. Douglas,' a Wisconsin leader advised Hammond, 'the Democratic party would have been swept from the Northern States as with a besom of destruction and not a vestige of the wreck would have been left.' [13] It was a shrewd hint. Why battle over formulæ without relevance to actualities? Let the South seek substance, not shadow, and there would be no pretext for a politicians' war.

Douglas' friends generally assumed that the Illinois victory would be but the prelude to the great battle of 1860. 'When is the time for your friends to raise the flag for 1860?' inquired an Ohio leader. Editors from Missouri to Virginia hoisted Douglas' name to the masthead. For years Daniel P. Rhodes measured every act by its effect upon Douglas' presidential aspirations. In 1857 he had burst forth that he was resolved 'to work for this object alone.' Now he sniffed the coming battle, set in motion the campaign for Ohio's delegation to the 1860 gathering at Charleston and wrote his distinguished cousin, 'If I am living I shall be there.' [14]

[12] Charleston *Courier*, Nov. 1, 3, 1858, giving Hammond's speech at Barnwell's Court House, S.C., Oct. 29, 1858. *Ibid.*, July 22, 1858, gives a Hammond speech at Beach Island, S.C., June 22, in which he had said that he 'doubted whether the body of the South would be willing to make an issue of disunion on a single presidential triumph of the adversary.' Merritt, *James Henry Hammond*, 124, quotes Laurence Orr, similarly.

[13] B. Kilborn to Hammond, Milwaukee, Nov. 23, 1858; copy in Douglas MSS.

[14] Wayne Griswold, Circleville, Ohio, Nov. 5; A. Musser, Carrolton, Mo., Nov. 17; James B.

But John W. Forney warned the Little Giant that his foes wanted to get him to Charleston only to take his life, and the people would not consent to enter a fight for delegates, only in the end to be ground under the Administration's heel. Broderick, of California, held with Forney for a battle outside the Democratic organization and the Native Americans felt out Douglas on accepting their nomination.[15]

These men were not far wrong as to Administration fears and intentions.[16] Enraged by the Illinois outcome, Buchanan determined to pursue Douglas with 'relentless fury,' and to remove from Federal office every Douglas sympathizer in the United States. Howell Cobb, who had been laying plans for the nomination, was raging 'like a tiger' and Douglas heard that the Georgian would 'shed his brains' to get him in the Charleston Convention so that the Administration could throttle him.[17]

But there were weighty considerations against Forney's policy. Judge Treat, of St. Louis, urged the necessity for fighting within the party; a triumph so glorious always carried with it the danger of imprudent excesses, and the Buchaneers' hopes rested on convincing the country that Douglas was a bolter. Therefore he must avoid Republican entanglements, keep in the front rank of party champions and let Buchanan, Cobb, Bright and Slidell be the schismatics. Treat thought Hammond's South Carolina speech 'removed all obstacles to harmony.' Douglas' Illinois victory should have shown the South that the Lincoln-Seward program could be defeated in the North, and that if the two sections were to avert a sectional contest, both must look to Douglas.[18]

Many friends urged Douglas to be 'quiet, circumspect and modestly assured.' Edwards Pierrepont wished him to steer clear of the slavery question and to assume his nomination as a matter of course.[19] 'If you could stand before the country for eighteen months as you now stand, 10,000 devils could not prevent your nomination nor your election,' Julius Granger wrote; but his real friends feared some imprudent act. 'Don't come here and pitch into all those *that deserve it*,' he implored. 'You are great in a row, but your rows are so devilish magnificent that you can't get over them the same day. Your fight has been a regular Bridge of Lodi affair, but don't for God's sake, forget that Waterloo came afterwards.'[20]

Murray McConnel predicted a Donnybrook Fair among Southern aspirants for the White House, and thought Douglas, by announcing with-

Steedman, Toledo, Ohio, Nov. 7; P. Henry Aylett, Richmond, Va., Nov. 17; Daniel P. Rhodes, Cleveland, June 15 [1857], Nov. 18, 1858; Douglas MSS.

[15] J. W. Forney, Philadelphia, Nov. 7; James B. Sheridan, Philadelphia, Dec. 8, quoting Broderick; William D. Murphy, New York, Nov. 27, 1858; Douglas MSS.

[16] Duff Green to Buchanan, New York City, Oct. 29, 1858; Buchanan MSS.

[17] James B. Steedman, Toledo, Ohio, Nov. 10, 1858, Douglas MSS. Steedman had sent a Federal office-holder to Washington to discover the inside situation, the emissary had seen Buchanan and Cobb and this was his report.

[18] Samuel Treat, St. Louis, Nov. 17, 1858; Douglas MSS.

[19] Edwards Pierrepont, New York, Nov. 6; John A. Sargeant, New York, Nov. 22; James A. Nisbet, Macon, Ga., Nov. 5, 1858; Douglas MSS.

[20] J. N. Granger, Washington, Nov. 12, 18, 1858; Douglas MSS.

drawal now could so increase the bitterness of Southern rivalry that he would be named himself, probably in 1860 and certainly in 1864. Most of the Little Giant's friends, however, opposed such an announcement on his part. 'Your enemies got that kind of a pledge out of you in 1856,' wrote Washington McLean, a pledge 'which done (*sic*) you infinite damage. . . . Do not let them again be successful, neither seek nor decline.' [21]

The Little Giant soon made his decision and debated only as to the best technique for carrying it out. Inactivity did not fit his nature and within two weeks of the election he was planning a trip through the South. He would travel down the Mississippi to New Orleans and to Cuba, thence back to Washington. This was a realistic move. The flood of congratulations was most pleasing but what did it really represent? Douglas' penetrating insight into Northern psychology enabled him to judge to what extent popular feeling could overcome political machinery, and to work out a reasonably satisfactory index for Northern delegate expectation. But had Lincoln been right in saying, in the Jonesboro debate, that Douglas' Freeport doctrine could pass muster south of the Ohio no better than could Lincoln's own views? So the Little Giant made plans for a journey of political as well as physical recuperation.

Before he left Chicago, he sought to clarify his views for the Southern people. Buchanan's clutch on the party machinery was the most serious obstacle to Douglas' translation of popular support into dependable delegates. None the less, he preferred the ills he knew to those he knew not, and vetoed the plan for a new party. The Chicago *Times* made authoritative editorial announcement that the Democrats of Illinois pledged 'fidelity to the organization, principles, and nominees of the Democratic party,' and that the Little Giant would submit himself entirely to the Charleston Convention, with implicit confidence in its decision.[22]

Stating that Douglas held 'no sentiments or wishes upon political questions which are not universally shared and asserted by the Democracy of Illinois,' the *Times* laid down the eleven points of Illinois belief upon the controverted slavery issue. The most important departure from the Ultra Southern viewpoint was that, while the Democracy of Illinois supported the Dred Scott decision in the sense that it sought to assure owners of slaves of an equality with owners of other property in being introduced into the Territories, property in slaves, 'like all other property, must be subject to all local laws of the Territory as do not infringe upon the Constitution of the United States.' If, after thus being placed on an equality with other property being introduced into a Territory, property in slaves should 'require higher and further affirmative legislation for its protection and security than is afforded to other property,' and the Territorial Legislature should not accord it, that would be 'a misfortune attending that

---

[21] Murray McConnel, Washington, Dec. 10; Washington McLean, Cincinnati, Dec. 15, 1858; Douglas MSS. For list of Southern presidential aspirants as early as January, 1858, see James H. Hammond to William Gilmore Sims, Washington, Jan. 20, March 24, 1858, quoted, Elizabeth Merritt, *James Henry Hammond*, Baltimore, 1923; 121.

[22] Chicago *Times*, Nov. 11, 1858; O. B. Ficklin, Charleston, Ill., Nov. 14, 1858; Douglas MSS.

description of property for which the Democratic party have no remedy and are not responsible.' [23]

This considered bid represented the utmost concession Douglas felt able to make to the South upon slavery in the Territories. Just before he left Chicago, he told the editor of the Chicago *Journal* that he had no peace to make with Buchanan because he had made no war. However, should a bill be introduced to reopen the slave trade or to establish a Congressional code for protecting property in slaves in the Territories, he would immediately oppose it. Buchanan and his Administration had 'reduced Negroes to the status of mules'; having done so, they must be content with legislation which would protect mules. Nor did he seem to Ray eager for the presidential race. 'He was still a young man, only forty-five years old, and could wait until the signs came right.' Then too, he knew that there were a hundred hidden rocks in the stream; that when he got to Washington, 'traps would be set for him by both parties, to sever him from the Southern Democracy or the Northern.' But he was 'going straight ahead, and consequences and gin-traps might take care of themselves.' [24]

The Douglases reached Springfield on November 22. A great throng greeted the Senator at the depot, a thirty-two-gun salute signaled his arrival, bonfires lit his way to the St. Nicholas Hotel and for two days Springfield held an old-time Democratic jubilee.[25] Then Douglas and Adèle made their way to Alton, where they took passage on the packet *City of Memphis* to New Orleans. At every landing Douglas was met with a crowd manifesting its confidence and approval in his course. Douglas' Memphis supporters made elaborate plans for his reception. Led by 'Lean Jimmy' Jones, J. Knox Walker, James K. Polk's nephew and Governor Matthews of Mississippi, a large committee went up the river to meet the *City of Memphis*. Sunday afternoon the steamboat laid up at the Memphis wharf, Douglas was pressed to speak to the people the next day, and agreed to do so.

There was need for him to offset the extremist views Jefferson Davis had just enunciated. Returning from New England, that Senator had addressed the Mississippi Legislature upon 'the dangers confronting the South,' terming Douglas' doctrine heresy. The Little Giant, having said he would not favor a Congressional code to support slavery in the Territories, would not do, and the South must look to Buchanan. Moreover, Davis, who had visited the White House, assured them that the President would 'not shrink a hair's breadth from the position he has taken,' but 'would take another step in advance.' Douglas' repudiation might result in electing a Black Republican President in 1860, but the South's remedy was secession from the Union, not submission to Douglas' candidacy.[26]

[23] Chicago *Times*, Nov. 11, 1858. This editorial was generally reprinted throughout the country.

[24] C. H. Ray to Elihu Washburne, Chicago, Nov. 22, 1858; Washburne MSS., Chicago Public Library. Ray, an ardent Republican, added that 'beyond that everlasting cackle about "my great principle" I found little to object to in his talk.' Medill to Colfax, quoted, Hollister, 123–24.

[25] *Illinois State Register*, Nov. 23, 25, 1858.

[26] Dunbar Rowland, *Jefferson Davis, Constitutionalist*, Jackson, Miss., 1923; III, 339–60.

While this insistence on a Congressional slave code gave the cue to the Ultras of both sections, there was prompt counter-attack by the Moderates, even in Mississippi, where Henry S. Foote issued a public letter rebuking Davis. 'A further step' by Buchanan could endanger the Union by forcing the election of a Black Republican President, but the South's obvious escape from 'such a grievous public calamity' was to rally around Douglas, 'a sterling, high-toned patriot' and the South's hope against Disunion.[27] This new debate while he was en route South made it more necessary than ever that Douglas warn the South of the limits of Northern Democratic co-operation and of the dangers of blind folly. This he undertook to do at Memphis.

Monday noon 'an immense crowd' gathered at Exchange Hall to greet the Little Giant. Introduced by Senator Jones as a friend of the South, Douglas took occasion to show the people that his words and his principles were 'the same in Tennessee as in Illinois.' 'As long as we live under a common political Constitution,' he insisted, 'the principles of that Constitution ought to be the same in every State. The creed which cannot be a national one must be wrong.' He had gone into his contest with Lincoln mainly 'to see if there was no common platform upon which both the North and the South might stand.' He reviewed some of the major issues of the late campaign, particularly Lincoln's House Divided doctrine, and his strictures on the Supreme Court. 'Before the contest was over,' Douglas said proudly, 'Mr. Lincoln was driven from every plank of his platform.'

Uniformity was not a national blessing; variety of climate and soil had created a variety of interest, 'hence it does not follow that slavery is as good for the North as for the South,' and each State must decide for itself. Deciding that slavery was not adapted to its soil and climate, Illinois had abolished it, 'but Illinois said to the South, work out your own salvation... To Tennessee, if you want slavery, have it, it is your right. Be content to exercise sovereign power yourself, and we will be friends.' The South should stand by the Constitution regardless of expediency; 'if you deem it treason for Abolitionists to appeal to the passions and prejudices of the North for the purpose of overriding these principles, how much less treason is it, my friends, for Southern men to appeal to the passions with the same end?'

The question of slavery in the Federal Territories had been 'the greatest disturbing element' in recent national history. In the North there had been a delusion that she had 'an exclusive right and interest to establish freedom for the Territories, while the same delusion has existed in the South with respect to her exclusive right and interest to establish slavery within them.' He went on that 'the Constitution recognized no such distinction of sectional

---

[27] Henry S. Foote to D. Mitchell, W. P. Anderson, etc., Jackson, Miss., Nov. 30, 1858, carried in Vicksburg, Miss., *Whig*, Dec. 5, 1858. The South could do this either by the Southern Democrats taking up Douglas, or by the intelligent Moderates of the South dropping the Democratic party and forming a completely new one, with Douglas as its leader. Foote felt sure that unless the Southern Moderates asserted themselves, Douglas could not be nominated at Charleston; 'nearly all the prominent Democratic leaders and astute managers of caucus machinery are utterly opposed to him. The presidential patronage would all be brought into deadly conflict with his pretensions.'

rights or interest. For either the North or the South to interfere to deprive Kansas of what she desires is a violation of the rights of the people of Kansas.' He had not opposed the Lecompton Constitution because of its slavery clause, but because he did not believe it the act and deed of the people of Kansas, and it was fundamental that 'the people have the right to decide the question of goodness or badness for themselves.'

He was careful to repeat his Freeport doctrine. Chief Justice Taney had held that slaves ought to be protected as other property under the Constitution, and that slave-holders could take them, as they could other property, into the Territories. But the actual question was, What was the condition of that property when it went into the Territories? Then it was subject to local law just as dry-goods were subject to local laws.

'Wherever climate, soil and production combine to encourage the use of slave labor,' he announced, 'the people will accept and protect it, and wherever these circumstances do not exist, the contrary result will follow.... It is visionary to talk of planting slavery where it is not wanted, and it is equally folly in the Northern fanatic to attempt to exclude it where it is wanted.... I have never thought proper to disguise the fact that, if the people desire slavery, they are entitled to have it, and I am content with the result. But I would not be instrumental in attempting to force a Constitution upon an unwilling people.' These principles afforded the only common ground upon which union and peace could be found. And these and union were necessary for America to fulfill her destiny.[28]

This sensible presentation of the considered attitude of the Northern Democracy brought a fine response from the country. Forney, who had been alarmed by the Ultras' demand for a slave code, was now reassured. A Western Democrat sent Douglas an account of John C. Calhoun's statement to him eighteen years before, that Congress had no power to protect slavery in a Territory — 'a *casus omissus* in the Constitution, for which there was no remedy' — an observation in direct line with Douglas' Freeport doctrine![29] Archibald Dixon wrote Douglas to fight on, Kentucky would be his in 1860. The Memphis *Appeal* declared that 'if such doctrines as these be treason, and their advocate a "traitor," and if the Southern people are ready and disposed to ostracise and cut loose from every Northern man who upholds them, then indeed has the time for Secession and dissolution come.' [30]

But the Southern Radicals considered Douglas' words highly dangerous because so plausible, and their speakers and papers redoubled their vilification and abuse of him. A paper at Port Gibson sneered that 'Douglas is his name, duplicity is the chief element in his character, he knows no country, no friendship, no party, no patriotism, nothing but Stephen A. Douglas.' A Davis editor opined that Douglas' election would be a remedy 'worse than the disease which it is proposed to guard against' — the election of a

[28] Memphis *Daily Appeal*, Nov. 30, 1858.

[29] W. W. Wick, Indianapolis, Dec. 8, 1858; Douglas MSS. Howard, of Indiana, had been with Wick in Washington, a July night of 1840, when Calhoun made the remembered remark.

[30] J. W. Forney, Philadelphia, Nov. 27; Archibald Dixon, Henderson, Ky., Dec. 2, 1858; Douglas MSS.; Memphis *Appeal* editorial, clipped in *Illinois State Register*, Nov. 27, 1858.

Republican President. Douglas did not lack newspaper support in the State, but the Ultras' bitter partisan attitude was responsible for the failure of the Mississippi Legislature, still in session at Jackson, to invite Douglas to address it.[31]

Thenceforth to New Orleans Douglas was everywhere received politely, often cordially, occasionally with great enthusiasm. He made no speeches in Mississippi, but when the steamboat stopped at Vicksburg he went ashore and saw 'with his own eyes 300 of those recently imported miserable beings in the slave-pens.' [32] The sight of these Negroes freshly smuggled in from the Gold Coast stiffened his determination not to yield to the new Southern demand for reopening the African slave trade.[32]

The Senator's New Orleans friends undertook to give him a grand reception. Pierre Soulé formed a committee and the *True Delta* trumpeted the occasion. When the steamer neared the wharves, Douglas was greeted with a salute and an illumination, escorted to the St. Charles Hotel by a crack military company and a great throng of people. There the Mayor welcomed him, Soulé applauded Douglas' recent course and he responded with unwonted modesty.[33] His rooms were crowded with politicians, most of whom were impressed with his frankness and his charm; so much so that indignant Ultras sneered that he was doing 'the lowest-down electioneering for the Presidency.' [34] Douglas' formal address on December 6, followed closely the lines of his Memphis speech, but added a statement regarding Cuba. It was folly to debate the acquisition of the island, which naturally belonged to the American continent, Douglas said, but he favored no filibuster: the acquisition must be on terms honorable to America, Cuba and Spain.[35]

From Louisiana the Douglases sought Havana, where Adèle's time was chiefly given to sight-seeing and recreation, but her husband also sought first-hand information about the real condition of Spain's unhappy province. Then they sailed for America, landing at New York two days before New Year's.

[31] Port Gibson, Miss., *Daily Southern Reveille*, Dec. 4; Jackson, Miss., *Mississippian State Gazette*, Dec. 8, 22, 1858. Major Ethelbert Barksdale, its editor, added that not three members of the Legislature failed to concur with the paper in its opposition to Douglas. The Vicksburg *Whig* and the *True Southron* defended the Illinois Senator.

[32] Rhodes, II, 371. Douglas had also seen some in Memphis — perhaps those offered for sale by the not yet famous Nathan Bedford Forrest. Carlinville, Ill., *Free Democrat*, Sept. 8, 1859, quotes Douglas about the Vicksburg slave-pen, and that 'there had been more slaves imported ... during the last year' than ever before in a year, even when the trade was legal.

[33] Sheahan, 524. Pierre Soulé, *et al.*, New Orleans, Dec. 2, 1858; Douglas MSS.; Douglas' response to invitation; retained copy, Martin F. Douglas MSS.

[34] Jackson *Mississippian State Gazette*, Dec. 8, 1858, letter signed 'A Mississippi Democrat,' New Orleans, Dec. 4. Particular offense was taken to the Douglas remark 'that nearly all aspirants for the Presidency had combined against him for no other purpose than to defeat him for that station, and that it was not because of his sentiments.' The writer added the hope that 'there will be no man go to the convention at Charleston from this State who will favor the nomination of S. A. Douglas or who will not be in favor of breaking up such a convention in the event of such a nomination.'

[35] New Orleans *True Delta*, Dec. 8, 1858.

Manhattan's Democracy gave Douglas an extraordinary ovation. A Philadelphia committee escorted him from New York to their city, where he was greeted at Independence Hall by the Mayor. The jubilee at Baltimore redoubled when Douglas received the telegram announcing his election by the Illinois Legislature. Buchanan henchmen pleased their master by reports that his enemy's visits had been failures and had 'crushed out the last of Douglasism' in Philadelphia and Baltimore. In truth, however, it was a triumphal procession. At Washington, thousands gathered at the station, accompanied the Senator to Minnesota Row and insisted on a speech. Douglas had won 'a complete and perfect triumph' with the rank and file of the Northern Democrats.[36]

But his reception by official Washington, ever a national blind spot, was as frigid as that by the people had been warm. Undertaking to make the Little Giant rue the day that he had dared to cross 'Old Obliquity,' the Buchanan cabal had opened the war as soon as Congress opened. For eleven years Douglas had been Chairman of the Senate Committee of Territories, a position of commanding importance in adolescent America. During his years in Congress, a dozen Territories had been organized and a dozen States had come into the Union; the whole technique of conferring statehood was his creation and his pride. This was the vital spot to which Buchanan and his Senatorial Machiavelli, John Slidell, directed their thrust. Thus when Douglas reached Washington he found Senator Green had his chairmanship. The deed had been done secretly in the Senate's Democratic caucus, the simple announcement being made that James S. Green, of Missouri, had been chosen Chairman of the Committee on Territories. No Senator gave any reason for the change until the next Summer, when Gwin, of California, said Douglas' Freeport doctrine had required this reprimand.[37]

This action evoked 'curses loud and bitter' from the Little Giant's friends. 'We have been outraged almost beyond endurance by the Democratic caucus of the Danite department,' an Illinois Democratic member wrote Lanphier; the decapitation, a 'piece of low-flung madness and malevolence,' meant 'farewell to all hope of harmony and all hopes of the success of the Charleston nominee in 1860.'[38] But far from destroying Douglas, 'this miserable meanness' made him the hero of the Northern Democracy. No one had believed the President's weak denial that he had ordered the swinging of the axe. All could see that the Administration war on Douglas grew more bitter every day. Washington filled with the talk that the two-thirds rule was Buchanan's 'last ray of hope' to keep Douglas from a Charleston victory.[39]

[36] Rhodes, II, 311. W. E. Lehman, Chairman of Committee, telegram, Philadelphia, Jan. 1, 1859; Douglas MSS. J. B. Baker, Philadelphia, Jan. 4; Levi K. Bowen, Baltimore, Jan. 6, 1859; Buchanan MSS. James B. Steedman, Toledo, Ohio, Jan. 5, 1859; Douglas MSS.

[37] Sheahan, 500, Dr. Gwin's speech was at Grass Valley, Cal.

[38] S. S. Marshall, Washington, Dec. 9, 1858; Patton MSS.

[39] James B. Steedman, Toledo, Ohio, Jan. 5, 1859; Douglas MSS. J. N. Morris, Washington, Dec. 18; I. C. Allen, Washington, Dec., 1858; Patton MSS.

Friends renewed their urgings that he be 'circumspect, discreet, sagacious,' not pitch into the Senators who had outraged him but 'treat the matter with dignified contempt.' [40] And he knew that Buchanan's blundering blow had helped rather than hurt him in the North; perhaps he also hoped that the bitterness of the Southern Ultras would be lessened; perhaps he merely had determined that his enemies must show their hand. But whatever the reason, all remarked the fact — Douglas kept silent upon the critical Territorial issue, indulged in no recriminations but took up the legislative routine.

Early in January he advocated the Pacific railroad bill, again before Congress. A little later, attending a caucus of Senate Democrats called to discuss a Cuban program, he reiterated that he was in favor of acquiring Cuba by any proper means. These efforts to keep his temper, seemingly out of character with Stephen A. Douglas, brought criticism that he was 'playing the game too low down.' A Kentucky stalwart wrote Crittenden that Douglas, in his attempt to prove himself 'a whole-souled Democrat,' had 'run himself out of breath trying to keep up,' and would be forced to take a bold stand — too late.[41]

Douglas' foes at both ends of the Avenue were irritated, and the rumor sped through Washington that, should an 'accident' remove him, the President would be quite pleased. Soon it was whispered that it had been determined at a caucus at Cobb's home that John Slidell should insult Douglas in the Senate bar, force the quarrel and shoot him down. One of Douglas' newspaper friends dispatched a note of warning. 'If you are pushed to the wall,' the correspondent advised, 'send for Tom Hawkins, of Louisville' — a famous shot of the 'Fifties. Douglas sent for Major Hawkins and the event showed that it was a prudent move.[42]   •

Trouble did ensue, but from Fitch, of Indiana, Bright's jackal. Buchanan sent to the Senate a long list of Danites and Douglas' personal enemies to be nominated for jobs in Illinois, a deliberate slap in Douglas' face. When the Senate was in executive session on them, the Little Giant said bluntly that many of the nominees were dishonest and corrupt — a charge, alas! too true.

Buchanan's nominee for United States Attorney at Chicago was the son of Senator Fitch, of Indiana. Douglas had not included young Fitch in his excoriation but the father twisted his remarks into an excuse for a wanton, unprovoked and unjustifiable affront to the Little Giant. Fitch was a huge, powerful fellow and a known marksman, but his language was so unpardonable that it could neither be misconstrued nor overlooked. Major Hawkins and Roger Pryor soon handed Fitch a note from Douglas, demanding that he withdraw the offensive language.

Senator Benjamin brought Fitch's response. Douglas deemed it unsatisfactory and was about to send a formal challenge but Pryor and Hawkins persuaded him to give the Indiana bully one further chance for peace.

[40] Albert Smith, Boston, Dec. 11, 1858; Douglas MSS.

[41] R. P. Letcher, Frankfort, Ky., Jan. 20, 26, 1858; Crittenden MSS.

[42] Stevens, 658, quoting letter to Chicago *Tribune* of George Alfred Townsend — 'Gath' — the correspondent involved.

The correspondence continued until Fitch finally made a clumsy withdrawal which, 'under the unanimous advice of his friends,' Douglas accepted as satisfactory. Throughout the affair, Pryor declared, the Senator 'conducted himself with the courage which was a distinguishing element of his character. Indeed, I never knew a man of more immovable firmness or of greater indifference to personal danger.'[43]

January was marked by Democratic meetings and conventions and by the expressions of State Legislatures upon national affairs. Kentucky's State Democratic Convocation repudiated the establishment of any new party test and refused to endorse Lecomptonism. Danites in the Illinois Legislature introduced a pro-Buchanan resolution but it was promptly voted down. There were 175,000 Ohio Democrats ready to vote for Douglas, men 'who would not stoop to ask favors of Mr. Buchanan even if they were hungry and naked.' And Douglas could be assured of the State's entire delegation.[44] The proprietor of a new Boston paper agreed with a New York leader that Douglas had the Democratic masses; 'all that is needful is to secure and retain the organization.'

In the South some of the violent had grown silent and others now proclaimed that they had 'always believed' Douglas right. The Speaker of North Carolina's House and other prominent men came out for him. Terming the Administration's Kansas policy 'a disgrace to the nation,' one of Green's chief Missouri lieutenants declared for Douglas.[45] His probable nomination was freely discussed and Ultra Southern journals began to take alarm. Even if Douglas should win at Charleston, thundered Jefferson Davis' chief home organ, it would be 'an act of humiliation utterly unpardonable' for Mississippi's Democracy to support him.[46]

In gathering a staff, Douglas was handicapped by the loss of that loyal friend and shrewd political psychologist Thomas L. Harris, who had died while his chief was on his Southern journey. But the Senator did not lack for substitutes. For a contact man to send out through the country, he selected A. D. Banks, a Virginia editor with long experience and a multitude of friendly contacts. John W. Forney and his allies fell to work in Pennsyl-

---

[43] Cincinnati *Enquirer*, Aug. 2, 1885, printing Indianapolis dispatch containing the Douglas-Fitch correspondence. For Pryor detail, see Roger A. Pryor to Judge Walter B. Douglas, of St. Louis, New York, Nov. 14, 1885, printed, Stevens, 663–64.

[44] W. A. Cocke, Louisville, Jan. 10; J. H. Harney, Louisville, Jan. 13; James B. Steedman, Toledo, Ohio, Jan. 5; Wayne Griswold, Circleville, Ohio, Jan. 18; D. P. Rhodes, Cleveland, Ohio, Jan. 20; Geo. P. Buell, Cincinnati, Jan. 24; George Gillaspy, Ottumwa, Iowa, Feb. 28, 1859; Douglas MSS. Isaac Cook, Chicago, Feb. 14, 1859; Buchanan MSS.

[45] Lewis Josselyn, Boston, Jan. 4; his paper was the Boston *North*; Peter Dunbar, Boston, Jan. 16; D. A. Smalley, Burlington, Vt., Feb. 1; J. C. Palmer, Hartford, Conn., Feb. 4; James T. Pratt, Rockhill, Conn., Feb. 15; C. C. Fellows, Centre Sandwich, N.H., Feb. 26; Wm. H. Ludlow, Sayville, L.I., N.Y., Jan. 28; C. S. Whitney, San Francisco, Feb. 18; C. R. Harris, Brandy Station, Va., Jan. 3; John E. Manley, Clarksville, Ark., Jan. 4; J. F. Simmons, Weldon, N.C., Jan. 22; A. L. Gillstrap, Bloomington, Mo., Jan. 22; Thos. S. Drew, Fort Smith, Ark., Jan. 24, 1859; Douglas MSS.

[46] *Mississippian State Gazette*, Jackson, Feb. 16, 1859.

vania and the Middle States. Dean Richmond and the New York Softs laid their lines for a Douglas delegation. Solomon Parsons renewed his political travels in New England and Douglas' Ohio friends became active.

Of the key men, perhaps none was shrewder than James W. Singleton, of Quincy, who discounted the surface signs, noted the local politicians' 'mad, blind and infamous servility' to the White House and advised Douglas that actually he was occupying an anomalous and highly dangerous situation.

Let him beware of pretended friends who, 'under the guise of disinterested friendship,' would sell off his chances for the smallest crumb of office. Let him beware the advice of any who urged him to withdraw from the coming race — this was 'the contrivance of an enemy.' He could not reconcile his rivals and had better drive them forth into open opposition. Douglas and his friends must go to work at once to control the gathering at Charleston; if then a Southern minority should bolt, the odium would be upon the seceders; 'there is no hope but in determined resistance, coupled with efficient organization.' [47]

Douglas' trouble with Fitch increased the Senate tension, and the Southern Ultras found it more and more difficult to maintain silence on the Freeport 'heresy.' On February 23 the storm broke and by that day's adjournment all hopes of agreement between Douglas and the Ultras had been riven by debate.

The first thunderbolt was hurled by Albert Gallatin Brown. A warm personal friend of Douglas, Brown agreed with him on practically every political issue except slavery. But an intense conviction as to the South's slave rights, to which was added the need to maintain himself in his bitter struggle with Jefferson Davis for party dominance in Mississippi, now led Brown to court an open break with the Little Giant. [48]

The Senate was considering a provocative Kansas amendment which Hale, of New Hampshire, had offered, probably in hope of precipitating the Democratic battle. Availing himself of the pretext, Brown began by announcing that he wished neither to cheat nor to be cheated in the 1860 contest, and intended to bring the Territorial question into the open. 'We have a right of protection for our slave property in the Territories,' he declared. 'The Constitution, as expounded by the Supreme Court, awards it. We demand it and we mean to have it.' Some Senators contended that this right depended on action by the Territorial Legislature, but Brown held that any such doctrine confused a power and a right. 'What I want to know is whether you will interpose against power and in favor of right,' he demanded. 'If the Territorial Legislature refuses to act, will you act?...

[47] J. W. Singleton, Quincy, Ill., Feb. 21, 1859; Douglas MSS.

[48] S. P. McCutchen, 'Albert Gallatin Brown,' MSS. Dissertation, University of Chicago Library, reveals the struggle between Brown and Davis for primacy in Mississippi. There was personal feeling as well as political rivalry between the two, and each sought to oust the other from power by taking a more and more advanced position on slavery. Their duel continued until Davis became President of the Confederacy. I am indebted to Dr. W. E. Dodd, of the University of Chicago, for calling my attention to Dr. McCutchen's dissertation. A. G. Brown, Terry Hinds Co., Miss., Sept. 10, 1859, Douglas MSS., speaks of his 'cordial personal friendship' for Douglas and his political agreement with him 'in all things save niggers.'

If it pass laws hostile to slavery, will you annul them and substitute laws favoring slavery in their stead?' He and his people had never entered any compromise 'which would release Congress from an obligation imposed on it by the Constitution of the United States,' and so he and they insisted upon 'positive, unqualified action.' If he could not obtain the rights guaranteed under the Constitution, as expounded by the Supreme Court, his mind would be 'forced irresistibly to the conclusion that the Constitution is a failure, and the Union a despotism, and then, Sir, I am prepared to retire from the concern.' [49]

Douglas began by saying that he admired Brown's frankness and candor, and he hoped to put his own opinions on the record in a manner that would acquit him 'of the slightest suspicion of desire to cheat or be cheated.' Under the Dred Scott decision, slaves were property on an equal footing with other property and consequently the owner of the slaves has the full right to emigrate to a Territory, and carry his slave property with him.

But to what extent was property, slaves included, subject to the Territory's local law? Douglas insisted the Territorial Legislatures had power over slave property 'to the same extent and no further' than over other property. Brown had contended that there was something peculiar in slave property requiring a protection beyond that other property needed. 'If so,' Douglas responded, 'it is the misfortune of those who own that species of property. He tells us that, if the Territorial Legislature fails to pass a slave code for the Territories... the absence of such legislation practically excludes slave property as effectually as a Constitutional prohibition would exclude it. I agree to that proposition. He says, furthermore, that it is competent for the Territorial Legislature, by the exercise of the taxing power and other functions within the limits of the Constitution, to adopt unfriendly legislation which practically drives slavery out of the Territory. I agree to that proposition. That is just what I said, and all I said, and just what I meant by my Freeport speech.'

Then Douglas took up the demand that if a Territorial Legislature would not enact a slave code, Congress must do it. Brown's conclusion was logical unless Douglas' own position were right. All men must agree that nonaction by the Territorial Legislature was practical exclusion. 'I never would vote for a slave code in the Territories by Congress,' he continued, 'and I have yet to learn that there is a man in a free State of this Union, of any party, who would.' Furthermore, no 'Democratic candidate can ever carry any one Democratic State of the North on the platform that it is the duty of the Federal Government to force the people of a Territory to have slavery when they do not want it.'

This brought Jefferson Davis to his feet. Douglas had asked whether the owner of a slave desiring to take his slave property into a Territory expected a greater measure of legal protection for that property than would be given property in dry-goods, liquors, horses or cattle. 'I say yes,' Davis answered. 'I would discriminate in the Territories wherever it is necessary to assert

[49] *Congressional Globe*, Thirty-Fifth Congress, Second Session, 1241 *et seq.*

the right of a citizen.' The South now claimed no more from the Federal Government than the men who had framed the Constitution were willing to concede. If Douglas were right and this were a doctrine unpopular in the North, then Davis' vote could be gotten for no candidate not willing thus to be defeated: 'We are not, with our eyes open, to be cheated.'

The mantle of John C. Calhoun seemed to have fallen on Jefferson Davis as he erected the constitutional arguments for this new extension of pro-slavery demands. He insisted that a Territory's right of Popular Sovereignty did not commence until its people were ready to form a Constitution and become a State. Until then the people of a Territory were merely tenants for the Federal Government, which itself held the Territory as trustee for its co-partners, the different States. Congress delegated its powers to the Territorial Legislatures, whose only power came through this delegation.

The Little Giant was rising from his chair to counter Davis' thin though plausible logistics but Mason, of Virginia, who first gained recognition, continued the Mississippian's argument.[50] When Douglas finally secured the floor, Mason demanded that he define a slave code. Douglas did so in the terms Brown himself had used. Green demanded to know whether Douglas would submit to a Territorial statute for the punishment of larceny which excepted the larceny of slaves. 'While all other property is dependent on the Territorial Legislature for protection,' Douglas answered, 'I hold that slave property must look to the same authority for its protection.'

His argument was bottomed on economic common sense rather than on legalism. 'If the people think that particular laws on the subject of property are beneficial to their interests,' he insisted, 'they will enact them. If they do not think such laws are wise, they will refrain from enacting them. They will protect slaves there provided they want slavery; and they will want slavery if the climate be such that the white man cannot cultivate the soil, so as to render Negro compulsory labor necessary. Hence it becomes a question of climate, of production, of self-interest, and not a question of legislation, whether slavery shall or shall not exist there.'

This passage-at-arms had an acrimonious climax when Davis charged hotly that Douglas was playing the demagogue, and was building up a political reputation 'by catering to the prejudice of a majority to exclude the property of a minority.' Douglas answered angrily that he mourned 'to see men from other sections of the Union pandering to a public sentiment against what I conceive to be common rights under the Constitution.' He was very certain that Congress should not force slavery on the people of the Territories against their will.

---

[50] His points were three: first, the Dred Scott decision established that Congress had no power to prohibit slavery in a Territory. Next, Douglas himself was on record that a Territory's legislative power was not inherent but derived. Finally, the people of a Territory could have no right to prohibit slavery; if they sought to do so by non-action, Congress must take appropriate action to prevent this wrong. Mason's argument was weak in its second premise. Douglas had admitted that the power of a Territorial Legislature was derived, but he had derived it not solely from the organic Act of Congress, but from the Constitution through the organic Act.

Davis termed Douglas 'full of heresy,' and warned that he could not get Mississippi's vote. Douglas said the time would come when Davis would seek quarter. 'I scorn your quarter,' Davis shouted fiercely. It was the final break between the realists and the heirs of John C. Calhoun.[51]

[51] Davis and Douglas had never liked one another, and their friction was often in evidence. Early in 1855, when Davis was Secretary of War, Douglas protested against having the promotion of George E. Pickett to an Army captaincy charged to Illinois' portion of the general patronage. Davis to Douglas, Washington, April, 1855, Douglas MSS., rebuked Douglas because Pickett, 'by his Conspicuous Gallantry in battle,' etc., had earned a reputation 'to which every American citizen may lay claim as the property of the whole country.' Pickett came from Richmond, Va., but had been named to West Point from the fifth Illinois District. It was his division which made the final charge at Gettysburg.

CHAPTER XXIII

THE STRUGGLE WITH THE ULTRAS

AFTER this the stream of American events flowed swiftly from crisis to climax to catastrophe. Pondering the war ensuing, one cannot escape the question: Need it all have been?

Superficially the record seems to support the conventional explanation of irrepressible conflict between blind forces fated to test their strength in blood. But it is easy to read cause and effect into episodes with merely a time relation; when one breaks the tough crust of the 'Fifties and the truth begins to piece together, Chance seems to have played as great a part as Fate in shaping the sequence of events.

It was the tragedy of the epoch that, in North and South alike, Extremist minorities manipulated the machinery of the parties, seized the tools of government and committed the two sections to a brothers' war. But often it seemed that the Moderates were about to quell the storm. As late as March of 1860 there was good chance to avert Secession. Had the mechanism for the Democratic presidential nomination been responsive to real party feeling, the Southern Ultras could not have won enough delegates to Charleston for their bolt to have been important. And Charleston really began the Civil War.

Through these months of frantic turmoil one sees Douglas employing his great powers for compromise and common sense — and almost winning. It required a combination of James Buchanan's hatred, the Fire-Eaters' frenzy and the caprice of Chance to bring his failure, with its dire consequences.

At that, there was more to the battle between Douglas and the Ultras than mere personal feud. A few, like Davis, personally disliked the Little Giant but some extremist leaders loved the man. Albert Gallatin Brown had a real personal affection. In the Georgia hustings, in 1860, someone asked Robert Toombs if Douglas really were a great man. The Georgian's great voice boomed back: 'There has been but one greater, and he the Apostle Paul.'[1]

Until the debate of February 23, Douglas hoped the Ultras would discuss the status of slave property in the Territories from the standpoint of common sense as well as of the Constitution. He knew a thoughtful examination of realities would show slavery an economic anachronism too costly for the South to maintain. Also the Ultras' platform seemed so hopeless of attainment and, if gained, so empty of reward, that it must have been brought forward chiefly for trading purposes.

While right as to economics, Douglas gave insufficient weight to the psychological compulsions behind the demand for a Congressional slave code. As with all Absolutist efforts, the Ultra program could not admit

[1] A. G. Brown, Terry, Hinds County, Miss., Sept. 10, 1859; Douglas MSS.; Pleasant A. Stovall, *Robert Toombs*, New York, 1892; 165.

concession or compromise. Then, too, no matter how thin and unsubstantial might be their logistics, the Ultra leaders knew full well that once they relaxed their agitation and the spell was broken, Moderates would replace them in office and in power.

While Davis, of Mississippi; Hunter, of Virginia; Iverson, of Georgia; Clement Clay, of Alabama, and Wigfall, of Texas, upheld the Ultra cause in the Senate, William L. Yancey, of Alabama, was its agitating genius on the hustings. For years he had been preaching full equal rights or withdrawal. The John the Baptist of Secession, Yancey was a platform power; imposing in appearance, he resembled John C. Calhoun in his restraint of statement and deliberation of speech: once grant his starting premise and the conclusion could not be assailed. Nor did he temper his expressions to geography but proclaimed his doctrine in Faneuil Hall. Second to Yancey as propagandists among the people were R. Barnwell Rhett, of the Charleston *Mercury*, and Edmund Ruffin, of Virginia. Buchanan's Federal office-holders, 'active, boisterous professional politicians,' were the drill sergeants for the faction's rank and file. So active were they that an Alabama Conservative complained to Douglas that they were 'trying to bring about a sort of reign of terror' to control the South.[2]

During the Summer of 1859 the Ultras agreed on a fighting program so extreme that the Democracy of the North could never accept it. This they knew, but part of their purpose was to use that rejection as new proof that the Ultra program was the South's protection. Its outlines, as disclosed to Douglas by Albert Gallatin Brown, were to demand at Charleston 'a platform explicitly declaring that slave property is entitled, in the Territories and on the high seas, to the same protection that is given to any other and every other species of property. Failing to get it, she will retire from the Convention. The South will demand of the Congress that it afford protection to her people in their lives, liberty and property. If Congress refuses,... we will as our right resist the Government and throw off its authority.'

Full equal rights — that was the flame point of agitation. Senator Hammond, of South Carolina, might be right that slavery's Territorial relations no longer presented any actual practical problem, but to the Fire-Eaters these realities did not matter: Southern Rights must be demanded to the last letter of the Constitution. 'Any assumption, direct or indirect, that a law-giver may in any way discriminate against slave property,' the Mississippi Senator insisted, 'is insulting to us as equals.' The Southern States were constitutionally entitled to full justice and equality, and 'I hope we shall all be damned together if we consent to take less.'[3]

But Douglas remained unpersuaded that the Ultras reflected the attitude of a majority of the Southern people. He had not forgotten how, in 1850, the Southern people had emphatically repudiated a Secession plan. Now his mail revealed the pattern of the Southern mind. While most of his 'famous friends' were silent, a myriad of lesser political lights replaced them. Then there was an amazing outpouring of opinion from merchants,

[2] J. W. Lapsley, Selma, Ala., Dec. 12, 1859; Douglas MSS.
[3] A. G. Brown, Terry, Hinds County, Miss., Sept. 10, 1859; Douglas MSS.

bankers, professional men and slave-holding planters endorsing Douglas' candidacy and platform. The masses had 'no sympathy with the Radicals,' wrote one observer; 'the Fire-Eaters' doctrine finds no echo in the people's hearts,' were typical observations.[4]

In addition to the Ultras, the candidate must overcome Buchanan's opposition and the alliance of the 'favorite sons.' At times Buchanan's hatred of the Little Giant reached the point at which the mention of Douglas' name almost gave him apoplexy. He made no bones about the fact that his whole policy was framed with the single purpose of effecting Douglas' overthrow at Charleston.[5] By late Spring, the proscription as to Douglas' friends was in full swing all through the North, and Slidell kept up a stream of suggestions as to men whose necks should feel the axe. At the same time the Administration men tried to seduce the Little Giant's delegates. In one district a contract for supplying the Navy with live-oak would be dangled; in another, land patent favors; in still others appointments as postmasters, marshals and collectors; everywhere the office-holding army sought to storm conventions and precipitate contests. Buchanan was a dull and flabby Samson, but he exhibited great energy and resource in pulling down the pillars of his temple and destroying his enemy along with his party, his country and himself.[6]

John Slidell headed 'Old Obliquity's' general staff for the war on Douglas. Tammany-trained, a master of political intrigue and ballot-box manipulation, the Louisiana Senator thrilled with the feel of power and cared little how he employed it. His chief aides were men of less ability but of comparable political morality. Jesse D. Bright now entered the final phases of a career

[4] Space does not admit of any full citation of the hundreds of such letters Douglas received in 1859. Typical letters are those of L. V. B. Martin, Tuscaloosa, Ala., June 28 (Martin was prosecuting attorney for the Tuscaloosa Judicial District); J. W. Lapsley, Selma, Ala., Dec. 2; W. E. Morton, Athens, Ga., Dec. 30; J. W. Singleton, Memphis, Dec. 10; John E. Robertson and William Carlisle, Ridgeway, S.C., Nov. 2; A. K. Richardson, Hog Mountain, Ga., Nov. 5, 1859; Douglas MSS.

[5] Abner S. Backus, Columbus, Ohio, June 8, 1859; Douglas MSS. Backus, a member of the Ohio Board of Public Works, went with a delegation to Washington in March to find out direct from the President what Douglas' friends in Federal posts might expect. Buchanan to Harriet Lane, Washington, May 14, 1859; James Buchanan MSS., Library of Congress: 'What means this ominous conjunction between Mr. Van Buren and Mr. Douglas at the New York Hotel?'

[6] Isaac McDaniels to Slidell, Rutland, Vt., April 12; J. G. Locke to Slidell, Rutland, Vt., March 16; Slidell to Buchanan, Washington, May 2, 1859; Buchanan MSS. Charles Upton, Salem, Mass., Jan. 13; James Gallagher, New Haven, Conn., July 14, 1859; Douglas MSS. But Gallagher, let out as Collector of the Port of New Haven 'for no other crime than defending the Democratic doctrine of Popular Sovereignty,' informed Douglas that his business would support his family, and that he would 'defy and despise this miserable whelp of an Administration.' George Plitt to Howell Cobb, Philadelphia, Sept. 25, 1859; Erwin MSS.; a letter marked 'entirely confidential,' reveals a typical Administration maneuver in New England. 'If Douglas is to be defeated,' Cobb's aide wrote, 'nothing should be left in *doubt*. Even a single delegate from New England might turn the scale one way or the other.' A certain Alfred Norton sought appointment as Collector of the Port of Edgartown, Mass. 'If it could be made at once, it would insure us a proper delegate to the Charleston Convention.' Furthermore, 'our *Live-Oak* friend, W. C. N. Swift, wants to be a delegate.'

which ended two years later in his expulsion from the Senate as a traitor. By his side was Dr. Fitch, his colleague and pliant tool. The blundersome Bigler sought to offset Forney in Buchanan's State. The cabal depended on Daniel S. Dickinson to tie up New York's delegation. They looked to Isaac Cook, Buchanan's defaulter-postmaster at Chicago, to make a show of opposition in Illinois.[7] H. M. Rice, of Minnesota, Slidell's lieutenant for the Northwest, boasted loudly that in no event could Douglas ever get Minnesota's delegation. Most of the Cabinet co-operated energetically and by early Summer the whole Federal machine was hard at work.[8]

As always, the presidentially ambitious combined to destroy the strongest man. Let each Southern candidate tie up his home State delegation and the Administration would steal from the Little Giant each Northern delegate whom a contract could secure or a postmastership pervert. By Summer the Administration press was blowing bubbles for a dozen favorite sons.

Virginia contributed two White House hopefuls: Senator R. M. T. Hunter, and Governor Henry A. Wise. Less able than Brown or Davis, Hunter upheld identical doctrine. Wise, who had hitherto agreed with Douglas, could have given the latter's Virginia friends enough assistance to have won the delegation. Unstable as well as brilliant, his ambition overcame him and the candidacy launched was for a time 'most pestilential' to Douglas' Southern chances. But Wise was addicted to unwise letters and soon wrote himself out of the race.[9]

Howell Cobb and Alexander H. Stephens were the Georgia hopefuls. Nine years before, Cobb had been one of the Georgia giants who battled for the Union; now he wrote intimates that, unless the North accepted the Ultra platform, 'the Union must go by the board,' and claimed that he was not a candidate. All the while, however, his brother was putting pressure on Toombs and Stephens to yield Cobb the State's delegation.[10] To this Toombs agreed, but Stephens was 'in an oyster shell,' and Douglas men in Georgia suspected him of 'playing for the accidency nomination at Charleston.' In June it looked as if the Georgia delegation would be for Stephens, but soon these prospects waned and Douglas was informed that if Toombs and Stephens aided, he could gain the delegation. He had some of his papers boom Stephens for Vice-President and tried to find out if the latter would accept. At length a vexed friend reported that 'Little Alec' hoped to step into the Presidency by some kind of luck or accident.[11]

[7] I. Cook to J. S. Black, Chicago, June 2, 1859; Black MSS.

[8] A. D. Banks, Cincinnati, May 1, 1859; Douglas MSS. 'Occasional,' writing in Philadelphia *Press*, Oct. 20, 1859, said that of the Cabinet only Floyd and Thompson were reluctant to enter the proscription policy.

[9] Cincinnati *Gazette*, Aug. 5, 1859, containing Wise letters; Natchez, Miss., *Daily Courier*, Aug. 15, 1859; Fred W. Hoffman, Schenectady, N.Y., Aug. 15; James B. Steedman, Toledo, Aug. 21, 1859; Douglas MSS.

[10] T. R. R. Cobb to Howell Cobb, Jefferson, Ga., Aug. 24; Howell Cobb to J. B. Lamar, Washington, Nov. 19, Dec. 5, 1859; Erwin MSS.

[11] James A. Nisbet, Macon, Ga., Aug. 23, Oct. 25, Dec. 1, 27; James Patillo, Milledgeville, Ga., Nov. 8; Geo. W. Lamar, Augusta, June 8; James B. Steedman, Toledo, Dec. 31, 1859; Douglas MSS.; D. P. Rhodes, Cleveland, July 15, 1859; Martin F. Douglas MSS.

Mississippi had a candidate in Jefferson Davis, who began to talk about 'a rapidly increasing feeling in favor of opening the African slave trade,' and the State's Ultras ranged themselves behind his ambitions. Brown was so discomfited that he nursed a boomlet of his own, whereat Davis sneered that opposition to Douglas was his trump card! Buchanan began to talk of Sam Houston, but Texas did not respond.[12]

The Little Giant's Tennessee campaign did well through the Summer. By September 'Lean Jimmy' Jones had high hopes of a Douglas delegation, and prepared to stump the State for him. During the Fall, however, the Slidell cabal aroused the ambitions of Andrew Johnson, then at the height of his power in Tennessee, and he entered the lists himself.[13]

While Kentucky was natural Douglas territory, the Buchaneers played both ends against the middle. Bright visited the State to start a boom for James Guthrie, Pierce's Secretary of the Treasury and now head of the Louisville and Nashville road. Several State papers came out for Guthrie and his ambitions became aroused. To insure that the other Kentucky faction would not turn to the Little Giant, the Administration sent H. M. Rice to stir up Vice-President Breckinridge. In short order the State's two Democratic factions were backing rival favorite sons.[14]

Douglas had done more than any other Senator to bring Oregon into the Union. Early in 1859, however, its newly elected Senator came East with a presidential boom in his grip. This was Joseph Lane, an Indiana adventurer who, capitalizing a Mexican War record and a rough rural eloquence, catapulted to power in Oregon Democratic politics. Lane was 'as Ultra a Southern Fire-Eater as Jefferson Davis,' and Bright sought to persuade Indiana to adopt him as a quasi-favorite son. When some Southern Fire-Eaters talked him up as a proper Northern candidate, Lane puffed up to unbelievable proportions.[15]

The Federal office-holders in New England gave some thought to bringing out Isaac Toucey, of Connecticut, but put in most of their time warming up the dying embers of Franklin Pierce's ambition. Douglas' lieutenants were much disturbed and Forney rushed to Concord to see what was what. George Sanders, who was still Navy Agent at New York, but had come back to Douglas, soon followed Forney there. But Pierce proved very firm in his declaration that 'under no circumstances would he accept the nomination if tendered him by acclamation' — his public life was closed. Still

[12] Jefferson Davis, Washington, May 17, 1859; C. C. Clay MSS., Duke University Library. 'Occasional,' Philadelphia *Press*, Aug. 30, 1859.

[13] George W. Bridges, Athens, Tenn., May 24; W. H. Carroll, Nashville, Aug. 27; Henry P. Stanton, Memphis, Aug. 28; James C. Jones, Memphis, Sept. 8, 1859; Douglas MSS.

[14] Washington McLean, Cincinnati, Feb. 21; A. D. Banks, Lexington, Ky., April 23; W. W. Wick, Indianapolis, Nov. 20, 1859; Douglas MSS.

[15] Washington McLean, Cincinnati, Feb. 21; A. M. Gibson, Portland, Ore., Oct. 19; W. W. Wick, Indianapolis, Nov. 20; A. W. Sweet, Lafayette, Ore., Nov. 27; James W. Nesmith, Salem, Ore., Nov. 28; J. A. Cravens, Hardensburg, Ind., Dec. 26, 1859, Douglas MSS., on Bright's Indiana movement for Joe Lane. Buchanan to John B. Floyd, Washington, Aug. 14, 1859; Buchanan MSS., Library of Congress: 'General Lane has sustained a sad blow in losing his State. I am sorry for it.'

his local lieutenants set up a skeleton organization, their Washington agent wrote that 'the talk is Douglas but the meaning is Pierce,' and Caleb Cushing plunged into delegate intrigue.[16]

This parade of candidates had back of it the shadow of the President. Shortly before his Cincinnati nomination, Buchanan had evaded a definite assurance that he only sought a single term.[17] Now, despite Inauguration statement and later testy denial, he kept offering name after name — even Robert J. Walker of Kansas fame! — and reports could not be quieted that he intended to offer himself at Charleston as a compromise between Douglas and the Ultras: he would save the Union — from himself![18]

Douglas' problem involved the persuasion of masses as well as checking White House maneuvers. The country over he must mobilize public sentiment and implement it with an organization strong enough to force the party mechanism to register the general will. In the North this meant wresting local party control from the hands of Buchanan's office-holders. In the South Douglas must both find agencies through which to get access to the people and must also organize the Conservatives into effective delegate-electing groups.

There were three Norths: New England, where the Democracy was dispirited and postmasters ruled with an iron hand; the Middle States, where the Democratic party machinery was reasonably free; then the West, where enthusiasm for the Little Giant shattered the bonds of patronage.

The Abolition, Prohibition and Know-Nothing movements had wreaked havoc on New England Democracy. The active Democratic politicians won few local offices and their livelihood depended on a thin gruel of Federal patronage. These professional Democrats held the post offices, sustained the party press, staffed the State Committees and packed the State Conventions. New England also numbered many thousands who were Democrats for faith, not revenue, but between campaigns these were dormant. Douglas' battle with the Southrons quickened the imagination of this group. Popular Sovereignty clubs sprang up and Douglas doctrine was offered as an antidote

---

[16] Eli S. Shorter, Eufaula, Ala., Sept. 7; Elon Comstock, New York, Oct. 24, 1859; Pierce MSS. Pierce to Eli Shorter, Andover, Mass., Sept. 22, 1859; New Hampshire Historical Society. J. W. Forney, Philadelphia, Sept. 25; J. L. Foster, Dover, N.H., Oct. 7, 1859; Douglas MSS. Foster, editor of the Dover *Gazette*, distrusted Forney's report. S. W. Jones to John H. George, Washington, Nov. 12, 19; John C. Wilson, Washington, Dec. 20, 1859; New Hampshire Historical Society MSS. Wilson writes: 'Our policy must be to nurse Douglas for the purpose of bringing forward our favorite at the right time.'

[17] James Buchanan to John Slidell, Washington, May 28, 1856, Breckinridge MSS., stating it was simply absurd for a man of sixty-five to declare he would not be a candidate for re-election in the seventieth year of his age if Providence should prolong his life.

[18] Buchanan to Jas. P. Barr, Washington, Aug. 8, 1859, Buchanan MSS.: '... I had supposed my purpose was well understood not again to become a candidate for the Presidency'; Cincinnati *Gazette*, Aug. 5, 1859, quoting Henry A. Wise letter: 'But you may rely upon it that Mr. Buchanan himself is a candidate, and all his patronage and power will be used to disappoint Douglas.' 'Occasional,' Philadelphia *Press*, June 25, July 4, 1859, for Buchanan's reconciliation with Walker, and talk of a Walker candidacy. *Ibid.*, July 24, 28, Aug. 30, 1859, for Buchanan's own candidacy.

to Buchanan blunders. This awakening had fresh impetus after the Spring elections in Connecticut, New Hampshire and Massachusetts gave an index of the devastating effect which Lecompton, the Cuban question and the Ultra demands had had on Democratic lines. The Douglas men now redoubled their activities and expected to win all the New England delegations, unless Cushing should snip off Maine.[19]

New York had always been a bugaboo; in each of the last two Democratic National Conventions its factional broils had probably cost Douglas the nomination, an outcome he now was determined to prevent. The first man he sent to New York was Thomas Dyer, of Chicago, who soon penetrated to the heart of the political complex. The basic situation was that inherited from the 'Forties — the Hards would accept no candidate favored by the Softs. Daniel S. Dickinson had personal presidential ambitions and Fernando Wood, head of Mozart Hall, that apparently sturdy but short-lived rival to Tammany, allied himself with the Hards. But Dyer found that Wood's interests were entirely personal, and concluded that the Dickinson enterprise would soon peter out.

William L. Marcy, the Softs' great leader of the 'Forties, was dead, and the reins had gone into the hands of Dean Richmond, a railroad magnate from extreme up-State. Vanderbilt's main lieutenant in building the New York Central, this new chief of faction was a competent and successful man of affairs who played politics both as a necessary element of railroad policy and because he found satisfaction in the game itself. Thoroughly dependable, he kept his own counsel, read the intrigues of rivals and organized his own forces with success. Richmond, who believed Douglas the only Democrat who could be elected, came to New York City in June, to present his plans to a small Douglas caucus. Dyer reported that Richmond was dependable and had the Empire State's Democratic machinery well in hand, and Douglas promptly put him in charge. Soon Young Men's Douglas Democratic Clubs began to be established, up-State leaders were committed and New York's delegation seemed about in the bag.[20]

Pennsylvania, with Buchanan's henchmen in every post office, presented more difficulty. Forney led the party revolt against Buchanan, his Philadelphia *Press* rang the tocsin and volunteers flocked to his standard. In April the Douglas Democrats held a State Convention and formed a committee to fight for the control for the Keystone delegation. After a Summer's hard work, they concluded that a few Douglas speeches would give the added strength needed to take the State.

For twenty years, Western Democrats had not resented the sobriquet of 'doughface,' for they had been conscious of more identity of economic interests with the South than with the North and had some contact with

---

[19] Solomon Parsons, Boston, March 18; John H. Pillsbury, Boston, March 23; Thos. Yeatman, New Haven, Conn., March 24; J. H. Clay Mudd, New York, April 9; Otis Bullard, Lowell, Mass., April 11; John Clark, Boston, July 28; E. W. Flagg, Bangor, Me., April 4; J. W. Schofield, Hartford, Conn., June 27; Thos. Dyer, New York, June 5, 1859; Douglas MSS.

[20] Thos. Dyer, New York, June 5; Aug. 6; John B. Haskin, New York, July 18; James C. Carlisle, New York, Aug. 13; George N. Sanders, Syracuse, N.Y., Sept. 15, 1859; Douglas MSS.

the slavery warp to the Southern social pattern. But the battle over Lecompton disturbed this comradely relation. After the February, 1859, Senate debate the Western Democrats felt, as Senator Pugh expressed it, that Buchanan had lost strongholds 'the enemy never was able to storm,' and refused to follow him any longer.[21]

'Now the mask is thrown off entirely,' Henry B. Payne, of Ohio, wrote Douglas. The 'insolence and infamous exaction' of the Fire-Eaters could no longer be endured. His first impulse had been to fight no more battles for the South — 'Let them have a Black Republican Administration, the blacker the better.' At any event it would dishonor the Northern Democracy either to accept a new plank or to drop the old one of Popular Sovereignty. If the Democratic party *must split* on this rock, he preferred it 'a thousand times to the disgrace and infamy of concession.' With the Democracy through the West, Daniel P. Rhodes was willing to give the South 'all that protection to property that we ask, no more, not one single bit,' and was resolved that Ohio should keep voting for Douglas at Charleston 'even after Brown shall have blown the party to flinders.' [22]

Indiana's Democratic party had been so machine-ridden that Douglas' friends lamented that there 'the scoundrels can defeat a foregone conclusion, and do it frequently.' But there were signs of a real party revolution. Thomas A. Hendricks took command of the Douglas campaign and the days of Bright and Fitch were numbered.[23]

Rhodes found that Wisconsin's delegation would be instructed for the Little Giant. Ex-Senator Stuart preached through Michigan that Democracy was dead in the Northwest unless Douglas was elected. Despite Senator Rice's fulminations, Minnesota's State Convention adopted an unequivocal Popular Sovereignty platform.[24] Iowa's Doughfaces had Senator George Washington Jones at their head, but Augustus Cæsar Dodge cast his lot with the Little Giant; a host of Conservative Democrats, particularly around Dubuque, saw in Popular Sovereignty a chance to redeem their State from Republican rule and Douglas' strength waxed greatly. Late in the Spring, however, it appeared that his boom had developed too quickly.[25]

[21] H. L. McGraw, Harrisburg, Pa., March 18; J. B. Sheridan, Philadelphia, April 23; J. W. Forney, Philadelphia, July 23, Sept. 25, 1859; Douglas MSS. George Pugh to Clement C. Clay, Cincinnati, June 5, 1859; C. C. Clay MSS., Pugh added, sarcastically, 'To what laurels is he not entitled?'

[22] H. B. Payne, Cleveland, April 12, July 22; James B. Steedman, Toledo, Aug. 21, 1859; Douglas MSS. D. P. Rhodes, Cleveland, July 15, 1859; Martin F. Douglas MSS. Unmistakably this was the feeling of Ohio's Democrats, a few vagabond office-holders excepted. When their State ticket was selected, every man on it was for Douglas; even the post-office politicians saw the handwriting on the wall.

[23] W. M. McCarty, Kellysville, Ind., Feb. 28; J. B. Danforth, Jr., Rock Island, March 14, reporting on Indiana trip; W. W. Wick, Indianapolis, June 16, July 25; W. E. Whittlesly, Evansville, Ind., Aug. 27; Aquilla Jones, Indianapolis, Sept. 27, 1859; Douglas MSS.

[24] D. P. Rhodes, June 22; J. R. Sharpstein, Milwaukee, Aug. 17; A. F. Bell, Ionia, Mich., Aug. 7; Earle S. Goodrich, St. Paul, Aug. 20; W. W. Gorman, St. Paul, Aug. 27; 1859; Douglas MSS. Goodrich, editor of the St. Paul *Pioneer and Democrat*, was made Chairman of the Minnesota State Democratic Committee.

[25] William Mills, Dubuque, March 12; J. B. Dorr, Dubuque, June 30, 1859; Douglas MSS.

In the South, the Fire-Eaters had conditioned the public mind to antagonism to the Little Giant, but in the Spring the Conservatives took hope that
if the people could know the facts the truth would set them free, and set
to work to get the facts before the people. Douglas soon experienced a heavy
Southern demand for reprints of his answer to Brown and Davis. The New
Orleans Moderates, led by Pierre Soulé, held a great mass meeting of conciliation. Despite the frantic efforts of Slidell and his Custom House coterie,
Miles Taylor, a Douglas man, was chosen for Congress in an up-State
Louisiana district, developments of real significance.[26]

There came a change effected in Alabama when an energetic editor took
command of the fight against Yancey and his Fire-Eaters. This was courageous John Forsyth, proprietor of the Mobile *Register*, called 'Little John,'
to distinguish him from his father and namesake of Jackson's day. Buchanan's Minister to Mexico, the younger Forsyth was badly treated by the
President and came home in insurgent mood. A man of character, he looked
with horror at the rocking chariot of Secession and turned to Douglas as
an alternative.

Forsyth realized that the Southern current was running fast against the
Little Giant, but did not believe it was running deep, and the task of breasting
it challenged and attracted him. Forsyth knew of no Southern figure who
could secure more than the Slave State vote, and that the South must
have a sound Free-State man to keep the issue from being purely sectional.
Up to the time of Buchanan's Lecompton folly Douglas had been the man
of all men for the race; could he now be reinstated in the South's esteem? [27]
He considered Douglas' record on every single item of the Negro question
except that of slavery in the Territories 'clear and beyond suspicion,' a letter
from the Little Giant cleared up Popular Sovereignty completely, and
Forsyth undertook to win Douglas and his principles a hearing in Alabama
and the Cotton South.

This work soon heartened the timid realists in Alabama; planters began
denouncing the Fire-Eaters and the cautious Fitzpatrick wrote Clement Clay
that the fight against Popular Sovereignty was an issue without substance.[28]
Many felt, like Hugh Wright, of northern Georgia, that 'if the present generation does not do you justice, Posterity will.' The Senator knew, however,
that he must move boldly and his friends must appeal 'from the politicians
to the people.' [29]

To succeed, such an appeal required skillful presentation and efficient
organization, and Douglas gave close attention to both requirements. The

[26] C. R. Collier, Petersburg, Va., March 1; John H. Gilmer, Richmond, March 2; F. W. Hart,
New River P.O., Va., March 2; W. Jones, Clayton, Ala., March 1; John A. Gilmer, Lexington,
N.C., April 13; John L. Peyton, Staunton, Va., May 4; John T. Reid, New Orleans, May 13;
Isaac Morse, New Orleans, July 28, 1859; Douglas MSS.

[27] John Forsyth, New York, March 26, 31, 1859; Douglas MSS.

[28] George F. Sallee, Mount Pleasant P.O., Ala., July 16, 1859, Douglas MSS.; Benjamin
Fitzpatrick, Wetumpka, Ala., Aug. 30, 1859; C. C. Clay MSS.

[29] James A. Nisbet, Macon, Ga., June 24; Hugh Wright, Rome, Ga., Sept. 29, 1859; Douglas
MSS.

first step in the publicity campaign was to make a pamphlet of his speech in the February 23 debate, with an appendix quoting statements within the decade by Davis, Brown, Quitman, Calhoun and other Southern leaders praising Popular Sovereignty. This damning document, circulated by the hundreds of thousands, had such effect on those who read it that, in the Cotton States, a curious canard arose that Brown had plotted the debate with Douglas so that the latter could register a triumph.[30]

Douglas' speech evoked several supporting pamphlets, the most notable of which was one written anonymously by Reverdy Johnson, of Maryland. Its authorship suspected, the Buchanan press loosed its batteries on Johnson. 'What a bankrupt Administration we have,' the latter wrote the Little Giant. 'To differ with the President is treason and he who does is reviled. I wonder if the fool will ever discover that in this he only makes his own course the more odious.'[31] The events of February stimulated Douglas' already burdensome correspondence, all of which he patiently examined and appraised. Although it was before the day of the promiscuous distribution of campaign photographs, he had a Boston commercial artist copy a Healy portrait and sent out a hundred of them, and a New York printmaker turned out a steel engraving of his Brandon birthplace.[32]

The newspaper problem had the Senator's careful attention. Hofer, his old friend of the New York *Staats-Zeitung*, moved to Cincinnati, bought into the *Volksfreund* there and began striking body blows for Douglas. A pro-Douglas Scandinavian paper was considered for Chicago. Rabbi Wise, of the *American Israelite*, urged his merits on the Jewish immigrants.[33] Chief in importance, however, was the Little Giant's work with the English language press. In these days newspapers could be started on little more than a hope and a promise, and several of the Senator's supporters bought out hostile journals or started new papers to offset them.[34]

Not until the Fall of 1859 did he secure proper New York support, but finally he made a convert of the *Times*, which was beginning to vie with Greeley's *Tribune* and Bennett's *Herald*. Its founder, proprietor and chief

---

[30] Albert Gallatin Brown, Terry, Hinds County, Miss., Sept. 10, 1859; in this letter the Mississippi Senator indignantly repudiated the suggestion that he had staged a sham battle. 'There was positively no arrangement, nothing akin to it,' he wrote. He had 'never expected nor deserved any response' from Douglas, but the other Northern candidates had been playing 'a game of hide and whoop' and he had wanted to show them up. A. D. Banks, Lexington, Ky., April 23, 1859, Douglas MSS., wrote that McLean had also set up Douglas' speech and printed 100,000 copies for distribution.

[31] Reverdy Johnson, Baltimore, March 2, 4, 25, 1859; Douglas MSS.

[32] C. H. Brainerd, Boston, April 2; John Cain, Rutland, Vt., Aug. 3, 1859; Douglas MSS. Brainerd, the commercial artist, charged $136 for his work. William L. S. Harrison, 80 Duane Street, New York, engraved Douglas' Brandon home.

[33] E. H. Orberg, Chicago, June 7; A. V. Hofer, Cincinnati, June 8, 18; B. A. Froseith, Chicago, June 18, 1859; Douglas MSS.

[34] C. K. Garvey, Topeka, Kan., April 2; Garvey was ready to start a Douglas paper whenever he got the word; he had the needed capital and 'asked no bonus, only friendship'; Oliver Jones, Aberdeen, Miss., Nov. 30, 1859; Douglas MSS. Jones had been so provoked with the fire-eating proclivities of the Aberdeen *Conservative* that he bought it out and wrote Douglas, 'I will be found pushing at the wheel.'

public figure was Henry J. Raymond, a foppish genius with a penchant for gold-headed canes, gray spats and personal oratory. A Seward man, Raymond was a little slow in warming up to Douglas. But William Henry Hurlbert, his main inside man, and at the time regarded as the paper's heart and brains, became intensely interested in the Little Giant's battle and brought Raymond and the *Times* into line. John W. Forney sent his Philadelphia *Press* a series of pungent letters from Washington, signed 'Occasional,' ridiculing Buchanan and disclosing the skeletons in the White House closet — all to the great irritation of the President. In the National Capital, the *States* kept up its fight for Popular Sovereignty, while the *Union* so vented its spleen on Douglas that the more intelligent Administrationists tried to convert it to neutrality.[35]

In the mid-West Washington McLean and the Cincinnati *Enquirer* continued friendly; the Cleveland *Plain Dealer*, Steedman's Toledo paper and Medary's old organ at Columbus did good service. Indiana papers turned with the Douglas tide. Sheahan, Lanphier and the other faithful kept up the Illinois barrage and strong journalistic support developed in Milwaukee, Detroit and St. Paul.

Nor did the Illinois Senator altogether lack Southern newspaper support. Harney and the Louisville *Democrat* did what they could in Kentucky. Pressed by 'Lean Jimmy' Jones, the Memphis *Appeal* swung stronger and stronger into line. Five papers in Arkansas supported him. In Mississippi, Barksdale's paper kept up its fulminations against Douglas, but several of the State's Conservative journals pressed for a square deal for the Senator. The New Orleans *True Delta* took delight in hurling bombshells at Slidell's gang and Forsyth's Mobile *Register* soon found support in other parts of Yancey's State.[36]

In Georgia, the Milledgeville *Federal Union* displayed increasing friendliness, James Gardner, of the Augusta *Constitutionalist*, fought the Little Giant's battles and a new paper was established at Savannah to support him. The Charleston *Mercury*, the Fire-Eaters' bible, denounced Douglas

[35] A. D. Banks, New York, Sept. 28, Oct. 19, 29; John W. Forney, Philadelphia, April 3, May 10, June 30; A. O. P. Nicholson, Washington, Nov. 10, 1859; Douglas MSS. Hurlbert was a real figure in New York journalism, although now chiefly remembered for his famous editorial, supposedly written while on a spree, containing the phrase, 'the elbows of the Quadrilateral.' The best sketch is that in *Dictionary of American Biography*, written by A. F. Harlow. Nicholson, who had edited the *Union* for Pierce and had still a money stake in it, opened negotiations with Senator Douglas, informing him that a *bona fide* change in ownership was taking place and that the attacks upon him would cease. 'I have seen and talked with Mr. Buchanan,' he added, 'and he readily acquiesces in the future policy of the paper indicated.' 'Occasional,' in Philadelphia *Press*, June 25, July 4, 24, 28, Aug. 29, 30, 1859.

[36] A. D. Banks, St. Louis, May 19, 1859; J. L. Jones, Memphis, Sept. 1; James W. Singleton, Little Rock, Dec. 29, 1859; Douglas MSS. Singleton reported the *Old Line Democrat* at Little Rock, the Madison *Journal*, El Dorado *Times*, Pine Bluff *Independent*, Van Buren *Press*, for Douglas. *Weekly Mississippian*, Jackson, Aug. 31, Sept. 28, Oct. 12, 1859, for Barksdale's views. Okalona, Miss., *Prairie News*, July 21, 1859, lists Corinth *Republican* as for Douglas. Other favoring papers included Macon *Beacon*, Aberdeen *Conservative*, Vicksburg *Whig*. J. J. Seibels, Washington, Aug. 26, 1859; Douglas MSS. Seibels, editor of the Montgomery *Confederation*, and a Fitzpatrick aide, swung to Douglas and came North to cement the new alliance.

as a traitor to the party and the South, announcing that it would support 'no man of whatever party, clique, creed or section' who stood on Douglas' platform, 'though he should be nominated by twenty Democratic conventions.' But the violence of such language had offsetting value beyond South Carolina's borders. Colonel Patrick Henry Aylette, editor of the Richmond *Enquirer*, believed in Douglas. Editor Glass worked unceasingly at Lynchburg, while west of the mountains Douglas became the favorite candidate. While the weight of Southern newspaper circulation was against him, Douglas had supporters in many Southern sanctums and their friendliness had effect.[37]

Early in the year George Ticknor, the New England *littérateur*, planned a book on Popular Sovereignty. A little later John Savage, a popular writer of the day, made Douglas an important figure in *Men of Our Times* and asked for a $500 loan.[38] The task of a campaign biography Douglas entrusted to James W. Sheahan's affectionate care. When the author submitted the manuscript of his first chapter, Douglas thought 'the dates, names, etc., about families... indelicate, if not trifling,' and went over Sheahan's proofs with a heavy hand. Still not satisfied, he sketched off his own outline of his family origin and early life.[39] In July the faithful Sheahan went to Washington to pick up loose ends.[40] But he met delay after delay in finishing his manuscript, and while he was rewriting and revising, Henry Flint, a young Chicago lawyer, rushed a collection of Douglas speeches through the press. Harper and Brother, who published Sheahan's official volume, did not get it from the bindery until the eve of the Charleston Convention.[41]

The organization process started in January, 1859. The candidate's enormous private correspondence was chiefly devoted to setting up local delegate-getting organizations and supervising their endeavors. One day he would send Forney a draft of resolutions for Democratic members of the New Jersey Legislature. The next he would pass upon the qualifications

[37] James Nisbet, Macon, Ga., Oct. 25; Douglas MSS.; *re* Milledgeville *Federal Union*; Charleston *Mercury* editorial clipped in Okalona, Miss., *Prairie News*, June 30, 1859.

[38] George Ticknor, Claremont, N.H., May 12; John Savage, Washington, Aug. 12, 1859; Douglas MSS. Ticknor, an Old-Line Whig, had become convinced that Douglas' platform of Popular Sovereignty afforded the only safety for the Union of the States. Thereupon he undertook to prove that by it the Union could be saved.

[39] Douglas to J. W. Sheahan, April 8, 16, 1859; originals in possession of Geo. H. Sheahan, Chicago. Sending this outline to Sheahan, Douglas enjoined the biographer to omit 'those minutiæ that may seem trifling and not worthy of record in a permanent work.' He also bluepenciled Sheahan's frequent repetition of the phrase 'marriage to a principle.' All these objections he sought to soften by adding, 'Pardon the freedom of my criticisms, for you know that I always invite criticism in my own productions as freely as I make them in others.' For the volume's frontispiece he selected a Brady photograph, 'the best yet taken.'

[40] John Pearson, Danville, Ill., Aug. 4, 1859; Douglas MSS. Pearson insisted that the 1844 speech on General Jackson's fine and the Chicago speech on the Compromise of 1850 must both be inserted in their entirety.

[41] Flint's volume was jointly issued by Derby and Jackson, of New York. At first it bore the signature 'By a Member of the Western Bar,' but in the 1860 edition Flint signed it. In 1863 Flint revised it to include the Little Giant's death and it was reissued by John E. Porter, of Philadelphia. Sheahan's book came out in Febraury, 1860. It went through several editions and was given a final revision in 1862.

of a potential Democratic candidate for Governor of Ohio. A third he would counsel the course of action for his group in Illinois and suggest appropriate resolves for the General Assembly of Missouri.[42] In April the actual field work began, through a series of detailed check-ups throughout the country, made by A. D. Banks, George N. Sanders, Thomas Dyer, General James W. Singleton, Daniel P. Rhodes, 'Lean Jimmy' Jones and others. One after another of these men toured the country and reported to Douglas, who occasionally went out himself.

Early in April Banks left on an extended trip West and South. Senator Pugh, who had just been through Missouri, Illinois and Indiana, met him in Cincinnati and reported that he had found an 'overwhelming and resistless' Douglas sentiment, and that the candidate only needed to swing one or two Southern States in line to win. After a series of conferences with Ohio leaders, Banks went on to St. Louis, where he conferred with Judge Treat, John Krum and other Douglas men and set up a quiet campaign for the Missouri delegation. 'Matters continue to improve,' he wrote his chief.[43] Thence he turned south for a trip through the Carolinas, Georgia, Tennessee and Virginia, meeting Douglas at Memphis to report those intimacies politicians do not commit to paper.

Douglas had gone South about the middle of May to inspect his children's Mississippi properties. While he avoided public speeches, he held several conferences en route, including one in Augusta with Georgia leaders. After a few days on the plantation, he started north, stopping off at Memphis, where he discussed Southern prospects with Senator Jones, the *Appeal* editors and others and made plans for a finish fight for the Tennessee delegation. Then he boarded a river packet north.[44]

In Chicago the Senator found that some of his Northwestern supporters seemed to sense a beginning disintegration of strength, due to the absence of any public pronouncement of his candidacy. J. B. Dorr, editor of a paper at Dubuque, came to Chicago to tell Sheahan his fears in the matter, and left with Sheahan a letter asking Douglas whether or not his friends could place him before the Charleston Convention. The Little Giant decided to use this letter as the occasion for a public declaration of his purposes. Friends who met him along the road as he sped to Washington noted that he looked as if he 'would "never say die" physically, intellectually, or politically.'[45] A few days after his arrival, newspapers published his letter to Mr. Dorr.

[42] Martin Ryerson, Newton, N.J., Feb. 22; H. B. Payne, Cleveland, Ohio, Feb. 25, April 12; Ferdinand Kennett, St. Louis, Mo., Feb. 28; Samuel Eaton, Tamaroa, Ill., Feb. 28, 1859; Douglas MSS.

[43] A. D. Banks, Lexington, Ky., April 23; Cincinnati, May 1; St. Louis, May 18; Cincinnati, June 6, 1859; Douglas MSS.

[44] W. T. Beale, Augusta, Ga., May 22; apparently Douglas had lost his coat and hat in Augusta; Beale forwarded them to Washington. Geo. W. Lamar, Augusta, June 8; Captain Dan Able, Memphis, June 4, 1859; Douglas MSS. Able's invitation to Douglas to go north on the steamer *J. H. Dickey* is endorsed 'accepted.' Memphis *Daily Appeal*, June 3, 4, 1859.

[45] W. W. Wick, Indianapolis, June 16, 1859; Douglas MSS. Wick's son had met Douglas at a stop en route and the father was quoting the son's description.

Before he could determine whether or not he would be a candidate, declared Douglas in carefully chosen words, he must know upon what issues the campaign would be fought. If, as he expected, the coming National Convention were to register the party's determination 'to adhere to the principles embodied in the Compromise of 1850, and ratified by the people in the presidential election of 1852, and reaffirmed in the Kansas-Nebraska Act of 1854, and incorporated into the Cincinnati platform in 1856, as expounded by Mr. Buchanan in his letter accepting the nomination, and approved by the people in his election,' Douglas' friends would be at liberty to present his name.

In the unlikely event, however, that 'the Democratic party should repudiate their time-honored principles, and in lieu of these interpolate into the creed of the party such new issues as the revival of the African Slave Trade, or a Congressional Slave Code for the Territories, or the doctrine that the Constitution of the United States either establishes or prohibits slavery in the Territories beyond the power of the people legally to control it as other property,' he declared, 'I could not accept the nomination if tendered to me.' [46]

To this announcement of extraordinary import, Douglas might well have added the explicit warning to the Ultras that the fruit of their extremity would be the election of a Black Republican President. A disturbed Buchanan wrote Slidell in rhetorical inquiry. 'Is he still in favor of the odious doctrine of Squatter Sovereignty?' The latter responded that Douglas had shown 'intolerable arrogance.' [47]

Through the North the Dorr letter was a bugle-call to Democrats, while in the South it nerved the Moderates to sterner battle with the Fire-Eaters. It did 'a glorious work' in Ohio; Bright's lieutenants, busy filling Indiana with the rumor that Douglas would show a craven spirit, were taken aback. The veteran Tom Corwin said that Douglas' 'frank sincerity and determination not to be misunderstood' were most refreshing. Editor Dorr thought that, after the 'bold and candid avowal,' the Iowa delegation would be instructed to vote for Douglas 'from first to last.' [48]

The South's leading Fire-Eaters were spurred to fresh attacks. Barksdale's paper sneered that Douglas would 'rather rule in Hell than serve in Heaven'; Rhett's Charleston *Mercury* preached a holy war against him; but this was an index, in reverse, of the Southern effect of the pronouncement. After a swing through Mississippi, Arkansas, Alabama, Georgia and Florida, a New Orleans politician reported that he found a general sentiment that the next President would be either Douglas or Seward, and that the

---

[46] Douglas to J. B. Dorr, Washington, June 22, 1859, printed in *Daily National Intelligencer*, Washington, June 24, 1859.

[47] Buchanan to Slidell, Lancaster, Pa., June 24; Slidell to Buchanan, Washington, July 3, 1859; Buchanan MSS.

[48] Cyrus Powers, Moravia, Cayuga County, N.Y., June 30; H. B. Payne, Cleveland, July 22; W. C. Hise, Lebanon, Ind., June 24; W. W. Wick, Indianapolis, July 7, giving his views and reporting interview with Corwin; J. B. Dorr, Dubuque, Iowa, June 30, 1859; Douglas MSS.

people very much preferred the Little Giant. 'Lean Jimmy' Jones sniffed the scent of battle and came east with General Singleton to help. Tennessee Moderates dug up and made much of a statement Polk had made in 1849 endorsing Popular Sovereignty; Breckinridge men in Tennessee and Kentucky began warming up to Douglas.

Even more significant was Forsyth's experience. To test out Alabama sentiment, he offered himself for the State Senate on a Douglas platform. The Ultra candidate denounced Douglas and his champion all over the district, at times so viciously that Forsyth hinted a challenge. While no public speaker, the editor of the *Register* took the stump and delivered fifteen speeches discussing Douglas' program. Far from apologizing for the Freeport doctrine, Forsyth boldly proclaimed it as right and proper. His crowds increased until near the end a thousand heard him every night. In the outcome this Douglas champion led the ticket. The strongest State's Rights county in a reputed Ultra State elected a Freeport doctrine candidate who had gotten the truth to the people.[49]

But a thread of warning ran through the jubilation. Steedman thought Douglas certain of nomination unless he himself defeated it. 'You must quit writing letters,' the shrewd Ohio editor insisted. 'Remember the fate of Clay. When I read your last letter, I thought I heard a voice say "Write not at all.".... Write no more *platform* letters.... Every man in the Nation knows precisely what your platform is.' [50]

By Summer the people seemed to have their minds made up to draft Douglas. His organization grew so fast that he was urged to open national headquarters in New York. The candidate was loath to do this; the day had not yet come when aspirants publicly sought the Presidency or pulled back the curtain to reveal the machinery of their ambition. But circumstances forced his hand. Late in the Summer Banks went to New York to open unofficial headquarters. A steering committee was organized, numbering such men as John Jacob Astor, Moses Taylor, August Belmont, Dean Richmond, Isaac Townsend, Walter Sherman, Hurlbert of the *Times*, George Sanders and a few others of prominence and strength. They set about raising a preliminary campaign fund and before long reported that sufficient money had been subscribed. The impatient Sanders thought

[49] *Weekly Mississippian*, Jackson, Aug. 3, 1859; Charleston *Mercury*, clipped in Okolona, Miss., *Prairie News*, June 30, 1859; James A. Nisbet, Macon, Ga., June 25; I. V. B. Martin, Tuscaloosa, Ala., June 28; I. D. Fuller, New Orleans, Sept. 5, reporting on recent Southern tour; George N. Sanders, New York, Aug. 17, telling of talk with Green; J. W. Singleton, New York, July 11, telling of his and Jones' advent to New York: 'Our sole object is to make political discourses and observations'; G. W. Jones, Nashville, Tenn., Sept. 2, 1859, sending Douglas reference to Polk Diary note of anticipated veto prepared for Wilmot Proviso: 'The people who inhabit or may inhabit the acquired Territories have alone the right to decide for themselves what their domestic institutions shall be, without the intervention or interference of Congress,' printed in Washington *Union*, April 25, 1850, now exhumed by Jones and reprinted through South; John Forsyth, Mobile, June 26, July 30, Aug. 4, 1859; Douglas MSS. There was another Alabama index in the bad defeat W. F. Samford, on a Yancey platform, suffered in seeking the governorship. 'Occasional,' Philadelphia *Press*, Aug. 30, 1859, for Breckinridge drift to Douglas in Tennessee, Kentucky and Ohio.

[50] James B. Steedman, Toledo, Ohio, Aug. 21, 1859; Douglas MSS.

Banks was too slow but soon admitted that the manager was making considerable headway.

Buchanan postmasters strove vainly to deprive Douglas of Vermont's support. 'The watch-fires are burning brightly,' a Massachusetts aide reported, 'the battlefield is well ranged, the sentinels are at their post and the countersign is Douglas and Popular Sovereignty.' Sure enough, the Douglas men elected their delegate slate at the Democratic State Convention at Worcester in September by more than two to one. Rhode Island planned a solid Douglas delegation. The Little Giant's Maine leaders secured two of the four delegates and procured a Popular Sovereignty platform.[51]

Of New York's delegates, chosen in September, there were some Dickinson men, postmasters and traitors, but 'forty-five of the seventy are right and there is the power.' Pierce was warned that if Douglas were nominated, 'he could not fail to carry New York.' Buchanan showered Richmond with White House invitations, but the New Yorker skillfully evaded them.[52]

If Ohio's Douglas Democracy won the Fall election, that would be a harbinger of Douglas' 1860 presidential vote. The candidate was continually consulted about the Ohio ticket and one of his ardent supporters was nominated for Governor. Republican dissensions increased Democratic hopes, and the campaign was hard-fought. The Ohio campaign managers tried to forestall White House sabotage by a written agreement with the Federal contingent for an honest joint effort for the State ticket. But Buchanan could not forego his hatred of Douglas, even though the cost of vengeance would be Chase's election to the Senate, in place of George Pugh. Late in the Summer the campaign leaders discovered that the postmaster brigade was whetting the knife of betrayal. Douglas determined to go there to campaign for his friends.[53]

During the Summer the Little Giant wrote another public letter which delighted the Irish immigrants but disquieted 'Lean Jimmy' Jones. 'I don't want you to write any more letters,' he chided. 'Many great men

[51] J. P. Atwood, Madison, Wis., Aug. 15; Atwood had gone to Burlington, Vt., for Douglas; Edward Riddle to George N. Sanders, Boston, Aug. 16, covered Sanders to Douglas, New York, Aug. 18; Johnson Gardner, Pawtucket, Mass., Sept. 5; Moses Bates, Plymouth, Mass., Sept. 19; Alexander Eddy, Chepachet, R.I., Aug. 23; Solomon Parsons, Boston, July 4, 1859; Douglas MSS. 'Occasional,' Philadelphia *Press*, July 4, 1859.

[52] A. D. Banks, New York, Sept. 25, 28, Oct. 19; H. B. Payne, Cleveland, Ohio, Oct. 20, describing confidential interview with Richmond on the latter's visit to Cleveland the day before; George N. Sanders, New York, Oct. 30, 1859; Douglas MSS. Elon Comstock to Franklin Pierce, New York, Oct. 24, 1859; Pierce MSS. Comstock, editor of the New York *Journal of Commerce*, sought to persuade Pierce to get in the race, and also disclosed that the Hards had Horatio Seymour in mind for a favorite son should Dickinson develop insufficient strength against Douglas for control of the New York delegation.

[53] Abner S. Backus, Columbus, Ohio, June 8; H. B. Payne, Cleveland, June 10; George W. Manypenny, Columbus, June 27; D. P. Rhodes, Cleveland, July 26; as to Bright's effort to prevent the Ohio invitation; George E. Pugh, Cincinnati, Aug. 13; A. S. Backus, Toledo, Sept. 25; as to Buchaneers violating the agreement; J. W. Forney, Philadelphia, Sept. 26, 1859; Douglas MSS.

have committed suicide in this way. Stand on your present record and let the people do the rest.'[54] Douglas did slow down on 'platform letters,' but committed a perhaps more grievous error, for in its September issue *Harper's Magazine* published an article by the Senator discussing Popular Sovereignty in the Territories.

Douglas' Senate critics had consistently charged that, while Popular Sovereignty as a policy might offer a practical solution to the sectional dispute, it had no philosophical foundation and the Constitution was on the side of the South. The February debate with Brown and Davis convinced Douglas that, to win theoreticians' support in the South, he must derive his doctrine from the Founding Fathers.

Thereupon he set to work gathering material for a speech which would show the legal right, as well as the practical good sense, of permitting 'the people of the Territories to govern themselves in all their domestic relations without the interference of the Federal Government.' He sent to the Library of Congress for Elliott's *Debates*, examined Calhoun's arguments with painstaking care and made a thorough search of the literature of the Continental Congress and of the Congress of the Confederation.[55]

This research convinced him 'that while the Colonists ceded to the Imperial Government the right to pass all laws which were imperial and not Colonial, they claimed for themselves the exclusive right of legislation in respect to their internal policy, slavery included.' He was impressed by a memoir Thomas Jefferson had prepared in 1774, and which the Continental Congress followed in its formal remonstrance to King and Parliament, reciting 'that the Colonial Legislatures repeatedly passed acts prohibiting the introduction of any more African slaves, and that the King withheld his consent.' Douglas was eager to dig up examples of the Colonial Acts Jefferson had mentioned, but time was short, other duties pressing, and he turned for aid to his friend George Bancroft, then revising his monumental history of the United States. 'Can you furnish me with a list of the enactments by Virginia, South Carolina, and each of the other colonies prohibiting or excluding slavery,' with dates and attending circumstances? Douglas asked. These facts would enable him 'to show that our Colonies claimed the right as Colonies to prohibit slavery.'[56] Now more pressing campaign necessities delayed research until the Senate's adjournment, but early in the Summer Douglas resumed his work and cast it in form for *Harper's*.

The article, which bore the formidable title 'Popular Sovereignty in

---

[54] B. O. Kean, Mobile, Ala., Sept. 7; J. C. Jones, Memphis, Tenn., Sept. 1, 1859; Douglas MSS.

[55] The Library of Congress register charges Douglas in 1859 with Calhoun's *Works*, *The Federalist*, Hollister's *Connecticut*, Gordon's *History of New Jersey*, Carey's *Slave Trade*, Stroud on Slavery, Elliott's *Debates*, McMahan's *History of Maryland*, and Bancroft's *History of the United States*, volumes II to VI inclusive.

[56] Douglas to George Bancroft, Washington, April 11, 1859; original in Brown University Library, Providence, R.I. Douglas also pointed out that the citations he wished were to enactments prior to 1774, 'for those of that year were merely retaliatory and therefore not the operation of a principle.' Bancroft must have responded, for, when published, Douglas' article called attention to a formidable list of Colonial statutes.

the Territories — The Dividing Line Between Federal and Local Authority,' created a sensation. To the modern reader it is clear but somewhat heavy argument. To the historian it is important because in it, for the first time, Douglas offered a constitutional foundation for Popular Sovereignty.

He insisted that there was a definite dividing line between Federal and local authority, which had been an important element of Colonial political philosophy during the century preceding independence. The Americans of the era preceding the Revolution 'acknowledged and affirmed their allegiance to the Crown,' but claimed the right 'to exercise and enjoy all the rights, privileges and immunities of self-government in respect to all matters and things which were local and not general — internal and not external — Colonial and not Imperial.' The Founding Fathers initially contended, not for independence, but 'to make their own local laws, form their own domestic institutions, and manage their own internal affairs in their own way, subject only to the Constitution of Great Britain as the paramount law of the Empire.'

This statement he buttressed with specific citations, some doubtless suggested by George Bancroft, of objections raised by Virginia and South Carolina to the English insistence upon 'forcing African slavery upon a dependent colony without her consent and in opposition to the wishes of her people.' When the Continental Congress of 1774 adopted a Bill of Rights, each Provincial Legislature specifically reserved 'the sole and exclusive right of regulating the internal policy and government' of the Colony, including the domestic institution of slavery.

Jefferson's 1784 plan of government for the Northwest Territory he termed a repudiation of the theory that all Colonies and Territories were the common property of the Empire and a substitution of the doctrine 'that the people of every separate political community (dependent Colonies, Provinces and Territories as well as sovereign States) have an inalienable right to govern themselves in respect to their internal polity.' This same theory was held by the framers of the Constitution and must be the basis for its interpretation.[57]

Douglas now turned his attention to demonstrating that the Federal Constitution did not automatically establish slavery in all Territories of the United States. From Taney's Dred Scott opinion, as from the Constitution itself, he showed Congress' inability either to enact or prohibit slavery in Territories or States. 'No word can be found in the Constitution,' Taney had said, 'which gives Congress a greater power over slave property, or which entitles property of that kind to less protection, than property

[57] Douglas further called attention to the fact that, in 1787 and for some decades thereafter, the word 'territory' referred to real-estate area or property, and unformed political communities were termed 'States' or 'new States' and not 'Territories.' Thus Madison in 1787 referred to the Committee of Detail of the Constitutional Convention the propriety of adding to the powers of the proposed Congress one 'to institute temporary governments for the new States arising therein.' The Founding Fathers obviously intended to confer upon these new communities on their way to become States the same rights of internal self-government given to the formally organized States.

of any other description,' and Douglas flung this statement in the face of the Ultras who were demanding a Congressional slave code.

From this point he argued that, in 1850, Congress had specifically refused to limit the right of Territorial Legislatures to pass on slavery. Citing the non-intervention doctrine in the Kansas-Nebraska bill and the Cincinnati platform, the Senator recalled how James Buchanan, accepting the presidential nomination, had firmly adopted, as founded upon principles as ancient as free government itself, the doctrine that 'the people of a Territory, like those of a State, shall decide for themselves whether slavery shall or shall not exist within their limits.'

All these measures and commitments, in Douglas' view, clearly established the dividing line between Federal and local authority upon the principle that every distinct political community was 'entitled to all the rights, privileges and immunities of self-government in respect to their local concerns and internal polity, subject only to the Constitution of the United States.'

With this closely reasoned argument the Little Giant believed that he had transformed Popular Sovereignty from a policy into a principle. Upon the people's right to choose he rested his case. But would the people choose the nominee at Charleston or would the politicians run the show?

CHAPTER XXIV

THE NORTHWEST ASSERTS ITSELF

THE *Harper's* article produced a national sensation. So eager were newspapers to use it that the Printing House of Franklin Square was forced to waive its copyright; Douglas, too, circulated thousands of pamphlet reprints. John Forsyth thought it made the Southern current flow more swiftly toward the Little Giant, and even such a Fire-Eater as Albert Gallatin Brown congratulated the author, 'You have made the best use of a bad cause.'[1]

The interventionists showered *Harper's* with rebuttals. Horace Greeley and George Ticknor Curtis sought space for a Republican answer, while Henry Hilliard, of Alabama, and other Southern Rights men clamored for their day in print.[2] 'Old Obliquity' set his side to work to counteract Douglas' article. As in 1858, he selected Jeremiah Sullivan Black to hurl the Administration's stink-pots, a task which that worthy undertook with alacrity. Not so many years before, Black had preached Popular Sovereignty as the 'great truth of the day.' But his life aspiration was to be appointed to the United States Supreme Court, there was now a vacancy and Douglas writers charged that ambition as well as changed opinion made the Attorney-General eager to please the President.[3] He soon issued, unsigned, a pamphlet which not only assailed Douglas' thesis but also reflected on the Senator's public record and private character.

Black had much praise from Buchanan men. Judge Woodward, of the Pennsylvania Supreme Court, wrote that while he, with Black, had formerly thought that 'the immigrant carried in the Territory all the sovereignty of an American citizen and had an inalienable right to admit or exclude slavery,' yet the Attorney-General's pamphlet marked 'a long step in advance.' Slidell thought Black's reply 'indeed an extinguisher'; Douglas' New York manager thought it was 'a skillfully devised libel' to befog the Southern mind. Reverdy Johnson felt that while the argument was 'fallacious throughout,' Black had done it so 'artistically' that it required a short, emphatic answer.[4]

Douglas was on the train for Ohio when this pamphlet was thrust in

---

[1] John Forsyth, New York, Sept. 1; Albert Gallatin Brown, Terry, Hinds County, Miss., Sept. 10, 1859; Douglas MSS.

[2] William A. Seaver, New York, Oct. 3, 1859; Douglas MSS. Seaver, the editor of *Harper's Magazine*, listed these and other offerings which the Magazine had declined.

[3] 'Occasional,' in Philadelphia *Press*, Oct. 15, 1859.

[4] Justice George W. Woodward, Philadelphia, Sept. 19, 1859; J. S. Black MSS. The South 'understands our institutions and our Constitution better than the wisest doctors of the North,' Judge Woodward continued; their superiority was not only of statesmanship but of manners and morals, and all 'due to their slavery as the ultimate cause.' John Slidell, New Orleans, Sept. 28, 1859; Buchanan MSS.; A. D. Banks, New York, Sept. 25; Reverdy Johnson, Philadelphia, Sept. 16, 1859; Douglas MSS.

his hands. It aroused his indignation, and in his speeches for Ohio's Democratic ticket, made at Cincinnati, Columbus and Wooster, he scornfully repelled the Attorney-General's personal aspersions and pointed out that, during the 1858 Illinois campaign, this Cabinet member of a Democratic Administration had written scurrilous letters to Democrats all over that State urging his defeat. What sort of a Democrat did that make Black? [5] As to this renewed Administration effort to drive him from the Democratic party, 'the thing cannot be done.'

Events of the last few years had brought Douglas to regard himself as a man upon whose shoulders had fallen the mantles of Webster and Clay. Each Ohio speech contained touching references to the memories of the Whig pacificators, and his appeal to the great Conservative masses to rebuke all extremists was moving and profound. He pointed out how in the North the Ultras sought intervention to prohibit slavery in the Territories, while in the South the Fire-Eaters demanded a Congressional slave code for unwilling Territories, neither of which programs could be accomplished without endangering the Union. Douglas' counter to the Ultras of both sections was Federal non-intervention. Increasingly he emphasized that slavery depended on climate, soil conditions and prevailing economic characteristics rather than upon constitutional laws. 'In Ohio it is a question only between the white man and the Negro,' he said, 'but if you go further South you will come to a place where it is a question between the Negro and the crocodile.'

After his return to Washington, he put his reply to Black into a formal pamphlet, Reverdy Johnson wrote a supporting article and Douglas gave both a wide circulation.[6] The New York *Times* had the full text of the Columbus speech sent it by telegraph, a journalistic achievement for the day, and also reprinted Douglas' and Johnson's pamphlets. A dozen papers in Virginia, North Carolina and Georgia approved Douglas' Cincinnati declaration. Southern Moderates wrote that his position was now all his personal friends could desire. The people of Alabama 'are beginning to open their eyes,' 'the Fire-Eaters — "the would-be Presidents" of the South — cannot force the people.' Banks sent word from New York, 'You have killed Black!' [7]

Late in September Adèle's approaching confinement forced the Senator to adjourn his personal attention to politics. On the last day of the month she gave birth to a daughter; there were complications, for six weeks Adèle suffered with puerperal fever and several times the physicians despaired of

[5] This was a telling shot. Chicago *Times*, clipped in Philadelphia *Press*, Oct. 19, 1859, tells how Black promptly wrote his Illinois familiars asking return of his 1858 letters to them!

[6] Douglas, Pamphlet, Washington, Oct. 1859; Reverdy Johnson, Baltimore, Oct. 31, 1859; Douglass MSS.

[7] A. D. Banks, New York, Sept. 25, Oct. 31, Nov. 1; B. O. Kean, Mobile, Ala., Sept. 16; J. H. Gilmer, Richmond, Va., Oct. 31; John Forsyth, Mobile, Ala., Nov. 1; John W. Forney, Philadelphia, Sept. 26, 1859; Douglas MSS. New York *Times*, Sept. 9, 13, Oct. 29, 1859. Banks ordered 20,000 copies of the paper containing the pamphlet, and sent them to lists of Southern legislators, State Convention members, etc.

her life. The baby, whom they named Ellen, seemed sturdy enough but died after about ten weeks.

Douglas canceled all conferences during Adèle's crisis and stayed by her bedside, taking time off only to send lieutenants a few indispensable instructions. Before the end of the month he himself was laid low with a violent attack of inflammatory rheumatism, later complicated with a renewal of his former afflictions of throat and chest. So persistent were these ills that the doctors urged him to go South to recuperate; it was mid-December before he recovered sufficiently for this prescription to be remitted.[8]

Thus the Douglases were late in joining in Washington's social season, which that year was unusually brilliant, as though all hoped that the deadly tensions of politics could be relieved by the amenities of teas, receptions, dinners and balls. But it was a hope disappointed, for the political battle cut athwart the lines of society. Adèle loyally espoused her husband's quarrels, 'cut' the most outrageous of his enemies and no longer appeared at Harriet Lane's unusually elaborate White House teas. But Adèle and Harriet had adjoining boxes at Ford's Theater, a juxtaposition which sometimes led to amusing *contretemps*. One evening a leading South Carolina Fire-Eater who had attacked Douglas entered the Douglas box to pay his respects to a guest there. 'Sir, you have made a mistake,' said Adèle, with frigid hauteur. 'Your visit is intended for next door.'[9]

The wonder was the Winter passed without bloody brawls in society, for passions flared high in both Houses of Congress. The tragic death of Senator Broderick in California in September had cast a shadow over the National Capital. Immediately after a hot political campaign in California between the Douglas and the Buchanan forces, Judge Terry, a dead-shot lieutenant of Dr. Gwin, picked a quarrel with and forced a duel on the brave but helpless Broderick, who fell a victim to his marksmanship. 'Duel,' all the Buchanan apologists explained.[10] The North was shocked by this tragedy, its papers denounced Terry, Gwin and the whole Buchanan Administration, and charged that they had shown their true colors by silencing with a pistol-shot an antagonist whose voice they could not answer. Writhing under these implications, Buchanan protested shrilly that he had no hand in it.[11] But many Popular Sovereignty Congressmen armed themselves and let it be known that they would shoot any attacker. Such was the soil in which the 1860 campaign was sown.

The Republicans became more and more apprehensive of a Douglas victory in the Democratic battle-royal. They had reason to fear his hold

---

[8] Douglas to McClernand, Washington, Oct. 1, 1859; McClernand MSS.; Douglas to Lanphier, Washington, Oct. 1, 1859; Patton MSS.; 'Occasional,' in Philadelphia *Press*, Nov. 7, 1859; Douglas to George N. Sanders, Washington, Dec. 15, 1859; Sanders MSS., Library of Congress.

[9] Mrs. Roger B. Pryor, *Reminiscences*, 98–99.

[10] The literature on the Broderick-Terry duel is voluminous; for brief accounts, see Rhodes, II, 330–35; Schouler, V, 428. Douglas had many reports on it from California friends.

[11] 'Occasional,' in Philadelphia *Press*, Oct. 15, 1859.

on the Northern voters. David Davis, Lincoln's friend, believed that, were the Little Giant nominated at Charleston, he would carry Illinois 'no matter how strongly Southern the platform may be on which he runs.' Strong fears of this character led the Northern Abolitionists to offer ingenuous arguments why the Democrats should select a Southern slave code candidate. Should the South accept Douglas, warned the *National Era*, chief Anti-Slavery paper in Washington, it would stimulate insurrection among the slaves; 'the triumph of the Republicans would leave the honor and spirit of the Oligarchy intact but their surrender to the Northern Doughfaces would be fatal.' [12]

A moment's glance at the Douglas side of the picture makes clear the reasons for Republican concern. Popular Sovereignty was sweeping Indiana, the frantic postmasters could do nothing about it and the Bright-Fitch machine was going to pieces. Douglas' Wooster speech represented the 'sentiments of ninety-one hundredths of the Democrats and thousands of the Republicans' of Ohio. New York reports continued good. In New England the Popular Sovereignty men thought they could take care of the embattled postmasters and feared only a Pierce boom. The ex-President, however, kept writing friends that it would annoy him for his name to go before the Charleston Convention 'under any possible combination of circumstances.' [13]

In the South the news was somewhat encouraging. Yancey in his speeches reprehended non-intervention but always referred to Douglas' 'manliness, boldness, and statesmanship.' From New York John Forsyth began a vigorous pamphlet war for the Little Giant. When Henry Hotze, the 'gallant and talented young gentleman' who ran Forsyth's Mobile paper in its owner's absence, discovered a particularly alarming Alabama concentration against Douglas, he 'brought all the guns of the *Register* to bear' and recovered the lost ground. But the Alabama Fire-Eaters took time by the forelock and secured an unofficial agreement upon Alabama's delegates-at-large to the Charleston Convention nine months before it was due to assemble. Even so, Hotze's brave fight gave the weakening Douglas men new courage. 'All that is necessary is to take a bold stand and we intend to do it,' a Selma leader wrote him. 'I really think the tide is on the turn,' wrote Forsyth upon his return to Alabama, 'the reaction will be strong in proportion to the flow.' Forsyth believed the battle in the South would develop into a continuation of the Illinois debates, and that Douglas, on his non-intervention platform, could not fail to win. [14]

[12] David Davis to H. E. Dummer, Bloomington, Ill., Feb. 20, 1860; Dummer MSS., Chicago Historical Society; *National Era*, Washington, quoted in Philadelphia *Press*, Oct. 8, 1859. *National Era*, May 19, 1859: Douglas' followers made up all but a corporal's guard of the Northern Democracy; *ibid.*, June 2, 1859, gives a similar apprehensive reflection.

[13] W. J. Elliot, Indianapolis, Oct. 10; Charles M. Aten, New Lisbon, Ohio, Oct. 13, 1859; Douglas MSS.; John Appleton, New Haven, Conn., Sept. 1, 1859; Buchanan MSS.; Pierce to Eli Shorter, Andover, Mass., Sept. 22, 1859; retained copy, Pierce MSS.

[14] Yancey quoted in clipping, New York, Sept. 2, 1859, enclosed B. O. Kean, Mobile, Ala., Sept. 7, 1859; Douglas MSS. The Alabama Fire-Eater told a dinner *vis-à-vis* that he admired Douglas highly and that it gave him great pain to differ with him. Forsyth's pamphlet war was

The Little Giant's own hopes ran high. 'All right in the West, and no mistake,' he jubilated to Sanders. 'Our friends in the South are in fine spirits, gaining every day and confident of success,' he informed McClernand. 'There will be no difficulty in Charleston.' [15]

At this point the strange figure of John Brown reappears in our narrative — John Brown, of Osawatomie, whom God had told to shoot down Southern settlers in cold blood. When last we saw him, in 1856, the old man was rejoicing over murder on the prairie.[16] Now on a cold October night three years later we find him leading an Abolition company in a sudden descent upon a sleeping Virginia town, hoping to arm the Negroes with pike and torch and to light the match to the Southern powder-mine.

In the years between Bleeding Kansas and Harper's Ferry, the Territory had become more peaceful, much to the disgust of Brown and his Northeastern sponsors. These latter were philanthropists, non-resisters, men of peace; Gerrit Smith, a chief among them — a handsome, florid-faced man of eloquence, charm and fine hospitality — was Vice-President of the American Peace Society and often presided at its meetings.[17] But for all their professed abhorrence of war, Smith and his associates proclaimed that there were instances in which blood-letting was unavoidable, notably the war against the slave system. They deemed the Kansas enterprise of the Emigrant Aid Society a holy war, in which both Border Ruffians and Federal soldiers were fair targets for their Sharps' rifles. Revolutionary possibilities were scented by Thomas Wentworth Higginson, another of their most noted leaders, who found the Kansas Abolition men 'just as

with William F. Samford, an Alabama politician, in 1858 an anti-Lecomptonite, who in 1859 had gone Fire-Eater and had unsuccessfully run for Governor on a Yancey platform. The Mobile *Mercury* published Samford's ten letters, the *Register* Forsyth's replies. These last were then put into a pamphlet by Lemuel Tower, of Washington; for photostats I am indebted to the Illinois State Historical Library. John Forsyth, Mobile, Oct. 9, for description of Hotze's campaign; Forsyth to A. D. Banks, Mobile, Oct. 16, asking for Douglas visit. James D. Smith, Selma, Ala., Oct. 31, 1859, Douglas MSS., for Selma meeting, typical of those in the campaign. Addresses were made by C. W. Lee, Alexander White, John W. Lapsley and James D. Smith. Henry Hotze was in truth a remarkable young man. He was not twenty at the time of the Douglas campaign. Three years later he was sent to England as an agent for the Confederacy, and developed into the South's most useful propagandist abroad, almost repairing the blunders of Mason, Slidell and Davis himself. For Hotze's subsequent career, see Frank Owsley, *King Cotton Diplomacy*, Chicago, 1931; 120, 166, 176, 179, 186, 188; Donaldson Jordan and Edwin J. Pratt, *Europe and the American Civil War*, Boston, 1933; 125, 166, 184–86.

15 Douglas to George N. Sanders, Washington, Sept. 22, 1859; original in Watertown, Conn., Library; Douglas to McClernand, Washington, Oct. 1, 1859, McClernand MSS. To Lanphier he wrote similarly: 'The prospects in the South are improving every day. We will have a strong party in the South when the convention meets.' Lanphier should exchange with the Mobile *Register*, which was making a glorious fight on the right line.' Douglas to Lanphier, Washington, Oct. 1, 1859; Patton MSS.

16 Cf. *supra*, 199–200.

17 'Occasional,' in Philadelphia *Press*, Oct. 21, 1859, tells how Smith, while a Congressman in Washington, 'delighted in the most elegant hospitalities, spending his money with a frequency and a freedom that was a subject of general remark.' Southerners liked him and classified him as an Abolitionist who should be tolerated.

ready to fight the U.S. Government as the Missourians.' After vainly seeking public appropriations for an Abolition army, they undertook to raise private funds therefor. John Brown kept in touch with them.[18]

Late in 1857 the Kansas chieftain plotted a descent upon Virginia and came East for help. He found Gerrit Smith and his associates ready to 'go *all* lengths' with him. The invasion was scheduled for the Spring of 1858 but there was an accident — Brown quarreled with his drill-master, and the latter turned informer, causing a hasty scurrying to cover. In March, 1859, the old man paid another visit to Smith's home at Peterboro, there was a gathering of the faithful, poems were read calling Brown a true Christian and expense money was raised. A company of whites and blacks went with him to Canada, where he perfected plans and arms and drafted a 'Provisional Constitution and Ordinance for the People of the United States.' Then, in August, using an alias, Brown leased a farm in western Maryland, a few miles from Harper's Ferry, the seat of a Government arsenal, and set to work drilling the soldiers of the Lord.[19]

'We may look any year, any month, any day' for a slave insurrection, Gerrit Smith proclaimed in a public letter. Admitting that such a revolt would probably fail, he asked: 'Is it so entirely certain that these insurrections will be put down promptly, and before they can be spread far? ...Remember that telegraphs and railroads can be rendered useless in an hour. Remember, too, that many who would be glad to face the insurgents, would be busy in transporting their wives and daughters to places where they would be safe from that worst fate which husbands and fathers can imagine for their wives and daughters.'[20]

On Sunday night, October 16, the Sword of Gideon smote Harper's Ferry. John Brown and a band of sixteen white men and five Negroes seized the railway bridge over the Potomac, cut the telegraph wires and dashed into the sleeping town. At first the invaders had things their own way and the town was quickly captured. Detachments of the force rushed into the countryside, rousing the gentry from their sleep and seizing sixty hostages, among them Colonel Lewis Washington, a grandnephew of the first President. But Brown was enormously disappointed that the Negroes he had come to save were reluctant to seize his cutlasses and pikes or to carry the torch about the countryside.

The next morning the local militia gathered, there was some shooting and the invaders abandoned the Armory for the fire hall or engine house. Washington, which heard of the invasion before news reached Richmond,

[18] T. W. Higginson, Worcester, Mass., Nov. 1; Gov. Ryland Fletcher, Montpelier, Vt., Nov. 4, 1856; Gerrit Smith MSS. Vermont did vote $20,000 but no other New England Legislature responded.

[19] Ralph Volney Harlow, 'Gerrit Smith and John Brown,' *American Historical Review*, XXXVIII, 32–60; Professor Harlow's article brings to light a great deal of important new evidence about Smith's and Higginson's general willingness to incite bloodshed and their part in the Harper's Ferry raid. Others who helped Brown finance treason were Theodore Parker, George L. Stearns and F. B. Sanborn.

[20] Smith to 'Jerry Rescue' Anniversary Committee, Peterboro, N.Y., Aug. 27, 1859; printed copy in Gerrit Smith MSS.

promptly dispatched a special train, bearing a Marine contingent under command of Colonel R. E. Lee, of the Regular Army. Lee brought with him as temporary aide young J. E. B. Stuart, a cavalry lieutenant on leave from Kansas. Early Tuesday morning Lee sent Stuart to the door of the engine house to promise a legal trial and demand surrender. Old Brown threatened that, if attacked, he would kill the hostages, Stuart parleyed but Colonel Washington cried out, 'Never mind us — fire.' Brown persisted, Stuart gave the signal and the Marines attacked. The white-bearded leader coolly defied danger. One son was killed and another wounded, but 'he felt the pulse of his dying son with one hand, held his rifle with the other and commanded his men with the utmost composure.' [21] Soon the door was broken in, Brown and his remaining confederates were wounded, overpowered and rushed to the Charles Town jail. Governor Wise, who soon reached the scene of treason, questioned Brown and pronounced him no maniac but 'a bundle of the best nerves I ever saw.'

Virginia acted promptly; a week after capture Brown was placed on trial, six days later he was adjudged guilty, on November 2 he was sentenced to death and a month later John Brown's life paid the penalty of the triple crimes of conspiracy, murder and treason. And there were some on the Pottawatomie who thought there was merit in Virginia hemp.[22]

'Like a fire bell in the night,' the slavery argument had terrified Thomas Jefferson forty years before. Like a fire bell in the night this example of Abolition fanaticism now aroused the whole United States. Brown's failure caused dismay among many Northern groups. Gerrit Smith promptly sent his son-in-law about the country to destroy any incriminating evidence, and burned all letters he had from Brown. Soon thereafter he seemed to go mad, recovering only when the Congressional investigating committees had reported and been dismissed. The less aggressive anti-slavery leaders reprehended the raid as a wrong means to effect a right result. But many Abolition preachers said in the pulpit that Brown was a martyr, and that the Virginia gallows were 'as glorious as a cross.' [23]

The Republican politicians were in a dilemma. To denounce John Brown would lose them the support of the emotional Anti-Slavery group already beginning to canonize the bloodthirsty old man. Yet they could not yet afford to endorse treason or to condone the invasion of a sovereign State. The course adopted was characteristic of politicians: pretending to regard Brown as a madman, they sought to lay the blame on Douglas and the Kansas-Nebraska bill. Administration Democrats were equally anxious

[21] Colonel Washington's testimony, quoted in B. H. Wise, *Life of Henry A. Wise*, 247.

[22] For details of the raid, trial and execution, see Elijah Avey, *Capture and Execution of John Brown*, Chicago, 1906; John Newton, *Captain John Brown of Harper's Ferry*, London, 1902; James Redpath, *Public Life of Captain John Brown, with an Autobiography*, Boston, 1860; William S. Robinson, *'Warrenton' Pen Portraits: Personal and Political Reminiscences, 1848-76*, Boston, 1877; John S. Wise, *The End of an Era*, Boston, 1902; O. G. Villard, *John Brown*, 391-557; John W. Thomason, Jr., *Jeb Stuart*, New York, 1930; 49-55; James C. Young, *Marse Robert*, New York, 1929; 67-70.

[23] Thomason, 57.

to damn Douglas; a Buchanan organ in Ohio alleged that among the letters found on Brown at Harper's Ferry was one from Douglas, enclosing a contribution of one thousand dollars to the cause![24] But the very day of Brown's capture, Douglas gave an interview drawing the moral of the invasion and pointing out that intervention from either section endangered the Union of the States.[25]

There was an immediate note of deep alarm from the South. 'This unnatural war upon Negro slavery in one section by another of the common country,' Governor Wise told the Virginia Legislature, 'inevitably drives to disunion of the States, embittered with all the vengeful hate of civil war.' Many Alabamians came to believe 'that there is no longer safety for them in the Union, and that the Harper's Ferry fray is but the beginning of the trial of blood that is made up after twenty years of argument.'

Within a few weeks of Brown's capture, however, the most immediate Southern apprehensions began to quiet, Virginia took Brown's trial with unusual calm and a new tone appeared in Douglas' Southern mail. As a proprietor of the Memphis *Appeal* expressed it, as soon as the Senate convened, Douglas must 'trace the Harper's Ferry treason as a legitimate consequence (as it is) of the doctrine taught by Seward and Lincoln.'[26] The Senator had waged such continual warfare against this 'House Divided,' 'Irrepressible Conflict' doctrine that his Southern supporters resumed their canvass. Forsyth pressed Douglas to come South to speak to the people. 'Our friends are increasing and our cause is growing,' he wrote on November 1. 'The crazy politicians will wake up to their mistake or I am greatly mistaken in the temper of the Southern people.' Senator Clement Clay, an Ultra of the Ultras, could not control the Democratic convention in his home county. Forsyth became convinced Yancey could not carry the State upon a separation program.[27]

And yet, after two years' testing, that great Secessionist had developed his Southern Rights technique to a fine point. It had been outlined in the Summer of 1858 in his famous 'Scarlet Letter' counseling against any further Southern effort to control the Democratic party. The South's true remedy was 'a diligent organization of her true men for prompt resistance to the next aggression.' Through Committees of Safety over the Cotton States, 'we shall fire the Southern heart, instruct the Southern mind, give courage to each other, and at the proper moment by one organized, concerted action we can precipitate the Cotton States into a revolution.'[28]

[24] Richard Yates to William Jayne, N.P., Nov. 8, 1859; Chicago Historical Society MSS.; *Ohio State Journal*, Columbus, Nov. 3, 1859, printed this forged letter, under purported date of Sept. 1, 1859, Washington, and signed 'Yours in the cause, S. A. D.'

[25] 'Occasional,' in Philadelphia *Press*, Oct. 20, 21, 1859.

[26] Wise, *Henry A. Wise*, 252–53. A. D. Banks, New York, Oct. 29; James Nisbet, Macon, Ga., Oct. 25; John H. Gilmer, Richmond, Va., Oct. 28; John Forsyth, Montgomery, Ala., Dec. 16; B. S. Dill, Memphis, Nov. 2, 1859; Douglas MSS.

[27] John Forsyth, Mobile, Nov. 1; J. C. Bradley, Huntsville, Ala., Nov. 10, 1859; Douglas MSS.

[28] Yancey to James S. Slaughter, Montgomery, Ala., June 15, 1858; clipping from Chattanooga *Advertiser*, in scrapbook owned by Mrs. J. H. Stanfield, Chattanooga, Tenn.

Yancey modified this plan in the Summer of 1859. Now he saw that if the Ultras stayed out of the Charleston Convention, the Cincinnati platform would be readopted and Douglas named to run upon it. Therefore the Fire-Eaters should go in and make a fight for a slave code plank in the platform. If they failed, 'the State's Rights wing should secede from the convention' and run a candidate of its own. If then a Black Republican should be elected President, the Southern States must withdraw from the Union before his inauguration.[29]

Douglas was repeatedly warned that Yancey's dearest object was to send a delegation to force 'the most unsound and disturbing heresies' into the party platform, failing which, he and his following would 'secede from the convention and endeavor to break it up in a row.'[30] The great agitator was 'full of political cunning' and more Alabama politicians leaped over the fence to join him. But now Yancey undertook to be elected to the United States Senate in place of Benjamin Fitzpatrick, whose term was about to expire. Governor Winston, the executive in office, was also a candidate. The chief effect of Yancey's candidacy was to delay the Legislature's vote and temporarily to tie Fitzpatrick's hands in the Secession argument. Douglas, however, was advised that Yancey was 'not half so popular in Alabama as he pretends to be,' and so it proved, for when the Assembly voted, the chief Fire-Eater came in third. Forsyth now believed more firmly than ever that the people of Alabama could also be persuaded to eschew Yancey's nostrum of Secession as a cure for abstract ills.[31]

'If we could get through the upper crust' of politicians and aspirants, a Tennessee editor advised Douglas, 'you would have but little difficulty in this section of the country.' But he had suffered a personal as well as political loss in that State — 'Lean Jimmy' Jones had died. Stricken in October, when told that there was no hope of recovery, he settled up his personal affairs and began to talk about Douglas, 'the truest and bravest of men, as pure a patriot as any living or dead.' A half-hour before death he whispered that outside his family he had but one aim in life — 'if Stephen A. Douglas is nominated, to canvass once more every county in Tennessee.'[32] The death of this veteran cast a damper on Douglas' Tennessee campaign. The remaining leaders lacked Jones' finesse and force, and were hard put to it to counter the Andrew Johnson favorite son campaign.

Louisiana's election early in November had mixed results. The New Orleans current was moving so strongly in Douglas' direction that Slidell resorted to a characteristic stratagem. He brought out a ticket representing itself to be 'purely independent, clear of Slidellism and Know-Nothingism,'

[29] Speech at Columbus, S.C., July, 1859, from scrapbook of James K. Polk, of Warrenton, N.C.

[30] B. O. Kean, Mobile, Nov. 1; J. W. Lapsley, Selma, Dec. 2, 1859; Douglas MSS.

[31] B. O. Kean, Mobile, Nov. 1; W. A. Smythe, Montgomery, Nov. 30, John Forsyth, Montgomery, Dec. 16, 1859; Douglas MSS.

[32] L. J. Dupree, O. H. Lide, Nathan Anderson, J. R. McClanahan, Memphis, Oct. 30; D. S. Dill, Memphis, Nov. 2; Henry C. Grossman, Macon, Miss., Nov. 12; James W. Singleton, Memphis, Dec. 10, 1859; Douglas MSS. Macon, Miss., *Beacon*, Nov. 10, 1859; Memphis *Appeal*, Nov. 13, 1859, printing letter of Dupree, Jones' son-in-law, telling of death-bed scenes.

but actually a group of Slidell's tools. The Douglas men, deceived, put out no slate of their own. Then Slidell brought forward a formal pro-Slidell ticket, the resulting campaign was a farce and less than six thousand votes were cast in place of a normal fifteen thousand. Out in the State, however, there was a real test; Miles Taylor, an open Douglas candidate for Congress, won handily, while so many anti-Slidell men were elected to the Legislature that that worthy's re-election to the Senate seemed impossible.[33]

Douglas' increasing Georgia strength alarmed the leading Fire-Eaters, who resorted to a trick to insure an anti-Douglas delegation. This new support for the Little Giant was 'of the quiet men and among the masses.' While at heart for him, Robert Toombs did not avow it; Herschel V. Johnson was suspiciously quiet and Alexander H. Stephens was busy with his own plans. But while Douglas' Georgia friends of high estate seemed paralyzed, such men as James A. Nisbet at Macon, James Patillo in south Georgia, George H. Lamar and James Gardner at Augusta and Ambrose Spencer at Savannah enlisted 'substantial old-panel Democrats' all over Georgia.

Senator Iverson's situation gave the Ultras more food for reflection. That Spring, when 'Little Alec' had announced his plan to quit public life in a 'Farewell Address' devoted to peace, prosperity and Union, Iverson had insolently countered by a speech on the text 'Slavery, it must and shall be preserved.' This had not sat so well with the people, and when the Legislature met Iverson faced strong opposition for re-election. Governor Johnson, his leading opponent, let it be known that he was 'on the same line with Douglas.' When the matter came to a vote, Iverson was retired.

The report of a Stephens-Douglas combination completed the Fire-Eaters' alarm. The Democratic State Executive Committee had already issued its call for a State Convention to be held in March to pick delegates to Charleston, but the Ultras, rigging up a temporary legislative majority, rushed through a bill calling a new State Democratic Convention to meet on December 8. This was packed by legislative Ultras, adopted a Yancey Slave Code platform to which all delegates must subscribe and 'presented' Howell Cobb as a candidate. This roused the Moderates. Meetings were held in many parts of the State, which repudiated the rump convention and named delegates to the regularly called gathering for March.

'The great majority of our people have lost interest in the Charleston nomination,' Nisbet reported. 'There is a deep, sullen, desponding state of feeling among our people who really desire the perpetuation of the Union. They see the Republican party under the control of extreme men and the Democratic party at the South pushed on to the extreme policy by Ultraists, and they fold their hands and say, "All is lost."' The slavery agitation was sinking in, 'death must ensue without powerful remedy.' Why not a Union party to arouse and rally patriots in North and South alike? And in the meanwhile, 'let your friends stand in hollow square at Charleston.' [34]

[33] H. Kennedy, New Orleans, Nov. 16; F. H. Clarke, New Orleans, Nov. 15, 1859; Douglas MSS.

[34] James A. Nisbet, Macon, Oct. 25; Dec. 1, 27; George H. Lamar, Augusta, Dec. 11, 1859; Douglas MSS. Nancy Telfair, *History of Columbus*, Columbus, Ga., 1929; 99–100. Ulrich B. Phillips, *Robert Toombs*, New York, 1913; 188.

During these Southern developments, the Douglas campaign encountered the usual alarms, upsets and successes in the other sections. Tammany, as usual, began playing a double game; but some Douglas men who had been large Wigwam contributors closed their purses, and the intrigue, while annoying, had no real consequence, for Dean Richmond had the New York delegate situation well in hand.[35] While the Iowa Democrats lost their State election, they fought well, had few bad wounds, were full of spirit and felt confident of victory in 1860. More and more moderate anti-slavery men in the Northwest were beginning to realize, as Senator Dodge put it, that Republican triumph nationally 'would subject our system to a frightful trial, to one from which may God in His mercy preserve it.' [36]

Ohio Democrats also lost their State election. Realizing the pivotal importance, the Republicans poured outside speakers into the State. Among the number was Abraham Lincoln, who spoke at Cincinnati, Columbus, Hamilton and Dayton, assailing Douglas and Popular Sovereignty. And as in Illinois, Buchanan's Federal office-holders not only refused to contribute to the Democratic campaign fund but wielded their treacherous knives on election day. For all this, in the outcome the Democrats did well. Ranney, their candidate for Governor, lost by a little less than 15,000 votes out of 400,000. To the gratification of the Little Giant's friends, the Democratic ticket showed an increased strength in each of the three places where he had made speeches, although in two of these Lincoln had also appeared. This convinced them that Douglas would carry Ohio for President.[37] By late November the Indiana Douglas men had three-fourths of the Charleston delegation, to say nothing of the coming State Convention.[38]

Douglas realized that every move in Illinois would have national repercussions. When the Danite Committee met in Springfield, October 1, to

[35] 'Occasional,' in Philadelphia *Press*, Oct. 15, 1859. Those placing embargoes on contributions included August Belmont, Watt Sherman, James Lee, S. L. W. Barlow, Schuyler Livingston and Royal Phelps. A. D. Banks, New York, Oct. 29, 31; George N. Sanders, New York, Oct. 30; J. A. McMasters, New York, Oct. 30, 1859; Douglas MSS.

[36] Augustus Cæsar Dodge, Burlington, Iowa, Nov. 10, 1859; Douglas MSS.

[37] James E. Cox, Mansfield, Ohio, Oct. 18; A. L. Backus, Columbus, Ohio, Oct. 18; H. B. Payne, Cleveland, Ohio, Oct. 20; D. P. Rhodes, Cleveland, Oct. 23; F. W. Murray, Delhi, Ohio, Nov. 30, 1859; Douglas MSS. Douglas spoke at three places, Columbus in Wayne County; Cincinnati in Hamilton County and Wooster in Franklin County. The 1858 and 1859 comparisons for these counties follow:

	Governor — 1859		Judge — 1858	
	Dennison, R.	Ranney, D.	Peck, R.	Bartley, D.
Wayne..............	2944	3285	2775	2828
Hamilton............	13,280	14,178	13,326	14,151
Franklin............	3762	4634	3735	4336

Lincoln spoke in Columbus twice on September 16, and on the next day made a two-hour speech at Dayton, a brief talk at Hamilton and that night a long address at Market House Square at Cincinnati.

[38] Aquilla Jones, Indianapolis, Nov. 2; Gordon Tanner, Indianapolis, Nov. 2; Gordon James, Indianapolis, Nov. 5; A. H. Brown, Indianapolis, Nov. 28, 1859; Douglas MSS. Brown figured seven of the eleven district conventions for Douglas. Delegates thus elected, plus the four from the State-at-large, would give the Little Giant eighteen of Indiana's twenty-six.

set the stage for a contesting delegation to Charleston, the Little Giant
sent Lanphier a detailed plan of battle for the Regulars, who must under
no circumstances recognize the Danites. Let the State Convention meet
in January, adopt a platform and name delegates, adjourning until June
the selection of a State ticket, so as to avoid any disturbance from disappointed aspirants. He rather liked Richardson's idea of naming the
State's twenty-two delegates all from the State-at-large, and of having
those selected 'the most prominent men with the best political record
on the slavery question that could be found in the State — men well known
to the whole country and especially favorably known to the South.' All
Douglas' friends wanted to go to South Carolina, but he kept insisting
that it was important for 'our leading men' to be selected.[39]

With the opening of Congress in December, the National Capital throbbed
with politics and the Nation throbbed with it. The various House factions
employed the contest over the Speakership to bring the slavery issue forward with the utmost violence. The Southern Ultra feeling was well expressed by Howell Cobb, who wrote a kinsman that, unless the North
changed its views completely, 'the Union must go by the boards.' The
South would never 'submit to the election of a Black Republican President'
and he did not think it should.
    A book by a Southern man precipitated the battle — *The Impending
Crisis* by one Hinton Rowan Helper, a 'poor white' from North Carolina,
expressing with convincing statistics but questionable rhetoric the wrong
done the South's non-slave-holding whites by the slave system. This economic *Uncle Tom's Cabin*, published in 1857, had secured but scant reading
from the Southern 'mud-sills' its author claimed he sought to influence, but
was taken up by the Republicans. The book itself and its party sponsorship
aroused the flaming rage of the Southern politicians, and its sale was prohibited in several States, including that of Helper's nativity.
    John Sherman, of Ohio, the initial Republican choice for Speaker, had
signed an endorsement of a pamphlet based on Helper's book. No sooner
was he brought forward than a Missouri Democrat offered a resolution that
no member who had endorsed such an insurrectionary book was fit to
be Speaker. With this, the House, unbound by rules and with a helpless clerk in the chair, turned itself into a disorderly debating society.
Abolitionist denunciations of slavery and Southern counter-threats of a
determination to 'shatter this Republic from turret to foundation stone'
unless full rights were given, punctuated the debate.
    Threats of physical altercation were frequent, challenges were offered
and refused, and one day a pistol fell from the pocket of a Northern speaker,
almost precipitating riot and bloodshed. Every man in both Houses had
armed himself 'with a revolver — some with two — and a bowie knife,' and
some had armed friends in the galleries.

    [39] Murray McConnel, Jacksonville, Ill., Sept. 29; Chas. H. Lanphier, Springfield, Ill., Dec.
16, 1859; Douglas MSS.; Douglas to McClernand, Washington, Oct. 1, 1859; McClernand MSS.;
Douglas to Lanphier, Washington, Oct. 1, 1859, Jan. 1, 1860; Patton MSS.

So bitter was the contest that one of the great banking family of Rothschild, who had come to America to study conditions, feared that the United States might soon break into bits. 'Political passions are pushed forward to a state of paroxysm,' he wrote home. 'The question of slavery will be buried forever, or else there will be separation... and perhaps civil war.'

The Douglas Democrats were in the direct line of fire and the extremists of both sections attacked them bitterly. The most violent Southern Ultras dramatically announced that they would vote for no Popular Sovereignty Democrat for Speaker, defiantly adding that they would not support Douglas for President were he the nominee of a dozen Charleston conventions, while the editor of Buchanan's new organ, the *Constitution*, said he would rather see John Sherman Speaker than an anti-Lecompton Democrat. 'I see you have got the nigger up in the House "aready,"' Lincoln's partner, Billy Herndon, gibed at McClernand, who had been elected to Harris' seat. 'Niggers are great institutions, are they not?'

But the Douglasites determined to enlighten the country as to 'all the obstructions to the triumph of the Democracy.' After giving their complimentary votes for one or two Northern Democrats, they concentrated on such Southern conservatives as Bocock, of Virginia; Rust, of Arkansas, and Hamilton, of Texas, all of whom stood on the Cincinnati platform and would support Douglas. The Little Giant's own delegation sought manfully to 'neutralize Southern prejudice and to establish a standard of forbearance and conciliation.' [40]

While waiting for the House to get organized, the Republicans did all the damage to Douglas that they could. William Kellogg, a Republican from Illinois, tried to warm up the old story of an 1858 plot between Greeley

---

[40] Howell Cobb to J. B. Lamar, Washington, Dec. 5, 1859; Erwin MSS. The full title of Helper's book was *The Impending Crisis of the South. How to Meet It*, New York, 1857. My copy, dated 1859, is imprinted '14th Thousand,' a large sale for the day. Its foundation was a comparison of the census figures for Northern and Southern States, showing how these last were continually falling behind in the economic competition and showing what a fearful disadvantage this placed upon the non-slave-holding white. It went into an excited argument against the slavocracy and demanded that 'oligarchical despotism must be overthrown; slavery must be abolished.' But the Negro must then be removed from the United States. This had been put into cheap abstracts for free distribution. The booklet had John Sherman's endorsement, along with many other Republican members of the House. Sherman later explained that he had endorsed it without reading it. Penningon, of New Jersey, finally elected Speaker, had not endorsed it. David Rankin Barbee, 'Hinton Rowan Helper,' *Tyler's Quarterly Historical and Genealogical Magazine*, XV, 144–72, casts doubt on Helper's authorship of the book, and suggests that Francis Preston Blair had a good deal to do with it. Mr. Barbee also amasses evidence to show Helper a good deal of a scamp. Rhodes, II, 374, 383, gives a vivid description of the scenes in the House in December, 1859, and January, 1860. Salomon de Rothschild, New York, Jan 3, 1860, MSS. Travel Letters, Baron Salomon de Rothschild, Bibliothèque Nationale, Paris, photostats in Library of Congress. For translation I am indebted to Miss Mildred Lamoreaux, of the University of Chattanooga. Hammond to Francis Lieber, Washington, April 19, 1860, quoted in Merritt, 133. Salter, *James W. Grimes*, 121; W. H. Herndon to McClernand, Springfield, Dec. 8, 1859; McClernand to Capt. John Henry, Washington, Jan. 14, 1860; retained copy, McClernand MSS. McClernand to Lanphier, Washington, Dec. 22, 27, 30, 1859; Patton MSS.

and Douglas, and McClernand and John A. Logan gave Kellogg a verbal
trouncing, with a physical one narrowly averted. This interchange aroused
joy in Illinois. This 'devil-up-ment,' one man chuckled, meant that Logan
'wanted to make his marks on a Kel-log.' [41]

Buchanan held his message for three weeks for the House to choose a
Speaker, but finally his patience gave out and he dispatched it to the Senate.
In addition to placing responsibility for the Harper's Ferry invasion on the
Republicans, the President mildly approved the extreme Southern slave
code position and urged Cuba's acquisition.   Growling angrily that the
message was 'damnable' and 'subversive of the settled ideas of the country since the formation of the Federal Government,' Douglas' aides recognized it as 'a malicious endeavor to do mischief.'   They realized that it
would embarrass his Southern friends but believed that, by its very extremity, the message would also crush out Northern Democratic opposition
to Douglas' choice.[42]

At first the news from the South did not bear out this judgment. 'The
most your friends fear in the South,' wrote a Kentuckian, 'is the politicians.
...Your strength is with the people.' [43] Nor was evidence lacking that the
Southern masses were anxious to break the politicians' hold. On the completion of the Louisville and Nashville Railroad, Louisville held a union
festival to honor Tennessee, the latter's Legislature journeyed to Frankfort,
whence the solons of the two States went on to the Ohio Capital at Columbus. There the three Legislatures held a joint session to register their determination that the Union be maintained.[44] This fear of strife and hope
for peace also had expression from some of the Cotton South's great slave-
holders, conservatives who were alarmed by the Fire-Eaters' dogma.
Meredith Calhoun, of Alabama, one of the largest slave-owners in the
South termed Douglas' doctrine of non-intervention 'a wall of fire between us
and the Abolitionists.' [45]

The epoch's tragedy, however, was that the political machinery prevented
the registration, against the will of the controlling group, of any other than
the most deep-seated and persistent public demand. Professional politicians
staffed and ran State and local committees, held caucuses, controlled conventions and parceled out party honors, offices and emoluments. A study
of comparative techniques of public control shows that our modern political

[41] T. W. S. Kidd, Springfield, Dec. 16, 1859; McClernand MSS. McClernand and Douglas
had 'made the whole body politic of the Black Republicans feel sore, even the legs of the party
(Honest Abe) felt sympathetic pains.'

[42] McClernand to Lanphier, Washington, Dec. 27, 29, 1859; Patton MSS.

[43] John Forsyth, Mobile, Dec. 24; J. W. Singleton, Memphis, Dec. 10, 1859; J. B. Cochran,
Shelbyville, Ky., March 4, 1860; Douglas MSS.

[44] Senate Journal, Tennessee, Jan. 9, 1860, for acceptance of Louisville invitation; Lewis
D. Campbell to T. W. Newman, Hamilton, Ohio, Jan. 30, 1860, giving resolutions adopted by
the City of Hamilton, hailing the visit 'as a harbinger of the era of fraternal feeling'; Tennessee
Senate Journal, Feb. 2, 1860, resolution of thanks by Tennessee to Kentucky and Ohio. Cf.
'Excursion Made by the Executives — Legislatures of Kentucky and Tennessee to Ohio,' a
pamphlet, printed in Cincinnati, in 1860.

[45] Joseph C. Bradley, Huntsville, Ala., April 6, 1860, quoting Meredith Calhoun; Douglas MSS.

machines are heavier, clumsier, more costly and considerably less effective than were their counterparts of the 'Fifties.

Patronage had an even greater impress and the appointing power was bolder and more ruthless in using it. This Federal set-up of postmasters, attorneys, marshals and their retainers had a disproportionate influence upon the party process in the sparsely settled areas of the agrarian South. Add to this the sincere Fire-Eating patriot with his parade of abstract wrongs and program of reform or revolution, and there was a perfect pattern of pressure politics — minority control of political decisions against the wishes of a rank and file not organized to compel obedience.

This curious divergence between the fiction of a government by public opinion and the fact of control by special groups was well illustrated by the case of Tennessee. Just about the time that its General Assembly journeyed to Kentucky and Ohio to promote the cause of Union, its State Democratic Convention on January 17 took action which in practical effect struck a blow at peace. The great planters of West Tennessee, the Memphis Moderates, Gideon Pillow and the old James K. Polk organization in Middle Tennessee and a vigorous group of farmers and workers in lower East Tennessee favored a Douglas delegation. But they had to reckon with the Johnson group's dislike of Gideon Pillow, Knox Walker and the other political heirs of Polk. Johnson himself was somewhat reluctant but because of local factional necessities finally gave consent and his son managed the affair.

Perhaps good management would have saved the day for Douglas, but 'Lean Jimmy' Jones was dead. General Pillow drafted the slavery planks of the platform so that they neither conflicted with Douglas' views nor compromised his friends. Suddenly Johnson's lieutenants sent the Platform Committee a resolution recommending him as Tennessee's choice for President. Pillow opposed but it carried in committee by twelve to ten and was reported to the convention. Then the Johnson forces approached the Douglas men, and an understanding was reached under which Johnson instructions were accepted, but the delegation was to come to Douglas if and when Johnson dropped out. Pursuant to this, Tennessee instructed for her plebeian Senator.[46]

Kentucky's outcome also showed the danger of depending on unorganized public sentiment. Douglas had about a third of the delegates to the State Convention, a speech in his behalf was received 'with thunderous applause,' his position was treated courteously in the platform and with some finesse he could have won the delegation. But his friends could not cope with Guthrie, who as President of the Louisville and Nashville was establishing that road as the political control of the State. Breckinridge's maladroit campaign was even less successful. Douglas pressed Guthrie hard in the critical ballot but the railroad politician won.[47]

[46] Gideon J. Pillow, Columbia, April 3, 1860; Douglas MSS.; Robert Johnson to Andrew Johnson, Nashville, Jan. 20, 22, 1860; Robert Johnson MSS., Library of Congress; Milton, *The Age of Hate*, 94.

[47] E. T. Holloway, Richmond, Ky., Jan. 18; Geo. N. Sanders, n.p., Jan.; J. B. Cochran, Shelbyville, Ky., March 4, 1860; Douglas MSS. Sanders quoted a letter from his sister, Mrs.

Alabama's delegates had been slated six months before its State Convention met in January. For some time prior to its assemblage, Forsyth's *Register* each day asked the Ultras: 'Will you abide the action of the Charleston Convention?' Most of the county delegations, however, had been packed by Ultras weeks before.

The great debate of the Alabama Convention occurred on the night of January 13. John Forsyth manfully stood up to the great Yancey, that night at the height of oratorical force, but the outcome was predetermined. The Fire-Eaters forced through a platform calling for a slave code plank at Charleston. The delegates were also ordered to bolt were such a plan refused. Public reaction against this action was of no avail.[48]

In Georgia the Stephens men now realized that they had been victims, along with Douglas, of the Legislature's rump convention, and made common cause with his followers to upset the fraud. Great meetings of protest were held and delegates were chosen for the legal State Convention of March 12. 'Little Alec' ended his deep silence and began to denounce 'with much bitterness' the war on Douglas, whom he would 'most cordially' support. Had Stephens taken this position the previous Summer the Georgia outcome might have been very different. Perhaps now it would have consequence.[49]

Douglas' chief lieutenants at Washington came increasingly to realize the grave national consequences of Douglas' defeat. 'Our country for the first time is in serious danger of civil commotions,' one lieutenant confidentially advised a friend. 'Unless the triumph of conservative and patriotic sentiment in the approaching presidential election delivers us from danger, the result must be disastrous.' But Douglas' election would establish a common denominator of agreement among Conservatives, and strengthen their hands by excluding the Ultras of both sections 'from patriotic association.'

No sooner did Douglas recover from his illness than he began performing such Herculean labors that he was in danger of breaking down again. Even so, he was bearing up like a hero 'under the concerted and continuous fire of his piebald persecutors.' The little group around Douglas became more and more confident. 'The North is almost unanimously for him,' wrote McClernand; Douglas was making rapid gains in the South and would be 'the second choice of many, if not all, of the Southern States.' A large majority of the convention would be for him, 'probably on the first ballot,' the platform would be under their control and would be national in tone. 'Douglas is now sweeping everything,' Logan wrote his wife. 'Unless some-

Lindsay, of Carroll County, Ky., whose husband had been at the convention and reported 'That all that was wanted to send Douglas delegates to Charleston was some of your management — you should have been there.' John A. Logan to Mrs. Logan, Washington, Jan. 7, 1860; Logan MSS.

[48] John Forsyth, Mobile, Dec. 24, 1859; Jan. 6, 13, 1860; Douglas MSS. E. C. Bullock, Eufaula, Ala., Dec. 30, 1859; H. L. Clay, Huntsville, Jan. 19, 1860, C. C. Clay MSS.

[49] James A. Nisbet, Macon, Jan. 9; Ambrose Spencer, Savannah, Jan. 14; S. I. Johnson, New York, April 20, 1860; Douglas MSS. Johnson quoted a letter he had received from Stephens that day.

thing turns up unforeseen, he will be President next.' Douglas too, felt better. 'Everything looks well here,' he advised the group at Springfield. 'Prospects better every day.' [50]

Now came helpful news from Illinois, where the Regulars' State Convention had met and framed a fine Douglas platform. In this Lanphier and the other Illinois lieutenants had acted with extreme caution. Knowing that their resolutions would be taken by the whole party as Douglas' final word on issues, they insisted that the Senator draft them himself. Douglas called in McClernand, the two wrote an outline, and forwarded it to Springfield. McClernand's accompanying letter insisted that great emphasis be put on the willingness of the Illinois Democracy to stand by the Charleston nominee, whoever he might be. 'We hold that no man can honorably go into this Charleston Convention who is not willing to abide by its action. This position disturbs the extremists of the South, who claim to be Democrats and repudiate Douglas. Let us take the highest ground upon this subject.' [51]

The convention, which met in the State Capital on January 4, unanimously instructed for Douglas and adopted his platform. Most of its planks ran along familiar lines.[52] In addition, the Convention viewed the John Brown conspiracy with 'inexpressible horror and indignation,' and termed it 'the natural consequence and logical result of the doctrines and teachings of the Republican party.' The Illinois delegates to Charleston were instructed to demand the readoption of the Cincinnati platform 'without additions or subtractions.' The convention likewise declared 'that no honorable man can accept a seat as a delegate in the National Democratic Convention or should be recognized as a member of the Democratic party, who will not abide the decisions of such Convention and support its nominees.' [53]

The Danite meeting a few days later was 'respectable' in numbers, and

[50] McClernand to Capt. John Henry, Washington, Jan. 1, 1860; retained copy, McClernand MSS.; McClernand to Lanphier, Washington, Jan. 3, 13; Douglas to Lanphier, Washington, Jan. 1, 1860; Patton MSS.; John A. Logan to Mrs. Logan, Washington, Jan. 7, 1860; Logan MSS., Library of Congress.

[51] C. H. Lanphier, Springfield, Dec. 16, 1859; Douglas MSS.; McClernand to Lanphier, Washington, Dec. 20, 26, 27; Douglas to Lanphier, Washington, Dec. 31, 1859, Jan. 1, 1860; Patton MSS.

[52] C. H. Lanphier, Springfield, Jan. 5, 1860; Douglas MSS. Sheahan, 455, for convention; *Illinois State Register*, Jan. 7, 1860; *Illinois State Journal*, Jan. 10, 1860, for platform text. One plank insisted that until party action at Charleston, the Cincinnati platform, 'Unaltered and unalterable,' remained 'the only authoritative exposition of Democratic doctrine.' Alarmed by the attempt to force new issues and tests upon the party, the Illinois Democracy reasserted and reaffirmed the Cincinnati platform; renewed the call for an effective Fugitive Slave Law; again pledged the party's faith and honor to the Kansas-Nebraska Act; recognized the Supreme Court's highest judicial authority and called on all good citizens to respect and obey its decisions; repelled imputations upon the Court's integrity, and urged that whenever Congress or State or Territorial Legislature should pass any law to prejudice any owner of slave or any other property, and the aggrieved party would bring his case before the United States Supreme Court, the Democracy of Illinois would 'cheerfully and faithfully respect and abide by the decision.'

[53] The personal endorsement of Douglas was not the latter's handiwork; he and McClernand had deliberately left it up to the convention. But Douglas had agreed with McClernand as to the plank about supporting the nominee. McClernand to Lanphier, Washington, Jan. 10, 1860; Patton MSS. J. W. Sheahan, Chicago, Jan. 16, 1860, Douglas MSS.

the bolters were of such a bitter temper that anyone suggesting that they not send a delegation to Charleston 'would have been thrown out of the window.' They named a full set of delegates and were confident these would be seated at Charleston.[54]

The news from other States of the Northwest was even more significant. When Ohio's Democratic district conventions met early in December, all Buchanan's postmasters, collectors, marshals and deputies were 'in the fire ranks' but the result was 'a terrible blow to the President.' Sixteen of the twenty-one districts instructed for Douglas and three of the other five chose delegates committed to him.[55]

The State convention completed the Administration rout. Payne set the stage, Ranney, Steedman, Backus and Rhodes played their parts and the whole affair was a Douglas triumph. 'All the Buchanan men in the State were there,' exulted Payne, 'and they numbered about sixty.' When the various Congressional districts presented their district delegate nominees for the convention's formal approval, Payne moved that before being elected the aspirants 'should come upon the stand and defend their position as to Douglas.' This was done amidst the greatest enthusiasm and every candidate himself or by proxy distinctly pledged himself to vote and labor for the Little Giant so long as his name was before the Charleston convention. Then, not satisfied with this, the delegates met, appointed committees to correspond with other Northwestern delegations and sent six or eight men to Indianapolis to help the good fight there.[56]

In Indiana, a critical sector in the Northwestern battle, 'Old Obliquity' had sinned away his day of grace. Bright, Fitch and their officialdom fought desperately but Douglas instructions in the county conventions foreshadowed the result.[57] A Buchanan confidential agent reported that sixty of Indiana's ninety-one counties had instructed for the Little Giant. The agent suggested a deal under which the Bright forces would not oppose a Douglas personnel if only the delegation be left uninstructed. This was promptly turned down, for the Douglas men were determined this time not to be cheated of their prize. From organization to instruction every convention question went in Douglas' favor. There was a shout of derision when the Bright men proposed Joe Lane and Douglas instructions carried by an overwhelming majority.

This triumph had been achieved 'without caucus, intrigues and management, without the services of political brokers, without trick or fraud of any kind or from any quarter.' All four delegates-at-large were enthusiastic Douglas men, as were seventeen of the twenty-four men from the districts.

[54] Cook to Buchanan, Chicago, Jan. 11, 1860; Buchanan MSS. Cook to J. S. Black, Chicago, Jan. 12, 1860; Black MSS. Virgil Hickox, Springfield, Jan. 11, 1860; Douglas MSS.

[55] A. L. Backus, Columbus, Dec. 3; James Black, Mount Vernon, Ohio, Dec. 5; H. B. Payne, Cleveland, Dec. 10; D. P. Rhodes, Cleveland, Dec. 11; J. B. Steedman, Toledo, Dec. 12, 1859; Douglas MSS.

[56] D. P. Rhodes, Cleveland, Jan. 7; H. B. Payne, Cleveland, Jan. 2, 9, 1860; Douglas MSS.

[57] H. Berry, Jr., Brookville, Ind., Dec. 3; E. M. Huntingdon, Terre Haute, Dec. 4; Thomas A. Hendricks, Indianapolis, Dec. 19; Winslow S. Pierce, Indianapolis, Dec. 19; W. C. Tarkington, Indianapolis, Dec. 19; W. W. Wick, Indianapolis, Dec. 20, 1859; Douglas MSS.

They would vote for Douglas, as a unit, 'first, last and forever.' This 'Solferino victory,' many thought, settled the Charleston nomination.[58]

Minnesota developments were almost equally heartening. Senator Rice had boasted that the Little Giant would never win its delegation; General Shields, Governor Gorman and other dependable Douglas men took the matter in hand, the Minnesota State Convention wrote a Popular Sovereignty platform and instructed for the Senator from Illinois. Shields purposely drafted a platform which would not alienate 'the most fastidious Southern men.' Six of the State's eight delegates were hardly on speaking terms with Rice, while as to the other two, 'with the overwhelming sentiment of the people ringing in his ears,' no man who dared vote against Douglas at Charleston could live politically in the State.[59]

The news from the two Pacific Coast States was disappointing. The Democratic party in both was so dominated by Federal patronage that these States were little more than pocket boroughs for the Administration. Senator Lane's sons-in-law went over Oregon denouncing Douglas as a Black Republican and boasting they would not vote for him under any circumstances. Given full power of removal, the Lane leaders exercised it so ruthlessly that no Federal office-holder could whisper that there was any good in Douglas without being thrust from office. This political terrorism caused the selection of a delegation to Charleston as Ultra as that from Texas.[60]

A new sun had risen in Democratic affairs in California — Milton S. Latham, who was elected to the murdered Broderick's Senate seat. When news of this reached Washington, McClernand wrote Lanphier excitedly that it meant that the Gwin dynasty had been overthrown; Latham was Douglas' friend and his election represented Douglas' solution for the California wrongs.[61] California's Democratic State Convention expressed a mild preference for Daniel S. Dickinson, but refused instructions for him and tabled overwhelmingly a resolution that Douglas was 'the last choice' of the State's Democracy. This outcome further encouraged some of the Little Giant's aides, but George Sanders feared California could 'not be relied on' and the event demonstrated that he was right.[62]

[58] *National Era*, Washington, Jan. 19, 1860; James W. Hughes, Indianapolis, Jan. 13, 1860; Buchanan MSS.; Winslow Pierce, Indianapolis, Jan. 7; Ezra Reed, Indianapolis, Jan. 12; Austin H. Brown, Indianapolis, Jan. 13; A. T. Hann, Columbus, Ind., Jan. 13; E. M. Miller, Indianapolis, Jan. 14; W. W. Wick, Indianapolis, Jan. 15; Norman Eddy, Indianapolis, Jan. 16; Wash McLean, Cincinnati, March 2; Ezra Read, Terre Haute, Ind., April 2, 1860; Douglas MSS.

[59] W. A. Gorman, St. Paul, Minn. Jan. 18, 29, 1860; Douglas MSS. James A. Shields to McClernand, Faribault, Minn., Feb. 11, 1860; McClernand MSS. Even so, the day after the adjournment one of the two Rice men left for Washington and the rumor got around that he would be appointed postmaster as soon as he broke instructions.

[60] Israel Bush, Salem, Oregon, March 5; Wesley Shannon, Salem, March 15; A. W. Sweet, Lafayette, March 26, 1860; Douglas MSS.

[61] Alfred Reddington, Sacramento, Cal., March 17, 1860; Douglas MSS. McClernand to Lanphier, Washington, Feb. 11, 1860; Patton MSS. 'Latham is Douglas' friend but has been forced by circumstances to work out his end in his own peculiar way. The rumor here is that Gwin seems to be paralyzed.'

[62] George N. Sanders, New York, March 6, 1860; Douglas MSS.

These 'rotten boroughs,' however, were not then considered as part of the Northwest. The action of Ohio, Indiana and Minnesota proved merely a foretaste of what the rest of the Northwest had made up its mind to do at Charleston. The Douglas sentiment in Michigan, Wisconsin and Iowa was so deepseated that the rank and file were not willing to choose any doubtful men, and the Senator was beset with questions as to the loyalty of this, that and the other leader.[63]

The Douglas wave swept on across the Northwest. The Democratic conventions in Michigan, Iowa and Wisconsin followed the Ohio and Indiana pattern, electing the staunchest sort of Douglas delegates, binding them under the unit rule and instructing them for the Little Giant. 'Hurrah for Michigan, Iowa and Wisconsin,' Lanphier wrote gleefully to McClernand. 'Are we getting ahead! With the Northwest solidly instructed, New England and New York promised and a peep into Maryland, we ought to be "praying proud."' [64]

'The Presidential struggle is growing more and more vehement,' McClernand advised the Springfield faithful. 'The fight is hand to hand. We are beating them.' [65]

[63] D. B. Cook, Niles, Mich., Jan. 10, 1860; Douglas MSS. Cook was editor of the Niles *Republican*, a Democratic paper. Douglas to Charles E. Stuart, Washington, Jan. 15, 1860; copy found in Jeremiah Sullivan Black MSS. Cook asked if ex-Senator Stuart could be trusted. Douglas responded cautiously, referring to his general rule 'not to interfere with the matter in any State, not even in Illinois, but to leave my friends in each State free to do as they pleased.' Judging from the place this letter was found, Stuart might have flirted with the Buchaneers, but in the event he was among the bravest of the brave at Charleston.

[64] Lanphier to McClernand, Springfield, Ill., Feb. 24, 1860; McClernand MSS. H. C. Dean, Mt. Pleasant, Ia., Feb. 8, Eben Prentis, Detroit, Mich., Feb. 22, 1860, Douglas MSS.

[65] McClernand to Lanphier, Washington, April 4, 1860; Patton MSS.

CHAPTER XXV

ON TO CHARLESTON

THESE Douglas victories in the Northwest affected sentiment all through the country. Asked what he thought of Douglas' chances at Charleston, Lincoln reviewed the Senator's almost impossible achievements in the Illinois campaign and commented, reminiscently, that such a man 'may play the devil at Charleston.' [1]

Douglas' managers at Washington sensed a change in Southern sentiment. They were advised that Andrew Johnson had gotten Tennessee instructions only after a deal with the Douglas men. 'Tennessee is in effect committed,' declared McClernand, 'and the delegates will no doubt be for Douglas in time to serve him efficiently and decisively.' There was 'no well-founded hope for the preservation of the existing Union' with honor to the South except through Douglas' candidacy, Miles Taylor, a Louisiana Congressman, declared in a public letter. Were he nominated, Taylor predicted that 'a mighty wave of patriotism and devotion to the Constitution' would sweep the North.

Soon Congressmen Rust, of Arkansas, and Reagan, of Texas, made formal Douglas speeches and a second Louisiana member prepared to announce for him. These were an index that, in the Southern States, the current was running strong. As McClernand put it, 'The people and the politicians are joining in battle against each other upon the Douglas question.' [2]

These events disconcerted and alarmed the Senate Fire-Eaters. Two months before, they had been confident that political legerdemain, presidential patronage and John Brown had destroyed Douglas' candidacy. But he had an alarming habit of coming back to life and the Ultras determined on another effort to draw and quarter him. The occasion selected was the debate over Douglas' own Senate resolutions proposing stringent legislation to protect the States against domestic invasion. Introduced early in January, the Little Giant used them to excoriate alike the Black Republican philosophy bottoming Brown's invasion and the Southern Ultra interventionist demands. This brought him under the fire of both extremes but most particularly fire from the Southern Senators. Jefferson Davis, James S. Green and Clement Clay assailed him in concert, charging that by ignoring the South's constitutional rights to equality, he was

---

[1] William Kellogg, speech in House of Representatives, March 13, 1860, reprinted in pamphlet *cit. supra.* Kellogg was quoting an interview William H. Gill, of the Leavenworth, Kansas, *Herald*, visiting Illinois, had with Lincoln. Kellogg read the interview as reprinted in Cincinnati *Enquirer*.

[2] McClernand to Lanphier, Washington, Jan. 3, 14, 19, 26, 1860; Patton MSS. Miles Taylor to Lewis Bush, Washington, Jan. 19, 1860, printed in Memphis *Appeal*, Feb. 10, 1860. These debates, covering several weeks, are to be found in *Congressional Globe*, Thirty-Sixth Congress, First Session, 325–658. This particular expression occurred January 13, 1860.

the real author of the national unrest, and that his motive was a frenzy to become President.

Douglas did not yield an inch. 'I am not seeking a nomination,' he declared solemnly. 'I am willing to take one, providing I can assume it on principles that I believe to be sound; but in the event of your making a platform that I could not conscientiously execute in good faith if I were elected, I will not stand upon it and be a candidate.... I have no grievances, but I have no concessions. I have no abandonment of position or principle; no recantation to make to any man or body of men on earth.' [3]

On another day he insisted 'that the Harper's Ferry crime was the natural, logical, inevitable result of the doctrines and teachings of the Republican party, as explained and enforced in their platform, their partisan presses, their pamphlets and books and especially in the speeches of their leaders in and out of Congress.' That party's great principle was 'violent, irreconcilable, eternal warfare upon the institution of slavery in America.' Its leaders might disavow Brown's *acts* at Harper's Ferry, but they must also disavow or cease uttering the doctrines which produced those acts.

Fessenden, who made the chief Republican reply, charged Douglas with moral obtuseness and hinted a political motive. Douglas resented this inference. His only object was 'to establish firmly the doctrine that each State is to do its own voting, establish its own institutions, make its own laws without interference, directly or indirectly, from any outside power.' He wished to put down outside interference and 'to repress this "irrepressible conflict."'

This juncture of the Ultras of both sections against Douglas seemed significant to the Moderates. 'What has brought about this reconciliation between the Fire-Eaters of the South and the Opposition?' a Nashville paper asked, 'Have they united to overthrow the great Democratic party of the country and precipitate a dissolution of the Union?' [4]

This was a shrewd hit, for the Southern Disunionists and the Northern Republicans, determined to eliminate all alternatives and 'to make an issue between Republican prohibition of slavery in the Territories, and Fire-Eating protection of it there,' had met 'in a common crusade against Douglas and his friends,' whose position alone could frustrate Ultra designs.[5]

Douglas' friends were anxious for him. One wrote, 'Laugh if you can.' George Sanders suggested that the Little Giant point out how Davis had

[3] Douglas' manly bearing in this encounter 'created a perfect furor of delight' through the Northern Democracy. *Illinois State Register*, Jan. 26, 1860. *National Era*, Washington, Jan. 19, 1860, the Abolition organ, chortled that the debate had 'all the raciness of a political family quarrel.' The attack on Douglas was 'an irrepressible outburst of sectional rancor at a moment when prudence would have dictated silence.' The Ultras 'feel conscious that they cannot do without Mr. Douglas, and yet their indignation at his course is so great that they cannot sit still and listen to the utterance of his rebellious sentiments.'

[4] Nashville *Patriot*, n.d. [probably January, 1860], in scrapbook of Mrs. J. H. Stanfield, Chattanooga, Tenn.

[5] McClernand to Lanphier, Washington, Feb. 9, 11, 1860; Patton MSS. Lanphier could have 'no conception of the damned villainy and wicked and dastardly persecutions to which we are subjected by the Ultras.'

changed his demands. During the California debate a decade earlier, John C. Calhoun had drawn up an amendment which was 'but a simple agreement to submit the slave question in the Territories to the Supreme Court.' Davis had then warmly supported the proposal; Douglas now, as always, adhered to it. Let him challenge Davis to explain why he now repudiated the Calhoun platform and demanded further Congressional legislation.[6]

Davis soon introduced a series of resolutions declaratory of the nature of the Federal compact from the extreme State's Rights viewpoint. These resolutions led to further passages at arms, but Davis did not press for an immediate vote, for the Southrons had decided to hold a caucus of the Democratic Senators and adopt a statement of party principle to injure Douglas' chances at Charleston.

Not all the Ultra Senators approved these resolutions, although Buchanan gave them his endorsement. 'All of them are wrong,' Toombs wrote. 'It is the very foolishness of folly to raise and make prominent such issues now. Hostility to Douglas is the sole motive of movers of this mischief.'[7]

Yet in March this caucus upheld Davis' resolutions as the true Democratic interpretation of the Constitution. 'The platform movement in the Senate is designed to keep down Douglas,' McClernand wrote Lanphier; 'the President is urging it on.'[8] But not all the Southern Senators approved the caucus program or its mover. Toombs reprehended it as merely a move against Douglas, and a very injudicious one. Andrew Johnson thought that Jefferson Davis, 'burning up with ambition, is nearer consumed by the internal heat than any man I ever saw.... What Jeff will do if he is not nominated God only knows!'[9]

Douglas parried the caucus thrust by saying that party dogma could be promulgated by no other organ than a National Convention. Until the Charleston Convention altered the Cincinnati platform, no trick caucus of a Senate cabal could declare new party law. The general reaction was that the Ultras had overreached themselves. 'That senatorial caucus is a trump card for us,' wrote John Forsyth. 'I can make it win a trick down here. Your foes are getting shaky in the knees.'[10]

---

[6] George N. Sanders, n.p., n.d. [internal evidence indicates New York, about Jan. 20, 1860]; Douglas MSS.

[7] *Congressional Globe*, Thirty-Sixth Congress, First Session, 658, for text. The critical one declared 'that neither Congress nor a Territorial Legislature, whether by indirect legislation or legislation of an indirect and unfriendly character, possesses power to annul or to impair the Constitutional right of any citizen to take his slave property into the common Territory, and there hold and enjoy the same while the Territorial condition remains.' On the contrary, the Federal Government had the clear duty to provide the needful protection of slave property as for other species of property. Toombs to A. H. Stephens, Washington, Feb. 10, 1860, in Ulrich B. Phillips, *Robert Toombs*, New York, 1913; 184. Toombs added that he also wanted Douglas beaten, but he did not 'want him and his friends crippled and driven off. Where are we to get as many or as good men in the North to supply their places?'

[8] McClernand to Lanphier, Washington, Feb. 23, 1860; Patton MSS.

[9] Milton, *The Age of Hate*, quoting Johnson to George W. Jones of Tennessee, Washington, March 19, 1860.

[10] John Forsyth, Mobile, Ala., March 9, 1860; Douglas MSS.

Southern reports, however, were confusing. The process of delegate selection continued to illustrate the disparity between public sentiment and political response, but in some States the people were speaking out more sharply. General Singleton thought Arkansas debatable until he discovered that its 'three or four ruling families' had made up their minds against Douglas and could not be unhorsed.[11] Texas likewise witnessed a complete Ultra triumph. These Texas Ultras had made effective use of the State printing, always a luscious morsel, in attaching editors to their support. Under the lead of Senator Wigfall's lieutenants, the Texans adopted the Alabama platform and their delegates were 'secretely pledged to withdraw from the convention' if they could not otherwise defeat Douglas.[12]

But Alabama opposition to the extremist platform kept increasing. The masses of the people were beginning to see in Popular Sovereignty 'our great defense against Congressional interference,' a far-sighted delegate wrote Douglas. 'We now have the power to control the county meetings,' and if only the Alabama State Convention could be held in April, Douglas delegates would be chosen. When Yancey's lieutenants undertook to hold platform ratification meetings in the counties, they found that 'the people don't stand to those resolutions.' Many uncommitted politicians concluded that the State would support Douglas after Charleston. In any event, he would be represented at Charleston by 'men of the right stamp' from Alabama.

John Forsyth agreed that the Little Giant was 'stronger a thousand times with the Southern people' than the Ultra politicians would admit. Let the North and West stand firm, he urged; accept no material interpolation in the Cincinnati platform, save perhaps an endorsement of the Dred Scott decision; when once a Southern Border State went over, the Ultra phalanx would be breached and 'the Southern spell is broken.[13]

Thanks to Jefferson Davis and his lieutenants, Mississippi was generally regarded as the bitterest of the Ultra States. Major Ethelbert Barksdale thundered in the *Mississippian* that 'she will not support Douglas upon any platform'; should the Charleston Convention prove 'so faithless and dishonest' as to name Douglas, 'all true Democrats will be bound by their faith to repudiate its action.' But some of her delegates to Charleston were uneasy, and one let it be known that while he intended first to vote for a Southern man, 'if he could not do better he would vote for Douglas and take the stump for him.' 'The people of this State have been most

[11] J. W. Singleton, Memphis, Dec. 10, Little Rock, Ark., Dec. 22, 1859; William P. Grace, Pine Bluff, April 14, 1860; Douglas MSS. Some of the delegates, like Thomas Flournoy, were individually ardent Douglas men but considered themselves bound.

[12] For State printing influence I am indebted to Dr. Charles W. Ramsdell, University of Texas; letter to author, Austin, Tex., Feb. 22, 1934. For Texas delegate pledge see George W. Pascal, San Antonio, Texas, April 17, 1860; Douglas MSS.

[13] J. T. Menefee, Tuskegee, Ala., Feb. 21; G. T. Horn, Mount Sterling, March 1c; Joseph C. Bradley, Huntsville, April 6; John M. Hollingsworth, Mobile, April 6; John Forsyth, Mobile, April 5, 1860; Douglas MSS. Menefee predicted the Alabama Ultras would 'have to back down... amid shame and disgrace.'

WEARING CALHOUN'S MANTLE: JEFFERSON DAVIS
Senator from Mississippi, and leader of the State's Rights
group in the parliamentary combat

egregiously hoodwinked by ambitious men who desire a dissolution of the Union' so as to get high offices, wrote an editor at Aberdeen, but the masses would cast an overwhelming vote for Douglas as the nominee.[14]

The regularly called Georgia Convention met on March 12, adopted conservative resolutions and appointed a full slate of delegates. These were mainly moderate men, several of whom, like James Gardner, the Augusta editor; Solomon Cohen, of Savannah; James L. Seward, of Thomasville, and W. B. Gaulden, of Huntsville, the largest owner of slaves in the South, were staunch Douglas men. The Ultra papers portrayed this outcome as 'a triumph of Douglas trickery over the will of the Democracy,' but it put a crimp in the boom for Howell Cobb. His brother advised him to 'let the bear fight come on with you out of the ring,' and he soon forbade the presentation of his name at Charleston. Alexander H. Stephens now advised friends that he felt the utmost confidence in Douglas' nomination and election, and only feared that, prompted 'by the Caliban of the White House,' Cobb would join a bolt. Disruptionists busied themselves getting up meetings and passing resolutions against Douglas. Douglas was advised that these had generally been 'small gatherings of factious, turbulent men who have arrogated to themselves the privilege of giving expression to the voice of the people; and so were not representative.

At first it seemed as though the two delegations would meet in bitter contest for the Georgia seats. Before the Convention opened, however, an arrangement was made whereby they were both admitted, dividing evenly the allotted vote. From the Little Giant's standpoint this was unfortunate, for every man of the rump delegation was bound against him, a small minority of the legal one had been put on to represent the Ultras, and on joint ballot the majority of the combined delegations was against him.[15] To cap the climax, the extremists later claimed unit rule instructions, to silence the voice of the important minority.

Surprisingly enough, Douglas had word from South Carolina that he had many friends in that State, particularly ex-Speaker Orr, who would control the approaching State Convention and who, upon Douglas' nomination, would give him 'a willing support,' and would 'sweep the State.'[16] Travelers through the Cotton States were surprised at Douglas' strength with the rank and file. So prevalent was the impression that the Little Giant would be nominated that professional gamblers in New Orleans were

[14] *Weekly Mississippian*, Jackson, March 21; Oliver Jones, Aberdeen, April 5, quoting Judge Gordon (or Gholson); R. D. Shropshire, Aberdeen, April 16, 1860; Douglas MSS. Shropshire, editor of the *Mississippi Conservative*, was himself going to Charleston to repudiate the Ultras' claim that they represented the rank and file of the people.

[15] Thomas R. R. Cobb to Howell Cobb, Athens, March 16; John B. Lamar to Howell Cobb, Macon, April 5, 1860; Erwin MSS. S. J. Anderson, New York, April 20, quoting letter he had from Stephens that day; J. A. Stewart, Atlanta, March 11; James Gardner, Augusta, April 13, 1860; Douglas MSS. Thomas Dyer, Memphis, Tenn., Mar. 21, 1860, M. F. Douglas MSS., reports on a two-day interview with Stephens: 'He is as outspoken for you as I am... He thinks you are the only man that can be elected... He would like very much to be put on the ticket with you for Vice-President.' Phillips, *Robert Toombs*, 189.

[16] Warren D. Wilkes, Laurens County, S.C., April 2, 1860; Douglas MSS.

offering five thousand dollars, even money, on it, with no takers.[17] Douglas himself believed the keen edge of Southern rancor was being dulled. 'There will be no serious difficulty in the South,' he wrote Peter Cooper in February, 'The last few weeks has worked a perfect revolution in that section. They all tell me and write me that all will be right if our Northern friends will fearlessly represent the wishes and feelings of the Democracy in their own States.'[18]

The determinations of the Border Slave States were of great importance. By March, some of Douglas' shrewder lieutenants learned that their January hopes as to Tennessee were illusory, that it was really 'decidedly against' him.[19] Kentucky however, exhibited symptoms of a reaction and Douglas was informed that he might get all its votes on the second ballot.[20]

There were five other Border State Conventions — North Carolina, Virginia, Maryland, Delaware and Missouri. The North Carolina Democrats met at Raleigh on March 9. Issue was joined when the Resolutions Committee took up a plank against Popular Sovereignty. The Douglas men fought it both in committee and on the floor, but were given explicit assurance that it was 'intended as an expression only of Territorial legislative authority over slavery,' a purely judicial question which would finally be decided by the Supreme Court. The plank was to put North Carolina's view on record and 'had no purpose to injure Douglas in the estimation of the State's Democracy or to impair his Charleston chances.' The convention refrained from imposing instructions or the unit rule, several delegates were Douglas men and four were counted for him on the first ballot.[21]

Virginia had two favorite sons but also had men all through the State who were for Douglas as soon as *pro forma* compliments had been paid to R. M. T. Hunter and Henry A. Wise. A Virginian had an article in *DeBow's Review* for January, 1860, lauding Douglas' position. Banks toured the State and reported that matters were 'looking steadily well.' When the State Convention declined to express a preference for any candidate, Wise announced that his name must not be presented. Hunter then became more active, but Washington heard there was a strong Douglas minority on the delegation.[22]

[17] D. D. Mitchell, St. Louis, March 2; Samuel Bridge, New Orleans, March 1, Louisville, April 11, 1860; Douglas MSS. Mitchell, who had wintered at New Orleans, found a prevailing opinion that no Ultra could be elected, but Douglas could and the South would take him.

[18] Douglas to Peter Cooper, Washington, Feb. 19, 1860. For photostat of this letter I am indebted to Mr. Stan V. Henkels, the well-known Philadelphia autograph dealer.

[19] George N. Sanders, New York, March 6, 1860; Douglas MSS.

[20] James McCreary, Richmond, Ky., April 8, 1860; Douglas MSS.

[21] J. J. Rea, Mackey's Ferry, N.C., Feb. 16, quoting Congressman Thomas Bragg that Douglas would be elected if nominated; P. H. Langdon, Raleigh, March 9; W. J. Hoke, Lincolnton, March 8; William White, Raleigh, March 12; H. W. Miller, Raleigh, April 20, 1860; Douglas MSS.

[22] Sam J. Mullens, Henry County, Va., Jan. 12; R. R. Collier, Petersburg, Jan. 14, describing his *DeBow's* article; A. D. Banks, Hampton, March 14; Charles Irvine, Danville, March 17,

When Maryland made her selections the Buchanan men jubilated that 'Douglas cannot get a vote.' Reverdy Johnson, however, polled the sixteen delegates and reported that ten were Douglas' friends, an outcome he thought quite satisfactory in view of Buchanan's unusual patronage concentration in the State.[23]

Delaware was little more than a pocket borough for the Saulsburys and the Bayards, and it was generally recognized that Senator Willard Saulsbury, the momentary boss, would 'cast the vote of the State' at Charleston. While personally not greatly concerned over slavery, these bosses had long affiliated with the ruling Southern group. None the less, Saulsbury promised Douglas' Delaware friends both to vote the delegation against the Ultra slave code plan and, as soon as Douglas received a majority, to let the Delaware delegation go for him.[24]

The Missouri struggle partook of as much of the Western as of the Border spirit. The Administration men wanted to instruct for Daniel S. Dickinson, but in March southeast Missouri began consolidating behind Douglas, the Buchaneers became alarmed, and they proposed to yield the candidate for Governor in return for Dickinson instructions. This offer, promptly refused, whetted the determination of the Little Giant's friends. Both Dickinson instructions and the unit rule were refused at the State Convention and ten or twelve of the eighteen delegates favored Douglas.[25]

The Middle States, quite as important as South or Border, represented a quite different problem of politics. Douglas had every reason to believe that he had already won New York, but a victory here must not only be first won but renewed nearly every week. Led by Mayor Fernando Wood, the myriad party foes of the Dean Richmond group made a drive to convince Douglas that the Richmond delegates planned betrayal, August Belmont, American agent of the Rothschilds, being a special target of attack. But Douglas' faith in Richmond and his allies was unshaken. His Senate fight with the Ultras had heated New York's political irons to white heat, and in January he visited Manhattan to weld them into an efficient instrument. Peter Cooper, the famous merchant, was disturbed and wrote Douglas that he must not credit the stories of bad faith. The latter responded cordially that he had 'implicit confidence' in their 'entire

Halifax County Court House, March 26; M. G. Harman, Staunton, April 9, 1860; Douglas MSS.; B. H. Wise, *Life of Henry A. Wise*, 263.

[23] L. K. Brown, Baltimore, March 23, 1860; Buchanan MSS. Jervey Spencer, Baltimore, Feb. 24, Reverdy Johnson, Baltimore, March 24, 1860; Douglas MSS.

[24] Samuel Townsend, Townsend P.O., New Castle County, Delaware, March 28, 1860; Douglas MSS. Townsend also caused the Delaware *Enquirer* to drop Breckinridge and take Douglas as its candidate.

[25] E. D. Mitchell, St. Louis, March 2; W. J. Elliott, Jefferson City, March 6, April 12; James L. Faucette, St. Louis, March 6; Faucette, a Douglas editor in St. Louis, received and rejected the Buchanan group's proposal, which came through the latter's agent, James M. Hughes; S. M. Yost, Lexington, Mo., March 7; John M. Krum, St. Louis, April 12; James McBride, St. Louis, April 12; James D. Eads, Warrensburg, Mo., April 13; Thomas L. Price, Jefferson City, April 14; D. A. January, St. Louis, April 16, 1860; Douglas MSS.

good faith.' Wood finally set up a contesting delegation but the Regulars developed into sure first-ballot Douglas votes.[26]

Buchanan had not hesitated to invade Illinois in 1858 with a complete counter-organization, and he had since maintained the Danites and was supporting their contesting delegation. Douglas therefore undertook a counter-move in Buchanan's home State. Embarrassed by Forney's extremist policies, the Little Giant could not get the proper set-up until after the Democratic State Convention. But this meeting, at Reading on March 3, revealed more Douglas strength than for 'either or all of the 3 B's' — Buchanan, Black or Bigler. It refused to endorse any of the Buchanan hopefuls or to impose the unit rule on the delegation, a substantial segment of which favored Douglas.[27]

With this tacit invitation, Douglas sought to develop the greatest possible amount of Pennsylvania support. Hendrick B. Wright, of Wilkes-Barre, a respected Democrat of conspicuous party record, large personal following and independent views, and himself a delegate to Charleston, took up Douglas' cause. His success was such that when the delegates sailed for Charleston, an apprehensive aide wrote Buchanan: 'The Devil must be itching to strangle some rascals on board.' [28]

The Buchanan contingent worked frantically to hold New Jersey. George Sanders wanted to checkmate these efforts. 'Jersey is now our battleground,' he wrote Douglas early in March, 'and must be carried.' The Little Giant did what he could and heard, soon after the Convention, that he had eight of the fourteen New Jersey delegates. A few days later, however, Hendrick B. Wright, of Pennsylvania, was informed that 'the greatest favor that could be done to Douglas' would be for him to go into New Jersey to proselyte the key man on its delegation. Apparently Wright was

[26] Fernando Wood, New York, Jan. 21; George N. Sanders, New York, Jan. 25, 1860; Douglas MSS. McClernand to Lanphier, Washington, Jan. 26, 1860; Patton MSS., telling of the journey. Douglas to Peter Cooper, Washington, Feb. 19, 1860; I am indebted to Mr. Stan V. Henkels, of Philadelphia, the autograph dealer, for a photostat of it. H. G. Warner, Rochester, N.Y., March 12; John Clancy, New York, April 12; Anthony Dutro, New York, April 12; Edward C. West, New York, April 16, 1860; Douglas MSS. Belmont said, 'I am the personal friend of Douglas and the personal friend of his personal friends, and will be with his friends at Charleston. Besides all of which he is the only man in the country we can elect.'

[27] W. G. Baer, Somerset, Pa., March 3; James H. Hopkins, Pittsburgh, March 19; C. W. (perhaps Cornelius Wendell), Philadelphia, March 8; H. B. Wright, Wilkes-Barre, March 30, 1860; Douglas MSS.

[28] William Montgomery to Hendrick B. Wright, Washington, March 5; J. R. Randall, Washington, March 26, 30; S. A. Douglas, Washington, April 1; John McReynolds, Harrisburg, April 11; H. B. Robinson, Philadelphia, April 11, 1860; Hendrick B. Wright MSS., Wyoming Historical and Geological Society, Wilkes-Barre, Pa. For notes from this fine collection of Pennsylvania papers I am indebted to Dr. Julian P. Boyd, then Secretary of the Society at Wilkes-Barre but now with the New York Historical Association at Fort Ticonderoga. Douglas approached Wright through Montgomery, a Congressman from Pennsylvania, who wrote him early in March pointing out how Douglas had taken the lead in procuring Wright's selection as President of the 1844 Democratic National Convention. Now the Little Giant, knowing how Buchanan had mistreated Wright, assured the latter of 'that situation which your commanding talents and high standing entitle you to receive.' For reports to Buchanan, see R. Tyler, Philadelphia, April 19, 1860; Buchanan MSS.

unsuccessful, for New Jersey voted against the Douglas men on nearly every test at Charleston.[29]

The delegate process in New England showed that an ounce of political machinery was worth a pound of public support. 'There is not a delegate from New England, who, if he honestly represents the Democracy, but will give his first and last vote for you' — so Douglas was advised by E. D. Beach, four times Democratic candidate for Governor of Massachusetts. But Buchanan made a large number of new Federal appointments in that section, and most of the new office-holders, before plucking the plums, 'were required not only to swear fealty to the President in all things but to renounce you and swear eternal hatred to all your friends.' Many of these new recruits to the patronage brigade had 'smuggled themselves into the Conventions,' and Douglas could look for a record-breaking betrayal.[30]

Promised retention of their jobs if they would beat Douglas, Federal appointees in Rhode Island packed a district convention or so but could not budge the Democratic rank and file. Before the State Convention met, the Buchananites offered to yield instructions without a struggle and 'there was a fair understanding' to that effect, but in the event, 'by some hocus-pocus which nobody seems to understand,' the instruction resolution was not offered and Douglas must console himself with assurances that the actual delegates would not desert.[31] Vermont was staunchly loyal. Of the sixteen men selected by Maine's March convention, eleven were thought for Douglas. While the Connecticut convention was sharply fought, his followers appeared in control and thought they had won the delegation.[32]

The major Northeastern disturbance was the effort to bring Franklin Pierce back into the ring. It is possible that the campaign to this end had some secret encouragement from the ex-President, but no valid evidence sustains the charge. In all probability the intrigues rested on the ambitions of such local Pierce lieutenants as John H. George, anxious to recover national power and importance, and even more on Caleb Cushing's

[29] J. D. Hoover to Pierce, Washington, Feb. 25; Pierce MSS., Library of Congress; George N. Sanders, New York, March 6, 1860; Douglas MSS. McClernand to Lanphier, Washington, March 30, 1860; Patton MSS. J. R. Thompson to Buchanan, Trenton, N.J., March 28; Buchanan MSS. William Montgomery to H. B. Wright, Washington, April 9, 1860; H. B. Wright MSS. Richard Brodhead, Washington, April 12, 13, 1860; H. B. Wright MSS.

[30] E. D. Beach, Springfield, Mass., April 12, 1860. Beach had gotten three thousand more votes for Governor in Massachusetts in 1856 than Buchanan had gotten for President.

[31] Clement Webster, Providence, R.I., March 7, April 14, 17; Johnson Gardener, Pawtucket, R.I., Jan. 10, April 16; George N. Sanders, New York, March 21, April, 15, 1860; Douglas MSS.; Webster was editor of the Providence *Post*. Sanders wanted Douglas to go to Rhode Island for speeches in its State campaign, saying that if he would do so with all his enthusiasm no combination could beat him at Charleston. Douglas did not go, but the Democratic candidate, an anti-Lecompton man, was elected.

[32] E. K. Smart, Camden, Maine, March 2; J. M. Schofield, Hartford, Conn., Jan. 2, 1860; Douglas MSS.

belief that he could usefully employ a Pierce boom for his own purposes. Pierce himself favored Jefferson Davis and whole-souledly endorsed the Mississippian's Southern Rights platform. If civil war came, Pierce wrote Davis, the fighting would not alone be along the border between the sections but also 'within our own borders, in our own streets,' between Abolitionists and defenders of the Constitution, and the Abolitionists would 'find occupation enough at home.'

While Pierce was spending the Winter months in the Bahamas, the old Pierce machine had the New Hampshire Democratic Convention adopt a Southern slave code platform. Pierce wrote home that he hoped New Hampshire would vote as a unit but his name must not be presented at Charleston. What he wrote Cushing is not completely known, but that worthy told all who would listen that the fight would narrow down to Douglas and Pierce. The Little Giant must have attached considerable importance to the intrigue, for in February he remarked to Senator Bigler that the man who beat Pierce at Charleston would be the nominee.[33]

The power of presidential patronage was most forcibly illustrated in Massachusetts. The Bay State's delegates to Charleston had been chosen at a State Convention in Worcester, in September, 1859. In full control of the Convention by a majority of about three to one, the Douglas men required each candidate for delegate to give an unequivocal pledge to support the Little Giant and his platform. Thus all the Massachusetts delegates were 'elected solely on the ground that they were and would be to the last friends of Douglas and Popular Sovereignty.' [34]

None had been more fervent in these oaths of fealty than James G. Whitney, a prominent Boston Democrat. Early in 1860, however, President Buchanan nominated Whitney to be Collector of the Port of Boston, and this worthy's prompt desertion of Douglas was but the payment of the asking price. Soon the new Collector was employing the rich patronage of his office to corrupt other delegates and was pulling every wire 'to have the vote of our delegation thrown as a unit' against the candidate he was pledged to support.

Informed of this treason, Douglas' Washington headquarters rushed a man to New England, who found the Administration 'raising Heaven and earth' to break down the delegations of that section. 'To that end

[33] Pierce to Davis, Amherst, Mass., Jan. 6; J. D. Hoover to Pierce, Washington, Feb. 25; Caleb Cushing to Pierce, Boston, Feb. 25; C. E. Potter to Pierce, Jersey City, March, n.d.; Pierce to Josiah Minot, Nassau, April 11, 1860; Pierce MSS., Library of Congress. New Hampshire *Patriot*, quoted *National Era*, Washington, Feb. 23, 1860. The resolution in question said among other things that if slave property were disturbed in a Federal Territory, 'it is the duty of the Congress of the U.S. to enact all laws which may be necessary for its security and protection.' Pierce to John H. George, Nassau, Feb. 16; John C. Wilson to George, Washington, Feb. 25; New Hampshire Historical Society MSS. William Bigler to Hendrick B. Wright, Washington, Feb. 6, 1860; Wright MSS. Bigler was quoting Douglas' remark to him.

[34] John W. Mahan, Boston, April 17, 1860; Douglas MSS. Mahan described the careful pledges required and given by all, even Cushing. But a Washington dispatch, 'that General Whitney and eight other Massachusetts delegates have turned traitors,' had occasioned great excitement in Boston.

and that alone,' the offices in the Boston Custom House and elsewhere were being distributed by the new Collector, 'under the direction of the Old Chief at Washington.' So bold was this effort that Douglas' own agent was tendered 'one of the best places under Collector Whitney,' if only he would cease work for the Little Giant.[35]

Another Worcester selection and pledge-maker had been Benjamin Franklin Butler, of Lowell, a politician extraordinary whose pendulous eyelids gave a sinister expression to his fat-padded face. The prince of demagogues, Butler had leaped into political power by pretending to champion the cause of labor. He had voted for Sumner for the Senate but turned to Popular Sovereignty and for months had been preening about as a loyal Douglas man. All through March he kept up this pretense, talking largely of how he was fighting the Little Giant's battles and of his confidence that the majority of the delegation would remain faithful. But Butler, who always had his eye upon the immediate main chance, soon lent an ear to Cushing; first he brought forward a shabby scheme for the delegation to give Cushing a complimentary vote on the first ballot at Charleston, 'so as to make him feel good.' At Charleston he went the full way of treason. Cushing, too, kept up the pretense that he would stand by Douglas. But in early March Douglas' confidential agent for New England believed that the majority of the Bay State delegates were still true to their pledges, and would be so at Charleston.[36]

The process by which the Buchanan Administration bartered Massachusetts Federal offices for delegate betrayals is important, not so much because the subsequent conduct of the Massachusetts delegation at Charleston singly determined the outcome there, but because activities of the Whitney-Butler-Cushing type well illustrated the general White House technique. Whenever the Administration could not defeat Douglas delegates in State or District Convention, the Cabinet and Senators in Washington and the attorneys, marshals and postmasters at home set to work to steal them away.

Jefferson Davis warned the New Hampshire delegates, as they passed through Washington, that they must desert Douglas. John C. Breckinridge gave a dinner to 'the harlotting portion of the Massachusetts delegation,' and Senator Slidell acted as the master of ceremonies for the Vice-President, who had become the Administration's main candidate.

[35] Joseph Smith, Boston, March 20, telling of Whitney's efforts; John W. Mahan, Boston, April 17: 'General Whitney especially' had been elected solely on the ground that he was a staunch Douglas man. Moses Bates, Plymouth, March 5, 1860, telling of trip to Massachusetts to stop the treason; Douglas MSS.

[36] Patrick Eagan, Lowell, Mass., Nov. 7, 1859, describes Butler's staunch Douglas views; Moses Bates, Plymouth, Mass., March 5, 1860, gives account of his interview with Butler; Douglas MSS. H. H. Coates, New York, Feb. 22, 1860, Douglas MSS., tells of a trip Butler, Whitney, C. W. N. Swift, our 'Live-Oak friend' of Connecticut, and John H. George, of New Hampshire, made to New York to try to take Dean Richmond along with them in their treachery. Davis to Franklin Pierce, Washington, June 13, 1860, Pierce MSS. J. W. Gray, Washington, April 17, 18, in Cleveland *Plain Dealer*, April 19, 1860. The Breckinridge dinner had taken place April 16.

Immediately after the Minnesota Convention, Senator Rice undertook to seduce that State's delegates from their allegiance, writing again and again that they must leave Douglas so as to 'get a man that can serve us.' The event showed the attractiveness of his bait, for at Charleston two of the eight Minnesotans deserted and post offices began to change hands.[37] Jesse D. Bright did what he could in Indiana but the delegation would not yield. Dean Richmond's men had fantastic propositions laid before them but they, too, had made up their minds. In several of the solid Douglas delegations from the Northwest, however, the Administration succeeded in corrupting a single delegate here and there, thus giving an appearance of insubstantiality to the Little Giant's strength. This enabled the Administration to broadcast the charge that the reported Northern fixity of conviction on Popular Sovereignty and its sponsor was pretense; that the Douglas delegations, bound by unit rules, had important anti-Douglas minorities, and that the Southern platform had almost as much strength among the Northern Democracy as did the Douglas heresy.

While this apparent Northern division was seen in its true lights both by the Douglas and Administration leaders, some sincere Southern State's Rights men were deceived by it. A Cincinnati newspaper correspondent en route to Charleston had an example of this when he asked an Alabama delegate why the Southerners could not see the impossibility of the Douglas men accepting the Yancey platform, that were they to do so, 'they would be beaten in every Northern State and every Northern township.' The Alabamian countered by asking if Fernando Wood, as 'sound a man' on Southern Rights as any in the South, had not been elected Mayor of the City of New York. Furthermore, would not the Democrats have carried Connecticut except for 'so much pandering to Douglasism'?[38] Were not many Northern delegates as much against Douglas and Popular Sovereignty as any Southerners? The only way to win a fight was to fight it out on principle. Let this be done and the North would stand 'squarely up for the Constitution and the South.'

Thus the chief effect of the Administration's efforts among Northern delegates was to join together more determinedly the three groups which made up the chief Douglas opposition: the Buchanan Administration leaders who opposed the Little Giant, both because of personal hatred and because they knew too well that, once he succeeded, their sun had set; the Southern political oligarchy, which similarly realized that a Douglas in the White House would bring into power in the South a new group which would take over the Federal patronage and strength there; and then finally, the

---

[37] H. M. Rice to John H. Stevens, Washington, April 4, 1860; Stevens MSS., Minnesota Historical Collection.

[38] Murat Halstead, *Caucuses of 1860*, Columbus, Ohio, 1860; 1, 4. Halstead, editor of the Cincinnati *Commercial*, took the dispatches he had sent his paper during the various national conventions of the year, added to them certain documentary material and certain personal observations, and put them in book form. It is one of the most valuable contemporary written records of the year. The particular dispatches from which this conversation is taken was dated Atlanta, April 17.

sincere Southern Rights doctrinaires, hundreds of really thoughtful Southern men who convinced themselves that the South's interests required the
full letter of constitutional rights. However mistaken these views might have
been, men of the type of Ruffin and Rhett believed them implicitly. Now
they seemed to sense, in the apparent division of Northern Democrats, real
popular support for their views.

The chief distress confronting the anti-Douglas cabal, however, was
the extreme difficulty of concentrating their strength upon a single candidate.
The White House had been successful in nearly every Southern and Border
State in quickening the Presidential hopes of the locally significant Democratic leaders, so much so indeed that the plethora of favorite sons eventually
prevented pooling Administration strength behind any single candidate.
The axiom, 'You can't beat somebody with nobody,' had pertinence then
as now, and during February and March the Administration cabal sought
strenuously to convert the candidacies of Guthrie, Hunter, Dickinson,
Lane, Cobb and Davis into efforts of more than home State importance.

Shortly before the convention gathered, the Ultra leaders made a strong
effort to center on Hunter, of Virginia, with Dickinson, of New York, as
running-mate. John Slidell, chief of the Administration Senatorial cabal,
adopted the boom, and for a week or so the movement seemed infused with
possibilities. Quite sure that Hunter would never really be a possibility,
George Sanders suggested that the Douglas forces ought to try to keep
Hunter down in the North while encouraging the Southern campaign for
him.[39]

The Little Giant and his aides did not stand idly by during these weeks
of gestation. His Washington headquarters, in the National Hotel, were
thronged with Governors, Senators, Congressmen, editors, diplomats and
delegates. On April 16, there was a rousing meeting with delegates from
twenty-four states, and speakers from all parts of the country. A tally of
first-ballot expectations yielded 155 votes, and there was 'not a wavering
man' from the West. [40]

The candidate now found himself 'so overwhelmed with calls and letters'
that he could not handle half the problems which pressed upon him. Unfriendly observers sneered that his agents were 'holding up the Vice-
Presidency to every man of ambition in the South, making all sorts of
pledges to others, looking after the spoils.' Doubtless the Vice-Presidential
bauble was dangled about a bit but it was not promiscuously promised, for
Douglas was anxious to have as running-mate a Southern man who would

[39] Martin Ryerson, Newton, N.J., Jan. 13; James Patillo, Milledgeville, Ga., March 22;
George N. Sanders, New York, April 2, 1860; Douglas MSS. J. D. Hoover to Franklin Pierce,
Washington, Feb. 25; Pierce MSS. William Bigler to Hendrick B. Wright, Washington, Feb. 6;
Richard Brodhead to Wright, Washington, April 12, 13, 1860; H. B. Wright MSS.

[40] The best contemporary account of Douglas' Washington headquarters activities is to be
found in the letters of J. W. Gray, Washington, April 16, 17, 19, in Cleveland *Plain Dealer*,
April 18, 19, 23, 1860. Gray, editor of the *Plain Dealer*, was an 'Adamantine,' as the Western
supporters of the Little Giant called themselves.

attract the energetic support of the Moderate party in that section. Late in 1859 he had written trusted friends in Georgia, Alabama and other Cotton States canvassing their confidential judgment whether Alexander H. Stephens or Benjamin Fitzpatrick would make the best running-mate.

Forsyth had 'very little choice' between Stephens and Fitzpatrick, while Nisbet preferred Stephens. Suggesting Herschel V. Johnson as an alternative, James Patillo added that, as soon as 'any good Southern man' was identified with Douglas on the ticket, Howell Cobb's capacity for mischief-making would be minimized. Soon several Douglas journals in the West began to trumpet 'Little Alec' for Vice-President. The evidence indicates that the Little Giant had become more concerned about Southern support in the campaign than in the convention.

His plans were obviously premised on the assumption that the gathering at Charleston would follow the normal pattern of these great political in- quests. This involved a leading candidate with a majority or near-majority of the delegates, opposed by a host of minor aspirants dividing the remaining votes. Could the leader increase his vote to the two-thirds needed for Demo- cratic nomination, or would his vote prove to be one cast in large part by delegates who would salve their consciences by a few ballots and then con- centrate on a dark horse? This was the normal nominating question and its answer normally depended on the stuff the initial majority was made of. If it consisted of determined men who would not yield, at length the favorite son delegations would abandon their local choices and accord the required two-thirds.[41]

Three weeks before the convention, many individual delegates let it be known that they would yield to him when they saw that they could not get their own man across. One declared that his interests were twofold — the protection of the rights of the South and the party's success in the election. Should he not be able to do both, his choice would go for the course which promised success. He liked neither Douglas' platform nor his campaign manner, yet expected to wind up voting for him because he could be elected President. This opinion represented that of a large portion of the men who would make up the Charleston Convention.[42]

Then, too, the delegation from nearly every Cotton State contained warm supporters of Judge Douglas. Most were bound to some local favorite, but as soon as that hopeful had been eliminated they would vote for their personal choice. Joseph R. Bradley and other Alabama delegates considered protesting to the Credentials Committee that their whole delegation had been illegally elected and should be thrown out. Thompson B. Flournoy,

[41] Douglas to Hendrick B. Wright, Washington, April 1, 1860; H. B. Wright MSS. J. D. Hoover to Franklin Pierce, Washington, Feb. 25, 1860; Pierce MSS. John Forsyth, Mobile, Ala., Dec. 24, 1859, April 5, 1860. The first letter was answering Douglas' letter of Dec. 16. James A. Nisbet, Macon, Ga., Dec. 27, 1859; James Patillo, Milledgeville, Ga., March 22; James Barr, Pittsburgh, Pa., Feb. 20, 1860; Douglas MSS. Barr had asked if Douglas wanted Houston, of Alabama. The letter is endorsed: 'Has no choice.'

[42] William Bigler, Washington, Feb. 6; J. R. Randall to Wright, Washington, March 26, 30, 1860; Wright MSS.

of Arkansas, a staunch Douglasite, was similarly bound — and hopeful. The Virginia, North Carolina, Kentucky and Tennessee delegations all had similar hostages, while second-choice Douglas support was reported in nearly every Cotton and Border State. Careful estimaters expected him to get ten first-ballot votes from the South, and that by the third or fourth ballot there would be such a swing to him that he would top the necessary two-thirds.

The Fire-Eaters undertook to meet this danger. Douglas had word from Texas that the delegation from the Lone Star State had secretly pledged to bolt the convention if he were nominated. Yancey persistently threatened the same remedy, as did the Davis Mississippians. The general staff of the Buchanan-Ultra combine, however, put no undue confidence in this suicide program, and felt that some other device was necessary, some convenient formula by which to sublimate these personal dissatisfactions into a parade of principles.

It was a time-honored method based upon a good understanding of mob psychology and often used in Democratic conventions. The point was to introduce, deliberately, an issue extraneous to the principal issue, but having possibilities of emotional exploitation. Debate on this would bring emotions to white heat, and even if they cooled, delegate attitudes would retain a permanent set, thus destroying all chance for compromise on the main question.

The particular issue through which the anti-Douglas cabal expected to crystallize the convention was that slavery in the Territories demanded affirmative Congressional protection. Kansas was the only Territory where the issue existed in practical form, there had never been over two hundred slaves there and in 1860 there were only two; New Mexico's Territorial Legislature had already adopted a slave code and thus the question was an empty abstraction. But such an abstraction represented the very type of verbal bauble most useful in ordering an emotional storm. It was not without psychological prevision that the Ultras laid their plans for a slave code fight.

Through February Douglas expected the pressure of moderating Southern opinion to influence the Cotton State delegations. But the Democratic caucus declarations revealed the real purpose of the Buchanan-Ultra cabal, and on March 10, Douglas wrote H. B. Payne, of Ohio, a shrewd, realistic thinker, analyzing the enemy movements. Payne instantly perceived that the Ultra effort was directed 'to bring the Southern sentiment to the point of demanding Davis' resolution as a *sine qua non*, making Congressional protection a test of orthodoxy and proscribing all who dissent.' In a word, it was to set the stage for Charleston.

The first act in the Fire-Eaters' drama would be to try to procure a majority of the convention's Committee on Resolutions which would report a platform calling for a Congressional slave code. Inasmuch as this Committee would be made up of one member from each State, Payne feared that the fifteen Slave States, together with Buchanan's rotten borough delegations from California and Oregon, might give the Ultras a majority of one on the Committee, and secure for them the majority report. He feared, too, that 'unless Pennsylvania goes with us in the convention,' the slave code plank might win on the convention floor.

If the Southern Ultras forced a slave code upon the party, what course should the Northwest pursue? Payne knew that the imposition of any such platform would prevent Douglas' name from even being presented. Even more, for the Northerners to succumb to such a platform 'would be destruction to us at home.' But if the Douglas delegates could force the re-adoption of the Cincinnati platform, unamended, the victory was already 'half-gained.' [43]

[43] H. B. Payne, Cleveland, Ohio, March 17, 1860; Douglas MSS.

CHAPTER XXVI

THE DEATH OF A PARTY

AMONG minor incitements which in mid-April led hundreds of delegates to journey to the Democratic inquest at Charleston was a curiosity to inspect that almost fabulous city. While not the titular capital of the Palmetto State — up-country jealousy had shifted that honor to Columbia, in the Piedmont — for a century Charleston had been a magnet for the wealth and leisure of the Southeastern coastal plain. Her leading families were often rich and always aristocratic, and her highly stratified society attracted the *nouveaux riches* who hoped for *entrée* to the most exclusive society upon the continent.

She had her own poets in Hayne and Timrod, her own Walter Scott in William Gilmore Simms, her evangel of the pen in Rhett of the *Mercury*, even her own accent, pronunciation and patois. Here, too, the code duello was raised to its highest American refinement. Most of her fine houses seemed to stand 'sidewaies, backward into their yards, and nearly endwaies, with their gables towards the street'; each dwelling of any pretension had a balcony or veranda to each story, each veranda unwaveringly facing east, as though the structures were looking wistfully at an envied England across the seas.[1]

The convention met just after the season for the azaleas at Drayton Hall and the magnolias at Middleton Gardens; the air was balmy, culture and aristocracy were everywhere apparent. To a few Northern sojourners whose social standing brought admittance to the charmed circle, Charleston's inhabitants seemed to 'incarnate every quality that graces humanity — most especially beauty, wit and hospitality.' The homes were luxurious and exclusive, and the streets were full of fine victorias and phaëtons, prancing horses and sporty traps and gigs. The men still had a dash of ruffled elegance and the ladies' clothes were richer and more sumptuous than perhaps anywhere else save New Orleans.[2] The city's physical surroundings, social customs and intellectual addictions were exotic, as though Charleston were an orchid upon America's social tree.

[1] U.S. Census for 1860, Preliminary Report, gives the city of Charleston a population of 40,578. Charleston County had 70,100, of which 29,188 were white, 37,290 Negro slaves and 3622 Negro freedmen. For dueling, see John Lyde Wilson, *The Code of Honor or Rules for the Government of Principals and Seconds in Dueling*, Charleston, 1858. Harriette Kershaw Leiding, *Old Charleston and South Carolina*, Philadelphia, 1931, 3–4, thinks the idea for the east-turned verandas had been brought over from San Domingo. See also Alice Huger Smith and D. E. Smith, *Dwelling Houses of Charleston, S.C.*, Philadelphia, 1917; 321, 347–48. The reason generally given for their uniform eastward facing is that they thus caught the prevailing breeze from the sea.

[2] F. O. Prince to Mrs. Stephen A. Douglas, Charleston, April 26, 1860; Douglas MSS. Cleveland *Plain Dealer*, April 21, 1860, clipping from the Charleston *Mercury*; Charleston *Daily Courier*, April 27, 1860.

The convention was to be held in the Hall of the South Carolina Institute, an association 'for the promotion of the Industrial Arts.' This fine two-story structure located on Meeting Street between St. Michael's and the Circular Church, was a spacious gathering place with good acoustics, holding about twenty-five hundred people. A stone's throw from it was Hibernia Hall, the scene of the annual St. Cecilia balls. Farther west on Meeting Street was the Charleston House, famous for its suave, well-trained slaves who would care for every want of the traveler. The Mills House, another well-known hostelry, was close at hand.[3]

Charleston had been rather pleased at her selection as the convention city because, in the last decade, she had begun to give considerable lip-service to the Democratic name. But still she took no stock in leveling party tenets and, even though the adjective white be interpolated, heartily disapproved Jefferson's dogma that all men were created free and equal.

Her selection, the closing episode of the Cincinnati Convention of 1856, was deemed at the time a pleasant compliment to King Cotton. Long before 1860, however, Northern Democrats regretted the thoughtless gesture. Shortly before the convention, Easterners who went to Charleston to make arrangements for the customary convention facilities discovered a distinctly unfriendly local atmosphere and sensed a local purpose 'to keep away Northern outsiders.' Some of the Douglas leaders discussed shifting the convention site, and George Sanders thought Douglas' nomination would be 'a frolic' at New Orleans. But when the matter was brought up in March at a preliminary gathering of the Democratic National Executive Committee in Washington, the Administration majority took refuge behind the convenient excuse that the National Committee had no power to make the change.[4]

The Douglas managers were forehanded in local arrangements. Upon the Indiana victory an agent sped to Charleston, where he leased Hibernia Hall for the Northwestern delegations. Other backers of the Little Giant went to the Mills House, the Southern Hotspurs gathered at the Charleston Hotel, and Buchanan's inside managers chartered a private mansion for the duration of the war.

So long had William A. Richardson, Douglas' veteran convention leader, and other lieutenants lingered at Washington that their chief's interests at Charleston suffered during the highly important days on the eve of battle.[5] Others of the Illinois faithful, led by O. B. Ficklin, and many Indiana and Ohio delegates came through Kentucky, Tennessee and the Cotton South.[6]

[3] Arthur Mazyck, *Guide to Charleston*, Charleston, S.C., 1875, 52–54, describes the Hall of the Institute as 'elegant and spacious.' It had been built in 1854. In December, 1860, it was the scene of the signing of the Ordinance of Secession, and was afterwards known as Secession Hall. The Charleston *Evening Post's* present building is erected on its site.

[4] George N. Sanders, New York, March 26, 30; Douglas MSS. McClernand to Lanphier, Washington, March 21, 1860; Patton MSS.

[5] McClernand to Lanphier, Washington, Feb. 23, 1860; Patton MSS. J. P. Jones, Charleston, S.C., April 20, 1860; Douglas MSS.: 'Our friends made a great mistake in remaining so long in Washington. They should have been here.'

[6] O. B. Ficklin, Charleston, Ill., April 19, 1860; Douglas MSS.

The trains entering Charleston from the west were the scenes of many arguments, as Southerners debated with one another or with Westerners. 'Douglas men were thick as blackberries' all through the region, one Georgian told Murat Halstead, a Republican editor of Cincinnati making his way to Charleston to 'cover' the convention, 'Let him be nominated, and there will be such a war whoop as never was heard in the land.' But a second Georgian insisted there was only one Douglas man in his district. Mississippians informed Indianians that 'Davis was a patriot, and Douglas was a traitor, damned little better than Seward.' Mississippi was scornful of Northern Democratic aid: the South could fight her own battles and protect her rights herself — out of the Union if not in it.[7]

The Charleston hotels began filling a week before the opening and each day increased the press of delegates, managers, Senators, politicians and hangers-on. 'The strong men of the South are here in force, as they always are upon such occasions,' reported Halstead; 'the South will have the intellect and the pluck to make its point.' When Yancey, who, rumor had it, was 'charged with a three-day speech against Douglas,' reached the city and held almost a royal court at the Charleston Hotel, it was freely predicted that no Douglasite could cope with him.[8]

The Charlestonians, disgusted when they saw the stuff of which their compatriots from Tammany, Philadelphia and Boston were made, attributed to all the Northerners the repellent characteristics of these plug-uglies and few were the invitations to their private homes. But there was politics as well as pride in this — the Charlestonians, female and male, lost no occasion to exhibit their disapproval of men who would not give the South her 'rights.'

Many Northerners were shocked by what they saw in the orchidaceous city. The great majority of Popular Sovereignty delegates were fine, clean, upstanding men, particularly the visitors from the Northwest. Chiefly these were lawyers, doctors, editors, business men and politicians of the better grade, men of substance, attainment and local respect. They peered curiously about the city, inspected the slave markets and interviewed the human merchandise. While they heard little of the whippings advertised by the Abolitionists, yet they were revolted at the spectacle of humans being sold like horses.[9]

The hotel lobbies intrigued the curious. There were 'great portly fellows with protuberant stomachs and puffy cheeks, thin hair and grizzly, dressed in glossy black and fine linen with the latest style of stove pipe hats and ponderous gold-headed canes.' With these was a good sprinkling of distinguished-looking men.[10]

The Douglas management converted Hibernia Hall to efficient service. The office space on the first floor was fixed up for the convenience of delegates and visitors; the smaller rooms contained long tables, many chairs,

[7] Halstead, 1-4.   [8] Ibid., 5, 6, 7.
[9] J. W. Gray in Cleveland, Ohio, Plain Dealer, April 20, 1860. Halstead, 13, says that the Sunday before the convention there was much drunkenness, mainly among 'roughs from the Northern Atlantic cities.'
[10] Halstead, 6.

pens, and writing material, and great stacks of Sheahan's book on Douglas. On the second floor were several hundred cots, each with white spreads and pillows. Even so, the delegates found that attendance at the convention was costing ten dollars a day, despite the utmost economy.[11]

The Douglas delegates from the North were pleased to find that a large part of the Southern attendants were for their candidate. John Forsyth led a group of Alabamans who had come to offset the Ultra boast that Douglas' nomination would mean the loss of that State in November. James Gardner, of the Augusta *Constitutionalist*, led a similar group from Georgia, and many of that State's delegation were willing to take Douglas with Stephens as his running mate. Many Mississippians and Louisianians were there to deny the imputation as to their States. Often a Fire-Eater talking too loudly of the certainty of Douglas losing some particular State would be challenged by a Southern Douglas man to 'put up or shut up.'[12]

No sooner had Yancey reached Charleston than the Ultras undertook to set up a Southern Rights caucus. At first only Alabama and Mississippi were involved and some of the delegations, like that from North Carolina, refused to have anything to do with it.[13] But the Ultras made every kind of appeal to the incoming Southern delegates and 'the poison of sectionalism' spread rapidly. On Friday night, April 20, representatives of six Southern delegations were brought into a meeting, where they resolved to stand on the Alabama platform 'and to bolt if Douglas is nominated.' But while the Ultra delegations proclaimed themselves 'nearly solid against Squatter Sovereignty,' they were quite unable to unite upon a candidate and for a while were 'wearing forlorn faces.'

The Buchanan leaders were hard at work 'to devise some plan to distract the convention.' 'The Government office-holders that have stolen into the convention,' wrote a Douglas editor, 'are giving us all the trouble we meet with from the North.' The Little Giant's leaders found, 'by actual count, 507 office-holders here... to misrepresent public sentiment in the North.' When the Massachusetts men arrived, Douglas headquarters quickly found most of them 'speculators and traders,' and called them 'Butler and his Boston harlots.' Fernando Wood, leading a contesting New York delegation, was invited into the conclave. It was determined that the Buchanan majority in the Pennsylvania delegation must impose the unit rule, a step which would cost Douglas eight votes.[14]

[11] Halstead, 5; McClernand to Lanphier, Washington, March 28, 1860; Patton MSS. J. W. Sheahan, New York, April 14, Murray McConnel, Charleston, April 22, 1860; Douglas MSS.

[12] J. J. Jones, Charleston, April 20; C. P. Culver, Charleston, April 21; John Clancy, Charleston, S.C., April 21, 1860; Douglas MSS. Jones was an important Tennessean, Clancy was Charles G. Halpine's partner in the conduct of the New York *Leader*. Halstead, 1–8. D. C. Humphreys was another of the 'outside pressure' from Alabama. Nisbet and Patillo were among the Georgians, Shropshire and Dill from Mississippi. All told, it was an impressive exhibit.

[13] Broadside, 'Robert P. Dick to the Democracy of the Fifth Congressional District of North Carolina,' Greensboro, N.C., Aug. 14, 1860.

[14] J. P. Jones, Charleston, April 20; C. P. Culver, Charleston, April 21; Murray McConnel, Charleston, April 22, 1860; Douglas MSS.; Halstead, 7, 8. W. M. Browne to Buchanan, Charles-

The Southern division on candidates upset Buchanan's lieutenants, who reported their alarm to Washington. Senator Slidell, Buchanan's chief intriguer, had almost ostentatiously remained at the Capital. Now, however, he determined to attend the convention in person. This news, announced Saturday, was generally interpreted to mean that the Administration was 'uneasy on the Douglas question.' [15]

Some of Douglas' managers predicted that if their candidate could have, on first ballot, even ten Southern votes, it would clinch his victory. The extremists continued unable to agree on a candidate. Even so, their bitter daily meetings were having increasing effect on the Dixie delegations, until on Saturday it was reported that Alabama, Georgia, Mississippi, Louisiana, Florida, Texas and Arkansas delegations had agreed to bolt if Douglas were chosen, and that parts of the Border States would follow them.

Every night the Ultra leaders would collect 'large and excited crowds' in the two main hotels, and would make violent speeches against Douglas and the Northern Democrats in general. Occasionally some Douglas follower would try to answer, only to be 'shouted and hissed down.' All over Charleston there was the most excited discussion, and the delegates' faces soon looked 'as if they were going into battle.' The Douglas men, who were making a desperate effort to be conciliatory, were amazed at the bitterness. The Ultras go so far, Murray McConnel reported, 'as to call us Abolitionists and say we had better stay at home and attend the Chicago Convention, where we legitimately belong.' [16]

Saturday morning the Democratic National Executive Committee met to award temporary credentials to the delegates. The only major contests were from the Illinois Danites and Fernando Wood's New-Yorkers. The Buchanan-Ultra combination had a one-vote majority at the day session, and talked of excluding the Regular delegations from Illinois and New York until the convention's Credentials Committee could pass on the flimsy contests. This warned the Douglas men that the party machinery would be against them every minute, and the Northwestern delegates discussed refusing to enter the convention. Late that afternoon Judge John M. Krum, of St. Louis, a Douglas delegate and National Committeeman, arrived on the scene. By his vote the Douglas forces reversed the morning's action. The Douglas men then adjourned the Committee *sine die*.

The Pennsylvania caucus that evening did not quite conform to the cabal's plans. The Douglas men threatened to leave the caucus and denounce it if the unit rule motion were insisted on. This had a chastening

ton, April 22, 1860; Buchanan MSS. Browne blamed the Southern confusion on Hunter, of Virginia, but termed Douglas 'utterly lost.' Massachusetts would be 'a unit against him.' J. W. Gray, Charleston, April 22, 30, in Cleveland *Plain Dealer*, April 27, May 4, 1860. But despite Northern jobholders and Southern Ultras, Gray predicted a first-ballot Douglas vote of 155.

[15] Halstead, 7.

[16] James E. Harvey to George Harrington, Charleston, April 21; Murray McConnel, Charleston, April 22; F. O. Prince to Mrs. Douglas, Charleston, April 26, 1860; Douglas MSS. Halstead, 7, 8. Charleston *Mercury*, reprinted in Cleveland, Ohio, *Plain Dealer*, April 21, 1860.

effect and the unit rule was not imposed. These minor victories sent up Douglas stock.[17]

That Charleston Sunday was no day of rest for the three headquarters. The Mills House was 'a little bedlam.' Yancey remained upstairs in his apartments at the Charleston Hotel. Northern delegates expressed surprise at his mild, bland manner, which reminded them somewhat of Fernando Wood's. Downstairs in the lobby a newspaper correspondent found Yancey's colleague and delegation chairman, Leroy P. Walker, a tall, fine-looking man with a thin, pale face. Also he noted that fiercest of Mississippi Ultras, Major Ethelbert Barksdale, a lean, intense-looking man, 'wiry as a cat,' together with F. R. Lubbuck, former Lieutenant-Governor of Texas, and some of Slidell's Louisiana aides.

A large, old-fashioned dwelling on King Street had become the headquarters of the Administration Senators. Here Halstead found the occupants interrupting their senatorial ease every now and then to talk impressively to doubtful delegates their lieutenants kept bringing in.

The Senators' talk was big with figures. Douglas could not possibly get more than 106 votes on the first ballot. He would never show such strength as he had at Cincinnati. Both the Richmond and the Wood delegations from New York were dead against him. Certainly he could never get a single vote from the President's home State. 'Massachusetts is against Douglas — dead and united against him.' New Hampshire was merely 'waiting to have him slaughtered' so that Franklin Pierce could be trotted forth. These statements, generally qualified with the saving clause, 'If there is truth in man,' were uttered and re-uttered with each delegate carried through. It was easy to see that the Senators hated Douglas most cordially.

It was an oddly assorted group; Senator Bayard, of Delaware, a full-faced man, with long brown curling hair parted in the middle, had discarded his vest and was smoking expensive cigars. Close to him was Jesse D. Bright, of Indiana, a heavy, closely shaven gentleman, with a yellow vest open to the breeze. Hatred of the Little Giant was 'the strongest passion of his soul,' but now he 'seems to be certain' of Douglas' approaching doom. Close by was Bigler, of Pennsylvania, rosy in face and rural in appearance, mopping his brow with his handkerchief. One of the visitors, not a Senator but anxious to be one, was a man with a little brown mustache beneath a sharp, crooked nose and a voice with 'the sound of a file on a cross-cut saw.' It was Ben Butler, of Massachusetts, about ready to throw off all disguise.

The others were constantly consulting John M. Slidell, the kingpin of them all. His features were well-cut but cherry red; like Bright, he seemed a business man, and was generally recognized in and out of Administration circles as 'the power behind the throne, greater than the throne itself.' His special mission to Charleston was to defeat Douglas, and that Sunday afternoon he wore a smile of satisfaction, for he had just finished a most satisfactory discussion with some New England delegates.

[17] Murray McConnel, Charleston, April 22, 1860; Douglas MSS.; Halstead, 7, 8. J. W. Gray, Charleston, April 22, in Cleveland *Plain Dealer*, April 27, 1860.

All that Sunday the Douglas men in Hibernia Hall were busy organizing their forces for the sharp test ahead. Among these the strong men from Illinois stood out. Richardson was a man of impressive strength. John A. McClernand was peaked in face and hooked of nose. John A. Logan, the pride of Egypt, was conspicuous for his dark, narrow face, black eyes and hair. O. B. Ficklin and 'For God's Sake' Linder were also there talking to visitors.

Ohio was represented by H. B. Payne, of Cleveland, an earnest, impressive man; Daniel P. Rhodes, George W. McCook, James B. Steedman, Congressman Clement L. Vallandigham, and Washington McLean. Ex-Senator Charles E. Stuart, of Michigan, was conspicuous and active. The chief leaders from Iowa were ex-Senator Dodge and B. M. Samuels, the latter particularly active and beloved. Another vigorous personality was 'Bill' Montgomery, a Pennsylvania Congressman.

One other man was conspicuous — George N. Sanders, 'a burly, piratical-looking person,' who seemed a bundle of nerves and smoked cigars 'with furious, incessant whiffs.' In 1856 this stormy petrel from Kentucky had gone with Buchanan, receiving as reward the rich post of Navy Agent at New York, which he still held, although mirth-seeking friends inquired politely of him whether he felt comfortable about the neck.[18]

The Douglas men had set up their organization for the fight on the convention floor. Richardson was commander-in-chief. Stuart was to be floor leader, a steering committee of two men from each State was being formed. Wherever possible these were delegates.[19]

When the delegates reached Institute Hall Monday morning they snickered a little at the fresco, above the stage, of three dumpish female figures.[20] But almost from the moment of the call to order, there was an angry snarl. The most extreme of the Ultras made a desperate effort to exclude the New York and Illinois Regulars until the Credentials Committee had reported, but the case was so weak that they lost, 257 to 48.[21]

The Douglas men were not so well pleased that evening, however, when word came that the Committee on Permanent Organization had selected Caleb Cushing for Permanent President. The Douglas men were in a bad position to make a fight on him and sullenly consented to his choice.

Cushing, who had a Websterian sense of the dramatic, arrayed himself in

[18] Halstead, 5, 6, 10, 11, 12, 13, 20, 21, 22; J. W. Gray, Charleston, April 23, in Cleveland *Plain Dealer*, April 28, 1860. Robert Dick, Greensboro, N.C., May 8, 1860; Douglas MSS. H. M. Phillips, Charleston, April 26, 1860, Buchanan MSS. Chicago *Times*, Sept. 30, 1863, reprints Douglas to B. M. Samuels, Washington, June 3, 1860, as to Vallandigham's 'fidelity and energy' at Charleston.

[19] C. P. Culver, Charleston, April 24, 1860; Douglas MSS. Stuart was made chairman, Dr. J. J. Jones, of Tennessee, secretary of this steering committee.

[20] Halstead, 4, 5. One, possibly Minerva, had a contemplative air; a second, who was mixing colors, seemed to be getting ready to do some painting; the third was about to plunge a dagger into a painted sea upon a painted globe.

[21] *Proceedings of the Democratic National Conventions of Charleston and Baltimore*, Cleveland, Ohio, 1860, 2–10, hereafter to be called *Proceedings*; Halstead, 18, 19.

black satin vest, gray trousers and brown coat. The delegates saw a man with a round, high head, straight, sharp nose, thin lips and cheeks but slightly wrinkled. They liked his clear, musical voice. From the outset he gave the appearance of fairness to decisions and carefully explained each ruling. But for all this cloak of surface impartiality, almost never was there disputed parliamentary issue on which this Massachusetts Democrat, who fifteen years before had bitterly denounced slavery, did not rule in favor of the Slave Code faction — and with such plausibility that the enraged Douglas men had the utmost difficulty in sustaining appeals from the chair.[22]

The Committee on Permanent Organization also recommended readoption of the rules of the 1852 and 1856 conventions, with the single amendment that the convention recognize the unit rule only when a State convention, in electing a delegation, had imposed the rule upon it. The Ultras flared up at once, but Richardson strode up and down the aisles, forehead furrowed, face glowing, collar wilted, marshaling the Douglas delegates and directing the forensic argument. When brought to roll call, the new rule won handsomely.[23] This meant that thirty or forty Douglas men in various delegations could vote their preference, and Stuart thought it 'a great point gained.'

Should the convention vote first on platform or on candidate? Slidell was understood to be set upon first nominating the candidate, but the Yancey Ultras demanded the platform first. The Little Giant's steering committee finally concluded to insist that platform adoption should precede balloting on a nominee. The convention then decisively so voted and some Northern leaders elatedly claimed a second upset to Slidell's program. Stuart, however, wrote Douglas regretfully that he was not at all sure that they had not made a mistake.

The Fire-Eaters' caucus Monday night was incandescent but inconclusive. Beyond agreeing on Davis' Senate resolutions for their platform statement, they wrought no program from their heat. Stuart sensed a somewhat more friendly feeling among Southern delegates, Ultra leaders being excepted. Some delegations would like to come over if only they could find some formula by which to maintain consistency, their main trouble being that they were 'bound hand and foot by their resolutions and declarations at home.' South Carolina's Ultras, following Rhett, had boycotted the preliminary conventions which chose that State's delegates, and so the men selected represented the conciliatory party. Its chairman, Colonel Orr, a former Speaker of the National House, a tall, portly man with brilliant eyes, was a constant visitor to Hibernia Hall, and the Ultras charged him with a consuming anxiety to be chosen Douglas' running-mate.

[22] C. P. Culver, Charleston, April 24, 1860; Douglas MSS.; Halstead, 26. J. W. Gray, Washington, May 6, in Cleveland *Plain Dealer*, May 8, 1860, wrote: 'But we did not know that we had unwittingly elected the veriest toady and tool of the Fire-Eaters... until we found that his decisions were the results of factious caucuses with the Yancey wing of the convention.'

[23] *Proceedings*, 11; Halstead, 25–28. The vote was 197 to 103. Moses Bates, Charleston, April 24, 1860, Douglas MSS., on the 'most zealous efforts' which had recovered some of the lost Massachusetts vote.

Tuesday's developments greatly increased the Douglas prestige, and Halstead took note that the Little Giant's friends had 'not only the strongest, compact body of delegates' but they were using the best tactics, while the Southerners were divided in council and deficient in judgment. The Ultra meeting Tuesday night reflected their desperation. One speaker so far forgot himself as to denounce the 'bob-tailed pony from Illinois.' The caucus fixed on the recent Senate Democratic caucus resolutions for their platform demands and announced they would disrupt the party if they did not get them.[24]

The convention's Committee on Credentials did not report until Wednesday afternoon, when majority and minority reports were brought in. The former, signed by all of the Committee except six Ultras, upheld the Illinois Regulars and the Dean Richmond New York delegates. The claims of Ike Cook's Danites had proved too flimsy even for the Ultras, but they wanted to seat both New York delegations with equal vote. The debate yielded one amusing revelation: Fernando Wood's delegation had first made the most solemn pledge to the Douglasites that, if admitted, they would vote solidly for the Little Giant. It was next 'developed by the parties in their defense, Alabama, Mississippi and Georgia, that they had bargained, sold and conveyed themselves over to these factional delegations.' The minority report lost by an overwhelming convention vote.[25]

The platform issue was the Ultras' last chance to blow up the convention. The Douglas men desired the readoption of the Cincinnati platform, and were willing to add an endorsement of Supreme Court authority and a declaration of willingness to abide by past or future decisions. The Southern Ultras, however, were determined 'to make it a point of honor' that the platform must not be capable of any construction short of 'sound Southern doctrine.' This meant affirmation of the Dred Scott decision and endorsement of a Congressional Slave Code.[26]

All Wednesday and Thursday Charleston seethed with rumors. The Committee on Resolutions was locked in a death battle. The convention itself passed the time by receiving a flood of pro-Southern resolutions and orations, all aimed at a Slave Code. The tenor of these, Halstead thought, was that the South 'insists upon the political execution of every Northern Democrat and the total destruction of the Democratic party.' [27]

It was almost noon Friday when the Committee on Resolutions filed into Institute Hall, its members looking ashen and haggard. The committeemen from California and Oregon had gone with those from the fifteen Slave States to give a Committee majority of one to the flat statement 'that

---

[24] Charles E. Stuart, Charleston, April 24; C. P. Culver, Charleston, April 24, 25, 1860; Douglas MSS. *Proceedings*, 19-24; Halstead, 10, 28, 29, 30.

[25] C. P. Culver, Charleston, April 25, 1860; Douglas MSS.; *Proceedings*, 24, 25. The vote was 210½ to 55.

[26] C. P. Culver, Charleston, April 25, 1860; Douglas MSS. Halstead, 30, 37. He heard Richardson would, by authority, withdraw Douglas' name if a Slave Code were adopted.

[27] Halstead, 38-42.

it is the duty of the Federal Government to protect, when necessary, the rights of person and property on the high seas, in the Territories or wherever else its Constitutional authority extends.' [28]

Henry B. Payne, of Ohio, presented the minority report. Affirming the Cincinnati platform, it made this addition as to slavery: 'That all questions in regard to the rights of property in States or Territories arising under the Constitution of the United States, are judicial in their character; and that the Democratic party is pledged to abide by and faithfully carry out such determination of these questions as has been made or may be made by the Supreme Court of the United States.' [29] There was also a third report — Ben Butler's one-man affair. This Massachusetts worthy attracted attention to himself by calling for the 1856 platform, with the sole addition of a plank urging Federal protection for naturalized citizens abroad.

These reports brought the long-awaited debate. Chairman W. W. Avery, of North Carolina, defended the Slave Code plank with a 'dreary' argument which had 'no visible effect.' [30] Henry B. Payne, of Ohio, made the minority plea. A Douglas friend for almost two decades, he was not a professional politician but a leader of the fine bar of Cleveland. An impressive speaker, he communicated to the convention a sense of the solemnity of the decision at hand.

Each of those who signed the minority report, he said earnestly, 'had felt in his conscience and in his heart that upon the result of our deliberations and the action of this convention, in all human probability, depended the fate of the Democratic party and the destiny of the Union.' Next he called attention to the relatively recent expressions of many Southern statesmen, Calhoun among them, to show that not so long ago the Southern conception of Popular Sovereignty had been identical with that now held by the North.

'The Northern mind is thoroughly imbued with the principle of Popular Sovereignty,' he continued. 'We ask nothing for the people of the Territories but what the Constitution allows them, for we say we abide by the decision of the Courts, who are the final interpreters of the Constitution.

[28] The majority platform provided for readopting the Cincinnati platform, with five additional resolutions, of which the one quoted in the text was the third. The others were: One, 'that Congress has no power to abolish slavery in the Territories; that the Territorial Legislature has no power to abolish slavery in any Territory nor to prohibit the introduction of slaves therein, nor any power to exclude slavery therefrom nor any power to destroy or to impair the right of property in slaves by any legislation whatever.' Second, 'that the enactments of State Legislatures to defeat the faithful execution of the Fugitive Slave law are hostile in character, subversive of the Constitution, and revolutionary in their effect.' The fourth was a statement about the Government's duty to protect the naturalized citizens at home or abroad. The fifth earnestly recommended acquiring Cuba 'at the earliest practicable period.' To these was added a whereas about a Pacific railroad, pledging the party to secure the passage of 'some bill' to that end.

[29] *Proceedings*, 37–39. The minority report did not disagree with majority resolution number two. Its Cuban plank insisted that the terms of acquisition 'shall be honorable to ourselves and just to Spain.' Its Pacific railroad plank was bold and forthright. It accepted the plank as to upholding the rights of naturalized citizens.

[30] Halstead, 45, 50. J. W. Gray, Charleston, April 30, in Cleveland *Plain Dealer*, May 4, 1860.

The Dred Scott decision, having been rendered since the Cincinnati platform was adopted, renders this proper. We will take that decision and abide by it like loyal, steadfast, true-hearted men.' The hall grew still as Payne asked: 'Are you, for a very abstraction, going to yield the chance of success?' Rather than this, he appealed to the South 'to put no weights on the North — to let them run this race unfettered and unhampered. If the appeal is answered, the North will do her duty in the struggle.'[31]

When he finished there was tremendous applause from the Northern delegations but silence from the Southern. Ben Butler then interposed a sneering attack on Payne. Barksdale, of Mississippi, and ex-Governor King, of Missouri, each spoke for an hour. The Ultras, however, were waiting for their great champion. That afternoon William Lowndes Yancey took the stage.

For him it was the culmination of a long struggle; as usual he was mild, good-humored, and by his mode of saying things almost disarmed the revolutionary import of what he said. It grew dark before he finished, the gas-jets were lit, and the combination of flashing lights, crowded hall and 'rapturous' Southern enthusiasm made it the apex of his career.

The Southern delegations, began their high priest, had come to Charleston with one great purpose — 'to save our Constitutional rights, if it lay in our power to do so.' They had been taunted with being in the minority and they knew that was the fact. Even so, their minority claimed the rights of a minority. 'The benefit of the Constitution was that it was made for the protection of minorities... That a majority should not rely upon their numbers and strength, but should look loyally into the written compact and see where the minority was to be respected and protected.' Should they accept the proposition of the Douglas platform, continued Yancey, it would 'bankrupt us of the South.' Therefore the time had come for Southern men to form a united front; surely defeat on principle was better than victory through fraud.

Not one Northern State which opposed the Slave Code was safely Democratic. The reason was that the advocates of the Northern platform had acknowledged that slavery existed neither by the law of nature nor that of God but only by State law; 'that it was wrong but that you were not to blame.' 'That was your position and it was wrong,' Yancey trumpeted in his powerful, silver tones. 'If you had taken the position directly that slavery was right, and therefore ought to be,... you would have triumphed, and anti-slavery would now have been dead in your midst.' But the North had not done so. The Abolitionist heresy had now spread into three different groups, the Black Republicans, the Free-Soilers, and Squatter Sovereignty men — but 'all representing the common sentiment that slavery is wrong. I say it in no disrespect, but it is a logical argument that your admission that slavery is wrong has been the cause of all this discord.'

Senator Pugh had been growing more and more agitated over these statements. When Yancey took his seat the Ohioan leaped to his feet, ex-

[31] Halstead, 45–46; Rhodes, II, 402, for character of Payne; Charleston *Mercury*, April 28, 29, 1860, for text references.

claiming loudly that he thanked God that at last a bold and honest man from the South had spoken and had revealed the full measure of Southern demands. But the South itself had been responsible for the downfall of the Northern Democracy. Their leaders had been slaughtered fighting for the South, and for what reward? It was that, after they had been reduced to a minority through defending the South, when they came to the convention in Charleston, 'the Northern Democracy were thrust back and told in effect they must put their hands on their mouths and their mouths in the dust.'

'Gentlemen of the South,' Pugh cried, in thrilling tones, 'you mistake us — you mistake us — we will not do it.' [32]

This blunt challenge produced 'profound excitement.' The Ohio Senator was known as an intimate of Douglas; he too had recently been the victim of anti-slavery opposition joined to the treachery of Buchanan's office-holders. All realized that this bold confrontation of the issue was no un-thoughted personal emotion, but meant that thus far would the North go — but no farther.

It was the moment for decision and the Popular Sovereignty leaders sought to bring on the determinative ballot. But they overestimated the fortitude of their followers — the hour was late, the delegates tired, hungry and rest-less, and there was no resisting the Buchanan-Ultra demand for adjourn-ment. So Pugh's speech was left suspended in midair and the convention adjourned until the next morning.

Far into the wee sma' hours of Saturday morning the Little Giant's aides discussed the situation. Some thought the day's debate had acted as a safety valve for the escape of pent-up steam. All knew that the Southern Ultras could not win their platform. Alabama and Mississippi insisted that once their planks were lost they would withdraw. Slidell was urging Louisiana to go along, but some objected that this would be committing suicide. The Georgia Moderates were opposed to going out.

But the convention atmosphere had been changing. The high cost of Charleston and the long-drawn-out convention had worn out the nerves and pockets of many of the Douglas men, who were going home by every train and steamer. By special order daily prayers were being given at St. Michael's for the victory of the Southern cause.[33] But this increase of an-tagonistic outside pressure merely made the Northwestern delegates more determined. They were told that Pugh's blunt challenge had made an impression on and was being 'highly spoken of by the most radical men of the South.' Richardson expressed himself full of hope.

George Sanders telegraphed Buchanan that Douglas would have a majority on first ballot, and reminded the President of the Little Giant's 'example at Cincinnati, by which alone you could have been nominated.' Buchanan

[32] Halstead, 47-49; Charleston *Mercury*, April 28, 29, 1860. J. W. Gray, Charleston, April 30, in Cleveland *Plain Dealer*, May 4, 1860: Pugh 'took the tuck out of him [Yancey] hand-somely.'

[33] Charleston *Daily Courier*, April 27, 1860.

must send for Douglas and offer his support, for he could not 'afford to be the last President of the United States.' [34]

Pugh claimed the floor the next morning to finish his interrupted speech. The Constitution, he insisted, had no warrant for a Slave Code, and the Northern Democrats could make no fight for one because they had already sacrificed their political lives for Southern Rights and could go no further. The truth of this he illustrated by pointing all through the hall to Northern victims of this battle, men who had been Senators and Congressmen but had been beaten because they had fought for the rights of the South.

The Northern Democracy was ready to stand by its old platform and its old faith, and would regret to have the South depart, but if the South would stay only on terms of a Slave Code, go she must. The Democracy of the Northwest was determined to make itself heard and felt; Northern Democrats were not children under the pupilage of the South, to be told to stand here and stand there and be moved at the South's beck and bidding. The North too had rights and she intended to maintain them. The hall was still as Pugh finished. Another great section had spoken. The fateful hour of decision had come.[35]

Suddenly there was a call for the previous question, putting an immediate end to debate. With this came bedlam. Cushing pounded incessantly for order, but so great was the uproar that those close to the chair could see, but not hear, the movement of his gavel. The Buchanan-Ultra combine was well aware of the Douglas purpose, and for more than an hour parliamentary points delayed the calling of the roll of States. Determined to fix the emotions of every wavering Southern delegate, the Buchanan Senators left no stone unturned to renew and to prolong the debate.

The previous question was finally withdrawn. Then Senator Bigler promptly introduced an ambiguous resolution and moved that the convention recommit the platform to the Committee. The Douglas men tried to defeat this new stratagem, but New York now determined to yield to the request for more delay, voted against the Northwest on recommitting, and the motion carried 152 to 151. Dean Richmond then swung back on instructing the Committee's report, and this branch of the Slidell scheme was defeated by over four to one.

Late Saturday afternoon the Platform Committee returned, again with three reports. The majority had altered the form but not the substance of its expression. The second of its new resolutions declared it 'the duty of the Federal Government, in all its departments, to protect, when necessary, the rights of persons and property in the Territories, and wherever else its Constitutional authority extends.' [36]

The minority report, read by Samuels, of Iowa, thus rephrased its statement: 'Inasmuch as difference of opinion exists in the Democratic party

[34] C. P. Culver, Charleston, April 28, 1860; Douglas MSS. Some Douglas men were betting ten to one on the Little Giant's choice. Halstead, 52–59. Sanders to Buchanan, telegram, Charleston, April 27, 1860, Buchanan MSS., 'I rely on your patriotism,' Sanders added. The message, sent collect, cost Buchanan $26.80!

[35] Halstead, 49–50. [36] *Proceedings*, 55–59.

as to the nature and extent of the powers of a Territorial Legislature and as to the powers and duties of Congress, under the Constitution of the United States, over the institution of slavery within the Territories, resolved that the Democratic party will abide by the decisions of the Supreme Court of the United States upon these questions of constitutional law.' Ben Butler again brought in his simple reaffirmation, but this time had persuaded the Committee members from New Jersey, Indiana and Minnesota to sign it with him.

Now came a debate 'dreadfully long and intolerably dull,' interspersed with points of order, motions to adjourn, and to lay the platform on the table.[37] The Ultras hoped to prevent the platform coming to a finish vote. Cushing 'had the floor farmed out and expected to make a speech himself.' The Buchanan-Ultra forces resorted to every possible tactic of delay to prevent a call for the previous question. Before a delegate could secure Cushing's recognition, he must first assure a messenger from the Chair that he did not rise to demand the previous question. These tactics finally disgusted John Milton, a delegate from Florida, who told his fellow Southerners that the South had been listened to attentively, had been fairly met in argument and should now cease to offer factitious opposition.

About this time Caleb Cushing made an error. A Missouri delegate sought recognition. Cushing's messenger interviewed and reported on the wrong Missourian. Thereupon Cushing recognized the clamant delegate from Missouri, who did demand the previous question and upset the apple-cart. Cushing, who was now in a very tight place, grew nervous and fidgety, but there was nothing he could do about it, and by 272 to 31, the convention declared itself ready to have the main question put. This done, the weary delegates again overbore the Douglas leaders and adjourned to Monday.

There was heavy rain that night and Sunday but this did not dampen the furious political maneuvering. The Southern Ultras now knew definitely that they could not force a Slave Code plank upon the party and the question of a bolt was upon them. Telegrams began to come in from Senators in Washington; Toombs insisted that Georgia follow Alabama out. Hammond got after the South Carolina 'Softs.' [38]

The Douglas leaders, reconciling themselves to the impending departure of the most intransigeant delegates, lamented it so little that some Ultras became suspicious that the Little Giant's forces were too willing. Accordingly some of Slidell's group set their hands to constructing a face-saving formula by which the Southern Extremists would be kept in the convention. That night it was reported that Alabama would be the only seceder — the other Southern Ultras 'would stay in and slaughter Douglas.' They also employed the Sabbath for earnest work on some 'hungry parasites' from the Northwest who wanted propositions. The Douglas men knew 'that Slidell and company were willing to buy all such fellows' and their ire reached boiling point.

[37] Halstead, 52–56; 68, 69.
[38] Halstead, 51; Hammond Diary, April 29; 'they did just what I ordered,' Hammond spread upon his Diary record, quoted in Merritt, 135.

Should the Slave Code platform carry by purchase, the Douglas North-westerners made up their minds to leave the convention and go home.[39]

Monday morning South Carolinians shouting for a Slave Code fill the balconies at Institute Hall, 'the convention wears a Southern aspect,' and the Northwestern delegates look a bit disheartened. But debate is over, and the main questions are quickly put. Ben Butler's platform, an amendment to the minority amendment, which comes up first, is defeated 198 to 105. Ultra points of order now delay but slightly the main question of substituting minority for majority report. The roll call is ordered; as it proceeds, the crowd sees that the Slave Code is lost. The clerk announces the vote of 165 to 132. Thus the convention puts aside the majority platform.[40]

Now Captain Ashe, of North Carolina, appeals to the North to yield their platform demand because it will lead to 'division and ruin.' But the balloting goes right on. The next question is upon the adoption of the minority report. Caleb Cushing insists on a separate vote on each item, involving a half-dozen roll calls of the States. The first is ordered and by a vote of 237½ to 65, the entire Cincinnati platform is reaffirmed. Now comes a motion to table the rest of the report. This loses, 188 to 81. The delegates from neither Alabama, Mississippi nor Arkansas answer their names when called.

Next comes the motion to adopt the second of the Douglas resolutions, that which binds the Democratic party to past and future Supreme Court decisions. Bedford Brown, of Mississippi, awakes to a realization that the crisis is at hand. He clambers upon his chair and makes an appeal, 'as piteous, as solemn, as agonizingly earnest as ever a man offered up for his life.' As he pours forth his soul, a reporter catches the eye of William L. Yancey. The Alabaman is pleased, his eye twinkles and he is 'smiling as a bridegroom.'

This brings another parliamentary tangle. William A. Richardson seeks recognition but an obstreperous Ultra refuses consent. Cries of protest are heard all over the convention; here is an olive branch, they shout, let us hear what Richardson has to say! The Douglas leader soon announces that his forces will be quite content with the Cincinnati platform unamended, if only their opponents will be similarly content.

The balloting proceeds amid great confusion. The second clause of the Douglas resolutions is defeated by the joint vote of the Douglas men and the remaining Southerners, but the delegations from the seven Cotton States remain silent in their seats. It is 'the frown of King Cotton.'

[39] Halstead, 58–60; 68–69. J. W. Gray, Charleston, April 30, in Cleveland *Plain Dealer*, May 4, 1860: 'Our only fear is they [the Southern Fire-Eaters] will not go... They are a nuisance to the party and the country, and the sooner they get out of both the better.'

[40] Analysis of this crucial roll call displayed the ravages which Buchanan's tactics had made on the Northern Popular Sovereignty strength. Though all New England save Massachusetts was solidly aye, 6 of Cushing's, Whitney's and Butler's State went for the Slave Code. New Jersey split 5 and 2; Pennsylvania, 12 and 15; and Delaware voted solidly for the Davis resolutions. In Maryland, too, 4½ of the 8 votes were Ultra; Missouri split 4 to 5, and all of both California and Oregon went for the Code.

Clause by clause the rest of the platform is quickly voted. Saulsbury, of Delaware, endeavors to testify his travail of spirit; Stuart, of Michigan, arises to pour oil upon the waters but irritates instead.

All during his remarks 'a tall, pale gentleman' stands upon his chair appealing for recognition. It is Leroy P. Walker, chairman of the Alabama delegation. He catches Cushing's eye, walks to the platform and announces that it is his duty to read a communication from the State of Alabama. A shudder of excitement goes over the convention. For the first time of the day there is profound stillness.

Alabama's chairman now reads his 'communication.' It recites the resolutions of the State Convention at Montgomery, which elected their delegation, expressly directing them to 'insist' on a Slave-Code plank; if this should be refused, the delegates were 'positively instructed to withdraw.' This point has now been reached and it is the duty of Alabama to withdraw, and no one now has any 'authority to represent Alabama upon the floor of the convention.' [41] With this the Alabama men stalk out. Glenn, of Mississippi, next rises, his face 'pale as ashes,' his eyes roll and he launches into a thrilling and impassioned speech, lasting twenty minutes. The North must go her way, he shouts, and the South will go hers. The ladies in the gallery smile and applaud his words.

Mississippi is followed by Louisiana, whose spokesman says that the principles the majority has adopted 'can never be the principle of the South.' Two Louisianians, however, remain. Colonel Orr's South Carolina 'Softs' can no longer withstand the carefully built-up pressure, but heed Senator Hammond's telegram and all but two of them announce their bolt. Now the Floridians arise, and then Texas, each with a protest. If the Northern delegates properly represent the principles of the Democratic party in that section, declares the Texas spokesman, 'we do not hesitate to declare that their principles are not only not ours but, if adhered to and enforced by them, will destroy the Union.'

Georgia's chairman asks and is granted leave to withdraw for consultation. An Arkansas member announces the departure of his delegation; some, however, refuse to go out. Senator Bayard, of Delaware, withdraws his delegation, while Saulsbury repeats that he does not know what to do. Announcement is made that the seceders will meet that night in St. Andrew's Hall. For an hour and a half the convention, in contradistinction to the gallery, has been profoundly silent. A New York leader moves adjournment until Tuesday morning, the convention agrees, and the delegates return to their hotels and headquarters. [42]

A large crowd gathers in the lobby of the Charleston Hotel. Yancey and Meek are showered with plaudits and congratulations, but Bradley, of their delegation, offers to bet large amounts of money that Douglas can carry Alabama by 20,000 majority. Finding no takers, he remarks in disgust: 'And yet I was compelled to leave the convention owing to *instructions*. Could any position be more ridiculous?'

[41] *Proceedings*, 55–60; Halstead, 72.
[42] Halstead, 61–68; 72–73; *Proceedings*, 60–65.

About this same time the Georgia delegates debate excitedly what shall be their course. The original Fire-Eaters and the Cobb men declare they will withdraw. Most of the conservative delegation term the Yancey bolt nothing but disunion *per se*, and thirteen determine to stay in the convention and act with it.[43]

Now is discerned a curious cross-current — some Ultras openly express regret that Texas, South Carolina, and Louisiana have joined in Alabama's bolt. This comes from some of the Buchanan men who are planning to name Joe Lane, of Oregon, the 'Constitutional' candidate, but find that the very act of bolting has made the seceders 'so red hot Southern' that Lane is out and they will nominate Jeff Davis or some other Southerner.[44]

That evening, the seceded delegates assemble at St. Andrew's Hall. They display a 'regular Fourth of July feeling' and everyone is rejoicing. The Ultras go through the motion of organizing a 'Constitutional Democratic convention,' but after several perfervid speeches and perfunctory motions, adjourn for a demonstration of their joy. Headed by a band, they now parade about the town in triumph, serenading R. Barnwell Rhett and Fernando Wood. There is joy in the seceders' hearts; at last they can make good their threats to disrupt the Democratic party, the last binding tie of Union. 'Perhaps even now,' Yancey tells them, 'the pen of the historian is nibbed to write the story of a new Revolution.' The crowd gives three cheers for a new Southern Republic.[45]

It may be appropriate at this point to seek to discern, if possible, the actual point upon which the bolt was based. The platform of the Buchanan-Ultra group insisted that it was the duty of the Federal Government, through affirmative Congressional legislation, to protect slave property within the Territories. The Douglas platform proposed to leave the matter to the decision of the Supreme Court of the United States. The Ultra platform gave active instrumentation to the extreme demands of the slave power. The Douglas platform declared that, should the Supreme Court decide that such affirmative legislation really was a duty, the Democratic party would faithfully uphold its decision.

This was the difference upon which the Southern Ultras bolted the Charleston Convention. An unwillingness to be satisfied with future decisions of the same Supreme Court which had held the Missouri Compromise uncon-

[43] *Proceedings*, 60, 65; Halstead, 61, 68; Washington Gibbons, Rochester, N.Y., May 10, 1860; Douglas MSS.; Gibbons is quoting to Douglas an account of a New York delegate who was in the hotel lobby and heard Bradley's offer and bitter gibe. James Patillo, Mitchell City, Ga., May 20, 1860; Douglas MSS.; Patillo was asked in the Georgia delegation rooms the night of the Alabama bolt. J. W. Gray, Charleston, May 2, in Cleveland *Plain Dealer*, May 5, 1860: 'There are monied men here from the South offering to take bets that Douglas will carry every Southern State.'

[44] Edward J. Pringle to Mrs. Rose Greenhow, Charleston, May 2, 1860; Greenhow Papers, State Department Archives. Mrs. Rose Greenhow had a secret file which was seized by Federal forces when she was arrested Aug. 23, 1860. Pringle, a Charleston lawyer and Secessionist, described to Mrs. Greenhow the attitude of the Ultras on the day of the Yancey bolt.

[45] Halstead, 74–76; 97, 100.

stitutional and Dred Scott a slave led the Southern Ultras to this determinative event which so swiftly breached the Union and precipitated a politicians' war.

Many Southern delegates did not feel that the Northern Democrats had been unfair. Robert P. Dick, of North Carolina, testified that they had 'manifested a spirit of conciliation and compromise.' As he saw it, the issue came down to one as to the construction of the Dred Scott decision, and both North and South should have been willing to leave it to the decision of the Supreme Court. When all was said and done, in his opinion the Northerners had 'made every fair proposition of compromise,' the Secessionists 'were alone in fault,' and the question was, at most, 'a mere abstraction.' The Southern extremists later claimed that they had bolted the doctrine of Popular Sovereignty but this was not the truth. 'The Northern men did not ask us to subscribe to their opinion on Popular Sovereignty,' declared Dick. W. W. Holden, another North Carolina delegate, left Charleston convinced that the leaders of the secession cared nothing about the platform but were 'Disunionists *per se.*' [46]

The decimated convention assembled somberly Tuesday morning. After the usual opening prayer, Judge Benning, the Georgia chairman, presented a notice that his delegation felt it a duty 'not to participate further.' Twenty-two of the Georgia delegates signed this communication; four of the minority of fifteen signed an appendix that they disapproved, but agreed 'that the vote of the majority should control our action,' the other eleven Georgians remained steadfast to the convention.[47]

The Tennessee and Virginia delegations now retired for consultation, as did parts of Kentucky, North Carolina and Maryland. McCook, of Ohio, now moved that the convention proceed, at two o'clock, to nominate a candidate for President. There was considerable delay, much speaking, finally the roll was called upon it and the motion won by a large vote.

During this ballot, Cushing availed himself of another opportunity to harm the Douglas cause. The Georgians who had remained faithful to the convention sought to vote but Cushing ruled that the secession of the others gave the loyal men no right to remain there. This decision roused bitter protest. Gaulden, the South's largest slave-holder, who was clinging to the party, denounced it as 'most suicidal and destructive'; the bolters did not represent the rank and file of the Georgia party, and the delegates who had stayed in 'remained to vote.' An appeal from the ruling lost, whereupon the remaining Georgians left — but Cushing and not Secession had thrust them forth! [48]

There was some disturbance when a Californian insulted the Douglas men and for a moment it looked as though this would precipitate a brawl.

[46] Channing, VI, 241; Dick Broadside. I. G. Tucker, Summit, N.C., May 30, 1860, Douglas MSS., quoting to Douglas letter to him from W. W. Holden.

[47] *Proceedings*, 66; James Patillo, Mitchell City, Ga., May 20, 1860; Douglas MSS.

[48] *Proceedings*, 69. Halstead, 78–79. The vote was 148 to 100. No roll call is given.

This attitude by Buchanan's pocket boroughs on the Coast greatly pleased the bolters, who expressed their gratitude by a serenade.[49]

Now came a critical fight staged on the question of the construction of the two-thirds rule. Monday night, when the delegations from Virginia, North Carolina, Kentucky and Tennessee caucused, the Hunter men in the Virginia group were highly sympathetic with the seceders, as were fractions from North Carolina and Tennessee. In the end, however, each delegation resolved not to join the bolt but to put forward a scheme under which Douglas could not possibly win.

The device these Borderers planned to use was to have Caleb Cushing proclaim from the Chair that, under the two-thirds rule as he construed it, to secure the nomination an aspirant must receive the votes, not merely of two-thirds of the remaining delegates but of two-thirds of the theoretical full convention strength — the total number of votes in the electoral college. There were 303 votes in the electoral college; two-thirds majority of this was 202. Only 248 electoral votes remained in the convention after the Southerners' secession; two-thirds majority of this was 166. Thus the desired ruling by Cushing would have the practical effect of transforming the two-thirds rule into a five-sixths rule, which would make Douglas' success quite impossible. The Borderers expected no difficulty in securing such a ruling from Caleb Cushing. They knew, too, that the Douglas men would appeal from the Chair's decision and that the appeal would be sustained unless the New York delegation, with its thirty-five votes, could be persuaded to go for this five-sixths rule.

The New York delegation was the key to Douglas' majority. When it was selected at the New York State Democratic Convention at Syracuse, in September, 1859, that convention also placed it under the unit rule. Seventy individuals were selected to cast the thirty-five votes, four from the State at large, the others elected by and representing the thirty-three Congressional districts. The largest single unit thereof was that for Manhattan, about twenty Tammany men, definitely out of sympathy with up-State sentiment. At the moment Fernando Wood was Mayor of New York, Mozart Hall, his Manhattan organization, dispensed the city patronage, Tammany was reduced to the crumbs from Buchanan's Federal table and so was anti-Douglas. About ten more delegates came from the southern tier, where Daniel S. Dickinson had his home and strength. These two groups co-operated and so on every poll of the New York delegation, about fifteen full votes were against the Little Giant.

The remaining forty New York delegates were grouped around half a dozen individual leaders. When the Douglas men set out to win the vote of the Empire State, they had had to enlist not only Dean Richmond, the great chieftain of the Buffalo area, but also Peter Cagger, Albany's King Democrat; Sanford E. Church, an important leader of that same area; Darius A. Ogden, S. L. M. Barlow, Edwin Creswell, Erastus Corning and one or two other minor potentates of other localities. Richmond had helped in the arrangements, and Cagger became the most earnest of Doug-

⁂ Edward J. Pringle, Charleston, May 2, 1860; Greenhow Papers; Halstead, 79.

las' supporters. The ten-vote margin of Douglas control in the delegation, however, was so slender that an upset was never out of the probabilities.

In addition to this, Dean Richmond and his associates felt an unusual responsibility. They were determined to exercise a moderating force upon convention animosities, and almost frantically sought some alternative to break-up and party defeat. From the time the convention started, as Sanford E. Church said later, New York 'yielded everything but personal honor in order to heal up the divisions of the convention.'

The New Yorkers had never forgotten the Baltimore Convention of 1844, when Martin Van Buren, their last great leader, had been deprived of the Presidential nomination by the two-thirds rule. Their 1860 leaders thought it 'outrageous, undemocratic, despotic, wrong,' and before they left for Charleston had discussed supporting a move to abolish it.

When the Border leaders came to the New-Yorkers with their rules proposal, Richmond, Cagger and Church thought it an outrage to be 'asked to increase the number necessary to nominate from two-thirds to five-sixths.' But Howard, of Tennessee, who led the negotiations for the Border men, urged that to do so would prevent the break-up of the convention. Furthermore, the leaders of the Tennessee, Kentucky, North Carolina, and Virginia delegations pledged that if New York would do this, the Border men would 'remain in the convention, stand by its action, and fight the seceders and disunionists' to the bitter end. The New-Yorkers held an excited caucus. 'In God's name,' Church finally exclaimed, 'let us sacrifice all we can for peace and harmony.' So New York undertook, 'as a peace offering,' to vote to sustain the expected ruling.

Tuesday morning Howard, of Tennessee, offered a motion that the President of the convention declare no one nominee until he should have received 'a number of votes equal to two-thirds of the votes of all the electoral college.' The Douglasites must not have been informed of the New York decision, for Richardson moved to table the motion. The roll call revealed the New-Yorkers' critical decision, for Richardson's motion lost, 141 to 111½.

Richardson, Stuart, McClernand, Samuels and other Northwestern leaders now sought to reconvert New York, but without effect. Then they fought desperately to uphold their interpretation of the rule according to precedents at Baltimore in 1848 and 1852, and Cincinnati in 1856. Each time, with poisonous politeness, Cushing ruled against them. On their final appeal, New York again sided with the Borderers and the five-sixths rule was imposed.[50]

Then the convention turned to the now hopeless task of selecting a candidate. It was before the day of the interminable 'he is the man who' type of nominating speech, or the highly organized 'demonstration.' In less than ten minutes, the names of Douglas, Guthrie, Dickinson, Hunter, Johnson and Lane were formally offered and the balloting commenced.

The first roll call yielded Douglas 145½ votes. While six short of a majority

---

[50] *Proceedings*, 164–65, give Church's speech at Baltimore describing the Charleston conferences on this point. For Southern joy see Edward J. Pringle, Charleston, May 2, 1860; Greenhow Papers.

of the electoral college strength, this was fifty-eight per cent of the total of 246½ votes cast. Next was Hunter, with 42 votes, while Guthrie was third, with 35. Andrew Johnson had Tennessee's 12, Dickinson, 7, Joe Lane, 6, Isaac Toucey, 2½, Jefferson Davis, 1½ and Franklin Pierce, 1.

The Douglas managers had suffered critical losses both from the Administration campaign to seduce Northern delegates, and also from the shrewd scheme of the Buchanan-Ultra coalition to raise Southern delegate emotions to white heat through the Slave Code debate. Six Maine delegates, casting three full votes, had on the very first tests disregarded their pledges to the conventions which elected them. Typical was the case of Henry W. Owen, of Bath, 'a little recreant' whom the Administrationists had 'smuggled' on the delegation, professing loyalty to the Little Giant. George F. Shepley, of Portland, Buchanan's district attorney, had made the most solemn protestations that he knew Maine's Democracy was for the Little Giant, that their party's whole future there depended on his nomination, and that he would vote for Douglas at Charleston 'at the hazard of being removed' from office — a pledge he forgot as soon as he reached the convention.[51]

The whole Massachusetts delegation had been selected for and individually pledged to Douglas at the State Convention at Worcester the preceding September. But the combined efforts of 'that arch-traitor' James Whitney, whom Buchanan had secured by the collectorship of the Port of Boston; Ben Butler, who threw off his mask completely at Charleston, and Caleb Cushing drew off a little over half of the delegation. One Douglas man was induced to stay at home so that his substitute could vote against the Little Giant. A second was promised an office on his return to Massachusetts. Sufficient inducements were held before six others to pull them away. The first nomination ballot showed seven and a half Massachusetts votes against Douglas and the figure never went below six.[52]

The twelve delegates who cast Connecticut's six votes at Charleston had all committed themselves to the Little Giant's leaders in that State. Yet on nearly every ballot at Charleston five were ranged against the Senator from Illinois.[53] But the Vermont, New Hampshire, and Rhode Island

[51] Owen's and Shepley's pledges to support Douglas at Charleston were described in detail to Douglas; J. C. McClintock, Belfast, Me., May 31, June 7; H. D. Rice, Augusta, Me., June 8; H. G. Jewett, Belfast, Me., June 7, 1860; Douglas MSS. Jewett added that Shepley 'passed through Washington on his way to Charleston and there you have the explanation.'

[52] D. W. Carpenter, of Greenfield, was persuaded to stay at home by Whitney. Noble was the name of his substitute, an anti-Douglas man. C. W. N. Swift, of New Bedford, was promised the office. James Riley and Isaac H. Wright, of Boston, delegates of the Fourth District, E. G. Williams, of Newburyport, and C. G. Clark, of Lynn, the Sixth District delegates, and George Johnson, of Bradford, a Seventh District delegate, were among the pledge-breakers. These seven, with Cushing, Butler and Whitney, account for ten of the fourteen consistent Massachusetts deserters. George H. Laflin, Pittsfield, May 4; Moses Bates, New York, May 7, Plymouth, May 18; John W. Mahan, Boston, May 10; Edwin B. Spinney, South Boston, May 15, June 2; A. N. Brown, Lowell, May 16; J. F. Whitney, Lee, May 31, 1860; Douglas MSS. B. F. Butler to J. B. Alden, Washington, Oct. 29, 1867, B. F. Butler MSS., Library of Congress: 'I voted in the Charleston Convention seven times for Judge Douglas... I then threw my vote away upon [Jefferson] Davis, as the representative man of the South.'

[53] These were cast by Colin M. Ingersoll, of New Haven; Samuel Arnold, of Haddam, W. D.

delegations remained staunch to the Little Giant to the end of the convention.

New York had done its damage on the vote on the five-sixths rule; throughout the presidential balloting its thirty-five votes were cast for Douglas. New Jersey, however, went heavily against him. Its delegates, provided with the excuse of having been instructed to vote for a favorite son for Vice-President, tried to stretch this into a unit rule on other questions. Cushing ruled with them but the Douglas men's appeal from the chair was sustained.[54]

Broken Pennsylvania pledges also disappointed the Douglas managers. The Little Giant had committals from twenty-four delegates, or twelve votes, out of the total of twenty-seven. Senator Bigler and the other Buchanan lieutenants were free with offers and with threats of proscription and began making inroads into Douglas' Pennsylvania ranks. The first nominating ballot showed that they had cut his strength to nine votes, which proved an irreducible minimum.[55]

Delaware was completely hostile from the outset. Douglas' friend Townsend had Senator Saulsbury's promise that the delegation would not vote for a Slave Code plank — but it did so. Saulsbury and three other Delaware delegates remained after Bayard and a satellite had joined the Yancey bolt. But while Saulsbury had also promised Townsend to bring the delegation to Douglas whenever the latter received a majority, Douglas never received a single vote from that State.[56]

The Maryland record was better. Robert J. Brent, of Baltimore, the Douglas leader on the Free State's delegation, had promised five of Maryland's eight electoral votes. From Charleston he reported that Douglas would have 'two original and unwavering full electoral votes from first to last.' His first ballot prediction was verified and before the balloting ended Douglas was getting four Maryland electoral votes.[57]

From the beginning Douglas received half of Missouri, but the other Southern States did not give him a single first ballot vote, dividing all their tallies between Guthrie, Hunter and the minor candidates. Many delegates from the Border States came to Charleston anxious to vote for Douglas, but during the convention gave way to a combination of resentment

Bishop and P. C. Calhoun, of Bridgeport, and E. Augustus Russell, of Middletown, M. Schofield, Hartford, Conn., May 3; James Gallagher, New Haven, May 9; A. G. Hasard, Hasardville, May 16, 1860; Douglas MSS. Schofield wrote: As to Bishop, 'In order to procure his seat in the convention, he was obliged to come down to an acknowledgement that Douglas was his preference, and if they would send him he would do all in his power to aid in your nomination.'

[54] *Proceedings*, 51.

[55] For example, Francis W. Hughes, of Pottsville, just before leaving for Charleston, pledged himself specifically and unequivocally to be for Douglas first, last and all the time — a pledge immediately broken. A. A. Plumer, of Franklin, was another whose memory was quite convenient. Charles Hottenstein (or Hotlestein, as *Proceedings*, 28, spells it), of Milton, likewise broke his pledge. C. L. Lamberton, Clairon, Pa., May 10; W. L. Helfenstein, Shamokin, Pa., May 15, June 15; Benjamin Patton, Philadelphia, May 15; J. L. Nutting, Schuylkill County, May 19; W. L. Dewart, Sunbury, Pa., May 15, 1860; Douglas MSS.

[56] Samuel Townsend, Townsend P.O., New Castle County, Delaware, March 28, 1860; Douglas MSS.

[57] R. J. Brent, Charleston, S.C., April 22, 1860; Douglas MSS.

at some of his floor leaders and of response to Ultra 'outside pressure.' Richardson, Pugh and Samuels won great favor with the Southerners and 'could have had great influence' with them had it not been for Stuart, Montgomery and McCook, men who became 'rather obnoxious to every man in the South who was disposed to favor' the Little Giant.

North Carolina's delegation was neither instructed nor under unit rule. Robert P. Dick, the Douglas stalwart in the delegation, expected that eventually six of North Carolina's electoral votes would go to the Little Giant, but during the early days at Charleston the other Douglas men either got disgusted and went home or proved 'afraid of the outside pressure,' and Douglas never received more than one full North Carolina vote.[58] This situation was typical of that of the Douglas delegates from Tennessee, Kentucky, Virginia and Arkansas.

Twelve ballots were taken that first day. The only incident of consequence occurred during the ninth ballot, when Senator Rice pulled two of his three purloined Minnesota delegates away from Douglas. Accordingly, A. J. Edgerton informed the chair that he and A. M. Fridley had decided to change from Douglas to Andrew Johnson. The chairman of the delegation objected, reading the resolution adopted by the Minnesota Convention directing him as chairman to cast Minnesota's whole vote for Douglas so long as he should consider it of advantage to that candidate. Samuels made the point of order that this resolution, under Cushing's Georgia ruling, had the force of instructions. The Chair countered by ruling that the delegates of Minnesota had 'the right to cast their votes as their consciences should dictate.' Thenceforth the two Minnesotans voted against their instructions and Rice wrote an intimate that they had acted 'nobly.' [59]

Doubtless the Buchanan Senators expected this defection to start the expected crumbling of the Douglas Northwest vote. But far from crumbling, Douglas' forces stood firm, 'there was no bear-baiting, brow-beating or bull-ragging that could budge them one inch.' The Ultras in and out of the convention were 'amazed at Douglas' strength.' [60] His vote mounted to 150½ on the day's last ballot. Guthrie was now second.[61]

That night, the seceding Ultras held their second session, this time in

[58] Thomas Goode Tucker, Summit, Hampton Co., N.C., May; Robt. P. Dick, Greensboro, N.C., May 17, 1860; Douglas MSS.

[59] *Proceedings*, 76–77, General James A. Shields to John A. McClernand, Faribault, Rice County, Minn., Feb. 11, 1860; McClernand MSS.; W. A. Gorman, St. Paul, Minn., Jan. 16, 29, 1860; Douglas MSS. Gorman reported that Fridley was not on speaking terms with Rice. Becker was one of Rice's friends, but in the convention 'he avowed himself for you as his first choice, over and over again, in the presence of the whole caucus of 90 delegates, which Shields heard also.' Gorman added, 'I have no confidence in his sincerity.' Edgerton was a friend of Rice. In his second letter Gorman reported that Becker had left for Washington on Jan. 28, and that it was rumored that he was about to be appointed postmaster at St. Paul. Rice worked through Becker on Edgerton and Fridley. H. M. Rice to John H. Stevens, of Glencoe, Minn., Washington, April 4; Charleston, May, n.d., 1860; Stevens Papers, Minnesota Historical Society Collection.

[60] Edward J. Pringle to Mrs. Rose Greenhow, Charleston, May 2, 1860; Greenhow Papers. J. W. Gray, Washington, May 6, in Cleveland *Plain Dealer*, May 8, 1860.

[61] The Kentuckian had 39½ to Hunter's 38. Andrew Johnson still had his 12.

Military Hall, where their deliberations were witnessed by a galaxy of the beauty and charm of Charleston. Senator Bayard presided and a full Ultra platform was adopted. They did not, however, nominate a presidential ticket, but determined to adjourn to meet in Richmond the second Monday in June.[62]

Wednesday's sessions demonstrated to nearly everyone that the convention was in a deadlock. Much to the Buchanan Senators' disgust, the Douglas men stood firm through all the heat and tumult and on the twenty-third ballot the Little Giant reached his greatest strength, 152½ votes, one more than a clear majority of the full electoral college strength. It was also within sixteen votes of two-thirds of the delegates remaining in the convention. The addition to Douglas' actual vote of the deserting delegates from Maine, Massachusetts, Connecticut, Minnesota and Pennsylvania would give him a two-thirds majority of actual voting delegates.

At last the Douglas men of the Border delegations were asserting themselves and Douglas had on this ballot a vote from Virginia, another from North Carolina, and a third from Tennessee. The delegates representing the Valley — Virginia's famous 'Tenth Legion' — announced that, after they had discharged any reasonable obligation to Senator Hunter, their constituents expected them to vote for Douglas. The Hunter chairman protested that although Virginia's convention had not imposed the unit rule, delegations from that State had cast their vote as a unit 'so long that it had become common law.' But this effort was too bald to get a ruling even from Caleb Cushing.[63]

Tennessee formally withdrew Andrew Johnson after the thirty-sixth ballot. This, however, was a Buchanan, not a Johnson move; no sooner was the tailor-statesman out of the way than every Administration vote in the North and Border was concentrated upon Guthrie, whose vote mounted to 64½.[64] But this Buchanan-Ultra effort to build a Guthrie boom went up against a stone wall — not a vote did Douglas lose.

When this effort failed to produce a stampede, a Maryland delegate moved that the convention adjourn to meet in Baltimore the first Monday in June. The Douglas men promptly tabled this move. The convention continued balloting, with Douglas not losing a vote and with Guthrie unable to gain.

[62] Halstead, 97–100.

[63] The two Virginia delegates were S. M. Yost, of Stanton, and S. H. Moffatt, of Harrisonburg. Douglas' Tennessee vote came from William R. Carroll, of Memphis, and Samuel McClanahan, of Jackson. Robert P. Dick of Greensboro, and Charles S. Winstead, of Roxboro, gave his North Carolina vote.

[64] Guthrie's votes were: Maine, 3; Massachusetts, 6; Connecticut, 2½; New Jersey, 4½; Pennsylvania, 17½; Maryland, 4; Missouri, 4½; Tennessee, 10½; Kentucky, 12. For Johnson's course, see Milton, *The Age of Hate*, 94–95. Whitthorne, the Tennessee chairman, had telegraphed him on April 29: 'Have you declared for Douglas in the event of the adoption of the minority report? Six or more States will withdraw. What ought Tennessee to do?' Johnson answered promptly and firmly, 'I recommend and acquiesce in the nomination, Nicholson, Wright and Avery concurring.' Later that same day he telegraphed again: 'I would hold out; acquiesce in the nomination.'

The Northwestern delegations grew more and more bitter. The New-Yorkers now saw that the Borderers were not willing to carry out their pledge.[65] For thirty-four ballots Douglas had had a clear majority; he had withdrawn himself from consideration four years before at the Cincinnati Convention the instant Buchanan received a majority. But the doctrine of majority rule meant nothing to the alliance at Charleston. When the embittered followers of the Little Giant finally realized the unyielding nature of the opposition, spectators 'saw tears of sorrow fall from the eyes of hard-featured Western men,' to whom Douglas' defeat was a personal catastrophe.[66]

But all were beginning to see the hopelessness of further balloting. A report spread about the hall that New York was about ready to favor a mild Slave Code plank. The galleries stirred with interest as Richardson, Stuart, McCook and other Douglas leaders nervously gathered for whispered conferences. After the fifty-seventh ballot the convention recessed.

The Southern Conservatives wanted time to organize a fight at home against the Fire-Eaters. The Douglas men saw no virtue in continuing the deadlock and decided to adjourn to Baltimore. Thursday morning, Russell, of Virginia, made a motion that the gathering reconvene at Baltimore on June 18. He further asked 'that it be respectfully recommended to the Democratic party of the several States to make provision for supplying all vacancies in their respective delegations, to this convention when it shall reassemble.' With this, balloting for a nominee was laid on the table, and adjournment was agreed to, 194 to 55.[67] As soon as Cushing's gavel sounded, the bitter delegates made haste to shake the dust of Charleston from their feet.

[65] But the Henry A. Wise segment of the Virginia delegation was becoming restive, and determined to vote a few more ballots for Hunter, and then to go to Douglas, giving him 7½ votes. See T. P. French, Richmond, Va., June 6, 1860, Douglas MSS.

[66] J. Howard, *Atlantic Monthly*, VIII, 211; William Garrott Brown, 'Lincoln's Rival,' *Atlantic Monthly*, LXXXIX, 234.

[67] *Proceedings*, 89–90; Halstead, 91–100.

CHAPTER XXVII

THE CONSERVATIVES AWAKE

THE forty-five days between the Charleston adjournment and Baltimore reassembly were filled with stirring political debate. During these six weeks two other party conventions were held and two presidential tickets launched, but the most important developments took place in the great battle among the Democratic rank and file.

This unprecedented recess raised intricate questions of party law. The delegations of eight Cotton States had formally 'absolved themselves' from all connection with the National Democratic party. The Charleston Convention had requested the appropriate party authorities in these eight States to make provision for supplying the vacancies in their delegations. These actions added several new issues to the existing dispute over a Slave Code for the Territories.

During this interregnum, Douglas considered carefully the desirability of withdrawing his name to prevent a party breach; he also examined the possibility of further platform modification which, while it might not meet Ultra demands, would quiet some sincere Southern apprehension without stultifying the Democracy of the North. But he had become the living symbol of a cause to which hundreds of leaders were irrevocably committed and in which hundreds of thousands of the party rank and file were enlisted, and so could not adopt a course of action with sole reference to his own ambitions. There was hardly a suggestion in the letters which poured in upon him that he yield the nomination. Alexander H. Stephens sent word both that he would not occupy first place and that the real mass of the Southern people desired nothing more than the Cincinnati platform.

Stephens reflected the Democratic conservative feeling that Douglas must fight to the end. Hendrick B. Wright, of Pennsylvania, pointed out that his withdrawal would result in the proscription of too many devoted and important men. Henry S. Foote insisted that a Republican victory would be 'fatal to the Union,' Douglas was the only Democrat who could be elected, and that 'to give up the contest now is to relinquish the cause of Union.'[1]

In mid-May, representatives of the Old-Line Whigs gathered at Baltimore in national convention. As a result, they put a ticket in the field to compete with the Douglas men for the favor of the Union-loving conservatives. This split the conservative vote and had perhaps tragic consequence. Yet this Whig action was an understandable outgrowth of the emotional fixations of the epoch. The demise of the Whig party had not ended the almost reverential affection hundreds of thousands of its members retained for the verbal symbol of its faded greatness. Many Northern Whigs rushed

[1] Hendrick B. Wright, Philadelphia, May 7; Henry S. Foote, Nashville, May 11; Thomas Dyer, Memphis, Tenn., May 11, 1860; Douglas MSS. Dyer quoted an interview with Stephens two days before. Johnson, 425.

to join the new Anti-Nebraska party and a smaller but important group overcame treasured prejudices and joined the Douglas Democracy. A large segment, however, could neither overcome their dislike of Democratic policies, nor subdue their animosities toward the Irish in the Democratic ranks. These die-hards formed the backbone of the Know-Nothings. Although routed in the North, this hybrid of secret order and political party retained some vitality in the South and the Border. Now in 1860 these Know-Nothing remnants made up the main body of the group which met at Baltimore May 9 to form the Constitutional Union party.

John Bell, of Tennessee, and John J. Crittenden, of Kentucky, with their twin loves of the Constitution with its slavery guaranties and the Union never to be dissolved, represented the Old-Line Whigs of the Border. Edward Everett and Rufus Choate, to whom Webster's Seventh of March speech remained the formula for solving sectional difficulties, represented New England conservatism. In the main the delegates were men of a passing generation, equally distrustful of the old Democracy and the new Republicanism.

The convention did not adopt a platform but contented itself with the statement that it supported 'the Constitution of the country, the Union of the States, and the enforcement of the laws.' There had been some talk of nominating Sam Houston, of Texas; in the event, however, he did not become formidable, Crittenden was passed by and the convention selected John Bell, with Everett, as running-mate. While both men were fitly expressive of the Whig tradition, their choice was but another index of the time-lag stamped upon their party's effort.[2]

These nominations served notice that the 1860 campaign would have at least as many tickets as did that of 1856. Then, however, despite the contest's triangularity, the Democracy had elected the President. But now a vindictive President and an envious Senate renewed a 'fierce and uncompromising' war on Douglas; they would not have harmony at Baltimore. The Senate Ultras were the fountain from which poured forth 'the bitter waters of envy and jealousy.' Jefferson Davis' Slave Code resolutions had been slumbering since February; now he furbished them up and on May 7 formally demanded their adoption.

Davis' face was ghastly white, his eyes sunken, his cheeks hollow, his nervous hands thin and bloodless and his hair prematurely gray. But his physical condition did not diminish the arrogance with which he hinted the South's secession unless she secured a Congressional Slave Code.

All knew that this was the first skirmish of Baltimore, and some of Douglas' friends urged him to 'give the infernal scoundrels the devil.' But when his main campaign leaders reached Washington from Charleston, they discussed the certainty that the Ultras would renew the attack, not only on issues but even more against Douglas personally. The Senator promised them that he 'would not be drawn into any debate except with Jeff Davis.'[3]

[2] Rhodes, II, 410; Coleman, *John J. Crittenden*, II, 182 *et seq.*

[3] S. J. Anderson, New York, May 26, 1860, Douglas MSS., for Senate fountain simile. Hal-

The Little Giant had had a return of his throat troubles and was far from well. He took several days to prepare his rejoinder and it was May 15 before he began his response. When he was about halfway through, his voice faltered so that he could hardly be heard. He agreed to an adjournment until Tuesday, when Pugh, of Ohio, reduced Douglas' physical strain by reading many of the documents and excerpts with which the argument was reinforced.

The Senator from Illinois pointed out that the Administration Senators had no right to prescribe any new party test — this could only be done by a Democratic National Convention, and that which had just recessed at Charleston had reaffirmed the Cincinnati platform. Then he warned the Fire-Eaters that they were insisting on doctrine quite as unfair and as dangerous as that of the Republicans. The Southern extremists, he exclaimed, 'are for non-interference so long as the people want slavery, so long as they will provide by law for its introduction and protection; but the moment the people say they do not want it and will not have it, then Congress must intervene and force the institution on an unwilling people. On the other hand, the Republican party is also for non-intervention, in certain contingencies.... So long as the people of a Territory prohibit slavery, the Abolitionists are for non-intervention and will not interfere at all; but whenever the people of a Territory say by their legislation that they do want it... then the Republicans are for intervening and for depriving them of it.... There is no difference in principle between intervention North and intervention South.'

If only the South would go forward on the old principles, 'the party can remain a unit and present an invincible and irresistible front to the Republican or Abolition phalanx at the North. So certain as you abandon non-intervention and substitute intervention, just so certain you yield a power into their hands which will sweep the Democratic party from the face of the globe.' The safety, peace and highest interests of the Nation required the preservation intact of the party on its old platform. Unanimity would never be secured on another. Once adopt Congressional intervention and 'you will make two sectional parties, hostile to each other, divided by the line that separates the Free from the Slave-holding States, and present a conflict that will be irrepressible, and will never cease until the one shall subdue the other or they shall agree to divide, in order that they may live in peace.'

But Davis would not yield so much as a comma of his demanded platform, while Douglas could go no further than he had gone. His forces had proposed at Charleston that the Democratic party would pledge itself to respect and be governed by the decisions, future as well as past, of the Supreme Court. This offer, which the Ultras had contemptuously rejected before bolting, represented every inch of compromise the Northern Democrats could make. For them to go any further meant deliberately surrendering

stead, 103. New York *Tribune*, April 14, 1860. W. D. Shepherd, Washington, May 10; W. A. Richardson, New York, May 17, 22, 1860; Douglas MSS. Richardson on May 22 referred to Douglas' conference with Stuart, Samuels, Vallandigham and himself.

all chance of winning an electoral vote or Congressional representation in every single Northern State.

The Buchanan-Ultra Senators knew this; they knew Douglas was offering them a program which would, in fact, protect their present slave-holding areas, although it might not give them the empty right to have a battalion of Federal soldiers to prevent the escape of the two slaves then in Kansas. Once more the Ultras spurned conciliation, thus making themselves the chief architects of misfortunes soon to be visited not only on themselves but also on millions of men and women who disapproved their course.

Douglas seemed to lose patience with his opponents' fine-spun theories. Davis, he said, 'has got one idea into his brain and he has magnified it so much that it is expanding till I'm afraid it will drive out almost all other ideas. It is that protection is the end of government.' But this was subject to certain limitations; Davis must not seek to carry his protection further than permitted by the Constitution; 'if he does, I cannot go with him beyond that point.'

Davis referred offensively to his antagonist's 'swelling manner' and 'egregious vanity' and accused him of trying to force upon the party, through delegates from Northern States which did not deliver and could not deliver electoral votes, a platform which the Democratic electoral vote-giving States despised, and himself, whom they would never accept. Calling attention to the electoral vote in 1852, reviewing what had taken place in the North since Pierce's election, Douglas insisted that it was 'not fair to try to disfranchise or deny equal rights to those Northern States who were uniformly Democratic until they were borne down fighting your battles to save you from an enemy.' Furthermore, 'my name would never have been presented at Charleston, except for the attempt to proscribe me as a heretic. . . . I was forced to allow my name to go there in self-defense: and I will now say that had any gentleman, friend or foe, received a majority of that convention over me, the lightning would have carried a message withdrawing my name.'

Davis had himself confessed, Douglas went on, that regardless of protection, slavery could not exist among a hostile people. The Senator from Mississippi was 'following a mere phantom in trying to get a recognition of the right of Congress to intervene for the protection of slavery in the Territories when the people do not want it. He, in effect, confesses that it is a mere phantom, an abstract theory, without results, without fruits; and why? He says that he admits that slavery cannot be forced on a hostile people. He says he has always regarded it as a question of soil, climate, and political economy. I so regard it.'

'I say we have a constitutional right to try it,' Davis interjected.

'Statesmen,' Douglas countered, 'do not always act on the principle that they will do whatever they have a right to do. A man has a right to do a great many silly things. A statesman has a right to perpetrate acts of consummate folly. But I do not know that it is a man's duty to do all that he has a right to do. Why are you not satisfied with these practical results?' he asked. 'Intervention, North or South, means disunion; non-intervention promises peace, fraternity, and perpetuity to the Union and to all our cherished institutions.' The insistence upon such demands as Yancey had made at Charleston would lead 'directly and inevitably' to a dissolution of the Union.

The next day Davis resented the 'insinuation' that he did not love the Union and charged that Douglas and not himself was the cause of strife. The South would have no more to do with 1856's 'rickety, double-constructed platform,' Davis said. He himself 'would sooner have an honest man on any sort of a rickety platform...than to have a man I did not trust on the best platform which could be made. A good platform and an honest man on it, is what we want.' Douglas reminded him sharply that the bolters at Charleston had seceded, not on the candidate but on the platform. 'If the platform is not a matter of much consequence, why press that question to the disruption of the party?' he inquired. 'Why did not you tell us in the beginning of this debate that the whole fight was against the man and not upon the platform?'

Douglas' manly argument created a sensation. The Ultras moved promptly to offset it, issuing an address calling upon the Southern people to keep up the battle and presenting a campaign plan. Under it, the bolting Southern delegations, without apology or pledge, must demand readmission; if not received, those Southerners who had not bolted must withdraw. Should the Yanceyites be readmitted, they were not to accept the situation but to demand a Territorial Code. Were this again refused, all the South, together with the Buchanan men from Pennsylvania, Indiana, New York, New Jersey, and New England, must protest violently and withdraw. To aid this strategy, the Richmond convention must undertake no business but must recess until the close of the battle of Baltimore. Only nineteen Senators and Representatives signed this document, but it presented a definite program for Ultra effort to widen the party breach.[4]

The leading Senate Ultras kept up their attacks on Douglas on the Senate floor, but their target was so exhausted by his speech that he went to bed for the rest of the week. The disappointed Ultras thereupon planned for the next Wednesday an attack so personal that Douglas could not help being involved. But two days before the day appointed, a disgusted Ultra tipped off the program to Richardson, who was in New York. Alarmed, the latter dispatched A. D. Banks to Washington to force Douglas to come to New York. 'Toombs, Wigfall and company intend to blackguard you — nothing more and nothing less,' he warned. 'For God's sake don't peril interests not only dear to you but to your friends and the country when you have nothing to gain, but everything to lose.'[5]

[4] *Congressional Globe*, Thirty-Sixth Congress, First Session, App., 313 *et seq.*, for text of Douglas' speech; *Globe*, First Session, 2103–56, for Douglas-Davis interchange; W. A. Richardson, New York, May 17; L. P. Bayne, Baltimore, May 16; R. T. Merrick, Chicago, May 27, 1860, Douglas MSS., for effectiveness of Douglas' speech; Henry T. Stanton, Memphis, May 23, for Davis' inconsistency; James W. Sheahan, Chicago, May 21, 1860, Douglas MSS., for Ultras' Address.

[5] W. A. Richardson, New York, May 17, 22, 1860; Douglas MSS. For Benjamin's tone toward Douglas, see Samuel P. Orth, *Five American Politicians*, Cleveland, Ohio, 1906, 401–02.

While Douglas did not accompany Banks to New York, his illness kept him home some of the time, and when he did attend he kept his temper well in hand and would not be goaded into meeting billingsgate in kind. The Ultra phalanx finally passed their resolutions, but Douglas' friends felt that the debates had yielded their champion a great victory.

While Douglas and Davis were concluding their Senate duel on May 16, the leaders of the Republican party were assembling in Chicago for their second national convention. Delegates were on hand from all the Free States and from Delaware, Maryland, Virginia, Kentucky and Missouri. Republicans had scented victory ever since the Charleston deadlock and party workers throughout the Northwest flocked to Chicago by the thousands. A 'wigwam,' said to hold ten thousand people, had been built for the occasion, but by the second day more than forty thousand visitors were on hand. Success was in the air and there was a general scramble to climb on the band wagon. Nearly all of the candidates planned outside pressure to influence delegate opinion. Although a band of leathern-lunged New York bravos made the welkin rings for Seward, Lincoln, the local favorite, had by far the best-organized claque.

The chief contenders for the nomination were William H. Seward, of New York, by now well convinced of the new party's vitality; Simon Cameron, one of Pennsylvania's most devious and unscrupulous machine bosses; the impeccable, humorless Salmon P. Chase, who divided the Ohio delegation with Ben Wade; Edward Bates, of St. Louis, an ex-Whig Borderer who made a strong appeal to Seward's more conservative opponents; and then Abraham Lincoln, Douglas' opponent in the Senate race in 1858.

Seward, the new party's most conspicuous statesman, was expected to be an easy victor. His doctrine of irrepressible conflict had fired the imagination of the rank and file and he would have won easily in a nation-wide primary. The leading party politicians from most of the Northern States were for him, that 'prince of politicians,' Thurlow Weed, was managing his campaign; William M. Evarts, Carl Schurz and Austin Blair were active lieutenants. The favorite Seward argument, 'Who else can get the money to finance a campaign?' seemed unanswerable.

This year, however, Horace Greeley, once copartner with Seward and Weed in ruling New York Republican destinies, was in conspicuous opposition.[6] Kept off the New York delegation, he inserted himself among the group from Oregon and went to Chicago with poison on his tongue. Greeley's chief argument was Seward's purported weakness in Pennsylvania and Indiana because of Know-Nothing opposition.

The anti-Seward leaders, however, reached Chicago without much hope of stopping him. Unable to get Ohio's solid vote, Chase was resigned to fate. Cameron gathered no strength outside of Pennsylvania. Francis P. Blair and his sons labored for Bates, but not many outside delegates were

---

[6] The editor of the *Tribune* had hungered for the Republican nomination for Lieutenant-Governor of New York; Weed had been otherwise committed, Seward would do nothing about it, and on Nov. 11, 1854, the wrathful Greeley dissolved their 'partnership.'

committed. The anti-Seward chiefs saw clearly that they must unite on a single candidate. Judge David Davis, whom Lincoln had put in charge of his convention interests, sensed the opportunity to concentrate the opposition about Illinois' favorite son. The Illinois Republicans demonstrated more ardently than ever, and Davis initiated secret negotiations.

Lincoln had a real claim upon the new party, for he shared with Seward the credit for contriving the formulæ which had given it continued life. Although Seward's emotion-arousing phrases, 'irrepressible conflict' and 'higher law' had heartened the party membership, their flavor of radicalism disturbed certain among them to whom victory was more important than the full flaunting of prejudice.

Lincoln's contribution had been shrewder. In 1857, when he laid the plans for his contest with Douglas, far-sighted Republican leaders could see, and conservative Southern Democrats frankly admitted, that extension of slavery in the Territories was about to become merely a moot question. The struggle in Kansas had ended with the Free-State men outnumbering the Pro-Slavery party four to one. Nebraska had never had a pro-slavery agitation. New Mexico had long ago adopted laws protecting slavery. With the elimination of the Territorial issue upon which the Republican party had been created, all reason for its continued existence would end.

And yet the Republican politicians, as is the common lot of politicians everywhere, were interested in power, income and office, and saw great merit to any party mechanism which could supply these desirabilities. If only the party could be supplied with new formulæ for maintaining the emotional consent of its members, not only could it preserve its present position but it could, perhaps, improve it. While the practical settlement of the Territorial slavery issue ended the question so far as it then legally existed, the emotional fixations of hundreds of thousands of Northern people were such that, while they would prefer a party to attack slavery in the States, yet they would support one which, while disclaiming either right or purpose of interfering with slavery there, would none the less carry a hidden threat to do so.

Lincoln's 'House Divided' statement fit this situation like a glove. Probably the shrewdest political formula ever constructed in America, its two propositions seemed to join in a harmonious whole, but when especial emphasis was given either, it altered the effect of the doctrine.

Abolitionists accented the statement that slavery would either 'be put in the course of ultimate extinction' or its advocates would make it lawful in all the States. This broad hint that the Southern Ultras would soon undertake to force slavery on the Northern States acted as a trumpet call to the North to prevent such aggression, and was an elixir for the Republican party.

The other aspect of the statement was an anodyne for the Conservatives. Such words as 'permanently' and 'ultimate' could be used to indicate Republican belief that the change would come slowly and in the day of another and perhaps distant generation. Those anxious to show Lincoln's and his party's conciliatory purpose here placed their emphasis. Although

Lincoln did not get to the Senate on his 'House Divided' doctrine, he did through it increase the zeal of active Abolitionists and at the same time quieted Conservative fears. Such a doctrine was an ideal formula for practical politicians and helped give the Republican party a new lease on life.[7]

Party leaders gave Lincoln definite establishment among the men who mattered in their national leadership. His despondency at the time of defeat was ephemeral, and in the early Winter of 1860 he accepted several Eastern speaking invitations. His sensationally successful Cooper Union lecture and his subsequent appearances in New England increased his self-confidence, and he concluded that he could win the nomination — even over Seward. As soon as Lincoln returned to Illinois he began pulling wires to win delegates. In some instances, as in Kansas, his work was clumsy, but in many others effective. There was a shrewd stroke at the Illinois State Republican Convention when John Hanks, Lincoln's uncle, strode in with some old split rails Lincoln might then have fashioned; the candidate was promptly labeled 'rail-splitter,' with ponderable effect.

The first day's session was consumed with organization maneuvers and an argument about whether or not the Republicans should yield to the radicals' demand that they readopt the Declaration of Independence, or ignore it, as the practical politicians, with their eyes on the Border States, demanded. A final burst of oratory brought its inclusion, but the platform preserved silence as to the Fugitive Slave Law and the Dred Scott case and skirted carefully about the edges of prohibition of slavery in Territories. It termed John Brown's raid on Harper's Ferry 'among the greatest of crimes,' denounced Buchanan for Lecompton, labeled Popular Sovereignty 'a deception and a fraud,' but its *pièce de résistance* was a vigorous tariff plank which was expected to attach Pennsylvania firmly to the new chariot.

With the second day Seward's lieutenants saw success in sight, but the leaders of the opposition were getting closer together. That night David Davis put through a deal securing Indiana, the price being a post in Lincoln's Cabinet. An hour or so afterward, he gathered Pennsylvania's second ballot vote with a promise of a Cabinet position for Simon Cameron — bargains which actually determined the outcome.

Seward's vote, on the first ballot Thursday, was 173⅓, or 60 less than a majority. Lincoln, with 102, had more than twice the strength of any of the other candidates. Pennsylvania switched to Lincoln on the next roll call, and his total reached 181. With the third effort the band-wagon was in full parade, and 'rail-splitter' receiving 231½ votes. Before this was announced, Ohio shifted four more votes and the man Douglas had beaten two years before became Republican candidate for President.[8]

[7] Mary Scrugham, *The Peaceable Americans of 1860–1861*, New York; 14–22.

[8] Rhodes, II, 412–27. For Greeley-Seward relations and their breach, Frederick Bancroft, *William H. Seward*, New York, 1900; I, 372; 528 *et seq.* Greeley, *Recollections of a Busy Life*, 315–20; 390; for Blair influence, Smith, II, 461; Halstead, 121–53. J. H. Bromley, 'The Nomination of Lincoln,' *Scribner's Magazine*, XIV, new series, 653: 'It was the commerce between Illinois, Indiana and Pennsylvania that night that made Mr. Lincoln President, and put Caleb B. Smith and Simon Cameron in his Cabinet.'

Several of Douglas' friends stayed through the Chicago turmoil. 'It is not half an hour since Lincoln's nomination,' wrote one. 'Your friends are as delighted as the Lincoln men themselves. You have beaten him once and will beat him again.'

The Seward men were sulphurous. 'It is a damned shame,' old Tom Corwin told a friend, 'that no statesman can get nominated and elected, but they must nominate some man who can hardly read or write.' George Sanders believed that the Sewardites, who had the Republican money, would 'not pay a dollar... toward the election' and Douglas would carry New York City by 50,000. 'It is easy enough to kill Lincoln!' Sheahan wrote Douglas, 'but opinions are divided here as to the propriety of doing anything to represent him as weak until *after* the Baltimore meeting.'

August Belmont thought Lincoln's choice would open the South's eyes to the 'necessity' of naming Douglas. 'With you we can carry New York and the Northwest entire,' believed Richardson. 'With anyone else we lose New York and the Northwest entire and forever. If we are to sink, like the story man of old, we had as well pull down the pillars and all perish together.' [9]

The feeling Richardson thus voiced was wide-spread among Northern Democratic leaders and was intensified by the resumption of Administration maneuvers to seduce further Northern Douglas delegates, and by the reign of terror the Ultras were attempting in the South. New England was again a Buchanan target, Edmund Burke and the other Buchanan editors were soon 'out-Heroding Herod in their dirty work.' Ultra lieutenants in Washington arrogantly notified the Little Giant's New England friends that they need not expect to force him on the South 'by any species of legerdemain.' [10]

The Ultras' chief effort, however, was to persuade Franklin Pierce's to enter the Baltimore mêlée. Caleb Cushing, John H. George and others pressed him to reconsider his decision and Jefferson Davis joined in the appeal. The South would unite on Pierce or any 'sound' man, the Mississippian added, but would as soon have a Free-Soiler as 'our little grog-drinking, electioneering demagogue.' But while Pierce was sympathetic with the Ultras, he insisted that Cushing 'provide against even a remote possibility' of his name being introduced at Baltimore. Furthermore, aside from postmasters and the kept Buchanan press, little pressure came upon him from New Hampshire, while the Concord *Patriot*, Pierce's own paper, was 'doing service boldly and manfully, 'in Douglas' behalf. [11]

[9] T. G. Wright, Chicago, May 18; August Belmont, New York, May 18; George N. Sanders, New York, May 19; T. R. Westbrook, Kingston, New York, May 19; W. H. Ludlow, Sayville, L.I., N.Y., May 28, for Seward soreness; K. W. Perrin, Toledo, Ohio, May 21, quoting Corwin's bitter remark; W. A. Gorman, St. Paul, Minn., May 24; J. W. Sheahan, Chicago, May 21; H. W. Starr, Burlington, Ia., May 25, 1860; Douglas MSS. Thomas H. Seymour to Franklin Pierce, Hartford, Conn., June 18, 1860; Pierce MSS. Lincoln was 'positively the weakest creature the Blacks could have put up.'

[10] Moses Bates, Plymouth, Mass., May 8; George C. Patterson to John Cain, Washington, May 14; Cain to Patterson, Rutland, Vt., May 19, 1860; Douglas MSS. Cain, editor of the Rutland *Herald*, pointed out the farce of the Southern Ultras 'bolting the convention because they could not control it,' adding that 'notwithstanding the Northern renegades bought up by the Administration,' Douglas was the choice of a majority of the party.

[11] Davis to Pierce, Washington, June 13, 1860; Pierce MSS., Library of Congress; Pierce

This reflected the general New England tenor. The Administration endorsement of the Yancey secession had lost Buchanan, Cushing and Slidell 'the good opinion of the entire Democracy' of Maine, postmasters alone excepted. Measures were promptly taken to bind the bolting delegates with new instructions too emphatic to be susceptible of evasion. Maine's Fourth District Democratic Committee called a convention, which met at Augusta on June 7. 'Without a dissenting voice,' it reinstructed 'the little recreant' Owen to vote for Douglas, adding a resolution that if he should not do so, their other delegate should cast both of the district's votes.[12] Douglas need have no fears of the faithful Connecticut delegates; 'we will stand as firm at Baltimore as we did at Charleston.' One of them, receiving an Administration offer, denounced its makers as a 'class of puppies who are barking at trees they cannot climb.'[13]

There was quite a struggle in Massachusetts. Cushing, Whitney, Butler and Swift and the other deserters had the money and the command of public offices. At first Moses Bates, Douglas' manager there, feared that the Buchaneers might wreak fresh havoc. But when he began a canvass of his State, he found that he had underestimated the rank and file's resentment against the traitors. Douglas had insistent pleas from leading Massachusetts Democrats to stand firm, 'make no compromise, offer no terms and accept none,' and a movement was promptly started to see to it that 'the traitors of the Massachusetts Democracy would yet receive the punishment they so justly merit.' Conventions were called in several districts. The two backsliders of one were instructed 'to vote in accordance with the wishes of their constituents.' A sell-out in another was told bluntly 'to alter his course or resign.'

The Administration tried to pack the meeting of the Jefferson Club, in South Boston, the evening of May 14, with henchmen from the Navy Yard and Custom House, but were outnumbered ten to one. Enthusiastically sustaining a faithful representative, a convention at Lee ordered a deserter to return to the ranks. At Lowell, Butler's home, all the young men were heart and soul for Douglas and not twenty Democratic foes could be found. The incensed Douglas men republished Ben Butler's letter of acceptance as gubernatorial nominee in 1858, making Popular Sovereignty his main campaign tenet. Nearly five thousand Democrats were on the floor and the galleries were overflowing at a mass meeting at Huntington Hall on June 1. The vast throng vindicated Popular Sovereignty and its champion and denounced Butler's breaking of his pledged word.

The high point of the Massachusetts campaign, however, was a great

to Caleb Cushing, New York, June 7; Sidney Webster to John H. George, New York, June 17, 1860; New Hampshire Historical Society MSS. J. L. Foster, Dover, N.H., May 7, 1860; Douglas MSS.

[12] James O'Donnell, Portland, Me., May 8; H. D. Rice, Rockland, May 12, Augusta, June 9; Elias Harmon, Biddeford, May 14; C. H. Campbell, Portland, May 16; Calvin Record, Auburn, May 17; J. C. McClintock, Belfast, May 31, Augusta, June 7; H. C. Jewett, Belfast, June 7, 1860; Douglas MSS.

[13] J. M. Schofield, Hartford, May 5, 23; James Gallagher, New Haven, May 9; W. M. Converse, Norwich, May 14; A. G. Hasard, Hasardville, May 16, 1860; Douglas MSS.

meeting in Boston, on June 9. 'The old cradle of liberty,' Faneuil Hall, was 'crammed to its utmost capacity' and the meeting was really 'glorious.' Reverdy Johnson, who came from Baltimore to make the principal speech, was in fine form and roused the audience to tremendous enthusiasm. With this great expression backing up the reinstruction of so many of the district delegates, the Douglas men expected Massachusetts to make a better showing at Baltimore.[14]

Soon after Charleston, indignant Pennsylvania Democrats took steps 'to have public sentiment proclaimed and the course of the seceders and the impracticables denounced,' and the next six weeks in Buchanan's State were marked with conventions, mass meetings, presentation of petitions and other expressions of the wishes of the party rank and file. These were insistent that Douglas 'remain firm and steadfast,' and he was told repeatedly that he had 'an army of true men' at his back. 'You have hardly any idea,' Hendrick B. Wright was advised, 'how almost unanimous the people are for Douglas — outside of the office-holders.' The Douglas delegates were fêted and gleeful but the others had 'a pretty rough time of it.'

The two delegates from the 'Wild Cat District' in which Senator Bigler resided, had been pledged to Douglas but had followed Bigler's orders there. A district convention reimposed instructions. When one of the recalcitrants endeavored to prevent this action, the convention passed its instructions a second time 'so as not to be misunderstood.'

The Democrats of Schuylkill County, so resented the forgetfulness of Delegate Hughes that several mass meetings denounced him and then a county convention instructed him to go for Douglas. The Democracy of Northumberland County held a convention to order Delegate Hottenstein 'either to obey the instructions or resign.' When that worthy sought to stop that action, a further resolution passed 'instructing him to vote for Douglas in convention and if he refused, to declare his place vacant and fill it with another person.'

A great Philadelphia meeting on the night of June 5 climaxed the Douglas campaign. Just at the time of assembly 'a tremendous storm of rain came up and for one hour the rain fell in torrents.' The deluge, however, did not dampen the enthusiasm; Concert Hall 'was crammed to suffocation,' two large overflow meetings were organized and the main gathering kept going until eleven o'clock. 'I never saw such enthusiasm in my life,' an experienced observer declared. Such developments carried conviction. Richardson, after spending a few days in the State, concluded that if the public voice could only reach the Buchanan delegates, Douglas would lose no Pennsylvania vote at Baltimore.[15]

[14] George H. Laflin, Pittsfield, Mass., May 4; Moses Bates, New York, May 7, Plymouth, Mass., May 18, Boston, June 11; John W. Mahan, Boston, May 10; Edwin B. Spinney, South Boston, May 15, June 2; A. N. Brown, Lowell, May 28; S. S. Drew, Lowell, June 6; E. A. Alger, Lowell, June 7; Reverdy Johnson, Baltimore, June 12; Johnson Gardiner, Pawtucket, R.I., May 3, June 14, 1860; Douglas MSS. The delegates reinstructed by district conventions were James Riley and Isaac H. Wright of Boston; George Johnson, of Bradford; E. G. Williams, of Newburyport; C. C. Clark, of Lynn, and D. N. Carpenter, of Greenfield.

[15] H. B. Robinson, Philadelphia, May 24, 26; Wm. Montgomery, Washington, May 29,

No other Middle Atlantic State witnessed such an active effort against recalcitrants. The Administration had the New Jersey situation tied in a knot. Senator Bayard's bolt might have 'forever damned him in Delaware,' but he and a companion seceder raised the Newcastle County Convention of February from a *sine die* adjournment and procured reappointments. Douglas' chief supporters in the State called a new convention and elected new delegates in the bolters' places. The Baltimore Custom House called a meeting to condemn the Douglas Maryland delegates, but the Senator's friends defeated the resolutions by a vote of five to one.[16]

Developments in the West afforded even less comfort to the Buchaneers. Senator Green, of Missouri, did announce that the Democrats of that State demanded a slave code, but the Douglas delegates stood by their guns. The Iowa prairies were 'aflame' for Douglas' nomination. One delegate was confronted, on his return from Charleston, with a Buchanan census appointment but contemptuously refused. 'The Iowa delegates are for you to the death,' one of them wrote the Little Giant; they knew that if he lost at Baltimore their party would be blotted out in Iowa. Ohio was fixed in its determination. There would be no change in Indiana, whose delegation would 'never compromise their favorite candidate nor yield to any but merely verbal modification of the platform.'

Minnesota received the faithful among its delegates with tremendous enthusiasm, but the turncoats would not come home. Governor Gorman electrified a tremendous St. Paul mass meeting with his excoriation of the faith-breakers. This set off a host of meetings over the State, at all of which Douglas and his platform were endorsed and the traitors were called on 'to resign and let the majority cast the whole vote.' These expressions Henry B. Payne believed sufficiently earnest and emphatic to satisfy the country as to the position the Northwest would occupy at Baltimore.[17]

But New York was the scene of the sharpest Northern fighting. Implemented with the Tammany-Dickinson minority of the delegation, the Buchanan-Ultra alliance set to work to break down the Douglas majority.

1860; H. B. Wright MSS. For Bigler district, C. L. Lamberton, Clarion, May 10; for the operations on Bolter Hughes, see William L. Helfenstein, Shamokin, May 15; Benjamin Patten, Philadelphia, May 15; J. L. Nutting, Schuylkill County, May 19; for proceedings against Hottenstein see W. L. Helfenstein, Shamokin, Pa., May 5, June 11; W. L. Dewart, Sunbury, May 15. For general account, Hendrick B. Wright, Philadelphia, May 7; J. W. Gilliam, Carlisle, May 11; John Davis, Davisville, May 30; C. H. Barrett, Clearfield County, May 21; W. A. Richardson, Quincy, Ill., May 30, reported on Pennsylvania visit. James B. Sheridan, Philadelphia, May 31; Daniel Dougherty, Philadelphia, June 7; W. C. Oakley, Girard, June 7, 1860; Douglas MSS.

[16] G. P. Halstead, Newark, N.J., June 4; Samuel Townsend, Townsend P.O., May 5, 31; Henry May, Baltimore, May 16; J. T. Ensor, Towsontown, May 24, 1860; Douglas MSS. L. K. Bowen, Baltimore, May 13, 1860, Buchanan MSS.

[17] R. J. Tunstall, St. Louis, June 5; Reuben Beers, Mt. Pleasant, Iowa, May 24; H. W. Starr, Burlington, May 25; J. B. Thomas, Independence, June 12; I. B. McDonald, Columbia City, Ind., May 5; W. W. Wick, Indianapolis, May 12; James B. Ryan, Indianapolis, May 16, Willis A. Gorman, St. Paul, May 14, 24; H. B. Payne, Cleveland, May 16, 1860; Douglas MSS. Cleveland *Plain Dealer*, May 28, 1860, editorial by J. W. Gray.

The chief of their schemes was to bring Horatio Seymour forward as New York's favorite son; other elements were to get a majority committed to receive the Yancey bolters and to insert a disguised slave code plank in the platform. The Seymour plot sprang from the fertile brains of Ben Butler, John H. George 'and the most accomplished traders in Washington,' and friends of Douglas became apprehensive that some of the old delegation majority were involved. Tammany called a mass meeting to promote it, while the Administration dispatched Judge Killiam, of the Treasury Department, to New York to aid the scheme.[18]

The Little Giant's chief managers soon awoke to these new dangers. Upon completing discussions with Douglas in Washington, William A. Richardson hastened to New York, found Dean Richmond, king-pin of their New York majority, unaffected by the new Buchanan maneuvers, and soon came to a satisfactory agreement with him about order of business at Baltimore. If there were 'any reliance in the word of men,' things were all right in New York. Richardson also warned Killiam, the Buchanan-Cobb envoy, that the question of Union and Disunion was clearly made up, he looked on Buchanan and Cobb as the leaders of the Disunion side and had 'no choice between a Secessionist and an Abolitionist.' [19]

Stuart, who went to Albany to feel the pulse of Cagger and Church, was pleased to find that 'the men who control affairs' were unshaken. Cagger soon wrote Douglas directly that the New York delegation would 'assent to no change either in the platform or the candidate.' [20]

Douglas' New York friends, 'perfectly electrified' by his tilt with Davis, planned a great meeting for Cooper Institute the night of May 22. F. B. Cutting, the chief speaker, made a fine, vigorous presentation, the resolutions were adopted 'with extraordinary approbation' and the meeting was 'an ovation; nothing like it has ever taken place in this city.' Seymour's boom was now expected to die a peaceful death.[21] On the heels of this triumph, Sanders, Belmont, Stebbins, West, John Jacob Astor and George Law set up a special committee 'to collect funds to pay extraordinary expenses.' A project to buy the *Times* from Henry Raymond fell through, but the paper continued friendly to Douglas, and Raymond telegraphed from Chicago not to commit the paper to Lincoln.[22]

[18] W. A. Richardson, New York, May 15, 1860; Douglas MSS.

[19] Moses Bates, New York, May 7; Hendrick B. Wright, Wilkes-Barre, Pa., May 14; H. B. Payne, Cleveland, Ohio, May 16, telling of conversation with Ludlow; A. D. Banks, New York, May 11; William A. Richardson, New York, May 13; New York, n.d. (*circa* May 24), 1860; Douglas MSS.

[20] C. E. Stuart, Albany, N.Y., May 14; August Belmont, New York, May 18, quoting letter from Cagger; Peter Cagger, Albany, N.Y., May 18, 1860; Douglas MSS. R. Tyler to Buchanan, Philadelphia, June 14, 1860, Buchanan MSS. Cagger 'is *mighty* for Douglas, but says *he will try to see me.*'

[21] John Clancy, New York, May 15; August Belmont, May 18; R. B. Connally, New York, May 23; S. J. Anderson, New York, May 26; W. A. Richardson, New York, n.d. (*circa* May 24), 1860; Douglas MSS. New York *Times*, May 23, 24, 1860.

[22] W. A. Richardson, New York, May 15, 17; George N. Sanders, New York, May 19, May 25, 1860; Douglas MSS.

Thus Douglas retained his New York majority — forty men who could be 'neither bribed, coaxed, frightened or abused into opposition'; who would, 'under no pretense, or for any cause, yield one inch.' Richardson wrote that if New York were wrong, he was 'the most cheated man in America.' [23]

The Cotton States Conservatives came to life during the weeks between Charleston and Baltimore and undertook to end the Ultras' political reign of terror. But the Secession managers had 'for several years past been allowed to retain in their hands the whole machinery of the party,' a power they had strengthened and consolidated. To assert themselves, the Moderates must select their captains, drill their recruits and improvise arms and ammunition to attack a well-prepared enemy — and one who, all the while, was vigorously belaboring the raw troops and disrupting its formations.

The divorce between political control and public feeling was now laid bare through most of the South.[24] Border State developments were in Douglas' favor. Virginia sentiment inclined toward him in early May. Several influential adverse papers mellowed. Western Virginia was outspoken. The Wise delegates were ready to cut short the farce of voting for Hunter. The seceders' convention, which assembled at Richmond on June 11, was poorly attended. The Richmond *Whig* declared that Douglas was the only Democrat who had 'the remotest chance to obtain the electoral vote of a single Northern State.'

Some of the Little Giant's Northern leaders insisted that approaches be made to Hunter. Wright, of Pennsylvania, believed the ambitious Virginian could be brought to terms, for 'men are men the world over — moved by impulses and operated upon by like motives.' Henry B. Payne wanted word gotten to Hunter that, if he would 'now play the man,' he could have anything he wanted from the Northwest in the future. Richardson undertook to see what could be done, but soon new Ultra issues came from the South to interfere.[25]

The first was a demand that the Baltimore Convention drop the slavery planks adopted at Charleston and substitute what was known as the 'Tennessee platform.' The gravamen of this was that the Federal Government had no power to introduce slavery into the Territories or exclude it from them, and no duty to perform there except 'to protect the rights of the owner from wrong and to restore fugitives from labor.' [26] This 'Tennessee platform' was susceptible to the interpretation equally that it did and did not call for a Congressional Slave Code. Many Ultras who had talked so stoutly at Charleston about their contempt for *double entendre* now found

[23] George N. Sanders, New York, May 20; William H. Ludlow, Sayville, L.I., N.Y., May 28; D. A. Ogden, New York, May 28; W. A. Richardson, New York, May 17, Quincy, Ill., May 30; August Belmont, New York, May 31; F. B. Cutting, New York, June 11, 1860; Douglas MSS.

[24] Henry S. Foote, Nashville, Tenn., May 11, 1860; Douglas MSS.

[25] James S. French, Alexandria, Va., May 5; S. B. French, Richmond, June 6; N. A. Thompson, Ashland, near Richmond, June 11; S. B. Major, South Boston, Va., June 12; Hendrick B. Wright, Philadelphia, May 7; H. B. Payne, Cleveland, May 16, 1860; Douglas MSS. Richmond *Whig*, quoted in *Illinois State Register*, June 11, 1860.

[26] *Proceedings*, 32.

ingenious reasons for urging this plank which yielded under pressure. Not all Ultras yielded to this scheme; one Virginian termed it 'miserable, double-faced, forked-tongued,' and some began to see that its promoters were merely seeking a new excuse to prostrate Douglas.

For all this, the project had effect; so much, indeed, that Editor Glass, of Lynchburg, wrote Douglas claiming that Richardson had promised at Charleston that after the nomination the Tennessee platform 'or the equivalent' would be adopted.[27] But before June 18 the Ultras subordinated the Tennessee platform to new demand of more explosive value — the readmission of the bolters, without re-election or pledge of support.

Douglas' strength improved in North Carolina, where the public seemed more and more disgusted with 'those rotten-hearted politicians who have but one idea — self-aggrandizement.' A county convention at Raleigh endorsed him warmly and seven of the ten electoral candidates declared for him. W. W. Holden, an influential delegate, thus put the situation: 'The choice is now between Douglas and defeat and sectional dissolution. God forbid that the madness of the North and our own blindness, prejudice and folly should ever compel us to this step. I voted fifty-seven times against Douglas at Charleston. I expect to vote for him at Baltimore.' [28]

There were signs of a change in Kentucky, and the Little Giant was assured that he would carry the State over Bell and a seceder by ten thousand votes.[29] Tennessee leaders, frightened at 'the whirlpool of Secession,' spoke bluntly of 'honest, deranged Jeff Davis' and 'that damned, corrupt, dishonest Slidell.' The chairman of the delegation was cheered to the echo when he made a speech saying that if Douglas were nominated he would support him. The Memphis *Appeal* did yeoman work; Editor Trousdale bought into the Nashville *Union* to convert it to proper use. Andrew Jackson's State seemed to be swinging into line.[30]

Cotton States conditions, however, showed no consistent pattern. The Conservatives in South Carolina, Mississippi and Texas seemed stunned. Those of Florida and Arkansas were a little more active. Louisiana, Alabama and Georgia witnessed almost public revolutions against Fire-Eater rule. The Texas Unionists must have followed Sam Houston into the Constitutional Union party, for the Wigfall group easily maintained Democratic control. In addition, there was evidence of the existence of a secret disunion party.[31]

[27] S. Bassett French, Whitby, near Richmond, May 5; James A. Parker, Richmond, May 23; R. H. Glass, Lynchburg, June 7, 1860; Douglas MSS.

[28] J. A. Fogg, Holly Grove, N.C., May 8; Robert P. Dick, Greensboro, May 17; William P. Richardson, Raleigh, May 19; Thomas Goode Tucker, Summit, May 30, sending excerpt from letter from Holden; H. W. Miller, Raleigh, June 14, 1860; Douglas MSS.

[29] S. S. English, Louisville, Ky., May 5; Frank Waters, Lexington, May 14, 1860; Douglas MSS. Kentucky *Statesman*, Lexington, May 11, 1860.

[30] R. A. McDonald, Columbia, Tenn., May 9, telling of speech of W. C. Whitthorne, the chairman, at Columbia, May 7; J. George Harris, Nashville, May 10, June 1; Henry S. Foote, Memphis, May 11; T. W. N. Bilbo, Nashville, May 24, 1860; Douglas MSS.

[31] A. L. Gilstrap, Bloomington, Mo., May 12; Douglas MSS. Gilstrap, a Douglas man, had been in Texas from 1857 to 1860.

The party machinery in Mississippi, according to a confidential description, was 'as perfectly separated from the interests and heart of the people as night from day.' The people prospered and paid little attention to the politicians. In consequence, 'our party affairs now amount to little more than juggling for office and the promotion of selfish ends. The press is generally in the hands of young and inexperienced men controlled by the ruling dynasty. When a scheme is put on foot, the *Mississippian* roars, and all the little county papers yelp, the cross-road and bar-room politicians take it up and so it goes; and if anyone opposes them, they raise the cry of Abolitionist and traitor, two words of awful import in this country.'

And yet the people of the State seemed to have a reserve power which they would use if a direct attack were made upon the Union. This deep-seated feeling among the Southern people was causing the tergiversation of the seceders, whose object was the dissolution of the Union but who did not dare make the direct issue. The Mississippi rank and file had not been excited by the Charleston bolt. Nearly all conceded that Douglas was the only Democrat who could beat the Republicans. And yet it was doubtful if the popular feeling could be brought to bear on the conventions, for Mississippi was 'bound hand and foot by as imperious a conclave of politicians as ever lorded it over a State.' [32]

South Carolina's delegation did not dare oppose Hammond's instructions. A convention of a sort in Florida commissioned its delegation to Richmond but not Baltimore. The two Arkansas delegates who had not bolted at Charleston planned to vote for Douglas at Baltimore. A district convention set up by the Arkansas Moderates named three new delegates to replace Charleston bolters; an Ultra convention commissioned the three seceders to both Richmond and Baltimore. [33]

Louisiana had a sharp contest. The New Orleans *True Delta* proclaimed the 'humiliation, astonishment and mortification' of the people at finding themselves placed in partnership with a 'plot to destroy the Union.' Pierre Soulé took the lead in calling for a new delegation, there were mass meetings of protest, at which 'men spoke out boldly.' The result was the election of delegates to a new State convention, where a slate of delegation to Baltimore was chosen, Senator Soulé at its head. Slidell's bolters, they insisted, did not represent Louisiana Democracy. [34]

Great efforts were made to redeem Georgia. An important group of Conservatives, 'filled with painful forebodings at the prospect of the Democratic party being slaughtered in the house of its friends,' addressed identic

---

[32] S. S. Fairchild, Grenada, Miss., May 19; the *Mississippian*, described by Fairchild, was Ethelbert Barksdale's paper at Jackson; Henry S. Foote, Nashville, Tenn., May 11, and James E. Sanders, Mobile, Ala., May 22, confirmed this estimate; Henry T. Stanton, Memphis, May 23; G. N. Hillyer, Natchez, Miss., June 1, 1860; Douglas MSS.

[33] W. F. Richstein, Cantonville, Md., May 16, quoting two Arkansas delegates. Blanton Duncan, Louisville, Ky., May 28, 1860, Douglas MSS., recounting conversation with Jils Johnson, an Arkansas delegate.

[34] New Orleans *True Delta*, from scrapbook of James K. Polk of Warrenton, N.C., *circa* May 15, 1860; T. McGinnis, New Orleans, May 10, 22; Thos. Burke, New Orleans, May 28, 1860; Douglas MSS.

letters to Stephens, Cobb and Toombs invoking their counsel. Stephens answered that non-intervention was 'the settled doctrine of the South' and that it was 'mischievous folly' to demand more than that the Supreme Court should settle disputes over abstract rights — let Georgia send delegates to Baltimore. More than this, he wrote lieutenants that Douglas was 'precisely the same man now' that he was in 1856, and aided efforts to arouse the Union men. 'We are overwhelmingly against the seceders,' he advised Western friends.

But Toombs applauded the Charleston bolt, saying that 'our greatest danger today is that the Union will survive the Constitution.' Howell Cobb insisted that the seceding Georgia delegates deserved their constituents' 'cordial approval and renewed confidence,' besought Georgia 'under no circumstances' to aid Douglas. The bolting delegates at first branded as an insult any suggestion that they go to Baltimore. Georgia sentiment, however, soon forced them to profess willingness to go to Baltimore as well as Richmond. But if admitted they intended to repeat their bolt.[35]

Georgia had its full quota of 'political charlatans and desperadoes,' who had committed themselves to disunion, and the Conservatives were divided in counsel and badly outmaneuvered. Instead of calling a new State Convention, they permitted a merger of Cobb men and Fire-Eaters to reassemble the old State Convention which, under the Ultras' control by a small margin, voted an unpalatable platform and sent its delegates to Baltimore by way of Richmond. Not until then did the Conservative segment call a new convention of their own. But Stephens had been outmaneuvered and the Conservatives acted too late.[36]

The struggle elsewhere in the South was not a circumstance to that in Yancey's State, where an 'astounding reaction' set in soon after the Charleston adjournment. Forsyth, Bradley, Humphreys, Seibels, James Smith and ex-Governor Winston met in Mobile on May 7 for a council of war. Repudiating as hostile to Democracy the Yancey Convention of January, 'its delegates, its acts, and its consequences,' they determined to organize 'the National Democracy of Alabama.' Soon they laid the foundation for a State-wide organization, and appealed to the counties to send representatives to a State convention. 'We have just begun to fight,' Forsyth wrote, 'and mean yet to drive the Yanceyites to the wall. They are very uneasy and we shall not spare them.'

[35] Cobb to Robert Collins, Washington, May 9; Toombs to Robert Collins, Washington, May 10; Toombs to Stephens, Washington, May 12, 16, 1860, quoted Toombs, Stephens, Cobb Correspondence, 571–79. Alexander H. Stephens, *A Constitutional View of the War Between the States*, Philadelphia, 1870; II, 677–84.

[36] Thomas Dyer, Memphis, May 11, describing interview with Stephens. Robert W. Sims, Atlanta, May 10, endorsed by V. A. Gaskill, both of whom had just had such a letter from Stephens. Washington McLean to Mrs. Douglas, Cincinnati, May 22, enclosing letter James Gardner to McLean, Augusta, May 18. S. J. Anderson, New York, May 26, quoting letter from Stephens; James Patillo, Mitchell City, Ga., May 20; James Gardner, Milledgeville, June 4; John W. Duncan, Atlanta, June 8; J. A. Stewart, Atlanta, June 11, 1860; Douglas MSS. Phillips, *Robert Toombs*, 189.

A powerful call was issued, signed by many influential men, with Governor Winston's name at the top.[37] The response was immediate. Mobile, Montgomery, Perry and other large counties took the lead in great meetings. All over the State determined Conservatives chose delegates.

The Yanceyites assumed the sonorous title of the 'Constitutional Party' and called a new convention to accredit their delegates to the seceders' 'national convention' at Richmond. The Conservatives were gleeful; theretofore, they charged, the Yanceyites had 'managed to keep from the people their real treasonable object of "precipitating the Cotton States into revolution."' But their Charleston bolt and Richmond purpose now exposed their hand.

Alabama never had a more hectic campaign. 'We are here in the midst almost of a revolution,' wrote the editor of the Alabama *Confederation*, who with other Conservatives boldly charged that the extremists knew well they would be politically dead 'should conservatism hold its proper preponderance.' The time was short but the Douglas move spread rapidly.[38]

The convention of the National Democratic party met at Selma on June 4. The size of the gathering, the representative character of the county delegations and the importance and earnestness of its leaders 'astonished its friends and sent terror and dismay into the ranks of the enemy.' Organizing with scrupulous regard for party forms, it adopted a platform that Douglas could stand on and sent a strong delegation of stalwart Unionists to Baltimore.

The Yanceyites, meeting in Montgomery the next day, found themselves in a dilemma. A large majority of their faction's county meetings had instructed to send delegates only to Richmond. But now it was found that fifteen counties had demanded Baltimore and that three refused to take part in a meeting which planned to recognize the seceders' convention. To forestall still further defections, the high priests of the Charleston Secession swallowed their words of repudiation and accredited their delegates first to Richmond and then to Baltimore.

The Douglasites gibed that 'the anti-Squatter Sovereigns have squatted.' The Yanceyites were in the ridiculous attitude 'of backing down and trying to sneak, beg or pray back into a convention they have so recently, so unmercifully denounced.' Their action, however, added another critical question to those to be decided at Baltimore. Would the Democrats, in national convention assembled, again 'admit this band of disorganizers

---

[37] The call, dated May 9, recited that, inasmuch as disorganization threatened 'the only national party, faithful to the Union,' all who favored 'the perpetuity of the institutions of the government, the integrity, power and authority of the Democratic party, who meet in county conventions to name delegates for a State Convention for Monday, June 4, which in turn should select delegates for Baltimore.

[38] Gilbert Hathaway, Mobile, Ala., May 6; Dr. George W. Graves, Uniontown, May 5; John Forsyth, Mobile, May 9, 16; James Smith, Selma, May 13; D. B. Canfield, Montgomery, May 18; James E. Sanders, Mobile, May 22; Joseph C. Bradley, D. C. Humphreys and others, Huntsville, May 22, 1860; Douglas MSS.

and disunionists' or would it seat the new delegation, which contended that it represented 'the true Democracy of Alabama?' [39]

Thus the North instructed most of its Douglas deserters to keep faith or resign. The Border States were moderating their opposition to the Little Giant. Three Cotton States cast doubt upon the Fire-Eaters' right to represent them. Could this belated counter-revolution save the party — and the Union — at Baltimore? Alexander H. Stephens, with clairvoyant vision, feared that it was too late. 'The party is split forever,' he told a friend. 'The only hope was at Charleston. If the party would be satisfied with the Cincinnati platform and would cordially nominate Douglas, we should carry the election; but I repeat to you that it is impossible.'

'The seceders intended from the beginning "to rule or ruin"' he wrote as the convention gathered, 'and when they find they cannot rule they will then ruin. They have about enough power for this purpose; not much more; and I doubt not but they will use it. Envy, hate, jealousy, spite — these make war in Heaven, which makes devils of angels and the same passions will make devils of men. The Secession movement was instigated by nothing but bad passions. Patriotism, in my opinion, has no more to do with it than love of God had with the other revolt.' Within a year, he said sadly, 'we shall be in a war, and the bloodiest in history.' [40]

[39] J. J. Seibels, Montgomery, June 5; J. T. Menefee, Tuskegee, June 6; Benjamin F. Porter, Sidney, June 6; D. C. Humphreys, Huntsville, June 7; Thomas Jones, Montgomery, June 9, 1860; Douglas MSS.

[40] Johnston and Brown, *Alexander H. Stephens*, 355–65.

CHAPTER XXVIII

THE SECOND BOLT

WITH the middle of June, Democratic eyes turned to Baltimore; some still hoped that the convention would yield a reunited Democracy, but Buchanan and his Ultra allies, fearful that the appeal to the people might yield Douglas a legal nomination, were planning a second bolt. Conforming to program, the seceders' gathering in Richmond on June 11 transacted no business and soon adjourned until June 25. R. Barnwell Rhett remained at Richmond to keep the embers warm and William L. Yancey led the active trouble-makers to Baltimore.

The impending Democratic disruption occasioned the greatest jubilation among the Republicans. Sensing in the Democratic *débâcle* the certainty of their own victory, they launched a campaign which set the record for color, spectacular demonstrations and shrewd maneuver.[1]

But this merely increased the determination with which the Northwest advanced on Baltimore. The week before the assembly, that city's hotels and saloons filled with visitors. Senators Bigler, Bright and Slidell came 'determined to break up the Democratic party rather than submit to the nomination of Douglas' and 'opened shop as they did at Charleston.' Their crew of Federal office-holders and controlled delegates was soon drilled in its parts in the new act of the Democratic tragedy. 'We will break up the convention unless...' was constantly upon their tongues. 'Let them break,' Editor Gray wrote his paper. 'The Douglas delegates are the same as they were at Charleston, only a little more so.'

The Douglas leaders arrived in no pleasant frame of mind. Richardson was more determined than ever. Stuart came with a grim set to his jaw. Montgomery, of Pennsylvania, was fighting mad. Pierre Soulé headed a new Louisiana delegation which, in addition to claiming legal title to represent that State, reflected its essentially Union-loving conservative sentiment. John Forsyth captained a similar Alabama group and James Seward led the Georgia Moderates. These Union Democrats from the South minced no words in characterizing the seceders as 'cotton fusileers, a crazy, lousy set of schismatics who no more represent the people South than Lloyd Garrison does the people North.'

The gathering hosts also included the Charleston seceders. At first 'very quiet, very demure' in demeanor, they begged readmission to the convention which they had done their best to disrupt.[2] But this surface meekness belied their real attitude. While they had laid aside 'the nice principles that drove them out of the convention at Charleston,' the Yanceyites

[1] Halstead, 154-55.

[2] J. W. Gray, Baltimore, June 17, to Cleveland *Plain Dealer*, June 20, 1860. Editor Gray further referred to 'these political pukes from the North who, with Administration bribes in their pockets, come here to oppose the known will of their constituents.' Halstead, 159.

'expressed no regret for the past and no hopes for the future.' 'Will you agree to abide by the action of the convention?' the Douglas men asked repeatedly, but the Ultras refused to answer. The truth was, a Douglas leader advised his chief, that the Southern Hotspurs, like the seventy ancient virgins in Byron's graphic description of the siege of Ismail, were 'anxiously wondering when the ravishing will begin.'[3]

The Front Street Theater was packed with delegates and spectators Monday morning when Caleb Cushing called for order and the convention resumed. The Permanent President first read a short statement of the parliamentary situation at the time of the Charleston adjournment and then the battle began.[4]

The question was over the admission of delegates and on this the Ultras promptly demanded their new program. No longer was it a slave code plank; now it was the unqualified readmission of the bolters. The Ultra sections of the Border State delegations, convinced of the usefulness of the new tactics of Buchanan-Ultra alliance, began to protest that State's Rights would be outraged both by the failure to readmit the bolters or to require of them any type of pledge.[5]

Howard, of Tennessee, moved that all delegates elected to the Charleston Convention be *ipso facto* admitted at Baltimore. Church, of New York, sought to refer to the convention's existing Committee on Credentials the title of all claimants to seats 'made vacant by the secession of the delegates at Charleston,' and insisted that everyone accepting a delegate's seat was 'bound in honor and good faith to abide by the action of this convention and support its nominees.' This evoked enthusiasm from the galleries and Cushing grew indignant.[6]

The New York delegation now withdrew for consultation, occasioning an excited buzz, for all knew that New York controlled the fate of the convention. All knew that Dean Richmond had stopped off in Washington just before the convention for a long conference with Douglas. What did this new move mean?[7]

After about half an hour the New-Yorkers returned and the debate resumed. Ultra speakers denied any convention right to exact loyalty to its nominee. Opposing a motion that Florida, Mississippi, Texas and Arkansas be forthwith admitted, Richardson related that a Florida delegate had lately told him that the Florida group had been accredited only to

---

[3] Robert P. Dick, Greensboro, N.C., Aug. 14, 1860, Broadside. C. L. Ward, Baltimore, noon, June 20, 1860; Douglas MSS.

[4] *Proceedings*, 93-97.

[5] The Ultra argument ran thus: The State is sovereign and so is the Democratic party of a State. Whenever the party of a particular Commonwealth, operating through a due and legal State Convention, shall have commissioned certain men to represent it in a National Convention, this latter body has no authority to supervise these delegates other than to become satisfied of the legitimacy of the electing agency and the actuality of their choice. Whether these delegates or the State party they represented intended to bolt the action of the convention was no concern of the national group but solely that of the individuals and State party concerned.

[6] *Proceedings*, 97-98; Halstead, 161-64.　　　　[7] Halstead, 159, 167.

Richmond. 'I want no delegates here who have not been accredited here!' the Douglas leader said bluntly. 'I do not propose to sit side by side with delegates who do not represent the people; who are not bound by anything when I am bound by everything.'

That evening Congressman Montgomery, of Pennsylvania, was even more plain-spoken. 'For the first time in the history of the Democratic party,' he declared, 'a number of delegations of sovereign States relinquished and resigned, by a solemn instrument in writing, their places as delegates upon the floor of the convention. They went out with a protest, not against a candidate but against the principles of the party.... They called a hostile convention in the city of Charleston, and sat side by side with us deliberating upon a nomination of candidates and the adoption of a platform.... Our convention was compelled, under the circumstances, in order to have those sovereign States represented, to adjourn. We did adjourn. What became of the gentlemen who seceded? They adjourned to meet at Richmond at another time. They did meet at Richmond.... They adjourned that convention and today they hold it *in terrorem* over us if we do not come to their terms.' These men might still have 'their original authority which constituted them delegates' to Charleston; but they had, 'by a paper which remains on file in this convention, resigned their places,' filed a protest against its proceedings, and 'are now in a hostile organization.'

'It is because I love the country and the Union that I am determined that any man who arrays himself in hostility to it shall not, by my consent, take a seat in this convention,' Montgomery exclaimed with intense feeling. 'I am opposed to disunion and I am opposed to the advocates of it. And I am opposed to secession either from this Union or from the Democratic Convention.' As the Ultras had filed protests that they would not support the principles of the Democratic party, 'it is high time, if they ask to come back, that they shall declare that they have changed their minds.' Montgomery's words were punctuated with tumultuous applause from the packed galleries. That first day the political thermometer reached a Charleston temperature.[8]

Later in the debate, M. R. West, a Connecticut delegate, recited how, only four short years before, the Cincinnati Convention adopted a Popular Sovereignty platform unanimously. But now the Southern Ultras 'ask us to turn about and place ourselves in a position which would be absolute death to our whole Democratic party of the North. We have fought the Black Republicans at home; we have been denounced from the pulpit and from the press and have been hissed in the streets. And now when we come here and ask you to reaffirm the same principles which every leading man of your party in Congress — in the House of Representatives and the Senate of the United States — have proclaimed, you even turn around and taunt us with being Black Republicans.'

The extra-curricular activities at Baltimore were spectacular and colorful. After the first night's adjournment, a Douglas band paraded to Reverdy Johnson's home to serenade that staunch conservative and many thousands

[8] Halstead, 161–71.

gathered to applaud Pierre Soulé's oratory. The crowd which attended the Ultra meeting in front of the Gilmore House punctuated every speech of lesser lights with demands for Yancey. At midnight he finally appeared and his silver tones aroused his votaries to fighting pitch.

Tuesday morning's convention action was speeded when Church withdrew his demand for a pledge of loyalty. Thereupon by unanimous vote all claims upon vacant seats were referred to the Committee on Credentials. The struggle there was fierce and protracted. The Northern members had a strong majority of the Committee, but made great efforts and took much time to reason with the Ultra members. The bolters were unyielding in their determination to come back on their own terms.

While the Committee wrangled, the convention quarreled. Border Ultra delegates were incensed at reports from the committee room that the majority was willing to seat any Ultras recommissioned without contest, but would not sacrifice the new Conservative delegations from Alabama and Louisiana. While they waited, the Douglas managers both renewed their organization, and, coming to understand the Ultras' anxiety to be ravished, were determined 'to precipitate nothing of which our opponents can complain.'

Word came Thursday morning that the Committee was ready to report, but before they arrived the floor in the center of the theater gave way. No one was seriously injured, and when the panic was quieted, Chairman Krum, of Missouri, read the majority report. The chief point at issue was the rival delegations from Alabama, Louisiana, Georgia and Arkansas. The majority of the Committee felt that the new Alabama Conservatives had the title to the seats, as did Pierre Soulé's Louisiana Moderates and the new segment from Arkansas. For Georgia it recommended dividing the total vote equally between the delegations representing the two recent State conventions. Stevens, of Oregon, presented the Ultra defense in a minority report in which eight other committeemen joined. His theme, the rights of the States, was applauded to the echo by the Ultras in the galleries.[9]

The call for the previous question brought a new sensation. The New-Yorkers had but recently caucussed and agreed to uphold the Committee report. But now several leaders asked for a recess for consultation. Everyone wondered what was going on in Richmond's mind. At four-thirty, William H. Ludlow informed the convention that the New-Yorkers needed still more time to debate the problem and the delegates reluctantly adjourned until Friday morning.

The Douglas men were sick at heart at this dénouement. The rumor ran like wildfire that Richmond, Church and Cagger had finally been persuaded 'to slaughter Douglas!' For several hours the air was blue as 'New York was profoundly anathematized' and all knew that on her verdict depended the whole convention fate.[10]

[9] C. L. Ward, Baltimore, May 20, 1860; Douglas MSS. For committee reports, see *Proceedings*, 113–21; Halstead, 174–83.
[10] Halstead, 183–85.

These events increased the bitterness of the Douglas men, who would sneer at Northern turncoats, 'What office has old Buchanan given you?' These would counter, 'What office has Douglas promised you?' Congressman Montgomery was attacked by a Pennsylvania Buchaneer but floored his assailant. The Ultras redoubled the violence of their street meetings; Yancey made two speeches that Thursday night.[11]

The extremist elements among the Border delegations caucussed in preparation for a bolt. Virginia, for example, voted 'by six to one' to secede. R. H. Glass wrote Douglas that the greater portions of the representatives from Tennessee, Kentucky, North Carolina and Maryland would follow suit, and the Administration's 'fractional portions of several Northern States' would accompany them. This would 'at once destroy the convention.' But even if the break-up were averted, Douglas' choice was 'utterly impossible,' and Glass advised him to send his friends a dispatch withdrawing his name after he had again received a majority convention vote.[12]

The Little Giant was not unaware of the influence of the new Ultra tactics on Border delegation emotions. Furthermore, he was quite willing to withdraw in favor of any other candidate who represented his general principles. Late Wednesday night, Douglas wrote Richardson placing the decision in the hands of his friends at Baltimore. He felt that the party was in imminent danger of being 'demoralized, if not destroyed, by the breaking-up of the convention.' This would ·expose the Nation to the perils of strife by interventionists North and South, each of whom 'appeals to the passions and prejudices of his own section against the peace of the whole country!' Hence it was a matter of high national concern that the doctrine of non-intervention 'be preserved at all hazards.' 'To maintain the principle,' Douglas would 'cheerfully and joyfully sacrifice' his own ambitions. Whenever his friends at Baltimore should decide that non-intervention could be maintained, 'and the country saved from the perils of Northern abolitionism and Southern disunion,' by uniting on another Union-loving Democrat, Douglas besought them 'to pursue that course.' They must 'act with an eye single to the safety and the welfare of the country.' To save the country from the rule of a sectional party would be the greatest reward he could ask.[13]

Richardson doubtless summoned a council to consider these instructions and a rumor flashed over Baltimore that authority of withdrawal was in his hands. But where were they to find a 'non-intervention and Union-loving Democrat' to take the Little Giant's place? His followers could not go to either Hunter, Lane or Breckinridge, all committed to intervention. Perhaps they could agree on Alexander H. Stephens or Horatio Seymour but not until the actual balloting. So Richardson determined to wait for an appropriate time to use the letter.[14]

[11] Halstead, 185–87.   [12] R. H. Glass, Baltimore, June 21, 1860; Douglas MSS.

[13] Douglas to Richardson, 'Private,' Washington, 11 P.M., June 20, 1860; *Proceedings*, 178–79.

[14] Rhodes, II, 431. Richardson later explained that the new Southern secession on the adoption of the majority credentials report 'put it out of his power to use Douglas' letter.'

The truth was that the demands of the Buchanan-Ultra alliance made compromise impossible. No other candidate favoring non-intervention was satisfactory to them. The New-Yorkers likewise found there was no escape from the dilemma presented by the new Ultra demands. As at Charleston, New York's vacillation was not entirely a mark of unreliability. Granted that her leaders were expert in practical politics, yet important leaders of American business were on the delegation, men anxious for national quiet and peace, and the practical politicians would go great lengths to make a compromise which would give the party a chance at the polls.

But the leaders, and particularly Dean Richmond, knew that to knuckle under to the Southern interventionists would destroy the Democratic party's chances in New York as in the rest of the North. New York could agree to let the uncontested Mississippi and Texas men back in, she might yield on Georgia, but 'to admit, without question or examination, the whole body of seceders,' was a demand to which New York could never yield.[15] The politicians, business men and financiers who controlled this delegation had sought some middle ground to save the party — but there was none. Therefore her caucus late Thursday night balloted on each item of the majority report and in each case determined to sustain it.

Apparently Douglas had no word from Richardson concerning his withdrawal, for at nine-thirty Friday morning he telegraphed Dean Richmond: 'If my enemies are determined to divide and destroy the Democratic party, and perhaps the country, rather than see me elected,' the New York leader must unite with other friends in dropping his name and uniting on a non-intervention, Union-loving Democrat. 'Consult freely and act boldly for the right.'[16]

The Ultra motion was finally brought to ballot Friday morning, the hall being in 'profound silence' while the roll was called. New York announced her vote 'promptly and decisively,' and her firm 'no' settled the fate of the effort to readmit Yancey and his bolters. The motion lost, $100\frac{1}{2}$ to 150, but the roll call revealed that the Northern delegates who before and at Charleston had yielded to Administration blandishments remained impervious to renewed instructions. The Popular Sovereignty men, on their part, gained slightly in New Jersey and Pennsylvania and registered a number of Southern Border votes against the readmission of the Yanceyites.[17]

The convention then balloted on the majority report, section by section, and in almost perfect silence. Mississippi was voted into the convention without contest; so was Texas. Then the Louisiana Conservatives were admitted, the roll-call vote being 153 to 98. The extremists of the Border delegations sat glowering in their chairs; the disruption of the convention was close at hand.

[15] Rhodes, II, 430; *Proceedings*, 164–65.

[16] Douglas to Richmond, Washington, June 22, 1860; Johnson, 426–27.

[17] The minority report's $100\frac{1}{2}$ votes included $2\frac{1}{2}$ from Maine; $1\frac{1}{2}$ from New Hampshire; $1\frac{1}{2}$ from Vermont; 8 from Massachusetts; $2\frac{1}{2}$ from Connecticut; 4 from New Jersey and 17 from Pennsylvania. *Proceedings*, 133, gives the detail of this critical roll call.

When Georgia's case came up, the Conservative contest was partially withdrawn. The Alabama verdict went to the delegation from the National Democratic party. Roll call after roll call, New York firmly announced her verdict in favor of the majority report. Dean Richmond was the focus of attention. Every few minutes someone came up to whisper in his ear and he would nod a decision. The convention was 'strangely silent'; for an hour and a half there had been neither hissing nor applause.

Soon Russell, of Virginia, sought to make an announcement. All knew this was the beginning of the second bolt but New York delayed the evil hour, causing a recess until seven o'clock that night. Now the majority leaders of the Empire State delegation debated Richmond's message from Douglas. Confronted with the situation with which Richardson had vainly grappled, they came to the same conclusion that the Little Giant's withdrawal would merely deliver the Northern Democratic party to destruction. That afternoon Baltimore flamed with the rumor that Richmond had a withdrawal message, but he denied it. It also was noised about that New York would now readmit all the original seceding delegations except Yancey's Alabamans. The Buchanan-Ultra allies, however, scorned any such compromise. New York could not satisfy the Ultras without 'passing under the yoke of Yancey,' and she would not consent to that humiliation.[18]

At the night session, the motion to reconsider was put on the table, New York's '35 votes no' being given in quick, sharp tones. There was now no chance of turning back. A Douglas delegate moved that the convention proceed to ballot upon a candidate for President. But Caleb Cushing would not put the motion, insisting instead on recognizing Russell. Douglas leaders protested but Cushing had made his own plans and overbore the objection. Thereupon Russell announced that a large majority of the Virginia delegation felt that, for reasons they would explain to Virginia's Democrats and to them alone, it was 'inconsistent with their convictions of duty to participate longer in its deliberations.' The larger part of the Virginians then departed. A North Carolina spokesman proclaimed that 'the rights of sovereign States' had been denied, and led a secession of sixteen of the State's twenty delegates. Half of Maryland withdrew, and the major portion of Tennessee and Kentucky retired for consultation. After proclaiming that California was there 'with a lacerated heart, bleeding and weeping over the downfall and destruction of the Democratic party,' an Administrationist led out its delegation, followed promptly by Stevens and the Oregon pocket-borough delegates.

These prearranged secessions brought notice from Harvey Watterson, of Tennessee, that there were some from the land of Jackson who would remain. Other Southerners refused to withdraw. 'Must we fight the men who stood on the platform at Cincinnati in 1856, and kick them off and break up the Democratic party?' asked Moffatt, of Virginia. Gaulden, the great Georgia slave-holder, was for 'non-intervention in the broadest sense of the term.' Five Tennessee delegates would stay to the end. A North Carolina delegate refused to bolt. Col. Nat C. Claiborne, of Missouri, a slave-holder, an-

[18] Halstead, 194–95, 227–29.

nounced that his State would go for Douglas by twenty-five thousand majority. Adjournment was then taken until Saturday.[19] The next morning's session produced further announcements. Nine Kentuckians would remain regardless of their fellows. The number of faithful Tennesseans grew from five to eleven men. The picture was clearer — only the Hunter, Joe Lane and Breckinridge Borderers had gone out.

But the Northern Administrationists were only awaiting appropriate pretext to follow suit. As soon as there was a renewed demand for ballot roll call, Caleb Cushing resigned his seat as presiding officer, quitted the chair, and prepared the Buchanan group in the Massachusetts delegation to stalk out. When he left the stage the Northwestern delegates cheered the change. David Tod, of Ohio, then took the chair, amid great applause.

Protected by a paid plug-ugly, Ben Butler rose to say that he was quitting the convention, because there has been a withdrawal in part of a majority of the States, and further 'upon the ground that I will not sit in a convention where the African slave trade — which is piracy by the laws of my country — is approvingly advocated.' [20]

Now came the speech of the day — perhaps of the entire convention — that of Pierre Soulé. The Louisianian's rolling, glittering, eagle eye, Napoleonic head and face, sharp, French-accented voice, 'and piercing, intense earnestness of manner commanded profound attention and fascinated all who saw and heard.' Soulé traced the whole trouble to politicians' lust for power. The South was afflicted with a crew of office-holders which considered that their offices had become their 'inalienable property.' Such men were the leaders in the present secession conspiracy. When Douglas' name was entered in the Presidential canvass, the extremist cabal, 'instead of bringing a candidate to oppose him,' undertook to ruin the party. The fruit of the battle was the present attempt to disrupt the party, accompanied by threats that if a Black Republican became President, these political adventurers would force their States to secede. Secession, however, meant disunion. All knew that John C. Calhoun had offered to accept the decision of the Supreme Court as to slavery rights, 'and where Calhoun could stand a Southern man need not fear to stand.' Louisiana would not risk her future and that of the Union 'upon impracticable issues and merely theoretical abstractions.' It was a brilliant speech and the convention cheered it to the echo.[21]

Now the delegates were ready to ballot. Out of a total of 190½ votes cast, Douglas received all but 17. Sanford Church then moved to declare him the nominee. This he supported with a forceful speech reviewing the course of the New York delegation. He described New York's abhorrence of the anti-Democratic two-thirds rule; yet so anxious was New York for party concord that she had yielded to the Borderers to make it a five-sixths rule. But the Border delegations had agreed to battle disunion to the end. All could now see their broken pledge. With the recess new demands were

[19] Halstead, 198–202.
[20] Halstead, 206. The bodyguard was a Boston prize-fighter named Price.
[21] Halstead, 206–07.

addressed to New York. 'When we were asked to admit, without question, or examination, the whole body of seceders who came here to our doors — not repentant, not determined to abide by our action, but demanding the surrender of our principles into their hands,' he exclaimed with feeling, 'when we were asked to do that, and besides give up our candidate and the candidate of the choice of the Democracy of New York... we said firmly, we cannot in honor comply with your demands.' [22]

But Church's motion was withheld for a second ballot, which yielded Douglas 181½ out of the total of 194½ votes cast.[23] Then the New York resolution passed without a dissenting vote. The choice of the candidate for Vice-President was informally committed to the Southern delegation. In the evening, the Southerners proposed Senator Benjamin Fitzpatrick, of Alabama, to be Douglas' running-mate.

At the close, Richardson made a speech announcing that Douglas would accept the nomination. In its course, he had the Clerk read the Senator's letter authorizing withdrawal, upon which the whole convention rose in its seats, waved their hats and cheered. Richardson added acidly, 'those gentlemen who have seceded from this convention placed it out of my power to use it. And the responsibility, therefore, is on them.' Then the Baltimore Convention adjourned, its members pledged to go into the field to fight fanaticism North and Secession South.[24]

There was an immediate epilogue. The new seceders could not wait for the scheduled resumption at Richmond on June 26, but held a session at once in Baltimore; as soon as Caleb Cushing came out of the regular convention he became its presiding officer. As he marched down the aisle the seceders whooped and shouted.[25] Ben Butler came close behind him, with Stevens, of Oregon, and other Administrationists, until it seemed that the convention was entirely made up of Buchanan office-holders from the North and Ultra seceders from the South.

After adopting the Charleston Ultra report for their platform, the seceders made John C. Breckinridge Presidential nominee, with Joe Lane, of Oregon, as running-mate. Then the delegates demanded Yancey, who amiably began to speak. His voice was clear as a bugle note but his speech was a disappointment. After a few cold remarks about the Union, he launched into an hour and a half's speech about Alabama politics. Hundreds began leaving the hall and Cushing tried vainly to flag him down.[26] Monday morning the seceders regathered in Richmond. Claiming to be the legal and constitutional Democracy of the country, the convention ratified actions taken by the rump meeting at Baltimore and adjourned.[27]

[22] *Proceedings*, 164–66, for motion and speech.

[23] For detail see *Proceedings*, 163–69; Halstead, 211.

[24] *Proceedings*, 170–81; Halstead, 216. Dwight L. Dumond, *The Secession Movement*, New York, 1931; 90, states that, on the motion to make the Douglas nomination unanimous, to get a two-thirds vote the Chair counted some withdrawn delegates who were in the back of the hall as spectators. He gives no source for the statement, however.

[25] Halstead, 219.

[26] *Ibid.*, 225–27. The vote was: Breckinridge, 74; Daniel S. Dickinson, 24.   [27] *Ibid.*, 231.

Murat Halstead, who had covered the various nominating conventions, concluded from them that the convention or caucus method was 'a system of swindling' by which the people were 'defrauded out of the effective exercise of the right of suffrage.' King Caucus was maintained by governmental corruption funds, every year cost the country $50,000,000, and 'if a Republican form of government is to be preserved in our confederacy, the people must make a bonfire of his throne.' [28]

This second Secession, over the pretext of the refusal to readmit a bolting delegation, was notice unmistakable that the Ultras had their minds made up to break up the Democratic party, although whether Buchanan and his lieutenants wanted to do more than defeat Douglas will remain a debated point. Neither group could have accomplished its purposes without the other's co-operation.

Douglas had been deeply concerned over this onrush to catastrophe, yet there was naught he could do about Buchanan, Bright, Bigler and Slidell, whose hate was such that they cared no whit what might be the cost of his destruction. But he must have marveled at the phantasy in the minds of Jefferson Davis, Albert Gallatin Brown, even Robert Toombs, which would lead them to positions of which disunion was the logical consequence. The Little Giant often plumbed the depths for motives. He knew that all these men did not hate him. Davis did and it was a mutual disaffection. But Toombs loved him, and Brown and several other Southern extremists considered him as great a man as America had ever produced. One must look elsewhere than personal dislike of Douglas for the curious alchemy which changed their minds to madness.

Some historians continue to give full weight to the contention that the Ultras would break up the Union for abstract principle. Others hold that the South had determined to make a last desperate stand for the maintenance of slave economics and the social system knit about it.

Now Life seldom affords completely simple explanations and the actuality is a plexus, not a syllogism. Some of the Ultras, ideologues like Rhett and Ruffin, sincerely alarmed at the drift of sentiment in the North, had convinced themselves that it was only a matter of time until the overwhelming population and economic and political strength of the North would be employed against the South and its mode of life. These men did not see the inescapable truth that the slave system was bound to pass anyway, that Douglas' program offered the best possible transition and that the South's real interests, as well as the country's, called for embracing the path of gradual adjustment. Men of this type were sincere but blind.

And yet, when one examines the available evidence as to the actual pattern of Southern thought and feeling, one finds that the great slave-holders had little sympathy with the men who provoked disruption, and that at no time prior to Lincoln's election did a majority of the Southern white people desire the Union breached. Rather, the breach was largely the work of the ideologues just mentioned, and perhaps more importantly, that of a

[28] Halstead, 232.

small but powerful group of political exploiters, men without much economic stake in maintaining the *status quo*, but with a compelling interest to keep themselves in office and in power. Such men had long run the Government. They had made up the majority of the Supreme Court, they had held a disproportionate weight in the Congress, particularly in the Senate. Their sons and nephews held the key posts in the Army and Navy and the Diplomatic Service. They could not lightly endure the prospect of having this power taken away.

Four years later, when Jefferson Davis was the head of the Confederate Government at Richmond, two Federal Commissioners asked him why the South had ever revolted. 'We did it,' he responded, 'to escape the rule of the majority.' For these men it was not an unequal gamble. If the South remained in the Union, they as individuals would lose their offices anyway. But if they could successfully establish a new nation, they could maintain their prestige and their power in this smaller confederacy. If their effort failed, they would lose only offices, honors and emoluments which in any event they could no longer have.

For Douglas to defeat the Republicans and install non-intervention as a national policy would not help their case. Then men of the stripe of Dean Richmond, George Pugh, H. B. Payne and Charles E. Stuart would officer and dominate the Northern Democracy, while the Southerners who would be admitted to their confidence and councils would be Unionists such as Stephens, Fitzpatrick, Orr, Flournoy, Forsyth, Soulé and Miles Taylor. Thus Douglas' election as President would bring to the party helm in the South a group to displace the Ultras. So they personally had everything to gain and nothing to lose by precipitating a constitutional revolution. If there came war and abolition of slavery, the Fire-Eating politicians would not be the chief sufferers, but the Unionists with great plantations, who sneered at the extremists' 'buttered thunder' and held them in contempt.

But whatever the reasons, the fact remained that, for a mere abstraction, the Ultras, in league with 'Old Obliquity,' had broken up the party and invited the Black Republicans to name the next President.

CHAPTER XXIX

THE CAMPAIGN OF 1860

UPON the adjournment at Baltimore, a Notification Committee placed the 'authentic evidence' of nomination in Douglas' hands. Soon thereafter, through a letter to the Committee, he laid the issues before the country. The candidate felt it necessary to meet boldly the attack upon the legitimacy of his nomination. While this was at best a matter of splitting hairs, the party had its full quota of those who laid great emphasis upon the regularity of party process. Indeed, the Baltimore bolters proclaimed that they themselves had legal title to the party machinery and name, and most of Buchanan's appointees joined in the chorus that the Little Giant had been nominated by a mob rather than by a convention.

Throughout his career, Douglas declared, it had been his 'inflexible purpose not to be a candidate, nor to accept the nomination in any contingency, except as the regular nominee of the National Democratic party, and in that case only upon condition that the usages as well as the principles of the party should be strictly adhered to.' He had made a careful examination of the official records of the Baltimore proceedings, and had found that his nomination had been made 'with great unanimity, in the presence, and with the concurrence, of more than two-thirds of the whole number of delegates, and in exact accordance with the long established usages of the party.' [1]

All through the campaign Buchanan-Ultra speakers made a great point about Douglas' bastard nomination, which they had bolted two conventions to get the grounds to make. It would seem, however, from an examination of prior Democratic practice that the Little Giant was correct in his contention that party usage applied the two-thirds rule as meaning 'two-thirds of the vote given,' rather than two-thirds of the entire electoral college strength.[2] In addition, the platform adopted at Charleston and reaffirmed at Baltimore represented 'a faithful embodiment of the time-honored principles of the Democratic party.' As such, he was proud to stand upon it.

The candidate next emphasized that a policy of non-intervention was necessary to preserve the Union and maintain the peace. For the country to do otherwise would result in two hostile parties, 'the one inflaming the passions and ambition of the North and the other of the South.' Along

---

[1] *Proceedings*, 182–83.

[2] Fite, 110–11; *Missouri Republican*, St. Louis, Aug. 9, 1860. Cass was nominated in 1848 by the vote of two-thirds of the 254 votes cast, although New York, with 36 votes, was present and did not vote. Never before 1860 had it been a party usage to have every State represented and reflected in the balloting. All had been present only in 1848 and 1856. For Breckinridge men's contentions, see Dumond, 89–91.

that road lay madness; Douglas' alternative was that the Constitution be 'maintained inviolate in all its parts.' The judicial authority must be sustained, its decision obeyed and faithfully executed. The law must be administered, the constitutional authorities upheld and unlawful resistance suppressed. Only thus could their generation transmit to .its successors the inheritance it had received in trust from the Founding Fathers.[3]

These brave words were written under circumstances of peculiar embarrassment, for Senator Benjamin Fitzpatrick, of Alabama, did not relish the prospect of a battle with the Ultras, and sent a somewhat obscure letter of declination. Thus the Democratic National Committee, when it met in Washington on June 25, must first liquidate this unexpected declination with the smallest possible loss of prestige.[4] By acclamation the Committee chose Herschel V. Johnson, a former Georgia Governor and a man of intellectual integrity and general respect. The new nominee accepted in a ringing speech laying on the Southern factionists full responsibility for the havoc their course had wrought.[5]

This was but one of many decisions the Committee had to make, for it was faced with almost as many problems as though it were organizing a new party. The great task was to erect the machinery for effective campaign organization. For Chairman they selected August Belmont, the great New York financier. American agent of the Rothschilds, Belmont had been consistently Democratic. He had staunchly supported the Little Giant, and the Committee hoped he could smite the Manhattan rock and cause campaign funds to flow. Miles Taylor, an able, energetic Louisianian, agreed that, as soon as he could go South to quicken action there, he would return to Washington to open headquarters. Richardson, Sibley, Richmond and the other committeemen worked out a skeleton program for the fight.

The party committees in the Southern States were in the hands of the Buchanan-Ultra alliance, and the Democratic electoral candidates had generally declared for Breckinridge. The Douglas men must build from the ground up in every Cotton and Border State; for weeks their energies were absorbed in overcoming legal obstacles, calling new conventions, organizing State committees and launching electoral tickets. By late Summer, however, they had strong electors in the field throughout the South. Alexander H. Stephens, for example, headed their Georgia list. The Administration also controlled the Democratic machinery in a few Northeastern States and in the two pocket boroughs on the Pacific Coast, in which the National Democrats had to set up new organizations. Elsewhere in the North it was the Buchanan-Ultra alliance which had to build the new local machinery.

---

[3] *Proceedings*, 183.   [4] Fitzpatrick's letter was dated Washington, June 25, 1860.

[5] *Proceedings*, 185–88. The truth was, Johnson said, that the Baltimore seceders 'were waging war against the distinguished man, and not for the maintenance of "the principle"; they were willing to jeopard the integrity of the Democratic party and the triumph of its cherished principles rather than see its will proclaimed in the nomination of its favorites.'

Mathematically, the election problem was quite simple. In 1856, Fremont had secured 114 electors. To succeed, Lincoln must retain the Fremont States and secure 38 additional electoral votes. His opportunity for doing so lay in Pennsylvania, 27; New Jersey, 7; Indiana, 13; Illinois, 11; Minnesota, 4; California, 4, and Oregon, 3. He did not absolutely have to win Pennsylvania's vote to be elected, but, practically speaking, he must carry it.[6]

As the nominee of a united party on the Cincinnati platform, Douglas would have been an extremely formidable competitor. On the other hand, had Breckinridge been the only Democratic candidate and running on the Slave Code platform, the only conceivable difference would have been that Lincoln would have carried in the Northern States by much larger majorities.[7] But now all but the blind could see that, with three other tickets dividing the opposition, the only hope of defeating Lincoln was to deprive him of a majority of the electoral college, in which contingency the members of the sitting House, voting by States, would choose from the three highest candidates. The Republicans had a majority of only fifteen State delegations. At one time Douglas believed that Lincoln, Bell and himself would be the top three, but outside observers figured Douglas out and Breckinridge in.[8] There was still another contingency — that the Senate, choosing the Vice-President from the two highest candidates, would promptly select Joe Lane. Should no President be elected by the House, Lane would become acting President!

Since Charleston, the Republicans had envisioned victory with its spoils, and were determined not to be deprived of it by any lack of electoral majority. Now they adapted their campaign to the specific purpose of carrying Pennsylvania, New Jersey, Indiana and Illinois. Raking up 1824's 'corrupt bargain' story, they portrayed in black colors the uncertainties of an interregnum and the unsatisfactory character of Joe Lane. It was an effective appeal.

Again they sought to minimize the Douglas issue of non-intervention by adopting a complaisant attitude toward Popular Sovereignty. It was true that the party had been organized to oppose it and that Chase, Sumner, Wade, Seward and Lincoln had made the welkin ring with their denunciations of it. But many saw, with Oliver P. Morton, of Indiana, that the issue on which Republicanism had been founded was disappearing, and that they 'must have a new issue' for its perpetuation. For some time Horace Greeley and Eli Thayer had urged the party to adopt 'real' Popular Sovereignty. Most of the party leaders realized that Popular Sovereignty had a firm hold on the hearts of nine-tenths of the American people.

Many Republican stumpers began talking about the merits of Popular

[6] The admission into statehood of Minnesota had increased the Republicans' need by four electoral votes.

[7] Baltimore *Daily Exchange*, Sept. 7, 1860; Rhodes, II, 433-35.

[8] Douglas to Lanphier, Washington, July 5, 1860; Patton MSS. New York *Tribune*, July 16, 1860: Lincoln, 15 States; Breckinridge, 12; Bell, 2; doubtful, 4. *Ibid.*, Oct. 4, 1860: Lincoln, 15; Breckinridge, 11; Douglas, 2; Bell, 1; doubtful, 4.

Sovereignty. Eli Thayer and F. P. Stanton campaigned New England for it with such effect that Salmon P. Chase, who in 1854's 'Appeal of the Independent Democrats' had denounced it as a monstrous fraud, now invited Thayer to Ohio to repeat these speeches. Before long Chase himself took up the issue, and proclaimed in Kentucky and Ohio that 'under the doctrine of non-interference and Popular Sovereignty, truly understood and properly applied, the question of slavery might be safely left to the people of the Territories.' [9]

The Republican campaign diet for Pennsylvania and New Jersey was the tariff — the bid direct to pocketbook. Nearly every party stumper recited the Democrats' 1856 platform favoring 'progressive free trade throughout the world,' a specter which greatly alarmed the Keystone voters, and Douglas was warned that 'the tariff possesses more interest to the working classes than the Negro question.' [10]

Lincoln himself spent most of the time in Springfield answering correspondence, greeting visitors and making an occasional response to a delegation. Efforts were made to elicit from him new expressions on the slavery issue but in vain. Soon after his nomination, he had an invitation to visit the scenes of his boyhood in Kentucky. Such a trip would be pleasant, he answered, 'but would it be safe? Would not the people lynch me?' During the campaign, however, Springfield was colorful and excited. The 'Wide-Awakes,' clad in their shining oil-cloth capes and bearing smoking torches, held meetings every day and sometimes all night. Every few days there was a parade, with a long procession of elaborately decorated wagons. The demand for campaign souvenirs was keen and the townfolk plied a thriving trade in Lincoln mauls and rails — any old rail served the purpose and brought a first-rate price.

All over the country the chief campaign color was afforded by the 'Wide-Awakes' and other marching clubs in semi-military uniform. In mid-September it was reported that there were 400,000 of young men whose colorful evolutions were a part of every Republican demonstration, and some Southerners saw in these joyous lads the cadre of an army of coercion. The rail-splitting idea also swept the North, and a Boston parade was signalized by a rail-splitters' battalion of men averaging six feet two in height. [11] The young men of the North were brought so actively into Re-

[9] *Congressional Globe*, Thirty-Fifth Congress, Second Session, 236–39, for one such Thayer speech; W. D. Foulke, *Oliver P. Morton*, Indianapolis, 1899; I, 64; New York *Times*, June 26, July 11, 1860; *Tri-Weekly Republican*, Springfield, Mass., Sept. 28, 1860; Cincinnati *Daily Commercial*, Sept. 14, 1860, for Thayer-Stanton speeches in New England; *ibid.*, Oct. 20, 1860, for Chase invitation to Thayer; *ibid.*, Nov. 2, 1860, for Chase's Popular Sovereignty speech at Covington, Ky.

[10] W. T. Helfenstein, New York, July 31, Pottsville, Pa., Sept. 5, 1860; Douglas MSS; Philadelphia *North American*, Sept. 3, 1860; Channing, VI, 249–50; Rhodes, II, 436.

[11] Channing, VI, 245–46; Lincoln to Samuel Haycroft, Springfield, Ill., June 4, 1860, cited, Herndon, I, 7; *Works*, VI, 21–22; 39; 51; 52–53; 69–70, give this and other letters to Haycroft, who was clerk of the Court of Hardin County; New York *Herald*, Aug. 13, 1860, prints Springfield correspondence quoting Lincoln to the effect that he would like to go South to discuss the Territorial question with the people, but they 'might be inclined to inflict lynch law upon his person.' *Ibid.*, Aug. 13, 14, 1860, editorially denounced Lincoln for this statement. Lincoln to

publican activities that Seward termed it 'a party chiefly of young men.'

The chief party figures all took the stump. In a powerful speech at St. Paul, Seward ridiculed the idea that the South would secede, saying that the Slave Power 'rails now with a feeble voice.... Nobody is afraid, nobody can be bought.' Carl Schurz too made light of the South's cries of alarm, and James Russell Lowell sneeringly termed them 'the old Mumbo Jumbo.' But Francis Lieber, who had lived many years in South Carolina, thought the threat 'made in good earnest.' [12]

Congress did what it could to create issues for the campaign. The House, with its Republican majority, passed a bill to admit Kansas under a free Constitution, repealed New Mexico's Slave Code, passed a Homestead bill and tried to raise the tariff. The Senate and the President negatived all these moves.

But the chief Congressional ammunition was furnished by the House's Committee investigation into Buchanan's patronage activities. Headed by John Covode, a Pennsylvania ex-Democrat, this body made Buchanan writhe in torment. The testimony showed how executive patronage and contracts, particularly for printing, had been employed to influence newspapers, Senate and House votes and political election. Particularly had this been the case in the struggle over Lecompton. Cornelius Wendell, former proprietor of the Washington *Union* and Buchanan printer and contributor, had been let out and was 'ready to tell all.' From 1854 to 1860, there had been $3,500,000 of public printing, at a profit of half that sum, most of which had gone into Buchanan newspaper and election expenses. Navy Yard matters were equally scandalous. The lengths to which Old Obliquity had used the power of the Government to defeat Douglas were thoroughly exposed.

No resolution of impeachment resulted, but 100,000 copies of the Covode report were published, and it was in the hands of every anti-Buchanan stumper during the campaign.[13]

The Republicans found the campaign tepid but the leaders and managers of the other tickets were feverishly active. The Constitutional Unionists began their organization in May. Shortly after their convention, some of their leaders drafted a scheme to withdraw the Bell-Everett ticket and unite on Douglas 'as the only man that can save the country.' [14] The

Haycroft, Springfield, Aug. 16, 1860, letter in possession of Mr. W. H. Courtney, Owensboro, Ky., said his quoted 'fear of a trap' was a mistake. Weber, MSS. Reminiscences, 104–08, for Springfield color; I. H. Bromley, 'The Nomination of Lincoln,' *Scribner's Magazine*, XIV, new series, 646; for other phases, see Rhodes, II, 439; Nicolay and Hay, 11, 284; New York *Herald*, Sept. 19, 1860, for Wide-Awakes; they first arose in the Connecticut State campaign in the Spring of 1860; the name, accidentally bestowed, quickly caught public fancy.

[12] Seward, Works, VI, 344; Lieber, *Life and Letters*, 313–14.

[13] The committee's report, a fat volume of 385 pages, is to be found, Reports of Committees Thirty-Sixth Congress, First Session, V. Buchanan complained of 'star chamber' proceedings and sent a message of protest, without effect. James Buchanan, *Works*, Philadelphia, 1910, X, 434, claims Wendell's testimony was false.

[14] Washington McLean, Cincinnati, May 24, 1860; Douglas MSS. Tom Crittenden, son of

scheme proved impracticable, chiefly because the rank and file of the Constitutional Union party, Old-Line Whigs and Native Americans, had set
preconceptions against Democrats in general and Douglas in particular.
The country over, however, there was an 'entente cordiale' between Bell
and Douglas men. Both groups believed Buchanan insincere in his protestations of devotion to the Union; 'the old scoundrel would rather burst this
government into pieces,' one wrote, 'than see either Bell or Douglas in the
White House.' They heard, with real alarm, that Buchanan, Davis and
others had entered into 'a deliberate contract... that if they should carry
all the Slave States and Oregon and California for Breckinridge,' then the
President would 'hand the Government, Army, Navy and all, over to him.'
Such fears stimulated the co-operation of the Douglas and Bell headquarters.
Blanton Duncan, of Louisville, one of the main go-betweens, kept in constant
touch with Douglas, August Belmont and Bell. The first test of their Southern co-operation came in the August State elections in Kentucky, North
Carolina and Missouri. The results were strikingly satisfactory. 'We
cleaned out the Vandals,' Duncan wrote the Little Giant; the Breckinridge
party was 'utterly prostrated.' Belmont jubilated that, with that start, if
only they could win New York, Douglas or Bell would be elected.[15]

The Breckinridge campaign had its unofficial headquarters in the White
House. The Administration machinery creaked into action with a ponderous procession of ratification meetings, resolutions and pronouncements by party pundits. Great pride was taken in the fact that Caleb
Cushing had been presiding when Breckinridge was named, and that 231
'regularly elected' delegates from nineteen States had participated in
his choice.[16] Cushing, Whitney, Butler and the New England turncoats
went to work. Daniel S. Dickinson, suffused with 'impotent wrath,' became active in New York.[17] Pierce let it be known that he would be gratified 'if our friends in all sections of the land could unite earnestly and
cordially in support of Mr. Breckinridge and General Lane.' Buchanan,

the Senator, who was chairman of the Union National Executive Committee, revealed the
scheme to McLean. It involved Senator Crittenden's resignation from the Senate and issuance
of a farewell address, 'warning the people of the dangers that now surround the Union,' and
urging his friends all over the Union to 'unite on Douglas.' Simultaneously 'the Union National
Executive Committee would pass a resolution calling upon Bell and Everett to resign in favor
of Douglas and the Union.'

[15] Blanton Duncan, Louisville, July 14, Aug. 14. Every Congressional district in Kentucky
had gone for the Union candidate, whose majority was 25,000. Gordon Tanner, Indianapolis,
Aug. 16; Henry L. Stanton, Maysville, Ky., Aug. 27, 1860; Douglas MSS. August Belmont
to Duncan, New York, Aug. 19; A. H. Stuart to Blanton Duncan, Staunton, Va., Aug. 23;
Jere Clemens to Bell, Huntsville, Ala., Oct. 1, 1860, John Bell MSS., Library of Congress.
Browning, Diary, I, 465, quoting Douglas on Buchanan's 'deliberate contract' to keep Lincoln
out of office. Richard and Lewis Collins, History of Kentucky, Covington, Ky., 1871, I, 84, for
that State's election figures.

[16] This figure represented, however, only 115½ electoral unit votes. But three States were
represented by complete delegations and the fifty-eight Northern representatives were merely
the Buchanan patronage fractions.

[17] Butler's main speech, at Lowell, Aug. 10, 1860, is in pamphlet form. August Belmont, New
York, June 25, 1860; Douglas MSS.

Cobb and the Cabinet became 'very earnest' in wielding the headsman's axe on 'noisy partisans' of Douglas.[18]

Some hostile contemporaries charged Buchanan with full participation in the initial phases of Secession and certainly the Ultras found him ever willing to respond to plans to break down the National Democracy. But madness ruled the hour, and this, added to a certain obliquity of moral perception which came from Buchanan's hatred of the Little Giant, would seem chiefly responsible for the President's disastrous policy. But the Ultra section of the alliance had no illusions. Some of their leaders told a Minnesotan that their initial hopes were of throwing the election into the House, through which they hoped to 'secure a larger share of power and Northern concessions.' A little later, however, they moved a step further. Three Southern Legislatures ordered the assembly of State Constitutional Conventions if a Republican were elected, and the charge was bluntly made in Cotton States and Border that the Ultras had forced the Democratic break-up so as to disrupt the Union.

In any event, it became increasingly apparent that Yanceyites, Administrationists, Douglas Democrats and supporters of John Bell agreed that any 'overt act' against Southern Rights would call for separation. There was some division as to whether Lincoln's election, under the forms of the Constitution, would constitute such an 'overt act.' The immediate Secessionists said legality was unimportant. 'I hope to God,' Yancey said at Memphis, 'there will be some man or set of men, whom Providence will rear in our midst,... that there will be some Washington arise who will be able to scourge them from the temple of freedom, even if he is called a traitor, an agitator or a rebel during the glorious process.' The Constitutional Unionists denounced the Fire-Eaters but admitted that they would not stand for coercion. Several Douglas papers in the South admitted there was a breaking point. Herschel V. Johnson himself declared that 'if the South shall persist in the policy which she has inaugurated,' he would 'follow her fortunes for weal or woe.' [19]

Perhaps this news from the South startled the President into seeing that the only hope of defeating Lincoln was to keep him from securing an electoral majority, which fusion alone could do. So far as mechanics went, this could be effected either by the concentration of candidacies or by the pooling of electoral tickets in particular States. The first course demanded withdrawal of two of the three tickets in behalf of the third, or by the elimination of all in favor of a new one. Neither was practicable.

[18] Pierce to B. F. Hallett, Hillsboro, N.H., June 29; Ephraim K. Smart to Pierce, Portland, Me., June 27; Isaac J. Stevens to Pierce, Washington, July 26; Pierce to Stevens, Andover, July 30, 1860; Pierce MSS. S. S. Cox to Lewis Cass, Columbus, Ohio, July 5; D. S. Dickinson, Binghamton, N.Y., June 30, asking for removals; Isaac Cook, Chicago, July 4, 1860; Buchanan MSS.

[19] For Southern Ultra attitude in late June, see T. T. Mann to Gov. Alexander Ramsey, Georgetown, D.C., July 2, 1860, Minnesota Historical Society MSS. For next phase, see *Kentucky Statesman*, Lexington, July 27, 1860, citing Atlanta *Advertiser* that if Lincoln won, 'let us with one heart and mind forget the past and go out of the Union together.' Dumond, 110 *et seq.*, has other illustrations.

The Buchanan-Ultra group, after bolting two conventions to destroy the Little Giant's chances, would under no circumstances consider fusing with him as candidate.[20] Would the majority waive in favor of a minority except for whose intransigeance the breach would not have occurred? Were it to do so in Breckinridge's behalf, the rank and file of the Douglas men in the North would go to Lincoln. Bell had little Northern Democratic appeal.

'If the withdrawal of my name would tend to defeat Mr. Lincoln,' Douglas declared, 'I would this moment withdraw it.' But this step would be useful only if there were, as a substitute, a Northern Democratic leader, who, by support of Non-intervention doctrine, could hold his own people. Had there been such a man, the New-Yorkers would have nominated him at Baltimore. Fusion on a doubtful man would release to Lincoln hundreds of thousands of Northern Democrats and doubly insure Republican success.

Some time in the Summer, Jefferson Davis sought to have all three candidates withdraw in favor of Horatio Seymour. Bell and Breckinridge both agreed. Douglas termed the plan 'impracticable.' If he were to withdraw, his Northern Democratic supporters 'would join in the support of Lincoln rather than of anyone who should supplant him.' It was soon announced that the Little Giant and his forces were against fusion 'all the way from Maine to California.' [21]

These belated pleas for fusion were the chief contribution of the Buchanan-Ultra party to the drama of the campaign. Douglas, however, threw to the winds a precedent which had existed since Washington's first election, and took the stump. In the first part of July the Little Giant seemed persuaded that he had a good chance to win. Richardson spent ten days in New England and came back with favorable predictions. Roseate reports came from the Northwest, while his Southern supporters were feverishly active. In the light of subsequent events it would seem likely that Douglas was keeping a stiff upper lip so as to sustain the Democratic organization in the North. Yet it was possible that he had deluded himself.

At any event, he wrote Lanphier early in July that 'we must make war boldly against the Northern Abolitionists and the Southern disunionists and give no quarter to either,' for 'the chances in our favor are immense in the East.' He did not ignore the possibility that the election would be thrown into the House of Representatives, but thought that, in such an event, the three high men would be Lincoln, Bell and himself. His supporters must cultivate friendly relations with the Bell-Everett supporters, but whatever happened, 'we can have no partnership with the bolters.' [22]

[20] There were a few interesting exceptions. Isaac J. Merritt to Pierce, Nassau, N.H., Aug. 24, 1860; Pierce MSS. Governor Isham G. Harris, of Tennessee, a Baltimore seceder, advised the Tennessee electors to vote for Douglas if Lincoln could thereby be defeated; Nashville *Union and American*, July 1, 1860.

[21] New York *Tribune*, Sept. 13, 1860, for Douglas statement; Wilson, *Slave Power*, II, 52. New York *Times*, Sept. 13, 1860. Washington *Constitution*, Aug. 25, 1860. Franklin Pierce to James Campbell, Amherst, Oct. 17, 1860; Pierce MSS.

[22] Douglas to Lanphier, Washington, July 5, 1860; Patton MSS. Pierre Soulé, New Orleans, July 27, 1860, Douglas MSS., reported a great ratification meeting there, and a fair prospect of carrying Louisiana and Alabama.

This energy and enthusiasm communicated itself to his chief lieutenants, who made ambitious campaign plans. Newspaper support was immediately surveyed. Hundreds of papers had hoisted Douglas' name to the masthead. In New York, however, the *Times*, while still assiduous in its news coverage, had declared for Lincoln, leaving Bennett's *Herald* the only Douglas paper, and its support was 'worse than its opposition.' In Chicago, Sheahan's *Times* was tottering to the grave. Cyrus H. McCormick soon combined his Chicago *Herald* with it, but Sheahan was let out and the merged *Times and Herald* gave a most ineffectual support. There was nothing to be done about it, however, and the Douglas managers perforce got along the best they could.[23]

The newspaper difficulties were met to some degree by a flood of pamphlets and by a copious supply of campaign lives. Sheahan's volume began to enjoy a large circulation, as did Flint's shorter book of speeches. The publishers of the 1858 debates naïvely admitted to Douglas that 'we put in the book more of Lincoln than Douglas simply because the Republican Committee desired it.' Even so, the book was selling three hundred to five hundred copies a day and the Senator had better 'have it made correct and endorse it.'[24]

Both candidate and Committee had shrewd plans for wooing the doubtful voter. August Belmont returned to New York quite enthusiastic. Tammany leaders quickly assured him they would support the Douglas ticket, and he believed that, though Fernando Wood was 'a most slippery fellow,' Dean Richmond would be able to handle him. The Sewardites were still sore over their rebuff at Chicago, and other factors made it look as if New York could be gathered into the fold.[25]

Belmont soon began his drive for funds, starting the list with a personal contribution of one thousand dollars. He set up an imposing finance committee and began soliciting the usual Manhattan donors. It took only a week for his eyes to open. By the end of the first month he was frantic. Not one dollar had been added to his own contribution and, unless some funds could be gotten, 'the whole machinery has to stop.' He wrote despairingly that Douglas could have no idea of the apathy with which the moneyed men regarded the campaign. Belmont had made a 'most urgent appeal' to George Law, who declined flatly to contribute. Aspinwall kept aloof. The New York Central group had not responded, although that road 'could well afford to pay $100,000 in order to carry the State.' Many

[23] Reid Sanders, New York, Aug. 10, 1860, Douglas MSS., for New York *Herald*; Isaac Cook to J. S. Black, Chicago, July 2, 1860; Black MSS. Sheahan to Lanphier, Chicago, July 28, Aug. 3, 1860; Patton MSS.: 'The sheriff was at the door and we had to sell or be sold,' Douglas had treated him cruelly, 'I owe him nothing in any way.'

[24] *Illinois State Register*, June 19, 1860; Foster, Follet and Company, to S. S. Cox, Columbus, Ohio, May 23; S. S. Cox, Columbus, Ohio, July 16, 1860; Douglas MSS.

[25] August Belmont, New York, June 25; C. M. Harmon, New York, July 18, 1860; Douglas MSS. Harmon, assistant editor of the *Express*, offered a scheme by which Douglas might get the Native American party's support in New York. G. J. Tucker, New York, June 29, 1860, Buchanan MSS., recites Wood's prompt announcement for Douglas.

THE LITTLE GIANT IN THE CHARACTER OF THE GLADIATOR.

A CARTOON OF THE CAMPAIGN OF 1860

of the important merchants, normally heavy contributors, were 'afraid to lose their Southern customers by siding with us.'

The worst of the situation was that the Douglas campaign would continue unable to get the needed money 'unless we can give to our merchants and politicians some assurance of success.' Tears must have mixed with ink as the great banker lamented that, '*if we could only demonstrate to all these lukewarm and selfish moneybags that we have a strong probability to carry the State of New York, we might get from them the necessary sinews of war.*' The emptiness of the war chest took the heart out of the Douglas campaign. Late in July, when Miles Taylor reached Washington to start active work on organization problems, he found money 'absolutely lacking' and everything at a standstill. Suspecting that Belmont was not loyal, the indignant Louisianian undertook to set up in New York, under Horace F. Clarke, a money-raising committee of his own. Its experiences convinced him of the validity of the Chairman's excuses.[26]

This condition had even graver consequences in the State campaigns. H. H. Sibley, Douglas' chief leader in the Northwestern States, reported that the people were very poor, the Federal patronage was now against them, and it would be 'absolutely necessary' for the Douglas campaigners to have outside campaign funds.

When they found campaign money 'non-existent,' the Minnesota Popular Sovereignty men undertook to run their canvass on a pauper's oath, traveling the State by horseback and making 'an almost fatal sacrifice of time and funds.' Their local resources were soon exhausted and Sibley sent an envoy to Belmont to renew the plea. The latter responded mournfully that it looked as though his National Committee could not raise for the whole country as much money as Minnesota alone required.[27]

Even more important was Maine, from whose State election in September came the phrase 'as goes Maine, so goes the nation.' Its Democratic leaders visited Douglas and Belmont and urged their case. 'Everything depends upon the election in Maine,' Miles Taylor wrote the candidate. Should the State ticket succeed there, it would convince the Southern people that they could defeat Republicanism by voting for Douglas. But Belmont's sad experiences in giving money for New England politics made him cold to the Maine overtures. Late in July, however, an important delegation visited Newport, where Belmont was vacationing; after a two-day conference he agreed to concentrate the National Committee's efforts on Maine, both by raising campaign funds and by persuading Douglas to make speeches in the State.

The Chairman returned to New York and summoned a meeting of the National Executive Committee for August 9. To his chagrin the only ones who showed up were the Connecticut and Pennsylvania members.

[26] August Belmont, New York, July 28; Miles Taylor, Washington, July 25, 29, Aug. 13, 1860; Douglas MSS.

[27] H. H. Sibley, Mendota, Minn., July 16; W. A. Gorman, St. Paul, July 14, 1860; Douglas MSS. C. C. Andrews to H. H. Sibley, St. Cloud, Minn., Aug. 27; Sibley to Belmont, St. Paul, Sept. 1; Belmont to Sibley, New York, Sept. 11, 1860; MSS. Minnesota Historical Collection.

The next night Belmont invited to his house all the Little Giant's rich supporters, and put the Maine question straight up to them. They agreed to put up half the desired amount if the Boston Douglas men would raise the balance. By strenuous exertions this last was done, and there were some sinews of war for a real Maine effort; the Democrats there promptly announced speaking dates for Douglas.[28]

This was the high-water mark of Douglas' campaign finance. The National Committee appealed to each Congressional district for one hundred dollars, but by mid-September 'not a single cent' had been received. No money could be collected for the New York campaign. Belmont began making desperate appeals to Blanton Duncan and other rich Southern Conservatives for funds 'to throw into New York from the South.' To Belmont's joy, these did respond with contributions, but the current could not be reversed and, to the last, the Douglas men had to battle with almost no campaign chest.[29]

Douglas endeavored so far as he could to offset the deficit in cash and organization through the effect of his 'electric presence' upon the voters themselves. To do so, however, required the shattering of a seventy-year tradition that Presidential candidates should not participate in their own campaigns. While these abstentions were superficial, the pretense was carefully kept up. Douglas seemed at first disposed to conform to the tradition.[30] But his impatience caused him to seek the thick of the fray. It was announced that it had been a long time since the Senator had seen his mother, and that he would soon visit her at Clifton Springs, New York. Altogether it took a month for the candidate to reach his destination, and long before the completion of this odyssey the Republican Campaign Committee began issuing almost daily handbills, signed 'S. D.'s Mother,' appealing for information about her wandering son.[31]

In Boston, Douglas was the guest of Harvard University at its annual alumni banquet. There was a public call upon him 'by way of serenade,'

[28] E. K. Smart, Lawrence, Mass., July 19; Camden, Me., July 26, Aug. 4; F. O. Prince, Boston, Aug. 10; S. R. Lyman, Portland, Me., Aug. 11; E. W. Flagg, Bangor, Aug. 11, 1860; Douglas MSS.

[29] Belmont to Sibley, New York, Sept. 11, 1860; MSS. Minnesota Historical Collection; Blanton Duncan, Louisville, Ky., Aug. 14, 1860; Douglas MSS. Belmont to Duncan, New York, Sept. 19, 1860; Bell MSS. Fresh borrowings of Douglas himself, together with the debt-ridden condition of his estate in 1861, indicate that he himself put up the funds for headquarters' expenses.

[30] New York *Times*, July 3, 1860. George N. Sanders, New York, July 15, 1860; Douglas MSS.: 'A thorough canvass is indicated as desirable.'

[31] Mr. Martin F. Douglas, of Greensboro, N.C., has several of these handbills. One of them reads: 'A Boy Lost! Left Washington, D.C., some time in July, to go home to his mother. He has not yet reached his mother, who is very anxious about him. He has been seen in Philadelphia, New York City, Hartford, Conn., at a clambake in Rhode Island. He has been heard from at Boston, Portland, Augusta, and Bangor, Me.... He is about five feet nothing in height and about the same in diameter the other way. He has a red face, short legs, and a large belly. Answers to the name of Little Giant, talks a great deal, very loud, always about himself. Has an idea that he is a candidate for President.'

and some of the Massachusetts Administrationists 'cuddled around' the Senator, urging fusion. But he was indignant. 'If you voted against me on principle, being for intervention,' he told B. F. Hallett, 'we cannot act together. If you voted against me out of personal hatred, I know very well how to act toward you.'[32]

From Boston the Senator made his way, via Saratoga Springs, and Troy, to his birthplace at Brandon, Vermont, where he and Adèle arrived Saturday, July 28, being greeted by a concourse of about a thousand people. Formally welcomed to the village of his birth, the Senator responded with an attractive speech of reminiscence. At first his hearers were unresponsive. Suddenly an old gentleman out in the crowd called, in a squeaky voice: 'How about that speech you made in Middlebury in which you said Vermont was a great State to be born in — provided you left it early in life?' Douglas said what he had meant was that a young man trying to make his way in life in Vermont encountered the 'opposition of great men with great minds, he had absolutely no chance here then, he has no chance now — if he wants to advance he must still go out where he encounters less intellectual opposition.' This clever retort swept the crowd by storm.

In Burlington he enjoyed another non-partisan reception. In his response, with an adroit defense of Popular Sovereignty, he described the privations and labors of a settler who had to make his own fences and 'split his own rails'; this brought a hearty shout from the Republicans. It was midnight when he reached Montpelier, but his stay there was made brilliant with illuminations, bonfires and fireworks. At Concord, New Hampshire, he spoke 'a little, just for exercise'; in Providence, he referred appropriately to Roger Williams and the struggle for religious liberty.[33]

August Belmont was awaiting him at Newport, Sanders came on from New York and Prince from Boston, campaign problems were thoroughly discussed and it was decided to make a desperate effort to redeem Maine. Thereupon Douglas went on to Bangor, Augusta and Portland. This invasion alarmed the Maine Republicans. James G. Blaine informed National Headquarters that they must have money to offset it: 'If you can do anything for us, do it quick, for Heaven's sake!' And Blaine was right, the Little Giant's presence had an electric effect upon the Democratic campaign, but events redressed the balance.[34]

---

[32] Oliver Stevens, Boston, July 12, 1860; Douglas MSS. New York *Times*, July 20, 21, 24, 28, 1860. Springfield *Tri-Weekly Republican*, July 23, 1860. For Hallett incident, see Burlington, Vt., *Weekly Times*, Aug. 1, 1860; clipping Boston correspondence of New York *Tribune*.

[33] Burlington, Vt. *Weekly Times*, Aug. 1, 1860, correspondence Brandon, July 28; memorandum of Speaker Henry T. Rainey, on Brandon incident; he had an account of it from a member of the audience. Bernice D. Ames, Brandon, July 28, 1860; Douglas MSS.; Burlington *Free Press*, July 30, 1860. Burlington *Weekly Times*, Aug. 1, 1860; Montpelier *Watchman*, Aug. 3, 1860, and *Vermonter*, XI, 99, for Montpelier speech and reception. Providence, R.I., *Post*, quoted *Illinois State Register*, Aug. 11, 1860, says the vast audience at Providence 'seemed in its motions like the waves of the sea.'

[34] Harry F. Lake, 'Influence of Douglas on the Life of Lincoln,' *Granite Monthly*, LX, 153, quoting Blaine to C. C. Fogg, Augusta, Me., Aug. 6, 1860. Fogg was Secretary of the National Republican Committee. Blaine wanted $2000. New York *Times*, Aug. 10, 14, 16, 1860.

In Boston, Douglas revealed to Senator Henry Wilson his belief that Lincoln would be elected, and that it was his own purpose to go South to 'urge the duty of all to submit to the verdict of the people and to maintain the Union.' [35] Sure enough, after a day or so in Washington he set out for Virginia to rally the Union men. Douglas had had a host of friends and followers in the Old Dominion, but Wise had found a way to be for Breckinridge, Letcher was 'acting oddly,' and General Singleton, who was visiting his old Virginia home, found the State 'completely overrun with political excitement.' But the conservative Democrats thought Virginia had disgraced herself at Baltimore, they felt that the time had come 'for men to act and cowards to shrink,' set up their own electoral ticket and put up a fight.[36]

Douglas' first speech was from the steps of the Norfolk City Hall, on August 25. 'I desire no man to vote for me,' he announced, 'unless he hopes and desires the Union maintained and preserved intact by the faithful execution of every act, every line and letter of the written Constitution which our fathers bequeathed to us.' He had not come South to 'purchase' the votes of the Southerners by promises contrary to his beliefs. He regarded sectional parties, South as well as North, 'as the great evil and curse of this country,' and had come there to see if there were not some common principle around which all Union-loving men might rally 'to preserve this glorious Union against Northern and Southern agitators.'

As he was warming to his theme of non-intervention, a slip of paper was handed him, reciting two questions from some Breckinridge electors. The first was: 'If Abraham Lincoln be elected President of the United States, will the Southern States be justified in seceding from the Union?'

'To this I emphatically answer no,' he said firmly. 'The election of a man to the Presidency by the American people in conformity with the Constitution of the United States *would not justify any attempt at dissolving this glorious confederacy.*'

'If they seceded from the Union upon the inauguration of Abraham Lincoln, before an overt act against their Constitutional rights, will you advise or vindicate resistance to the decision?' was the second. To this he answered 'that it is the duty of the President of the United States, and of all others in authority under him, to enforce the laws of the United States, passed by Congress and as the Courts expound them; and I, as in duty bound by my oath of fidelity to the Constitution, *would do all in my power to aid the Government of the United States in maintaining the supremacy of the laws against all resistance to them, come from whatever quarter it might.*'

[35] Wilson, *Slave Power*, II, 699; Johnson, 431.

[36] Wise, 264–65; S. M. Yost, Alexandria, Va., July 1; G. A. Hamil, July 10; James S. Carlisle, of Charleston, Va., Baltimore, July 11; A. D. Banks, Hampton, July 15: 'Seceders are alarmed and propose terms already. The only ones your friends will listen to is a proposition to take one ticket instructed to vote for the candidate who gets the most electoral votes at the North. This Letcher, Richie and others advise and agree to.' S. B. Major, South Boston, Halifax Cy., July 15; Robert J. Lacey, Heathsville, Aug. 21, 1860; Douglas MSS. James W. Singleton to Joseph Sherrard, Aug. 25, 1860, letter loaned by Mrs. Singleton Osburn, of Charles Town, W.Va.

The Constitution had a remedy for every grievance. 'The mere inauguration of a President of the United States,... without an overt act on his part,... is not such a grievance as would justify revolution or secession.' But for the Southern disunionists, Douglas exclaimed, he would have beaten Lincoln in every State but Vermont and Massachusetts. It was nothing short of insult for these disunionists now to come forward and ask aid in dissolving the Union. 'I tell them "no — never, on earth!"' [37]

These answers caused a sensation through the South. Rhett's *Mercury* called Douglas 'a regular old John Adams Federalist and Consolidationist.' A flock of Southern pamphlets denounced the 'Doctrine of Coercion,' and even in southern Illinois there were rumblings of resentment, with John A. Logan storming around, 'ugly and full of fight.' [38] None the less, in Petersburg, his next stopping-place, the Little Giant insisted that America had no evil for which the Constitution and the laws 'do not furnish a remedy, no grievance that can justify disunion.' [39]

Now he turned to North Carolina, where at first any effort had seemed quite hopeless. But Robert P. Dick, the Douglas committeeman, abandoned his law practice and set to work to stem the tide. The State election proved 'an awful damper' to the Ultras, Dick called a Douglas State Convention for Raleigh, August 30, and the Little Giant agreed to attend. [40] He found Senator Clingman at Raleigh, to propose a fusion of Breckinridge and Douglas electors in the State, which the latter promptly negatived. The North Carolina Senator also objected to the Norfolk speech, and urged Douglas to modify his views.

That next day there was an enormous crowd to hear the Little Giant. Again his Union speech was interrupted with questions. 'I am in favor of executing, in good faith, every clause and provision of the Constitution and of protecting every right under it,' he responded. 'Yes, friends, I would hang every man higher than Haman who would attempt to resist by force the execution of any provision of the Constitution which our fathers made and bequeathed to us.' He spoke feelingly of the West's position in the feud between the two older sections; 'you cannot sever this Union unless you cut the heartstrings that bind father to son, daughter to mother and brother to sister in all our new States and Territories.' [41]

[37] *Southern Argus*, Norfolk, Aug. 25, 26, 1860, as clipped in Wheeler Scrapbook, Illinois State Historical Library; New York *Herald*, Aug. 27, 1860, giving special, Norfolk, Aug. 26; New York *Times*, Aug. 29, 1860; New York *Tribune*, Sept. 8, 1860, quoted Douglas as saying at Norfolk that 'no longer was he the Little Giant of Illinois but the little sucker.' Wilson, II, 699. Wertenbaker, 220, quotes the Norfolk *Argus*, Sept. 27, 1860, that Douglas was received 'with great respect' but no enthusiasm.

[38] Charleston *Mercury*, Sept. 3, 1860. A typical pamphlet was 'Doctrine of Coercion,' by William D. Porter, Tract No. 2, the 1860 Association. W. A. Richardson, Jr., MS. Diary and Scrapbook, Quincy, Ill., gives what Richardson, Senior, related to his wife in September, 1860, about Logan.

[39] Wilson, II, 699, 700. Stevens, 623, for Petersburg remark.

[40] I. F. Simmons, Weldon, N.C., June 26; R. P. Dick, Greensboro, Aug. 2; H. W. Mills, Raleigh, Aug. 8, 14; G. L. Pennington, Newbern, Aug. 16; William White, Raleigh, Aug. 17, 1860; Douglas MSS.

[41] H. W. Miller, Raleigh, Aug. 8, 1860; Douglas MSS.; Clingman, *Speeches and Writings,*

Soon after Douglas returned to Washington, word came that Maine had gone decisively Republican. It now began to dawn on the Northern postmasters, collectors, attorneys, marshals and the like that their factitious folly at Charleston and Baltimore, even though in obedience to the White House orders, was about to destroy their political lives.

The result was a new demand for fusion on a State basis. The project, in its usual form was to merge the three electoral tickets, giving Douglas, Bell and Breckinridge each a portion of the electors.[42] The New Jersey pressure began early, Douglas' veto was disregarded and a joint ticket was set up. In Pennsylvania, the weight of patronage secured a major share of the joint ticket for Breckinridge. New York witnessed desperate efforts to arrange a scheme of fusion.[43] But Douglas felt that fusion with seceders merely added dishonor to defeat. Speaking at Baltimore on September 6, he proclaimed the Union in danger; there was 'a mature plan through the Southern States' to break it up, and the Ultra leaders desired Lincoln elected 'so as to have an excuse for disunion.' Under these circumstances he deemed it folly to talk about fusion with Secessionists, because 'every disunionist in America is a Breckinridge man.' These men should know what it was they proposed to do; 'States that secede cannot screen themselves under the pretense that resistance to their acts' would be making war upon sovereign States. 'Sovereigns cannot commit treason. Individuals may.'[44]

A week later Douglas and Herschel V. Johnson spoke to 30,000 in a great meeting at Jones Wood, in New York City. Breckinridge and fusion were the Little Giant's especial target. If his Kentucky competitor favored 'enforcing the laws against disunionists, seceders, Abolitionists and all other classes of men, in the event the election does not result to suit him,' Douglas was willing for fusion. But he was 'utterly opposed' to any combination 'with any man or any party who will not enforce the laws, maintain the Constitution and preserve the Union in all contingencies.' There was deafening applause when he added: 'I wish to God we had an Old Hickory now alive in order that he might hang Northern and Southern traitors on the same gallows.'[45]

512 *et seq.* Raleigh *Standard,* Sept. 5, 1860; Newbern *Progress,* Sept. 5, 1860. Lyman Trumbull, 'Celebrated Men of the Day,' *Belford's Magazine,* V, 225, quotes Douglas as also saying: 'I trust the Government will show itself strong enough to perform that final deed—hang a traitor.' New York *Times,* Sept. 5, 1860, Richmond correspondence, stated that Douglas, stopping at Richmond on his way back was greeted with an ovation reminiscent of those given Henry Clay.

42 W. M. Converse, Norwich, Conn., Aug. 6, 1860, Douglas MSS., proposed electors be instructed to vote for Douglas and Johnson, but if the State's vote would not elect them, 'they shall be at liberty to cast it for anyone that will defeat Lincoln.' J. T. Menefee, Tuskegee, Ala., Aug. 31, 1860, Douglas MSS., reported the proposal of David Clopton for Ultra electors to be withdrawn in Louisiana, Missouri and Indiana, while Douglas electors were eliminated in Virginia, Tennessee and Alabama. Douglas did not accept.

43 Geo. B. Halstead, Newark, July 13, James M. Scovel, Camden, Dec. 10, 1860; Douglas MSS. Eighteen of the New York electors were Douglas, ten Bell, seven Breckinridge. Rhodes, II, 453. *Cabinet Maker,* Boston, Sept. 27, 1860, a Douglas campaign paper edited by E. O. Foss, demanded consolidation of the three anti-Lincoln tickets in Massachusetts.

44 Baltimore *Daily Exchange,* Sept. 7, 1860; New York *Times,* Sept. 7, 1860; Orth, 434.

45 New York *Weekly Herald,* Sept. 15, 1860. The meeting was on Sept. 14.

Bell and Douglas speakers amplified their charges with lists of out-standing Breckinridge supporters openly advocating disunion. A public letter from L. M. Keitt, of South Carolina, was branded as unvarnished treason. Yancey consistently refused to say whether he was for or against the Union, but went to New York to defend 'the great right that rises above all — revolution.' [46] When Jefferson Davis stopped off in Phila-delphia, James Campbell told him Lincoln would carry the State and be elected, but that the Democrats would have the Senate and the House and Lincoln could do nothing. 'If you permit Mr. Lincoln to serve his term out,' Campbell continued, 'I pledge my life that his successor will be a Democrat.' 'I love this old Union,' Davis replied, but would not commit himself about Secession.[47]

John C. Breckinridge was a disappointment as a candidate. A Kentucky lady called him 'all ruffles and no shirt,' the Memphis *Appeal* thought him a 'mountebank.' The truth was that he hoped to avoid declaring his position. But the pressure grew so great that at length he was forced to break his silence, saying in a speech at Lexington that 'the man does not live who has power to couple my name successfully with disloyalty to the Constitution and the Union.' But he uttered no word as to the questions which had been addressed to him as well as to Douglas.[48]

In September, the Little Giant undertook a new canvass to influence the October State elections in Pennsylvania and Indiana, where Douglas, Bell and Breckinridge men were supporting single State tickets. He spoke at Easton, Reading, Pittsburgh, and Erie, and it was plain that he was fighting to save the Union.[49] He was eager to be helpful in Ohio, where his followers were putting up a masterful battle against odds, and the Administration's separate set-up had yielded naught more than 'an empty organization of the office-holders, unable to command 3000 votes.' Yet when he reached Cincinnati, he was so hoarse and exhausted that he could not speak to the thousands who had gathered to hear him.[50]

[46] W. G. Brownlow, speech at Knoxville, Tenn., Oct. 18, 1860, printed in *Sketches of the Rise, Progress and Decline of Secession*, Philadelphia, 1862, 191 *et seq.*, listed among others; Jefferson Davis; L. M. Keitt, R. B. Rhett and J. L. Orr, of South Carolina; and Yancey, J. T. Morgan, J. L. M. Curry and Governor Pettus, of Alabama. Charleston *Mercury*, July 20, 1860, carried a letter of L. M. Keitt saying that, if Lincoln won, 'loyalty to the Union will be treason to the South.' Memphis *Appeal*, July 19, 1860; Newbern, N.C., *Progress*, Aug. 16, 1860, for Yancey's silence on Secession; New York *Herald*, Oct. 11, 1860, for his speech at Cooper Union, Oct. 10.

[47] P. J. Hoban, in Philadelphia *Public Ledger*, Dec. 7, 1889, giving Campbell's statement of his interview with Davis in the Continental Hotel in the summer of 1860. Campbell to Frank-lin Pierce, Philadelphia, Oct. 22, 1860; Pierce MSS.: 'We must again rule the country.... There can be no real danger to the South or her institutions.'

[48] V. B. Young, Owensboro, Ky., Feb. 4, 1861, Douglas MSS., quoting Mrs. Linn Boyd on Breckinridge; Memphis *Appeal*, Sept. 4, 1860; Montgomery, Ala., *Mail*, clipping in Wheeler scrapbook, Illinois State Historical Library, quotes Johnson Hooper, its editor, interviewing Breckinridge 'the day of the Lexington speech,' that the secession of any State 'ends the Federa-tive system; all the delegated powers revert.' New York *Herald*, Sept. 6, 1860.

[49] New York *Tribune*, Sept. 10; New York *Times*, Sept. 27, 1860.

[50] J. H. Smith, Columbus, June 27; Washington McLean, Cincinnati, June 30, 1860; Douglas MSS. Chicago *Times and Herald*, Oct. 9, 1860, for Douglas' condition at Cincinnati.

The next day, however, the Little Giant insisted on going on to Indiana. That State was in a ferment, but the trend was apparent. 'The world out here hurrahs for Douglas and Johnson,' a young settler noted, 'Buchanan stock is not worth anything in this market and the first Breckinridge man I find I'll send to Barnum.' In Indianapolis, he was greeted with a great day parade and night torchlight procession, and despite his physical condition Douglas addressed an enormous crowd.[51]

Douglas next paid a brief visit to Illinois, where the Republicans were circulating all sorts of fantastic canards. He had 'received the sacraments from the hands of the Pope,' and 'no sound, true American can support him.' He had called Henry Clay a 'rascal.' He was 'a habitual drunkard.' 'The Rothschilds wanted to elect him President, so as to control him' — so the stories went.

At Chicago, on October 5, however, the Senator had a great reception, a parade four miles long, and an exhibition of the 'Douglas Invincibles.' But he spoke plainly. 'I'm no alarmist,' he said, but 'I believe that this country is in more danger now than at any other moment since I have known anything of public life. It is not personal ambition that has induced me to take the stump this year. I say to you who know me that the Presidency has no charms for me. I do not believe that it is my interest as an ambitious man to be President this year if I could. But I do love this Union. There is no sacrifice on earth that I would not make to preserve it.'[52]

Douglas was in Cedar Rapids, Iowa, when a telegram came from John W. Forney announcing that the Republicans had elected their Governor in Pennsylvania. A little later he had a dispatch from Indiana telling of the Republican victory there. 'Mr. Lincoln is the next President,' he remarked to Sheridan, his secretary. 'We must try to save the Union. I will go South.'[53]

Douglas was quite right about it: the results in Pennsylvania and Indiana insured Lincoln's election. Some of Buchanan's Pennsylvania in-

[51] *Driftwind Magazine*, VII, 152, for letter William Nye, Aug. 30, 1860. Aquilla Jones, Indianapolis, July 26; Gordon Tanner, Indianapolis, Aug. 16; W. W. Wick, Indianapolis, Aug. 28; Austin H. Brown, Indianapolis, Sept. 2, 1860; Douglas MSS. For handbill issued by Dr. Winslow S. Pierce, for Indianapolis parade, I am indebted to Mrs. Frederick Krull, of Indianapolis; Chicago *Times and Herald*, Oct. 9, 1860, for Douglas' condition and speech at Indianapolis.

[52] William S. McCormick to James Campbell, Chicago, Aug. 8, 1860; MSS. McCormick Historical Association; Philip A. Hoyne, Chicago, Sept. 2; R. D. Goodell, Joliet, Ill., Sept. 3, 1860; Douglas MSS. Carlinville *Free Democrat*, July 5, 1860; Montezuma, Ga., Republican, Oct. 10, 1860, reprinting Chicago *Press and Tribune's* eleven reasons for believing Douglas a Catholic. Carrollton, Ill., *Press*, Sept. 20, 1860; and Carlinville *Free Democrat*, Sept. 27, 1860, charging Douglas with saying, in the 1844 Congressional campaign, that Clay was a rascal. Walter Barrett, Clearfield, Pa., Dec. 3, 1860, Douglas MSS. gives drunkenness charge. Charles H. Winder, New York, July 7, 1860, Buchanan MSS., as to Rothschild 'plot.' Chicago *Times and Herald*, Oct. 6, 1860, for Chicago speech. Illinois *State Register*, June 25, 1860. William Eldon Baringer, *Campaign Technique in Illinois — 1860*; *Transactions*, Illinois State Historical Society for 1932, 203–77, gives much detail of the campaign. Isabel Wallace, *Life and Letters of General W. H. L. Wallace*, Chicago, 1910; 90 *et seq.*, for Douglas' Chicago reception.

[53] Wilson, II, 700; Forney, Eulogy on Douglas; Curtin had carried Pennsylvania by 32,000 majority. Henry S. Lane, the Republican candidate, had won in Indiana by 9759 votes.

timates had really fought for their State ticket. But the chief Administration men in Indiana so hated Douglas and his followers that they deserted Thomas A. Hendricks on the eve of the election. Senator Bright gave the cue and it was estimated that ten thousand Administration men voted for Lane, the Republican candidate for Governor, and elected him.[54]

There remained but one slim chance for defeating Lincoln. This was New York, where the Douglas men were making a desperate fight. Late in October, George Sanders held a meeting of all 'the solid men of the city and the strong men of the State.' Dean Richmond was there, with Horatio Seymour, Peter Cooper and Sanford Church. They concluded that the State would be safe if Tammany and Fernando Wood proved true to them, and would give a 60,000 majority in New York City. This last minute effort would take money, but money was now in sight; 'We require $100,-000,' Sanders reported, 'and expect to raise at least $200,000.' The New York campaign made headway, and just before the election Sanders informed his chief that 'our city is now at white heat, the result doubtful. We are gaining so rapidly that it is impossible to foretell the result.' [55] The event, however, was to prove that they had begun too late.

Before turning South, Douglas had to fill a few other Northwestern engagements. He hastened to Milwaukee, where he gripped his hearers with the disclosure of the details of the momentous White House interview when he had reminded Buchanan that General Jackson was dead. His trip southward through Illinois was a veritable ovation. A great throng greeted him at Bloomington and a crowd of five thousand cheered him at Springfield. Alton had 'an immense turn out.' [56]

The Senator's first actual Slave State speech was at St. Louis on October 19. He spoke on the levee, which was ablaze and crowded with people. 'I am not here tonight to ask for your votes for the Presidency,' he said, and those who heard him marked the weariness of his voice and the fatigue

[54] N. E. Paine, Philadelphia, Aug. 21; W. S. Hirst, Harrisburg, Oct. 12, 1860; Buchanan MSS. Blanton Duncan, Louisville, Ky., Oct. 14, 1860, giving estimate of 10,000 Breckinridge votes for Lane, the Republican candidate; J. B. Nowland, Jeffersonville, Ind., Oct. 15, 1860, Douglas MSS: 'Your Southern friends would like to know how their professed friends in Indiana are going. They have gone over to Lincoln, britches and all.' Louisville *Daily Democrat*, Oct. 14, 1860, charged Bright with voting for Lane; 'Bright himself has not denied it.... He advised it in a public speech, as note from letter to William M. French, editor of the Jeffersonville *Republican*, signed by four men asking if Bright did not on Monday last say "We must beat this anti-Lecompton Douglas Democratic party. You may begin tomorrow if you please, but it must be done." French responded that he had heard the speech and that Bright had said the Douglas party would be defeated, adding: "When shall we begin the work? Tomorrow, if you please. You can find no better time."'

[55] August Belmont to Blanton Duncan, New York, Aug. 19, 1860; Bell MSS.; George N. Sanders, New York, Oct. 18, 1860; Douglas MSS. Sanders thought 'if we had three weeks more upon them, we would beat them 50,000.' *National Intelligencer*, Washington, Nov. 1, 1860, printed the report that William B. Astor had contributed $1,000,000 to the New York fusion campaign.

[56] Chicago *Times and Herald*, Oct. 14, 1860, for Douglas' Milwaukee speech; Milwaukee *Daily Enquirer*, Oct. 15, 1860. *Illinois State Register*, Oct. 8, 1860, gives Douglas' Western itinerary.

of his face. 'I am not one of those who believe that I have any more personal interest in the Presidency than any other good citizen in America. I am here to make an appeal to you on behalf of the Union and the peace of the country.' [57]

The next night a little party boarded a river steamer for Memphis. It consisted of Mrs. Douglas, faithful as she was beautiful, James B. Sheridan, Douglas' loyal secretary, and the Senator himself, worn to the breaking point but determined to carry on. Since the middle of July he had been on the hustings, making a speech a day, sometimes two or three, inside halls and in the open air, from the back of railroad trains and upon river wharves. His endurance amazed his friends, some of whom said that he possessed 'the very constitution of the United States.' When Douglas' journey was announced in the Cotton States, threats of physical violence were published, but he was not deterred.

Memphis was an appropriate place for beginning his new Southern campaign, because western Tennessee, eastern Arkansas, and northern Mississippi had taken the lead in setting up Douglas electoral tickets in the respective States. The Little Giant's friends had been particularly active in Tennessee; William H. Polk and Harvey Watterson became Douglas electors-at-large, strong district electors were chosen, a campaign daily was established at Nashville and the Volunteer State resounded with the campaign.[58]

Ultra papers farther South were terming his tour 'the most impudent, the most disgraceful, the most indefensible' of his acts during the campaign, but the West Tennesseans 'became utterly mad with excitement' upon his arrival, and the Senator was 'literally lifted through the assemblage.' His speech the next day was an ovation. At Jackson, Tenn., he talked to 10,000. In Nashville the greatest crowd of two decades cheered him to the echo, although Yancey, of Alabama, who spoke there that same evening, had a rough time of it. En route to Chattanooga occurred the first of several incidents which convinced him that attempts were being made to wreck the trains on which he was riding.[59] He arrived safely, however, the

[57] T. M. Rice, Jefferson City, Mo., June 26; L. J. Taylor, Princeton, July 9; D. T. Brigham, Keokuk, Iowa, July 28, 1860; Douglas MSS.: Despite Senator Green's opposition, an efficient electoral ticket was in the field and Douglas would carry the State. Chicago *Times and Herald*, Oct. 24, 1860, *Illinois State Register*, Oct. 18, 19, 23, 1860.

[58] Josiah Fisher, Pocahontas, Ark., July 13; C. H. Wheeler, New Baltimore, Va., July 11, 1860, Douglas MSS., quoting John Carnall, Fort Smith, Ark., on electoral ticket; Vicksburg *Whig*, July 4, 1860, has call for Douglas State Convention at Holly Springs, July 30. The Mississippi electoral ticket there announced was strong, B. N. Kinyon, 'one of the ablest men in North Mississippi,' took the stump for Douglas. Samuel P. Walker, Memphis, July 9; W. L. Green, Memphis, July 17, 1860, Douglas MSS. So strong was Douglas sentiment in Memphis that a German language paper, the *Democrat*, was started in his behalf; for its history see Memphis *Avalanche*, July 10, 1867. Harvey M. Watterson, Nashville, Aug. 4, 1860, Douglas MSS., had gotten out the Nashville *Daily Evening Democrat*, which 'shall be published so long as there is a button on our coats.'

[59] Memphis *Appeal*, Oct. 20, 23, 24, 25, 1860. Nashville *Patriot*, Oct. 27, 1860. For Nashville references I am indebted to Mr. Maxwell Benson, of that city. Natchez, Miss., *Free Trade*, Oct. 25, 1860, Philadelphia *Press*, Oct. 29, 1860, for denunciations and threats. Memphis

surrounding country had turned out *en masse* and the bustling little city on the Tennessee seemed 'possessed of two spirits — the spirit of politics and the rectified spirit of alcohol.' Douglas' descent from the train occasioned 'an outburst of deafening salutations,' and his address was cheered to the echo.[60]

A great State-wide demonstration was staged in Atlanta on Oct. 30. Herschel V. Johnson had proved a disappointment in the Georgia campaign, but 'the bright Damascus blade of Alexander H. Stephens' began flashing in the battle. Under Georgia law, a majority was necessary for carrying an electoral ticket. When it became apparent that the Douglas men could not get a majority, they campaigned to throw the State to Bell.[61] Stephens introduced Douglas at Atlanta with an eloquent tribute. The latter revealed that prior to the Charleston Convention he had asked the Illinois delegation, if it found his own nomination impossible, 'to do all in their power to secure this honor for his friend Mr. Stephens.' [62] Douglas now accompanied Governor Johnson to Macon, where he shared a speech with Herschel V. Johnson and a reception with the charming Adèle.[63]

Soon the little party turned to Alabama to urge that Lincoln's election would not require withdrawal. The Summer's struggle had been a gruelling one for the Douglas leaders. The Governor, all but one of the ex-Governors, the two Senators and all but one of the State's Congressmen had announced for Breckinridge. Forsyth and his group bravely but vainly stumped the State. 'I fear that we are in the midst of a revolution,' Douglas was advised. 'The storm rages to such a madness that it is beyond the control of those who raised it. Our own people are becoming frantic and what is to be done?' [64]

A great torchlight procession greeted Douglas on his arrival in Montgomery, but the crowd had its hostile members, and when the Little Giant and the welcoming committee alighted at their hotel, rotten tomatoes and eggs were thrown at him. These missed their target but hit some of the committee.

The next day Douglas spoke from the steps of the State Capitol, his appeal being for Alabama to take second thought about Secession. His

---

Appeal, Oct. 28, 1860, Chicago *Times and Herald*, Nov. 12, 1860, and Johnson, 439, for tamperings with trains.

[60] Knoxville, Tenn., *Chronicle*, Oct. 31, 1860, report signed K. N. Pepper, Jr., Proofsheet in Johnson MSS., Greeneville, Tenn.

[61] James Gardner, Augusta, Ga., July 7. William De Graffenreid, Macon, July 10; Gardner to George N. Sanders, Augusta, July 15; S. I. Anderson, New York, July 22, quoting Stephens. Gardner, Augusta, Aug. 2, 5, 1860, Douglas MSS.

[62] Foote, *Casket of Reminiscences*, 19.

[63] Personal reminiscence of the late Mrs. Sarah Fort Milton, the author's grandmother, who came from Milledgeville to attend the reception. Mrs. Douglas graciously presented her with a rose.

[64] Pierre Soulé, New Orleans, July 27, describes Mobile ratification meeting of July 21, with 3000 present. Joseph C. Bradley, Huntsville, Aug. 31, telling of Foote's speech to the same number near Huntsville the day before; D. C. Humphreys, Huntsville, Oct. 28, Nov. 3; John Forsyth, Mobile, Oct. 30, 1860; Douglas MSS.

huge audience was loath for him to close, shouting 'Go on! Go on!' That night he boarded the steamboat, which was to carry him to Selma. Thousands gathered on the wharf to shout for Douglas. Finally he appeared on the upper deck to give a word of parting. With this, hundreds rushed on the steamer, and the deck gave way under the pressure, dropping the speaker, his wife and all the others down to the lower deck. For a moment it seemed there had been a fearful catastrophe. Douglas was badly bruised and had an injured leg. Mrs. Douglas was so seriously wrenched and shaken that she could not go on to Selma. But the Senator went on to another ovation at Selma, where he repeated his defense of the Union.[65] John Forsyth and a welcoming committee met the Douglas steamer forty miles from Mobile. That evening a large crowd cheered his plea that Alabama had more security within than without the Union. It was the night before the great election.

The Little Giant spent the next day quietly, 'seemed to be less excited by the election, and to think less of it, than perhaps any other man in the city.' That evening he sat with Forsyth in the *Register* office, reading the dispatches from the North. Long before midnight both knew that Lincoln had won.

The question immediately arose as to what the *Register* should say the next morning. Forsyth read an editorial favoring the assemblage of a State Convention to discuss Alabama's course. Douglas earnestly urged him not to print it. Forsyth agreed, but insisted that the only way the Alabama Unionists could manage the Secession current was to appear to go along, elect their own friends to the convention and control it when it met. Douglas argued that if the Union men could not prevent a convention, they certainly could not control it when held. But Forsyth had made up his mind and the editorial went in.

Thereupon Douglas made his way back to his hotel — its name, ominously enough, was the Battle House. Sheridan noted that he seemed 'more hopeless than I had ever before seen him.' [66] And well he might, for that night Secession had been born.

[65] Montgomery *Weekly Confederation*, Nov. 9, 1860; Alabama *State Sentinel*, Selma, Nov. 7, 1860; Chicago *Times and Herald*, Nov. 12, 1860; Johnson, 439; F. A. Gulledge, in Montgomery *Advertiser*, Oct. 18, 1933.

[66] Mobile *Register*, quoted *Illinois State Register*, Nov. 22, 1860. Wilson, *Slave Power*, II, 700, quoting letter from Sheridan.

CHAPTER XXX

THE COTTON STATES SECEDE

WHILE Lincoln had received a majority of the electoral votes and thus had won the Presidency, he had about a million fewer popular votes than his opponents combined.[1] Douglas' popular vote, a little over two-thirds that of Lincoln, afforded eloquent testimonial to his hold on the hearts of Northern Democrats. But his electoral strength was less than that of either Breckinridge or Bell, a commentary on the queer tricks of the American presidential system, under which a small vote, focused in certain States, can yield an electoral strength considerably greater than that won by a large but dispersed vote.[2]

An analysis of the returns, however, indicated the general wish for Union and peace. Bell carried Tennessee, Kentucky, and Virginia, while Douglas won Missouri and New Jersey. The two Conservatives received a majority of the vote in Georgia, Louisiana and Maryland, and in no Southern State save Texas was it less than forty per cent. Douglas came within 12,000 votes of defeating Lincoln in Illinois, within 557 votes of topping him in California, and over the entire Northwestern group of Illinois, Indiana, Iowa, Ohio, Michigan, Wisconsin and Minnesota, he received forty-three per cent of the vote cast. The North had given the Republican party no unmistakable mandate to refuse to compromise the disturbing sectional issues.[3]

The South, too, did not vote for Secession. Fifty-four per cent of the Border State voters preferred a National to a sectional candidate, as did forty-six per cent of those of the Cotton States, indicating that the people of the South were by no means unanimously willing to breach the Union for an abstraction. The outcome could, indeed, mean that about half the Southern

[1] The popular vote was: Lincoln, 1,857,610; Douglas, 1,365,967; Breckinridge, 847,953; Bell, 590,631. The electoral vote was: Lincoln, 180; Breckinridge, 72; Bell, 39; Douglas, 12.

[2] Nine of Douglas' twelve electoral votes came from Missouri, the other three from New Jersey, where his loyal followers concentrated on their own Douglas ticket, electing those three who were also on the fusion list. *American Almanac*, 1861, gives Missouri's vote as Douglas, 58,801; Bell, 58,372; Breckinridge, 31,317; Lincoln, 17,028. The Douglas electors in New Jersey received 62,801 to 58,324 for the Lincoln men. James M. Scovel, Camden, N.J., Dec. 10, 1860; Douglas MSS. A Pennsylvania Democratic electoral ticket, with nine Douglas men on it, named before the Baltimore Convention, was withdrawn when separate Douglas and Breckinridge tickets were put up. Then when the Breckinridge ticket was withdrawn, the old ticket came back but the separate Douglas ticket remained. The official fusion ticket vote is all credited to Breckinridge: Lincoln, 268,030; Douglas, 16,765; Breckinridge, 178,871; Bell, 12,776. Fusion lost in New York by 50,475. The expected New York City fusion majority shriveled to 29,000. Fusion lost Rhode Island by 5000.

[3] The Douglas-Bell percentages of the Northwestern States were: Illinois, 48; Ohio, 45; Indiana, 44; Iowa, 44; Wisconsin, 43; Michigan, 42; Minnesota, 34. Douglas lost Illinois to Lincoln, despite the Bell and Breckinridge tickets, by only 12,000 out of a total of 335,000 votes. In Iowa he received 55,000; in Indiana, 115,000; in Michigan, 65,000; in Wisconsin, 65,000; in Minnesota, 11,000; in Ohio, 187,000.

voters preferred the Union, with eventual emancipation, to slavery without the Union.[4]

Lincoln's party had won control of neither House nor Senate. Provided the Southern members stayed in their seats, before the new President could have even a postmaster, he must secure confirmation from a Senate opposed to him. Douglas, Stephens, Crittenden and other Union leaders so regarded the practical effects of Lincoln's election.

In New Orleans, the Little Giant reminded his Southern friends that a President could do only that which the law authorized him to do. If Lincoln failed in his duties, he would 'soon find himself a prisoner before the high court of impeachment.' No new legislation was necessary for protecting slavery, nor was there the least danger of new legislation against slavery, because neither House could pass any bill aimed to injure the Southerners, 'UNLESS *a portion of the Southern Senators and Representatives absent themselves.*'

Let the South stay in the Union and the President would be 'utterly powerless for evil,' Douglas continued. Surely a partisan President, 'tied hand and foot, and powerless for good or evil without the consent and support of his political opponents, should be an object of pity and commiseration rather than of fear and apprehension by a brave and chivalrous people.' Four years would pass quickly and then the ballot box would furnish 'a peaceful, legal and constitutional remedy' for any grievances or evils. He could see, therefore, 'no just cause, no reasonable ground,' for rash and precipitate action, with its consequences of revolution, anarchy and bankruptcy.[5]

The Douglases soon began the steamboat journey up the Mississippi. When the *James Battle* tied up to the Vicksburg wharf, a large crowd assembled to ask that the Senator address them. Responding with the arguments of his New Orleans letter, the crowd cheered again and again. That Union sentiments were still appreciated at the most important point in Mississippi seemed to him a good omen.[6]

---

[4] In the States soon to secede, 856,524 people voted. Of these, 345,919 voted for Bell, and 72,084 for Douglas, or about 48 per cent of the total vote cast. This percentage of total votes ran, by Cotton States: Louisiana, 55; Georgia, 51; Arkansas, 46; Alabama, 45; Florida, 40; Mississippi, 40; Texas, 23. Cf. also Scrugham, 51–52; Channing, VI, 251. *Kentucky Statesman*, Lexington, Dec. 4, 1860, gives Kentucky figures: Bell, 66,058; Breckinridge, 53,143; Douglas, 25,652. Bell carried Breckinridge's home county.

[5] Mobile *Register*, clipped in *Illinois State Register*, Nov. 22, 1860; Mrs. Douglas joined her husband at Mobile and the two went to New Orleans on the mail steamer *Alabama*. New York *Times*, Nov. 15, 1860, describes Douglas' arrival in New Orleans. *Missouri Republican*, Nov. 17, 1860, printed letter from New Orleans Committee, Nov. 12, and Douglas' reply, Nov. 13.

[6] Vicksburg *Whig*, Nov. 17, 1860. New York *Times*, Nov. 15, 1860, had a New Orleans dispatch that the Senator was 'exceedingly ill' in some Mississippi town, but the Vicksburg paper reported him in good health and spirits. A. A. Burwell, Vicksburg, Nov. 16, 1860, Douglas MSS., Douglas' remarks on the levee that had 'produced an intense enthusiasm.' While Mississippi was customarily accredited to Disunion, 'the sentiment of the mass of the people is not. in favor of such a movement.' Professor P. L. Rainwater, of the University of Mississippi, who has made a careful study of Mississippi sentiment in late 1860 and early 1861, is convinced that a majority of the people of Jefferson Davis' State did not want to secede.

And yet by the time the Senator reached Vicksburg the Secession parade had commenced, with South Carolina in the lead. South Carolina still clung to the custom of choosing presidential electors by the Legislature, and so the Legislature's assemblage for that purpose could also be employed to begin the revolution according to the forms of law.

In September some Charlestonians organized 'The 1860 Association,' an instrumentation of Yancey's plea for 'one organized concerted action,' and it soon gained important Southern support. Early in October, Governor Gist sent a confidential letter to the Executive of each Slave State urging concert of action: South Carolina would follow if a single State seceded; she would take the lead herself if assured of a companion. Later in the month he met with South Carolina's leading Secessionists and agreed on a detailed program. When the Legislature met, November 5, he recommended quitting an unendurable Union. With Lincoln's election the Federal Grand Jury refused to function, the United States District Judge dramatically closed court and resigned and the two United States Senators renounced their commissions. A week later the Legislature called a convention to consider 'the dangers incident to the position of the State in the Federal Union.' Charleston then staged a gala celebration, and many speeches were addressed to 'citizens of the Southern republic.' [7]

One reason for this swift action was to strengthen the Ultras' hands in other States, where several diverse schools of thought existed among the State's Rights men. The real Ultras, Immediate Separationists, formed the best-organized group. Whatever their propaganda technique, their chiefs expected no overt act on the part of the new Administration, but feared a new Union party in the South. Expecting that the Cotton South would soon siphon the slaves out of the Border States, they saw the day when these would be abolitionized, making the lot of Cotton States all the more hopeless. These true Ultras cared little for new constitutional guaranties, but would remain in the Union only if it adopted something resembling Calhoun's doctrine of concurrent majorities. Some looked to the right of revolution to justify withdrawal, while others sought sanction in the Constitution's vatic silences.

They were opposed by the Co-operationists, who were in turn divided into those who wanted immediate separation, but in concert; those who desired to present to the North an ultimatum of their demands, with the hope that it would be accepted, and those who would make no move until there had been some 'overt act.' [8] The Co-operationists were strong and made a

---

[7] Nicolay and Hay, II, 305, for 'The 1860 Association'; Confederate Archives MSS., War Department, Washington, for Gist October correspondence with other Southern Governors. Gist called the Legislature on Oct. 12, for selecting electors and to 'take action for the safety and protection of the State.' On Nov. 6, South Carolina's Legislature elected Breckinridge and Lane electors; on Nov. 10, a committee recommended a convention bill, and on Nov. 13, it became a law.

[8] Dumond, 117–34, makes these distinctions. There can be no doubt of the fear that the non-slave-holding whites would cease to support the peculiar institution. Judge George W. Woodward to J. S. Black, Pittsburgh, Pa., Nov. 18, 1860; Black MSS.: 'An Abolition party is to be built up in the South through patronage.... A raid here and there and a local insurrection now

powerful argument. But the Immediate Separationists, controlling the executive machinery in most of the Cotton States, used it both to take the States out separately, as rapidly as local conditions permitted, and to effect unity of action through the interchange of State Commissioners, who constituted almost a diplomatic service for the Ultras. This group of officially accredited agitators and secession technicians became active in every Slave State, and within a month of Lincoln's election the fires of revolution had been lit all through the Cotton South.

Time was of the essence of the situation. Buchanan, whom the Secessionists considered 'at heart right and with us,' would remain in office until March 4.[9] But even if not a sympathizer, they felt that such was his irresolution that he would take no effective step to hinder the break-up of the Union. By speeding the separation of two or three States, the remainder must choose between casting their lot with neighbors or remaining part of a hostile and coercive Government, an alternative which would quicken the velocity of secession.[10]

The lengths to which the Immediate Separationists went to set fire to the apprehensions of the people struck consternation to the hearts of those who wanted to ponder the problem. 'I think the Union is gone,' Herschel V. Johnson advised Douglas soon after the election. 'South Carolina will secede, and whether they will or not, she will drag the Cotton States with her very soon.' Another Georgia Conservative observed that the Ultras had raised the cry of mad-dog and the 'people will kill the dog in a panic.'[11]

The Georgia Legislature invited T. R. R. Cobb, brother of Howell, Robert Toombs and Alexander H. Stephens to present their recommendations. Cobb argued shrewdly that Georgia could make better terms 'out of the Union than in it.' Toombs spoke on the night of November 13. 'I ask you to give me the sword,' he shouted. 'If you do not give it to me, as God lives, I will take it myself.' Let the Legislature forthwith enact an Ordinance of Secession and, if a referendum were necessary, let the people have the choice, on the ballot, of 'Submission to Abolition Rule' or 'Resistance.'

Stephens, who spoke the next evening, was earnestly grave. The South would put herself in the wrong to resist merely 'because a man had been constitutionally elected.' It was said Lincoln's policy would destroy the

and then are to be achieved... until one after another concludes, "well, slavery is a bad thing — slavery is a sin against God and man.... Let's vote for the anti-slavery candidates."' But several saw in the success of disunion this same menace. Thomas M. Peters, Moulton, Ala., Jan. 16: 'Upon any other principle save force, we shall have Black Republicanism here as fierce as it is in Chicago itself before the lapse of a quarter of a century.' Charles S. Drake, St. Louis, Mo., Jan. 16, 1861, Douglas MSS.: If they succeeded in Secession, the South would face irretrievable ruin, for 'slavery would not exist there twenty-five years hence. Ten years would not lapse before the institution would become oppressive even to the Cotton States, and they would be seeking how to check its enlargement.'

[9] Jacob Thompson to Howell Cobb, Washington, Jan. 16, 1861; Erwin MSS.

[10] *The War of the Rebellion: A Compilation of the Official Records of the Union and Confederate Armies*, Washington, 1880–1901 (hereafter to be referred to as *O.R.*), Series IV, I, 20, 46–47.

[11] H. V. Johnson, Spiers Turnout, Jefferson County, Ga., Nov. 25; John E. Winston to H. B. Stone (of New York), Columbus, Ga., Nov. 21, 1860; Douglas MSS.

South's rights, but 'let us not anticipate a threatened evil.' Lincoln was powerless; both Houses of Congress were against him; why disrupt the ties of Union when his hands were tied? Toombs had asked: 'Would we submit to Black Republican rule?' Stephens answered that he 'never would submit to Black Republican *aggression* upon our constitutional rights'; but new safeguards could be secured within the Union.

The Legislature should insist on the Georgia platform of 1850 — perfect equality between all the States. Georgia could withdraw if this were violated, but she must 'wait for an overt act of aggression.' There was now much talk of the personal liberty laws of certain Northern States, and some had 'violated their plighted faith.' But the question was newly raised and formal demand for redress had never been made on the faithless States.[12]

Stephens warned that the Legislature had no power to pass an Ordinance of Secession; it must refer the question to the people and must 'wait to hear from the men at the crossroads.' However much derided, Popular Sovereignty was the foundation of American institutions, the people had made the Constitution 'and they alone can rightfully unmake it.' 'I am afraid of conventions,' Toombs interjected. Stephens was afraid of none 'legally chosen by the people.' Toombs did not 'wish the people to be cheated.' Stephens thought Toombs' own proposition 'had a considerable smack of unfairness not to say cheat'; who in Georgia would vote 'submission to Abolition rule?'[13]

This onrushing revolution distressed President Buchanan and most of his Northern supporters, who had so long proclaimed the North altogether wrong in the sectional controversy that now they were caught in the net of their own emotional fixations. The Northerners who wrote Buchanan were chiefly men who had acquired their mental patterns decades earlier, and could regard the present scene only in the light of the past.

For example, Judge Woodward, of the Pennsylvania Supreme Court, who regarded himself 'a Northern man of common sense,' believed slavery was 'a special blessing to the people of the United States,' and wrote Attorney-General Black that he 'could not, in justice, condemn the South for withdrawing from the Union.' The truth was that the South had been 'loyal to the Union formed by the Constitution — Secession is not disloyalty to that, for that no longer exists — the North has extinguished it.' The Administration should urge the Southern States 'to bear and forbear a little longer,' but if they would not do so, 'let them go in peace — I wish Pennsylvania could go with them.'[14] The Attorney-General read this letter to the Cabinet,

[12] A listener shouted to Stephens that the argument was already exhausted. He countered that 'you have never called the attention of the Legislature of those States to this subject, that I am aware of.' The Reverend George Moore Payne, Kittery, Me., Jan. 12, 1861, Douglas MSS.; 'The South complains of grievances' but only a very few at the North know of what they do complain.

[13] *Harper's Pictorial History*, 1866; 19–21.

[14] Judge George W. Woodward to J. S. Black, Pittsburgh, Pa., Nov. 18, 1860; Black MSS. Woodward's belief was that the whole trouble sprang from the Abolitionists, 'with all those Boston infidels whom Unitarianism had thrown up to the surface.' Woodward was a United States District Judge from 1841 to 1851. Polk nominated him to a vacancy on the United States

where it 'excited universal admiration and *approbation* for its eloquence and its truth,' and the President was anxious to publish it to the world.[15]

The fact that Buchanan applauded such views, added to his irresolution, led Radical Republicans to say that he was almost as much involved in Secession as were Cobb, Thompson, Slidell and Yancey. These critics seldom gave sufficient weight to the inherent difficulties of Buchanan's situation. As Black saw it in November, if the President made any show of force, the Cotton States would 'all be in a blaze instantly.' If no force were used, and the early seceders could show the other Slave States 'the road to independence and freedom from Abolition rule without fighting their way,' each Slave State would before long secede. The North had already turned against Buchanan, and the South would do so as quickly as he refused to 'abandon his sworn duty of seeing the laws fully executed.' Even so, the Administration's conduct was so unsatisfactory that one of its former well-wishers wrote Franklin Pierce: 'Has there ever been such a dismal and disgraceful failure as that of Buchanan's Presidency?' [16]

But probably ineptitude more than turpitude bottomed Buchanan's course from Lincoln's election to inauguration. His sympathy for the Ultras was doubtless in large part sincerely felt. While his hatred of Douglas had made him the chief architect of the Democratic ruin, Buchanan never admitted his own part in it, for the dead hand of the past directed the mind of the President.

One memory should have served him — that of Andrew Jackson in the Nullification crisis. Buchanan had been, in his way, a Jacksonian; and the latter had written him: 'I met Nullification at its threshold.' [17] Douglas, Bell and their campaign speakers had charged and Buchanan was clearly warned of the Secession plan.

Late in October, Winfield Scott, General-in-Chief of the Army, laid before Buchanan his 'Views' of the situation. Its political section bordered on

Supreme Court, but Buchanan had another candidate and, Polk believed, caused Woodward's rejection by the Senate. Polk, *Diary*, I, 138-96. In 1852 Woodward went on the Pennsylvania Supreme Court. T. H. Seymour to Franklin Pierce, Hartford, Conn., Dec. 5, 1860; Pierce MSS.: 'The Union is about gone already.... We have deferred cutting throats long enough.... I should like to begin with Abolitionists at once.' John B. Floyd Diary, entry for Nov. 8, 1860, printed in E. A. Pollard. ('A Distinguished Southern Journalist'), *Robert E. Lee*, New York, 1871, 789 *et seq.*, relates a talk the Secretary of War had with Senator Lane, of Oregon, that day, in which Breckinridge's running-mate had said that nothing was now left to the South but 'resistance or dishonor.' When his own services would be useful, he would 'offer them unhesitatingly to the South!'

[15] Black to Woodward, Washington, Nov. 24, 1860; copy in Black MSS. Black wisely restrained publication. Furthermore, the Attorney-General made certain reservations to his own endorsement. Woodward had somewhat overstated the effect of Northern bigotry. The worst factor was 'that we now seem to have a majority in the Northern States of men who are perfectly willing to take advantage of any prejudice, whether they approve it or not, which will give them votes enough to carry them into power.'

[16] Black to Woodward, *cit. supra*: J. L. O'Sullivan to Pierce, New York, Feb. 7, 1861; Pierce MSS. *Harper's Pictorial History*, 18, quoted Laurence M. Keitt, a South Carolina Congressman, as declaring in a Washington speech in December that Buchanan 'was pledged to Secession and would be held to it.'

[17] Curtis, *James Buchanan*, I, 185, gives Jackson's letter to Buchanan.

the absurd, but its military advice was sound. There were nine important Federal fortresses within the Southern States, six of which were bare of troops, while the other three had only skeleton garrisons; let all be manned so that no surprise attack or *coup de main* could succeed. The President, however, paid no attention to this advice.[18]

But Buchanan was anxious. The day after the election he remarked that it looked as though disunion were inevitable; 'his reason told him there was great danger, yet his feelings repelled the convictions of his mind.' On November 9, at a Cabinet meeting, he brought up the 'alarming condition of the country,' and suggested a plan for calling a general Constitutional Convention to propose some compromise. Should the North decline, the South 'would stand justified before the whole world for refusing longer to remain in a Confederacy where her rights were so shamefully violated.'

All the members applauded this proposal, but on other points the division between North and South was basic. Cass advocated using force to prevent a State from seceding. Jeremiah Sullivan Black earnestly urged strengthening the garrisons at Charleston. Toucey and Holt sided with them. The Southern members were bitterly hostile to these ideas. Howell Cobb, who had been seconding Secession with 'earnestness, singleness of purpose and resolution,' told the Cabinet that he 'thought disunion inevitable and, under certain circumstances, most desirable.' Jacob Thompson warned that the first show of force would 'instantly make Mississippi a unit in favor of disunion.' John B. Floyd, the Virginia Secretary of War, was already negotiating to sell South Carolina ten thousand old Federal muskets.

At a Cabinet the next day Buchanan read an elaborate document which 'inculcated submission to Lincoln's election, and intimated the use of force' to halt Secession. This brought 'extravagant commendation' from Cass, Black, Holt and Toucey, but the Southerners violently dissented.[19] Cobb and Thompson telegraphed Jefferson Davis, who was in Mississippi, to come to Washington 'immediately' and he responded. When the President read him the message, Davis objected to certain sections, whereupon Buchanan 'very kindly' accepted all his modifications.[20]

On November 17, the President asked the Attorney-General's opinion as to the powers with which he was equipped to meet the emergency. Black

---

[18] Winfield S. Scott, 'Views,' New York, Oct. 29, 1860; printed in *Mr. Buchanan's Administration*, New York, 1866 (Buchanan's anonymously issued self-defense); 287 *et seq*. The nine forts were Moultrie and Sumter, at Charleston; Pickens and McRae, at Pensacola; Jackson and St. Philip, below New Orleans; Morgan, in Mobile Harbor; Pulaski, below Savannah, and Fortress Monroe, at Hampton Roads. *National Intelligencer*, Washington, Oct. 1, 1862, contains Buchanan's defense. *Ibid.*, Nov. 12, 1862, for Scott's reply.

[19] Floyd, Diary, entries for Nov. 7–10, inclusive. Cobb's views as of late October are given, W. H. Trescott to R. B. Rhett, Washington, Nov. 1, 1860, printed in Nicolay and Hay, II, 317–19. Trescott, a South Carolinian, was Assistant Secretary of State under Cass. For Floyd's negotiations with South Carolina representatives on the sale of Federal muskets, see Thomas F. Drayton to Governor Gist, Charleston, S.C., Nov. 3, 6, 8, 16; Washington, Nov. 19 (two letters), New York, Nov. 23; Trescott to Drayton, Washington, Nov. 19, 1860, Confederate Archives MSS. Texas had 'engaged 20,000 of these muskets.'

[20] Davis, *Rise and Fall*, I, 57–59.

replied later that the Constitution contained neither sanction for a State's Secession, nor legal means by which the Federal Government could coerce a State. But there was no question of the President's constitutional power to see to it that the laws were faithfully executed.[21]

About this time, Edwin M. Stanton, an able but excitable Pennsylvania Democratic lawyer, was asked to come to Washington to discuss the question: 'Can a State be coerced?' From the time of his arrival the President's resistance to the Secession group seemed to increase.[22]

Buchanan's message, read in Congress on December 4, was almost a mosaic of the conflicting views. It laid strong emphasis upon the wrongs which the South had endured at the hands of the North, and suggested a national convention to secure a remedial agreement. But those who founded the Government were not, 'at its creation, guilty of the absurdity of providing for its own dissolution.... Secession is neither more nor less than revolution.' The Federal Government had an unquestioned property right in her forts, magazines and arsenals in South Carolina, the commanding officer there had been ordered to act upon the defensive, and if attack should be made, 'the responsibility for the consequences would rightfully rest upon the assailants.' But the message ended with a long argument to prove that the United States had no constitutional authority to coerce a State. The message 'shows conclusively,' Senator Seward declared, 'that it is the duty of the President to execute the laws — unless somebody opposes it; and that no State has a right to go out of the Union — unless it wants to.'[23]

South Carolina's convention was not to be elected until December 6, and the delegates were not to assemble until December 17. But upon the exposure of Executive self-contradiction, the Palmetto State Legislature set to work in earnest giving secondary legal establishment to the Secession effort. The leaders of her revolution, insisting that the Federal Constitution sanctioned their conduct, sought to breach it in a most constitutional way. Under their theory, until the convention met and passed a formal ordinance, South Carolina would remain a part of the Union, and no official demand for surrender of the forts could be made.

Early in December some Charleston leaders began to fear that they had fired the public temper too quickly, and that a mob might try to overwhelm the handful of men in the forts. At this particular stage, such a move would bring prompt Federal reinforcements and the revolution might be nipped in

[21] *Opinions of the Attorneys-General*, Washington, v.d.; IX, 517; Curtis, *James Buchanan*, II, 321.

[22] *Atlantic Monthly*, XXVI, 468, quoting Henry L. Dawes in the Boston *Congregationalist*; 'Mr. Stanton was sent for by Mr. Buchanan to answer the question, "Can a State be coerced"?' Jacob Thompson to Howell Cobb, Washington, Jan. 16, 1861, Erwin MSS.: 'Old Buck, at heart, is right and with us. But after Stanton came in, I have seen him gradually giving way.' Trescott to Drayton, Washington, Nov. 19; Drayton to Gist, Washington, Nov. 19, 1860, Confederate Archives MSS.: Trescott advised Drayton, confidential agent of the State of South Carolina, that Buchanan would do 'what he believes to be his duty,' but that so long as Cobb and Thompson remained in the Cabinet, all might be 'confident that no action has been taken which seriously affects the position of any Southern State.'

[23] Richardson, *Messages*, V, 626–53; F. W. Seward, II, 480.

the bud. Governor Gist now assured the President that South Carolina desired no collision before separation, and urged him to send no reinforcements to the Charleston forts, otherwise on him would rest the responsibility 'of lighting the torch of discord.'

Buchanan acquiesced in Gist's informal truce, but not without inner turmoil. When a Federal warship returned unexpectedly from foreign station, the President toyed with the idea of sending her to Charleston with troops and supplies. The South Carolina Congressmen then called at the White House to promise that, 'provided' reinforcements were not sent, there would be no attack before legal separation. The Chief Executive agreed.

The Secretary of War then dispatched an officer to Charleston to instruct Major Anderson, in command of the Federal forts, that a collision must be avoided. The officer added that Washington felt assured no attack would be made, but none the less ordered Anderson to hold possession of the forts and. if attacked, to defend them 'to the last extremity.' The commander was also authorized, if he thought danger imminent, to concentrate his command into whichever fort he believed best defensible.

The Union men in Washington watched these scenes with growing anger. John A. McClernand concluded that Buchanan intended either to sacrifice Anderson's force or to use their defenseless situation to force Congress to recognize South Carolina's independence. 'The curses of all future ages will be heaped upon him,' the indignant Westerner exploded. 'God's grace could scarcely save him from endless and infinite damnation.' [24]

Howell Cobb now determined that the time had come for him to take the formal, public lead in the Secession movement. On December 6 he published an address asserting that, after March 4, the Federal Government would cease to have the slightest claim 'on the South's confidence or loyalty'; the time had come 'to announce and maintain your independence out of the Union, for you will never again have equality and justice in it.' Two days later he resigned. [25]

This dénouement must have shocked the President, for a day or so thereafter he startled Floyd by saying: 'I would rather be in the bottom of the Potomac tomorrow than that these forts in Charleston should fall into the hands of those who intend to take them. It will destroy me, Sir, and, Mr. Floyd, if that thing occurs it will cover your name with an infamy that all time can never efface, for it is in vain that you will attempt to show that you have not some complicity in handing over those forts to those who take them.' The Virginian was quick to summon assistance, and Jefferson Davis, Mason and Hunter, of Virginia, and others visited the White House to urge: 'Let there be no force.' At length the poor old man agreed to return to his prior policy. [26]

[24] Nicolay and Hay, II, 383–88; *O.R.*, I, 117; McClernand to Lanphier, Washington, Dec. 27, 1860; Patton MSS.

[25] Washington *Constitution*, Dec. 12, 1860, carried both Cobb's appeal to the South and his letter of resignation.

[26] Floyd's speech in Richmond, New York *Herald*, Jan. 17, 1861.

Lewis Cass, who, for all his years and his Buchanan service, was still a good Union man, demanded, at several Cabinet sessions, that the forts be strengthened. Buchanan finally answered that he would not do it, his mind was made up and he would take the responsibility. Cass promptly resigned.[27] This seemed to rouse the President to a sense of the danger in which he was placed because of his political and personal affection for the South and her leaders. He shifted Black to the State Department, named Edwin M. Stanton Attorney-General and there was a little more force in the Government.[28]

But this shift in focus was not achieved overnight. Jacob Thompson had not followed Cobb in resignation. When Mississippi appointed him its Commissioner to North Carolina, Senator Clingman was amazed that the President would permit a Cabinet officer to urge Secession, but Thompson insisted that his chief wished him to go and hoped he might succeed.[29]

By the time Congress met, the Legislatures of Mississippi, Florida and Alabama had ordered the election of Constitutional Conventions. Georgia's General Assembly had appropriated $1,000,000 to arm the State and had also called a delegate election. Governor Houston, of Texas, refused to summon an extra session, but the raging Ultras called an unofficial convention and prepared to throw legality to the wind. Many of the prime movers in the revolution employed the halls of the Capital as a sounding-board for a recital of the wrongs done the South. Reciting the schedule of convention dates for State action, Iverson, of Georgia, predicted that by the fourth of March, five Southern States would have declared their independence and three other Cotton States would soon follow. He warned, too, that if Houston did not yield, some Texas Brutus would arise 'to rid his country of the hoary-headed incubus.' Whatever happened, they were determined 'to go out — peaceably if we can, forcibly if we must.'[30]

Soon these Congressional Ultras announced that the argument was exhausted, 'all hope of relief in the Union extinguished,' and 'the honor, safety and independence of the Southern people required the organization of a Southern Confederacy.' Therefore 'the primary object of each slave-holding State ought to be its speedy and absolute separation from a Union with hostile States.'[31]

On December 17, South Carolina's Convention gathered at Columbia.

[27] Curtis, II, 397–98, for Cass-Buchanan correspondence. Philadelphia *Press*, March 4, 1883, has an interview with Jacob Thompson stating that Cass quickly regretted this action and asked Thompson to see the President to recall it.

[28] 'The Diary of a Public Man,' *North American Review*, CXXIX, 262, entry for Feb. 28. Hereafter to be referred to as 'Public Man.' The author of this diary is anonymous. Professor Frank M. Anderson, of Dartmouth, who has studied the authorship, thinks it was Amos Kendall. 'Public Man' had immense sources of information, and his diary constitutes an invaluable intimate record of Washington at this time.

[29] Clingman, *Speeches and Writings*, 526–27.

[30] *Congressional Globe*, Thirty-Sixth Congress, Second Session, 11 *et seq.*

[31] Washington *Constitution*, Dec. 15, 1860. About half the Southern Senators and Representatives signed this appeal. A startling document saw publication that same day — a proclamation from the President appointing January 4 a national day of humiliation.

An epidemic raging in that city occasioned an adjournment to Charleston, where the Ordinance of Secession — in form, the repeal of the resolution of adhesion to the Constitution in 1789 — was actually drafted and adopted. The historic moment came a little after noon on December 20. Then Rhett's *Mercury* issued an extra, bells rang, salute-guns thundered and a great parade signalized the news of the birth of the 'Independent Commonwealth of South Carolina.' For the final act of signing, the convention adjourned to Institute Hall, where eight months earlier the Democratic party had received its death thrust. There the Ordinance was signed with solemn and impressive ceremony.[32]

In Washington that afternoon James Buchanan laid aside the cares of state to attend the wedding ceremony of some young friends. There was some point in his going; the report was all over town that he was pale with fear and divided his time between weeping and praying, but he insisted to Mrs. Roger Pryor that he had 'not lost an hour's sleep nor a single meal.' The reception after the ceremony was disturbed by loud shouts outside. Mrs. Pryor found Laurence Keitt dancing around, wild with joy, shouting, 'Thank God! Oh! Thank God! South Carolina has seceded. Here's the telegram. I feel like a boy let out of school.' Hastily re-entering the room, she whispered to the President, who looked stunned, fell back in his chair and gasped for his carriage to be called. A moment more and he was on his way to the White House, the picture of despair.[33]

This confronted the President quite directly with disunion. Perhaps it also meant war, for it terminated the unofficial truce and Buchanan did not know at what moment the authorities of the State might undertake to storm the forts in Charleston Harbor. Francis W. Pickens, who had succeeded to the governorship the day the convention met, sent word to the President that, unless the Federal Government would cease improvements on the forts and would surrender Sumter, the Governor could not 'answer for the consequences.'

Buchanan had dispatched Caleb Cushing to South Carolina, to forestall the dread Act of Secession. The President's agent reached Charleston the day that the convention voted the Ordinance. Governor Pickens told him bluntly there was no hope for the Union. Cushing's cup of humiliation overflowed when the Secessionists requested him to take part in their pageant, and he returned to Washington giving every evidence 'of having been broken down by sheer fright.' [34]

The South Carolina Convention now dispatched three Commissioners to Washington to negotiate for the transfer of Federal property in the State. News of their appointment alarmed Douglas and his aides, who expected that of course the President would refuse to receive them, which would precipitate an overt act by South Carolina. Then Governor Wise, of Virginia, and his men would 'march on Washington and seize it.' 'Don't be

---

[32] 'Bulletin No. 1,' Charleston *Mercury*, Dec. 20, 1860, issued at one-fifteen P.M.

[33] Mrs. Pryor, *Reminiscences*, 110–13. New York *Tribune*, Dec. 17, 1860.

[34] Nicolay and Hay, III, 6–13. 'Public Man,' 132, terms Cushing's mission 'a most mischievously foolish performance.'

deceived,' McClernand wrote Lanphier, 'civil war is immediately impending.'

Even so, many believed that the most prominent of the three Commissioners, former Speaker James L. Orr, was 'honestly trying to make the best of what he felt to be a wretched business.' They arrived in Washington expecting to be received by the President. The latter's state of mind at this time was pitiable; he 'could not and would not know the fact' of South Carolina's separation, yet a White House intimate soon told the Commissioners that the Chief Executive 'would receive them and confer with them,' and an hour was appointed for their call.[35] But strange news from Charleston caused postponement.

The Secession city had been full of rumors of scaling ladders being prepared for a descent on Moultrie. Major Anderson felt there was imminent danger, and on the night of December 26, he transferred his meager forces to Sumter, in the middle of the harbor; although unfinished, it was a powerful fortification and in it even a handful might resist successfully. The Secessionists were wild with anger. Governor Pickens sent a demand that Anderson return to Moultrie, which that officer declined.[36]

Men were 'paralyzed' when this news reached Washington. 'War is upon us,' McClernand wrote gloomily. In view of Buchanan's flabbiness, all acquitted him of having ordered the sudden movement. Douglas heard that Ben Wade and kindred Radical Republicans, as anxious as the Secessionists to prevent compromise, had intrigued with some of Anderson's subordinates. But Douglas added that Lincoln was 'incapable of such an act.' Others thought Floyd had deliberately given orders to make an armed explosion inevitable, so as to draw in the Border States.[37]

The South Carolina Commissioners sent word to the President that the Government had broken its pledge. The Secretary of War demanded that Anderson be ordered back to Moultrie. Black, Holt, and Stanton resisted stoutly and Buchanan wavered irresolutely. Floyd was spurred by more than Southern sympathies. That week his part in breaches of trust involving almost a million dollars had been disclosed, and Buchanan had promptly asked him to resign. This Charleston tempest now afforded him excuse to pitch his departure upon grounds of principle, and on December 28 he resigned, claiming that the President had subjected him 'to a violation of solemn pledges and plighted faith.' [38]

[35] McClernand to Lanphier, Washington, Dec. 25, 1860; Patton MSS. Orr's associates were R. W. Barnwell and J. H. Adams. 'Public Man,' 129, thought that Orr, who called on him on Dec. 28, was 'at heart as good a Union man as anybody in Connecticut or New York.' Thompson to Cobb, Washington, Jan. 16, 1861; Erwin MSS.

[36] 'Public Man,' 126. Samuel Wylie Crawford, The Genesis of the Civil War, New York 1887; 102–12, for details of Moultrie-Sumter transfer.

[37] McClernand to Lanphier, Washington, Dec. 27, 1860; Patton MSS. 'Public Man,' 1860, 126–30; in Douglas' remarks to 'Public Man,' he added: 'Besides, it is quite incompatible with what I have heard from him' — hastily checked himself to amend 'what I have heard of his program.' Seward told Orr that Anderson's movement was a mistake, and that he was anxious for pressure to be brought on Buchanan to order Anderson back to Moultrie. Ibid., 262, for Floyd rumor.

[38] Rhodes, III, 123–28. The peculations arose from the financial difficulties of a firm of

A blending of weakness and obstinacy, mixed with an apparent enjoyment of dissimulation and petty craft, were particularly prominent in Buchanan's actions at this critical period. He now asked Postmaster-General Holt to add the War Department to his regular assignment. Jacob Thompson took his resignation to the White House and placed it in Buchanan's hands, telling him that Holt's appointment meant 'the adoption of his line of policy, which makes my withdrawal a necessity.' 'Not at all,' said Buchanan, who promised that 'no order should be issued without being first considered and decided in Cabinet.' [39]

The Unionists in Washington would not believe that Buchanan would so compromise the Federal dignity as to receive the South Carolina Commissioners. When someone hinted it, Douglas retorted: 'He will never dare to do that.' His informant persisted. 'If there is such a rumor afoot,' Douglas countered, 'it was put afoot by him, Sir; by his own express proceedings. He likes to have people deceived in him — he enjoys treachery, Sir, enjoys it as other men do a good cigar — he likes to sniff it up, Sir, to relish it.' [40]

But Buchanan had only postponed his appointment with Orr and his associates until he could learn what had happened at Charleston. By December 28, when he did receive them, Washington had learned that the Charleston Arsenal had been seized, Moultrie and Pinckney had been stormed and batteries were being built to bear on Sumter. None the less, the President told the South Carolinians that he would transmit their request to Congress. The Commissioners, however, announced with truculence that South Carolina could enter into no conversation until Sumter had been surrendered.

Buchanan submitted this demand to his Cabinet and read the draft of his proposed answer, reiterating his lack of power to coerce, disavowing Anderson's movement and regretting that the Commissioners had suspended negotiations. Black, Holt and Stanton listened with amazement, but found the President inflexibly determined. That night they counseled, and the next morning Black informed the Northern Cabinet members that both he and Stanton were determined to resign. When Toucey took this news to the White House, Buchanan crumpled, sent for Black and gave him permission to criticize and modify the answer. In the resulting memorandum, Black opposed the reiteration of any non-coercion doctrine, insisted that the President contradict the idea that he had made a pledge to South Carolina, reprehended the failure to strengthen Sumter and said that Anderson, who

---

Army contractors, for whose aid Floyd gave War Department acceptances for services yet unperformed. When these transactions came to Buchanan's attention in the Spring of 1860, Floyd promised him to issue no more, but did not keep his word. Later, there was a crisis and to prevent Floyd's 'retirement in disgrace,' one of his relatives, a confidential clerk in the Interior Department, substituted $870,000 of the War Department acceptances for Indian trust bonds. Buchanan learned of the theft December 22 and asked Floyd to resign. The ex-Secretary was later indicted for 'malversation in office,' but the indictment was quashed on a minor flaw. Black thought him merely recklessly imprudent. He gained no cent from the affair. Nicolay and Hay, III, 65–75, for Cabinet crisis.

[39] Thompson to Cobb, Washington, Jan. 16, 1861; Erwin MSS.
[40] 'Public Man,' 130.

had 'saved the country when its day was darkest and its perils most extreme,' must not be repudiated.

Although under this spur Buchanan amended his response, his letter had an apologetic tone, referring again to his willingness to submit South Carolina's claims to Congress. But it did refuse to withdraw the troops, and proclaimed it the President's duty 'to defend Fort Sumter as a portion of the public property of the United States against hostile attacks from whatever quarter they may come.' [41]

Now Buchanan sent word to Orr that if the demands were rephrased so as to accord the President a proper respect, he was disposed to accede to them. The South Carolinians rewrote their letter, Buchanan's confidential agent approved it and on January 3 sent it on to the White House. Jacob Thompson now submitted the rough draft of a message the President could send to Congress transmitting South Carolina's demands. Howell Cobb, foreseeing the Charleston complications, had sketched out and sent to Thompson the sort of message he would like dispatched. But the Mississippian found that, whatever the President's agreement with their views, he 'had not the nerve and backbone' to do so.

What destroyed Buchanan's 'nerve and backbone'? Perhaps it was fresh pressure from the Northern members of the Cabinet: 'Neither Black, Holt nor Stanton have any common sense,' Thompson wrote Cobb, 'and hence all of the President's difficulties.' Furthermore, Buchanan had 'the horrors for fear of impeachment,' and the withdrawal of Southern Senators would make it all the easier to be done. At any event, the Commissioners' letter was returned to them, with an unsigned endorsement that the President declined to receive it. Believing themselves both duped and insulted, they prepared a sulphurous response recounting Buchanan's duplicity and departed for Charleston. [42]

Upon Holt's advent at the War Office, Sumter was discussed again and the Cabinet decided 'to send a messenger to Major Anderson to learn his true condition and wishes.' General Scott convinced Holt that a steamer carrying recruits and supplies 'could steal into Sumter without discovery or collision' — if the movement could be kept secret. They kept their plans from the Cabinet, for, as Thompson soon wrote Cobb, 'they all knew I would resign for such an order and thus blow the order.' A commercial steamer, the *Star of the West*, was secretly chartered in New York and two hundred recruits and supplies were put on board. It was three or four days before Holt could get the President to say the final word, but on January 5 the ship sailed. Thompson found out about it and the night before the relief steamer arrived off Charleston sent word to the South Carolinians to be prepared. He likewise charged that the President and Holt had 'played the meanest trick on me in the world,' and resigned. [43]

[41] *O.R.*, I, 118, for text of Buchanan's reply, dated Dec. 31, 1860. J. S. Black, *Essays and Speeches*, New York, 1871, 14–17, prints his memorandum to Buchanan, Dec. 30, 1860.

[42] Thompson to Cobb, Washington, Jan. 16, 1861; Erwin MSS.: 'I sketched out a programme of a message for the President to write according entirely with your suggestions in your letter.' 'Public Man,' 132–33; 269.

[43] Thompson to Cobb, Washington, Jan. 16, 1861; Erwin MSS.

The South Carolinians had been working feverishly on Morris Island, constructing a battery to command the ship channel, but did not have it in shape for service until January 6. Early on January 9 the *Star of the West* began feeling its way toward Sumter. The new battery fired a warning shot but the side-wheeler put on full steam. The Stars and Stripes were hoisted to the masthead, the hail of shells increased. At length Moultrie's batteries opened up. Anderson and his officers rushed to the Sumter parapet; should they now open on Moultrie and thus begin the Civil War? Before they could reach a decision, the *Star of the West* turned and made for the sea.[44]

All this while, the Secession effort had gone forward in nearly every Cotton *Pickin'* State. As will be seen, the velocity of their program was intensified by Republican rejection of the Crittenden Compromise. Furthermore the Immediate Separationists had an unofficial general staff, a quasi-official diplomatic corps and an effective plan of campaign. They were immensely aided by the velocity with which public feeling swept from discussion to emotional hysteria. In addition, the Co-operationists, having widely variant purposes and programs, and being sneered at as 'Submissionists' and 'galvanized Republicans,' were distinctly on the defensive.

In November the State Commissioners were the active Secession managers; the next month the Cotton State Senators and Congressmen assumed the formal leadership. By early January this group worked out a three-phase program: each State should be seceded with all possible dispatch; a convention at Montgomery, not later than February 15, should organize a Southern Confederacy; the South's Senators and Representatives should remain in Congress until March 4, to 'keep the hands of Mr. Buchanan tied,' and prevent the Republicans from strengthening the incoming Administration.[45]

There was some doubt that the members of this Secession staff had any agreement upon ultimate plan and purpose.[46] But whatever their inward doubts, the program was given immediate application. It was, however, modified in one particular. The leaders in the States laid such stress on constitutional Secession that they objected to members remaining in Congress after their State had quitted the Federal tie. The Washington cabal yielded, and the halls of the Capitol resounded with the swan songs of departing members.

Mississippi's hotheads were 'hurrying over the precipice of irretrievable ruin,' and by early December her Conservatives lost hope of stemming the

---

[44] Crawford, 123; 136–37; Nicolay and Hay, III, 87–101.

[45] D. L. Yulee to Joseph Finegan, Washington, Jan. 7, 1861, *O.R.*, I, 443–44. These resolutions were signed by Davis and Brown, of Mississippi; Hemphill and Wigfall, of Texas; Slidell and Benjamin, of Louisiana; Iverson and Toombs, of Georgia; Johnson, of Arkansas; Clay, of Alabama, and Yulee and Mallory, of Florida. Davis, Slidell and Mallory were to carry them into effect. 'Public Man,' 264, quotes a statement of Benjamin early in January 'that the Confederate Congress would assemble at Montgomery before Feb. 15, and choose a President, so that Lincoln should find himself confronted, when he took oath in March, by a complete government, extending at least over eight States, and offering peace or war to his choice.'

[46] 'Public Man,' 133–34.

torrent. The delegate campaign was listless, the vote was small and only about a dozen counties sent Co-operationist delegates. One who observed the State Convention at Jackson concluded that 'Wise men are fools, fools laugh and folly rules the hour.' The Ordinance of Secession swept through the convention and on January 9, Mississippi claimed to be an independent State.[47] The next day Florida 'resumed her freedom,' by a vote of 62 to 7.

Alabama's delegate election was poorly attended, the people seemed to regard Secession as a 'foregone conclusion' and Ultra candidates won by default in many counties. John Forsyth felt that, with Douglas' defeat, the Union cause had been lost. Had only there been 'some great soul to rally and lead the South,' it would not have rushed blindly into Secession. But 'our leaders are the authors of the public mischief and are themselves on trial. I have the feeling, but God has not endowed me with the power equal to so grand an epoch.'[48]

The center of opposition was in the Tennessee Valley area, where the people demanded that the convention submit its Ordinance to a general plebiscite. Indeed, Clement Clay's home county instructed its delegates to withdraw 'if the Ordinance of Secession was not submitted' to a popular vote.[49]

In the convention tests, the Conservatives mustered 45 votes to 54 for the Secessionists. When the Ordinance was passed, a few Conservatives signed it to prevent 'serious divisions among the people,' but thirty-nine delegates refused to sign it because no referendum by the people had been provided. Jere Clemens said bluntly that the Ordinance was 'treason,' but he was a son of Alabama and would 'walk into revolution' with her.

Alabama's Ordinance also called a meeting of delegates representing all the Slave States to be held at Montgomery on February 4. Though designed for the definite purpose of forming a Southern Confederacy, some of the Alabama Conservatives hoped against hope that this Congress might result in a request for redress of grievances and thus hold open the door to reunion.[50]

Georgia was the real key to the Southern revolution. She had quite a contest over the election of delegates and her Conservatives fought on to the end. Georgia, however, was affected by the velocity with which Secession feeling developed. The people were 'frenzied by the politicians,' and the Ultras began discussing what quality of rope to use when they lynched Alexander H. Stephens.[51]

[47] J. S. Johnson, Carrollton, Miss., Dec. 11; B. N. Kinyon, Jacinto, Dec. 17, 1860; J. W. Williams, Holly Springs, Jan. 18, 1861; Douglas MSS.; Dumond, 200.

[48] John Forsyth, Mobile, Dec. 28, 1860. Geo. W. Lamar, Augusta, Jan. 19, 1861; Douglas MSS. He was opposed to the State's Secession, had seven sons who would be involved, all his property was in Negroes and land, but if the Ordinance passed, 'then I am for it — right or wrong, as a duty which I owe to Georgia.'

[49] H. L. Clay to C. C. Clay, Huntsville, Jan. 11, 1861; Clay MSS.

[50] Journal of the Constitutional Convention of the State of Alabama, Montgomery, 1861; 72–80. J. W. Lapsley, Selma, Ala., Jan. 14, 1861; Douglas MSS.

[51] Journal of the Mississippi Convention... 1861, 197, report of Judge W. L. Harris, Mississippi State Commissioner to Georgia. Robert Collins, Macon, Ga., Jan. 12, 1861; Dr. T. S. Powell, Atlanta, Dec. 25; J. A. Stewart, Atlanta, Dec. 25; L. S. Bennett, Savannah, Dec. 26, 1860; Douglas MSS.

Although some doubt was thrown upon the fairness of the delegate elections, many of the State's most distinguished leaders were elected to the convention. Leading the battle for immediate Secession were Robert Toombs, Howell Cobb, Senator Iverson and Governor Joseph E. Brown. Ranged against them were Alexander H. Stephens and his brother Linton; Benjamin H. Hill, just budding into fame, and Herschel V. Johnson. When a resolution for immediate Secession was introduced, Herschel V. Johnson proposed a substitute calling for consultation at a conference of all the Slave States and including a program of safeguards and reforms. But the Immediate Separationists would brook no compromise. They cut off debate on Johnson's motion by demanding the previous question, which they carried by a vote of 166 to 130.

The struggle continued a few days longer. Milledgeville was tense with excitement, men were armed and anything might happen. Stephens tried to argue, but was cried down from the galleries and the floor. On the night of the final debate, young girls were warned not to go to the Capitol, because riot and bloodshed were likely. The Ordinance carried by 208 to 89, and there was a great parade. Herschel V. Johnson knelt in the home of a friend, praying for the folly of the people of his State.[52]

Cobb's friends advised him that the South's gratitude would soon be 'evinced in a manner gratifying to you and honorable to them.' The Georgia Convention appointed him at the head of its delegation to the convention at Montgomery, where he was expected to be chosen President of the forming Confederacy. But a brave editor in LaGrange could not forgive the way 'we have been fifed and drummed and voted out of the Union.'[53]

Louisiana had formerly been regarded as a Conservative State. Wherever they were strong, the Douglas men exerted their influence, with fair success, to elect Conservative delegates, and determined to insist both upon a convention of the States for joint action and on a referendum, believing the Union 'certain of a majority of the popular vote.'[54] By the time her convention assembled, however, five Cotton States had seceded, the ground was cut from beneath the Conservatives' feet, and the Ordinance of Secession passed by a large vote. The Ultras jubilated that the Yankees were 'all a set of cringing cowards' who would fight only when there was money in it.[55]

Houston's obstinacy forced the Texas Secessionists to a long delay. As soon as the Legislature met in regular session, he was pushed out of the way,

[52] For suspicion of delegate election fraud, see *Journal of the Convention of the People of Georgia, 1861*, 27, giving vote of 168 to 127, rejecting resolution of inquiry. Thompson to Cobb, Washington, Jan. 16, 1861; Erwin MSS. New York *Tribune*, Jan. 21, 1861, Milledgeville correspondence. Personal recollections of Mrs. Sarah Fort Milton: she was warned not to attend the final debate for there would be bloodshed that night. Her two younger brothers marched in the Secession parade, her elder brother and her mother stayed at home. Governor Johnson visited them there, the lights were extinguished and the three knelt together in prayer.

[53] A. C. Magrath to Cobb, Charleston, S.C., Jan. 18, 1861; Erwin MSS. James Patillo, Camilla, Ga., Feb. 12, 1861; Douglas MSS. LaGrange, Ga., *Reporter*, Jan. 25, clipped in *National Intelligencer*, Washington, Feb. 6, 1861.

[54] Thomas Cottman, Donaldsville, La., Jan. 13, 1861; Douglas MSS.

[55] *Official Journal, Proceedings of the Convention of the State of Louisiana, 1861*, 5–18. Jane Martin Johns, *Personal Recollections, 1849–1865*, Decatur, Ill., 1912; 88 *et seq.*

the Ultras' irregular acts were legalized and a convention was called. This met on January 28 and the next day declared the State free.[56]

During the interval between the passage of these ordinances and the assembly of the Congress at Montgomery, each Governor employed his military forces to seize whatever Federal property he could find. Fort after fort went into possession of the Secessionists, until finally only four remained in Federal hands. Appropriations flowed from the Legislatures, arms were bought and volunteers enrolled. 'We are in the hands of the revolutionary cabals,' wrote an Alabaman who a year before had been in the van but was now left far behind. 'It is red against Black Republicans.' [57]

All was now set for the final scene. On February 4 the delegates from six Cotton States gathered at Montgomery. The only debate was on the quickest way to form a new government. Howell Cobb was made Chairman of the convention. Committees were appointed to draft a Provisional Constitution, which was modeled upon the Federal Constitution being abandoned. Within three days this document was presented to the convention and became the charter for the governance of the 'Confederate States of America.' [58]

The great question, of course, was who would be President of the new republic. Georgia expected this honor; the Empire State of the South, she had been the most reluctant of the Cotton States to go with Secession; in Howell Cobb, Robert Toombs and Alexander H. Stephens, she had probably the three ablest figures in Southern life. But she also had division of strength as to the claims of Cobb and Toombs, a schism which proved fatal — plus, it was rumored, a heavy drinking bout of the brilliant but unstable Toombs on the night before the election. South Carolina took the lead in urging another, Georgia's claims were passed by and Jefferson Davis, of Mississippi, was unanimously elected. As a sop to Georgia, Stephens was made Vice-President.

Still the gentlemen at Montgomery seemed persuaded that the Union could be broken without calling upon the god of battles. They soon chose three commissioners to visit Washington to negotiate for the surrender of Federal property, naming as their leader John Forsyth, of Mobile. Forsyth accepted the commission without much hope, for he knew that 'a giant union could not be broken without a giant struggle.' The general view, however, was that expressed by T. R. R. Cobb, in a letter to his wife saying that the chances were 'decidedly against war. There may be a little collision and confusion, but no bloody war.' [59]

---

[56] J. J. Dickson, McKinney, Tex., Jan. 9, 1861; Douglas MSS. The Texas Convention vote was 166 to 8. An election, held some time later, approved Secession, 146,129 to 14,697.

[57] A. M. Samford, letter to Tuskegee, Ala., *Republican*, clipped in *National Intelligencer*, Washington, Feb. 6, 1861.

[58] Under it the President was to serve a seven-year term, and be ineligible for re-election. 'We the people' was omitted and it was made a Confederacy of States, sovereign and independent. It did not say anything about the rights of Secession or deny coercion. Its Provisional Congress was to be made up of the members of the convention itself!

[59] John Forsyth, Mobile, Ala., Dec. 28, 1860, Douglas MSS., for expression cited. T. R. R. Cobb to Mrs. Cobb, Montgomery, Feb. 7, 1861; Southern Historical Association *Publications*, 1907.

CHAPTER XXXI

LINCOLN REJECTS COMPROMISE

PROBABLY no division point in the human record is harder to determine than that at which an event moved across the threshold of choice to the area of certainty. It would seem that, prior to the disruption of the Democracy, civil war was not inevitable. Except for the weight of Administration influence in Southern Democratic conventions, together with the President's prostitution of his office and power to corrupt and seduce Northern delegates, Douglas would almost certainly have been nominated at Charleston by two-thirds of the electoral college strength, Bell would have withdrawn and the campaign between Douglas and Lincoln would have been clear-cut.

As it was, while everyone recognized the certainty of Lincoln's election, nearly a million and a half Northern men cast their votes for the Little Giant. Had Douglas, the non-interventionist, with a program of gradual economic and social adjustment, confronted Lincoln, the interventionist, on his doctrine of 'House Divided,' it seems almost too plain for argument that the former would have become President. In that event there would have occurred no immediate Secession or appeal to arms.

But these might-have-beens belong to the hypothetics of history. Another group of probabilities arises as to the compromises refused during the short session of the Thirty-Sixth Congress. In view of the imponderables of party constraints and emotions, it is probable that Lincoln's election reduced the chances for peaceful maintenance of the Union to a minor fraction, somewhere from a tenth to a third, of what they had been before the Democratic break-up. And yet until the firing on Sumter the Northern people did not consent to coercion. Up to Lincoln's inauguration, a large majority in that section applauded the various projects of compromise, and if given the opportunity, it seems almost certain that the North would have approved either the Crittenden, Douglas or Corwin compromise by overwhelming vote.

The North's great merchants, bankers and industrialists were panic-stricken at the prospect of Secession and war. The South began severing commercial ties, orders were canceled, and Eastern factors, wholesalers and bankers faced the prospect of the loss of the many millions normally carried, as the South was a heavy importer of short-term capital. This 'derangement of business' brought Republican businessmen up short.

'"Almighty Dollar" is beginning to raise its voice higher than public sentiment,' de Rothschild noted early in December. 'The factories are closing down from lack of work, trade has ceased and thousands of laborers are without employment.' 'The political revolution' had already taken place, and the Baron's Continental background led him to expect that a real war 'of the proletarian without work against the proprietor' would follow.[1]

[1] Baron de Salomon de Rothschild to his wife, New York, Dec. 14, 1860; Rothschild MSS. The Baron was convinced that a fatal flaw in the Federal Constitution was the idea that political

These events had a great effect on the minds of the people. In December 'Boston, by the ballot box, spoke for peace,' and the Democrats carried elections in several other cities that had gone heavily for Lincoln the month before. New York was disturbed. Eminent men addressed conciliation meetings, and Mayor Fernando Wood actually proposed that New York City secede with the South, to become a free port of entry like Bremen or Hamburg.[2] Apart from its army of office-holders, many of whom were waiting the chance to jump the fence, Mr. Buchanan's 'Constitutional Democracy' was of slight importance in forming the Northern mind.[3] The Douglas Democrats, however, were of major consequence. Events had somewhat disorganized them. Some were of the mind of John A. Logan and sympathized with the Secession program; a much larger number agreed with the clearer-visioned Lanphier that 'we must not be put in the fix of antagonism to the Union in any shape.'

They thought Buchanan had blundered badly, but agreed that it was better to let resistance by force come from the Seceders, and would favor no program of force until negotiation had been clearly exhausted. 'The Democracy are for the Union and are in favor of giving to the South all the rights they are entitled to by virtue of the Constitution,' Sheahan wrote Douglas, interpreting the feeling of the Northern Democracy. They were willing to go further and define these rights more exactly through constitutional amendment — 'but this must be done in the Union.' August Belmont felt that conciliation alone could save the Border, any other policy involved 'complete disintegration,' but if conciliation failed he would reluctantly grasp the sword.[4]

Before mid-December, the Little Giant and his intimates concluded that, if the Border States could be saved, the Union would endure and the seceders would return 'slowly but certainly.' They saw clearly that the Secession of the States controlling the mouth of the Mississippi River would be a major

power could be entrusted to the people without their surely seeking economic power to complete it: 'If for years you have tried to win the popular masses,... if you have said and repeated a thousand times, and convinced them that they are... the infallible sovereigns, how will you prove to them now that they are wrong... in making themselves master of your possessions?'

[2] Newburyport, Mass., petition to Congress, copy in Douglas MSS., Feb. 4, 1861. Curtis, II, 354; Channing, VI, 292. 'Public Man,' 140, quotes Lincoln's apt remark to him on Wood's fantastic proposition: 'I reckon it will be some time before the front door sets up housekeeping for itself.' Hamilton Fish to Senator William Pitt Fessenden, New York, Dec. 11, 1860; Fessenden MSS., Library of Congress. The Reverend Henry J. Van Dyke, 'The Character and Influence of Abolitionism,' Sermon, Brooklyn, Dec. 9, 1860, Pamphlet, is an index of Northern reaction against the Abolitionists, 'chief cause of the present strife.' Richard Vaux, Philadelphia, Dec. 12, 1860, Douglas MSS.

[3] Black to Woodward, Washington, Nov. 24, 1860; copy in Black MSS.

[4] 'Public Man,' 139-40; Virgil Hickox, Springfield, Ill., Jan. 8, 1861; Douglas MSS.; Lanphier to McClernand, Springfield, Dec. 19, 1860; McClernand MSS.; John W. Krum, St. Louis, Dec. 19, 1860; Douglas MSS.; Sheahan, Chicago, Dec. 17; Belmont to Herschel V. Johnson, New York, Dec. 30; to Douglas, Dec. 31, 1860, Feb. 11, 1861; Douglas MSS. Belmont to John Forsyth, New York, Nov. 22, Dec. 19, 1860; *Belmont Correspondence*, privately printed, 1890: 23-25; 36-39.

disaster to the Northwest, which could not 'submit to disunion except as an unavoidable necessity.'

Douglas himself was particularly emphatic that the Northwest must 'never acknowledge the *right of a State to secede and cut us off from the ocean and the world, without our consent.*' He knew that the prospects were gloomy and that the hope of compromise was faint. None the less, he would refuse to invoke force 'until all efforts at peaceable adjustment have been made and have failed.'

But while Douglas did 'not yet despair of the Union,' the first three weeks of Congress convinced him that the real obstacle to effective adjustment was the Republican party. Many of their leaders thought they could maintain 'a permanent Republican ascendancy in the Northern States, but not in the whole Union!' Because of this they 'desired war and disunion under the pretext of saving the Union' — if only it could be done 'without making them responsible before the people.'[5]

The Little Giant was quite right that upon the Republicans depended the success or failure of compromise. 'The Republican party today is as uncompromising as the Secessionists in South Carolina,' Senator Seward wrote Thurlow Weed at the opening of Congress.[6] 'This inflexibility resulted from no new evidences of Northern approval of the Chicago platform.[7] Rather, the Republican lieutenants and drill sergeants, who were expecting the loaves and fishes of Federal office, feared that any compromise of the platform would probably destroy their party, and were determined that at all hazards the party be preserved. This they demanded of their Senators and Representatives in Washington, and these yielded, some quite willingly, to their importunities.

The Republicans had discounted Douglas' Secession warnings as campaign rodomontade, and seemed unable to comprehend the effect the election of the author of the House Divided doctrine would have on the Southern mind. But when the victorious minority realized that the Cotton States meant business, three different reactions developed.

One group had such a horror of war that it favored peaceable separation. Horace Greeley, for example, could not bear the thought of one section of the country 'pinned to the residue by bayonets.' *Tribune* editorials declared that whenever the fifteen Slave States, or even eight Cotton States, made up their minds to retire, 'we shall insist that they be permitted to go in peace.' Henry Ward Beecher said at Boston that he did not care if the Cotton States departed. The day before Lincoln's inauguration, Senator Sumner said that 'nothing would be so horrible, so wicked or so senseless as a war.' This group

---

[5] *Illinois State Register*, Dec. 4, 1860; Douglas reached Washington Dec. 1. McClernand to Lanphier, Washington, Dec. 10, 25, and n.d., 1860; Patton MSS.; Douglas to Lanphier, Washington, Dec. 25, 1860; Patton MSS. Illinois Democracy faithfully carried out the Douglas instructions. A State convention on Jan. 16 adopted strong compromise, Union resolutions. *Illinois State Register*, Jan. 22, 1861.

[6] Seward to Weed, Washington, Dec. 3, 1860; quoted in Weed, II, 308.

[7] J. W. Kane, Pittsburgh, Pa., Dec. 22, 1860; Douglas MSS.: 'The Republican party would not have a majority today in any State of the Union if the election were to come off tomorrow.'

disliked the idea of coercing a State, and felt that the practical difficulties were staggering. Federal Judges had resigned, Federal Grand Juries would not serve, collectors, attorneys and other functionaries were absent; how practicable was it to send Massachusetts men to serve as South Carolina grand jurors?[8]

Another Republican segment desired some compromise to maintain the Union without war. Thurlow Weed, a man of more depth than Seward, his *alter ego*, began a public campaign for compensation for fugitive slaves, and for the restoration of the Missouri Compromise line. The New York *Times* and the *Courier and Enquirer* advocated Weed's plan. Important Republican merchants organized a 'conciliatory demonstration,' to put squarely on 'the more Extreme Republicans' full responsibility for 'any disastrous result.' Thus a large and growing Republican section was 'anxious to settle the whole party matter by any concession not too wounding to pride nor destructive to all claim of consistency.'[9]

But a third element was equally unwilling 'to let the wayward sisters depart in peace' or to yield the Chicago platform. Some thought that, as Lincoln had been honorably elected, it was up to the South to accept him; many feared that any compromise of Republican doctrine would precipitate party disaster. Many men in the North regarded Secession as treason, and lauded the example of Andrew Jackson. These men's vocabulary, however, was also employed by the party mechanicians. Most of these desired some formula by which the Republican party could preserve both the Union and itself. But if they must choose between saving the party, at the cost of civil war, and saving the Union through sacrificing the party, they placed party first.

No sooner had Weed begun his editorials than protests flowed in that compromise 'would be fatal,' that to hold any parley with slavery would mean 'lowering our flag, giving up our principles and *destroying the Republican party.*' To compromise, the Republican Senators and Representatives were warned, 'would lay us out colder than a wedge.' 'The Republican pulse beats high for war,' a second reported, 'but a backdown to Traitors and Slavery will ruin our party and prospects.' The whole idea of compromise, one man wrote Senator Trumbull, had been 'concocted purposely to bring about the destruction of the Republican party.' Any departure from the Chicago platform, insisted another, 'would be the annihilation of the party.'[10]

[8] New York *Tribune*, Nov. 9, 16, 19, for Greeley editorials; *ibid.*, Nov. 30, 1860, for quotation of Beecher's speech in Boston, Nov. 27. 'Public Man,' 278, for Sumner's statement.

[9] For Weed plan see New York *Tribune*, Nov. 27; Albany *Evening Journal*, Nov. 30, Dec. 1; New York *Times*, Nov. 28, Dec. 1; New York *Courier and Enquirer*, Nov. 26, Dec. 4, 1860; Hamilton Fish to W. P. Fessenden, New York, Dec. 11, 1860; Fessenden MSS.; E. B. Hart to Howell Cobb, New York, Dec. 20, 1860; Erwin MSS.

[10] A. P. Granger to 'Friend Weed,' Syracuse, N.Y., Dec. 1, 1860; for copy, I am indebted to Mr. Franklin J. Meine, of Chicago Book and Art Auctions, Inc.; italics author's. C. K. Judson, Freeport, Ill., Jan. 17, 1861, Alvin Armstrong, Boston, Feb. 12, 1861; Washburne MSS., Library of Congress. Coleman Gaines and John H. Crow, Pleasant Plains, Ill., Feb. 22, 1861; Wait Talcott, Mattoon, Ill., Dec. 16, 1860; Trumbull MSS.

As soon as Congress received the President's message, the Conservatives, with Crittenden and Douglas in the lead, sought machinery for compromise. The House move was first. On December 5, Boteler, of Virginia, moved and by a vote of 145 to 38 the House authorized a Select Committee of one member from each State. Every negative vote was cast by Republicans, an ominous portent. Pennington, the Republican Speaker, named no Northern Douglas Democrats on this Committee of Thirty-Three, selected only two Bell men from the Border, and wherever possible appointed Douglas Democrats from the Cotton South — appointments John A. McClernand denounced as a 'parliamentary atrocity.' The Speaker's choice for chairman was Thomas Corwin, of Ohio, whose opposition to the Mexican War was still remembered in the South.[11] Upon this partisan action, the Florida and South Carolina committeemen refused to serve and several other Southern members did not attend its meetings, and the Republicans buried deep every conciliation measure introduced. Corwin later backed a mild compromise, but the Committee's final report was another case of the mountain laboring to bring forth a mouse.

The Senate's initial action was little more encouraging. Powell, of Kentucky, moved on December 6 that a Committee of Thirteen be appointed, and the Conservatives urged this course but the Republican Senators held up passage until December 18.

The Conservatives wanted the Committee really to represent the various sections and attitudes, and Powell's motion called for the appointment of five Republicans, three Northern Democrats and five Southerners. Vice-President Breckinridge named Seward, Ben Wade, Collamer, Doolittle and Grimes for the first group; Douglas, Rice and Bigler represented the Northern Democrats. Crittenden, Powell, Hunter, Toombs and Davis were named for the South.

Crittenden's Compromise, formally laid before the Senate the day the Committee of Thirteen was set up, sought chiefly to settle the status of slavery in the Territories. It would divide the area from Missouri River to California along the line of 36° 30'; to the north Territorial slavery would be forever prohibited; to the south it would be protected by Congressional legislation. Whenever any area was ready to enter statehood, it should be admitted free or slave as its people determined.

All this was to be assured by unalterable constitutional amendment. Crittenden would also deprive Congress of power to abolish slavery in the District of Columbia so long as it existed in Maryland and Virginia, or to abolish it in the forts, arsenals and other places under Congress' special jurisdiction within the Slave States, or to interfere in the interstate slave trade. A fourth amendment would establish the machinery by which the slave-owner would be paid, by the county at fault, the value of any slave taken from him by 'violence, intimidation or rescue.' Accompanying resolutions would pledge Congress to request from Northern States repeal of offensive 'Personal Liberty' laws, while Congress itself would proceed to

[11] *Congressional Globe*, Thirty-Sixth Congress, Second Session, I, 6; Dumond, 155–57; McClernand to Lanphier, Washington, Dec. 10, 1860; Patton MSS.

eliminate from the Fugitive Slave Act those points of recovery procedure which had upset the North.[12]

In a few days Douglas introduced a proposal to give constitutional application to Popular Sovereignty, but in such a way as to protect the South's legitimate rights. It would prohibit Congressional legislation on slavery in the Territories; the existing status as to each present Territory should remain unchanged until it reached a population of fifty thousand, when it would be given full self-government as to its domestic institutions. As soon as it attained the population to entitle it to a member in the House, it should automatically be made a State. His plan called for the concurrent vote of two-thirds of both Houses of Congress before new territory might be acquired, and demanded guaranty of adequate enforcement of the Fugitive Slave laws.[13]

The Crittenden and Douglas Compromises made a deep impress on the North. Congress was soon flooded with approving memorials, petitions and resolutions. Private assurances were even more significant. Crittenden heard from Old-Line Whigs, Douglas from Conservative Democrats, both from Moderate Republicans from all over the North, and the word was that not 'one in ten of the men of the North and Northwest would not be satisfied with any fair and honorable solution.' [14]

But would the Crittenden or Douglas plan be accepted by the South? Alexander H. Stephens thought all that was needed was 'a little time and further forbearance.' 'No wise man can fail to see that this question of differences about the Territories is all a mere quibble,' a North Carolinian wrote Douglas; the South knew that the location of the Territories in controversy would make them free, but pled for 'the abstract right.' Thus the North could save the Union without loss of honor, by according the South these guaranties.[15]

Tennessee's Union men were enheartened. The Douglas Committee kept alive their campaign paper so as to battle against Secession, and it promptly announced Jackson's toast, 'the Federal Union, it must be preserved,' as its motto. None the less, revolutionary feeling grew, and Felix K. Zollicoffer, of Nashville, advised Douglas that Tennessee could be kept

[12] Coleman, II, 224–37.

[13] Douglas introduced this proposal on December 23, immediately following the rejection by the Committee of Thirteen of the Crittenden program. Senate Reports, Thirty-Sixth Congress, Second Session, Report 288, being the Journal of the Committee of Thirteen, 8–11.

[14] Coleman, II, 240–49, for list of some of the petitions sent to Crittenden for presentation to the Senate. *Ibid.*, 237–40, for letters of John A. Dix, Edward Everett, Elisha Whittlesey, Robert C. Winthrop and Amos A. Lawrence. Cyrus H. McCormick to P. H. Watson, Chicago, Jan. 8; W. S. McCormick to T. Berry, Chicago, Jan. 20; to John Churchman, Chicago, Feb. 6, 1861; McCormick Historical Association MSS.; Cyrus H. McCormick to Douglas, Chicago, Dec. 28, 1860; Robert Dale Owen, Indianapolis, Feb. 14, 1861; T. M. Gray, Greenfield, Ohio, Dec. 24, 1860; Samuel Gross, Bloomville, Ohio, Jan. 27, 1861; John Brodhead, Philadelphia, Jan. 9, 1861; Douglas MSS.; August Belmont to Herschel V. Johnson, New York, Dec. 30, to Douglas, New York, Dec. 26, 30, 31, 1860; Douglas MSS.

[15] Stephens to William Epler (of Omaha, Neb.), Crawfordsville, Ga., Dec. 24, 1860; Illinois State Historical Library MSS. J. M. Marshall, Mt. Airy, N.C., Jan. 10; H. M. Pritchard, Charlotte, Jan. 15, 1861; Douglas MSS.

from Secession only through some plan of compromise. Douglas' own proposition, which he termed 'a bold, direct, comprehensive, pertinent plan of masterly statesmanship,' could save the country.[16] While the deep South was less encouraging, when the Committee of Thirteen first took up consideration of the Crittenden proposal, both Jefferson Davis and Robert Toombs declared that the Cotton States would accept it.[17]

The Committee of Thirteen met informally on December 21, but the next day settled down to serious business. Davis proposed and the Committee agreed to present no recommendation which did not receive the approval of a majority both of the five Republican members and of the eight Democrats and Conservatives. Davis was wise in this, for, lacking the support of a majority of the two groups, no plan the Committee might adopt could win in Congress or in the country.

The Crittenden Compromise now came before the Thirteen. The restoration of the Missouri Compromise was the keystone of the whole structure. Every Southern member, including Davis and Toombs, representing the Cotton States, declared that, provided the Republicans would 'tender and sustain' it, they would accept it. But when the five Republicans flatly refused, the two Cotton State Senators went with them, because it would merely deceive the country for the Committee to adopt a proposal the Republicans unitedly opposed. The Republicans voted favorably only upon Crittenden's planks for changing such sections of the Fugitive Slave Act as offended the North. Thus the Republicans on the Committee killed the Compromise.

Douglas now made his own proposal. The Conservatives approved it, but this was of no consequence in view of the united opposition of the Republican group. The Little Giant felt that no readjustment would restore and preserve peace 'which does not banish the slavery question from Congress forever.' Crittenden's Compromise would do this, and his own plan would have given 'assurance of permanent peace.' But the Republicans refused both plans.[18]

Seward now brought forward the Republican offer, which involved four things: to support a constitutional amendment to deprive Congress of power 'to abolish or interfere with slavery in the States.' Next, Congress would amend the Fugitive Slave Act so that the fugitive would be granted a trial by jury. Again, Congress would ask the Northern States to repeal

[16] W. R. Hurley, Nashville, Tenn., Dec. 10, 1860; Joseph Ramsey, Wartrace, Jan. 17, 1861; Felix K. Zollicoffer, Nashville, Dec. 31, 1860; Douglas MSS.

[17] J. O. Harrison, New Orleans, Jan. 31, 1861; Douglas MSS. *Congressional Globe*, Thirty-Sixth Congress, Second Session, 270, for Toombs, Jan. 7, 1861: 'I said to the Committee of Thirteen, and I say here, that, with other satisfactory provisions, I would accept it.' *Ibid.*, App., 41, for Douglas' speech, Jan. 3, 1861; *ibid.*, 1391, for Douglas' remarks March 2, 1861: 'Senator Davis himself, when on the Committee of Thirteen, was ready at all times to compromise on the Crittenden proposition.... Mr. Toombs was also.' *Ibid.*, 1390, for confirmation by Pugh.

[18] Douglas to Lanphier, Washington, Dec. 25, 1860; Patton MSS. Douglas thought the chief merits of his own plan were that 'while it takes the slavery question out of Congress forever, and secures the rights of self-government to the white male inhabitants, it also covers all the points in controversy and gives assurance of permanent peace.' Journal of Committee of Thirteen, 3–17, for votes on these rejections.

'their Personal Liberty Acts which contravene the Constitution or the laws.' Finally, 'Congress should pass an efficient law for the punishment of all persons engaged in the armed invasion of any State from another.'

These four items left the main issue — slavery in the Territories — untouched, and so fell far short of an acceptable compromise. The Southern members could accept naught less than the Crittenden Compromise — the Republicans would not yield. On December 28, the Committee of Thirteen confessed its failure and dissolved.

Responsibility for the defeat of the Crittenden or Douglas Compromise rested squarely on the five Republican Senators. Had it been adopted, probably no Cotton State save South Carolina would have seceded. Upon the Republican party, therefore, rested the responsibility for the refusal of compromise and the soon ensuing outbreak of civil war.[19]

Why did these five Republican Senators unitedly force the defeat of the Compromise? Partly because of the importunities of their political aides, but a large portion of the answer must be sought at Springfield, beneath the brooding brows of the President-elect.

'The Union is at the mercy of the President-elect — even before the inauguration,' General Scott had written Crittenden on November 12. 'His silence may be fatal.' And yet, as in the campaign, Lincoln parried all efforts to procure from him a public statement to quiet Southern apprehensions by replying that his record 'is in print, and open to all who will read.'[20] Several earnest efforts were made to persuade Lincoln to adhere to one of the real compromise plans, and to demonstrate to the country that he intended to give a national administration by inviting to his Cabinet several Union men from the South.

Early in December, the *Illinois Journal*, for which the President-elect still contributed or inspired leading editorials, began to print articles complimenting some of the compromise leaders. On December 11, however, Lincoln wrote William Kellogg, the Illinois member of the Committee of Thirty-Three, to 'entertain no proposition for a compromise in regard to the extension of slavery. The instant you do they have us under again: All our labor is lost, and sooner or later must be done over.... The tug has to come, and better now than later.' Two days later he warned a second Republican member from Illinois to 'hold firm as a chain of steel' against 'propositions for compromise of any sort on slavery extension.'[21]

[19] Rhodes, II, 41–42, concludes: 'No fact is clearer than that the Republicans in December defeated the Crittenden Compromise; few historic probabilities have better evidence to support them than the one which asserts that the adoption of this measure would have prevented the Secession of the Cotton States, other than South Carolina, and the beginning of the Civil War in 1861.'

[20] Winfield Scott to Crittenden, New York, Nov. 12, 1860; Crittenden MSS. Lincoln to William S. Speer; to George D. Prentice, to Truman Smith, to Samuel Haycroft, to N. P. Paschall, *Works*, VI, 66–83, reveal his invariable response. Villard, *Memoirs*, I, 145; Henry Villard was Springfield correspondent for the Associated Press during the interregnum. Lincoln, he says, 'could not be got to say what he would do in the face of Southern Secession.' *cf.* New York *Tribune*, Nov. 10, *Herald*, Nov. 22, 1860.

[21] Nicolay and Hay, III, 259. The second letter was to Elihu Washburne.

This was his state of mind on December 15 when Edward Bates visited him, and that determined anti-slavery Borderer, whom Lincoln asked that day to enter his Cabinet, did nothing to moderate it. Almost immediately the *Illinois Journal* altered its editorial attitude, and declared that the Republicans *must* stand by the Chicago platform, that Secession would not be allowed, that the Union would be preserved, 'peaceably if we can — forcibly if we must.' [22]

Early in December Senator Crittenden dispatched an emissary to Springfield. The resulting conference was quite 'indefinite and unsatisfactory.' The Conservative envoy urged that, to save the Union and establish his own fame, Lincoln should organize a national and representative Cabinet. 'Does any man think that I will take to my bosom an enemy?' countered the President-elect, amending his words, on remonstrance, to 'any man who voted against me.' [23]

A second major compromise effort came from the Seward group, who felt that compromise was preferable to war. At Seward's instance, Lincoln invited Thurlow Weed to Springfield. Seward's *alter ego* left New York with some hopes that Lincoln would cast his lot with the Conservative Republicans in favoring his proposal of compromise. But Lincoln merely commented that 'it would do some good or much mischief.' [24]

But Weed did procure from Lincoln a memorandum suggestion for the Republican leaders in Congress, involving an unalterable constitutional amendment to prevent Congress from interfering with slavery in the States; asking repeal of offensive Personal Liberty Acts, and so strengthening the Fugitive Slave Act that Seward's associates would not agree to it.[25]

Seward called a conference of the Republican members of the Committee of Thirteen, together with Trumbull and Fessenden. They found little in Lincoln's suggestion that had not already been covered in the four resolutions they had offered in the Committee of Thirteen, while one section of it would divide the Republicans in Congress as a whole. Therefore it was never laid before the Committee of Thirteen.[26]

Another important mission to Springfield came from President Buchanan himself. The envoy chosen was General Duff Green, whose prominence dated from the days of Andrew Jackson, and an uncle of Ninian Edwards,

[22] *Illinois Journal*, Dec. 13, 17, 19, 1860. C. H. Lanphier to Douglas, Springfield, Dec. 19, 1860; Douglas MSS. Bates came upon Dec. 15, 'and was housed with Lincoln all day.' Between Thursday the 13th and Monday the 17th, the *Journal* made a complete change of front and set its face firmly against compromise. 'Stand firm — Be True' was its Dec. 17 editorial. 'Peaceably if we can — forcibly if we must' was its language on Dec. 19. *Journal*, Jan. 24, 1861, for its harmony with the views of the President-elect.

[23] George Robertson to Crittenden, Washington, Dec. 16, 1860; Crittenden MSS. The envoy is described, in Robertson's report to Crittenden, as 'B.' Efforts to identify him have failed.

[24] E. B. Hart to Howell Cobb, New York, Dec. 20, 1860; Erwin MSS. Thurlow Weed, *Autobiography*, Boston, 1883; 604–14. Weed returned again and again to the idea of putting Southern Unionists in the Cabinet, and Lincoln finally agreed to write John A. Gilmer, of North Carolina, stating his views and offering Gilmer a Cabinet seat if he approved of them. Weed bore the letter to Gilmer, who eventually declined.

[25] Seward to Lincoln, Washington, Dec. 26, 1860, Nicolay and Hay, III, 262–64.

[26] *Ibid.*, III, 263.

whose wife was a sister of Mary Todd Lincoln. When the Southerners on the Committee of Thirteen offered to take Crittenden's Compromise if the Republicans would, and these refused to yield, Buchanan, Davis and Toombs sent Green to Springfield to urge Lincoln to come to Washington immediately. He would be received 'with all the respect due to the President-elect,' and Buchanan would most cordially unite with him 'in the measures necessary to preserve the Union.'

Green reached Springfield on December 28. Lincoln refused the invitation to come to Washington, and explained why he could not accept the Crittenden plan. While the restoration of the Missouri Compromise line 'would quiet for the present the agitation of the slavery question,' sectional difficulties would soon be renewed by the seizure and attempted annexation of Mexico. The real question at issue between the North and the South was slavery 'propagandism'; the Republican party was opposed to the South upon that issue and he was with his own party; it had elected him and he 'intended to sustain his party in good faith.' General Green appealed for a letter from Lincoln agreeing that Congress should refer 'the measures for the preservation of the Union to the action of the people in the several States.' Lincoln promised such a letter the next morning.[27]

No letter came and Green returned to Washington bitter over his experiences. He did not know that Lincoln had prepared a letter but had dispatched it to Trumbull, in Washington. Only if 'our discreet friends' agreed it could 'do no harm' should it be given to Green. This letter, which was never handed to Green, began bluntly, 'I do not desire any amendment of the Constitution.' However, as questions of amending the organic law rightfully belonged to the American people, 'I should not feel justified nor inclined to withhold from them, if I could, a fair opportunity of expressing their will thereon through either of the modes expressed in the instrument.'

He next declared 'that the maintenance inviolate of the rights of the States, and especially the right of each State to order and control its own domestic institutions according to its own judgment exclusively, is essential to that balance of powers on which the perfection and endurance of our political fabric depend.' In addition, he denounced 'the lawless invasion by armed force of the soil of any State or Territory, no matter under what pretext, as the gravest of crimes.' But there was not a word about the interstate slave trade, no hint of the District of Columbia, no whisper of the Missouri Compromise line, and no real reassurance could be had from it.

Yet the close of the letter set forth that Lincoln consented to its publication 'only upon the condition that six of the twelve United States Senators for the States of Georgia, Alabama, Mississippi, Louisiana, Florida and Texas 'would sign a postscript written beneath his own signature.

---

[27] New York *Herald*, Jan. 3, 1861, for interview with Green, in fact written by the latter. Duff Green to Buchanan, Springfield, Dec. 28, 1860; Buchanan MSS.; Duff Green, *Facts and Suggestions*, New York, 1866; 225 *et seq.* The *Herald* interview, however, quoted *ibid.*, 230, states that Green believed Lincoln 'desires a satisfactory adjustment.'

This addendum read: 'We recommend to the people of the States we represent respectively, to suspend all action for dismemberment of the Union, at least until some act deemed violative of our rights shall be done by the incoming Administration.' [28]

Why did Lincoln turn his face so sternly against any effective compromise? So far as can be judged from Lincoln's letters and the reports of conferences with him, at no time from November to March did he depart from an inflexible determination not to concede slavery any increase of area.[29] As well as can be judged, his chief objection to the Crittenden Compromise was not that it would protect slavery in the existing area south of 36° 30'. Lincoln realized that New Mexico was the only Territory there. Crittenden's original compromise had covered territory 'now held.' Powell added, with Crittenden's consent, the phrase 'or hereafter acquired.' Lincoln declared that a constitutional amendment with such an after-acquired clause would precipitate all sorts of filibustering, wars of aggression and seizures of territory to the south, and soon the slavery battle would recommence.

Apparently the President-elect ignored Douglas' provision to give the North a sure veto upon any unwanted addition to the national domain, by requiring that two-thirds of each House of Congress must agree to any accession. Additionally, Douglas' proposal neither formally dedicated any new area to slavery nor changed the status in existing Territories. Furthermore, certain sections of the Republican party had adopted Popular Sovereignty as a proper formula for solving the Territorial problem and were now urging the Douglas Compromise. But these facts did not influence Lincoln. 'Douglas is sure to be again trying to bring in his "Popular Sovereignty."' Have none of it,' he wrote Kellogg, and did not change his position on it.

'Lincoln's bellicose demonstrations,' observed McClernand, 'have brought the Republicans here up to the war point.' But they also convinced the Cotton South that compromise would not be offered, and depressed the Union men in the Border States. Then, too, the Republican leadership refused to admit that there was any wrong to the South to correct or any

[28] *Works*, VI, 87–89, for Lincoln's letter to Trumbull, Springfield, Dec. 28, 1860, and enclosure to General Duff Green. Lincoln wrote Trumbull that Green was 'here endeavoring to draw a letter out of me.' He also advised the Senator that 'you need not mention that the second clause of the letter is copied from the Chicago platform.' New York *Herald*, Jan. 8, 1861. Green's book, published in 1866, brought Radical Republican attack upon his reliability as a witness. There is no doubt that Green did have a high estimate of his own importance. But St. George Sioussat, 'Duff Green's "England and the United States,"' *Proceedings*, American Antiquarian Society, October, 1930, believes that his 'statements of fact are usually found to be trustworthy.'

[29] The author has made careful search for record or intimation that Lincoln did change his attitude, even temporarily. Except for one incident, about Dec. 31, 1860, of which note will soon be taken, no such information has been found. John G. Nicolay, Lincoln's secretary during these weeks in Springfield, kept certain manuscript notes about the interviews at that time. Miss Helen Nicolay, his daughter, has examined these notes. She informs me that they reveal no added information.

grievance to discuss. Ben Wade's speech in the Senate on December 17 probably did more to inflame the South than a dozen Secession pronouncements. 'With the verdict of the people given in favor of the platform upon which our candidates have been elected,' Wade had said, 'so far as I am concerned, I would suffer anything to come before I could compromise that away.'

The 'war tone' of Lincoln and his group, wrote the Louisville *Courier*, had blasted all hope of reconciliation 'almost ere it was born.'[30] 'Our people very generally begin to feel that the Union is lost,' a Conservative Tennessean wrote Douglas. Early in December, Governor Wise, of Virginia, announced that he favored 'fighting in the Union' rather than out of it, but the Republican course rapidly metamorphosed Conservative sentiment in the Old Dominion.[31] Lincoln's December attitude tremendously stimulated the Secession movement.

The cause of compromise was finally lost when Lincoln refused to yield, but Crittenden and Douglas would not concede defeat. From the start the country had looked to Douglas to lead the fight. 'Save our country,' came the message from all parts of the Union. 'Remember us who have stood by you.'[32]

The Little Giant realized that the country was in 'imminent danger,' entered actively into the Senate debate, and McClernand wrote proudly that he had 'fought a dozen of his assailants in the Senate . . . and worsted the whole of them.' He pressed for the appointment of the Committee of Thirteen; then, when it was voted and the Crittenden proposal came before it, Douglas earnestly seconded the Kentuckian's plan. No sooner was the Crittenden proposal rejected than the Northwestern leader brought forward his own. When the Republicans vetoed it too, still he refused to give up all hope.[33]

The intense hope of the friends of Union kept these champions at their tasks. James Madison, on his deathbed, had said that the advice nearest to his heart was that the Union 'be cherished and perpetuated.' 'This feeling still possessed the masses of the people, and Douglas and Crittenden knew that if a real compromise plan could only be gotten to the masses, it would carry the North overwhelmingly. As soon as the Committee reported its failure, they asked the Senate to authorize the submission of compromise amendments to the people themselves, through the constitutionally provided method of summoning a general convention. Republican leaders

[30] *Congressional Globe*, Thirty-Sixth Congress, Second Session, I, 99–104. Louisville, Ky., *Courier*, Dec. 27, 1860; New Orleans *Picayune*, Dec. 27, 1860.

[31] McClernand to Lanphier, Washington, Dec. 25, 1860; Patton MSS. August Belmont, New York, Dec. 25; F. K. Zollicoffer, Nashville, Dec. 31, 1860; C. F. Collier, Richmond, Va., Jan. 14; T. F. Fauntleroy, Jr., Winchester, Jan. 14, 1861; Douglas MSS. B. H. Wise, 267–68.

[32] H. W. Miller, Raleigh, N.C., Nov. 28; J. H. Gilmer, Richmond, Va., Nov. 30; H. B. Harris, Louisa County, Va., Dec. 5; Thos. L. Foust, Charlottesville, Va., Dec. 13; Herschel V. Johnson, Spiers Turnout, Jefferson County, Ga., Nov. 25, 1860; Douglas MSS.

[33] Douglas to W. S. Prentice, Washington, Dec. 5, 1860; Illinois State Historical Library MSS.; McClernand to Lanphier, Washington, Dec. 12, 1860; Patton MSS.; Felix K. Zollicoffer, Nashville, Tenn., Dec. 31, 1860; Douglas MSS.

contended that the North had endorsed the Chicago platform at the last election. 'Better that all platforms be scattered to the winds,' Douglas told the Senate, on January 3; 'better that every public man and politician in America be consigned to political martyrdom; better that all political organization be broken up, than that the Union be destroyed and the country plunged into civil war.'

In addition, he denied that the Northern people had voted for the Chicago platform. But if the Republican Senators and Representatives were so certain of it, why did they fear a national convention? If they had no purpose of initiating a destructive war on Southern institutions, why did they stand so inflexibly against all the proposals of real settlement? They could not hide behind the excuse that they themselves had offered a real adjustment, for their compromise had been a plain fraud, which had offered an assurance on a point where no danger was feared, but had been silent on the points of real apprehension.[34]

If the South's fears were really groundless, he asked the Republicans, 'is it not a duty you owe to God and your country to relieve their anxiety and remove all causes of discontent?' The fact that assurance was proposed on one point and refused on the others, did authorize the presumption that they intended to use the Federal power, as Lincoln's House Divided doctrine proclaimed, with a view of slavery's 'ultimate extinction in all States, old as well as new, North as well as South.'

Had the Republicans deliberately undertaken to use all their ingenuity to make a plan to drive the South into revolution and disunion, Douglas said scathingly, they could have devised no better course 'than the offering of that one amendment to the Constitution and rejecting all others which are infinitely more important to the safety and domestic tranquillity of the slave-holding States.'

He agreed that Secession was unlawful, unconstitutional and criminal; 'South Carolina had no right to secede — but she has done it.' Legally the Federal jurisdiction remained but its possession had been lost. Only three courses could be followed: reunion through mutual compromise, peaceable separation, and forcible maintenance by war. 'Are we prepared *in our hearts* for war with our own brethren and kindred?' he asked.

Pressing home the fearful alternatives to compromise, he made it plain that he was ready himself to act as if he 'had never given a vote or uttered a word, or had an opinion,' upon slavery and the Territories. He repeated his warning that 'a war upon a political issue, waged by the people of eighteen States against the people and domestic institutions of fifteen sister-States, is a fearful and revolting thought.' Any political party which refused to allow the people themselves to determine 'between revolution and war, on the one side, and obstinate adherence to a party platform on the other,' assumed a fearful responsibility.

And yet he never yielded as to Secession. He would go to the limits of

[34] James Madison's dying words, as written down by his wife; Stan V. Henkels, Jr., Catalogue No. 1478; 26. For Douglas speech, see *Congressional Globe*, Thirty-Sixth Congress, Second Session, App., 35 *et seq*.

the Constitution to maintain the South's just rights, 'but if the Southern States attempt to secede, I am in favor of their having just so many slaves and just so much slave territory as they can hold at the point of a bayonet and no more.' The South must not expect the Northwest to be neutral. States in the interior of the continent could 'never consent to be shut within the circle of a Chinese Wall erected and controlled by others.'

Up to this time Seward had taken no part in the debate. But he was known to have been designated Secretary of State, and a packed Senate Chamber listened to his speech of January 12. He offered no more immediate relief than the Republicans had proposed to the Committee of Thirteen, but vaguely suggested that in a year or so a national convention should be called to consider amendments to the Constitution. The Republican Radicals did not like his soft tone, but the Secessionists claimed it destroyed the last hope of compromise.[35]

Some of the Conservatives had hoped that Seward would endorse the effort to submit the compromise to the people, which 'would give peace at once to the country.' And had this plan for a plebiscite been adopted, it would have carried the country overwhelmingly.[36] But the Republican Senators soon gave the *coup de grâce* to all further talk of compromise. Crittenden still had his resolution before the Senate. On January 16, an amendment offered by Clark, a New Hampshire Republican, came up for vote. 'The provisions of the Constitution are ample for the preservation of the Union,' it declared, 'and the protection of all the material interests of the country; it needs to be obeyed rather than amended.' This the Republicans carried by a vote of 25 to 23, six Southern members refusing to answer when the roll was called. The Border Senators were indignant. Andrew Johnson turned in his seat to rebuke Benjamin. Crittenden charged bluntly that six Southern men were responsible for the defeat.[37]

Five days later, all the Cotton State Senators except Wigfall withdrew and the revolt of the deep South was an accomplished fact. But would the Border States follow them out? Douglas and Crittenden still insisted that there were hopes of adjustment.[38] Virginia, Tennessee and North

[35] *Congressional Globe*, Thirty-Sixth Congress, Second Session, 341 *et seq.*, for the speech. Pierce, *Sumner*, IV, 17: 'I supplicated him [Seward] to give countenance to no scheme of compromise!' Richmond, Va., *Enquirer*, Jan. 15, 1861.

[36] Rhodes, III, 148, declares: 'No doubt can now exist and but little could have existed in January, 1861, that if it had been submitted to the people it would have carried the Northern States by a great majority; that it would have received the preponderating voice of all the Cotton States but South Carolina.' Greeley, *Recollections*, 397: 'It would have prevailed by a tremendous majority.'

[37] *Congressional Globe*, Thirty-Sixth Congress, Second Session, 409, for this vote. The six were Slidell and Benjamin, of Louisiana; Iverson, of Georgia; Johnson, of Arkansas; Wigfall and Hemphill, of Texas. Of these, all but the Arkansas member had voted for Powell's amendment. On the Republican side it must not be thought that the Clark amendment did not represent a general party tone. Northern Legislatures were passing violent resolves against 'rebellion and Treason.' Michigan repudiated compromise with 'traitors,' Ohio offered her 'entire power and resources' to punish traitors. *Cf. House Miscellaneous Documents*, Thirty-Sixth Congress, Second Session for these and other resolutions.

[38] Raleigh, N.C., *Register*, Jan. 19, 1861, for Crittenden telegram.

Carolina were the chief battlegrounds. North Carolina was to lead off with an election on January 28. On February 4, Virginia was to elect a State Convention. Five days later Tennessee would decide.

Although the North Carolina Conservatives feared defeat because 'the facts are kept from the people,' they made a determined effort, and the election resulted in a decisive defeat for the Secessionists. Not only was a majority of Union delegates elected, but the very holding of the convention lost by a small vote.[39]

The defiant attitude of the Republicans in Congress had driven many Virginia Union men into Secession support, and the masses were rapidly drifting to the point 'where men cease to reason and the most desperate councils alone seem to fill the festering public mind.' The greatest foe of Union was 'a feeling of despair on the part of those best inclined to help.'

But the Unionists went bravely forward, Douglas' and Crittenden's telegrams and letters from Washington and a supplementary Fugitive Slave bill which Douglas introduced and urged on January 28, proving chief factors in the Virginia campaign. Senator Mason, whose sympathies were with Secession, denounced the Little Giant's messages as a 'puny, pusillanimous attempt to hoodwink' the people. 'I never intend to give up hope of saving this Union so long as there is a ray left,' Douglas answered feelingly. 'Why break up the Union upon an abstraction?'[40] Following the election Douglas was informed: 'Your call on Virginia has been heard and answered through the ballot box.'

The weather on election day was 'terrible,' but the Union men turned out and the result was a 'Waterloo defeat' for the Secessionists. The convention, which was to meet on February 13, would contain 'at least three-fourths Union men.' But Secession was dead in Virginia only if the Republican party would 'do justice to the South.' 'Having performed our duty,' Douglas was informed, 'we expect you to see, according to promise, that the Union itself is saved from destruction by the Conservative elements.'[41]

---

[39] *Appleton's Annual Cyclopædia*, 1861, 538, gives 82 Conservatives and 38 Secessionists as having been elected. The anti-convention majority was 651. W. S. Chappin, Carthage, N.C., Feb. 1; Daniel McDougald, Somerville, Feb. 5, 1861; Douglas MSS.

[40] *Congressional Globe*, Thirty-Sixth Congress, Second Session, 586 *et seq.*, 661 *et seq.*, gives Douglas' bill and speeches. His supplementary Fugitive Slave bill provided that if the fugitive should insist that he was really a free man, he could have a jury trial in a Federal Court. If the claimant to a slave lost the fugitive through violence, the Federal Government should pay him damages, which it would then recover from the county of the offense. Albert Taylor Bledsoe, Washington, Feb. 6, 1861, Douglas MSS.: 'Your last great and glorious speech... will do you more honor, in the eyes of posterity, than a thousand presidencies.' Dr. Bledsoe was later the most acute defender of the legal justification of Southern grievances and secession. At this time, however, he approved Douglas' policies and wrote the latter that no political event had given him 'so bitter a pang as the failure of your nomination.' For contrary later view, *cf.* *Southern Review*, IX, 809–10.

[41] Ellis B. Schnabel, Richmond, Jan. 5; A. M. Kelley, Petersburg, Jan. 29. Josiah Stevens, Portsmouth, Va., Feb. 4, 1861; Douglas MSS. Douglas, Crittenden, Boteler and Harris to James Barbour, Washington, Jan. 25, printed in Richmond *Whig*, Jan. 29, 1861. Douglas to Barbour, Washington, Jan. 27, printed in *Illinois State Register*, Feb. 2, 1861. Robert G. Green, Lynchburg, Feb. 7; James B. Dorman, Lexington, Feb. 24; Robert W. Baylor, Charlestown,

Tennessee Conservatives went to work as soon as her Legislature ordered a convention election. William H. Polk, Harvey Watterson and other stalwart Douglas followers announced for delegate. Shortly before the election Polk telegraphed to know if there was any chance for adjustment. 'Our hope for the Union firm,' Douglas and Crittenden responded. 'Take courage from Old Virginia. Save Tennessee and the Union is safe.'

When the Memphis *Appeal*, which had gone for Secession, declared that Douglas had come to favor 'the immediate withdrawal of the remaining States ... as a peace measure,' the Senator denied this 'unaccountable error.' The Border States must remember that the North had its own extremists, and that nothing would gratify them so much or so aid their success 'as the secession of Tennessee and the Border States.' Let these States remain steadfast, uniting with Northern Conservatives in a just and honorable compromise, peace and friendship would soon return, the Cotton States would come back 'and the Union be rendered perpetual.' [42]

With such arguments, Polk, Watterson and other Conservatives met the Secessionists. The people of Tennessee defeated the convention by a majority of 12,000, and the Union delegate slate led by five times that figure. But again the verdict did not mean unconditional Union.[43]

Without other explanation, later events would make it seem that Douglas and Crittenden either deliberately deluded the Border State Conservatives or were themselves blind to the plain facts of the case. But the truth of the matter was that they were negotiating with Seward and other Republican leaders.

The night before their appeal to Virginia, the two Union Senators had a long private conference with Seward and Dixon, of Connecticut, to come 'to some definite arrangement on our present national difficulties.' Rumors of new compromise hopes became widespread. Weed renewed his editorial appeals. Greeley, who had long since gone over bag and baggage to the Ben Wade coercionists, exhibited alarm and began talking about 'betrayal.' Seward, in a speech on January 31, intimated that he was 'ready to renounce Republican principles for the sake of the Union.' [44]

Feb. 4: 'We are indebted to you for the conservative spirit which Virginia has indicated this day through the ballot box. If you had withdrawn from the canvass last Fall, Virginia would now be out of the Union.' James Barbour, Culpeper, Feb. 26, 1861; Douglas MSS.

[42] Memphis *Daily Appeal*, Jan. 30, 1861; Douglas to the editors of the *Appeal*, Washington, Feb. 2, 1861, reprinted in *National Intelligencer*, Feb. 8; Cleveland *Plain Dealer*, Feb. 7, 1861. John L. Hopkins, Chattanooga, Nov. 9, 1860; Douglas MSS.

[43] Wm. H. Polk, telegram, Columbia, Tenn., Feb. 5; Douglas and Crittenden to Polk, Washington, Feb. 5; Jesse Thompson, Chattanooga, Feb. 9. Harvey Watterson, McMinnville, Tenn., Feb. 15; 'My majority is more than 500 over the strongest Breckinridge man in the district'; A. M. Tillman, Nashville, Feb. 20, 1861; Douglas MSS. Nicolay and Hay, IV, 250.

[44] Thomas Fitnam to Buchanan, Washington, Jan. 25, 1861; Buchanan MSS. Fitnam had his information that morning from Congressman John A. Gilmer, of North Carolina, who had added: 'They can do it if they will.' New York *Tribune*, Jan. 29, 1861, editorial: 'We have positive information from Washington that a compromise on the basis of Mr. Crittenden's issue is sure to be carried through Congress either this week or the next, provided a *very few more Republicans* can be got to enlist in the enterprise.... Several gentlemen who have hitherto enjoyed the

A second, and perhaps even more important, factor in Douglas' mind was an intimation that Lincoln was now about ready to yield to the restoration of the Missouri line. On January 18, the *Missouri Democrat*, the Republican organ in St. Louis, made the categorical statement that, in a recent conference in which both Northern and Southern men had participated, the President-elect had agreed that, if to do so 'would preserve the Union and restore harmony,' he was willing to divide the territory 'we *now own* by the line of 36° 30'.' During a discussion as to after-acquired territory, Lincoln negatived the prohibition of any acquisition, but declared that the vote of two-thirds of the States ought to admit new territory.[45] Edward Bates, who had been to Springfield for a second conference with Lincoln, confirmed to Douglas' friend Judge Treat that the views expressed in the *Democrat* represented what Lincoln was now willing to undertake. This news Treat hastened to Douglas in Washington, urging him to introduce a new constitutional amendment along these precise lines.[46]

Without doubt the Senator discussed this new suggestion with Seward and the Compromise Republicans. The steady procession of Ordinances of Secession, the farewells of the Cotton States Senators, the continued Republican refusal to submit the compromise to the people, were having a bad effect on Northern opinion, and there was increasing pressure for the Republican members to subordinate party to Union.

The conciliatory Republican element now dispatched a representative to Springfield to invite Lincoln to come to Washington immediately to help draft an acceptable compromise. The man selected was William Kellogg, Illinois Republican Congressman and that State's member of the Committee of Thirty-Three. Leonard Swett, whom Lincoln had sent over the North and East to make a first-hand investigation of public feeling, left for Springfield, to urge Lincoln, 'at the request of a large number of leading Republicans, to repair to Washington at once.' [47]

But even before Kellogg's arrival, the President-elect had become 'inflexible' again. The Lincoln organ at Springfield published an editorial saying that compromise was out of the question, and after his interview with Kellogg, Lincoln told Orville H. Browning that Crittenden's amendment should not be made, because 'far less bloodshed would result from an effort to maintain the Union and the Constitution than from disruption and the formation of two confederacies.' A few days later a New York paper quoted him as saying: 'I will suffer death before I will consent or will advise my friends to consent to

confidence of the Republican party are actively engaged in the endeavor to convert their colleagues to their new faith.' *Ibid.*, Feb. 5, 1861. *Congressional Globe*, Thirty-Sixth Congress, Second Session, 656, for Seward speech. 'Public Man,' 135. About that time Senator Cameron, of Pennsylvania, said he too would preserve the Union 'by any sacrifice of feeling, and I may say of principle.'

[45] *Missouri Democrat*, St. Louis, Jan. 18, 1861, printing letter signed R. S. H. The correspondent added that Lincoln had said, as to personal liberty bills, 'that he had never read one of them but if these were as represented to be by Southern men, they certainly ought to be repealed.'

[46] Samuel Treat, St. Louis, Jan. 18, 1861; Douglas MSS.

[47] New York *Herald*, Jan. 21, 1861.

any compromise.' And the President-elect repeated to Seward: 'On the territorial question... I am inflexible.' [48]

How much Lincoln's 'I am inflexible' proceeded from his essential conviction that extension of the area of slavery was sinful — and it must be said that there is no doubt that he had this sincere feeling, whether or not he then went further to balance its sinfulness against the perhaps greater sinfulness of a brothers' war — and how much from the fear that, with any compromise, they have us under again,' cannot be objectively determined. In all probability, there is merit to the contemporary judgment of one who knew Lincoln well and had a personal respect for him — none other than Stephen A. Douglas.

Shortly before Inauguration he was asked if Lincoln were not 'a lamentably weak and pliable character.' 'No, he is not that, Sir,' Douglas responded. 'But he is eminently a man of the atmosphere which surrounds him. He has not yet got out of Springfield, Sir.... He does not know that he is President-elect of the United States. He does not see that the shadow he casts is any bigger now than it was last year. It will not take him long to find it out when he has got established in the White House. But he has not found it out yet.' [49]

[48] New York *Herald*, Jan. 21, 1861, for Kellogg and Swett trips to Springfield and their purposes. *Illinois Journal*, Jan. 15, 1861, for editorial. Browning, *Diary*, I, 453; New York *Herald*, Jan. 28, 1861, for the President-elect's statement. *Illinois Journal*, Feb. 7, 1861, repudiating Kellogg's compromise, said he spoke for himself alone. Lincoln to Seward, Springfield, Feb. 1, 1860, Nicolay and Hay, III, 260.

[49] 'Public Man,' 261.

CHAPTER XXXII

HOLDING LINCOLN'S HAT

ON FEBRUARY 4, 1861, the Commissioners to a Peace Convention gathered in Washington. The assembly was at the instance of Virginia, to whose authorities John Tyler, the venerable ex-President, had appealed for such action, and whose Legislature invited all the States to send delegates 'to unite with Virginia in an earnest effort to adjust the present unhappy controversies.'[1] To insure peace during the convention's deliberations, she dispatched commissioners to both Buchanan and the Governors of the seceded States, asking them to abstain from any acts 'calculated to produce a collision of arms between the States and the Government of the United States.'[2]

By February public opinion in the Cotton South was so inflamed that hopes of reunion were fast disappearing. The Crittenden Compromise represented not the maximum but the minimum of Cotton States' demands, but the Republican refusal of this minimum extinguished nearly all remaining hopes. 'If the Union is to be preserved, it must be done now or never,' an Alabama Conservative warned Douglas. 'The Union sentiment grows weaker and weaker every day.' Even after the passage of her Ordinance, many Georgia Conservatives hoped that God would deliver them from a government gotten up 'to accommodate Robert Toombs, Howell Cobb, and such men as Iverson.' But the larger part were without hope. 'The stubborn and determined course of the Abolitionists has so irritated the Union men of our section,' Douglas was informed, 'that they have become Ultra Secessionists. Even Mr. Stephens has given up the ship.'[3]

The North misinterpreted the Border State elections. The anti-secessionists in North Carolina, Virginia and Tennessee had campaigned under the title of the Union Party, but the word meant one thing along the Border and another in the North. Northern Legislatures coupled tenders of force to the Federal Government with expressions of gratitude to the 'Southern patriots.' But Tennessee's General Assembly countered by declaring that she would, 'as one man, resist such invasion of the soil of the South, at all hazards and to the last extremity.' The Governor of Kentucky remonstrated against coercion. Virginia was ready to resist. Missouri inclined toward the Union, but Kentucky's Secession sentiment increased. For all this, the Northern Republicans would not realize that the election

---

[1] Quoted, Dumond, 227–28. The resolutions further urged, as a basis for reunion, the Crittenden Compromise with an after-acquired clause.

[2] *Ibid.* Tyler was sent as delegate to Buchanan, Judge John Robertson to the seceded States. Buchanan said he had no constitutional right to make such a pledge, but soon asked Congress to pass no hostile legislation during the convention. The seceded States answered with professions of peaceful intent but determination to maintain independence.

[3] Augustus H. Wright, Montgomery, Ala., Feb. 6; James A. Hamilton, Athens, Ga., Feb. 4; L. S. Bennett, Savannah, Ga., Feb. 5, 1861; Douglas MSS.

outcomes in North Carolina, Virginia, and Tennessee meant only that these States had not abandoned hope of compromise.[4]

At any event, Virginia's invitation was coldly received in the North. Some Republican States accepted the proffer and promptly regretted it, others sent commissioners for the express purpose of preventing settlement, and Michigan, Wisconsin and Minnesota refused to respond at all.[5]

The twenty-one States finally represented named their commissioners on no uniform basis, hence the conference resorted to the State as the unit of voting, which put the seven Slave States at a disadvantage.[6] Several Northern delegations were entirely Republican. The New York group was so split that their State did not vote on several important resolutions. Ohio men were instructed to seek adjournment for sixty days. The New England commissioners, Rhode Island excepted, came with mischief in their eyes.[7]

It was not until February 9 that the delegation from the twenty-first State appeared. The sessions, conducted in secret, continued through the month. John Tyler was made President, James Guthrie headed its compromise committee, and the delegates, including many men of present or future prominence, represented sufficient ability to find a formula of compromise if only the will to do it had been present.[8]

This assemblage stimulated compromise leaders in Congress to further efforts. Congressman Kellogg, of Illinois, branded a fellow Republican who interrupted his compromise speech 'as a mere partisan ready to sacri-

[4] Resolutions cited, Dumond, 246, 207, 222, 224. Thomas L. Price, Jefferson City, Mo., Jan. 29: Price, leader of the Douglas men in the Missouri Legislature, also sent the Little Giant word that their group had taken steps and 'James S. Green cannot be re-elected to the Senate.' The actual election did not come until March 18, but then the prediction was fulfilled. William Douglas, Booneville, Feb. 14, 1861; Douglas MSS.

[5] The six Cotton States sent their delegates to Montgomery. Word could not be gotten to California and Oregon in time for them to name commissioners. Texas and Arkansas sent none because they too were preparing to secede.

[6] Dumond, 243-44.

[7] Leonard Alleman, Milton, Pa., Feb. 2, 1861; Douglas MSS. Governor Curtin had wanted to name some Democrats but the Legislature, heavily Republican, had threatened that unless he would promise not to name Democrats, it would select the delegation itself. McClernand to Lanphier, Feb. 18, 1861; Patton MSS. The Illinois Legislature 'ought to be politically damned for all eternity' for sending such a delegation. None the less, Stephen T. Logan had 'powerfully contributed to carry the plan over the head of the active and malignant opposition of Trumbull.' L. E. Chittenden, Recollections of President Lincoln and His Administration, New York, 1893; 19.

[8] For delegate list, see L. E. Chittenden, Report of the Peace Convention in 1861, New York, 1864 (hereafter to be termed Peace Convention); 465. On it one finds the names of such men as Senator Fessenden, of Maine; George S. Boutwell, of Massachusetts; David Dudley Field, James B. Wadsworth, Erastus Corning and Francis Granger, of New York; ex-Governor James Pollock and David Wilmot, of Pennsylvania; Reverdy Johnson, of Maryland; Tyler, William C. Rives and James A. Seddon, of Virginia; Chief Justice Thomas Ruffin, of North Carolina; Samuel Milligan, ex-Congressman George W. Jones, and Felix K. Zollicoffer, of Tennessee; ex-Senator William O. Butler, James B. Clay, son of Henry Clay, Guthrie and ex-Governor Charles A. Wickliffe, of Kentucky; Salmon P. Chase and Thomas Ewing, of Ohio; Caleb B. Smith, Lincoln's designate for Secretary of Interior, from Indiana; Stephen T. Logan, John M. Palmer and Burton C. Cook, of Illinois; Senators Harlan and Grimes, of Iowa; and Thomas Ewing, Jr., of Kansas.

fice his country for party,' and exclaimed that he was willing to join Conservative men of all parties in an effort to save the country. John A. McClernand dramatically clasped hands with him and the House and galleries shook with applause.[9]

The Border State delegates were split into a major group, to which the Crittenden Compromise was eminently satisfactory, and a Radical minority, represented by Seddon, of Virginia, and Ruffin, of North Carolina. At the start, Radical Republicans cried that Ohio, Indiana and Rhode Island were 'caving in' and that there was 'danger' of Illinois. Thereupon they bestirred themselves to redress the balance by having Michigan and Wisconsin send belated delegations of 'true, unflinching men' — or, as Zach Chandler put it, '*stiff-backed* men or none' — in order to 'save the Republican party from rupture.' [10]

But before long this 'caving in' was checked by the establishment of a Republican 'caucus' to pass on all proposals. The voting procedure stilled the voice of the Conservative minority in several Northern delegations. The votes of Maine, New Hampshire, Vermont, Massachusetts, Connecticut and Iowa were cast against every important conciliatory proposal. New York did not vote at all on the six main propositions. These facts, together with the abstention of Michigan, Wisconsin and Minnesota, were taken by the Border Conservatives as an added proof that the Republican party would not compromise for peace.[11] Even so, the conciliators left no path to compromise unexplored and the convention remained in session until Inauguration Eve.

Douglas now saw all too well that nothing would come from private conferences with Seward; that the Republicans would not yield without word from Springfield, if at all, and that no such word would come. The month before, he had contrasted the three alternatives of compromise, peaceable separation and war. Now that the last compromise effort had failed, he feared that 'no earthly power could tell the extent or the end of the calamities ahead.'

Neither war nor Disunion, Douglas felt, would 'afford any additional guaranties or protection either in the States or the Territories; while separation and independence would annul all the securities and safeguards contained in the Constitution... and aggravate the irritation and increase the

[9] Douglas to John Tyler, Washington, Feb. 8, 1861; MSS. in Essex Institute, Salem, Mass. Douglas tendered the convention a formal reception on Feb. 12. McClernand to Lanphier, Washington, Feb. 8, 1861; Patton MSS.

[10] *Congressional Globe*, Thirty-Sixth Congress, Second Session, II, 1247, printing Chandler to Governor Austin Blair, Feb. 11, 1861, and Bingham to Blair, Feb. 15, 1861. On Feb. 9, Massachusetts and New York delegates had asked Chandler and Bingham to telegraph Blair for Michigan to send a delegation to the conference. 'They admit that we were right and that they were wrong; that no Republican State should have sent delegates; but they are here and cannot get away.' Elisha E. Hundley, Detroit, Mich., Feb. 7, 1861; Douglas MSS.

[11] Chittenden, *Peace Convention*. Careful reading of this volume of 621 pages leaves one with a feeling of hopelessness at the doctrinaire stubbornness of the Radical Republicans and the Radical segment of the Border State delegations. Each preferred war to giving an inch.

insecurity by bringing the land of refuge to the door of the fugitive.' He also thought it was impossible to overstress the economic evils consequent upon disunion. 'It would destroy that freedom of trade, transit and intercourse which has always been deemed one of the greatest blessings of the Union. It would annihilate that *uniformity* in the regulations of commerce, navigations and tariffs which was the chief inducement of the formation of a Federal Constitution.' The conflicting systems which would result would be 'destructive of the great interests of commerce, navigation and trade; and alike prejudicial to the merchant, to the manufacturer and the agriculturist.' Separation would lead to constant dispute 'all along the interior border, and upon the navigable rivers and on all the lines of transit and trade,' which would be bound to result in war. Dissolution, whether peaceful or warlike, could not fail to be 'most disastrous to the interests, happiness and prosperity of the great masses of the people in every portion of the country.' [12]

And yet, if political separation became unavoidable, Douglas believed that it would become the solemn duty of the people to see if the two divisions of the old Union could not agree, in advance, 'upon such terms of political separation and commercial union' as would insure peace, friendship, reciprocal advantage and mutual benefit. He was emphatic that peaceful separation was preferable to war — 'provided the terms are so fair, reciprocal and mutually beneficial as to insure permanent peace.' But without such terms peaceful separation could not be had. [13]

Douglas now tried his own hand at a statement of 'fair, reciprocal and mutually beneficial terms.' He had a ready-made matrix in an article he had drafted, a few weeks before, proposing to bring Canada, Mexico, and the Central American Republics into a *Zollverein* with the United States. [14]

[12] This description of Douglas' views I quote and condense from an extraordinary manuscript of some forty pages found in the Douglas MSS. at Greensboro. It is undated, but in it Douglas speaks of the 'Confederate States' which dates it after Feb. 8, 1861. The first half is in the handwriting of Adèle Douglas, the remainder in that of the Senator himself.

[13] Douglas' memorandum insisted that 'there can never be peace between the people of the upper and lower Mississippi so long as the one attempts to exercise jurisdiction to the seclusion of the other over any portion of the river; or obstructs, impairs or interferes with the rights of free navigation on terms of entire equality with its own citizens. There can never be peace so long as goods and merchandise, imported at the ports of the one confederacy, for sale and consumption in the other, or subjected to the payment of duties and taxes, under the operation of laws in whose enactment they have no voice, and in the proceeds of which they have not an equal participation. There can be no peace so long as there be any restriction, hindrance or encumbrance upon commerce, trade, transit, and intercourse which is not common to the citizens of both.' There are hints of this memorandum in Douglas' subsequent speech of March 12, 1861. William H. Russell to the London *Times*, Washington, April 1, 1861, printed, Russell, *The Civil War in America*, Boston, 1861; 18, conveys a hint of it.

[14] Ever since his European tour in 1853, Douglas had been impressed with the North German Customs Union. When the project of a Continental Customs Alliance came to his mind, he turned with his usual energy to collecting statistics and worked it out into an article of considerable detail. A draft of this paper fell into the hands of James Madison Cutts, Jr., his brother-in-law, who published it in 1889. On July 5, 1911, Senator Shively, of Indiana, offered a copy of the Cutts pamphlet for republication as a Government document. It is to be found as Senate Document No. 61, serial 6107, Sixty-Second Congress, First Session. I have compared, paragraph by

Using this as a basis, he drafted tentative terms for the 'recognition of the independence of the Confederate States on the fundamental condition of a Union for commercial purposes, between them and the United States, indissoluble except on common consent.'

Douglas' terms divided into two groups, the first to establish uniform economic regulation for the two republics, and the second to set up machinery for their application and enforcement. All laws and regulations concerning trade, commerce and navigation, tariff duties, patents and copyrights should be 'uniform and common to both republics.' Again there should be absolute freedom of navigation, trade and transport in and between all States and Territories of the two republics.

He would confer the power to make laws for the Commercial Union upon 'a Council, to be composed of one member from each State of the two Republics.' One member was to be chosen for a seven-year term by the Legislature of each State of the two countries, and they were to be classified that one-seventh would be replaced each year.[15] This Council was to pass its laws, ordinances and decrees only with 'the concurrence of a majority of the councillors present from each Republic.' It should have a president and other officers and was to be economically supreme.

The Commercial Union would then collect tariff duties for both Republics, following initially the schedules of either the tariff of 1846 or that of 1857. The first charge on these collections would be the payment of the public debt of the old United States. After this had been serviced, the balance would be distributed between the two nations, on a population basis, in which the slave ratio of three-fifths would be preserved.

Perhaps the most important section was 'that the Allied Republics guarantee the integrity of the territorial limits of each other against invasion and external violences.' But neither Republic was to be permitted to add new area without the other's consent, the boundaries of each must, at the beginning, be distinctly defined, and must 'never be changed without the consent of both.'[16] So long as the Union were maintained in its common economic aspects, Douglas thought it by no means certain that the great body of the American people might not soon conclude that it was possible for them to be prosperous and happy, 'even if their members of Congress should assemble at two places instead of one.'

This ingenious plan called for such intelligence and social judgment that Douglas never projected it beyond his own private circle. To the historian, the document's chief value is that it affords further example of Douglas' economic realism and of the lengths to which he would go to maintain peace.

Washington was excited over rumors that Congress might either refuse or not be permitted to declare Lincoln the constitutionally chosen President.

paragraph and sentence by sentence, this published paper and the Douglas peace plan. The actual peace proposals are new entirely, in lengthy sections in Douglas' own hand.

[15] In the first drafting of this section, a five-year term was provided, and no classification. A revision, occurring immediately afterwards in the manuscript, put it as above.

[16] This restriction on the power of unilateral expansion is found in the revision.

There was loose talk that the Capital would be seized, the President-elect assassinated or the Inauguration broken up.

'Can there not be found men bold and brave enough in Maryland,' asked a Richmond paper, 'to unite with Virginians in seizing the Capital in Washington?' Upon Buchanan's rebuff to the South Carolina Commissioners, some 'choice spirits' discussed carrying him off 'to a secure place,' so that Breckinridge would become acting President.[17] A little later it was whispered in the Cotton South, 'the mine is laid, the fuse ready, the *coup d'état* prepared' — Washington would be seized and Lincoln never inaugurated.[18]

The best historical judgment is that no such plot was ever actually instrumented by any responsible Southern group, and that the wild talk that went around was mere gasconade. And yet in early February the more uncompromising Republicans predicted bloodshed at the barriers. Northern delegates to the Peace Convention were informed that Virginia had proposed the Washington gathering only to lull the North into a false sense of security.' By March the conspirators would seize Washington and prevent the inauguration.[19]

'This Capital is in undoubted peril,' the *Tribune's* Washington correspondent wrote. Seward and Scott believed there were plots to seize the Capital, and one night in mid-January Washington was awakened 'by the roll of artillery carriages, the prancing of horses, the clanking of sabers and the sound of trumpets — forty cars full of United States troops had arrived!' Prompted secretly by Buchanan's Attorney-General, the House set up a Special Committee to investigate the plots.[20]

Lincoln apprehended that inauguration was 'not the most dangerous point,' but 'rather, what should be done if, on the day appointed for canvassing the vote, the two Houses refused to meet, or met without a quorum.' But Vice-President Breckinridge was resolved to permit no trifling. General Scott posted troops over the city and in the Capitol. The canvass, on February 13, passed without incident; Douglas quickened it by moving that certain

---

[17] Richmond *Examiner*, Dec. 25, 1860; 'Public Man,' 131, entry for Dec. 29, 1860. 'Public Man' noted that Wigfall and Floyd were in it. Ward Hill Lamon, *Recollections of Abraham Lincoln*, Washington, 1911 (the first edition was printed in 1895); 264–65.

[18] Jane Martin Johns, *Personal Recollections, 1849–1865*, 88 *et seq.*

[19] Chittenden, *Recollections*, 26–31, gives a description of the 'conspiracy,' and quotes Adam Gurowski's remarks to a group of Northern delegates. Gurowski, a Polish *émigré* who had come to America following the European revolutionary troubles of 1848, quickly became an active anti-slavery agitator and through the Civil War had the ear and reflected the views of Sumner, Wade and the Republican Radicals.

[20] New York *Tribune*, Jan. 3, 1861, dispatch of J. S. Pike; Seward to his wife, Washington, Dec. 29, 1860, F. W. Seward, II, 488, 497; Seward to Lincoln, Dec. 29, 1860; Nicolay and Hay, III, 264–65. For Buchanan's orders to Scott, see Simon Cameron to Lincoln, Washington, Jan. 3, 1861, Nicolay and Hay, III, 250–51; for Scott's actions, *O.R.*, Series III, 1, 36; William M. Browne to Howell Cobb, Washington, Jan. 15, 1861, Erwin MSS.: 'General Scott thinks that Virginia and Maryland may try to seize the Capital and prevent the inauguration of Mr. Lincoln.... Scott and Holt dictate and the President decrees.' For Committee's investigation, Henry Wilson, *Atlantic Monthly*, XXVI, 467. For Committee Report, with considerable interesting testimony, see Thirty-Sixth Congress, Second Session, Reports of House Committees, Report no. 79.

pro-forma recitations be omitted and Breckinridge announced in a profound silence that Lincoln had been 'duly elected President of the United States for the four years beginning on the fourth day of March, 1861.' [21]

Lincoln left Springfield for the Capital two days before his election was declared. Initially he had planned to take the direct rail route through western Virginia, but reports that there would be an attempt to seize him en route caused him to change to a more northern itinerary.[22] An equal reason, perhaps, was his desire to respond to invitations from Northern cities and legislatures.

His farewell at Springfield was fitting, but the Conservatives were shocked by his Indianapolis comparison of the Southern idea of Union to free love and the Northern to regular marriage. His speeches at Cincinnati were taken by the Democracy there as little short of a declaration of war against the South. 'There is nothing going wrong,' he told the Ohio Legislature, at Columbus. 'There is nothing that really hurts anybody.' At Pittsburgh and again at Cleveland he declared: 'There is no crisis but an artificial one.' These statements indicated to the country that he woefully underestimated the crisis, but one who called on him in New York City found Lincoln 'more troubled by the outlook than he thought discreet to show.' [23]

There was a more serious tone to the last few speeches. 'The Government will not use force,' he said in Philadelphia, 'unless force is used against it.' Again, at Harrisburg, after Governor Curtin's militia had passed in review, Lincoln said that the country should never witness bloodshed in fraternal strife with his consent.

Allan Pinkerton and other private detectives, employed by a railroad to ferret out expected Secession sabotage, convinced road officials that Lincoln would be in danger in a daylight passage through Baltimore. The railroad president took Pinkerton to Lincoln, in Philadelphia, to relate how a mob would stop the cars, the police would furnish no protection and an Italian barber named Ferrandini would dash upon the coach and assassinate the President-elect. About this time Frederick W. Seward arrived from Washington with a warning letter from the Senator, his father, confirmed by information from General Scott.

[21] Lincoln to Seward, Springfield, Jan. 3, 1861. *Works*, VI, 90–91; Chittenden, *Recollections*, 38. Cf. also *O.R.*, Series III, 1, 80, for Scott's orders for the day.

[22] *National Intelligencer*, Feb. 6, 1861, printing letter of John W. Garrett, President of the Baltimore and Ohio, to J. G. Berret, Mayor of Washington, Feb. 1, 1861, claiming that these rumors of trouble along his road were 'the simple inventions of those who are agents in the West for other lines.'

[23] Nicolay and Hay, III, 294; George N. Sanders, Cincinnati, Feb. 12, 1861; Douglas MSS.; Henry J. Raymond, *President Lincoln and His Administration*, New York, 1865; 131, 160, prints all these speeches. *Works*, VI, 110–64, gives speeches at Springfield, Feb. 11; Indianapolis, Feb. 11 and 12; Cincinnati, two speeches Feb. 12; Columbus, Feb. 13; Steubenville, Ohio, Feb. 14; Syracuse, Feb. 18; Utica, Feb. 18; Albany, Feb. 18, three speeches; Troy, Feb. 19; Poughkeepsie, Feb. 19; Hudson, Feb. 19; Peekskill, Feb. 19; New York City, Feb. 19, 20; Trenton, N.J., Feb. 21, two speeches; Philadelphia, Feb. 21, two speeches; and Feb. 22, one speech at Philadelphia; Harrisburg, Feb. 22, two speeches. 'Public Man,' 139–40, for interview with Lincoln in New York, Feb. 20.

Lincoln then agreed that, after filling his Harrisburg engagements, he would let his friends smuggle him through Baltimore. The evening of February 22, a special train rushed him from Harrisburg, his sole companion being the giant Ward H. Lamon. In Philadelphia Lincoln and Lamon were transferred to a sleeping-car on the night train for Washington, Lincoln hiding his identity by a felt hat, pulled well over his eyes, and a large shawl. There was no incident at Baltimore; at six the next morning the President-elect descended at Washington.[24] This triumph over the 'plot' delighted Pinkerton, who telegraphed associates that 'Plums' had brought 'Nuts' through in safety. That same day, however, the remainder of the Lincoln party made the Baltimore passage in broad daylight without disturbance of any kind.

For ten years Lamon 'implicitly believed in the reality of the atrocious plot which these spies were supposed to have detected and thwarted.' Then, however, he put the acid test to Pinkerton's 'conspiracy' evidence, and found that there was 'literally nothing to sustain the accusation,' that there had been no conspiracy, and that the whole thing was a mare's nest gotten up by the vainglorious detective.[25]

Lincoln's friends were distressed over his unseemly entry into the National Capital. One noted in his diary that Seward, as well as he himself, thought it 'in every imaginable way a distressing and ill-advised thing.' Douglas thought the Blairs had persuaded General Scott of 'the cock and bull story of the Italian assassins.' Stanton sneered at the way Lincoln had 'crept into Washington' and termed him 'a low, cunning clown.' [26]

Soon after Lincoln reached Washington, the delegates to the Peace Convention called on him. Some of the Southerners were surprised that the President-elect talked with them pleasantly and with much shrewd sense.[27]

By this time, however, the convention's impotence had become apparent to all. On February 27, it adopted a series of recommendations to Congress, and adjourned. The extension of the Missouri Compromise line carried on the final vote only because divisions in three delegations kept them from voting. Virginia voted against it, and Tyler publicly repudiated it. [28] Although laid before both Houses of Congress, it received scant attention there. From the first, the Republicans regarded the whole Peace Convention idea as 'a device of traitors and conspirators again to cheat the North.' Epitomiz-

[24] Ward H. Lamon, *The Life of Abraham Lincoln*, Boston, 1872; 511–26, gives a detailed account of this journey. Lamon's book is said to have been chiefly written by Chauncey F. Black, son of Jeremiah Sullivan Black. But Lamon denied this, even writing Black, ' this is *my* book,' and defending its accuracy. Internal evidence convinces me that Lamon did impress upon the account of the journey through Baltimore his own intimate knowledge of details.

[25] *Ibid.*, 513–17, for Lamon's analysis of the detective's 'evidence.' Nicolay and Hay, III, 311 *et seq.*; Chittenden, *Recollections*, 58–65; Alexander K. McClure, *Lincoln and Men of War Time*, Philadelphia, 1892; 43; Blaine, I, 280. Lamon, *Recollections*, 40–47, written in 1895, omits the 1872 volume's analysis of the emptiness of the conspiracy charge.

[26] 'Public Man,' 259–62.   [27] Chittenden, *Recollections*, 71–77.

[28] *Peace Convention*, 440–52. A second section, regarding the acquisition of new territory required the assent of a majority of the Senators from the slave-holding and from the free States. This carried 11 to 8.

ing the viewpoint of the Radicals, Chandler, of Michigan, said that 'without a little blood-letting this Union will not be... worth a rush.' On March 4, when Douglas finally secured Senate action, the Peace Convention plan received only seven votes.[29]

In making this fight Douglas was but carrying out his earlier promises to the Borderers. The Arkansas Convention, for example, when it organized on March 4, found the Conservatives in control by five votes. 'May we hope for settlement in the Union?' they telegraphed the Little Giant.[30] Doubtless his wish to maintain the peace effort bottomed his introduction of a resolution proposing a constitutional amendment guaranteeing that the Federal Government would never disturb slavery in the Slave States.

On the last night of the session, and at Lincoln's instance, the Republicans got behind this resolution and both Senate and House adopted it.[31] In his Inaugural Lincoln approved this action and, except for the firing on Sumter, it probably would have become a part of the Constitution. But the Thirteenth Amendment which was actually adopted freed the slaves.

The evening Lincoln reached Washington, Douglas called upon him at Willard's Hotel, and for half an hour the two men talked with 'deep, solemn earnestness.' When Douglas rose to leave, he took Lincoln's hand and looked him earnestly in the face. 'You and I have been for many years politically opposed to each other,' he said, 'but in our devotion and attachment to the Constitution and Union we have never differed — in this we are one — this must and shall not be destroyed.'

He had called that evening to tell Lincoln that he was on the side of the Union, and pledge himself and his friends to aid and sustain any effort to save the Union 'with all our strength and energy we will aid you,' he went on. 'Our Union must be preserved. Partisan feeling must yield to patriotism. I am with you, Mr. President, and God bless you.'

Lincoln's eyes streamed with tears, he wrung his opponent's hand and exclaimed: 'God bless you, Douglas... O, how you have cheered and warmed my heart. The danger is great but with such words and such friends why should we fear? Our Union cannot be destroyed. With all my heart I thank you. The people with us and God helping us all will yet be well. God bless you, Douglas, I can't forget it.' As the door closed, Lincoln exclaimed to another visitor: 'What a noble man Douglas is!'[32]

[29] Chittenden, *Recollections*, 20, so quotes Senator Foot, of Vermont. *Congressional Globe*, Thirty-Seventh Congress, Second Session, 1405.

[30] S. F. Clark, Fort Smith, Feb. 8; W. A. Counts, Little Rock, Feb 24; David Walker and J. H. Spierman, telegram, Little Rock, March 4; T. F. Curry, telegram, Little Rock, March 5, 1861; Douglas MSS.

[31] John Fiske, *History of the United States*, Boston, 1899, 370; Green, *Notes and Reflections*, 232.

[32] MS. record made by ex-Governor James A. Pollock, of Pennsylvania, of the Douglas-Lincoln interview. MS. now in Lincoln Collection, Brown University Library, Providence, R.I. For text see *Journal*, Illinois State Historical Society, XXXIII, 168–69. David Rankin Barbee, 'One Day in Lincoln's Life,' Washington *Post*, Feb. 11, 1934, relates that Adèle Douglas promptly called on Mrs. Lincoln, after which 'nearly everybody of position, either social or political, called.'

This interview led to a series of intimate conferences between the Senator and the President-elect. From then until early in April, Lincoln discussed his problems and plans with Douglas, and was increasingly responsive to the latter's efforts to persuade him to a policy of forbearance. Already the opposing forces within the Republican party were in a desperate struggle to determine which group should dominate their new President. Seward was in the forefront of the Conservatives, while the Radicals, with Chase and Montgomery Blair as their chief Cabinet figures, had important Congressional support in Sumner, Ben Wade and Thad Stevens. Delegations representing the two groups beset Lincoln. Douglas exerted himself to keep the Radicals from securing control of Lincoln's mind. On the evening of February 27 he had a 'private, earnest talk' with Lincoln, and besought him to recommend the 'instant calling of a national convention,' but could not get him to the point of decision.[33]

Another Conservative who saw Lincoln the next day found the President-elect still full of the idea of a conspiracy; Sumner had been trying to scare him, apparently with success. 'I should say he is at his wits' end,' this interviewer noted, 'if he did not seem to me to be so thoroughly aware of the fact that some other people are in that condition.' [34]

The day before Inauguration, Lincoln read Douglas some sections of his Inaugural. The speech, now about in final draft, had been softened in response to Seward's insistence.[35] Douglas was satisfied with the denial of the validity of the Acts of Secession, remarking: 'It will do for all Constitutional Democrats to brace themselves against.' He was equally pleased with Lincoln's declaration that, while he intended to see that the laws were faithfully executed, there would be 'no invasion, no using of force against or among the people anywhere.'

The great majority of the Northern people of both parties would support Lincoln in this policy, he thought. Also it would 'give the people time to recover their senses at the South.' Following this interview, Douglas told a confidant 'in the strongest language' that he intended to support Lincoln 'in a temperate, resolute Union policy.' He would regard the President's adoption of such a policy as a virtual vindication of his own program. Further-

---

[33] 'Public Man,' 268. The next day, when Douglas related the interview to 'Public Man,' the latter noted 'it is impossible not to feel that he [Douglas] really and truly loves his country in a way not too common, I fear, now in Washington.'

[34] 'Public Man,' 265–67. Lincoln remarked of Sumner that he 'is just my idea of a Bishop.'

[35] Nicolay and Hay, III, 319 et seq. Lincoln gave it to Seward to read on Feb. 23. Seward objected strongly to two paragraphs in which Lincoln said that, after being made President on the Chicago platform, 'one so elected is not at liberty to shift his position.... I hold myself bound by duty, as well as impelled by inclination, to follow, within the Executive sphere, the principles therein declared.' In Seward's opinion these would cause Maryland and Virginia immediately to withdraw, 'and we shall within ninety, perhaps sixty, days be obliged to fight the South for this Capital, with a divided North for our reliance.' In that event, 'the dismemberment of the Republic would date from the inauguration of a Republican Administration.' He knew 'the tenacity of party friends' but they knew nothing of the peril. Let Lincoln follow the example of Jefferson's first Inaugural. Lincoln wisely omitted the two objectionable paragraphs. The fine closing was likewise a Seward note.

more, should it succeed, it would eventually destroy the political power of the Republican party.[36]

That same day two of Douglas' distinguished Southern friends told him that the South could not endure the disgrace of a Republican in the White House. The era of compromise would end the day the South took up arms against the Government, Douglas warned them; 'you and your institution will perish together.' [37]

General Scott made elaborate preparations to prevent disturbance on Inauguration Day, but none occurred. The Republicans, on their part, had made great efforts to have the ceremonies solemn and imposing. The city filled with militia from the Northern States, companies of the Republican Wide-Awakes and a larger army of patriotic Republicans who had come looking for post offices.

Inauguration morning was cloudy and raw. The various processions and ceremonies were awkward and poorly made, but a crowd of about thirty thousand gathered in front of the steps to the Capitol to see Lincoln sworn in and hear his address.[38] Both outgoing and incoming Presidents seemed ill at ease during the giving of the oath, while Chief Justice Taney was uncontrollably agitated.

Douglas had heard new rumors of impending troubles. 'I shall be there,' he said, 'and if any man attacks Lincoln, he attacks me too!' It was his purpose 'to leave no doubt on anyone's mind of his determination to stand by the new Administration in the performance of its first great duty to maintain the Union.' With great difficulty he made his way to the front of the crowd and stood a little behind the incoming President. A rickety little table had been provided for Lincoln, who could hardly find room on it for his hat. With a smile, Douglas reached forward, took the bothersome headpiece, and held it during the address. An observer noted that 'it was a trifling act, but a symbolic one, and not to be forgotten.'

The new President was 'pale and very nervous,' but as he went forward Douglas nodded frequently, and a friend standing close by overheard his muttered comments: 'Good,' 'That's fair,' 'No backing out there,' 'That's a good point.'

When the President reached his closing paragraphs, he was visibly affected and 'threw a tone of strange but genuine pathos' into his poetic appeal. As soon as he ended, Douglas rushed forward and congratulated him.[39]

---

[36] 'Public Man,' 379–80. But John Forsyth to Robert Toombs, Washington, March 8, 1861, Pickett MSS., claims Douglas said he defended Lincoln's Inaugural as a peace measure 'for the purpose of fixing that construction on it, and of tomahawking it afterwards if it [the Lincoln Administration] departed from it.'

[37] *Weekly Illinois Journal*, Springfield, Jan. 21, 1863, quoting from speech of Mr. Eastman, of Chicago, made at a Union demonstration in the Hall of Representatives, Springfield, Jan. 9, 1863.

[38] Villard, *Memoirs*, I, 158; Nicolay and Hay, III, 324–25.

[39] Howard, 212; Orth, 438; 'Public Man,' 383–85. But Henry Watterson, who was among the spectators, thought Lincoln composed; he too noticed Douglas' symbolic courtesy.

That evening the President and Mrs. Lincoln went to the Inaugural Ball. 'Such an assemblage of strange costumes, male and female, was never seen before.' Lincoln looked exhausted and uncomfortable. Mrs. Lincoln, dressed in blue, with a feather in her hair, was highly flushed. By her side, and 'very civil and attentive, was Stephen A. Douglas, who had escorted her as a further mark of his loyalty to the Union and its new President. The Ultras were 'very bitter' about the way Douglas had stood by the President. The day, they admitted, 'had not been a good one for the disruptionists.' [40]

Lincoln's Cabinet was almost equally divided between Conservatives and Radicals. Seward, who had at the last moment withdrawn his acceptance, reconsidered and became Secretary of State. Chase took the direction of the Treasury and Bates became Attorney-General. Caleb Smith, of Indiana, was made Secretary of the Interior, and Simon Cameron, of Pennsylvania, Secretary of War; thus the President redeemed the two pledges which had brought him the Chicago nomination. Gideon Welles, a conservative, white-bearded Connecticut editor, was made Secretary of the Navy. Montgomery Blair, of Maryland, became Postmaster-General and chief of Republican patronage.[41]

The first morning of the new Administration the President was confronted with the reality of Fort Sumter, when Holt handed him a communication from Major Anderson, explaining that the Confederate authorities had deprived the garrison of any local food supplies, and that he could not hold out much over three weeks more.[42]

The Cabinet — and the North — was divided into two schools of thought about the problem. The Radical Republicans favored an immediate attempt at resupply, even should this precipitate war. These men thought the new Confederacy would crumble upon the first show of force, because a small junta had caused all the trouble, and the Southern people would have no heart in a conspirators' war.

It was true that a comparatively small cabal had played the decisive part in the initial stages of Secession. But the Radicals failed to recognize that Lincoln's election had amazingly accelerated Secession feeling among the Conservatives, and as has often occurred in American annals, quickly mobilized majority consent for a program initiated by a minority faction.

The second Cabinet group, to which the Conservatives threw their strength, believed that, given peace and adequate time, the Union could be reconstituted. The actual situation backed up their view. The Confederates had seized all the Federal forts except Sumter in Charleston Harbor and Fort Pickens in Pensacola Bay, which now represented symbolic rather than actual National authority. Would it not be better to withdraw their small garrisons from these forts, so as to prevent immediate hostilities and secure the Border States?

---

[40] 'Public Man,' 385, 387–88.

[41] Nicolay and Hay, III, 345–74, for Seward correspondence and background of the various appointments.

[42] Nicolay and Hay, III, 376–77; Rhodes, III, 212.

Through most of March, Lincoln's mind was torn between these alternatives, callers noted his 'haggard, worn look' — and, indeed, he must make about as trying a decision as a man was ever called upon to make. Seward knew there were no military reasons for keeping Sumter and had no doubt that it would soon be evacuated. Lincoln's own mind was uncertain. On March 7, he told a caller that if Sumter were abandoned, he would have to leave the White House the same day. But a little later he told Douglas that he intended to evacuate the fort, and that all his Cabinet except Blair concurred.[43]

The Little Giant was doing everything in his power to aid the Conservatives. The Senate was in special session to pass upon Lincoln's nominations. Douglas sought to gain support there for a conciliatory course, for he knew that such a program was essential to secure the Border States.[44]

Lincoln's Inaugural disturbed the Southern Unionists. Virginia Union leaders stressed the fact that the Secessionists' only hope was an armed collision.[45] Were the North Carolina election to be held now, Douglas was informed, the convention program would carry by ten thousand votes. Similar word came from Tennessee and Kentucky.

The Virginia Convention remained a potent factor; although it had declined Secession, despite all the efforts of the Conservatives, it had remained in session. The Administration efforts sought to reassure the convention and to persuade it to adjourn *sine die*. On March 9, Seward sent unofficial assurances that on no account would Anderson be reinforced. A rumor that Lincoln planned to abandon the fort 'nerved the hearts' of the Unionists. On March 11, a secret ballot of the convention yielded a majority of twenty-three Unionists — 'men not to be frightened' — against Secessionists of all sorts.

'Virginia is sadly in our way and would to God we could kick her out,' a Maryland Hotspur complained to Howell Cobb. 'She is a degenerate old State.' He and his allies felt that a stubborn Governor, and the example of Virginia, had kept Maryland from seceding.

Thus it was not without reason that the Border leaders urged Douglas to use his influence to persuade the President that he could disarm the Secessionists by removing the Federal forces from Sumter and Pickens. Several advised that 'public opinion' was effecting more than Lincoln could do 'with an army with banners.' 'All we ask of Mr. Lincoln is to give us a fair field and not to mar our prospects by a forcible interference.... We cannot stand a moment against our enemies if force should be used in any shape. If fighting is begun, we are all swept into the vortex of disunion.' [46]

---

[43] Public Man,' 488–93. New York *Herald*, March 10, 1861, said Sumter was to be abandoned.

[44] W. B. Sayles, Richmond, Va., March 3, Savannah, Ga., March 11, 1861; Douglas MSS. 'The man that prevents the first blood-shed,' Sayler wrote from Savannah, 'saves the country.'

[45] Joseph R. Bradley, Huntsville, Ala., March 8; James R. Holt, Lynchburg, Va., March 10: George Blow, Jr., Richmond, March 13; Felix McClosky, Richmond, March 14; Quint Busby, Raleigh, N.C., March 11, 1861; Douglas MSS. The North Carolinian added that through the seceders' failure in the convention campaign, the people 'have learned for the first time in a series of years their power over politicians and party organizations.'

[46] A. M. Reilly, Pettersburg, March 12; James R. Holt, Lynchburg, March 10, 1861; Douglas

Douglas sought to check the unfavorable effect of Lincoln's speech in the Border States. On March 6, Clingman, in a Senate speech, attacked the Inaugural as 'a preachment which must lead to war.' Douglas countered that, on the contrary, 'it is a peace offering rather than a war message.' The President had guaranteed the faithful execution of the Fugitive Slave Act, and, so far as seceded States were concerned, Lincoln proposed to act only in accordance with such legislation as Congress should pass to equip and direct him.[47] Douglas' analysis went far to reassure the Border. 'Your interpretation,' they advised him, 'has again placed us erect.' Lincoln told Douglas that he 'agreed with all its views and sympathized with its spirit.'

All the President wanted, he went on, was to remove the points of present irritation 'so that the people might grow cool, and reflect on the general position all over the country.' With this, a general demand would arise for a national convention, at which the difficulties could be radically treated. In the meanwhile, he did not see why the Executive need attempt to retake the Federal forts.

'I am just as ready to reinforce the garrisons at Sumter and Pickens, or to withdraw them,' he continued, 'as I am to see the amendment adopted protecting slavery in the Territories or prohibiting slavery in the Territories. What I want is to get done what the people desire to have done, and the question for me is how to find that out exactly.' [48]

Word filtered in from Montgomery that the Confederacy had its troubles. Toombs, whom Davis had made Secretary of State, was saying on all occasions that 'Cotton is King,' and had the wildest ideas that England and France would immediately accord recognition. But Memminger, the head of the Treasury, feared that unless something was done to procure a solid basis of credit abroad, the Confederacy could not much longer carry on the ordinary processes of government.[49] More than this, the people of Secessia were disappointed at the lack of action. Some of Davis' advisers concluded that unless blood spilled it would be hard to cement the new government. But the Confederate President wanted the North to open fire.

On March 12 Douglas began a debate designed to force the Radical Republicans either to accept or to attack Lincoln's peace policy. He reviewed at length the legal status of Federal authority in the South. As the laws stood, the Executive could not use the army and the navy to enforce the law in the Southern States. What would be involved in the use of force? He had

MSS.; Levi K. Bowen to Howell Cobb, Baltimore, March 18, 1861; Erwin MSS. 'Public Man,' 487, for Seward's assurance to Virginia Convention.

[47] For press reaction to Inaugural, see Richmond *Enquirer*, March 5, 1861: 'Civil war must now come.' Richmond *Whig*, March 5, 1861: Lincoln's policy 'will meet with the stern and unyielding resistance of a United South.' For Douglas' speech, *Congressional Globe*, Thirty-Seventh Congress, Special Session of the Senate, of March 4, 1861; 1436 *et seq*.

[48] Hamilton C. Jones, Raleigh, March 10; Quint Busby, Raleigh, March 11, 1861; Douglas MSS.; 'Public Man,' 493–94. Sanders to Reverdy Johnson, London, Aug. 11, 1866; Andrew Johnson MSS.

[49] 'Public Man', 485–86.

secured estimates from competent military authorities as to the troop requirements in the event of war. At least 285,000 men would be needed to compel submission and it would cost at least $316,000,000 to keep them in the field for a year. How could eighteen States ever pay the cost of subjugating fifteen?[50] The Republicans sat silent as he talked, smiling contemptuously. When he finished, Henry Wilson, of Massachusetts, attacked him as the country's outstanding alarmist. Douglas lost his temper and taunted the Republican Radicals with desiring the Union dissolved. The Republicans were unyielding, the few Northern Democrats were impotent but the galleries applauded wildly.

It was significant that, all through this debate, 'it was perfectly obvious' that the Republican who answered Douglas knew that the Little Giant was 'really uttering the sentiments and sketching the policy of the President.' Indeed, Hale and Wilson were about willing to admit that Douglas reflected Lincoln's policy and to go on and 'attack the White House.'

In mid-March, Douglas seemed on the way to becoming the President's main Senate supporter. Whenever word came of the evacuation of Sumter, as was momentarily expected, the Little Giant would register a great political triumph. 'We shall then see collisions which will bring out the innermost truths as to the political chart of the new Administration,' a diarist noted. This would almost certainly 'lead to the complete reorganization of our political parties, if indeed it stops there.'[51] Thus the Little Giant continued to hold Lincoln's hat.

[50] *Congressional Globe*, Thirty-Seventh Congress, Special Session, of the Senate of March 4, 1861; 1461 *et seq.* for this speech and ensuing debates.
[51] 'Public Man,' 494–96.

CHAPTER XXXIII

DEATH OF A HERO

WHILE Douglas sought vainly to commit the Republican Senators to conciliation, Lincoln seemed to have decided to make an energetic effort to hold Fort Pickens in Pensacola Bay and to withdraw from Fort Sumter in Charleston Harbor. Pickens could be easily reinforced from the sea, and the *Brooklyn*, with several hundred soldiers aboard, had been lying off the fort, refraining from landing them only because of an unofficial armistice arranged between the Buchanan Administration and the two Florida Senators.

On March 12, Lincoln, who had no precise information about this agreement, dispatched orders to throw the troops on the *Brooklyn* into Pickens at once. Then he asked his constitutional advisers: 'Assuming it to be possible to now provision Fort Sumter, under all the circumstances is it wise to attempt it?'

Seward answered that withdrawal's effect on the Border States would far outweigh the loss of a fort, while the effort to supply would certainly lead to 'war, by our own act, without an adequate object, after which reunion will be hopeless.' Cameron, Welles, Smith and Bates agreed that it was inadvisable. Chase wrote that, if the enterprise would occasion civil war and 'involve an immediate necessity for the enlistment of armies and the expenditure of millions,' he was against it. Montgomery Blair thought that Buchanan's policy had already made war inevitable. Furthermore, the Secessionists 'for the most part believe *that the Northern men are deficient in the courage necessary to maintain the government*'; were Sumter evacuated, that would seem added proof. The relief effort was necessary to show that the North would fight to preserve the Union.[1]

As soon as the meeting broke up, the Postmaster-General told his father what had happened; the latter hastened to the White House and asked Lincoln whether abandonment had been definitely decided upon. The President answered, that, of the Cabinet, 'all except your son' had advised the course and he thought it would be followed. Blair objected that the people would disapprove such a policy, it would 'destroy the formation of the Republican party,' and probably impeachment would follow.[2]

Unsettled by this remonstrance, Lincoln sent two missions to feel out the situation at Sumter and at Charleston. The first was that of Captain

---

[1] Crawford, 347–58; Nicolay and Hay, III, 385–88; Rhodes, III, 214 *et seq.*; Bates, *Diary* 177–80. Seward made a powerful argument for the political expediency of evacuation as a move which 'would enable the Unionists in the Slave States to maintain' themselves. Cameron concluded that no practical benefit would accrue from the effort. Bates was 'willing to evacuate Fort Sumter, rather than be an active party in the beginning of civil war.' On March 13, General Scott had written a memorandum for Secretary of War Cameron, giving the opinion that 'an abandonment of the fort in a few weeks sooner or later would appear... to be a pure necessity.'

[2] Francis P. Blair to General Samuel W. Crawford; quoted in Crawford, 364.

Gustavus V. Fox, of the Navy, who thought Sumter could be reinforced by a sudden sortie from the sea, and wanted Lincoln to put him in charge of such an expedition. After Fox assured Governor Pickens that his object was peaceful, the latter gave him a pass to Sumter. Major Anderson felt it impracticable to attempt relief without a large land force, the garrison's food was almost exhausted and he could not hold out after noon on April 15.[3]

The President next sent Stephen A. Hurlbut and Ward H. Lamon to Charleston. Hurlbut, who was a friend of that staunch Unionist, James L. Petigru, was to find out whether a strong Union party actually existed in the Cotton South. Lamon came ostensibly to examine post-office accounts. Petigru quickly disabused Hurlbut of the idea of a strong Union party. Lamon told Governor Pickens that Lincoln planned to evacuate Sumter, gave Anderson the same impression, and, on returning to Washington, wrote Pickens that he would soon return to remove the garrison.[4]

With these reports, Lincoln again sought a definite decision. His mind still went to the withdrawal of the garrison as soon as he had news that Fort Pickens had been reinforced. The members of the Cabinet went to the White House on March 28 for Lincoln's first State dinner. At its close the President drew them aside and read, with great emotion, a memorandum from General Scott recommending the immediate evacuation of Pickens as well as Sumter. This raised a storm of protest.[5]

Lincoln ordered immediate preparation at New York of an expedition to relieve Sumter, this force 'to be ultimately used or not, according to circumstances.' Cabinet opinion definitely shifted. While Seward still favored yielding Sumter, he would 'at once, and at every cost, prepare for a war at Pensacola and Texas.' Chase now favored relieving both forts, regardless of war, and Welles thought the Government must 'assert and maintain its authority.' A secret force was accordingly prepared to relieve Pickens.

Lincoln now undertook to make a bargain with Virginia for the evacuation of Sumter. Shortly after the Cabinet meeting of March 29, he had Seward send a messenger to Richmond to ask George W. Summers, the leader of the Unionist delegates in the Constitutional Convention, to come to Washington for a conference. Summers pleaded important business and sent John B. Baldwin, another Union delegate, in his stead.

After reviewing the several refusals of the Union majority in the convention to pass a Secession Ordinance, Lincoln proposed that, if his visitor would 'get that Union majority to adjourn and go home without passing the Ordinance of Secession, so anxious am I for the preservation of the peace of this country, and to save Virginia and the other Border States from

---

[3] Crawford, 369–73.

[4] Nicolay and Hay, III, 389–92; Crawford, 373–74; Lamon, *Recollections*, 68–79. Lamon asked Pickens if he would permit the ingress of a Federal war vessel to remove the garrison. The Governor replied that 'no war vessel could be allowed to enter the harbor on any terms.' Hurlbut reported to Lincoln, March 27, 1861, that Petigru had told him separate nationality was 'a fixed fact' in the Southern mind.

[5] *O.R.*, I, 200–01; Crawford, 363. Scott's memorandum recited that the evacuation of Sumter 'would be charged to *necessity*, and the holding of Fort Pickens would be adduced in support of that view.'

going out, that I will take the responsibility of evacuating Fort Sumter, and take the chance of negotiating with the Cotton States.' Startled, Baldwin asked: 'Adjourn it how? Do you mean *sine die?*' When Lincoln answered in the affirmative, Baldwin declared he would not agree; Lincoln must call a national convention and order his forces withdrawn from Pickens as well as Sumter. The offer was never brought before the Virginia Convention.[6]

The President now found that his instructions of March 12 about landing troops to reinforce Pickens had not been carried out. Lincoln, who had expected to make simultaneous announcement that Pickens was secure, and that Sumter would be abandoned, was terribly upset.[7] He promptly dispatched an officer overland to Pensacola with peremptory instructions, and urged haste on the second expedition to Pickens. Most important of all, he made up his mind to send the other expedition to Sumter, and thus to cast the die of war.[8]

Now he ordered an official of the State Department to Charleston. On April 8, the latter read to Governor Pickens this statement: 'I am directed by the President of the United States to notify you to expect an attempt will be made to supply Fort Sumter with provisions only, and that, if such attempt be not resisted, no effort to throw men, arms or ammunition, will be made, without further notice or in case of an attack upon the fort.' [9]

In sending this notice, Lincoln redeemed a pledge Seward had given in the course of unofficial negotiations with the Confederate Commissioners.

[6] This account is based on testimony before the Joint Committee of Reconstruction, Thirty-Ninth Congress, First Session, in 1866. John Minor Botts, a Virginia Unionist, there testified that he had visited the White House on April 7, 1861, three days after the Lincoln-Baldwin interview, and that the President had then related the conversation to him and his offer to Virginia. Baldwin, who also testified, insisted that Lincoln had made 'no pledge, no offer, no promise of any sort,' but did admit the request to adjourn the convention and his own question about *sine die* and Lincoln's response. Botts' book, *The Great Rebellion*, New York, 1866, 195–202, f.n., contains corroborative evidence that Lincoln had made an offer, and had said that he 'would give a fort for a State' any time. Nicolay and Hay, III, 426–28.

[7] Lincoln Message to Congress on July 4, 1861: 'Starvation was not yet upon the [Sumter] garrison, and ere it would be reached, Fort Pickens might be reinforced. This fact would be a clear indication of policy, and would better enable the country to accept the evacuation of Fort Sumter as a military necessity. An order was at once directed to be sent for the landing of troops from the Steamship *Brooklyn* into Fort Pickens.... The first return news from the order was received just one week before the fall of Sumter. The news itself was that the officer commanding the *Sabine*, to which vessel the troops had been transferred from the *Brooklyn*, acting upon some quasi-armistice of the last Administration (and of the existence of which the present Administration, up to the time the order was dispatched, had only too vague and uncertain rumors to give attention), had refused to land the troops. To now reinforce Fort Pickens before a crisis would be reached at Fort Sumter was impossible.'

[8] Dr. Charles W. Ramsdell, of the University of Texas, letter to author, June 18, 1934, suggests his strong suspicion that Lincoln's course as to Sumter was from the outset aimed at getting the Confederates to fire the first gun. Lamon's report of his Charleston visit, Dr. Ramsdell thinks, showed Lincoln that the Confederates would open fire if any sort of a relief expedition were sent; therefore the effort 'to send food to starving men.' If so, the Confederates fell into the trap. *Cf.* Browning, *Diary*, I, 465; 475–76.

[9] Crawford, 396.

These came to Washington early in March. Should the President refuse to receive them formally, they were instructed to accept an informal conversation, but under no circumstances to countenance any Federal jurisdiction, civil or military, within the limits of the Confederacy.[10] Soon after their arrival they reported to Montgomery that Seward felt that he had brought the Republican party to triumph, the enjoyment of which was now periled. Therefore he 'must save the party and save the Government in its hands. To do this, war must be averted, the Negro question must be dropped, the irrepressible conflict ignored, and a Union party to embrace the Border Slave States inaugurated'; after these had been saved 'by moderation and justice,' the people of the Cotton States, unwillingly led into Secession, would repudiate their false leaders and reconstruction would follow.[11] But Seward must have time to work out this program.

When the Commissioners had Senator Hunter, of Virginia, call on Seward to arrange for an interview, the Secretary said not to press him on it; only refusal could follow. But if time were given, there would be a better chance for peace. Accordingly the Confederates prepared a memorandum outlining the conditions for a twenty-day respite in their formal demand. When Hunter presented it, Seward was 'perceptibly embarrassed and uneasy.' The next day he handed Hunter a note saying that it would not be in his power to receive the Commissioners. The latter then submitted a formal demand for an interview, knowing that Seward's answer would put an end to all hopes of peace.

At this juncture, Justice Nelson, of the United States Supreme Court, entered the picture. A New York Unionist, he reprehended Secession, but felt that whatever was done to assert Federal authority should be done in accordance with the Constitution. Lately he had sought to determine the limits within which Federal authority could be exerted, and now he called on Seward to recount his views. During the conversation the Secretary of State mentioned his embarrassment over the Confederate Commissioners' demand. At once Nelson consulted his colleague, Justice Campbell, still an Alabama Unionist, and the two urged Seward to answer the Confederate note with assurance of forbearance. Seward became excited and said that, 'if Jefferson Davis had known the state of things here, he would not have sent those Commissioners; the evacuation of Sumter is as much as the Administration can bear.'

Campbell who had not heard of this possibility, undertook to halt the Commissioners' demand.[12] This he did, and, with Montgomery's approval, for the next three weeks Seward and the Confederates passed word back and forth through Justice Campbell, as to the evacuation of Sumter, and Lincoln had some knowledge of this backstairs relationship.[13]

[10] The three men were John Forsyth, of Alabama; Martin J. Crawford, of Georgia; and A. B. Roman, of Louisiana; they were appointed Feb. 15, 1861, by a resolution of the Provisional Confederate Congress. Their instructions, prepared by the Confederate State Department, were signed by Robert Toombs and dated Montgomery, Feb. 27, 1861.

[11] Forsyth and Crawford to Toombs, Washington, March 8, 1861; Pickett MSS.

[12] J. A. Campbell, 'Facts of History,' MSS., quoted in Crawford, 328 *et seq.*

[13] Nicolay and Hay, IV, 33 *et seq.*, giving memorandum of John G. Nicolay.

Seward told Campbell on March 15 that Sumter would be evacuated within five days, and that there would be no change as to Pickens. When the evacuation did not occur, Seward explained that 'Governments could not move with bank accuracy.' On March 30, Campbell called on Seward again with a telegram from Governor Pickens about Lamon's unfulfilled promises. Lincoln, much concerned, sent word that Lamon had no authority, and Seward handed the Justice a memorandum 'that the President may desire to supply Fort Sumter, but will not undertake to do so without first giving notice to Governor Pickens.'

When Lincoln's agent called upon Governor Pickens at Charleston, Campbell protested to Seward of bad faith. In answer, he received an unsigned message, in Seward's hand: 'Faith as to Sumter fully kept; wait and see.' The Commissioners now demanded the reply to their interview request, and Seward furnished them a copy of his memorandum dated March 15, refusing any relations with them. Justice Campbell, who felt that he had been outrageously tricked, resigned from the Supreme Court and went South.[14]

It is hard to explain these dealings. For months Seward clung to the obsession that he could outmaneuver the Southerners; before Lincoln went in, he was negotiating with Montgomery through Dr. Gwin, of California. After the arrival of the Commissioners, John Forsyth told Douglas that Seward flattered himself that he 'was using and could control them.' [15]

After the middle of March, Douglas' own contact with the White House seemed broken, perhaps because he saw Lincoln veering toward war. At any event, on March 25 the Little Giant advised a Virginia Conservative that he had 'no political affinity with the Administration,' and from then until middle April his relations with Lincoln seemed suspended. But the Senator continued to be pressed for help by the Border Conservatives. North Carolinians advised that, if the Administration would withdraw from Sumter, 'if its policy is peace and that policy is promptly carried out,' they could overwhelm the Secessionists. But the uncertainty was bringing Union men 'to despair and doubt the faith of the Administration.' [16] The vacillation about Sumter had sorely perplexed the Virginia Conservatives, and Douglas was informed of the dangers which surrounded them. 'There are times when a man's life is in his own hands,' one wrote, 'any day may be my last.' None the less, as late as April 4 the Unionist delegates defeated, 88 to 45, a motion to bring in a Secession Ordinance.[17]

[14] Crawford, 340; Connor, *Life of Campbell*, 109–48; Bancroft, *Seward*, II, 107–120; 129–30; 140–42. Official Correspondence, Confederate Commissioners, Pickett MSS., March 3 to April 8, 1861.

[15] Crawford, 319–20, quoting letter from Gwin to himself; 'Public Man,' 394; Gideon Welles, *Diary*, Boston, 1913, I, 34.

[16] For Douglas' expression as to lack of political affinity, see Thos. H. Gilmer, Richmond, Va., March 28, 1861, Douglas MSS., quoting Douglas' letter to him of March 25. Robt. P. Dick, Greensboro, N.C., March 7; John A. Gilmer, Greensboro, March 18; H. W. Miller, Raleigh, March 31, 1861; Douglas MSS.

[17] Crawford, 340; Connor, *Life of Cambell*, 109–48; Bancroft, *Seward*, II, 107–120; 129–30; 140–42. Official Correspondence, Confederate Commissioners, Pickett MSS., March 3 to April 8, 1861.

One item from the Border could not have failed to please the Little Giant: the Missouri Legislature had retired Green, his bitter enemy, from the Senate. Not only this, but Indiana turned down Fitch, Bright's ally; California repudiated Dr. Gwin and Oregon returned Joe Lane to private life. Douglas might be excused a feeling of satisfaction at this belated verdict of the people upon the Buchaneers.[18]

With April, Douglas seemed to realize that there was no further chance for compromise or peaceful separation, and that now it was imperative that the Administration act decisively and effectually to reconstitute the Union. Lincoln's dispatch of the expedition to Sumter added to this conviction. On April 10, the Senator warned Gideon Welles that a terrible civil war was now inevitable, due to the Administration's vacillation, and urged 'immediate and decisive measures.'

When Welles asked him to talk to Seward, Douglas looked at him with 'mingled astonishment and incredulity,' and asked if Welles had not known that 'Seward has had an understanding with these men. If he has any influence with them, why don't he use it?' But he did accompany Welles to Seward's office, where he told the two Cabinet members that they must take his word for the information he gave, for he could not name his informant. But the 'Fire-Eaters were going to fire on Sumter.' Seward heard this statement calmly, took a pinch of snuff, and said that he would speak to the President about it.[19]

Seward at the time was smarting under a White House rebuke. A few days earlier he had given Lincoln a paper entitled 'Some thoughts for the President's consideration.' At the end of a month the Administration was 'yet without a policy either domestic or foreign.' One must be adopted immediately, and executed either by the President, who must 'be all the time active in it,' or by some member of his Cabinet. 'It is not in my especial province,' Seward concluded, 'but I never seek to evade nor assume responsibility.'

As to domestic affairs, the Secretary of State would 'change the question before the public from one upon slavery, or about slavery, for a question upon Union or disunion.' Sumter's relief was in some way bound up in the public mind with slavery, and therefore that fort should be promptly abandoned, the blame being put on the Buchanan Administration. But Seward would 'simultaneously defend and reinforce all the forts in the Gulf,' and institute a blockade. This course would 'raise distinctly the question of Union or disunion,' and allow the shift of the issue from slavery. In the foreign field, Seward proposed that the Government immediately demand explanations from Spain, France, Russia and Great Britain, because of recent movements in the Caribbean. Should they not give satisfactory

[18] James C. Faucette, Jefferson City, Mo., March 18; James D. Eads, Warrensburg, Mo., March 23, 1861; Douglas MSS.: 'I think the people of Indiana, Missouri, California and Oregon have treated the traitors about right politically. But if they had got their just deserts they would have been hanged long ago. In my opinion a worse set of men never lived in any country or in any age than the late friends of President James Buchanan.'

[19] Russell, *The Civil War in America*, 18; dispatch to London *Times*, Washington, April 1, 1861; Welles, *Diary*, I, 32 *et seq.*

explanations, the President must 'convene Congress and declare war against them.' This would reunite the country.

Lincoln's reply, in form kindly, was in fact a sharp rebuke. The domestic policy thus far pursued had been precisely that urged by Seward, except that it no longer involved abandoning Sumter. He did not see why Sumter could be abandoned because it was involved with the slavery issue, while Pickens could be reinforced as a Union issue. As to a foreign war, his irony was decisive: 'If this must be done, I must do it.' In other words, he and not Seward was President.[20]

Lincoln's notice to Governor Pickens had been telegraphed to Montgomery by General G. T. Beauregard, of Louisiana, a brother-in-law of Senator Slidell, whom Davis had placed in command at Charleston. The General, whose batteries were ready to reduce Sumter, asked orders. The Davis Cabinet was in a dilemma. Lincoln's notice had been framed to give the expedition the form of an errand of humanity rather than of war.

'The firing on that fort,' Toombs told the Cabinet, 'will inaugurate a civil war greater than any the world has yet seen; and I do not feel competent to advise you.' But Davis was also told that 'unless you sprinkle blood in the face of the people of Alabama, they will be back in the old Union in less than ten days.' So Beauregard was instructed that the fort must surrender or be reduced.[21]

So he sent three aides to Sumter, bearing an evacuation demand. Anderson refused, but remarked that in five days his food would be exhausted and he would have to withdraw anyway. Beauregard was then authorized by Montgomery 'to avoid the effusion of blood' if Anderson would specify when he would evacuate.

This brought a second Confederate offer, under which, at the end of five days, the garrison could withdraw with full honors of war. The Federal commander agreed to evacuate at noon on April 15, 'should I not receive prior to that time controlling instructions from my Government, or additional supplies.' Without referring the answer to Beauregard, the aides — two of them Secessionist politicians — rejected it as 'manifestly futile.' The next morning the Confederate War Department telegraphed Beauregard to know what had become of the proposed compromise. By that time, however, the Confederate batteries were raining shells on Sumter and the Civil War had begun.[22]

Major Anderson then had in Sumter nine officers and seventy-four enlisted men, to serve forty-eight guns. The Confederates had against

[20] Lincoln, *Works*, VI, 234–37. Seward's 'Thoughts' were dated April 1, 1861, and Lincoln replied the same day.

[21] Crawford, 421. Nicolay and Hay, IV, 456.

[22] Nicolay and Hay, IV, 45 *et seq.*; Crawford, 425. The three aides were James Chestnut, Sr., an ex-Senator from South Carolina; Stephen D. Lee, later a Confederate General, and Roger A. Pryor, of Virginia. A star shell, signal for the general bombardment, was fired by Captain George S. James, at Fort Johnson. Then the venerable Edmund Ruffin, the Virginia prophet of Secession, attached to a battery on Cummings Point, pulled the lanyard for the first shell against the fort itself. Senator Wigfall, of Texas, was also on Beauregard's staff.

him seven thousand officers and men, serving forty-seven mortars and guns. The Federals fed that last day on rice gathered from the storeroom floor. Their guns were without screws, scales or tangents, they had no fuses for their shells, no cartridge bag for their powder, and their fate was fore-doomed.[23]

Some of the ships of the relief expedition arrived off the Charleston bar the night Beauregard's guns opened. But there had been a severe storm, the naval officers agreed that open boats could not live in the harbor chan-nel, and the relieving forces made no move to relieve. For thirty-four hours guns thundered, and yet no one on either side was killed. But the Confederate shells started a breach, soon an infantry assault would be in order, and when Senator Wigfall came to offer evacuation, Anderson ca-pitulated on the very terms he had offered to accept two days before.[24]

On April 13, President Lincoln received a committee from the Virginia Convention, which had come to appeal to him for a peaceful policy. That day, he told them, there were reports that the Seceders had fired on Fort Sumter, and he would 'repel force by force.' He would not attempt to collect the Federal taxes by armed invasion, but he would protect the Govern-ment's property with troops. The Virginians returned to Richmond con-vinced that war could no longer be forestalled.

All day Saturday Washington was in ferment. The Cabinet met early Sunday morning, officers of the Army and Navy were consulted, militia laws examined and troop quotas assigned the various States. On word from Charleston that Major Anderson had capitulated, Lincoln drafted a pro-clamation calling on the treasonable combinations to disperse, and sum-moning seventy-five thousand men to three months' service, to repress rebellion and repossess the Federal forts and property.

Late that afternoon when George Ashmun, a Republican Congressman from Massachusetts, called at the White House, Lincoln expressed 'his earnest desire for the support of the best men of the country.' Obviously at the President's request, Ashmun sped to the home of Stephen A. Douglas, unfolded his mission and urged Douglas: 'Go at once to the President, and take him by the hand and tender him all the aid you can give.' Adèle put her hands on Douglas' shoulders and urged him to go, and he said decisively that he would.[25]

[23] Russell, *Civil War*, 40–41; Nicolay and Hay, IV, 48–49.

[24] Crawford, 427–48. Casualties, however, occurred on the 14th, as Anderson was lowering his flag and was saluting it with a hundred guns. One gun exploded, powder blew up and there were two killed and several severely wounded.

[25] Probably the most dependable account of this interview is that by S. P. Hanscom, printed as an editorial in the *National Republican*, Washington, Sept. 16, 1866, occasioned by the dedica-tion of the Douglas monument at Chicago. New York *Tribune*, Oct. 31, 1864, contains a letter from Ashmun to Isaac N. Arnold, an Illinois Congressman, dated Springfield, Mass., Oct. 15, 1864, in which Ashmun gives an account, generally identical with that of Hanscom, of the Douglas interview. Holland, 300–02, has an account, apparently based on Ashmun's letter. Nicolay and Hay, IV, 80 *et seq.*, has an account without source references; this last account claims that Douglas, 'through a friend, signified his desire for an interview.'

The Senator drove with Ashmun to the White House. Lincoln received him 'with outstretched hands and with a benignant smile,' and handed him a draft of the proclamation which would be published the next morning.

'Seventy-five thousand men will not be sufficient,' Douglas declared. 'I would make it two hundred thousand.'[26] A map was brought and he pointed out and marked the strategic points which should at once be strengthened, especially Washington, Fortress Monroe, Harper's Ferry and Cairo, Illinois, whose proper protection might require most of the men in the call. Impressed, Lincoln asked him to repeat these views to General Scott. Douglas went on to impress the essentials of the strategic situation, with Lincoln 'an earnest and gratified listener.' He warned that there would be trouble bringing Federal troops through Baltimore and showed the President an alternative route by Perryville, Havre de Grace and Annapolis.[27]

When, after two hours of earnest discussion, Douglas took his departure, Ashmun remarked:[28]

'You have done justice to your own reputation, and to the President, and the country must know it. The proclamation will go by telegraph all over the country in the morning, and an account of this interview must go with it. I shall send it either in my own language or yours. I prefer that you should give your own version.' Douglas immediately replied: 'Drive to your room at Willard's and I will give it shape.' In a short while he wrote out a dispatch which was given to the Associated Press and published over the country the next morning.

'Mr. Douglas called on the President, and had an interesting conversation on the present condition of the country,' it stated. 'The substance of the conversation was that, while Mr. Douglas was unalterably opposed to the Administration on all its political issues, he was prepared to sustain the President in the exercise of all his constitutional functions to preserve the Union, and maintain the Government and defend the Federal capital. A firm policy and prompt action was necessary. The Capital of our country was in danger and must be defended at all hazards, and at any expense of men and money. He spoke of the present and future without reference to the past.'

The Little Giant now put his hand to the plow. Publication of his Associated Press dispatch brought many anxious inquiries. He telegraphed a Missouri friend that 'without having been consulted or endorsing any

[26] Nicolay and Hay, IV, 80, states that Douglas arrived between seven and eight o'clock and that 'these two remarkable men sat in confidential interview, without a witness, nearly two hours.' Ashmun, *loc. cit.*, states that he was present during the discussion. The Washington *Republican* account infers Ashmun's presence as a spectator.

[27] I have reconstructed this interview from Ashmun's letter, Hanscom's editorial, Holland, Nicolay and Hay; J. Howard, *Atlantic Monthly*, Aug., 1861, 202; giving Lincoln's statement, a few days later: 'If it is well to appoint brigadier-generals from the civil list, I can imagine few men better qualified for such a position than Judge Douglas. For myself I know I have not much military knowledge, and I think Douglas has.' Interview of Judge William Ewing, in Quincy, Ill. *Optic*, reprinted in Danville, Ill., *Democrat*, Nov. 6, 1907.

[28] Four years later, to the day and hour, John Wilkes Booth assassinated Lincoln.

particular measure, I am for my country and against all assailants.' A puzzled lieutenant objected that Missouri did not endorse Lincoln's war policy and surely Douglas could not. 'I deprecate war,' he promptly answered, 'but if it must come I am with my country and for my country under all circumstances and in every contingency.' When John W. Forney asked him what course to follow, Douglas answered: 'There can be but two parties, the party of patriots and the party of traitors. We belong to the first.' [29]

The firing on Sumter brought a surge of Northern patriotic emotion which almost assumed the proportions of a holy crusade. Men wore badges of loyalty, every house hung out the national flag, pulpits were dressed with the Stars and Stripes and Sunday School children wore bunting buttons.

The attitude of the Northern Democrats was that of their section. John Cochrane, of Tammany, wanted 'to crush the rebellion.' Daniel S. Dickinson, who had helped the Ultras split the Democratic party, consigned the Secessionists to perdition. James Buchanan, who had done more to insure the conflict than any other American, declared that 'The North will sustain the Administration almost to a man; and it ought to be sustained at all hazards.' Ben Butler metamorphosed into a Massachusetts brigadier.[30]

During these weeks the Cotton South was in transports of delight. Davis' Cabinet greeted Lincoln's call for troops with 'bursts of laughter,' and the Secretary of War predicted that by May 1 the Confederate flag would float over the old Capitol at Washington. Already the Confederates had thirty-five thousand men in the field, but they put their main reliance on King Cotton, which was sure to 'exert an influence mightier than armies or navies.' [31]

The Border States must now either aid the 'coercion' of the deep South or join the war on the Union. If the Confederacy would but 'strike a blow,' Roger A. Pryor told the Charlestonians on April 11, it would 'put Virginia in the Southern Confederacy in less than an hour by the Shrewsbury clock.' Sure enough, upon Lincoln's call for troops Governor Letcher informed him: 'You have chosen to inaugurate civil war.' On April 17, by a vote of 88 to 55, the Virginia Convention passed its Ordinance of Secession.

Those Virginians who had been seeking Union through compromise complained bitterly that 'We could have saved the country but for the fatuity and cowardice of this infernal Administration.' Now they hoped that the god of battles 'would crush to the earth and consign to eternal perdition, Mr. Lincoln, his Cabinet and all aiders and abettors of this cruel, needless, cor-

[29] Douglas to T. E. Courtenay, Washington, April 15; James L. Faucette to Douglas, St. Louis, April 15; Douglas to Faucette, Washington, April 17, printed in Quincy, Ill., *Herald*, and *Illinois State Register*, both April 22, 1861. Remark to Forney quoted, Lyman Trumbull, 'Celebrated Men of the Day,' *Belford's Magazine*, V, 225.

[30] E. A. Pollard, *The Lost Cause*, New York, 1866; 113-15; Curtis, II, 543, quotes Buchanan to John A. Dix, Lancaster, Pa., April 19, 1861.

[31] Montgomery dispatch in New York *Tribune*, April 15, 1861; Pollard, *Davis*, 112-16.

rupt betrayal of the Conservative men in the South.'[32] Richmond was now made the Capital of the Confederacy.

Tennessee would not 'furnish a man for purposes of coercion,' Governor Harris telegraphed Washington. While at first John Bell thought it Tennessee's duty 'to maintain the sanctity of her soil from the hostile tread of any party,' within a week he urged the State to stand by the South. Soon Tennessee entered into a military league with the Confederacy, and declared her independence, basing this action on the right of revolution. At the ballot box, separation was sustained by more than two to one.[33]

The Governor of Arkansas proclaimed that his people would 'defend to the last extremity their honor, lives and property against Northern mendacity and usurpation.' The Arkansas Constitutional Convention reassembled, to pass an Ordinance of Secession with only one dissenting vote.[34]

Governor Ellis, of North Carolina would 'be no party to... this war upon the liberties of a free people.' After some delay, a Constitutional Convention was assembled and on May 20 unanimously passed a Secession Ordinance.[35]

North Carolina's was the last Confederate accession. Kentucky's Legislature took the position that she would remain neutral, and Lincoln took great care to prevent too great offense being given her spirit. Her June Congressional elections yielded a stalwart Union delegation. Two months later she chose a new Legislature definitely Union in sentiment. That Fall Confederate troops invaded the State, thus ending all danger of her secession.[36]

Two months before, Missouri's voters had rejected Secession by 80,000 majority. Now Governor Claiborne F. Jackson, termed Lincoln's requisition 'inhuman and diabolical' and refused to supply troops. But Frank Blair, son of Francis and brother of Montgomery, offered and Washington accepted four regiments of home guards, opening a struggle between Jackson and Blair for Missouri public sentiment. Before long Blair's strength was manifest, and in the Summer the Missouri Constitutional Convention deposed Jackson from the Governor's office and Missouri was fixed as a loyal State.

Washington's physical location meant that troops for her defense must come through Maryland, and it was imperative to prevent her secession. The Governor was thoroughly loyal and would not call the Legislature. Lincoln's call for troops, however, forced his hand and he summoned a session but urged that Maryland assume 'a neutral position.' The Legislature pro-

[32] Pollard, *Davis*, 109; John H. Gilmer, Richmond, April 17, 1861; Douglas MSS.; Rhodes, III, 274, for Virginia delegate vote. The election, on May 23, resulted in 128,884 for secession, and 32,134 against it.

[33] Isham G. Harris to Simon Cameron, Nashville, April 30, 1861, printed in *O.R.*, Series III, I, 106; *Appleton's Annual Cyclopædia*, 1861, 678. The vote was 104,913 to 47,238.

[34] *O.R.*, Series III, I, 124; *Appleton's Annual Cyclopædia*, 1861, 23.

[35] *O.R.*, Series III, I, 99, gives Ellis' letter to Cameron. *Appleton's Annual Cyclopædia*, 1861, 539; the North Carolina Convention vote against submission of the Ordinance to the people was 72 to 34.

[36] *O.R.*, Series III, I, 98; Edward Conrad Smith, *The Borderland in the Civil War*, New York, 1927; 263-312.

tested against the war but declined to call a convention and took no steps to secede. That Fall her elections went heavily Union.

None the less, Maryland was the scene of the first actual casualties of the war. Washington was bare of defenders, and Lincoln was desperately anxious for troops from the North. On April 19, when the Sixth Massachusetts Regiment was transferring between stations in Baltimore, a fierce mob attacked, and the men had to leave their cars and fight their way through the streets. The Baltimore authorities then appealed to Lincoln to send no more troops through the State. He could not do this, but altered the route for the next few regiments, bringing them to Washington by the route Douglas had suggested.[37]

Douglas exerted himself to strengthen the organization of the national defense. He had several more interviews with Lincoln, and Scott consulted freely with him about Army problems. The rumor became widespread that Lincoln had determined to make the Little Giant a brigadier-general. When a friend asked the President about it, he said he had no reason to believe Douglas would accept such a position, but 'I can imagine few men better qualified.' Three years later he told Orville H. Browning that he had intended to make Douglas his General-in-Chief.[38]

The question of field command bothered both Lincoln and Scott. The latter was old and obese but there was no question of his utter loyalty. When a committee from the Virginia Convention called on Scott on April 20 to offer him the supreme command of their forces, he responded: 'I have served my country under the flag of the Union for more than fifty years, and as long as God permits me to live, I will defend that flag with my sword, even if my own native State assails it.' Senator Douglas called on him a few minutes later and found him 'writing his orders for the defense and safety of the American capital.'

Scott's choice for the active command of the Federal forces had fallen on another Virginian, Colonel Robert Edward Lee, an engineer, with a fine record and reputation. Lee disliked slavery, felt that the Union was meant to be perpetual and that Secession was 'nothing but revolution.' Lincoln asked Francis Preston Blair to offer him the command of the Army. 'I look upon Secession as anarchy,' Lee answered. 'If I owned four million of slaves at the South, I would sacrifice them all to the Union. But how can I draw my sword upon Virginia, my native State?' Two days later he resigned from the United States Army. On April 22 he accepted the command of Virginia's military forces.[39]

---

[37] *Appleton's Annual Cyclopædia*, 1861, 446; Rhodes, III, 197; 275 *et seq.* On May 9, Federal troops came through the city without disturbance.

[38] Forney, I, 424 *et seq.*; J. Howard, Jr., *Atlantic Monthly*, VIII, 212; Ewing statement of Browning-Lincoln interview, *cit. supra.* Forney, I, 121, 226, states: 'By authority' that Lincoln had in mind giving Douglas a high military command or putting him in the Cabinet.

[39] Offer to Scott and his words of refusal described in Douglas' speech at Bellaire, Ohio, Wheeling, Va., *Intelligencer*, April 23, reprinted in Philadelphia *Press*, April 26, 1861; E. D. Townsend, *Anecdotes of the Civil War*, New York, 1884; 91. Clifford I. Millard, of Norfolk, states that the family of General Joseph E. Johnston, in Norfolk, are convinced that the Federal

By this time, word had come from Illinois which convinced Douglas that he could do more good in the West than in Washington. Governor Yates called a special session of the Illinois Legislature, but there were mutterings in Egypt, with danger of an actual insurrection. Lanphier and other Douglas Democrats telegraphed the Little Giant that there were 'grave reasons' why he must be in Springfield when the Legislature met. He laid the matter before Lincoln, who knew, as well as Douglas, the immense importance of the Northwest to the Union. The decision was for Douglas to go West. They shook hands in affectionate farewell and parted for the last time.[40]

The railroad line north through Baltimore was still broken, and the Douglases were forced to take the Baltimore and Ohio through western Virginia. They missed train connections at Bellaire, Ohio, just below Wheeling, Virginia. News that the Little Giant was at the hotel spread like wildfire, a throng gathered and he was beset for a speech. Thousands poured in on special trains from western Virginia, and Douglas' words that afternoon were sober and thoughtful. 'The very existence,' he said, 'of the people in this great valley depends upon maintaining inviolate and forever that great right secured by the Constitution, of freedom of trade, of transit, and of commerce, from the center of the continent to the ocean that surrounds it.' The question was not only one of Union or disunion, but 'of order, of the stability of the government; of the peace of communities. The whole social system is threatened with destruction.'

'Unite as a band of brothers,' he plead, 'and rescue your Government and its capital and your country from the enemies who have been the author of your calamity.' Glancing at the Ohio River, he exclaimed that 'this great valley must never be divided. The Almighty has so arranged the mountain, and the plain, and the water-courses as to show that this valley in all time shall remain one and indissoluble. Let no man attempt to sunder what Divine Providence has rendered indivisible.'

At the close, he was anxiously asked if it were true that General Scott had resigned. In answer, Douglas repeated the General's words to the Virginia offer and the crowd broke into frenzied cheers. The speech had a powerful reaction through Western Virginia, which held few slaves and had long-standing grievances against the Tidewater. Within a few weeks its loyalists initiated a movement to create a new Commonwealth, and soon West Virginia was knocking at the doors of Congress for admission as a State.[41]

---

command was offered to General Johnston after Lee had declined it. *Congressional Globe*, Fortieth Congress, Second Session, 1270, gives speech of Simon Cameron, Feb. 19, 1868, saying that Lee called on a 'gentleman who had my entire confidence and intimated that he would like to have the command of the army.... The place was offered to him unofficially.... It was accepted by him verbally.' J. W. Jones, *Life of Lee*, New York, 1875, 141, quoting Lee to Reverdy Johnson, Feb. 25, 1868, denying Cameron's statement. *National Intelligencer*, Aug. 9, 1868, quotes a letter of Montgomery Blair giving his father's statement of Lee's declaration, as carried in the text above.

40 Telegram described by Charles H. Lanphier, Springfield, Oct. 25, 1876, printed, Chicago *Times*, Oct. 31, 1876. Herndon, *Lincoln*, II, 249, f.n., Forney, I, 225.

41 Philadelphia *Press*, April 26, 1861, reprinting account of Douglas' speech in Wheeling *Intelligencer*; Channing, VI, 320 *et seq.*, for the grievances of western Virginia.

It was evening when Douglas reached Columbus, but a crowd gathered before his hotel and demanded a word from him. He was only half-dressed, but appeared in the window, and through the darkness came his deep, sonorous appeal for united defense of the Union. When he closed with a pledge to support President Lincoln, a deep 'Amen' went up from the crowd.[42]

The next day he was in Indianapolis, and he spoke from a hotel balcony. 'Our country is in danger,' he said, 'our Capital besieged and piracy invited to prey upon our commerce.' The Northwest could never consent to have its access to the ocean cut off by any Secession, and it was the duty of all its citizens, 'Democrats and Republicans, to rise up and unsheathe the sword in defense of our constitutional rights, and never sheathe it until they are secure.'[43]

The Little Giant reached Springfield on April 25 and found that Lanphier had been right about the grave disaffection in southern Illinois, and John A. Logan told him: 'You have sold out the Democratic party but, by God, you can't deliver it!'[44] The Union leaders were depending on the Little Giant's influence. 'If he speaks *right*,' Judge David Davis wrote Lamon, 'the people in Illinois will be an entire unit.' That night the Hall of Representatives was crowded as never before.[45]

The circumstances were impressive, and the earnest passion of his plea gave it an extraordinary force and appeal. As he neared his climax, the perspiration streamed down his face, the veins of his neck and forehead stood out and the very Hall of the House seemed to tremble with his words. During one such passage a man rushed into the Chamber bearing a national flag, and the audience was roused into the wildest enthusiasm.

It was 'with a heart filled with sadness and grief' that he spoke. For the first time since the adoption of the Constitution, there was 'a widespread conspiracy' to destroy the Government and hostile armies were marching on the Capital. What should Illinois do?

The people of the great valley of the Mississippi had peculiar interests and inducements in the struggle, he insisted. They could never sanction being isolated from the seacoast and made 'dependent provinces upon the powers that thus choose to isolate us.' Therefore, if war came, 'it is a war of self defense on our part. It is a war... in defense of those great rights of freedom of trade, commerce and intercourse from the center to the circumference of our great continent.'

It was the duty of the assembled legislators 'to lay aside, for the time being, your party creeds and party platforms; to dispense with your party organizations and partisan appeals; to forget that you were ever divided,

[42] Douglas to Lanphier, telegram, Bellaire, Ohio, April 22, 1861; Patton MSS. J. D. Cox, *Military Reminiscences of the Civil War*, New York, 1900; I, 5–6.

[43] *Illinois State Register*, April 25, 1861, quoting Indianapolis speech.

[44] Lanphier, Chicago *Times*, Oct. 31, 1876. Logan returned to Egypt, where he sought to prevent the organization of an Illinois regiment called for from that district. A little later, mainly through the persuasion of John A. McClernand, Logan concluded to raise a regiment himself. Before long he was vigorously pro-war.

[45] Davis to 'Dear Hill' (W. H. Lamon), Lincoln, Ill., April 24, 1861; original in Huntington Library.

until you have rescued the Government and the country from their assailants.'

His hearers knew that he was 'thoroughly national,' and had never pandered to the prejudice and passion of his own section against the minority section of the South. His hearers knew, he said, with a catch in his voice, that he had 'struggled almost against hope to avert the calamities of war and to effect a reunion and reconciliation.' Providence alone could reveal the issue of the struggle, 'bloody — calamitous,' he feared it would be, and the North must not yield to resentment or vengeance, 'much less to the desire for conquest or ambition.' He himself saw 'no path of ambition open in a bloody struggle for triumphs over my countrymen.'

Douglas' close was highly affecting. 'To discuss these topics,' he said with feeling, 'is the most painful duty of my life. It is with sad heart — with a grief I have never before experienced — that I have to contemplate this fearful struggle. But I believe in my conscience that it is a duty we owe ourselves, and our children, and our God, to protect this Government and that flag from every assailant, be he who he may.'

This speech was applauded, from beginning to end, by men of all parties. Its results were immediate and enduring. As John Wentworth put it, like Patrick Henry in the Revolution, Douglas had 'roused his countrymen as one man to the defense of their flag.' Through it, Douglas secured 'perfect unanimity on all measures in support of the Government.' In years to come it was realized that, but for the Little Giant, there would have been 'civil war in Illinois from Cairo north to the doorsteps of Springfield.' Instead, Douglas 'put 500,000 men into the Union Army, and 50,000 from Illinois alone.' [46]

During his two days at Springfield, Douglas sought to attach to the Union every man he could. One of those whom he influenced, Douglas' family record declares, was U. S. Grant, an ex-officer of the United States Army, a Democrat, whose wife held slaves in Missouri. Grant, according to their story, had about decided to accept a Confederate commission, but Douglas 'dissuaded' him. A little later Grant accepted appointment by Governor Yates, of Illinois, as mustering officer for State troops. One can idly wonder whether the outcome of the war would have been altered had Lee accepted Lincoln's invitation, and had Grant gone on to the South.[47]

[46] *Illinois State Register*, April 27; New York *Tribune*, May 1, 1861, for text. The Illinois Legislature published it in pamphlet form and hundreds of thousands of copies were distributed. Isaac N. Arnold, *Lincoln*, 201, for Cullom; Horace White to Robert M. Douglas, New York, Dec. 9, 1909; Martin F. Douglas MSS. General W. H. L. Wallace to Mrs. Wallace, Springfield, Ill., April 25, 1861; W. H. L. Wallace MSS. Browning, *Diary*, I, 465. *Missouri Republican*, St. Louis, Jan. 28, 1862; Congressman Richard Yates, speech in House of Representatives, Washington, June 14, 1920, *Congressional Record*, Sixty-Sixth Congress, 8453-54. David Davis to 'Dear Hill,' [Ward H. Lamon] Bloomington, Ill., May 6, 1861, Huntington Library MSS.: 'Douglas is on the topmost wave, but Trumbull is not invited.' Apparently only John A. Logan remained sullen about it. The next night, as Douglas and his wife walked on the railroad station platform, waiting for the Chicago train, Logan walked by cursing. Lanphier, Chicago *Times*, Oct. 31, 1876, and Linder, *Reminiscences*, 345.

[47] This story, one of the firm and well-detailed traditions of the Douglas family in Greensboro, has been communicated to me both by Martin F. Douglas and Robert Dick Douglas, each

Arriving in Chicago on May 1, Douglas was escorted to the Wigwam and greeted by a cheering throng of all parties. His theme was the need for loyalty in the midst of treason. The Southern Ultras had designed 'to create a purely sectional vote to demonstrate that the two sections could not live together.' They would carry the South, the North would elect Lincoln, 'then a united South was to assail a divided North and gain an easy victory.' 'There are but two sides to the question,' he said dramatically, 'and every man must be on the side of the United States or against it. There can be none but *patriots or traitors*.' [48] Douglas' labor had exhausted him, a severe attack of rheumatism sent him to bed, but he wrote the Chairman of the Illinois Democratic State Committee, 'that a man cannot be a true Democrat unless he is a loyal patriot.' [49]

Those first few days at Chicago brought Douglas no surcease of anxiety. His over-extension in land purchases, his heavy mortgages upon his property, first for the Buchanan campaign in 1856 and then for his own political expenses in 1858, were made all the more distressful by the financial crisis of Secession. Now large mortgages were maturing and it was proving impossible to renew them.[50]

The combination of financial harassments and the physical exhaustion from his Union efforts laid the Little Giant in bed. At first it seemed only a severe attack of rheumatism, but soon he had a serious relapse with high fever. 'Douglas is very ill,' Sheahan wrote Lanphier, 'and I am afraid is past all surgery.' Sheahan had said nothing about it in the paper, 'because I hate to write that he is in danger, and truth would demand that.' While some improvement was noted, Adèle was deeply disturbed and sent to Washington for Dr. Thomas Miller, her husband's special physician, who arrived on May 27, accompanied by Mrs. Douglas' mother and younger

of whom had it from their father, Robert Martin Douglas. The latter, in an article in the *Youth's Companion*, Dec. 19, 1912, skirted about the edges of the matter. In 1867, Robert M. Douglas and h s b other Step'en A., Jr., went to North Carolina to look after property there. Robert was e ghteen years old. The next year he became private secretary for Governor W. W. Holden. In March, 1869, according to his published account, he called on Grant at the White House in behalf of a friend, but at the end of the interview Grant asked, 'What can I do for you personally?' The published account then continued that Douglas thanked the President but said frankly that he did not think it would be advisable to accept any office the President could afford to give a man of his youth. Grant then hesitated and asked him if he would not care to go abroad. This he declined. That evening young Douglas called on the Grants, Mrs. Grant said she was sorry he had declined the position of Secretary with the President. Douglas was startled for Grant had not offered it, but he did offer it and Douglas accepted. The record of the conversation, as preserved by Robert M. Douglas' sons, was that the interview had come as a result of a telegram Grant had sent young Douglas at Greensboro. The family account is that Grant, in opening his offer, said that he owed Stephen A. Douglas the greatest debt of gratitude of any man in his life. 'I was about to accept a Confederate commission,' Grant said to young Douglas, 'your father dissuaded me from accepting it. All my career I owe to him, and nothing is too good for his son. How would you like to be Minister to Austria?'

[48] Chicago *Post*, May 2, 1861. New York *Tribune*, June 13, 1861.

[49] *Illinois State Register*, July 1, 1861, quoting Douglas to Virgil Hickox, Chicago, May 10, 1861.

[50] Johnson, 488.

brother. Daniel P. Rhodes hastened from Cleveland and the Douglas rooms at the Tremont House took on the appearance of a hospital. The malady baffled medical skill, much of the time Douglas was delirious, yet his mind was taken with the Nation's ills rather than his own. 'Telegraph to the President and let the column move on,' he cried on one occasion. The high fevers continued, and on May 31 his recovery was despaired of.[51]

Sunday morning Adèle called in Bishop Duggan, the leading Catholic prelate of the district, to offer spiritual comfort. According to newspaper dispatches, the Bishop soon asked him whether he had been baptized according to the rites of any church. Douglas answered no. 'Do you desire to have mass said after the ordinances of the Holy Catholic Church?' the cleric continued. 'No, sir,' Douglas was said to have answered, 'when I desire it, I will communicate with you freely.' [52]

There is, however, an intimate record to the contrary effect. The Bishop had a young friend, William J. Onahan, who aided him in correspondence and clerical matters. On June 3, a few hours after Douglas' demise, Onahan noted in his private diary: 'From what I can learn, he was received into the Church before his death and participated in her holy rites.' At any event, Bishop Duggan, 'in full canonicals,' preached the Douglas funeral service.[53]

Sunday afternoon Douglas rallied slightly, but that night sank rapidly. All realized that death was close at hand. About five Monday morning he asked that the windows be opened and the blinds thrown back. He took on new life for a moment, but soon sank back on the pillow and said, with a pause between each word: 'Death — death — death...'

About five, Adèle put her arms about his neck and asked if he had any message for his mother, sister and the two boys. 'Tell them,' he said, with an effort, 'to obey the laws and support the Constitution of the United

[51] Douglas to Virgil Hickox, Chicago, May 10, 1861; M. F. Douglas MSS.; Sheahan to Lanphier, Chicago, May 17, 1861; Patton MSS.; *Illinois State Register*, May 20, 1861, quoting Chicago papers of May 8; Chicago *Post*, May 27, 1861; *Illinois Journal*, May 28, 1861; William J. Onahan, M.S. Diary entry for May 31, 1861; for photostats of these and subsequent entries, I am indebted to Mr. Onahan's daughter, Mrs. Daniel J. Gallery, of Chicago.

[52] Johnson, 489, for muttering in delirium. New York *Herald*, June 6, 1861; Philadelphia *Press*, June 8, 1861; *Frank Leslie's Illustrated Newspaper*, New York, June 15, 1861, for account of Douglas' declination of Bishop Duggan's offer.

[53] William J. Onahan, MSS. Diary, entry for June 3, 1861. In 1918 Mr. Onahan wrote some articles of reminiscences, in which he stated that Douglas had died a Catholic. This statement was disputed, and then he answered: 'I may say that I have the most unequivocal testimony of the truth of what I assert. The physician who was in attendance, Dr. Hare, afterwards for a long time my own physician, and a Sister of the Good Shepherd, who, at the time, was at the Tremont House, both corroborate my assertion.' The Reverend Father G. J. Garraghan, S.J., of St. Louis University, has been most gracious in seeking further information on this matter for me. He is 'not ready to hold that the matter is proved beyond doubt,' yet he thinks it probable that Douglas was received in membership, chiefly because 'Catholic clergymen may not perform the liturgical burial rites of the Church over non-Catholics.' The most dependable funeral account, that of the Chicago *Times*, June 8, 1861, states that 'the clergy were in full canonicals, and their impressive services were a fitting close to the grand and solemn demonstration.' For the Bishop to be clad even in partial rubrical garb implied that he performed the Catholic burial rite. Yet the evidence is inferential only, and Father Garraghan has been able to discover 'no direct statement on the point from the Bishop or any of his clergy.'

States.' Adèle sat by him, holding his right hand and sobbing convulsively. Rhodes whispered he was afraid Douglas was not comfortable. The dying man answered, with an effort: 'He — is — very — comfortable.' The day came up calm and peaceful. A little after nine there were a few faint breaths and a convulsive shudder; Douglas passed from time into eternity.[54]

The North was shocked at the news. Washington's public buildings were draped in mourning and the White House was elaborately festooned in black. The War Department issued a general order, probably drafted by Lincoln, that all regimental colors be draped in mourning in honor of this man 'who nobly discarded party for his country.'[55]

Word came from Seward that the illustrious dead belonged to the Nation and should be buried in Washington. But Illinois would not hear to it. Governor Yates, Senator Trumbull, John A. McClernand, Gustave Koerner, Jesse K. Dubois and others gathered at Springfield and wired the Mayor of Chicago a protest. Lanphier, who loved him like a brother, telegraphed Sheahan: 'The State claims what is left.'[56]

In the event Illinois had its way. Douglas' casket lay in state in Bryant Hall from Tuesday through Thursday, and over seventy thousand people passed by in grief-stricken respect. On Friday they held the funeral. Business was suspended all over the city, which was shrouded in mourning. About ten thousand formed in procession and marched four miles to the open grave. While it passed, all the bells in the city were tolled and minute guns were fired. Reaching Oakenwald, the soldiers formed a hollow square in the grove and Bishop Duggan, clad in the robes of his episcopate, delivered the funeral oration and performed the last rites.

Thus the place where Douglas hoped to establish the home for his declining years became his home in death. Five years later it was made the site for a great monument. There to this day a marble shaft seeks the skies; atop is the heroic figure of the Little Giant, done in bronze by Leonard Volk's loving hands; on its base is written: 'Tell them to obey the laws and support the Constitution of the United States.'[57]

When news of Douglas' death reached Alexander H. Stephens, he wrote

[54] Philadelphia *Press*, June 8, 1861.

[55] General Orders No. 29, War Department, Adjutant General's Office, Washington, June 4, 1861. Major D. B. Sanger, Division Signal Officer, First Cavalry Division, Fort Bliss, Texas, who has examined the curious language of this order, thinks Lincoln likely its author. I am indebted to Major Sanger for a copy of his manuscript paper before the Mississippi Valley Historical Society, Chicago, 1933.

[56] Yates, etc., telegram, Springfield, June 3, 1861; M. F. Douglas MSS. Lanphier to Sheahan, telegram, Springfield, June 3, 1861; Douglas MSS.

[57] Chicago *Post*, June 6, 1861; *Illinois State Register*, June 7, 1861, for Bryant Hall incidents; William J. Onahan, MS. Diary, entry for June 7, 1861; Chicago *Times*, June 8, 1861; Chicago *Tribune*, June 8, 1861, had Bishop Duggan in 'half canonicals' and said there was no religious service at the grave. Chicago *Times*, June 8, and Chicago *Post*, June 8, and *Illinois State Register*, June 10, 1861, had the Bishop clad in the robes of his office, and a service at the grave. Chicago *Times*, Sept. 7, 1866, describes the statue and the acquisition of the site, from Mrs. Douglas, by the State of Illinois, for $25,000. It was the last unmortgaged property Douglas had.

that he 'almost wished he had died sooner or lived longer.' And as the years passed, Stephens became more and more convinced that it was indeed a great calamity that the Little Giant had not succeeded in his great endeavor to preserve the Union without war. Douglas, Stephens said twenty years later, 'was Napoleonic in firmness, compactness and power. The grasp, breadth, reach and readiness of Douglas' mind was marvelous. In an offhand running debate, Douglas was without an equal.' Stephens himself had 'stood by and believed in the living Douglas, and as time advanced he had grown firmer in his opinion that Douglas was right. If the extremists of the South had not prevented, Douglas would have prevailed; the Civil War would not have occurred and the Union would have been preserved. Douglas' true place in history... is that of the foremost patriot and statesman of his time.' [58]

[58] Alexander H. Stephens to Herschel V. Johnson, Crawfordsville, Ga., June 10, 1860; Illinois State Historical Society MSS. For Stephens' views in 1881, see Quincy, Ill., *Journal*, Nov. 20, 1902, reprinting interview in Omaha *World Herald*, with Judge J. H. Brooks of Lincoln, Neb. Brooks had a long talk with Stephens in 1881. The Georgian discussed Calhoun, Clay and Webster briefly, but when he came to speak of Douglas, Judge Brooks related: 'He threw off reserve and with an enthusiasm that he had not displayed before, grew exceedingly eloquent.' In defining Douglas' 'true place in history,' Stephens added that it was one which the Little Giant 'will doubtless never get.'

FINIS

BIBLIOGRAPHY

BIBLIOGRAPHY

THE author has consulted hundreds of manuscript letters, books, pamphlets, proceedings, reports, magazines and newspapers as to specific episodes, all of which are referred to and appropriately described in footnotes at the place of citation. Those sources here listed for the reader's convenient reference are those several times consulted. Because of space limitations, no attempt has been made to list here pamphlet sources except those of frequent consultation.

MANUSCRIPTS

Baird, Glenn Earl, 'The Southern Tours of Stephen A. Douglas,' MSS. Thesis, University of Chicago Library.
Bell, John, MSS., Library of Congress.
Black, Jeremiah Sullivan, MSS., Library of Congress.
Blair, Francis Preston, MSS., Library of Congress.
Breckinridge, John C., MSS., Library of Congress.
Breese, Sidney, MSS., Illinois Historical Society.
Buchanan, James, MSS., Historical Society of Pennsylvania, Philadelphia, and Library of Congress.
Caton, John Dean, MSS., Library of Congress.
Chicago Historical Society MSS.
Church of Latter Day Saints, Manuscript History, Salt Lake City, Utah.
Clay, Clement C., MSS., Duke University Library, Durham, N.C.
Clay, Henry, MSS., Library of Congress.
Confederate Archives, MSS., State Department, Washington.
Corcoran, W. W., MSS., Library of Congress.
Crittenden, John J., MSS., Library of Congress.
Dixon, Archibald, Family MSS., Mrs. Julia Dixon Clarke, Henderson, Ky.
Douglas, M. F., MSS., Mr. Martin F. Douglas, Greensboro, N.C.
Douglas, Robert Dick (listed as Douglas MSS.), University of Chicago Library.
Douglas, Stephen A., 'Autobiography,' MS., in possession of Mr. Martin F. Douglas, Greensboro, N.C.
Erwin MSS. (Howell Cobb papers), Miss Mary Erwin, Athens, Ga.
Fell, Jesse W., MSS., Henry Huntington Library, San Marino, Calif.
George, John H., MSS., New Hampshire Historical Society, Concord, N.H.
Greenhow, Kate, MSS., State Department Archives, Washington, D.C.
Gwin, William H., 'Memoirs on History of United States, Mexico and California.' MSS., Bancroft Library, Berkeley, Cal.
Illinois State Historical Library MSS.
Johnson, Andrew, MSS., Library of Congress.
Johnson, Robert, MSS., Library of Congress.
Marcy, William L., MSS., Library of Congress.
McClernand, John A., MSS., Major William J. Butler, Springfield, Ill.
McCutchen, S. P., Albert Gallatin Brown, MSS. Dissertation, University of Chicago Library.
Minnesota Historical Society, MSS., St. Paul, Minn.
Missouri Historical Society, MSS., Columbia, Mo.
Onahan, William J., MSS. Diary, in possession of Mrs. Daniel J. Gallery, Chicago.

Patton MSS. (Papers of Charles H. Lanphier), Mr. William Lanphier Patton and Dr. Charles Lanphier Patton, Springfield, Ill.
Phillips, Philip, MSS., Library of Congress.
Pierce, Franklin, MSS., Library of Congress.
Pierce, Franklin, MSS., New Hampshire Historical Society, Concord, N.H.
Rothschild, Baron Salomon de, Family Letters, MSS. Photostats, Library of Congress.
Sanders, George N., MSS., Library of Congress.
Seymour, Glenn G., 'The Political Principles of Stephen A. Douglas,' MSS. Dissertation, Charleston, Ill.
Sheahan, James W., MSS., Mr. George H. Sheahan, Chicago.
Sibley, H. H., MSS., Minnesota Historical Society, St. Paul.
Smith, Gerrit, MSS., Peterboro, New York.
Stevens, John H., MSS., Minnesota Historical Society, St. Paul.
Treat, Samuel, MSS., Historical Society of Missouri, St. Louis, Mo.
Trumbull, Lyman, MSS., Library of Congress.
Van Buren, Martin, MSS., Library of Congress.
Washburne, Elihu B., MSS., Library of Congress.
Webster, Daniel, MSS., Library of Congress.
Welles, Gideon, MSS. Diary, Library of Congress.
Whitthorne, W. C., Diary, MSS., Columbia, Tenn.
Wright, Hendrick B., MSS., Wyoming Historical and Geological Society, Wilkes-Barre, Pa.

NEWSPAPERS, PERIODICALS AND PAMPHLETS

Abraham Lincoln Association Bulletins, Nos. 27, 28, 35.
Albany, N.Y., *Evening Journal*, 1860.
American Historical Association Reports.
American Historical Review.
American Law Review, XLVI.
Appleton's Annual Cyclopedia, 1861.
Atlantic Monthly, VIII, XXVI, LXXIX.
Baltimore *Daily Exchange*, 1860.
Baltimore *Sun*, 1852, 1860.
Belford's Magazine, V.
Belleville, Ill., *Advocate*, 1858.
Bloomington, Ill., *Pantagraph*, 1854, 1858.
Boston *Times*, 1851–52.
Carlinville, Ill., *Free Democrat*, 1857–60.
Charleston, S.C., *Courier*, 1858, 1860.
Charleston, S.C., *Mercury*, 1859–60.
Chicago *Press and Tribune*, 1857–58.
Chicago *Times*, 1854–60, 1866, 1876.
Chicago *Times and Herald*, 1860–61.
Chicago *Tribune*, 1854.
Cincinnati *Enquirer*, 1853, 1856.
Cincinnati *Gazette*, 1853, 1856, 1858–59.
Cleveland *Plain Dealer*, 1855, 1857–60.
Congressional Globe, 28th to 37th Congresses.
Cox, S. S., Eulogy on Douglas, *Annual Report*, Smithsonian Institution, 1863.
Curti, Merle E., 'George N. Sanders—American Patriot of the Fifties,' *South Atlantic Quarterly*, XXVII.
DeBow's *Review*, XV.

Dick, Robert P., Broadside, 'To the Democracy of the Fifth Congressional District of North Carolina,' Greensboro, N.C., Aug. 14, 1860.
Douglas, Stephen A., 'Popular Sovereignty,' *Harper's Monthly Magazine*, September, 1857.
Driftwind Magazine, VII.
Granite Monthly, LX.
Harper's Monthly Magazine, LXXXVII.
Herriott, F. I., 'James W. Grimes Versus the Southrons,' *Annals of Iowa*, VI.
Herriott, F. I., 'Senator Stephen A. Douglas and the Germans in 1854,' Illinois State Historical Society *Transactions*, 1912.
Hodder, Frank H., 'Propaganda as a Source for American History,' *Mississippi Valley Historical Review*, IX.
Hodder, Frank H., 'Railroad Background of the Kansas-Nebraska Act,' *Mississippi Valley Historical Review*, XII.
Hodder, Frank H., 'Some Phases of the Dred Scott Case,' *Mississippi Valley Historical Review*, XVI.
Hodder, Frank H., 'Genesis of the Kansas-Nebraska Act,' State Historical Society of Wisconsin, *Proceedings*, 1912.
Illinois Journal, Springfield, 1853–61.
Illinois State Historical Society *Journal*.
Illinois State Historical Society *Transactions*.
Illinois State Register, Vandalia, 1834–37.
Illinois State Register, Springfield, 1838–61.
Jackson, Miss., *Weekly Mississippian*, 1854, 1857–60.
Kansas Historical Collections, Topeka, Kan., v.d.
Lawrence, Kan., *Herald of Freedom*, 1855.
Learned, H. B., 'The Relation of Philip Phillips to the Repeal of the Missouri Compromise,' *Mississippi Valley Historical Review*, VIII.
Lewiston, Ill., *Fulton Democrat*, 1858.
Lexington, Ky., *Statesman*, 1854, 1860.
McConnel, George Murray, 'Recollections of Stephen A. Douglas,' Illinois State Historical Society *Transactions*, Springfield, 1901.
Memphis, Tenn., *Appeal*, 1852, 1854–58.
Mississippi Valley Historical Review.
Mobile, Ala., *Register*, 1860–61.
Nashville, Tenn., *Union and American*, 1860.
Nebraska Historical Society *Transactions*, II.
New Orleans, La., *True Delta*, 1850–60.
New York *Courier and Enquirer*, 1860.
New York *Evening Post*, 1856.
New York *Herald*, 1852, 1854, 1856–61.
New York *Independent*, 1857.
New York *Journal of Commerce*, 1857–58.
New York *Times*, 1854, 1858, 1860–61.
New York *Tribune*, 1850, 1854–60.
Norfolk, Va., *Southern Argus*, 1860.
North American Review, CXXIX. 'Diary of a Public Man,' 1860–61.
Ohio Archaeological and Historical Quarterly, XXXIV.
Philadelphia *Press*, 1857–60.
'Popular Sovereignty — The Reviewer Reviewed by a Southern Inquirer,' Washington, 1859.
Richmond, Va., *Enquirer*, 1861.

Richmond, Va., *Examiner*, 1858.
Richmond, Va., *Whig*, 1860–61.
Searle, George N., 'The Supreme Court of the United States in 1853–4.' *American Law Register*, October, 1854.
Sheahan, James W., 'Eulogy on Stephen A. Douglas,' Pamphlet, Chicago, July 3, 1861.
Southern Historical Society, *Publications*, 1907.
Southern Review, IX.
St. Louis, *Missouri Democrat*, 1861.
St. Louis, *Missouri Republican*, 1852, 1854, 1858, **1860, 1862.**
Transactions of Illinois State Historical Society.
Tribune Almanac and Political Register, 1857–59.
Trinity College Historical Papers, XVII–XIX.
United States Democratic Review, XXX.
Vicksburg, Miss., *Whig*, 1858, 1860.
Washington *National Era*, 1854, 1859–60.
Washington *National Intelligencer*, 1858, 1860–**62.**
Washington *Sentinel*, 1854–55.
Washington *Star*, 1857.
Washington *States*, 1858.
Washington *Union*, 1848, 1852, 1854, 1856–58.
White, Horace, *Abraham Lincoln in 1854.* Address, Springfield, Jan. 30, 1908.
White, Horace. Address, 'Abraham Lincoln in 1854,' Illinois State Historical Society *Transactions*, 1908.
Winchester, Ill., *Times*, 1909, 1930.

BOOKS

Ackerman, William K., *Early Illinois Railroads.* Chicago, 1884.
Adams, Charles F., Jr., *Richard H. Dana.* 2 vols., Boston, 1890.
Adams, John Quincy, *Memoirs.* 12 vols., Philadelphia, 1874–77.
Alfriend, Frank H., *Life of Jefferson Davis.* Cincinnati, 1868.
Allen, Alexander V. G., *Life and Letters of Phillips Brooks.* 2 vols., New York, 1900.
Angle, Paul M., editor, *New Letters and Papers of Lincoln.* Boston, 1930.
Arnold, Isaac N., *Early Chicago and Illinois Bar.* Chicago, 1880.
Auchampaugh, Phillip G., *James Buchanan and His Cabinet.* Lancaster, Pa., 1926.
Avery, Elijah, *Capture and Execution of John Brown.* Chicago, 1906.
Bancroft, Frederic, *Slave Trading in the Old South.* Baltimore, 1931.
Bancroft, Frederic, *Life of William H. Seward.* 2 vols., New York, 1900.
Barker, H. E., *Mary Todd.* Springfield, 1917.
Barnes, Thurlow Weed, *Memoirs of Thurlow Weed.* 2 vols., Boston, 1884.
Belmont, August, *Letters, Speeches and Addresses.* New York, 1890.
Belmont, August, *Private Correspondence*, New York, 1890.
Beveridge, Albert J., *Abraham Lincoln, 1809–1858.* 2 vols., Boston, 1928.
Black, Jeremiah Sullivan, *Essays and Speeches.* New York, 1885.
Blaine, James G., *Twenty Years of Congress.* 2 vols., Norwich, Conn., 1884–86.
Botts, John M., *The Great Rebellion.* New York, 1866.
Boyd, Minnie C., *Alabama in the Fifties.* New York, 1931.
Bridge, Horatio, *Personal Recollections of Nathaniel Hawthorne.* New York, 1893.
Brown, William G., *The Lower South in American History.* New York, 1902.
Browning, Orville H., T. C. Pease and J. G. Randall, editors, *Diary.* 2 vols., Springfield, Ill., 1925; 33.
Brownson, Howard G., *History of the Illinois Central Railroad to 1870.* Urbana, Ill., 1915.

Burgess, John W., *The Civil War and the Constitution*. 2 vols., New York, 1901.
Calhoun, John C., Richard K. Crallé, editor, *A Disquisition on Government*. Columbia, S.C., 1852.
Calhoun, John C., Richard K. Crallé, editor, *Works*. 6 vols., New York, 1851-56.
Carpenter, W. H., and T. S. Arthur, *History of Illinois*. Philadelphia, 1854.
Carr, Clark E., *Stephen A. Douglas*. Chicago, 1909.
Channing, Edward, *History of the United States*. 6 vols., New York, 1905-29.
Chesnut, Mary B., *A Diary From Dixie*. New York, 1905.
Chittenden, L. E., *Recollections of President Lincoln*. New York, 1891.
Chittenden, L. E., *Report of the Peace Convention in 1861*, New York, 1864.
Claiborne, J. F. H., *Life and Correspondence of John A. Quitman*. 2 vols., New York, 1860.
Clarke, S. J., *History of McDonough County, Illinois*. Chicago, 1878.
Clay, Mrs. Clement C., Ada Sterling, Ed., *A Belle of the 'Fifties*. New York, 1905.
Coates, Wm. R., *History of Cuyahuga County and the City of Cleveland*. Chicago and New York, 1924.
Cole, Arthur C., *Centennial History of Illinois* — Vol. III — *The Era of the Civil War, 1848-1870*. Springfield, 1919.
Colton, Calvin, *Last Seven Years of Henry Clay*. New York, 1856.
Colton, Calvin, Ed., *Private Correspondence of Henry Clay*. New York, 1856.
Colvin, Leigh, *Prohibition in the United States*. New York, 1926.
Congdon, Charles T., *Reminiscences of a Journalist*. Boston, 1880.
Connelley, William E., *James Henry Lane*. Topeka, Kansas, 1899.
Connor, Henry G., *Life of John A. Campbell*. Boston, 1920.
Craven, Avery, *Edmund Ruffin*. New York, 1933.
Crawford, Samuel W., *The Genesis of the Civil War*. New York, 1887.
Curtis, Benjamin R., *A Memoir of Benjamin Robbins Curtis*. 2 vols., Boston, 1879.
Curtis, George Ticknor, *Life of Daniel Webster*. 2 vols., Boston, 1878.
Cutts, J. Madison, *Constitutional and Party Questions*. New York, 1866.
Davidson, Alexander, and Bernard Stuvé, *History of Illinois*. Springfield, 1873.
Davis, Varina, *Jefferson Davis, A Memoir*. 2 vols., New York, 1890.
Democratic National Committee, *Proceedings of Charleston and Baltimore Conventions*, Cleveland, Ohio, 1860.
Denman, Clarence P., *The Secession Movement in Alabama*. Montgomery, 1933.
Dew, Thomas Roderick, et al., *Pro-Slavery Argument*. Philadelphia, 1853.
Dickinson, John R., *Speeches, etc., of Daniel S. Dickinson*. 2 vols., New York, 1867.
Dittrick, Howard, Compiler, *Pioneer Medicine in the Western Reserve*. Cleveland, 1932.
Dixon, Mrs. S. B., *A True History of the Missouri Compromise and Its Repeal*. Cincinnati, 1899.
Dubois, J. T., and G. S. Mathews, *Galusha A. Grow*. New York, 1900.
DuBose, John, *The Life and Times of William Lowndes Yancey*. Birmingham, Ala., 1892.
Dumond, Dwight L., *The Secession Movement*. New York, 1931.
Ettinger, Amos A., *The Mission to Spain of Pierre Soulé*. New Haven, 1932.
Fiske, John, *History of the United States*. Boston, 1899.
Fite, Emerson D., *The Presidential Campaign of 1860*. New York, 1911.
Flint, Henry M., *Life of Stephen A. Douglas*. Philadelphia, 1863.
Foote, Henry S., *A Casket of Reminiscences*. Washington, 1872.
Ford, Thomas, *History of Illinois*. Chicago, 1854.
Forney, John W., *Anecdotes of Public Men*. 2 vols., New York, 1881.
Fuess, Claude M., *Caleb Cushing*. 2 vols., New York, 1923.
Fuess, Claude M., *Daniel Webster*. 2 vols., New York, 1930.
Gardner, William, *Stephen A. Douglas*. Boston, 1905.

Garrett, William, *Reminiscences of Public Men in Alabama*. Atlanta, 1872.
Gates, Paul W., *The Illinois Central Railroad and Its Colonization Work*. Cambridge, Mass., 1934.
Gihon, John H., *Geary and Kansas*. Philadelphia, 1857.
Goodspeed, Thomas Wakefield, *University of Chicago Biographical Sketches*. Chicago, 1925.
Gouverneur, Marian, *As I Remember*. New York, 1911.
Greeley, Horace, *Recollections of a Busy Life*. New York, 1868.
Green, Duff, *Facts and Suggestions*. New York, 1866.
Hale, Edward Everett, *Kansas and Nebraska*. Boston, 1854.
Halstead, Murat, *Caucuses of 1860*. Columbus, Ohio, 1860.
Hambleton, James P., *Henry A. Wise*. Richmond, 1856.
Hamlin, Charles Eugene, *The Life and Times of Hannibal Hamlin*. Cambridge, 1899.
Harvey, Peter, *Reminiscences and Anecdotes of Daniel Webster*. Boston, 1877.
Haskell, Fritz, *Winchester Centennial Souvenir*. Winchester, Ill., 1930.
Helper, Hinton R., *The Impending Crisis*. New York, 1857.
Hilliard, Henry, *Political Pen Pictures at Home and Abroad*. New York, 1893.
Hinsdale, Burke, *Horace Mann*. New York, 1898.
Holland, J. G., *Life of Lincoln*. Springfield, Mass., 1866.
Hollister, Orando J., *Schuyler A. Colfax*. New York, 1886.
Holst, Hermann E. von, *John C. Calhoun*. Boston, 1882.
Holst, Hermann E. von, *Constitutional and Political History of the United States*. 7 vols., Chicago, 1877–92.
Howland, Louis, *Stephen A. Douglas*. New York, 1920.
Iglehart, N. P., *History of the Douglas Estate*. Chicago, 1869.
Irelan, John Robert, *History of the Administration of James Buchanan*. Chicago, 1888.
Irelan, John Robert, *History of Life, Administration and Times of Millard Fillmore*. Chicago, 1888.
Irelan, John Robert, *History of Life, Administration and Times of Franklin Pierce*. Chicago, 1888.
Irelan, John Robert, *History of Life, Administration and Times of James K. Polk*. Chicago, 1888.
Irelan, John Robert, *History of Life, Administration and Times of Zachary Taylor*. Chicago, 1888.
Jervey, Theodore D., *Robert Y. Hayne and His Times*. New York, 1909.
Johns, Jane Martin, *Personal Recollections, 1849–1865*. Decatur, Ill., 1912.
Johnson, Allen, *Life of Stephen A. Douglas*. New York, 1908.
Johnson, Zachary T., *The Political Principles of Howell Cobb*. Nashville, Tenn., 1928.
Jones, J. W., *Life and Letters of Robert Edward Lee*. New York, 1875.
Jordan, Donaldson and Edwin J. Pratt, *Europe and the American Civil War*. Boston, 1931.
Journal of the Convention of the People of Georgia, 1861.
Journal of the Mississippi Convention… 1861.
Journal, Official Proceedings of the State of Louisiana, 1861.
Lamon, Ward Hill, *Life of Abraham Lincoln*. Boston, 1872.
Lamon, Ward Hill, *Recollections of Abraham Lincoln*. Washington, 1911.
Lanman, Charles, *Private Life of Daniel Webster*. New York, 1856.
Lawrence, William, *Life of Amos A. Lawrence*. Boston, 1880.
Leiding, Harriette Kershaw, *Old Charleston and South Carolina*. Philadelphia, 1931.
Lincoln's Works (John G. Nicolay and John Hay, editors). 12 vols., New York, 1905.
Linder, Usher F., *Reminiscences of the Early Bench and Bar of Illinois*. Chicago, 1879.
Lusk, D. W., *Eighty Years of Illinois*. Springfield, 1889.

Lynch, Jeremiah, *A Senator of the Fifties — David C. Broderick*. San Francisco, 1911.
Martineau, Harriet, *Society in America*. New York, 1837.
Mazyck, Arthur, *Guide to Charleston*. Charleston, S.C., 1875.
McClure, Alexander K., *Abraham Lincoln and Men of War Times*. Philadelphia, 1892.
McCormac, Eugene I., *James K. Polk*. New York, 1918.
Merriam, George S., *Life and Times of Samuel Bowles*. 2 vols., New York, 1885.
Merrit, Elizabeth, *James Henry Hammond*. Baltimore, 1923.
Milton, George Fort, *The Age of Hate*. New York, 1930.
Montgomery, H., *The Life of Major-General Zachary Taylor*. Auburn, New York, 1854.
Munford, Beverly B., *Virginia's Attitude Toward Slavery and Secession*. New York, 1909.
Nevins, Allan, *John C. Frémont*. 2 vols., New York, 1928.
Newton, John, *Captain John Brown of Harper's Ferry*. London, 1902.
Newton, Joseph Fort, *Lincoln and Herndon*. Cedar Rapids, Iowa, 1910.
Nichols, Roy F., *The Democratic Machine, 1850–1854*. New York, 1923.
Nichols, Roy F., *Franklin Pierce*. Philadelphia, 1931.
Nicolay, John G., and John Hay, *Abraham Lincoln: A History*. 10 vols., New York, 1890.
Olmsted, Frederic Law, *A Journey in the Seaboard Slave States*. 2 vols., New York, 1856.
Orth, Samuel P., *Five American Politicians*. Cleveland, 1906.
Owsley, Frank, *King Cotton Diplomacy*. Chicago, 1931.
Palmer, John M., *Personal Recollections*. Cincinnati, Ohio, 1901.
Parrington, Vernon Louis, *Main Currents in American Thought*. 3 vols., New York, 1927.
Parton, James, *Life of Andrew Jackson*. 3 vols., New York, 1860.
Peck, J. W., *Gazetteer of Illinois*. Jacksonville, Ill., 1834.
Phillips, Isaac, Ed., *Abraham Lincoln, By Some Men Who Knew Him*. Bloomington, Ill., 1910.
Phillips, Ulrich B., *American Negro Slavery*. New York, 1918.
Phillips, Ulrich B., *A History of Transportation in the Eastern Cotton Belt to 1860*. New York, 1908.
Phillips, Ulrich B., *Life and Labor in the Old South*. Boston, 1929.
Phillips, Ulrich B., *Robert Toombs*. New York, 1913.
Polk, James K., *Diary*. 4 vols., Chicago, 1910.
Pollard, Edward A., *Life of Jefferson Davis*. Philadelphia, 1869.
Pollard, Edward A., *Robert E. Lee*, New York, 1871.
Pollard, Edward A., *The Lost Cause*. New York, 1867.
Poore, Ben: Perley, *Reminiscences*. Philadelphia, 1886.
Prentis, Noble L., *Kansas Miscellanies*. Topeka, 1889.
Pryor, Mrs. Roger A., *Reminiscences of Peace and War*. New York, 1904.
Ray, P. Orman, *The Repeal of the Missouri Compromise, Its Origin and Authorship*. Cleveland, 1909.
Raymond, Henry J., *The Life and Public Services of Abraham Lincoln*. New York, 1864.
Raymond, Henry J., *President Lincoln and His Administration*. New York, 1865.
Redpath, James, *Public Life of Captain John Brown, With an Autobiography*. Boston, 1860.
Rhodes, James Ford, *History of the United States, 1850–1909*. 9 vols., New York, 1893–1907.
Richardson, James D., *Messages and Papers of the Presidents*. 10 vols., New York, 1896–99.

Robinson, William S., *Warrenton Pen Portraits, Personal and Political Reminiscences, 1848-76.* Boston, 1877.
Roman, Alfred, *The Military Operations of General Beauregard.* 2 vols., New York, 1884.
Rowland, Dunbar, *Jefferson Davis, Constitutionalist.* 10 vols., Jackson, Miss., 1923.
Russell, W. H., *The Civil War in America.* Boston, 1861.
Sandburg, Carl, and Paul M. Angle, *Mary Lincoln, Wife and Widow.* New York, 1932.
Sangamo County, History of, Chicago, 1881.
Schouler, James, *History of the United States.* 7 vols., New York, v.d.
Schurz, Carl, *Life of Henry Clay.* 2 vols., Boston, 1887.
Scisco, Louis Davis, *Political Nativism in New York State.* New York, 1901.
Scrugham, Mary, *The Peaceable Americans of 1860-61.* New York, 1921.
Sears, Louis Martin, *John Slidell.* Durham, N.C., 1925.
Seward, Frederick W., *William H. Seward.* 2 vols., New York, 1891.
Seward, William H. (George E. Baker, editor), *Works.* 5 vols., Boston, 1883.
Sheahan, James W., *The Life of Stephen A. Douglas.* New York, 1860.
Sherman, William T., *Personal Memoirs.* 2 vols., New York, 1875.
Smith, Edward C., *The Borderland in the Civil War.* New York, 1927.
Smith, Justin H., *The Annexation of Texas,* New York, 1913.
Smith, Justin H., *The War With Mexico.* 2 vols., New York, 1919.
Smith, William E., *The Francis Preston Blair Family in Politics.* 2 vols., New York, 1933.
Sparks, Edwin, Ed., *Lincoln-Douglas Debates.* Springfield, Ill., 1908.
Stanton, Henry B., *Random Recollections.* New York, 1886.
Stephens, Alexander H., *A Constitutional View of the War Between the States.* 2 vols., Philadelphia, 1868-70.
Stevens, Frank E., *Life of Stephen A. Douglas.* Springfield, Ill., 1923.
Thayer, Eli, *A History of the Kansas Crusade.* New York, 1889.
Thayer, William R., *Life and Letters of John Hay.* 2 vols., Boston, 1908.
Townsend, E. D., *Anecdotes of the Civil War.* New York, 1884.
Turnley, Parmenas Taylor, *Letters of Parmenas.* London, 1863.
Tyler, Samuel, *Memoir of Roger Brooke Taney.* Baltimore, 1876.
United States Census Reports, for 1850.
Villard, Henry, *Memoirs.* 2 vols., Boston, 1904.
Villard, Oswald Garrison, *John Brown.* Boston, 1910.
Wallace, Isabel, *Life and Letters of General W. H. L. Wallace.* Chicago, 1910.
War of the Rebellion: A Compilation of the Official Records of the Union and Confederate Armies (O.R.). Four series, 113 vols., Washington, v.d.
Warden, Robert B., *Stephen Arnold Douglas.* Columbus, Ohio, 1860.
Warren, Charles, *The Supreme Court in United States History.* 3 vols., Boston, 1924.
Welles, Gideon, *Diary.* 3 vols., Boston, 1911.
Wertenbaker, Thomas J., *Norfolk, Historic Southern Seaport.* Durham, N.C., 1931.
Whittier, John, *Poetical Works.* 7 vols., Boston, 1888.
Willis, Henry P., *Stephen A. Douglas.* Philadelphia, 1910.
Wilson, Henry, *History of the Rise and Fall of the Slave Power in America.* 3 vols., Boston, 1872-77.
Wilson, John Lyde, *The Code of Honor, or Rules for the Government of Principals and Seconds in Duelling.* Charleston, 1858.
Wise, Barton H., *Life of Henry A. Wise, 1806-1876.* New York, 1899.
Wise, John S., *The End of an Era.* Boston, 1899.
Woodward, Walter C., *Political Parties in Oregon.* Portland, 1913.
Wright, Mrs. D. Giraud (Louise Wigfall), *A Southern Girl in '61.* New York, 1905.
Young, James C., *Marse Robert.* New York, 1929.

INDEX

INDEX